THE SEAN O'CASEY READER

SEAN O'CASEY

THE SEAN O'CASEY READER

PLAYS, AUTOBIOGRAPHIES, OPINIONS

Edited, *with an Introduction,* by
Brooks Atkinson

1968 · ST. MARTIN'S PRESS · *New York*
MACMILLAN · *London* · *Toronto* · *Melbourne*

Contents

Introduction   xi

Chronology of the O'Casey Works   viii

Plays   I

    JUNO AND THE PAYCOCK   3

    THE PLOUGH AND THE STARS   63

    THE SILVER TASSIE   133

    WITHIN THE GATES   205

    PURPLE DUST   285

    RED ROSES FOR ME   365

    COCK-A-DOODLE DANDY   435

    BEDTIME STORY   505

    THE DRUMS OF FATHER NED   529

Autobiographies   601

    From I KNOCK AT THE DOOR:

    "A Child is Born"   603

    "First the Green Blade"   611

    "The Castle Ball"   615

    "The Hill of Healing"   616

    "His Da, His Poor Da"   621

    "His Father's Wake"   625

    "The Street Sings"   629

    "Crime and Punishment"   636

From PICTURES IN THE HALLWAY:

"Comin' of Age"   645
"Bring Forth the Best Robe"   649
"The Shame Is a Thief and a Robber"   656
"Alice, Where Art Thou?"   663
"To Him That Hath Shall Be Given"   671
"Touched by the Theatre"   679
"I Strike a Blow for You, Dear Land"   689

From DRUMS UNDER THE WINDOWS:

"At the Sign of the Pick and Shovel"   701
"Prometheus Hibernica"   717

From INISHFALLEN, FARE THEE WELL:

"Mrs. Casside Takes a Holiday"   729
"The Raid"   745
"Blessed Bridget O'Coole"   757
"Where Wild Swans Nest"   761
"The Temple Entered"   771
"Inishfallen, Fare Thee Well"   787

From ROSE AND CROWN:

"London Apprentice"   793
"The Silver Tassie"   795
"The Friggin Frogs"   806
"Feathering His Nest"   816
"Black Oxen Passing By"   833
"Ship in Full Sail"   835
"Within the Gates"   842

From SUNSET AND EVENING STAR:

"Childerness"   851
"Deep in Devon"   859
"Red Laugh of War"   867
"Shaw's Corner"   874
"And Evening Star"   890

Opinions (also, a short story)   895

"Under the Greenwood Tree He Died"   897
"Bonfire Under a Black Sun"   917
"Shakespeare Among the Flags"   937
"The Bald Primaqueera"   941
"Crabbed Age and Youth"   953
"The Day the Worker Blows a Bugle"   959
"Not Waiting for Godot"   965
"I Wanna Woman"   967
"Purple Dust in Their Eyes"   983

A Sean O'Casey Bibliography   993
Index   1001

Chronology of the O'Casey Works

1918†   SONGS OF THE WREN / *verses*

1918†   MORE WREN SONGS / *verses*

1918†   THOMAS ASHE / *pamphlet*

1918†   THE SACRIFICE OF THOMAS ASHE / *pamphlet*

1919†   THE STORY OF THE IRISH CITIZEN ARMY / *history*

1923*   THE SHADOW OF A GUNMAN / *full-length play*

1923*   CATHLEEN LISTENS IN / *one-act play*

1924*   JUNO AND THE PAYCOCK / *full-length play*

1924*   NANNIE'S NIGHT OUT / *one-act play*

1926*   THE PLOUGH AND THE STARS / *full-length play*

1929*   THE SILVER TASSIE / *full-length play*

1933*   WITHIN THE GATES / *full-length play*

1934†   WINDFALLS / *short stories, poems, and the following two plays*

1934†   THE END OF THE BEGINNING / *one-act play*

1934†   A POUND ON DEMAND / *one-act play*

1937†   THE FLYING WASP / *essays*

1939†   I KNOCK AT THE DOOR / *autobiography*

1940*   THE STAR TURNS RED / *full-length play*

1940†   PURPLE DUST / *full-length play*

1942†   RED ROSES FOR ME / *full-length play*

1942†   PICTURES IN THE HALLWAY / *autobiography*

1946†   OAK LEAVES AND LAVENDER / *full-length play*

1946† Drums Under the Windows / *autobiography*

1949† Cock-a-Doodle Dandy / *full-length play*

1949† Inishfallen, Fare Thee Well / *autobiography*

1951† The Hall of Healing / *one-act play*

1951† Bedtime Story / *one-act play*

1951† Time to Go / *one-act play*

1952† Rose and Crown / *autobiography*

1954† Sunset and Evening Star / *autobiography*

1955* The Bishop's Bonfire / *full-length play*

1956† The Green Crow / *essays*

1959* The Drums of Father Ned / *full-length play*

1961† Behind the Green Curtains / *play in three scenes*

1961† Figuro in the Night / *one-act play*

1961† The Moon Shines on Kylenamoe / *one-act play*

1962† Feathers from the Green Crow / *stories, essays, songs and plays*

1963† Under a Colored Cap / *essays*

1967† Blasts and Benedictions / *stories and essays*

* DATE OF PRODUCTION
† DATE OF PUBLICATION

Five of O'Casey's earliest one-act plays were never published. They are "The Robe of Rosheen," 1918; "The Frost in the Flower," 1919; "The Harvest Festival," 1920; "The Crimson in the Tri-Color," 1921; and "The Cooing of the Doves," 1923.

Introduction

I

Thirteen days before Sean O'Casey died on September 18, 1964, at the age of eighty-four, a friend who was visiting him intercepted a telephone call. The call was from a London newspaperman who wanted to interview O'Casey. "Tell him I'm talking only to God," O'Casey replied with his familiar grin. When someone asked him on one of his last birthdays how he felt, he repeated something he had written about himself in his youth: "Tired, but joyous, praising God for His rightness and the will towards joy in the hearts of men."

Those remarks are interesting for two reasons. One: Although he described himself as a rationalist he was preoccupied with religion. His vocabulary was as rich in religious words and phrases as if he had been an evangelist. Two: He was an optimist about the human race. "Merry," "rejoice," "laughter," "dance," "song," "love" are words he used repeatedly. Since he was also cantankerous and petulant and since he struck out with terrible wrath against people and institutions that he regarded as harmful, it may seem arbitrary to describe him as a radiant man. The people he singled out for oblivion—W. H. Auden, Noel Coward, James Agate, Beverley Nichols, George Orwell, Denis Johnston, Kenneth Tynan—could hardly be expected to appreciate his radiance. Nor the Irish and British critics: he not only ran them down but he trampled on them repeatedly. In a large area of life he was contrary-minded and he wrote some very bitter prose.

But it was faith in life, love for his family and friends, and belief in a cheerful destiny that kept him going through a life of indigence and several personal catastrophes. He was affectionate, generous, and loyal towards those he loved and respected. His hatreds were confined to people and institutions that, in his opinion, impeded or impaired the normal joyousness of human existence. Among the advertising cards inside a Second Avenue bus in New York I was once surprised and delighted to find a quotation from O'Casey: "I have found life an enjoyable, enchanting, active and sometimes terrifying experience, and I've enjoyed it completely. A lament in one ear, maybe, but always a song in the other." This turned out to be a quotation from one of the hundreds of personal letters he wrote to hundreds of anonymous admirers, particularly in the United States, of which he was especially fond. O'Casey was a believer; it is a temptation to misuse a religious term and call him an Old Believer. That was his strength as a writer. The fire was in his hatred. The strength was in his love.

He was a frail man, afflicted all his life with ulcerated eyes that resulted in almost total blindness in his last years. He suffered from lumbago that made movement painful; he had bronchial and respiratory troubles that consigned him to nursing homes repeatedly. But he left a prodigious body of exuberant work. Beginning at the age of thirty-eight, when his first writings were published ("Songs of the Wren" and "The Story of Thomas Ashe") he wrote twelve full-length plays, fifteen one-act plays, six volumes of autobiography and four volumes of poems, short stories, reviews, articles and jeremiads. Although the literary forms changed, the basic point of view remained consistent.

II

He was born in a Dublin tenement on March 30, 1880, and baptized in a Protestant church as John Casey. Although the family was poor, his parents were cultivated people. Michael Casey, the father, was employed by a religious organization and had a big library that contained many religious books. When his son John was only three years old, Michael Casey died from injuries caused by a fall from a ladder he was using to reach the top shelf of his bookcases. The mother, Susan, was a woman of great sweetness and fortitude. She bore her husband thirteen children, only five of whom lived to be adults. Susan lived in tenements to the age of eighty without losing her kindness, pride, and inner grace. She appears throughout the first volume of O'Casey's autobiography, "I Knock at the Door." There is a second sketch of her in the last volume, "Sunset and Evening Star." She is also Mrs. Breydon, the mother in "Red Roses for Me," which is in many respects an autobiographical play.

Because of the painful disease in his eyes O'Casey could not attend school regularly. But throughout his long lifetime he had a passion for learning. In his youth he read widely in the classics and in the Bible. (At the age of eighty-four he was still learning by listening to the Schools Program of the British Broadcasting Corporation.) He went to work when he was an adolescent as a department store clerk, an experience entertainingly described in "Pictures in the Hallway." Among his many random occupations was digging with pick and shovel. That was what he was doing when his first play, "The Shadow of a Gunman," was acted at the Abbey Theatre. (Total royalties from that production—£4.)

Although the family seems to have had middle-class standards of behavior, O'Casey was a natural rebel. He was never satisfied with the status quo. One of his early enthusiasms was the Gaelic language which was an important aspect of Irish nationalism. Caught up in the romantic hurly-burly of that cause, he gaelicized his name into Sean O'Cathasaigh, which he later simplified to O'Casey. When Jim Larkin led the long strike against the trolley monopoly in Dublin in 1913, O'Casey became an admirer and assistant. O'Casey was also thrilled by the Easter Rising against the British in 1916. He served for a time as secretary of the Irish Citizen Army and wrote articles supporting the cause. His early published writings derived from the labor movement and the rebellion. In addition to the "Songs of the Wren" and "The Story of Thomas Ashe," who was a martyr to the movement, he wrote "The Story of the Citizen Army." In his autobiography, written many years later, he said he belonged to the world of discontent, resentment, and resistance.

But he had enough surplus energy to enjoy life even during the years when it was difficult to earn a bare living. He wrote and sang songs in an appealing Irish voice. As a youth he sang hymns in church with an enthusiasm that left an impression on other churchgoers; and when the moment for voluntary prayers came he could be counted on for one that was long and fervent. At the age of ten he rehearsed Shakespeare with his brother, who was an amateur actor; and at fifteen he played Henry VI in an amateur production on the stage that later became the Abbey Theatre. He also played in Boucicault's "The Shaughraun" in a professional cast in which he replaced a regular actor.

Using odd sheets of paper of different sizes that he picked up here and there and ink that he made, he also wrote three plays that he submitted to the Abbey. They were all rejected. But they compelled the Abbey management to take an interest in this strange workman with an independent point of view. O'Casey had attended performances at the Abbey only twice, once to see Shaw's "Androcles and the Lion." "Not far from being a good play," the Abbey management said about the first one that O'Casey had submitted. Lady Gregory, a wonderful woman who was one of O'Casey's three heroines (his mother and his wife being the other two), told him after reading his third play: "I believe there is something in you, and your strong point is characterization." If it had not been for W. B. Yeats, who was the most powerful voice in the council, the Abbey might have produced the third play, which was called "The Crimson and the Tri-Color."

O'Casey's fourth play, "The Shadow of a Gunman," was produced by the Abbey in 1923 when O'Casey was forty-three years of age and supporting himself as a common laborer. The next play, produced in 1924, was "Juno and the Paycock," which is a world classic; and the third was produced in 1926, "The Plough and the Stars," also a classic and, in my opinion, O'Casey's finest play. Those two roaring plays are steeped in the Irish tenement life that O'Casey had known intimately all his life with its poverty, irresponsibility, temperament, kindness, treachery and civil war; the characters exude vitality, and the dialogue is racy, pungent, and comic. Certain phrases from "Juno and the Paycock" have become part of our literary currency—Captain Boyle's repeated remark that "the whole world's in a terrible state of chassis"; and Joxer's shiftless adjective "darlin'," as in "A darlin' funeral, a daarlin' funeral" or "a darlin' song, a daarlin' song." Mrs. Tancred's scream of agony is another famous and piercing speech: "Sacred Heart o' the Crucified Jesus, take away our hearts o' stone . . . and give us hearts o' flesh! . . . Take away this murdherin' hate . . . an' give us Thine eternal love!"

When those two plays were first produced and were acted also in other parts of the world O'Casey became famous and successful. Although he continued writing for thirty-five years, none of his later plays had the impact of those two. Eventually he came to resent the fact that he was most widely known as the author of those two early plays, and many years later he said that they would survive only as historical documents and that "Cock-a-Doodle Dandy," written in 1949 when he was sixty-nine years old, was his best play. Despite the variety, vitality, high aspirations and originality of most of the later plays, "Juno and the Paycock" and "The Plough and the Stars" in my opinion retain the highest rank because of the comic extravagance of the dialogue, the mercurial temperament of the characters, and the earthiness of the themes. The plays leaped fresh out of O'Casey's daily experience. Given the liveliness of his own personality, he could never be dull or prosaic. But when he left Ireland in self-imposed exile in 1926 he left the environment that had fed his mind and stimulated his spirit for forty-six years. He also left a band of Irish actors whose speech and gusto have not been equaled. For the rest of his professional life O'Casey needed actors as exuberant as Arthur Sinclair, Barry Fitzgerald, F. J. Mc-Cormick, Arthur Shields, Maire O'Neill, Sara Allgood, Eileen Crowe and the other lively members of that matchless company. When O'Casey was writing his later plays—particularly "Cock-a-Doodle Dandy"—it seems to me that he was still hearing in his mind those lilting voices that could transmute temperamental remarks into explosive comedy or tragedy. If most of the later plays are difficult to act, it is because that unique band of actors is no longer in existence.

O'Casey had created an unhackneyed and non-academic style of theatre. From reading Shakespeare, from acting in Boucicault and, let us not forget, out of his own vivid talent, he had learned how to combine comedy and tragedy into a single instrument. "I tell you, life is not one thing but many things, a wide branching flame, grand and good to see, dazzling to the eye of no-one loving it," says Ayamonn in the autobiographical "Red Roses for Me." Some traditionalists, like T. S. Eliot, regarded O'Casey's intuitive style as an impure art form of which they disapproved. Some complained that the plays were so diffuse that they could not understand what O'Casey was getting at or on which side he stood. All his life he was condescended to by traditional academicians. But theatre-goers all over the world have never had any difficulty in understanding and appreciating "Juno and the Paycock" and "The Plough and the Stars," which are intensifications of experience and part of the vernacular of the theatre.

In 1928 O'Casey wrote "The Silver Tassie." Nothing was the same for him after that. Labeled a tragi-comedy, it is a play about the price the common people have to pay for the cruelty and stupidity of war. Of the four acts three continue the familiar liveliness of the O'Casey style. The second act is a sketch of battlefields written in the expressionistic style of chants and dance movement. Since "Juno and the Paycock" and "The Plough and the Stars" saved the Abbey Theatre from bankruptcy, O'Casey had a right to expect the Abbey to stage his next play. But it did not. In an insufferably patronizing and belittling letter, Yeats said among other things: "You have no subject. You are not interested in the Great War."

Instead of accepting the rejection humbly, O'Casey turned it into a public scandal that must have been as traumatic an experience for Yeats and the Abbey Theatre council as the rejection had been for him. He always had a talent for making sensational exits on high moral principles. He had resigned from the Council of the Irish Citizen Army when a vote went against him. He emigrated from Ireland in the mood of a martyr; on that occasion he said of himself: "He was a voluntary and settled exile from every creed, from every party and from every literary clique." Now he made reconciliation with the Abbey impossible by the vehemence of his rebuke to Yeats. But it seems to me that he was well justified in rejecting Yeats' pompous comments. "The Silver Tassie" is an original drama on an enlightened theme, and its point of view is civilized and humane. Bernard Shaw thought highly of "The Silver Tassie": "What a hell of a play!" he exclaimed enthusiastically. After seeing the London production the next year, Lady Gregory wrote in her journal: "I am convinced we ought to have taken it and done our best to put it on and make such cuts of the bad language as he would allow." Yeats later admitted that the rejection was a mistake. "The Silver Tassie" states forcefully the evangelical point of view that became the basic theme of the rest of O'Casey's life.

In his next play, "Within the Gates" (1933) he took the deep plunge into a dramatic form that was the equivalent of allegory—part dance, part song, nearer to ballet and music than to the simpler form of his early plays. Now he was trying to deal less with people than with philosophical essences. "The closer we approach to actual life, the further we move away from the drama," he wrote in 1934 when "Within the Gates" was acted in New York. "If a play is what it ought to be it must be a religious function, whether it is played before a community of thousands or a community of ten." Although "Within the Gates" sets the theatre some serious problems in staging, it is worth the effort. There is an abundance of mercy and compassion in this complex morality play, as illustrated by the poignant character of the Bishop. What the Bishop learns about life is tender and humiliating. Although "Within the Gates" has a pagan exterior, it has a religious code of values. O'Casey is against cant, sanctimoniousness, arbitrariness, and everything that diminishes the energy and scope of life—everything that inhibits "dancing in the gold and purple pavilions of laburnum and lilac" which represented the beauty of life to him.

"Red Roses for Me" (published in 1942; produced in 1943) is a beautifully written drama with interpolated songs and dances that in large part tells O'Casey's own story in terms of romantic tragedy. "Purple Dust" (published in 1940; produced in 1944) is one of his most popular plays. It makes satiric comedy out of the loutishness of Irish peasants and the superciliousness of some wealthy Britishers. Since the form is simple, this play is easy to act.

"Cock-a-Doodle Dandy" is the best constructed of the plays written in a fantastic style. Against a background of quarrelsome Irish men, impulsive Irish women and the inevitable parish priest with his obsequious followers, O'Casey created the mythic figure of the Cock to represent the joyful spirit of life and to draw an invidious comparison with the avarice, fears, superstition and callousness of human beings. When it was produced in London in 1959, Granville Barker (son of the illustrious theatre man who admired "The Silver Tassie") wrote some admiring comments: "A rollicking fantasy that burns with compassion and crackles with wit." In both form and theme it represents the tremendous vitality of O'Casey's spirit and his unequaled gift for shining language. I saw this play in a production that could not express the buoyancy and the virtuosity of the script. But "Cock-a-Doodle Dandy" need not remain a victim of the theatre's literal-mindedness. Some director with access to a first-rate acting company (as Peter Brook had in the British company that played "Marat/de Sade") could make something gay and glorious out of this text. It has certain deficiencies. In comparison with "Juno and the Paycock" and "The Plough and the Stars" it shows O'Casey's increasing preoccupation with ideas rather than people. He was becoming the teacher instead of the poet. The characters are symbols rather than people. But in view of the literary vitality, humane principle, and melodious language of the play, the burden of proof is on the theatre. Although the comedians of the Abbey Theatre are no longer in existence, some troupe ought to be able to act "Cock-a-Doodle Dandy" eloquently.

O'Casey wrote two more full length plays—"The Bishop's Bonfire" (produced in 1955), and "The Drums of Father Ned" (produced in 1959). "The Bishop's Bonfire" makes rowdy comedy out of the loutishness of some Irish people after the style of "Purple Dust." Published under the rubric of

"A Sad Play Within the Tune of a Polka," it lampoons the stuffiness of formal religion. When it was produced in Dublin at the Gaiety Theatre it extracted more venom than usual from the Dublin critics and disturbed some members of the audience. But it was a solid success that showed how much interest the Irish people still took in their pugnacious emigré who invariably gave them a good thumping. O'Casey's whooping rejoinder to the outcries of the Irish critics appears in this book.

"The Drums of Father Ned," which O'Casey described as "This comedy's but an idle, laughing play/About things encumbering Ireland's way," became as much a cause célèbre as "The Silver Tassie," although for a different reason. It was to have been part of the Dublin International Theatre Festival during the Tostal celebration of 1958; a play made from Joyce's "Ulysses" was to have been a companion piece. But several months before the festival was to open, the Archbishop of Dublin announced that he would not perform the Votive Mass if plays by O'Casey and Joyce were to be acted. Since this was tantamount to a boycott of the Tostal by the most powerful man in Dublin, the Council hastily rejected "The Drums of Father Ned," as well as "Ulysses." Not to be outdone by a bishop, O'Casey put a resounding ban on further performances of his plays in Ireland—on the stage or radio. He could hurl a thunderbolt as fiercely as anyone.

"The Drums of Father Ned" would have been particularly appropriate because it makes comedy out of some harum-scarum antics at a Tostal festival. Father Ned, who does not appear in the play, beats a drum in support of a more joyous Ireland than Church or state permit. The young people, in whom O'Casey always had a mystic faith, take the festival away from their cautious elders and put their hearts and shoulders into feats of merriment. "Lassies an' lads, it's time to go, for more life, more laughter, a sturdier spirit and a stronger heart," says the mayor's exuberant though incorrigible son. "Father Ned is on the march."

In addition to the full-length plays O'Casey wrote fifteen one-act plays. "Bedtime Story" is the only one included in this book. He discarded the earliest one-acts from his collected works; presumably he did not regard them as up to the standard to which he aspired. Many of the one-acts are knock-about pieces like the small plays that used to be called "curtain-raisers." They are examples of O'Casey's fondness for the hearty laugh of theatrical enjoyment. In 1961, when he was eighty-one years of age, he published three short plays under the title of the first play—"Behind the Green Curtains." Written in three scenes, "Behind the Green Curtains" is another broadside attack on the joylessness of Ireland under the thumbs of the Church and religious bigots. "Catholics, Protestants and you unbelievers seem to be frightened fools," says the most generous-hearted woman in the play.

The second play, "Figuro in the Night," is a harlequinade directed at what O'Casey calls "The Ferocious Chastity of Ireland,"—entertaining to read, difficult to stage. "The Moon Shines on Kylenamoe" is a one-act skit that contrasts the self-assurance of a British bureaucrat with the suspicion, animosity, and malice of some Irish country people.

All these three last plays convey the wholesomeness of O'Casey's mind, the ingenuity of his imagination, and the brightness of his spirit. Although they lack the sustained mockery of "Bedtime Story," they express the extraordinary grace of his old age. His eyesight was fading so fast that he had to be read to and his health was infirm. But the spirit that began in a Dublin tenement remained indomitable.

I have left to the last my comments on O'Casey's only humorless play— "The Star Turns Red," which was put on by a left-wing group in London in 1940. It was O'Casey's salute to Communism. From an artistic point of view it is dogmatic and sterile, like most party-line plays. But it has one significant factor: again there are religious undertones, or so it seems to me: "The star turned red is still the star of him who came as a man's pure prince of peace," says one of the characters in the last act of this apocalyptic play. O'Casey's Communism should be discussed because it was just about as original in form as "Within the Gates" or "Cock-a-Doodle Dandy." There was less of political Communism in it than O'Casey's personal rebelliousness and humanitarianism. Jesus was a Communist, by O'Casey's standards. In his opinion Keats, Shelley, and Dickens were Communists; so was Whitman, and just about anyone he admired. "Any man who is honest and gives all he can to the community is a Communist," O'Casey said. When his children were growing up he once remarked to me: "I am not trying to convert them to Communism. I don't think anyone has the right to try to control the minds of his children. I urge them to make up their own minds. But, of course, I'm hoping that they will turn out to be Communists."

Since he made this comment during one of the most frigid moments of the Cold War when Great Britain and the United States were almost hysterically anti-Communist, the remark seemed to me comically eccentric. Because I could never take his Communism seriously, I wondered if his children could, since they represent a skeptical generation. I asked his daughter, Shivaun, what she thought. His Communism did not seem eccentric to her. "Sean was a humanitarian, a Communist and a pure spirit," she replied. "He saw a long way into the future and saw things improving all the time. . . . I miss talking to him now; it seems as if a great piece of life and knowledge has gone." She added that "he knew very well what was happening in Russia and China, and saw that his ideals were being arrived at quicker there than in other countries, particularly the capitalistic ones." In O'Casey's home, familiarity bred love and devotion.

But I am a member of the skeptical generation on this issue. O'Casey was never a member of the Communist Party. I think his non-membership in a party he actively supported was significant. It indicated not only his fundamental independence, but also his congenital distrust of any organization that required so much discipline, whether it was a political party or the Roman Catholic Church. He was incapable of accepting discipline from any external source. There is not much about Lenin or Stalin in his comments on Communism.

Never a man to do anything by halves, he supported Communism uncritically. He wrote articles for the *London Daily Worker* until his eyesight made it necessary to reduce his writing commitments. Although he never went to Moscow he proclaimed it his Holy City with the jubilance of a convert. He paid homage to Moscow as "a flame to light the way of all men towards the people's ownership of the earth; where revolution stands in man's holy fire, and in the rich mosaic of a red wall." In what he wrote for the *New Times* in Moscow his style could be uncharacteristically humble; he accepted Communist propaganda as reality. He denied that there was censorship in Russia because, as he pointed out, it was not mentioned in the "History of the Communist Party." He grandly dismissed as a bore a disillusioned British woman who told him that when she and her husband were working in some Commissariat in Moscow her husband was picked up by the OGPU and disappeared permanently. O'Casey concluded that probably her husband had taken this portentous way of escaping from a wife he couldn't stand any longer.

After "The Star Turns Red" O'Casey never wrote another propaganda play, although there is a self-righteous Communist in "Oak Leaves and Lavender," which is otherwise an amusing play about some of the crotchets of the home life of England during World War II. With the exception of "The Star Turns Red" and "Oak Leaves and Lavender," it seems to me that O'Casey abided by his own philosophy: "As a man the revolutionist playwright is much the same as the drama critic: he has to get better from an illness by sending for a doctor; his personal problems cannot be solved by a constant reading of the Communist Manifesto; so when he's writing a play, the dramatist is neither Tory nor Communist, but only a playwright, setting down his characters as he knew them, giving, if he can, added depth, height and lilt to the words he makes them speak."

O'Casey's Communism had a flamboyant style. But it must have perplexed orthodox Communists. As usual, he made his own rules and preserved his personal independence.

III

In 1939, when he and his family were living in Totnes, Devon, and he was still writing plays, O'Casey published the first volume of his autobiography, "I Knock at the Door," which chronicled the first ten years of his life in Dublin. It is a masterpiece of recollection, mood, perception and writing. Before he finished the autobiography in 1954, he had written six volumes. In "Sean O'Casey, the Man and His Work," which is the best book on the subject, David Krause has described the time spans of the various volumes as follows: "I Knock at the Door" (1939) 1880–1890; "Pictures in the Hallway" (1942) 1891–1904; "Drums Under the Windows" (1946) 1905–1916; "Inishfallen, Fare Thee Well" (1949) 1916–1926; "Rose and Crown" (1952) 1926–1934; "Sunset and Evening Star" (1954) 1934–1953. In 1956 the six volumes were collected in two volumes and published under the generic title of "Mirror in My House."

The autobiographies are not an orderly record of O'Casey's life, complete with names, dates, and records. They are offered as a conscious work of art. O'Casey tells the story of his life in terms of a grand myth, like Joyce's "Ulysses," and, in some elusive manner, the Old Testament, as if his own life were a footnote to the mythology of mankind, part of the "sad, sweet silent music of humanity." In the early volumes the chief character is called Johnny Casside, but he becomes Sean O'Casside in the third volume and finally Sean O'Casey. The chronology is often confusing. The author repeatedly returns to scenes that he has left, or he anticipates other scenes without explanation. He is concerned, not with facts, but with the vicissitudes and wonders of life.

Although the autobiographies are primarily concerned with basic subjects, like children, homes, schools, debts, people, pubs, theatres, history, they are written in a key of high emotion by a man caught up in the ecstasy of words—long, rushing sentences that describe a wide range of human experience. The point of view is detached, as if the volumes were fiction, but the style is overwhelmingly personal. Some of it is fantastically comic; some of it is fiercely proud; some of it explodes with anger. It is also, I think, a lonely book by a man separated from the centers of activity and recalling with nostalgia things that happened long ago.

The first two volumes of the autobiographies have been very successfully recast into the form of stage readings by Paul Shyre, an American admirer of O'Casey, and brilliantly staged by Stuart Vaughan. Sitting behind lecterns on plain stages, some of the most talented American actors have on several occasions created memorable evenings by reading sections of "I Knock at the Door" and "Pictures in the Hallway." Arranged in a simple, classical form, the stage readings have turned out to be tender and comic in the best style of O'Casey. The autobiographies are also the basic material from which a film about O'Casey, "Young Cassidy," was made in 1965. Since the part of O'Casey was acted by a vigorous, swashbuckling young man, Rod Taylor, the film did not have much literal resemblance to the autobiographies.

As Mrs. Gogan says in "The Plough and the Stars": "There's always the makin's of a row in th' mention of religion," and religion keeps cropping up throughout the autobiographies. Men of the cloth receive a lot of attention—the Reverend E. M. Griffin, whom O'Casey revered second only to his mother in his youth and whose photograph is the frontispiece to the third volume; also, Dr. Michael O'Hickey and Dr. Walter McDonald, both of whom defied their ecclesiastical superiors on matters of principle and in the O'Casey lexicon became martyrs. Only a religious man who had lost the innocence of his youthful faith could take such an evangelical interest in religion as O'Casey did. It is, incidentally, significant that he dedicated "The Drums of Father Ned" to the memories of five priests, all of whom defied the Church in some act of insubordination. O'Casey admired them. Gestures of defiance usually won O'Casey's approval. He was a veteran in that field.

IV

In his last years Sean O'Casey was a thin man, with sharp features, lusterless eyes, a fighting jaw, an entrancing Irish voice and a gay spirit. He lived a warm and intimate family life in the third floor flat of a house on a hill in Torquay, Devon. Although the flat was small it was brightly decorated. Perhaps because of his impaired vision, he liked brilliant colors, and took particular pleasure in the decoration of all the places where he lived, including his room in the Dublin tenement. The bright colors extended to his dress. When Shivaun was eight years old she made a gaily-colored cap or "beanie" for him at school—yellow, red, and navy blue. Since the cap kept O'Casey's head warm in winter he continued to wear it. Shivaun made him three or four more, and then people all over the world sent him so many bizarrely decorated caps that he soon had a large collection and could choose a cap to fit his mood every day. Out of a Mexican blanket, Shivaun also made him a red house coat that he wore in the cold weather. He had always worn jerseys and sweaters, but when he married, Eileen introduced him to the turtle-necked sweater, which became the badge of his tribe—the working man. As he stumbled cautiously around the flat, smoking Evinmore tobacco in a battered pipe, he looked like a cross between a chief rabbi and a giddy bishop.

To say that he was fortunate in his family life would be to imply that

he was not primarily responsible for it. But he was. Family came first in his order of values. In 1927 when he was forty-seven years of age, he married Eileen Reynolds Carey, who was then in her early twenties and was playing Nora in a London production of "The Plough and the Stars." He was or had been a Protestant; she was a Catholic, and they were married by a Catholic priest. His marriage was about the best thing that ever happened to him. When they married he was famous as author of "Juno and the Paycock" and "The Plough and the Stars." He had reason to assume that the rest of his life would be equally exciting and profitable, and his bride was also well established in her own right as an actress. She lived in a comfortable flat of her own.

Their life did not turn out to be as bountiful as they probably expected. They had hardly married before the angry controversy over "The Silver Tassie" broke out, and O'Casey was in serious financial trouble almost at once. But Eileen, an attractive woman with great strength and force of character, was equal to every crisis the family had to cope with for the rest of their lives. They had three children—Breon, born in 1928, Niall, born in 1936 (died in 1956) and Shivaun, born in 1939. (O'Casey's poignant requiem to Niall, "Under a Greenwood Tree," appears in this volume.) If O'Casey and his wife had been complaisant people they could probably have organized a secure professional life in the theatre world of London. Both of them were talented and well known. But after a few years of moving from one flat to another they left London and settled down in Totnes, Devon, to be near Dartington Hall School where the children were educated. Children outranked career in the family code of values.

During these years when he was writing plays and his autobiographies he also wrote innumerable essays, articles, stories and poems which are collected in four of his most caustic volumes: "The Flying Wasp" (1937), "The Green Crow" (1956), "Under a Colored Cap" (1963) and "Blasts and Benedictions" (1967, posthumous). In "The Green Crow" he observed that some Latin writer once said that "If a crow could feed in quiet, it would have more meat." He added that he, who came to be known as The Green Crow, would doubtless have had more meat if he had kept his "big beak shut." But he could never back away from a fight. The words, the epithets, the derision flew in all directions, and most people ran for cover.

The frontispiece of the original edition of "Pictures in the Hallway" consists of a studio photograph of O'Casey in his twenties. Neatly attired in gray trousers and a dark vest and jacket, his hands in his trousers pockets, the pugnacious Gaelic Leaguer lounges on a carved studio table and takes a cocky look into the eye of the camera. Very grand; very sure of himself; everything is there except the humor, which made all the difference between a bore and a great humanitarian. The frontispiece of the original edition of "The Bishop's Bonfire" is a black-and-white reproduction of Breon O'Casey's painting of his father. In his old age, under a capacious round field hat, holding an open book in his left hand, O'Casey has the stern look of a reproachful prophet. Again, the humor is missing. But the humor is of fundamental importance. Humor indicates an acceptance of the imperfection of life; humor is the adjustment to human realities. All his life O'Casey professed to be surprised when people took exception to his fulminations. For he was personally a modest man. His attitude towards life and his conception of his place in it are well expressed in a letter he wrote to Harold Macmillan, his friend and publisher, in 1951:

"I cannot expect, nor do I expect, that everyone should like and agree with my 'judgment.' I don't think 'judgment' to be the right word about what I state or seem to imply in play or biography. They are opinions only; honest ones, taken after thought and long and wide experience of men and things; but they are, for all that, far from being infallible. Only God or Time can vindicate the judgment of man. To me one thing alone is certain—we are all one in the tremendous and glorious bond of humanity. Jew, Gentile, bond and free, Tory and Communist can never break away from this grand bond. We are born, we die and we must do the best we can between the day of birth and the night of death."

When he reached his eighties his vision had deteriorated so rapidly that he could see nothing except the difference between light and dark. "All the hundreds of books around me are dumb," he said, though without self-pity. Now he was totally dependent on others to read to him; and chiefly on Eileen, who was everything to him, even more than she had been before. The width of his life contracted accordingly. In better days they had read the *London Daily Worker* and *The Times* of London every day, and frequently the *Manchester Guardian,* and they had subscribed to two Irish newspapers. When he could no longer read they reduced the daily newspapers to *The Times* and one Dublin paper. Those were all Eileen had time to read in addition to parts of books and articles in periodicals that contained things he wanted to know about. He depended on the radio for daily news.

But he never surrendered. He remembered that Beethoven wrote his greatest symphonies when he was deaf; that Prescott was half-blind when he wrote "History of the Conquest of Mexico" and that Renoir went on painting when he was so rheumatic that he had to tie the brush to his hand. O'Casey kept on learning about music and other things by listening to instructive programs on BBC radio. He never considered himself too old to be instructed about anything from any source. Although he had plenty of pride he was never too proud to learn something new. As he went swirling (his word) around the streets of the St. Marychurch part of Torquay, the beauties and complexities of life astounded him. It seemed to him that life was so fantastic that writers and artists did not need to invent anything more remarkable.

A little less than a month before he died he wrote a mocking condemnation of the theatre of cruelty under the sardonic title "The Bald Primaqueera," which was a parody of the title of Eugène Ionesco's "The Bald Prima Donna." It is included in this book. The prose style of O'Casey's epilogue is a little labored, as if he were pushing himself just beyond his strength; the style does not have the reverberant energy of "Bonfire Under a Black Sun" (which is also included in this book). But his faith in life is as sweet and exultant as ever. Still hating the nay-sayers, he still believes in the basic goodness of humanity. He continues to translate everything and everybody out of the tiny particular into the grand mythology of life which he still loved and revered.

Over the forty-six years of his literary career the quality of his writing was uneven. Although he wrote the most glorious English of his era—the English nearest in color and strength to the Elizabethan—the content did not always support the imagery. But he was creative and imaginative and he was spiritually alive until the last moment. He had the moral courage of an idealist. Whatever his religious ideas may have been, I think God had reason to be proud of Sean O'Casey.

BROOKS ATKINSON

plAys

JUNO AND THE PAYCOCK

A Tragedy in Three Acts

(1924)

✤ ✤ ✤

CHARACTERS IN THE PLAY

"Captain" Jack Boyle
Juno Boyle, *his wife*
Johnny Boyle ⎱
Mary Boyle ⎰ *their children*
"Joxer" Daly
Mrs. Maisie Madigan
"Needle" Nugent, *a tailor*
Mrs. Tancred

⎱ *Residents in the Tenement*

Jerry Devine
Charles Bentham, *a school teacher*
An Irregular Mobilizer
Two Irregulars
A Coal-block Vendor
A Sewing Machine Man
Two Furniture Removal Men
Two Neighbours

SCENE

ACT I · The living apartment of a two-roomed tenancy of the Boyle family, in a tenement house in Dublin.

ACT II · The same.

ACT III · The same.

A few days elapse between Acts I and II, and two months between Acts II and III.

During Act III the curtain is lowered for a few minutes to denote the lapse of one hour.

Period of the play, 1922.

ACT I

The living-room of a two-room tenancy occupied by the Boyle family in a tenement house in Dublin. Left, a door leading to another part of the house; left of door a window looking into the street; at back a dresser; farther to right at back, a window looking into the back of the house. Between the window and the dresser is a picture of the Virgin; below the picture, on a bracket, is a crimson bowl in which a floating votive light is burning. Farther to the right is a small bed partly concealed by cretonne hangings strung on a twine. To the right is the fireplace; near the fireplace is a door leading to the other room. Beside the fireplace is a box containing coal. On the mantelshelf is an alarm clock lying on its face. In a corner near the window looking into the back is a galvanized bath. A table and some chairs. On the table are breakfast things for one. A teapot is on the hob and a frying-pan stands inside the fender. There are a few books on the dresser and one on the table. Leaning against the dresser is a long-handled shovel— the kind invariably used by labourers when turning concrete or mixing mortar. Johnny Boyle is sitting crouched beside the fire. Mary with her jumper off—it is lying on the back of a chair—is arranging her hair before a tiny mirror perched on the table. Beside the mirror is stretched out the morning paper, which she looks at when she isn't gazing into the mirror. She is a well-made and good-looking girl of twenty-two. Two forces are working in her mind—one, through the circumstances of her life, pulling her back; the other, through the influence of books she has read, pushing her forward. The opposing forces are apparent in her speech and her manners, both of which are degraded by her environment, and improved by her acquaintance—slight though it be—with literature. The time is early forenoon.

Mary [*looking at the paper*].   On a little bye-road, out beyant Finglas, he was found.

> [*Mrs. Boyle enters by door on right; she has been shopping and carries a small parcel in her hand. She is forty-five years of age, and twenty years ago she must have been a pretty woman; but her face has now assumed that look which ultimately settles down upon the faces of the women of the working-class; a look of listless monotony and harassed anxiety, blending with an expression of mechanical resistance. Were circumstances favourable, she would probably be a handsome, active and clever woman.*

Mrs. Boyle.   Isn't he come in yet?

Mary.   No, mother.

Mrs. Boyle.   Oh, he'll come in when he likes; struttin' about the town like a paycock with Joxer, I suppose. I hear all about Mrs. Tancred's son is in this mornin's paper.

Mary. The full details are in it this mornin'; seven wounds he had—one entherin' the neck, with an exit wound beneath the left shoulder-blade; another in the left breast penethratin' the heart, an' . . .

Johnny [*springing up from the fire*]. Oh, quit that readin', for God's sake! Are yous losin' all your feelin's? It'll soon be that none of you'll read anythin' that's not about butcherin'!

[*He goes quickly into the room on left.*]

Mary. He's gettin' very sensitive, all of a sudden!

Mrs. Boyle. I'll read it myself, Mary, by an' by, when I come home. Everybody's sayin' that he was a Diehard—thanks be to God that Johnny had nothin' to do with him this long time. . . . [*Opening the parcel and taking out some sausages, which she places on a plate*] Ah, then, if that father o' yours doesn't come in soon for his breakfast, he may go without any; I'll not wait much longer for him.

Mary. Can't you let him get it himself when he comes in?

Mrs. Boyle. Yes, an' let him bring in Joxer Daly along with him? Ay, that's what he'd like, an' that's what he's waitin' for—till he thinks I'm gone to work, an' then sail in with the boul' Joxer, to burn all the coal an' dhrink all the tea in the place, to show them what a good Samaritan he is! But I'll stop here till he comes in, if I have to wait till to-morrow mornin'.

Voice of Johnny inside. Mother!

Mrs. Boyle. Yis?

Voice of Johnny. Bring us in a dhrink o' wather.

Mrs. Boyle. Bring in that fella a dhrink o' wather, for God's sake, Mary.

Mary. Isn't he big an' able enough to come out an' get it himself?

Mrs. Boyle. If you weren't well yourself you'd like somebody to bring you in a dhrink o' wather. [*She brings in drink and returns.*]

Mrs. Boyle. Isn't it terrible to have to be waitin' this way! You'd think he was bringin' twenty poun's a week into the house the way he's going on. He wore out the Health Insurance long ago, he's afther wearin' out the unemployment dole, an', now, he's thryin' to wear out me! An' constantly singin', no less, when he ought always to be on his knees offerin' up a Novena for a job!

Mary [*tying a ribbon fillet-wise around her head*]. I don't like this ribbon, ma; I think I'll wear the green—it looks betther than the blue.

Mrs. Boyle. Ah, wear whatever ribbon you like, girl, only don't be botherin' me. I don't know what a girl on strike wants to be wearin' a ribbon round her head for, or silk stockins on her legs either; it's wearin' them things that make the employers think they're givin' yous too much money.

Mary. The hour is past now when we'll ask the employers' permission to wear what we like.

Mrs. Boyle. I don't know why you wanted to walk out for Jennie Claffey; up to this you never had a good word for her.

Mary. What's the use of belongin' to a Trades Union if you won't stand up for your principles? Why did they sack her? It was a clear case of victimization. We couldn't let her walk the streets, could we?

Mrs. Boyle. No, of course yous couldn't—yous wanted to keep her company. Wan victim wasn't enough. When the employers sacrifice wan victim, the Trades Unions go wan betther be sacrificin' a hundred.

Mary. It doesn't matther what you say, ma—a principle's a principle.

Mrs. Boyle. Yis; an' when I go into oul' Murphy's tomorrow, an' he gets to know that, instead o' payin' all, I'm goin' to borry more, what'll he say when I tell him a principle's a principle? What'll we do if he refuses to give us any more on tick?

Mary. He daren't refuse—if he does, can't you tell him he's paid?

Mrs. Boyle. It's lookin' as if he was paid, whether he refuses or no.

> [*Johnny appears at the door on left. He can be plainly seen now; he is a thin, delicate fellow, something younger than Mary. He has evidently gone through a rough time. His face is pale and drawn; there is a tremulous look of indefinite fear in his eyes. The left sleeve of his coat is empty, and he walks with a slight halt.*

Johnny. I was lyin' down; I thought yous were gone. Oul' Simon Mackay is thrampin' about like a horse over me head, an' I can't sleep with him— they're like thunder-claps in me brain! The curse o'—God forgive me for goin' to curse!

Mrs. Boyle. There, now; go back an' lie down again, an' I'll bring you in a nice cup o' tay.

Johnny. Tay, tay, tay! You're always thinkin' o' tay. If a man was dyin', you'd thry to make him swally a cup o' tay! [*He goes back.*

Mrs. Boyle. I don't know what's goin' to be done with him. The bullet he got in the hip in Easter Week was bad enough, but the bomb that shatthered his arm in the fight in O'Connell Street put the finishin' touch on him. I knew he was makin' a fool of himself. God knows I went down on me bended knees to him not to go agen the Free State.

Mary. He stuck to his principles, an', no matther how you may argue, ma, a principle's a principle.

Voice of Johnny. Is Mary goin' to stay here?

Mary. No, I'm not goin' to stay here; you can't expect me to be always at your beck an' call, can you?

Voice of Johnny. I won't stop here be myself!

Mrs. Boyle. Amn't I nicely handicapped with the whole o' yous! I don't know what any o' yous ud do without your ma. [*To Johnny*] Your father'll be here in a minute, an' if you want anythin', he'll get it for you.

Johnny. I hate assin' him for anythin'. . . . He hates to be assed to stir. . . . Is the light lightin' before the picture o' the Virgin?

Mrs. Boyle. Yis, yis! The wan inside to St. Anthony isn't enough, but he must have another wan to the Virgin here!

> [*Jerry Devine enters hastily. He is about twenty-five, well set, active and earnest. He is a type, becoming very common now in the Labour Movement, of a mind knowing enough to make the mass of his associates, who know less, a power, and too little to broaden that power for the benefit of all. Mary seizes her jumper and runs hastily into room left.*

Jerry [*breathless*]. Where's the Captain, Mrs. Boyle, where's the Captain?

Mrs. Boyle. You may well ass a body that: he's wherever Joxer Daly is— dhrinkin' in some snug or another.

Jerry. Father Farrell is just afther stoppin' to tell me to run up an' get him to go to the new job that's goin' on in Rathmines; his cousin is foreman o' the job, an' Father Farrell was speakin' to him about poor Johnny an' his father bein' idle so long, an' the foreman told Father Farrell to send the Captain up an' he'd give him a start—I wondher where I'd find him?

Mrs. Boyle. You'll find he's ayther in Ryan's or Foley's.

Jerry. I'll run round to Ryan's—I know it's a great house o' Joxer's.

> [*He rushes out.*

Mrs. Boyle [*piteously*]. There now, he'll miss that job, or I know for what! If he gets win' o' the word, he'll not come back till evenin', so that it'll be too late. There'll never be any good got out o' him so long as he goes with that shouldher-shruggin' Joxer. I killin' meself workin', an' he sthruttin' about from mornin' till night like a paycock!

> [*The steps of two persons are heard coming up a flight of stairs. They are the footsteps of Captain Boyle and Joxer. Captain Boyle is singing in a deep, sonorous, self-honouring voice.*

The Captain. Sweet Spirit, hear me prayer! Hear . . . oh . . . hear . . . me prayer . . . hear, oh, hear . . . Oh, he . . . ar . . . oh, he . . . ar . . . me . . . pray . . . er!

Joxer [*outside*]. Ah, that's a darlin' song, a daaarlin' song!

Mrs. Boyle [*viciously*]. Sweet spirit hear his prayer! Ah, then, I'll take me solemn affeydavey, it's not for a job he's prayin'!

> [*She sits down on the bed so that the cretonne hangings hide her from the view of those entering.*
> [*The Captain comes slowly in. He is a man of about sixty; stout, grey-haired and stocky. His neck is short, and his head looks like a stone ball that one sometimes sees on top of a gate-post. His cheeks, reddish-purple, are puffed out, as if he were always repressing an almost irrepressible ejaculation. On his upper lip is a crisp, tightly cropped moustache; he carries himself with the upper part of his body slightly thrown back, and his stomach slightly thrust forward. His walk is a slow, consequential strut. His clothes are dingy, and he wears a faded seaman's-cap with a glazed peak.*

Boyle [*to Joxer, who is still outside*]. Come on, come on in, Joxer; she's gone out long ago, man. If there's nothing else to be got, we'll furrage out a cup o' tay, anyway. It's the only bit I get in comfort when she's away. 'Tisn't Juno should be her pet name at all, but Deirdre of the Sorras, for she's always grousin'.

> [*Joxer steps cautiously into the room. He may be younger than the Captain but he looks a lot older. His face is like a bundle of crinkled paper; his eyes have a cunning twinkle; he is spare and loosely built; he has a habit of constantly shrugging his shoulders with a peculiar twitching movement, meant to be ingratiating. His face is invariably ornamented with a grin.*

Joxer. It's a terrible thing to be tied to a woman that's always grousin'. I don't know how you stick it—it ud put years on me. It's a good job she has to be so ofen away, for [*with a shrug*] when the cat's away, the mice can play!

Boyle [*with a commanding and complacent gesture*]. Pull over to the fire, Joxer, an' we'll have a cup o' tay in a minute.

Joxer. Ah, a cup o' tay's a darlin' thing, a daaarlin' thing—the cup that cheers but doesn't . . .

> [*Joxer's rhapsody is cut short by the sight of Juno coming forward and confronting the two cronies. Both are stupefied.*

Mrs. Boyle [*with sweet irony—poking the fire, and turning her head to glare at Joxer*]. Pull over to the fire, Joxer Daly, an' we'll have a cup o' tay in a minute! Are you sure, now, you wouldn't like an egg?

Joxer. I can't stop, Mrs. Boyle; I'm in a desperate hurry, a desperate hurry.

Mrs. Boyle. Pull over to the fire, Joxer Daly; people is always far more comfortabler here than they are in their own place.

[*Joxer makes hastily for the door. Boyle stirs to follow him; thinks of something to relieve the situation—stops, and says suddenly*: Joxer!

Joxer [*at door ready to bolt*]. Yis?

Boyle. You know the foreman o' that job that's goin' on down in Killesther, don't you, Joxer?

Joxer [*puzzled*]. Foreman—Killesther?

Boyle [*with a meaning look*]. He's a butty o' yours, isn't he?

Joxer [*the truth dawning on him*]. The foreman at Killesther—oh yis, yis. He's an oul' butty o' mine—oh, he's a darlin' man, a daarlin' man.

Boyle. Oh, then, it's a sure thing. It's a pity we didn't go down at breakfast first thing this mornin'—we might ha' been working now; but you didn't know it then.

Joxer [*with a shrug*]. It's betther late than never.

Boyle. It's nearly time we got a start, anyhow; I'm fed up knockin' round, doin' nothin'. He promised you—gave you the straight tip?

Joxer. Yis. "Come down on the blow o' dinner," says he, "an' I'll start you, an' any friend you like to brin' with you." "Ah," says I, "you're a darlin' man, a daaarlin' man."

Boyle. Well, it couldn't come at a betther time—we're a long time waitin' for it.

Joxer. Indeed we were; but it's a long lane that has no turnin'.

Boyle. The blow up for dinner is at one—wait till I see what time it 'tis.

[*He goes over to the mantelpiece, and gingerly lifts the clock.*

Mrs. Boyle. Min' now, how you go on fiddlin' with that clock—you know the least little thing sets it asthray.

Boyle. The job couldn't come at a betther time; I'm feelin' in great fettle, Joxer. I'd hardly believe I ever had a pain in me legs, an' last week I was nearly crippled with them.

Joxer. That's betther an' betther; ah, God never shut wan door but He opened another!

Boyle. It's only eleven o'clock; we've lashins o' time. I'll slip on me oul' moleskins afther breakfast, an' we can saunther down at our ayse. [*Putting his hand on the shovel*] I think, Joxer, we'd betther bring our shovels?

Joxer. Yis, Captain, yis; it's betther to go fully prepared an' ready for all eventualities. You bring your long-tailed shovel, an' I'll bring me navvy. We mighten' want them, an', then agen, we might: for want of a nail the shoe was lost, for want of a shoe the horse was lost, an' for want of a horse the man was lost—aw, that's a darlin' proverb, a daarlin' . . .

> [*As Joxer is finishing his sentence, Mrs. Boyle approaches the door and Joxer retreats hurriedly. She shuts the door with a bang.*

Boyle [*suggestively*]. We won't be long pullin' ourselves together agen when I'm working for a few weeks.   [*Mrs. Boyle takes no notice.*

Boyle. The foreman on the job is an oul' butty o' Joxer's; I have an idea that I know him meself. [*Silence*] . . . There's a button off the back o' me moleskin trousers. . . . If you leave out a needle an' thread I'll sew it on meself. . . . Thanks be to God, the pains in me legs is gone, anyhow!

Mrs. Boyle [*with a burst*]. Look here, Mr. Jacky Boyle, them yarns won't go down with Juno. I know you an' Joxer Daly of an oul' date, an' if you think you're able to come it over me with them fairy tales, you're in the wrong shop.

Boyle [*coughing subduedly to relieve the tenseness of the situation*]. U-u-u-ugh!

Mrs. Boyle. Butty o' Joxer's! Oh, you'll do a lot o' good as long as you continue to be a butty o' Joxer's!

Boyle. U-u-u-ugh!

Mrs. Boyle. Shovel! Ah, then, me boyo, you'd do far more work with a knife an' fork than ever you'll do with a shovel! If there was e'er a genuine job goin' you'd be dh'other way about—not able to lift your arms with the pains in your legs! Your poor wife slavin' to keep the bit in your mouth, an' you gallivantin' about all the day like a paycock!

Boyle. It ud be betther for a man to be dead, betther for a man to be dead.

Mrs. Boyle [*ignoring the interruption*]. Everybody callin' you "Captain", an' you only wanst on the wather, in an oul' collier from here to Liverpool, when anybody, to listen or look at you, ud take you for a second Christo For Columbus!

Boyle. Are you never goin' to give us a rest?

Mrs. Boyle. Oh, you're never tired o' lookin' for a rest.

Boyle. D'ye want to dhrive me out o' the house?

Mrs. Boyle. It ud be easier to dhrive you out o' the house than to dhrive you into a job. Here, sit down an' take your breakfast—it may be the last you'll get, for I don't know where the next is goin' to come from.

Boyle. If I get this job we'll be all right.

Mrs. Boyle. Did ye see Jerry Devine?

Boyle [*testily*]. No, I didn't see him.

Mrs. Boyle. No, but you seen Joxer. Well, he was here lookin' for you.

Boyle. Well, let him look!

Mrs. Boyle. Oh, indeed, he may well look, for it ud be hard for him to see you, an' you stuck in Ryan's snug.

Boyle. I wasn't in Ryan's snug—I don't go into Ryan's.

Mrs. Boyle. Oh, is there a mad dog there? Well, if you weren't in Ryan's you were in Foley's.

Boyle. I'm telling you for the last three weeks I haven't tasted a dhrop of intoxicatin' liquor. I wasn't in ayther wan snug or dh'other—I could swear that on a prayer-book—I'm as innocent as the child unborn!

Mrs. Boyle. Well, if you'd been in for your breakfast you'd ha' seen him.

Boyle [*suspiciously*]. What does he want me for?

Mrs. Boyle. He'll be back any minute an' then you'll soon know.

Boyle. I'll dhrop out an' see if I can meet him.

Mrs. Boyle. You'll sit down an' take your breakfast, an' let me go to me work, for I'm an hour late already waitin' for you.

Boyle. You needn't ha' waited, for I'll take no breakfast—I've a little spirit left in me still!

Mrs. Boyle. Are you goin' to have your breakfast—yes or no?

Boyle [*too proud to yield*]. I'll have no breakfast—yous can keep your breakfast? [*Plaintively*] I'll knock out a bit somewhere, never fear.

Mrs. Boyle. Nobody's goin' to coax you—don't think that.

[*She vigorously replaces the pan and the sausages in the press.*]

Boyle. I've a little spirit left in me still. [*Jerry Devine enters hastily.*]

Jerry. Oh, here you are at last! I've been searchin' for you everywhere. The foreman in Foley's told me you hadn't left the snug with Joxer ten minutes before I went in.

Mrs. Boyle. An' he swearin' on the holy prayer-book that he wasn't in no snug!

Boyle [*to Jerry*]. What business is it o' yours whether I was in a snug or no? What do you want to be gallopin' about afther me for? Is a man not to be allowed to leave his house for a minute without havin' a pack o' spies, pimps an' informers cantherin' at his heels?

Jerry. Oh, you're takin' a wrong view of it, Mr. Boyle; I simply was anxious to do you a good turn. I have a message for you from Father Farrell: he says that if you go to the job that's on in Rathmines, an' ask for Foreman Managan, you'll get a start.

Boyle. That's all right, but I don't want the motions of me body to be watched the way an asthronomer ud watch a star. If you're folleyin' Mary aself, you've no pereeogative to be folleyin' me. [*Suddenly catching his thigh*] U-ugh, I'm afther gettin' a terrible twinge in me right leg!

Mrs. Boyle. Oh, it won't be very long now till it travels into your left wan. It's miraculous that whenever he scents a job in front of him, his legs begin to fail him! Then, me bucko, if you lose this chance, you may go an' furrage for yourself!

Jerry. This job'll last for some time too, Captain, an' as soon as the foundations are in, it'll be cushy enough.

Boyle. Won't it be a climbin' job? How d'ye expect me to be able to go up a ladder with these legs? An', if I get up aself, how am I goin' to get down agen?

Mrs. Boyle [*viciously*]. Get wan o' the labourers to carry you down in a hod! You can't climb a laddher, but you can skip like a goat into a snug!

Jerry. I wouldn't let myself be let down that easy, Mr. Boyle; a little exercise, now, might do you all the good in the world.

Boyle. It's a docthor you should have been, Devine—maybe you know more about the pains in me legs than meself that has them?

Jerry [*irritated*]. Oh, I know nothin' about the pains in your legs; I've brought the message that Father Farrell gave me, an' that's all I can do.

Mrs. Boyle. Here, sit down an' take your breakfast, an' go an' get ready; an' don't be actin' as if you couldn't pull a wing out of a dead bee.

Boyle. I want no breakfast, I tell you; it ud choke me afther all that's been said. I've a little spirit left in me still.

Mrs. Boyle. Well, let's see your spirit, then, an' go in at wanst an' put on your moleskin trousers!

Boyle [*moving towards the door on left*].   It ud be betther for a man to be dead! U-ugh! There's another twinge in me other leg! Nobody but meself knows the sufferin' I'm goin' through with the pains in these legs o' mine!

> [*He goes into the room on left as Mary comes out with her hat in her hand.*

Mrs. Boyle.   I'll have to push off now, for I'm terrible late already, but I was determined to stay an' hunt that Joxer this time.   [*She goes off.*

Jerry.   Are you going out, Mary?

Mary.   It looks like it when I'm putting on my hat, doesn't it?

Jerry.   The bitther word agen, Mary.

Mary.   You won't allow me to be friendly with you; if I thry, you deliberately misundherstand it.

Jerry.   I didn't always misundherstand it; you were often delighted to have the arms of Jerry around you.

Mary.   If you go on talkin' like this, Jerry Devine, you'll make me hate you!

Jerry.   Well, let it be either a weddin' or a wake! Listen, Mary, I'm standin' for the Secretaryship of our Union. There's only one opposin' me; I'm popular with all the men, an' a good speaker—all are sayin' that I'll get elected.

Mary.   Well?

Jerry.   The job's worth three hundred an' fifty pounds a year, Mary. You an' I could live nice an' cosily on that; it would lift you out o' this place an' . . .

Mary.   I haven't time to listen to you now—I have to go.

> [*She is going out, when Jerry bars the way.*

Jerry [*appealingly*].   Mary, what's come over you with me for the last few weeks? You hardly speak to me, an' then only a word with a face o' bitherness on it. Have you forgotten, Mary, all the happy evenins that were as sweet as the scented hawthorn that sheltered the sides o' the road as we saunthered through the country?

Mary.   That's all over now. When you get your new job, Jerry, you won't be long findin' a girl far betther than I am for your sweetheart.

Jerry.   Never, never, Mary! No matther what happens, you'll always be the same to me.

Mary.   I must be off; please let me go, Jerry.

Jerry. I'll go a bit o' the way with you.

Mary. You needn't, thanks; I want to be by meself.

Jerry [*catching her arm*]. You're goin' to meet another fella; you've clicked with someone else, me lady!

Mary. That's no concern o' yours, Jerry Devine; let me go!

Jerry. I saw yous comin' out o' the Cornflower Dance Class, an' you hangin' on his arm—a thin, lanky strip of a Micky Dazzler, with a walkin'-stick an' gloves!

Voice of Johnny [*loudly*]. What are you doin' there—pullin' about everything!

Voice of Boyle [*loudly and viciously*]. I'm puttin' on me moleskin trousers!

Mary. You're hurtin' me arm! Let me go, or I'll scream, an' then you'll have the oul' fella out on top of us!

Jerry. Don't be so hard on a fella, Mary, don't be so hard.

Boyle [*appearing at the door*]. What's the meanin' of all this hillabaloo?

Mary. Let me go, let me go!

Boyle. D'ye hear me—what's all this hillabaloo about?

Jerry [*plaintively*]. Will you not give us one kind word, one kind word, Mary?

Boyle. D'ye hear me talkin' to yous? What's all this hillabaloo for?

Jerry. Let me kiss your hand, your little, tiny, white hand!

Boyle. Your little, tiny, white hand—are you takin' leave o' your senses, man?   [*Mary breaks away and rushes out.*

Boyle. This is nice goins on in front of her father!

Jerry. Ah, dhry up, for God's sake!   [*He follows Mary.*

Boyle. Chiselurs don't care a damn now about their parents, they're bringin' their fathers' grey hairs down with sorra to the grave, an' laughin' at it, laughin' at it. Ah, I suppose it's just the same everywhere —the whole worl's in a state o' chassis! [*He sits by the fire*] Breakfast! Well, they can keep their breakfast for me. Not if they were down on their bended knees would I take it—I'll show them I've a little spirit left in me still! [*He goes over to the press, takes out a plate and looks at it*] Sassige! Well, let her keep her sassige. [*He returns to the fire, takes up the teapot and gives it a gentle shake*] The tea's wet right enough.

   [*A pause; he rises, goes to the press, takes out the sausage, puts it on the pan, and puts both on the fire. He attends the sausage with a fork.*

Boyle [*singing*]:
> When the robins nest agen,
> And the flowers are in bloom,
> When the Springtime's sunny smile seems to banish all sorrow an'
>> gloom;
> Then me bonny blue-ey'd lad, if me heart be true till then—
> He's promised he'll come back to me,
> When the robins nest agen!

> [*He lifts his head at the high note, and then drops his eyes to the pan.*

Boyle [*singing*]:
> When the . . .

> [*Steps are heard approaching; he whips the pan off the fire and puts it under the bed, then sits down at the fire. The door opens and a bearded man looking in says:*

You don't happen to want a sewin' machine?

Boyle [*furiously*].   No, I don't want e'er a sewin' machine!
> [*He returns the pan to the fire, and commences to sing again.*

Boyle [*singing*]:

> When the robins nest agen,
> And the flowers they are in bloom,
> He's . . .

> [*A thundering knock is heard at the street door.*
Boyle.   There's a terrible tatheraraa—that's a stranger—that's nobody belongin' to the house.   [*Another loud knock.*

Joxer [*sticking his head in at the door*].   Did ye hear them tatherarahs?

Boyle.   Well, Joxer, I'm not deaf.

Johnny [*appearing in his shirt and trousers at the door on left; his face is anxious and his voice is tremulous*].   Who's that at the door; who's that at the door? Who gave that knock—do'ye yous hear me—are yous deaf or dhrunk or what?

Boyle [*to Johnny*].   How the hell do I know who 'tis? Joxer, stick your head out o' the window an' see.

Joxer.   An' mebbe get a bullet in the kisser? Ah, none o' them thricks for Joxer! It's betther to be a coward than a corpse!

Boyle [*looking cautiously out of the window*].   It's a fella in a thrench coat.

Johnny.   Holy Mary, Mother o' God, I . . .

Boyle.   He's goin' away—he must ha' got tired knockin'.

[*Johnny returns to the room on left.*

Boyle.   Sit down an' have a cup o' tay, Joxer.

Joxer.   I'm afraid the missus ud pop in on us agen before we'd know where we are. Somethin's tellin' me to go at wanst.

Boyle.   Don't be superstitious, man; we're Dublin men, an' not boyos that's only afther comin' up from the bog o' Allen—though if she did come in, right enough, we'd be caught like rats in a thrap.

Joxer.   An' you know the sort she is—she wouldn't listen to reason—an' wanse bitten twice shy.

Boyle [*going over to the window at back*].   If the worst came to the worst, you could dart out here, Joxer; it's only a dhrop of a few feet to the roof of the return room, an' the first minute she goes into dh'other room I'll give you the bend, an' you can slip in an' away.

Joxer [*yielding to the temptation*].   Ah, I won't stop very long anyhow. [*Picking up a book from the table*] Whose is the buk?

Boyle.   Aw, one o' Mary's; she's always readin' lately—nothin' but thrash, too. There's one I was lookin' at dh'other day: three stories, The Doll's House, Ghosts, an' The Wild Duck—buks only fit for chiselurs!

Joxer.   Didja ever rade *Elizabeth, or Th' Exile o' Sibayria?* . . . Ah, it's a darlin' story, a daarlin' story!

Boyle.   You eat your sassige, an' never min' *Th' Exile o' Sibayria.*

[*Both sit down; Boyle fills out tea, pours gravy on Joxer's plate, and keeps the sausage for himself.*

Joxer.   What are you wearin' your moleskin trousers for?

Boyle.   I have to go to a job, Joxer. Just afther you'd gone, Devine kem runnin' in to tell us that Father Farrell said if I went down to the job that's goin' on in Rathmines I'd get a start.

Joxer.   Be the holy, that's good news!

Boyle.   How is it good news? I wondher if you were in my condition, would you call it good news?

Joxer.   I thought . . .

Boyle.   You thought! You think too sudden sometimes, Joxer. D'ye know, I'm hardly able to crawl with the pains in me legs!

Joxer. Yis, yis; I forgot the pains in your legs. I know you can do nothin' while they're at you.

Boyle. You forgot; I don't think any of yous realize the state I'm in with the pains in me legs. What ud happen if I had to carry a bag o' cement?

Joxer. Ah, any man havin' the like of them pains id be down an' out, down an' out.

Boyle. I wouldn't mind if he had said it to meself; but, no, oh no, he rushes in an' shouts it out in front o' Juno, an' you know what Juno is, Joxer. We all know Devine knows a little more than the rest of us, but he doesn't act as if he did; he's a good boy, sober, able to talk an' all that, but still . . .

Joxer. Oh ay; able to argufy, but still . . .

Boyle. If he's runnin' afther Mary, aself, he's not goin' to be runnin' afther me. Captain Boye's able to take care of himself. Afther all, I'm not gettin' brought up on Virol. I never heard him usin' a curse; I don't believe he was ever dhrunk in his life—sure he's not like a Christian at all!

Joxer. You're afther takin' the word out o' me mouth—afther all, a Christian's natural, but he's unnatural.

Boyle. His oul' fella was just the same—a Wicklow man.

Joxer. A Wicklow man! That explains the whole thing. I've met many a Wicklow man in me time, but I never met wan that was any good.

Boyle. "Father Farrell," says he, "sent me down to tell you." Father Farrell! . . . D'ye know, Joxer, I never like to be beholden to any o' the clergy.

Joxer. It's dangerous, right enough.

Boyle. If they do anything for you, they'd want you to be livin' in the Chapel. . . . I'm goin' to tell you somethin', Joxer, that I wouldn't tell to anybody else—the clergy always had too much power over the people in this unfortunate country.

Joxer. You could sing that if you had an air to it!

Boyle [*becoming enthusiastic*]. Didn't they prevent the people in " '47" from seizin' the corn, an' they starvin'; didn't they down Parnell; didn't they say that hell wasn't hot enough nor eternity long enough to punish the Fenians? We don't forget, we don't forget them things, Joxer. If they've taken everything else from us, Joxer, they've left us our memory.

Joxer [*emotionally*]. For mem'ry's the only friend that grief can call its own, that grief . . . can . . . call . . . its own!

Boyle. Father Farrell's beginnin' to take a great intherest in Captain Boyle; because of what Johnny did for his country, says he to me wan day. It's a curious way to reward Johnny be makin' his poor oul' father work. But that's what the clergy want, Joxer—work, work, work for me an' you; havin' us mulin' from mornin' till night, so that they may be in betther fettle when they come hoppin' round for their dues! Job! Well, let him give his job to wan of his hymn-singin', prayer-spoutin', craw-thumpin' Confraternity men!

[*The voice of a coal-block vendor is heard chanting in the street.*

Voice of Coal Vendor. Blocks . . . coal-blocks! Blocks . . . coal-blocks!

Joxer. God be with the young days when you were steppin' the deck of a manly ship, with the win' blowin' a hurricane through the masts, an' the only sound you'd hear was, "Port your helm!" an' the only answer, "Port it is, sir!"

Boyle. Them was days, Joxer, them was days. Nothin' was too hot or too heavy for me then. Sailin' from the Gulf o' Mexico to the Antanartic Ocean. I seen things, I seen things, Joxer, that no mortal man should speak about that knows his Catechism. Ofen, an' ofen, when I was fixed to the wheel with a marlin-spike, an' the wins blowin' fierce an' the waves lashin' an' lashin', till you'd think every minute was goin' to be your last, an' it blowed, an' blowed—blew is the right word, Joxer, but blowed is what the sailors use. . . .

Joxer. Aw, it's a darlin' word, a daarlin' word.

Boyle. An', as it blowed an' blowed, I often looked up at the sky an' assed meself the question—what is the stars, what is the stars?

Voice of Coal Vendor. Any blocks, coal-blocks; blocks, coal-blocks!

Joxer. Ah, that's the question, that's the question—what is the stars?

Boyle. An' then, I'd have another look, an' I'd ass meself—what is the moon?

Joxer. Ah, that's the question—what is the moon, what is the moon?

[*Rapid steps are heard coming towards the door. Boyle makes desperate efforts to hide everything; Joxer rushes to the window in a frantic effort to get out; Boyle begins to innocently lilt "Oh, me darlin' Jennie, I will be thrue to thee", when the door is opened, and the black face of the Coal Vendor appears.*

The Coal Vendor. D'yes want any blocks?

Boyle [*with a roar*]. No, we don't want any blocks!

Joxer [*coming back with a sigh of relief*]. That's afther puttin' the heart across me—I could ha' sworn it was Juno. I'd betther be goin', Captain; you couldn't tell the minute Juno'd hop in on us.

Boyle. Let her hop in; we may as well have it out first as at last. I've made up me mind—I'm not goin' to do only what she damn well likes.

Joxer. Them sentiments does you credit, Captain; I don't like to say anything as between man an' wife, but I say as a butty, as a butty, Captain, that you've stuck it too long, an' that it's about time you showed a little spunk.

⇒ How can a man die better than facin' fearful odds,
   For th' ashes of his fathers an' the temples of his gods?

Boyle. She has her rights—there's no one denyin' it, but haven't I me rights too?

Joxer. Of course you have—the sacred rights o' man!

Boyle. Today, Joxer, there's goin' to be issued a proclamation be me, establishin' an independent Republic, an' Juno'll have to take an oath of allegiance.

Joxer. Be firm, be firm, Captain; the first few minutes'll be the worst:—if you gently touch a nettle it'll sting you for your pains; grasp it like a lad of mettle, an' as soft as silk remains!

Voice of Juno outside. Can't stop, Mrs. Madigan—I haven't a minute!

Joxer [*flying out of the window*]. Holy God, here she is!

Boyle [*packing the things away with a rush in the press*]. I knew that fella ud stop till she was in on top of us!   [*He sits down by the fire.*
                    [*Juno enters hastily; she is flurried and excited.*

Juno. Oh, you're in—you must have been only afther comin' in?

Boyle. No, I never went out.

Juno. It's curious, then, you never heard the knockin'.
                    [*She puts her coat and hat on bed.*

Boyle. Knockin'? Of course I heard the knockin'.

Juno. An' why didn't you open the door, then? I suppose you were so busy with Joxer that you hadn't time.

Boyle. I haven't seen Joxer since I seen him before. Joxer! What ud bring Joxer here?

Juno. D'ye mean to tell me that the pair of yous wasn't collogin' together here when me back was turned?

Boyle. What ud we be collogin' together about? I have somethin' else to think of besides collogin' with Joxer. I can swear on all the holy prayer-books . . .

Mrs. Boyle. That you weren't in no snug! Go on in at wanst now, an' take off that moleskin trousers o' yours, an' put on a collar an' tie to smarten yourself up a bit. There's a visitor comin' with Mary in a minute, an' he has great news for you.

Boyle. A job, I suppose; let us get wan first before we start lookin' for another.

Mrs. Boyle. That's the thing that's able to put the win' up you. Well, it's no job, but news that'll give you the chance o' your life.

Boyle. What's all the mystery about?

Mrs. Boyle. G'win an' take off the moleskin trousers when you're told!

[*Boyle goes into room on left.*

[*Mrs. Boyle tidies up the room, puts the shovel under the bed, and goes to the press.*

Mrs. Boyle. Oh, God bless us, looka the way everything's thrun about! Oh, Joxer was here, Joxer was here!

[*Mary enters with Charlie Bentham; he is a young man of twenty-five, tall, good-looking, with a very high opinion of himself generally. He is dressed in a brown coat, brown knee-breeches, grey stockings, a brown sweater, with a deep blue tie; he carries gloves and a walking-stick.*

Mrs. Boyle [*fussing round*]. Come in, Mr. Bentham; sit down, Mr. Bentham, in this chair; it's more comfortabler than that, Mr. Bentham. Himself'll be here in a minute; he's just takin' off his trousers.

Mary. Mother!

Bentham. Please don't put yourself to any trouble, Mrs. Boyle—I'm quite all right here, thank you.

Mrs. Boyle. An' to think of you knowin' Mary, an' she knowin' the news you had for us, an' wouldn't let on; but it's all the more welcomer now, for we were on our last lap!

Voice of Johnny inside. What are you kickin' up all the racket for?

Boyle [*roughly*]. I'm takin' off me moleskin trousers!

Johnny. Can't you do it, then, without lettin' th' whole house know you're takin' off your trousers? What d'ye want puttin' them on an' takin' them off again?

Boyle. Will you let me alone, will you let me alone? Am I never goin' to be done thryin' to please th' whole o' yous?

Mrs. Boyle [*to Bentham*]. You must excuse th' state o' th' place, Mr. Bentham; th' minute I turn me back that man o' mine always makes a litther o' th' place, a litther o' th' place.

Bentham. Don't worry, Mrs. Boyle; it's all right, I assure . . .

Boyle [*inside*]. Where's me braces; where in th' name o' God did I leave me braces? . . . Ay, did you see where I put me braces?

Johnny [*inside, calling out*]. Ma, will you come in here an' take da away ou' o' this or he'll dhrive me mad.

Mrs. Boyle [*going towards the door*]. Dear, dear, dear, that man'll be lookin' for somethin' on th' day o' Judgement. [*Looking into room and calling to Boyle*] Look at your braces, man, hangin' round your neck!

Boyle [*inside*]. Aw, Holy God!

Mrs. Boyle [*calling*]. Johnny, Johnny, come out here for a minute.

Johnny. Ah, leave Johnny alone, an' don't be annoyin' him!

Mrs. Boyle. Come on, Johnny, till I inthroduce you to Mr. Bentham. [*To Bentham*] My son, Mr. Bentham; he's afther goin' through the mill. He was only a chiselur of a Boy Scout in Easter Week, when he got hit in the hip; and his arm was blew off in the fight in O'Connell Street. [*Johnny comes in.*] Here he is, Mr. Bentham; Mr. Bentham, Johnny. None can deny he done his bit for Irelan', if that's goin' to do him any good.

Johnny [*boastfully*]. I'd do it agen, ma, I'd do it agen; for a principle's a principle.

Mrs. Boyle. Ah, you lost your best principle, me boy, when you lost your arm; them's the only sort o' principles that's any good to a workin' man.

Johnny. Ireland only half free'll never be at peace while she has a son left to pull a trigger.

Mrs. Boyle. To be sure, to be sure—no bread's a lot betther than half a loaf. [*Calling loudly in to Boyle*] Will you hurry up there?

[*Boyle enters in his best trousers, which aren't too good, and looks very uncomfortable in his collar and tie.*

Mrs. Boyle. This is me husband; Mr. Boyle, Mr. Bentham.

Bentham. Ah, very glad to know you, Mr. Boyle. How are you?

Boyle. Ah, I'm not too well at all; I suffer terrible with pains in me legs. Juno can tell you there what . . .

Mrs. Boyle. You won't have many pains in your legs when you hear what Mr. Bentham has to tell you.

Bentham. Juno! What an interesting name! It reminds one of Homer's glorious story of ancient gods and heroes.

Boyle. Yis, doesn't it? You see, Juno was born an' christened in June; I met her in June; we were married in June, an' Johnny was born in June, so wan day I says to her, "You should ha' been called Juno," an' the name stuck to her ever since.

Mrs. Boyle. Here, we can talk o' them things agen; let Mr. Bentham say what he has to say now.

Bentham. Well, Mr. Boyle, I suppose you'll remember a Mr. Ellison of Santry—he's a relative of yours, I think.

Boyle [*viciously*]. Is it that prognosticator an' procrastinator! Of course I remember him.

Bentham. Well, he's dead, Mr. Boyle . . .

Boyle. Sorra many'll go into mournin' for him.

Mrs. Boyle. Wait till you hear what Mr. Bentham has to say, an' then, maybe, you'll change your opinion.

Bentham. A week before he died he sent for me to write his will for him. He told me that there were two only that he wished to leave his property to: his second cousin, Michael Finnegan of Santry, and John Boyle, his first cousin, of Dublin.

Boyle [*excitedly*]. Me, is it me, me?

Bentham. You, Mr. Boyle; I'll read a copy of the will that I have here with me, which has been duly filed in the Court of Probate.

[*He takes a paper from his pocket and reads:*

6th February 1922

This is the last Will and Testament of William Ellison, of Santry, in the County of Dublin. I hereby order and wish my property to be sold and divided as follows:—

£20 to the St. Vincent de Paul Society.

£60 for Masses for the repose of my soul (5s. for each Mass).

The rest of my property to be divided between my first and second cousins.

I hereby appoint Timothy Buckly, of Santry, and Hugh Brierly, of Coolock, to be my Executors.

(*Signed*) WILLIAM ELLISON.
HUGH BRIERLY.
TIMOTHY BUCKLY.
CHARLES BENTHAM, N.T.

Boyle [*eagerly*]. An' how much'll be comin' out of it, Mr. Bentham?

Bentham. The Executors told me that half of the property would be anything between £1500 and £2000.

Mary. A fortune, father, a fortune!

Johnny. We'll be able to get out o' this place now, an 'go somewhere we're not known.

Mrs. Boyle. You won't have to trouble about a job for awhile, Jack.

Boyle [*fervently*]. I'll never doubt the goodness o' God agen.

Bentham. I congratulate you, Mr. Boyle.   [*They shake hands.*

Boyle. An' now, Mr. Bentham, you'll have to have a wet.

Bentham. A wet?

Boyle. A wet—a jar—a boul!

Mrs. Boyle. Jack, you're speakin' to Mr. Bentham, an' not to Joxer.

Boyle [*solemnly*]. Juno . . . Mary . . . Johnny . . . we'll have to go into mournin' at wanst. . . . I never expected that poor Bill ud die so sudden. . . . Well, we all have to die some day . . . you, Juno, to-day . . . an' me, maybe, to-morrow. . . . It's sad, but it can't be helped. . . . Requiescat in pace . . . or, usin' our oul' tongue like St. Patrick or St. Bridget, Guh sayeree jeea ayera!

Mary. Oh, father, that's not Rest in Peace; that's God save Ireland.

Boyle. U-u-ugh, it's all the same—isn't it a prayer? . . . Juno, I'm done with Joxer; he's nothin' but a prognosticator an' a . . .

Joxer [*climbing angrily through the window and bounding into the room*]. You're done with Joxer, are you? Maybe you thought I'd stop on the roof all the night for you! Joxer out on the roof with the win' blowin' through him was nothin' to you an' your friend with the collar an' tie!

Mrs. Boyle. What in the name o' God brought you out on the roof; what were you doin' there?

Joxer [*ironically*]. I was dhreamin' I was standin' on the bridge of a ship, an' she sailin' the Antartic Ocean, an' it blowed, an' blowed, an' I lookin' up at the sky an' sayin', what is the stars, what is the stars?

Mrs. Boyle [*opening the door and standing at it*]. Here, get ou' o' this, Joxer Daly; I was always thinkin' you had a slate off.

Joxer [*moving to the door*]. I have to laugh every time I look at the deep-sea sailor; an' a row on a river ud make him sea-sick!

Boyle. Get ou' o' this before I take the law into me own hands!

Joxer [*going out*]. Say aw rewaeawr, but not good-bye. Lookin' for work, an' prayin 'to God he won't get it!   [*He goes.*

Mrs. Boyle. I'm tired tellin' you what Joxer was; maybe now you see yourself the kind he is.

Boyle. He'll never blow the froth off a pint o' mine agen, that's a sure thing. Johnny . . . Mary . . . you're to keep yourselves to yourselves for the future. Juno, I'm done with Joxer. . . . I'm a new man from this out. . . .

> [*Clasping Juno's hand, and singing emotionally:*

O, me darlin' Juno, I will be thrue to thee;
Me own, me darlin' Juno, you're all the world to me.

CURTAIN

ACT II

The same, but the furniture is more plentiful, and of a vulgar nature. A glaringly upholstered armchair and lounge; cheap pictures and photos everywhere. Every available spot is ornamented with huge vases filled with artificial flowers. Crossed festoons of coloured paper chains stretch from end to end of ceiling. On the table is an old attaché case. It is about six in the evening, and two days after the First Act. Boyle, in his shirt-sleeves, is voluptuously stretched on the sofa; he is smoking a clay pipe. He is half asleep. A lamp is lighting on the table. After a few moments' pause the voice of Joxer is heard singing softly outside at the door—"Me pipe I'll smoke, as I dhrive me moke—are you there, Mor . . . ee . . . ar . . . i . . . teee!"

Boyle [*leaping up, takes a pen in his hand and busies himself with papers*].
Come along, Joxer, me son, come along.

Joxer [*putting his head in*]. Are you be yourself?

Boyle. Come on, come on; that doesn't matther; I'm masther now, an' I'm goin' to remain masther. [*Joxer comes in.*

Joxer. How d'ye feel now, as a man o' money?

Boyle [*solemnly*]. It's a responsibility, Joxer, a great responsibility.

Joxer. I suppose 'tis now, though you wouldn't think it.

Boyle. Joxer, han' me over that attackey case on the table there. [*Joxer hands the case.*] Ever since the Will was passed I've run hundhreds o' dockyments through me hans—I tell you, you have to keep your wits about you. [*He busies himself with papers.*

Joxer. Well, I won't disturb you; I'll dhrop in when . . .

Boyle [*hastily*]. It's all right, Joxer, this is the last one to be signed to-day. [*He signs a paper, puts it into the case, which he shuts with a snap, and sits back pompously in the chair.*] Now, Joxer, you want to see me; I'm at your service—what can I do for you, me man?

Joxer. I've just dhropped in with the £3 : 5s. that Mrs. Madigan riz on the blankets an' table for you, an' she says you're to be in no hurry payin' it back.

Boyle. She won't be long without it; I expect the first cheque for a couple o' hundhred any day. There's the five bob for yourself—go on, take it, man; it'll not be the last you'll get from the Captain. Now an' agen we have our differ, but we're there together all the time.

Joxer. Me for you, an' you for me, like the two Musketeers.

Boyle. Father Farrell stopped me to-day an' tole me how glad he was I fell in for the money.

Joxer. He'll be stoppin' you ofen enough now; I suppose it was "Mr." Boyle with him?

Boyle. He shuk me be the han' . . .

Joxer [*ironically*]. I met with Napper Tandy, an' he shuk me be the han'!

Boyle. You're seldom asthray, Joxer, but you're wrong shipped this time. What you're sayin' of Father Farrell is very near to blasfeemey. I don't like any one to talk disrespectful of Father Farrell.

Joxer. You're takin' me up wrong, Captain; I wouldn't let a word be said agen Father Farrell—the heart o' the rowl, that's what he is; I always said he was a darlin' man, a daarlin' man.

Boyle. Comin' up the stairs who did I meet but that bummer, Nugent. "I seen you talkin' to Father Farrell," says he, with a grin on him. "He'll be folleyin' you," says he, "like a Guardian Angel from this out"—all the time the oul' grin on him, Joxer.

Joxer. I never seen him yet but he had that oul' grin on him!

Boyle. "Mr. Nugent," says I, "Father Farrell is a man o' the people, an', as far as I know the History o' me country, the priests was always in the van of the fight for Irelan's freedom."

Joxer [*fervently*]:
  Who was it led the van, Soggart Aroon?
  Since the fight first began, Soggart Aroon?

Boyle. "Who are you tellin'?" says he. "Didn't they let down the Fenians, an' didn't they do in Parnell? An' now . . ." "You ought to be ashamed o' yourself," says I, interruptin' him, "not to know the History o' your country." An' I left him gawkin' where he was.

Joxer. Where ignorance's bliss 'tis folly to be wise; I wondher did he ever read the Story o' Irelan'.

Boyle. Be J. L. Sullivan? Don't you know he didn't.

Joxer. Ah, it's a darlin' buk, a daarlin' buk!

Boyle. You'd betther be goin', now, Joxer; his Majesty, Bentham, 'll be here any minute, now.

Joxer. Be the way things is lookin', it'll be a match between him an' Mary. She's thrun over Jerry altogether. Well, I hope it will, for he's a darlin' man.

Boyle. I'm glad you think so—I don't. [*Irritably*] What's darlin' about him?

Joxer [*nonplussed*]. I only seen him twiced; if you want to know me, come an' live with me.

Boyle. He's too dignified for me—to hear him talk you'd think he knew as much as a Boney's Oraculum. He's given up his job as teacher, an' is goin' to become a solicitor in Dublin—he's been studyin' law. I suppose he thinks I'll set him up, but he's wrong shipped. An' th' other fella— Jerry's as bad. The two o' them ud give you a pain in your face, listenin' to them; Jerry believin' in nothin', an' Bentham believin' in everythin'. One that says all is God an' no man; an' th' other that says all is man an' no God!

Joxer. Well, I'll be off now.

Boyle. Don't forget to dhrop down afther awhile; we'll have a quiet jar, an' a song or two.

Joxer. Never fear.

Boyle. An' tell Mrs. Madigan that I hope we'll have the pleasure of her organization at our little enthertainment.

Joxer. Righto; we'll come down together. [*He goes out.*

[*Johnny comes from room on left, and sits down moodily at the fire. Boyle looks at him for a few moments, and shakes his head. He fills his pipe.*

Voice of Juno at the door. Open the door, Jack; this thing has me nearly kilt with the weight.

[*Boyle opens the door. Juno enters carrying the box of a gramophone, followed by Mary carrying the horn and some parcels. Juno leaves the box on the table and flops into a chair.*

Juno. Carryin' that from Henry Street was no joke.

Boyle. U-u-ugh, that's a grand-lookin' insthrument—how much was it?

Juno. Pound down, an' five to be paid at two shillins a week.

Boyle. That's reasonable enough.

Juno. I'm afraid we're runnin' into too much debt; first the furniture, an' now this.

Boyle. The whole lot won't be much out of £2000.

Mary. I don't know what you wanted a gramophone for—I know Charlie hates them; he says they're destructive of real music.

Boyle. Desthructive of music—that fella ud give you a pain in your face. All a gramophone wants is to be properly played; its thrue wondher is only felt when everythin's quiet—what a gramophone wants is dead silence!

Mary. But, father, Jerry says the same; after all, you can only appreciate music when your ear is properly trained.

Boyle. That's another fella ud give you a pain in your face. Properly thrained! I suppose you couldn't appreciate football unless your fut was properly thrained.

Mrs. Boyle [*to Mary*]. Go on in ower that an' dress, or Charlie'll be in on you, an' tea nor nothing'll be ready. [*Mary goes into room left.*

Mrs. Boyle [*arranging table for tea*]. You didn't look at our new gramophone, Johnny?

Johnny. 'Tisn't gramophones I'm thinking of.

Mrs. Boyle. An' what is it you're thinkin' of, allanna?

Johnny. Nothin', nothin', nothin'.

Mrs. Boyle. Sure, you must be thinkin' of somethin'; it's yourself that has yourself the way y'are; sleepin' wan night in me sisther's, an' the nex' in your father's brother's—you'll get no rest goin' on that way.

Johnny. I can rest nowhere, nowhere, nowhere.

Mrs. Boyle.   Sure, you're not thryin' to rest anywhere.

Johnny.   Let me alone, let me alone, let me alone, for God's sake.

[*A knock at street door.*

Mrs. Boyle [*in a flutter*].   Here he is; here's Mr. Bentham!

Boyle.   Well, there's room for him; it's a pity there's not a brass band to play him in.

Mrs. Boyle.   We'll han' the tea round, an' not be clustered round the table, as if we never seen nothin'.

[*Steps are heard approaching, and Juno, opening the door, allows Bentham to enter.*

Juno.   Give your hat an' stick to Jack, there . . . sit down, Mr. Bentham . . . no, not there . . . in th' easy chair be the fire . . . there, that's betther. Mary'll be out to you in a minute.

Boyle [*solemnly*].   I seen be the paper this mornin' that Consols was down half per cent. That's serious, min' you, an' shows the whole counthry's in a state o' chassis.

Mrs. Boyle.   What's Consols, Jack?

Boyle.   Consols? Oh, Consols is—oh, there's no use tellin' women what Consols is—th' wouldn't undherstand.

Bentham.   It's just as you were saying, Mr. Boyle . . .

[*Mary enters, charmingly dressed.*

Bentham.   Oh, good evening, Mary; how pretty you're looking!

Mary [*archly*].   Am I?

Boyle.   We were just talkin' when you kem in, Mary; I was tellin' Mr. Bentham that the whole counthry's in a state o' chassis.

Mary [*to Bentham*].   Would you prefer the green or the blue ribbon round me hair, Charlie?

Mrs. Boyle.   Mary, your father's speakin'.

Boyle [*rapidly*].   I was jus' tellin' Mr. Bentham that the whole counthry's in a state o' chassis.

Mary.   I'm sure you're frettin', da, whether it is or no.

Mrs. Boyle.   With all our churches an' religions, the worl's not a bit the betther.

Boyle [*with a commanding gesture*].Tay!

[*Mary and Mrs. Boyle dispense the tea.*

Mrs. Boyle.   An' Irelan's takin' a leaf out o' the worl's buk; when we got the makin' of our own laws I thought we'd never stop to look behind

us, but instead of that we never stopped to look before us! If the people
ud folley up their religion betther there'd be a betther chance for us—
what do you think, Mr. Bentham?

Bentham. I'm afraid I can't venture to express an opinion on that point,
Mrs. Boyle; dogma has no attraction for me.

Mrs. Boyle. I forgot you didn't hold with us: what's this you said you
were?

Bentham. A Theosophist, Mrs. Boyle.

Mrs. Boyle. An' what in the name o' God's a Theosophist?

Boyle. A Theosophist, Juno, 's a—tell her, Mr. Bentham, tell her.

Bentham. It's hard to explain in a few words: Theosophy's founded on
The Vedas, the religious books of the East. Its central theme is the
existence of an all-pervading Spirit—the Life-Breath. Nothing really
exists but this one Universal Life-Breath. And whatever even seems to
exist separately from this Life-Breath, doesn't really exist at all. It is
all vital force in man, in all animals, and in all vegetation. This Life-
Breath is called the Prawna.

Mrs. Boyle. The Prawna! What a comical name!

Boyle. Prawna; yis, the Prawna. [*Blowing gently through his lips*]
That's the Prawna!

Mrs. Boyle. Whist, whist, Jack.

Bentham. The happiness of man depends upon his sympathy with this
Spirit. Men who have reached a high state of excellence are called Yogi.
Some men become Yogi in a short time, it may take others millions of
years.

Boyle. Yogi! I seen hundhreds of them in the streets o' San Francisco.

Bentham. It is said by these Yogi that if we practise certain mental exercises that we would have powers denied to others—for instance, the
faculty of seeing things had happen miles and miles away.

Mrs. Boyle. I wouldn't care to meddle with that sort o' belief; it's a very
curious religion, altogether.

Boyle. What's curious about it? Isn't all religions curious?—if they
weren't, you wouldn't get any one to believe them. But religions is passin'
away—they've had their day like everything else. Take the real Dublin
people, f'rinstance: they know more about Charlie Chaplin an' Tommy
Mix than they do about SS. Peter an' Paul!

Mrs. Boyle. You don't believe in ghosts, Mr. Bentham?

Mary.   Don't you know he doesn't, mother?

Bentham.   I don't know that, Mary. Scientists are beginning to think that what we call ghosts are sometimes seen by persons of a certain nature. They say that sensational actions, such as the killing of a person, demand great energy, and that that energy lingers in the place where the action occurred. People may live in the place and see nothing, when someone may come along whose personality has some peculiar connection with the energy of the place, and, in a flash, the person sees the whole affair.

Johnny [*rising swiftly, pale and affected*].   What sort o' talk is this to be goin' on with? Is there nothin' betther to be talkin' about but the killin' o' people? My God, isn't it bad enough for these things to happen without talkin' about them!   [*He hurriedly goes into the room on left.*

Bentham.   Oh, I'm very sorry, Mrs. Boyle; I never thought . . .

Mrs. Boyle [*apologetically*].   Never mind, Mr. Bentham, he's very touchy.
            [*A frightened scream is heard from Johnny inside.*

Mrs. Boyle.   Mother of God, what's that?

            [*He rushes out again, his face pale, his lips twitching, his limbs trembling.*

Johnny.   Shut the door, shut the door, quick, for God's sake! Great God, have mercy on me! Blessed Mother o' God, shelter me, shelther your son!

Mrs. Boyle [*catching him in her arms*].   What's wrong with you? What ails you? Sit down, sit down, here, on the bed . . . there now . . . there now.

Mary.   Johnny, Johnny, what ails you?

Johnny.   I seen him, I seen him . . . kneelin' in front o' the statue . . . merciful Jesus, have pity on me!

Mrs. Boyle [*to Boyle*].   Get him a glass o' whisky . . . quick, man, an' don't stand gawkin'.   [*Boyle gets the whisky.*

Johnny.   Sit here, sit here, mother . . . between me an' the door.

Mrs. Boyle.   I'll sit beside you as long as you like, only tell me what was it came across you at all?

Johnny [*after taking some drink*].   I seen him. . . . I seen Robbie Tancred kneelin' down before the statue . . . an' the red light shinin' on him . . . an' when I went in . . . he turned an' looked at me . . . an' I seen the wouns bleedin' in his breast. . . . Oh, why did he look at me like that? . . . it wasn't my fault that he was done in. . . . Mother o' God, keep him away from me!

Mrs. Boyle.   There, there, child, you've imagined it all. There was nothin' there at all—it was the red light you seen, an' the talk we had put all the rest into your head. Here, dhrink more o' this—it'll do you good. . . . An', now, stretch yourself down on the bed for a little. [*To Boyle*] Go in, Jack, an' show him it was only in his own head it was.

Boyle [*making no move*].   E-e-e-e-eh; it's all nonsense; it was only a shadda he saw.

Mary.   Mother o' God, he made me heart lep!

Bentham.   It was simply due to an over-wrought imagination—we all get that way at times.

Mrs. Boyle.   There, dear, lie down in the bed, an' I'll put the quilt across you . . . e-e-e-eh, that's it . . . you'll be as right as the mail in a few minutes.

Johnny.   Mother, go into the room an' see if the light's lightin' before the statue.

Mrs. Boyle [*to Boyle*].   Jack, run in an' see if the light's lightin' before the statue.

Boyle [*to Mary*].   Mary, slip in an' see if the light's lightin' before the statue.   [*Mary hesitates to go in.*

Bentham.   It's all right; Mary, I'll go.

[*He goes into the room; remains for a few moments, and returns.*

Bentham.   Everything's just as it was—the light burning bravely before the statue.

Boyle.   Of course; I knew it was all nonsense.   [*A knock at the door.*

Boyle [*going to open the door*].   E-e-e-e-eh.

[*He opens it, and Joxer, followed by Mrs. Madigan, enters. Mrs. Madigan is a strong, dapper little woman of about forty-five; her face is almost always a widespread smile of complacency. She is a woman who, in manner at least, can mourn with them that mourn, and rejoice with them that do rejoice. When she is feeling comfortable, she is inclined to be reminiscent; when others say anything, or following a statement made by herself, she has a habit of putting her head a little to one side, and nodding it rapidly several times in succession, like a bird pecking at a hard berry. Indeed, she has a good deal of the bird in her, but the bird instinct is by no means a melodious one. She is ignorant, vulgar and forward, but her heart is generous withal. For instance, she would help a neighbour's sick child; she would probably kill the child, but her intention would be to cure it; she would be more at home helping a drayman to lift a fallen horse. She is dressed in a rather soiled grey dress and a vivid purple blouse; in her hair is a huge comb, ornamented with huge coloured beads. She enters with a gliding step, beaming smile and nodding head. Boyle receives them effusively.*

Boyle. Come on in, Mrs. Madigan; come on in; I was afraid you weren't comin'. . . . [*Slyly*] There's some people able to dhress, ay, Joxer?

Joxer. Fair as the blossoms that bloom in the May, an' sweet as the scent of the new-mown hay. . . . Ah, well she may wear them.

Mrs. Madigan [*looking at Mary*]. I know some as are as sweet as the blossoms that bloom in the May—oh, no names no pack dhrill!

Boyle. An' now I'll inthroduce the pair o' yous to Mary's intended: Mr. Bentham, this is Mrs. Madigan, an oul' back-parlour neighbour that if she could help it at all, ud never see a body shuk!

Bentham [*rising, and tentatively shaking the hand of Mrs. Madigan*]. I'm sure it's a great pleasure to know you, Mrs. Madigan.

Mrs. Madigan. An' I'm goin' to tell you, Mr. Bentham, you're goin' to get as nice a bit o' skirt in Mary, there, as ever you seen in your puff. Not like some of the dhressed-up dolls that's knockin' about lookin' for men when it's a skelpin' they want. I remember, as well as I remember yestherday, the day she was born—of a Tuesday, the 25th o' June, in the year 1901, at thirty-three minutes past wan in the day be Foley's clock, the pub at the corner o' the street. A cowld day it was too, for the season o' the year, an' I remember sayin' to Joxer, there, who I met comin' up th' stairs, that the new arrival in Boyle's ud grow up a hardy chiselur if it lived, an' that she'd be somethin' one o' these days that nobody suspected, an' so signs on it, here she is to-day, goin' to be married to a young man lookin' as if he'd be fit to commensurate in any position in life it ud please God to call him!

Boyle [*effusively*]. Sit down, Mrs. Madigan, sit down, me oul' sport. [*To Bentham*] This is Joxer Daly, Past Chief Ranger of the Dear Little Shamrock Branch of the Irish National Foresters, an oul' front-top neighbour, that never despaired, even in the darkest days of Ireland's sorra.

Joxer. Nil desperandum, Captain, nil desperandum.

Boyle. Sit down, Joxer, sit down. The two of us was ofen in a tight corner.

Mrs. Boyle. Ay, in Foley's snug!

Joxer. An' we kem out of it flyin', we kem out of it flyin', Captain.

Boyle. An' now for a dhrink—I know yous won't refuse an oul' friend.

Mrs. Madigan [*to Juno*]. Is Johnny not well, Mrs. . . .

Mrs. Boyle [*warningly*]. S-s-s-sh.

Mrs. Madigan. Oh, the poor darlin'.

Boyle. Well, Mrs. Madigan, is it tea or what?

Mrs. Madigan. Well, speakin' for meself, I jus' had me tea a minute ago, an' I'm afraid to dhrink any more—I'm never the same when I dhrink too much tay. Thanks, all the same, Mr. Boyle.

Boyle. Well, what about a bottle o' stout or a dhrop o' whisky?

Mrs. Madigan. A bottle o' stout ud be a little too heavy for me stummock afther me tay. . . . A-a-ah, I'll thry the ball o' malt.

[*Boyle prepares the whisky.*

Mrs. Madigan. There's nothin' like a ball o' malt occasional like—too much of it isn't good. [*To Boyle, who is adding water*] Ah, God, Johnny, don't put too much wather on it! [*She drinks.*] I suppose yous'll be lavin' this place.

Boyle. I'm looking for a place near the sea; I'd like the place that you might say was me cradle, to be me grave as well. The sea is always callin' me.

Joxer. She is callin', callin', callin', in the win' an' on the sea.

Boyle. Another dhrop o' whisky, Mrs. Madigan?

Mrs. Madigan. Well, now, it ut be hard to refuse seein' the suspicious times that's in it.

Boyle [*with a commanding gesture*]. Song! . . . Juno . . . Mary . . . "Home to Our Mountains"!

Mrs. Madigan [*enthusiastically*]. Hear, hear!

Joxer. Oh, tha's a darlin' song, a daarlin' song!

Mary [*bashfully*]. Ah no, da; I'm not in a singin' humour.

Mrs. Madigan. Gawn with you, child, an' you only goin' to be marrid; I remember as well as I remember yestherday,—it was on a lovely August evenin', exactly, accordin' to date, fifteen years ago, come the Tuesday folleyin' the nex' that's comin' on, when me own man—*the Lord be good to him*—an' me was sittin' shy together in a doty little nook on a counthry road, adjacent to The Stiles. "That'll scratch your lovely, little white neck," says he, ketchin' hould of a danglin' bramble branch, holdin' clusters of the loveliest flowers you ever seen, an' breakin' it off, so that his arm fell, accidental like, roun' me waist, an' as I felt it tightenin', an' tightenin', an' tightenin', I thought me buzzom was every minute goin' to burst out into a roystherin' song about

The little green leaves that were shakin' on the threes,
The gallivantin' buttherflies, an' buzzin' o' the bees!"

Boyle. Ordher for the song!

Juno. Come on, Mary—we'll do our best.

[*Juno and Mary stand up, and choosing a suitable position, sing
simply "Home to Our Mountains".
[They bow to company, and return to their places.*

Boyle [*emotionally, at the end of song*]. Lull . . . me . . . to . . .
rest!

Joxer [*clapping his hands*].Bravo, bravo! Darlin' girulls, darlin' girulls!

Mrs. Madigan. Juno, I never seen you in betther form.

Bentham. Very nicely rendered indeed.

Mrs. Madigan. A noble call, a noble call!

Mrs. Boyle. What about yourself, Mrs. Madigan?

[*After some coaxing, Mrs. Madigan rises, and in a quavering voice
sings the following verse:*

If I were a blackbird I'd whistle and sing;
I'd follow the ship that my thrue love was in;
An' on the top riggin', I'd there build me nest,
'An' at night I would sleep on me Willie's white breast!

[*Becoming husky, amid applause, she sits down.*

Mrs. Madigan. Ah, me voice is too husky now, Juno; though I remember the time when Maisie Madigan could sing like a nightingale at
matin' time. I remember as well as I remember yestherday, at a party
given to celebrate the comin' of the first chiselur to Annie an' Benny
Jimeson—who was the barber, yous may remember, in Henrietta Street,
that, afther Easter Week, hung out a green, white an' orange pole, an',
then, when the Tans started their Jazz dancin' whipped it in agen, an'
stuck out a red, white an' blue wan instead, givin' as an excuse that a
barber's pole was strictly non-political—singin' "An' You'll Remember
Me", with the top notes quiverin' in a dead hush of pethrified attention,
folleyed be a clappin' o' hans that shuk the tumblers on the table, an'
capped by Jimeson, the barber, sayin that it was the best rendherin' of
"You'll Remember Me" he ever heard in his natural!

Boyle [*peremptorily*]. Ordher for Joxer's song!

Joxer. Ah no, I couldn't; don't ass me, Captain.

Boyle. Joxer's song, Joxer's song—give us wan of your shut-eyed wans.

[Joxer settles himself in his chair; takes a drink; clears his throat; solemnly closes his eyes, and begins to sing in a very querulous voice:

She is far from the lan' where her young hero sleeps,
An' lovers around her are sighing   *[He hesitates.*
An' lovers around her are sighin' . . . sighin' . . . sighin' . . .
                                                         [A pause.

Boyle [imitating Joxer]:

And lovers around her are sighing!

What's the use of you thryin' to sing the song if you don't know it?

Mary.   Thry another one, Mr. Daly—maybe you'd be more fortunate.

Mrs. Madigan.   Gawn, Joxer; thry another wan.

Joxer [starting again]:

I have heard the mavis singin' his love song to the morn;
I have seen the dew-dhrop clingin' to the rose jus' newly born; but
. . . but . . . *[frantically]* To the rose jus' newly born . . . newly
born . . . born.

Johnny.   Mother, put on the gramophone, for God's sake, an' stop Joxer's bawlin'.

Boyle [commandingly].   Gramophone! . . . I hate to see fellas thryin' to do what they're not able to do.

[Boyle arranges the gramophone, and is about to start it, when voices are heard of persons descending the stairs.

Mrs. Boyle [warningly].   Whisht, Jack, don't put it on, don't put it on yet; this must be poor Mrs. Tancred comin' down to go to the hospital—I forgot all about them bringin' the body to the church to-night. Open the door, Mary, an' give them a bit o' light.

[Mary opens the door, and Mrs. Tancred—a very old woman, obviously shaken by the death of her son—appears, accompanied by several neighbours. The first few phrases are spoken before they appear.

First Neighbour.   It's a sad journey we're goin' on, but God's good, an' the Republicans won't be always down.

Mrs. Tancred.   Ah, what good is that to me now? Whether they're up or down—it won't bring me darlin' boy from the grave.

Mrs. Boyle.   Come in an' have a hot cup o' tay, Mrs. Tancred, before you go.

Mrs. Tancred. Ah, I can take nothin' now, Mrs. Boyle—I won't be long afther him.

First Neighbour. Still an' all, he died a noble death, an' we'll bury him like a king.

Mrs. Tancred. An' I'll go on livin' like a pauper. Ah, what's the pains I suffered bringin' him into the world to carry him to his cradle, to the pains I'm sufferin' now, carryin' him out o' the world to bring him to his grave!

Mary. It would be better for you not to go at all, Mrs. Tancred, but to stay at home beside the fire with some o' the neighbours.

Mrs. Tancred. I seen the first of him, an' I'll see the last of him.

Mrs. Boyle. You'd want a shawl, Mrs. Tancred; it's a cowld night, an' the win's blowin' sharp.

Mrs. Madigan [*rushing out*]. I've a shawl above.

Mrs. Tancred. Me home is gone now; he was me only child, an' to think that he was lyin' for a whole night stretched out on the side of a lonely counthry lane, with his head, his darlin' head, that I often kissed an' fondled, half hidden in the wather of a runnin' brook. An' I'm told he was the leadher of the ambush where me nex' door neighbour, Mrs. Mannin', lost her Free State soldier son. An' now here's the two of us oul' women, standin' one on each side of a scales o' sorra, balanced be the bodies of our two dead darlin' sons. [*Mrs. Madigan returns, and wraps a shawl around her.*] God bless you, Mrs. Madigan. . . . [*She moves slowly towards the door*] Mother o' God, Mother o' God, have pity on the pair of us! . . . O Blessed Virgin, where were you when me darlin' son was riddled with bullets, when me darlin' son was riddled with bullets! . . . Sacred Heart of the Crucified Jesus, take away our hearts o' stone . . . an' give us hearts o' flesh! . . . Take away this murdherin' hate . . . an' give us Thine own eternal love! [*They pass out of the room.*

Mrs. Boyle [*explanatorily to Bentham*]. That was Mrs. Tancred of the two-pair back; her son was found, e'er yesterday, lyin' out beyant Finglas riddled with bullets. A Die-hard he was, be all accounts. He was a nice quiet boy, but lattherly he went to hell, with his Republic first, an' Republic last an' Republic over all. He often took tea with us here, in the oul' days, an' Johnny, there, an' him used to be always together.

Johnny. Am I always to be havin' to tell you that he was no friend o' mine? I never cared for him, an' he could never stick me. It's not because he was Commandant of the Battalion that I was Quarther-Masther of, that we were friends.

Mrs. Boyle. He's gone now—the Lord be good to him! God help his poor oul' creature of a mother, for no matther whose friend or enemy he was, he was her poor son.

Bentham. The whole thing is terrible, Mrs. Boyle; but the only way to deal with a mad dog is to destroy him.

Mrs. Boyle. An' to think of me forgettin' about him bein' brought to the church to-night, an' we singin' an' all, but it was well we hadn't the gramophone goin', anyhow.

Boyle. Even if we had aself. We've nothin' to do with these things, one way or t'other. That's the Government's business, an' let them do what we're payin' them for doin'.

Mrs. Boyle. I'd like to know how a body's not to mind these things; look at the way they're afther leavin' the people in this very house. Hasn't the whole house, nearly, been massacreed? There's young Dougherty's husband with his leg off; Mrs. Travers that had her son blew up be a mine in Inchegeela, in Co. Cork; Mrs. Mannin' that lost wan of her sons in ambush a few weeks ago, an' now, poor Mrs. Tancred's only child gone west with his body made a collandher of. Sure, if it's not our business, I don't know whose business it is.

Boyle. Here, there, that's enough about them things; they don't affect us, an' we needn't give a damn. If they want a wake, well, let them have a wake. When I was a sailor, I was always resigned to meet with a wathery grave; an' if they want to be soldiers, well, there's no use o' them squealin' when they meet a soldier's fate.

Joxer. Let me like a soldier fall—me breast expandin' to th' ball!

Mrs. Boyle. In wan way, she deserves all she got; for lately, she let th' Die-hards make an open house of th' place; an' for th' last couple of months, either when th' sun was risin' or when th' sun was settin', you had C.I.D. men burstin' into your room, assin' you where were you born, where were you christened, where were you married, an' where would you be buried!

Johnny. For God's sake, let us have no more o' this talk.

Mrs. Madigan. What about Mr. Boyle's song before we start th' gramophone?

Mary [*getting her hat, and putting it on*]. Mother, Charlie and I are goin' out for a little sthroll.

Mrs. Boyle. All right, darlin'.

Bentham [*going out with Mary*]. We won't be long away, Mrs. Boyle.

Mrs. Madigan. Gwan, Captain, gwan.

Boyle. E-e-e-eh, I'd want to have a few more jars in me, before I'd be in fettle for singin'.

Joxer. Give us that poem you writ t'other day. [*To the rest*] Aw, it's a darlin' poem, a daarlin' poem.

Mrs. Boyle. God bless us, is he startin' to write poetry!

Boyle [*rising to his feet*]. Ee-e-e-eh.

> [*He recites in an emotional, consequential manner the following verses:*
>
> Shawn an' I were friends, sir, to me he was all in all.
> His work was very heavy and his wages were very small.
> None betther on th' beach as Docker, I'll go bail,
> 'Tis now I'm feelin' lonely, for to-day he lies in jail.
> He was not what some call pious—seldom at church or prayer;
> For the greatest scoundrels I know, sir, goes every Sunday there.
> Fond of his pint—well, rather, but hated the Boss by creed
> But never refused a copper to comfort a pal in need.

E-e-e-eh. [*He sits down.*

Mrs. Madigan. Grand, grand; you should folly that up, you should folly that up.

Joxer. It's a daarlin' poem!

Boyle [*delightedly*]. E-e-e-eh.

Johnny. Are yous goin' to put on th' gramophone to-night, or are yous not?

Mrs. Boyle. Gwan, Jack, put on a record.

Mrs. Madigan. Gwan, Captain, gwan.

Boyle. Well, yous'll want to keep a dead silence.

> [*He sets a record, starts the machine, and it begins to play "If you're Irish, come into the Parlour". As the tune is in full blare, the door is suddenly opened by a brisk, little bald-headed man, dressed circumspectly in a black suit; he glares fiercely at all in the room; he is "Needle" Nugent, a tailor. He carries his hat in his hand.*

Nugent [*loudly, above the noise of the gramophone*]. Are yous goin' to have that thing bawlin' an' the funeral of Mrs. Tancred's son passin' the house? Have none of yous any respect for the Irish people's National regard for the dead? [*Boyle stops the gramophone.*

Mrs. Boyle. Maybe, Needle Nugent, it's nearly time we had a little less respect for the dead, an' a little more regard for the livin'.

Mrs. Madigan. We don't want you, Mr. Nugent, to teach us what we learned at our mother's knee. You don't look yourself as if you were dyin' of grief; if y'ass Maisie Madigan anything, I'd call you a real thrue Diehard an' live-soft Republican, attendin' Republican funerals in the day, an' stoppin' up half the night makin' suits for the Civic Guards!

[*Persons are heard running down to the street, some saying, "Here it is, here it is." Nugent withdraws, and the rest, except Johnny, go to the window looking into the street, and look out. Sounds of a crowd coming nearer are heard; portion are singing:*

To Jesus' Heart all burning
With fervent love for men,
My heart with fondest yearning
Shall raise its joyful strain.
While ages course along,
Blest be with loudest song
The Sacred Heart of Jesus
By every heart and tongue.

Mrs. Boyle. Here's the hearse, here's the hearse!

Boyle. There's t'oul' mother walkin' behin' the coffin.

Mrs. Madigan. You can hardly see the coffin with the wreaths.

Joxer. Oh, it's a darlin' funeral, a daarlin' funeral!

Mrs. Madigan. W'd have a betther view from the street.

Boyle. Yes—this place ud give you a crick in your neck.

[*They leave the room, and go down. Johnny sits moodily by the fire.*

[*A young man enters; he looks at Johnny for a moment.*

The Young Man. Quarther-Masther Boyle.

Johnny [*with a start*]. The Mobilizer!

The Young Man. You're not at the funeral?

Johnny. I'm not well.

The Young Man. I'm glad I've found you; you were stoppin' at your aunt's; I called there but you'd gone. I've to give you an ordher to attend a Battalion Staff meetin' the night afther to-morrow.

Johnny. Where?

The Young Man. I don't know; you're to meet me at the Pillar at eight o'clock; then we're to go to a place I'll be told of to-night; there we'll meet a mothor that'll bring us to the meeting. They think you might be able to know somethin' about them that gave the bend where Commandant Tancred was shelterin'.

Johnny.   I'm not goin', then. I know nothing about Tancred.

The Young Man [*at the door*].   You'd betther come for your own sake—remember your oath.

Johnny [*passionately*].   I won't go! Haven't I done enough for Ireland! I've lost me arm, an' me hip's desthroyed so that I'll never be able to walk right agen! Good God, haven't I done enough for Ireland?

The Young Man.   Boyle, no man can do enough for Ireland!

[*He goes.*

[*Faintly in the distance the crowd is heard saying:*

Hail, Mary, full of grace, the Lord is with Thee;
Blessed art Thou amongst women, and blessed, etc.

CURTAIN

ACT III

The same as Act II. It is about half-past six on a November evening; a bright fire burns in the grate; Mary, dressed to go out, is sitting on a chair by the fire, leaning forward, her hands under her chin, her elbows on her knees. A look of dejection, mingled with uncertain anxiety, is on her face. A lamp, turned low, is lighting on the table. The votive light under the picture of the Virgin gleams more redly than ever. Mrs. Boyle is putting on her hat and coat. It is two months later.

Mrs. Boyle.   An' has Bentham never even written to you since—not one line for the past month?

Mary (*tonelessly*).   Not even a line, mother.

Mrs. Boyle.   That's very curious. . . . What came between the two of yous at all? To leave you so sudden, an' yous so great together. . . . To go away t' England, an' not to even leave you his address. . . . The way he was always bringin' you to dances, I thought he was mad afther you. Are you sure you said nothin' to him?

Mary. No, mother—at least nothing that could possibly explain his givin' me up.

Mrs. Boyle. You know you're a bit hasty at times, Mary, an' say things you shouldn't say.

Mary. I never said to him what I shouldn't say, I'm sure of that.

Mrs. Boyle. How are you sure of it?

Mary. Because I love him with all my heart and soul, mother. Why, I don't know; I often thought to myself that he wasn't the man poor Jerry was, but I couldn't help loving him, all the same.

Mrs. Boyle. But you shouldn't be frettin' the way you are; when a woman loses a man, she never knows what she's afther losin', to be sure, but, then, she never knows what she's afther gainin', either. You're not the one girl of a month ago—you look like one pinin' away. It's long ago I had a right to bring you to the doctor, instead of waitin' till to-night.

Mary. There's no necessity, really, mother, to go to the doctor; nothing serious is wrong with me—I'm run down and disappointed, that's all.

Mrs. Boyle. I'll not wait another minute; I don't like the look of you at all. . . . I'm afraid we made a mistake in throwin' over poor Jerry. . . . He'd have been betther for you than that Bentham.

Mary. Mother, the best man for a woman is the one for whom she has the most love, and Charlie had it all.

Mrs. Boyle. Well, there's one thing to be said for him—he couldn't have been thinkin' of the money, or he wouldn't ha' left you . . . it must ha' been somethin' else.

Mary [*wearily*]. I don't know . . . I don't know, mother . . . only I think . . .

Mrs. Boyle. What d'ye think?

Mary. I imagine . . . he thought . . . we weren't . . . good enough for him.

Mrs. Boyle. An' what was he himself, only a school teacher? Though I don't blame him for fightin' shy of people like that Joxer fella an' that oul' Madigan wan—nice sort o' people for your father to inthroduce to a man like Mr. Bentham. You might have told me all about this before now, Mary; I don't know why you like to hide everything from your mother; you knew Bentham, an' I'd ha' known nothin' about it if it hadn't bin for the Will; an' it was only to-day, afther long coaxin', that you let out that he's left you.

Mary. It would have been useless to tell you—you wouldn't understand.

Mrs. Boyle [*hurt*]. Maybe not. . . . Maybe I wouldn't understand. . . . Well, we'll be off now.

> [*She goes over to door left, and speaks to Boyle inside.*

Mrs. Boyle. We're goin' now to the doctor's. Are you goin' to get up this evenin'?

Boyle [*from inside*]. The pains in me legs is terrible! It's me should be poppin' off to the doctor instead o' Mary, the way I feel.

Mrs. Boyle. Sorra mend you! A nice way you were in last night—carried in in a frog's march, dead to the world. If that's the way you'll go on when you get the money it'll be the grave for you, an asylum for me and the Poorhouse for Johnny.

Boyle. I thought you were goin'?

Mrs. Boyle. That's what has you as you are—you can't bear to be spoken to. Knowin' the way we are, up to our ears in debt, it's a wondher you wouldn't ha' got up to go to th' solicitor's an' see if we could ha' gotten a little o' the money even.

Boyle [*shouting*]. I can't be goin' up there night, noon an' mornin', can I? He can't give the money till he gets it, can he? I can't get blood out of a turnip, can I?

Mrs. Boyle. It's nearly two months since we heard of the Will, an' the money seems as far off as ever. . . . I suppose you know we owe twenty pouns to oul' Murphy?

Boyle. I've a faint recollection of you tellin' me that before.

Mrs. Boyle. Well, you'll go over to the shop yourself for the things in future—I'll face him no more.

Boyle. I thought you said you were goin'?

Mrs. Boyle. I'm goin' now; come on, Mary.

Boyle. Ey, Juno, ey!

Mrs. Boyle. Well, what d'ye want now?

Boyle. Is there e'er a bottle o' stout left?

Mrs. Boyle. There's two o' them here still.

Boyle. Show us in one o' them an' leave t'other there till I get up. An' throw us in the paper that's on the table, an' the bottle o' Sloan's Liniment that's in th' drawer.

Mrs. Boyle [*getting the liniment and the stout*].   What paper is it you want—the *Messenger?*

Boyle.   *Messenger!* The *News o' the World!*

[*Mrs. Boyle brings in the things asked for, and comes out again.*

Mrs. Boyle [*at door*].   Mind the candle, now, an' don't burn the house over our heads. I left t'other bottle o' stout on the table.

> *She puts bottle of stout on table. She goes out with Mary. A cork is heard popping inside.*
>
> [*A pause; then outside the door is heard the voice of Joxer lilting softly:* "Me pipe I'll smoke, as I dhrive me moke . . . are you . . . there . . . Mor . . . ee . . . ar . . . i . . . teee!" *A gentle knock is heard, and after a pause the door opens, and Joxer, followed by Nugent, enters.*

Joxer.   Be God, they must be all out; I was thinkin' there was somethin' up when he didn't answer the signal. We seen Juno an' Mary goin', but I didn't see him, an' it's very seldom he escapes me.

Nugent.   He's not goin' to escape me—he's not goin' to be let go to the fair altogether.

Joxer.   Sure, the house couldn't hould them lately; an' he goin' about like a mastherpiece of the Free State counthry; forgettin' their friends; forgettin' God—wouldn't even lift his hat passin' a chapel! Sure they were bound to get a dhrop! An' you really think there's no money comin' to him afther all?

Nugent.   Not as much as a red rex, man; I've been a bit anxious this long time over me money, an' I went up to the solicitor's to find out all I could—ah, man, they were goin' to throw me down the stairs. They toul' me that the oul' cock himself had the stairs worn away comin' up afther it, an' they black in the face tellin' him he'd get nothin'. Some way or another that the Will is writ he won't be entitled to get as much as a make!

Joxer.   Ah, I thought there was somethin' curious about the whole thing; I've bin havin' sthrange dhreams for the last couple o' weeks. An' I notice that that Bentham fella doesn't be comin' here now—there must be somethin' on the mat there too. Anyhow, who, in the name o' God, ud leave anythin' to that oul' bummer? Sure it ud be unnatural. An' the way Juno an' him's been throwin' their weight about for the last few months! Ah, him that goes a borrowin' goes a sorrowin'!

Nugent.   Well, he's not goin' to throw his weight about in the suit I made for him much longer. I'm tellin' you seven pouns aren't to be found growin' on the bushes these days.

Joxer. An' there isn't hardly a neighbour in the whole street that hasn't lent him money on the strength of what he was goin' to get, but they're after backing the wrong horse. Wasn't it a mercy o' God that I'd nothin' to give him! The softy I am, you know, I'd ha' lent him me last juice! I must have had somebody's good prayers. Ah, afther all, an honest man's the noblest work o' God! [*Boyle coughs inside.*]

Joxer. Whisht, damn it, he must be inside in bed.

Nugent. Inside o' bed or outside of it, he's goin' to pay me for that suit, or give it back—he'll not climb up my back as easily as he thinks.

Joxer. Gwan in at wanst, man, an' get it off him, an' don't be a fool.

Nugent [*going to door left, opening it and looking in*]. Ah, don't disturb yourself, Mr. Boyle; I hope you're not sick?

Boyle. Th' oul' legs, Mr. Nugent, the oul' legs.

Nugent. I just called over to see if you could let me have anything off the suit?

Boyle. E-e-e-eh, how much is this it is?

Nugent. I's the same as it was at the start—seven pouns.

Boyle. I'm glad you kem, M. Nugent; I want a good heavy top-coat—Irish frieze, if you have it. How much would a top-coat like that be, now?

Nugent. About six pouns.

Boyle. Six pouns—six an' seven, six an' seven is thirteen—that'll be thirteen pouns I'll owe you.

[*Joxer slips the bottle of stout that is on the table into his pocket. Nugent rushes into the room, and returns with suit on his arm; he pauses at the door.*

Nugent. You'll owe me no thirteen pouns. Maybe you think you're bether able to owe it than pay it!

Boyle [*frantically*]. Here, come back to hell ower that—where're you goin' with them clothes o' mine?

Nugent. Where am I goin' with them clothes o' yours? Well, I like your damn cheek!

Boyle. Here, what am I goin' to dhress meself in when I'm goin' out?

Nugent. What do I care what you dhress yourself in! You can put yourself in a bolsther cover, if you like.

[*He goes towards the other door, followed by Joxer.*

Joxer. What'll he dhress himself in! Gentleman Jack an' his freize coat!

[*They go out.*

Boyle [*inside*].   Ey, Nugent; ey, Mr. Nugent, Mr. Nugent!

> [*After a pause Boyle enters hastily, buttoning the braces of his moleskin trousers; his coat and vest are on his arm; he throws these on a chair and hurries to the door on right.*]

Boyle.   Ey, Mr. Nugent, Mr. Nugent!

Joxer [*meeting him at the door*].   What's up, what's wrong, Captain?

Boyle.   Nugent's been here an' took away me suit—the only things I had to go out in!

Joxer.   Tuk your suit—for God's sake! An' what were you doin' while he was takin' them?

Boyle.   I was in bed when he stole in like a thief in the night, an' before I knew even what he was thinkin' of, he whipped them from the chair an' was off like a redshank!

Joxer.   An' what, in the name o' God, did he do that for?

Boyle.   What did he do it for? How the hell do I know what he done it for?—jealousy an' spite, I suppose.

Joxer.   Did he not say what he done it for?

Boyle.   Amn't I afther tellin' you that he had them whipped up an' was gone before I could open me mouth?

Joxer.   That was a very sudden thing to do; there mus' be somethin' behin' it. Did he hear anythin', I wondher?

Boyle.   Did he hear anythin'?—you talk very queer, Joxer—what could he hear?

Joxer.   About you not gettin' the money, in some way or t'other?

Boyle.   An' what ud prevent me from gettin' th' money?

Joxer.   That's jus' what I was thinkin'—what ud prevent you from gettin' the money—nothin', as far as I can see.

Boyle [*looking round for bottle of stout, with an exclamation*].   Aw, holy God!

Joxer.   What's up, Jack?

Boyle.   He must have afther lifted the bottle o' stout that Juno left on the table!

Joxer [*horrified*].   Ah no, ah no; he wouldn't be afther doin' that now.

Boyle.   An' who done it then? Juno left a bottle o' stout here, an' it's gone —it didn't walk, did it?

Joxer. Oh, that's shockin'; ah, man's inhumanity to man makes countless thousands mourn!

Mrs. Madigan [*appearing at the door*]. I hope I'm not disturbin' you in any discussion on your forthcomin' legacy—if I may use the word—an' that you'll let me have a barny for a minute or two with you, Mr. Boyle.

Boyle. [*uneasily*]. To be sure, Mrs. Madigan—an oul' friend's always welcome.

Joxer. Come in the evenin', come in th' mornin'; come when you're assed, or come without warnin', Mrs. Madigan.

Boyle. Sit down, Mrs. Madigan.

Mrs. Madigan [*ominously*]. Th' few words I have to say can be said standin'. Puttin' aside all formularies, I suppose you remember me lendin' you some time ago three pouns that I raised on blankets an' furniture in me uncle's?

Boyle. I remember it well. I have it recorded in me book—three pouns five shillins from Maisie Madigan, raised on articles pawned; an', item: fourpence, given to make up the price of a pint, on th' principle that no bird ever flew on wan wing; all to be repaid at par, when the ship comes home.

Mrs. Madigan. Well, ever since I shoved in the blankets I've been perishing with th' cowld, an' I've decided, if I'll be too hot in th' nex' world aself, I'm not goin' to be too cowld in this wan; an' consequently, I want me three pouns, if you please.

Boyle. This is a very sudden demand, Mrs. Madigan, an' can't be met; but I'm willin' to give you a receipt in full, in full.

Mrs. Madigan. Come on, out with th' money, an' don't be jack-actin'.

Boyle. You can't get blood out of a turnip, can you?

Mrs. Madigan [*rushing over and shaking him*]. Gimme me money, y'oul reprobate, or I'll shake the worth of it out of you!

Boyle. Ey, houl' on, there; houl' on, there! You'll wait for your money now, me lassie!

Mrs. Madigan [*looking around the room and seeing the gramophone*]. I'll wait for it, will I? Well, I'll not wait long; if I can't get th' cash, I'll get th' worth of it.   [*She catches up the gramophone.*

Boyle. Ey, ey, there, wher'r you goin' with that?

Mrs. Madigan. I'm goin' to th' pawn to get me three quid five shillins; I'll brin' you th' ticket, an' then you can do what you like, me bucko.

Boyle.   You can't touch that, you can't touch that! It's not my property, an' it's not ped for yet!

Mrs. Madigan.   So much th' betther. It'll be an ayse to me conscience, for I'm takin' what doesn't belong to you. You're not goin' to be swankin' it like a paycock with Maisie Madigan's money—I'll pull some o' th' gorgeous feathers out o' your tail!   [*She goes off with the gramophone.*

Boyle.   What's th' world comin' to at all? I ass you, Joxer Daly, is there any morality left anywhere?

Joxer.   I wouldn't ha' believed it, only I seen it with me own two eyes. I didn't think Maisie Madigan was that sort of woman; she has either a sup taken, or she's heard somethin'.

Boyle.   Heard somethin'—about what, if it's not any harm to ass you?

Joxer.   She must ha' heard some rumour or other that you weren't goin' to get th' money.

Boyle.   Who says I'm not goin' to get th' money?

Joxer.   Sure, I don't know—I was only sayin'.

Boyle.   Only sayin' what?

Joxer.   Nothin'.

Boyle.   You were goin' to say somethin'—don't be a twisther.

Joxer [*angrily*].   Who's a twisther?

Boyle.   Why don't you speak your mind, then?

Joxer.   You never twisted yourself—no, you wouldn't know how!

Boyle.   Did you ever know me to twist; did you ever know me to twist?

Joxer [*fiercely*].   Did you ever do anythin' else! Sure, you can't believe a word that comes out o' your mouth.

Boyle.   Here, get out, ower o' this; I always knew you were a prognosticator an' a procrastinator!

Joxer [*going out as Johnny comes in*].   The anchor's weighed, farewell, ree . . . mem . . . ber . . . me. Jacky Boyle, Esquire, infernal rogue an' damned liar.

Johnny.   Joxer an' you at it agen?—when are you goin' to have a little respect for yourself, an' not be always makin' a show of us all?

Boyle.   Are you goin' to lecture me now?

Johnny.   Is mother back from the doctor yet, with Mary?

[*Mrs. Boyle enters; it is apparent from the serious look on her face that something has happened. She takes off her hat and coat without a word and puts them by. She then sits down near the fire, and there is a few moments' pause.*

Boyle. Well, what did the doctor say about Mary?

Mrs. Boyle [*in an earnest manner and with suppressed agitation*]. Sit down here, Jack; I've something to say to you . . . about Mary.

Boyle [*awed by her manner*]. About . . . Mary?

Mrs. Boyle. Close that door there and sit down here.

Boyle [*closing the door*]. More throuble in our native land, is it? [*He sits down.*] Well, what is it?

Mrs. Boyle. It's about Mary.

Boyle. Well, what about Mary—there's nothin' wrong with her, is there?

Mrs. Boyle. I'm sorry to say there's a gradle wrong with her.

Boyle. A gradle wrong with her! [*Peevishly*] First Johnny an' now Mary; is the whole house goin' to become an hospital! It's not consumption, is it?

Mrs. Boyle. No . . . it's not consumption . . . it's worse.

Johnny. Worse! Well, we'll have to get her into some place ower this, there's no one here to mind her.

Mrs. Boyle. We'll all have to mind her now. You might as well know now, Johnny, as another time. [*To Boyle*] D'ye know what the doctor said to me about her, Jack?

Boyle. How ud I know—I wasn't there, was I?

Mrs. Boyle. He told me to get her married at wanst.

Boyle. Married at wanst! An' why did he say the like o' that?

Mrs. Boyle. Because Mary's goin' to have a baby in a short time.

Boyle. Goin' to have a baby!—my God, what'll Bentham say when he hears that?

Mrs. Boyle. Are you blind, man, that you can't see that it was Bentham that has done this wrong to her?

Boyle [*passionately*]. Then he'll marry her, he'll have to marry her!

Mrs. Boyle. You know he's gone to England, an' God knows where he is now.

Boyle. I'll folly him, I'll folly him, an' bring him back, an' make him do her justice. The scoundrel, I might ha' known what he was, with his yogees an' his prawna!

Mrs. Boyle. We'll have to keep it quiet till we see what we can do.

Boyle. Oh, isn't this a nice thing to come on top o' me, an' the state I'm in! A pretty show I'll be to Joxer an' to that oul' wan, Madigan! Amn't I afther goin' through enough without havin' to go through this!

Mrs. Boyle. What you an' I'll have to go through'll be nothin' to what poor Mary'll have to go through; for you an' me is middlin' old, an' most of our years is spent; but Mary'll have maybe forty years to face an' handle, an every wan of them'll be tainted with a bitther memory.

Boyle. Where is she? Where is she till I tell her off? I'm tellin' you when I'm done with her she'll be a sorry girl!

Mrs. Boyle. I left her in me sister's till I came to speak to you. You'll say nothin' to her, Jack; ever since she left school she's earned her livin', an' your fatherly care never throubled the poor girl.

Boyle. Gwan, take her part agen her father! But I'll let you see whether I'll say nothin' to her or no! Her an' her readin'! That's more o' th' blasted nonsense that has the house fallin' down on top of us! What did th' likes of her, born in a tenement house, want with readin'? Her readin's afther bringin' her to a nice pass—oh, it's madnin', madnin', madnin'!

Mrs. Boyle. When she comes back say nothin' to her, Jack, or she'll leave this place.

Boyle. Leave this place! Ay, she'll leave this place, an' quick too!

Mrs. Boyle. If Mary goes, I'll go with her.

Boyle. Well, go with her! Well, go, th' pair o' yous! I lived before I seen yous, an' I can live when yous are gone. Isn't this a nice thing to come rollin' in on top o' me afther all your prayin' to St. Anthony an' The Little Flower! An' she's a Child o' Mary, too—I wonder what'll the nuns think of her now? An' it'll be bellows'd all over th' disthrict before you could say Jack Robinson; an' whenever I'm seen they'll whisper, "That's th' father of Mary Boyle that had th' kid be th' swank she used to go with; d'ye know, d'ye know?" To be sure they'll know—more about it than I will meself!

Johnny. She should be dhriven out o' th' house she's brought disgrace on!

Mrs. Boyle. Hush, you, Johnny. We needn't let it be bellows'd all over the place; all we've got to do is to leave this place quietly an' go somewhere where we're not known, an' nobody'll be th' wiser.

Boyle. You're talkin' like a two-year-oul', woman. Where'll we get a place ou' o' this?—places aren't that easily got.

Mrs. Boyle. But, Jack, when we get the money . . .

Boyle. Money—what money?

Mrs. Boyle. Why, oul' Ellison's money, of course.

Boyle. There's no money comin' from oul' Ellison, or any one else. Since you've heard of wan throuble, you might as well hear of another. There's no money comin' to us at all—the Will's a wash-out!

Mrs. Boyle. What are you sayin', man—no money?

Johnny. How could it be a wash-out?

Boyle. The boyo that's afther doin' it to Mary done it to me as well. The thick made out the Will wrong; he said in th' Will, only first cousin an' second cousin, instead of mentionin' our names, an' now any one that thinks he's a first cousin or second cousin t'oul' Ellison can claim the money as well as me, an' they're springin' up in hundreds, an' comin' from America an' Australia, thinkin' to get their whack out of it, while all the time the lawyers is gobblin' it up, till there's not as much as ud buy a stockin' for your lovely daughter's baby!

Mrs. Boyle. I don't believe it, I don't believe it, I don't believe it!

Johnny. Why did you say nothin' about this before?

Mrs. Boyle. You're not serious, Jack; you're not serious!

Boyle. I'm tellin' you the scholar, Bentham, made a banjax o' th' Will; instead o' sayin', "th' rest o' me property to be divided between me first cousin, Jack Boyle, an' me second cousin, Mick Finnegan, o' Santhry", he writ down only, "me first an' second cousins", an' the world an' his wife are afther th' property now.

Mrs. Boyle. Now I know why Bentham left poor Mary in th' lurch; I can see it all now—oh, is there not even a middlin' honest man left in th' world?

Johnny [to Boyle]. An' you let us run into debt, an' you borreyed money from everybody to fill yourself with beer! An' now you tell us the whole thing's a washout! Oh, if it's thrue, I'm done with you, for you're worse than me sisther Mary!

Boyle. You hole your tongue, d'ye hear? I'll not take any lip from you. Go an' get Bentham if you want satisfaction for all that's afther happenin' us.

Johnny. I won't hole me tongue, I won't hole me tongue! I'll tell you what I think of you, father an' all as you are . . . you . . .

Mrs. Boyle. Johnny, Johnny, Johnny, for God's sake, be quiet!

Johnny. I'll not be quiet, I'll not be quiet; he's a nice father, isn't he? Is it any wondher Mary went asthray, when . . .

Mrs. Boyle. Johnny, Johnny, for my sake be quiet—for your mother's sake!

Boyle. I'm goin' out now to have a few dhrinks with th' last few makes I have, an' tell that lassie o' yours not to be here when I come back; for if I lay me eyes on her, I'll lay me hans on her, an' if I lay me hans on her, I won't be accountable for me actions!

Johnny. Take care somebody doesn't lay his hands on you—y'oul' . . .

Mrs. Boyle. Johnny, Johnny!

Boyle [*at door, about to go out*]. Oh, a nice son, an' a nicer daughter, I have. [*Calling loudly upstairs*] Joxer, Joxer, are you there?

Joxer [*from a distance*]. I'm here, More . . . ee . . . aar . . . i . . . tee!

Boyle. I'm goin' down to Foley's—are you comin'?

Joxer. Come with you? With that sweet call me heart is stirred; I'm only waiting for the word, an' I'll be with you, like a bird!

[*Boyle and Joxer pass the door going out.*

Johnny [*throwing himself on the bed*]. I've a nice sisther, an' a nice fa-ther, there's no bettin' on it. I wish to God a bullet or a bomb had whipped me ou' o' this long ago! Not one o' yous, not one o' yous, have any thought for me!

Mrs. Boyle [*with passionate remonstrance*]. If you don't whisht, Johnny, you'll drive me mad. Who has kep' th' home together for the past few years—only me? An' who'll have to bear th' biggest part o' this throuble but me?—but whinin' an' whingin' isn't goin' to do any good.

Johnny. You're to blame yourself for a gradle of it—givin' him his own way in everything, an' never assin' to check him, no matther what he done. Why didn't you look afther th' money? why . . .

[*There is a knock at the door; Mrs. Boyle opens it; Johnny rises on his elbow to look and listen; two men enter.*

First Man. We've been sent up be th' Manager of the Hibernian Furnish-ing Co., Mrs. Boyle, to take back the furniture that was got a while ago.

Mrs. Boyle. Yous'll touch nothin' here—how do I know who yous are?

First Man [*showing a paper*]. There's the ordher, ma'am. [*Reading*] A chest o' drawers, a table, wan easy an' two ordinary chairs; wan mirror; wan chestherfield divan, an' a wardrobe an' two vases. [*To his comrade*] Come on, Bill, it's afther knockin'-off time already.

Johnny. For God's sake, mother, run down to Foley's an' bring father back, or we'll be left without a stick. [*The men carry out the table.*

Mrs. Boyle. What good would it be?—you heard what he said before he went out.

Johnny. Can't you thry? He ought to be here, an' the like of this goin' on. [*Mrs. Boyle puts a shawl around her, as Mary enters.*

Mary. What's up, mother? I met men carryin' away the table, an' everybody's talking about us not gettin' the money after all.

Mrs. Boyle. Everythin's gone wrong, Mary, everythin'. We're not gettin' a penny out o' the Will, not a penny—I'll tell you all when I come back; I'm goin' for your father. [*She runs out.*

Johnny [*to Mary, who has sat down by the fire*]. It's a wondher you're not ashamed to show your face here, afther what has happened.

    [*Jerry enters slowly; there is a look of earnest hope on his face. He looks at Mary for a few moments.*

Jerry [*softly*]. Mary! [*Mary does not answer.*

Jerry. Mary, I want to speak to you for a few moments, may I?
    [*Mary remains silent; Johnny goes slowly into room on left.*

Jerry. Your mother has told me everything, Mary, and I have come to you. . . . I have come to tell you, Mary, that my love for you is greater and deeper than ever. . . .

Mary [*with a sob*]. Oh, Jerry, Jerry, say no more; all that is over now; anything like that is impossible now!

Jerry. Impossible? Why do you talk like that, Mary?

Mary. After all that has happened.

Jerry. What does it matter what has happened? We are young enough to be able to forget all those things. [*He catches her hand*] Mary, Mary, I am pleading for your love. With Labour, Mary, humanity is above everything; we are the Leaders in the fight for a new life. I want to forget Bentham, I want to forget that you left me—even for a while.

Mary. Oh, Jerry, Jerry, you haven't the bitter word of scorn for me after all.

Jerry [*passionately*]. Scorn! I love you, love you, Mary!

Mary [*rising, and looking him in the eyes*]. Even though . . .

Jerry. Even though you threw me over for another man; even though you gave me many a bitter word!

Mary. Yes, yes, I know; but you love me, even though . . . even though . . . I'm . . . goin' . . . goin' . . . [*He looks at her questioningly, and fear gathers in his eyes.*] Ah, I was thinkin' so. . . . You don't know everything!

Jerry [*poignantly*]. Surely to God, Mary, you don't mean that . . . that . . . that . . .

Mary. Now you know all, Jerry; now you know all!

Jerry. My God, Mary, have you fallen as low as that?

Mary. Yes, Jerry, as you say, I have fallen as low as that.

Jerry. I didn't mean it that way, Mary . . . it came on me so sudden, that I didn't mind what I was sayin'. . . . I never expected this—your mother never told me. . . . I'm sorry . . . God knows, I'm sorry for you, Mary.

Mary. Let us say no more, Jerry; I don't blame you for thinkin' it's terrible. . . . I suppose it is. . . . Everybody'll think the same . . . it's only as I expected—your humanity is just as narrow as the humanity of the others.

Jerry. I'm sorry, all the same. . . . I shouldn't have troubled you. . . . I wouldn't if I'd known. . . . If I can do anything for you . . . Mary . . . I will. [*He turns to go, and halts at the door.*

Mary. Do you remember, Jerry, the verses you read when you gave the lecture in the Socialist Rooms some time ago, on Humanity's Strife with Nature?

Jerry. The verses—no; I don't remember them.

Mary. I do. They're runnin' in me head now—

An' we felt the power that fashion'd
All the lovely things we saw,
That created all the murmur
Of an everlasting law,
Was a hand of force an' beauty,
With an eagle's tearin' claw.

Then we saw our globe of beauty
Was an ugly thing as well,
A hymn divine whose chorus
Was an agonizin' yell;
Like the story of a demon,
That an angel had to tell;

Like a glowin' picture by a
Hand unsteady, brought to ruin;
Like her craters, if their deadness
Could give life unto the moon;
Like the agonizing horror
Of a violin out of tune.

[*There is a pause, and Devine goes slowly out.*

Johnny [*returning*].   Is he gone?

Mary. Yes.   [*The two men re-enter.*

First Man.   We can't wait any longer for t'oul' fella—sorry, Miss, but we
have to live as well as th' nex' man.   [*They carry out some things.*

Johnny.   Oh, isn't this terrible! . . . I suppose you told him everything
. . . couldn't you have waited for a few days? . . . he'd have stopped
th' takin' of the things, if you'd kep' your mouth shut. Are you burnin' to
tell every one of the shame you've brought on us?

Mary [*snatching up her hat and coat*].   Oh, this is unbearable!

[*She rushes out.*

First Man [*re-entering*].   We'll take the chest o' drawers next—it's the
heaviest.   [*The votive light flickers for a moment, and goes out.*

Johnny [*in a cry of fear*].   Mother o' God, the light's after goin' out!

First Man.   You put the win' up me the way you bawled that time. The
oil's all gone, that's all.

Johnny [*with an agonizing cry*].   Mother o' God, there's a shot I'm after
gettin'!

First Man.   What's wrong with you, man? Is it a fit you're takin'?

Johnny.   I'm after feelin' a pain in me breast, like the tearin' by a bullet!

First Man.   He's goin' mad—it's a wondher they'd leave a chap like that
here by himself.

[*Two Irregulars enter swiftly; they carry revolvers; one goes over to
Johnny; the other cover the two furniture men.*

First Irregular [*to the men, quietly and incisively*].   Who are you?—what
are yous doin' here?—quick!

First Man.   Removin' furniture that's not paid for.

Irregular.   Get over to the other end of the room an turn your faces to the
wall—quick!

[*The two men turn their faces to the wall, with their hands up.*

Second Irregular [*to Johnny*]. Come on, Sean Boyle, you're wanted; some of us have a word to say to you.

Johnny. I'm sick, I can't—what do you want with me?

Second Irregular. Come on, come on; we've a distance to go, an' haven't much time—come on.

Johnny. I'm an oul' comrade—yous wouldn't shoot an oul' comrade.

Second Irregular. Poor Tancred was an oul' comrade o' yours, but you didn't think o' that when you gave him away to the gang that sent him to his grave. But we've no time to waste; come on—here, Dermot, ketch his arm. [*To Johnny*] Have you your beads?

Johnny. Me beads! Why do you ass me that, why do you ass me that?

Second Irregular. Go on, go on, march!

Johnny. Are yous goin' to do in a comrade?—look at me arm, I lost it for Ireland.

Second Irregular. Commandant Tancred lost his life for Ireland.

Johnny. Sacred Heart of Jesus, have mercy on me! Mother o' God, pray for me—be with me now in the agonies o' death! . . . Hail, Mary, full o' grace . . . the Lord is . . . with Thee.

> [*They drag out Johnny Boyle, and the curtain falls. When it rises again the most of the furniture is gone. Mary and Mrs. Boyle, one on each side, are sitting in a darkened room, by the fire; it is an hour later.*

Mrs. Boyle. I'll not wait much longer . . . what did they bring him away in the mothor for? Nugent says he thinks they had guns . . . is me throubles never goin' to be over? . . . If anything ud happen to poor Johnny, I think I'd lose me mind. . . . I'll go to the Police Station, surely they ought to be able to do somethin'.

> [*Below is heard the sound of voices.*

Mrs. Boyle. Whisht, is that something? Maybe, it's your father, though when I left him in Foley's he was hardly able to lift his head. Whisht!

> [*A knock at the door, and the voice of Mrs. Madigan, speaking very softly*]: Mrs. Boyle, Mrs. Boyle.   [*Mrs. Boyle opens the door.*

Mrs. Madigan. Oh, Mrs. Boyle, God an' His Blessed Mother be with you this night!

Mrs. Boyle [*calmly*]. What is it, Mrs. Madigan? It's Johnny—something about Johnny.

Mrs. Madigan. God send it's not, God send it's not Johnny!

Mrs. Boyle. Don't keep me waitin', Mrs. Madigan; I've gone through so much lately that I feel able for anything.

Mrs. Madigan. Two polismen below wantin' you.

Mrs. Boyle. Wantin' me; an' why do they want me?

Mrs. Madigan. Some poor fella's been found, an' they think it's, it's . . .

Mrs. Boyle. Johnny, Johnny!

Mary [*with her arms round her mother*]. Oh, mother, mother, me poor, darlin' mother.

Mrs. Boyle. Hush, hush, darlin'; you'll shortly have your own throuble to bear. [*To Mrs. Madigan*] An' why do the polis think it's Johnny, Mrs. Madigan?

Mrs. Madigan. Because one o' the doctors knew him when he was attendin' with his poor arm.

Mrs. Boyle. Oh, it's thrue, then; it's Johnny, it's me son, me own son!

Mary. Oh, it's thrue, it's thrue what Jerry Devine says—there isn't a God, there isn't a God; if there was He wouldn't let these things happen!

Mrs. Boyle. Mary Mary, you musn't say them things. We'll want all the help we can get from God an' His Blessed Mother now! These things have nothin' to do with the Will o' God. Ah, what can God do agen the stupidity o' men!

Mrs. Madigan. The polis want you to go with them to the hospital to see the poor body—they're waitin' below.

Mrs. Boyle. We'll go. Come, Mary, an' we'll never come back here agen. Let your father furrage for himself now; I've done all I could an' it was all no use—he'll be hopeless till the end of his days. I've got a little room in me sisther's where we'll stop till your throuble is over, an' then we'll work together for the sake of the baby.

Mary. My poor little child that'll have no father!

Mrs. Boyle. It'll have what's far betther—it'll have two mothers.

A Rough Voice shouting from below. Are yous goin' to keep us waitin' for yous all night?

Mrs. Madigan [*going to the door, and shouting down*]. Take your hour, there, take your hour! If yous are in such a hurry, skip off, then, for nobody wants you here—if they did yous wouldn't be found. For you're the same as yous were undher the British Government—never where yous are wanted! As far as I can see, the Polis as Polis, in this city, is Null an' Void!

Mrs. Boyle. We'll go, Mary, we'll go; you to see your poor dead brother, an' me to see me poor dead son!

Mary. I dhread it, mother, I dhread it!

Mrs. Boyle. I forgot, Mary, I forgot; your pool oul' selfish mother was only thinkin' of herself. No, no, you mustn't come—it wouldn't be good for you. You go on to me sister's an' I'll face th' ordeal meself. Maybe I didn't feel sorry enough for Mrs. Tancred when her poor son was found as Johnny's been found now—because he was a Diehard! Ah, why didn't I remember that then he wasn't a Diehard or a Stater, but only a poor dead son! It's well I remember all that she said—an' it's my turn to say it now: What was the pain I suffered, Johnny, bringin' you into the world to carry you to your cradle, to the pains I'll suffer carryin' you out o' the world to bring you to your grave! Mother o' God, Mother o' God, have pity on us all! Blessed Virgin, where were you when me darlin' son was riddled with bullets, when me darlin' son was riddled with bullets? Sacred Heart o' Jesus, take away our hearts o' stone, and give us hearts o' flesh! Take away this murdherin' hate, an' give us Thine own eternal love! [*They all go slowly out.*

[*There is a pause; then a sound of shuffling steps on the stairs outside. The door opens and Boyle and Joxer, both of them very drunk, enter.*

Boyle. I'm able to go no farther. . . . Two polis, ey . . . what were they doin' here, I wondher? . . . Up to no good, anyhow . . . an' Juno an' that lovely daughter o' mine with them. [*Taking a sixpence from his pocket and looking at it*] Wan single, solitary tanner left out of all I borreyed. . . . [*He lets it fall.*] The last o' the Mohicans. . . . The blinds is down, Joxer, the blinds is down!

Joxer [*walking unsteadily across the room, and anchoring at the bed*]. Put all . . . your throubles . . . in your oul' kit-bag . . . an' smile . . . smile . . . smile!

Boyle. The counthry'll have to steady itself . . . it's goin' . . . to hell. . . . Where'r all . . . the chairs . . . gone to . . . steady itself, Joxer. . . . Chairs'll . . . have to . . . steady themselves. . . . No matther . . . what any one may . . . say. . . . Irelan' sober . . . is Irelan' . . . free.

Joxer [*stretching himself on the bed*]. Chains . . . an' . . . slaveree . . . that's a darlin' motto . . . a daaarlin' . . . motto!

Boyle. If th' worst comes . . . to th' worse . . . I can join a . . . flyin' . . . column. . . . I done . . . me bit . . . in Easther Week . . .

had no business . . . to . . . be . . . there . . . but Captain Boyle's Captain Boyle!

Joxer. Breathes there a man with soul . . . so . . . de . . . ad . . . this . . . me . . . o . . . wn, me nat . . . ive l . . . an'!

Boyle [*subsiding into a sitting posture on the floor*] Commandant Kelly died . . . in them . . . arms . . . Joxer. . . . Tell me Volunteer Butties . . . says he . . . that . . . I died for . . . Irelan'!

Joxer. D'jever rade Willie . . . Reilly . . . an' his own . . . Colleen . . . Bawn? It's a darlin' story, a daarlin' story!

Boyle. I'm telling you . . . Joxer . . . th' whole worl's . . . in a terr . . . ible state o' . . . chassis!

CURTAIN

THE PLOUGH AND THE STARS

A Tragedy in Four Acts

(1926)

To the gay laugh of my mother
at the gate of the grave

❦ ❦ ❦

CHARACTERS IN THE PLAY

JACK CLITHEROE (*a bricklayer*), *Comman-*
  dant in the Irish Citizen Army
NORA CLITHEROE, *his wife*
PETER FLYNN (*a labourer*), *Nora's uncle*
THE YOUNG COVEY (*a fitter*), *Clitheroe's*   *Residents in*
  cousin   *the Tenement*
BESSIE BURGESS (*a street fruit-vendor*)
MRS. GOGAN (*a charwoman*)
MOLLSER, *her consumptive child*
FLUTHER GOOD (*a carpenter*)
LIEUT. LANGON (*a Civil Servant*), *of the Irish Volunteers*
CAPT. BRENNAN (*a chicken butcher*), *of the Irish Citizen*
  Army
CORPORAL STODDART, *of the Wiltshires*
SERGEANT TINLEY, *of the Wiltshires*
ROSIE REDMOND, *a daughter of "the Digs"*
A BAR-TENDER
A WOMAN
THE FIGURE IN THE WINDOW

SCENE

ACT I · The living-room of the Clitheroe flat in a Dublin
  tenement.

ACT II · A public-house, outside of which a meeting is being held.

ACT III · The street outside the Clitheroe tenement.

ACT IV · The room of Bessie Burgess.

TIME · Acts I and II, November 1915; Acts III and IV, Easter Week, 1916. A few days elapse between Acts III and IV.

ACT I

The home of the Clitheroes. It consists of the front and back drawing-rooms in a fine old Georgian house, struggling for its life against the assaults of time, and the more savage assaults of the tenants. The room shown is the back drawing-room, wide, spacious, and lofty. At back is the entrance to the front drawing-room. The space, originally occupied by folding doors, is now draped with casement cloth of a dark purple, decorated with a design in reddish-purple and cream. One of the curtains is pulled aside, giving a glimpse of front drawing-room, at the end of which can be seen the wide, lofty windows looking out into the street. The room directly in front of the audience is furnished in a way that suggests an attempt towards a finer expression of domestic life. The large fireplace on right is of wood, painted to look like marble (the original has been taken away by the landlord). On the mantelshelf are two candlesticks of dark carved wood. Between them is a small clock. Over the clock is hanging a calendar which displays a picture of "The Sleeping Venus". In the centre of the breast of the chimney hangs a picture of Robert Emmet. On the right of the entrance to the front drawing-room is a copy of "The Gleaners", on the opposite side a copy of "The Angelus". Underneath "The Gleaners" is a chest of drawers on which stands a green bowl filled with scarlet dahlias and white chrysanthemums. Near to the fireplace is a settee which at night forms a double bed for Clitheroe and Nora. Underneath "The Angelus" are a number of shelves containing saucepans and a frying-pan. Under these is a table on which are various articles of delf ware. Near the end of the room, opposite to the fireplace is a gate-legged table, covered with a cloth. On top of the table a huge cavalry sword is lying. To the right is a door which leads to a lobby from which the staircase leads to the hall. The floor is covered with a dark green linoleum. The room is dim except where it is illuminated from the glow of the fire. Through the window of the room at back can be seen the flaring of the flame of a gasolene lamp giving light to workmen repairing the street. Occasionally can be heard the clang of crowbars striking the sets. Fluther Good is repairing the lock of door, Right. A claw-hammer is on a chair beside him, and he has a screw-driver in his hand. He is a man of forty years of age, rarely surrendering to thoughts of anxiety, fond of his "oil" but determined to conquer the habit before he dies. He is square-jawed and harshly featured; under the left eye is a scar, and his nose is bent from a smashing blow received in a fistic battle long ago. He is bald, save for a few peeping tufts of reddish hair around his ears; and his upper lip is hidden by a scrubby red moustache, embroidered here and there with a grey hair. He is dressed in a seedy black suit, cotton shirt with a soft collar, and wears a very respectable little black bow. On his head is a faded jerry hat, which, when he is excited, he has a habit of knocking farther back on his head, in a series of taps. In an argument he usually fills with sound and fury generally signifying a row. He is in his shirt-sleeves at present, and wears a soiled white apron, from a pocket in which sticks a carpenter's two-foot rule. He has just finished the job of putting on a new lock, and, filled with satisfaction, he is opening and shutting the door, enjoying the completion of a work well done. Sitting at the fire, airing a white shirt, is Peter Flynn. He is a little, thin bit of a man, with a face shaped like a lozenge; on his cheeks and under his chin is a straggling wiry beard of a dirty-white and lemon hue. His face invariably wears a look of animated anguish, mixed with irritated defiance, as if everybody was at war with him, and he at war with everybody. He is cocking his head in a way that suggests resentment at the presence of Fluther, who pays no attention to him, apparently, but is really furtively watching him. Peter is clad in a singlet, white whipcord knee-breeches, and is in his stocking-feet.

A voice is heard speaking outside of door, Left [it is that of Mrs. Gogan].

Mrs. Gogan [*outside*].   Who are you lookin' for, sir? Who? Mrs. Clith-eroe? . . . Oh, excuse me. Oh ay, up this way. She's out, I think: I seen her goin'. Oh, you've somethin' for her; oh, excuse me. You're from Arnott's. . . . I see. . . . You've a parcel for her. . . . Righto. . . . I'll take it. . . . I'll give it to her the minute she comes in. . . . It'll be quite safe. . . . Oh, sign that. . . . Excuse me. . . . Where? . . . Here? . . . No, there; righto. Am I to put Maggie or Mrs.? What is it? You dunno? Oh, excuse me.

> [*Mrs. Gogan opens the door and comes in. She is a doleful-looking little woman of forty, insinuating manner and sallow complexion. She is fidgety and nervous, terribly talkative, has a habit of taking up things that may be near her and fiddling with them while she is speaking. Her heart is aflame with curiosity, and a fly could not come into nor go out of the house without her knowing. She has a draper's parcel in her hand, the knot of the twine tying it is untied. Peter, more resentful of this intrusion than of Fluther's presence, gets up from the chair, and without looking around, his head carried at an angry cock, marches into the room at back.*]

Mrs. Gogan [*removing the paper and opening the cardboard box it contains*].   I wondher what's that now? A hat! [*She takes out a hat, black, with decorations in red and gold.*] God, she's goin' to th' divil lately for style! That hat, now, cost more than a penny. Such notions of upperosity she's gettin'. [*Putting the hat on her head*] Oh, swank, what!

> [*She replaces it in parcel.*]

Fluther.   She's a pretty little Judy, all the same.

Mrs. Gogan.   Ah, she is, an' she isn't. There's prettiness an' prettiness in it.

I'm always sayin' that her skirts are a little too short for a married woman. An' to see her, sometimes of an evenin', in her glad-neck gown would make a body's blood run cold. I do be ashamed of me life before her husband. An' th' way she thries to be polite, with her "Good mornin', Mrs. Gogan," when she's goin' down, an' her "Good evenin', Mrs. Gogan," when she's comin' up. But there's politeness an' politeness in it.

Fluther. They seem to get on well together, all th' same.

Mrs. Gogan. Ah, they do, an' they don't. The pair o' them used to be like two turtle doves always billin' an' cooin'. You couldn't come into th' room but you'd feel, instinctive like, tha; they'd just been afther kissin' an' cuddlin' each other. . . . It often made me shiver, for, afther all, there's kissin' an' cuddlin' in it. But I'm thinkin' he's beginnin' to take things more quietly; the mystery of havin' a woman's a mystery no longer. . . . She dhresses herself to keep him with her, but it's no use—afther a month or two, th' wondher of a woman wears off.

Fluther. I dunno, I dunno. Not wishin' to say anything derogatory, I think it's all a question of location: when a man finds th' wondher of one woman beginnin' to die, it's usually beginnin' to live in another.

Mrs. Gogan. She's always grumblin' about havin' to live in a tenement house. "I wouldn't like to spend me last hour in one, let alone live me life in a tenement," says she. "Vaults," says she, "that are hidin' th' dead, instead of homes that are sheltherin' th' livin'." "Many a good one," says I, "was reared in a tenement house." Oh, you know, she's a well-up little lassie, too; able to make a shillin' go where another would have to spend a pound. She's wipin' th' eyes of th' Covey an' poor oul' Pether—everybody knows that—screwin' every penny she can out o' them, in ordher to turn th' place into a babby-house. An' she has th' life frightened out o' them; washin' their face, combin' their hair, wipin' their feet, brushin' their clothes, thrimmin' their nails, cleanin' their teeth—God Almighty, you'd think th' poor men were undhergoin' penal servitude.

Fluther [*with an exclamation of disgust*]. A-a-ah, that's goin' beyond th' beyonds in a tenement house. That's a little bit too derogatory.

> [*Peter enters from room, Back, head elevated and resentful fire in his eyes; he is still in his singlet and trousers, but is now wearing a pair of unlaced boots—possibly to be decent in the presence of Mrs. Gogan. He places the white shirt, which he has carried in on his arm, on the back of a chair near the fire, and, going over to the chest of drawers, he opens drawer after drawer, looking for something; as he fails to find it he closes each drawer with a snap; he pulls out pieces of linen neatly folded, and bundles them back again any way.*]

Peter [*in accents of anguish*]. Well, God Almighty, give me patience!

[*He returns to room, Back, giving the shirt a vicious turn as he passes.*

Mrs. Gogan. I wondher what he is foostherin' for now?

Fluther. He'd adornin' himself for th' meeting to-night. [*Pulling a handbill from his pocket and reading*] "Great Demonstration an' torchlight procession around places in th' city sacred to th' memory of Irish Patriots, to be concluded by a meetin', at which will be taken on oath of fealty to th' Irish Republic. Formation in Parnell Square at eight o'clock." Well, they can hold it for Fluther. I'm up th' pole; no more dhrink for Fluther. It's three days now since I touched a dhrop, an' I feel a new man already.

Mrs. Gogan. Isn't oul' Peter a funny-lookin' little man? . . . Like somethin' you'd pick off a Christmas Tree. . . . When he's dhressed up in his canonicals, you'd wondher where he'd been got. God forgive me, when I see him in them, I always think he must ha' had a Mormon for a father! He an' th' Covey can't abide each other; th' pair o' them is always at it, thryin' to best each other. There'll be blood dhrawn one o' these days.

Fluther. How is it that Clitheroe himself, now, doesn't have anythin' to do with th' Citizen Army? A couple o' months ago, an' you'd hardly ever see him without his gun, an' th' Red Hand o' Liberty Hall in his hat.

Mrs. Gogan. Just because he wasn't made a Captain of. He wasn't goin' to be in anything where he couldn't be conspishuous. He was so cocksure o' being made one that he bought a Sam Browne belt, an' was always puttin' it on an' standin' at th' door showing it off, till th' man came an' put out th' street lamps on him. God, I think he used to bring it to bed with him! But I'm tellin' you herself was delighted that that cock didn't crow, for she's like a clockin' hen if he leaves her sight for a minute.

[*While she is talking, she takes up book after book from the table, looks into each of them in a near-sighted way, and then leaves them back. She now lifts up the sword, and proceeds to examine it.*

Mrs. Gogan. Be th' look of it, this must ha' been a general's sword. . . . All th' gold lace an' th' fine figaries on it. . . . Sure it's twiced too big for him.

Fluther. A-ah; it's a baby's rattle he ought to have, an' he as he is with thoughts tossin' in his head of what may happen to him on th' day o' judgement.

[*Peter has entered, and seeing Mrs. Gogan with the sword, goes over to her, pulls it resentfully out of her hands, and marches into the room, Back, without speaking.*

Mrs. Gogan [*as Peter whips the sword*]. Oh, excuse me! . . . [*To Fluther*] Isn't he th' surly oul' rascal!

Fluther. Take no notice of him. . . . You'd think he was dumb, but when you get his goat, or he has a few jars up, he's vice versa.

[*He coughs.*

Mrs. Gogan [*she has now sidled over as far as the shirt hanging on the chair*]. Oh, you've got a cold on you, Fluther.

Fluther [*carelessly*]. Ah, it's only a little one.

Mrs. Gogan. You'd want to be careful, all th' same. I knew a woman, a big lump of a woman, red-faced an' round-bodied, a little awkward on her feet; you'd think, to look at her, she could put out her two arms an' lift a two-storied house on th' top of her head; got a ticklin' in her throat, an' a little cough, an' th' next mornin' she had a little catchin' in her chest, an' they had just time to wet her lips with a little rum, an' off she went.   [*She begins to look at and handle the shirt.*

Fluther [*a little nervously*]. It's only a little cold I have; there's nothing derogatory wrong with me.

Mrs. Gogan. I dunno; there's many a man this minute lowerin' a pint, thinkin' of a woman, or pickin' out a winner, or doin' work as you're doin', while th' hearse dhrawn be th' horses with the black plumes is dhrivin' up to his own hall door, an' a voice that he doesn't hear is mutherin' in his ear, "Earth to earth, an' ashes t' ashes, an' dust to dust."

Fluther [*faintly*]. A man in th' pink o' health should have a holy horror of allowin' thoughts o' death to be festherin' in his mind, for—[*with a frightened cough*] be God, I think I'm afther gettin' a little catch in me chest that time—it's a creepy thing to be thinkin' about.

Mrs. Gogan. It is, an' it isn't; it's both bad an' good. . . . It always gives meself a kind o' thresspassin' joy to feel meself movin' along in a mournin' coach, an' me thinkin' that, maybe, th' next funeral 'll be me own, an' glad, in a quiet way, that this is somebody else's.

Fluther. An' a curious kind of a gaspin' for breath—I hope there's nothin' derogatory wrong with me.

Mrs. Gogan [*examining the shirt*]. Frills on it, like a woman's petticoat.

Fluther. Suddenly gettin' hot, an' then, just as suddenly, gettin' cold.

Mrs. Gogan [*holding out the shirt towards Fluther*]. How would you like to be wearin' this Lord Mayor's nightdhress, Fluther?

Fluther [*vehemently*]. Blast you an' your nightshirt! Is a man fermentin' with fear to stick th' showin' off to him of a thing that looks like a shinin' shroud?

Mrs. Gogan. Oh, excuse me!

[*Peter has again entered, and he pulls the shirt from the hands of Mrs. Gogan, replacing it on the chair. He returns to room.*

Peter [*as he goes out*]. Well, God Almighty, give me patience!

Mrs. Gogan [*to Peter*]. Oh, excuse me!

[*There is heard a cheer from the men working outside on the street, followed by the clang of tools being thrown down, then silence. The glare of the gasolene light diminishes and finally goes out.*

Mrs. Gogan [*running into the back room to look out of the window*]. What's the men repairin' th' streets cheerin' for?

Fluther [*sitting down weakly on a chair*]. You can't sneeze but that oul' one wants to know th' why an' th' wherefore. . . . I feel as dizzy as bedamned! I hope I didn't give up th' beer too suddenly.

[*The Covey comes in by door, Right. He is about twenty-five, tall, thin, with lines on his face that form a perpetual protest against life as he conceives it to be. Heavy seams fall from each side of nose, down around his lips, as if they were suspenders keeping his mouth from falling. He speaks in a slow, wailing drawl; more rapidly when he is excited. He is dressed in dungarees, and is wearing a vividly red tie. He flings his cap with a gesture of disgust on the table, and begins to take off his overalls.*

Mrs. Gogan [*to the Covey, as she runs back into the room*]. What's after happenin', Covey?

The Covey [*with contempt*]. Th' job's stopped. They've been mobilized to march in th' demonstration to-night undher th' Plough an' th' Stars. Didn't you hear them cheerin', th' mugs! They have to renew their political baptismal vows to be faithful in seculo seculorum.

Fluther [*forgetting his fear in his indignation*]. There's no reason to bring religion into it. I think we ought to have as great a regard for religion as we can, so as to keep it out of as many things as possible.

The Covey [*pausing in the taking off of his dungarees*]. Oh, you're one o' the boys that climb into religion as high as a short Mass on Sunday mornin's? I suppose you'll be singin' songs o' Sion an' songs o' Tara at th' meetin', too.

Fluther. We're all Irishmen, anyhow; aren't we?

The Covey [*with hand outstretched, and in a professional tone*]. Look here, comrade, there's no such thing as an Irishman, or an Englishmen, or a German or a Turk; we're all only human bein's. Scientifically speakin', it's all a question of the accidental gatherin' together of molly-cewels an' atoms.

[*Peter comes in with a collar in his hand. He goes over to mirror, Left, and proceeds to try to put it on.*]

Fluther. Mollycewels an' atoms! D'ye think I'm goin' to listen to you thryin' to juggle Fluther's mind with complicated cunundhrums of mollycewels an' atoms?

The Covey [*rather loudly*]. There's nothin' complicated in it. There's no fear o' th' Church tellin' you that mollycewels is a stickin' together of millions of atoms o' sodium, carbon, potassium o' iodide, etcetera, that, accordin' to th' way they're mixed, make a flower, a fish, a star that you see shinin' in th' sky, or a man with a big brain like me, or a man with a little brain like you!

Fluther [*more loudly still*]. There's no necessity to be raisin' your voice; shoutin's no manifestin' forth of a growin' mind.

Peter [*struggling with his collar*]. God, give me patience with this thing. . . . She makes these collars as stiff with starch as a shinin' band o' solid steel! She does it purposely to thry an' twart me. If I can't get it on th' singlet, how, in th' Name o' God, am I goin' to get it on th' shirt?

The Covey [*loudly*]. There's no use o' arguin' with you; it's education you want, comrade.

Fluther. The Covey an' God made th' world, I suppose, wha'?

The Covey. When I hear some men talkin' I'm inclined to disbelieve that th' world's eight-hundhred million years old, for it's not long since th' fathers o' some o' them crawled out o' th' sheltherin' slime o' the sea.

Mrs. Gogan [*from room at back*]. There, they're afther formin' fours, an' now they're goin' to march away.

Fluther [*scornfully*]. Mollycewels! [*He begins to untie his apron*] What about Adam an' Eve?

The Covey. Well, what about them?

Fluther [*fiercely*]. What about them, you?

The Covey. Adam an' Eve! Is that as far as you've got? Are you still thinkin' there was nobody in th' world before Adam an' Eve? [*Loudly*] Did you ever hear, man, of th' skeleton of th' man o' Java?

Peter [*casting the collar from him*]. Blast it, blast it, blast it!

Fluther [*viciously folding his apron*]. Ah, you're not goin' to be let tap your rubbidge o' thoughts into th' mind o' Fluther.

The Covey. You're afraid to listen to th' thruth!

Fluther. Who's afraid?

The Covey. You are!

Fluther. G'way, you wurum!

The Covey. Who's a worum?

Fluther. You are, or you wouldn't talk th' way you're talkin'.

The Covey. Th' oul', ignorant savage leppin' up in you, when science shows you that th' head of your god is an empty one. Well, I hope you're enjoyin' th' blessin' o' havin' to live be th' sweat of your brow.

Fluther. You'll be kickin' an' yellin' for th' priest yet, me boyo. I'm not goin' to stand silent an' simple listenin' to a thick like you makin' a maddenin' mockery o' God Almighty. It 'ud be a nice derogatory thing on me conscience, an' me dyin', to look back in rememberin' shame of talkin' to a word-weavin' little ignorant yahoo of a red flag Socialist!

Mrs. Gogan [*she has returned to the front room, and has wandered around looking at things in general, and is now in front of the fireplace looking at the picture hanging over it*]. For God's sake, Fluther, dhrop it; there's always th' makin's of a row in th' mention of religion . . . [*Looking at picture*] God bless us, it's a naked woman!

Fluther [*coming over to look at it*]. What's undher it? [*Reading*] "Georgina: The Sleepin' Vennis". Oh, that's a terrible picture; oh, that's a shockin' picture! Oh, th' one that got that taken, she must have been a prime lassie!

Peter [*who has also come over to look, laughing, with his body bent at the waist, and his head slightly tilted back*]. Hee, hee, hee, hee, hee!

Fluther [*indignantly, to Peter*]. What are you hee, hee-in' for? That' a nice thing to be hee, hee-in' at. Where's your morality, man?

Mrs. Gogan. God forgive us, it's not right to be lookin' at it.

Fluther. It's nearly a derogatory thing to be in th' room where it is.

Mrs. Gogan [*giggling hysterically*]. I couldn't stop any longer in th' same room with three men, afther lookin' at it!   [*She goes out.*

[*The Covey, who has divested himself of his dungarees, throws them with a contemptuous motion on top of Peter's white shirt.*

Peter [*plaintively*]. Where are you throwin' them? Are you thryin' to twart an' torment me again?

The Covey. Who's thryin 'to twart you?

Peter [*flinging the dungarees violently on the floor*]. You're not goin' to make me lose me temper, me young Covey.

The Covey [*flinging the white shirt on the floor*]. If you're Nora's pet, aself, you're not goin'to get your way in everything.

Peter [*plaintively, with his eyes looking up at the ceiling*]. I'll say nothin'. . . . I'll leave you to th' day when th' all-pitiful, all-merciful, all-lovin' God 'll be handin' you to th' angels to be rievin' an' roastin' you, tearin' an' tormentin' you, burnin' an' blastin' you!

The Covey. Aren't you th' little malignant oul' bastard, you lemon-whiskered oul' swine!

> [*Peter runs to the sword, draws it, and makes for the Covey, who dodges him around the table; Peter has no intention of striking, but the Covey wants to take no chances.*

The Covey [*dodging*]. Fluther, hold him, there. It's a nice thing to have a lunatic like this lashin' around with a lethal weapon!

> [*The Covey darts out of the room, Right, slamming the door in the face of Peter.*

Peter [*battering and pulling at the door*]. Lemme out, lemme out; isn't it a poor thing for a man who wouldn't say a word against his greatest enemy to have to listen to that Covey's twartin' animosities, shovin' poor, patient people into a lashin' out of curses that darken his soul with th' shadow of th' wrath of th' last day!

Fluther. Why d'ye take notice of him? If he seen you didn't, he'd say nothin' derogatory.

Peter. I'll make him stop his laughin' an' leerin', jibin' an' jeerin' an' scari-fyin' people with his cornerboy insinuations! . . . He's always thryin' to rouse me: if it's not a song, it's a whistle; if it isn't a whistle, it's a cough. But you can taunt an' taunt—I'm laughin' at you; he, hee, hee, hee, hee, heee!

The Covey [*singing through the keyhole*]:

> Dear harp o' me counthry, in darkness I found thee,
> The dark chain of silence had hung o'er thee long—

Peter [*frantically*]. Jasus, d'ye hear that? D'ye hear him soundin' forth his divil-souled song o' provocation?

The Covey [*singing as before*]:
> When proudly, me own island harp, I unbound thee,
> An' gave all thy chords to light, freedom an' song!

Peter [*battering at door*]. When I get out I'll do for you, I'll do for you, I'll do for you!

The Covey [*through the keyhole*]. Cuckoo-oo!

[*Nora enters by door, Right. She is a young woman of twenty-two, alert, swift, full of nervous energy, and a little anxious to get on in the world. The firm lines of her face are considerably opposed by a soft, amorous mouth and gentle eyes. When her firmness fails her, she persuades with her feminine charm. She is dressed in a tailor-made costume, and wears around her neck a silver fox fur.*

Nora [*running in and pushing Peter away from the door*]. Oh, can I not turn me back but th' two o' yous are at it like a pair o' fightin' cocks! Uncle Peter . . . Uncle Peter . . . UNCLE PETER!

Peter [*vociferously*]. Oh, Uncle Peter, Uncle Peter be damned! D'ye think I'm goin' to give a free pass to th' young Covey to turn me whole life into a Holy Manual o' penances an' martyrdoms?

The Covey [*angrily rushing into the room*]. If you won't exercise some sort o' conthrol over that Uncle Peter o' yours, there'll be a funeral, an' it won't be me that'll be in th' hearse!

Nora [*between Peter and the Covey, to the Covey*]. Are yous always goin' to be tearin' down th' little bit of respectability that a body's thryin' to build up? Am I always goin' to be havin' to nurse yous into th' hardy habit o' thryin' to keep up a little bit of appearance?

The Covey. Why weren't you here to see th' way he run at me with th' sword?

Peter. What did you call me a lemon-whiskered oul' swine for?

Nora. If th' two o' yous don't thry to make a generous altheration in your goin's on, an' keep on thryin' t' inaugurate th' customs o' th' rest o' th' house into this place, yous can flit into other lodgin's where your bowsey battlin' 'ill meet, maybe, with an encore.

Peter [*to Nora*]. Would you like to be called a lemon-whiskered oul' swine?

Nora. If you attempt to wag that sword of yours at anybody again, it'll have to be taken off you an' put in a safe place away from babies that don't know th' danger o' them things.

Peter [*at entrance to room, Back*]. Well, I'm not goin' to let anybody call me a lemon-whiskered oul' swine.   [*He goes in.*

Fluther [*trying the door*]. Openin' an' shuttin' now with a well-mannered motion, like a door of a select bar in a high-class pub.

Nora [*to the Covey, as she lays table for tea*]. An', once for all, Willie, you'll have to thry to deliver yourself from th' desire of provokin' oul' Pether into a wild forgetfulness of what's proper an' allowable in a respectable home.

The Covey. Well, let him mind his own business, then. Yestherday, I caught him hee-hee-in' out of him an' he readin' bits out of Jenersky's *Thesis on th' Origin, Development, an' Consolidation of th' Evolutionary Idea of th' Proletariat.*

Nora. Now, let it end at that, for God's sake; Jack 'll be in any minute, an' I'm not goin' to have th' quiet of his evenin' tossed about in an everlastin' uproar between you an' Uncle Pether. [*To Fluther*] Well, did you manage to settle th' lock, yet, Mr. Good?

Fluther [*opening and shutting door*]. It's betther than a new one, now, Mrs. Clitheroe; it's almost ready to open and shut of its own accord.

Nora [*giving him a coin*]. You're a whole man. How many pints will that get you?

Fluther [*seriously*]. Ne'er a one at all, Mrs. Clitheroe, for Fluther's on th' wather waggon now. You could stan' where you're stannin' chantin', "Have a glass o' malt, Fluther; Fluther, have a glass o' malt," till th' bells would be ringin' th' ould year out an' th' New Year in, an' you'd have as much chance o' movin' Fluther as a tune on a tin whistle would move a deaf man an' he dead.

> [*As Nora is opening and shutting door, Mrs. Bessie Burgess appears at it. She is a woman of forty, vigorously built. Her face is a dogged one, hardened by toil, and a little coarsened by drink. She looks scornfully and viciously at Nora for a few moments before she speaks.*

Bessie. Puttin' a new lock on her door . . . afraid her poor neighbours ud break through an' steal. . . . [*In a loud tone*] Maybe, now, they're a damn sight more honest than your ladyship . . . checkin' th' children playin' on th' stairs . . . gettin' on th' nerves of your ladyship. . . . Complainin' about Bessie Burgess singin' her hymns at night, when she has a few up. . . . [*She comes in half-way on the threshold, and screams*] Bessie Burgess 'll sing whenever she damn well likes!

> [*Nora tries to shut door, but Bessie violently shoves it in, and, gripping Nora by the shoulders, shakes her.*

Bessie. You little over-dressed throllope, you, for one pin I'd paste th' white face o' you!

Nora [*frightened*]. Fluther, Fluther!

Fluther [*running over and breaking the hold of Bessie from Nora*]. Now, now, Bessie, Bessie, leave poor Mrs. Clitheroe alone; she'd do no one any harm, an' minds no one's business but her own.

Bessie. Why is she always thryin' to speak proud things, an' lookin' like a mighty one in th' congregation o' th' people!

[*Nora sinks frightened on to the couch as Jack Clitheroe enters. He is a tall, well-made fellow of twenty-five. His face has none of the strength of Nora's. It is a face in which is the desire for authority, without the power to attain it.*

Clitheroe [*excitedly*].   What's up? what's afther happenin'?

Fluther.   Nothin', Jack. Nothin'. It's all over now. Come on, Bessie, come on.

Clitheroe [*to Nora*].   What's wrong, Nora? Did she say anything to you?

Nora.   She was bargin' out of her, an' I only told her to g' up ower o' that to her own place; an' before I knew where I was, she flew at me like a tiger, an' thried to guzzle me!

Clitheroe [*going to door and speaking to Bessie*].   Get up to your own place, Mrs. Burgess, and don't you be interferin' with my wife, or it'll be th' worse for you. . . . Go on, go on!

Bessie [*as Clitheroe is pushing her out*].   Mind who you're pushin', now. . . . I attend me place o' worship, anyhow . . . not like some o' them that go to neither church, chapel nor meetin'-house. . . . If me son was home from th' threnches he'd see me righted.

[*Bessie and Fluther depart, and Clitheroe closes the door.*

Clitheroe [*going over to Nora, and putting his arm around her*].   There, don't mind that old bitch, Nora, darling; I'll soon put a stop to her interferin'.

Nora.   Some day or another, when I'm here be meself, she'll come in an' do somethin' desperate.

Clitheroe [*kissing her*].   Oh, sorra fear of her doin' anythin' desperate. I'll talk to her to-morrow when she's sober. A taste o' me mind that'll shock her into the sensibility of behavin' herself!

[*Nora gets up and settles the table. She sees the dungarees on the floor and stands looking at them, then she turns to the Covey, who is reading Jenersky's "Thesis" at the fire.*

Nora.   Willie, is that th' place for your dungarees?

The Covey [*getting up and lifting them from the floor*].   Ah, they won't do th' floor any harm, will they?   [*He carries them into room, Back.*

Nora [*calling*].   Uncle Peter, now, Uncle Peter; tea's ready.

[*Peter and the Covey come in from room, Back; they all sit down to tea. Peter is in full dress of the Foresters: green coat, gold braided; white breeches, top boots, frilled shirt. He carries the slouch hat, with the white ostrich plume, and the sword in his hands. They eat for a few moments in silence, the Covey furtively looking at Peter with scorn in his eyes. Peter knows it and is fidgety.*

The Covey [*provokingly*].   Another cut o' bread, Uncle Peter?
[*Peter maintains a dignified silence.*

Clitheroe.   It's sure to be a great meetin' to-night. We ought to go, Nora.

Nora [*decisively*].   I won't go, Jack; you can go if you wish.   [*A pause.*

The Covey.   D'ye want th' sugar, Uncle Peter?

Peter [*explosively*].   Now, are you goin' to start your thryin' an' your twartin' again?

Nora.   Now, Uncle Peter, you musn't be so touchy; Willie has only assed you if you wanted th' sugar.

Peter.   He doesn't care a damn whether I want th' sugar or no. He's only thryin' to twart me!

Nora [*angrily, to the Covey*].   Can't you let him alone, Willie? If he wants the sugar, let him stretch his hand out an' get it himself!

The Covey [*to Peter*].   Now, if you want the sugar, you can stretch out your hand and get it yourself!

Clitheroe.   To-night is th' first chance that Brennan has got of showing himself off since they made a Captain of him—why, God only knows. It'll be a treat to see him swankin' it at th' head of the Citizen Army carryin' th' flag of the Plough an' th' Stars. . . . [*Looking roguishly at Nora*] He was sweet on you, once, Nora?

Nora.   He may have been. . . . I never liked him. I always thought he was a bit of a thick.

The Covey.   They're bringin' nice disgrace on that banner now.

Clitheroe [*remonstratively*].   How are they bringin' disgrace on it?

The Covey [*snappily*].   Because it's a Labour flag, an' was never meant for politics. . . . What does th' design of th' field plough, bearin' on it th' stars of th' heavenly plough, mean, if it's not Communism? It's a flag that should only be used when we're buildin' th' barricades to fight for a Workers' Republic!

Peter [*with a puff of derision*].   P-phuh.

The Covey [*angrily*].   What are you phuhin' out o' you for? Your mind is th' mind of a mummy. [*Rising*] I betther go an' get a good place to have a look at Ireland's warriors passin' by.
[*He goes into room, Left, and returns with his cap.*

Nora [*to the Covey*].   Oh, Willie, brush your clothes before you go.

The Covey.   Oh, they'll do well enough.

Nora.   Go an' brush them; th' brush is in th' drawer there.

> [*The Covey goes to the drawer, muttering, gets the brush, and starts to brush his clothes.*

The Covey [*singing at Peter, as he does so*]:

> Oh, where's th' slave so lowly,
> Condemn'd to chains unholy,
> Who, could he burst his bonds at first,
> Would pine beneath them slowly?

> We tread th' land that . . . bore us,
> Th' green flag glitters . . . o'er us,
> Th' friends we've tried are by our side,
> An' th' foe we hate . . . before us!

Peter [*leaping to his feet in a whirl of rage*].   Now, I'm tellin' you, me young Covey, once for all, that I'll not stick any longer these tittherin' taunts of yours, rovin' around to sing your slights an' slandhers, reddenin' th' mind of a man to th' thinkin' an' sayin' of things that sicken his soul with sin! [*Hysterically; lifting up a cup to fling at the Covey*] Be God, I'll—

Clitheroe [*catching his arm*].   Now then, none o' that, none o' that!

Nora.   Uncle Pether, Uncle Pether, UNCLE PETHER!

The Covey [*at the door, about to go out*].   Isn't that th' malignant oul' varmint! Lookin' like th' illegitimate son of an illegitimate child of a corporal in th' Mexican army!   [*He goes out.*

Peter [*plaintively*].   He's afther leavin' me now in such a state of agitation that I won't be able to do meself justice when I'm marchin' to th' meetin'.

Nora [*jumping up*].   Oh, for God's sake, here, buckle your sword on, and go to your meetin', so that we'll have at least one hour of peace!
                    [*She proceeds to belt on the sword.*

Clitheroe [*irritably*].   For God's sake hurry him up ou' o' this, Nora.

Peter.   Are yous all goin' to thry to start to twart me now?

Nora [*putting on his plumed hat*].   S-s-sh. Now, your hat's on, your house is thatched; off you pop!   [*She gently pushes him from her.*

Peter [*going, and turning as he reaches the door*].   Now, if that young Covey—

Nora.   Go on, go on.   [*He goes.*

> [*Clitheroe sits down in the lounge, lights a cigarette, and looks*

thoughtfully into the fire. Nora takes the things from the table, placing them on the chest of drawers. There is a pause, then she swiftly comes over to him and sits beside him.

Nora [*softly*].   A penny for them, Jack!

Clitheroe.   Me? Oh, I was thinkin' of nothing.

Nora.   You were thinkin' of th' . . . meetin' . . . Jack. When we were courtin' an' I wanted you to go, you'd say, "Oh, to hell with meetin's," an' that you felt lonely in cheerin' crowds when I was absent. An' we weren't a month married when you began that you couldn't keep away from them.

Clitheroe.   Oh, that's enough about th' meetin'. It looks as if you wanted me to go, th' way you're talkin'. You were always at me to give up th' Citizen Army, an' I gave it up; surely that ought to satisfy you.

Nora.   Ay, you gave it up—because you got th' sulks when they didn't make a Captain of you. It wasn't for my sake, Jack.

Clitheroe.   For your sake or no, you're benefitin' by it, aren't you? I didn't forget this was your birthday, did I? [*He puts his arms around her*] And you liked your new hat; didn't you, didn't you?
                              [*He kisses her rapidly several times.*

Nora [*panting*].   Jack, Jack; please, Jack! I thought you were tired of that sort of thing long ago.

Clitheroe.   Well, you're finding out now that I amn't tired of it yet, anyhow. Mrs. Clitheroe doesn't want to be kissed, sure she doesn't? [*He kisses her again*] Little, little red-lipped Nora!

Nora [*coquettishly removing his arm from around her*].   Oh, yes, your little, little red-lipped Nora's a sweet little girl when th' fit seizes you; but your little, little red-lipped Nora has to clean your boots every mornin', all the same.

Clitheroe [*with a movement of irritation*].   Oh, well, if we're goin' to be snotty!   [*A pause.*

Nora.   It's lookin' like as if it was you that was goin' to be . . . snotty! Bridlin' up with bittherness, th' minute a body attempts t'open her mouth.

Clitheroe.   It is any wondher, turnin' a tendher sayin' into a meanin' o' malice an' spite!

Nora.   It's hard for a body to be always keepin' her mind bent on makin' thoughts that'll be no longer than th' length of your own satisfaction.
                              [*A pause.*

Nora [*standing up*].   If we're goin' to dhribble th' time away sittin' here like a pair o' cranky mummies, I'd be as well sewin' or doin' something about th' place.

> [*She looks appealingly at him for a few moments; he doesn't speak. She swiftly sits down beside him, and puts her arm around his neck.*]

Nora [*imploringly*].   Ah, Jack, don't be so cross!

Clitheroe [*doggedly*].   Cross? I'm not cross; I'm not a bit cross. It was yourself started it.

Nora [*coaxingly*].   I didn't mean to say anything out o' the way. You take a body up too quickly, Jack. [*In an ordinary tone as if nothing of an angry nature had been said*] You didn't offer me me evenin' allowance yet.

> [*Clitheroe silently takes out a cigarette for her and himself and lights both.*]

Nora [*trying to make conversation*].   How quiet th' house is now; they must be all out.

Clitheroe [*rather shortly*].   I suppose so.

Nora [*rising from the seat*].   I'm longin' to show you me new hat, to see what you think of it. Would you like to see it?

Clitheroe.   Ah, I don't mind.

> [*Nora suppresses a sharp reply, hesitates for a moment, then gets the hat, puts it on, and stands before Clitheroe.*]

Nora.   Well, how does Mr. Clitheroe like me new hat?

Clitheroe.   It suits you, Nora, it does right enough.

> [*He stands up, puts his hand beneath her chin, and tilts her head up. She looks at him roguishly. He bends down and kisses her.*]

Nora.   Here, sit down, an' don't let me hear another cross word out of you for th' rest o' the night.   [*They sit down.*

Clitheroe [*with his arms around her*].   Little, little, red-lipped Nora!

Nora [*with a coaxing movement of her body towards him*].   Jack!

Clitheroe [*tightening his arms around her*].   Well?

Nora.   You haven't sung me a song since our honeymoon. Sing me one now, do . . . please, Jack!

Clitheroe.   What song? "Since Maggie Went Away"?

Nora.   Ah, no, Jack, not that; it's too sad. "When You Said You Loved Me."

[*Clearing his throat, Clitheroe thinks for a moment, and then begins to sing. Nora, putting an arm around him, nestles her head on his breast and listens delightedly.*

Clitheroe [*singing verses following to the air of "When You and I Were Young, Maggie"*]:

Th' violets were scenting th' woods, Nora,
  Displaying their charm to th' bee,
When I first said I lov'd only you, Nora,
  An' you said you lov'd only me!

Th' chestnut blooms gleam'd through th' glade,
    Nora,
  A robin sang loud from a tree,
When I first said I lov'd only you, Nora,
  An' you said you lov'd only me!

Th' golden-rob'd daffodils shone, Nora,
  An' danc'd in th' breeze on th' lea,
When I first said I lov'd only you, Nora,
  An' you said you lov'd only me!

Th' trees, birds, an' bees sang a song, Nora,
  Of happier transports to be,
When I first said I lov'd only you, Nora,
  An' you said you lov'd only me!   [*Nora kisses him.*

[*A knock is heard at the door, Right; a pause as they listen. Nora cling closely to Clitheroe. Another knock, more imperative than the first.*

Clitheroe.   I wonder who can that be, now?

Nora [*a little nervous*].   Take no notice of it, Jack; they'll go away in a minute.   [*Another knock, followed by a voice.*

Voice.   Commandant Clitheroe, Commandant Clitheroe, are you there? A message from General Jim Connolly.

Clitheroe.   Damn it, it's Captain Brennan.

Nora [*anxiously*].   Don't mind him, don't mind, Jack. Don't break our happiness. . . . Pretend we're not in. Let us forget everything to-night but our two selves!

Clitheroe [*reassuringly*].   Don't be alarmed, darling; I'll just see what he wants, an' send him about his business.

Nora [*tremulously*].   No, no. Please, Jack; don't open it. Please, for your own little Nora's sake!

Clitheroe [*rising to open the door*].   Now don't be silly, Nora.

> [*Clitheroe opens door, and admits a young man in the full uniform of the Irish Citizen Army—green suit; slouch green hat caught up at one side by a small Red Hand badge; Sam Browne belt, with a revolver in the holster. He carries a letter in his hand. When he comes in he smartly salutes Clitheroe. The young man is Captain Brennan.*

Capt. Brennan [*giving the letter to Clitheroe*].   A dispatch from General Connolly.

Clitheroe [*reading. While he is doing so, Brennan's eyes are fixed on Nora, who droops as she sits on the lounge*].   "Commandant Clitheroe is to take command of the eighth battalion of the I.C.A. which will assemble to proceed to the meeting at nine o'clock. He is to see that all units are provided with full equipment; two days' rations and fifty rounds of ammunition. At two o'clock A.M. the army will leave Liberty Hall for a reconnaissance attack on Dublin Castle.—Com.-Gen. Connolly."

Clitheroe.   I don't understand this. Why does General Connolly call me Commandant?

Capt. Brennan.   Th' Staff appointed you Commandant, and th' General agreed with their selection.

Clitheroe.   When did this happen?

Capt. Brennan.   A fortnight ago.

Clitheroe.   How is it word was never sent to me?

Capt. Brennan.   Word was sent to you. . . . I meself brought it.

Clitheroe.   Who did you give it to, then?

Capt. Brennan [*after a pause*].   I think I gave it to Mrs. Clitheroe, there.

Clitheroe.   Nora, d'ye hear that?   [*Nora makes no answer.*

Clitheroe [*there is a note of hardness in his voice*].   Nora . . . Captain Brennan says he brought a letter to me from General Connolly, and that he gave it to you. . . . Where is it? What did you do with it?

Nora [*running over to him, and pleadingly putting her arms around him*].   Jack, please, Jack, don't go out to-night an' I'll tell you; I'll explain everything. . . . Send him away, an' stay with your own little red-lipp'd Nora.

Clitheroe [*removing her arms from around him*].   None o' this nonsense, now; I want to know what you did with th' letter?

> [*Nora goes slowly to the lounge and sits down.*

Clitheroe [*angrily*]. Why didn't you give me th' letter? What did you do with it? . . . [*He shakes her by the shoulder*] What did you do with th' letter?

Nora [*flaming up*]. I burned it, I burned it! That's what I did with it! Is General Connolly an' th' Citizen Army goin' to be your only care? Is your home goin' to be only a place to rest in? Am I goin' to be only somethin' to provide merry-makin' at night for you? Your vanity'll be th' ruin of you an' me yet. . . . That's what's movin' you: because they've made an officer of you, you'll make a glorious cause of what you're doin', while your little red-lipp'd Nora can go on sittin' here, makin' a companion of th' loneliness of th' night!

Clitheroe [*fiercely*]. You burned it, did you? [*He grips her arm*] Well, me good lady——

Nora. Let go—you're hurtin' me!

Clitheroe. You deserve to be hurt. . . . Any letter that comes to me for th' future, take care that I get it. . . . D'ye hear—take care that I get it!

> [*He goes to the chest of drawers and takes out a Sam Browne belt, which he puts on, and then puts a revolver in the holster. He puts on his hat, and looks towards Nora. While this dialogue is proceeding, and while Clitheroe prepares himself, Brennan softly whistles "The Soldiers' Song".*]

Clitheroe [*at door, about to go out*]. You needn't wait up for me; if I'm in at all, it won't be before six in th' morning.

Nora [*bitterly*]. I don't care if you never come back!

Clitheroe [*to Capt. Brennan*]. Come along, Ned.

> [*They go out; there is a pause. Nora pulls the new hat from her head and with a bitter movement flings it to the other end of the room. There is a gentle knock at door, Right, which opens, and Mollser comes into the room. She is about fifteen, but looks to be only about ten, for the ravages of consumption have shrivelled her up. She is pitifully worn, walks feebly, and frequently coughs. She goes over to Nora.*]

Mollser [*to Nora*]. Mother's gone to th' meetin', an' I was feelin' terrible lonely, so I come down to see if you'd let me sit with you, thinkin' you mightn't be goin' yourself. . . . I do be terrible afraid I'll die sometime when I'm be meself. . . . I often envy you, Mrs. Clitheroe, seein' th' health you have, an' th' lovely place you have here, an' wondherin' if I'll ever be sthrong enough to be keepin' a home together for a man. Oh, this must be some more o' the Dublin Fusiliers flyin' off to the front.

[*Just before Mollser ceases to speak, there is heard in the distance the music of a brass band playing a regiment to the boat on the way to the front. The tune that is being played is "It's a Long Way to Tipperary"; as the band comes to the chorus, the regiment is swinging into the street by Nora's house, and the voices of the soldiers can be heard lustily singing the chorus of the song.*]

It's a long way to Tipperary, it's a long way to go;
It's a long way to Tipperary, to th' sweetest girl I know!
Goodbye Piccadilly, farewell Leicester Square.
It's a long, long way to Tipperary, but my heart's right there!

[*Nora and Mollser remain silently listening. As the chorus ends and the music is faint in the distance again, Bessie Burgess appears at door, Right, which Mollser has left open.*]

Bessie [*speaking in towards the room*]. There's th' men marchin' out into th' dhread dimness o' danger, while th' lice is crawlin' about feedin' on th' fatness o' the land! But yous'll not escape from th' arrow that flieth be night, or th' sickness that wasteth be day. . . . An' ladyship an' all, as some o' them may be, they'll be scattered abroad, like th' dust in th' darkness!

[*Bessie goes away; Nora steals over and quietly shuts the door. She comes back to the lounge and wearily throws herself on it beside Mollser.*]

Mollser [*after a pause and a cough*]. Is there anybody goin', Mrs. Clitheroe, with a titther o' sense?

CURTAIN

ACT II

A commodious public-house at the corner of the street in which the meeting is being addressed from Platform No. 1. It is the south corner of the public-house that is visible to the audience. The counter, beginning at Back about one-fourth of the width of the space shown, comes across *two-thirds of the length of the stage, and, taking a circular sweep, passes out of sight to Left. On the counter are beer-pulls, glasses, and a carafe. The other three-fourths of the Back is occupied by a tall, wide, two-paned window. Beside this window at the Right is a small, box-like, panelled snug. Next to the snug is a double swing door, the entrance to that particular end of the house. Farther on is a shelf on which customers may rest their drinks. Underneath the windows is a cushioned seat. Behind the counter at Back can be seen the shelves running the whole length of the counter. On these shelves can be seen the end (or the beginning) of rows of bottles. The Barman is seen wiping the part of the counter which is in view. Rosie is standing at the counter toying with what remains of a half of whisky in a wine-glass. She is a sturdy, well-shaped girl of twenty; pretty, and pert in manner. She is wearing a cream blouse, with an obviously suggestive glad neck; a grey tweed dress, brown stockings and shoes. The blouse and most of the dress are hidden by a black shawl. She has no hat, and in her hair is jauntily set a cheap, glittering, jewelled ornament. It is an hour later.*

Barman [*wiping counter*]. Nothin' much doin' in your line to-night, Rosie?

Rosie. Curse o' God on th' haporth, hardly, Tom. There isn't much notice taken of a pretty petticoat of a night like this. . . . They're all in a holy mood. Th' solemn-lookin' dials on th' whole o' them an' they marchin' to th' meetin'. You'd think they were th' glorious company of th' saints, an' th' noble army of martyrs thrampin' through th' sthreets of paradise. They're all thinkin' of higher things than a girl's garthers. . . . It's a tremendous meetin'; four platforms they have—there's one o' them just outside opposite th' window.

Barman. Oh, ay; sure when th' speaker comes [*motioning with his hand*] to th' near end, here, you can see him plain, an' hear nearly everythin' he's spoutin' out of him.

Rosie. It's no joke thryin' to make up fifty-five shillin's a week for your keep an' laundhry, an' then taxin' you a quid for your own room if you bring home a friend for th' night. . . . If I could only put by a couple of quid for a swankier outfit, everythin' in th' garden ud look lovely—

Barman. Whisht, till we hear what he's sayin'.

[*Through the window is silhouetted the figure of a tall man who is speaking to the crowd. The Barman and Rosie look out of the window and listen.*]

The Voice of the Man. It is a glorious thing to see arms in the hands of Irishmen. We must accustom ourselves to the thought of arms, we must accustom ourselves to the sight of arms, we must accustom ourselves to the use of arms. . . . Bloodshed is a cleansing and sanctifying thing, and the nation that regards it as the final horror has lost its manhood. . . . There are many things more horrible than bloodshed, and slavery is one of them!

[*The figure moves away towards the Right, and is lost to sight and hearing.*

Rosie. It's th' sacred thruth, mind you, what that man's afther sayin'.

Barman. If I was only a little younger, I'd be plungin' mad into th' middle of it!

Rosie [*who is still looking out of the window*]. Oh, here's the two gems runnin' over again for their oil!

[*Peter and Fluther enter tumultuously. They are hot, and full and hasty with the things they have seen and heard. Emotion is bubbling up in them, so that when they drink, and when they speak, they drink and speak with the fullness of emotional passion. Peter leads the way to the counter.*

Peter [*splutteringly to Barman*]. Two halves . . . [*To Fluther*] A meetin' like this always makes me feel as if I could dhrink Loch Erinn dhry!

Fluther. You couldn't feel any way else at a time like this when th' spirit of a man is pulsin' to be out fightin' for th' thruth with his feet thremblin' on th' way, maybe to th' gallows, an' his ears tinglin' with th' faint, far-away sound of burstin' rifle-shots that'll maybe whip th' last little shock o' life out of him that's left lingerin' in his body!

Peter. I felt a burnin' lump in me throat when I heard th' band playin' "The Soldiers' Song", rememberin' last hearin' it marchin' in military formation, with th' people starin' on both sides at us, carryin' with us th' pride an' resolution o' Dublin to th' grave of Wolfe Tone.

Fluther. Get th' Dublin men goin' an' they'll go on full force for anything that's thryin' to bar them away from what they're wantin', where th' slim thinkin' counthry boyo ud limp away from th' first faintest touch of compromization!

Peter [*hurriedly to the Barman*]. Two more, Tom! . . . [*To Fluther*] Th' memory of all th' things that was done, an' all th' things that was suffered be th' people, was boomin' in me brain. . . . Every nerve in me body was quiverin' to do somethin' desperate!

Fluther. Jammed as I was in th' crowd, I listened to th' speeches pattherin' on th' people's head, like rain fallin' on th' corn; every derogatory thought went out o' me mind, an' I said to meself, "You can die now,

Fluther, for you've seen th' shadow-dhreams of th' past leppin' to life in th' bodies of livin' men that show, if we were without a titther o' courage for centuries, we're vice versa now!" Looka here. [*He stretches out his arm under Peter's face and rolls up his sleeve.*] The blood was BOILIN' in me veins!

[*The silhouette of the tall figure again moves into the frame of the window speaking to the people.*

Peter [*unaware, in his enthusiasm, of the speaker's appearance, to Fluther*]. I was burnin' to dhraw me sword, an' wave an' wave it over me——

Fluther [*overwhelming Peter*]. Will you stop your blatherin' for a minute, man, an' let us hear what he's sayin'!

Voice of the Man. Comrade soldiers of the Irish Volunteers and of the Citizen Army, we rejoice in this terrible war. The old heart of the earth needed to be warmed with the red wine of the battlefields. . . . Such august homage was never offered to God as this: the homage of millions of lives given gladly for love of country. And we must be ready to pour out the same red wine in the same glorious sacrifice, for without shedding of blood there is no redemption!

[*The figure moves out of sight and hearing.*

Fluther [*gulping down the drink that remains in his glass, and rushing out*]. Come on, man; this is too good to be missed!

[*Peter finishes his drink less rapidly, and as he is going out wiping his mouth with the back of his hand he runs into the Covey coming in. He immediately erects his body like a young cock, and with his chin thrust forward, and a look of venomous dignity on his face, he marches out.*

The Covey [*at counter*]. Give us a glass o' malt, for God's sake, till I stimulate meself from th' shock o' seein' th' sight that's afther goin' out!

Rosie [*all business, coming over to the counter, and standing near the Covey*]. Another one for me, Tommy; [*to the Barman*] th' young gentleman's ordherin' it in th' corner of his eye.

[*The Barman brings the drink for the Covey, and leaves it on the counter. Rosie whips it up.*

Barman. Ay, houl' on there, houl' on there, Rosie!

Rosie [*to the Barman*]. What are you houldin' on out o' you for? Didn't you hear th' young gentleman say that he couldn't refuse anything to a nice little bird? [*To the Covey*] Isn't that right, Jiggs? [*The Covey says nothing.*] Didn't I know, Tommy, it would be all right? It takes Rosie to size a young man up, an' tell th' thoughts that are thremblin' in his mind. Isn't that right, Jiggs?

[*The Covey stirs uneasily, moves a little farther away, and pulls his cap over his eyes.*]

Rosie [*moving after him*]. Great meetin' that's gettin' held outside. Well, it's up to us all, anyway, to fight for our freedom.

The Covey [*to Barman*]. Two more, please. [*To Rosie*] Freedom! What's th' use o' freedom, if it's not economic freedom?

Rosie [*emphasizing with extended arm and moving finger*]. I used them very words just before you come in. "A lot o' thricksters," says I, "that wouldn't know what freedom was if they got it from their mother." . . . [*To Barman*] Didn't I, Tommy?

Barman. I disremember.

Rosie. No, you don't disremember. Remember you said, yourself, it was all "only a flash in th' pan." Well, "flash in th' pan, or no flash in th' pan," says I, "they're not goin' to get Rosie Redmond," says I, "to fight for freedom that wouldn't be worth winnin' in a raffle!"

The Covey. There's only one freedom for th' workin' man: conthrol o' th' means o' production, rates of exchange, an' th' means of disthribution. [*Tapping Rosie on the shoulder*] Look here, comrade, I'll leave here to-morrow night for you a copy of Jenersky's *Thesis on the Origin, Development, an' Consolidation of the Evolutionary Idea of the Proletariat.*

Rosie [*throwing off her shawl on to the counter, and showing an exemplified glad neck, which reveals a good deal of a white bosom*]. If y'ass Rosie, it's heartbreakin' to see a young fella thinkin' of anything, or admirin' anything, but silk thransparent stockin's showin' off the shape of a little lassie's legs!   [*The Covey, frightened, moves a little away.*

Rosie [*following on*]. Out in th' park in th' shade of a warm summery evenin', with your little darlin' bridie to be, kissin' an' cuddlin' [*she tries to put her arm around his neck*], kissin' an' cuddlin', ay?

The Covey [*frightened*]. Ay, what are you doin'? None o' that, now; none that. I've something else to do besides shinannickin' afther Judies!

[*He turns away, but Rosie follows, keeping face to face with him.*

Rosie. Oh, little duckey, oh, shy little duckey! Never held a mot's hand, an' wouldn't know how to tittle a little Judy! [*She clips him under the chin.*] Tittle him undher th' chin, tittle him undher th' chin!

The Covey [*breaking away and running out*]. Ay, go on, now; I don't want to have any meddlin' with a lassie like you!

Rosie [*enraged*]. Jasus, it's in a monasthery some of us ought to be, spendin' our holidays kneelin' on our adorers, tellin' our beads, an' knockin' hell out of our buzzums!

The Covey [*outside*]. Cuckoo-oo!

[*Peter and Fluther come in again, followed by Mrs. Gogan, carrying a baby in her arms. They go over to the counter.*

Peter [*with plaintive anger*]. It's terrible that young Covey let me pass without proddin' at me! Did you hear him murmurin' "cuckoo" when we were passin'?

Fluther [*irritably*]. I wouldn't be everlastin' cockin' me ear to hear every little whisper that was floatin' around about me! It's my rule never to lose me temper till it would be dethrimental to keep it. There's nothin' derogatory in th' use o' th' word "cuckoo", is there?

Peter [*tearfully*]. It's not th' word; it's th' way he says it: he never says it straight out, but murmurs it with curious quiverin' ripples, like variations on a flute!

Fluther. Ah, what odds if he gave it with variations on a thrombone! [*To Mrs. Gogan*] What's yours goin' to be, ma'am?

Mrs. Gogan. Ah, a half o' malt, Fluther.

Fluther [*to Barman*]. Three halves, Tommy.
[*The Barman brings the drinks.*

Mrs. Gogan [*drinking*]. The Foresthers' is a gorgeous dhress! I don't think I've seen nicer, mind you, in a pantomime. . . . Th' loveliest part of th' dhress, I think, is th' osthrichess plume. . . . When yous are goin' along, an' I see them wavin' an' noddin' an' waggin', I seem to be lookin' at each of yous hangin' at th' end of a rope, your eyes bulgin' an' your legs twistin' an' jerkin', gaspin' an' gaspin' for breath while yous are thryin' to die for Ireland!

Fluther. If any o' them is hangin' at the end of a rope, it won't be for Ireland!

Peter. Are you goin' to start th' young Covey's game o' proddin' an' twartin' a man? There's not many that's talkin' can say that for twenty-five years he never missed a pilgrimage to Bodenstown!

Fluther. You're always blowin' about goin' to Bodenstown. D'ye think no one but yourself ever went to Bodenstown?

Peter [*plaintively*]. I'm not blowin' about it; but there's not a year that I go there but I pluck a leaf off Tone's grave, an' this very day me prayer-book is nearly full of them.

Fluther [*scornfully*].   Then Fluther has a vice versa opinion of them that put ivy leaves into their prayer-books, scabbin' it on th' clergy, an' thryin' to out-do th' haloes o' th' saints be lookin' as if he was wearin' around his head a glittherin' aroree boree allis! [*Fiercely*] Sure, I don't care a damn if you slep' in Bodenstown! You can take your breakfast, dinner, an' tea on th' grave in Bodenstown, if you like, for Fluther!

Mrs. Gogan.   Oh, don't start a fight, boys, for God's sake; I was only sayin' what a nice costume it is—nicer than th' kilts, for, God forgive me, I always think th' kilts is hardly decent.

Fluther.   Ah, sure, when you'd look at him, you'd wondher whether th' man was makin' fun o' th' costume, or th' costume was makin' fun o' th' man!

Barman.   Now, then, thry to speak asy, will yous? We don't want no shoutin' here.

> [*The Covey followed by Bessie Burgess comes in. They go over to the opposite end of the counter, and direct their gaze on the other group.*

The Covey [*to Barman*].   Two glasses o' malt.

Peter.   There he is, now; I knew he wouldn't be long till he folleyed me in.

Bessie [*speaking to the Covey, but really at the other party*].   I can't for th' life o' me undherstand how they can call themselves Catholics, when they won't lift a finger to help poor little Catholic Belgium.

Mrs. Gogan [*raising her voice*].   What about poor little Catholic Ireland?

Bessie [*over to Mrs. Gogan*].   You mind your own business, ma'am, an' stupefy your foolishness be gettin' dhrunk.

Peter [*anxiously*].   Take no notice of her; pay no attention to her. She's just tormentin' herself towards havin' a row with somebody.

Bessie.   There's a storm of anger tossin' in me heart, thinkin' of all th' poor Tommies, an' with them me own son, dhrenched in water an' soaked in blood, gropin' their way to a shattherin' death, in a shower o' shells! Young men with th' sunny lust o' life beamin' in them, layin' down their white bodies, shredded into torn an' bloody pieces, on th' althar that God Himself has built for th' sacrifice of heroes!

Mrs. Gogan.   Isn't it a nice thing to have to be listenin' to a lassie an' hangin' our heads in a dead silence, knowin' that some persons think more of a ball of malt than they do of th' blessed saints.

Fluther.   Whisht; she's always dangerous an' derogatory when she's well oiled. Th' safest way to hindher her from havin' any enjoyment out of her spite, is to dip our thoughts into the fact of her bein' a female person that has moved out of th' sight of ordinary sensible people.

Bessie. To look at some o' th' women that's knockin' about, now, is a thing to make a body sigh. . . . A woman on her own, dhrinkin' with a bevy o' men, is hardly an example to her sex. . . . A woman dhrinkin' with a woman is one thing, an' a woman dhrinkin' with herself is still a woman—flappers may be put in another category altogether—but a middle-aged married woman makin' herself th' centre of a circle of men is as a woman that is loud an' stubborn, whose feet abideth not in her own house.

The Covey [*to Bessie*]. When I think of all th' problems in front o' th' workers, it makes me sick to be lookin' at oul' codgers goin' about dhressed up like green-accountred figures gone asthray out of a toy-shop!

Peter. Gracious God, give me patience to be listenin' to that blasted young Covey proddin' at me from over at th' other end of th' shop!

Mrs. Gogan [*dipping her finger in the whisky, and moistening with it the lips of her baby*]. Cissie Gogan's a woman livin' for nigh on twenty-five years in her own room, an' beyond biddin' th' time o' day to her neighbours, never yet as much as nodded her head in th' direction of other people's business, while she knows some as are never content unless they're standin' senthry over other people's doin's!

> [*Bessie is about to reply, when the tall, dark figure is again silhouetted against the window, and the voice of the speaker is heard speaking passionately.*

Voice of Speaker. The last sixteen months have been the most glorious in the history of Europe. Heroism has come back to the earth. War is a terrible thing, but war is not an evil thing. People in Ireland dread war because they do not know it. Ireland has not known the exhilaration of war for over a hundred years. When war comes to Ireland she must welcome it as she would welcome the Angel of God!

> [*The figure passes out of sight and hearing.*

The Covey [*towards all present*]. Dope, dope. There's only one war worth havin': th' war for th' economic emancipation of th' proletariat.

Bessie. They may crow away out o' them; but it ud be fitther for some o' them to mend their ways, an' cease from havin' scouts out watchin' for th' comin' of th' Saint Vincent de Paul man, for fear they'd be nailed lowerin' a pint of beer, mockin' th' man with an angel face, shinin' with th' glamour of deceit an' lies!

Mrs. Gogan. An' a certain lassie standin' stiff behind her own door with her ears cocked listenin' to what's being said, stuffed till she's sthrained with envy of a neighbour thryin' for a few little things that may be got be hard sthrivin' to keep up to th' letther an' th' law, an' th' practices of th' Church!

Peter [*to Mrs. Gogan*].   If I was you, Mrs. Gogan, I'd parry her jabbin' remarks be a powerful silence that'll keep her tantalizin' words from penethratin' into your feelin's. It's always betther to leave these people to th' vengeance o' God!

Bessie.   Bessie Burgess doesn't put up to know much, never havin' a swaggerin' mind, thanks be to God, but goin' on packin' up knowledge accordin' to her conscience: precept upon precept, line upon line; here a little, an' there a little. But [*with a passionate swing of her shawl*], thanks be to Christ, she knows when she was got, where she was got, an' how she was got; while there's some she knows, decoratin' their finger with a well-polished weddin' ring, would be hard put to it if they were assed to show their weddin' lines!

Mrs. Gogan [*plunging out into the centre of the floor in a wild tempest of hysterical rage*].   Y' oul' rip of a blasted liar, me weddin' ring's been well earned be twenty years be th' side o' me husband, now takin' his rest in heaven, married to me be Father Dempsey, in th' Chapel o' Saint Jude's, in th' Christmas Week of eighteen hundhred an' ninety-five; an' any kid, livin' or dead, that Jinnie Gogan's had since, was got between th' bordhers of th' Ten Commandments! . . . An' that's more than some o' you can say that are kep' from th' dhread o' desthruction be a few drowsy virtues, that th' first whisper of temptation lulls into a sleep, that'll know one sin from another only on th' day of their last anointin', an' that use th' innocent light o' th' shinin' stars to dip into th' sins of a night's diversion!

Bessie [*jumping out to face Mrs. Gogan, and bringing the palms of her hands together in sharp claps to emphasize her remarks*].   Liar to you, too, ma'am, y' oul' hardened thresspasser on other people's good nature, wizenin' up your soul in th' arts o' dodgeries, till every dhrop of respectability in a female is dhried up in her, lookin' at your ready-made manœuverin' with th' menkind!

Barman.   Here, there; here, there; speak asy there. No rowin' here, no rowin' here, now.

Fluther [*trying to calm Mrs. Gogan*].   Now Jinnie, Jinnie, it's a derogatory thing to be smirchin' a night like this with a row; it's rompin' with th' feelin's of hope we ought to be, instead o' bein' vice versa!

Peter [*trying to quiet Bessie*].   I'm terrible dawny, Mrs. Burgess, an' a fight leaves me weak for a long time afterwards. . . . Please, Mrs. Burgess, before there's damage done, thry to have a little respect for yourself.

Bessie [*with a push of her hand that sends Peter tottering to the end of the shop*]. G'way, you little sermonizing, little yella-faced, little consequential, little pudgy, little bum, you!

Mrs. Gogan [*screaming*]. Fluther, leggo! I'm not goin' to keep an unresistin' silence, an' her scattherin' her festherin' words in me face, stirrin' up every dhrop of decency in a respectable female, with her restless rally o' lies that would make a saint say his prayer backwards!

Bessie [*shouting*]. Ah, everybody knows well that th' best charity that can be shown to you is to hide th' thruth as much as our thrue worship of God Almighty will allow us!

Mrs. Gogan [*frantically*]. Here, houl' th' kid, one o' yous; houl' th' kid for a minute! There's nothin' for it but to show this lassie a lesson or two. . . . [*To Peter*] Here, houl' th' kid, you. [*Before Peter is aware of it, she places the infant in his arms.*]

Mrs. Gogan [*to Bessie, standing before her in a fighting attitude*]. Come on, now, me loyal lassie, dyin' with grief for little Catholic Belgium! When Jinnie Gogan's done with you, you'll have a little leisure lyin' down to think an' pray for your king an' counthry!

Barman [*coming from behind the counter, getting between the women, and proceeding to push them towards the door*]. Here, now, since yous can't have a little friendly argument quietly, you'll get out o' this place in quick time. Go on, an' settle your differences somewhere else—I don't want to have another endorsement on me licence.

Peter [*anxiously, over to Mrs. Gogan*]. Here, take your kid back, ower this. How nicely I was picked, now, for it to be plumped into me arms!

The Covey. She knew who she was givin' it to, maybe.

Peter [*hotly to the Covey*]. Now, I'm givin' you fair warnin', me young Covey, to quit firin' your jibes an' jeers at me. . . . For one o' these days, I'll run out in front o' God Almighty an' take your sacred life!

Barman [*pushing Bessie out after Mrs. Gogan*]. Go on, now; out you go.

Bessie [*as she goes out*]. If you think, me lassie, that Bessie Burgess has an untidy conscience, she'll soon show you to th' differ!

Peter [*leaving the baby down on the floor*]. Ay, be Jasus, wait there, till I give her back her youngster! [*He runs to the door.*] Ay, there, ay! [*He comes back.*] There, she's afther goin' without her kid. What are we goin' to do with it, now?

The Covey. What are we goin' to do with it? Bring it outside an' show everybody what you're afther findin'!

Peter [in a panic to Fluther]. Pick it up, you, Fluther, an' run afther her with it, will you?

Fluther. What d'ye take Fluther for? You must think Fluther's a right gom. D'ye think Fluther's like yourself, destitute of a tither of undherstandin'?

Barman [imperatively to Peter]. Take it up, man, an' run out afther her with it, before she's gone too far. You're not goin' to leave th' bloody thing here, are you?

Peter [plaintively, as he lifts up the baby]. Well, God Almighty, give me patience with all th' scorners, tormentors, an' twarters that are always an' ever thryin' to goad me into prayin' for their blindin' an' blastin' an' burnin' in th' world to come! *[He goes out.*

Fluther. God, it's a relief to get rid o' that crowd. Women is terrible when they start to fight. There's no holdin' them back. *[To the Covey]* Are you goin' to have anything?

The Covey. Ah, I don't mind if I have another half.

Fluther [to Barman]. Two more, Tommy, me son.
[The Barman gets the drinks.

Fluther. You know, there's no conthrollin' a woman when she loses her head.

[Rosie enters and goes over to the counter on the side nearest to Fluther.

Rosie [to Barman]. Divil a use o' havin' a thrim little leg on a night like this; things was never worse. . . . Give us a half till to-morrow, Tom, duckey.

Barman [coldly]. No more to-night, Rosie; you owe me for three already.

Rosie [combatively]. You'll be paid, won't you?

Barman. I hope so.

Rosie. You hope so! Is that th' way with you, now?

Fluther [to Barman]. Give her one; it'll be all right.

Rosie [clapping Fluther on the back]. Oul' sport!

Fluther. Th' meetin' should be soon over, now.

The Covey. Th' sooner th' betther. It's all a lot o' blasted nonsense, comrade.

Fluther. Oh, I wouldn't say it was all nonsense. Afther all, Fluther can remember th' time, an' him only a dawny chiselur, bein' taught at his mother's knee to be faithful to th' Shan Van Vok!

The Covey. That's all dope, comrade; th' sort o' thing that workers are fed on be th' Boorzwawze.

Fluther [*a little sharply*]. What's all dope? Though I'm sayin' it that shouldn't: [*catching his cheek with his hand, and pulling down the flesh from the eye*] d'ye see that mark there, undher me eye? . . . A sabre slice from a dragoon in O'Connell Street! [*Thrusting his head forward towards Rosie*] Feel that dint in th' middle o' me nut!

Rosie [*rubbing Fluther's head, and winking at the Covey*]. My God, there's a holla!

Fluther [*putting on his hat with quiet pride*]. A skelp from a bobby's baton at a Labour meetin' in th' Phœnix Park!

The Covey. He must ha' hitten you in mistake. I don't know what you ever done for th' Labour movement.

Fluther [*loudly*]. D'ye not? Maybe, then, I done as much, an' know as much about th' Labour movement as th' chancers that are blowin' about it!

Barman. Speak easy, Fluther, thry to speak easy.

The Covey. There's no necessity to get excited about it, comrade.

Fluther [*more loudly*]. Excited? Who's gettin' excited? There's no one gettin' excited! It would take something more than a thing like you to flutther a feather o' Fluther. Blatherin', an', when all is said, you know as much as th' rest in th' wind up!

The Covey. Well, let us put it to th' test, then, an' see what you know about th' Labour movement: what's the mechanism of exchange?

Fluther [*roaring, because he feels he is beaten*]. How th' hell do I know what it is? There's nothin' about that in th' rules of our Thrades Union!

Barman. For God's sake, thry to speak easy, Fluther.

The Covey. What does Karl Marx say about th' Relation of Value to th' Cost o' Production?

Fluther [*angrily*]. What th' hell do I care what he says? I'm Irishman enough not to lose me head be follyin' foreigners!

Barman. Speak easy, Fluther.

The Covey. It's only waste o' time talkin' to you, comrade.

Fluther. Don't be comradin' me, mate. I'd be on me last legs if I wanted you for a comrade.

Rosie [*to the Covey*]. It seems a highly rediculous thing to hear a thing that's only an inch or two away from a kid, swingin' heavy words about he doesn't know th' meanin' of, an' uppishly thryin' to down a man like Misther Fluther here, that's well flavoured in th' knowledge of th' world he's livin' in.

The Covey [*savagely to Rosie*]. Nobody's askin' you to be buttin' in with your prate. . . . I have you well taped, me lassie. . . . Just you keep your opinions for your own place. . . . It'll be a long time before th' Covey takes any insthructions or reprimandin' from a prostitute!

Rosie [*wild with humiliation*]. You louse, you louse, you! . . . You're no man. . . . You're no man . . . I'm a woman, anyhow, an' if I'm a prostitute aself, I have me feelin's. . . . Thryin' to put his arm around me a minute ago, an' givin' me th' glad eye, th' little wrigglin' lump o' desolation turns on me now, because he saw there was nothin' doin'. . . . You louse, you! If I was a man, or you were a woman, I'd bate th' puss o' you!

Barman. Ay, Rosie, ay! You'll have to shut your mouth altogether, if you can't learn to speak easy!

Fluther [*to Rosie*]. Houl' on there, Rosie; houl' on there. There's no necessity to flutther yourself when you're with Fluther. . . . Any lady that's in th' company of Fluther is goin' to get a fair hunt. . . . This is outside your province. . . . I'm not goin' to let you demean yourself be talkin' to a tittherin' chancer. . . . Leave this to Fluther—this is a man's job. [*To the Covey*] Now, if you've anything to say, say it to Fluther, an', let me tell you, you're not goin' to be pass-remarkable to any lady in my company.

The Covey. Sure I don't care if you were runnin' all night afther your Mary o' th' Curlin' Hair, but, when you start tellin' luscious lies about what you done for th' Labour movement, it's nearly time to show y'up!

Fluther [*fiercely*]. Is it you show Fluther up? G'way, man, I'd beat two o' you before me breakfast!

The Covey [*contemptuously*]. Tell us where you bury your dead, will you?

Fluther [*with his face stuck into the face of the Covey*]. Sing a little less on th' high note, or, when I'm done with you, you'll put a Christianable consthruction on things, I'm tellin' you!

The Covey. You're a big fella, you are.

Fluther [*tapping the Covey threateningly on the shoulder*]. Now, you're temptin' Providence when you're temptin' Fluther!

The Covey [*losing his temper, and bawling*]. Easy with them hands, there, easy with them hands! You're startin' to take a little risk when you commence to paw the Covey!

> [*Fluther suddenly springs into the middle of the shop, flings his hat into the corner, whips off his coat, and begins to paw the air.*

Fluther [*roaring at the top of his voice*]. Come on, come on, you lowser; put your mits up now, if there's a man's blood in you! Be God, in a few minutes you'll see some snots flyin' around, I'm tellin' you. . . . When Fluther's done with you, you'll have a vice versa opinion of him! Come on, now, come on!

Barman [*running from behind the counter and catching hold of the Covey*]. Here, out you go, me little bowsey. Because you got a couple o' halves you think you can act as you like. [*He pushes the Covey to the door*] Fluther's a friend o' mine, an' I'll not have him insulted.

The Covey [*struggling with the Barman*]. Ay, leggo, leggo there; fair hunt, give a man a fair hunt! One minute with him is all I ask; one minute alone with him, while you're runnin' for th' priest an' th' doctor.

Fluther [*to the Barman*]. Let him go, let him go, Tom: let him open th' door to sudden death if he wants to!

Barman [*to the Covey*]. Go on, out you go an' do th' bowsey somewhere else.   [*He pushes the Covey out and comes back.*

Rosie [*getting Fluther's hat as he is putting on his coat*]. Be God, you put th' fear o' God in his heart that time! I thought you'd have to be dug out of him. . . . Th' way you lepped out without any of your fancy side-steppin'! "Men like Fluther," say I to meself, "is gettin' scarce nowadays."

Fluther [*with proud complacency*]. I wasn't goin' to let meself be malignified by a chancer. . . . He got a little bit too derogatory for Fluther. . . . Be God, to think of a cur like that comin' to talk to a man like me!

Rosie [*fixing on his hat*]. Did j'ever!

Fluther. He's lucky he got off safe. I hit a man last week, Rosie, an' he's fallin' yet!

Rosie. Sure, you'd ha' broken him in two if you'd ha' hitten him one clatther!

Fluther [*amorously, putting his arm around Rosie*]. Come on into th' snug, me little darlin', an' we'll have a few dhrinks before I see you home.

Rosie. Oh, Fluther, I'm afraid you're a terrible man for th' women.

> [*They go into the snug as Clitheroe, Captain Brennan, and Lieut. Langon of the Irish Volunteers enter hurriedly. Captain Brennan carries the banner of The Plough and the Stars, and Lieut. Langon a green, white, and orange Tri-colour. They are in a state of emotional excitement. Their faces are flushed and their eyes sparkle; they speak rapidly, as if unaware of the meaning of what they said. They have been mesmerized by the fervency of the speeches.*

Clitheroe [*almost pantingly*]. Three glasses o' port!
> [*The Barman brings the drinks.*

Capt. Brennan. We won't have long to wait now.

Lieut. Langon. Th' time is rotten ripe for revolution.

Clitheroe. You have a mother, Langon.

Lieut. Langon. Ireland is greater than a mother.

Capt. Brennan. You have a wife, Clitheroe.

Clitheroe. Ireland is greater than a wife.

Lieut. Langon. Th' time for Ireland's battle is now—th' place for Ireland's battle is here.

> [*The tall, dark figure again is silhouetted against the window. The three men pause and listen.*

Voice of the Man. Our foes are strong, but strong as they are, they cannot undo the miracles of God, who ripens in the heart of young men the seeds sown by the young men of a former generation. They think they have pacified Ireland; think they have foreseen everything; think they have provided against everything; but the fools, the fools, the fools!— they have left us our Fenian dead, and, while Ireland holds these graves, Ireland, unfree, shall never be at peace!

Capt. Brennan [*catching up The Plough and the Stars*]. Imprisonment for th' Independence of Ireland!

Lieut. Langon [*catching up the Tri-colour*]. Wounds for th' Independence of Ireland!

Clitheroe. Death for th' Independence of Ireland!

The Three [*together*]. So help us God!

> [*They drink. A bugle blows the Assembly. They hurry out. A pause. Fluther and Rosie come out of the snug; Rosie is linking Fluther, who is a little drunk. Both are in a merry mood.*

Rosie. Come on home, ower o' that, man. Are you afraid or what? Are you goin' to come home, or are you not?

Fluther.   Of course I'm goin' home. What ud ail me that I wouldn't go?

Rosie [*lovingly*].   Come on, then, oul' sport.

Officer's Voice [*giving command outside*].   Irish Volunteers, by th' right, quick march!

Rosie [*putting her arm round Fluther and singing*]:
> I once had a lover, a tailor, but he could do nothin' for me,
> An' then I fell in with a sailor as strong an' as wild as th' sea.
> We cuddled an' kissed with devotion, till th' night from th' mornin'
>   had fled;
> An' there, to our joy, a bright bouncin' boy
> Was dancin' a jig in th' bed!
>
> Dancin' a jig in th' bed, an' bawlin' for butther an' bread.
> An' there, to our joy, a bright bouncin' boy
> Was dancin' a jig in th' bed!
>   [*They go out with their arms round each other.*

Clitheroe's Voice [*in command outside*].   Dublin Battalion of the Irish Citizen Army, by th' right, quick march!

CURTAIN

ACT III

The corner house in a street of tenements: it is the home of the Clitheroes. The house is a long, gaunt, five-story tenement; its brick front is chipped and scarred with age and neglect. The wide and heavy hall door, flanked by two pillars, has a look of having been charred by a fire in the distant past. The door lurches a little to one side, disjointed by the continual and reckless banging when it is being closed by most of the residents. The diamond-paned fanlight is destitute of a single pane, the framework alone remaining. The windows, except the two looking into the front parlour [Clitheroe's room], are grimy, and are draped with fluttering and soiled fragments of lace curtains. The front parlour windows are hung with rich, compara-

tively, casement cloth. Five stone steps lead from the door to the path on the street. Branching on each side are railings to prevent people from falling into the area. At the left corner of the house runs a narrow lane, bisecting the street, and connecting it with another of the same kind. At the corner of the lane is a street lamp.

As the house is revealed, Mrs. Gogan is seen helping Mollser to a chair, which stands on the path beside the railings, at the left side of the steps. She then wraps a shawl around Mollser's shoulders. It is some months later.

Mrs. Gogan [*arranging shawl around Mollser*]. Th' sun'll do you all th' good in th' world. A few more weeks o' this weather, an' there's no knowin' how well you'll be. . . . Are you comfy, now?

Mollser [*weakly and wearily*]. Yis, ma; I'm all right.

Mrs. Gogan. How are you feelin'?

Mollser. Betther, ma, betther. If th' horrible sinkin' feelin' ud go, I'd be all right.

Mrs. Gogan. Ah, I wouldn't put much pass on that. Your stomach maybe's out of ordher. . . . Is th' poor breathin' any betther, d'ye think?

Mollser. Yis, yis, ma; a lot betther.

Mrs. Gogan. Well, that's somethin' anyhow. . . . With th' help o' God, you'll be on th' mend from this out. . . . D'your legs feel any sthronger undher you, d'ye think?

Mollser [*irritably*]. I can't tell, ma. I think so. . . . A little.

Mrs. Gogan. Well, a little aself is somethin'. . . . I thought I heard you coughin' a little more than usual last night. . . . D'ye think you were?

Mollser. I wasn't, ma, I wasn't.

Mrs. Gogan. I thought I heard you, for I was kep' awake all night with th' shootin'. An' thinkin' o' that madman, Fluther, runnin' about through th' night lookin' for Nora Clitheroe to bring her back when he heard she'd gone to folly her husband, an' in dhread any minute he might come staggerin' in covered with bandages, splashed all over with th' red of his own blood, an' givin 'us barely time to bring th' priest to hear th' last whisper of his final confession, as his soul was passin' through th' dark doorway o' death into th' way o' th' wondherin' dead. . . . You don't feel cold, do you?

Mollser. No, ma; I'm all right.

Mrs. Gogan. Keep your chest well covered, for that's th' delicate spot in you . . . if there's any danger, I'll whip you in again. . . . [*Looking up the street*] Oh, here's th' Covey an' oul' Pether hurryin' along. God

Almighty, sthrange things is happenin' when them two is pullin' together.

[*The Covey and Peter come in, breathless and excited.*

Mrs. Gogan [*to the two men*]. Were yous far up th' town? Did yous see any sign o' Fluther or Nora? How is things lookin'? I hear they're blazin' away out o' th' G.P.O. That th' Tommies is sthretched in heaps around Nelson's Pillar an' th' Parnell Statue, an' that th' pavin' sets in O'Connell Street is nearly covered be pools o' blood.

Peter. We seen no sign o' Nora or Fluther anywhere.

Mrs. Gogan. We should ha' held her back be main force from goin' to look for her husband. . . . God knows what's happened to her—I'm always seein' her sthretched on her back in some hospital, moanin' with th' pain of a bullet in her vitals, an' nuns thryin' to get her to take a last look at th' crucifix!

The Covey. We can do nothin'. You can't stick your nose into O'Connell Street, an' Tyler's is on fire.

Peter. An' we seen th' Lancers——

The Covey [*interrupting*]. Throttin' along, heads in th' air; spurs an' sabres jinglin', an' lances quiverin', an' lookin' as if they were assin' themselves, "Where's these blighters, till we get a prod at them?" when there was a volley from th' Post Office that stretched half o' them, an' sent th' rest gallopin' away wondherin' how far they'd have to go before they'd feel safe.

Peter [*rubbing his hands*]. "Damn it," says I to meself, "this looks like business!"

The Covey. An' then out comes General Pearse an' his staff, an', standin' in th' middle o' th' street, he reads th' Proclamation.

Mrs. Gogan. What proclamation?

Peter. Declarin' an Irish Republic.

Mrs. Gogan. Go to God!

Peter. The gunboat *Helga's* shellin' Liberty Hall, an' I hear the people livin' on th' quays had to crawl on their bellies to Mass with th' bullets that were flyin' around from Boland's Mills.

Mrs. Gogan. God bless us, what's goin' to be th' end of it all!

Bessie [*looking out of the top window*]. Maybe yous are satisfied now; maybe yous are satisfied now. Go on an' gets guns if yous are men— Johnny get your gun, get your gun, get your gun! Yous are all nicely shanghaied now; th' boyo hasn't a sword on his thigh now! Oh, yous are all nicely shanghaied now!

Mrs. Gogan [*warningly to Peter and the Covey*].   S-s-sh, don't answer her. She's th' right oul' Orange bitch! She's been chantin' "Rule, Britannia" all th' mornin'.

Peter.   I hope Fluther hasn't met with any accident, he's such a wild card.

Mrs. Gogan.   God grant it; but last night I dreamt I seen gettin' carried into th' house a sthretcher with a figure lyin' on it, stiff an' still, dhressed in th' habit of Saint Francis. An', then, I heard th' murmurs of a crowd no one could see sayin' th' litany for th' dead; an' then it got so dark that nothin' was seen but th' white face of th' corpse, gleamin' like a white wather-lily floatin' on th' top of a dark lake. Then a tiny whisper thrickled into me ear, sayin', "Isn't the face very like th' face o' Fluther?" an' then, with a thremblin' flutther, th' dead lips opened, an', although I couldn't hear, I knew they were sayin', "Poor oul' Fluther, afther havin' handed in his gun at last, his shakin' soul moored in th' place where th' wicked are at rest an' th' weary cease from throublin'."

Peter [*who has put on a pair of spectacles, and has been looking down the street*].   Here they are, be God, here they are; just afther turnin' th' corner—Nora an' Fluther!

The Covey.   She must be wounded or something—he seems to be carryin' her.

> [*Fluther and Nora enter. Fluther has his arm around her and is half leading, half carrying her in. Her eyes are dim and hollow, her face pale and strained-looking; her hair is tossed, and her clothes are dusty.*

Mrs. Gogan [*running over to them*].   God bless us, is it wounded y'are, Mrs. Clitheroe, or what?

Fluther.   Ah, she's all right, Mrs. Gogan; only worn out from thravellin' an' want o' sleep. A night's rest, now, an' she'll be as fit as a fiddle. Bring her in, an' make her lie down.

Mrs. Gogan [*to Nora*].   Did you hear e'er a whisper o' Mr. Clitheroe?

Nora [*wearily*].   I could find him nowhere, Mrs. Gogan. None o' them would tell me where he was. They told me I shamed my husband an' th' women of Ireland be carryin' on as I was. . . . They said th' women must learn to be brave an' cease to be cowardly. . . . Me who risked more for love than they would risk for hate. . . . [*Raising her voice in hysterical protest*] My Jack will be killed, my Jack will be killed! . . . He is to be butchered as a sacrifice to th' dead!

Bessie [*from upper window*].   Yous are all nicely shanghaied now! Sorra mend th' lasses that have been kissin' an' cuddlin' their boys into th' sheddin' of blood! . . . Fillin' their minds with fairy tales that had no

beginnin', but, please God, 'll have a bloody quick endin'! . . . Turnin'
bitther into sweet, an' sweet into bitther. . . . Stabbin' in th' back th'
men that are dyin' in th' threnches for them! It's a bad thing for any one
that thries to jilt th' Ten Commandments, for judgements are prepared
for scorners an' sthripes for th' back o' fools! [*Going away from window
as she sings:*]

> Rule, Britannia, Britannia rules th' waves,
> Britons never, never, never shall be slaves!

Fluther [*with a roar up at the window*].   Y'ignorant oul' throllope, you!

Mrs. Gogan [*to Nora*].   He'll come home safe enough to you, you'll find,
Mrs. Clitheroe; afther all, there's a power o' women that's handed over
sons an' husbands to take a runnin' risk in th' fight they're wagin'.

Nora.   I can't help thinkin' every shot fired 'll be fired at Jack, an' every
shot fired at Jack'll be fired at me. What do I care for th' others? I can
think only of me own self. . . . An' there's no woman gives a son or a
husband to be killed—if they say it, they're lyin', lyin', against God, Nature, an' against themselves! . . . One blasted hussy at a barricade told
me to go home an' not be thryin' to dishearten th' men. . . . That I
wasn't worthy to bear a son to a man that was out fightin' for freedom.
. . . I clawed at her, an' smashed her in th' face till we were separated.
. . . I was pushed down th' street, an' I cursed them—cursed the rebel
ruffians an' Volunteers that had dhragged me ravin' mad into th' sthreets
to seek me husband!

Peter.   You'll have to have patience, Nora. We all have to put up with
twarthers an' tormentors in this world.

The Covey.   If they were fightin' for anything worth while, I wouldn't
mind.

Fluther [*to Nora*].   Nothin' derogatory 'll happen to Mr. Clitheroe. You'll
find, now, in th' finish up it'll be vice versa.

Nora.   Oh, I know that wherever he is, he's thinkin' of wantin' to be with
me. I know he's longin' to be passin' his hand through me hair, to be
caressin' me neck, to fondle me hand an' to feel me kisses clingin' to his
mouth. . . . An' he stands wherever he is because he's brave? [*Vehemently*] No, but because he's a coward, a coward, a coward!

Mrs. Gogan.   Oh, they're not cowards anyway.

Nora [*with denunciatory anger*].   I tell you they're afraid to say they're
afraid! . . . Oh, I saw it, I saw it, Mrs. Gogan. . . . At th' barricade in
North King Street I saw fear glowin' in all their eyes. . . . An' in th'
middle o' th' sthreet was somethin' huddled up in a horrible tangled heap.
. . . His face was jammed again th' stones, an' his arm was twisted

round his back. . . . An' every twist of his body was a cry against th' terrible thing that had happened to him. . . . An' I saw they were afraid to look at it. . . . An' some o' them laughed at me, but th' laugh was a frightened one. . . . An' some o' them shouted at me, but th' shout had in it th' shiver o' fear. . . . I tell you they were afraid, afraid, afraid!

Mrs. Gogan [*leading her towards the house*].   Come on in, dear. If you'd been a little longer together, th' wrench asundher wouldn't have been so sharp.

Nora.   Th' agony I'm in since he left me has thrust away every rough thing he done, an' every unkind word he spoke; only th' blossoms that grew out of our lives are before me now; shakin' their colours before me face, an' breathin' their sweet scent on every thought springin' up in me mind, till, sometimes, Mrs. Gogan, sometimes I think I'm goin' mad!

Mrs. Gogan.   You'll be a lot betther when you have a little lie down.

Nora [*turning towards Fluther as she is going in*].   I don't know what I'd have done, only for Fluther. I'd have been lyin' in th' streets, only for him. . . . [*As she goes in*] They have dhriven away th' little happiness life had to spare for me. He has gone from me for ever, for ever. . . . Oh, Jack, Jack, Jack!

> [*She is led in by Mrs. Gogan as Bessie comes out with a shawl around her shoulders. She passes by them with her head in the air. When they have gone in, she gives a mug of milk to Mollser silently.*]

Fluther.   Which of yous has th' tossers?

The Covey.   I have.

Bessie [*as she is passing them to go down the street*].   You an' your Leadhers an' their sham-battle soldiers has landed a body in a nice way, havin' to go an' ferret out a bit o' bread God knows where. . . . Why aren't yous in th' G.P.O. if yous are men? It's paler an' paler yous are gettin'. . . . A lot o' vipers, that's what th' Irish people is!   [*She goes out.*

Fluther.   Never mind her. . . . [*To the Covey*] Make a start an' keep us from th' sin o' idleness. [*To Mollser*] Well, how are you to-day, Mollser, oul' son? What are you dhrinkin', milk?

Mollser.   Grand, Fluther, grand, thanks. Yis, milk.

Fluther.   You couldn't get a betther thing down you. . . . This turn-up has done one good thing, anyhow; you can't get dhrink anywhere, an' if it lasts a week, I'll be so used to it that I won't think of a pint.

The Covey [*who has taken from his pocket two worn coins and a thin strip of wood about four inches long*].   What's th' bettin'?

Peter. Heads, a juice.

Fluther. Harps, a tanner.

[*The Covey places the coins on the strip of wood, and flips them up into the air. As they jingle on the ground the distant boom of a big gun is heard. They stand for a moment listening.*

Fluther. What th' hell's that?

The Covey. It's like th' boom of a big gun!

Fluther. Surely to God they're not goin' to use artillery on us?

The Covey [*scornfully*]. Not goin'! [*Vehemently*] Wouldn't they use anything on us, man?

Fluther. Aw, holy Christ, that's not playin' th' game!

Peter [*plaintively*]. What would happen if a shell landed here now?

The Covey [*ironically*]. You'd be off to heaven in a fiery chariot.

Peter. In spite of all th' warnin's that's ringin' around us, are you goin' to start your pickin' at me again?

Fluther. Go on, toss them again, toss them again. . . . Harps, a tanner.

Peter. Heads, a juice.   [*The Covey tosses the coins.*

Fluther [*as the coins fall*]. Let them roll, let them roll. Heads, be God!

[*Bessie runs in excitedly. She has a new hat on her head, a fox fur round her neck over her shawl, three umbrellas under her right arm, and a box of biscuits under her left. She speaks rapidly and breathlessly.*

Bessie. They're breakin' into th' shops, they're breakin' into th' shops! Smashin' th' windows, battherin' in th' doors, an' whippin' away everything! An' the Volunteers is firin' on them. I seen two men an' a lassie pushin' a piano down th' sthreet, an' th' sweat rollin' off them thryin' to get it up on th' pavement; an' an oul' wan that must ha' been seventy lookin' as if she'd dhrop every minute with th' dint o' heart beatin', thryin' to pull a big double bed out of a broken shop-window! I was goin' to wait till I dhressed meself from th' skin out.

Mollser [*to Bessie, as she is going in*]. Help me in, Bessie; I'm feelin' curious.

[*Bessie leaves the looted things in the house, and, rapidly returning, helps Mollser in.*

The Covey. Th' selfishness of that one—she waited till she got all she could carry before she'd come to tell anyone!

Fluther [*running over to the door of the house and shouting in to Bessie*]. Ay, Bessie, did you hear of e'er a pub gettin' a shake up?

Bessie [*inside*]. I didn't hear o' none.

Fluther [*in a burst of enthusiasm*]. Well, you're goin' to hear of one soon!

The Covey. Come on, man, an' don't be wastin' time.

Peter [*to them as they are about to run off*]. Ay, ay, are you goin' to leave me here?

Fluther. Are you goin' to leave yourself here?

Peter [*anxiously*]. Didn't yous hear her sayin' they were firin' on them?

The Covey and Fluther [*together*]. Well?

Peter. Supposin' I happened to be potted?

Fluther. We'd give you a Christian burial, anyhow.

The Covey [*ironically*]. Dhressed up in your regimentals.

Peter [*to the Covey, passionately*]. May th' all-lovin' God give you a hot knock one o' these days, me young Covey, tuthorin' Fluther up now to be tiltin' at me, an' crossin' me with his mockeries an' jibin'!

[*A fashionably dressed, middle-aged, stout woman comes hurriedly in, and makes for the group. She is almost fainting with fear.*

The Woman. For Gawd's sake, will one of you kind men show any safe way for me to get to Wrathmines? . . . I was foolish enough to visit a friend, thinking the howl thing was a joke, and now I cawn't get a car or a tram to take me home—isn't it awful?

Fluther. I'm afraid, ma'am, one way is as safe as another.

Woman. And what am I gowing to do? Oh, isn't this awful? . . . I'm so different from others. . . . The mowment I hear a shot, my legs give way under me—I cawn't stir, I'm paralysed—isn't it awful?

Fluther [*moving away*]. It's a derogatory way to be, right enough, ma'am.

Woman [*catching Fluther's coat*]. Creeping along the street there, with my head down and my eyes half shut, a bullet whizzed past within an inch of my nowse. . . . I had to lean against the wall for a long time, gasping for breath—I nearly passed away—it was awful! . . . I wonder, would you kind men come some of the way and see me safe?

Fluther. I have to go away, ma'am, to thry an' save a few things from th' burnin' buildin's.

The Covey. Come on, then, or there won't be anything left to save.
[*The Covey and Fluther hurry away.*

Woman [*to Peter*].   Wasn't it an awful thing for me to leave my friend's house? Wasn't it an idiotic thing to do? . . . I haven't the slightest idea where I am. . . . You have a kind face, sir. Could you possibly come and pilot me in the direction of Wrathmines?

Peter [*indignantly*].   D'ye think I'm goin' to risk me life throttin' in front of you? An' maybe get a bullet that would gimme a lame leg or something that would leave me a jibe an' a jeer to Fluther an' th' young Covey for th' rest o' me days!

> [*With an indignant toss of his head he walks into the house.*

The Woman [*going out*].   I know I'll fall down in a dead faint if I hear another shot go off anyway near me—isn't it awful!

> [*Mrs. Gogan comes out of the house pushing a pram before her. As she enters the street, Bessie rushes out, follows Mrs. Gogan, and catches hold of the pram, stopping Mrs. Gogan's progress.*

Bessie.   Here, where are you goin' with that? How quick you were, me lady, to clap your eyes on th' pram. . . . Maybe you don't know that Mrs. Sullivan, before she went to spend Easther with her people in Dunboyne, gave me sthrict injunctions to give an accasional look to see if it was still standin' where it was left in th' corner of th' lobby.

Mrs. Gogan.   That remark of yours, Mrs. Bessie Burgess, requires a little considheration, seein' that th' pram was left on our lobby, an' not on yours; a foot or two a little to th' left of th' jamb of me own room door; nor is it needful to mention th' name of th' person that gave a squint to see if it was there th' first thing in th' mornin', an' th' last thing in th' stillness o' th' night; never failin' to realize that her eyes couldn't be goin' wrong, be sthretchin' out her arm an' runnin' her hand over th' pram, to make sure that th' sight was no deception! Moreover, somethin's tellin' me that th' runnin' hurry of an inthrest you're takin' in it now is a sudden ambition to use th' pram for a purpose that a loyal woman of law an' ordher would stagger away from!

> [*She gives the pram a sudden push that pulls Bessie forward.*

Bessie [*still holding the pram*].   There's not as much as one body in th' house that doesn't know that it wasn't Bessie Burgess that was always shakin' her voice complainin' about people leavin' bassinettes in th' way of them that, week in an' week out, had to pay their rent, an' always had to find a regular accommodation for her own furniture in her own room. . . . An' as for law an' ordher, puttin' aside th' harp an' shamrock, Bessie Burgess'll have as much respect as she wants for th' lion an' unicorn!

Peter [*appearing at the door*].   I think I'll go with th' pair of yous an' see th' fun. A fella might as well chance it, anyhow.

Mrs. Gogan [*taking no notice of Peter, and pushing the pram on another step*]. Take your rovin' lumps o' hands from pattin' th' bassinette, if you please, ma'am; an', steppin' from th' threshold of good manners, let me tell you, Mrs. Burgess, that's it's a fat wondher to Jennie Gogan that a lady-like singer o' hymns like yourself would lower her thoughts from sky-thinkin' to sthretch out her arm in a sly-seekin' way to pinch anything dhriven asthray in th' confusion of th' battle our boys is makin' for th' freedom of their counthry!

Peter [*laughing and rubbing his hands together*]. Hee, hee, hee, hee, hee! I'll go with th' pair o' yous an' give yous a hand.

Mrs. Gogan [*with a rapid turn of her head as she shoves the pram forward*]. Get up in th' prambulator an' we'll wheel you down.

Bessie [*to Mrs. Gogan*]. Poverty an' hardship has sent Bessie Burgess to abide with sthrange company, but she always knew them she had to live with from backside to breakfast time; an' she can tell them, always havin' had a Christian kinch on her conscience, that a passion for thievin' an' pinchin' would find her soul a foreign place to live in, an' that her present intention is quite th' lofty-hearted one of pickin' up anything shaken up an' scatthered about in th' loose confusion of a general plundher!

[*By this time they have disappeared from view. Peter is following, when the boom of a big gun in the distance brings him to a quick halt.*]

Peter. God Almighty, that's th' big gun again! God forbid any harm would happen to them, but sorra mind I'd mind if they met with a dhrop in their mad endeyvours to plundher an' desthroy.

[*He looks down the street for a moment, then runs to the hall door of the house, which is open, and shuts it with a vicious pull; he then goes to the chair in which Mollser had sat, sits down, takes out his pipe, lights it and begins to smoke with his head carried at a haughty angle. The Covey comes staggering in with a ten-stone sack of flour on his back. On the top of the sack is a ham. He goes over to the door, pushes it with his head, and finds he can't open it; he turns slightly in the direction of Peter.*]

The Covey [*to Peter*]. Who shut th' door? . . . [*He kicks at it*] Here, come on an' open it, will you? This isn't a mot's hand-bag I've got on me back.

Peter. Now, me young Covey, d'ye think I'm goin' to be your lackey?

The Covey [*angrily*]. Will you open th' door, y'oul'—

Peter [*shouting*]. Don't be assin' me to open any door, don't be assin' me to open any door for you. . . . Makin' a shame an' a sin o' th' cause that good men are fightin' for. . . . Oh, God forgive th' people that, instead o' burnishin' th' work th' boys is doin' to-day with quiet honesty an' patience, is revilin' their sacrifices with a riot of lootin' an' roguery!

The Covey. Isn't your own eyes leppin' out o' your head with envy that you haven't th' guts to ketch a few o' th' things that God is givin' to His chosen people? . . . Y'oul' hypocrite, if everyone was blind you'd steal a cross off an ass's back!

Peter [*very calmly*]. You're not going to make me lose me temper; you can go on with your proddin' as long as you like; goad an' goad an' goad away; hee, hee, heee! I'll not lose me temper.

> [*Somebody opens door and the Covey goes in.*

The Covey [*inside, mockingly*]. Cuckoo-oo!

Peter [*running to the door and shouting in a blaze of passion as he follows the Covey in*]. You lean, long, lanky lath of a lowsey bastard. . . . [*Following him in*] Lowsey bastard, lowsey bastard!

> [*Bessie and Mrs. Gogan enter, the pride of a great joy illuminating their faces. Bessie is pushing the pram, which is filled with clothes and boots; on the top of the boots and clothes is a fancy table, which Mrs. Gogan is holding on with her left hand, while with her right hand she holds a chair on the top of her head. They are heard talking to each other before they enter.*

Mrs. Gogan [*outside*]. I don't remember ever havin' seen such lovely pairs as them, [*they appear*] with th' pointed toes an' th' cuban heels.

Bessie. They'll go grand with th' dhresses we're afther liftin', when we've stitched a sthray bit o' silk to lift th' bodices up a little bit higher, so as to shake th' shame out o' them, an' make them fit for women that hasn't lost themselves in th' nakedness o' th' times.

> [*They fussily carry in the chair, the table, and some of the other goods. They return to bring in the rest.*

Peter [*at the door, sourly to Mrs. Gogan*]. Ay, you. Mollser looks as if she was goin' to faint, an' your youngster is roarin' in convulsions in her lap.

Mrs. Gogan [*snappily*]. She's never any other way but faintin'!

> [*She goes to go in with some things in her arms, when a shot from a rifle rings out. She and Bessie make a bolt for the door, which Peter, in a panic, tries to shut before they have got inside.*

Mrs. Gogan. Ay, ay, ay, you cowardly oul' fool, what are you thryin' to shut th' door on us for?

> [*They retreat tumultuously inside. A pause; then Captain Brennan*

comes in supporting Lieutenant Langon, whose arm is around Bren-nan's neck. Langon's face, which is ghastly white, is momentarily convulsed with spasms of agony. He is in a state of collapse, and Brennan is almost carrying him. After a few moments Clitheroe, pale, and in a state of calm nervousness, follows, looking back in the direction from which he came, a rifle, held at the ready, in his hands.

Capt. Brennan [*savagely to Clitheroe*]. Why did you fire over their heads? Why didn't you fire to kill?

Clitheroe.   No, no, Bill; bad as they are they're Irish men an' women.

Capt. Brennan [*savagely*].   Irish be damned! Attackin' an' mobbin' th' men that are riskin' their lives for them. If these slum lice gather at our heels again, plug one o' them, or I'll soon shock them with a shot or two meself!

Lieut. Langon [*moaningly*].   My God, is there ne'er an ambulance knockin' around anywhere? . . . Th' stomach is ripped out o' me; I feel it—o-o-oh, Christ!

Capt. Brennan.   Keep th' heart up, Jim; we'll soon get help, now.

[*Nora rushes wildly out of the house and flings her arms round the neck of Clitheroe with a fierce and joyous insistence. Her hair is down, her face is haggard, but her eyes are agleam with the light of happy relief.*

Nora.   Jack, Jack, Jack; God be thanked . . . be thanked. . . . He has been kind and merciful to His poor handmaiden. . . . My Jack, my own Jack, that I thought was lost is found, that I thought was dead is alive again! . . . Oh, God be praised for ever, evermore! . . . My poor Jack. . . . Kiss me, kiss me, Jack, kiss your own Nora!

Clitheroe [*kissing her, and speaking brokenly*].   My Nora; my little, beautiful Nora, I wish to God I'd never left you.

Nora.   It doesn't matter—not now, not now, Jack. It will make us dearer than ever to each other. . . . Kiss me, kiss me again.

Clitheroe.   Now, for God's sake, Nora, don't make a scene.

Nora.   I won't, I won't; I promise, I promise, Jack; honest to God. I'll be silent an' brave to bear th' joy of feelin' you safe in my arms again. . . . It's hard to force away th' tears of happiness at th' end of an awful agony.

Bessie [*from the upper window*].   Th' Minsthrel Boys aren't feelin' very comfortable now. Th' big guns has knocked all th' harps out of their hands. General Clitheroe'd rather be unlacin' his wife's bodice than standin' at a barricade . . . An' th' professor of chicken-butcherin' there, finds he's up against somethin' a little tougher even than his own chickens, an' that's sayin' a lot!

Capt. Brennan [*up to Bessie*].   Shut up, y'oul' hag!

Bessie [*down to Brennan*].   Choke th' chicken, choke th' chicken, choke th' chicken!

Lieut. Langon.   For God's sake, Bill, bring me some place where me wound 'll be looked afther. . . . Am I to die before anything is done to save me?

Capt. Brennan [*to Clitheroe*].   Come on, Jack. We've got to get help for Jim, here—have you no thought for his pain an' danger?

Bessie.   Choke th' chicken, choke th' chicken, choke th' chicken!

Clitheroe [*to Nora*].   Loosen me, darling, let me go.

Nora [*clinging to him*].   No, no, no, I'll not let you go! Come on, come up to our home, Jack, my sweetheart, my lover, my husband, an' we'll forget th' last few terrible days! . . . I look tired now, but a few hours of happy rest in your arms will bring back th' bloom of freshness again, an' you will be glad, you will be glad, glad . . . glad!

Lieut. Langon.   Oh, if I'd kep' down only a little longer, I mightn't ha' been hit! Everyone else escapin', an' me gettin' me belly ripped asundher! . . . I couldn't scream, couldn't even scream. . . . D'ye think I'm really badly wounded, Bill? Me clothes seem to be all soakin' wet. . . . It's blood . . . My God, it must be me own blood!

Capt. Brennan [*to Clitheroe*].   Go on, Jack, bid her good-bye with another kiss, an' be done with it! D'ye want Langon to die in me arms while you're dallyin' with your Nora?

Clitheroe [*to Nora*].   I must go, I must go, Nora. I'm sorry we met at all. . . . It couldn't be helped—all other ways were blocked be th' British. . . . Let me go, can't you, Nora? D'ye want me to be unthrue to me comrades?

Nora.   No, I won't let you go. . . . I want you to be thrue to me, Jack. . . . I'm your dearest comrade; I'm your thruest comrade. . . . They only want th' comfort of havin' you in th' same danger as themselves. . . . Oh, Jack, I can't let you go!

Clitheroe.   You must, Nora, you must.

Nora.   All last night at th' barricades I sought you, Jack. . . . I didn't think of th' danger—I could only think of you. . . . I asked for you everywhere. . . . Some o' them laughed. . . . I was pushed away, but

I shoved back. . . . Some o' them even sthruck me. . . . An' I screamed an' screamed your name!

Clitheroe [*in fear her action would give him future shame*]. What possessed you to make a show of yourself, like that? . . . What way d'ye think I'll feel when I'm told my wife was bawlin' for me at th' barricades? What are you more than any other woman?

Nora. No more, maybe; but you are more to me than any other man, Jack. . . . I didn't mean any harm, honestly, Jack. . . . I couldn't help it. . . . I shouldn't have told you. . . . My love for you made me mad with terror.

Clitheroe [*angrily*]. They'll say now that I sent you out th' way I'd have an excuse to bring you home. . . . Are you goin' to turn all th' risks I'm takin' into a laugh?

Lieut. Langon. Let me lie down, let me lie down, Bill; th' pain would be easier, maybe, lyin' down. . . . Oh, God, have mercy on me!

Capt. Brennan [*to Langon*]. A few steps more, Jim, a few steps more; thry to stick it for a few steps more.

Lieut. Langon. Oh, I can't, I can't, I can't!

Capt. Brennan [*to Clitheroe*]. Are you comin', man, or are you goin' to make an arrangement for another honeymoon? . . . If you want to act th' renegade, say so, an' we'll be off!

Bessie [*from above*]. Runnin' from th' Tommies—choke th' chicken. Runnin' from th' Tommies—choke th' chicken!

Clitheroe [*savagely to Brennan*]. Damn you, man, who wants to act th' renegade? [*To Nora*] Here, let go your hold; let go, I say!

Nora [*clinging to Clitheroe, and indicating Brennan*]. Look, Jack, look at th' anger in his face; look at th' fear glintin' in his eyes. . . . He himself's afraid, afraid, afraid! . . . He wants you to go th' way he'll have th' chance of death sthrikin' you an' missin' him! . . . Turn round an' look at him, Jack, look at him, look at him! . . . His very soul is cold . . . shiverin' with th' thought of what may happen to him. . . . It is his fear that is thryin' to frighten you from recognizin' th' same fear that is in your own heart!

Clitheroe [*struggling to release himself from Nora*]. Damn you, woman, will you let me go!

Capt. Brennan [*fiercely, to Clitheroe*]. Why are you beggin' her to let you go? Are you afraid of her, or what? Break her hold on you, man, or go up, an' sit on her lap! [*Clitheroe trying roughly to break her hold.*

Nora [*imploringly*]. Oh, Jack. . . . Jack. . . . Jack!

Lieut. Langon [*agonisingly*]. Brennan, a priest; I'm dyin', I think, I'm dyin'!

Clitheroe [*to Nora*]. If you won't do it quietly, I'll have to make you! [*To Brennan*] Here, hold this gun, you, for a minute.

> [*He hands the gun to Brennan.*

Nora [*pitifully*]. Please, Jack. . . . You're hurting me, Jack. . . . Honestly. . . . Oh, you're hurting . . . me! . . . I won't, I won't, I won't! . . . Oh, Jack, I gave you everything you asked of me. . . . Don't fling me from you, now!

> [*He roughly loosens her grip, and pushes her away from him. Nora sinks to the ground and lies there.*

Nora [*weakly*]. Ah, Jack. . . . Jack. . . . Jack!

Clitheroe [*taking the gun back from Brennan*]. Come on, come on.

> [*They go out. Bessie looks at Nora lying on the street, for a few moments, then, leaving the window, she comes out, runs over to Nora, lifts her up in her arms, and carries her swiftly into the house. A short pause, then down the street is heard a wild, drunken yell; it comes nearer, and Fluther enters, frenzied, wild-eyed, mad, roaring drunk. In his arms is an earthen half-gallon jar of whisky; streaming from one of the pockets of his coat is the arm of a new tunic shirt; on his head is a woman's vivid blue hat with gold lacing, all of which he has looted.*

Fluther [*singing in a frenzy*]:

> Fluther's a jolly good fella! . . . Fluther's a jolly good fella
> Up th' rebels! . . . That nobody can deny!

> [*He beats on the door.*

Get us a mug or a jug, or somethin,' some o' yous, one o' yous, will yous, before I lay one o' yous out! . . . [*Looking down the street*] Bang an' fire away for all Fluther cares. . . . [*Banging at door*] Come down an' open th' door, some of yous, one o' yous, will yous, before I lay some o' yous out! . . . Th' whole city can topple home to hell, for Fluther!

> [*Inside the house is heard a scream from Nora, followed by a moan.*

Fluther [*singing furiously*]:

> That nobody can deny, that nobody can deny,
> For Fluther's a jolly good fella, Fluther's a jolly good fella,
> Fluther's a jolly good fella . . . Up th' rebels! That nobody can deny!

> [*His frantic movements cause him to spill some of the whisky out of the jar.*

Blast you, Fluther, don't be spillin' th' precious liquor! [*He kicks at the door.*] Ay, give us a mug or a jug, or somethin', one o' yous, some o' yous, will yous, before I lay one o' yous out!

[*The door suddenly opens, and Bessie, coming out, grips him by the collar.*

Bessie [*indignantly*].   You bowsey, come in ower o' that. . . . I'll thrim your thricks o' dhrunken dancin' for you, an' none of us knowin' how soon we'll bump into a world we were never in before!

Fluther [*as she is pulling him in*].   Ay, th' jar, th' jar, th' jar!

[*A short pause, then again is heard a scream of pain from Nora. The door opens and Mrs. Gogan and Bessie are seen standing at it.*

Bessie.   Fluther would go, only he's too dhrunk. . . . Oh, God, isn't it a pity he's so dhrunk! We'll have to thry to get a docthor somewhere.

Mrs. Gogan.   I'd be afraid to go. . . . Besides, Mollser's terrible bad. I don't think you'll get a docthor to come. It's hardly any use goin'.

Bessie [*determinedly*].   I'll risk it. . . . Give her a little of Fluther's whisky. . . . It's th' fright that's brought it on her so soon. . . . Go on back to her, you.

[*Mrs. Gogan goes in, and Bessie softly closes the door. She is moving forward, when the sound of some rifle shots, and the tok, tok, tok of a distant machine-gun bring her to a sudden halt. She hesitates for a moment, then she tightens her shawl round her, as if it were a shield, then she firmly and swiftly goes out.*

Bessie [*as she goes out*].   Oh, God, be Thou my help in time o' throuble. An' shelter me safely in th' shadow of Thy wings!

CURTAIN

ACT IV

The living-room of Bessie Burgess. It is one of two small attic rooms [the other, used as a bedroom, is to the Left], the ceiling slopes up towards the back, giving to the apartment a look of compressed confinement. In the centre of the ceiling is a small skylight. There is an unmistakable air of poverty bordering on destitution. The paper on the walls is torn and soiled, particularly near the fire where the cooking is done, and near the wash-stand where the washing is done. The fireplace is to the Left. A small arm-chair near fire. One small window at Back. A pane of this window is starred by the entrance of a bullet. Under the window to the Right is an oak coffin standing on two kitchen chairs. Near the coffin is a home-manufactured stool, on which are two lighted candles. Beside the window is a worn-out dresser on which is a small quantity of delf. Tattered re-mains of cheap lace curtains drape the window. Standing near the window on Left is a brass standard-lamp with a fancy shade; hanging on the wall near the same window is a vividly crimson silk dress, both of which have been looted. A door on Left leading to the bedroom. Another opposite giving a way to the rest of the house. To the Left of this door a common washstand. A tin kettle, very black, and an old saucepan inside the fender. There is no light in the room but that given from the two candles and the fire. The dusk has well fallen, and the glare of the burning buildings in the town can be seen through the window, in the distant sky. The Covey and Fluther have been playing cards, sitting on the floor by the light of the candles on the stool near the coffin. When the curtain rises the Covey is shuffling the cards, Peter is sitting in a stiff, dignified way beside him, and Fluther is kneeling beside the window, cautiously looking out. It is a few days later.

Fluther [*furtively peeping out of the window*]. Give them a good shuffling. . . . Th' sky's gettin' reddher an' reddher. . . . You'd think it was afire. . . . Half o' th' city must be burnin'.

The Covey. If I was you, Fluther, I'd keep away from that window. . . . It's dangerous, an', besides, if they see you, you'll only bring a nose on th' house.

Peter. Yes; an' he knows we had to leave our own place th' way they were riddlin' it with machine-gun fire. . . . He'll keep on pimpin' an' pimpin' there, till we have to fly out o' this place too.

Fluther [*ironically*]. If they make any attack here, we'll send you out in your green an' glory uniform, shakin' your sword over your head, an' they'll fly before you as th' Danes flew before Brian Boru!

The Covey [*placing the cards on the floor, after shuffling them*]. Come on, an' cut.   [*Fluther comes over, sits on floor, and cuts the cards.*

The Covey [*having dealt the cards*]. Spuds up again.

                         [*Nora moans feebly in room on Left.*

Fluther. There, she's at it again. She's been quiet for a long time, all th' same.

The Covey. She was quiet before, sure, an' she broke out again worse than ever. . . . What was led that time?

Peter. Thray o' Hearts, Thray o' Hearts, Thray o' Hearts.

Fluther. It's damned hard lines to think of her dead-born kiddie lyin' there in th' arms o' poor little Mollser. Mollser snuffed it sudden too, afther all.

The Covey. Sure, she never got any care. How could she get it, an' th' mother out day an' night lookin' for work, an' her consumptive husband leavin' her with a baby to be born before he died!

Voices in a lilting chant to the Left in a distant street. Red Cr . . . oss, Red Cr . . . oss! . . . Ambu . . . lance, Ambu . . . lance!

The Covey [*to Fluther*]. Your deal, Fluther.

Fluther [*shuffling and dealing the cards*]. It'll take a lot out o' Nora— if she'll ever be th' same.

The Covey. Th' docthor thinks she'll never be th' same; thinks she'll be a little touched here. [*He touches his forehead.*] She's ramblin' a lot; thinkin' she's out in th' counthry with Jack; or gettin' his dinner ready for him before he comes home; or yellin' for her kiddie. All that, though, might be th' chloroform she got. . . . I don't know what we'd have done only for oul' Bessie: up with her for th' past three nights, hand runnin'.

Fluther. I always knew there was never anything really derogatory wrong with poor oul' Bessie. [*To Peter, who is taking a trick*] Ay, houl' on, there, don't be so damn quick—that's my thrick.

Peter. What's your trick? It's my thrick, man.

Fluther [*loudly*]. How is it your thrick?

Peter [*answering as loudly*]. Didn't I lead th' deuce!

Fluther. You must be gettin' blind, man; don't you see th' ace?

Bessie [*appearing at door of room, Left; in a tense whisper*]. D'ye want to waken her again on me, when she's just gone asleep? If she wakes will yous come an' mind her? If I hear a whisper out o' one o' yous again, I'll . . . gut yous!

The Covey [*in a whisper*]. S-s-s-h. She can hear anything above a whisper.

Peter [*looking up at the ceiling*]. Th' gentle an' merciful God'll give th' pair o' yous a scawldin' an' a scarifyin' one o' these days!

[*Fluther takes a bottle of whisky from his pocket, and takes a drink.*

The Covey [*to Fluther*]. Why don't you spread that out, man, an' thry to keep a sup for to-morrow?

Fluther. Spread it out? Keep a sup for to-morrow? How th' hell does a fella know there'll be any tomorrow? If I'm goin' to be whipped away, let me be whipped away when it's empty, an' not when it's half full! [*To Bessie, who has seated herself in an armchair at the fire*] How is she, now, Bessie?

Bessie. I left her sleeping quietly. When I'm listenin 'to her babblin', I think she'll never be much betther than she is. Her eyes have a hauntin' way of lookin' in instead of lookin' out, as if her mind had been lost alive in madly minglin' memories of th' past. . . . [*Sleepily*] Crushin' her thoughts . . . together . . . in a fierce . . . an' fanciful . . . [*She nods her head and starts wakefully*] idea that dead things are livin', an' livin' things are dead. . . . [*With a start*] Was that a scream I heard her give? [*Reassured*] Blessed God, I think I hear her screamin' every minute! An' it's only there with me that I'm able to keep awake.

The Covey. She'll sleep, maybe, for a long time, now. Ten there.

Fluther. Ten here. If she gets a long sleep, she might be all right. Peter's th' lone five.

The Covey. Whisht! I think I hear somebody movin' below. Whoever it is, he's comin' up.

> [*A pause. Then the door opens and Captain Brennan comes into the room. He has changed his uniform for a suit of civvies. His eyes droop with the heaviness of exhaustion; his face is pallid and drawn. His clothes are dusty and stained here and there with mud. He leans heavily on the back of a chair as he stands.*]

Capt. Brennan. Mrs. Clitheroe; where's Mrs. Clitheroe? I was told I'd find her here.

Bessie. What d'ye want with Mrs. Clitheroe?

Capt. Brennan. I've a message, a last message for her from her husband.

Bessie. Killed! He's not killed, is he!

Capt. Brennan [*sinking stiffly and painfully on to a chair*]. In th' Imperial Hotel; we fought til th' place was in flames. He was shot through th' arm, an' then through th' lung. . . . I could do nothin' for him— only watch his breath comin' an' goin' in quick, jerky gasps, an' a tiny sthream o' blood thricklin' out of his mouth, down over his lower lip. . . . I said a prayer for th' dyin', an' twined his Rosary beads around his fingers. . . . Then I had to leave him to save meself. . . . [*He shows some holes in his coat*] Look at th' way a machine-gun tore at me coat, as I belted out o' th' buildin' an' darted across th' sthreet for shelter. . . . An' then, I seen The Plough an' th' Stars fallin' like a shot as th' roof crashed in, an' where I'd left poor Jack was nothin' but a leppin' spout o' flame!

Bessie [*with partly repressed vehemence*]. Ay, you left him! You twined his Rosary beads round his fingers, an' then you run like a hare to get out o' danger!

Capt. Brennan. I took me chance as well as him. . . . He took it like a man. His last whisper was to "Tell Nora to be brave; that I'm ready to meet my God, an' that I'm proud to die for Ireland." An' when our General heard it he said that "Commandant Clitheroe's end was a gleam of glory." Mrs. Clitheroe's grief will be a joy when she realizes that she has had a hero for a husband.

Bessie. If you only see her, you'd know to th' differ.

[*Nora appears at door, Left. She is clad only in her nightdress; her hair, uncared for some days, is hanging in disorder over her shoulders. Her pale face looks paler still because of a vivid spot on the tip of each cheek. Her eyes are glimmering with the light of incipient insanity; her hands are nervously fiddling with her night-gown. She halts at the door for a moment, looks vacantly around the room, and then comes slowly in. The rest do not notice her till she speaks.*]

Nora [*in a quiet and monotonous tone*]. No . . . Not there, Jack. . . . I can feel comfortable only in our own familiar place beneath th' bramble tree. . . . We must be walking for a long time; I feel very, very tired. . . . Have we to go farther, or have we passed it by? [*Passing her hand across her eyes*] Curious mist on my eyes. . . . Why don't you hold my hand, Jack. . . . [*Excitedly*] No, no, Jack, it's not. Can't you see it's a goldfinch. Look at th' black-satiny wings with th' gold bars, an' th' splash of crimson on its head. . . . [*Wearily*] Something ails me, some-thing ails me. . . . Don't kiss me like that; you take my breath away, Jack. . . . Why do you frown at me? . . . You're going away, and [*frightened*] I can't follow you. Something's keeping me from moving. . . . [*Crying out*] Jack, Jack, Jack!

Bessie [*who has gone over and caught Nora's arm*]. Now, Mrs. Clitheroe, you're a terrible woman to get up out of bed. . . . You'll get cold if you stay here in them clothes.

Nora. Cold? I'm feelin' very cold; it's chilly out here in th' counthry. . . . [*Looking around frightened*] What place is this? Where am I?

Bessie [*coaxingly*]. You're all right, Nora; you're with friends, an' in a safe place. Don't you know your uncle an' your cousin, an' poor oul' Fluther?

Peter [*about to go over to Nora*].   Nora, darlin, now——

Fluther [*pulling him back*].   Now, leave her to Bessie, man. A crowd'll only make her worse.

Nora [*thoughtfully*].   There is something I want to remember, an' I can't. [*With agony*] I can't, I can't, I can't! My head, my head! [*Suddenly breaking from Bessie, and running over to the men, and gripping Fluther by the shoulders*] Where is it? Where's my baby? Tell me where you've put it, where've you hidden it? My baby, my baby; I want my baby! My head, my poor head. . . . Oh, I can't tell what is wrong with me. [*Screaming*] Give him to me, give me my husband!

Bessie.   Blessin' o' God on us, isn't this pitiful!

Nora [*struggling with Bessie*].   I won't go away for you; I won't. Not till you give me back my husband. [*Screaming*] Murderers, that's what yous are; murderers, murderers!

Bessie.   S-s-sh. We'll bring Mr. Clitheroe back to you, if you'll only lie down an' stop quiet. . . . [*Trying to lead her in*] Come on, now, Nora, an' I'll sing something to you.

Nora.   I feel as if my life was thryin' to force its way out of my body. . . . I can hardly breathe . . . I'm frightened, I'm frightened, I'm frightened! For God's sake, don't leave me, Bessie. Hold my hand, put your arms around me!

Fluther [*to Brennan*].   Now you can see th' way she is, man.

Peter.   An' what way would she be if she heard Jack had gone west?

The Covey [*to Peter*].   Shut up, you, man!

Bessie [*to Nora*].   We'll have to be brave, an' let patience clip away th' heaviness of th' slow-movin' hours, rememberin' that sorrow may endure for th' night, but joy cometh in th' mornin'. . . . Come on in, an' I'll sing to you, an' you'll rest quietly.

Nora [*stopping suddenly on her way to the room*].   Jack an' me are goin' out somewhere this evenin'. Where I can't tell. Isn't it curious I can't remember. . . . Maura, Maura, Jack, if th' baby's a girl; any name you like, if th' baby's a boy! . . . He's there. [*Screaming*] He's there, an' they won't give him back to me!

Bessie.   S-sss-h, darlin', s-ssh. I won't sing to you, if you're not quiet.

Nora [*nervously holding Bessie*].   Hold my hand, hold my hand, an' sing to me, sing to me!

Bessie.   Come in an' lie down, an' I'll sing to you.

Nora [*vehemently*].   Sing to me, sing to me; sing, sing!

Bessie [*singing as she leads Nora into room*]:
    Lead, kindly light, amid th' encircling gloom,
       Lead Thou me on.
    Th' night is dark an' I am far from home,
       Lead Thou me on.
    Keep Thou my feet, I do not ask to see
    Th' distant scene—one step enough for me.

    So long that Thou hast blessed me, sure Thou still
       Wilt lead me on;   [*They go in.*

Bessie [*singing in room*]:
    O'er moor an' fen, o'er crag an' torrent, till
       Th' night is gone.
    An' in th' morn those angel faces smile
    That I have lov'd long since, an' lost awhile!

The Covey [*to Brennan*]. Now that you've seen how bad she is, an' that we daren't tell her what has happened till she's betther, you'd best be slippin' back to where you come from.

Capt. Brennan. There's no chance o' slippin' back now, for th' military are everywhere: a fly couldn't get through. I'd never have got here, only I managed to change me uniform for what I'm wearin'. . . . I'll have to take me chance, an' thry to lie low here for a while.

The Covey [*frightened*]. There's no place here to lie low. Th' Tommies'll be hoppin' in here, any minute!

Peter [*aghast*]. An' then we'd all be shanghaied!

The Covey. Be God, there's enough afther happenin' to us!

Fluther [*warningly, as he listens*]. Whisht, whisht, th' whole o' yous. I think I heard th' clang of a rifle butt on th' floor of th' hall below. [*All alertness.*] Here, come on with th' cards again. I'll deal.
              [*He shuffles and deals the cards to all.*

Fluther. Clubs up. [*To Brennan*] Thry to keep your hands from shakin', man. You lead, Peter. [*As Peter throws out a card*] Four o' Hearts led.

    [*The door opens and Corporal Stoddart of the Wiltshires enters in full war kit; steel helmet, rifle and bayonet, and trench tool. He looks around the room. A pause and a palpable silence.*

Fluther [*breaking the silence*]. Two tens an' a five.

Corporal Stoddart. 'Ello. [*Indicating the coffin*] This the stiff?

The Covey. Yis.

Corporal Stoddart.   Who's gowing with it? Only one allowed to gow with it, you know.

The Covey.   I dunno.

Corporal Stoddart.   You dunnow?

The Covey.   I dunno.

Bessie [*coming into the room*].   She's afther slippin' off to sleep again, thanks be to God. I'm hardly able to keep me own eyes open. [*To the soldier*] Oh, are yous goin' to take away poor little Mollser?

Corporal Stoddart.   Ay; 'oo's agowing with 'er?

Bessie.   Oh, th' poor mother, o' course. God help her, it's a terrible blow to her!

Fluther.   A terrible blow? Sure, she's in her element now, woman, mixin' earth to earth, an' ashes t'ashes an' dust to dust, an' revellin' in plumes an' hearses, last days an' judgements!

Bessie [*falling into chair by the fire*].   God bless us! I'm jaded!

Corporal Stoddart.   Was she plugged?

The Covey.   Ah, no; died o' consumption.

Corporal Stoddart.   Ow, is that all? Thought she moight 'ave been plugged.

The Covey.   Is that all? Isn't it enough? D'ye know, comrade, that more die o' consumption than are killed in th' wars? An' it's all because of th' system we're livin' undher?

Corporal Stoddart.   Ow, I know. I'm a Sowcialist moiself, but I 'as to do my dooty.

The Covey [*ironically*].   Dooty! Th' only dooty of a Socialist is th' emancipation of th' workers.

Corporal Stoddart.   Ow, a man's a man, an 'e 'as to foight for 'is country, 'asn't 'e?

Fluther [*aggressively*].   You're not fightin' for your counthry here, are you?

Peter [*anxiously, to Fluther*].   Ay, ay, Fluther, none o' that, none o' that!

The Covey.   Fight for your counthry! Did y'ever read, comrade, Jenersky's *Thesis on the Origin, Development, an' Consolidation of th' Evolutionary Idea of the Proletariat*?

Corporal Stoddart.   Ow, cheese it, Paddy, cheese it!

Bessie [*sleepily*].   How is things in th' town, Tommy?

Corporal Stoddart. Ow, I fink it's nearly hover. We've got 'em surrounded, and we're clowsing in on the bloighters. Ow, it was only a little bit of a dawg-foight.

> [*The sharp ping of the sniper's rifle is heard, followed by a squeal of pain.*

Voices to the Left in a chant. Red Cr . . . oss, Red Cr . . . oss! Ambu . . . lance, Ambu . . . lance!

Corporal Stoddart [*excitedly*]. Christ, that's another of our men 'it by that blawsted sniper! 'E's knocking abaht 'ere, somewheres. Gawd, when we gets th' bloighter, we'll give 'im the cold steel, we will. We'll jab the belly aht of 'im, we will!

> [*Mrs. Gogan comes in tearfully, and a little proud of the importance of being directly connected with death.*

Mrs. Gogan [*to Fluther*]. I'll never forget what you done for me, Fluther, goin' around at th' risk of your life settlin' everything with th' undhertaker an' th' cemetery people. When all me own were afraid to put their noses out, you plunged like a good one through hummin' bullets, an' they knocking' fire out o' th' road, tinklin' through th' frightened windows, an' splashin' themselves to pieces on th' walls! An' you'll find, that Mollser, in th' happy place she's gone to, won't forget to whisper, now an' again, th' name o' Fluther.

Corporal Stoddart. Git it aht, mother, git it aht.

Bessie [*from the chair*]. It's excusin' me you'll be, Mrs. Gogan, for not stannin' up, seein' I'm shaky on me feet for want of a little sleep, an' not desirin' to show any disrespect to poor little Mollser.

Fluther. Sure, we all know, Bessie, that it's vice versa with you.

Mrs. Gogan [*to Bessie*]. Indeed, it's meself that has well chronicled, Mrs. Burgess, all your gentle hurryin's to me little Mollser, when she was alive, bringin' her somethin' to dhrink, or somethin' t'eat, an' never passin' her without liftin' up her heart with a delicate word o' kindness.

Corporal Stoddart [*impatiently, but kindly*]. Git it aht, git it aht, mother.

> [*The Covey, Fluther, Brennan, and Peter carry out the coffin, followed by Mrs. Gogan.*

Corporal Stoddart [*to Bessie, who is almost asleep*]. 'Ow many men is in this 'ere 'ouse? [*No answer. Loudly*] 'Ow many men is in this 'ere 'ouse?

Bessie [*waking with a start*]. God, I was nearly asleep! . . . How many men? Didn't you see them?

Corporal Stoddart. Are they all that are in the 'ouse?

Bessie. Oh, there's none higher up, but there may be more lower down. Why?

Corporal Stoddart. All men in the district 'as to be rounded up. Somebody's giving 'elp to the snipers, and we 'as to take precautions. If I 'ad my woy, I'd make 'em all join hup, and do their bit! But I suppowse they and you are all Shinners.

Bessie [*who has been sinking into sleep, waking up to a sleepy vehemence*]. Bessie Burgess is no Shinner, an' never had no thruck with anything spotted be th' fingers o' th' Fenians; but always made it her business to harness herself for Church whenever she knew that God Save the King was goin' to be sung at t'end of th' service; whose only son went to th' front in th' first contingent of the Dublin Fusiliers, an' that's on his way home carryin' a shatthered arm that he got fightin' for his King an' counthry!

> [*Her head sinks slowly forward again. Peter comes into the room; his body is stiffened and his face is wearing a comically indignant look. He walks to and fro at the back of the room, evidently repressing a violent desire to speak angrily. He is followed in by Fluther, the Covey, and Brennan, who slinks into an obscure corner of the room, nervous of notice.*

Fluther [*after an embarrassing pause*]. Th' air in th' sthreet outside's shakin' with the firin' o' rifles an' machine-guns. It must be a hot shop in th' middle o' th' scrap.

Corporal Stoddart. We're pumping lead in on 'em from every side, now; they'll soon be shoving up th' white flag.

Peter [*with a shout*]. I'm tellin' you either o' yous two lowsers 'ud make a betther hearse-man than Peter; proddin' an' pokin' at me an' I helpin' to carry out a corpse!

Fluther. It wasn't a very derogatory thing for th' Covey to say that you'd make a fancy hearse-man, was it?

Peter [*furiously*]. A pair o' redjesthered bowseys pondherin' from mornin' till night on how they'll get a chance to break a gap through th' quiet nature of a man that's always endeavourin' to chase out of him any sthray thought of venom against his fella-man!

The Covey. Oh, shut it, shut it, shut it!

Peter. As long as I'm a livin' man, responsible for me thoughts, words, an' deeds to th' Man above, I'll feel meself instituted to fight again' th' sliddherin' ways of a pair o' picaroons, whisperin', concurrin', concoctin', an' conspirin' together to rendher me unconscious of the life I'm thryin' to live!

Corporal Stoddart [*dumbfounded*].   What's wrong, Daddy; wot 'ave they done to you?

Peter [*savagely to the Corporal*].   You mind your own business! What's it got to do with you, what's wrong with me?

Bessie [*in a sleepy murmur*].   Will yous thry to conthrol yourselves into quietness? Yous'll waken her . . . up . . . on . . . me . . . again.

[*She sleeps.*

Fluther.   Come on, boys, to th' cards again, an' never mind him.

Corporal Stoddart.   No use of you gowing to start cawds; you'll be gowing out of 'ere, soon as Sergeant comes.

Fluther.   Goin' out o' here? An' why're we goin' out o' here?

Corporal Stoddart.   All men in district to be rounded up, and 'eld in till the scrap is hover.

Fluther.   An' where're we goin' to be held in?

Corporal Stoddart.   They're puttin 'em in a church.

The Covey.   A church?

Fluther.   What sort of a church? Is it a Protestan' Church?

Corporal Stoddart.   I dunnow; I suppowse so.

Fluther [*dismayed*].   Be God, it'll be a nice thing to be stuck all night in a Protestan' Church!

Corporal Stoddart.   Bring the cawds; you moight get a chance of a goime.

Fluther.   Ah, no, that wouldn't do. . . . I wondher? [*After a moment's thought*] Ah, I don't think we'd be doin' anything derogatory be playin' cards in a Protestan' Church.

Corporal Stoddart.   If I was you I'd bring a little snack with me; you moight be glad of it before the mawning. [*Sings*]:

I do loike a snoice mince poy,
I do loike a snoice mince poy!

[*The snap of the sniper's rifle rings out again, followed simultaneously by a scream of pain. Corporal Stoddart goes pale, and brings his rifle to the ready, listening.*

Voices chanting to the Right.   Red Cro . . . ss, Red Cro . . . ss! Ambu . . . lance, Ambu . . . lance!

[*Sergeant Tinley comes rapidly in, pale, agitated, and fiercely angry.*

Corporal Stoddart [*to Sergeant*].   One of hour men 'it, Sergeant?

Sergeant Tinley.   Private Taylor; got 'it roight through the chest, 'e did; an 'ole in front of 'im as 'ow you could put your fist through, and 'arf 'is back blown awoy! Dum-dum bullets they're using. Gang of Hassassins potting at us from behind roofs. That's not playing the goime: why down't they come into the owpen and foight fair!

Fluther [*unable to stand the slight*].   Fight fair! a few hundhred scrawls o' chaps with a couple o' guns an' Rosary beads, again' a hundhred thousand thrained men with horse, fut, an' artillery . . . an' he wants us to fight fair! [*To Sergeant*] D'ye want us to come out in our skins an' throw stones?

Sergeant Tinley [*to Corporal*].   Are these four all that are 'ere?

Corporal Stoddart.   Four; that's all, Sergeant.

Sergeant Tinley [*vindictively*].   Come on, then; get the blighters aht. [*To the men*] 'Ere, 'op it aht! Aht into the streets with you, and if a sniper sends another of our men west, you gow with 'im! [*He catches Fluther by the shoulder*] Gow on, git aht!

Fluther.   Eh, who are you chuckin', eh?

Sergeant Tinley [*roughly*].   Gow on, git aht, you blighter.

Fluther.   Who are you callin' a blighter to, eh? I'm a Dublin man, born an' bred in th' city, see?

Sergeant Tinley.   I down't care if you were Broin Buroo; git aht, git aht.

Fluther [*halting as he is going out*].   Jasus, you an' your guns! Leave them down, an' I'd beat th' two o' yous without sweatin'!

> [*Peter, Brennan, the Covey, and Fluther, followed by the soldiers, go out. Bessie is sleeping heavily on the chair by the fire. After a pause, Nora appears at door, Left, in her nightdress. Remaining at door for a few moments she looks vaguely around the room. She then comes in quietly, goes over to the fire, pokes it, and puts the kettle on. She thinks for a few moments, pressing her hand to her forehead. She looks questioningly at the fire, and then at the press at back. She goes to the press, opens it, takes out a soiled cloth and spreads it on the table. She then places things for tea on the table.*]

Nora.   I imagine th' room looks very odd somehow. . . . I was nearly forgetting Jack's tea. . . . Ah, I think I'll have everything done before he gets in. . . . [*She lilts gently, as she arranges the table.*]

> Th' violets were scenting th' woods, Nora,
>   Displaying their charms to th' bee,

When I first said I lov'd only you, Nora,
An' you said you lov'd only me.

Th' chestnut blooms gleam'd through th' glade, Nora,
A robin sang loud from a tree,
When I first said I lov'd only you, Nora,
An' you said you lov'd only me.

[*She pauses suddenly, and glances around the room.*

Nora [*doubtfully*]. I can't help feelin' this room very strange. . . .
What is it? . . . What is it? . . . I must think. . . . I must thry to
remember. . . .

Voices chanting in a distant street. Ambu . . . lance, Ambu . . . lance!
Red Cro . . . ss, Red Cro . . . ss!

Nora [*startled and listening for a moment, then resuming the arrangement of the table*]:

Trees, birds, an' bees sang a song, Nora,
Of happier transports to be,
When I first said I lov'd only you, Nora,
An' you said you lov'd only me.

[*A burst of rifle fire is heard in a street near by, followed by the
rapid rok, tok, tok of a machine-gun.*

Nora [*staring in front of her and screaming*]. Jack, Jack, Jack! My baby,
my baby, my baby!

Bessie [*waking with a start*]. You divil, are you afther gettin' out o' bed
again!

[*She rises and runs towards Nora, who rushes to the window,
which she frantically opens.*

Nora [*at window, screaming*]. Jack, Jack, for God's sake, come to me!

Soldiers [*outside, shouting*]. Git away, git away from that window,
there!

Bessie [*seizing hold of Nora*]. Come away, come away, woman, from
that window!

Nora [*struggling with Bessie*]. Where is it; where have you hidden it?
Oh, Jack, Jack, where are you?

Bessie [*imploringly*]. Mrs. Clitheroe, for God's sake, come away!

Nora [*fiercely*]. I won't; he's below. Let . . . me . . . go! You're thryin'
to keep me from me husband. I'll follow him. Jack, Jack, come to your
Nora!

Bessie. Hus-s-sh, Nora, Nora! He'll be here in a minute. I'll bring him to you, if you'll only be quiet—honest to God, I will.

[*With a great effort Bessie pushes Nora away from the window, the force used causing her to stagger against it herself. Two rifle shots ring out in quick succession. Bessie jerks her body convulsively; stands stiffly for a moment, a look of agonized astonishment on her face, then she staggers forward, leaning heavily on the table with her hands.*

Bessie [*with an arrested scream of fear and pain*]. Merciful God, I'm shot, I'm shot, I'm shot! . . . Th' life's pourin' out o' me! [*To Nora*] I've got this through . . . through you . . . through you, you bitch, you! . . . God, have mercy on me! . . . [*To Nora*] You wouldn't stop quiet, no, you wouldn't, you wouldn't, blast you! Look at what I'm afther gettin', look at what I'm afther gettin' . . . I'm bleedin' to death, an' no one's here to stop th flowin' blood! [*Calling*] Mrs. Gogan, Mrs. Gogan! Fluther, Fluther, for God's sake, somebody, a doctor, a doctor!

[*She staggers frightened towards the door, to seek for aid, but, weakening half-way across the room, she sinks to her knees, and bending forward, supports herself with her hands resting on the floor. Nora is standing rigidly with her back to the wall opposite, her trembling hands held out a little from the sides of her body, her lips quivering, her breast heaving, staring wildly at the figure of Bessie.*

Nora [*in a breathless whisper*]. Jack, I'm frightened. . . . I'm frightened, Jack. . . . Oh, Jack, where are you?

Bessie [*moaningly*]. This is what's afther comin' on me for nursin' you day an' night. . . . I was a fool, a fool, a fool! Get me a dhrink o' wather, you jade, will you? There's a fire burnin' in me blood! [*Pleadingly*] Nora, Nora, dear, for God's sake, run out an' get Mrs. Gogan, or Fluther, or somebody to bring a doctor, quick, quick, quick! [*As Nora does not stir*] Blast you, stir yourself, before I'm gone!

Nora. Oh, Jack, where are you?

Bessie [*in a whispered moan*]. Jesus Christ, me sight's goin'! It's all dark, dark! Nora, hold me hand!

[*Bessie's body lists over and she sinks into a prostrate position on the floor.*

Bessie. I'm dyin', I'm dyin' . . . I feel it. . . . Oh God, oh God! [*She feebly sings*]

I do believe, I will believe
That Jesus died for me;

That on th' cross He shed His blood,
From sin to set me free. . . .
I do believe . . . I will believe
. . . Jesus died . . . me;
. . . th' cross He shed . . . blood,
From sin . . . free.

[*She ceases singing, and lies stretched out, still and very rigid. A pause. Then Mrs. Gogan runs hastily in.*

Mrs. Gogan [*quivering with fright*]. Blessed be God, what's afther happenin'? [*To Nora*] What's wrong, child, what's wrong? [*She sees Bessie, runs to her and bends over the body*] Bessie, Bessie! [*She shakes the body*] Mrs. Burgess, Mrs. Burgess! [*She feels Bessie's forehead*] My God, she's as cold as death. They're afther murdherin' th' poor inoffensive woman!

[*Sergeant Tinley and Corporal Stoddart enter agitatedly, their rifles at the ready.*

Sergeant Tinley [*excitedly*]. This is the 'ouse. That's the window!

Nora [*pressing back against the wall*]. Hide it, hide it; cover it up, cover it up!

Sergeant Tinley [*going over to the body*]. 'Ere, what's this? Who's this? [*Looking at Bessie*] Oh Gawd, we've plugged one of the women of the 'ouse.

Corporal Stoddart. Whoy the 'ell did she gow to the window? Is she dead?

Sergeant Tinley. Oh, dead as bedamned. Well, we couldn't afford to toike any chawnces.

Nora [*screaming*]. Hide it, hide it; don't let me see it! Take me away, take me away, Mrs. Gogan!

[*Mrs. Gogan runs into room, Left, and runs out again with a sheet which she spreads over the body of Bessie.*

Mrs. Gogan [*as she spreads the sheet*]. Oh, God help her, th' poor woman, she's stiffenin' out as hard as she can! Her face has written on it th' shock o' sudden agony, an' her hands is whitenin' into th' smooth shininess of wax.

Nora [*whimperingly*]. Take me away, take me away; don't leave me here to be lookin' an' lookin' at it!

Mrs. Gogan [*going over to Nora and putting her arm around her*]. Come on with me, dear, an' you can doss in poor Mollser's bed, till we

gather some neighbours to come an' give th' last friendly touches to
Bessie in th' lonely layin' of her out.

> [*Mrs. Gogan and Nora go slowly out.*

Corporal Stoddart [*who has been looking around, to Sergeant Tinley*].
Tea here, Sergeant. Wot abaht a cup of scald?

Sergeant Tinley.   Pour it aht, Stoddart, pour it aht. I could scoff hany-
thing just now.

> [*Corporal Stoddart pours out two cups of tea, and the two soldiers
> begin to drink. In the distance is heard a bitter burst of rifle and
> machine-gun fire, interspersed with the boom, boom of artillery.
> The glare in the sky seen through the window flares into a fuller
> and a deeper red.*

Sergeant Tinley.   There gows the general attack on the Powst Office.

Voices in a distant street.   Ambu . . . lance, Ambu . . . lance! Red
Cro . . . ss, Red Cro . . . ss!

> [*The voices of soldiers at a barricade outside the house are heard
> singing;*

They were summoned from the 'illside,
They were called in from the glen,
And the country found 'em ready
At the stirring call for men.
Let not tears add to their 'ardship,
As the soldiers pass along,
And although our 'eart is breaking,
Make it sing this cheery song.

Sergeant Tinley and Corporal Stoddart [*joining in the chorus, as they sip
the tea*]:

Keep the 'owme fires burning,
While your 'earts are yearning;
Though your lads are far away
They dream of 'owme;
There's a silver loining
Through the dark cloud shoining,
Turn the dark cloud inside out,
Till the boys come 'owme!

CURTAIN

THE SILVER TASSIE

A Tragi-Comedy in Four Acts

(1929)

STAGE VERSION

TO

EILEEN

with the yellow daffodils
in the green vase

NOTES

The Croucher's make-up should come as close as possible to a death's head, a skull; and his hands should show like those of a skeleton's. He should sit somewhere *above* the group of Soldiers; preferably to one side, on the left, from view-point of audience, so as to overlook the Soldiers. He should look languid, as if very tired of life.

The group of Soldiers—Act Two—should enter in a close mass, as if each was keeping the other from falling, utterly weary and tired out. They should appear as if they were almost locked together.

The Soldiers' last response to the Staff-Wallah's declaration, namely, "To the Guns!" should have in these three words the last high notes of "The Last Post".

The song sung at the end of the play should be given to the best two [or one] singers in the cast. If, on the other hand, there be no passable singer among the players, the song should be omitted.

Perhaps a more suitable Spiritual than "Sweet Chariot" would be chosen for Harry to sing. For instance, "Keep Inchin' Along", or "Keep Me from Sinkin' Down".

The Chants in the play are simple Plain Song. The first chant is given in full as an example of the way in which they are sung. In the others, the dots . . . indicate that the note preceding them should be sustained till the music indicates a change. There are three parts in each chant: the Intonation; the Meditation; and the Ending. After a little practice, they will be found to be easy to sing. The Soldiers having the better voices should be selected to intone the chants, irrespective of the numbers allotted to them as characters in the book of the play.

❦ ❦ ❦

CHARACTERS IN THE PLAY
(As they appear)

SYLVESTER HEEGAN
MRS. HEEGAN, *his wife*
SIMON NORTON
SUSIE MONICAN
MRS. FORAN
TEDDY FORAN, *her husband*
HARRY HEEGAN, D.C.M., *Heegan's son*
JESSIE TAITE
BARNEY BAGNAL
THE CROUCHER
1ST SOLDIER
2ND SOLDIER
3RD SOLDIER
4TH SOLDIER
THE CORPORAL
THE VISITOR
THE STAFF-WALLAH
1ST STRETCHER-BEARER
2ND STRETCHER-BEARER
1ST CASUALTY
2ND CASUALTY
SURGEON FORBY MAXWELL
THE SISTER OF THE WARD

SCENE

ACT I · Room in Heegan's home.

ACT II · Somewhere in France (*later on*).

ACT III · Ward in a Hospital (*a little later on*).

ACT IV · Room in Premises of Avondale Football Club
(*later on still*).

ACT I

The eating, sitting, and part sleeping room of the Heegan family. A large window at back looks on to a quay, from which can be seen the centre mast of a steamer, at the top of which gleams a white light. Another window at right looks down on a side street. Under the window at back, plumb in the centre, is a stand, the legs gilded silver and the top gilded gold; on the stand is a purple velvet shield on which are pinned a number of silver medals surrounding a few gold ones. On each side of the shield is a small vase holding a bunch of artificial flowers. The shield is draped with red and yellow ribbons. To the left of the stand is a bed covered with a bedspread of black striped with vivid green. To the right of the stand is a dresser and chest of drawers combined. The fireplace is to the left. Beside the fireplace is a door leading to a bedroom, another door which gives access to the rest of the house and the street, on the right. At the corner left is a red coloured stand resembling an easel, having on it a silver-gilt framed picture photograph of Harry Heegan in football dress, crimson jersey with yellow collar and cuffs and a broad yellow belt, black stockings, and yellow football boots. A table on which are a half-pint bottle of whisky, a large parcel of bread and meat sandwiches, and some copies of English illustrated magazines.

Sylvester Heegan and Simon Norton are sitting by the fire. Sylvester Heegan is a stockily built man of sixty-five; he has been a docker all his life since first the muscles of his arms could safely grip a truck, and even at sixty-five the steel in them is only beginning to stiffen.

Simon Norton is a tall man, originally a docker too, but by a little additional steadiness, a minor effort towards self-education, a natural, but very slight superior nimbleness of mind, has risen in the Company's estimation and has been given the position of checker, a job entailing as many hours of work as a docker, almost as much danger, twice as much responsibility, and a corresponding reduction in his earning powers. He is not so warmly, but a little more circumspectly dressed than Sylvester, and in his manner of conduct and speech there is a hesitant suggestion of greater refinement than in those of Sylvester, and a still more vague indication that he is aware of it. This timid semi-conscious sense of superiority, which Simon sometimes forgets, is shown frequently by a complacent stroking of a dark beard which years are beginning to humiliate. The night is cold, and Simon and Sylvester occasionally stretch longingly towards the fire. They are fully dressed and each has his topcoat and hat beside him, as if ready to go out at a moment's notice. Susie Monican is standing at the table polishing a Lee-Enfield rifle with a chamois cloth; the butt of the rifle is resting on the table. She is a girl of twenty-two, well-shaped limbs, challenging breasts, all of which are defiantly hidden by a rather long dark blue skirt and bodice buttoning up to the throat, relieved by a crimson scarf around her neck, knotted in front and falling down her bosom like a man's tie. She is undeniably pretty, but her charms are almost completely hidden by her sombre, ill-fitting dress, and the rigid manner in which she has made her hair up declares her unflinching and uncompromising modesty. Just now she is standing motionless, listening intently, looking towards the door on right.

Mrs. Heegan is standing at the window at right, listening too, one hand pulling back the curtain, but her attention, taken from the window, is attracted to the door. She is older than Sylvester, stiffened with age and rheumatism; the end of her life is unknowingly lumbering towards a rest: the impetus necessity has given to continual toil and striving is beginning to slow down, and everything she has to do is done with a quiet mechanical persistence. Her inner ear cannot hear even a faint echo of a younger day. Neither Sylvester nor Simon has noticed the attentive attitude of Mrs. Heegan or Susie, for Sylvester, with one arm outstretched crooked at the elbow, is talking with subdued intensity to Simon.

Sylvester.   I seen him do it, mind you. I seen him do it.

Simon.   I quite believe you, Sylvester.

Sylvester.   Break a chain across his bisseps! [*With pantomime action*] Fixes it over his arm . . . bends it up . . . a little strain . . . snaps in two . . . right across his bisseps!

Susie.   Shush you, there!

> [*Mrs. Heegan goes out with troubled steps by door. The rest remain still for a few moments.*]

Sylvester.   A false alarm.

Simon.   No cause for undue anxiety; there's plenty of time yet.

Susie [*chanting as she resumes the polishing of rifle*]:

> Man walketh in a vain shadow, and disquieteth himself in vain:
> He heapeth up riches, and cannot tell who shall gather them.

> [*She sends the chant in the direction of Sylvester and Simon, Susie coming close to the two men and sticking an angry face in between them.*]

Susie.   When the two of yous stand quiverin' together on the dhread day of the Last Judgement, how will the two of yous feel if yous have nothin' to say but "he broke a chain across his bisseps"? Then the two of you'll know that the wicked go down into hell, an' all the people who forget God!

[*She listens a moment, and leaving down the rifle, goes out by door left.*

Sylvester. It's persecutin', that tambourine theology of Susie's. I always get a curious, sickenin' feelin', Simon, when I hear the Name of the Supreme Bein' tossed into the quietness of a sensible conversation.

Simon. The day he won the Cross Country Championship of County Dublin, Syl, was a day to be chronicled.

Sylvester. In a minor way, yes, Simon. But the day that caps the chronicle was the one when he punched the fear of God into the heart of Police Constable 63 C under the stars of a frosty night on the way home from Terenure.

Simon. Without any exaggeration, without any exaggeration, mind you, Sylvester, that could be called a memorable experience.

Sylvester. I can see him yet [*he gets up, slides from side to side, dodging and parrying imaginary blows*] glidin' round the dazzled Bobby, cross-ey'd tryin' to watch him.

Simon [*tapping his pipe resolutely on the hob*]. Unperturbed, mind you, all the time.

Sylvester. An' the hedges by the road-side standin' stiff in the silent cold of the air, the frost beads on the branches glistenin' like toss'd-down diamonds from the breasts of the stars, the quietness of the night stimulated to a fuller stillness by the mockin' breathin' of Harry, an' the heavy, ragin' pantin' of the Bobby, an' the quickenin' beats of our own hearts afraid, of hopin' too little or hopin' too much.

[*During the last speech by Sylvester, Susie has come in with a bayonet, and has commenced to polish it.*

Susie. We don't go down on our knees often enough; that's why we're not able to stand up to the Evil One: we don't go down on our knees enough. . . . I can hear some persons fallin' with a splash of sparks into the lake of everlastin' fire. . . . An account of every idle word shall be given at the last day. [*She goes out again with rifle.*

Susie [*bending towards Simon and Sylvester as she goes*]. God is listenin' to yous; God is listenin' to yous!

Sylvester. Dtch, dtch, dtch. People ought to be forcibly restrained from constantly cannonadin' you with the name of the Deity.

Simon. Dubiety never brush'd a thought into my mind, Syl, while I was waitin' for the moment when Harry would stretch the Bobby hors dee combaa on the ground.

Sylvester [*resuming his pantomime actions*]. There he was staggerin', beatin' out blindly, every spark of energy panted out of him, while Harry feinted, dodg'd, side-stepp'd, then suddenly sail'd in an' put him asleep with . . .

Simon. A right-handed hook to the jaw! ⎫
Sylvester. A left-handed hook to the jaw! ⎭ [*together*].

Sylvester [*after a pause*]. A left-handed hook to the jaw, Simon.

Simon. No, no, Syl, a right-handed hook to the jaw.

> [*Mrs. Foran runs quickly in by the door with a frying-pan in her hand, on which is a steak. She comes to the fire, pushing, so as to disturb the two men. She is one of the many gay, careworn women of the working-class.*

Mrs. Foran [*rapidly*]. A pot of clothes is boilin' on the fire above, an' I knew yous wouldn't mind me slappin' a bit of a steak on here for a second to show him, when he comes in before he goes away, that we're mindful of his needs, an' I'm hopeful of a dream to-night that the sea's between us, not lookin' very haggard in the mornin' to find the dream a true one. [*With satisfied anticipation*]
For I'll be single again, yes, I'll be single again;
An' I eats what I likes, . . . an' I drinks what I likes,
An' I likes what I likes, when I'm——
[*Stopping suddenly*] What's the silence for?

Sylvester [*slowly and decidedly*]. I was at the fight, Simon, an' I seen him givin' a left-handed hook to the jaw.

Mrs. Foran. What fight?

Simon [*slowly and decidedly*]. I was there too, an' I saw him down the Bobby with a right-handed hook to the jaw.

Mrs. Foran. What Bobby? [*A pause.*

Sylvester. It was a close up, an' I don't know who'd know better if it wasn't the boy's own father.

Mrs. Foran. What boy . . . what father?

Sylvester. Oh, shut up, woman, an' don't be smotherin' us with a shower of questions.

Susie [*who has entered on the last speech, and has started to polish a soldier's steel helmet*]. Oh, the miserableness of them that don't know the things that belong unto their peace. They try one thing after another, they try everything, but they never think of trying God. [*Coming nearer to them.*] Oh, the happiness of knowing that God's hand has pick'd you out for heaven. [*To Mrs. Foran*] What's the honey-pot kiss of a lover to the kiss of righteousness and peace?

[*Mrs. Foran, embarrassed, goes over to window.*

Susie [*turning to Simon*].   Simon, will you not close the dandy door of the public-house and let the angels open the pearly gates of heaven for you?

Sylvester.   We feel very comfortable where we are, Susie.

Susie.   Don't mock, Sylvester, don't mock. You'd run before a great wind, tremble in an earthquake, and flee from a fire; so don't treat lightly the still, small voice calling you to repentance and faith.

Sylvester [*with appeal and irritation*].   Oh, do give over worryin' a man, Susie.

Susie.   God shows His love by worrying, and worrying, and worrying the sinner. The day will come when you will call on the mountains to cover you, and then you'll weep and gnash your teeth that you did not hearken to Susie's warning. [*Putting her hands appealingly on his shoulders*] Sylvester, if you pray long enough, and hard enough, and deep enough, you'll get the power to fight and conquer Beelzebub.

Mrs. Foran.   I'll be in a doxological mood to-night, not because the kingdom of heaven'll be near me, but because my husband'll be far away, and to-morrow [*singing*]:

  I'll be single again, yes, single again;
  An' I goes where I likes, an' I does what I likes,
  An' I likes what I likes now I'm single again!

Simon.   Go on getting Harry's things ready, Susie, and defer the dosing of your friends with canticles till the time is ripe with rest for them to listen quietly.

> [*Simon and Sylvester are very self-conscious during Susie's talk to them. Simon empties his pipe by tapping the head on the hob of the grate. He then blows through it. As he is blowing through it, Sylvester is emptying his by tapping it on the hob; as he is blowing it Simon taps his again; as Simon taps Sylvester taps with him, and then they look into the heads of the pipes and blow together.*

Susie.   It must be mercy or it must be judgement: if not mercy to-day it may be judgement to-morrow. He is never tired of waiting and waiting and waiting; and watching and watching and watching; and knocking and knocking and knocking for the sinner—you, Sylvester, and you, Simon—to turn from his wickedness and live. Oh, if the two of you only knew what it was to live! Not to live leg-staggering an' belly-creeping among the pain-spotted and sin-splashed desires of the flesh; but to live, oh, to live swift-flying from a holy peace to a holy strength, and from holy strength to a holy joy, like the flashing flights of a swallow in the deep beauty of a summer sky.

        [*Simon and Sylvester shift about, self-conscious and uneasy.*

Susie [*placing her hand first on Simon's shoulder and then on Sylvester's*]. The two of you God's elegant swallows; a saved pair; a loving pair strong-wing'd, freed from the gin of the snarer, tip of wing to tip of wing, flying fast or darting swift together to the kingdom of heaven.

Simon [*expressing a protecting thought to Sylvester*]. One of the two of us should go out and hunt back the old woman from the perishing cold of watching for the return of Harry.

Sylvester. She'll be as cold as a naked corpse, an' unstinted watchin' won't bring Harry back a minute sooner. I'll go an' drive her back. [*He rises to go*] I'll be back in a minute, Susie.

Simon [*hurriedly*]. Don't bother, Syl, I'll go; she won't be farther than the corner of the street; you go on toasting yourself where you are. [*He rises*] I'll be back in a minute, Susie.

Mrs. Foran [*running to the door*]. Rest easy the two of you, an' I'll go, so as to give Susie full time to take the sin out of your bones an' put you both in first-class form for the kingdom of heaven.   [*She goes out.*

Susie. Sinners that jeer often add to the glory of God: going out, she gives you, Sylvester, and you, Simon, another few moments, precious moments—oh, how precious, for once gone, they are gone for ever—to listen to the warning from heaven.

Simon [*suddenly*]. Whisht, here's somebody coming, I think?

Sylvester. I'll back this is Harry comin' at last.

        [*A pause as the three listen.*

Sylvester. No, it's nobody.

Simon. Whoever it was 's gone by.

Susie. Oh, Syl, oh, Simon, don't try to veil the face of God with an evasion. You can't, you can't cod God. This may be your last chance before the pains of hell encompass the two of you. Hope is passing by; salvation is passing by, and glory arm-in-arm with her. In the quietness left to you go down on your knees and pray that they come into your hearts and abide with you for ever. . . . [*With fervour, placing her left hand on Simon's shoulder and her right hand on Sylvester's, and shaking them*] get down on your knees, get down on your knees, get down on your knees and pray for conviction of sin, lest your portion in David become as the portion of the Canaanites, the Amorites, the Perizzites and the Jebusites!

Sylvester. Eh, eh, Susie; cautious now—you seem to be forgettin' yourself.

Simon. Desist, Susie, desist. Violence won't gather people to God. It only ingenders hostility to what you're trying to do.

Sylvester. You can't batter religion into a man like that.

Simon. Religion is love, but that sort of thing is simply a nullification of religion.

Susie. Bitterness and wrath in exhortation is the only hope of rousing the pair of yous into a sense of coming and everlasting penalties.

Sylvester. Well, give it a miss, give it a miss to me now. Don't try to claw me into the kingdom of heaven. An' you only succeed in distempering piety when you try to mangle it into a man's emotions.

Simon. Heaven is all the better, Susie, for being a long way off.

Sylvester. If I want to pray I do it voluntarily, but I'm not going to be goaded an' goaded into it.

Susie. I go away in a few days to help to nurse the wounded, an' God's merciful warnings may depart along with me, then sin'll usher the two of you into Gehenna for all eternity. Oh, if the two of you could only grasp the meaning of the word eternity! [*Bending down and looking up into their faces*] Time that had no beginning and never can have an end—an' there you'll be—two cockatrices creeping together, a desolation, an astonishment, a curse and a hissing from everlasting to everlasting. [*She goes into room.*

Sylvester. Cheerful, what! Cockatrices—be-God, that's a good one, Simon!

Simon. Always a trying thing to have to listen to one that's trying to push the kingdom of God into a reservation of a few yards.

Sylvester. A cockatrice! Now where did she manage to pick up that term of approbation, I wonder?

Simon. From the Bible. An animal somewhere mentioned in the Bible, I think, that a serpent hatched out of a cock's egg.

Sylvester. A cock's egg! It couldn't have been the egg of an ordinary cock. Not the male of what we call a hen?

Simon. I think so.

Sylvester. Well, be-God, that's a good one! You know Susie'll have to be told to disintensify her soul-huntin', for religion even isn't an excuse for saying that a man'll become a cockatrice.

Simon. In a church, somehow or other, it seems natural enough, and even in the street it's all right, for one thing is as good as another in the wide-open ear of the air, but in the delicate quietness of your own home it, it——

Sylvester.   Jars on you!

Simon.   Exactly!

Sylvester.   If she'd only confine her glory-to-God business to the festivals, Christmas, now, or even Easter, Simon, it would be recommendable; for a few days before Christmas, like the quiet raisin' of a curtain, an' a few days after, like the gentle lowerin' of one, there's nothing more . . . more—

Simon.   Appropriate. . . .

Sylvester.   Exhilaratin' than the singin' of the Adestay Fidellis.

Simon.   She's damned pretty, an' if she dressed herself justly, she'd lift some man's heart up, an' toss down many another. It's a mystery now, what affliction causes the disablement, for most women of that kind are plain, an' when a woman's born plain she's born good. I wonder what caused the peculiar bend in Susie's nature? Narrow your imagination to the limit and you couldn't call it an avocation.

Sylvester [*giving the head of his pipe a sharp, quick blow on the palm of his hand to clear it*].   Adoration.

Simon.   What?

Sylvester.   Adoration, Simon, accordin' to the flesh. . . . She fancied Harry and Harry fancied Jessie, so she hides her rage an' loss in the love of a scorchin' Gospel.

Simon.   Strange, strange.

Sylvester.   Oh, very curious, Simon.

Simon.   It's a problem, I suppose.

Sylvester.   An inconsolable problem, Simon.

[*Mrs. Foran enters by door, helping in Mrs. Heegan, who is pale and shivering with cold.*

Mrs. Heegan [*shivering and shuddering*].   U-u-uh, I feel the stream of blood that's still trickling through me old veins icifyin' fast; u-uh.

Mrs. Foran.   Madwoman, dear, to be waitin' out there on the quay an' a wind risin' as cold as a stepmother's breath, piercin' through your old bones, mockin' any effort a body would make to keep warm, an' [*suddenly rushing over to the fireplace in an agony of dismay, scattering Simon and Sylvester, and whipping the frying-pan off the fire*]—The steak, the steak; I forgot the blasted steak an' onions fryin' on the fire! God Almighty, there's not as much as a bead of juice left in either of them. The scent of the burnin' would penetrate to the street, an' not one of you'd stir a hand to lift them out of danger. Oh, look at the condition they're in. Even the gospel-gunner couldn't do a little target practice by helpin' the necessity of a neighbour. [*As she goes out*] I can hear the love for your neighbours almost fizzlin' in your hearts.

Mrs. Heegan [*pushing in to the fire, to Simon and Sylvester*].   Push to the right and push to the left till I get to the fosterin' fire. Time eatin' his heart out, an' no sign of him yet. The two of them, the two of my legs is numb . . . an' the wind's risin' that'll make the sea heave an' sink under the boat to-night, under shaded lights an' the submarines about. [*Susie comes in, goes over to window, and looks out.*] Hours ago the football match must have been over, an' no word of him yet, an' all drinkin' if they won, an' all drinkin' if they lost; with Jessie hitchin' on after him, an' no one thinkin' of me an' the maintenance money.

Sylvester.   He'll come back in time; he'll have to come back; he must come back.

Simon.   He got the goals, Mrs. Heegan, that won the last two finals, and it's only fair he'd want to win this, which'll mean that the Cup won before two——

Sylvester [*butting in*].   Times hand runnin'.

Simon.   Two times consecutively before, makin' the Cup the property of the Club.

Sylvester.   Exactly!

Mrs. Heegan.   The chill's residin' in my bones, an' feelin's left me just the strength to shiver. He's overstayed his leave a lot, an' if he misses now the tide that's waitin', he skulks behind desertion from the colours.

Susie.   On Active Service that means death at dawn.

Mrs. Heegan.   An' my governmental money grant would stop at once.

Susie.   That would gratify Miss Jessie Taite, because you put her weddin' off with Harry till after the duration of the war, an' cut her out of the allowance.

Sylvester [*with a sickened look at Simon*].   Dtch, dtch, dtch, the way the women wag the worst things out of happenings! [*To the women*] My God Almighty, he'll be back in time an' fill yous all with disappointment.

Mrs. Heegan.   She's coinin' money workin' at munitions, an' doesn't need to eye the little that we get from Harry; for one evening hurryin' with him to the pictures she left her bag behind, an' goin' through it what would you think I found?

Susie. A saucy book, now, or a naughty picture?

Mrs. Heegan. Lion and Unicorn standin' on their Jew ay mon draw. With all the rings an' dates, an' rules an' regulations.

Simon. What was it, Mrs. Heegan?

Mrs. Heegan. Spaced an' lined; signed an' signatured; nestlin' in a blue envelope to keep it warm.

Sylvester [*testily*]. Oh, sing it out, woman, an' don't be takin' the value out of what you're goin' to tell us.

Mrs. Heegan. A Post Office Savings Bank Book.

Sylvester. Oh, hairy enough, eh?

Simon. How much, Mrs. Heegan?

Mrs. Heegan. Pounds an' shillings with the pence missin'; backed by secrecy, an' security guaranteed by Act of Parliament.

Sylvester [*impatiently*]. Dtch, dtch. Yes, yes, woman, but how much was it?

Mrs. Heegan. Two hundred an' nineteen pounds, sixteen shillings, an' no pence.

Sylvester. Be-God, a nice little nest-egg, right enough!

Susie. I hope in my heart that she came by it honestly, and that she remembers that it's as true now as when it was first spoken that it's harder for a camel to go through the eye of a needle than for a rich person to enter the kingdom of heaven.

Simon. And she hidin' it all under a veil of silence, when there wasn't the slightest fear of any of us bein' jealous of her.

> [*A tumult is heard on the floor over their heads, followed by a crash of breaking delf. They are startled, and listen attentively.*]

Mrs. Heegan [*breaking the silence*]. Oh, there he's at it again. An' she sayin' that he was a pattern husband since he came home on leave, merry-making with her an' singin' dolorously the first thing every mornin'. I was thinkin' there'd be a rough house sometime over her lookin' so well after his long absence . . . you'd imagine now, the trenches would have given him some idea of the sacredness of life!

> [*Another crash of breaking delfware.*]

Mrs. Heegan. An' the last week of his leave she was too fond of breakin' into song in front of him.

Sylvester. Well, she's gettin' it now for goin' round heavin' her happiness in the poor man's face.

> [*A crash, followed by screams from Mrs. Foran.*]

Susie. I hope he won't be running down here as he often does.

Simon [*a little agitated*]. I couldn't stay here an' listen to that; I'll go up and stop him: he might be killing the poor woman.

Mrs. Heegan. Don't do anything of the kind, Simon; he might down you with a hatchet or something.

Simon. Phuh, I'll keep him off with the left and hook him with the right. [*Putting on his hat and coat as he goes to the door.*] Looking prim and careless 'll astonish him. Monstrous to stay here, while he may be killing the woman.

Mrs. Heegan [*to Simon as he goes out*]. For God's sake mind yourself, Simon.

Sylvester [*standing beside closed door on right with his ear close to one of the panels, listening intently*]. Simon's a tidy little man with his fists, an' would make Teddy Foran feel giddy if he got home with his left hook. [*Crash.*] I wonder is that Simon knockin' down Foran, or Foran knockin' down Simon?

Mrs. Heegan. If he came down an' we had the light low, an' kept quiet, he might think we were all out.

Sylvester. Shush. I can hear nothin' now. Simon must have awed him. Quiet little man, but when Simon gets goin'. Shush? No, nothin' . . . Something unusual has happened. Oh, oh, be-God!

> [*The door against which Sylvester is leaning bursts suddenly in. Sylvester is flung headlong to the floor, and Mrs. Foran, her hair falling wildly over her shoulders, a cut over her eye, frantic with fear, rushes in and scrambles in a frenzy of haste under the bed. Mrs. Heegan, quickened by fear, runs like a good one, followed by Susie, into the room, the door of which they bang after them. Sylvester hurriedly fights his way under the bed with Mrs. Foran.*]

Mrs. Foran [*speaking excitedly and jerkily as she climbs under the bed*]. Flung his dinner into the fire—and started to smash the little things in the room. Tryin' to save the dresser, I got a box in the eye. I locked the door on him as I rushed out, an' before I was half-way down, he had one of the panels flyin' out with—a hatchet!

Sylvester [*under the bed—out of breath*]. Whythehell didn'tyou sing out beforeyousent thedoor flyin' inontop o' me!

Mrs. Foran. How could I an' I flyin' before danger to me—life?

Sylvester. Yes, an'you'vegot meinto a nice extremity now!

Mrs. Foran. An' I yelled to Simon Norton when he had me—down, but the boyo only ran the faster out of the—house!

Sylvester. Oh, an' the regal-like way he went out to fight! Oh, I'm findin' out that everyone who wears a cocked hat isn't a Napoleon!

[*Teddy Foran, Mrs. Foran's husband, enters by door, with a large, fancy, vividly yellow-coloured bowl, ornamented with crimson roses, in one hand and a hatchet in the other. He is big and powerful, rough and hardy. A man who would be dominant in a public-house, and whose opinions would be listened to with great respect. He is dressed in the khaki uniform of a soldier home on leave.*]

Teddy. Under the bed, eh? Right place for a guilty conscience. I should have thrown you out of the window with the dinner you put before me. Out with you from under there, an' come up with your husband.

Susie [*opening suddenly door right, putting in her head, pulling it back and shutting door again*]. God is looking at you, God is looking at you!

Mrs. Foran. I'll not budge an inch from where I am.

Teddy [*looking under the bed and seeing Sylvester*]. What are you doin' there encouragin' her against her husband?

Sylvester. You've no right to be rippin' open the poor woman's life of peace with violence.

Teddy [*with indignation*]. She's my wife, isn't she?

Mrs. Foran. Nice thing if I lose the sight of my eye with the cut you gave me!

Teddy. She's my wife, isn't she? An' you've no legal right to be harbourin' her here, keepin' her from her household duties. Stunned I was when I seen her lookin' so well after me long absence. Blowin' her sighin' in me face all day, an' she sufferin' the tortures of hell for fear I'd miss the boat!

Sylvester. Go on up to your own home; you've no right to be violatin' this place.

Teddy. You'd like to make her your cheery amee, would you? It's napoo, there, napoo, you little pip-squeak. I seen you an' her goin' down the street arm-in-arm.

Sylvester. Did you expect to see me goin' down the street leg-in-leg with her?

Teddy. Thinkin' of her Ring-papers instead of her husband. [*To Mrs. Foran*] I'll teach you to be rippling with joy an' your husband goin' away! [*He shows the bowl.*] Your weddin' bowl, look at it; pretty, isn't it? Take your last eyeful of it now, for it's goin' west quick!

Susie [*popping her head in again*].   God is watching you, God is watching you!

Mrs. Foran [*appealingly*].   Teddy, Teddy, don't smash the poor weddin' bowl.

Teddy [*smashing the bowl with a blow of the hatchet*].   It would be a pity, wouldn't it? Damn it, an' damn you. I'm off now to smash anything I missed, so that you'll have a gay time fittin' up the little home again by the time your loving husband comes back. You can come an' have a look, an' bring your mon amee if you like.

[*He goes out, and there is a pause as Mrs. Foran and Sylvester peep anxiously towards the door.*

Sylvester.   Cautious, now cautious; he might be lurking outside that door there, ready to spring on you the minute you show'd your nose!

Mrs. Foran.   Me lovely little weddin' bowl, me lovely little weddin' bowl!
[*Teddy is heard breaking things in the room above.*

Sylvester [*creeping out from under the bed*].   Oh, he is gone up. He was a little cow'd, I think, when he saw me.

Mrs. Foran.   Me little weddin' bowl, wrapp'd in tissue paper, an' only taken out for a few hours every Christmas—me poor little weddin' bowl.

Susie [*popping her head in*].   God is watching—oh, he's gone!

Sylvester [*jubilant*].   Vanished! He was a little cow'd, I think, when he saw me.   [*Mrs. Heegan and Susie come into the room.*

Mrs. Foran.   He's makin' a hash of every little thing we have in the house, Mrs. Heegan.

Mrs. Heegan.   Go inside to the room, Mrs. Foran, an' if he comes down again, we'll say you ran out to the street.

Mrs. Foran [*going into room*].   My poor little weddin' bowl that I might have had for generations!

Susie [*who has been looking out of the window, excitedly*].   They're comin': a crowd with a concertina; some of them carrying Harry on their shoulders, an' others are carrying that Jessie Taite too, holding a silver cup in her hands. Oh, look at the shameful way she's showing her legs to all who like to have a look at them!

Mrs. Heegan.   Never mind Jessie's legs—what we have to do is to hurry him out in time to catch the boat.

[*The sound of a concertina playing in the street outside has been heard, and the noise of a marching crowd. The crowd stop at the house. Shouts are heard—"Up the Avondales!"; "Up Harry Heegan*

*and the Avondales!" Then steps are heard coming up the stairs,
and first Simon Norton enters, holding the door ceremoniously wide
open to allow Harry to enter, with his arm around Jessie, who is
carrying a silver cup joyously, rather than reverentially, elevated, as
a priest would elevate a chalice. Harry is wearing khaki trousers, a
military cap stained with trench mud, a vivid orange-coloured jersey
with black collar and cuffs. He is twenty-three years of age, tall, with
the sinewy muscles of a manual worker made flexible by athletic
sport. He is a typical young worker, enthusiastic, very often boisterous, sensible by instinct rather than by reason. He has gone to the
trenches as unthinkingly as he would go to the polling booth. He
isn't naturally stupid; it is the stupidity of persons in high places that
has stupefied him. He has given all to his masters, strong heart,
sound lungs, healthy stomach, lusty limbs, and the little mind that
education has permitted to develop sufficiently to make all the rest
a little more useful. He is excited now with the sweet and innocent
insanity of a fine achievement, and the rapid lowering of a few
drinks.*

[*Jessie is twenty-two or so, responsive to all the animal impulses
of life. Ever dancing around, in and between the world, the flesh,
and the devil. She would be happy climbing with a boy among
the heather on Howth Hill, and could play ball with young men
on the swards of the Phoenix Park. She gives her favour to the
prominent and popular. Harry is her favorite: his strength and
speed have won the Final for his club, he wears the ribbon of the
D.C.M. It is a time of spiritual and animal exaltation for her.*

[*Barney Bagnal, a soldier mate of Harry's, stands a little shyly near
the door, with a pleasant, good-humoured grin on his rather
broad face. He is the same age as Harry, just as strong, but not so
quick, less finely formed, and not so sensitive; able to take most
things quietly, but savage and wild when he becomes enraged. He
is fully dressed, with topcoat buttoned on him, and he carries
Harry's on his arm.*

Harry [*joyous and excited*].   Won, won, won, be-God; by the odd goal in
five. Lift it up, lift it up, Jessie, sign of youth, sign of strength, sign of
victory!

Mrs. Heegan [*to Sylvester*].   I knew, now, Harry would come back in
time to catch the boat.

Harry [*to Jessie*].   Leave it here, leave it down here, Jessie, under the
picture, the picture of the boy that won the final.

Mrs. Heegan. A parcel of sandwiches, a bottle of whisky, an' some magazines to take away with you an' Barney, Harry.

Harry. Napoo sandwiches, an' napoo magazines: look at the cup, eh? The cup that Harry won, won by the odd goal in five! [*To Barney*] The song that the little Jock used to sing, Barney, what was it? The little Jock we left shrivellin' on the wire after the last push.

Barney. "Will ye no come back again?"

Harry. No, no, the one we all used to sing with him, "The Silver Tassie". [*Pointing to cup*] There it is, the Silver Tassie, won by the odd goal in five, kicked by Harry Heegan.

Mrs. Heegan. Watch your time, Harry, watch your time.

Jessie. He's watching it, he's watching it—for God's sake don't get fussy, Mrs. Heegan.

Harry. They couldn't take their beatin' like men. . . . Play the game, play the game, why the hell couldn't they play the game? [*To Barney*] See the President of the Club, Dr. Forby Maxwell, shaking hands with me, when he was giving me the cup, "Well done, Heegan!" The way they yell'd and jump'd when they put in the equalizing goal in the first half!

Barney. Ay, a fluke, that's what it was; a lowsey fluke.

Mrs. Heegan [*holding Harry's coat up for him to put it on*]. Here, your coat, Harry, slip it on while you're talkin'.

Harry [*putting it on*]. All right, keep smiling, don't fuss. [*To the rest*] Grousing the whole time they were chasing the ball; an' when they lost it, "Referee, referee, offside, referee . . . foul there; ey, open your eyes, referee!"

Jessie. And we scream'd and shouted them down with "Play the game, Primrose Rovers, play the game!"

Barney. You ran them off their feet till they nearly stood still.

Mrs. Foran [*has been peeping twice in timidly from the room and now comes in to the rest*]. Somebody run up an' bring Teddy down for fear he'd be left behind.

Sylvester [*to Harry*]. Your haversack an' trench tools, Harry; haversack first, isn't it?

Harry [*fixing his haversack*]. Haversack, haversack, don't rush me. [*To the rest*] But when I got the ball, Barney, once I got the ball, the rain began to fall on the others. An' the last goal, the goal that put us one ahead, the winning goal, that was a-a-eh-a stunner!

Barney. A beauty, me boy, a hot beauty.

Harry. Slipping by the back rushing at me like a mad bull, steadying a moment for a drive, seeing in a flash the goalie's hands sent with a shock to his chest by the force of the shot, his half-stunned motion to clear, a charge, and then carrying him, the ball and all with a rush into the centre of the net!

Barney [*enthusiastically*]. Be-God, I did get a thrill when I seen you puttin' him sittin' on his arse in the middle of the net!

Mrs. Foran [*from the door*]. One of yous do go up an' see if Teddy's ready to go.

Mrs. Heegan [*to Harry*]. Your father'll carry your kit-bag, an' Jessie'll carry your rifle as far as the boat.

Harry [*irritably*]. Oh, damn it, woman, give your wailin' over for a minute!

Mrs. Heegan. You've got only a few bare minutes to spare, Harry.

Harry. We'll make the most of them, then. [*To Barney*] Out with one of them wine-virgins we got in "The Mill in the Field", Barney, and we'll rape her in a last hot moment before we set out to kiss the guns!

> [*Simon has gone into room and returned with a gun and a kit-bag. He crosses to where Barney is standing.*

Barney [*taking a bottle of wine from his pocket*]. Empty her of her virtues, eh?

Harry. Spill it out, Barney, spill it out. . . . [*Seizing Silver Cup, and holding it towards Barney*] Here, into the cup, be-God. A drink out of the cup, out of the Silver Tassie!

Barney [*who has removed the cap and taken out the cork*]. Here she is now. . . . Ready for anything, stripp'd to the skin!

Jessie. No double-meaning talk, Barney.

Susie [*haughtily, to Jessie*]. The men that are defending us have leave to bow themselves down in the House of Rimmon, for the men that go with the guns are going with God.

> [*Barney pours wine into the cup for Harry and into a glass for himself.*

Harry [*to Jessie*]. Jessie, a sup for you. [*She drinks from the cup.*] An' a drink for me. [*He drinks.*] Now a kiss while our lips are wet. [*He kisses her.*] Christ, Barney, how would you like to be retreating from the fairest face and [*lifting Jessie's skirt a little*]—and the trimmest, slimmest little leg in the parish? Napoo, Barney, to everyone but me!

Mrs. Foran. One of you go up, an' try to get my Teddy down.

Barney [lifting Susie's skirt a little]. Napoo, Harry, to everyone but——

Susie [angrily, pushing Barney away from her]. You khaki-cover'd ape, you, what are you trying to do? Manhandle the lassies of France, if you like, but put on your gloves when you touch a woman that seeketh not the things of the flesh.

Harry [putting an arm round Susie to mollify her]. Now, Susie, Susie, lengthen your temper for a passing moment, so that we may bring away with us the breath of a kiss to the shell-bullied air of the trenches. . . . Besides, there's nothing to be ashamed of—it's not a bad little leggie at all.

Susie [slipping her arm round Harry's neck, and looking defiantly at Barney]. I don't mind what Harry does; I know he means no harm, not like other people. Harry's different.

Jessie. You'll not forget to send me the German helmet home from France, Harry?

Susie [trying to rest her head on Harry's breast]. I know Harry, he's different. It's his way. I wouldn't let anyone else touch me, but in some way or another I can tell Harry's different.

Jessie [putting her arm round Harry under Susie's in an effort to dislodge it.] Susie, Harry wants to be free to keep his arm round me during his last few moments here, so don't be pulling him about!

Susie [shrinking back a little]. I was only saying that Harry was different.

Mrs. Foran. For God's sake, will someone go up for Teddy, or he won't go back at all!

Teddy [appearing at door]. Damn anxious for Teddy to go back! Well, Teddy's goin' back, an' he's left everything tidy upstairs so that you'll not have much trouble sortin's things out. [*To Harry*] The Club an' a crowd's waitin' outside to bring us to the boat before they go to the spread in honour of the final. [*Bitterly*] A party for them while we muck off to the trenches!

Harry [after a slight pause, to Barney]. Are you game, Barney?

Barney. What for?

Harry. To go the spread and hang the latch for another night?

Barney [taking his rifle from Simon and slinging it over his shoulder]. No, no, napoo desertin' on Active Service. Deprivation of pay an' the rest of your time in the front trenches. No, no. We must go back!

Mrs. Heegan. No, no, Harry. You must go back.

Simon,

Sylvester, } [*together*]. You must go back.

and Susie

Voices of crowd outside. They must go back!

[*The ship's siren is heard blowing.*

Simon. The warning signal.

Sylvester. By the time they get there, they'll be unslinging the gangways!

Susie [*handing Harry his steel helmet*]. Here's your helmet, Harry.

[*He puts it on.*

Mrs. Heegan. You'll all nearly have to run for it now!

Sylvester. I've got your kit-bag, Harry.

Susie. I've got your rifle.

Simon. I'll march in front with the cup, after Conroy with the concertina.

Teddy. Come on: ong avong to the trenches!

Harry [*recklessly*]. Jesus, a last drink, then! [*He raises the Silver Cup, singing*]:

Gae bring to me a pint of wine,
And fill it in a silver tassie;

Barney [*joining in vigorously*]:

. . . . a silver tassie.

Harry:

That I may drink before I go,
A service to my bonnie lassie.

Barney:

. . . . bonnie lassie.

Harry:

The boat rocks at the pier o' Leith,
Full loud the wind blows from the ferry;
The ship rides at the Berwick Law,
An' I must leave my bonnie Mary!

Barney:

. . . . . . leave my bonnie Mary!

Harry:

The trumpets sound, the banners fly,
The glittering spears are ranked ready;

Barney:

 . . . glittering spears are ranked ready:

Harry:

The shouts of war are heard afar,
The battle closes thick and bloody.

Barney:

 . . . . . . closes thick and bloody.

Harry:

It's not the roar of sea or shore,
That makes me longer wish to tarry,
Nor shouts of war that's heard afar—
It's leaving thee, my bonnie lassie!

Barney:

 . . . leaving thee, my bonnie lassie!

Teddy. Come on, come on.   [*Simon, Sylvester, and Susie go out.*

Voices outside:

Come on from your home to the boat;
Carry on from the boat to the camp.

> [*Teddy and Barney go out. Harry and Jessie follow; as Harry reaches the door, he takes his arm from round Jessie and comes back to Mrs. Heegan.*

Voices outside. From the camp up the line to the trenches.

Harry [*shyly and hurriedly kissing Mrs. Heegan*]. Well, goodbye, old woman.

Mrs. Heegan. Good-bye, my son.

> [*Harry goes out. The chorus of "The Silver Tassie", accompanied by a concertina, can be heard growing fainter till it ceases. Mrs. Foran goes out timidly. Mrs. Heegan pokes the fire, arranges the things in the room, and then goes to the window and looks out. After a pause, the loud and long blast of the ship's siren is heard. The light on the masthead, seen through the window, moves slowly away, and Mrs. Heegan with a sigh, "Ah dear", goes over to the fire and sits down. A slight pause, then Mrs. Foran returns to the room.*

Mrs. Foran. Every little bit of china I had in the house is lyin' above in a mad an' muddled heap like the flotsum an' jetsum of the seashore!

Mrs. Heegan [*with a deep sigh of satisfaction*]. Thanks be to Christ that we're after managin' to get the three of them away safely.

CURTAIN

ACT II

In the war zone: a scene of jagged and lacerated ruin of what was once a monastery. At back a lost wall and window are indicated by an arched piece of broken coping pointing from the left to the right, and a similar piece of masonry pointing from the right to the left. Between these two lacerated fingers of stone can be seen the country stretching to the horizon where the front trenches are. Here and there heaps of rubbish mark where houses once stood. From some of these, lean, dead hands are protruding. Further on, spiky stumps of trees which were once a small wood. The ground is dotted with rayed and shattered shell-holes. Across the horizon in the red glare can be seen the criss-cross pattern of the barbed wire bordering the trenches. In the sky sometimes a green star, sometimes a white star, burns. Within the broken archway to the left is an arched entrance to another part of the monastery, used now as a Red Cross Station. In the wall, right, near the front is a stained-glass window, background green, figure of the Virgin, white-faced, wearing a black robe, lights inside making the figure vividly apparent. Further up from this window is a life-size crucifix. A shell has released an arm from the cross, which has caused the upper part of the figure to lean forward with the released arm outstretched towards the figure of the Virgin. Underneath the crucifix on a pedestal, in red letters, are the words: PRINCEPS PACIS. *Almost opposite the crucifix is a gunwheel to which Barney is tied. At the back, in the centre, where the span of the arch should be, is the shape of a big howitzer gun, squat, heavy underpart, with a long, sinister barrel now pointing towards the front at an angle of forty-five degrees. At the base of the gun a piece of wood is placed on which is chalked,* HYDE PARK CORNER. *On another piece of wood near the entrance of the Red Cross Station is chalked,* NO HAWKERS OR STREET CRIES PERMITTED HERE. *In the near centre is a brazier in which a fire is burning. Crouching above, on a ramp, is a soldier whose clothes are covered with mud and splashed with blood. Every feature of the scene seems a little distorted from its original appearance. Rain is falling steadily; its fall worried now and again by fitful gusts of a cold wind. A small organ is heard playing slow and stately notes as the curtain rises.*

After a pause, the Croucher, without moving, intones dreamily:

Croucher. And the hand of the Lord was upon me, and carried me out
    in the spirit of the Lord, and set me down in the midst of a valley.
    And I looked and saw a great multitude that stood upon their feet,
    an exceeding great army.
    And he said unto me, Son of man, can this exceeding great army be-
    come a valley of dry bones?

[*The music ceases, and a voice, in the part of the monastery left standing, intones:* Kyr . . . ie . . . e . . . eleison. Kyr . . . ie . . . e . . . eleison, *followed by the answer:* Christe . . . eleison.

Croucher [*resuming*]. And I answered, O Lord God, thou knowest. And he said, prophesy and say unto the wind, come from the four winds a breath and breathe upon these living that they may die.

[*As he pauses the voice in the monastery is heard again;* Gloria in excelsis Deo et in terra pax hominibus bonae voluntatis.

Croucher [*resuming*]. And I prophesied, and the breath came out of them, and the sinews came away from them, and behold a shaking, and their bones fell asunder, bone from his bone, and they died, and the exceeding great army became a valley of dry bones.

[*The voice from the monastery is heard, clearly for the first half of the sentence, then dying away towards the end:* Accendat in nobis Dominus ignem sui amoris, et flammam aeternae caritatis.

[*A group of soldiers come in from fatigue, bunched together as if for comfort and warmth. They are wet and cold, and they are sullen-faced. They form a circle around the brazier and stretch their hands towards the blaze.*

1st Soldier. Cold and wet and tir'd.

2nd Soldier. Wet and tir'd and cold.

3rd Soldier. Tir'd and cold and wet.

4th Soldier [*very like Teddy*]. Twelve blasted hours of ammunition transport fatigue!

1st Soldier. Twelve weary hours.

2nd Soldier. And wasting hours.

3rd Soldier. And hot and heavy hours.

1st Soldier. Toiling and thinking to build the wall of force that blocks the way from here to home.

2nd Soldier. Lifting shells.

3rd Soldier. Carrying shells.

4th Soldier. Piling shells.

1st Soldier. In the falling, pissing rine and whistling wind.

2nd Soldier. The whistling wind and falling, drenching rain.

3rd Soldier. The God-dam rain and blasted whistling wind.

1st Soldier. And the shirkers sife at home coil'd up at ease.

2nd Soldier.   Shells for us and pianos for them.

3rd Soldier.   Fur coats for them and winding-sheets for us.

4th Soldier.   Warm.

2nd Soldier.   And dry.

1st Soldier.   An' 'appy.   [*A slight pause.*

Barney.   An' they call it re-cu-per-at-ing!

1st Soldier [*reclining near the fire*].   Gawd, I'm sleepy.

2nd Soldier [*reclining*].   Tir'd and lousy.

3rd Soldier [*reclining*].   Damp and shaking.

4th Soldier [*murmuringly, the rest joining him*].   Tir'd and lousy, an' wet an' sleepy, but mother call me early in the morning.

1st Soldier [*dreamily*].   Wen I thinks of 'ome, I thinks of a field of dysies.

The Rest [*dreamily*].   Wen 'e thinks of 'ome, 'e thinks of a field of dysies.

1st Soldier [*chanting dreamily*]:
    I sees the missus paryding along Walham Green,
    Through the jewels an' silks on the costers' carts,
    Emmie a-pulling her skirt an' muttering,
    "A balloon, a balloon, I wants a balloon",
    The missus a-tugging 'er on, an' sying,
    "A balloon, for shime, an' your father fighting:
    You'll wait till 'e's 'ome an' the bands a-plying!"   [*He pauses.*
[*Suddenly*]   But wy'r we 'ere, wy'r we 'ere—that's wot we wants to know!

2nd Soldier.   God only knows—or else, perhaps, a redcap.

1st Soldier [*chanting*]:
    Tabs'll murmur, 'em an' 'aw, an' sy: "You're 'ere because you're
    Point nine double o, the sixth platoon an' forty-eight battalion,
    The Yellow Plumes that pull'd a bow at Crecy,
    And gave to fame a leg up on the path to glory;
    Now with the howitzers of the Twenty-first Division,
    Tiking life easy with the Army of the Marne,
    An' all the time the battered Conchie squeals,
    'It's one or two men looking after business'."

3rd Soldier.   An' saves his blasted skin!

1st Soldier [*chanting*].   The padre gives a fag an' softly whispers:
    "Your king, your country an' your muvver 'as you 'ere."

An' last time 'ome on leave, I awsks the missus:
"The good God up in heaven, Bill, 'e knows,
An' I gets the seperytion moneys reg'lar." [*He sits up suddenly.*
But wy'r we 'ere, wy'r we 'ere,—that's wot I wants to know!

The Rest [*chanting sleepily*]. Why 's 'e 'ere, why 's 'e 'ere—that's wot 'e wants to know!

Barney [*singing to the air of second bar in chorus of "Auld Lang Syne"*]. We're here because we're here, because we're here, because we're here!

[*Each slides into an attitude of sleep—even Barney's head droops a little. The Corporal, followed by the Visitor, appears at back. The Visitor is a portly man with a rubicund face; he is smiling to demonstrate his ease of mind, but the lines are a little distorted with an everpresent sense of anxiety. He is dressed in a semi-civilian, semi-military manner—dark worsted suit, shrapnel helmet, a haversack slung round his shoulder, a brown belt round his middle, black top boots and spurs, and he carries a cane. His head is bent between his shoulders, and his shoulders are crouched a little.*

Visitor. Yes, to-morrow, I go a little further. Penetrate a little deeper into danger. Foolish, yes, but then it's an experience; by God, it's an experience. The military authorities are damned strict—won't let a . . . man . . . plunge!

Corporal. In a manner of speakin', sir, only let you see the arses of the guns.

Visitor [*not liking the remark*]. Yes, no; no, oh yes. Damned strict, won't let a . . . man . . . plunge! [*Suddenly, with alarm*] What's that, what was that?

Corporal. Wha' was what?

Visitor. A buzz, I thought I heard a buzz.

Corporal. A buzz?

Visitor. Of an aeroplane.

Corporal. Didn't hear. Might have been a bee.

Visitor. No, no; don't think it was a bee. [*Arranging helmet with his hands*] Damn shrapnel helmet; skin tight; like a vice; hurts the head. Rather be without it; but, regulations, you know. Military authorities damn particular—won't let a . . . man . . . plunge!

Visitor [*seeing Barney*]. Aha, what have we got here, what have we got here?

Corporal [*to Barney*]. 'Tshun! [*To the Visitor*] Regimental misdemeanour, sir.

Visitor [*to Barney*]. Nothing much, boy, nothing much?

Barney [*chanting softly*]:
    A Brass-hat pullin' the bedroom curtains
    Between himself, the world an' the Estaminay's daughter,
    In a pyjama'd hurry ran down an' phon'd
    A Tommy was chokin' an Estaminay cock,
    An' I was pinch'd as I was puttin' the bird
    Into a pot with a pint of peas.

Corporal [*chanting hoarsely*]:
    And the hens all droop, for the loss has made
    The place a place of desolation!

Visitor [*reprovingly, to the Corporal*]. Seriously, Corporal, seriously, please. Sacred, sacred: property of the citizen of a friendly State, sacred. On Active Service, serious to steal a fowl, a cock. [*To Barney*] The uniform, the cause, boy, the corps. Infra dignitatem, boy, infra dignitatem.

Barney. Wee wee.

Visitor [*pointing to reclining soldiers*]. Taking it easy, eh?

Corporal. Done in; transport fatigue; twelve hours.

Visitor. Um, not too much rest, corporal. Dangerous. Keep 'em moving much as possible. Too much rest—bad. Sap, sap, sap.

Corporal [*pointing to the left*]. Bit of monastery left intact. Hold services there; troops off to front line. Little organ plays.

Visitor. Splendid. Bucks 'em up. Gives 'em peace.
    [*A Staff Officer enters suddenly, passing by the Visitor with a springing hop, so that he stands in the centre with the Visitor on his right and the Corporal on his left. He is prim, pert, and polished, superfine khaki uniform, gold braid, crimson tabs, and gleaming top-boots. He speaks his sentences with a gasping importance.*

Corporal [*stiffening*]. 'Shun! Staff!

Soldiers [*springing to their feet—the Croucher remains as he is, with a sleepy alertness*]. Staff! 'Shun!

Corporal [*bellowing at the Croucher*]. Eh, you there: 'shun! Staff!

Croucher [*calmly*]. Not able. Sick. Privilege. Excused duty.

Staff-Wallah [*reading document*]:
    Battery Brigade Orders, F.A., 31 D 2.
    Units presently recuperating, parade eight o'clock P.M.

Attend Lecture organized by Society for amusement
    and mental development, soldiers at front.
Subject: Habits of those living between Frigid Zone
    and Arctic Circle.
Lecturer: Mr. Melville Sprucer.
Supplementary Order: Units to wear gas-masks.
As you were.

> *The Staff-Wallah departs as he came with a springing hop. The
> Visitor and the Corporal relax, and stroll down towards the R.C.
> Station. The soldiers relax too, seeking various positions of
> ease around the fire.*

Visitor [*indicating R.C. Station*]. Ah, in here. We'll just pop in here
for a minute. And then pop out again.

> [*He and the Corporal go into the R.C. Station. A pause.*

1st Soldier [*chanting and indicating that he means the Visitor by looking
in the direction of the R.C. Station*]:
    The perky bastard's cautious nibbling
    In a safe, safe shelter at danger queers me.
    Furiously feeling he's up to the neck in
    The whirl and the sweep of the front-line fighting.

2nd Soldier [*chanting*]:
    In his full-blown, chin-strapp'd, shrapnel helmet,
    He'll pat a mug on the back and murmur,
    "Here's a stand-fast Tauntonshire before me",
    And the mug, on his feet, 'll whisper "yessir".

3rd Soldier [*chanting*]:
    Like a bride, full-flush'd, 'e'll sit down and listen
    To every word of the goddam sermon,
    From the cushy-soul'd, word-spreading, yellow-streaked dud.

Barney [*chanting*]. Who wouldn't make a patch on a
    Tommy's backside.   [*A pause.*

1st Soldier. 'Ow long have we been resting 'ere?

2nd Soldier. A month.

3rd Soldier. Twenty-nine days, twenty-three hours and [*looking at watch*]
twenty-three minutes.

4th Soldier. Thirty-seven minutes more'll make it thirty days.

Croucher:
    Thirty days hath September, April, June, and
      November—

November—that's the month when I was born—
  November.
Not the beginning, not the end, but the middle of
  November.
Near the valley of the Thames, in the middle of
  November.
Shall I die at the start, near the end, in the middle
  of November?

1st Soldier [*nodding towards the Croucher*]. One more scrap, an'
'e'll be Ay one in the kingdom of the bawmy.

2nd Soldier. Perhaps they have forgotten.

3rd Soldier. Forgotten.

4th Soldier. Forgotten us.

1st Soldier. If the blighters at the front would tame their grousing.

The Rest. Tame their grousing.

2nd Soldier. And the wounded cease to stare their silent scorning.

The Rest. Passing by us, carried cushy on the stretchers.

3rd Soldier. We have beaten out the time upon the duck-board.

4th Soldier. Stiff standing watch'd the sunrise from the firestep.

2nd Soldier. Stiff standing from the firestep watch'd the sunset.

3rd Soldier. Have bless'd the dark wiring of the top with curses.

2nd Soldier. And never a ray of leave.

3rd Soldier. To have a quiet drunk.

1st Soldier. Or a mad mowment to rustle a judy.

> [*3rd Soldier takes out a package of cigarettes; taking one himself he
> hands the package round. Each takes one, and the man nearest to
> Barney, kneeling up, puts one in his mouth and lights it for him.
> They all smoke silently for a few moments, sitting up round the
> fire.*

2nd Soldier [*chanting very earnestly and quietly*]:
  Would God I smok'd an' walk'd an' watch'd th'
  Dance of a golden Brimstone butterfly,
  To the saucy pipe of a greenfinch resting
  In a drowsy, brambled lane in Cumberland.

1st Soldier:
  Would God I smok'd and lifted cargoes
  From the laden shoulders of London's river-way;

Then holiday'd, roaring out courage and movement
To the muscled machines of Tottenham Hotspur.

3rd Soldier:

To hang here even a little longer,
Lounging through fear-swell'd, anxious moments;
The hinderparts of the god of battles
Shading our war-tir'd eyes from his flaming face.

Barney:

If you creep to rest in a clos'd-up coffin,
A tail of comrades seeing you safe home;
Or be a kernel lost in a shell exploding—
It's all, sure, only in a lifetime.

All Together:

Each sparrow, hopping, irresponsible,
Is indentur'd in God's mighty memory;
And we, more than they all, shall not be lost
In the forgetfulness of the Lord of Hosts.

[*The Visitor and the Corporal come from the Red Cross Station.*]

Visitor [*taking out a cigarette-case*]. Nurses too gloomy. Surgeons too serious. Doesn't do.

Corporal. All lying-down cases, sir. Pretty bad.

Visitor [*who is now standing near the crucifix*]. All the more reason make things merry and bright. Lift them out of themselves. [*To the soldiers*] See you all to-morrow at lecture?

1st Soldier [*rising and standing a little sheepishly before the Visitor*]. Yessir, yessir.

The Rest. Yessir, yessir.

The Visitor. Good. Make it interesting. [*Searching in pocket*] Damn it, have I none? Ah, saved.

[*He takes a match from his pocket and is about to strike it carelessly on the arm of the crucifix, when the 1st Soldier, with a rapid frightened movement, knocks it out of his hand.*]

1st Soldier [*roughly*]. Blarst you, man, keep your peace-white paws from that!

2nd Soldier. The image of the Son of God.

3rd Soldier. Jesus of Nazareth, the King of the Jews.

1st Soldier [*reclining by the fire again*]. There's a Gawd knocking abaht somewhere.

4th Soldier. Wants Him to be sending us over a chit in the shape of a bursting shell.

The Visitor. Sorry put it across you. [*To Corporal*] Too much time to think. Nervy. Time to brood, brood; bad. Sap. Sap. Sap. [*Walking towards where he came in*] Must return quarters; rough and ready. Must stick it. There's a war on. Cheerio. Straight down road instead of round hill: shorter?

Corporal. Less than half as long.

The Visitor. Safe?

Corporal. Yes. Only drop shells off and on, cross-roads. Ration party wip'd out week ago.

The Visitor. Go round hill. No hurry. General Officer's orders, no unnecessary risks. Must obey. Military Authorities damned particular— won't let a . . . man . . . plunge!

> [*He and the Corporal go off. The soldiers in various attitudes are asleep around the fire. After a few moments' pause, two Stretcher-Bearers come in slowly from left, carrying a casualty. They pass through the sleeping soldiers, going towards the Red Cross Station. As they go they chant a verse, and as the verse is ending, they are followed by another pair carrying a second casualty.*

1st Bearers [*chanting*]:
Oh, bear it gently, carry it softly—
A bullet or a shell said stop, stop, stop.
It's had its day, and it's left the play,
Since it gamboll'd over the top, top, top.
It's had its day and it's left the play,
Since it gamboll'd over the top.

2nd Bearers [*chanting*]:
Oh, carry it softly, bear it gently—
The beggar has seen it through, through, through.
If it 'adn't been 'im, if it 'adn't been 'im,
It might 'ave been me or you, you, you.
If it 'adn't been 'im, if it 'adn't been 'im,
It might 'ave been me or you.

Voice [*inside R.C. Station*]. Easy, easy there; don't crowd.

1st Stretcher-Bearer [*to man behind*]. Woa, woa there, Bill, 'ouse full.

Stretcher-Bearer [*behind, to those following*]. Woa, woa; traffic blocked.
[*They leave the stretchers on the ground.*

The Wounded on the Stretchers [*chanting*]:

Carry on, carry on to the place of pain,
Where the surgeon spreads his aid, aid, aid.
And we show man's wonderful work, well done,
To the image God hath made, made, made,
And we show man's wonderful work, well done,
To the image God hath made!

When the future hours have all been spent,
And the hand of death is near, near, near,
Then a few, few moments and we shall find
There'll be nothing left to fear, fear, fear,
Then a few, few moments and we shall find
There'll be nothing left to fear.

The power, the joy, the pull of life,
The laugh, the blow, and the dear kiss,
The pride and hope, the gain and loss,
Have been temper'd down to this, this, this,
The pride and hope, the gain and loss,
Have been temper'd down to this.

1st Stretcher-Bearer [*to Barney*]. Oh, Barney, have they liced you up because you've kiss'd the Colonel's judy?

Barney. They lit on me stealin' Estaminay poulthry.

1st Stretcher-Bearer. A hen?

2nd Stretcher-Bearer. A duck, again, Barney?

3rd Stretcher-Bearer. A swan this time.

Barney [*chanting softly*]:
A Brass-hat pullin' the bedroom curtains
Between himself, the world an' the Estaminay's daughter,
In a pyjama'd hurry ran down and phon'd
A Tommy was chokin' an Estaminay cock;
An' I was pinch'd as I was puttin' the bird
Into a pot with a pint of peas.

1st Stretcher-Bearer. The red-tabb'd squit!

2nd Stretcher-Bearer. The lousy map-scanner!

3rd Stretcher-Bearer. We must keep up, we must keep up the morale of the awmy.

2nd Stretcher-Bearer [*loudly*]. Does 'e eat well?

The Rest [*in chorus*]. Yes, 'e eats well!

2nd Stretcher-Bearer. Does 'e sleep well?

The Rest [*in chorus*]. Yes, 'e sleeps well!

2nd Stretcher-Bearer. Does 'e whore well?

The Rest [*in chorus*]. Yes, 'e whores well!

2nd Stretcher-Bearer. Does 'e fight well?

The Rest [*in chorus*]. Napoo; 'e 'as to do the thinking for the Tommies!

Voice [*from the R.C. Station*]. Stretcher Party—carry on!

> [*The Bearers stoop with precision, attach their supports to the stretchers, lift them up and march slowly into the R.C. Station, chanting.*

Stretcher-Bearers [*chanting*]:
> Carry on—we've one bugled reason why—
> We've 'eard and answer'd the call, call, call.
> There's no more to be said, for when we are dead,
> We may understand it all, all, all.
> There's no more to be said, for when we are dead,
> We may understand it all.

> [*They go out, leaving the scene occupied by the Croucher and the soldiers sleeping around the fire. The Corporal re-enters. He is carrying two parcels. He pauses, looking at the sleeping soldiers for a few moments, then shouts.*

Corporal [*shouting*]. Hallo, there, you sleepy blighters! Number 2, a parcel; and for you, Number 3. Get a move on—parcels!

> [*The Soldiers wake up and spring to their feet.*

Corporal. For you, Number 2. [*He throws a parcel to 2nd Soldier.*] Number 3.   [*He throws the other parcel to 3rd Soldier.*

3rd Soldier [*taking paper from around his parcel*]. Looks like a bundle of cigarettes.

1st Soldier. Or a pack of cawds.

4th Soldier. Or a prayer-book.

3rd Soldier [*astounded*]. Holy Christ, it is!

The Rest. What?

3rd Soldier. A prayer-book!

4th Soldier. In a green plush cover with a golden cross.

Croucher. Open it at the Psalms and sing that we may be saved from the life and death of the beasts that perish.

Barney. Per omnia saecula saeculorum.

2nd Soldier [*who has opened his parcel*].   A ball, be God!

4th Soldier.   A red and yellow coloured rubber ball.

1st Soldier.   And a note.

2nd Soldier [*reading*].   To play your way to the enemies' trenches when you all go over the top. Mollie.

1st Soldier.   See if it 'ops.

> [*The 2nd Soldier hops the ball, and then kicks it from him. The Corporal intercepts it, and begins to dribble it across the stage. The 3rd Soldier tries to take it from him. The Corporal shouts "Offside, there!" They play for a few minutes with the ball, when suddenly the Staff-Wallah springs in and stands rigidly in centre.*

Corporal [*stiff to attention as he sees the Staff-Wallah*].   'Shun. Staff!

> [*All the soldiers stiffen. The Croucher remains motionless.*

Corporal [*shouting to the Croucher*].   You: 'shun. Staff!

Croucher.   Not able. Sick. Excused duty.

Staff-Wallah [*reading document*]:
> Brigade Orders, C/X 143. B/Y 341. Regarding gas-masks. Gas-masks to be worn round neck so as to lie in front 2½ degrees from socket of left shoulder-blade, and 2¾ degrees from socket of right shoulder-blade, leaving bottom margin to reach ¼ of an inch from second button of lower end of tunic. Order to take effect from 6 A.M. following morning of date received. Dismiss!
> > [*He hops out again, followed by Corporal.*

1st Soldier [*derisively*].   Comprenneemoy.

3rd Soldier.   Tray bong.

2nd Soldier [*who is standing in archway, back, looking scornfully after the Staff-Wallah, chanting*]:
> Jazzing back to his hotel he now goes gaily,
> Shelter'd and safe where the clock ticks tamely.
> His backside warming a cushion, down-fill'd,
> Green clad, well splash'd with gold birds red-beak'd.

1st Soldier:
> His last dim view of the front-line sinking
> Into the white-flesh'd breasts of a judy;
> Cuddling with proud, bright, amorous glances
> The thing salved safe from the mud of the trenches.

2nd Soldier:
> His tunic reared in the lap of comfort

Peeps at the blood-stain'd jackets passing,
Through colour-gay bars of ribbon jaunty,
Fresh from a posh shop snug in Bond Street.

Croucher:

Shame and scorn play with and beat them,
Till we anchor in their company;
Then the decorations of security
Become the symbols of self-sacrifice.

[*A pause.*

2nd Soldier:

A warning this that we'll soon be exiles
From the freedom chance of life can give,
To the front where you wait to be hurried breathless,
Murmuring how, how do you do, to God.

3rd Soldier:

Where hot with the sweat of mad endeavour,
Crouching to scrape a toy-deep shelter,
Quick-tim'd by hell's fast, frenzied drumfire
Exploding in flaming death around us.

2nd Soldier:

God, unchanging, heart-sicken'd, shuddering,
Gathereth the darkness of the night sky
To mask His paling countenance from
The blood dance of His self-slaying children.

3rd Soldier:

Stumbling, swiftly, cursing, plodding,
Lumbering, loitering, stumbling, grousing,
Through mud and rain and filth and danger,
Flesh and blood seek slow the front line.

2nd Soldier:

Squeals of hidden laughter run through
The screaming medley of the wounded
Christ, who bore the cross, still weary,
Now trails a rope tied to a field gun.

[*As the last notes of the chanting are heard the Corporal comes rapidly in; he is excited but steady; pale-faced and grim.*

Corporal. They attack. Along a wide front the enemy attacks. If they break through it may reach us even here.

Soldiers [*in chorus as they all put on gas-masks*]. They attack. The enemy attacks.

Corporal.   Let us honour that in which we do put our trust.

Soldiers [*in chorus*]:
> That it may not fail us in our time of need.

> [*The Corporal goes over to the gun and faces towards it, standing on the bottom step. The soldiers group around, each falling upon one knee, their forms crouched in a huddled act of obeisance. They are all facing the gun with their backs to the audience. The Croucher rises and joins them.*

Corporal [*singing*]:
> Hail, cool-hardened tower of steel emboss'd
> With the fever'd, figment thoughts of man;
> Guardian of our love and hate and fear,
> Speak for us to the inner ear of God!

Soldiers:
> We believe in God and we believe in thee.

Corporal:
> Dreams of line, of colour, and of form;
> Dreams of music dead for ever now;
> Dreams in bronze and dreams in stone have gone
> To make thee delicate and strong to kill.

Soldiers:
> We believe in God and we believe in thee.

Corporal:
> Jail'd in thy steel are hours of merriment
> Cadg'd from the pageant-dream of children's play;
> Too soon of the motley stripp'd that they may sweat
> With them that toil for the glory of thy kingdom.

Soldiers:
> We believe in God and we believe in thee.

Corporal:
> Remember our women, sad-hearted, proud-fac'd,
> Who've given the substance of their womb for shadows;
> Their shrivel'd, empty breasts war tinselléd
> For patient gifts of graves to thee.

Soldiers:
> We believe in God and we believe in thee.

Corporal:
> Dapple those who are shelter'd with disease,
> And women labouring with child,

And children that play about the streets,
With blood of youth expiring in its prime.

Soldiers:
We believe in God and we believe in thee.

Corporal:
Tear a gap through the soul of our mass'd enemies;
Grant them all the peace of death;
Blow them swiftly into Abram's bosom,
And mingle them with the joys of paradise!

Soldiers:
For we believe in God and we believe in thee.

[*The sky has become vexed with a crimson glare, mixed with yellow streaks, and striped with pillars of rising brown and black smoke. The Staff-Wallah rushes in, turbulent and wild, with his uniform disordered.*

Staff-Wallah:
The enemy has broken through, broken through, broken through!
Every man born of woman to the guns, to the guns.

Soldiers:
To the guns, to the guns, to the guns!

Staff-Wallah:
Those at prayer, all in bed, and the swillers drinking deeply in the
    pubs.

Soldiers:
To the guns, to the guns.

Staff-Wallah:
All the batmen, every cook, every bitch's son that hides
A whiff of courage in his veins,
Shelter'd vigour in his body,
That can run, or can walk, even crawl—
Dig him out, dig him out, shove him on—

Soldiers:
To the guns!

[*The Soldiers hurry to their places led by the Staff-Wallah to the gun. The gun swings around and points to the horizon; a shell is swung into the breech and a flash indicates the firing of the gun, searchlights move over the red glare of the sky; the scene darkens, stabbed with distant flashes and by the more vivid flash of the gun* which the Soldiers load and fire with rhythmical movements while the scene is closing. Only flashes are seen; no noise is heard.

CURTAIN

ACT III

The upper end of an hospital ward. At right angles from back wall are two beds, one covered with a red quilt and the other with a white one. From the centre of the head of each bed is an upright having at the top a piece like a swan's neck, curving out over the bed, from which hangs a chain with a wooden cross-piece to enable weak patients to pull themselves into a sitting posture. To the left of these beds is a large glass double-door which opens on to the ground: one of the doors is open and a lovely September sun, which is setting, gives a glow to the garden.

Through the door two poplar trees can be seen silhouetted against the sky. To the right of this door is another bed covered with a black quilt. Little white discs are fixed to the head of each bed: on the first is the number 26, on the second 27, and on the third 28. Medical charts hang over each on the wall. To the right is the fireplace, facing down the ward. Farther on, to the right of the fire, is a door of a bathroom. In the corner, between the glass door and the fire, is a pedestal on which stands a statue of the Blessed Virgin; under the statue is written, "Mater Misericordiae, ora pro nobis". An easy-chair, on which are rugs, is near the fire. In the centre is a white, glass-topped table on which are medicines, drugs, and surgical instruments. On one corner is a vase of flowers. A locker is beside the head, and a small chair by the foot of each bed. Two electric lights, green-shaded, hang from the ceiling, and a bracket light with a red shade projects from the wall over the fireplace. It is dusk, and the two lights suspended from the ceiling are lighted. The walls are a brilliant white.

Sylvester is in the bed numbered "26"; he is leaning upon his elbow looking towards the glass door.

Simon, sitting down on the chair beside bed numbered "27", is looking into the grounds.

Sylvester [*after a pause*].   Be God, isn't it a good one!

Simon.   Almost, almost, mind you, Sylvester, incomprehensible.

Sylvester.   To come here and find Susie Monican fashion'd like a Queen of Sheba. God moves in a mysterious way, Simon.

Simon.   There's Surgeon Maxwell prancing after her now.

Sylvester [*stretching to see*].   Heads together, eh? Be God, he's kissing her behind the trees! Oh, Susannah, Susannah, how are the mighty fallen, and the weapons of war perished!

> [*Harry Heegan enters crouched in a self-propelled invalid chair; he wheels himself up to the fire. Sylvester slides down into the bed, and Simon becomes interested in a book that he takes off the top of his locker. Harry remains for a few moments beside the fire, and then wheels himself round and goes out as he came in; Sylvester raises himself in the bed, and Simon leaves down the book to watch Harry.*

Sylvester.   Down and up, up and down.

Simon.   Up and down, down and up.

Sylvester.   Never quiet for a minute.

Simon.   Never able to hang on to an easy second.

Sylvester.   Trying to hold on to the little finger of life.

Simon.   Half-way up to heaven.

Sylvester.   And him always thinking of Jessie.

Simon.   And Jessie never thinking of him.

> [*Susie Monican, in the uniform of a V.A.D. nurse, enters the ward by the glass door. She is changed, for it is clear that she has made every detail of the costume as attractive as possible. She has the same assertive manner, but dignity and a sense of importance have been added. Her legs, encased in silk stockings, are seen (and shown) to advantage by her short and smartly cut skirt. Altogether she is now a very handsome woman. Coming in she glances at the bed numbered 28, then pauses beside Sylvester and Simon.*

Susie.   How is Twenty-eight?

Simon and Sylvester [*together*].   Travelling again.

Susie.   Did he speak at all to you?

Sylvester.   Dumb, Susie, dumb.

Simon.   Brooding, Susie; brooding, brooding.

Sylvester.   Cogitatin', Susie; cogitatin', cogitatin'.

Susie [*sharply, to Sylvester*]. It's rediculous, Twenty-six, for you to be in bed. The Sister's altogether too indulgent to you. Why didn't you pair of lazy devils entice him down to sit and cogitate under the warm wing of the sun in the garden?

Sylvester. Considerin' the low state of his general health.

Simon. Aided by a touch of frost in the air.

Sylvester. Thinkin' it over we thought it might lead——

Simon. To him getting an attack of double pneumonia.

Sylvester and Simon [*together*]. An' then he'd go off like—[*they blow through their lips*] poof—the snuff of a candle!

Susie. For the future, during the period you are patients here, I am to be addressed as "Nurse Monican", and not as "Susie". Remember that, the pair of you, please.

> [*Harry wheels himself in again, crossing by her, and, going over to the fire, looks out into grounds.*

Susie [*irritatedly, to Sylvester*]. Number Twenty-six, look at the state of your quilt. You must make an effort to keep it tidy. Dtch, dtch, dtch, what would the Matron say if she saw it!

Simon [*with a nervous giggle*]. He's an uneasy divil, **Nurse Monican.**

Susie [*hotly, to Simon*]. Yours is as bad as his, Twenty-seven. You mustn't lounge on your bed; it must be kept perfectly tidy [*she smoothes the quilts*]. Please don't make it necessary to mention this again. [*To Harry*] Would you like to go down for a little while into the garden, Twenty-eight?   [*Harry crouches silent and moody.*

Susie [*continuing*]. After the sober rain of yesterday it is good to feel the new grace of the yellowing trees, and to get the fresh smell of the grass.
> [*Harry wheels himself round and goes out by the left.*

Susie [*to Sylvester as she goes out*]. Remember, Twenty-six, if you're going to remain in a comatose condition, you'll have to keep your bed presentable.   [*A pause.*

Sylvester [*mimicking Susie*]. Twenty-six, if you're going to remeen in a comatowse condition, you'll have to keep your bed in a tidy an' awdahly mannah.

Simon. Dtch, dtch, dtch, Twenty-seven, it's disgriceful. And as long as you're heah, in the capacity of a patient, please remember I'm not to be addressed as "Susie", but as "Nurse Monican".

Sylvester. Twenty-seven, did you tike the pills the doctah awdahed?

Voice of Susie, left. Twenty-six!

Sylvester. Yes, Nurse?

Voice of Susie. Sister says you're to have a bawth at once; and you, Twenty-seven, see about getting it ready for him.

[*A fairly long pause.*

Sylvester [*angrily*]. A bawth: well, be God, that's a good one! I'm not in a fit condition for a bath! [*Another pause.*

Sylvester [*earnestly, to Simon*]. You haven't had a dip now for nearly a week, while I had one only the day before yesterday in the late evening: it must have been you she meant, Simon.

Simon. Oh, there was no dubiety about her bellowing out Twenty-six, Syl.

Sylvester [*excitedly*]. How the hell d'ye know, man, she didn't mix the numbers up?

Simon. Mix the numbers up! How could the woman mix the numbers up?

Sylvester. How could the woman mix the numbers up! What could be easier than to say Twenty-six instead of Twenty-seven? How could the woman mix the numbers up! Of course the woman could mix the numbers up!

Simon. What d'ye expect me to do—hurl myself into a bath that was meant for you?

Sylvester. I don't want you to hurl yourself into anything; but you don't expect me to plunge into a bath that maybe wasn't meant for me?

Simon. Nurse Monican said Twenty-six, and when you can alter that, ring me up and let me know.

[*A pause; then Simon gets up and goes toward bathroom door.*

Sylvester [*snappily*]. Where are you leppin' to now?

Simon. I want to get the bath ready.

Sylvester. You want to get the bawth ready! Turn the hot cock on, and turn the cold cock on for Number Twenty-six, mixin' them the way a chemist would mix his medicines—sit still, man, till we hear the final verdict.

[*Simon sits down again. Susie comes in left, and, passing to the door leading to grounds, pauses beside Simon and Sylvester.*

Susie [*sharply*]. What are the two of you doing? Didn't I tell you, Twenty-six, that you were to take a bawth; and you, Twenty-seven, that you were to get it ready for him?

Sylvester [*sitting brightly up in bed*].   Oh, just goin' to spring up, Nurse Monican, when you popped in.

Susie.   Well, up with you, then, and take it. [*To Simon*] You go and get it ready for him.   [*Simon goes into the bathroom*.

Sylvester [*venturing a last hope as Susie goes towards the entrance to grounds*].   I had a dip, Nurse, only the day before yesterday in the late evening.

Susie [*as she goes out*].   Have another one now, please.

   [*The water can be heard flowing in the bathroom, and a light cloud of steam comes out by the door which Simon has left open*.

Sylvester [*mimicking Susie*].   Have another one, now, please! One to be taken before and after meals. The delicate audacity of the lip of that one since she draped her shoulders with a crimson cape!

   [*Simon appears and stands leaning against the side of the bathroom door*.

Simon [*gloating*].   She's steaming away now, Sylvester, full cock.

Sylvester [*scornfully, to Simon*].   Music to you, the gurgling of the thing, music to you. Gaugin' the temperature for me. Dtch, dtch, dtch [*sitting up*], an' hospital's the last place that God made. Be damn it, I wouldn't let a stuffed bird stay in one!

Simon.   Come on, man, before the hot strength bubbles out of it.

Sylvester [*getting out of bed*].   Have you the towels hot an' everything ready for me to spring into?

Simon [*with a bow*].   Everything's ready for your enjoyment, Sir.

Sylvester [*as he goes towards the bathroom*].   Can't they be content with an honest to God cleanliness, an' not be tryin' to gild a man with soap and water.

Simon [*with a grin, as Sylvester passes*].   Can I do anything more for you, Sir?

Sylvester [*almost inarticulate with indignation, as he goes in*].   Now I'm tellin' you, Simon Norton, our cordiality's gettin' a little strained!

   [*Harry wheels himself in, goes again to the fireplace, and looks into grounds. Simon watches him for a moment, takes a package of cigarettes from his pocket and lights one*.

Simon [*awkwardly, to Harry*].   Have a fag, Harry, oul' son?

Harry.   Don't want one; tons of my own in the locker.

Simon.   Like me to get you one?

Harry. I can get them myself if I want one. D'ye think my arms are lifeless as well as my legs?

Simon. Far from that. Everybody's remarking what a great improvement has taken place in you during the last few days.

Harry. Everybody but myself.

Simon. What with the rubbing every morning and the rubbing every night, and now the operation to-morrow as a grand finally, you'll maybe be in the centre of the football field before many months are out.

Harry [*irritably*]. Oh, shut up, man! It's a miracle I want—not an operation. The last operation was to give life to my limbs, but no life came, and again I felt the horrible sickness of life only from the waist up. [*Raising his voice*] Don't stand there gaping at me, man. Did you never before clap your eyes on a body dead from the belly down? Blast you, man, why don't you shout at me, "While there's life there's hope"!

> [*Simon edges away to his corner. Susie comes in by the glass door and goes over to the table.*

Harry [*to Susie*]. A package of fags. Out of the locker. Will you, Susie?

> [*Susie goes to Harry's locker, gets the cigarettes and gives them to him. As he lights the cigarette, his right arm gives a sudden jerk.*

Susie. Steady. What's this?

Harry [*with a nervous laugh*]. Barred from my legs it's flowing back into my arms. I can feel it slyly creeping into my fingers.

Voice of Patient, out left [*plaintively*]. Nurse!

Susie [*turning her head in direction of the voice*]. Shush, you Twenty-three; go asleep, go asleep.

Harry. A soft, velvety sense of distance between my fingers and the things I touch.

Susie. Stop thinking of it. Brooding checks the chance of your recovery. A good deal may be imagination.

Harry [*peevishly*]. Oh, I know the different touches of iron [*he touches the bed-rail*]; of wood [*he touches the chair*]; of flesh [*he touches his cheek*]; and to my fingers they're giving the same answers—a feeling of numb distance between me and the touches of them all.

Voice of Patient, out left. Nurse!

Susie. Dtch, dtch. Go asleep, Twenty-three.

Voice, out left. The stab in the head is worse than ever, Nurse.

Susie. You've got your dose of morphia, and you'll get no more. You'll just have to stick it.

[*Resident Surgeon Forby Maxwell enters from the grounds. He is about thirty years of age, and good-looking. His white overalls are unbuttoned, showing war ribbons on his waistcoat, flanked by the ribbon of the D.S.O. He has a careless, jaunty air, and evidently takes a decided interest in Susie. He comes in singing softly.*

Surgeon Maxwell:

Stretched on the couch, Jessie fondled her dress,
That hid all her beauties just over the knee;
And I wondered and said, as I sigh'd, "What a
    shame,
That there's no room at all on the couch there for me."

Susie [*to Surgeon Maxwell*].   Twenty-three's at it again.

Surgeon Maxwell.   Uh, hopeless case. Half his head in Flanders. May go on like that for another month.

Susie.   He keeps the patients awake at night.

Simon.   With his "God have mercys on me", running after every third or fourth tick of the clock.

Harry.   'Tisn't fair to me, 'tisn't fair to me; I must get my bellyful of sleep if I'm ever going to get well.

Surgeon Maxwell.   Oh, the poor devil won't trouble any of you much longer. [*Singing*]:
Said Jess, with a light in the side of her eyes,
"A shrewd, mathematical fellow like you,
With an effort of thought should be able to make
The couch wide enough for the measure of two."

Susie.   Dtch, dtch, Surgeon Maxwell.

Surgeon Maxwell [*singing*]:
I fixed on a plan, and I carried it through,
And the eyes of Jess gleam'd as she whisper'd to
    me:
"The couch, made for one, that was made to hold two,
Has, maybe, been made big enough to hold three!"

[*Surgeon Maxwell catches Susie's hand in his. Sylvester bursts in from the bathroom and rushes to his bed, colliding with the Surgeon as he passes him.*

Surgeon Maxwell.   Hallo, hallo there, what's this?

Sylvester [*flinging himself into bed, covering himself rapidly with the clothes, blowing himself warm*].   Pooh, pooh, I feel as if I was sittin' on the doorstep of pneumonia! Pooh, oh!

Surgeon Maxwell [*to Sylvester*].   We'll have a look at you in a moment, Twenty-six, and see what's wrong with you.

> [*Sylvester subsides down into the bed, and Simon edges towards the entrance to grounds, and stands looking into the grounds, or watching Surgeon Maxwell examining Sylvester.*

Surgeon Maxwell [*to Harry, who is looking intently out into the grounds*].   Well, how are we to-day, Heegan?

Harry.   I imagine I don't feel quite so dead in myself as I've felt these last few days back.

Surgeon Maxwell.   Oh, well, that's something.

Harry.   Sometimes I think I feel a faint, fluttering kind of a buzz in the tops of my thighs.

Surgeon Maxwell [*touching Harry's thigh*].   Where, here?

Harry.   No; higher up, doctor; just where the line is that leaves the one part living and the other part dead.

Surgeon Maxwell.   A buzz?

Harry.   A timid, faint, fluttering kind of a buzz.

Surgeon Maxwell.   That's good. There might be a lot in that faint, fluttering kind of a buzz.

Harry [*after a pause*].   I'm looking forward to the operation to-morrow.

Surgeon Maxwell.   That's the way to take it. While there's life there's hope [*with a grin and a wink at Susie*]. And now we'll have a look at Twenty-six.

> [*Harry, when he hears "while there's life there's hope", wheels himself madly out left; half-way out he turns his head and stretches to look out into the grounds, then he goes on.*

Susie.   Will the operation to-morrow be successful?

Surgeon Maxwell.   Oh, of course; very successful.

Susie.   Do him any good, d'ye think?

Surgeon Maxwell.   Oh, blast the good it'll do him.

> [*Susie goes over to Sylvester in the bed.*

Susie [*to Sylvester*].   Sit up, Twenty-six, Surgeon Maxwell wants to examine you.

Sylvester [*sitting up with a brave effort but a woeful smile*]. Righto. In the pink!

> [*Surgeon Maxwell comes over, twirling his stethoscope. Simon peeps round the corner of the glass door.*]

Susie [*to Surgeon Maxwell*]. What was the cause of the row between the Matron and Nurse Jennings? [*To Sylvester*] Open your shirt, Twenty-six.

Surgeon Maxwell [*who has fixed the stethoscope in his ears, removing it to speak to Susie*]. Caught doing the tango in the Resident's arms in the Resident's room. Naughty girl, naughty girl. [*To Sylvester*] Say "ninety-nine".

Sylvester. Ninety-nine.

Susie. Oh, I knew something like that would happen. Daughter of a Dean, too.

Surgeon Maxwell [*to Sylvester*]. Say "ninety-nine".

Sylvester. Ninety-nine. U-u-uh, it's gettin' very cold here, sitting up!

Surgeon Maxwell [*to Sylvester*]. Again. Don't be frightened; breathe quietly.

Sylvester. Ninety-nine. Cool as a cucumber, Doctor. Ninety-nine.

Surgeon Maxwell [*to Susie*]. Damn pretty little piece. Not so pretty as you, though.

Sylvester [*to Surgeon Maxwell*]. Yesterday Doctor Joyce, givin' me a run over, said to a couple of medical men that were with him lookin' for tips, that the thing was apparently yieldin' to treatment, and that an operation wouldn't be necessary.

Surgeon Maxwell. Go on; ninety-nine, ninety-nine.

Sylvester. Ninety-nine, ninety-nine.

Surgeon Maxwell [*to Susie*]. Kicks higher than her head, and you should see her doing the splits.

Sylvester [*to Surgeon Maxwell*]. Any way of gettin' rid of it'll do for me, for I'm not one of them that'll spend a night before an operation in a crowd of prayers.

Susie. Not very useful things to be doing and poor patients awaiting attention.

Surgeon Maxwell [*putting stethoscope into pocket*]. He'll do all right; quite fit. Great old skin. [*To Sylvester*] You can cover yourself up, now. [*To Susie*] And don't tell me, Nurse Susie, that you've never felt a thrill or left a bedside for a kiss in a corner. [*He tickles her under the arm.*] Kiss in a corner, Nurse!

Susie [*pleased, but coy*].   Please don't, Doctor Maxwell, please.

Surgeon Maxwell [*tickling her again as they go out*].   Kiss in a corner; ta-ra-ra-ra, kiss in a corner!   [*A pause.*

Sylvester [*to Simon*].   Simon, were you listenin' to that conversation?

Simon.   Indeed I was.

Sylvester.   We have our hands full, Simon, to keep alive. Think of sinkin' your body to the level of a hand that, ta-ra-ra-ra, would plunge a knife into your middle, haphazard, hurryin' up to run away after a thrill from a kiss in a corner. Did you see me dizzied an' wastin' me time pumpin' ninety-nines out of me, unrecognized, quiverin' with cold an' equivocation!

Simon.   Everybody says he's a very clever fellow with the knife.

Sylvester.   He'd gouge out your eye, saw off your arm, lift a load of vitals out of your middle, rub his hands, keep down a terrible desire to cheer lookin' at the ruin, an' say, "Twenty-six, when you're a little better, you'll feel a new man!"

[*Mrs. Heegan, Mrs. Foran, and Teddy enter from the grounds. Mrs. Foran is leading Teddy, who has a heavy bandage over his eyes, and is dressed in the blue clothes of military hospitals.*

Mrs. Foran [*to Teddy*].   Just a little step here, Ted; upsh! That's it; now we're on the earth again, beside Simon and Sylvester. You'd better sit here.   [*She puts him sitting on a chair.*

Sylvester [*to Mrs. Heegan, as she kisses him*].   Well, how's the old woman, eh?

Mrs. Heegan.   A little anxious about poor Harry.

Simon.   He'll be all right. To-morrow'll tell a tale.

Susie [*coming in, annoyed*].   Who let you up here at this hour? Twenty-eight's to have an operation to-morrow, and shouldn't be disturbed.

Mrs. Heegan.   Sister Peter Alcantara said we might come up, Nurse.

Mrs. Foran [*loftily*].   Sister Peter Alcantara's authority ought to be good enough, I think.

Mrs. Heegan.   Sister Peter Alcantara said a visit might buck him up a bit.

Mrs. Foran.   Sister Peter Alcantara knows the responsibility she'd incur by keeping a wife from her husband and a mother from her son.

Susie.   Sister Peter Alcantara hasn't got to nurse him. And remember, nothing is to be said that would make his habit of introspection worse than it is.

Mrs. Foran [*with dignity*]. Thanks for the warnin', Nurse, but them kind of mistakes is unusual with us.

> [*Susie goes out left, as Harry wheels himself rapidly in. Seeing the group, he stops suddenly, and a look of disappointment comes on to his face.*

Mrs. Heegan [*kissing Harry*]. How are you, son?

Mrs. Foran. I brought Teddy, your brother in arms, up to see you, Harry.

Harry [*impatiently*]. Where's Jessie? I thought you were to bring her with you?

Mrs. Heegan. She's comin' after us in a moment.

Harry. Why isn't she here now?

Mrs. Foran. She stopped to have a word in the grounds with someone she knew.

Harry. It was Barney Bagnal, was it? Was it Barney Bagnal?

Teddy. Maybe she wanted to talk to him about gettin' the V.C.

Harry. What V.C.? Who's gettin' the V.C.?

Teddy. Barney. Did he not tell you? [*Mrs. Foran prods his knee.*] What's up?

Harry [*intensely, to Teddy*]. What's he gettin' it for? What's he gettin' the V.C. for?

Teddy. For carryin' you wounded out of the line of fire. [*Mrs. Foran prods his knee.*] What's up?

Harry [*in anguish*]. Christ Almighty, for carryin' me wounded out of the line of fire!

Mrs. Heegan [*rapidly*]. Harry, I wouldn't be thinkin' of anything till we see what the operation'll do to-morrow.

Simon [*rapidly*]. God, if it gave him back the use even of one of his legs.

Mrs. Foran [*rapidly*]. Look at all the places he could toddle to, an' all the things he could do then with the prop of a crutch.

Mrs. Heegan. Even at the worst, he'll never be dependin' on anyone, for he's bound to get the maximum allowance.

Simon. Two quid a week, isn't it?

Sylvester. Yes, a hundred per cent total incapacitation.

Harry. She won't come up if one of you don't go down and bring her up.

Mrs. Heegan. She's bound to come up, for she's got your ukelele.

Harry. Call her up, Simon, call her up—I must see Jessie.

[*Simon goes over to the door leading to the grounds, and looks out.*]

Mrs. Foran [*bending over till her face is close to Harry's*]. The drawn look on his face isn't half as bad as when I seen him last.

Mrs. Heegan [*bending and looking into Harry's face*]. Look, the hollows under his eyes is fillin' up, too.

Teddy. I'm afraid he'll have to put Jessie out of his head, for when a man's hit in the spine . . . [*Mrs Foran prods his knee.*] What's up, woman?

Harry [*impatiently, to Simon*]. Is she coming? Can you see her anywhere?

Simon. I see someone like her in the distance, under the trees.

Harry. Call her; can't you give her a shout, man?

Simon [*calling*]. Jessie. Is that you, Jessie? Jessie-e!

Mrs. Heegan [*to Harry*]. What time are you goin' under the operation?

Harry [*to Simon*]. Call her again, call her again, can't you!

Simon [*calling*]. Jessie, Jessie-e!

Teddy. Not much of a chance for an injury to the spine, for . . .

Mrs. Foran [*putting her face close to Teddy's*]. Oh, shut up, you!

Harry. Why did you leave her in the grounds? Why didn't you wait till she came up with you?

Mrs. Foran [*going over to Simon and calling*]. Jessie, Jessie-e!

Jessie's Voice, in distance. Yehess!

Mrs. Foran [*calling*]. Come up here at once; we're all waitin' for you!

Jessie's Voice. I'm not going up!

Mrs. Foran [*calling*]. Bring up that ukelele here at once, miss!

Jessie's Voice. Barney'll bring it up!

[*Harry, who has been listening intently, wheels himself rapidly to where Simon and Mrs. Foran are, pushing through them hurriedly.*]

Harry [*calling loudly*]. Jessie! Jessie! Jessie-e!

Mrs. Foran. Look at that, now; she's runnin' away, the young rip!

Harry [*appealingly*].   Jessie, Jessie-e!

[*Susie enters quickly from left. She goes over to Harry and pulls him back from the door.*

Susie [*indignantly*].   Disgraceful! Rousing the whole ward with this commotion! Dear, dear, dear, look at the state of Twenty-eight. Come along, come along, please; you must all go at once.

Harry.   Jessie's coming up for a minute, Nurse.

Susie.   No more to come up. We've had enough for one night, and you for a serious operation to-morrow. Come on, all out, please.

[*Susie conducts Mrs. Heegan, Mrs. Foran, and Teddy out left.*

Mrs. Foran [*going out*].   We're goin', we're goin', thank you. A nice way to treat the flotsum and jetsum of the battlefields!

Susie [*to Harry*].   To bed now, Twenty-eight, please. [*To Simon*] Help me get him to bed, Twenty-seven.

[*Susie pushes Harry to his bed, right; Simon brings portion of a bed-screen which he places around Harry, hiding him from view.*

Susie [*turning to speak to Sylvester, who is sitting up in bed, as she arranges screen*].   You're going to have your little operation in the morning, so you'd better go to sleep too.

[*Sylvester goes pale and a look of dismay and fear crawls over his face.*

Susie.   Don't funk it now. They're not going to turn you inside out. It'll be over in ten minutes.

Sylvester [*with a groan*].   When they once get you down your only hope is in the infinite mercy of God!

Simon.   If I was you, Sylvester, I wouldn't take this operation too seriously. You know th' oul' song—Let Me like a Soldier Fall! If I was you, I'd put it completely out of me mind.

Sylvester [*subsiding on to the pillow—with an agonised look on his face*].   Let me like a soldier fall! Did anyone ever hear th' equal o' that! Put it out of me mind completely! [*He sits up, and glares at Simon.*] Eh, you, look! If you can't think sensibly, then thry to think without talkin'! [*He sinks back on the pillow again.*] Let me like a soldier fall. Oh, it's not a fair trial for a sensible man to be stuck down in a world like this!

[*Sylvester slides down till he lies prone and motionless on the bed. Harry is in bed now. Simon removes the screen, and Susie arranges Harry's quilt for the night.*

Susie [*to Simon*].   Now run and help get the things together for supper.

[*Simon goes out left.*] [*Encouragingly to Harry*] After the operation, a stay in the air of the Convalescent may work wonders.

Harry. If I could mingle my breath with the breeze that blows from every sea, and over every land, they wouldn't widen me into anything more than the shrivell'd thing I am.

Susie [*switching off the two hanging lights, so that the red light over the fireplace alone remains*]. Don't be foolish, Twenty-eight. Wheeling yourself about among the beeches and the pines, when the daffodils are hanging out their blossoms, you'll deepen your chance in the courage and renewal of the country.

[*The bell of a Convent in grounds begins to ring for Compline.*]

Harry [*with intense bitterness*]. I'll say to the pine, "Give me the grace and beauty of the beech"; I'll say to the beech, "Give me the strength and stature of the pine". In a net I'll catch butterflies in bunches; twist and mangle them between my fingers and fix them wriggling on to mercy's banner. I'll make my chair a Juggernaut, and wheel it over the neck and spine of every daffodil that looks at me, and strew them dead to manifest the mercy of God and the justice of man!

Susie [*shocked*]. Shush, Harry, Harry!

Harry. To hell with you, your country, trees, and things, you jibbering jay!

Susie [*as she is going out*]. Twenty-eight!

Harry [*vehemently*]. To hell with you, your country, trees, and things, you jibbering jay!

[*Susie looks at him, pauses for a few moments, as if to speak, and then goes out.*

[*A pause; then Barney comes in by door from grounds. An overcoat covers his military hospital uniform of blue. His left arm is in a sling. Under his right arm he carries a ukelele, and in his hand he has a bunch of flowers. Embarrassed, he goes slowly to Harry's bed, drops the flowers at the foot, then he drops the ukelele there.*

Barney [*awkwardly*]. Your ukelele. An' a bunch of flowers from Jessie.
[*Harry remains motionless on the bed.*

Barney. A bunch of flowers from Jessie, and . . . your . . . ukelele.

[*The Sister of the Ward enters, left, going to the chapel for Compline. She wears a cream habit with a white coif; a large set of Rosary beads hangs from her girdle. She pauses on her way, and a brass Crucifix flashes on her bosom.*

Sister [*to Harry*].   Keeping brave and hopeful, Twenty-eight?

Harry [*softly*].   Yes, Sister.

Sister.   Splendid. And we've got a ukelele too. Can you play it, my child?

Harry.   Yes, Sister.

Sister.   Splendid. You must play me something when you're well over the operation. [*To Barney*] Standing guard over your comrade, Twenty-two, eh?

Barney [*softly and shyly*].   Yes, Sister.

Sister.   Grand. Forasmuch as ye do it unto the least of these my brethren, ye do it unto me. Well, God be with you both, my children. [*To Harry*] And Twenty-eight, pray to God, for wonderful He is in His doing toward the children of men.

> [*Calm and dignified she goes out into the grounds.*

Barney [*pausing as he goes out left*].   They're on the bed; the ukelele, and the bunch of flowers from . . . Jessie.

> [*The Sisters are heard singing in the Convent the hymn of Salve Regina.*

Sisters:

> Salve Regina, mater misericordiae;
> Vitae dulcedo et spes nostra, salve!
> Ad te clamamus, exules filii Hevae;
> Ad te suspiramus, gementes et flentes in hac lacrymarum valle.
> Eia ergo Advocata nostra,
> Illos tuos misericordes oculos ad nos converte,
> Et Jesum, benedictum fructum ventris tui—

Harry.   God of the miracles, give a poor devil a chance, give a poor devil a chance!

Sisters:

> Nobis post hoc exsilium ostende,
> O clemens, o pia, o dulcis Virgo Maria!

CURTAIN

ACT IV

A room of the dance hall of the Avondale Football Club. At back, left,
cutting corners of the back and side walls, it is the arched entrance, divided
by a slim pillar, to the dance hall. This entrance is hung with crimson and
black striped curtains; whenever these are parted the dancers can be seen
swinging or gliding past the entrance if a dance be taking place at the time.
Over the entrance is a scroll on which is printed: "Up the Avondales!" The
wall back has a wide, tall window which opens to the garden, in which the
shrubs and some sycamore trees can be seen. It is hung with apple-green
casement curtains, which are pulled to the side to allow the window to be
open as it is at present. Between the entrance to hall and the window is a
Roll of Honour containing the names of five members of the Club killed in
the war. Underneath the Roll of Honour a wreath of laurel tied with red
and black ribbon. To the front left is the fireplace. Between the fireplace
and the hall entrance is a door on which is an oval white enamel disc with
"Caretaker" painted on it. To the right a long table, covered with a green
cloth, on which are numerous bottles of wine and a dozen glasses. On the
table, too, is a telephone. A brown carpet covers the floor. Two easy and one
ordinary chairs are in the room. Hanging from the ceiling are three lanterns;
the centre one is four times the length of its width, the ones at the side are
less than half as long as the centre lantern and hang horizontally; the lan-
terns are black, with a broad red stripe running down the centre of the
largest and across those hanging at each side, so that, when they are lighted,
they suggest an illuminated black cross with an inner one of gleaming red.
The hall is vividly decorated with many coloured lanterns, looped with
coloured streamers.

When the scene is revealed the curtains are drawn, and the band can be
heard playing a fox-trot. Outside in the garden, near the window, Simon
and Sylvester can be seen smoking, and Teddy is walking slowly up and
down the path. The band is heard playing for a few moments, then the
curtains are pulled aside, and Jessie, with Barney holding her hand, comes
in and walks rapidly to the table where the wine is standing. They are
quickly followed by Harry, who wheels himself a little forward, then stops,
watching them. The curtains part again, and Mrs. Heegan is seen watching
Harry. Simon and Sylvester, outside, watch those in the room through the
window. Barney wears a neat navy-blue suit, with a rather high, stiff collar
and black tie. Pinned on the breast of his waistcoat are his war medals,
flanked by the Victoria Cross. Harry is also wearing his medals. Jessie has
on a very pretty, rather tight-fitting dance frock, with the sleeves falling
widely to the elbow, and cut fairly low on her breast. All the dancers, and
Harry too, wear coloured, fantastically shaped paper hats.

Jessie [*hot, excited, and uneasy, as with a rapid glance back she sees the curtains parted by Harry*].   Here he comes prowling after us again! His watching of us is pulling all the enjoyment out of the night. It makes me shiver to feel him wheeling after us.

Barney.   We'll watch for a chance to shake him off, an' if he starts again we'll make him take his tangled body somewhere else. [*As Harry moves forward from the curtained entrance*] Shush, he's comin' near us. [*In a louder tone to Jessie*] Red wine, Jessie, for you, or white wine?

Harry.   Red wine first, Jessie, to the passion and the power and the pain of life, an' then a drink of white wine to the melody that is in them all!

Jessie.   I'm so hot.

Harry.   I'm so cold; white wine for the woman warm to make her cold; red wine for the man that's cold to make him warm!

Jessie.   White wine for me.

Harry.   For me the red wine till I drink to men puffed up with pride of strength, for even creeping things can praise the Lord!

Barney [*gently to Harry, as he gives a glass of wine to Jessie*].   No more for you now, Harry.

Harry [*mockingly*].   Oh, please, your lusty lordship, just another, an' if I seek a second, smack me well. [*Wheeling his chair viciously against Barney*] Get out, you trimm'd-up clod. There's medals on my breast as well as yours! [*He fills a glass.*]

Jessie.   Let us go back to the dancing, Barney. [*Barney hesitates.*] Please, Barney, let us go back to the dancing!

Harry.   To the dancing, for the day cometh when no man can play. And legs were made to dance, to run, to jump, to carry you from one place to another; but mine can neither walk, nor run, nor jump, nor feel the merry motion of a dance. But stretch me on the floor fair on my belly, and I will turn over on my back, then wriggle back again on to my belly; and that's more than a dead, dead man can do!

Barney.   Jessie wants to dance, an' so we'll go, and leave you here a little.

Harry.   Cram pain with pain, and pleasure cram with pleasure. I'm going too. You'd cage me in from seeing you dance, and dance, and dance, with Jessie close to you, and you so close to Jessie. Though you wouldn't think it, yes, I have—I've hammer'd out many a merry measure upon a polish'd floor with a sweet, sweet heifer. [*As Barney and Jessie are moving away he catches hold of Jessie's dress*] Her name? Oh, any name will do—we'll call her Jessie!

Jessie.   Oh, let me go. [*To Barney*] Barney, make him let me go, please.

[*Barney, without a word, removes Harry's hand from Jessie's dress. Jessie and Barney then go out to the dance hall through the curtained entrance. After a while Mrs. Heegan slips away from the entrance into the hall. After a moment's pause Harry follows them into the hall. Simon and Sylvester come in from the garden, leaving Teddy still outside smoking and walking to and fro in the cautious manner of the blind. Simon and Sylvester sit down near the fire and puff in silence for a few moments.*

Sylvester [*earnestly*].   I knew it. I knew it, Simon—strainin' an' strainin' his nerves; driftin' an' driftin' towards an hallucination!

Simon.   Jessie might try to let him down a little more gently, but it would have been better, I think, if Harry hadn't come here to-night.

Sylvester.   I concur in that, Simon. What's a decoration to an hospital is an anxiety here.

Simon.   To carry life and colour to where there's nothing but the sick and helpless is right; but to carry the sick and helpless to where there's nothing but life and colour is wrong.   [*The telephone bell rings.*

Sylvester.   There's the telephone bell ringing.

Simon.   Oh, someone'll come in and answer it in a second.

Sylvester.   To join a little strength to a lot of weakness is what I call sensible; but to join a little weakness to a lot of strength is what I call a . . .

Simon.   A cod.

Sylvester.   Exactly.   [*The telephone continues to ring.*

Sylvester.   There's that telephone ringin' still.

Simon.   Oh, someone 'll come in and answer it in a second.
              [*Teddy has groped his way to French window.*

Teddy.   The telephone's tinklin', boys.

Sylvester.   Thanks, Teddy. We hear it, thanks. [*To Simon*] When he got the invitation from the Committay to come, wearin' his decorations, me an' the old woman tried to persuade him that, seein' his condition, it was better to stop at home, an' let me represent him, but [*with a gesture*] no use!   [*Teddy resumes his walk to and fro.*

Simon.   It was natural he'd want to come, since he was the means of winning the Cup twice before for them, leading up to their keeping the trophy for ever by the win of a year ago.

Sylvester.   To bring a boy so helpless as him, whose memory of agility an' strength time hasn't flattened down, to a place wavin' with joy an' dancin', is simply, simply——

Simon. Devastating, I'd say.

Sylvester. Of course it is! Is that god-damn telephone goin' to keep ringin' all night? [*Mrs. Foran enters from hall quickly.*

Mrs. Foran. Miss Monican says that one of you is to answer the telephone, an' call her if it's anything important.

Sylvester [*nervously*]. I never handled a telephone in my life.

Simon. I chanced it once and got so hot and quivery that I couldn't hear a word, and didn't know what I was saying myself.

Mrs. Foran. Have a shot at it and see.
[*The three of them drift over to the telephone.*

Sylvester. Chance it again, Simon, an' try to keep steady.
[*As Simon stretches his hand to the receiver.*

Sylvester. Don't rush, don't rush, man, an' make a mess of it. Take it in your stride.

Simon [*pointing to receiver*]. When you lift this down, you're connected, I think.

Sylvester. No use of thinkin' on this job. Don't you turn the handle first?

Simon [*irritably*]. No, you don't turn no handle, man!

Mrs. Foran. Let Simon do it now; Simon knows.

[*Simon tremblingly lifts down the receiver, almost letting it fall.*

Sylvester. Woa, woa, Simon; careful, careful!

Simon [*speaking in receiver*]. Eh, hallo! Eh, listen there. Eh, hallo! listen.

Sylvester. You listen, man, an' give the fellow at the other end a chance to speak.

Simon. If you want me to manipulate the thing, let me manipulate it in tranquillity.

Mrs. Foran [*to Sylvester*]. Oh, don't be puttin' him out, Sylvester.

Simon [*waving them back*]. Don't be crushing in on me; give me room to manipulate the thing. [*Dead silence for some moments.*

Mrs. Foran. Are you hearin' anything from the other end?

Simon. A kind of a buzzing and a roaring noise.

[*Sylvester suddenly gives the cord a jerk and pulls the receiver out of Simon's hand.*

[*Angrily*] What the hell are you trying to do, man? You're after pulling it right out of my mit.

Sylvester [*heatedly*].   There was a knot or a twist an' a tangle in it that was keepin' the sound from travellin'.

Simon.   If you want me to work the thing properly, you'll have to keep yourself from interfering. [*Resuming surlily*] Eh, hallo, listen, yes? Ha! ha! ha! ha! Yes, yes, yes. No, no, no. Cheerio! Yes. Eh, hallo, listen, eh. Hallo.

Sylvester.   What is it? What're they sayin'?

Simon [*hopelessly, taking the receiver from his ear*].   I don't seem to be able to hear a damn sound.

Sylvester.   An' Holy God, what are you yessin' and noin' and cheerioin' out of you for then?

Simon.   You couldn't stand here like a fool and say nothing, could you?

Sylvester.   Show it to me, Simon, show it to me—you're not holdin' it at the proper angle.

Mrs. Foran.   Give it to Syl, Simon; it's a delicate contrivance that needs a knack in handlin'.

Sylvester [*as he is taking the receiver from Simon and carefully placing it to his ear*].   You have always to preserve an eqwee-balance between the speakin' mouth and the hearin' ear. [*Speaking into receiver*] Hallo! Anybody there at the other end of this? Eh, wha's that? Yes, yes, I've got you [*taking the receiver from his ear and speaking to Simon and Mrs. Foran*]: Something like wine, or dine, or shine, or something—an' a thing that's hummin'.

Simon.   I can see no magnificent meaning jumping out of that!

Mrs. Foran.   They couldn't be talkin' about bees, could they?

Sylvester [*scornfully*].   Bees! No, they couldn't be talkin' about bees! That kind of talk, Mrs. Foran, only tends to confuse matters. Bees! Dtch, dtch, dtch—the stupidity of some persons is . . . terrifyin'!

Simon.   Ask them quietly what they want.

Sylvester [*indignantly*].   What the hell's the use of askin' them that, when I can hear something only like a thing that's hummin'?

Mrs. Foran.   It wouldn't be, now, comin', or even bummin'?

Sylvester.   It might even possibly be drummin'. Personally, Mrs. Foran, I think, since you can't help, you might try to keep from hinderin'.

Simon.   Put it back, Syl, where it was, an' if it rings again, we'll only have to slip quietly out of this.

Mrs. Foran. Yes, put it back, an' say it never rang.

Sylvester. Where was it? Where do I put it back?

Simon. On that thing stickin' out there. Nice and gently now.

[*Sylvester cautiously puts receiver back. They look at the telephone for a few moments, then go back to the fire, one by one. Sylvester stands with his back to it; Simon sits in a chair, over the back of which Mrs. Foran leans.*]

Mrs. Foran. Curious those at the other end of the telephone couldn't make themselves understood.

Simon. Likely they're not accustomed to it, and it's a bit difficult if you're not fully conscious of its manipulation.

Sylvester. Well, let them study an' study it then, or abide by the consequences, for we can't be wastin' time teachin' them.

[*The curtains at entrance of dance hall are pulled aside, and Teddy, who has disappeared from the garden a little time before, comes in. As he leaves the curtains apart, the dancers can be seen gliding past the entrance in the movements of a tango. Teddy comes down, looks steadily but vacantly towards the group around the fire, then goes over carefully to the table, where he moves his hand about till it touches a bottle, which he takes up in one hand, feeling it questioningly with the other.*]

Simon. How goes it, Teddy?

Teddy [*with a vacant look towards them*]. Sylvester—Simon—well. What seest thou, Teddy? Thou seest not as man seeth. In the garden the trees stand up; the green things showeth themselves and fling out flowers of divers hues. In the sky the sun by day and the moon and the stars by night—nothing. In the hall the sound of dancing, the eyes of women, grey and blue and brown and black, do sparkle and dim and sparkle again. Their white breasts rise and fall, and rise again. Slender legs, from red and black, and white and green, come out, go in again—nothing. Strain as you may, it stretches from the throne of God to the end of the hearth of hell.

Simon. What?

Teddy. The darkness.

Simon [*knowing not what to say*]. Yes, oh yes.

Teddy [*holding up a bottle of wine*]. What colour, Syl? It's all the same, but I like the red the best.

Mrs. Foran [*going over to Teddy*]. Just one glass, dear, and you'll sit down quietly an' take it in sips.

[*Mrs. Foran fills a glass of wine for Teddy, leads him to a chair, puts him sitting down, and gives the glass of wine carefully to him. The band in the hall has been playing, and through the parted curtains the dancers are seen gliding past. Jessie moves by now in the arms of Barney, and in a few moments is followed along the side of the hall by Harry wheeling himself in his chair and watching them. Mrs. Foran and the two men look on and become more attentive when among the dancers Susie, in the arms of Surgeon Maxwell, Jessie partnered with Barney, and Harry move past.*]

Sylvester [*as Susie goes by*]. Susie Monican's lookin' game enough tonight for anything.

Simon. Hardly remindful of her one-time fear of God.

Sylvester [*as Jessie goes by followed by Harry*]. There he goes, still followin' them.

Simon. And Jessie's looking as if she was tired of her maidenhood, too.

Mrs. Foran. The thin threads holdin' her dress up sidlin' down over her shoulders, an' her catchin' them up again at the tail end of the second before it was too late.

Simon [*grinning*]. And Barney's hand inching up, inching up to pull them a little lower when they're sliding down.

Mrs. Foran. Astonishin' the way girls are advertisin' their immodesty. Whenever one of them sits down, in my heart I pity the poor men havin' to view the disedifyin' sight of the full length of one leg couched over another.

Teddy [*forgetful*]. A damn nice sight, all the same, I think.

Mrs. Foran [*indignantly*]. One would imagine such a thought would jar a man's mind that had kissed goodbye to the sight of his eyes.

Teddy. Oh, don't be tickin' off every word I say!

Mrs. Foran [*after an astonished pause, whipping the glass out of Teddy's hand*]. Damn the drop more, now, you'll get for the rest of the evenin'.

[*The band suddenly stops playing, and the couples seen just then through the doorway stop dancing and look attentively up the hall. After a slight pause, Harry in his chair, pushed by Susie, comes in through the entrance; his face is pale and drawn, his breath comes in quick faint gasps, and his head is leaning sideways on the back of the chair. Mrs. Heegan is on one side of Harry, and Surgeon Maxwell, who is in dinner-jacket style of evening dress, wearing his medals, including the D.S.O., walks on the other. Harry is wheeled*] *over near the open window. Barney and Jessie, standing in the entrance, look on and listen.*

Maxwell.   Here near the window. [*To Mrs. Heegan*] He'll be all right, Mrs. Heegan, in a second; a little faint—too much excitement. When he recovers a little, I'd get him home.

Harry [*faintly but doggedly*].   Napoo home, napoo. Not yet. I'm all right. I'll spend a little time longer in the belly of an hour bulgin' out with merriment. Carry on.

Maxwell.   Better for you to go home, Heegan.

Harry.   When they drink to the Club from the Cup—the Silver Tassie— that I won three times, three times for them—that first was filled to wet the lips of Jessie and of me—I'll go, but not yet. I'm all right; my name is yet only a shadow on the Roll of Honour.

Mrs. Heegan.   Come home, Harry; you're gettin' your allowance only on the understandin' that you take care of yourself.

Harry.   Get the Cup. I'll mind it here till you're ready to send it round to drink to the Avondales—on the table here beside me. Bring the Cup; I'll mind it here on the table beside me.

Maxwell.   Get the Cup for him, someone.

　　　[*Simon goes to the hall and returns with the Cup, which he gives to Harry.*

Harry [*holding the Cup out*].   A first drink again for me, for me alone this time, for the shell that hit me bursts for ever between Jessie and me. [*To Simon*] Go on, man, fill out the wine!

Maxwell [*to Simon*].   A little—just a glass. Won't do him any harm. [*To Harry*] Then you'll have to remain perfectly quiet, Heegan.

Harry.   The wine—fill out the wine!

Simon [*to Harry*].   Red wine or white?

Harry.   Red wine, red like the faint remembrance of the fires in France; red wine like the poppies that spill their petals on the breasts of the dead men. No, white wine, white like the stillness of the millions that have removed their clamours from the crowd of life. No, red wine; red like the blood that was shed for you and for many for the commission of sin! [*He drinks the wine.*] Steady, Harry, and lift up thine eyes unto the hills. [*Roughly to those around him*] What are you all gaping at?

Maxwell.   Now, now, Heegan—you must try to keep quiet.

Susie.   And when you've rested and feel better, you will sing for us a Negro Spiritual, and point the melody with the ukelele.

Mrs. Heegan. Just as he used to do.

Sylvester. Behind the trenches.

Simon. In the Rest Camps.

Mrs. Foran. Out in France.

Harry. Push your sympathy away from me, for I'll have none of it. [*He wheels his chair quickly towards the dance hall.*] Go on with the dancing and keep the ball a-rolling. [*Calling loudly at the entrance*] Trumpets and drum begin! [*The band begins to play.*] Dance and dance and dance. [*He listens for a moment.*] Sink into merriment again, and sling your cares to God! [*He whirls round in the chair to the beat of the tune. Dancers are seen gliding past entrance.*] Dear God, I can't. [*He sinks sideways on his chair.*] I must, must rest. [*He quietly recites:*]

> For a spell here I will stay,
> Then pack up my body and go—
> For mine is a life on the ebb,
> Yours a full life on the flow!

> [*Harry goes over to far side of window and looks out into garden. Mrs. Heegan is on his right and Teddy on his left; Simon and Sylvester a little behind, looking on. Mrs. Foran to the right of Mrs. Heegan. Surgeon Maxwell and Susie, who are a little to the front, watch for a moment, then the Surgeon puts his arm round Susie and the pair glide off into the dance hall.*]

> [*When Surgeon Maxwell and Susie glide in to the motions of the dance through the entrance into the dance hall, the curtains are pulled together. A few moments' pause. Teddy silently puts his hand on Harry's shoulder, and they both stare into the garden.*]

Simon. The air'll do him good.

Sylvester. An' give him breath to sing his song an' play the ukelele.

Mrs. Heegan. Just as he used to do.

Sylvester. Behind the trenches.

Simon. In the Rest Camps.

Mrs. Foran. Out in France.

Harry. I can see, but I cannot dance.

Teddy. I can dance, but I cannot see.

Harry. Would that I had the strength to do the things I see.

Teddy. Would that I could see the things I've strength to do.

Harry.   The Lord hath given and the Lord hath taken away.

Teddy.   Blessed be the name of the Lord.

Mrs. Foran.   I do love the ukelele, especially when it goes tinkle, tinkle, tinkle in the night-time.

Sylvester.   Bringin' before you glistenin' bodies of blacks, coilin' themselves an' shufflin' an' prancin' in a great jungle dance; shakin' assegais an' spears to the rattle, rattle, rattle an' thud, thud, thud of the tom-toms.

Mrs. Foran.   There's only one possible musical trimmin' to the air of a Negro Spiritual, an' that's the tinkle, tinkle, tinkle of a ukelele.

Harry.   The rising sap in trees I'll never feel.

Teddy.   The hues of branch or leaf I'll never see.

Harry.   There's something wrong with life when men can walk.

Teddy.   There's something wrong with life when men can see.

Harry.   I never felt the hand that made me helpless.

Teddy.   I never saw the hand that made me blind.

Harry.   Life came and took away the half of life.

Teddy.   Life took from me the half he left with you.

Harry.   The Lord hath given and the Lord hath taken away.

Teddy.   Blessed be the name of the Lord.

> [*Susie comes quickly in by entrance, goes over to the table and, looking at several bottles of wine, selects one. She is going hurriedly back, when, seeing Harry, she goes over to him.*

Susie [*kindly*].   How are you now, Harry?

Harry.   All right, thank you.

Susie.   That's good.

> [*Susie is about to hurry away, when Mrs. Foran stops her with a remark.*

Mrs. Foran [*with a meaning gesture*].   He's takin' it cushy till you're ready to hear him singin' his Negro Spiritual, Miss.

Susie.   Oh, God, I'd nearly forgotten that. They'll be giving out the balloons at the next dance, and when that fox-trot's over he'll have to come in and sing us the Spiritual.

Mrs. Heegan.   Just as he used to do.

Simon.   Behind the trenches.

Sylvester.   In the Rest Camps.

Mrs. Foran.   Out in France.

Susie.   As soon as the Balloon Dance is over, Harry, out through the garden and in by the front entrance with you, so that you'll be ready to to start as they all sit down. And after the song, we'll drink to the Club from the Silver Tassie.

> [*She hurries back to the hall with the bottle of wine.*

Mrs. Foran.   I'm longin' to hear Harry on the ukelele.

Harry.   I hope I'll be able to do justice to it.

Mrs. Heegan.   Of course you will, Harry.

Harry [*nervously*].   Before a crowd. Forget a word and it's all up with you.

Simon.   Try it over now, softly; the sound couldn't carry as far as the hall.

Sylvester.   It'll give you confidence in yourself.

Harry [*to Simon*].   Show us the ukelele, Simon.

> [*Simon gets the ukelele and gives it to Harry.*

Teddy.   If I knew the ukelele it might wean me a little way from the darkness.

> [*Harry pulls a few notes, tuning the ukelele, then he softly sings.*

Harry:
> Swing low, sweet chariot, comin' for to carry me home,
> Swing low, sweet chariot, comin' for to carry me home.
> I looked over Jordan, what did I see, comin' for to carry me home?
> A band of angels comin' after me—comin' for to carry me home.

> [*A voice in the hall is heard shouting through a megaphone.*

Voice.   Balloons will be given out now! Given out now—the balloons!

Mrs. Foran [*excitedly*].   They're goin' to send up the balloons! They're going to let the balloons fly now!

Harry [*singing*]:
> Swing low, sweet chariot, comin' for to carry me home.
> Swing low, sweet chariot, comin' for to carry me home.

Mrs. Foran [*as Harry is singing*].   Miss Monican wants us all to see the flyin' balloons.

> [*She catches Teddy's arm and runs with him into the hall.*

Simon.   We must all see the flyin' balloons.

Mrs. Heegan [*running into hall*].   Red balloons and black balloons.

Simon [*following Mrs. Heegan*].   Green balloons and blue balloons.

Sylvester [*following Mrs. Heegan*].   Yellow balloons and puce balloons.

> [*All troop into the hall, leaving the curtains apart, and Harry alone with his ukelele. Through the entrance various coloured balloons that have been tossed into the air can be seen, mid sounds of merriment and excitement.*

Harry [*softly and slowly*].   Comin' for to carry me home.

> [*He throws the ukelele into an armchair, sits still for a moment, then goes to the table, takes up the Silver Cup, and wheels himself into the garden.*

> [*After a pause Barney looks in, then enters pulling Jessie by the hand, letting the curtains fall together again. Then he goes quickly to window, shuts and bolts it, drawing-to one half of the curtains, goes back to Jessie, catches her hand again, and tries to draw her towards room on the left. During the actions that follow the dance goes merrily on in the hall.*

Jessie [*holding up a broken shoulder-strap and pulling back towards the hall*].   Barney, no. God, I'd be afraid he might come in on us alone.

> [*Hands part the curtains and throw in coloured streamers that encircle Jessie and Barney.*

Barney.   Damn them! . . . He's gone, I tell you, to sing the song an' play the ukelele.

Jessie [*excited and afraid*].   See, they're watching us. No, Barney. You mustn't. I'll not go! [*Barney seizes Jessie in his arms and forces her towards the door on the left.*] You wouldn't be good. I'll not go into that room.

Barney.   I will be good, I tell you! I just want to be alone with you for a minute.

> [*Barney loosens Jessie's other shoulder-strap, so that her dress leaves her shoulders and bosom bare.*

Jessie [*near the door left, as Barney opens it*].   You've loosened my dress —I knew you weren't going to be good. [*As she kisses him passionately*] Barney, Barney—you shouldn't be making me do what I don't want to do!

Barney [*holding her and trying to pull her into room*].   Come on, Jessie, you needn't be afraid of Barney—we'll just rest a few minutes from the dancing.

> [*At that part of the window uncurtained Harry is seen peering in.*

He then wheels his chair back and comes on to the centre of the window-frame with a rush, bursting the catch and speeding into the room, coming to a halt, angry and savage, before Barney and Jessie.

Harry.   So you'd make merry over my helplessness in front of my face, in front of my face, you pair of cheats! You couldn't wait till I'd gone, so that my eyes wouldn't see the joy I wanted hurrying away from me over to another? Hurt her breast pulling your hand quick out of her bodice, did you? [*To Jessie*] Saved you in the nick of time, my lady, did I? [*To Barney*] Going to enjoy yourself on the same little couch where she, before you formed an image in her eye, acted the part of an amateur wife, and I acted the part of an amateur husband—the black couch with the green and crimson butterflies, in the yellow bushes, where she and me often tired of the things you're dangling after now!

Jessie.   He's a liar, he's a liar, Barney! He often tried it on with coaxing first and temper afterwards, but it always ended in a halt that left him where he started.

Harry.   If I had my hands on your white neck I'd leave marks there that crowds of kisses from your Barney wouldn't moisten away.

Barney.   You half-baked Lazarus, I've put up with you all the evening, so don't force me now to rough-handle the bit of life the Jerries left you as a souvenir!

Harry.   When I wanted to slip away from life, you brought me back with your whispered "Think of the tears of Jess, think of the tears of Jess", but Jess has wiped away her tears in the ribbon of your Cross, and this poor crippled jest gives a flame of joy to the change; but when you get her, may you find in her the pressed-down emptiness of a whore!

Barney [*running over and seizing Harry*].   I'll tilt the leaking life out of you, you jealous, peering pimp!

Jessie [*trying to hold Barney back*].   Barney, Barney, don't! don't!

Harry [*appealingly*].   Barney, Barney! My heart—you're stopping it!

Jessie [*running to entrance and shouting in*].   Help! help! They're killing each other!

[*In the hall the dance stops. Surgeon Maxwell runs in, followed by Susie, Simon, Sylvester, Mrs. Foran, Mrs. Heegan, and lastly Teddy finding his way over to the window. Dancers gather around entrance and look on.*

[*Surgeon Maxwell, running over, separates Barney from Harry.*

Maxwell. What's this? Come, come—we can't have this sort of thing going on.

Mrs. Heegan. He was throttlin' him, throttlin' a poor helpless creature, an' if anything happens, he and that painted slug Jessie Taite 'll be held accountable!

Maxwell. This can't be allowed to go on. You'll have to bring him home. Any more excitement would be dangerous.

Mrs. Heegan. This is what he gets from Jessie Taite for sittin' on the stairs through the yawnin' hours of the night, racin' her off to the play an' the pictures, an' plungin' every penny he could keep from me into presents for the consolidation of the courtship!

Maxwell. Bring the boy home, woman, bring the boy home.

Sylvester [*fiercely to Jessie*]. And money of mine in one of the gewgaws scintillatin' in her hair!

Jessie. What gewgaw? What gewgaw?

[*Coloured streamers are thrown in by those standing at entrance, which fall on and encircle some of the group around Harry.*

Sylvester. The tiarara I gave you two Christmases ago with the yellow berries and the three flutterin' crimson swallows!

Harry [*faintly and bitterly, with a hard little laugh*]. Napoo Barney Bagnal and napoo Jessie Taite. A merry heart throbs coldly in my bosom; a merry heart in a cold bosom—or is it a cold heart in a merry bosom? [*He gathers a number of the coloured streamers and winds them round himself and chair.*] Teddy! [*Harry catches Teddy by the sleeve and winds some more streamers round him.*] Sing a song, man, and show the stuff you're made of!

Maxwell [*catching hold of Mrs. Heegan's arm*]. Bring him home, woman. [*Maxwell catches Sylvester's arm.*] Get him home, man.

Harry. Dear God, this crippled form is still your child. [*To Mrs. Heegan*] Dear mother, this helpless thing is still your son. Harry Heegan, me, who, on the football field, could crash a twelve-stone flyer off his feet. For this dear Club three times I won the Cup, and grieve in reason I was just too weak this year to play again. And now, before I go, I give you all the Cup, the Silver Tassie, to have and to hold for ever, evermore. [*From his chair he takes the Cup with the two sides hammered close together, and holds it out to them.*] Mangled and bruised as I am bruised and mangled. Hammered free from all its comely shape. Look, there is Jessie writ, and here is Harry, the one name safely separated from the other. [*He flings it on the floor.*] Treat it kindly. With care it may be opened out, for Barney there to drink to Jess, and Jessie there to drink to Barney.

Teddy. Come, Harry, home to where the air is soft. No longer can you stand upon a hill-top; these empty eyes of mine can never see from one. Our best is all behind us—what's in front we'll face like men, dear comrade of the blood-fight and the battlefront!

Harry. What's in front we'll face like men! [*Harry goes out by the window, Sylvester pushing the chair, Teddy's hand on Harry's shoulder, Mrs. Heegan slowly following. Those left in the room watch them going out through the garden, turning to the right till they are all out of sight. As he goes out of window*] The Lord hath given and man hath taken away!

Teddy [*heard from the garden*]. Blessed be the name of the Lord!

[*The band in the hall begins to play again. Those in hall begin to dance.*

Maxwell. Come on, all, we've wasted too much time already.

Susie [*to Jessie, who is sitting quietly in a chair*]. Come on, Jessie— get your partner; [*roguishly*] you can have a quiet time with Barney later on.

Jessie. Poor Harry!

Susie. Oh nonsense! If you'd passed as many through your hands as I, you'd hardly notice one. [*To Jessie*] Jessie, Teddy Foran and Harry Heegan have gone to live their own way in another world. Neither I nor you can lift them out of it. No longer can they do the things we do. We can't give sight to the blind or make the lame walk. We would if we could. It is the misfortune of war. As long as wars are waged, we shall be vexed by woe; strong legs shall be made useless and bright eyes made dark. But we, who have come through the fire unharmed, must go on living. [*Pulling Jessie from the chair*] Come along, and take your part in life! [*To Barney*] Come along, Barney, and take your partner into the dance!

[*Barney comes over, puts his arm round Jessie, and they dance into the hall. Susie and Surgeon Maxwell dance together. As they dance the Waltz "Over the Waves", some remain behind drinking. Two of these sing the song to the same tune as the dance.*

Maxwell:
Swing into the dance,
Take joy when it comes, ere it go;

For the full flavour of life
Is either a kiss or a blow.
He to whom joy is a foe,
Let him wrap himself up in his woe;
For he is a life on the ebb,
We a full life on the flow!

[*All in the hall dance away with streamers and balloons flying.
Simon and Mrs. Foran sit down and watch the fun through the
entrance. Mrs. Foran lights a cigarette and smokes. A pause as they
look on.*

Mrs. Foran. It's a terrible pity Harry was too weak to stay an' sing his
song, for there's nothing I love more than the ukelele's tinkle, tinkle in
the night-time.

CURTAIN

WITHIN THE GATES

(1933)

STAGE VERSION

If possible, the Curtain intervening between the opening of the play and the scenes following, should be one showing the Park Gates, stiff and formal, dignified and insolent. The bars should shine with the silver gleam of aluminium paint, and cross or diagonal bars should be a deep and sombre black. All space between the bars should be dark—but not too dark—green. The gates proper are flanked by generous panels of a vivid yellow, representing the piers, lower than the bars, and topped by copings of orange-coloured panels. This curtain, when it is pulled back, represents the opening of the gates; and, when it falls back into its place, represents the closing of the gates: or, the outline of the gates may be suggested on the curtain.

The above idea of a front curtain was derived from Eugene O'Neill's suggestion of a front curtain for his great play, *Mourning Becomes Electra*.

✤ ✤ ✤

CHARACTERS IN THE PLAY

The Dreamer
Older Chair Attendant
Younger Chair Attendant
The Bishop
The Bishop's Sister
The Atheist
The Policewoman
1st Nursemaid
2nd Nursemaid
A Guardsman
A Gardener
1st Evangelist
2nd Evangelist
The Young Woman
A Young Salvation Army Officer
The Old Woman
A Man wearing a Bowler Hat
The Man with the Stick (*afterwards, an umbrella*)
Man wearing a Trilby Hat
Man wearing a Straw One (*afterwards, a cap*)
A Crowd of the Down-and-Out

    A Chorus of Young Men and Maidens

SCENE I · Within a Park. On a Spring Morning.

SCENE II · Within a Park. On a Summer Noon.

SCENE III · Within a Park. On an Autumn Evening.

SCENE IV · Within a Park. On a Winter's Night.

SCENE I

Spring. Morning.

Within a Park on a Spring morning.

A clear, light-blue sky, against which are shown, in places, the interlaced dark-brown branches of trees, dotted with green, yellow, and red buds.

The green sward in front slopes up towards the back, but in no way high enough to prevent a view of the spaciousness of the Park behind. In the centre of the slope are a few wide steps leading to the top, where, a little to one side, stands a War Memorial in the form of a steel-helmeted soldier, the head bent on the breast, skeleton-like hands leaning on the butt-end of a rifle. Bushes allow the figure to be seen only from the waist up. The body and arms of the figure are shaped in a sharply defined way; the hat a wide circle; and the features are cut in long, sharp, and angular lines. The figure stands out grey against the blue sky and the green shrubs, and seems to be shrinking back from the growing interests brought into being by new life and her thrusting activities.

The rise of the slope is sprinkled with large, formalized figures of daffodils.

At the foot of the slope are paths branching to the right and to the left, that on the left flowing into a wider one encircling the Park lake, from which can be occasionally heard the cries of the water-fowl swimming on the water or preening themselves on the banks.

Birds are heard singing in a subdued but busy way, as they search for food or build their nests.

Formally shaped chairs are here and there, and one or two stiff and dignified-looking benches are near the foot of the slope. They are painted so as to mingle with the colours of the scene, and are hardly noticeable. The scheme of colour is a delicate green and light blue, patterned by the yellow daffodils and the bare, bud-dotted branches of the trees.

As the gates are opening, the Dreamer enters, and passes through them into the Park. He is gazing with an intensely dreaming expression at a paper which he holds in his left hand. His right hand, holding a short pencil, moves in a gentle, dreamy way, beating time, as he murmurs the opening bars of "Our Mother the Earth is a Maiden Again". He crosses out as the Chorus enters, singing, followed by various people, who move about at the back, up, down, and about the paths, without jostle or confusion.

A Chorus of Young Boys and Girls, representing trees and flowers, enter, singing.

First, a girl whose skirt represents a white crocus, veined with blue; next, a boy in black on whose breast is a stylized pattern of a beech-tree leaf; then a girl whose skirt represents a blue cornflower; next, a boy on whose

*breast is a formally shaped oak leaf; then a girl whose skirt represents a
daffodil; next, a boy on whose breast is the pattern of a maple leaf.*

*The Chorus remain in front, while the crowd move about as they listen,
or when they join in the singing.*

Chorus [*singing*]:
  Our mother the Earth is a maiden again, young, fair, and a maiden
    again.
  Our mother the Earth is a maiden again, she's young, fair, and a
    maiden again.
  Her thoughts are a dance as she seeks out her Bridegroom, the Sun,
    through the lovely confusion of singing of birds, and of blossom
    and bud.
  She feels the touch of his hand on her hair, on her cheeks; in the
    budding of trees,
  She feels the kiss of his love on her mouth, on her breast, as she
    dances along,

Crowd [*joining in*]:
  Through the lovely confusion of singing of birds, and of blossom and
    bud.
  Her thoughts are a dance as she seeks out her Bridegroom, the Sun,
    through the lovely confusion of singing of birds, and of blossom
    and bud.

Chorus:
  She hears the fiercely sung song of the birds, busy building new
    homes in the hedge;
  She hears a challenge to life and to death as she dances along,

Crowd [*joining in*]:
  Through the lovely confusion of singing of birds, and of blossom
    and bud.
  Her thoughts are a dance as she seeks out her Bridegroom, the Sun,
    through the lovely confusion of singing of birds, and of blossom
    and bud.

Chorus and Crowd:
  Our mother the Earth is a maiden again, young, fair, and a maiden
    again.

    [*While the last line is being sung, the Crowd and the Chorus go
    out by different ways, leaving only the two Chair Attendants dust-
    ing the chairs and arranging them. One is young and thin and the
    other is old and stocky, and both are in the last lap of physical de-
    cay. One has a stiff right leg, and the other has a stiff left one. They*

are dressed in long, khaki-coloured cotton coats, and wear peaked caps.

Older One. 'Ow's the poor old leg, todye, Godfrey?

Young One. Oh Gord! 'Ow's yours?

Older One. Aw—sime wye, with honours! I seen that poet chap atryin' to cadge a chire again; sits dahn on one till 'e sees me comin' in the distance.

Young one [not listening—pensively]. Wot'll we do when we file to be able to walk! 'En this singin' gets me dahn. 'Eartless for a crahwd to sing when a man's in misery.

Older One [testily]. Don't let us think of them things! It's our destiny. But I 'ates that poet chap; I 'ates 'im! 'Ate 'is liveliness. Fair cheek 'e 'as. A bum—that's wot 'e 'is. Wouldn't do a dye's work for Gord Almighty. I'd say it to 'is fice, I would.

Young One. Look aht! 'Ere 'e is.

[*The Dreamer comes down the grass slope, crosses over, and sits down on a bench. He watches the Two Attendants. He is a young man, lithely built, though a little thin and pale now from a hard time; but he carries himself buoyantly. His features are rugged; his eyes bright, sometimes flashing in an imaginative mood, but usually quiet and dreamy-looking. His head is covered with a soft black, broad-brimmed hat, and he is wearing a tightly-belted trench mackintosh. Outside the trench coat, around his neck, is a light, vivid orange scarf.*

Dreamer [suddenly]. Here, you two derelict worshippers of fine raiment —when are you going to die?

Older One [angrily]. Mind your own business, see! We 'as more right to life than you 'as. We work—you don't—eh, Godfrey?

Young One. My oath, we 'as!

Dreamer. No one has a right to life who doesn't fight to make it greater. I've watched you fawning on the bishop and on every good coat that sits down on a chair.

Young One. You mind your own business!

[*The Young Woman comes down the slope and crosses the sward to go out to the left. She has a preoccupied and rather anxious look on her face, and appears to be searching for someone.*

[*She is very pretty, and her figure would make most young men immediately forget the seventh commandment. Her face is a little pale, but this paleness is hidden by a cautious and clever make-up. She has an intelligent look, which is becoming a little worn by contact with the selfishness and meanness of the few clients that have patronised her; for these, though unable to resist the desire to have her, hate her subconsciously before they go with her, and consciously detest her when their desires have been satisfied. She has read a little, but not enough; she has thought a little, but not enough; she is deficient in self-assurance, and is too generous and sensitive to be a clever whore, and her heart is not in the business.*

[*Convent tales of punishments reserved for the particular sins tangled round sex expression have left in her mind lusty images of hellfire. She is dressed in a black tailored suit, topped by a scarlet hat. On the hat is an ornament, in black, of a crescent; and the hip of her dress is decorated with a scarlet one. The Dreamer sees her, rises, and is about to follow her. She stops and faces him.*

Young Woman.   I am troubled; I am anxious; please don't follow me.

Dreamer.   I shall follow after loveliness all the days of my life.

Young Woman.   Not just now, please; I do not want you. [*She turns to go; he follows slowly. She turns, to say hysterically*] Go away, please!

[*She goes out. He returns, crestfallen, to his seat on the bench. The Attendants snigger.*

Older One.   The likes of 'er ain't for the likes of 'im.

Young One [*to the Dreamer*].   A fine choke-off, wha'?
[*Dreamer rises, catches each by the coat-collar, and shakes them.*

Dreamer [*roughly*].   Ye lost ones! Will ye starve and droop and die without a dream? Even the lame and the halt can hunt out a shrine! Will ye mock at the better ones who refuse to die like sheep?

Attendants [*together*].   Eh, there, leggo! Someone call a perliceman!

[*The Atheist comes in from a path above, sees the angry scene, and hurries down to stop it.*

Atheist [*catching the Dreamer by the arm*].   Now then, friend, now then; let withered life die in its own sour way, without pushing it to a sudden and unprovided end!

Dreamer [*pushing the Attendants from him—one to the right, the other to the left*].   Away, and cower in your corner, till life hoodooes you out of the misery you both love! Away, the pair of you, who make a nightmare of the dream of God!

[*The Attendants slink off, one to the right, the other to the left. The Dreamer and the Atheist sit on the bench together.*

Atheist [*warningly*].   Take care, friend: you'd pay as high a penalty for hurting hopelessness as you would for a life of promise or one of proved production.

Dreamer.   I know; I lost my temper. Never mind that now. I've seen her; she passed by here just before you came.

Atheist [*rising*].   Passed by 'ere? I'm off in the opposite direction.

Dreamer [*stopping him*].   No fear of meeting her; she won't come back. I tried to keep her, but she wouldn't stay a second.

Atheist.   Oh, lay off the young lass, Dreamer. Let 'er go 'er own wye—up the hill of life or dahn it.

Dreamer.   She's too lonely to be left alone, Ned; and too pretty; intelligent, too, as you say.

Atheist [*impatiently*].   I know all that! She 'as a fine mind, if she'd only use it the right way. But it's forever darting forward, back; to the left to-day, to the right to-morrow—no 'uman being could stand it. I'm glad I'm only her step-da.

Dreamer.   Who is, and where is, her real daddy?

Atheist.   Stoodent of theology, the story goes: fell in love with a pretty housemaid, and she responded. When the mother knew what was abaht to happen, she knocked at the college gate, but was driven off. When a few years old, the kid was shoved into a church institootion, where the nuns, being what she was—a child of sin—, paid her special attention; an' the terrors an' dangers of hell became the child's chief enjoyment!

Dreamer.   Good God! [*Earnestly*] Ned, we must never ease off the fight for a life that is free from fear!

Atheist.   Never, Dreamer, never. Then the mother married an Irish dragoon, a brave, decent man, Dreamer, home from the front on leave; had a starlit time with the warrior for a week; then the dragoon disappeared in one of those vanishing advances from the front line an' the widow settles dahn on 'er pension.

Dreamer.   Then she fastened on to you, eh?

Atheist.   To tell the truth, it was I fastened on to 'er. Even when I met 'er, she was still the kind of woman would make a man long for something to 'appen—you know, Dreamer?

Dreamer.   Ay, I know—too damned well!

Atheist.   Then I delivered the child from the church institootion, sayin' I was the father. I did my best for 'er, takin' awye a supernatural 'eaven from over 'er 'ead, an' an unnatural 'ell from under 'er feet; but she never quite escaped. D'ye know, one time, the lass near knew the whole of Pine's *Age of Reason* off by 'eart!

Dreamer. And did you bring her into touch with song?

Atheist. Song? Oh, I had no time for song!

Dreamer. You led her from one darkness into another, man. [*He rises and walks about—angrily*] Will none of you ever guess that man can study man, or worship God, in dance and song and story! [*Appealingly*] Ah, Ned, if you could but see her with the eyes of youth, you would not let her live so lonely.

Atheist. I helped her all I could. Out of the earnings of a first-class carpenter, I gave 'er a good education, an' taught 'er a lot myself; but it was all no good—she refused to think as I did. The 'ome's broken up, now, and I'm not eager to try to get it together agine.

Dreamer. How broken up?

Atheist. You see, when the maid came close to womanhood, the mother turned religious, an' begun to 'ate the kid, sayin' that while the kid was there, 'er sin was ever in front of 'er fice. Then she took to drink an' violence.

Dreamer. A sweet home for a girl coming also to womanhood!

Atheist. After a long time of patient endoorance, one day the girl ups an', withaht a word, goes; an' a month after, I goes too; so 'ere she is, her whole life a desire for a bright time of it; an' 'ere I am, a speaker rending the strands of superstition's web thet keeps poor men from movin'.

Dreamer. Give the lovely lass one more chance, speaker; live the last years of your life with loveliness.

Atheist. Not damn likely; the longer I'm by myself, the more I likes it.

[*While they have been speaking the last few words, the Man with the Stick has appeared on the slope above.*

Man with Stick [*calling down to Atheist*]. 'Ave you got tonight's speech ready, Ned?

Atheist [*taking note-book from a pocket*]. Not yet, Bill.

Man with Stick. Get a move on: we 'as to bounce the idea of a Gord from men's minds, so make it strong.

[*The Two Chair Attendants limp in, carrying a chair between them. They set it down, stand panting for a while, then the Older One begins to give it a dust, the Man with the Stick watching them contemptuously, and dubiously shaking his grey head.*

Man with Stick [*going close to Older Attendant*]. 'Ere, 'ave you an inquirin' mind, friend?

Older One. Eh? Wot?

Man with Stick. I asks if you 'as an inquirin' mind. [*He taps the chair with the stick*]. Wot is this? A chair. Does thet tell you all abaht it? No. Wot's it myde of? Wood. Nah, if it was myde of cork it would be lighter; but if it was myde of lead it would be 'eavier—see?

Older One. Ay?

Man with Stick. Ay? Not ay, but wye?

Older One. Wye? Wot wye?

Man with Stick [*impatiently*]. Wot wye! Listen, man. [*Hitting the chair with stick.*] Wood; 'ard. Nah wye's the chair 'ard? Is it doo to density, or is it not?

Older One. I don't ask no questions of chairs.

Young One. We 'as to attend to our werk, see?

Man with Stick [*woe in his voice*]. No brrine!

[*The two Nursemaids, the Under One pushing the fine pram, appear behind Man with the Stick.*

Younger Nursemaid [*imperiously*]. Gangway there!

[*The pram strikes his heels, and he jumps aside, his mouth opening for an angry exclamation; but when he sees the splendid pram, he closes it without saying a word. The Upper Nursemaid picks out a chair farthest from the others. The Chair Attendants run over bearing a chair between them for the Under Maid, and the Older One dusts both the chairs vigorously.*

Older One [*after dusting*]. Now, miss. Nice day, miss.

Upper Nursemaid [*shortly*]. Very nice.

Older One. To cart such a byeby abaht's a responsible thing, I'd say, miss.

Upper Nursemaid [*stiffly*]. I suppose so. I don't feel it. [*She sees his dirty hand is resting on the pram.*] Take that dirty paw off the pram at once! This is a countess's baby!

Older One [*pulling his hand away as if the pram was red-hot*]. Oh, excuse me, miss. I forgot for the minute!

Upper Nursemaid [*loftily*]. Go away; we're season tickets; go away!

[*The Attendant slinks off from the pram as the Bishop, followed by his Sister, appears coming down the slope from behind the Memorial. The Policewoman strolls in from the path on the left.*

Atheist [*mockingly—over to the Nursemaids*]. Must be careful of a countess's byeby!

Upper Nursemaid [*with great dignity*]. A countess's byeby's a considery-tion, I'd like you all to know.

[*The Bishop and his Sister come down among the crowd. The Bishop is a heavily built man of sixty or so. His head, his feet, and hands are large; his voice, once deep and sonorous, has become a little husky. The pretentious briskness of his movements is an attempt to hide from others the fact that he is beginning to fail. He is anxious to show to all he meets that he is an up-to-the-present-minute clergyman, and that those who wear the stole are, on the whole, a lusty, natural, broad-minded, cheery crowd. He is in a black cassock, wears a purple stock round his neck, and his head is covered with a purple biretta or a scarlet one. A black ribbon is round his neck, and from the ends of this, which meet on his chest, hangs a large red cross, on which is a white figure of the Saviour.*

[*His Sister is a few years younger, grey-haired, stiff, and formal. She has more common sense than her brother, but, while there is a suggestion of good-nature about the Bishop, there is no suggestion whatever of softness about the form or manner of his Sister. Her dress is of grey stuff, stiff like steel.*

Bishop [*breezily*]. Hello, boys; good morning, Constable. [*To Nurse-maids*] Hello, girls!

Attendants [*together*]. 'Ello, your reverence.

Policewoman [*with a dignified salute*]. Morning, sir.

Bishop [*buoyantly*]. Glorious nip of crispness in the air of a Spring morning, isn't there?

Policewoman. Exhilarating, I'd say.

Older One. Gits a man goin'.

Younger One [*lilting*]. Yes, let me like a soldier fall, dideray diderum dideree.

Bishop. Flowers appear on the earth; the time of singing of birds is come, and the voice of the turtle is heard in the land—God speaking of Spring, friends!

Policewoman. Quate, sir.

Young One. 'Its it off nacely, sir.

Dreamer [*to the Bishop*].   Not God, but a poet speaking of Spring, sir. Render to God the things that are God's and to the poet the things that are his.

Bishop [*to the Dreamer—smilingly*].   God is in all, and God is all things, sir.

Atheist [*combatively*].   Would the reverend en' learned gentleman tell us poor people 'oo is Gord, wot 'e is, en' where 'e is located?

Policewoman [*to the Atheist, stiffly*].   You keep your almighty arguments for your meetings.

Older One [*viciously*].   'Ear, 'ear!

Bishop [*to Policewoman—graciously*].   Never mind, Constable; there are always those who never will give thanks to God for life.

Dreamer.   Always, when there are those who have no life for which to thank Him.

> [*Two prowling Evangelists come shuffling in. Each has a frame strapped to his body from which rise two upright pieces between which is a poster, looking like a square banner over their heads. On the first one, in red, is the phrase Once to Die, and on the second, in black, Then the Judgement.*

> [*The First Evangelist has a lemon-shaped head, staring, stupid-looking eyes, shrunken cheeks, surly lines round a wide mouth, and ears that stick out from the side of his head.*

> [*The Second has a big head, coarse face, heavy, hanging lips, and a small snubby nose. As he chants, he continually blinks his eyes. Both are shabbily dressed, and look, for all the world, like sullen, long-forgotten clowns. They shuffle in among the disputants, each pointing to the warning posters over their heads.*

1st Evangelist.   Once to Die.

2nd Evangelist.   After that The Judgement.

1st Evangelist [*chanting*]:
> Is it well with thy soul?
> Is it well, is it well with thy soul?

2nd Evangelist [*chanting*]:
> It is well with my soul.
> It is well, it is well with my soul.

> [*They chant themselves out, looking back to gather the others into the warning they give.*

Atheist [*mockingly—to the Bishop*].   Two more Richmonds in the field!

Young One [*encouraging the Bishop*].   Never you mind 'im or them, sir;
—go on torking abaht the Spring en' the birds!

> [*The birds sing merrily.*

Bishop [*joyously*].   Listen! The busy birds warbling a sylvan sonata.
Facing out life with a song! No shaking of the head here in denial of
God's goodness and glory. Sursum corda—lift up your hearts!

Dreamer.   We lift them up unto the birds.

Older One [*gushingly*].   The birds bring a man 'ope. Even with the
doo 'eavy on the grass, a feller begins to feel spry en' elevated when
they stert their chirruping.

Policewoman.   Not a daht abaht it.

Bishop's Sister.   Gilbert, come and look at the swans.

Bishop [*with conviction—to the Policewoman*].   Do you know, Constable, that, to an observing mind, it seems to be conclusive that the most
beautiful part of God's creation—apart from man, of course—

Policewoman.   Quate—setting man en' woman aside for a moment.

Bishop.   Quite. The most beautiful part of God's manifold creation is,
undoubtedly, the birds!

> [*The Bishop lifts his head and looks up at the sky; then the
> Policewoman does the same, and, lastly, the two Chair Attendants
> lift their heads and crane their necks in an upward look.*

Bishop.   Brave little birds.

Policewoman.   Beautiful little birds.

Attendants [*together*].   Beautiful, innocent little birds.

Man with Stick [*suddenly leaning forward—imperatively*].   'Ere, 'ow do
birds resist the lawrs of gravitation? Come, quick—the lot of you—
think!   [*They all lower their heads again, together.*

Young One [*enthusiastically*].   Never you mind 'im, sir. Wot you says
reminds man that Gord watches even over the fall of the sparrer!

Atheist [*mockingly*].   Ay, an' the fall of the 'awk on the sparrer to tear
it to pieces!

Older One [*hotly*].   You shut your rotten mouth, will you! Warnt to 'ear
yourself torkin', torkin', do you? Try to look at things in perspective,
carn't you? Wot's you or me in the general scheme of things, eh? Speck
o' dust, blide o' grass, a nought, a nothing. Wish Jimmy Douglas of the
Daily Express was 'ere to 'ear you. 'E's the man would stun you both
with truth! [*To his fellow Attendant*] Wot d'ye sye, Godfrey?

Young One.   'E's a man as knows 'oo's 'oo en' wot's wot.

Older One.   You bet 'e does. 'Ow on a 'olidye, sitting by the sea, under the stars, wot 'e sawr en' wot 'e 'eard. 'Ow 'e marvelled at the star dust 'e could see en' the star dust 'e couldn't see; en' 'ow 'e was filled with terror en' fear as 'e 'eard the clock of eternity ticking!

Dreamer.   It won't be long, old man, till you hear the clock of eternity ticking!

Older One [*stormily*].   Wot if it won't? It ain't the end, is it?

Dreamer [*rising from the bench—fervently*].   Kill off the withered mind, the violently-stupid, O Lord, who having nothing to give, have nothing to get!

Bishop's Sister [*pulling Bishop's cassock*].   Gilbert, do come to watch the swans!

Older One [*catching hold of Dreamer's sleeve—violently*].   Thinkin' thet life doesn't keep agoing on when it ends! I yells it aht, I yells it aht—death's only the gytewye to a fuller en' a nobler life!

Dreamer [*angrily shaking off the Attendant's hold*].   Take that dead hand off me! There are some here equal in value to a countess's baby. [*He shoves the Attendant roughly from him so that he lurches back against the pram.*] Be off, and die, and keep a holy distance from the quick and the lively!

Young One [*bawling to the Older One*].   'Erbert, eh, mind the countess's byeby!

Atheist [*mockingly—to the Nursemaid*].   Lady, lady, this is no place for a countess's byeby!

Policewoman [*going to the Nursemaid*].   'E's right; better conduct it to a calmer locality.

[*The two Nursemaids rise hurriedly, cross over the sward, preceded by the Policewoman, and disappear with the pram behind the trees to the left.*

Bishop's Sister [*plucking at his cassock*].   You see, Gilbert! A bishop should be in the midst of the incense, in the sanctuary, safe away from the sour touch of common humanity.

Bishop [*jovially*].   Nonsense, dear! I lose no dignity in getting close to the common people. Get them to talk with us; laugh and joke with us; and then we can expect them to pray with us.

Atheist [*over to the Bishop*].   Prayer? For what? To whom?
    Old memories, faiths infirm and dead,

Ye fools; for which among you deems
His prayer can alter green to red,
Or stones to bread?

Bishop's Sister [*pulling the Bishop away*]. You but mould mockery from the profane thoughts of others. Come and watch the swans. Remember what happened to you in your student days!

[*The Bishop, at the last phrase, stiffens, his face clenches, and he goes off with his Sister without another word.*

Atheist [*as the Bishop is pulled out*]. He 'as a better charnce with the swans than 'e 'as with us!

Man with Stick [*calling from top of slope*]. 'Ere, are you comin' to look up wot it says in *The Origin of the Idea of a God*?

Atheist [*rising to go*]. Must be off, Dreamer. Will you come a bit of the way?

Dreamer. No; I've got a song shaping in my mind, and I must think it out: Song of the Down-and-Out.

Atheist [*indifferently*]. Oh, hymn for the unemployed?

Dreamer. No, no; not the unemployed. They remain men in their misfortune. I keen those who whine through to-day and dread to-morrow; who would for ever furl the flag of life; who fear any idea common thought hasn't had time to bless; those who have a sigh for a song and a sad sigh for a drumbeat.

Atheist. A fair crowd, Dreamer. Well, so-long for the present.

Dreamer. See you at the old place, and we'll have coffee and a sandwich?

Atheist. I'll be there.

[*He goes off with the Man with the Stick. The Dreamer takes out a note-book, and writes in it. The Gardener appears behind, trimming the shrubs with a pair of shears. The Dreamer then strolls up to watch him, the two Chair Attendants put some chairs in order.*

Older One [*attempting brightness*]. I listened to the wireless last night, Godfrey.

Young One. 'Eard anything worth while?

Older One. Part of Pageant of England. Wunnerful! Mide me feel prahd to be en Englishman!

Young One. Wot was it abaht?

Older One.   The guys as was once kings en stytesmen wot mide us all wot we is. Mide me thrill, it did, to 'ear the sahnd of Drike's drum!

Young One.   'Oo's drum?

Older One.   Drike's. The bloke wot beat the Spanish Armyda, en' drove them back to Spine. A ghost-drum is alwyes 'eard beatin' whenever England's in dineger.

Young One [*scornfully*].   Superstition!

[*In the distance are heard faint sounds of the sombre music of the Down-and-Out chant, saddened with the slow beat of a muffled drum. The Attendants stand stiff, a look of fright on their faces.*

Attendants [*together*].   The drum-beat of the Down-and-Out!

Older One [*to his companion*].   Wot'r you stiffenin' for?

Young One [*tensely*].   I warn't stiffenin'. [*A pause.*] Wot'r you styrin' at?

Older One [*tensely*].   I warn't styrin'. Didja hear anything?

Younger One [*tensely*].   No, nothing; did you?

Older One.   Nothing.

[*They go slowly by each other, one to the left, the other to the right, and go out—a deeper limp coming into each lame leg, keeping time to the distant chant and drum-beat.*

[*The Dreamer is watching the Gardener working, handling the blossoms.*

Dreamer.   Happy man to be handling the purple, blue, and yellow of the blossoms.

Gardener.   Let them live and let them die, for I'm not thinking of blossoms at all.

Dreamer.   What are you thinking of then?

Gardener.   Of a dance I take a sweet little lass to, when the sun goes in and the stars come out.

Dreamer.   I envy you the handling of a flower by day and of a girl by night.

Gardener.   When the dance ends, I go to her little flat, her very own flat, where [*he lilts*] She'll be the honeysuckle, I'll be the bee!

Dreamer.   I hope a bee that never leaves a sting behind.

Gardener.   You should see her—a beauty! Thinks I'll marry her; I'm too young to marry yet. Mad to have a kid—matrimony's signature tune;

but not for me, though. An odd lass. A little too serious. Says she wants a chance sometimes to sit and wonder.

Dreamer [*musingly*].   I hear a song in what you've said.

Gardener [*surprised*].   A song? In what?

Dreamer.   In the flowers, heaven, and the girl.

Gardener.   You do, do you? Funny!

> [*The Gardener goes on arranging the flowers, while the Dreamer slowly goes off till he is hidden behind the shrubs. After a pause, the Gardener begins to sing.*

A fig for th' blossoms th' biggest vase can hold,
The flow'rs that face the world shy, the ones that face it bold.
Men may praise them and worship them as something fine and rare,
Lounging through their gorgeous perfumes so deftly hidden there.
But I'll never wonder though some in glee disclose
The white of whitest lily, the red of reddest rose;
For I'll fold in my arms a girl as bright as she is gay,
And tonight the primrose path of love will be a wonder way!

> [*Couples, linking arms, enter from different points, mix and cross by each other, parade about, keeping time with the tune as they join in the singing. The Gardener moves out of sight. The Young Woman is seen moving hurriedly among the couples, taking no heed of the singing, weaving a way through the couples without spoiling the ordered movements, but she doesn't keep in time with the lilt. She looks anxious, and appears to be searching for someone. She disappears while the song is being sung.*

The Crowd of Couples [*singing*]:
When Adam first corner'd Eve, he stood bewildered there,
For he saw beauty shining through a mist of golden hair;
But Eve quickly coaxed him on, and show'd him woman's way,
And so the lover and his lass are king and queen to-day!

So here's to the lasses who bow in beauty's fane,
Who kiss in costly parlour or kiss in country lane;
Let man bend his back to work or bend down his knee to pray,
Still the primrose path of love will ever be a wonder way!

> [*When the couples go, the only ones left are the Guardsman and the Nursemaid, and the Man with the Stick. The Nursemaid and the Guardsman, who has his arm round her, go to a bench. He sits down, and as the Nursemaid proceeds to do the same, he catches her, and sweeps her on to his knee. The Man with the Stick, who had been at the butt of the slope shaking his head contemptuously*

at the singing, now comes down to where the couple is seated, and swings his stick in disdain.

Man with Stick [*scornfully—swinging the stick*].   Nonsense! A lot of it is all nonsense, nonsense!

Guardsman.   Lot of wot?

Man with Stick.   Babble abaht life! Life, man, life! Before we can get sense into it, we've gotta know its meaning: wot it is, where it came from, where it goes.

Guardsman.   Where wot goes?

Man with Stick.   Life, man, life!

Nursemaid [*indignantly*].   You push off. We want to be left alone. We've important things to talk abaht, so push off, please!

Man with Stick [*taken aback*].   Oh? If you ain't eager to learn the truth, I'll push off—[*he sees the Two Evangelists approaching, displaying their placards*] now! [*Muttering as he goes*] Bumptious, brazen ignorance!

[*The Two Evangelists prowl forward, looking left and right for sinners. They spy the Guardsman and the Nursemaid, and shuffle over slowly to them.*]

1st Evangelist [*to the Couple*].   Remember, brother and sister, it's a terrible thing when it comes.

Guardsman.   Wot is? When wot comes?

1st Evangelist.   Death, brother, Death!

2nd Evangelist.   An' after death The Judgement!

1st Evangelist.   Oh, be converted before it is too late.

2nd Evangelist.   Before it is too, too late, too late.

1st Evangelist.   It may be upon you to-day, in an hour, in a moment.

Guardsman.   Wot mye?

1st Evangelist.   Death, brother, death!

Nursemaid [*indignantly*].   We want to be left alone. We've important business to talk about an' do, so push off, please.

1st Evangelist.   Left alone! Devil's desire that, sister. You won't be left alone in hell.

Guardsman [*rising angrily, and pushing them away*].   Here, git! We wants privacy, so git!

Nursemaid [*rising from bench as he is about to sit down again, having got rid of the Evangelists*]. Let's sit dahn on th' grass, 'Arry—it's more comfortable.

Guardsman. So it is.

> [*They recline on the slope. He puts his arms round her, kisses her, and is about to kiss again, when the Policewoman appears opposite, and stares reprovingly at them. She goes over to them.*

Policewoman. You can't do the like of that 'ere. Control yourselves. It doesn't allow such conduct in a public place.

Guardsman [*embarrassed, but trying to be defiant*]. Wot dorsen't?

Policewoman [*sharply*]. Th' lawr, young man, the lawr!

> [*The Couple rise, and go off embarrassed, followed by the Police-woman. As they go off, the Young Woman and the Atheist appear at the top of the slope, and come down it.*

Guardsman [*to the Nursemaid, as they go off*]. As I was asayin', th' orderly officer says to me, Private Odgerson, says 'e, seein' as you're a man of intelligence, says 'e, en' th' best shot in the battalion, 'e says, we warnt your edvice, 'e says, in a kinda fix we're in—

Young Woman [*indicating a bench to the Atheist*]. I'll sit down on a seat, Dad, for a minute. My legs are giving way under me. Let me sit down a second.

Atheist [*irritably—as they sit down*]. You shouldn't have rushed after me the way you did. En' 'urry up—I've gotta read up some things in *The Origin of the Idea of a God*.

Young Woman [*between breaths*]. I was afraid, if I didn't run, I'd lose sight of you, and I wanted to see you.

Atheist [*as he helps the Young Woman to sit down*]. Damn stupid to rush yourself into a heart attack.

Young Woman [*frightened*]. There's a shadow passing over my eyes again! [*Grasping the Atheist's arm*] Dad, I'm afraid I'm far from well.

Atheist [*soothingly*]. Just a little flutter from over-exertion, that's all. All our hearts jump at times.

Young Woman [*vehemently*]. I tell you it's deeper than that, an' I'll croak suddenly, sooner or later. The other night I had a man with me, an' when I was half stripped it came on me as he was coming over to paw me. In a mist I saw the fright in his eyes, saw him huddling his clothes on an' hurrying away. Then I fell down. In a faint I fell down, till the morning came an' brought up the woman below to find me still in a faint where I fell down.

Atheist.   Excitement, over-excitement.

Young Woman [*hysterically*].   If I have to die, I'll die game; I'll die dancing!

Atheist.   Hush! Not so loud—we're in a park.

Young Woman [*persuasively catching hold of his arm*].   I want you to help me, Dad; I'll go mad if I have to live alone any longer.

Atheist [*firmly*].   No, no; no more of that. Live your own life. I'm not your father, so cut out the daddy business.

Young Woman [*moving closer to him*].   You crept into a father's place when you took me away from the nuns who were moulding my life round the sin of my mother. You made me call you Dad when you saved me from their crosses, their crowns, and their canes, and lifted my hands up in salute to the sun and the moon and the stars. [*She puts an arm around him.*] You'll give me one more chance, won't you? You will, you will!

Atheist [*restlessly*].   I did that twice before, and, as soon as you felt well, you hurried off, leaving me with rooms I didn't want and furniture I couldn't sell.

Young Woman [*leaning wearily against his shoulder*].   I can't live alone any longer, Dad. When I lie down in bed and stretch out in search of sleep, the darkness reddens into a glow from the fire that can never be quenched.

Atheist [*impatiently*].   Oh, the old, false, foolish fear again!

Young Woman.   Green-eyed, barrel-bellied men glare and grin at me; huge-headed, yellow-eyed women beckon to me out of the glow from the fire that can never be quenched. Black-feathered owls, with eyes like great white moons, peck at me as they fly through the glow from the fire that can never be quenched. Save me, Dad, oh, save me!

Atheist [*scornful and angry*].   The hell en' red-fire for ever talk of the nuns! They frame the world en' fill life with it, till we eat, sleep, work, en' play for ever in the smoke of hell!

Young Woman [*humbly*].   It will be only for awhile, Dad, for I'm going to marry the Gardener. He's not much, but, at least, he is safety, and, maybe, peace too.

Atheist [*impatiently*].   For Gord's sike put 'im aht of your little 'ead, girl! 'E 'as much intention of marryin' you as I have.

Young Woman.   We're to go to a dance to-night, and afterwards we'll settle everything.

Atheist [*positively*].   I'm tellin' you all 'e wants is a good en' warm time
free o' cost.

> [*A handsome young Salvation Army Officer enters from the right
> above, crosses slope, and comes down towards a seat some distance
> away from the Young Woman and the Atheist. He is trying to read
> a book as he walks along. He is wearing a yellow mackintosh, which
> is open, showing the red jersey of a Staff Officer. The Officer
> glances at the Young Woman as he passes, and she returns the
> look. He sits down on a seat and steals a furtive look at the Young
> Woman. He meets her eyes and lowers his glance to the ground.
> He again glances at her, at her face, and then at her legs.*

Young Woman [*turning her thoughts away from the Officer, and pressing
close to the Atheist, as she puts an arm coaxingly round his neck*].
You'll do what I ask you, this once, Dad, only this once, won't you?

Atheist [*firmly removing her arm from around his neck*].   No, never
again. Swing along on your own sweet way, and leave your dad out of
it.

Young Woman [*tensely*].   You won't? You won't, Dad?

Atheist [*in a tone of finality*].   No, I won't!

> [*There is a pause, during which the Young Woman, with tight-
> ened lips and a sullen look in her eyes, stares in front of her.*

Young Woman [*suddenly thrusting her face close to the Atheist's*].   I
believe in God, see! And that in the beginning He created heaven and
earth.

Atheist [*moving his face away from the Young Woman's*].   I see, I see.

Young Woman [*following the face of the Atheist with her own, while the
Salvation Army Officer listens intently to what she is saying*].   And in
the resurrection of the dead, when they that have done good shall go
into life everlasting, and they that have done evil into everlasting fire!

> [*The Atheist rises from the bench without a word, and goes up
> the centre path to the slope, and passes out.*

Young Woman [*rising, follows him part of the way, and speaks loudly
after him*].   And I believe that God's near them who need His help,
and helps them who ask His help—see!

S.A. Officer [*softly and prayerfully*].   God be praised!

> [*The Young Woman returns to the bench, sinks down on it, and
> begins to cry softly and resentfully. The Salvation Army Officer after
> a moment's hesitation comes over, looking with a shy interest at the*

pretty legs displayed by a disarranged skirt, and then slowly sits down beside her.

S.A. Officer [*earnestly*].   No need to cry, sister, for no one trusts to God in vain.

Young Woman [*resentfully*].   Oh, go away; I'm miserable, for he that's gone is the only real friend I have in the world.

S.A. Officer.   God is your only friend.

Young Woman.   I've not called upon Him for years, and He will not hasten to hear me now.

S.A. Officer [*putting his hand gently on her knee*].   God would empty heaven of His angels rather than let the humblest penitent perish.

Young Woman [*in low tones*].   If I ask for help, will He hear?

S.A. Officer.   He will hear.

Young Woman.   And hearing, will He listen?

S.A. Officer.   Hearing, He will listen.

Young Woman [*grasping his arm appealingly*].   And listening, will He grant what the sinner asks, to save the sinner from a life of sin?

S.A. Officer [*fervently, as he caresses her knee*].   God is able to save to the uttermost all them that come to Him.

Young Woman [*earnestly, after a few moments' thought*].   I'll pray and pray and pray till all that's done's annulled, and all that is to do is blessed by God's agreement.

S.A. Officer [*fervently and softly*].   God be praised, sister!

Young Woman [*becoming conscious that he is caressing her knee*].   Oh, God, don't do that, please! You'll make a ladder, and silk stockings aren't easy to get.

[*She pushes his hand away, pulls down her skirt, and looks at him questioningly. He stands up, embarrassed, and fidgets with his cap.*

S.A. Officer [*nervously*].   I must go on, now, to our meeting. Will you come? [*She is silent.*] No? Some other time, then. I should like to keep in touch with you. Very much indeed. Sister, you are not very far from God. Good-bye.

Young Woman [*in a tired voice, void of interest*].   Good-bye.

[*He turns up the centre path, looks back for a moment at the Young Woman, then crosses the slope, and goes out. She leans her arm on the arm of the bench, and shades her eyes wearily with her hand. After a few moments have passed, the Gardener enters car-*

rying a tall, slender Maypole, painted black. On the top of the pole is a hoop from which hang long green, blue, and rich yellow ribbons. He fixes it in the centre of the sward. The Young Woman, with a long sigh, raises her head, sees the Gardener. She runs over to him, and flings her arms around his neck.

Gardener [*astonished*]. What has brought you here? Aren't you working?

Young Woman. No, I've given it up.

Gardener. Why?

Young Woman. You know well enough, you know well enough. How often have I told you that the swine of a manager brings good-looking girls, one at a time, to a silent storeroom to sort chemises, and then sends his slimy paw flickering around under their skirts. When he made a clutch at me, I came away.

Gardener [*peevishly*]. Oh, you should have fenced him off as every girl does with a man like that. What are you going to do if you can't get another job?

Young Woman [*coaxingly*]. That's why I wanted to speak to you. You'll have to live with me; I'm frightened, I'm frightened to live alone any longer.

Gardener [*suspiciously*]. Live with you—how live with you?

Young Woman [*with calm confidence*]. Marry me, Ned. You want me or you do not want me. I'm not going to be just a dance number for you any longer. Do you want me or do you not?

Gardener [*nervously*]. Look here, Jannice, I'm busy getting ready for some damned fools to practise folk-dancing. They're trying to make England merry again. So I've no time to talk to you now, dear.

Young Woman [*impetuously*]. Do you want me or do you not want me?

Gardener [*coaxingly*]. Of course, I want you, but we can talk about this to-night.

Young Woman. No, now; what we say now will last our lives out. There will only be our two selves—for awhile; we needn't have a kid till we can afford one. [*Appealingly*] You will, you will, Ned; this means everything to me, everything.

> [*At the beginning of the Young Woman's appeal, the Man with the Stick appears on the slope above, and halts to listen.*]

Gardener. A kid! Oh, be sensible, woman, for God's sake! We can't talk of these things here.

Young Woman [*vehemently*]. Oh, be a man, Ned, be a man, and, if you want a thing, take a risk to get it! I want something for what I mean to give. Answer me—is it yes or no!

Gardener [*roughly removing her arms*]. Buzz off, I tell you. I'll see you to-night.

Young Woman. Answer the question: yes or no, yes or no, yes or no!

Gardener [*with a shout*]. No!

> [*The Young Woman looks at him silently for a few moments, then turns away, and goes out, her face tense, but her lips quivering. The Gardener returns his attention to the Maypole.*

Man with Stick [*from top of slope*]. You've lost something, friend, you've lost a lot. If I was young as you, I'd ha' carried 'er 'ome!

Gardener [*resentfully*]. Mind your own affairs. I've got my werk to do.

Man with Stick [*extending the stick towards the Maypole*]. 'Ere, d'ye know what that there pole is a symbol of—what it represents?

Gardener [*surlily*]. No, en' don't want to know.

Man with Stick. You oughter then; knowledge is power, my friend. It represents life, new life about to be born; fertility; th' urge wot was in the young lass you hunted away.

Gardener [*mockingly*]. You don't say!

Man with Stick. Ay; en' Pharaoh 'ad one, en' on May Day used to pull it up with golden cords, en' orl the people darnced rahnd it.

Gardener. 'Ow d'ye know? You weren't there.

Man with Stick. Scholars were, man. Ask any scholar, en' 'e'll tell you the sime.

Gardener [*stepping back to view the Maypole*]. I'm not concerned with what Pharaoh did or didn't do.

> [*A group of lively Boys and Girls run in, and catch in their hands the ribbons hanging from the Maypole. They are dressed in fancy folk-dress. They dance round the pole, keeping time to the first part of the folk-tune "Haste to the Wedding". Then they suddenly stop as the Young Woman enters from the direction by which she left, closely followed by the Policewoman. The Young Woman is sobbing softly. The Gardener and the Man with the Stick stare at them. They cross over.*

Policewoman [*complacently*]. I caught you in the act that time, my lyedy.

Young Woman [*sobbing*]. It was he spoke to me, miss; on my word of honour, it was he spoke to me first.

Policewoman. On your word of honour! Tell that to the magistrite when you're in front of 'im. If I'm eny kind of a guesser, you'll not solicit eny more young en' innocent men for a month to come.

> [*The two of them pass out. The Gardener and the Man with the Stick stare after them. The Folk-Dancers begin again, and dance through the second part of the tune, "Haste to the Wedding".*]

THE GATES CLOSE

SCENE II

Summer noon. The same as the preceding one on a noonday in summer. The colours now are mainly golden glows, tinged with a gentle red. The green on the sward still lingers, but it, too, is tinted with a golden yellow. Instead of daffodils, big-faced hollyhocks, yellow, white, and red, peep out at life from the shrubbery. The Memorial, touched by the sun, now resembles a giant clad in gleaming steel.

The Dreamer enters as the gates open, and passes through them into the Park. He has a thoughtful look on his face, and is gazing at a piece of manuscript in his hand. His right hand moves gently as he beats time with the song that is being sung. People are moving about, all gay with a sensuous enjoyment of the loveliness of the day. They are singing at the top of their bent. The Dreamer passes through them, and goes out.

People [*singing*]:
> Ye who are haggard and giddy with care, busy counting your profit
>   and losses,
> Showing the might of your name unto God in the gay-coloured page
>   of a cheque book;
> Storing the best of your life in a drawer of your desk at the office:
>
> Bellow good-bye to the buggerin' lot 'n come out

To bow down the head 'n bend down the knee to the bee, the bird, 'n
    the blossom,
Bann'ring the breast of the earth with a wonderful beauty!

Ye who are twisting a prayer from your thoughts in the dimness and
    gloom of the churches,
Lighting your candle-petitions away to chalk-coloured virgins and
    martyrs,
Racking your life for the hope of a cosy corner in heaven:

All Crowd Together:
    Bellow, etc.

Some of the Crowd:
    Ye who in senates, and Parliaments, talk, talk on through the day 'n
        the night-time,
    Talk, and still talk, and still talk, and talk on through the hundreds of
        centuries passing,
    Till the wide ear of the wide world is deafen'd with wisdom!

    Bellow, etc.

> [*When the song has ended, the Atheist, the Man wearing the
> Trilby Hat, and the Man with the Stick are seen arguing together.
> On a bench towards the back sit the two Nursemaids, between them
> the pram enfolding the countess's baby. The Bishop is on a seat
> nearer the front. He has been reading a book, but this is now lying
> open on his knee, and he is bending forward to hear the better what
> is being said by the disputants. The two Chair Attendants are lying,
> half asleep, at the foot of the slope.*]

Man wearing Trilby.   An 'eathen song! Say wot you like, you'll find every
man at 'eart is religious.

Atheist.   Look, brother, no question can be solved by a generalization. All
men are not religious no more'n all men are liars. The more a man uses 'is
mind, the less 'e uses Gord.

Man wearing Trilby.   If we was to set aside Deity, we'd let loose all manner of evil among ourselves—everyone knows that. There'd be no authority nowhere.

Bishop [*speaking over to them*].   Our friend is right: there must be the
few who rule and the many whose duty it is to obey, or there would be
an end to order.

Atheist [*to the Bishop*].   It 'as been the few rebels life gave us, the ones
who forgot to obey, that have rushed the world ahead! You think of
Copernicus, Galileo, 'n Darwin—rebels against the thought en' dooty of

the time. [*He points an accusing finger at the Bishop.*] There isn't a single rebel in your calendar of saints!

Bishop. Nonsense, friend.

Man with Stick [*with a long-drawn, impatient sigh*]. Aw, wot's the use of arguin' with 'im!

Atheist [*to Bishop*]. 'Ere, d'ye believe that the ten commandments constitoot a competent rule of life en' conduct?

Bishop [*smiling indulgently*]. I'd venture to say they do, sir.

Man wearing Trilby. I'd sye so, too.

Nursemaid [*joining in*]. Of course they does.

Atheist [*mockingly*]. Christian countries don't seem to think so, then, for even England, dooring the last thirty years, 'as myde over two thousand lawrs, covering sixteen thousand pages of cep imperial octavo, a tidy addition to the lawr of loving your neighbour as yourself, sir.

Man with Stick [*gleefully*]. En' they ain't finished miking them yet!

Man wearing Trilby. Where's your authority for thet?

Man with Stick [*angrily*]. Where's your authority for wot you sye?

Man wearing Trilby [*firmly*]. The Bible, sir; the 'Oly Book, every word inspired, every verse infallible.

Attendants [*together*]. 'Ear, 'ear!

Nursemaid [*with calm conviction*]. Even from time immemorial, the Bible 'as myde truth pline to all people.

Man with Stick [*taking a few steps to go in disgust, and returning to thrust his face close to that of the Man wearing the Trilby*]. Aw, come on, Jenner; I'm off—no brrains! [*He taps his stick heatedly on the ground, and makes to go; he hesitates for a moment, then returns and comes close to Man wearing Trilby.*] 'Ere, d'ye believe the Bible where it syes the whyle swallowed Jonah?

Man wearing Trilby. 'Course I does.

Man with Stick. You does!

Nursemaid. En' wye wouldn't 'e?

Man wearing Trilby [*tapping Man with Stick on the chest*]. If the Bible said Jonah swallowed the whyle, I'd believe it; but I'm not asked to believe anything so absurd.

Man with Stick [*catching the Atheist's arm, and drawing him away*]. Aw, come on, man! We're just wastin' our knowledge 'ere. [*They go off.*

Attendants [*as they are going—together*].   Booh!

Bishop [*raising a hand to silence the boohing*].   Friends, let our misguided brothers go in peace. [*To Man wearing Trilby*] I shouldn't harp too much on the whale story, friend; it's but an allegory, you know.

Man wearing Trilby [*indignantly*].   Is that all you know about it! The Bible says the whyle swallowed Jonah, son of Amittae. It's a plyne fact, en' you should be ashymed to derny it. [*He crosses to go out; halts; and turns to glare at the Bishop.*] Tyke warnin', you, at wot 'appened to Jonah, son of Amittae, for you're worse'n 'e was!   [*He goes out.*

Nursemaid [*consolingly—to Bishop*].   Never mind 'im, sir; 'e don't know wot 'e's asaying of.

Older One.   Ignorance torkin'.

Young One.   Just ignorance.

Bishop [*cheerfully*].   Never mind! [*He goes over to the Nursemaids.*] Aha, here we have the fair countess's baby. No guile here. The world hasn't been long enough yet with the young lamb. [*To Upper Nursemaid*] And where's your boy-friend—that gallant guardsman I've seen you with so often?

Nursemaid [*after a moment's hesitation*].   We ain't on speaking terms, sir; he misbehaved himself by takin' walks with another girl.

> [*The head and half the body of the Guardsman has appeared above the bushes at top of the slope. He stares down at the Nursemaid, dodging down whenever he thinks anyone might see him.*

Bishop.   Oh? Maybe he is sorry.

Under Nursemaid [*to Bishop*].   'E is, sir. It's agettin' 'im dahn. [*To Upper Nursemaid*] I'd try to forgive 'im, Greeta, even if 'e was to blime. You never knows wot a quarrel 'll lead to—mye mean a parting for ever!

Bishop.   In this life, we have to forgive many things.

Under Nursemaid.   Besides, 'e asserted thet it was 'is sister.

Upper Nursemaid [*indignantly*].   'Is sister! I seen them in the bushes when 'e was atuckin' 'er into 'im. No; I'm determined to be adamant. I don't allow for deception. When 'e knew how to respect me, 'e 'ad me; when 'e doesn't, 'e 'asn't; en' I'm determined to be adamant!

Under Nursemaid [*catching a glimpse of the soldier's head as it pops up and down—excitedly*].   'E's behind the 'edge awatching us, Greeta! Oh, 'is fice 'as altered, worn en' unhappy like—Greeta, 'ave a 'eart: 'e is suffering!

Bishop.   Do be kind to him, dear.

Under Nursemaid. I feel for 'im when I see the sorrowful look in 'is eyes. You are 'ard, Greeta.

Upper Nursemaid [*rising and tidying the pram, preparatory to moving away*]. A little suffering'll do 'im good. No, Reeta; unless 'e writes en' apologizes humbly; unless 'e writes en' explines; unless 'e writes en' asks me to forgive 'im, 'e'll never 'ave a chance of being with yours truly agine!

> [*She goes off, pushing the pram, stiff and dignified, never glancing at where the head of the Guardsman is gaping over the bushes. She is followed by the other Nursemaid, shaking her head, and sending a sympathetic glance to the soldier. When they have gone, the Guardsman comes down the slope to follow; but the Bishop halts him by catching his arm in a friendly way.*

Bishop [*sympathetically*]. Friend, a little kindly advice to you: write a humble letter of apology to your sweetheart. Then there'll be harmony, and everything in the garden'll look lovely. [*Smilingly*] Your conduct calls for an apology, you know.

Guardsman [*coldly*]. Ow, does it? [*Angrily*] En' wot the 'ell is it to you wether it does or not? Powkin' your big nose into other people's business. You keep off my affyres, see!

> [*He goes angrily off after the Nurses, leaving the good Bishop embarrassed.*

Older One [*with almost tearful sympathy*]. Wot a shime, sir! You see wot 'appens when religion's lost. Upsets the mind. There ought to be some lawr to mike people respect religion.

Young One. We goes to church reglar, don't we, 'Erbert? We was brought up thet wye, wasn't we, 'Erbert? Respectful like.

Bishop [*feelingly*]. I know; I guessed it from the first.

Older One [*slyly*]. Where's the lyedy as is always with you, sir?

Bishop [*slyly, too*]. I gave her—what do you call it?—I gave her the slip, to-day. My sister, you know; she's too cautious; afraid I'll come to harm by being familiar with the common people.

Older One. Harm! Ahar har! [*He chuckles at the idea.*] Harm!

Young One. Nice thing to see a clergyman merry an' bright, an' ready to tork to 'umble men, like us—isn't it, 'Erbert?

Older One. I concur with thet.

Bishop [*gaily*]. Oh, the Church isn't altogether so solemn an institution as many people seem to think—she can laugh, sing, and skip—at a suitable time, at a suitable time.

Older One.   I always said the clergy was 'uman—didn't I, Godfrey?

Young One.   Often en' often.

Older One [*confidently*].   We've a friend 'ere—d'ye know thet, Godfrey?

Young One.   The gentleman's got a kind 'eart, I'd sye.

Older One.   You've only got to look at 'is fine fice to see thet. [*Affectionately linking his arm in that of the Bishop, an act which makes the Bishop stiffen a little in doubt.*] At the moment, sir, the pire of us is in a bad wye, a bad wye; we 'ave lost our jobs, en' don't know wot to do. A pahnd or two, now, would 'elp a lot—wouldn't it, Godfrey?

Young One.   I'd sye so.

Bishop [*growing stiffer, and withdrawing his arm from the contact of the Older Attendant's*].   No, no, please. My sister deals with all matters of help to the needy. Apply to her. If she approves, she'll assist you. One must be careful in the dispensation of charity.

Older One [*peevishly*].   Aw, your sister wouldn't be no good to us! She wouldn't listen right. She'd warnt to know the why en' wherefore of everything.

Bishop [*firmly*].   And rightly so, friend. The giving away of money is a great responsibility. She'd be very angry if I did what you ask.

Older One.   She'd never know, sir. Me nor Godfrey would never sye a word—would we, Godfrey?

Young One.   We'd keep it dark, orlright.

Bishop [*decisively*].   No no; a rule is a rule, so let us change the subject.
[*A silent pause.*

Older One [*bitterly*].   Chynge the subject! En' why did you coax innercent people into queuein' up behind the idea of the clergy bein' 'uman? [*Hotly*] Whaja warnt to force your company on them as didn't warnt it!

Young One.   I knew it all along. The clergy alwyes fail when they're asked a pline question.

Older One [*indignantly*].   'Op en' skip en' jump! Here's one as 'opes they'll 'op outa this place! [*The Bishop sits down on a bench, takes out his book, and begins to read again.*] Ow, we're goin' to read, are we? Well, if I was asittin' on a bench, en' got a 'int to go, I'd push off—wouldn't you, Godfrey?

Young One. Quick!

Bishop [*with quiet determination*]. I choose this place in which to rest, and I shall go when I think it dignified to do so.

[*He resumes his reading.*

Older One [*recklessly and loudly—to the Young One*]. Know wot I'd like to do, Godfrey, honest? Gambol a gime with en 'eifer in front of a clergyman, strite, I would! Show 'im a little of the gaiety of life, strite, I would!

Young One. Don't know as it would shock them, 'Erbert—I bet they 'as their 'ectic moments on the sly!

Older One. You bet they 'as! Wot do they do in their palaces when the lamps is lighted en' the blinds is drawn? We eats, they eats; we drinks, they drinks; we sleeps, they sleeps; but wot do they do in their palaces when the lamps is lighted en' the blinds is drawn?

[*The Young Woman enters, and, after a glance at the Bishop, sits down on a bench directly opposite him. She takes out mirror and puff from her handbag, and gives her face a few deft touches.*

Young One [*giving a few stiff steps of a dance—echoing the Older Attendant*]. Ay, wot do they do in their palaces when the lamps is lighted en' the blinds is drawn!

Older One [*poking him in the side to draw his attention to the Young Woman*]. Look, Godfrey, oh, look! Wot a peach! 'Ow would you like to tuck 'er up at night, Godfrey?

[*Lines of ugly joy swarm over their faces at the delightful thought, while they stare brazenly at the Young Woman. Suddenly, in the near distance, is heard the roll of a muffled drum, and the mournful chant of the Down-and-Out. The scene seems to grow dark and the air chilly. The two Attendants stiffen, and lines of fright chase away the lines of joy from their faces. The Young Woman, frightened too, turns pale, half rises from her seat, and stares into the distance.*

Down-and-Out [*chanting in the near distance*]:

Life has pass'd us by to the loud roll of her drum,

With her waving flags of green and yellow held high,

All starr'd with the golden, flaming names of her most mighty children. [*The chant fades away.*

[*The two Attendants slink out, bent-backed and silent, one to the right, the other to the left, as the chant fades away. The Young Woman, shivering, sinks slowly down on to the seat again. There is a pause. She is very attractive, sitting there in her tailor-made coat and her bright hat. Her slim legs looking slimmer in their elegant silk stockings are for all to see from the knees down. The Bishop suddenly sighs, closes the book he has been reading, puts it in his pocket, and, turning a little round, sees the Young Woman. He looks at her pretty face, thoughtfully bent towards the ground, at her neatly dressed body, and, finally, his eyes linger a little over the slim legs visible from the knees down. An old interest seems to stir in him as he looks at her. Ashamed, he turns his head away for a few moments. He looks at her again, first at her face, then at her body, and then, more consciously, at her legs. He turns his gaze away again and moves uneasily in his seat, lets his head sink forward till his chin rests on his breast. He lifts his head and looks at her; she turns at the same time, and they stare at each other for a moment; then the Bishop's head sinks down on his breast again.*

[*Suddenly the Young Woman rises swiftly, as if she had come to a sudden resolution, hurries to where the Bishop is, sits down on the bench beside him, and, catching his arm, speaks to him imploringly.*

Young Woman [*appealingly*]. I want you to help me. You are near to God, but I am out of reach.

Bishop [*frightened*]. Oh, my child, I'm afraid I can help only those whom I know.

Young Woman. Listen to me, listen to me, first. My heart is bad, and doctors say that death may seize me at any moment, and take me out of life. There's a young man who loves me, and is going to marry me, but I want you to come with me to see him, and make him marry me at once.

Bishop [*bewildered*]. But I know nothing about you or about him.

Young Woman. You will, please, you must; you are a man after God's own heart—you'll help a young girl whose one chance is help at once.

Bishop [*frightened to be seen talking to the girl—looking round him nervously*]. Why do you run to the priest for help only when you begin to feel the terrible consequences of your shame?

Young Woman [*irritated at the Bishop's thought*]. Oh, I'm not going to have a kid, man, if that's what you mean. Nothing like that for me yet, thank you! It's because I'd love to have one that I came to you;—to save me from falling into the condition that could never give me one.

Bishop. But you can't discuss such things with a man and a perfect stranger, girl.

Young Woman. You're neither a man nor a stranger: you are a priest of the most high God.

Bishop [*frightened and petulant*]. Oh, be sensible, girl! Go and talk these things with your father and mother.

Young Woman [*bitterly*]. I never knew my father, and my mother drinks, and hates me.

Bishop [*reprovingly*]. You mustn't talk like that about your mother. Whatever she may be, she should be sacred to you.

Young Woman [*impatiently*]. Sacred to me! A mother can be sacred only when she makes herself sacred to her children;—can't you understand that, man?

Bishop [*coldly*]. I have no help to offer you, and I must ask you to go away, please.

Young Woman [*impulsively sitting down beside him*]. Do listen to me, please do, Lord Bishop. I've seen you laughing and talking with common people, and it gave me heart to speak to you.

Bishop [*in his best manner; putting his hand on her knee and patting it*]. Go and live with your mother, and show her you realize what a mother really is. Work steadily, cultivate thrifty habits, and in a few years' time you'll be able to face marriage far more brightly and firmly than you could possibly face it now.

Young Woman [*trembling and agitated, pushing his hand from her knee*]. Oh, piping out of you the same old rot that I've heard a thousand times—mother, work, and thrift! [*Indignantly*] If you knew what a rip she was, I wonder if you'd like to live with her? I wonder, if you were a girl, and good-looking, would you bray about the happiness of work? [*Raising her voice a little*] Do you know why I had to fly out of the two last jobs I was in, had to—d'ye hear—had to fly out of them?

Bishop [*taking a book from his pocket and beginning to read—coldly*]. I do not want to know the reason.

Young Woman [*vehemently*]. Because I wouldn't let the manager see how I looked with nothing on. Oh, you hide behind your book when facts frighten you. There's many an old graven image has made a girl dance out of her job and chance the streets, sooner than strip herself for his benefit, with nine hours a day and three pounds a week added on to the pleasure.

Bishop [*from behind his book*]. You mustn't annoy me in this way. Please leave me in peace.

Young Woman [*vehemently*]. It's the truth. Can't you put your book down for a second and listen? [*She pushes the book aside.*] Come with me to the shop, and I'll bring you face to face with the man!

Bishop [*beginning to read again*]. Be good enough to go away, please.

Young Woman [*imploringly*]. Please listen to me! Are you afraid to find a lie in what you think to be the truth, or the truth in what you think to be a lie? Come and tell the manager you're my friend, and make him give me back the job I have had to leave. Oh, do, do, please!

[*The Bishop still remains behind the shelter of his book.*

Young Woman [*after a pause*]. Won't you help me?

Bishop [*in cold and final tones*]. No.

Young Woman [*with quiet bitterness*]. I suppose you'd have helped me had I let you go on handling my knee.

Bishop [*in cold and tense voice*]. If you don't go away at once, I'll have you handed over to the police for annoying me!

[*The Young Woman sits silent and shocked for a few moments, looking fixedly at the Bishop.*

Young Woman [*mockingly*]. Oh, hand me over to a policeman, would you? I see. Easy way of getting over a difficulty by handing it over to a policeman. [*She stands up.*] Get back, get back, please; gangway, gangway, there—policemen making a gangway for Jesus Christ! [*The Bishop stiffens himself behind his book. With intense scorn and bitterness*] You and your goodness are of no use to God! If Christ came again, He'd have to call, not the sinners, but the righteous to repentance. Go out into the sun, and pick the yellow primroses! Take your elegant and perfumed soul out of the stress, the stain, the horrid cries, the noisy laugh of life; and go out into the sun to pick the yellow primroses! When you go to where your God is throned, tell the gaping saints you never soiled a hand in Jesu's service. Tell them a pretty little lass, well on her way to hell, once tempted you to help her; but you saved yourself by the calm and cunning of a holy mind, an' went out into the sun to pick the yellow primroses, leaving her, sin-soddened, in the strain, the stain, the horrid cries, an' the noisy laugh of life. Tell them you were ever calm before the agony in other faces, an', an' the tip of your finger never touched a brow beaded with a bloody sweat!

[*The horrified Bishop suddenly closes his book, and rises from his seat to go away, but the Young Woman with a vigorous push from her hand, sends him sitting down in the seat again.*

Young Woman [*passionately, thrusting her face close to the Bishop's*]. A tired Christ would be afraid to lean on your arm. Your Christ wears a bowler hat, carries a cane, twiddles his lavender gloves, an' sends out gilt-edged cards of thanks to callers. Out with you, you old shivering sham, an' go away into the sun to pick the yellow primroses!

[*As the Young Woman is speaking her last few sentences the Old Woman enters. She is pale and haggard, and vicious lines harden the look of her mouth. Her hair is white, but her black eyes are still undimmed by age. Her thin body is still upright, showing that in her youth she was slim and vigorous, and her face still shelters traces of what were once very good looks. Her boots, though polished, are old and broken, and everything about her, though old and patched and shabby, is clean and neat. Constant, quiet drinking has made her a little incoherent in her thoughts. In one hand she carries a small wreath of red poppies and laurel leaves, which has a bunch of violets where the wreath is tied together by a bow of black ribbon. She has heard the voice of the Young Woman, and comes down to where the girl is speaking, gripping her roughly by the arm as the Young Woman is about to go away from the Bishop.*

Old Woman [*to the Young Woman*].   Putting yourself again on the market for men, are you? Piling up money, and not a penny nor the thought of a penny for your lonely and suffering mother. [*As the Young Woman tries to free herself*] No use your trying to get away. [*She drops the wreath on the ground, and holds the girl tighter.*] I have you and I hold you till I get a little to help me on in life for a day or two!

Young Woman [*doggedly*].   I haven't any money; and, even if I had, I wouldn't part with a penny to you, for all you want it for is drink!

Old Woman [*furiously*].   Drink! Hear that now! Is it any wonder God has given her a heart that may go phut any minute! [*Over to the Bishop*] Hear what she says, you? That I want the money for drink!

Young Woman [*with a frightened laugh*].   Let me go, will you? If my heart does go phut, I'll go game, see! Pass out dancing—see?

[*The Old Woman claws at the girl's hat, pulls it off, and flings it on the ground.*

Old Woman [*wildly*].   Want the money for drink, do I? I'll tear every stitch on you into ribbons!

Young Woman [*appealing*].   Please, please, Mother, don't ruin the few little decent things I have to wear!

[*The Bishop gets up from his seat, goes over to the struggling Women, and tries to separate them.*

Bishop [*trying to restore peace*].   For shame, for shame! Mother and daughter,—for shame, for shame!

[*As soon as she hears the Bishop's voice the Old Woman releases her hold on the girl, and stares at the Bishop. The Young Woman, excited and exhausted, sinks into a seat a little distance away. The Bishop returns the Old Woman's look for a moment, and then rather hastily returns to his seat and resumes the reading of his book.*

The Old Woman's eyes follow the Bishop and, after a moment's hesitation, she comes up close to him.

Old Woman [*looking fixedly at the Bishop—murmuringly*].   Your voice has a strange echo in it. Behind that wizened face is hidden a look of the first young man who conquered me on a Sunday night, after the ora pro nobis people had pulled down their blinds and were slinking into sleep. There under a yellow moon, among the shadows by a grove of birch trees, on a bed of flattened bluebells, one of the prettiest fillies that ever wore a skirt was jockeyed into sin, and out of the rapture and the risk came this girl who dares to fancy men more than she does her own mother. [*Suddenly*] Is your name Gilbert?

Bishop [*over the top of his book—looking very uneasy*].   Go away, you wretched and forgotten creature. My name is not Gilbert!

Old Woman [*still staring at him—murmuring*].   I'm not much to look at now; but the man who first got the better of me's a big jack-a-dandy in the church, for I saw him once in a holy procession, helping to sing a canticle, a purple cape hanging from his shoulders. [*Suddenly pushing the Bishop's book aside*] Eh, you, is your name Gilbert?

Bishop [*roughly*].   Get away, get away, woman. My name is not Gilbert. Get away, get away, I tell you!

[*The Old Woman goes over to the Young Woman, limping, sitting on a seat. The Bishop leans forward with his elbows on his knees and his head in his hands.*

Old Woman [*to the Young Woman—whiningly*].   Why don't you try to be decent to your poor mother? She won't trouble you for long. I feel a few more months will see the end of me.

Young Woman [*savagely*].   I'd dance and sing if I thought you'd die in an hour!

Old Woman [*wildly*].   You'd dance and sing if I died in an hour? Hear that, now? Dance and sing? How can God listen to such a saying and not strike you dead? [*Over to the Bishop*] Didja hear what she said?—dance and sing if I died in an hour? Come over and bruise her hopes with a grim curse from God.

Bishop [*his hands covering his face*].   Oh, hush, hush, woman; hush and go home.

Old Woman [*wrathful at the Bishop's indifference*].   Hush, hush, and go home you! Hear what she said to me, said to her mother? Dance if I died in an hour, and you take her part. You ought to be driven helter-skelter out of everything holy. Hush you, and go home, with your ora pro pugeree mugeree rigmarolum! [*Turning violently on the Young Woman*]

In league with you, is he? [*She seizes hold of the Young Woman and shakes her violently.*] Dance if I was dead to-day, or died to-morrow, would you?

Young Woman [*terrified*]. Mother, mind; don't—I didn't mean anything!

Old Woman [*shaking her more violently still*]. I think of nothing but drink, do I not?

Young Woman [*hysterically*]. My heart, my heart—you'll be the death of me!

> [*The Dreamer appears on the slope above and looks on at those below.*

Old Woman [*fiercely flinging her back so that the girl falls on her knees*]. I'll teach you a little of the duty a daughter owes to her mother!

> [*She raises a hand to strike the girl, but the Dreamer, who has come close, seizes her, and prevents her arm from falling. The Bishop rises, makes a step forward to interfere, but stops in hesitation.*

Dreamer [*gently shaking the Old Woman*]. Now then, now then— what's this?

> [*The Young Woman pulls herself on to a seat. She is panting for breath. She reclines down on the bench, closing her eyes, while trying to regain her breath.*

Young Woman [*her eyes closed—between breaths*]. Get her away; send her away, for God's sake!

Dreamer [*firmly conducting the Old Woman out*]. Go away; go home, old woman, better go home. Let the old pray by the fire, and leave a way for the young to live.

Old Woman [*murmuringly, as she goes out*]. No pity in the young; only waiting for time to hustle us off. [*She brushes with her hand the laurel wreath she has picked up from the ground.*] The bad present, and the good absent; the shame living, and the pride buried; gone from my grasp and my sight in the flame and smoke of the war. Oh, Jesus, is there no rest to be found anywhere!

> [*The Old Woman goes out, and the Dreamer, returning to the Young Woman, sees the Bishop beckoning to him. He goes to him.*

Bishop [*anxiously*]. Do you think she'll be all right?

Dreamer. Yes; she'll be herself again in a few minutes.

Bishop [*handing the Dreamer three pound notes*]. Steal over and slip these in her handbag. Don't mention me. I've no real interest in her, you understand? Still I pity her in a way. I must go now. It's all the money I have with me. I'll return this way again, later on. [*He turns to go, wheels, and grasps the Dreamer's arm tight.*] Please don't be anyway cruel to her. She is—God's child.

Dreamer.　I'll watch her till she has recovered.

Bishop.　Thanks.

> [*The Bishop goes up the slope. The Dreamer steals over to where the Young Woman is reclining on the bench. He takes up her handbag; sees the Bishop's back is turned; slips one of the notes into his pocket, and the other two into the handbag. When the Bishop reaches the top of the slope, he turns back to look at the Young Woman. The Dreamer waves a hand reassuringly, and the Bishop goes out. The Dreamer goes to the Young Woman, and sits down beside her.*

Dreamer [*to the Young Woman*].　Feeling a little better now?

Young Woman [*still panting a little*].　Bit better now. It's my heart—goes curious now when anything happens. Please sit down beside me for a minute or two.

Dreamer.　For a year and a day, if you like.
> [*He sits beside her and takes her hand in his and strokes it.*

Young Woman [*bitterly*].　I'll go off in one of these attacks yet. Nice thing to have for a mother, isn't she? I love the dear silver that shines in her hair! Feeling better, now, anyhow. [*Slyly*] Well, how do you like the hand?

Dreamer.　Lovely—like a blue-veined, pink-tipp'd lily.

Young Woman [*taking her hand away*].　Well, let it go for a minute, till I straighten myself up a little.

> [*She arranges her hat, smoothes the folds of her skirt, gives a few touches to her blouse, and sits down again.*

Young Woman.　I'm a little more presentable now.

Dreamer [*moving a hand semi-circularly over her breasts*].　There's a wrinkle or two in your blouse still.

Young Woman [*taking his hand away*].　Now, now! Dad's spoken about you. Not the real Dad,—never saw my real father; don't even know who or what he was. Hard lines, isn't it?

Dreamer.　It doesn't matter very much now, dear.

Young Woman.　My second Dad—the Atheist, you know—calls you a poet. How do you live?

Dreamer. Oh, I sell an odd article, or, maybe, a song or a story, and so manage to live an austere life. But oughtn't you to go home and have a rest? I'll see you safe there.

Young Woman [*slyly*]. Tuck me up, and sing me to sleep with one of your songs?

Dreamer [*earnestly*]. I'd love to! [*He rises and catches her by an arm.*] Come! Don't let this rosy chance be pulled to bits by prudence. Come, sweet lass, and let's transmute vague years of life into a glowing hour of love!

Young Woman [*pulling her arm free, and speaking somewhat sharply*]. Not so quick, please! Men are always ready to rush a pretty woman into love, looking for joy, and behold, trouble. Supposing I go and give, what do I get?

Dreamer. I'll pay your merry kindness with a song.

Young Woman [*a little scornfully*]. A song! A puff of scented air! You're out on the hunt for bargains, young man. Go with a priest for a prayer and with a poet for a song! It's a poor offer, young sir.

Dreamer [*sitting beside her. Earnestly—close to the Young Woman's face*]. Young lady, many great queens and many grand ladies have joyfully snared themselves in the golden meshes of a poet's song!

Young Woman [*laughingly*]. Well, I'm neither a great queen nor a grand lady; I'm not even a clergyman's daughter.

Dreamer. To me you're a great lady and a grand queen, and it was for you I wrote the song.

Young Woman [*a little recklessly*]. Well, let's see if your little song can snare the hapless heart of a pretty little maiden.

Dreamer. Wait till we get to your flat, so that I can kiss you between the verses.

Young Woman. Oh, you're travelling quick along your own little road, young singer. Sing it now or sing it never.

Dreamer [*resignedly*]. Oh, all right, then. We'll call it by your name— what is it?

Young Woman. Just Jannice.

Dreamer. What a pretty name! Well, we'll call the song just *Jannice.*

[*He gives a shy little cough and sings. He is standing now, with one foot on the seat of the bench*];

    Her legs are as pliant and slim
    As fresh, golden branches of willow;

I see lustre of love on each limb,
Looking down from the heights of a pillow!
Looking down from the heights of a pillow!

Tossed by a soft breeze in the spring,
The blooms of an apple tree billow;
And her breasts are as lovely to me,
Looking down from the heights of a pillow,
Looking down from the heights of a pillow!

Gay, white apple-blossoms her breast,
Her legs golden branches of willow;
I'd enjoy for a year and a day
Looking down from the heights of a pillow,
Looking down from the heights of a pillow!

Dreamer [*after a pause—expectantly*].   Well?

Young Woman [*not satisfied, but pleased withal on account of the praise that is in it*].   A pretty song, young singer, but its grace and meaning are hardly a fit for me. I cannot live, or even hope, on the sweet sound of a song. Have you nothing else to offer?

Dreamer [*reluctantly*].   I could give you a pound.

Young Woman.   A pound! A small gift of gold for a grand lady or a great queen! Have you nothing more?

Dreamer [*rather wearily*].   A few shillings for a meal to-day and a meal to-morrow.

Young Woman [*laying a hand almost affectionately on his arm. He covers her hand with his*].   Keep the little you have for yourself, young singer, for your life seems uncertain as my own.

[*The Bishop has strolled in, and now sits on the bench opposite, apparently reading his book, but really watching the Young Woman. She gives him a hasty, scornful glance.*]

Dreamer [*tightening his grip on her hand*].   Well, at least, let me walk across the park with you.

Young Woman [*releasing her hand, and rising*]   No, no; I don't want you. Why do you keep insisting that I need you with me?

Dreamer.   I am thinking, not of your need, but of my own, Jannice.

[*The young Salvation Army Officer enters, and comes down the slope slowly. He keeps looking at the Young Woman.*]

Young Woman [*to Dreamer*].   That is selfish. Your way, young singer, though bright with song, is dim with danger. At the end of the way, I might find myself even lower than I am. There is no peace with you. [*She indicates the Salvation Army Officer.*] Here is a real friend who offers peace as a child might offer a friend a new-blown daisy.

Dreamer. His voice is not the voice of peace, but of fear.

> [*The Young Woman goes to meet the young Salvation Army Officer.*

Young Woman [*gaily*]:

> Good morrow, good morrow, young sir;
> Let's sanction this bold, sunny weather,
> By lying aside in the shade,
> And cooling warm feelings together!

S.A. Officer [*seriously*]. God's blessing on you, sister, though your thoughtless manner is fashioned to the woe of the world.

Young Woman [*putting her arms round the neck of the Salvation Army Officer—recklessly*]. Oh, come out of the gloom for a moment, dear! Come into the sun, and kiss me with the kisses of thy mouth!

S.A. Officer [*gently removing the arms of the Young Woman*]. Our ways are not your ways, sister; we have been led to turn our eyes aside from the gaudy beckoning of the world's vanities.

Young Woman [*a little abashed*]. Sometimes it is very hard to choose. If I lodge where you do, can your people be my people, and your God my God?

S.A. Officer [*eagerly*]. Ah, if you only will it, sister, it is so! Out of self, into Christ, into glory! It is as simple as that, sister.

Bishop [*over to the Salvation Army Officer—sharply*]. The saints didn't find it quite so simple, my young friend.

S.A. Officer [*to Young Woman*]. Never heed him, sister. He would hide God's countenance with a cloud of ritual. Come with me: the yoke is easy; the burden light.

Young Woman. To peace?

S.A. Officer. To peace that is perfect, and peace everlasting.

Young Woman. I will go a little way to hear more of the peace that seems so far away. [*She takes the arm of the Salvation Army Officer, and bows mockingly to the Bishop.*] Good-bye, old man, who, saving yourself, had no time to save others.

> [*The Bishop does not reply, but sits sadly on the bench looking down towards the ground. The Dreamer sits sadly on the bench opposite, watching the Young Woman go with the Salvation Army Officer. The air of "Jannice" is heard softly, either on flute or fiddle.*

*The Salvation Army Officer and the Young Woman go slowly up
the slope. When they reach the top, and are about to go off, the
Young Woman turns and looks down towards the Dreamer.*

Young Woman [*down to the Dreamer*].   I have not quite forgotten your
sweet song, young singer!   [*The two go out.*

THE GATES CLOSE

SCENE III

*The same part of the Park on an Autumn evening. The sky now is a
deep rich crimson, faintly touched at the horizon with golden yellow;
while the upper part has a plainly-visible and sweeping border of purple
and mauve. The leaves of the trees are red and yellow, the trunks a rich
bronze. Now and again, one of them flutters to the ground. At the
back, against the slope, are a number of tall, gaunt sunflowers, something
like those shown to us by Van Gogh. The figure of the Soldier now shows
a deep black against the crimson hue of the sky. Chairs having coloured
cloth seats and backs are here and there.*

*The Two Attendants, looking more haggard and decayed than ever,
are lying, apparently asleep, on the slope.*

*Before the gates open, a band, somewhere in the Park, is heard playing
"Land of Hope and Glory". The music is quite clear and definite, but when
the Park is in view the music becomes fainter, as if it was being played
at some distance away. The music ceases when the Young Woman and
the Dreamer appear.*

Older One [*suddenly rousing up and leaning on his elbow to listen*].
"Land of 'Ope en' Glory"! There's not much of the glory left, en' none
of the 'ope. [*He nudges his sleeping companion.*] Eh, Godfrey, 'ear
wot they're playin'? [*Younger Attendant grunts sleepily.*] "Land of
'Ope en' Glory"! Wot d'ye think of that?

Young One [*in a sleepy mutter*].   Aw, wot they plays don't concern us.

Older One [*somewhat sharply*].   'Course it concerns us! Why aren't we part of the 'ope en' the glory? There's that Dreamer, the Atheist, the Man with the Stick, and that gay-dressed young 'eifer goin' abaht good en' proper, denyin' of Gord en' all as is His; en' 'ere we are, two God-fearin', upright men, en' wot's the misery for? [*The Young Attendant takes no notice, so he pokes him.*] Two God-fearin' men, Godfrey, I syes.

Young One [*drowsily*]. Yeh; two God-fearin' young men, ri' enough. I wanna go asleep.

Older One [*bending over and giving him a shake—impatiently*]. Not tykin' no interest in public affaires helps us dahn. Is there a Gord or ain't there? [*His head falls on his breast for a few moments, and he falls back a little in sleepiness, but jerks himself upright again.*] Wot I said before, I syes again: There'll be nothing left if we lift th' pahnd off th' gold stannard. [*He shakes the Younger Attendant again.*] I 'olds we're ruined if we go off th' gold stannard! [*He sinks slowly down on the slope, weary, and full of sleep.*] [*A pause.*

Young One [*suddenly sitting up*]. En' I syes no! Give the British pahnd a charnce in the world's market. While we keep on sterling, we lose our gold in masses. I 'olds we're ruined, if we don't go off the stannard. [*He sinks down.*

Older One [*sleepily*]. I 'olds we're ruined if we does!

[*They both apparently sink into sleep as the Young Woman and the Dreamer appear above, and come down the slope, passing the sleeping figures by. She is pale, but her eyes are asparkle, though she has the Dreamer by the arm, and leans a little on him.*

Young Woman [*as she is coming down*]. I shouldn't have taken the wine, Dreamer. It has made me unsteady, inclining me to see the world fairer than I should.

Dreamer. It was good wine, then. You see clearly, for wine is the mirror of the heart.

Young Woman. I feel uneasy, feeling so much joy.

Dreamer [*setting her on a seat*]. Wait for me here, Jannice. I must cash the cheque I got this morning. I won't be from you over half an hour.

Young Woman. I wish you wouldn't go, dear Dreamer. Alone, I feel afraid of myself. [*A little roguishly*] Supposing when you are gone, Salvation's Officer comes and I go with him?

Dreamer. I'm not afraid of him: there's no peace or joy for you where he is. To him, peace may bring joy; to such as you, only joy can give you peace.

Young Woman. Still, stay here, Dreamer. I've two pounds I found suddenly in my bag this morning.

Dreamer. Keep them. I'll go. The music of the band will keep you company till I come again. A kiss!

[*He kisses her, and goes, waving back from the top of the slope, while she reclines a little sleepily on the seat, as the Man wearing the Trilby comes hurriedly in, followed as quickly by the Man with the Stick; he is followed a little more slowly by the Atheist, a Man wearing a Bowler Hat, and a Man wearing a Straw Hat—commonly called "a boater". They come together, and form an arguing group. Each, excepting the Atheist, carries a big newspaper under an arm.*

Man with Stick [*calling to Man wearing Trilby*]. Eh, stand your ground! If we wants knorledge, we must ask questions.

Man wearing Trilby [*halting, and letting the rest come up to him*]. Let there be an end of mockery, then.

Man wearing Bowler. Yes; let's conduct the debate with decorum.

Man with Stick. I wasn't mockin' enyone—I was only mockin' Genesis.

Man wearing Trilby. Well, Genesis is part of me, en' I'm part of Genesis.

Man with Stick [*looking at the sky, and giving a long, impatient sigh*]. Uuh!

Atheist [*gently to Man wearing Trilby*]. You see, friend, your arguments for existence of a Gord can't be the cause of belief, for the reason that the belief was there before them; and this belief was born into the mind of primitive man by ignorance and fear.

Man wearing Straw Hat. So you say!

Atheist [*turning to him*]. And so say the most eminent anthropologists we have. [*To Man wearing Trilby*] You, my friend, are arguing for the arguments usually set forth to prove the belief, and not for the belief itself which existed before the arguments—see?

Man with Stick. 'E don't warnt to see!

Man wearing Trilby. All I syes is use your eyes, use your ears, use your brine, en' wot's the explyenation of all the wunnerful things we sees 'en 'ears arahnd us—on the earth en 'above us in the sky—en' I syes Gord myde them orl!

Man with Stick [*impatiently*]. Ah, wot we warnt to know, man, is who myde Gord!

Man wearing Straw Hat [*pushing in truculently*]. 'E always existed!

In the beginning all things was myde by 'im, en 'withaht 'im was not enything myde wot was myde!

Man with Stick [*with another look at the sky*]. Aw, aw—we're back to Genesis again!

Atheist [*quietly and firmly*]. There never was a beginning, friend. Nothing 'as been myde, en' everything's been evolved out of matter, energy, en' force; forms chynging, but substance remineing the syme.

Man with Stick [*tapping the ground affirmatively*]. 'Course they 'as.

Man wearing Trilby [*hesitant*]. Yes; in a way, yes; but even Einstein syes—

Man with Stick [*interrupting fiercely*]. Aw, we're not responsible for wot Einstein syes!

Atheist [*deprecatingly—to Man with Stick*]. Patience, brother.

Man wearing Trilby. Wot first created this matter en' this energy en' this force you speak abaht? If it was always, 'ow was it always, en' where was it always? We gets nowhere when we syes thet wot's to come comes aht of wot is, en' wot is, is aht of wot was: it only mystifies a man; so I syes in the beginning, before enything wot is was, was Gord, en' it was 'e manipulated energy en' force to mike us wot we are.

Young Woman [*who has been listening abstractedly for some time— running a little unsteadily over to them, and pushing her way into the group*]. And aren't you fellows a fine example of what we are! [*To Atheist*] No beginning? As it was in the beginning, is now, and ever shall be; world without end. Amen. See?

Man with Stick [*indignantly*]. You mustn't interrupt, young woman! Your mind isn't able to comprehend wot we're torking abaht.

Young Woman. And yours is? Why, the wisdom each of you has, taken together, would fit on a spoon. [*She pushes them about a little wildly.*] Oh, go away, you little chirrupers, and leave the Park to peace. Let a quiet place enjoy the quietness it gives.

Atheist [*moving off*]. The discussion's ended, gentlemen, for the present. Go and read your papers. [*He goes off.*]

> [*The four men, Man with Stick, Man wearing Trilby, Man wearing Bowler, and Man wearing Straw Hat, sit down on the seats having coloured cloth seats and backs. The seats are so placed that if a line was drawn to each of them, the lines would make an X. They take the papers from under their arms, spread them out, and begin to read. Each of the newspapers on the page facing outwards has one large word only. One has* Murder, *another* Rape,

another Suicide, on the fourth Divorce. The Young Woman returns, still a little unsteady, to the bench. As the men read, the Band is heard softly playing "London Bridge is Falling Down". As the tune is played for the second time, the Man wearing the Straw Hat sings the words half to himself.

Man wearing Straw Hat [*singing*]:
  London Bridge is falling down, falling down, falling
      down,
  London Bridge is falling down, my fair lady.

Man wearing Bowler [*with complacent dignity—singing*]:
  Build it up with gold and silver, gold and silver, gold
      and silver,
  Build it up with gold and silver, my fair lady.

Young Woman [*singing with distinct note of denial*]:
  Gold and silver will not do, will not do, will not do,
  Gold and silver will not do, my fair lady.

Man wearing Straw Hat [*singing a little sadly*]:
  Gold and silver's grown a god, grown a god, grown
      a god,
  Gold and silver's grown a god, my fair lady.

Young Woman [*standing up, stamping her foot, and singing fiercely*]:
  Let it fall to pieces then, pieces then, pieces then,
  Let it fall to pieces then, my fair lady!

Older One [*rising from the slope to lean on his elbow—in a protesting, whining snarl*]. Wot's yous warnt to make such a row when two poor men is tryin' to sleep awye the worries of the world!
                    [*The Older Attendant sinks down to sleep again.*

Young Woman [*mockingly—after watching the Readers for a few moments*]. Let every sound be hushed, for the oblate fathers are busy reading the gospel for the day. Furnishing their minds with holy thoughts, and storing wisdom there. Let us pray! Oh, Lucifer, Lucifer, who has caused all newspapers to be written for our learning—stars of the morning and stars of the evening—grant we may so read them that we may always find a punch in them, hot stuff in them, and sound tips in them; so that, outwardly in our bodies and inwardly in our souls, we may get closer and closer to thee! [*Indignantly*] Why the hell don't you all say Amen!

Man wearing Trilby [*to Young Woman*]. Hush, woman: we want quietness when our minds are busy.

Young Woman [*rising and moving about among the Readers recklessly*].

I've had a few drinks, but what about it! A short life and a merry one! My heart's due to stop beating any minute now, but what about it! [*She contemplates the Readers.*] Devoted, body and soul, to the love of learning. Listen: Jannice is going to die dancing. [*Vehemently*] Are all you damn perishers deaf and dumb?

Man wearing Bowler [*with irritation*].   Oh, go away; we want to read in peace.

Young Woman [*singing softly, but a little drunkenly*]:
Stirr'd by a soft breeze in the Spring,
The blooms of an apple tree billow;
And her breast is as fragrant to me,
Looking down from the height of a pillow,
Looking down from the height of a pillow!

> [*She coughs, becomes a little breathless, and presses a hand to her side.*

I'm a sick woman. [*She bends her head down on her breast.*] Death has touched me, and is telling me to be ready; take your things off, and come with me. [*Defiantly*] I'll not give in, I'll not hold back. And when I go, should God's angels beckon me up or push me down, I'll go game. [*Horrified*] Jesu, Son of Mary, what'm I saying? I'll fold all the things done in this life round me like a mantle, and wait for judgement.

> [*She sinks down on a seat, and stares thoughtfully in front of her.*

Man with Stick [*reading from behind the paper marked Murder*].   The condemned man, who is to be hanged for cutting a woman into bits, ate a hearty breakfast, spent an edifying time with the chaplain, smoked a cigarette while being pinioned, and walked with a goose-step to the gallows.

Rest of the Readers [*in chorus*].   Walked with a goose-step to the gallows.

Man with Straw Hat [*reading from behind the paper marked Suicide*]. The dead man left a letter saying, I have ruined thousands and have made many mad; I have shaken hands with Dukes and Duchesses; before I put the pistol-point to my ear and scatter my brains, I kiss the pictures of my little darlings; knowing that, while all men condemn, all men will understand.

Rest of the Readers [*in chorus*].   All men will understand.

Young Woman [*getting up from the bench with a half-hysterical laugh*].   Never say die till you're dead! [*She looks at the Readers.*] Rape, murder, and suicide! A bit of a change from the life of the saints.

[*Loudly to the Readers*] What will you fellows do when you die, and have to leave it all behind you?

The Readers [*in chorus*].   Go away, young woman—we want quietness.

Man wearing Bowler [*reading from behind the paper marked Divorce*]. The housemaid said she climbed the ivy, got to the verandah, looked in through the window, saw the co-respondent in bed, the respondent in her camisole trotting towards the bed; then came darkness, and she would leave the judge and jury to guess the rest.

Rest of the Readers [*in chorus*].   Leave the learned judge and jury to guess the rest.

> [*While the last phrase is being chorused by the Readers, the Bishop appears on the slope above, looking down anxiously at the Young Woman.*

Bishop [*from the slope above*].   Jannice!

Young Woman [*up to the Bishop*].   Are you following me still? [*Angrily*] Go away, go away and leave me in peace! Let me run my race in my own way. Don't be mousing after me.

Bishop [*pleadingly*].   I want to help you, Jannice; let me help you!

Young Woman [*loudly*].   Go away, I tell you; I want no God's grenadier running after me. [*In a half-scream*] Go away! [*The Bishop goes back to the Memorial, and the Young Woman again contemplates the Readers.*] What are you all seeking? You look like a silent gang of monkeys searching for fleas!

The Readers [*in chorus*].   Go away; we want to read our papers in peace!

Young Woman [*softly and thoughtfully*].   Most important thing, too, is peace; most important. Peace most pure and peace most perfect, due to the children of the Prince of Peace. [*Recklessly*] But what have I to do with peace! When I come to the temple of peace, the veil of the temple turns to steel! Is there no one far enough from the way of the world to take an interval of rest, and have a look at me? [*The tune of "The Danube Waltz" has been heard for a few moments before, played softly by the Band. She begins to dance to the tune, in and out among the Readers.*] Now, you deaf and dumb perishers, have a look at a lovely pair of legs, if you're not blind as well! [*She lifts her skirts as she dances, and makes her movements keep time with the tune. The Readers look over the tops of their papers and watch her.*] All interested now? Well, what do you think of them—saucy, eh? [*Slapping her left leg*] This one's lovely. [*Slapping the right one*] This divine! [*She stops breathless, and scans them scornfully. The music slowly fades away. Breathless and scornful*] You bunch of high-minded toads, don't look at me long, for there's only venom for a woman in the things ye think of her. The dear joy of a sin ye turn to a sting and a bruising. [*She half sinks on a seat.*] Oh, my heart, my heart's restless again! [*She speaks in a lower tone to the Readers.*] In your looking after a woman there is no kindliness; before ye no image of loveliness, neither can ye hear the sound of a song as ye follow her, for your desire's but a venomous heat and a shame and a bruising!

> [*She sinks down, pale, breathless, and frightened, on the seat. The Readers return their reading; and take no more notice of her.*

Man wearing Bowler [*reading from behind his paper*]. The great cricketer, unbuckling his pads, said, You may take it from me that out there somewhere is a supreme, infinitely wise mind, which we call God, behind everything. God won't let the English people dahn. He'll keep our wicket up, and the bat of faith will drive the bad ball of unbelief far away over the boundary of England!

Man with Stick [*with scornful disgust*]. Wot the 'ell does a cricketer know abaht them abstruse things!

Young Woman [*who has been moving uneasily on the bench*]. I can't breathe, I can't breathe! [*She pulls the neck of her bodice open.*] It's on me again, but I'll go game, I'll go game. Eyes front up or down! [*The Bishop begins to come down slowly towards the Young Woman. In a panic of fear*] Dance, sing, and strip for the fun of the thing— that's all they want from a woman! A sigh, a sob of pain, a thought higher than their own from a woman, and they're all hurrying home. [*Turning towards the Readers*] God damn you, will none of you stir to help when you see a Christian in danger! [*She calls out in a semiscream*] Dreamer, Dreamer—where's the Dreamer!

> [*She sinks down half fainting on the bench. The Bishop comes quickly to her, now, and chafes her hands. The Readers have risen from their seats, have folded up their newspapers, and now come to where the Young Woman and the Bishop are, forming a semicircle around them.*

Bishop [*gently and fervently.*] Jannice, my little Jannice, I've come to help you; everything will be all right soon. [*Addressing the Readers*] Don't gather round, friends. Leave the girl to me. I'll watch over her. [*As they don't stir—sharply*] Leave us alone, I say, and don't stand there, staring like apes! [*All but the Man with the Stick go silently and slowly out. To Man with the Stick*] Didn't you hear me tell you to go away, man?

Man with Stick [*indignantly*]. 'Oo are you to sye come en' 'e cometh, en' go en' 'e goeth? Wot she warnts is a doctor, en' not a pryer!

Bishop [*in a burst of fury—using some of the strength of his younger days, and pushing him out roughly*]. Oh, go to hell!

[*He returns to the Young Woman as she recovers slightly, looking up at him without any confidence in her look.*

Bishop [*returning a little to formal speech, but softly, and with feeling*]. You are ill, my child; and you are lonely. You have forgotten God for a few moments, but He sends you His help in time of trouble; and, through me, unworthy messenger, a share of His sympathy and love.

[*He sits down beside her. She recovers a little, sits up, and stretches out a hand to him, which he takes in his own, and strokes gently.*

Young Woman [*with a sigh of relief*]. I'm glad you came. I was very lonely. My heart's beating a bit steadier now, thank God.

Bishop [*gently patting her hand*]. That's good, now; that's good.

Young Woman [*regaining confidence*]. A lot steadier now. I think it's more fear than anything else. I've had a hard time of it; and I get into a panic whenever my heart gives a double-time beat. I feel nearly normal again.

Bishop [*encouragingly*]. That's good. Keep calm for a little while and you'll soon be all right.

Young Woman. I'm waiting for the Dreamer. He'll be here shortly, and then I'll be safe again.

Bishop [*still stroking her hand—a little coldly*]. My child, I shouldn't think too much of the Dreamer, or make a friend of him. The things he writes give scandal, and tend to undermine morality and overthrow tradition. He is a bad influence, my child.

Young Woman [*taking her hand out of the Bishop's—firmly*]. I won't hear a word said against the Dreamer. He was the only one from whom I got courage and help. The Atheist, when he acted as my dad, was kind, too, in his own self-interested way. [*She looks innocently into the Bishop's face.*] I never saw my real father. Mother often said he had a high place in your church; but he never had the courage to come and claim his child.

Bishop [*coldly*]. From what I saw of her, your mother isn't to be trusted.

Young Woman [*emphatically*]. Well, the Dreamer is. He is as poor as I am, but he gaily shares with me his money and his joy. So, you see, he is more important to me than the God you praise.

Bishop [*shocked*].   You mustn't say such things, my child! I am here to help you, showing how kind and gentle God can be to—er—a straying lamb seeking in devious ways to find a way back to the waiting flock.

Young Woman [*fretfully*].   Oh, the flock doesn't care a damn whether I'm in or out, man. The flock! So long as they get their four meals a day, with a gay hour after, and a cosy fire in the winter, they'll never stretch a neck to see where a ram or a ewe has wandered.

Bishop [*soothingly*].   Well, never mind, now, and don't let your thoughts irritate you into any excitement, child. What you need most, now, is rest, and a chance to live a sober and a quiet life.

Young Woman [*more irritably than ever*].   And follow the commandments of God—always trying to crimp people into piety. You cross, crown, and anchor boys expect the very linnets to sing hymns in their spare time. The Salvation Army Officer, too, has the same gloomy glimpse of life. Miserere, miserere, all the way to heaven!

Bishop.   Hush. Forget everything but your own helplessness; and don't get excited.

Young Woman [*vehemently*].   I have to get a little farther away from the devil before I try to get a little nearer to God. I've a long way to travel yet before the white and holy candles are lit, and the golden incense scattered.

Bishop.   My child, the sinner is always nearer to God than the sinner dares to think.

Young Woman [*a little hysterically*].   Amen, and let us get to business. Make me safe and make me happy, and I'll give sweet thanks to God. Why've you been following me about for days? I sought you once, and you sent me empty away. Why do you want to help me now? [*Indicating sleeping Attendants*] Why don't you try to help those poor sleeping devils there?

Bishop [*a little impatiently*].   Oh, it would be waste of time to think of them.

Young Woman.   They're still God's children, aren't they?

Bishop [*more impatiently*].   We'll see about them another time. You seem to be an interesting case—young and intelligent. You don't seem to be an ordinary—eh—what shall I say?

Young Woman [*bitterly.*]   Oh, a whore! You may as well say it as think it. [*The Bishop is shocked at the girl's bluntness. He stiffens, and stays silent. Looking intently at the Bishop's face*] What was it made you light on me, I wonder? There are hundreds of girls, some of them better, some of them worse, than me, and it's curious that I should be the lucky dip. [*The Bishop remains silent.*] Well, go on; open up the overture, and play us something nice.

Bishop [*trying to control his impatience*]. My child, your present way of life is an evil one. I wish to give you a chance to turn aside from it; so please try to be decently attentive, and listen seriously to what I am about to say.

Young Woman [*with a half-suppressed giggle.*] Wine's beginning to take effect again. I had a wild time all this week with the Dreamer. He got an advance on a book that's to be published soon, and he's gone for another advance now. [*She prods the Bishop's breast.*] If he comes back before our treaty's signed, I'm off, and you won't see me again till what he gets is gone: so go ahead, and strike a light, and let us see the way we're walking.

Bishop [*with gloomy indignation*]. I can't listen any longer to these frivolous remarks. You have no pity for yourself. You have gone too far away for any helping hand to reach. I will leave you alone. [*He rises from the bench to go.*] I have done my best. I will leave you alone.

Young Woman [*catching his cassock—pleadingly*]. No, no; don't go away. I will listen; I will listen quietly; I promise. Be kind, and help me. I do want to try to do what is lawful and right. In God's name, be kind, dear Bishop.

Bishop [*rather sternly*]. Listen, child, then, and be serious. When trying to help you, I must be careful of what others may think.

Young Woman. Why have you to be careful? Can't you yourself pray, or push yourself out of the fear of what may be said about you? What does it matter how many say a man's a sinner if God thinks him a saint?

Bishop [*very annoyed*]. I can't waste time going into those questions now. You said you were going to be serious. Well, then, one more flippant word and I leave you, never to turn a thought to you again.

Young Woman [*earnestly*]. I will be serious; I promise. I fix my face, and am serious. I'll do anything you ask me to do.

[*She pulls gently at his cassock, and he slowly resumes his seat on the bench beside her.*

Bishop [*with some embarrassment*]. I'm about to say something now which, I fear, will sound very unpleasant to you, perhaps even harsh and ungenerous; something that will bite deeply into all that you may think to be a pleasure. [*He puts a hand gently and appealingly on her shoulder.*] God alone knows, my dear daughter, how deep is my desire to save you!

Young Woman [*with calm and innocent confidence*]. Oh, with your power and position, you should be able to push me into a job that wouldn't make the change such a sad one.

Bishop [*taking his hand from her shoulder, and speaking harshly*]. I wouldn't think of getting you a place till, after a year or two of trial, I felt certain you had learned how to behave yourself.

[*A pause and a tense silence.*

Young Woman [*with a stifled sob of humiliation*]. I see. [*A pause.*] How am I to live through the two years?

Bishop [*forcing himself to speak harshly*]. I've arranged that a pious Sisterhood should receive you into their Hostel, where the Reverend Mother will care for you, watch over you, and help you to live with becoming circumspection. In return, when you begin to feel at home, you can make yourself useful to the good Sisters.

Young Woman [*with tightened lips*]. I see.

[*The Policewoman enters, crosses in front of the Young Woman and the Bishop, and looks fixedly and wonderingly at the pair of them. The Young Woman looks down at her feet and the Bishop stares in front of him.*

Policewoman [*speaking towards the Bishop*]. Nice die, m'lud.

Bishop. I beg your pardon?

Policewoman. Said it was a nice die, m'lud.

Bishop [*stammeringly*]. Oh yes, quite; lovely day, beautiful day; yes, indeed, a very beautiful day. [*The Policewoman, watching them as long as possible, goes slowly out. Appealingly*] Why do you keep silent? Take your chance, take your last chance; for God's sake take your last chance. [*The Young Woman sits silent.*] Do you hear me? The offer I have made is a good offer. In it is peace, and a fair hope of better things to come. Go on, girl, speak; make up your mind, make up your mind.

Young Woman [*rising with hysterical laughter that rouses the sleeping Attendants, who lean on their elbows, watching*]. Wine's beginning to take effect again. Your old mind must be worn out thinking of such a wonderful plan. He lifted me up and set me down in the midst of a holy sisterhood. Refugium peccatorum, but not for me, thank you kindly. [*She bows mockingly to the Bishop.*] Chained fast to prayer and firm to fasting! [*She puts her face near the Bishop's.*] Not for me, thank you kindly!

Bishop [*with intense feeling*]. What will you do when your good looks go, and you lose the means to earn your bread?

Young Woman [*with a snarling look on her face as she thrusts it close to the Bishop's*]. Die, I dare say, while you heap up hopes in the books of a bank, and carry your faith about in a coffin!

> [*She hurriedly opens her handbag, takes out two notes, and holds them close to the Bishop's nose. The Two Attendants are now alert, and are watching intently.*

Young Woman [*viciously*]. See, old purple buttons—the last two between all I need and me! [*She rolls each into the shape of a crumpled ball, and calls to the Attendants.*] Eh, you there—up, and see what God has sent you! [*She flings a crumpled note to each of them. They open them, smooth them out, and put them joyously into their pockets. To the Bishop—recklessly*] I fling my wealth away! [*She points a finger at the Bishop's nose.*] Faith in God, old purple buttons, faith in God! Be merry, man, for a minute, for you'll be a long time dead! [*The Bishop, full of sorrow and disappointment, mixed with shame, bends forward on the seat, and rests his head in his hands. The Young Woman dances round with mock stateliness as she sings words to the tune of "Little Brown Jug". The Two Chair Attendants, as far as their game legs will allow, imitate her in a reckless manner, beating out time, one with his good right leg, and the other with his good left one. Singing and dancing round with mock stateliness*]:

> Sing and dance, dance and sing,
> Brief life should be a joyous thing;
> The minds that are to troubles wed
> Are fit to host but with the dead!
> Ha ha ha, you and me, till we both have ceased to be,
> Sling out woe, hug joy instead.
> For we will be a long time dead!

Chair Attendants [*joining vigorously in*]:
> Sling aht woe, 'ug joy instead,
> For we will be a long time dead!

Young Woman [*singing*]:
> Life is born and has its day,
> Sings a song, then slinks away;
> Speaks a word—the word is said,
> Then hurries off to join the dead!
> Ha ha ha, you and me, till we both have ceased to be,
> Sling out woe, hug joy instead,
> For we will be a long time dead!

Attendants [*joining in*]:
> Sling aht woe, 'ug joy instead,
> For we will be a long time dead!

> [*During the singing of the second verse of the song the Atheist has made his appearance on the top of the slope, and stands there watching what is going on below. As the Young Woman is ending the latter verse of the song, the drum-beat and chant of the Down-and-Out is heard in the near distance, coming nearer and nearer. The Chair Attendants hear it, stiffen with fear, and end the chorus weakly. Then the Young Woman recognizes it, and stands stiff, frightened, while she listens intently. Together.*] The drum-beat and chant of the Down-and-Out!

> [*The scene grows dark and chilly, and even the Bishop shivers, though the Atheist seems not to notice the change. The sky seems to turn a cold grey, and against it the Down-and-Out pass by. They are all grey, vague figures of young and old men and women, hopelessness graven on every grey face. They go by in a rather slow shuffling march, chanting their miserere to the monotonous tap, tap of the drum-beat. They go behind the Atheist, but he stands there, indifferent to march or chant. The Attendants sink down to their knees, one on the right of the grass sward, the other to the left of it.*

Down-and-Outs [*chanting*]:
> We challenge life no more, no more, with our dead faith, and our
>   dead hope;
> We carry furl'd the fainting flag of a dead hope and a dead faith.
> Day sings no song, neither is there room for rest beside night in her
>   sleeping;
> We've but a sigh for a song, and a deep sigh for a drum-beat.
> Oh where shall we go when the day calls?
> Oh where shall we sleep when the night falls?
> We've but a sigh for a song, and a deep sigh for a drum-beat!

> [*The Down-and-Out pass out, their song fading out in the repetition of the line, "We've but a sigh for a song, and a deep sigh for a drum-beat".*]

Bishop [*pointing towards where the Down-and-Out have gone*]. There go God's own aristocracy, the poor in spirit! Their slogan, Welcome be the Will of God; their life of meek obedience and resignation in that state of poverty unto which it has pleased God to call them, a testimony that God's in His heaven, all's well with the world. [*To the Attendants*]

Join them, my sons. [*To Young Woman*] Join them, my daughter, in the spirit of penitence and prayer!

Atheist [*from the slope above*].   Jannice, stand firm, and remember that you are the bride of the Dreamer. Tell him that the world shall be, not what his God wills, but what fighting man can make it. Tell him you have given life a dance and the Dreamer has given life a song!

Bishop [*coming close to the Young Woman, who is leaning for help on the back of a bench*].   They came close, my child, they came close. They will get you some day, if you do not let me save you now.

Young Woman [*with a quivering lip*].   No!

Attendants [*together*].   Save us, sir; save us!

[*The Bishop takes no notice of them.*

Bishop [*bending over the Young Woman*].   The day is fair, my daughter, the day is fair; but what of the night, when youth has faded, and the shadows fall, and the heart is lonely?

Young Woman [*tonelessly, but defiantly*].   When youth has gone, when night has fallen, and when the heart is lonely, I will stand and stare steady at a God who has filled the wealthy with good things and has sent the poor empty away.

Bishop [*sorrowfully*].   Don't say such things, child. Come with me, I beg you to come with me.

Young Woman [*with tight lips*].   No.

[*The Bishop looks sadly at her for a moment, then turns and goes slowly up the slope.*

[*The Young Salvation Army Officer followed by other members of the Army, all in uniform, peaked caps and red jerseys, come in, and group themselves in a half-circle, near the centre, to the left of the grass sward. One of them has a trombone, another a cornet, and a third, a big drum. Beside them is raised the red and blue and yellow banner of the sect. A small, box-like stand is placed on the grass, so that a speaker may be raised a little above the crowd. Around them gather various people, among them the Man wearing a Bowler Hat, the Man wearing a Straw Hat, the Man wearing a Trilby, the Nursemaid with her Guardsman, the Attendants, and the Man with the Stick, who stands off, nearer to the Atheist, as if for protection. The Young Salvation Army Officer stands out to watch the Bishop going slowly up the slope. When he reaches the top, he turns, and speaks pleadingly down to the Young Woman.*

Bishop [*making a quiet sign of the cross*].   My poor child, I ask you, in the Name of God—come!

Young Woman [*firmly, though her lips quiver a little*].   No!

> [*The Bishop looks sadly at her for a moment, and then turns, goes by the Atheist, and passes out. The Young Woman reclines weakly back on the bench, silent and desolate-looking. The scene brightens and the birds sing once more. The Young Salvation Army Officer goes over close to the Young Woman.*

S.A. Officer to Young Woman.   The ritualist has left you in your need, but the evangelist is here to comfort and help you—if you will. Dear sister, set your foot, by faith, on the path that leads to the land that is fairer than day; where the Father waits to prepare you a dwelling-place—a house not made with hands, eternal in the heavens.

> [*She is silent, and stirs not. He quietly signals to the musicians, and they softly play the tune, "There were Ninety and Nine", the rest of the Army and some of the crowd singing the words.*

Crowd:
> There were ninety and nine that safely lay
> In the shelter of the fold,
> But one was out on the hills away,
> Far off from the gates of gold,
> Away on the mountains wild and bare,
> Away from the tender Shepherd's care;
> Away from the tender Shepherd's care.

S.A. Officer to Young Woman.   You, sister. But the Lord was anxious, and would not be satisfied with His ninety and nine who were safe. So He set out to find His lost sheep—you, dear sister, you!

> [*He again quietly signals the musicians, who play the air again, while the rest sing the words.*

Crowd:
> But none of the ransomed ever knew
> How deep were the waters crossed,
> Nor how dark was the night that the Lord pass'd through,
> Ere He found His sheep that was lost.
> Out in the desert He heard its cry—
> Sick and helpless and ready to die;
> Sick and helpless and ready to die.

> [*The Young Woman is visibly affected. She rises from the bench, and half turns towards where the Salvation Army members are*

grouped. The Young Salvation Army Officer, seeing this, lays a hand gently on her shoulder.

S.A. Officer [*with uplifted eyes—prayerfully*]. There is a young sinner with us now who needs the pardon Christ can give. Let her come to the foot of the cross. She must struggle down to the cross before she can climb up to the crown. Brothers and sisters, let us pray that she may turn from her sin, and be saved! [*As he is speaking the Dreamer appears on the top of the slope above, gets in front of the Atheist, and stands to look at what is happening.*] Save this wandering lamb, O God, and bring her safely home!

Salvationists [*in chorus*]. Save her, great and most merciful Redeemer!

S.A. Officer. That the trumpets of the angels may have a new note in their sounding!

Salvationists [*in chorus*]. Save her, great and most merciful Redeemer!

S.A. Officer. That the crown of thorns on the head of the crucified one may shine as the sun in the season of summer!

Salvationists [*in chorus*]. Save her, great and most merciful Redeemer!

S.A. Officer. That the nails in His hands and His feet may gleam like the moon at the full in the season of harvest!

Young Woman [*in a frightened voice*]. Ah, save me from the fire that is never quenched, and give me peace!

Dreamer [*from the slope above*]. Jannice, Jannice, the Dreamer calls!

> [*The air of "Jannice" is faintly heard, as if from a distance. The Young Woman stands listening, and the look of fright fades from her face.*

S.A. Officer [*up to the Dreamer*]. Go your wild way, young man; for our sister has shut herself away from the pride and vanity of your thoughtless life.

Dreamer [*to S.A. Officer*]. The rose that once has opened can never close again. [*To the Young Woman*] Jannice, here is peace; peace unharmed by the fire of life. I have what will give another month of gay and crowded life; of wine and laughter; joy in our going out and our coming in; and the dear pain from the golden flame of love. Jannice, the Dreamer calls!

> [*The tune of "Jannice" is heard much more clearly now. The Young Woman has retreated away from the Salvationist group; now the Young Salvation Army Officer holds out his arms to her, but she backs away from him and half turns towards the Dreamer.*

S.A. Officer [*sadly*]. Let us all pray silently and together against the power trying to draw our young sister from the offer of redemption.

[*The Attendants fall on their knees, and with outspread fingers cover their faces. The Men Salvationists remove their caps and bend their heads in an attitude of prayer. The Woman Salvationists do the same, but do not remove their bonnets. The Young Salvation Army Officer takes off his cap, and covers his face with one hand. The tune of "Jannice" is heard clearly.*

Dreamer [*taking a step down the slope*]. Jannice, the Dreamer calls you to the deep kiss and clutch of love; to sing our song with the song that is sung by a thousand stars of the evening!

[*The Young Woman moves slowly away from the praying group, gradually quickens her movement, till finally she runs to be clasped in the arms of the Dreamer; while the Atheist looks down on the Salvationists with a slight twist of mockery disarranging his lips.*

[*The Young Salvation Army Officer glances up, and sees that the Young Woman is about to go with the Dreamer. He bends his head on his breast—a picture of disappointment, and, maybe, of vanity cheated of its due. The Musicians, replacing their caps on their heads, play the tune of "Ninety and Nine" very softly, and the rest sing the words as softly, too, for the tune of "Jannice" has faded away as the Young Woman goes into the arms of the Dreamer, as the Dreamer and the Young Woman pass out on their way together.*

Oh, sad is the fate of the lamb who strays
Far off from her Shepherd's care,
Leaving fair fields where the sunlight plays
For the gloom of the mountains bare;
Oh, sad is the Shepherd seeking his sheep,
To find that his lov'd one is nowhere there;
To find that his lov'd one is nowhere there!

THE GATES CLOSE

SCENE IV

A Winter's night in the Park. The colour of the sky is a deep black, brightening from the centre to the horizon to a rich violet, deepening to a full purple hue. To the right, where the purple sky begins to sink into the darkness, is a group of stars; one red, the other golden, and a third, silver. The trees are quite bare of leaves, and their branches form a pattern against the purple parts of the sky.

Light from an electric lamp behind the War Memorial shines on the head and shoulders of the figure, making them glow like burnished aluminum; and the bent head appears to be looking down at the life going on below it.

A Group of Men are standing to the right, looking as if they were directly under the stars. They are the Man wearing a Trilby, the Man wearing a Bowler Hat, the Man who wore a Straw One, but now is wearing a Tweed Cap, the Man with the Stick, and some others. They are all wearing topcoats or mackintoshes, and their collars are pulled up as high as they can go around their throats. The Man with the Stick now carries an Umbrella. As the scene is opening, the latter part of the bugle-call, The Last Post, is heard sounding in the far distance.

Man wearing Cap [*to the Others*].   Wot's that, now?

Man wearing Bowler.   Sounds like *The Last Post.*

Man wearing Trilby.   It is *The Last Post.*

Man wearing Cap.   Wunner where's it from?

Man wearing Trilby.   From the barracks up Kensington way. You can 'ear any sound pline on a still, clear night like this one.

Man wearing Bowler.   Creepy sound, 'asn't it? Alwyes mikes me think of grives when I 'ears it.

Man with Umbrella.   En' wot if it does? A grive's as common as a crydle, man, en' we've no caurse to be afride of either.

Man wearing Cap.   It's easy to talk, but a grive's a grive; en' with winter 'ere, en' the Park nearly desolyte, the sahnd of *The Last Post* 'as en eerie effect on me.

Man wearing Trilby [*suddenly*].   'Ere 'e is agine! Like 'Amlet's ghost. Wot interest 'as 'e in the girl, I wunner?

Man with Umbrella.   Up to no good, I bet. No bishop ever is. Keep back in the gloom so as 'e won't see.   [*They retire a little.*

    [*The Bishop comes down the slope, looking from right to left, then stopping to look behind him. His face is grey, and a deep look of worry lines it. He is followed by his Sister, who looks stern and appears to be annoyed.*

Bishop's Sister [*with suppressed anger*]. Gilbert, for goodness' sake, have sense. Why do you trouble yourself like this for a trollop?

Bishop [*angrily*]. Don't call her by that name; I won't have it, I won't have it!

Bishop's Sister. You're a fool, Gilbert! She never was your child; and even if she ever had a claim, she ceased to be your child when we put her into the Institution.

Bishop. Even if she ceased to be my child, she, nevertheless, remains a child of God; she still has her claim to the kingdom of heaven. I must not forget that now; I must never forget that again!

Bishop's Sister. If you go on like this much longer, Gilbert, you'll find yourself becoming ridiculous to respectable and important opinion.

Bishop [*vehemently*]. That has been my besetting sin all along—fear of the respectable opinion of others. I renounce it now! She herself has said, What does it matter how many think a man to be a sinner if God believes him to be a saint. That's what she said—to my very face.

Bishop's Sister. Just like the impudent and semi-blasphemous thing such as she would say!

Bishop [*impatiently*]. Don't waste time talking, woman. [*Catching her arm*] Look at that figure out there in the shadows. [*He points with his finger*]. Can you see? Is it she?

Bishop's Sister [*freeing her arm*]. I refuse to look! What has happened to you, Gilbert, after all these years of forgetfulness? Why do you suddenly so concern yourself with such a trivial thing.

Bishop. A human soul is not a trivial thing.

Bishop's Sister. Some souls are, and well you know it, and she is one of them. I tell you this fancy solicitude of yours is just a sentimental fear of something done years ago in a foolish moment. I tell you, such a soul is a trivial thing to be a torment to you.

Bishop [*sadly*]. Not hers, but our souls, I'm afraid, are the trivial things in the sight of God, and in the minds of brave men. [*Fiercely*] But mine's going to be trivial no longer! I go to seek her, and don't follow me.

Bishop's Sister [*doggedly*]. I will follow you! You're not sensible enough to be left alone.

Bishop [*angrily*]. Go home, woman. Being too sensible has been my curse all along. By trying to save my honoured soul, I am losing it. Go home, woman, and let me find a way to my girl and my God!

[*He hurries away among the trees to the left, and, after a moment's hesitation, his Sister follows him. The Man with the Umbrella comes out from the group, and peers after them. The others, too, come out of the gloom and join the Man with the Umbrella in staring towards the direction in which the Bishop and his Sister have gone. As they stare, the Guardsman and the Nursemaid, arm-in-arm, enter from the opposite direction, and, seeing the men staring, are interested, so they join the group of peerers.*]

Man with Umbrella [*pointing with his umbrella*]. There they go, one after the other—foller my leader like. Thet sister of 'is'll 'ave to keep a close eye on 'er brother. At 'is age too, runnin' after a girl as might 'ave been 'is daughter!

Guardsman [*wonderingly*]. 'Oo?

Man wearing Trilby. Now, now; the gentleman 'as no evil aims in 'is afollowing 'er. I 'eard 'im sye 'e warnted to save 'is soul en' 'ers.

Guardsman [*wonderingly*]. 'Oo's soul, wot soul?

Man with Umbrella [*contemptuously*]. Soul! There ain't no soul. Wot you 'ave in your mind is mind; the mind wot conquers time, spice, en' material conditions.

Man wearing Trilby. En' when did mind begin, en' 'oo myde it?

Man with Umbrella. Nothing begins, man; things like mind simply appear, sudden like; when, 'ow, or where, we don't know.

Guardsman [*impatiently*]. But what was it arunning after the girl?

Man with Umbrella. That clergyman fella 'oo's been runnin' rahnd tryin' to mike free with ordinary people.

Guardsman [*indignantly*]. 'Im, is it? Th' bloke wot tried to interfere once with me en' my girl. Why didn't some of you tell 'im orf?

Nursemaid [*chucking his arm*]. Aw, come on, Harry.

Guardsman [*impatiently to Nursemaid*]. Wyte a minute, carn't you! [*To the group*] Wot prevented you from atellin' 'im orf? I'd ha' done it. Our company sergeant-major's a fire terror, 'e is. Gives you a feelin' 'e 'ites everyone, 'e does, en' wishes you was dead. But whenever 'e gets me on the rawr, I tells 'im orf, I do, s'elp me!

Man with Umbrella [*with amused scorn*]. You does, does you?

Guardsman [*getting warm to his subject*]. T'other dye, Guardsman Odgerson, 'e syes, wot's th' meanin' of your bed not bein' properly folded?

Git your poor mind movin', 'e roars, fer Gord's syke, en' sye wye your bed's not properly folded, 'e syes.

Nursemaid. 'E's en ign'rant barstid, 'e is; we all knows 'im.

Guardsman [*mimicking how he did it*]. I gits 'old of a byenet en' chises 'im rahnd the barrack square till I was caught up by the picket!

Man wearing Trilby. A serious thing to do in the Awmy.

Guardsman. When I was on the carpet before the Myjor, 'e did look fierce. Serious breach of discipline, 'e syes. But, 'e syes, considering the provocytion, 'e syes, admonished, 'e syes, I think will meet the cyse. Agoin' aht, 'e syes to me, private, served 'im right, Guardsman Odgerson; pity you didn't give 'im a jeb, 'e syes—I know th' bugger!

Nursemaid. A real torf, the myjor, 'e is; a proper torf. Come on, Harry.

Guardsman. Wyte a minute, carn't you.

Man wearing Trilby. Well, I won't wyte no longer for the Atheist to come en' amuse us with his relativity ideas. I knew 'e wouldn't fyce us aht, for everyone knows spice is one thing en' time is another.

Man with Umbrella. It's not 'im's afryde to come; it's you're afryde to stye. Spice-time gives a noo meanin' to th' universe. Spice is relative to time, en' time is relative to spice—there's nothin' easier to understand.

Man wearing Trilby [*dubiously*]. Yes, quite; I gets thet, but—

Man with Umbrella [*interrupting impatiently*]. Wyte, 'old on a second. Don't question me, yet. Listen carefully; let your mind foller wot I sye, en' you'll get th' idear.

Guardsman. Listen cautiously to wot th' gentleman's asyein'—'e knows wot 'e's torking abaht.

Nursemaid [*tugging at the Guardsman's sleeve*]. Aw, c'm on, Harry; you knows I 'as to be back by ten.   [*The Guardsman takes no notice.*

Man with Umbrella [*pompously*]. Now try to remember that all th' old idears of the cosmos—Greek for all things th' 'uman mind knows of—are buried with Copernicus, Kepler, Newton, en' all that crew.

Guardsman [*emphatically*]. 'Course they is, en' deep too.

Man with Umbrella. Now we all know that the clock created time, en' the measuring-rod created spice, so that there is really neither spice nor time; but there is such a thing as spice-time. See? Get that?

Man wearing Trilby [*with confidence*]. Quite; that much is perfectly clear.

Man with Umbrella. Right. Now, suppose that one night, when we all slept, th' universe we knows sank down to the size of a football, en' all the clocks began to move a thousand times quicker,—no, slower—it wouldn't mike the slightest difference to us, for we wouldn't realize that any difference 'ad tyken plice, though each of us would live a thousand times longer, en' man couldn't be seen, even under a microscope.

Guardsman [*jocularly.*]   Could a woman be seen under a microscope?

Man wearing Cap [*to Guardsman*].   Levity's outa plice, friend, when men are trying to think out th' truth of things.

Guardsman.   But 'ow could th' world sink dahn to th' size of a football? Doesn't seem a sife thing to me.

Man with Umbrella [*with cold dignity.*]   I said *if* it did, friend.

Guardsman [*trying to find a way out*].   Yes; but if a man couldn't be seen under a microscope, wot abhat 'is kids?

Man with Umbrella.   I simply styted a hypothenuse, friend.

Man wearing Cap [*to Guardsman*].   It's only en hypothenuse, you understand? [*To Man with Umbrella*] But it's en impossible one, I think. D'ye mean that under your hypothenuse, en hour of the clock would stretch aht into ten years of time?

Man with Umbrella.   Exactly that in spice-time; en 'undred years if you like.

Man wearing Cap.   Wot? Then in your spice-time, a man doin' eight hours would be workin' for eight 'undred years!

Guardsman [*to Man with Umbrella*].   You're barmy, man! Wot abhat th' bloke doin' penal servitude fer life? When is 'e agoin' to get aht? You're barmy, man!

Nursemaid [*to Guardsman—chucking his arm*].   Are you comin', Harry? If you don't 'urry, I'll 'ave to go, en' you'll 'ave to go withaht even a firewell squeeze.

Man with Umbrella [*annoyed—to Guardsman*].   Look, friend, if I was you, I'd go with the girl; for it's pline your mind 'asn't been educyted yet to grasp the complicyted functions of wot we know as spice-time problems.

Guardsman [*with heat*].   'Oo 'asn't a mind? 'Oo're you to sye I 'asn't a mind? I 'asn't a mind as would warnt to tern th' world into a football. It's a punch on the jawr you warnts for thinkin' people warnts the world to be a football. Wye's there different thoughts in every mind, en' different rules in every country? Becorse people like you 'as th' world turned upside dahn! Wot do I mean when I syes th' world is upside dahn? Why, I means th' whole world is upside dahn, en' ennyone as 'as a mind'll unnerstend me!

Man with Umbrella [*to Guardsman*]. Wite a minute, wite a minute—you've got it all wrong.

Nursemaid [*anxiously—pulling Guardsman's arm*]. Come awye, do! They'll get you with their tork right on the carpet, in front of the colonel; so mind yourself, for I warn you, en' everyone knows as 'ow it ain't never allowed by the War Office to tork politics—soldiers is above them things.

Guardsman [*freeing himself—stormily*]. I won't let no blighter sye as 'ow I ain't got no eddicytion to tork of things! [*To Group*] Where would you muckers be if it warnt for us swaddies, eh? Poor swaddies rovin' the world, pickin' up fevers, to keep you sife at 'ome, en' 'appy. 'Oo is it does it, I asks? [*He strikes his chest.*] We blighters, us blokes!

Man with Trilby. Tike it easy, soldier; tike it easy.

Guardsman [*more stormily still*]. O'o was it, en' 'oo is it is holdin' dahn Africar en' Indiar, en' teachin' 'em 'ow to behive theirselves proper, eh? [*He strikes his breast.*] We blighters, us poor blokes!

Nursemaid [*butting it hotly*]. Yes, en' we done a thing or two for the Chinks of China, too!

Guardsman. Too true, we did!

Nursemaid [*dragging the Guardsman away*]. Come on, come aht—we're wastin' our time torkin' to these silly old cacklers!

Guardsman [*as he is being pulled out*]. If it warn't my dooty to see my gal 'ome sife, I'd mike you muckers do a right-about-wheel en' quick march off the field; I would, en' proper, too, blimey; if I was to spend a month in clink for it, s'help me, I would!

　　　　　　　　　　　[*He and the Nursemaid pass out of view.*

Man with Umbrella. There's en example, a fine example of militarism for us!

Man wearing Bowler [*deprecatingly*]. He wasn't altogether to blime. It was en unfortunate hypothenuse to set before ignorent minds; en', to me, wholly ahtside respect to things unknowable, which should be left with 'Im 'oo mide things comprehensible en' incomprehensible. Introducin' the universe as a football was a regrettable en' might become a dinegerous conception, even as a mere hypothenuse, as you might sye.

　　　[*While the Man wearing the Bowler Hat has been speaking, the Old Woman comes in slowly and wearily, and now and again gives an unsteady step, as if she had a little drink taken. She plods along till she is beside the Group of Men. She stops and looks rather vacantly at them. She carries a laurel wreath tied with red ribbon.*

Old Woman [*tonelessly*].   Anyone here see a young girl pass? My daughter; a poor one; yes, indeed, regardless of her poor mother. A scarlet crescent on the hip of a black dress; a black one on the side of a scarlet hat. My dearest daughter. A good mother I've been; some say too good; but she doesn't care, never thinks of me. [*To the Group*] Did she pass you by?

Man wearing Bowler.   I shouldn't worry, ma'am; she'll soon be in good hands—the Bishop is seeking for her.

Old Woman [*cocking an ear*].   The Bishop? That villain! He took her part against me—against her own mother. What does he want with her?

Man wearing Bowler.   Don't know, ma'am; he seemed to be anxious to find her.

Old Woman [*musingly*].   My first husband is now a man like him. Somewhere he stands before an altar jewelled with candlelight, wearing a crimson cassock and a golden cope. And a mean heart is hiding under them. He left me alone. Somewhere he's powerful and pompous; in some place or other he's brightly hidden away where I can't reach. [*She sighs.*] Everything golden is going into the bellies of the worms.

Man wearing Cap.   Maybe the Bishop could help you, ma'am.

Old Woman.   Him? He'd help no one. God can, though. I never have to raise my voice, for God can hear a whisper better than a thunderclap. Yet a little while, and He'll level down to nothing the stir that still remains around us; for everything golden is going into the bellies of the worms.

Man wearing Trilby.   If I was you, ma'am, I'd go home and have a rest.

Old Woman.   There can be no rest nor work nor play where there is no life, and the golden infancy of England's life is tarnishing now in the bellies of the worms. But God can save us, maybe, even at this late hour.

Man with Umbrella [*mockingly*].   Gord's a poor prop for enny one to lean on, ma'am.

Old Woman [*awake and lively at once*].   Who said that about God? [*To Man with Umbrella—fiercely*] You did, you, you worm! Is it any wonder we're all as we are, and I'm as I am? Provoking God to hide His goodness and His mercy. Go away you—[*She raises an arm as if to strike him. He stretches out the hand holding the umbrella to guard himself, and she, with an unexpected jerk, snatches it from him and flings it from her.*] Ah, you'd strike an old woman, would you; and with a weapon, too? [*With bitterness*] And to think that all our hero soldiers died that such as you might live! [*She catches sight of the wreath she is carrying.*] May this little token ease the anger of the dead. [*She wanders over till she is facing the base of the War Memorial. She remains silent before it for a few moments, with head bent; then speaks tonelessly and sadly.*] A few more moments of time, and Spring'll be dancing among us again; dancing in gold and purple pavilions of laburnum an' lilac; the birds'll be busy at building small worlds of their own in the safe an' snug breast of the hedges; the girls will go rambling round, each big with the thought of the life in the loins of the young men; but those who are gone shall sink into stillness, deep under the stillness that shelters the dead!

Man wearing Trilby [*removing his hat*].   May they all rest in peace!

Man wearing Bowler [*removing his hat*].   Amen!

> [*The Old Woman lifts the wreath she is carrying, high above her head, much in the same way a priest elevates the Host. Man with Umbrella has picked it up.*

Old Woman [*lifting her head till she faces the Memorial Figure*].   O soldier in bronze, cold guard of remembrance for those who rode out on swift horses to battle, and fell, I lay at thy feet this circle of green and ribbon of red as a signal of shame unto those who've forgotten the dead. [*She bends down and lays the wreath at the foot of the Memorial. Then she sings softly and quietly, without moving, the following verse. Singing*]:

> When souls are lin'd out on th' cold Judgement Day,
> To stand shaking and sad in sin's wild disarray;
> When pardon is lost, and all hopes lie in ruin,
> May God give a thought to an Irish Dragoon!

Voices [*singing*]:

> May God give a thought to an Irish Dragoon!

Old Woman [*singing*]:

> Who fought on hills high and who fought in lands low,
> Till a blustering bullet came swift from a foe,
> And left me alone, though I'll follow full soon
> The path blaz'd to death by an Irish Dragoon!

Voices [*singing*]:

> The path blaz'd to death by her Irish Dragoon!
> [*She turns down and slowly comes towards the Group of Men, singing as she goes.*

Old Woman [*singing*]:

> Though God makes the brightest of mornings look sad,
> Though He's taken from me all the joys I once had;

Though He deny all, let Him grant me one boon,
To sleep when I die with my Irish Dragoon!

Voices [*singing*]:
To sleep when she dies with her Irish Dragoon!

[*As she crosses while singing the last line, the Bishop, followed by his Sister, comes in from the opposite side, his face full of anxiety and dejection. He and the Old Woman meet when they reach the Group of Men.*

Old Woman [*lifting her head, and seeing the Bishop*]. Ah, his reverence, the Bishop! Looking for my daughter, too. And what may you want with her, your reverence?

Bishop's Sister [*getting in front of the Bishop—to Old Woman*]. Get away, woman! He isn't looking for your daughter. She would be the last person he would wish to meet!

Old Woman. Aha, are you another of the night-strollers seeking lightsome contacts in the gloomier parts of the Park?

Bishop's Sister [*furiously*]. How dare you say such a thing! How dare you even hint at such a desire in me, you tumble-down, wicked woman! I do not tread the ways of sin like you or your daughter!

Old Woman. Indeed you don't; but you could, you know, without a risk. No harm could ever come to you.

Bishop's Sister. I am what you never were, never can be—a good woman!

Old Woman. Your misfortune, madam; but there's some compensation in being a stony monument to good conduct and virtue.

Bishop [*coming forward in front of his Sister*]. Go away, you wretched woman, and cease from annoying a Bishop's sister!

Old Woman [*a little confusedly*]. Oh, yes, a bishop; I forgot. Tell me, do you, at festivals, wear a crimson cassock and a golden cope?

Bishop. What I wear concerns you not; so go away.

Old Woman. You've been looking for a girl, haven't you? The one with a red crescent on the hip of a black dress, and a black one to the side of a scarlet hat? She's my daughter.

Bishop [*somewhat sharply*]. I wasn't seeking any girl, woman. No girl at all. I once tried to help your daughter, but it was useless. So I washed my hands of her completely and for ever.

Man wearing Trilby [*coming forward*]. You've forgotten, I think, sir. Remember you asked me if I saw her, some little time ago?

Bishop [*hesitantly*]. No, no; I did not.

Bishop's Sister [*quickly*]. If he asked for anyone, it must have been I he was looking for.

Man wearing Trilby [*embarrassed and confused*]. Yes, of course, ma'am; my mistake. [*He retires again.*

Old Woman [*meditatively—to the Bishop*]. There's a hidden hum in your old voice that carries a wisp of remembrance to me. [*Suddenly*] Is your name Gilbert?

Bishop [*hastily*]. No, no; it is not. Nothing like it either.

Bishop's Sister [*quickly*]. His name is not Gilbert! [*To the world at large*] What are the police doing that undesirable persons are allowed to annoy and molest people in this way!

Bishop [*to old Woman*]. Go away from us, woman. If our politics were what they should be, you wouldn't be permitted to wander about interfering with people enjoying the innocent pleasures of the Park!

Old Woman [*scornfully*]. Pleasures and politics! Your politics are husks that only swine will eat; your power shelters behind a battlement of hunger; your religion's as holy as a coloured garter round a whore's leg: truth's bent in two, and hope is broken. [*Mournfully*] O Jesus! is there no wisdom to be found anywhere! All gone with the golden life of England into the bellies of the worms!

[*While she has been saying the last few sentences, she has been going out slowly, with tired steps, and now passes from view.*

Bishop [*turning towards the Group of Men, and trying to appear in no way affected by his scene with the Old Woman*]. Shocking example, friends, of what a woman can become! Under the influence of drink, I'm afraid. But go on with your discussion, gentlemen—it is a fine thing to see working men trying to elevate and develop their minds.

Man wearing Cap. We've finished it, sir. We have had enough of argument for one dye. We were about to go home when the Old Woman made her appearance.

Bishop's Sister [*to the Men*]. We were going homewards, too, gentlemen, when, as you saw, the half-insane creature interfered with us. Good night to you all. Come along, Gilbert.

Bishop [*suddenly catching his Sister by the arm, and pointing away from himself—agitatedly*]. Look! That girl going down the path there! Is that she? She'll be passing through the light from a lamp in a second, and my old eyes are too dim to be sure. [*A short pause.*] Now! Quick, quick, look, can't you!

Bishop's Sister [*angrily*]. I won't, I won't look. Think of what you're trying to do, Gilbert: help and kindness are but tortures to girls of her kind and class. Please be sensible and come home!

[*He shakes off a hand she has placed on his arm, and hurries out in the direction of where he thinks he had seen the girl. His Sister remains motionless where she is for a few moments, and then, distractedly, follows him out.*

Man wearing Trilby.   See, we were right after all: his name is Gilbert, en' 'e is looking for the girl. There's something curious in it all.

Man with Umbrella.   May be something curious in it, but nothing strynge —you don't know bishops as well as I do.

Man wearing Bowler.   Odd how, after denying it, she called him Gilbert; en' 'e, forgetting wot 'e said a second before, called aht to 'er to tell 'im if the passing figure was the girl 'e sought.

Man wearing Cap.   Aware of nothing save wot was in their minds—like a man not feeling or hearing ennything when he's unconscious.

Man with Umbrella.   Nonsense, man; 'course you can feel en' 'ear when you're unconscious. You're unconscious when you're asleep, but you still 'ave the faculty of 'earin' en' feeling.

Man wearing Cap.   No, sir, no; all the so-called senses are dormant in a styte of unconsciousness.

Man with Umbrella.   Wot abhat en alawm clock agoing off first thing in the mawning?

Man wearing Cap.   You 'ear it only when you become conscious of its striking.

Man in Bowler.   'Ow does it wyeken you up, then?

Man wearing Cap.   It doesn't wyeken you up, it can't wyeken you up till you become conscious of its sahnd. You understand thet, surely?

Man wearing Bowler.   I understand, but I don't agree. Wot I sye is, while I'm asleep, which is a styte of unconsciousness, I 'ear.

Man with Umbrella.   'Course 'e 'ears!

Man wearing Cap.   The styte of unconsciousness implies a condition un-accompanied by conscious experience. We experience something when we 'ear; 'ow then can we, when we're unconscious, pass into the experience of 'earing?

Man with Umbrella.   You're confusing the issue: let's decide first wot is 'earing: now wot do we mean when we say we 'ear?

Man wearing Cap.   The sense of 'earing exists simply as the sense of feeling exists, manifested, for instance, in pleasure or pine, though we know thet pine is non-existent, strictly speaking.

Man wearing Bowler [*scornfully*]. Pine non-existent? Oh, don't be silly, man!

Man with Umbrella [*with disgust*]. Aw, 'e's a giving us Christian Science now!

Man wearing Bowler. Mean to sye you carn't feel the jeb of a pin or the sting of a wasp?

Man wearing Cap. You can, if you want to feel them.

Man with Umbrella. Can if you—but no one warnts to feel them. Aw! We're back again at where we sterted.

Man wearing Bowler [*to the Man with Umbrella*]. Wite a minute, wite a minute; impatience 'll never get at the truth of things. [*To the Man wearing Cap*] Suppose you cut your finger, wouldn't you feel pine?

Man wearing Cap. I'm not going to suppose ennything of the kind. As mind willed pine into existence, so mind c'n will pine awye again.

Man with Umbrella [*with impatience*]. Aw!

Man wearing Bowler [*to the Man with Umbrella*]. Wite a minute, wite a minute. [*To the Man wearing Cap*] You said thet if you cut your finger you wouldn't feel pine?

Man wearing Cap. I never said ennything of the kind.

Man with Umbrella. Never said ennything of the kind? But we 'eard you syeing it just now, man!

Man wearing Cap. I argued in a general wye, en' I refuse to be refuted by a trivial particular, the genesis of which I deny: immaterially speaking, you carn't cut your finger.

Man with Umbrella [*with consternation*]. Immaterially speaking—carn't cut your finger—oh, mister, mister!

Man wearing Bowler [*suddenly interrupting*]. Hush, hush; look—she's coming; the girl the Bishop warnted; coming with the Dreamer!

[*They all cease talking, and look towards the point indicated by the Man wearing the Bowler Hat.*

[*After a moment or two the Young Woman enters with the Dreamer. She is leaning heavily on his arm. Her breathing is quick; her face is very pale, and in her eyes is a fixed look of fear. The lie of her clothing shows that she has dressed hastily. She is dressed as before, in black, slashed with crimson.*

[*The Dreamer wears a vivid orange scarf thrown carelessly round his neck and shoulders. He leads the Young Woman to a bench opposite to where the Group of Men is standing, and gently helps her to sit down on it. There is a hushed pause for a few moments.*

Young Woman [*tremulously*].   I'm bad, Dreamer; please go and find the Bishop for me. [*She mechanically arranges her dress.*] My clothes seem to be on me every way and any way. [*With a wan smile*] You hurried me into them, Dreamer, as quick as you hurried me out of them! Things are twisting before my eyes. [*Frightened*] Get the Bishop, go for the Bishop!

Dreamer.   Aren't you safer in the arms of the Dreamer than you are at the Bishop's feet?

Young Woman [*tonelessly*].   While I had life—yes; but I feel close to death now, and I have a lot to answer for, Dreamer.

Dreamer [*vehemently*].   Not you, fair lass; not you! A few smiles bestowed on the unworthy is all that you have to answer for. It is those who disordered your life with their damned whims; those who have left a lovely thing lonely and insecure; who have neglected to nurture the rare: it is we, dear lass, who will have to answer for all these things!

Young Woman.   You were always kind, Dreamer, and, at least, you led me to where I heard a song. Be kind to me still, and bring the Bishop here.

[*The Dreamer goes over to the Group of Men who are watching him and the Young Woman.*

Dreamer [*to the Men*].   Have any of you seen the Bishop lately?

Man wearing Trilby.   'E was 'ere a short time ago. [*He points at the Young Woman.*] En' 'e was looking for 'er.

Dreamer.   If any of you see him, send him here—the spot where the Memorial is, near the Bird Sanctuary—please.

Man wearing Bowler.   As we go 'ome, if we see 'im, we'll send 'im along.

[*They go out by different ways, and the Dreamer goes back to the Young Woman.*

Dreamer.   On their way home, if they see him, the men will send the Bishop here.

Young Woman [*agitated*].   You go, too, Dreamer—none of them might meet the Bishop. Oh, please do!

Dreamer.   I don't like to leave you alone, Jannice.

Young Woman [*with a faint smile*].   You will soon have to leave me

alone, whether you like it or no. I will be quite safe here. No one will
bother me now.

Dreamer.   Don't stir then till I come back.

[*He takes her hand in his, gently kisses it, and goes up the slope,
and out.*

[*The Young Woman sits on the bench, staring straight before her,
looking lonely and unhappy. She remains alone in the scene for a
few moments; then the Bishop's Sister comes on to the top of the
slope, looking from side to side, as if in search of someone. As she
appears above, the Old Woman comes in from the shadows on the
left below. She is greatly bent, and walks with slow and dragging
feet. She shivers as she looks about and catches sight of the lonely
figure sitting on the bench. She shuffles over to it.*

Old Woman [*peering at the figure*].   Have you seen a Bishop strolling
about anywhere here recently? He's a friend of mine. I am in sore straits,
having no home now, and he may be willing to help me. [*She pauses for
an answer, but gets none.*] A man, a comfortable man wearing a cassock
adorned with purple buttons, with a scarlet cap on his head. Why don't
you answer? [*She peers more closely at the figure, and recognizes the
Young Woman.*] Oh, it's you, is it? So here you are, looking very pale,
and as if you were settling down for death. Remember now the way you
treated your poor mother! No fancy dreams in front of you now—only
the last things staring you in the face!

[*The Bishop's Sister has heard the Old Woman talking, has
watched her while she spoke, and now comes down the slope towards them.*

Young Woman [*doggedly—with a vicious look at the Old Woman*].
Anyhow, if I go, I'll go game, and die dancing!

Old Woman [*with some exultation in her voice*].   Looks as if it would be
me who would be dancing over your grave, my merry lady!

[*The Young Woman rises from the bench, and walks unsteadily
away from the Old Woman, meeting the Bishop's Sister, who has
come down the slope. The Young Woman retreats a few steps from
her, so that she is between them both, where she stands shivering.*

Bishop's Sister [*to the Young Woman*].   So I've found you just before the
Bishop could come to you. Waiting for his help and pity, are you? Be off
out of the Park, and hide yourself, you shameless thing, or I'll send the
police to take you out!

Old Woman [*getting in front of the Young Woman, and bowing low in
mockery before the Bishop's Sister*].   Salaam, mem pukka memsahib,

salaam, and pardon her and pardon me and pardon us all for getting in the way of thy greatness; and grant us grace to have faith in thy dignity and importance, per benedicite pax hugger muggery ora pro puggery rigmarolum!

Bishop's Sister [*venomously*].   The pair of you ought to be stretched out naked on the ground so that decent women could trample the life out of you!

Old Woman [*confidently*].   Gallant men would lift us up on to our feet again.

Bishop's Sister [*violently*].   Sympathy for such as you would be a sin. The soft and gentle hand of pity must be changed to the punishing hand of bronze!

Old Woman [*remonstrating*].   Oh, sister, sister!

Bishop's Sister [*furiously*].   How dare you call me sister!

Old Woman [*reflectively*].   How savage women can be when God has been unkind and made us plain, so that no man can find a vision in our face.

[*In the distance is heard the beat of the drum and the faint murmur of the Down-and-Out chant. The Three Women become rigid, and listen intently.*

[*Down the slope come the tottering Attendants, followed by the Two Evangelists, bent, and with unsteady legs. All their faces are full of fear. They come into the centre, an Evangelist and an Attendant going behind the Bishop's Sister, and an Evangelist and an Attendant behind the Young Woman.*

Evangelists and Attendants [*in chorus, as they come down the slope*]. With drum-beat and chant the Down-and-Out are close upon us!

Bishop's Sister [*with merry rancour*].   Soon they will encompass you round about; and there will be no way of escape, even for the lady of the good looks!

The Bishop appears on the slope above. He stands so that the light from a lamp falls on him, a sad and dignified figure in his cassock with its purple buttons, and the scarlet biretta on his head. He stretches out an arm over those below, extending two fingers of a hand in blessing, and says in sad and low tones, almost intoning the words:

Bishop.   Benedicti vos a Domino, qui fecit coelum et terram.

[*He comes slowly down the slope, backed by the chant, louder now,*

*of the Down-and-Outs, and the Young Woman rushes over to him,
and falls on her knees.*

Young Woman [*imploringly*]. Bless me, even me, oh! my father!

[*With a shiver and a quivering lip, the Bishop stretches an arm over
her, extends his fingers to bless her, but his arm falls slowly to his
side again, and he remains silent.*

[*The Dreamer now appears on the slope, and stands in the light
where the Bishop had stood before, looking at those below him. The
Bishop walks away from the kneeling Young Woman, and stands in
the centre, with a group on his right and another on his left.*

1st Evangelist. We have danced no dance, neither have we sought the
beauty of any woman; we have sung no songs, nor have we ever made
merry in our hearts.

2nd Evangelist. We have honoured pain; bound up joy with sighing; and
multiplied sorrows that men might know Thy mercy and Thy kindness.

Bishop. Grant them pardon, O Lord, and bring them peace!

Dreamer. Let them sink into the grave, O Lord, and never let their like
appear on the face of the earth again.

1st Evangelist. Stricken, we struck not back; we blessed them that cursed
us; and prayed for them that took no note of our misery and want.

Bishop. Grant them pardon, O Lord, and bring them peace!

Dreamer. Let brambles, O Lord, grow thick where they are buried deep;
let the fox and the vixen guard their cubs in the midst of the brambles;
and let children sing and laugh and play where these have moaned in
their misery!

[*The Down-and-Outs are here now, spreading over the slope above,
and making to come down; but the Dreamer with outstretched arms
bars the way. On their way, and just before coming in on to the
slope, they are heard singing.*

Down-and-Outs [*chanting*]:
Life has pass'd us by to the loud roll of her drum,
With her waving flags of yellow and green held high,
All starr'd with the golden, flaming names of her most mighty chil-
dren.
Oh, where shall we go when the day calls?
Oh, where shall we sleep when the night falls?
We've but a sigh for a song, and a deep sigh for a drum-beat!

[*Their chant changes into a menacing hum, like that of a swarm of*

*wasps, to the tune of the chant, as the rest speak to each other. The
Young Woman goes unsteadily over to the Bishop.*

Young Woman [*imploring*].   Let me not mingle my last moments with
this marching misery!

Bishop [*to Young Woman—slow, but with decision*].   You must go where
they go, and their sighing shall be your song!

Down-and-Outs [*chanting*]:
   She must be merry no more; she must walk in the midst of the mourn-
      ful;
   Who've but a sigh for a song, and a deep sigh for a drum-beat!

   [*The Young Woman has stiffened with resentment as she has listened, and now stands facing the Dreamer, looking at him for
   encouragement.*

Dreamer [*to Young Woman*].   Turn your back swift on the poor, purple-
button'd dead-man, whose name is absent from the book of life. Offer not
as incense to God the dust of your sighing, but dance to His glory, and
come before His presence with a song!

Young Woman [*with reckless defiance*].   I'll go the last few steps of the
way rejoicing; I'll go, go game, and I'll die dancing!

Dreamer [*exultantly*].   Sing them silent, dance them still, and laugh
them into an open shame!

   [*Faintly, as if the tune was heard only in the minds of the Dreamer
   and the Young Woman, the notes of a dance tune are heard, coming
   from the subdued playing of a flute and other instruments. The
   Young Woman and the Dreamer dance to the melody, she a little
   unsteadily. They dance for about a minute, then the movements of
   the Young Woman become a little uncertain; she staggers, recovers
   herself, dances again, but with faltering steps. The music of the
   dance becomes fainter.*

Young Woman [*frightened*].   Dreamer, Dreamer, I'm fainting—I think
I'm going to die.

Dreamer [*fiercely*].   Sing them silent; dance them still; laugh them into an
open shame!

Down-and-Outs [*chanting and coming down a little by the centre*].
   She must be merry no more; she must be set in the midst of the
      mournful,
   Who've but a sigh for a song, and a deep sigh for a drum-beat.

Dreamer [*fiercely, with his face close to the Young Woman's*].   Sing
them silent; dance them still; laugh them into an open shame!

Bishop [*prayerfully as they dance*].   O Lord, who taketh pleasure in Thy people, let this dance be unto Thee as a merry prayer offered by an innocent and excited child!

> [*The tune of the dance is now mournful, and the Dreamer is almost carrying the Young Woman in his arms. They dance in this way for a few moments, then the head of the Young Woman falls limp, and the Dreamer lifts her in his arms, carries her to a soft spot on the green sward, and lays her down there.*

Young Woman [*almost in a whisper*].   I die, Dreamer, I die, and there is fear in my heart.

Dreamer [*tenderly*].   Fear nothing: courage in the hearts of men and women is what God needs most; and He will find room for one scarlet blossom among a thousand white lilies!

> [*The Bishop goes unsteadily to where the Young Woman is lying. He kneels beside her, and takes one of her hands in his.*

Young Woman [*to the Bishop*].   Guide the hand you hold into making the sign of the cross, that I may whisper my trust in the golden mercy of God!

> [*The Bishop guides her hand as she makes the sign of the cross. She lies still and silent. The Down-and-Out come down the rest of the way, changing the waspish hum of their voices to the dolorous chant of their miserere. They spread out, enveloping the Evangelists, the Attendants, and the Old Woman.*

Down-and-Outs [*chanting*]:

> We challenge life no more, no more, with our dead faith and our dead hope;
> We carry furl'd the fainting flags of a dead hope and a dead faith.
> Day sings no song, neither is there room for rest beside night in her sleeping:
> We've but a sigh for a song, and a deep sigh for a drum-beat!

> > [*They force the Dreamer back a few paces at first; but exerting his strength, he forces a way through them, scattering them to right and left, as he chants his vigorous song of defiance and resolution.*

Dreamer:

> Way for the strong and the swift and the fearless:
> Life that is stirr'd with the fear of its life, let it die;
> Let it sink down, let it die, and pass from our vision for ever.
> Sorrow and pain we shall have, and struggle unending:
> We shall weave courage with pain, and fight through the struggle unending.

Way for the strong and the swift and the fearless:
Life that is stirr'd with the fear of its life, let it die;
Let it sink down, let it die, and pass from our vision for ever!

[*The Dreamer goes up the slope. When he reaches the top, he turns, looks down at the still form of the Young Woman. The Bishop's Sister stands apart, and watches the Bishop kneeling beside the form of the Young Woman. She goes over, after a moment's pause, and gently touches the Bishop's shoulder.*

Bishop [*looking up at his Sister*]. Go home, go home, for Christ's sake, woman, and ask God's mercy on us all!

[*She looks at the kneeling figure for a moment, then, turning, she goes out without a word.*

Bishop [*in low and grief-stricken tones*]. She died making the sign of the cross!

Dreamer [*looking down to where the Young Woman is lying*]. You fought the good fight, Jannice; and you kept the faith: Hail and farewell, sweetheart; for ever and for ever, hail and farewell!

[*The Dreamer turns, and begins to go out slowly. The sky's purple and black changes to a bright grey, pierced with golden segments, as if the sun was rising, and a new day about to begin. The music, sounding low, of the song he sang to her, is heard; in the middle of the melody the gates begin to close slowly, coming together on the last few notes of the tune.*

THE GATES CLOSE

PURPLE DUST

A Wayward Comedy in Three Acts

(1940)

TO

SHIVAUN

✵ ✵ ✵

CHARACTERS IN THE PLAY

CYRIL POGES
BASIL STOKE
SOUHAUN, *Cyril's mistress*
AVRIL, *Basil's mistress*
BARNEY, *their manservant*
CLOYNE, *their maidservant*
O'KILLIGAIN, *a foreman stonemason*
1ST WORKMAN
2ND WORKMAN
3RD WORKMAN
REVEREND GEORGE CANON CHREEHEWEL,
    P.P. of Clune na Geera
POSTMASTER
YELLOW-BEARDED MAN
THE FIGURE
THE BULL

SCENE

ACT I · A room in an old Tudor mansion in Clune na Geera.

ACT II · The same.

ACT III · The same.

TIME · The present.

ACT I

SCENE: *A wide, deep, gloomy room that was once part of the assembly or living room of a Tudor-Elizabethan mansion. The floor is paved with broad black and dull red flagstones. The walls are timbered with oak beams, and beams of the same wood criss-cross each other, forming the roof, so that the room looks somewhat like a gigantic cage. The beams are painted, alternately, black and white so as to show they are there and to draw attention to their beauty; but the paint makes them too conspicuous and, therefore, ugly.*

On the right is a huge open fireplace, overhung by a huge hood. In the centre of the fireplace is a big iron arm with a swinging cross-piece thrust out like a crane; from this cross-piece hangs a thick chain to which a big shining copper kettle is attached. At the back are two rather narrow arched doorways, one towards the right, the other towards the left. Between these are two long, deep, mullioned windows. At the right, nearly opposite the fireplace, is a wider arched doorway leading to the entrance hall. Near the fireplace are two straight-backed seats, like infantile church pews, each big enough only to hold one person. A small Elizabethan or Jacobean table is somewhere near the centre of the room. On this table is a vase in which are a collection of violets and primroses, mostly primroses.

It is about seven o'clock of an autumn morning, fine, crisp, and fair.

Three workmen are seen in the room, two with shovels and one with a pickaxe. One with a shovel and the one with the pickaxe are standing near the archway leading to the entrance hall; the other, with a shovel, is beside the wide fireplace, looking curiously at it. The 1st Workman is a tall, lean man with a foxy face; the 2nd Workman is tall too, and strongly built; he has a dreamy look, and has a dark trim beard faintly touched with grey; the 3rd Workman is stouter than the others, and not so tall. They are all roughly dressed in soiled clothes, and wear high rubber boots.

1st Workman [*near the fireplace*]. Well, of all th' wondhers, to come to live in a house that's half down and it's wanin' over. Thrickin' th' rotten beams into a look o' sturdiness with a coat o' white and black paint, an' they for long a dismal dwellin', even for the gnawin' beetle an' th' borin' worm.

3rd Workman [*with the pickaxe*]. They like that sort of thing.

1st Workman. An' th' maid was tellin' me they're goin' to invest in hins an' cows, an' make th' place self-supportin'.

3rd Workman. An' th' two o' them business men, rollin' in money.

1st Workman. Women you're not married to cost a lot to keep; an' th' two with them'll dip deep into the oul' men's revenue. Goin' over to London done them a world o' good.

3rd Workman.   Irish, too, an' not a bit ashamed o' themselves.

1st Workman.   Ashamed is it? Isn't th' oulder one proclaimin' she's straight derived from th' Duke of Ormond?

3rd Workman.   An' we knowin' th' two o' them well as kids with patched petticoats an' broken shoes, runnin' round th' lanes o' Killnageera.

1st Workman.   God be good to her, anyway, for bringin' a bit o' th' dod-dherers' money to where it's needed.

3rd Workman.   Th' two poor English omadhauns won't have much when th' lasses decide it's time for partin'.

2nd Workman [*who has been silently leaning on his shovel, looking dreamily ahead of him*].   That day'll hasten, for God is good. Our poets of old have said it often: time'll see th' Irish again with wine an' ale on th' table before them; an' th' English, barefoot, beggin' a crust in a lonely sthreet, an' th' weather frosty.

1st Workman.   Afther a reckless life, they need th' peace o' th' country.

3rd Workman [*assuming a listening attitude*].   They're stirrin'.

[*Mr. Cyril Poges, Souhaun, and Barney come in by one entrance at the back; Avril, Basil Stoke, and Cloyne from the other; they dance in what they think to be a country style, and meet in the centre, throwing their legs about while they sing. Avril has a garland of moonfaced daisies round her neck and carries a dainty little shepherd's crook in her hand; Cyril Poges, a little wooden rake with a gaily-coloured handle; Souhaun has a little hoe, garlanded with ribbons; Cloyne, a dainty little hayfork; Barney, a little reaping-hook; and Basil Stoke, a slim-handled little spade. Each wears a white smock having on it the stylised picture of an animal; on Poges's, a pig; on Basil's, a hen; on Souhaun's, a cow; on Avril's, a duck; on Cloyne's, a sheep; on Barney's, a cock.*

[*Poges is a man of sixty-five years of age. He was, when young, a rather good-looking man, but age has altered him a lot. He is now inclined to be too stout, with a broad chest and too prominent belly; his face is a little too broad, too ruddy, and there are perceptible bags of flesh under his eyes. He has a large head; getting bald in front; though behind and over his ears the hair is long, fairly thick, and tinged with grey. He has a fussy manner, all business over little things; wants his own way at all times; and persuades himself that whatever he thinks of doing must be for the best, and expects every-*

one else to agree with him. He is apt to lose his temper easily, and to shout in the belief that that is the only way to make other people fall in with his opinions. He has now persuaded himself that in the country peace and goodwill are to be found; and expects that everyone else should find them there too. Under the smock he is dressed in morning clothes, and he wears a tall hat.

[*Basil Stoke is a long, thin man of thirty, with a rather gloomy face which he thinks betokens dignity, made gloomier still by believing that he is something of a philosopher. His cheeks are thin and their upper bones are as sharp as a hatchet. He is clean-shaven, and the thin hair on his half-bald head is trimly brushed back from his forehead. His eyes are covered with a pair of large horn-rimmed glasses. Under the smock he is dressed in jacket, plus-fours, and he wears a cap.*

[*Souhaun is a woman of thirty-three years of age. She must have been a very handsome girl and she is still very good-looking, in a more matronly way. She has the fine figure of her young friend Avril, but her arms and her legs have grown a little plumper. She is still attractive enough to find attention from a good many men, when her young friend is out of the way. She wears, under the smock, what a lady would usually wear in the morning.*

[*Cloyne is a stoutly-built, fine-looking girl of twenty-six or so, and wears the servant's dress under her smock, and has a smart servant's cap on her head.*

[*Barney is a middle-aged man with a discontented face and a muttering manner. Under his smock he wears the usual dress of a butler.*

[*Avril is dressed, under her smock, in gay pyjamas.*

Poges [*singing*]:
Rural scenes are now our joy:
Farmer's boy,
Milkmaid coy,
Each like a newly-painted toy,

All:
In the bosky countrie!

Avril [*singing*]:
By poor little man the town was made,
To degrade
Man and maid;
God's green thought in a little green shade
Made the bosky countrie!

All [*chorus*]:
>   Hey, hey, the country's here,
>   The country's there,
>   It's everywhere!
>   We'll have it, now, last thing at night,
>   And the very first thing in the morning!

Basil [*singing*]:
>   Our music, now, is the cow's sweet moo,
>   The pigeon's coo,
>   The lark's song too,
>   And the cock's shrill cock-a-doodle-doo,

All:
>   In the bosky countrie!
>   [*chorus*]
>   Hey, hey, the country's here,
>   The country's there,
>   It's everywhere!
>   We'll have it, now, last thing at night,
>   And the very first thing in the morning!

>   [*As they are singing the last lines of the chorus for the second time,
>   those who have come in by the left entrance go out by the right one;
>   and those who have come in by the right entrance go out by the left
>   one. The workmen stand silent for a few moments, watching the
>   places where the singers disappeared.*]

1st Workman. Well, God help the poor omadhauns! It's a bad sign to see people actin' like that, an' they sober.

3rd Workman. A sthrange crowd, they are, to come gallivantin' outa the city to a lonely an' inconsiderate place like this.

1st Workman. At home, now, they'd be sinkin' into their first sleep; but because they're in the counthry they think the thing to do is to get up at the crack o' dawn.

3rd Workman. An' they killin' themselves thryin' to look as if the counthry loved them all their life.

1st Workman. With the young heifer gaddin' round with next to nothin' on, goadin' the decency an' circumspection of the place.

3rd Workman. An' her eyes wiltin' when she sees what she calls her husband, an' widenin' wondherfully whenever they happen to light on O'Killigain.

1st Workman. A handsome, hefty young sthripling, with a big seam in his arm that he got from a bullet fired in Spain.

3rd Workman. For ever fillin' the place with reckless talk against the composure of the Church in the midst of the way things are now.

2nd Workman. Ay, an' right he is, if ears didn't shut when his mind was speakin'.

1st Workman [*to 2nd Workman*]. If I was you I'd be dumb as well, for Canon Chreehewel's mad to dhrive him outa th' place, with all who hear him.

2nd Workman [*fervently*]. There's ne'er another man to be found as thrue or as clever as him till you touch a city's centre; an' if he goes, I'll go too.

1st Workman [*a little derisively*]. Me brave fella.

3rd Workman. It's what but they're thryin' to be something else beside themselves.

1st Workman. They'd plunge through any hardship to make themselves believe they are what they never can become.

2nd Workman [*dolorously*]. An' to think of two such soilifyin' females bein' born in Ireland, an' denizenin' themselves here among decent people!

3rd Workman. Whissht; here's the boss, O'Killigain.

[*O'Killigain comes in from the side entrance, with a short straight-edge in his hand. He is a tall, fair young man twenty-five or twenty-six years old. He has a rough, clearly-cut face; dogged-looking when he is roused, and handsome when he is in a good humour, which is often enough. He is clean-shaven, showing rather thick but finely-formed lips. His hair, though cut short, is thick and striking. When he speaks of something interesting him, his hands make graceful gestures. He has had a pretty rough life, which has given him a great confidence in himself; and wide reading has strengthened that confidence considerably. He is dressed in blue dungarees and wears a deep yellow muffler, marked with blue decoration, round his neck. He is humming a tune as he comes in, and goes over towards the men.*]

O'Killigain [*lilting, as he comes in*]:
   They may rail at this life, from the hour I began it,
   I found it a life full of kindness and bliss;
   And until they can show me some happier planet,
   More social and bright, I'll content me with this.

   [*To the men*] 'Morra, boys.

All the Men. 'Morra, Jack.

O'Killigain [*with a gesture pointing to where he thinks the people of the house may be*]. Up yet?

1st Workman. Up is it? Ay, an' dancin' all about the place.

O'Killigain. Bright colours, in cloth and paint, th' ladies want, they say; jazz pattherns, if possible, say the two dear young ladies: well, they'll want pretty bright colours to cheer up this morgue.

3rd Workman. It's a strange thing, now, that a man with money would like to live in a place lonesome an' cold enough to send a shiver through a year-old dead man!

O'Killigain. Because they think it has what they call a history. Everything old is sacred in every country. Give a house a history, weave a legend round it, let some titled tomfool live or die in it—and some fool mind will see loveliness in rottenness and ruin.

1st Workman. A nephew of the Duke of Ormond, they say, dhrank himself to death in it, and the supernumary wife of the older codger says she's a direct descendant of the nephew; and she says they've come from the darkness an' danger of England to settle down in what is really their proper home.

O'Killigain. And they're goin' to have the spoons and forks an' knives done with what they say is the Ormond crest; Ormond's motto will shine out from their notepaper; and this tumble-down oul' shack is to be christened Ormond Manor.

2nd Workman [*savagely*]. The English gett, hurryin' off with the ensign privilege of an Irish gentleman!

3rd Workman. Isn't it sthrange how many'll fall for a mere name? Remember oul' Miss MacWilliam who used to faint with ecstasy the times she told the story of sittin' for a second in the King o' Denmark's chair; an' oul' Tom Mulligan who swaggered round for years afther the son o' the Earl of Skibbereen had accidentally spit in his eye!

O'Killigain. Well, men, we'd better make a start.

1st Workman [*warningly*]. Shush! Here's the flower o' Finea!

[*Avril comes in from the left entrance. She is a pretty girl of twenty-one or so, inclined, at times, to be a little romantic, and is very much aware of her good looks. She is far from being unintelligent, but does little and cares less about developing her natural talents. Her eyes are large and expressive, but sometimes sink into a hardened lustre. She is inclined to think that every good-looking young fellow, rich or poor, should fall for her pretty face and figure, and is a little worried if one of them doesn't. She adopts a free-and-easy and very unnatural attitude when she is talking to workmen. She is dressed now in gay scarlet trousers, widening at the ends, and very tight around her hips and bottom; low-cut black silk bodice, slashed with crimson, half hidden by a red-and-white striped scarf thrown carelessly round her shoulders—and black shoes. She trips over in a slow dancing way to where the workmen are standing, and as she comes in she lilts the first verse of* The Maid of Bunclody.

Avril [*close to the workmen*].   Top o' the mornin', boys!

O'Killigain [*humouring her*].   Same to you, miss, an' many of them, each of them fairer an' finer than the finest of all that ever brought the soft light o' the dawn at the peep o 'day into your openin' eyes.

Avril.   It's meself that hopes you like the lovely house you're renovatin'?

O'Killigain.   An' tell me who wouldn't like the lovely house we're renovatin'? It's a dark man he'd be, without a stim o' light, an' destitute o' feelin'.

1st Workman [*enthusiastically*].   Sure, miss, it's dumb with many wondhers we've all been for years that no one o' the well-to-do laid hands suddenly on the house to give it the glory again that musta been here throughout the jewel'd days of the times gone by!

Avril.   When it's thoroughly restored it'll be a pleasure an' a pride to the whole district.

O'Killigain [*with just a touch of sarcasm in his voice*].   Sure, when we're done with it wouldn't it be fit for the shelther an' ayse an' comfort of Nuad of the Silver Hand, were he with us now, or of the great Fergus himself of the bright bronze chariots?

Avril.   Or even the nephew of Ormond's great Duke, the warlike ancestor of my very own friend an' distant cousin?

O'Killigain.   An' all the people here who are anything'll be mad with envy that they hadn't seized holt of it to make it what it'll soon be shown to be! [*Avril lilts a reel and dances lightly about the room. The 1st and 3rd Workmen join in the lilting of the air. As she is passing O'Killigain he catches her excitedly and whirls her recklessly round the room till she is breathless, while the two men quicken the time of the lilting. To Avril while she stands breathlessly before him*] Bow to your partner. [*Avril bows to him and he bows to her. Indicating the two men who lilted the tune of the reel*] Bow, bow to the bards.

[*She bows to the two men, and when she has bent to the bow, O'Killigain gives her a sharp skelp on the behind. She straightens herself with a little squeal of pain and a sharp cry of indignation, and faces him angrily.*

Avril [*indignantly*]. You low fellow, what did you dare do that for! How dare you lay your dirty hands on a real lady! That's the danger of being friendly with a guttersnipe! Wait till you hear what Mr. Basil Stoke'll say when he hears what you've done. Get out of the room, get out of the house—go away, and never let your ugly face be seen here again!

O'Killigain [*with some mockery in his voice*]. Sure, I meant no harm, miss; it was simply done in the excitement of the game. [*To 1st Workman*] Wasn't it, now, Bill?

3rd Workman. Ay was it, miss. Sure, th' poor man lost his caution in the gaiety and the gayer tune.

O'Killigain. I did it all in play; I thought you'd like it.

Avril [*sarcastically*]. Oh, did you? Well, I didn't like it, and I don't allow anyone to take advantage of any effort I make to treat workmen as human beings.

2nd Workman [*maliciously*]. If I was asked anything, I'd say I saw a spark of pleasure in the flame of pain that came into her eyes when she was hot!

Avril [*furiously—to the men*]. Be off, you, and let me speak alone to this young man! I don't require any explanation from such as you; so be off, and I'll deal with this fellow! [*The three workmen slide away out of the scene. With a gentler tone in her voice*] Never, never do a thing like that again, young man.

O'Killigain [*with mocking earnestness*]. Never again, young lady. You looked so handsome, gay, and young that my thoughts became as jaunty an' hilarious as your little dancin' feet.

Avril. Never again, mind you—especially when others are here to stand and gape. [*She goes over and feels the muscle of his arm*]. There's too much power in that arm to give a safe and gentle blow to a poor young girl.

O'Killigain. Ashamed I am of the force that sent a hand to hit a girl of grace, fit to find herself walkin' beside all the beauty that ever shone before the eyes o' man since Helen herself unbound her thresses to dance her wild an' willin' way through the sthreets o' Throy!

Avril. It's I that know the truth is only in the shine o' the words you shower on me, as ready to you as the wild flowers a love-shaken, innocent girl would pick in a hurry outa the hedges, an' she on her way to Mass.

O'Killigain. Is it afther tellin' me that you are, an' your own words dancin' out as fair an' fine as the best o' mine?

Avril. An' why wouldn't they, now, an' me that sang me song, first runnin' me years in, an' runnin' them out, in th' fields an' roads that skirted the threes an' hills o' Killnageera? But is there an Irishman goin' who hasn't a dint o' wondher in his talkin'?

O'Killigain. I never met many who had it; but I got the touch of makin' a song from me mother, who—[*proudly*]—once won a grand gold medal at a Feis for a song of her own, put together between the times of bringin' up six children an' puttin' an odd flower on the grave of the one that died.

Avril. You must sing me a few of your songs sometime.

O'Killigain. Now, if you'd like to listen, an' you think that the time is handy.

Avril. Not now; we might be disturbed; but some evening, somewhere away from here.

O'Killigain. I will, an' welcome; some of them, too, that have been set in a little book, lookin' gay an' grand, for all the world to see. Come; listen— [*in a mocking whisper*]—and brave the wrath of the gouty, doughty Basil Stoke.

Avril [*with a toss of her head*]. That thing! [*With bitter contempt*] A toddler thricking with a woman's legs; a thief without the power to thieve the thing he covets; a louse burrowing in a young lioness's belly; a perjurer in passion; a gutted soldier bee whose job is done, and still hangs on to life!

O'Killigain [*embracing her tightly*]. Tonight, or tomorrow night, then, beside the blasted thorn three.

Avril [*with fright in her voice*]. The blasted thorn tree! Oh, not there, not there—for evil things sit high, sit low in its twisty branches; and lovers, long ago, who leaned against it lost their love or died. No, no, not there: a saint himself would shudder if he had to pass it on a dusky night, with only a sly chit of a moon in the sky to show the way.

O'Killigain. Oh, foolish girl, there never can be evil things where love is living. Between the evil things an' us we'll make the sign of the rosy cross, an' it's blossomin' again the dead an' dhry thing will be, an' fruit will follow. We are no' saints, and so can abide by things that wither, without shudder or sigh, let the night be dark or dusky. It is for us to make dying things live once more, and things that wither, leaf and bloom again. Fix your arm in mine, young and fair one, and face for life.

Avril [*after a little hesitation*]. Undher the thorn three then, with you.

[*As the sound of voices is heard he holds her tight for a few mo-*

ments, kisses her several times, then lets her go. He goes over and examines a wall where a telephone is evidently being put in.

[*Avril, all demure, stands at the other end of the room watching him.*

[*Souhaun, followed by Poges and Basil, comes into the room. She is carrying a large-two-handled earthenware jug in her right hand, and two coloured cushions under her left arm. Cyril Poges is carrying a large coloured picture of himself in a gold frame; and Basil Stoke too is bearing a picture of himself in a silver frame; he has a hammer sticking out of his side pocket. Cloyne follows them in with a six-step A ladder. Poges and Stokes are wearing gum-boots reaching to their thighs, and bright scarves round their necks.*

[*Poges and Basil rest the pictures against a wall.*

Souhaun [*to Avril*]. Oh, here you are, with Mr. O'Killigain. We were wondering where you were. We've a lot to do, dear, before we can get the house comfortable, so don't keep Mr. O'Killigain from his work. [*She leaves the jug down in a corner.*] Filled with gay flowers, Cyril, this jug'll be just the thing on your quattrocento desk-bureau.

Poges. Lovely, darling. [*To O'Killigain*] We've been for a run over the fields, O'Killgain; lovely; feel as fresh as a daisy after it. [*Indicating the boots*] Great comfort, these boots, in the long damp grass. Saw a swarm of rabbits—quaint creatures.

Basil. With these and rubber hats and rubber coats, we'll be able to weather anything. I've got the hammer. Have you got the nails?

Poges. I forgot them. I'll get them now.

Basil. And I'll get the string.   [*One goes out left, and the other right.*

Souhaun [*to Cloyne*]. Hold this curtain stuff end, Cloyne, till we see its width.

[*Cloyne holds one end of the stuff while Souhaun holds the other. O'Killigain, pretending to be interested, bends over Cloyne and, stretching out a hand to handle the stuff, half puts his arm around Cloyne's neck, who is very well pleased.*

O'Killigain. Finely woven as a plover's wing, it is. No way odd it ud look as a cloak for the lovely Emer; an', if it hung from th' sturdy shouldhers of Queen Maev herself, she'd find a second glory!

Souhaun [*displeased at his covert attention to Cloyne*]. Over here, Cloyne, please; hold this end.

[*Souhaun and Cloyne change places, and O'Killigain bends over Souhaun.*

Avril [*to O'Killigain*]. I must have a chat with that man working for you who knows everything worth knowing about Ireland's past and present, Mr. O'Killigain.

O'Killigain [*very seriously*]. And please, miss, don't try to make fun of him. Touch him not with a jibe, for he's a wandherin' king holdin' th' ages be th' hand.

Souhaun. How could a common worker be a king, O'Killigain?

O'Killigain. Easier than for a king to be a common worker. Th' king o' a world that doesn't exist was a carpenter.

Avril. Where is the real world to be found, then?

O'Killigain. Where I have found it often, an' seek to find it still.

Avril. And where's that place to be found?

O'Killigain. With the bittherness an' joy blendin' in a pretty woman's hand; with the pity in her breast; in th' battlin' beauty of her claspin' arms; an' rest beside her when th' heart is tired.

Cloyne. Sure, it's only makin' fun of us all he is.

O'Killigain. Softer an' safer than St. Patrick's breastplate is a woman's breast to save a man from the slings of life. [*Singing softly, moving a little away. Slyly towards the women*:]

> Come in, or go out, or just stay at the door.
> With a girl on each arm an' one standin' before;
> Sure, the more that I have, the more I adore,
> For there's life with the lasses,
> Says Rory O'More!
>
> Oh, courtin's an illigant, gorgeous affray,
> When it's done in the night, or just done in the day;
> When joy has been spent, sure, there's joy still in store;
> For there's life with the lasses,
> Says Rory O'More!
>
> When all has been done, though nothin's been said,
> Deep in the green grass, or at home in the bed;
> To ev'ry brave effort we'll yield an encore;
> For there's life with the lasses,
> Says Rory O'More!

[*As he ends his song, Poges and Basil return, the one with the nails, the other with the string-wire.*

Poges [*to O'Killigain—briskly*]. The garage is well in hand, isn't it, O'Killigain?

O'Killigain [*who has tapped the wall, and is shaking his head*]. Yes, well in hands.

Poges [*enthusiastically*]. Good man; when it's done I'll get a first-class artist over from London to paint and make it exactly like a little Tudor dwelling, so that it won't in any way distort the beauty of the fine old house. What do you say, O'Killigain? [*O'Killigain is silent.*] Eh?

O'Killigain. I didn't speak.

Basil [*who has moved over, and is looking ecstatically up at an end wall*]. Early Tudor, I think; yes, Early Tudor, I'll swear. A great period, a great period. Full of flow, energy, colour, power, imagination, and hilarity.

O'Killigain [*tapping the wall beside him—ironically*]. And this is Middle Tudor—not a doubt about it.

Poges [*looking ecstatically at the other end wall*]. Late Tudor this one, I'm sure. Ah, England had no equal then. Look at the Lionheart, eh? Smashed the infidel, smashed him out of Jerusalem into the desert places. What was his name, follower of the Prophet? You remember, Hegira, the white stone, or was it a black stone?—oh, what was the bounder's name?

Souhaun [*helpfully*]. Tuttuttankamen, dear?

Poges [*scornfully*]. Tuttuttankamen! My God, woman, he was only the other day!

Avril [*more helpfully.*] The Mahdi, dear?

Poges [*more scornfully*]. The Mahdi! [*Plaintively*]. Is there no one here knows a line of the history of his country!

Basil [*with complacent confidence*]. Genghis Khan.

Poges [*emphatically*]. Genghis Khan! That was the name of the bounder driven from Jerusalem by the Lionhearted Richard. A warrior, a hero. And maybe he was actually in this very house. It's all very moving. [*To O'Killigain*] I imagine I hear the clank, clank, clank of armour when I walk the rooms, and see the banners and banneroles, with their quaint designs, fluttering from the walls! Don't you feel the lovely sensation of—er—er—er—old, unhappy, far-off things, and battles long ago? [*O'Killigain is silent.*] [*Insistently*] Don't you feel something of all that, O'Killigain, eh?

O'Killigain [*quietly*]. I let the dead bury their dead.

Souhaun. Oh, don't worry Mr. O'Killigain, Cyril; he's a workaday worker, and neither understands nor takes an interest in these things.

Poges. Nonsense; O'Killigain's an intelligent man, and is only too glad to learn a little about the finer things of life; and to think of great things past and gone is good—isn't that so?

O'Killigain. Occasionally, perhaps; but not to live among them. Life as it is, and will be, moves me more.

Poges. Come, come; we mustn't be always brooding upon the present and the future. Life is too much with us, O'Killigain; late and soon, getting and spending, we lay waste our powers. But you've never read good old Wordsworth, I suppose?

O'Killigain. As a matter of fact, I have.

Poges. You have? Well, that promotes a fellowship between us, eh? Great man, great man; but a greater poet, eh?

O'Killigain [*with some vehemence*]. A tired-out oul' blatherer; a tumbledown thinker; a man who made a hiding-place of his own life; a shadow parading about as the sun; a poet, sensitive to everything but man; a bladder blown that sometimes gave a note of music; a fool who thought the womb of the world was Wordsworth; a poet who jailed the striving of man in a moral lullaby; a snail to whom God gave the gleam of the glowworm; a poet singing the song of safety first!

Poges [*irritated*]. Oh! Is that the result of the new schooling? I'm afraid very few will agree with you, my friend. Well, well, we've more to do than discuss the merit of a poet; so hasten on the work of building the garage, like a good man.

O'Killigain [*bowing ironically*]. I go, sir.   [*He goes out.*

Poges [*to the others*]. Isn't that a shocking example of bad taste and ignorance? [*To Souhaun*] There's one of your fine countrymen for you, dear.

Souhaun. Well, Cyril dear, you know you were just trying to show off to him. A few little quotations, drummed into you at school, is all you know of Wordsworth. You're never tired of saying that poetry isn't your cup of tea.

Poges [*angry*]. Modern poetry, modern poetry isn't my cup of tea; and I don't care who knows it. But I don't deny the past. Tradition—that is our strength in time of trouble; tradition, follow the traditions, the only things that count in a cultured man's life. Keep as close as we can to the beauties of the past—the, the glory that was Rome and the grandeur that was Greece—Shakespeare knew what he was talking about when he said that.

Basil. Well, by living in this old historic house we're keeping close to the old traditions.

Souhaun [*dubiously*].   It's beginning to feel a little cold and damp to me.

Poges [*astonished and indignant*].   Cold? What are you talking about? Damp? Nonsense. Were it warmer, it would begin to feel uncomfortable. What do you say, Cloyne?

Cloyne [*who has been dusting the walls with a long-handled duster*].   I feel quite cosy, sir; though there is a bit of a breeze blowing down the chimney.

Poges [*shivering a little*].   Eh? Cosy, eh? Of course you do; we all do. Think, too, of the loveliness all round us: river, lake, valley, and hill. [*Lilting*] Angels, often pausing here, doubt if Eden were more fair. Here we have the peace of Eden.

Souhaun.   And you must admit, dear, that we Irish are a simple, hearty, honest, and obliging people.

Basil [*enthusiastically*].   They're dears. All I've met of them are dears; so quaint and charming—they are sweet. They need control, though; they need control.

Poges.   I agree. All the Irish are the same. Bit backward perhaps, like all primitive peoples, especially now, for they're missing the example and influence of the gentry; but delightful people all the same. They need control, though; oh yes, they need it badly.

Basil.   We must get to really know the country; it's one thing to be sensitive about the country scene, and quite another to understand it.

Poges [*heartily*].   Quite right, Basil. We must get to know the country so that everything in it is natural to us. [*Lilting*] To plough and to sow, to reap and to mow, and to be a farmer's boy-oy-oy. The different trees, for example, to call them by their names the instant we see them.

Avril.   In winter or summer.

Poges.   Quite. In the summer by their fruits.

Avril.   Trees don't have fruits, Cyril.

Poges.   Of course not. I mean barks and branches. It will be a joy to say to some ignorant visitor from the city: That tree? Oh, that's just an oak; and that one there by the river is a—a—

Avril.   Gooseberry tree, Cyril.

Poges.   A lilac, or something. [*To Avril*] Don't be funny. This is a serious matter.

Cloyne.   We mustn't forget the hens, either, sir.

Poges. Hens? Yes, of course—the hens. A fine idea. Yes, we'll have to have hens; a first-class strain, though: nothing else would be of any use.

Cloyne. A first-class strain, of course.

Poges. And a cow as well.

Avril. A cow might be dangerous.

Poges. Dangerous? Nonsense; if he was, then we'd simply have to keep him in a cage. [*He sets up the step-ladder, mounts it, and holds up his picture against the wall.*] How does that look?

Souhaun [*taking no notice*]. First of all, we must get to know the nature and names of all the wild flowers of the district.

Poges [*letting the picture rest on the ground, and turning to the rest*]. Especially the wild flowers that Shakespeare loved—the—the—er—er—[*his eye catches sight of primroses in a little vase on the table*]—the primrose, for instance; you know—the primrose by the river's brim, a yellow primrose was to him, but it was nothing more; though we all actually know all there is to be known about the little primrose.

Basil [*letting his picture rest on the ground, leaning over the top so that he at one end of the room and Poges at the other look like preachers in pulpits, panelled with their own portraits*]. That's just ignorant complacency, Cyril. Of course, if we regard, assume, or look at the plant purely as a single entity, then a primrose is a primrose, and there's nothing more to be said about it.

Poges. Well, you can't assume or regard the primrose as an elm tree, can you, old boy?

Basil [*quickly*]. Don't interrupt me for a minute, please. If we take the primrose, however, into our synthetical consideration, as a whole, or, *a priori*, as a part, with the rest of the whole of natural objects or phenomena, then there is, or may be, or can be a possibility of thinking of the flower as of above the status, or substance, or quality of a fragment; and, consequently, correlating it with the whole, so that, to a rational thinker, or logical mind, the simple primrose is, or may become, what we may venture to call a universal. See?

Poges [*bewildered*]. Eh? Oh yes, yes; no, no; yes, yes: eh, what?

Souhaun [*to Cloyne*]. Cloyne, you'd better go and look after the fires in our room. [*Cloyne rises and goes out.*

Avril [*with mockery in her voice*]. Hush, listen all—great men are speaking!

Poges [*to Basil*]. Eh, what the devil are you trying to say, man?

Avril [*with triumphant mockery*].   Ah, Cyril, you're caught!

Poges [*indignantly*].   Caught? Who's caught? Me? Nonsense, girl. He has simply compounded a fact with a fallacy. Can I see? Have I eyes? Yes. Very well, then. I see a flower with a root, leaves, and a blossom; I ask myself, What is it? I answer, A flower; I ask, What is it called? I answer, A primrose.

Basil [*languidly*]. So you say, sir.

Poges [*vehemently*].   So everyone says, sir!

Basil [*leaning forward towards Poges*].   And what is a flower, sir?

Poges [*furiously*].   A flower? Good God, sir, a plant; a contrivance springing out of the earth; a vegetating combination of root, leaves, and blossom.

Souhaun.   Calmly, Cyril, calmly.

Basil [*leaning back and closing his eyes wearily*].   I knew you'd just say that, sir. Words; you're merely using words. Try to think, sir, of a primrose, not as a primrose, but as a simple object, and as a substance outside of yourself.

Poges [*half frantic*].   Damn it, man, don't I know that a primrose isn't a substance inside of myself! Tell us how a man is to think of a primrose except as a primrose. He can't think of it as the dear little, sweet little shamrock of Ireland, can he? It is indeed a pitiful humiliation to have to listen to a half-educated fool!

Basil [*angry at last—setting the picture aside and taking a threatening step towards Poges, Avril stepping in front to restrain him*].   A fool! Do you say I am a fool, sir? Is a man versed in all the philosophies of the world to be called a fool!

Avril.   Basil, dear!

Souhaun [*getting in front of Poges*].   Cyril, darling, do remember that we are having just a little friendly discussion about a common country flower!

Avril [*ironically*].   Basil is only trying to share his great knowledge with us.

Poges.   He calls that knowledge, does he?

Souhaun.   We must remember that Basil passed through Oxford, dear.

Poges.   I don't care if he crept under it or flew over it; he's not going to punish me with what he picked up there.

Basil [*a little tearfully*].   Considering that I have read every word written by Hume, Spinoza, Aristotle, Locke, Bacon, Plato, Socrates, and Kant, among others, I think my views ought to receive some respect from an ignorant man.

Poges [*boastfully*]. I was reared any old how; and here I am today, a money'd man, able to say to almost any man, come, and he cometh, and to almost any other man, go, and he goeth—and quick too; able to shake hands with lords and earls, and call them by their Christian names. This —[*he touches his forehead*]—and these—[*he holds out his hands*]—did it all, without an inherited penny to help! [*He looks balefully at Basil.*] And that's more than some of them can say. And I never passed through Oxford!

Souhaun [*soothingly—to Basil*]. Come, now, go away for a few minutes, till he's calm again.

Basil [*tearfully and wrathfully*]. Souhaun and you can see, Avril, that the virtue of respect and ready veneration that every right-minded Englishman has for the classic colleges has gone completely out of him.

Souhaun [*soothingly.*] There now, there now; it'll all come back soon.

Basil [*almost weeping*]. Whenever he got the chance he hurried me down to Oxford to meet this professor and that doctor, itching all over to obtain a degree *honoris causa,* in any faculty of Divinity, Science, Literature, Medicine, or Law!

Poges [*scornfully*]. And most of them anxious for tips from the Stock Exchange. Go away, man, and weep in silence. [*He lifts his picture up against the wall.*] We have something else to do. Here, how does that look there?

Souhaun [*gently pushing Basil out of the room*]. There, go, dear, till you recover yourself.

Basil [*going out—loudly*]. Quisabit grunniodem expectio porcum—what can one expect from a pig but a grunt?

Poges [*with the picture against the wall*]. There, how does that look here? [*Pityingly*] Poor fool; juvenile mind, Souhaun, juvenile mind. But snappy enough, when he likes, and I, by cunning investment, having doubled his income for him. Ingratitude. [*Impatiently*] Well, how does this look here?

Souhaun. I think the opposite wall would be more suitable, dear.

Avril. Where it is, is best, mother.

Poges. Make up your minds, make up your minds!

Souhaun. Where it is, dear.

Poges. How is it for height?

Souhaun. A little higher.

Avril. A little lower.

Poges. One of you, one of you!

Souhaun. A little to the right, now.

Avril. A little to the left, now.

Poges [*lowering the picture to the ground*]. Which is it? How is it? What is it!   [*Cloyne comes in with a newspaper in her hand.*

Cloyne [*to Poges*]. Your newspaper, sir—the *Financial Universe.*

> [*She leaves it on the table, and goes out again. Poges breaks open his paper, and is about to look at it when Barney appears at the left entrance. A sound of cackling is heard outside, and the loud lowing of a cow, and the crowing of cocks.*

Poges [*with the paper half spread before him*]. What the hell's that?

Barney. There's a man outside wants to know if you want any entherprisin' hins?

Poges. Any what?

Barney. Any hins, entherprisin' hins?

Poges [*impatiently*]. What the devil would I want with hins enterprising or unenterprising?

Barney. He says it's all over the counthry that you're searchin' high an' low for entherprisin' hins.

Cloyne [*appearing at the right entrance*]. There's two men here wantin' to know if you'd buy some prime an' startlin' cocks, goin' cheap?

1st Workman [*appearing beside Barney, and shoving him aside to get in front*]. Excuse me, sir, but there's a friend o' mine just arrived with a cow that ud do any man good to see; a baste with a skin on her as shiny an' soft as the down on a first-class angel's wing; an' uddhers that'll make any man hard put to it to fetch enough pails to get the milk she gives!

Poges. Hins, cocks, and cows! [*To 1st Workman*] What the hell do you take me for—a farmer's boy, or what?

Souhaun. It's all out of what you said about having hens and a cow in the place. [*To Cloyne*] And you, you little fool, must have gossiped it all over the district!

Cloyne. The only one I mentioned it to was Mr. O'Killigain.

1st Workman [*coming over to Poges*]. Listen, sir, whisper, now: Sthrike for th' honour of St. Patrick, while the iron's hot, for the cow. An' whisper, don't, for the love o' God, have anything to do with the hins an' cocks they're thryin' to palm off on you—there isn't one o' them that isn't th' essence of a false pretendher!

Souhaun [*angrily—to Cloyne*]. I won't have you gossiping to O'Killigain, spending time with him you ought to give getting the house in shape! The idea of discussing our private affairs with O'Killigain! If you think that O'Kelligain has taken a fancy to you, you never made a bigger mistake, my girl.

Cloyne [*indignantly*]. Indeed, ma'am? Well, if Mr. O'Killigain bids me the time o' day, I'll do the same, without any permission from you, ma'am!

Barney [*impatiently*]. An' what am I goin' to say to the man who's brought th' entherprisin' hins?

Poges [*shouting*]. Pack him off about his business! [*Barney goes out.*

[*To Cloyne*] And you do the same to the man who brought the startling cocks!

Souhaun [*to Cloyne*]. And no more trespassing on the good nature of O'Killigain, either!

Cloyne [*turning and facing Souhaun swiftly as she is going out*]. There's a withering old woman, not a hundred miles from where I am, who ought to take her own advice, an' keep from thryin' her well-faded thricks of charm on poor Mr. O'Killigain herself! [*She goes out.*

Poges [*loudly and complainingly*]. Oh, stop these unseemly disputes in a house that ought to know only peace and dignity! Can't you try to act as the *les grand dames* and the *les grander monsieurs* must have acted when they moved about here in this beautiful Tudor house. While we're in it, let us forget the vile world and all its ways. [*Angrily—to 1st Workman, who has been tugging at his sleeve for the last few moments*] What the hell do you want, man?

1st Workman [*earnestly, almost into Poges's ear*]. Listen, whisper, sir; take the bull be th' horns, an' get the cow, before she's gone. An' as for entherprisin' hins, or cocks that'll do you credit, leave it to me, sir, an' you'll go about with a hilarious look in your eyes!

Poges [*catching 1st Workman by the shoulders, in a rage, and pushing him out of the room, and down the passage*]. Get out, get out, you fool, with your hins and cocks and cows!

Souhaun [*quickly—to Avril, when Poges has disappeared round the entrance*]. Go on up, and flatter and comfort your old fool by ridiculing my old fool; and, when he's half himself again, wanting still more comfort and flattery, wheedle a cheque out of the old prattler.

Avril [*jumping up*].   Splendid idea!   [*She runs off out.*

Souhaun [*calling after her*].   A good one, mind you!

> [*Poges comes back fuming, and brushing his coat where it touched the 1st Workman.*

Poges.   Are we to have no peace down here where peace was born? [*He takes up the paper again and begins to read it.*] Uum. Ha, tin shares up again. Good. [*He buries his face in the paper.*] If it weren't for the damned taxes.

> [*1st and 3rd Workmen peer around corner of the left entrance; then they come over quickly and smoothly to where Poges is buried in his paper, the 1st Workman standing on his left hand and the 3rd Workman on his right.*

1st Workman [*persuasively—towards Poges's paper*].   Listen, here, sir: if it's genuine poulthry you want, that lay with pride an' animation, an' not poor, insignificant fowls that set about th' business o' layin' like a member o' Doyle Eireann makin' his maiden speech, I have a sthrain o' pullets that'll give you eggs as if you were gettin' them be steam!

Poges [*angrily—glancing over the top of his paper*].   Go away, go away, man, and don't be driving me mad!

3rd Workman [*towards Poges's paper*].   Oh, the lies that some can tell to gain their own ends! Sure, sir, everyone knows that his poor hins are harmless; only venturin' to lay when heavy thundher frightens them into a hasty sign o' life! But it's meself can give you what you want, with a few lively cocks thrown in, to help them on with the work of furnishing nourishment to the whole world.

Poges.   Go away; when I want poultry, I'll get into touch with the experts in the Department of Agriculture.

1st Workman [*horrified—partly to Poges and partly to Souhaun*].   Oh, listen to that, now! Didja hear that, ma'am? The Department of Agriculture, is it? Wisha, God help your innocence, sir. Sure, it's only a tiny time ago that the same Department sent down a special sthrong covey o' cocks to improve the sthrain, an' only afther a short probation, didn't they give the hins hysterics?

Poges.   Hysterics? Good God!

3rd Workman.   Ay, an' hadn't the frightened farmers to bring guns to bear on the cocks when they found their hins scatthered over hill an' dale, lyin' on their backs with their legs in the air, givin' their last gasp, an' glad to get outa the world they knew so well! The few mighty ones who survived were that stunned that there wasn't an egg in th' place for years!

Poges [*good-humouredly catching the men by the arm and leading them to the left entrance*]. Now, now, men, I'm busy; I've some very important business to think about and can't be bothered with hins!

1st Workman [*as they go out*]. Another time, sir; but don't think of the Department in this important matther: they'll send you hins'll paralyse the cocks, or cocks that'll paralyse the hins! [*They go out.*

Poges [*returning, and reading the paper*]. Childlike people, the Irish, aren't they? Hysterical hins! Dr. What's-his-name, the fellow who said all man is moved by streams of thought that never enter his head—well, he'd find something to study down here. Well, it's delightful to be in a lovely house, in a lovely country, with nothing to think of but hysterical hins! [*He suddenly concentrates on something in the paper.*] I must have some of those shares. [*He runs to the telephone and joggles and shakes it.*] What can be the matter with this Exchange?—I can't hear a sound! [*To Souhaun*] Call one of the workmen, will you? I must get through to London at once.

   [*Souhaun runs out to call a workman. In a moment or two the 2nd Workman comes into the room.*

2nd Workman. Is it me you want, sir?

Poges. Not you especially; I just want to know if you know, or anyone in the county knows, why I can't connect with the Exchange?

2nd Workman. Oh, is that all, sir?

Poges [*snappily*]. Is that all! Isn't it enough, fool!

2nd Workman [*sharply*]. Who th' hell are you callin' a fool to?

Poges [*placatingly but with some impatience*]. My good man, please let me know if you can say why the Exchange doesn't answer my call.

2nd Workman. Ask anyone from one end o' the counthry to the other, or even O'Killigain himself, if Philib O'Dempsey's a fool, an' see what they'll say. A sound mind, armed with a firm education for seven long years in a steady school, an' now well fit to stand his ground in any argument, barrin' th' highest philosophies of the greatest minds mendin' th' world!

Poges. My good man, I only asked you a simple question.

2nd Workman [*ignoring the remark*]. Comin' over here, thinkin' that all the glory an' grandeur of the world, an' all the might of man, was stuffed into a bulgin' purse, an' stickin' their tongue out at a race that's oldher than themselves by a little like a thousand years, greater in their be-ginnin' than they are in their prime; with us speakin' with ayse the mighty languages o' the world when they could barely gurgle a few sounds, sayin' the rest in the movement of their fingers.

Poges [*shouting in rage*].   Go to the devil, man, and learn manners!

2nd Workman [*going on vehemently, but moving slowly to one of the entrances*].   Hammerin' out handsome golden ornaments for flowin' cloak an' tidy tunic we were, while you were busy gatherin' dhried grass, an' dyin' it blue, to hide the consternation of your middle parts; deco-ratin' eminent books with glowin' colour an' audacious beauty were we, as O'Killigain himself will tell you, when you were still a hundhred score o' years away from even hearin' of the alphabet. [*Beside the entrance*] Fool? It's yourself's the fool, I'm sayin', settlin' down in a place that's only fit for the housin' o' dead men! Settlin' here, are you? Wait till God sends the heavy rain, and the floods come!   [*He goes out.*

Poges [*to Souhaun*].   There's Erin, the tear and the smile in her eye for you! The unmannerly ruffian! Venomous, too—wanting me to wait till the floods come! Cheeking me up to my very face!

Souhaun.   Well, it's not a royal face, is it? You'll have to learn to be re-spectful to the people if you want them to be respectful to you.

Poges [*sarcastically*].   I'll be most deferential in the future. [*Stormily—to 1st Workman appearing at the entrance*] Well, what do you want?

1st Workman.   Excuse, but I sailed in, hearin' you were in a difficulty, an' I wanted to see if I could help.

Poges.   Well, I want to know where's the man who is responsible for put-ting in this 'phone?

1st Workman.   Why, is there anything wrong with it, sir?

Poges [*stormily*].   Everything's wrong with it, man! I can't get on to the Exchange.

1st Workman.   Sure, that's aysily explained: it's not connected yet.

Poges.   It was to be connected first thing this morning. When will it be connected?

1st Workman [*cautiously*].   Oh, now, that depends, sir.

Poges.   Depends? Depends on what?

1st Workman.   On how long it'll take to get the sthrame o' sound from here flowin' safely to whatever other end there may be fixed for it to be heard in.

Poges [*impatiently*].   Get O'Killigain, get him to come here at once.

1st Workman.   Sure, that's the Postmaster's job—Mr. O'Killigain has nothing to do with it.

Poges [*shouting*].   Then get me the man that has something to do with it!

Souhaun [*who has been looking at the coloured curtain stuff and spreading it out*].   Now, Cyril, see what you think: Is the red with the green stripe or the green with the red stripe the most suitable to go with the walls?

[*The sound of horses trotting is heard outside, becoming plainer, till the sound ceases somewhere close to the house.*

Poges [*to Souhaun—with irritation.*]   For goodness' sake, one thing at a time. [*To 1st Workman*] Go and get the man that's doing this job.

1st Workman.   I'm afraid you'll have to thravel a long way if you want to get him, sir; you see, he had to go to pay his last respects to a dead cousin; but never fear, he won't be gone beyond a couple of hours, unless something out o' the ordinary keeps him away the whole o' the evenin' an' th' strongest part o' th' night.

[*Poges sinks down on one of the seats, silent and confounded.*

Cloyne [*appearing at back entrance*].   Th' horses are here now, sir.

Poges [*sitting up*].   Horses? What horses?

Cloyne.   The horses Mr. Basil an' Miss Avril ordhered to come here.

Souhaun.   Basil and Avril are going out for a little canter, Cyril.

Poges [*peevishly.*]   But this is not the time to be thinking of amusement; we have to get the house into some shape. Ask O'Killigain to come here.

Souhaun [*to Cloyne*].   Yes, get O'Killigain, Cloyne; he has a good eye, and will be able to judge which of these curtain stuffs should go on the windows.

[*Cloyne goes. O'Killigain appears at the left entrance with an anxious look on his face.*

O'Killigain.   Who's going to ride these horses that are outside?

Souhaun [*haughtily*].   Miss Avril and her friend Mr. Basil Stoke are going to ride them.

O'Killigain.   I suppose you know these horses are mettlesome creatures, and need riders at home in the saddle?

Souhaun [*more haughtily still*].   Miss Avril and her friend learned the art in a London riding-school, and exercised frequently in Richmond Park; so your kind solicitude is unnecessary, sir.

O'Killigain [*viciously*]. Richmond Park isn't Clune na Geera, ma'am. The horses there are animals; the horses here are horses. [*Avril comes tripping in, dressed in jersey and jodhpurs, and is followed by Basil, dressed in a dark-green kind of hunting coat, buckskin breeches, and big gleaming top-boots with spurs; he carries a whip in his hand, and a high, handsome, shining tall hat on his head. With a frightened look at Basil*] Good God! [*He turns on his heel and walks out again.*

Basil [*with complacent conceit—to Souhaun*]. The old ways coming back again to the old house, Souhaun.

Souhaun [*rapturously*]. Isn't it grand, dear? Don't forget to go through the village.

Avril [*joyously*]. Basil has been so kind, Souhaun, dear; he has given me a grand cheque.

Souhaun [*giving Basil a kiss and winking at Avril*]. Basil, you're a darling!

Poges [*grumpily*]. Be careful how you handle those horses.

Basil [*haughtily—to Poges*]. Did you say anything, sir?

Poges [*with some heat*]. I said be careful how you handle those horses!

Basil [*with a mocking bow*]. Thank you, sir; we'll do our best. [*To Avril*] Come, darling.

[*Avril trips out, and Basil follows her in a way that he deems to be stately.*

Poges. I hope they'll do no damage, now.

Souhaun. Oh, never fear; Basil sits the saddle like a centaur.

[*The movement of horses' hooves is heard, then a trot, getting fainter till it dies away.*

Poges [*exasperated*]. God send he doesn't frighten the horse. More decent of him had he remained here to get this telephone going. They all seem to be determined here to keep us away from every semblance of civilisation! [*To Souhaun—stormily*] Will you, for God's sake, try to get O'Killigain to do something to get this thing in order? [*He goes over to where Souhaun is busy with the curtains and pulls the curtains out of her hands, then flings them on the floor.*] D'ye hear, d'ye hear what I'm saying to you, woman?

Souhaun [*losing patience and seizing him, and shaking him roughly*]. What d'ye think you're doing, you old dim-eyed, old half-dead old fool! I'll disconnect you as well as the telephone if you don't learn to behave yourself! You settled on coming here, and you'll put up with the annoyances!

Poges [*protestingly*]. Eh, eh, there! It was you who persuaded me to come to this god-forsaken hole!

Souhaun [*shaking him more fiercely*]. You're a liar, I didn't! It was you yourself who were always pining to see the little squirrels jigging about on the trees, and see the violets and primroses dreaming in the budding stir of spring! [*She pushes him violently from her.*] Another snarly sound out of you, and I'm off to live alone.

Poges [*gloomily*]. You can well afford to be independent now, since, like a fool, I settled five hundred a year on you.

[*During this contest Cloyne has appeared at the left entrance and now gives a judicious cough.*

Souhaun [*quickly—to cover dispute from Cloyne*]. We'll decide on this stuff, then, for the curtains, Cyril, dear.

Poges. It'll look delightful, darling. [*Pretending to see Cloyne for the first time.*] Oh, what do you want?

Cloyne. Canon Chreehewel's outside an' would like to have a few words with you, if you're not too busy.

Poges [*showing irritation*]. Oh, these priests, these priests! Thick as weeds in this poor country. Opposed to every decent thought that happens not to have come from them. Ever on guard to keep the people from growing out of infancy. No one should give them the slightest encouragement. Oh, if the misguided people would only go back to the veneration of the old Celtic gods, what a stir we'd have here! To the delightful, if legendary, loveliness of—er—er—er—what's his name, what's her name, what's their name? I have so often said it, so often in my mind, the chief, or one of the chief gods of the ancient Celts?

Souhaun. Was it Gog or Magog, dear?

Poges [*with fierce scorn*]. Oh, no, no, no; try to think a little, if you really want to assist me. Can't you remember that Gog and Magog were two Philistinian giants killed by David, or Jonathan, or Joshua, or Joab, or Samson, or someone? It's the old Celtic god I have in mind, the one—what was his name?

Souhaun. Gulliver?

Poges. Oh no; not Gulliver!

Souhaun. Well, I don't know the hell who it was.

Poges [*slapping his thigh exultantly*]. Brobdingnag! That was the fellow —the fellow that ate the nine nuts—or was it seven?—plucked from the tree hanging over the well near the world's end.

Cloyne. What am I to say to the Canon, sir?

Poges. What does he want; did you ask him what he wants?

Cloyne. He says he just wants to drop a word or two of thanks for the fifty pounds you sent him.

[*A murmur of voices is heard outside. It comes nearer and the sound seems excited.*

Poges [*listening*].What's that, now?

1st Workman's Voice [*outside*]. Keep his head up.

3rd Workman's Voice [*outside*]. You're home, sir, you're home now.

[*They come in supporting Basil by the arms, followed by the 2nd Workman, holding Basil's coat-tail. Basil is pale, and has a frightened look on his face. His lovely coat is spattered with mud and, in some places, torn. The 1st Workman is carrying the tall hat, now looking like a battered concertina.*

Poges [*anxiously*]. What's this; what's happened?

1st Workman [*soothingly*]. He's all right, sir; just a little shock. We seen him crawling towards the house an' went to his help. His horse flung him. [*Whispering to Poges*] He shouldn't be let on anything more mettlesome than a rocking-horse, sir.

Souhaun [*running to Basil*]. Are you much hurt, Basil, dear?

Basil [*brokenly*]. Bruised, bruised from head to foot.

Poges [*with irritation*]. Well, why the hell didn't you stay here and help me to get the telephone fixed?

Basil. Why didn't you hold me back by force? Oh, why did you let me go!

Souhaun [*anxiously*]. Where's Avril?

Basil [*ignoring her query*]. Oh, I should never have ventured upon an Irish horse! Irresponsible, irresponsible, like the people. When he wouldn't go, I gave him just a little jab with the spur—[*moaningly*]—and the brute behaved like a wild animal, just like a wild animal!

1st Workman [*soothingly—to Souhaun*]. He's not hurt much, ma'am; came down in th' grass on his poor bum.

Souhaun. But where's Avril? [*Shaking Basil's shoulder*] Where's Avril?

Basil. Gone!

Souhaun. Gone?

Basil. Away with O'Killigain. He came bounding up to help Avril and abused me for falling off. Then they cantered away together. [*Loudly and a little shrilly*] Naked and unashamed, the vixen went away with O'Killigain!

[*Plaster falls and a hole appears in the ceiling, almost directly over the fireplace; then a thin rope, with a bulb attached to its end, comes dangling down, followed by the face of a heavily Yellow-bearded Man, who thrusts his head as far as it can go through the hole.*

Yellow-bearded Man [*to those below*].   Hay, hay there; is this where yous want the light to go?

Poges [*with a vexatious yell when he sees where the rope hangs*].   No it isn't, no it isn't, you fool! [*Indicating a place near the centre and towards the back*] There, there's where it's wanted! Where my desk will be! Oh, they're knocking down more than they're building up!

Yellow-bearded Man [*soothingly*].   Don't worry; just a little mistake in measurement, sir. Never fear, we'll hit th' right spot one o' these days! The one thing to do, sir, is to keep cool.

[*He takes his head out of the hole and disappears, leaving Poges furious.*

Poges [*shouting up at the hole*].   Who are you to order me to keep cool? I won't keep cool. I refuse to keep cool!

Souhaun [*to Poges*].   Here, help me in with poor Basil till he drinks some brandy and lies down for a little.

[*Poges takes one arm, Souhaun takes the other, and they lead Basil out of the room.*

Poges [*to Basil—helping him out*].   I hope you realise the sterling trouble you give people by your damned refusal to recognise your limitations!

Basil [*petulantly*].   Carry me out, man; carry me out!

Cloyne [*as they pass*].   What am I to do with the Canon, sir?

Poges [*ferociously.*]   Tell him I'll give him another cheque if he gets the telephone fixed for me before the night is out!

[*Basil, Souhaun, and Poges go out by the left entrance; Cloyne by that on the right, leaving the men standing together in a corner of the room.*

2nd Workman [*pensively*].   Th' spirit of th' Grey o' Macha's in our Irish horses yet!

1st Workman [*excitedly*].   Did yous hear that, eh? Did yous hear what he just let dhrop? That the lassie o' th' house went off with O'Killigain riding naked through the locality!

2nd Workman. Stark naked she was, too. Didn't I know well be th' cut of her jib that she was a hop, step, an' lep of a lassie! An' right well she looked too!

1st Workman. Th' sight near left me eyes when I seen her go prancin' out without as much as a garther on her to keep her modesty from catchin' cold.

3rd Workman. This'll denude the disthrict of all its self-denyin' decency.

1st Workman [*excitedly jumping upon a seat to get nearer to the hole in the ceiling*]. Cornelius, eh, there, Cornelius!
[*The yellow-bearded head is thrust through the hole again.*]

Yellow-bearded Man. What's up?

1st Workmen. Didja hear th' terrible thing that's afther happenin'?

Yellow-bearded Man. No; what terrible thing?

1st Workman. The lassie o' th' house's gone careerin' all over th' counthry on horseback with only her skin as a coverin'!

Yellow-bearded Man [*horrified*]. G'way!

3rd Workman [*up to him*]. An' th' poor men workin' in th' fields had to flee to th' ditches to save th' sight of their eyes from th' shock o' seein' her!

Yellow-bearded Man [*with aggravated anguish in his voice*]. Oh, isn't it like me to be up here outa sight o' th' world, an' great things happenin'!

CURTAIN

ACT II

The same as in the preceding Act.

The two portraits, one of Stoke, the other of Poges, are now hanging on the wall at back, between the windows. Bright-green curtains, broadly striped with red, are on the windows. A Jacobean armchair has been added to the two stiff pew-like seats beside the fireplace. The table is to the left, so that two mattresses, one beside the other, can be seen, with their heads against the wall and their feet towards the front. On these, wrapped round with rugs and blankets, are Poges and Stoke. Some thick rolled-up floor rugs are lying against the wall. A bunch of pampas grass is in the earthenware jug standing on the table. The rejected crimson curtain stuff is lying over one of the pew-like seats. A walking-stick—Basil's—is leaning against the wall, near to where he is lying.

It is about half-past seven on a cold and misty morning. A few misty beams of sunlight are coming in through the windows, paling the light of a lighted lantern standing between the two beds.

The two men are twisting about uneasily on the mattresses; when Poges twists to the right, Basil twists to the left, and vice versa. Then Poges, wearing a blue beret with a black bow at the side, lifts his head a little and glances over at Basil. He is in that drowsy state felt by a man who has spent long hours of the night trying to get to sleep and failing to do so.

Before the scene is disclosed, the hooting of owls is heard first; then the faint lowing of cattle, grunting of swine, crowing of cocks, bleating of sheep; then, vigorously from various directions the whistling of the chorus of The Farmer's Boy.

Poges [*after he has twisted about several times—half to himself, half to Basil*]. Good God, isn't it cold! [*Basil is silent.*] Eh, Basil, are you awake? How d'ye feel now?

Basil *with a faint groan.* Stiff as hell still! It's a mercy I'm alive. And, on the top of it, Avril to make a laughing-stock of me by enjoying herself with O'Killigain.

Poges [*sympathetically*]. It was damned mean of her, Basil. She's inclined that way, I'm afraid. You'll have to keep a strong hand over her, my boy.

Basil [*with a deep groan*]. I can't—now.

Poges. Why can't you, man?

Basil. A month before we came here I did a very foolish thing.

Poges. Oh?

Basil [*mournfully*]. Settled five hundred a year on her for life.

Poges. Oh! [*A fairly long pause.*] Basil, Basil, I did the same to Souhaun!

Basil. We're done for, Cyril.

Poges [*in a sprightly way*]. No, no; a month in the country'll make us young again. We'll be as lively as goats in no time. Besides, we can always cautiously hint at an increase in the settlement.

Basil [*gloomily*].   With the workers always striking for higher wages, it'll have to remain a hint.

Poges [*as gloomily*].   It's damnable, Basil. If much more is given to them, how's a poor man to live? [*He sinks back on the mattress and pulls the clothes over his head. Outside a cock crows loudly, followed by the call of a cuckoo. Clicking his tongue exasperatedly—from under the clothes.*] Dtch, dtch, dtch! Isn't it a good thing those birds aren't in the house! [*The cock crows again, much louder this time, and the cuckoo calls again. Popping his head from under the clothes.*] Damn that cock and cuckoo! Did you hear that cock crowing, Basil, and the cuckoo calling?

Basil.   Deafening, aren't they! And the owls, too, all the night. Jungle noises!

Poges.   The country's not going to be so quiet as I thought. Still, I'm glad we came.

Basil.   So am I, really. These sounds are just part of the country's attractions—pleasant and homely.

Poges.   And stimulating, Basil, stimulating. Look at the sunlight coming in through the windows—another dawn, Basil; another life. Every day in the country brings another chance of living a new life.

Basil [*enthusiastically*].   And we're going to live it, eh, what, Cyril?

Poges [*enthusiastically*].   Oh, boy, ay!
        [*Souhaun appears at the back entrance, left, and Avril at entrance to the right. Both are wearing fur coats over their night-dresses, and shiver a little.*

Souhaun [*plaintively*].   For goodness' sake, will you two men get up and do something. Cloyne's fallen down in a dark passage and hurt her wrist, and she can't do much.

Poges.   Oh?

Avril.   And something will have to be done to heat the rooms—we were almost frozen last night.

Poges.   Ah! Well, we weren't scorched with the heat either.

Souhaun.   Well, stir yourselves, and you'll soon get warm. O'Killigain and his men are already at work, and will want to be coming in and out of here.
        [*The cock crows louder than ever, and is joined by many more, a few of them at a great distance, so that the sounds are heard but faintly; these are mingled with the barking of dogs, the lowing of cattle, the bleating of sheep, the twittering of birds, the grunting of pigs, and the cackling of hens.*

Avril. There, you hear; everything's alive but you two.

Poges. Well, we'll be in the midst of them all in a second.

[*The two women withdraw. Basil and Poges, with the clothes wrapped round them, sit up, and dive down again. After a second or two they sit bolt-upright again, and again dive down.*

Poges [*shivering*]. Ooooh, Basil, cold!

Basil [*shivering*]. Bitter, bitter! What would I not give now for a cosy flat; a cosier bed; and a blazing hot-water bottle!

[*They lie quiet for a short time.*

Poges. There's nothing for it but to plunge out of the summer into the black and bitter winter.

Basil. You say the word.

Poges. Ready! Steady! Go!

They climb laboriously out of the beds. When they get out, it can be seen that they have been fully dressed, even to their heavy top-coats and scarves wound round their necks.

Poges [*blowing on his hands and rubbing them*]. Ooooh, crisp, isn't it? Healthy, though. Ooooh! Where the hell's that Barney, that he hasn't a fire lighted for us? Oooh! One would want to be on his tail all day. [*Shouting*] Barney, Barney! [*Barney comes in holding some logs in the crook of his right arm, and a lantern in his left hand. Cloyne follows, with some paper and a bellows. Her left wrist is bandaged. Barney is wearing a topcoat, and has a muffler round his neck. Cloyne, too, is wearing a heavy coat. They both go over to the fireplace. As they come in*] Ah, here we are. Bit nippy, Barney; sharp, but beneficial. [*To Cloyne*] You'll have to be more careful with the steps and passages. Mind your feet coming in, mind your head going out. Oooooh! [*To Basil*] You better slip off, and give the others any help you can. [*As Basil is going*] What about your walking-stick?

Basil [*moving stiffly*]. I must try to do without it—about the house, any-way.

He takes the lantern that is beside his bed, and goes out, limping a little.

Poges [*to the other two*]. Well, what do the pair of you think of the country, eh? And the house? Better than any your old Kings of Tarara had, eh?

Cloyne [*effusively*]. I'm sure it'll be lovely, sir, when we settle down.

[*Poges has been jerking his arms about in an effort to drive the cold from his body. Cloyne begins to fold the clothes on the beds, and tidy them up.*

Poges. Of course it will. We'll enjoy it all; we'll feel younger; we will *be* younger. The air, fresh air, pure air, exhilarating air, will be able to get at us. [*He sucks in his breath and blows it out again.*] Ooooh! Soon we won't know ourselves. We'll eat better, sleep better; flabby muscles will become firm, and we'll realise that we are alive, alive, alive-O. Think of the walks we'll have; so much to see, so much to hear, so much to smell; and then to come back, nicely tired, to such a lovely house. A life for the gods!

Cloyne. Wondherful, wondherful, sir.

Poges. Now I must be off to swallow down a cup of tea, for there's a lot to be done, a lot to be done yet.   [*He hurries off out of the room.*

Cloyne. The poor oul' codger!

Barney. Comin' down to this back o' God-speed place for rest an' quietness! Afther all that science has thried to do for us, goin' back to lantherns an' candles. Th' only electric light he'll allow in a Tudor house is one over his own desk! Runnin' in the face o' God Almighty's goodness—that's what it is.

Cloyne. They'll get tired of it before us.

Barney. I can tell you, I'm tired of it already. Looka the place we're livin' in: doors everywhere shaped like doors o' dungeons; passages dark as hell when it was first formed; crackin' your head when you're goin' in, and breakin' your toe when you're goin' out; an' I'm tellin' you, it's only beginnin'.

Cloyne. It might be worse.

Barney [*striking a match to light the paper*]. We're goin' to be worse, I'm tellin' you.

Cloyne. We can't be worse than we are.

Barney [*as the flames of the paper die down*]. There's no chance o' kindlin' here. Why did you say, then, that we might be worse?

Cloyne. Well, so, indeed, an' we might.

Barney. How can we be worse, woman, when we're as bad as we can be?

Cloyne. Simply be bein' worse than we were.

Barney. How can we be worse than we were, when we're as bad as we can be, now.

Cloyne. You'll see we'll be worse before we're betther.

Barney. Damn these logs! Isn't that what I'm sthrivin' to dhrive into your head?

Cloyne. What are you sthrivin' to drhive into me head?

Barney. That we'll be worse than we were before we're as bad as we are now, an' in a week's time we'll be lookin' back with a sigh to a time, bad as it could be then, that was betther than the worst that was on top of us now.

[*Poges bustles in again. The heavy topcoat is gone and he is now dressed in bright-blue shorts, emerald-green jersey, brown shoes, and the scarf is still round his neck. He has a cup of tea in his hand, and he is sipping it as he comes into the room. He is miserably cold, but he puts on a brisk air, sorting it out in his mind that to be cold in the country is natural, to be ignored as far as possible, and to be countered by a smiling face, a brisk manner, and the wearing of brilliant clothes denoting freedom of movement and utter disregard of the common rules of convention. He is feeling far from comfortable, but thinks this shouldn't be shown; for the colder you are, and the more uncomfortable you feel, the brisker you must be, and the hardier you'll get.*]

Poges. Here we are again! Ready for anything now. [*Losing his gay attitude when he sees that the fire isn't lighted.*] Isn't the fire lighted yet? What are you doing, Barney? Being in the country's no reason why we should be frozen to death.

Barney. I can't get a spark out of it, afther all me sthrivin'.

Poges [*testily*]. You can't light logs with a bit of paper, man. Oh, use your brains, Barney, use your brains.

Barney. An' what else have I got to light them with?

Poges. Small sticks, man; put some small sticks under them.

Barney. An' will you tell me where I'm goin' to get the small sticks? Isn't the nearest shop a dozen miles away?

Poges. Well, if there's no sticks, sprinkle a little paraffin on them.

Barney [*sarcastically*]. An' where am I goin' to get the paraffin? There's no oil wells knockin' about here.

Poges [*severely*]. Don't be funny. You've got to remember you're in the country now.

Barney. Isn't it meself that's gettin' to know it well!

Poges. We've got to do things for ourselves: there's no chance of pushing a button to get things done here.

Barney.   Sure, I'm beginnin' to think you're right.

Poges.   Can't you see that those logs are too big?

Barney.   I think I do, unless me sight's goin' curious.

Poges [*hotly*].   Well, then, why don't you do it!

Barney.   Arra, do what?

Poges [*loadly*].   Make them smaller, man!

Barney [*calmly and sarcastically*].   An' how?

Poges.   And how? Why, with an axe, of course.

Barney [*losing his temper—loudly*].   An' where's the axe, an' where's the axe?

Poges.   There must be an axe knocking about somewhere.

Barney.   There's nothin' knockin' about here but a bitther breeze whirlin' through the passages that ud make the very legs of a nun numb!

Cloyne [*trying to mollify things*].   Sure, the poor man's back-broken an' heart-broken thryin' to kindle it, sir.

Poges [*who has been waving his arms and stamping his feet while his teeth chatter—turning fiercely on Cloyne*].   You mind your own business, girl! [*Seeing her putting the mattresses by the wall.*] Have we got to sleep down here again tonight?

Cloyne.   Ay, an' yous have. Th' other rooms are too damp still. Sure, Mr. O'Killigain says that it'll take a month of fierce fires to dhry them out.

Poges [*testily*].   Mr. O'Killigain says this, and Mr. O'Killigan says that! I'm getting tired of what Mr. O'Killigain says. If we have to sleep here, you or Barney'll have to stay up all night keeping the fire going, or we'll be frozen in our sleep. [*His eyes catches sight of the telephone. He goes over to it and lifts the receiver.*] Not a sound! No, oh no; not a bit of a hurry. [*Angrily to Cloyne*] Go out, girl, and send in the boy who's working at this telephone. [*With a low moan*] Ireland!

> [*Cloyne goes out by the doorway on the right leading to the entrance hall. After a few seconds the loud lowing of a cow is heard, followed by a scream from Cloyne, who rushes frantically back into the room, pale and trembling.*

Cloyne [*breathlessly rushing back into the room, falling on the floor, and catching Poges wildly by the legs*].   Save me! Stuck his head into me face, th' minute I opened the door. Mother o' God, I'll never see th' light of another day with th' fright I got!

Poges [*alarmed*].   What is it, what is it, woman?

Cloyne [*almost incoherent*].   A bull, a wild bull, out in th' enthrance hall!

Barney [*frantically*].   A wild bull! We're all desthroyed.

Poges [*trying to release himself from Cloyne's hold*].   Let me go, girl! Let me go, or I can't defend myself. If he comes in here, the whole of us'll be horned!

Cloyne [*frantically*].   My legs have given undher me. Let me hold on to you, sir—it's me only hope!

Poges [*to Barney*].   Put the table to the doorway, man, and help to bar him out—quick, quick, man! And a mattress. [*To Cloyne while Barney is pushing the table and a mattress to the door*]   Why didn't you clap the door in his face, you fool?

Cloyne.   Wasn't he half into the hall before I'd the door half open! Oh, sir, what are we goin' to do? Oh, please go, sir, an' thry an' shove him out!   [*The bellow of the animal is heard outside in the hall.*

Poges [*half dead with panic*].   My God, woman, you can't shove bullocks about! [*Shouting*] Souhaun, there's a wild bull in the house! Help, O'Killigain, help. [*To Barney*]   Run, run, man, and get Mr. Stoke to bring down the gun. Oh, go quick, man! An' keep well out of range. [*Barney runs off. Shouting*] O'Killigain, help! Can't you let me go, girl?

Cloyne [*still clinging to him*].   Carry me off, sir, please. Don't leave me here to die alone! Maybe he won't be able to climb the stairs afther us. Oh, when I came to th' counthry, I never thought there'd be wild animals on th' door-step!

[*Basil appears at one of the entrances at the back; he moves forward stealthily and extends a gun to Poges.*

Basil [*nervous*].   What is it, what is it?

Poges.   A bull, out in the hall.

Basil.   Who let him in? Damn it, such carelessness! You must be on guard in the country, you know. Here, take the gun, man.

Poges [*angrily—to Basil*].   Come out, come out in the open, man, and be ready to use the gun if he comes into the room! [*Shoving the gun from him.*] You use it, man; weren't you an A.R.P. man?

Basil [*indignantly*].   I never did anything more than clay-pigeon shooting! Let whoever let the damned animal in, let the damned animal out! [*He pokes Poges with the gun.*] Here, take this, and down him—you're nearer the bull than I am.

Poges [*angrily*].   I'm not a toreador, am I? And don't point, don't point

the gun at me! Lower the barrel, man; oh, lower the barrel! D'ye want
me to die two deaths at once? What's the advantage of your passing
through Oxford if you can't face a bull with a gun in your hand? Be a
man, man, and not a mouse.

Basil [*keeping well in the passage, and only showing his nose*]. Telephone the police, the fire brigade, or something.

Poges [*violently*]. Don't you know the kind of a country we're in! There's
no police, no fire brigade, no telephone! Come here, if you won't use the
gun, and help me carry this girl away out of danger.

> [*The cow puts a stylised head, with long curving horns, over the
> barricade and lets out a loud bellow. Cloyne spasmodically tugs the
> legs of Poges, making him lose his balance so that he topples to the
> floor, after a frantic effort to save himself.*

Cloyne. Oooh, sir, save me!

Poges [*with a wild shout as he is falling*]. My God, he's on top of us!
We're done for! Help!

> [*Basil throws the gun into the room and runs for his life.*

Barney [*in the far distance*]. Sing out, sir, if you want any assistance!

> [*Someone is heard stirring outside where the animal is; this stir is
> followed by the voice of the 1st Workman shooing the cow out of
> the hall. After a few moments, Poges slowly sits up and listens.*

1st Workman [*shouting outside*]. Eh, oick, oick, eh, yeh gett; ay, ay, oick
oick!

> [*Poges gets up on to his feet, shaking a little, and going over, picks
> up the gun and, steadying himself on it, stands over the prostrate
> Cloyne, who is almost in a faint, bundled up on the floor, with her
> face hidden in her hands. Shortly after, the 1st Workman appears at
> the entrance with a bucket of coal and some sticks. He looks over
> the table, astonished to see the prostrate Cloyne, and Poges standing
> near with a gun in his hand.*

Poges [*stormily*]. Where the hell did that bull come from? who owns
her? who let that bull come tearing into a private house?

1st Workman. Bull, sir? Oh, that wasn't a bull, sir. [*He pushes the table
back to its place.*] Jest a harmless innocent cow, sir. Frightened the poor
girl, now, did it? [*Cunningly*] But I see it didn't frighten you, sir.

Poges [*flattered*]. No, no, not me. [*To Cloyne*] Here, girl, get up on
your feet. [*Loudly*] It wasn't a bull; I knew it couldn't be a bull! and it's
gone, so get up. [*Putting down the gun.*] Get up! [*With the help of the
1st Workman and Poges, Cloyne gets up on her feet.*] There now, be off

with you. Get Miss Avril to give you a stiff glass of whiskey, and you'll be all right. And take this gun back to Mr. Basil.

[*He picks up the gun and hands it to the shaking Cloyne.*]

Cloyne. Oh, sir, this place is worse than a jungle in th' desert!

Poges. Go on, go on! I thought you Irish were a brave people.

[*He is shaky himself, but he stiffens himself to conceal the tremors.*]

Cloyne [*going out with the gun*]. For ages now, it's bulls I'll be dhreamin' of, an' there's ne-er a lock on me door either!

Poges. Fainting, shouting, screaming, and running about for nothing! No nerves, no nerves, no spirit; no coolness in a crisis.

1st Workman [*craftily*]. An' did they all think it was a bull, sir? An' you stood your ground. Looka that now. Prepared for anything, sir.

Poges [*taking it all in*]. The other fellow, Mr. Basil, ran for his life; think of that—ran for his life!

1st Workman. Did he, now?

Poges. British, too, think of that; surprising and disappointing, very. [*Briskly and a little anxiously*] Still, I must acquaint the police. I can't have cows or bulls wandering about the rooms of Ormond Manor.

1st Workman [*who has started to light the fire*]. One o' th' ladies sent me in to light a fire for you. [*Placatingly*] Sure, sir, she was only the cow me friend brought this mornin' so that, when you had a minute, you could run out an' look her over. A fine animal, sir. She got loose an' wandhered in when she found th' door open. She's betther than th' best that was in th' cattle raid o' Cooley.

[*Souhaun comes in by a back entrance followed by Avril. She is carrying a black vase, striped with blue, and has a jazzy overall on one of her arms. Avril carries a blue bowl, striped with black. They are carrying them very carefully, as if they were very precious indeed.*]

Souhaun. What's all this commotion about a bull? We had to stop Basil from trying to throw himself out of a window!

Avril. And Barney got out on top of the roof.

Poges. Oh, nothing, nothing at all; a stray cow in the garden mooed, and Basil lost his head and Cloyne lost her feet.

Avril. But Barney, when he was rushing past, said that you were out here roaring for help!

1st Workman. Roarin' for help, is it? Indeed an' he wasn't, for I can testify to that, but standin' here, cool as you like, he was, waitin' for the worst.

Souhaun. Well, if we're to stay in the country, we'll have to get used to all kinds of animals, big and small.

Poges [*shaking his head*]. I'm convinced now that poor Basil can't be wholly English. There's a weak joint somewhere.

Souhaun [*leaving the overall on a seat*]. There's your overall, dear, to wear when you're working, and we're taking your precious Annamese vase and Cambodian bowl to our room for safety, till everything's straight.

Poges. Oh, that's right, if anything happened to either of them, I'd pass out. Lift the vase up, dear, till I see it a second. [*She lifts it up.*] Oh, Lord, isn't it lovely? [*To Avril*] The Cambodian bowl too. [*She lifts it over her head.*] A little too high, dear; just go down on one knee. [*She does so.*] Aaah! Precious, precious! The chaste form, the tender planes, the refined colouring; the exquisite design, the *tout ensemble*—they go down into the undiscoverable deeps of the heart!

1st Workman. Arra, be God, indeed an' they do, sir.

Avril [*languishingly*]. A background of eau-de-nil would set them off to their full advantage.

Souhaun [*cocking her eye at them*]. Oh no, Avril; Chinese white's the pure and proper background for them.

Avril. Eau-de-nil.

Souhaun. Chinese white, dear.

Poges. Neither. Chrome yellow's the tone. A warm and pure cloak, as it were, for the chaste bodies of the vase and the bowl. [*He goes over and touches them tenderly.*] My darling treasures! Take them off, and lay them down with circumspection. Mind the step going out.

> [*Souhaun and Avril go slowly and stately out, carrying the vase and the bowl as if they were precious relics.*

1st Workman [*to Poges who has come over to the fireplace where a fine fire is blazing now*]. There y'are, sir; a fire that'll warm y' up an' make your mind easy.

Poges [*stretching out his hands to the fire*]. Good, great, grand! Are you the workman who knows all the stories and legends of Ireland since the world began?

1st Workman. No, no, not me, sir; it's Philib you mean—th' powerful man with th' powerful beard. [*Touching his forehead*] Some say he isn't all there, but a wondherful man, ay, indeed, is Philib. Does a man good to talk to him.

Poges. I'll have a chat with him, the first chance I get.

1st Workman [*looking round the room with a ravishing air*]. This is a wondherful house, so it is. It's an honour to be workin' in it. Afther hundhreds o' years standin' in frost, rain, an' snow, frontin' th' winds o' the world, it's a marvel it isn't flat on its face, furnishin' only an odd shelther for a sthray fox; but here it stands, an' we all waitin' for a windy winther ud stagger it an' send it tottherin' down.

Poges [*indignantly*]. Tottherin' down! What d'ye mean, tottherin' down? The place is as firm as a lighthouse. Tottherin' down, indeed!

1st Workman [*repelling the idea that he thought of such a thing*]. Tottherin' down, is it? Now who, in th' name o' God, save a sure an' safe fool ud think it was tottherin' down? Not me, now; oh no, not me. Tottherin' down me neck! Isn't the grand oul' house goin' to show, soon an' sudden, a sign of what a fine residence it was when the quality harnessed their horses for a hunt be the risin' rim o' th' dawn, or sat down in their silks an' satins to their evenin' meal in the shadowy shine o' th' golden candles!

Poges. Purple nights and golden days, my friend. [*He sighs.*] Aah!

1st Workman [*with a long, deep, imitative sigh*]. Aah! We'll never set eyes on the like o' them again, sir; th' sparklin' carriages comin' an' goin', th' steeds throttin' nicely an' neatly, or movin' at a gallop, always elegant, on a visit to me lord here, or me lady there, with th' sky above in a fair swoon o' pride for th' fine things movin' about below; an' they full o' grace, an' decked out in the grandeur o' th' West Indies an' th' East Indies, sobered down a thrifle for use in a Christian counthry, the women's bosoms asway with jewels, like a tendher evenin' sky, alive with stars. An' th' gentlemen, just a dim step down, but elegant too, in finery fair, with ruffles an' lace, with cutaway coats an' vests embroidhered, each holdin' a cane to keep them steady, an' all halo'd with scents to ring them round from th' smell o' th' poor an' dingier world at work or play!

Poges [*enthusiastically*]. Those were handsome days. [*He fixes a plume of pampas grass in his beret.*] When shall we look upon their like again? [*He folds the crimson curtain stuff round him as if it were a cavalier's cloak.*] The lawns and ramparts still are here, and we shall be the men! [*He snatches up Basil's walking-stick.*] The plume in the hat, the velvet cloak over the shoulder, the tapering rapier in the hand! [*He makes a vicious lunge at the 1st Workman, who narrowly dodges the pass.*] Die, varlet!

1st Workman [*remonstratively*].   Eh, eh, there; careful, sir, be careful! Be careful how yeh prod!

Poges [*leaning on the stick as if it were a sword—sorrowfully*].   Where are the kings and queens and warriors now? Gone with all their glory! The present day and present men? Paltry, mean, tight, and tedious. [*Disgustedly*] Bah!

1st Workman.   What are we now, what are we all, but a tired thribe thryin' to do nothin' in th' shortest possible time? Worn away we are, I'm sayin', to shreds and shaddas mouldin' machines to do everything for us. Tired, is it? Ay, tired an' thremblin' towards th' edge of th' end of a life hardly worth livin'!

Poges [*gloomily pacing up and down*].   Not worth living, not worth living.

1st Workman [*with greater energy*].   Time ago, an' we gave a ready ear to one speakin' his faith in God an' his neighbour; but now, there's so many gabbers goin' that there's hardly a listener left. Sure, that in itself is as sharp a punishment as a lease o' hell for a long vacation. It's meself is sayin' ourselves came late, but soon enough to see the finery fade to purple dust, an' the glow o' th' quality turn to murmurin' ashes.

Poges [*striking the attitude of a clumsy cavalier*].   We won't let them perish completely! We'll keep the stern old walls standing. We'll walk where they walked, sit where they sat, and sleep where they slept!

1st Workman.   An' talk as they talked too.

Poges [*wildly*].   Our pride shall be their pride, our elegance their elegance, and the banner of the Ormonds shall fly from the battlements again! The King, the King, God bless him!

1st Workman [*warningly*].   I wouldn't say too much about the King, sir; we're a little touchy about kings down here in Clune na Geera.

> [*From outside is heard a scream from Souhaun and a squeal from Avril; then the sound of running feet, and the crash of breaking chinaware. After a moment or so, Souhaun pitches into the room from the left entrance at back, and Avril from the right one. Souhaun is holding the top rim of the vase in her hand, and Avril the butt of the bowl. When he sees the damage, the 1st Workman slinks off.*

Poges [*furiously*].   What the hell's all this?

Avril [*breathlessly*].   Rats!

Souhaun [*breathlessly*].   Gigantic creatures!

Avril.   Here.

Souhaun. There.

Both [together]. Everywhere!

Poges [in anguish]. Oh, look at what's left of my Annamese vase and Cambodian bowl! A hundred pounds of the best for each, and then only when I happened to catch the cunning Keeper drunk in the Bazaar of Singapore. What the hell were the pair of you thinking of?

Souhaun. Rats.

Avril. Here, there, and everywhere.

Poges [wildly]. You evil-handed dolts to destroy my two best treasures! You'll pay for them, you'll pay for them!

Avril [scornfully]. We'd look well thinking of them, and we running for our lives.

Souhaun. You can imagine what it was when Basil is up there now on guard with the gun.

Poges [mockingly]. Oh, he's the boy to shoot down wild animals. [*Imploringly*] For God's sake go up and take the gun off him or he'll send a bullet through the body of some human being! And for the future, you and your friend keep your awkward hands off any treasures I may have left.

Souhaun [scornfully]. Treasures! Who told you that the Annamese vase and your old Cambodian bowl were treasures?

Poges. Everyone who saw them, woman!

Souhaun. Ay, to humour you. Well, let me tell you they weren't more valuable than a second-hand vase or bowl bought at a Woolworth sale. That's the fact, and it's best to know it.

Poges [with quiet emphasis]. And who gave you that information?

Avril. Couldn't anyone, not a fool, see what they were the minute they saw them?

Souhaun. The minute Mr. O'Killigain set eyes on them, he said that they went from Derby in thousands to Singapore and Saigon for suckers to buy them!

Poges [with furious scorn]. Oh, indeed, did he? Oh, an authority on what kind of art d'ye call it in Clune na Geera? I'll test them. I'll send them to the Curator of the Wallace Collection. We'll see. Mr. O'Killigain —good God!

[*He takes the pieces from Avril and Souhaun and puts them on the table. Cloyne appears at an entrance at back with a troubled look on her face.*]

Cloyne. Here, they've gone and dumped the garden tools an' the roller right in front of the hall door! And the roller's so close that when you want to go out or come in you have to climb over it.

Poges. Tell whoever brought them to bring them to the back and put them in the shed, fool!

Cloyne. How can I tell him an' the lorry's gone?

Poges [*furiously*]. And why didn't you tell him before he went?

Cloyne. An' didn't I now? He just said that the back was threnched be the workmen an' he hadn't time to build pontoon bridges.

Poges. What a country! What a people! [*Viciously—to Souhaun*] And you encourage them, because you and your friend Avril are Irish too!

Souhaun. If you ask me, you're not such a shining paragon of goodness yourself.

Poges [*explosively*]. I believe in efficiency! I demand efficiency from myself, from everyone. Do the thing thoroughly and do it well: that's English. The word given, and the word kept: that's English. [*Roaring*] And I'm an Englishman!

Souhaun. You are indeed, God help you!

Cloyne. An' what are we goin' to do about the garden tools an' th' roller?

Souhaun [*in a bustling and dominant way, catching up the jazz-patterned overall and putting it on Poges*]. Here, if we waste any more time talking, the house will never be ready to live in. Put this on, and go and bring the roller from the front door through here, out of the way, to the back. When you've done that, bring the garden tools to the back too, and let us see your grand English efficiency at work while I and Avril do some of the hundred things remaining to be done.

> [*She gives him a push from her, and she and Avril hurry away out by one of the back entrances.*

Cloyne [*warningly*]. It seems a heavy roller, sir, so mind you don't sthrain yourself when you're pullin' it.

Poges [*testily*]. Go away, go away, girl; I'm not an invalid. [*Cloyne goes. Poges moves over to the blazing fire and stretches out his hands to the flame. The 2nd Workman comes in by left entrance at back wheeling a barrow filled with bricks. He is a powerful man of fifty, with gleaming eyes and wide and strong beard. As he comes nearer, Poges turns to give him greeting. Warmly*] Good day, good sir; it's a cold day that's in it, surely.

2nd Workman [*eyeing Poges curiously*]. Ay is it, for them who has to brave it, an' can't stand all day in front of a sturdy fire like a kingly Pharaoh.

Poges [*a little nonplussed*]. Quite, yes, yes, quite. Everyone tells me the place round here is a rich storehouse of history, legend, and myth?

2nd Workman [*with a little scorn in his voice*]. It's a little they know an' little they care about those things. But the place has her share o' histhory an' her share o' wondhers.

Poges [*flatteringly*]. And I'm told you have a rare stock of them yourself.

2nd Workman. Ay, indeed, I have me share o' wondhers, new an' old.

Poges [*trying to be Irish*]. Looka that, now. Arra, whisht, an' amn't I told it's strange stories you do be tellin' of the noble things done by your fathers in their days, and in the old time before them.

2nd Workman [*sinking into a meditative mood*]. When less than a score of the Fianna brought back the King of England prisoner, invaded Hindostan, an' fixed as subjects the men of all counthries between our Bay o' Dublin and the holy river that gave to holy John the holy wather to baptize our Lord.

Poges [*astonished*]. I never heard that one before.

2nd Workman [*with murmuring scorn*]. An' where would th' like o' you hear it, man? That was in the days o' Finn Mac Coole, before his hair was scarred with a hint o' grey; the mighty Finn, I'm sayin', who stood as still as a stone in th' heart of a hill to hear the cry of a curlew over th' cliffs o' Erris, the song of the blackbird, the cry o' the hounds hotfoot afther a boundin' deer, the steady wail o' the waves tumblin' in on a lonely shore; the mighty Finn who'd surrendher an emperor's pomp for a place with the bards, and the gold o' the King o' Greece for a night asleep be the sthream of Assaroe!

Poges [*solemnly*]. A great man, a great man, surely; a great man gone for ever.

2nd Workman [*sharply*]. He's here for ever! His halloo can be heard on the hills outside; his spear can be seen with its point in the stars; but not with an eye that can see no further than the well-fashioned edge of a golden coin.

Poges [*moving back a step—a little awed*]. You see these things, do you?

2nd Workman. I hear sthrange things be day, an' see sthrange things be night when I'm touched be the feel of the touch of the long-handed Lugh. When the Dagda makes a gong o' the moon, an' the' Sword o' Light shows the way to all who see it.

Poges. Aah!

2nd Workman. Then every rib o' grass grows into a burnished fighter that throws a spear, or waves a sword, an' flings a shield before him. Then Ireland crinkles into a camp, an' kings an' sages, queens an' heroes, saints an' harpers stare me in the face, an' bow, an' pass, an' cry out blessing an' vict'ry too, for Heber's children, with the branch of greatness waving in their hands!

Poges [*sadly*]. And there it ends!

2nd Workman [*giving Poges a drowsy glance*]. I'm thinkin' it might have been well for some if the end an' all was there; but it sthretches out to the sight of a big dim ship with a followin' fleet in the great dim distance, with a stern-fac'd man in the blue-gold coat of the French Armee, standin' alone on th' bridge of the big dim ship, his eyes fixed fast on the shore that was fallin' undher the high-headed, rough-tumblin' waves o' the sea!

Poges [*awed into interest—murmuringly*]. A big dim ship and a following fleet, carrying a man in the blue-gold coat of the French Armee— who was he, and when was that, now?

2nd Workman. Th' man was Wolfe Tone, and the time was yestherday.

Poges. Yesterday!

2nd Workman. The man was there, but the fleet was a golden dhream, always comin' in an' ever goin' out o' th' Bay o' Banthry!

> [*O'Killigain has come in at the commencement of the 2nd Workman's musing, unnoticed by the dreaming worker, and barely noticed by the interested Poges, listening intently to what is being said, and a little awed by the influence of the 2nd Workman. O'Killigain comes softly over, and stands a little behind but close to the dreaming workman.*]

Poges [*bending towards the 2nd Workman*]. And who was the man in the blue-gold coat of the French Armee?

2nd Workman. He was a great Irish soldier and a great Irish friend to the people of no property in Ireland.

O'Killigain [*very softly*]. And there are others.

2nd Workman [*softly too, but not so softly*]. And there are others; for through the roads of the four green fields goes Shane the Proud, with his fine head hidden, waving away his more venturesome friends from the horns of a bull, the hoofs of a horse, the snarl of a dog, an' th' smile of an Englishman.

Poges [*going back a step*]. The smile of an Englishman!

2nd Workman [*unheeding the interruption*]. An' in the midst of them all is Parnell standing still; unheeding he stands with a hand on his breast, his white face fixed on the East, with his wine-coloured eyes flashin' hathred to England!

O'Killigain [*very softly*]. And there are others.

2nd Workman [*with a glance at O'Killigain*]. They came later, an' haven't wandhered fully back to where they cleared a way for a gropin' people, but they will come, an' stare us into the will to take our own again.

Poges [*detaching himself from the spell*]. And do none other of those you know, good man, see the things that you see?

2nd Workman. Barrin' a few an' O'Killigain there, they see these things only as a little cloud o' purple dust blown before the wind.

Poges. That's very sad.

2nd Workman. Barrin' O'Killigain there an' a few, what is it all now but a bitther noise of cadgin' mercy from heaven, an' a sour handlin' o' life for a cushion'd seat in a corner? There is no shout in it; no sound of a slap of a spear in a body; no song; no sturdy winecup in a sturdy hand; no liftin' of a mighty arm to push back the tumblin' waters from a ship just sthrikin' a storm. Them that fight now fight in a daze o' thradin'; for buyin' an' sellin', for whores an' holiness, for th' image o' God on a coin; while th' men o' peace are little men now, writin' dead words with their tiny pens, seekin' a tidy an' tendher way to the end. Respectable lodgers with life they are, behind solid doors with knockers on them, an' curtained glass to keep the stars from starin'!

> [*The 2nd Workman stoops, lifts the shafts of the barrow, and is about to go out.*

Poges [*to 2nd Workman—placatingly*]. My own great-grandfather was Irish, I'm told, and my grandmother was a kind of a Scotswoman.

2nd Workman [*going out with the barrow slowly*]. That's not such a lot, an' you're not sure of any of it either.

Poges. What a strange, odd man! I couldn't get half of what he was trying to say. Are there many like him?

O'Killigain. Millions of them, though few of them have tongues so musical.

Poges. He rather took to me, I think, and looks upon me as a friend.

O'Killigain [*ironically*]. He looks upon you, and all Englishmen, as a rascal, a thief, and a big-pulsed hypocrite.

Poges [*indignantly*].   Good God, but that's pure ignorance. Where would the world be without us?

O'Killigain.   The giddy globe would wobble, slow down, stand still, and death would come quick to us all.

Poges [*a little puzzled by this remark*].   Eh? Quite. Well, no, not so bad as that, you know, but near it, damned near it.

   [*Souhaun runs in with a look of dark annoyance on her face.*

Souhaun.   Oh, look at you standing here still, and so much to be done— [*her voice rises*]—so much to be done, so much to be done! I asked you to get the roller away from the door an hour ago, and here's Barney after twisting his wrist trying to climb over it standing in the same old place! [*She catches him by the overall.*] Come, for God's sake, and take the damn thing out of the way!

Poges [*pulling her hand away from the overall—angrily*].   Oh, have some decency, order, and dignity, woman! Can't you see I'm having a serious discussion with O'Killigain? [*He turns swiftly on O'Killigain.*] We, sir, are a liberty-loving people, and have always striven to preserve perfect— perfect, mind you—freedom of thought, not only in our own land, but throughout the whole world; but that anyone should be permitted to hold opinions such as are held by that lunatic just gone out, and are apparently held by you, sir, too, is a perfect scandal and disgrace!

Souhaun.   Oh, there's no use of you trying to ride your high horse here in Clune na Geera!

Poges [*stormily*].   I'm not trying to ride my high horse here in Clune na Geera! What is said in Clune na Geera is a matter of very little importance indeed. But every right-minded man the world over knows, or ought to know, that wherever we have gone, progress, civilisation, truth, justice, honour, humanity, righteousness, and peace have followed at our heels. In the Press, in the Parliament, in the pulpit, or on the battlefield, no lie has ever been uttered by us, no false claim made, no right of man infringed, no law of God ignored, no human law, national or international, broken.

O'Killigain [*very quietly*].   Oh, for God's sake, man, don't be pratin' like a pantaloon priest!

Souhaun [*trying to push Poges from the room—impatiently*].   Go out and get the garden roller!

Poges [*loudly*].   I say, sir, that Justice is England's old nurse; Righteousness and Peace sit together in her common-room, and the porter at her gate is Truth!

O'Killigain [*quietly, but sarcastically*]. An' God Himself is England's butler!

Poges [*roaring with rage*]. That's a vile slander, sir!

O'Killigain. Whether it is or no doesn't matter much, for in a generation or so the English Empire will be remembered only as a half-forgotten nursery rhyme!

Poges [*fiercely as Souhaun is pushing him out*]. An opinion like that deserves the jail!

Souhaun [*giving him a last strong push out into one of the back entrances*]. Oh, go on! [*She goes over towards O'Killigain and stands looking shyly and a little archly at him.*] What a naughty man you are to provoke him into such a tantrum! [*After a slight pause.*] I hear terrible things about you, Mr. O'Killigain.

O'Killigain. Oh?

Souhaun. That you are a great man for the girls!

O'Killigain. A pretty girl shows me a sign that God is smilin'.

Souhaun [*archly*]. It's well I need the gay an' youthful gloss of pretty Avril, or it's shelterless I'd be from all your stormy moods!

O'Killigain [*gallantly*]. When I look at you close I see you a week or two oldher than your younger friend, an' when you go as bright about the house, an' dhress as gay as she does, you look like an earlier summer kissin' a tardy spring goodbye.

Souhaun. More than twenty years younger than the old fool Poges I am of course. It's ridiculous for me to be with him. I have a nice little income of my own now, and it's like a young bird I feel that has just got command of its restless wings. [*She pauses for a moment.*] You really do believe that I am as pretty as Avril? You're not just teasing me, are you?

O'Killigain. Not I. You are one o' th' fine sights of this world. [*He lilts:*]
There are many fair things in this world as it goes,
The blue skies of summer, th' flushing red rose,
But of all th' fair, blossoming things that men see,
A comely-built lass is th' nearest to me,
A comely-built lass is th' dearest to me!

And you are a comely-built lass.

Souhaun [*coming near to him and stroking his arm*]. Your poor arm, wounded for the sake of others. What's your name?

O'Killigain. My name? O'Killigain, of course.

Souhaun. No, no, your more familiar name; the name your girl would call you by?

O'Killigain. Jack.

Souhaun [*lingering over it*]. Jack. What a dear name, Jack! What a dear name—[*she suddenly stands on tiptoe and kisses him*]—Jack!

> [*She is running out by the entrance on the right when she bumps into Poges laboriously pulling in a gigantic roller as high in diameter as he is tall. The heavy iron side-discs are vividly painted in panels of red, white, blue, green, and yellow. When the roller is pulled into the room, it can be seen that the 1st Workman is pushing it behind.*]

Poges [*angrily, as Souhaun bumps into him*]. Eh, eh, there, look where you are going, can't you?

Souhaun [*amazed at the size of the roller*]. God bless us, Cyril, what on earth's that you're carting into the house?

Poges [*petulantly*]. Can't you see what it is? The roller you told me to bring through here to the back. The roller, the roller I bought to roll the lawn.

Souhaun. But it's too big, man.

Poges. No, it isn't too big. The man who sold it to me said that the bigger it was, the more effective it would be.

Souhaun. But you'll never be able to pull a mighty thing like that.

Poges. And what's to prevent me from pulling it? Amn't I pulling it now? A child of ten could pull it, the man said; well-balanced, you know, the man said. Easy to pull, and easier to propel, the man said.

Souhaun. You've just been taken in, Cyril. The thing's altogether too big. [*To the 1st Workman*] Isn't it?

1st Workman. It looks a size too large to me, ma'am.

Poges. The grass in this district needed a special big roller to level it, the man said, and this was the roller to level it.

1st Workman. Sure, that roller ud level a hill.

O'Killigain. The grass'll give way undher that, right enough.

Souhaun. The cheek of declaring that a child of ten could pull it like a toy.

1st Workman. G'way, ma'am, an' did he really say that now?

Poges. One pull over the lawn with that roller would be enough for the season, the man said.

O'Killigain. An', faith, so it would, an' for every season afther too.

1st Workman. Sure, an' wouldn't a specially powerful horse himself wilt undher a thing like that! Whoever gave you that, man, musta taken it off an oul' steam-roller.

[*The 3rd Workman appears at entrance to right and proceeds to take an enjoyable interest in what is happening.*

3rd Workman. Mother o' God, looka what he's after buyin' be th' name of a roller! Isn't it a shame, now, to have imposed on a poor, simple, inoffensive man with a vehicle like that!

Poges [*defiantly*]. It's a bargain, I know it's a bargain; the man said it's a bargain.

Souhaun [*mockingly*]. The man said, the man said—ay, and you swallowed everything the man said.

O'Killigain [*to 1st Workman*]. Give Mr. Poges a hand to take this machine out of the sight of mortal men.

Poges [*obstinately*]. I'll take it myself, thank you all. Once you got the knack of balancing it, the man said, you could turn it with your little finger, and I believe what the man said.

O'Killigain [*to 3rd Workman*]. Here, you go on back to your work; go on, off you go!

[*He follows the 3rd Workman out of the room. Poges gives a mighty push to the roller, propelling it slowly to one of the entrances at the back. The 1st Workman goes over and helps him to push it.*

Poges [*fiercely—to 1st Workman*]. Let go, you! I'll manœuvre it myself. Let go, I tell you!

1st Workman [*as fiercely—to Poges*]. Can't you see, man, the declivity runnin' down the passage that'll lead you, if the roller once gets outa hand, into God knows where?

Poges [*with a roar into the face of the 1st Workman*]. Let go! [*The 1st Workman, startled, suddenly lets go his hold on the roller and the roller shoots forward down the declivity, Poges going with it, like a flash of lightning. Heard as he is careering down the passage—with anguish in his voice*] Help!

[*There is a pause of a few moments, then a thud is heard, followed by a rumbling crash of falling bricks and mortar; then silence again.*

Souhaun [*with vehement rage—running out*]. The blasted fool! He has rocked the house and killed himself and hasn't made his will!

1st Workman [*staring down the passage*]. Right through the wall he's gone! [*He runs to where the hole is in the ceiling, gets a seat and stands on it. Calling up to the hole*] Eh, Cornelius, eh, quick!

[*The face of the Yellow-bearded Man appears at the hole, and he thrusts down his head as far as it will go.*

Yellow-bearded Man. Well, what's up now?

1st Workman [*excitedly*]. The oul' man, the oul' fool, has gone right through the wall with the roller, an' shook the house—bang!

Yellow-bearded Man. Didn't I think it was an earthquake! [*Testily*] An' don't be tellin' me these things while I'm up here. Can't you wait till I'm down in th' world o' men, and can enjoy these things happenin'!

[*He angrily takes his head out of the hole. The 1st Workman gets down from the seat and runs out by entrance on right.*

1st Workman [*running out*]. Mr. O'Killigain, Jack, eh, Jack!

[*Souhaun returns, followed by Cloyne and Barney leading in the frightened Poges, powdered with the dust of the falling mortar. Souhaun arranges a mattress for him on which he squats, supported by pillows.*

Souhaun. You were warned, you were warned, and you would have your own way. It's fortunate you are, indeed, that none of your bones is broken.

Poges [*moaningly*]. Brandy, get me some brandy. [*Barney goes out and comes back with a glass, brandy, and soda-water. He fills out a glassful and gives it to Poges. After he has drunk the brandy—to Cloyne and Barney*] Go way, you two, and don't stand there gaping at me! [*They go. Musingly*] What a rascal that man must be who sold me the roller! In this simple country, among a simple people, where the very air is redolent with fairy lore, that such a dangerous and materialistic mind should be lurking!

Souhaun. For God's sake, man, talk sense.

Poges [*shaking his head sorrowfully*]. A gay and charming people, but irresponsible, utterly irresponsible.

[*O'Killigain appears at the right entrance with a cloudy look on his face.*

O'Killigain. Look here, that Basil of yours is goin' about the grounds carrying a fully-cocked gun at a dangerous angle. He'll do harm. Send someone to take it off him, or I'll twist it out of his hands myself! And you'll want to be more careful yourself, or you'll have th' oul' house down!

Poges [*indignantly*]. Oh, what a conceited fool that fellow is—going about to do dangerous damage for want of a little common sense and caution. I don't believe he ever fired a gun in his life. [*To Souhaun*] Go out, dear, and take it off him, before he shoots somebody—and go quick! [*Souhaun runs out by the entrance on the right, and O'Killigain is following her when Poges speaks to him, and halts him at the entrance.*] Oh yes, Mr. O'Killigain, a word please. [*He drinks some more brandy.*] Er, just a word. People are saying—there's a rumour going about that you and—and Miss Avril are—are, well, seen together at times.

O'Killigain. Well?

Poges. Well? Damn it, man, she's a lady, Mr. Stoke's a gentleman, and you're only a—a tradesman!

O'Killigain. Well?

Poges. Well? Oh, don't be welling me! The week she was away from here was bad enough, and very suspicious. She had the damned cheek to say she was with you.

O'Killigain. So she was.

Poges. So she was, was she? Well, it's dishonourable, and it will have to stop.

O'Killigain. And who'll stop it?

Poges [*firmly*]. I and Mr. Stoke will stop it.

O'Killigain [*quietly*]. You pair of miserable, old, hypocritical, wizened old getts, I'd like to see you trying!

Poges [*choking with rage*]. Get out of the house, and come here no more! I'll write to your parish priest! I'll—[*A shot rings out in the grounds outside.*] Good God, the fool has shot somebody!

    [*O'Killigain goes off in a hurry. There is a pause. Then the yellow-bearded face is thrust through the hole in the ceiling as far as it can go, and shouts down at Poges sitting like Buddha on the mattress:*

Yellow-bearded Man [*down to Poges*]. He's shot her, shot her dead, the poor little innocent creature! Th' charmin' little thing full o' gaiety an' go!

Poges [*very frightened, up to the Yellow-bearded Man*]. Shot who, shot who, man? Is it the young lass?

Yellow-bearded Man. Without warnin' he done it, without a flicker of an eyelid he sent her into the unknown!

Poges [*murmuring in agony*]. Avril! Oh, my God, little Avril. The curse of the Irish thorn-tree is on us! The little lass gone. [*Near swooning*]

Cut down like a coloured bubble! The fairies must be manœuvring, and
they'll get me next, maybe. Sweet little Avril the first to go!

Yellow-bearded Man [*savagely*].   Twenty-five pounds, an' not a penny
less, he'll pay for it, or I'll have the heavy law on him. I'd ha' let you have
her at first for the twenty, but in some compensation for th' agony of
seein' the poor thing sink down into death, I'll have to get the other five,
or I'll have the heavy law on him!

Poges [*sitting up suddenly*].   What are you talking about, man? What's
shot, who's killed?

Yellow-bearded Man.   Be th' way, you don't know that that lean, skulkin'
friend o' yours has shot dead me poor little innocent, poor little cow!
[*Sarcastically*] He thought it was a bull!

Poges [*bewildered*].   Oh, what a terrible country to have anything to do
with! My precious vase is gone, my beautiful bowl is broken; a wall's
demolished, and an innocent animal's shot dead: what an awful country
to be living in! A no-man's land; a waste land; a wilderness!

CURTAIN

ACT III

*Before the room appears, the sounds of falling rain and swishing winds
are heard; and these go on, at intervals, throughout the scene.*

   *The same as in the preceding act; but some more articles of furniture
have been added to the room. Between the entrance to the right at the
back, and the right wall, stands what is said to be a Jacobean china-cabinet,
filled with old pieces of china. At each side of the larger entrance on the
right stands an armoured figure, comical-looking things, with long sharp
points protruding where the man's nose (if a man were inside the suit)
would certainly be; each figure, standing stiff, holds a long halbert well
out from his body. Over these are, crossed, pennons, green and blue, fixed
on the wall.*

   A blazing fire is in the fireplace. No one is in the room. After a moment

Poges, dressed in his jazz-patterned overall, with a paper in his hand, runs in and rushes over to the telephone.

Poges [*into the mouthpiece—hurriedly*]. Get me—Oh, good evening, good evening. This is Mr. Poges, Ormond Manor. Get me St. Paul, London: 123. The house is getting on all right, thank you. Be quick, please. [*Warmly*] There's no—seems—in it; I am in a hurry. Oh, the ladies are quite well, sir. No, no, no; I don't want to go to an all-night dance to hear Irish songs sung! I want St. Paul! Eh? No, St. Peter won't do; please don't try to be funny; I am on very serious business. Get me the number I want at once! [*He takes the mouthpiece from his mouth and gives vent to a roaring growl of anger.*] Whether it won't matter a hundred years from now isn't the point, sir. [*Shouting*] Damn it, get me St. Paul! [*Bursting with rage*] No wonder I use bad language. Is this the way business is done here? No wonder this country's as it is. What's wrong with it? [*Roaring*] Everything's wrong with it! You what? You hope my stay here will help to civilise me a little! [*He looks stupefied; then he slams the receiver on the hook. Almost instantly the 'phone rings. He whips off the receiver again and puts it to his ear.*] What the hell does this—Eh? Who are you? St. Paul? Good God! This is Poges, Bradford. Oh, it's an awful place. People helpless, superstitious, and ignorant. I want you to get me five hundred shares in the Welldonian Cement Co.; shares are bound to jump, the minute the bombing starts seriously. They have jumped? Ah. What, a fiver a share, now? Well, get me two fifty. What? Not one to be had? [*Clicking his tongue*] Dtch, dtch. Run on them, eh? One wouldn't imagine there'd be so many trying to cash in on splintered bodies. The world, the world, Bradford! Yes, yes, of course; if there's any going, snap them up. Righto. Goodbye.

> [*He hangs up the receiver. Barney appears at the entrance on the right.*

Barney. Canon Chreehewel would like to speak to you, sir.

Poges. Right; send the Canon in to me.

> [*Barney goes; and, in a second or so, the Canon comes in. He is inclined to be portly, has rather a hard face, head bald at the front, with bushy greying hair at the back of his head and over his ears. He is wearing a soft hat, sodden with rain, which he puts on the end of the table when he comes in; and a long dark cloak, glistening with rain too. He comes over eager—to Poges, with a smile on his face, and outstretched hand.*

Canon. Ah, my dear friend, I'm so glad to have a chance of a word with you. How are you liking Clune na Geera?

Poges. Splendid, though the weather has been cold and very wet. Take your cloak off.

Canon [*taking off his cloak. When his cloak is off, it can be seen that his clothes fit nicely*]. Isn't it a nuisance; and we're in for more of it, by all accounts. If it goes on much more, the district will be a dismal swamp.

Poges [*indicating a seat*]. Sit down, Canon, sit down. Glass of sherry?
[*The Canon sits, and Poges sits too, opposite the Canon.*

Canon. No, thanks. I drink rarely. [*Apologetically*] Good example, you know. Well, welcome, my dear sir, to our district. You have a very beautiful house here. An old house, but a fine one. It is almost a sacred thing to keep an old thing from dying, sir; for whatsoever things are just, whatsoever things are honest, whatsoever things are pure, whatsoever things are lovely and of good report, are invariably found close to, and, sometimes, intimately enclosed in the life and being of ages that have passed, and in the life of men and women who have gone away before us.

Poges [*gratified*]. I wholeheartedly agree with you, reverend sir. I feel it, I know it.

Canon. With all its frills, its frivolities, its studied ceremonial, however gaily-coloured its leisure may have been, the past had in it the core of virtue; while the present swirl of young life, I'm saying, with its feverish sthrut of pretended bravery, its tawdry carelessness about the relation and rule of religion to man, with all its frantic sthretching of pleasure into every second of life, contains within it a tawny core of fear that is turning darker with every chime of the passing hours!
[*The rain and wind are plainly heard.*

Poges [*leaning towards the Canon—eagerly*]. We must lengthen our arm back to the past and pluck back some of the good things that haven't gone away as far from us as the dead who knew them.

Canon. A worthy enterprise, dear sir, and I hope you and your good people will be a help to us here to bring some of the slow movement of the past into the reckless and Godless speed of the present. [*He leans over towards Poges till their heads nearly touch.*] You and yours can do much to assist the clergy to keep a sensible check on the lower inclinations of the people, a work which should be near the heart of every sensible and responsible man with a stake in the country.

Poges. I'll do all I can. [*Leans back with an air of business importance*] From the practical point of view, how am I to help?

Canon [*dropping a little into the idiom of the district*]. Help us to curtail th' damned activity of the devilish dance halls! Open a dance hall, and in a month or less the innocent disthrict becomes worse than your Leicester Square in London when the night has fallen. If the dance halls are allowed to go ahead without the conthrol of the clergy an' responsible people, God will go from Clune na Geera!

Poges [*shocked*]. Good God! Such a condition of things among a simple, charming, and pastoral people amazes me.

Canon [*warming to it*]. Arra, wouldn't it sicken you, when the hot days come, to see fools of oul' men an' fools of oul' women too, settin' a bad example, goin' about nearly naked, in their coloured shorts, an' brazen-fac'd lasses mixed among them in low-cut bodices, defiant short skirts, or shorter trousers, murdherin' modesty with a restless an' a reckless hand!

Poges. A lamentable state of affairs entirely, sir.

Canon [*rising and going over close to Poges—intensely*]. An' like Eden, sir, we've a snake in our garden too!

Poges. Oh!

Canon. O'Killigain!

Poges. Ah! [*The wind and the rain are plainly heard.*

Canon. Guard your womenfolk from him, for no woman is safe with that man. He publicly defends the wearing of low-necked blouses by brazen hussies; he stands be the practice of courting couples walking the highways and byways be night. Why, one moonlight night, meetin' my curate dhrivin' home a lasciviously-minded girl, O'Killigain tore the stick from the curate's hand an' smashed it into pieces! A dangerous man, my dear sir, a most dangerous man.

Poges [*a little nervously*]. I'm what you'd call a foreigner down here, and so couldn't interfere with O'Killigain personally; but what I can do to help you, I certainly will, in any other way.

Canon. Thank you—I guessed you would. Your fifty pounds have helped a lot already. And now I've taken up a lot of your time and must go. [*He takes up his hat.*] By the way, how's the workman I sent you getting along?

Poges. Which one?

Canon. The one doing your electric light—a yellow-bearded fellow.

Poges [*emphatically*]. Oh, he's getting along splendidly!

Canon. I'm glad to hear it. A good fellow—a Knight of St. Columbus.

Poges. Well, now, I never knew Columbus was a saint.

Canon [*smiling indulgently*]. Oh yes indeed; a great Irish saint.

Poges. I always thought he was an American.

Canon. An American; who?

Poges. Christopher Columbus.

Canon [*smiling*]. Oh, there were two Columbuses, one Irish and the other—er—American.

> [*As the Canon is about to move away, Avril, followed by Souhaun, dances into the room from an entrance at the back. She is dressed in low-cut blouse, short tailor-made skirt, and soft leather high boots moulded to her calves and reaching to just below her knees; and looks, indeed, a very tempting and desirable young hussy. She has a mackintosh over her arm. Souhaun, too, is dressed in very short shorts of a vivid crimson and a black V-necked jersey, looking as enticing, in a more mature way, as young Avril herself. Poges is a little embarrassed, but the good Canon does not flicker an eyelid. Souhaun whips off Poges's overall and shows him in a green jersey and brown shorts.*]

Souhaun. You mustn't receive the Canon, dear, in an overall!

Avril. I say, Cyril, old boy, when are we going to get that damned bathroom? It's a bit thick trying to have a bath in a basin.
> [*She sees the Canon and stops to gaze at him.*]

Poges [*introducing her*]. Mr. Stoke's—er—wife—Miss Avril, Canon. [*Introducing Souhaun*] My—er—wife, Miss Souhaun.

Canon [*bowing graciously—to Avril*]. My dear young lady. [*To Souhaun*] Madam, I'm very pleased to know you.

Avril [*nodding to Canon—to Poges*]. Well, when are we going to have a decent bathroom, old cock o' th' walk?

Poges [*deprecatingly*]. The Canon's here, Avril.

Canon [*jovially*]. Youthful spirits, sir, youthful spirits.

Poges. We'll have a bathroom if we can fit one in without injuring the harmony of the old house. The Tudor period never saw a bathroom. This generation's getting soft, Canon; we want hardening.

Avril. Bunkum!

Poges [*indignantly*]. It's anything but bunkum! Shakespeare had to do without one.

Souhaun. But surely, dear, you must know that the Tudor people knew nothing about the use of steam?

[*Basil now appears at an entrance at the back, and when he sees the company, he stays there and listens. He is dressed in a yellow jersey and black shorts. No one notices him.*

Poges [*petulantly*]. Steam! We stand here, in the centre, not of a house, but of a great civilisation, and you mention steam!

Souhaun. In the centre of a hot bath, dear, I can remain in the centre of your civilisation.

Basil [*joining in—looking like a statue in the doorway*]. Not precisely, Souhaun, for it would require, or at least postulate, a full and concentrated retirement through the avenues of thought back to the time of which the visible surroundings are vividly, but quiescently reminiscent. The conception of the conscious thoughts, interrelating with the—with the outward and inward action and reaction of all—or most of the bodily senses, incorporating the outward vision of sight with the inward vision of the inward conception of the—of the fragmentary stumuli—er—stimuli, into a perfect and harmonious whole; a thing, if I may be allowed to say so, if not impossible, is at least improbable, sitting down, or indeed even standing up, in the middle of a hot bath.

Avril [*with mock enthusiasm*]. Hooray!

Poges [*to the Canon*]. Mr. Stoke, Canon; cousin to the uncle of a K.G., and passed through Oxford.

Canon. Really? Well, well, remarkable connections. [*In the far distance a faint clap of thunder is heard; the Canon cocks his ear to listen.*] I must be off. Bad sign. The soft rain that's falling may change to a downpour, and I've a long way to go.

[*Canon puts on his cloak. Barney and Cloyne come in carrying a heavy Jacobean chair between them.*

Souhaun. Ah, the Jacobin chair. [*Indicating the way*] Out in the entrance hall, Barney.

Poges. Let's look at it a second. [*Barney and Cloyne pause.*] Ah, Canon, old things take a lot of beating.

Canon. They do, they do, sir. Well, I must go now.

Poges [*halting him*]. One second, sir. [*He goes to the table, writes a cheque, and hands it to the Canon.*] Another little trifle to keep things going, Canon.

Canon. Twenty-five pounds! Oh, thank you, and God bless you, my very dear sir.

Souhaun. You must come to dinner some night.

Canon. I will, I will, with pleasure; goodbye all.

[*Midst a murmur of goodbyes the Canon goes out.*

Poges [*indignantly*]. Never showed the slightest interest in the Jacobin chair. Ignorance; Irish ignorance! [*Angrily—to Cloyne and Barney, who are holding the chair like a salesman displaying a piece of silk*] Bring the damned thing into the entrance hall, will you, and don't stand there like fools!

[*Cloyne, in her hurry, jerks the chair from Barney's hold and it bumps to the floor.*

Poges. Oh, butter-fingers, d'ye want to destroy it? That's a Jacobin chair, man, a Jacobin chair!

Barney [*with a yell as he carries out the chair with Cloyne*]. Well, if I let a damned chair fall, I didn't knock a wall down!

Poges. Impudent rascal. The more you do for them the less they think of you! [*He bustles into his overall again.*] Now to business. What'll we do first? The rugs?

Souhaun. There's no use of trying the rugs till you get your quattro-cento bureau in position. Then we'll be able to see if the colour of the rugs suits the bureau.

[*Avril has put on her mackintosh and sidled over to the entrance on right, leading to the hall, and is about to slip out when Basil darts to her side and catches her arm.*

Basil. Where are you slipping off to?

Avril. I'm going for a brisk walk along the bank of the brimming river. I'm fed-up carrying things about to get this foolish old house in order.

Poges. In this weather? Nonsense!

Basil. A good idea; I'll go with you, darling.

Avril [*with a malevolent look at him*]. Wouldn't you like to, eh? Take my advice and don't! [*To Poges*] Ay, in this weather.
       [*She goes quickly, leaving Basil, undecided, looking after her.*

Basil [*bitterly*]. She's going to go with O'Killigain!

Souhaun. Nonsense. She can't be out of your sight for a minute but you imagine the girl's with O'Killigain. The rain'll soon send her back. [*To Poges*] You see about locking the bureau, while I get the men to carry it in for you.   [*Poges goes by one of the entrances at the back.*

Basil [*going towards entrance at back*]. I tell you the jade's gone after O'Killigain.

Souhaun [*warningly*]. If I were you, Basil, I shouldn't press hard after little Avril; you are a little too consequential to please her always.

Basil [*maliciously—as he goes out*]. And you, me lady, are a lot too old to please O'Killigain at any time!

[*Souhaun stands stiff for a few moments; then she goes quickly to the entrance to the hall and is seen beckoning for one of the workmen.*

Souhaun [*calling*]. One of you, come here, please.

[*The 2nd Workman comes into the room and stands near the entrance, looking quietly at Souhaun.*

Souhaun. Send Mr. O'Killigain in to me, please.

2nd Workman. He's gone to the station to see afther a wagon-load o' bricks.

Souhaun [*slowly, after a pause*]. By himself?

2nd Workman [*after a pause*]. With th' handsome young woman. [*A pause.*] You're a handsome woman yourself; you're Irish too; an' y'ought to be sensible.

Souhaun [*slowly—a little surprised*]. Am I not sensible, good man?

2nd Workman [*earnestly*]. Your shinin' eyes can always say you are; an' soon you'll tire o' nestin' in a dusty nook with the hills outside an' th' roads for walkin'.

Souhaun. I will, will I?

2nd Workman [*with his eyes looking steadily in hers*]. Ay will you, an' dance away from a smoky bragger who thinks th' world spins round on th' rim of a coin; you'll hurry away from him, I'm sayin', an' it's a glad heart'll lighten th' journey to a one'll find a place for your little hand in th' white clouds, an' a place for your saucy head in th' blue o' th' sky.

Souhaun [*with a touch of mockery*]. Yourself, for instance?

2nd Workman. It's waitin' warm, he'll be, to please you, highly, an' show you wondhers of a manly manner.

Souhaun [*laughing, with a little catch in the laugh*]. A daughter of the Ormond with a workman!

2nd Workman [*raising his head proudly and looking steadily at her*]. An oldher name is an O'Dempsey, an' an oldher glory's in the name than the honour thrown to th' Earl o' Ormond when he crouched for favour at the English feet!

[*The 2nd Workman looks at Souhaun and Souhaun looks at the*

2nd Workman *for a moment, then she turns and goes slowly out by right entrance at back.*

3rd Workman [*appearing at the back left entrance*]. Here, Philib, what'r you doin'? You're to give us a hand to get in the oul' codger's bureau.

> [*The two of them go out by the entrance to the left at back. After a second or two, the sounds of scuffling and of voices are heard just outside the narrow entrance through which the two men have gone out, then Poges comes in with an anxious look on his face, turns and concentrates his gaze on the entrance. Presently the end of a big gilded desk-bureau comes in sight round the corner, with the three workmen puffing, pulling, pushing, and scuffling it along, each giving orders to the other two, to the concern of poor old Poges. When the bureau comes to the entrance, it can be seen to be a very tight fit.*

1st Workman. A little to the ayste, there, a little more to the ayste, can't yous!

2nd Workman. No, west, west; can't yous see it'll jam if yous cant it to the ayste? To th' west, I'm tellin' yous!

Poges [*anxiously*]. Easy, boys, easy, now; take care, take great care; that's a thing you won't meet every day, you know. I had an anxious time while it was coming over.

3rd Workman [*taking no notice of Poges*]. Where th' hell are yous shovin'? Are yous blind, or wha'? No squirming'll get it in that way. [*Recklessly*] Here, throw th' thing up on its hind legs an' let her go!

Poges [*loudly and anxiously*]. Eh, there, eh; steady, steady. Careful how you handle that. It's not a thing to throw up on its hind legs. I can't have a precious thing like that scratched and mangled. That's a quattrocento piece of furniture, and there isn't another piece like it in the world.

1st Workman [*to the others*]. Hear what the gentleman's sayin' to yous! Amn't I tired tellin' yous yous ud look long before yous ud find such a piece o' furniture in th' whole o' Clune na Geera? Yous can't fling a thing like this about the way you'd fling about an oul' kitchen chair. [*To Poges*] Amn't I right, sir?

Poges. Yes, yes; quite right, my man. Thousands of people would give a fortune to possess a thing like that bureau. So gently, boys, gently. The slightest scratch will do irreparable damage.

1st Workman. See, boys, it's a quattrocento lump o' furniture, an' so needs gentle handlin'. [*To 2nd Workman*] You, Philib, there, give it a sudden swing to the ayste, an' while she's swingin' we'll shoot her ahead.

2nd Workman [*angrily*]. How am I goin' to give her a sudden swing to the ayste when there's no purchase to get a grip of her? Squattrocento or nottrocento, I'm not goin' to let it whip a slice outa my hand!

3rd Workman [*thoughtfully*]. Th' only way to get it in proper is to get a sledge-hammer an' knock down some o' th' archway.

Poges [*indignantly*]. Knock down some of the archway! You'll do no such thing! You'll be suggesting that the house should be knocked down next. There's no sledge-hammer to be brought within sight of this precious bureau. [*Leaning over towards the men*] Listen: this is a piece of quattrocento—understand that, the whole of you, please!

1st Workman [*to the others*]. There, now, what did I tell yous? Yous hear what the gentleman says.

Poges. It ought to go in easily, if you knew your job. The driver of the furniture van looked at this entrance and told me not to worry, that the bureau would slide in without the slightest trouble.

1st Workman [*scornfully*]. Is it Larry Lunigan said that, now, did he? Don't mind anything Larry Lunigan says, sir. If your head was split he'd say it was only a scratch, to keep your heart up.

3rd Workman. Even if you were dead he'd tell your wife to wait, an' say you never could be sure of anything. An' we're not furniture shifters, sir.

Poges. Well, I'm sure of one thing: that bureau is coming into this room, and coming in without a scratch.

3rd Workman. 'Course it is.

1st Workman. Time an' patience'll do it.

Poges [*looking closely at the bureau—in anguish*]. Oh, my God, there's the stone wall eating into its edge! Get it away, pull it out, shove it in, you fools! [*As they shove*] Wait, wait!

1st Workman [*soothingly*]. I shouldn't worry, sir; a shavin' or two off is th' worst that can happen to it.

Poges. Wait, wait a second. I'll go and get some cushions and pillows to guard the sides from the wall.

[*He runs out by the adjoining entrance for the cushions.*]

1st Workman. J'ever see such an oul' fustherer in your life? You'd think the thing was on its way to the kingdom of heaven th' way he's cryin' over it.

3rd Workman. With a look on his ugly oul' gob like the tune th' oul' cow died of.

1st Workman. A quattrocento, mind you, says he.

3rd Workman. Seven hundred years an' more old, says he. Well, it's near time it met its death anyhow.

1st Workman. Here, let's get it in before he comes back billowin' with cushions. It's well able to take a knock or two.

2nd Workman. Here's th' crowbar he wouldn't let us use. [*He lifts up a big crowbar.*] We'll inch it in be main strength. Now, boys, get your shoulders to the quattrocento while I heave with th' bar! [*To the 1st Workman*] Start a shanty, Bill, to give us encouragement.

1st Workman [*chanting quickly, while they all brace themselves*]:
What shall we do with th' dhrunken sailor,
What shall we do with th' dhrunken sailor,
What shall we do with th' dhrunken sailor,
Early in th' mornin'?

All [*together—shoving and tugging vehemently*]:
Pull away, an' up she rises,
Pull away, an' up she rises,
Pull away, an' up she rises,
Early in th' mornin'!

> [*Poges rushes in with some cushions in his arms. He is frantic when he sees what the men are doing. As he rushes in he is accompanied by a peal of thunder, louder than the last, but still fairly faint. As he comes to a halt near the bureau the peal ends.*]

Poges [*enraged*]. What, in the devil's name, are you trying to do? Do you want to burst it to bits? Oh, why did I ever bring my poor quattrocento to a country like this! Shove it from the wall, shove it from the wall till I put a cushion in!

1st Workman. Sure, it won't go far enough away from the wall to fit a cushion, man.

Poges [*frantically*]. Do what you're told, do what you're told. [*He drops the cushions, seizes the edge of the bureau and tries to pull it from the wall.*] Here, somebody, help me!

> [*Before he is aware of it, the 1st Workman leaps on to the top of the bureau to cross over to him, his heavy hobnailed boots scraping the top of it.*]

Poges [*shouting at him*]. Get down, get down, man!

1st Workman [*astonished*].   Amn't I only comin' across to help you.

Poges [*yelling at him*].   That's a quattrocento, that's a quattrocento, man!

1st Workman.   Sure, I know it is.

Poges.   Then get off it, get off it—sticking your hobnailed boots through and through it!

1st Workman [*lifting up a foot so that the sole of the boot can be seen*]. Is it that, sir? Sure, th' nails are worn so soft an' smooth they wouldn't mark th' wing of a buttherfly.

Poges [*roaring*].   Get down, get down at once!
          [*The 1st Workman jumps off the bureau back among his mates.*

2nd Workman [*muttering loudly*].   It ud be a godsend to some I know if they opened their eyes to th' signs an' wondhers showin'.

Poges.   Now, no talk; and don't do anything till I give the order.

Men.   All right, sir; go ahead; we're waitin'.

Poges.   When I say go, you swing it to the right, while I swing to the left. Are you all ready?

1st Workman.   Ready an' waitin' an' willin'.

Poges.   Go!
          [*They all swing to the left, and Poges's foot is caught between the bureau and the archway. He lets a squeal out of him.*

Poges [*in anguish*].   Release my foot, my foot's caught! Why did you all swing left? Don't you know right from left?

3rd Workman.   You should have said ayste, sir.

Poges.   Shove it off, shove it from my foot!

1st Workman [*placing the crowbar between archway, against the column, and the bureau*].   Now, boys, all together—heave yo-ho! [*There is a mighty heave from them, one with the bar, the others with their shoulders. The bureau moves slowly; a crack is heard; the column snaps with the push of the bar against it and falls over the bureau, which suddenly shoots forward right into the middle of the room, the men stumbling after it. The men look triumphantly at the bureau, the 1st Workman leaning on the crowbar like a warrior leaning on his spear. Poges rubs his foot and contemplates the damage to the bureau and the entrance.*] There she is for you now, sir; right where you want her to be.

3rd Workman.   I knew well patience ud do it in the end.

Poges.   Oh, look at the bureau and look at the entrance!

1st Workman [*confidently*].   Oh, a spot o' cement an' a lick o' white paint'll make th' entrance look as young as ever again.

> [*Souhaun comes in, followed by Cloyne and Barney, who are carrying a rug between them. They leave it on the floor. Basil is wearing very wide plus-fours.*

Souhaun.   We're getting the house into some kind of order at last. [*She sees the damage.*] Oh, who's caused all the wreckage?

Poges [*sarcastically*].   Your very clever countrymen, dear.

Basil [*mockingly*].   And the high opinion they have of themselves.

2nd Workman.   There is sweet music in the land, but not for th' deaf; there is wisdom too, but it is not in a desk it is, but out in th' hills, an' in the life of all things rovin' round, undher th' blue sky.

Poges [*angrily and despairingly*].   Take this broken column away and be off to your work again. Leave us, leave us, before the house falls!

> [*The workmen take away the column and go out by entrance leading to the hall.*

Souhaun.   Let us try the rugs, for God's sake! I can't go out o' th' room but there's damage done. [*Cloyne and Barney spread on the floor a rug scattered over with brightly-coloured geometrical patterns. Cloyne and Barney then go out; the rest stare at the rug.*] Rather gay-looking for the floor of a Tudor house, dear.

Basil [*decidedly*].   Too bright and too modern.

Poges.   Where? how? why?

Basil.   The Tudors, my dear sir, were a sensible and sober people, and wouldn't tolerate anything that was vulgar, or shall I say, conspicuous.

Souhaun [*with some mockery*].   You see, darling, it was taste, and not steam, that was everything in those days.

Basil.   Quite, Souhaun; taste was the Tudor—er—er—*monumentum aere perennius.*

Poges.   I don't know everything, my dear sir; but I do know something about the period that this house—er—exemplifies; in fact, the period was so riotous in colour that the men's breeches had one leg blue, the other leg red, or vice versa.

Basil [*with a patronising laugh*].   Ah, old boy, that wasn't the Tudor period.

Poges.   What period was it, then?

Souhaun.   The Hiawatha period.

Poges [*indignantly—to Souhaun*]. This is no joke, please. [*To Basil*] What period was it, then?

Basil [*airily*]. Not the Tudor period, certainly; no, certainly not, old boy.

Poges [*contemptuously*]. Pshaw! You don't know it yourself.

> [*From the entrance at back the 2nd Workman appears wheeling a barrow filled with bricks. Passing by the disputants, on his way to the hall entrance, he wheels the barrow over a rug.*

Poges [*shouting at him*]. Where the hell are you going with your dirty barrow?

2nd Workman [*dropping the shafts of the barrow and turning to answer Poges*]. I'm bringin' a barrow o' bricks to O'Killigain, sir.

Basil. Oh, he's back, is he?

Poges. What the hell do you think you're doing, man?

2nd Workman. Amn't I afther tellin' you, I'm bringin' a barrow o' bricks to O'Killigain?

Poges. What d'ye mean, trundling your dirty barrow over a handsome rug laid out for inspection?

2nd Workman. What d'ye want me to do? Take th' barrow o' bricks up in me arms an' fly over it?

Basil [*with great dignity*]. Take it away at once, sir, and don't show impertinence to your betters.

2nd Workman [*eyeing Basil with scorn*]. Jasus, looka what calls itself a betther man than me!

> [*O'Killigain appears at the entrance leading to the hall.*

Poges [*earnestly—to the 2nd Workman*]. My man, you're cheeking a cousin of a K.G. whose family goes back to—to—[*turning to Basil*]—William the Conqueror, isn't it?

Basil [*stiffening—with proud complacency*]. Further back, old boy—Alfred; the last man of the last family fell at the battle of Hastings.

Poges [*impressively*]. There, you see.

Souhaun [*with a sign of mockery in her voice*]. And the ancient gentleman passed through Oxford, too.

O'Killigain [*from the archway*]. The city of dissolute might!

2nd Workman [*with mock deference*]. D'ye tell me that, now? Why didn't you make me aware of all that glory before I began to speak? Isn't it an alarmin' thing to hear of the ancientology of a being that I took to be an ordinary man! An' what might be the ancient gentleman's ancient name?

Poges. Basil Horatio Nelson Kaiser Stoke.

2nd Workman. A right worthy name. It mayn't have a musical sound, but it has a steady one. There's no flightiness in that name. An' now, would you like to know mine?

Poges [*amusedly*]. Here, be off with you to your work; as if your name mattered much.

2nd Workman. Me name's O'Dempsey, of the clan that were lords of Offaly ere his ancient highness here was a thousand years from bein' born; a clan that sthretches back as far as the time before an Englishman thought of buildin' a weedy shelther; an' further back to a day or two afther th' one when the sun herself was called upon to shine.

[*He takes hold of the shafts of the barrow preparatory to starting off.*

Poges [*contemptuously*]. You don't look it, my poor man!

2nd Workman [*as he wheels the barrow out*]. I feel it; an' th' river's risin'.

Poges [*severely—to O'Killigain*]. You really oughtn't to allow, much more encourage, this silly, ignorant, and superstitious conceit among your men; it is something close to scandalous!

O'Killigain [*quoting*]. They go their own gait: looking carelessly in the faces of presidents and governors, as to say, *Who are you?*

Poges [*imperatively*]. Well, it's not going to be heard in this house! The bobtag and ragtail must be made to keep their free-and-easy manners at a distance. Dignity reigns here.

[*A louder peal of thunder is heard in the distance, and the room darkens a little.*

O'Killigain. It's raining.

Poges. Eh?

O'Killigan. It's raining hard.

Souhaun [*shivering*]. And growing cold.

O'Killigain. And old things are perishing.

2nd Workman [*appearing at entrance*]. We're knocking off, O'Killigain, for the rain is heavier an' the winds are keen.

O'Killigain. You do well to knock off, for it is waste of time to try to butthress up a tumbling house.

Souhaun [*over to the 2nd Workman*]. The house'll be lonesome without you.

2nd Workman. Come, then, an' abide with the men o' th' wide wathers, who can go off in a tiny curragh o' thought to the New Island with th' outgoin' tide, an' come back be th' same tide sweepin' in again!

Poges [*mockingly—to Souhaun, clapping her on the back*]. There's a high and hearty invitation to you, my lady!

[*Avril comes in and dances over to Basil.*

Souhaun [*gleefully poking Poges in the ribs—to 2nd Workman*]. A long sail on the widening waters, no less; what gift is offered when the tide returns, good man?

2nd Workman. With firm-fed men an' comely, cordial women there'll be laughter round a red fire when the mists are risin', when th' roads an' fields are frosty, an' when th' nights is still.

Souhaun [*in a mocking voice—to Poges*]. There now, dear, is there anything more in the world than these that you can give?

Poges [*with pretended dismay*]. He has me beaten; what am I going to do at all, at all?

2nd Workman. A portion, too, with them who, ruddy-faced, were first in battle, with crimson cloak, white coat, an' silver belt studded with splendour by a cunning hand; a portion, too, with them of paler faces an' dhressed in dimmer clothes, who, fearless, stepped a straight way to th' gallows, silent an' darin' in th' midst of a yelled-out Sassenach song!

Souhaun [*trying to speak mockingly, but developing a slight catch in her voice; for she has been moved by the 2nd Workman's words*]. Where is the lady who would be slow to give a man with such a coaxing way an invitation to her pillow?

Avril [*who sees her friend is affected. She comes closer to her, and touches her on the arm*]. Souhaun, Souhaun, come an' show me your newest dhresses, an' don't stay listenin' to his thrancin' talk. Don't leave me alone with them.

Souhaun [*shaking off Avril's hand. Falling into the Irish idiom*]. Let me be, girl, for it's right an' lovely listenin' to a voice that's makin' gold embroidery out o' dancin' words.

Poges [*angry and a little nervous*]. It's time to put an end to all this nonsense!

O'Killigain [*ignoring Poges's angry exclamation—to Avril*]. An' you, young girl, sweet bud of an out-spreading three, graft yourself on to the living, and don't stay hidden any longer here. Come where the rain is heavy, where the frost frets, and where the sun is warm. Avril, pulse of me heart, listen to me, an' let longin' flood into your heart for the call of life. The young thorn-three withered away now, can awaken again, an' spread its fragrance around us. Spit out what's here, an' come where love is fierce an' fond an' fruitful. Come, lass, where there's things to say an' things to do an' love at the endings!

2nd Workman. Jack has spoken fair, an' there's no handsome hindrance near to stop yous. What's here but a creakin' grandeur an' poor witherin' talk; salt food without a dhrink to go with it; an' a purple dhryness turnin' timidly to dust!

O'Killigain [coming close to Avril]. Aren't my words a star in your ear, lass? Haven't you heard them? They've hit your young breast, lass. Come with me, I say; come away from where rich ignorance is a blessing, an' foolishness a gift from God! Come to th' house on th' hill: the door is open, the fire's alight on the hearth, and the table's laid with a clean white cloth.

Avril. Let another go in by the door; let another eat at the table; let another sit by the fire. Why didn't you come for me, O'Killigain, before the young thorn-tree had shed its blossom, and before the stems began to die?

O'Killigain. I'd other things to do. While you were livin' your lesser life, an' singin' your dowdy songs, I was fightin' in Spain that you might go on singin' in safety an' peace. [*He grips her arm*] I've come for you, now, me love.

Avril [emotionally and anxious]. I cannot go where things are said and things are done, for love has had no voice in the beginning of them! [*She tries to free her arm*] Oh, Jack, let me go—you're hurting me!

O'Killigain. It's O'Killigain gives the pressure of comfort and of care. D'ye mind th' hurt when th' hurt's th' hurt of love?

Avril [passionately]. Yes, I do! Oh, no, no; I don't, O'Killigain! I don't, I don't! Your pressure on my arm presses on my heart, too. Oh, go away an' leave me lonely!

[*She breaks away and runs to Souhaun, who puts an arm around her.*

O'Killigain. Avril, come out of th' guttherin' candlelight here to where th' wind puts a flush on the face, ruffles th' hair, and brings a catch to the breath; come to th' one you want; come to th' man who needs you!

2nd Workman [to Souhaun]. An' you, Souhaun, sturdy lily o' Clune na Geera, come into the love that can fix or flutther th' stars o' th' sky an' change th' shinin' moon into a lamp for two. Come to th' one you need; come to th' man who wants you!

Souhaun [*half joking, all in earnest*]. If you only had a horse handy, I'd ride away with you!

2nd Workman [*quietly*]. He's outside waitin'. A loan from Mr. O'Killigain. An animal can gallop glorious the livelong day undher th' sound of a steady voice an' th' touch of a steady hand.

Souhaun [*greatly moved*]. N-no!

2nd Workman [*firmly*]. Yes.

Basil [*rising out of astonishment—to Poges, angrily*]. How long are you ready to stick this, man? Send these impudent fellows away!

Poges [*as if awaking from a stupor—furiously to the two men*]. Get out, the two of you! We haven't lived long enough here to be touched with your insanity! Get out!

Souhaun [*to 2nd Workman—gently*]. I'll see; I'll do whatever Avril advises. [*To Avril*] Come, dear, till we think out a wonderful answer.

O'Killigain [*to Avril as she is going out*]. Be ready: I'll call, and come to take you when the river rises!   [*He goes out.*

2nd Workman [*to Souhaun as she is going out after Avril*]. I'll wait outside be th' good gallopin' horse till th' snowy-breasted pearl comes to shimmer on me shouldher.   [*He goes out after O'Killigain.*

Poges [*furious and mocking*]. When the river rises! Come with me and be my love! Come into the garden, Maud. Were ever fools so foolish!

Basil [*in angry glee*]. And the fellow with the galloping horse outside! Boot, saddle, and away! I never expected to see and hear the like, even in this odd country. [*Slapping Poges on the back—jokingly*] You'd better watch out for the sound of the galloping horse!

Poges [*slapping Basil on the back*]. And you keep an ear open for O'Killigain's call when the river rises!

Basil [*in a mock tragical voice*]. Beware the sound of a galloping horse!

Poges [*in the same manner*]. Beware of O'Killigain's call!

> [*Poges goes over to the bureau, opens a drawer, takes some papers out of it, and looks at them; then he sits down at the bureau, and arranges things in order to write a letter.*

Basil. And, for God's sake, did you hear that vulgar fellow chatting about making the moon do something or other?

Poges [*arranging things on the bureau*].   Poor crazy fool. They're all a
bit demented. Must be the climate. Most amusing.

Basil [*gloomily*].   Yes, amusing up to a point, but hardly reassuring; no.
[*He comes nearer to Poges.*] I don't like it, Poges.

Poges [*a little startled*].   Eh?

Basil.   Well, it isn't exactly comfortable to be living in a community of
crazy people, is it? It may even become dangerous.

Poges [*sitting up straight*].   That's a serious thought, Stoke. Now that
you mention it, I do feel the insidious influence of the place. We might
become demented too.

Basil.   If they allowed us to live long enough.

Poges.   Good God, what a thought! I must have a talk with you about
this when I finish this letter.

Basil.   You saw for yourself how this influence is even affecting the girls.

Poges [*emphatically*].   The girls? There you are wrong, Stoke. No, no,
not the girls, man. They were just humbugging the poor fools. Nonsense; not the girls.

Basil [*about to go out*].   You watch. Come up to our room when you've
finished the letter, will you?

Poges.   At once. [*Basil goes out. Poges takes some paper, and writes the
date on the top right corner. Then he pauses, and evidently begins to
think of what has happened. Shaking his head slowly from side to side
—musingly*]. Erin, the tear and the smile in thine eye.

> [*He clears his throat with a cough, and settles down to write. The
> room becomes darker. He has hardly been writing a minute when a
> curious face appears round the corner of the entrance leading to
> the hall. It is the stout little face of a little man dressed in neat
> black clothes covered with a saturated fawn-coloured mackintosh.
> Big spectacles cover his eyes. A huge fiery-red beard spreads over
> his chest like a breastplate, reaching to his belly, and extending out
> from his body like a fan turned downwards. He wears a black jerry
> hat. When he speaks he is found to have a little voice. He carries a
> blackthorn stick in his hand. As he peeps round he sees Poges at
> the bureau, and pulls in his head again. He thrusts it forward
> again, steps out, and comes into full view. He pulls his coat straight
> with a jerk and smoothes his trousers, and then comes with a trot
> into the room, right over to Poges, bends over towards him, and
> greets him in a hearty manner. He is the Postmaster of the village.*]

Postmaster.   An honour it is, sir, to meet the owner of such a fine house.

A house with a histhory. A house where the genthry joined themselves to merriment and danced th' stars to sleep! [*He dances clumsily round the room, singing*] See me dance the polka, see me dance the polka, see me dance the polka, as I have done before. [*He suddenly stops and comes close to Poges.*] I hope I see you well, sir? I bear a message from the Postmaster.

Poges [*amazed*]. I am well, thank you; and what is your message from the Postmaster?

Postmaster. When I was outside, an' heard you coughin', it's well I knew be th' sound of th' cough that the cough was th' cough of a gentleman.

Poges [*impatiently*]. Yes, yes; but what is your message?

Postmaster. Well, as genuine gentleman, you'll be th' first to agree that a Postmaster with a small wife an' a large family, an' hardly any salary—I near forgot to mention that—hardly any salary at all, if the thruth was told, as a thrue gentleman, you'll agree that a man like that is handicapped, an' has a claim on a gentleman's sympathy.

Poges. But I can't make his wife bigger or his family smaller, can I?

Postmaster. Sure, I know you can't, an' that's not what the Postmaster's complainin' about. [*He leans over Poges.*] But th' poor man needs sleep, he needs his share o' sleep.

Poges [*humouring him—thinking his visitor is out of his mind*]. Yes, yes; of course, the poor man needs sleep. We all need sleep. That's a fine stick you have in your hand, sir; can I see it?

Postmaster [*holding up the stick and stretching it away from Poges*]. Ay, ay, fine blackthorn. There y'are; look at it as long as you like— [*warningly*]—but don't lay a finger on it. There's a stick could give a man a crack a man ud remember!

Poges [*nervous*]. Oh? I can't see it well from here; let me take it in my hand for a moment.

Postmaster. Sorra a second you're goin' to have it in your hand. That stick has never been outa me father's hand an' it has never been outa mine. D'ye know why?

Poges. No, friend, I don't.

Postmaster. Guess, now, guess.

Poges [*smiling sweetly*]. I haven't the slightest idea, friend; I couldn't guess.

Postmaster. This's th' very stick that me oul' fellow made a swipe at Parnell with—th' scandaliser of Ireland's holy name, a swipe that, had it got home, ud a laid Parnell up for a month o' Sundays! Now, as a thrue gentleman, wouldn't you say I was right?

Poges. Yes, yes; quite right.

Postmaster. Well, havin' settled that, let's settle th' other: amn't I right in sayin' that every man should have his share o' sleep?

Poges. Yes, yes; of course.

Postmaster. Well, then, amn't I right in sayin' that th' poor Postmaster should have his share o' sleep too?

Poges. To be sure. [*Rising from his seat*] Now, I must be going. [*A fairly loud clap of thunder is heard, followed by the sound, first of a trotting horse, then of one going off at a gallop. They listen till the sounds die in the distance.*] A horse going off at a gallop. [*He makes a move away*] I must go to see what's wrong.

Postmaster [*waving him back with the stick*]. Wait a minute—I'm not done yet. You've just said the poor Postmaster should have his share o' sleep—didn't you?

Poges [*impatiently*]. Yes, yes, friend.

Postmaster. I knew you'd say that. [*He stretches out his hand to Poges.*] Lave it there. [*He shakes hands with Poges.*] Now I won't have to be keepin' one eye open an' me ear glued to the bell, for fear of a toll call or a thrunk call, afther ten o'clock at night, an' I settlin' down for a cosy sleep.

Poges [*the truth dawning on him*]. Oh, so you're the Postmaster, are you? So it was you who delayed me when I wanted St. Paul?

Postmaster. Didn't you know that?

Poges. The telephonic system here is an all-night one, isn't it?

Postmaster. 'Course it is, but that says nothin'.

Poges [*decidedly*]. Look here, my man; I'm a business man, and have to make calls at all hours of the night; I can't be thinking of every man having an honest night's sleep.

Postmaster. 'Course you can't; it's only the poor Postmaster that you've got to keep in mind.

Poges [*severely*]. Look here, my man, as long as I pay for the service, the service will have to be supplied. Good day.

Postmaster. There isn't a gentleman in th' whole disthrict ud think, except in th' case o' sudden death or disasther, of givin' a tinkle afther th' hand o' th' clock had passed the figure of half-past nine o' night.

Poges. Take yourself and your stick away out of the house, man!

Postmaster [*mimicking him*]. Take yourself and your stick away outa the house, man. Is it comin' down here to teach us good manners an' feelin' y'are, an' you puttin' a surly gob on you when you're asked to fall in with the sensible an' thried institutions of the neighbourhood?

> [*While they have been talking together, the room has darkened still more, and Poges sharply tugs the string that puts on the light; the wind has risen and can be heard occasionally blowing through the trees outside, and even shaking the old house.*]

Poges [*in a rage*]. Go on, get out!

> [*As he says this, a long, loud peal of thunder is heard.*]

Postmaster. D'ye hear that? There won't be many thrunk calls goin' for a while, an' th' poor Postmaster'll have a sweeter night's sleep than some I know. [*He bends towards Poges.*] When—the river—rises!

> [*The room has darkened; the wind rises; the one light in the room flickers. The Postmaster and Poges watch it. Then the Postmaster turns to go, but halts when a Figure of a man is seen standing at the entrance leading to the hall. He is dressed from head to foot in gleaming black oilskins, hooded over his head, just giving a glimpse of a blue mask, all illumined by the rays of flickering lightning, so that The Figure seems to look like the spirit of the turbulent waters of the rising river. The Postmaster goes back, startled, till he is beside Poges, and the two men stand and stare at the ominous Figure. Basil, Barney, and Cloyne appear at the entrances at back, each holding a lighted lantern in his and her hand. They are very frightened. They too hold up their lanterns and stare at The Figure.*]

Basil. The river is rising!

Barney. Risin' high!

Cloyne. An' will overwhelm us all!

The Figure [*in a deep voice*]. The river has broken her banks and is rising high; high enough to come tumbling in on top of you. Cattle, sheep, and swine are moaning in the whirling flood. Trees of an ancient heritage, that looked down on all below them, are torn from the power of the place they were born in, and are tossing about in the foaming energy of the waters. Those who have lifted their eyes unto the hills are firm of foot, for in the hills is safety; but a trembling perch in the highest place on the highest house shall be the portion of those who dwell in the valleys below!

[*The lightning ceases for a moment; the entrance becomes dark, and The Figure disappears.*

Poges [*frantic*]. What shall we do? what must we do? what can we do?

Basil [*in anguish*]. We're lost!

Cloyne [*sinking down on her knees*]. King o' th' Angels, save us!

Barney [*clasping his hands*]. Amen! A nice pass we've come to when we have to call for help in a Tudor house! [*To Basil and Poges*] It's the evil livin' of you two buckos that has brought this disaster upon us!

Poges [*bawling*]. Souhaun, Souhaun! O'Killigain, help!

Basil [*roaring at Poges.*] You made us come down here!

Poges [*roaring at Basil*]. You're a liar, it was you!

Postmaster [*bringing down the blackthorn stick with a bang on the quattrocento bureau*]. Eh, order, order, law an' order there; steady! Measures o' safety to be taken. [*Thrusting his stick towards Poges— sharply*] Has the highest room in the house a way to the roof—quick!

Poges [*answering at once*]. Yes.

Cloyne [*in anguish*]. Th' roof—oh, my God!

Postmaster [*rapidly*]. Up with us all with bread and wine, with fire-wood and coal, and an axe. Up!

Poges. An axe?

Postmaster. To hack whatever suitable furniture we can get into a raft if we're swirled off th' roof. [*Driving Cloyne and Barney before him*] Up!

Poges [*loudly*]. Souhaun, Souhaun, where's Souhaun?

Basil [*impatiently*]. Come on, and come up.

[*Avril comes in from one of the back entrances. She is covered with a green mackintosh, and a coloured scarf, peasant-wise, is over her head. She carries a small case. She passes between the two men without a word, and stands still near the entrance leading to the hall, looking out before her.*

Poges [*staring at her*]. What are you doing here? What are you watching? [*Avril stands still and silent.*] Where's Souhaun, where's Souhaun?

Avril [*quietly—without looking round*]. She's gone.

Poges. Gone? How? Where?

Avril [*quietly—still not moving*]. Gone with the wind; gone with the waters; gone with the one man who alone saw something in her!

Poges [*raging*]. What, with that loud-mouthed, ignorant, superstitious, low-born, half-mad Irishman! Oh, she's nicely rooked me! She was with him on the galloping horse that galloped away, was she? Oh, she's nicely rooked a simple, honest, loving-hearted, foolish man! She's gone, is she?

Avril. An' well it would be if I was with her.

Poges. You damned slut, are you in your mind as bad as she is?

Avril [*indicating Basil*]. The mind that went with him is as bad as the mind that went with you.

Basil [*sneeringly*]. You lost the chance you had to get away from it.

Avril. He said he'd come when the river rises.

O'Killigain [*outside—loudly*]. Avril!

Avril [*with a start of joy*]. O'Killigain! O'Killigain!

[*O'Killigain appears, his trench coat drenched and his hair soaking, at the entrance.*

O'Killigain. My barque is waiting, love; come!
[*Avril picks up the case and runs to O'Killigain.*

Basil. Honest, decent woman, she carries the booty of her friends in her pack!

Avril [*quietly*]. I gave more than I got, you gilded monkey. It's winnowed of every touch of life I'd be if I stayed with th' waste of your mind much longer. [*She taps the case.*] Th' thrinkets I wormed out of you are all here, an' here they stay, for th' wages were low for what was done for you.

Poges [*sneering*]. And gentleman O'Killigain will happier be with a harlot's fortune!

O'Killigain [*good-humouredly*]. Of course he will. Th' good things of this life are good for all, an' a pretty girl looks handsomer in arms that are fit and fond to hold her. You have had your day, like every dog. Your Tudors have had their day, and they are gone; and th' little heap o' purple dust they left behind them will vanish away in th' flow of the river. [*To Avril*] Come, love, to my little house up on th' hill.

[*He goes out with Avril. After a moment the sound of oars are heard splashing the waters, and O'Killigain is heard singing.*

O'Killigain [*singing: other voices, outside, join in the chorus*]:
Come from the dyin' an' fly from th' dead,
Far away O!

An' now, with th' quick, make your home an' your bed,
With a will an' a way, away O!

Then away, love, away,
Far away O!
To live any life that is looming ahead,
With a will an' a way, away O!

Away from all mouldherin' ashes we row,
Far away O!
Takin' th' splendour of livin' in tow,
With a will an' a way, away! O

Then away, love, away,
Far away O!
Where th' lightning of life flashes vivid we go,
With a will an' a way, away O!

> [*Poges stands still, listening till the song fades away in the distance. Suddenly Basil clutches his arm.*

Basil [*frantically*].   Look, the waters are tumbling towards us! Run, man!
> [*He tears up the passage while Poges follows more slowly.*

Poges [*going out*].   My poor little quattrocento, the waters are about to cover thee! My comfort's gone, and my house of pride is straining towards a fall. Would to God I were in England, now that winter's here!

> [*He disappears down the passage as the green waters tumble into the room through the entrance from the hall.*

CURTAIN

RED ROSES FOR ME

A Play in Four Acts

(1942)

CHARACTERS IN THE PLAY

MRS. BREYDON
AYAMONN BREYDON, *her son*
EEADA ⎤
DYMPNA ⎬ *Mrs. Breydon's neighbours in the house*
FINNOOLA ⎦
SHEILA MOORNEEN, *Ayamonn's sweetheart*
BRENNAN O' THE MOOR, *owner of a few oul' houses*
A SINGER, *a young man with a good voice*
ROORY O'BALACAUN, *a zealous Irish Irelander*
MULLCANNY, *a mocker of sacred things*
REV. E. CLINTON, *Rector of St. Burnupus*
SAMUEL, *verger to the church*
INSPECTOR FINGLAS, *of the Mounted Police, and the Rector's churchwarden*
1ST MAN ⎤
2ND MAN ⎬ *neighbours in the next house to Breydons'*
3RD MAN ⎦

DOWZARD ⎤ *members of St. Burnupus' Select Vestry*
FOSTER ⎦
A LAMPLIGHTER
1ST RAILWAYMAN
2ND RAILWAYMAN

SCENE

ACT I · Two-roomed home of the Breydons.

ACT II · The same.

ACT III · A Dublin street, beside a bridge over the river Liffey.

ACT IV · Part of the grounds round the Protestant Church of St. Burnupus. In this Act the curtain is lowered for a few minutes to denote the passing of a few hours.

TIME · A little while ago.

ACT I

*The front one of two rather dilapidated rooms in a poor working-class
locality. The walls, whitewashed, are dwindling into a rusty yellowish
tinge. The main door, leading to the hall, is at the back, a little towards
the right. The fireplace is in the right-hand wall, and a brilliant fire is
burning in the large, old-fashioned grate. In the centre of the room is an
old ebony-hued table on which stands a one-wick oil-lamp, its chimney
a little smoky from the bad oil in the reservoir. Some books lie on the
table, some paper, coloured chalks, a pen, and a small bottle of ink. In the
left wall, up towards the back, is the door leading to the second room. Below this door is a horsehair sofa showing signs of old age. On it, to the
head, is a neatly folded bundle of sheets and blankets, showing that it is
used as a bed during the night. To the left of the main door at back is a
large basket used by actors when on tour. On the other side of this door is
an ordinary kitchen dresser on which some of the crockery is on the ledge,
for the upper shelf is filled with a row of books, by the look of them
second-hand. Over the basket, on the wall, is tacked a childlike brightly-
coloured pastel of what is meant to be a copy of one of Fra Angelico's
angels blowing a curved and golden trumpet; and beside it is a small
coloured reproduction of Constable's "Cornfield". In the same wall, towards the back, is a large, tall window, nearly reaching the ceiling, and,
when one is in front of it, the top of a railway signal, with transverse arms,
showing green and red lights, can be seen. Under this window, on a
roughly made bench, stand three biscuit tins. In the first grows a geranium,
in the second, musk, and in the third, a fuchsia. The disks of the geranium
are extremely large and glowing; the tubular blooms of the golden musk,
broad, gay, and rich; and the purple bells of the fuchsia, surrounded by
their long white waxy sepals, seem to be as big as arum lilies. These crimson, gold, and purple flowers give a regal tint to the poor room. Occasionally in the distance can be heard the whistle of an engine, followed by
its strenuous puffing as it pulls at a heavy rake of goods wagons. A chair
or two stand about the room.*

*It is towards the evening of a mid-spring day, and the hour would make
it dusk, but it is darker than that, for the sky is cloudy and rain is falling
heavily over the city.*

*Ayamonn and his mother are in the room when the scene shows itself.
He is tall, well built, twenty-two or so, with deep brown eyes, fair hair,
rather bushy, but tidily kept, and his face would remind an interested observer of a rather handsome, firm-minded, thoughtful, and good-humoured
bulldog. His mother is coming up to fifty, her face brownish, dark eyes
with a fine glint in them, and she bears on her cheeks and brow the
marks of struggle and hard work. She is dressed in a black jacket, fitting*

close, marred by several patches, done very neatly, dark-blue skirt, a little faded, and rather heavily-soled boots. At the moment this is all covered with a rich blue velvet cloak, broidered with silver lace, and she is sitting on a kitchen chair covered with a dark-red, rather ragged cloth.

Ayamonn wears a bright-green silk doublet over which is a crimson velvet armless cloak bordered with white fur. The back part of the cloak is padded so as to form a big hump between his shoulders. Across his chest is a dark-green baldric from which hangs a scabbard. A cross-hilted sword is in his hand. On his head he has a black felt hat with narrow turned-up rims. A black band goes round the hat, and a crimson feather sticks up from it. His legs are in heavy, black, working corduroy trousers, and he wears heavy hobnailed boots. She and he are in an intensely listening attitude.

Mrs. Breydon [*whispering over to Ayamonn*]. She's gone; wanted to borra something else, I suppose. They're feverish with borrowing in this blessed house!

Ayamonn. Damn her for a troublesome fool! Where's this I was when the knock came?

Mrs. Breydon. I was just goin' to say
    Ay, an' for much more slaughter after this,
    O God! forgive my sins, and pardon thee!

Ayamonn [*looking at the floor*]. Oh yes! [*He recites*]—
    What, will th' aspiring blood of Lancaster
    Sink to the ground? I thought it would have mounted. [*He holds
        the sword aloft, and stares at it*]
    See how my sword weeps for the poor king's death!
    O, may such purple tears be always shed
    For those that wish the downfall of our house!
    If any spark of life be yet remaining,
    [*He stabs at the floor*] Down, down to hell; and say I sent thee thither!

        [*A knuckle-knock is heard at the door. Ayamonn and Mrs. Breydon
        stiffen into a silent listening attitude. A fine baritone voice, husky
        with age, is heard speaking outside.*

Voice. Is anyone in or out or what? [*Louder raps are given as Ayamonn steals over, and places his back to the door.*] Eh, in there—is there anyone movin', or is the oul' shack empty?

Mrs. Breydon [*in a whisper*]. Oul' Brennan on the Moor. He was here before, today. He's got his rent for his oul' houses, an' he wants to be told again that the Bank of Ireland's a safe place to put it.

Ayamonn [*warningly*]. Ssshush!

Voice. No answer, eh? An' me afther seein' a light in th' window. Maybe they are out. For their own sakes, I hope they are; for it's hardly an honourable thing to gainsay a neighbour's knock.

[*The sound of feet shuffling away is heard outside, and then there is silence for a few moments.*

Mrs. Breydon. He's gone. He's always a bit lively the day he gets his rents. How a man, with his money, can go on livin' in two rooms in a house an' sthreet only a narrow way betther than this, I don't know. What was he but an oul' painter an' paperhanger, starvin' to save, an' usin' his cunnin' to buy up a few oul' houses, give them a lick o' paint, and charge the highest rent for th' inconvenience of livin' in them!

Ayamonn. I wish he'd keep himself and his throubles far away from me now. I've higher things to think of and greater things to do than to be attached to the agony of an old fool for ever afraid a fistful of money'll be snatched away from him. Still, he isn't a miser, for he gives kids toys at Christmas, and never puts less than half a crown on the plate in church on Sundays.

Mrs. Breydon. So well he may!

Ayamonn. What was he sayin' when he was here before?

Mrs. Breydon. Oh, th' usual question of askin' me what I thought about the Bank of Ireland; mutterin' about somebody not payin' the rent; and that his birthday's due tomorrow.

Ayamonn [*looking at the chair*]. I'll have to get a loan of a chair with arms on, and someway make them golden to do the thing proper in the Temperance Hall; and I'll paint for the back of it, on thin cardboard, a cunning design of the House of Lancaster, the red rose, so that it'll look like a kingly seat.

Mrs. Breydon. Th' killin' o' th' king be th' Duke o' Gloster should go down well, an' th' whole thing should look sumptuous.

Ayamonn. So it will. It's only that they're afraid of Shakespeare out of all that's been said of him. They think he's beyond them, while all the time he's part of the kingdom of heaven in the nature of everyman. Before I'm done, I'll have him drinking in th' pubs with them!

Mrs. Breydon. I don't know that he'll go well with a Minstrel Show.

Ayamonn. He'll have to go well. If only King Henry doesn't rant too much, saw the air with his hands, and tear his passion to tatthers. The old fool saw someone do it that way, and thinks it must be right. [*With a sigh*] I daren't attempt to recite my part now, for Oul' Brennan on the Moor's waitin' and listenin' somewhere down below; so I'll just get it off by heart. How old does he say he'll be tomorrow?

Mrs. Breydon. Only seventy-six, he says, an' feelin' as if he was lookin' forward to his twenty-first birthday.

Ayamonn. Well, he won't have long to wait.

Mrs. Breydon [*slyly*]. He was muttherin', too, about some air or other on the oul' piano he has at home.

Ayamonn [*springing up from where he has been sitting*]. It's one o' mine he's put an air to! [*He rushes from the room and returns in a few moments.*] He's not there; gone home, I suppose. [*Irritably*] I wish you'd told me that at first.

Mrs. Breydon. I'd thry to rest a little, Ayamonn, before you go to work. You're overdoing it. Less than two hours' sleep today, and a long night's work before you. Sketchin', readin', makin' songs, an' lear.in' Shakespeare: if you had a piano, you'd be thryin' to learn music. Why don't you stick at one thing, an' leave the others alone?

Ayamonn. They are all lovely, and my life needs them all.

Mrs. Breydon. I managed to get on well enough without them. [*A pause. She goes over to the window and tenderly touches the fuchsia.*] There's this sorryful sthrike, too, about to come down on top of us.

Ayamonn [*sitting in the red-covered chair and reading Shakespeare— quietly and confidently*]. There'll be no strike. The bosses won't fight. They'll grant the extra shilling a week demanded.

Mrs. Breydon [*now fingering the musk*]. I thought this Minstrel Show was being run to gather funds together?

Ayamonn [*impatiently*]. So it is, so it is; but only in case the strike may have to take place. I haven't much to do with it, anyway. I'm with the men, spoke at a meeting in favour of the demand, and that's all.

Mrs. Breydon. You'll underhermine your health with all you're doin', tearin' away what's left of your time be runnin' afther——

[*She checks herself, and becomes silent.*

Ayamonn [*lowering his book to his lap—angrily*]. Go on—finish what you started to say: runnin' afther who?

Mrs. Breydon. Nobody, nobody.

Ayamonn. Runnin' afther Sheila Moorneen—that's what was in your mind to say, wasn't it?

Mrs. Breydon. If it was aself; is there a new law out that a body's not to think of her own thoughts.

Ayamonn [*sharply*].   What have you got against the girl?

Mrs. Breydon.   Nothing. As a girl, I'd say she's a fine coloured silken shawl among a crowd of cotton ones. A girl I'd say could step away from the shadowy hedges where others slink along, tiltin' her head as she takes the centre of the road for the entherprisin' light o' day to show her off to everyone. Still——   [*She stops speaking again.*

Ayamonn.   Ay, but still what? You've a maddenin' way of never finishing some of your sentences.

Mrs. Breydon [*braving it out*].   She's a Roman Catholic; steeped in it, too, the way she'd never forgive a one for venturin' to test the Pope's pronouncement.

Ayamonn.   And who wants to test the Pope's pronouncement? Life and all her vital changes'll go on testing everything, even to the Pope's pronouncement. D'ye think I've laboured as I have, and am labourin' now, to furnish myself with some of the greatness of the mighty minds of the past, just to sink down into passive acceptance of the Pope's pronouncement? Let the girl believe what she may, reverence what she can: it's her own use of her own mind. That she is fair to look upon, charming to talk with, and a dear companion, is well and away enough for me, were she even a believer in Mumbo Jumbo, and had a totem pole in her front garden.

Mrs. Breydon.   There's worse still than that in it.

Ayamonn.   Worse, is there? An' what may that be?

Mrs. Breydon.   She's th' child of a sergeant in the Royal Irish Constabulary, isn't she?

Ayamonn.   Well, she can't help it, can she?

Mrs. Breydon.   I know that; but many have murmured again' a son of mine goin' with the child of a man crouchin' close to their enemy.

Ayamonn.   Everything, it seems, is against her, save herself. I like herself, and not her faith; I want herself, and not her father.

Mrs. Breydon.   The bigger half of Ireland would say that a man's way with a maid must be regulated by his faith an' hers, an' the other half by the way her father makes his livin'.

Ayamonn.   And let the whole world join them! Fair she is, and her little ear's open to hear all that I thry to say, so, were she the child of darkness aself, I'd catch her hand and lead her out and show her off to all men.

Mrs. Breydon.   She wouldn't be a lot to look at afther she'd wended her way through poverty with you for a year an' a day.

Ayamonn. She gives no honour to gold; neither does her warm heart pine for silks and satins from China and Japan, or the spicy isles of Easthern Asia. A sober black shawl on her shoulders, a simple petticoat, and naked feet would fail to find her craving finer things that envious women love.

Mrs. Breydon. Ah, go on with you, Ayamonn, for a kingly fool. I'm tellin' you th' hearts of all proper girls glow with the dhream of fine things; an' I'm tellin' you, too, that the sword jinglin' on th' hip of Inspector Finglas, the red plume hangin' from his menacin' helmet, an' th' frosty silver sparklin' on his uniform, are a dazzle o' light between her tantalised eyes an' whatever she may happen to see in you.

Ayamonn. Tell me something else to add to my hope.

Mrs. Breydon. Go on readin', an' don't bother to listen to your mother.

Ayamonn [*going over and gently putting his hands on her shoulders*]. I do listen, but I am drifting away from you, Mother, a dim shape now, in a gold canoe, dipping over a far horizon.

Mrs. Breydon [*with a catch in her voice*]. I did an' dared a lot for you, Ayamonn, my son, in my time, when jeerin' death hurried your father off to Heaven.

Ayamonn. It's I who know that well: when it was dark, you always carried the sun in your hand for me; when you suffered me to starve rather than thrive towards death in an Institution, you gave me life to play with as a richer child is given a coloured ball. [*He gently lifts up her face by putting a hand under her chin.*] The face, the dear face that once was smooth is wrinkled now; the eyes, brown still, that once were bright, have now been dimmed by a sthrained stare into the future; the sturdy back that stood so straight, is bending. A well-tried leaf, bronzed with beauty, waiting for a far-off winter wind to shake it from the tree.

Mrs. Breydon [*gently removing his hand from her chin*]. I have a tight hold still. My back can still bear many a heavy burden; and my eyes, dimmer now than once they were, can still see far enough. Well, I betther take this fancy robe from off me, lest it give me gorgeous notions.

> [*She takes off her robe, and leaves it carefully folded on the basket, then goes over and arranges the fire. Ayamonn looks thoughtfully out of the window, then takes off cloak, sword, and hat, leaving them carefully on the basket.*

Ayamonn [*musingly*]. He'll hardly come tonight in this rain. If he does, I'll get him to read the King's part, and do mine over again.

Mrs. Breydon. Who's to come tonight?

Ayamonn. Mullcanny: he's searching Dublin for a book he wants to give me; and, if he got it, he was to bring it tonight—*The Riddle of the Universe.*

Mrs. Breydon. That's another one I wouldn't see too much of, for he has the whole neighbourhood up in arms against his reckless disregard of God, an' his mockery of everything solemn, set down as sacred.

Ayamonn. Oh, Tim is all right. The people are sensible enough to take all he says in good part; and a black flame stands out in a brightly-coloured world.

Mrs. Breydon. You don't know them, if you say that; he'll meet with a mishap, some day, if he doesn't keep his mouth shut.

Ayamonn. Nonsense.

[*She has quietly slipped a shawl around her, and is moving to the door so silently as to seem to want to prevent Ayamonn from notic-ing her movements, when the door opens and Eeada, Dympna, Finnoola, and several men, appear there. The three women come a little way into the room; the men stay around the door. All their faces are stiff and mask-like, holding tight an expression of dumb resignation; and are traversed with seams of poverty and a hard life. The face of Eeada is that of an old woman; that of Dympna, one coming up to middle age; and that of Finnoola, one of a young girl. Each shows the difference of age by more or less furrows, but each has the same expressionless stare out on life.*

[*Dympna is carrying a statue of the Blessed Virgin, more than two feet high, in her arms. The figure was once a glory of purest white, sparking blue, and luscious gilding; but the colours have faded, the gilt is gone, save for a spot or two of dull gold still lingering on the crown. She is wearing a crown that, instead of being domed, is castellated like a city's tower, resembling those of Dublin; and the pale face of the Virgin is sadly soiled by the grime of the house. The men are dressed in drab brown, the women in a chill grey, each suit or dress having a patch of faded blue, red, green, or pur-ple somewhere about them.*

Eeada [*to Mrs. Breydon*]. Could you spare a pinch or two of your Hud-son's soap, Mrs. Breydon, dear, to give the Blessed Virgin a bit of a wash? [*To all in general*] Though I've often said it's th' washin' that's done away with the bonnie blue of th' robe an' th' braver gold of its bordhers an' th' most o' th' royalty outa th' crown. Little Ursula below's savin' up her odd pennies to bring Her where She'll fine a new blue robe, an' where they'll make the royalty of th' gilt glow again; though whenever she's a shillin' up, it's needed for food an' firin'; but we never yet found Our Lady of Eblana averse to sellin' Her crown an' Her blue robe to provide for Her people's need. [*Mrs. Breydon gives half a packet of soap powder. Gratefully*] Thank you, ma'am, an' though y'are of a different persuasion, Our Blessed Lady of Eblana's poor'll bless you an' your fine son for this little tribute to Her honour and circumspect appearance before the world.

The Rest [*murmuring*]. Ay will She, an' that's a sure thing.

> [*They open a way for Eeada to pass out, with Dympna carrying the statue, following in a kind of simple procession. Mrs. Breydon is moving slowly after them.*]

Ayamonn [*who has noticed her under his eyes*]. You're not going out again, surely—on a night like this, too?

Mrs. Breydon. Not really; only down the road to Mrs. Cashmore's. She's not too well; I promised I'd dhrop in, and see to a hot dhrink or something for her before she wandhered off to sleep.

Ayamonn [*irritably*]. You think more of other homes than you do of your own! Every night for the past week you've been going out on one silly mission or another like an imitation sisther of charity.

Mrs. Breydon. I couldn't sit quiet knowin' the poor woman needed me. I'd hear her voice all through the night complainin' I never came to give her a hot dhrink, settle her bed soft, an' make her safe for th' lonely hours of th' slow-movin' night.

Ayamonn. A lot they'd do for you if you happened to need help from them.

Mrs. Breydon. Ah, we don't know. A body shouldn't think of that, for such a belief would dismay an' dismantle everything done outside of our own advantage. No harm to use an idle hour to help another in need.

Ayamonn. An' wear yourself out in the process?

Mrs. Breydon [*with a sigh*]. I'll wear out, anyway, sometime, an' a tired ould body can, at least, go to its long rest without any excuse.

> [*As she opens the door to go out, Sheila appears on the threshold. She is a girl of about twenty-three, fairly tall, a fine figure, carrying herself with a sturdiness never ceasing to be graceful. She has large, sympathetic brown eyes that dim, now and again, with a cloud of timidity. Her mouth is rather large but sweetly made; her hair is brown and long, though now it is gathered up into a thick*]

coil that rests on the nape of her neck. She is dressed in a tailor-made suit of rich brown tweed, golden-brown blouse, and a bright-blue hat. These are now covered with a fawn-coloured mackintosh, darkened with heavy rain, and a hastily folded umbrella is dripping on to the floor. She comes in shyly, evidently conscious of Mrs. Breydon's presence; but fighting her timidity with a breezy and jovial demeanour. Mrs. Breydon tries, but can't keep a little stiffness out of her greeting.

Sheila. Oh! good evening, Mrs. Breydon. What a night! I'm nearly blown to bits; and the rain—oh, the wind and the weather!

Mrs. Breydon. You must be perished. Take off your mac, and come over to the fire. Get Ayamonn to make you a cup o' tea, and bring you back to life again.

Sheila. No, really; I'm burning—the battle with the wind and the rain has made me warm and lively.

Ayamonn. Hey ho, the wind and the rain, for the rain it raineth every day. Sit down and take the weight off your legs.

Sheila. Not worth while, for I can't stop long. [*To Mrs. Breydon*] Going out on a night like this, Mrs. Breydon?

Ayamonn [*hastily*]. She has to go: got an urgent call from a poor sick neighbour.

Sheila [*hesitatingly*]. What is it? Could . . . could I do it for you?

Ayamonn [*decidedly*]. No, no, you couldn't. The woman knows my mother. It's only to see her safe and warm in bed for the night; Mother won't be long.

Mrs. Breydon. Good night, Miss Sheila; perhaps you'll be here when I come back.

Sheila. I don't think so. I must go almost at once.

Mrs. Breydon. Well, good night, then.

[*She goes out, and Ayamonn goes over to Sheila, kisses her, and helps her off with the mac.*

Sheila. You shouldn't let your mother go out on a night like this—she's no longer a young woman.

Ayamonn. I don't like to interfere with her need to give help to a neighbour. She likes it, and it does her good.

Sheila. But the rain's coming down in sheets, and she's got but a thin shawl round her shoulders.

Ayamonn [*impatiently*]. Oh, she hasn't very far to go. Let's think of greater things than the pouring rain and an old woman on her way to smooth pillows on a sick bed. Look!—[*he feels her skirt*]—the hem's wringing. Better dry it at the fire. Turn round and I'll unfasten it for you.

Sheila [*forcing his hand away*]. It's nothing—you are thinking now of your own pleasure. You weren't so eager to see me when I was knocking at the door a while ago.

Ayamonn. You! But it was Old Brennan o' the Moor that was there.

Sheila. Before him, I was there. He hammered at the door too.

Ayamonn [*angry with himself*]. And I thinking the rapping was that of a pestering neighbour! I might have guessed it wasn't, it was so gentle.

Sheila. After trying to slip in unnoticed, there I was left with the whole house knowing I was at the door, and when I ran down, I heard them yelling that the stylish-dressed pusher was trying to get into Breydon's again! A nice time I'll have with my people when they hear it.

Ayamonn. I was doing my Shakespeare part, and didn't want disturbance, so there I was, standing stiff and breathless like a heron in a pond, keeping my dear one away from me! [*Going over and taking her in his arms*] Well, it's all over now, and here you are in my arms, safe and sure and lovely.

Sheila [*struggling away from him*]. No, it's not all over; and don't press me so hard; don't ruffle me tonight, for I feel a little tired.

Ayamonn [*peevishly*]. Tired again? Well, so am I, more than a little tired; but never too tired to put a sparkle into a welcome for a loved one.

Sheila. Oh, Ayamonn, I do want you to be serious for one night.

Ayamonn. Very well, very well, Sheila. [*He moves away from her, and stands at the other side of the fire.*] Let us plan, then, of how we can spin joy into every moment of tomorrow's day.

Sheila. That's why I hurried here to see you—I can't be with you tomorrow. [*There is a long pause.*]

Ayamonn. Why can't you be with me tomorrow?

Sheila. The Daughters of St. Frigid begin a retreat tomorrow, to give the Saint a warm devotion, and Mother insists I go.

Ayamonn. And I insist that you go with me. Is the Saint Frigid more to you than the sinner Ayamonn? Would you rather go to the meeting than come to see me? [*A pause.*] Would you, would you, Sheila?

Sheila [*in a hesitant whisper*]. God forgive me, I'd rather come to see you.

Ayamonn. Come then; God will be sure to forgive you.

Sheila. I daren't. My mother would be at me for ever if I failed to go. I've told you how she hates me to be near you. She chatters red-lined warnings and black-bordered appeals into my ears night and day, and when they dwindle for lack of breath, my father shakes them out of their drowsiness and sends them dancing round more lively still, dressed richly up in deadly black and gleaming scarlet.

Ayamonn. Sheila, Sheila, on the one day of the month when I'm free, you must be with me. I wouldn't go to a workers' meeting so that I might be with you.

Sheila. There's another thing, Ayamonn—the threatened strike. Oh, why do you meddle with those sort of things!

Ayamonn. Oh, never mind that, now. Don't be like a timid little girl ensconced in a clear space in a thicket of thorns—safe from a scratch if she doesn't stir, but unable to get to the green grass or the open road unless she risks the tears the thorns can give.

Sheila. Oh, Ayamonn, for my sake, if you love me, do try to be serious.

Ayamonn [*a little wildly*]. Oh, Sheila, our time is not yet come to be serious in the way of our elders. Soon enough to browse with wisdom when Time's grey finger puts a warning speck on the crimson rose of youth. Let no damned frosty prayer chill the sunny sighs that dread the joy of love.

Sheila [*wildly*]. I won't listen, Ayamonn, I won't listen! We must look well ahead on the road to the future. You lead your life through too many paths instead of treading the one way of making it possible for us to live together.

Ayamonn. We live together now; live in the light of the burning bush. I tell you life is not one thing, but many things, a wide branching flame, grand and good to see and feel, dazzling to the eye of no-one loving it. I am not one to carry fear about with me as a priest carries the Host. Let the timid tiptoe through the way where the paler blossoms grow; my feet shall be where the redder roses grow, though they bear long thorns, sharp and piercing, thick among them!

Sheila [*rising from the chair—vehemently*]. I'll listen no more; I'll go. You want to make me a spark in a mere illusion. I'll go!

Ayamonn. Rather a spark from the althar of God, me girl; a spark that flames on a new path for a bubbling moment of life, or burns a song into the heart of a poet.

Sheila. I came here as a last chance to talk things quiet with you, but you won't let me; so I'll go. [*As he seizes her in his arms*] Let me go! [*Pleadingly*] Please, Ayamonn, let me go!

Ayamonn. I tell you it is a gay sight for God to see joy shine for a moment on the faces of His much-troubled children.

Sheila [*fearfully*]. Oh, don't bring God's name into this, for it will mean trouble to the pair of us. And your love for me lasts only while I'm here. When I'm gone, you think more of your poor painting, your poor oul' Ireland, your songs, and your workers' union than you think of Sheila.

Ayamonn. You're part of them all, in them all, and through them all; joyous, graceful, and a dearer vision; a bonnie rose, delectable and red. [*He draws her to him, presses her hard, lifts her on to his lap, and kisses her.*] Sheila, darling, you couldn't set aside the joy that makes the moon a golden berry in a hidden tree. You cannot close your ear to the sweet sound of the silver bell that strikes but once and never strikes again!

[*The door opens, and the head of Brennan o' the Moor looks into the room. It is a bald one, the dome highly polished; the face is wrinkled a lot, but the eyes are bright and peering. A long white beard gives him a far-away likeness to St. Jerome. He is dressed in a shabby-genteel way, and wears a long rain-soaked mackintosh. A faded bowler hat is on his head.*

Brennan. Oh, dear, dear, dear me!

[*He comes into the room showing that his back is well bent, though he still has a sturdy look about him. A strap around his body holds a melodeon on his back. Sheila and Ayamonn separate; he rises to meet the old man, while she stares, embarrassed, into the fire.*

Ayamonn. Now what th' hell do you want?

Brennan [*taking no notice of Ayamonn's remark—taking off his hat in a sweeping bow*]. Ah, me two sweet, snowy-breasted Dublin doves! Me woe it is to come ramblin' in through marjoram moments scentin' the serious hilarity of a genuine courtin' couple. I'm askin' now what's the dear one's name, if that isn't thresspassin' on others who are in a firmer condition of friendship? Though, be rights, it's a fair an' showy nose-gay I should be throwin' through a shyly opened window into the adorable lady's lap.

Sheila [*shyly*]. Me name is Sheila.

Brennan. Sheila is it? Ay, an' a Sheila are you. Ay, an' a suitable one too, for there's a gentle nature in the two soft sounds, an' a silver note in the echo, describin' grandly the pretty slendher lass me two ould eyes are now beholdin'.

Ayamonn [*going over and catching him by an arm to guide him out*]. I can't see you now, old friend, for the pair of us are heavily harnessed to a question that must be answered before either of us is a day older.

Brennan. Sure I know. An' isn't it only natural, too, that young people should have questions to ask and answers to give to the dewy problems that get in th' way of their dancin' feet?

Ayamonn [*impatiently*]. Come again, old friend, when time has halted us for an hour of rest.

Brennan. It isn't me, I'm sayin', that would be dense enough to circumvent your longin' to be deep down in the silent consequence of regardin' each other without let or hindrance. [*He goes toward Sheila, eagerly, pulling Ayamonn after him.*] It's easy seen, sweet lady, that you're well within the compass of your young man's knowledge, an' unaware of nothin', so I may speak as man to lady, so with cunnin' confidence, tell me what you think of the Bank of Ireland?

Ayamonn. Oh, for goodness' sake, old man. Sheila's no intherest in the Bank of Ireland. She cares nothing for money, or for anything money can buy.

Brennan [*staring at Ayamonn for a moment as if he had received a shock*]. Eh? Arra, don't be talkin' nonsense, man! Who is it daren't think of what money can buy? [*He crosses to the door in a trot on his toes, opens it, looks out, and closes it softly again. Then he tiptoes back to Sheila, bends down towards her, hands on knees, and whispers hoarsely*] I've just a little consideration of stocks and bonds nestin' in the Bank of Ireland, at four per cent—just enough to guard a poor man from ill, eh? Safe an' sound there, isn't it, eh? [*To Ayamonn*] Now, let the fair one speak out on her own. [*Twisting his head back to Sheila.*] Safe there as if St. Pether himself had the key of where the bonds are stationed, eh?

Sheila. I'm sure they must be, sir.

Brennan [*with chuckling emphasis*]. Yehess! Aren't you the sensible young lady; sure I knew you'd say that, without fear or favour. [*Turning towards Ayamonn.*] What do you say? You're a man, now, of tellin' judgement.

Ayamonn. Oh, the state would have to totther before you'd lose a coin.

Brennan [*gleefully*]. Go bang, absolutely bang! Eh?

Ayamonn. Go bang!

Brennan. Bang! [*To Sheila*] Hear that, now, from a man climbin' up to scholarship? Yehess! Stony walls, steely doors, locks an' keys, bolts an' bars, an' all th' bonds warm an' dhry, an' shinin' safe behind them.

Sheila. Safe behind them.

Brennan [*gleefully*]. Ay, so. An' none of it sthrollin' into Peter's Pence. [*Chuckling.*] Wouldn't the Pope be mad if he knew what he was missin'! Safe an' sound. [*To Ayamonn*] You think so, too, eh?

Ayamonn. Yes, yes.

Brennan [*soberly*]. Ay, of course you do. [*To Sheila—indicating Ayamonn*] A good breed, me sweet an' fair one, brought up proper to see things in their right light.

Ayamonn [*catching him impatiently by the arm*]. And now, old friend, we have to get you to go.

Brennan. Eh?

Ayamonn. To go; Sheila and I have things to talk about.

Brennan [*suddenly*]. An' what about the song, then?

Ayamonn. Song?

Brennan. Th' one for the Show. Isn't that what brought me up? At long last, afther hard sthrainin', me an' Sammy have got the tune down in tested clefs, crotchets, an' quavers, fair set down to be sung be anyone in thrue time. An' Sammy's below, in his gay suit for the Show, waitin' to be called up to let yous hear th' song sung as only Sammy can sing it.

Ayamonn. Bring him up, bring him up—why in hell didn't you tell me all this before?

Brennan [*stormily*]. Wasn't I thryin 'all the time an' you wouldn't let a man get a word in edgeways. [*Gesturing towards Sheila*] He'll jib at singin' in front of her. [*He whispers hoarsely towards Sheila.*] He's as shy as a kid in his first pair o' pants, dear lady.

Ayamonn [*impatiently pushing him out of the room*]. Oh, go on, go on, man, and bring him up.   [*Brennan goes out.*

Sheila [*earnestly*]. Wait till I'm gone, Ayamonn; I can't stop long, and I want to talk to you so much.

Ayamonn [*a little excited*]. Oh, you must hear the song, Sheila; they've been working to get the air down for a week, and it won't take a minute.

Sheila [*angrily*]. I've waited too long already! Aren't you more interested in what I want to say than to be listening to some vain fool singing a song?

Ayamonn [*a little taken aback*].   Oh, Sheila, what's wrong with you to-night? The young carpenter who'll sing it, so far from being vain, is as shy as a field-mouse, and you'll see, when he starts to sing, he'll edge his face away from us. You do want to hear it, Sheila, don't you?

Sheila [*appealingly*].   Let it wait over, Ayamonn; I can come to hear it some other time. I do want to say something, very serious, to you about our future meetings.

Ayamonn [*hastily*].   All right then; I'll hurry them off the minute the song's sung. Here they are, so sit down, do, just for one minute more.

[*But she goes towards the door, and reaches it just as Old Brennan returns shoving in before him a young man of twenty-three, shy, and loth to come in. He is tall, but his face is pale and mask-like in its expression of resignation to the world and all around him. Even when he shows he's shy, the mask-like features do not alter. He is dressed in a white cut-away coat, shaped like a tailed evening dress, black waistcoat over a rather soiled shirt-front, frilled, and green trousers. He carries a sheet of manuscript music in his hand. Brennan unslings his melodeon from his back, fusses the young Singer forward; bumping against Sheila, who has moved towards the door, he pushes her back with a shove of his backside; and puts Ayamonn to the other end of the room with a push on the shoulder.*]

Brennan [*as he pushes Sheila*].   Outa th' way, there! Stem your eagerness for a second, will yous? All in good time. Give the man a chance to get himself easy. [*As he pushes Ayamonn*] Farther back, there, farther back! Give the performer a chance to dispose himself. Isn't he a swell, wha'? The centre group's to be dhressed the same way, while th' corner men'll be in reverse colours—green coats, black trousers, an' white vest, see? Th' whole assembly'll look famous. Benjamin's lendin' all the set o' twelve suits for five bob, 'cause o' th' reason we're runnin' the Show for. [*To Sheila—in a hoarse whisper*] You stare at the fire as if he wasn't here. He's extravagant in shyness, an' sinks away into confusion at the stare of an eye—understand?

[*She slowly, and a little sullenly, sits down to stare into the fire. The door is opened, and in comes Roory O'Balacaun with a small roll of Irish magazines under an arm. He is a stout middle-aged man, dressed in rough homespun coat, cap, and knee-breeches, wearing over all a trench coat.*]

Roory.   Here y'are, Ayamonn, me son, avic's th' Irish magazines I got me friend to pinch for you. [*He looks at the Singer.*] Hello, what kind of a circus is it's goin' on here?

Ayamonn. Mr. Brennan Moore here's organising the singers for the Minsthrel Show to help get funds in case we have to go on sthrike, Roory.

Roory. I'm one o' th' men meself, but I don't stand for a foreign Minsthrel Show bein' held, an' the Sword of Light gettin' lifted up in th' land. We want no coon or Kaffir industry in our country.

Brennan [*indignantly*]. Doesn't matter what you stand for before you came here, you'll sit down now. Thry to regard yourself as a civilised member of the community, man, an' hold your peace for th' present. [*To the Singer*] Now, Sam, me son o' gold, excavate the shyness out of your system an' sing as if you were performin' before a Royal Command!

Roory [*with a growl*]. There's no royal commands wanted here.

Brennan [*with a gesture of disgusted annoyance*]. Will you for goodness' sake not be puttin' th' singer out? I used the term only as an allegory, man.

Roory. Allegory man, or allegory woman, there's goin' to be no royal inthrusions where the Sword o' Light is shinin'.

Ayamonn. Aw, for Christ's sake, Roory, let's hear the song!

Brennan [*to the Singer, who has been coughing shyly and turning sideways from his audience*]. Now, Sam, remember you're not in your working clothes, an' are a different man, entirely. Chin up and chest out. [*He gives a note or two on the melodeon*]. Now!

Singer [*singing*]:
>   A sober black shawl hides her body entirely,
>   Touch'd by th' sun and th' salt spray of the sea;
>   But down in th' darkness a slim hand, so lovely,
>   Carries a rich bunch of red roses for me.

>   [*He turns away a little more from his audience, and coughs shyly.*]

Brennan [*enthusiastically*]. Sam, you're excellin' yourself! On again, me oul' son!

Singer [*singing*]:
>   Her petticoat's simple, her feet are but bare,
>   An' all that she has is but neat an' scantie;
>   But stars in th' deeps of her eyes are exclaiming
>   I carry a rich bunch of red roses for thee!

Brennan [*after giving a few curling notes on the melodeon*]. A second Count McCormack in th' makin! An' whenever he sung *Mother Mo*

Chree, wasn't there a fewroory in Heaven with the rush that was made to lean over an hear him singin' it!

[*While Brennan has been speaking, the door has opened, and Mullcanny now stands there gaping into the room. He is young, lusty, and restless. He is wearing fine tweeds that don't fit too well; and his tweed cap is set rakishly on his head. He, too, wears a mackintosh.*

Mullcanny. Is this a home-sweet-away-from-home hippodhrome, or what?

Brennan [*clicking his tongue in annoyance*]. Dtchdtchdtch!

Mullcanny. An' did I hear someone pratin' about Heaven, an' I coming in? [*To Brennan—tapping him on the shoulder*] Haven't you heard, old man, that God is dead?

Brennan. Well, keep your grand discovery to yourself for a minute or two more, please. [*To the Singer*] Now, Sam, apologisin' for th' other's rudeness, the last verse, please.

Singer [*singing*]:
  No arrogant gem sits enthron'd on her forehead,
  Or swings from a white ear for all men to see;
  But jewel'd desire in a bosom, most pearly,
  Carries a rich bunch of red roses for me!

Brennan [*after another curl of notes on the melodeon*]. Well, fair damsel and gentlemen all, what do you think of the song and the singer?

Ayamonn. The song was good, and the singer was splendid.

Mullcanny. What I heard of it wasn't bad.

Singer [*shyly*]. I'm glad I pleased yous all.

Roory [*dubiously*]. D'ye not think th' song is a trifle indecent?

Mullcanny [*mockingly*]. Indecent! And what may your eminence's specification of indecency be? [*Angrily*] Are you catalogued, too, with the Catholic Young Men going about with noses long as a snipe's bill, sthripping the gayest rose of its petals in search of a beetle, and sniffing a taint in the freshest breeze blowing in from the sea?

Brennan [*warningly*]. Lady present, lady present, boys!

Roory. It ill becomes a thrue Gael to stand unruffled when either song or story thries to introduce colour to the sabler nature of yearnin's in untuthored minds.

Brennan [*more loudly*]. Lady present, boys!

Sheila [*rising out of the chair and going towards the door*]. The lady's going now, thank you all for the entertainment. [*To Ayamonn*] I won't stay any longer to disturb the important dispute of your friends.

Ayamonn [*going over to her*]. Don't be foolish, Sheila, dear; but if you must go, you must. We'll see each other again tomorrow evening.

Sheila [*firmly*]. No, not tomorrow, nor the next night either.

Ayamonn [*while Brennan plays softly on the melodeon to hide embarrassment*]. When then?

Sheila. I can't tell. I'll write. Never maybe. [*Bitterly*] I warned you this night might be the last chance of a talk for some time, and you didn't try to make use of it!

Ayamonn [*catching her arm*]. I made as much use of it as you'd let me. Tomorrow night, in the old place, near the bridge, the bridge of vision where we first saw Aengus and his coloured birds of passion passing.

Sheila [*wildly*]. I can't; I won't, so there—oh, let me go!

[*She breaks away from him, runs out, and a silence falls on the room for a few moments.*

Roory [*breaking the silence*]. Women is strange things! Elegant animals, not knowin' their own minds a minute.

Brennan [*consolingly*]. She'll come back, she'll come back.

Ayamonn [*trying to appear unconcerned*]. Aw, to hell with her!

Singer [*faintly*]. Can I go now?

Brennan. Wait, an' I'll be with you in a second.

Mullcanny [*to Ayamonn*]. I just dropped in to say, Ayamonn, that I'll be getting Haeckel's *Riddle of the Universe* tomorrow, afther long searching, and I'll let you have it the minute it comes into my hand.

[*The door is suddenly flung open, and Eeada, followed by Dympna and Finnoola, with others, mingled with men behind them, rushes into the room in a very excited state. She comes forward, with her two companions a little behind, while the rest group themselves by the door.*

Eeada [*distractedly*]. It's gone She is, an' left us lonesome; vanished She is like a fairy mist of an early summer mornin'; stolen She is be some pagan Protestan' hand, envious of the love we had for our sweet Lady of Eblana's poor!

Chorus. Our Lady of Eblana's gone!

Ayamonn. Nonsense; no Protestant hand touched Her. Where was She?

Dympna. Safe in Her niche in th' hall She was, afther Her washin', lookin' down on the comin's an' goin's of Her strugglin' children: an' then we missed Her, an' th' niche was empty!

Chorus. Our Lady of Eblana's gone!

Single Voice. An' dear knows what woe'll fall on our poor house now.

Brennan. An' a good job, too. [*Passionately*] Inflamin' yourselves with idols that have eyes an' see not; ears, an' hear not; an' have hands that handle not; like th' chosen people settin' moon-images an' sun-images, cuttin' away the thrue and homely connection between the Christian an' his God! Here, let me and me singer out of this unholy place!

> [*He pushes his way through the people, followed by the Singer, and goes out.*

Eeada [*nodding her head, to Ayamonn*]. All bark, but no bite! We know him of old: a decent oul' blatherer. Sure, doesn't he often buy violets and snowdhrops, even, for little Ursula, below, tellin' her she mustn't put them before a graven image, knowin' full well that that was th' first thing she'd hurry home to do. An' she's breakin' her young heart below, now, because her dear Lady has left her. [*Suspiciously*] If oul' Brennan had a hand in Her removal, woe betide him.

Mullcanny [*mocking.*] Couldn't you all do betther than wasting your time making gods afther your own ignorant images?

Ayamonn [*silencing him with a gesture*]. That's enough, Paudhrig. [*To Eeada*] Tell little Ursula not to worry. Her Lady'll come back. If your Lady of Eblana hasn't returned by tonight, I'll surrender my sleep afther my night's work to search for Her, and bring Her back safe to Her niche in the hall. No one in this house touched Her.

Eeada. An' you'll see She'll pay you back for your kindness, Ayamonn— [*looking at Mullcanny*]—though it's little surprised I'd be if, of her own accord, She came down indignant, an' slipped off from us, hearin' the horrid talk that's allowed to float around this house lately.

Mullcanny [*mocking*]. Afraid of me, She was. Well, Ayamonn, I've some lessons to get ready, so I'll be off. I'll bring you the book tomorrow. [*To the crowd—mocking*] I hope the poor Lady of Eblana's poor'll find Her way home again.   [*He goes out through a surly-faced crowd.*

Ayamonn [*to Eeada*]. Don't mind Mullcanny. Good night, now; and don't worry about your dear statue. If She doesn't come back, we'll find another as bright and good to take Her place.

Eeada [*growling*]. The fella that's gone'll have a rough end, jeerin' things sacred to our feelin'.

> [*They all go out, and Ayamonn is left alone with Roory. Ayamonn*

takes off his doublet, folds it up, and puts it back in the basket. He goes into the other room and comes back with oilskin coat and thigh-high leggings. He puts the leggings on over his trousers.

Ayamonn [*putting on the leggings*]. Th' shunting-yard'll be a nice place to be tonight. D'ye hear it?
> [*He listens to the falling rain, now heavier than ever.*

Roory. Fallin' fast. That Mullcanny'll get into throuble yet.

Ayamonn. Not he. He's really a good fellow. Gave up his job rather than his beliefs—more'n many would do.

Roory. An' how does he manage now?

Ayamonn. Hammering knowledge into deluded minds wishing to be civil servants, bank clerks, an' constables who hope to take the last sacraments as sergeants in the Royal Irish Constabulary or the Metropolitan Police.

Roory. By God, he's his work cut out for him with the last lot!
> [*The door is again opened and Eeada sticks her head into the room.*

Eeada. Your mother's just sent word that the woman she's mindin's bad, an' she'll have to stay th' night. I'm just runnin 'round meself to make your mother a cup o' tea.

Ayamonn [*irritably*]. Dtch dtch—she'll knock herself up before she's done! When I lock up, I'll leave the key with you for her, Eeada.
> [*He lights a shunter's lantern and puts out the lamp.*

Eeada. Right y'are.   [*She goes.*

Roory. What kid was it sketched th' angel on th' wall?

Ayamonn. Oh, I did that. I'd give anything to be a painter.

Roory. What, like Oul' Brennan o' th' Moor?

Ayamonn. No, no; like Angelico or Constable.

Roory [*indifferently*]. Never heard of them.

Ayamonn [*musingly*]. To throw a whole world in colour on a canvas though it be but a man's fine face, a woman's shape asthride of a cushioned couch, or a three-bordered house on a hill, done with a glory; even delaying God, busy forgin' a new world, to stay awhile an' look upon their loveliness.

Roory. Aw, Ayamonn, Ayamonn, man, put out your hand an' see if you're awake! [*He fiddles with the books on the table.*] What oul' book are you readin' now?

Ayamonn [*dressed now in oilskin leggings and coat, with an oilskin sou'-wester on his head, comes over to look at the book in Roory's hand, and shines the lantern on it*]. Oh, that's Ruskin's *Crown of Wild Olive*—a grand book—I'll lend it to you.

Roory. What for? What would I be doin' with it? I've no time to waste on books. Ruskin. Curious name; not Irish, is it?

Ayamonn. No, a Scotsman who wrote splendidly about a lot of things. Listen to this, spoken before a gathering of business men about to build an Exchange in their town.

Roory. Aw, Ayamonn—an Exchange! What have we got to do with an Exchange?

Ayamonn [*impatiently*]. Listen a second, man! Ruskin, speakin' to the business men, says: "Your ideal of life is a pleasant and undulating world, with iron and coal everywhere beneath it. On each pleasant bank of this world is to be a beautiful mansion; stables, and coach-houses; a park and hot-houses; carriage-drives and shrubberies; and here are to live the votaries of the Goddess of Getting-on—the English gentleman——"

Roory [*interrupting*]. There you are, you see, Ayamonn—th' English gentleman!

Ayamonn. Wait a second—Irish or English—a gentleman's th' same.

Roory. 'Tisn't. I'm tellin' you it's different. What's in this Ruskin of yours but another oul' cod with a gift of the gab? Right enough for th' English, pinin' afther little things, ever rakin' cindhers for th' glint of gold. We're different—we have th' light.

Ayamonn. You mean th' Catholic Faith?

Roory [*impatiently*]. No, no; that's there, too; I mean th' light of freedom; th' tall white candle tipped with its golden spear of flame. The light we thought we'd lost; but it burns again, sthrengthenin' into a sword of light. Like in th' song we sung together th' other night. [*He sings softly*]:

Our courage so many have thought to be agein',
Now flames like a brilliant new star in th' sky;
And Danger is proud to be call'd a good brother,
For Freedom has buckled her sword on her thigh.

Ayamonn [*joining in*]:
Then out to th' place where th' battle is bravest,
Where th' noblest an 'meanest fight fierce in th' fray,
Republican banners shall mock at th' foemen,
An' Fenians shall turn a dark night into day!

[*A pause as the two of them stand silent, each clasping the other's hand. Ayamonn opens the door to pass out.*

Roory [*in a tense whisper*]. Th' Fenians are in force again, Ayamonn; th' Sword o' Light is shinin'!
[*They go out, and Ayamonn closes the door as the Curtain falls.*

CURTAIN

ACT II

The same as in Act I.

It is about ten o'clock at night. The rain has stopped, and there is a fine moon sailing through the sky. Some of its rays come in through the window at the side.

Ayamonn, in his shirt-sleeves, is sitting at the table. He has an ordinary tin money-box in his hand, and a small pile of coppers, mixed with a few sixpences, are on the table beside him. He is just taking the last coin from the slit in the box with the aid of a knife-blade. His mother is by the dresser piling up the few pieces of crockery used for a recent meal. The old one-wick lamp is alight, and stands on the table near to Ayamonn. Several books lie open there, too.

Ayamonn. There's th' last one out, now. It's quite a job getting them out with a knife.

Mrs. Breydon. Why don't you put them in a box with a simple lid on?

Ayamonn. The harder it is to get at, the less chance of me spending it on something more necessary than what I seek. [*He counts the money on the table.*] One bob—two—three—an' sixpence—an' nine—three an' ninepence; one an' threepence to get yet—a long way to go.

Mrs. Breydon. Maybe, now, th' bookseller would give you it for what you have till you can give him th' rest.

Ayamonn [*in agony*]. Aw, woman, if you can't say sense, say nothing!

Constable's reproductions are five shillings second-hand, an' he that's sell-ing is the bastard that nearly got me jailed for running off with his Shakespeare. It's touch an' go if he'll let me have it for the five bob.

Mrs. Breydon [*philosophically*]. Well, seein' you done without it so long, you can go without it longer.

Ayamonn [*with firm conviction*]. I'll have it the first week we get the extra shilling the men are demandin'.

Mrs. Breydon. I shouldn't count your chickens before they're hatched.

Ayamonn [*joking a little bitterly*]. Perhaps our blessed Lady of Eblana's poor will work a miracle for me.

Mrs. Breydon [*a little anxiously*]. Hush, don't say that! Jokin' or seri-ous, Ayamonn, I wouldn't say that. We don't believe in any of their Blessed Ladies, but as it's somethin' sacred, it's best not mentioned. [*She shuffles into her shawl.*] Though it's a queer thing, Her goin' off out of Her niche without a one in th' house knowin' why. They're all out huntin' for Her still.

[*The door opens, and Brennan comes in slowly, with a cute grin on his face. He has a large package, covered with paper, under his arm.*

Brennan. Out huntin' still for Her they are, are they? Well, let them hunt; She's here! A prisoner under me arm!

Mrs. Breydon [*indignantly*]. Well, Mr. Brennan Moore, it's ashamed of yourself you should be yokin' th' poor people to throubled anxiety over their treasure; and little Ursula breakin' her heart into th' bargain.

Ayamonn. It's god-damned mean of you, Brennan! What good d'ye think you'll do by this rowdy love of your own opinions—forcing tumult into the minds of ignorant, anxious people?

Brennan [*calmly*]. Wait till yous see, wait till yous see, before yous are sorry for sayin' more. [*He removes the paper and shows the lost image transfigured into a figure looking as if it had come straight from the shop: the white dress is spotless, the blue robe radiant, and the gold along its border and on the crown is gleaming. He holds it up for admiration. Triumphantly*] There, what d'ye think of Her now? Fair as th' first grand tinge of th' dawn, She is, an' bright as th' star of the evenin'.

Mrs. Breydon. Glory be to God, isn't She lovely! But hurry Her off, Brennan, for She's not a thing for Protestant eyes to favour.

Ayamonn [*a little testily*]. Put it back, Brennan, put it back, and don't touch it again.

Brennan. Isn't that what I'm going to do? Oh, boy alive, won't they get th' shock o' their lives when they see Her shinin' in th' oul' spot. [*He becomes serious.*] Though, mind you, me thrue mind misgives me for decoratin' what's a charm to the people of Judah in th' worship of idols; but th' two of you is witness I did it for the sake of the little one, and not in any tilt towards honour to a graven image.

Mrs. Breydon [*resignedly*]. It's done now, God forgive us both, an' me for sayin' She's lovely. Touchin' a thing forbidden with a startled stir of praise!

Ayamonn. Put it back, put it back, man, and leave it quiet where you got it first.

[*Brennan goes out, looking intently out, and listening, before he does so.*

Mrs. Breydon. He meant well, poor man, but he's done a dangerous thing. I'll be back before you start for work. [*With a heavy sigh.*] It won't take us long to tend her for the last time. The white sheets have come, th' tall candles wait to be lit, an' th' coffin's ordhered, an' th' room'll look sacred with the bunch of violets near her head. [*She goes out slowly—as she goes*] Dear knows what'll happen to th' three children.

[*Ayamonn sits silent for a few moments, reading a book, his elbows resting on the table.*

Ayamonn [*with a deep sigh—murmuringly*]. Sheila, Sheila, my heart cries out for you! [*After a moment's pause, he reads:*]
But I am pigeon-livered, an' lack gall
To make oppression bitther; or, ere this,
I should have fatted all th' region kites
With this slave's offal: Bloody, bawdy villain!
Oh, Will, you were a boyo; a brave boyo, though, and a beautiful one!

[*The door opens and Old Brennan comes in, showing by his half-suppressed chuckles that he is enjoying himself. He wanders over the room to stand by the fire.*

Brennan [*chuckling*]. In Her old place She is, now, in Her new coronation robe; and funny it is to think it's the last place they'll look for Her.

Ayamonn. I'm busy, now.

Brennan [*sitting down by the fire*]. Ay, so you are; so I see; busy readin'. Read away, for I won't disturb you; only have a few quiet puffs at th' oul' pipe. [*A pause.*] Ah, then, don't I wish I was young enough to bury meself in th' joy of readin' all th' great books of th' world. Ah! but when I was young, I had to work hard.

Ayamonn. I work hard, too.

Brennan. 'Course you do! Isn't that what I'm sayin'? An' all th' more credit, too, though it must be thryin' to have thoughtless people comin' in an' intherferin' with the golden movements of your thoughts.

Ayamonn. It's often a damned nuisance!

Brennan. 'Course it is. Isn't that what I'm sayin'? [*As the door opens*] An' here's another o' th' boobies entherin' now. [*Roory comes in, and shuts the door rather noisily.*] Eh, go easy, there—can't you see Ayamonn's busy studyin'?

Roory [*coming and bending over Ayamonn*]. Are you still lettin' oul' Ruskin tease you?

Ayamonn [*angrily*]. No, no; Shakespeare, Shakespeare, this time! [*Springing from his chair*] Damn it, can't you let a man alone a minute? What th' hell d'ye want now?

Brennan [*warningly*]. I told you he was busy.

Roory [*apologetically*]. Aw, I only came with the tickets you asked me to bring you for the comin' National Anniversary of Terence Bellew MacManus.

Ayamonn. All right, all right; let's have them.

Roory. How many d'ye want? How many can you sell?

Ayamonn. Give me twelve sixpennies; if the sthrike doesn't come off I'll easily sell that number.

Roory [*counting out the tickets which Ayamonn gathers up and puts into his pocket*]. I met that Mullcanny on the way with a book for you; but he stopped to tell a couple of railwaymen that the Story of Adam an' Eve was all a cod.

Brennan [*indignantly*]. He has a lot o' the people here in a state o' steamin' anger, goin' about with his bitther belief that the patthern of a man's hand is nearly at one with a monkey's paw, a horse's foot, th' flipper of a seal, or th 'wing of a bat!

Ayamonn. Well, each of them is as wonderful as the hand of a man.

Roory. No, Ayamonn, not from the Christian point of view. D'ye know what they're callin 'him round here? Th' New Broom, because he's always sayin' he'll sweep th' idea of God clean outa th' mind o' man.

Brennan [*excited*]. There'll be dire damage done to him yet! He was goin' to be flattened out be a docker th' other day for tellin' him that a man first formin' showed an undoubted sign of a tail.

Ayamonn. Ay, and when he's fully formed, if he doesn't show the tail, he shows most signs of all that goes along with it.

Roory. But isn't that a nice dignity to put on th' sacredness of a man's conception!

Brennan [*whisperingly*]. An' a lot o' them are sayin', Ayamonn, that your encouragement of him should come to an end.

Ayamonn. Indeed? Well, let them. I'll stand by any honest man seekin' th' truth, though his way isn't my way. [*To Brennan*] You, yourself, go about deriding many things beloved by your Catholic neighbours.

Brennan. I contest only dangerous deceits specified be the Council o' Thrent, that are nowhere scheduled in th' pages of the Holy Scriptures.

Roory. Yes, Ayamonn, it's altogether different; he just goes about blatherin' in his ignorant Protestant way.

Brennan [*highly indignant*]. Ignorant, am I? An' where would a body find an ignorance lustier than your own, eh? If your Council o' Thrent's ordher for prayers for the dead who are past help, your dismal veneration of Saints an' Angels, your images of wood an' stone, carved an' coloured, have given you the image an' superscription of a tail, th' pure milk of the gospel has made a man of me, God-fearin', but stately, with a mind garlanded to th' steady an' eternal thruth!

> [*While they have been arguing, Mullcanny has peeped round the door, and now comes into the room, eyeing the two disputants with a lot of amusement and a little scorn. They take no notice of him.*

Roory. Sure, man, you have the neighbourhood hectored with your animosity against Catholic custom an' Catholic thought, never hesitatin' to give th' Pope even a deleterious name.

Brennan [*lapsing, in his excitement, into a semi-Ulster dialect*]. We dud ut tae yeh in Durry, on' sent your bravest floatin' down dud in th' wathers of th' Boyne, like th' hosts of Pharaoh tumblin' in the rush of th' Rud Sea! Thut was a slup in th' puss tae your Pope!

Mullcanny. You pair of damned fools, don't you know that the Pope wanted King Billy to win, and that the Vatican was ablaze with lights of joy afther King James's defeat over the wathers of the Boyne?

Roory. You're a liar, he didn't!

Brennan. You're a liar, it wasn't!

> [*They turn from Mullcanny to continue the row with themselves.*

Brennan. Looksee, if I believed in the ministhration of Saints on' Angels, I'd say thut th' good Protestant St. Puthrick was at the hud of what fell out at Durry, Aughrim, on' th' Boyne.

Roory [stunned with the thought of St. Patrick as a Protestant]. Protestant St. Pathrick? Is me hearin' sound, or what? What name did you mention?

Brennan. I said St. Puthrick—th' evangelical founder of our thrue Church.

Roory. Is it dhreamin' I am? Is somethin' happenin' to me, or is it happenin' to you? Oh, man, it's mixin' mirth with madness you are at thinkin' St. Patrick ever looped his neck in an orange sash, or tapped out a tune on a Protestant dhrum!

Brennan [contemptuously]. I refuse to argue with a one who's no' a broad-minded mon. Abuse is no equivalent for lugic—so I say God save th' King, an' tae hull with th' Pope!

Roory [indignantly]. You damned bigot—to hell with th' King, an' God save th' Pope!

Mullcanny [to Ayamonn]. You see how they live in bittherness, the one with the other. Envy, strife, and malice crawl from the coloured slime of the fairy-tales that go to make what is called religion. [*Taking a book from his pocket*] Here's something can bear a thousand tests, showing neatly how the world and all it bears upon it came into slow existence over millions of years, doing away for ever with the funny wonders of the seven days' creation set out in the fairy book of the Bible.

Ayamonn [taking the book from Mullcanny]. Thanks, Pether, oul' son; I'm bound to have a good time reading it.

Mullcanny. It'll give you the true and scientific history of man as he was before Adam.

Brennan [in a woeful voice]. It's a darkened mind that thries tae lower us to what we were before th' great an' good God fashioned us. What does ony sensible person want to know what we were like before the creation of th' first man?

Ayamonn [murmuringly]. To know the truth, to seek the truth, is good, though it lead to th 'danger of eternal death.

Roory [horror-stricken—crossing himself]. Th' Lord between us an' all harm!

Brennan [whispering prayerfully]. Lord, I believe, help Thou mine unbelief.

Mullcanny [*pointing out a picture in the book*].   See? The human form unborn. The tail—look; the os coccyx sticking a mile out; there's no getting away from it!

Brennan [*shaking his head woefully*].   An' this is holy Ireland!

Roory [*lifting his eyes to the ceiling—woefully*].   Poor St. Pathrick!

Mullcanny [*mockingly*].   He's going to be a lonely man soon, eh? [*To Ayamonn*] Keep it safe for me, Ayamonn. When you've read it, you'll be a different man. [*He goes to the door*] Well, health with the whole o' you, and goodbye for the present.   [*He goes out.*]

Roory.   Have nothin' to do with that book, Ayamonn, for that fellow gone out would rip up the floor of Heaven to see what was beneath it. It's clapped in jail he ought to be!

Brennan.   An' th' book banned!

Ayamonn.   Roory, Roory, is that th' sort o' freedom you'd bring to Ireland with a crowd of green branches an' th' joy of shouting? If we give no room to men of our time to question many things, all things, ay, life itself, then freedom's but a paper flower, a star of tinsel, a dead lass with gay ribbons at her breast an' a gold comb in her hair. Let us bring freedom here, not with sounding brass an' tinkling cymbal, but with silver trumpets blowing, with a song all men can sing, with a palm branch in our hand, rather than with a whip at our belt, and a headsman's axe on our shoulders.

> [*There is a gentle knock at the door, and the voice of Sheila is heard speaking.*

Sheila [*outside*].   Ayamonn, are you there? Are you in?

Brennan [*whispering*].   The little lass; I knew she'd come back.

Ayamonn.   I don't want her to see you here. Go into the other room— quick. [*He pushes them towards it.*] An' keep still.

Roory [*to Brennan*].   An' don't you go mockin' our Pope, see?

Brennan [*to Roory*].   Nor you go singlin' out King Billy for a jeer.

Ayamonn.   In with yous, quick!

Brennan.   I prophesied she'd come back, didn't I, Ayamonn? that she'd come back, didn't I?

Ayamonn.   Yes, yes; in you go.

> [*He puts them in the other room and shuts the door. Then he crosses the room and opens the door to admit Sheila. She comes in, and he and Sheila stand silently for some moments, she trying to look at him, and finding it hard.*

Sheila [*at last*].   Well, haven't you anything to say to me?

Ayamonn [*slowly and coldly*].   I waited for you at the bridge today; but you didn't come.

Sheila.   I couldn't come; I told you why.

Ayamonn.   I was very lonely.

Sheila [*softly*].   So was I, Ayamonn, lonely even in front of God's holy face.

Ayamonn.   Sheila, we've gone a long way in a gold canoe over many waters, bright and surly, sometimes sending bitter spray asplash on our faces. But you were ever listening for the beat from the wings of the angel of fear. So you got out to walk safe on a crowded road.

Sheila.   This is a cold and cheerless welcome, Ayamonn.

Ayamonn.   Change, if you want to, the burning kiss falling on the up-turned, begging mouth for the chill caress of a bony, bearded Saint. [*Loudly*] Go with th' yelling crowd, and keep them brave, and yell along with them!

Sheila.   Won't you listen, then, to the few words I have to say?

Ayamonn [*sitting down near the fire, and looking into it, though he leaves her standing*].   Go ahead; I won't fail to hear you.

Sheila.   God knows I don't mean to hurt you, but you must know that we couldn't begin to live on what you're earning now—could we? [*He keeps silent.*] Oh, Ayamonn, why do you waste your time on doing foolish things?

Ayamonn.   What foolish things?

> [*A hubbub is heard in the street outside; voices saying loudly "Give him one in the bake" or "Down him with a one in th' belly"; then the sound of running footsteps, and silence.*

Sheila [*when she hears the voices—nervously*].   What's that?

Ayamonn [*without taking his gaze from the fire*].   Some drunken row or other.   [*They listen silently for a few moments.*

Ayamonn.   Well, what foolish things?

Sheila [*timid and hesitating*].   You know yourself, Ayamonn: trying to paint, going mad about Shakespeare, and consorting with a kind of people that can only do you harm.

Ayamonn [*mockingly prayerful—raising his eyes to the ceiling*].   O Lord, let me forsake the foolish, and live; and go in the way of Sheila's understanding!

Sheila [*going over nearer to him*].   Listen, Ayamonn, my love; you know what I say is only for our own good, that we may come together all the sooner. [*Trying to speak jokingly*] Now, really, isn't it comical I'd look if I were to go about in a scanty petticoat, covered in a sober black shawl, and my poor feet bare! [*Mocking*] Wouldn't I look well that way!

Ayamonn [*quietly*].   With red roses in your hand, you'd look beautiful.

Sheila [*desperately*].   Oh, for goodness' sake, Ayamonn, be sensible! I'm getting a little tired of all this. I can't bear the strain the way we're going on much longer. [*A short pause.*] You will either have to make good, or——   [*She pauses.*

Ayamonn [*quietly*].   Or what?

Sheila [*with a little catch in her voice*].   Or lose me; and you wouldn't like that to happen.

Ayamonn.   I shouldn't like that to happen; but I could bear the sthrain.

Sheila.   I risked a big row tonight to come to tell you good news: I've been told that the strike is bound to take place; there is bound to be trouble; and, if you divide yourself from the foolish men, and stick to your job, you'll soon be a foreman of some kind or other.

Ayamonn [*rising from his seat and facing her for the first time*].   Who told you all this? The Inspector?

Sheila.   Never mind who; if he did, wasn't it decent of him?

Ayamonn.   D'ye know what you're asking me to do, woman? To be a blackleg; to blast with th' black frost of desertion the gay hopes of my comrades. Whatever you may think them to be, they are my comrades. Whatever they may say or do, they remain my brothers and sisters. Go to hell, girl, I have a soul to save as well as you. [*With a catch in his voice*] Oh, Sheila, you shouldn't have asked me to do this thing!

Sheila [*trying to come close, but he pushes her back*].   Oh, Ayamonn, it is a chance; take it, do, for my sake!

[*Rapid footsteps are heard outside. The door flies open and Mullcanny comes in, pale, frightened, his clothes dishevelled, and a slight smear of blood on his forehead. His bowler hat is crushed down on his head, his coat is torn, and his waistcoat unbuttoned, showing his tie pulled out of its place. He sinks into a chair.*

Ayamonn.   What's happened? Who did that to you?

Mullcanny.   Give's a drink, someone, will you?

[*Ayamonn gets him a drink from a jug on the dresser.*

Mullcanny.   A gang of bowseys made for me, and I talking to a man.

Barely escaped with my life. Only for some brave oul' one, they'd have laid me out completely. She saved me from worse.

Ayamonn. How th' hell did you bring all that on you?

Mullcanny [*plaintively*]. Just trying to show a fellow the foolishness of faith in a hereafter, when something struck me on the head, and I was surrounded by feet making kicks at me!

[*A crash of breaking glass is heard from the other room, and Brennan and Roory come running out of it.*

Roory. A stone has done for th' window! [*He sees Mullcanny.*] Oh, that's how th' land lies, is it? Haven't I often said that if you go round leerin' at God an' His holy assistants, one day He's bound to have a rap at you!

Brennan. Keep away from that window, there, in case another one comes sailin' in.

[*Immediately he has spoken, a stone smashes in through the window. Brennan lies down flat on the floor; Mullcanny slides from the chair and crouches on the ground; Roory gets down on his hands and knees, keeping his head as low as possible, so that he resembles a Mohammedan at his devotions; Sheila stands stiff in a corner, near the door; and Ayamonn, seizing up a hurley lying against the dresser, makes for the door to go out.*

Brennan. I guessed this was comin'.

Ayamonn [*angrily*]. I'll show them!

Sheila [*to Ayamonn*]. Stop where you are, you fool!

[*But Ayamonn pays no attention to the advice and hurries out of the door.*

Roory [*plaintively and with dignity—to Mullcanny*]. This is what you bring down on innocent people with your obstinate association of man with th' lower animals.

Mullcanny [*truculently*]. Only created impudence it is that strives to set yourselves above the ape's formation, genetically present in every person's body.

Brennan [*indignantly*]. String out life to where it started, an' you'll find no sign, let alone a proof, of the dignity, wisdom, an' civility of man ever having been associated with th' manners of a monkey.

Mullcanny. And why do children like to climb trees, eh? Answer me that?

Roory [*fiercely*]. They love it more where you come from than they do here.

Sheila [*from her corner*].   It's surely to be pitied you are, young man, lettin' yourself be bullied by ignorant books into believing that things are naught but what poor men are inclined to call them, blind to the glorious and eternal facts that shine behind them.

Mullcanny [*pityingly*].   Bullied be books—eternal facts—aw! Yous are all scared stiff at the manifestation of a truth or two. D'ye know that the contraction of catharrh, apoplexy, consumption, and cataract of the eye is common to the monkeys? Knowledge you have now that you hadn't before; and a lot of them even like beer.

Roory.   Well, that's something sensible, at last.

Brennan [*fiercely*].   Did they get their likin' for beer from us, or did we get our likin' of beer from them? Answer me that, you, now; answer me that!

Roory.   Answer him that. We're not Terra Del Fooaygeeans, but sensible, sane, an' civilised souls.

Mullcanny [*gleefully*].   Time's promoted reptiles—that's all; yous can't do away with the os coccyges!

Brennan.   Ladies present, ladies present.

Roory [*creeping over rapidly till his face is close to that of Mullcanny's—fiercely*].   We stand on the earth, firm, upright, heads cocked, lookin' all men in th' face, afraid o' nothin'; men o' goodwill we are, abloom with th' blessin' o' charity, showin' in th' dust we're made of, th' diamond-core of an everlasting divinity!

Sheila [*excitedly*].   Hung as high as Gilderoy he ought to be, an' he deep in the evil of his rich illusions, spouting insults at war with th' mysteries an' facts of our holy faith!

Brennan [*to Sheila*].   Hush, pretty lady, hush. [*To the others*] Boys, boys, take example from a poor oul' Protestant here, never lettin' himself be offended be a quiver of anger in any peaceable or terrified discussion. Now, let that last word finish it; finis—the end, see?

Roory [*angrily—to Brennan*].   Finis youssell, you blurry-eyed, wither-skinned oul' greybeard, singin' songs in th' public streets for odd coppers, with all th' boys in th' Bank of Ireland workin' overtime countin' all you've got in their front room! Finis you!

Brennan [*indignantly*].   An office-boy, in a hurry, wouldn't stop to pick up from th' path before him the few coins I have. An' as for being withered, soople as you I am, hands that can tinkle a thremblin' tune out of an oul' melodeon, legs that can carry me ten miles an' more, an' eyes that can still see without hardship a red berry shinin' from a distant bush!

[*The door opens and Ayamonn and his mother come in. She runs over to the blossoms at the window, tenderly examining the plants growing there—the musk, the geranium, and the fuchsia.*

Mrs. Breydon [*joyfully*].   Unharmed, th' whole of them. Th' stone passed them by, touchin' none o' them—thank God for that mercy!

Ayamonn.   What th' hell are you doin' on your knees? Get up, get up. [*They rise from the floor shamefacedly.*] Th' rioters all dispersed. [*To Mullcanny*] Mother was th' oul' one who saved you from a sudden an' unprovided death. An' th' Blessed Image has come back again, all aglow in garments new. Listen!

[*A murmur of song has been heard while Ayamonn was speaking, and now Eeada, Dympna, Finnoola, and the Men appear at the door —now wide open—half backing into the room singing part of a hymn softly, their pale faces still wearing the frozen look of resignation; staring at the Image shining bright and gorgeous as Brennan has made it for them, standing in a niche in the wall, directly opposite the door. Eeada, Dympna, Finnoola, and the Men singing softly—*
Oh! Queen of Eblana's poor children,
Bear swiftly our woe away;
An' give us a chance to live lightly
An hour of our life's dark day!
Lift up th' poor heads ever bending,
An' light a lone star in th' sky,
To show thro' th' darkness, descending,
A cheerier way to die.

Eeada [*coming forward a little*].   She came back to Her poor again, in raiment rich. She came back; of Her own accord. She came to abide with Her people.

Dympna.   From her window, little Ursula looked, and saw Her come in; in th' moonlight, along the street She came, stately. Blinded be the coloured light that shone around about her, the child fell back, in a swoon she fell full on the floor beneath her.

1st Man.   My eyes caught a glimpse of Her too, glidin' back to where She came from. Regal an' proud She was, an' wondrous, so that me eyes failed; me knees thrembled an' bent low, an' me heart whispered a silent prayer to itself as th' vision passed me by, an' I fancied I saw a smile on Her holy face.

Eeada.   Many have lived to see a strange thing this favoured night, an' blessin' will flow from it to all tempered into a lively belief; and maybe, too, to some who happen to be out of step with the many marchin' in th' mode o' thruth. [*She comes a little closer to Mrs. Breydon. The others, backs turned towards the room, stand, most of them outside the door, a few just across the threshold, in a semicircle, heads bent as if praying, facing towards the Image.*] Th' hand of a black stranger it was who sent the stones flyin' through your windows; but ere tomorrow's sun is seen, they will be back again as shelther from th' elements. A blessin' generous on yous all—[*pause*]—except th' evil thing that stands, all stiff-necked, underneath th' roof!

Mullcanny [*mockingly*].   Me!

Sheila [*fiercely*].   Ay, you, that shouldn't find a smile or an unclenched hand in a decent man's house!

Mullcanny.   I'll go; there's too many here to deal with—I'll leave you with your miracle.

Ayamonn.   You can stay if you wish, for whatever surety of shelther's here, it's open to th' spirit seeking to add another colour to whatever thruth we know already. Thought that has run from a blow will find a roof under its courage here, an' a fire to sit by, as long as I live an' th' oul' rooms last!

Sheila [*with quiet bitterness*].   Well, shelter him, then, that by right should be lost in the night, a black night, an' bitterly lonely, without a dim ray from a half-hidden star to give him a far-away companionship; ay, an' a desolate rest under a thorny and dripping thicket of lean and twisted whins, too tired to thry to live longer against th' hate of the black wind and th' grey rain. Let him lie there, let him live there, forsaken, forgotten by all who live under a kindly roof and close to a cosy fire!

Mullcanny [*with pretended alarm*].   Good God, I'm done, now! I'm off before worse befall me. Good night, Ayamonn.

Ayamonn.   Good night, my friend.   [*Mullcanny goes out.*

Brennan.   We're keepin' decent people out of their beds—so long, all.

Roory.   I'll be with you some o' th' way, an' we can finish that argument we had. Good night all.

[*He and Brennan go out together, closing the door after them. Sheila stands where she was, sullen and silent.*

Mrs. Breydon.   Shame on you, Sheila, for such a smoky flame to come from such a golden lamp! [*Sheila stays silent.*] Tired out I am, an' frightened be th' scene o' death I saw today. Dodge about how we may, we come to th' same end.

Ayamonn [*gently leading her towards the other room*].   Go an' lie down, lady; you're worn out. Time's a perjured jade, an' ever he moans a man must die. Who through every inch of life weaves a patthern of vigour an' elation can never taste death, but goes to sleep among th' stars, his withered arms outstretched to greet th' echo of his own shout. It will be for them left behind to sigh for an hour, an' then to sing their own odd songs, an' do their own odd dances, to give a lonely God a little company, till they, too, pass by on their bare way out. When a true man dies, he is buried in th' birth of a thousand worlds.

[*Mrs. Breydon goes into the other room, and Ayamonn closes the door softly behind her. He comes back and stands pensive near the fire.*

Ayamonn [*after a pause*].   Don't you think you should go too?

Sheila [*a little brokenly*].   Let me have a few more words with you, Ayamonn, before we hurry to our separation.

Ayamonn [*quietly*].   There is nothing more to be said.

Sheila.   There's a lot to be said, but hasty time won't stretch an hour a little out to let the words be spoken. Goodbye.

Ayamonn [*without turning his head*].   Goodbye.

[*Sheila is going slowly to the door when it partly opens, and half the head of Eeada peeps around it, amid an indistinct murmur as of praying outside.*

Eeada [*in half a whisper*].   Th' Protestan' Rector to see Mr. Breydon. [*The half of her head disappears, but her voice is heard saying a little more loudly*] This way, sir; shure you know th' way well, anyhow.

[*The door opening a little more, the Rector comes in. He is a handsome man of forty. His rather pale face wears a grave scholarly look, but there is kindness in his grey eyes, and humorous lines round his mouth, though these are almost hidden by a short, brown, pointed beard, here and there about to turn grey. His black clothes are covered by a warm black topcoat, the blackness brightened a little by a vivid green scarf he is wearing round his neck, the fringed ends falling over his shoulders. He carries a black, broad-brimmed, soft clerical hat and a walking-stick in his left hand. He hastens towards Ayamonn, smiling genially, hand outstretched in greeting.*

Rector.   My dear Ayamonn.   [*They shake hands.*

Ayamonn [*indicating Sheila*].   A friend of mine, sir—Sheila Moorneen. [*Moving a chair.*] Sit down, sir.

[*The Rector bows to Sheila; she returns it quietly, and the Rector sits down.*

Rector. I've hurried from home in a cab, Ayamonn, to see you before the night was spent. [*His face forming grave lines*] I've a message for you—and a warning.

> [*The door again is partly opened, and again the half head of Eeada appears, mid the murmurs outside, unheard the moment the door closes.*

Eeada. Two railwaymen to see you, Ayamonn; full house tonight you're havin', eh?

> [*The half head goes, the door opens wider, and the two railwaymen come into the room. They are dressed drably as the other men are, but their peaked railway uniform caps (which they keep on their heads) have vivid scarlet bands around them. Their faces, too, are like the others, and stonily stare in front of them. They stand stock still when they see the Rector.*

1st Railwayman [*after a pause*]. 'Scuse us. Didn' know th' Protestan' Minister was here. We'll wait outside till he goes, Ayamonn.

Ayamonn. Th' Rector's a dear friend of mine, Bill; say what you want, without fear—he's a friend.

1st Railwayman [*a little dubiously*]. Glad to hear it. You know th' sthrike starts tomorrow?

Ayamonn. I know it now.

2nd Railwayman. Wouldn' give's th' extra shillin'. Offered us thruppence instead—th' lowsers! [*Hastily—to Rector*] 'Scuse me, sir.

1st Railwayman [*taking a document from his breast pocket*]. An' th' meetin's proclaimed.

Rector [*to Ayamonn*]. That's part of what I came to tell you.

1st Railwayman [*handing document to Ayamonn*]. They handed that to our Committee this evening, a warrant of warning.

Rector [*earnestly—to Ayamonn*]. I was advised to warn you, Ayamonn, that the Authorities are prepared to use all the force they have to prevent the meeting.

Ayamonn. Who advised you, sir—th' Inspector?

Rector. My churchwarden, Ayamonn. Come, even he has good in him.

Ayamonn. I daresay he has, sir; I've no grudge against him.

Rector [*convinced*]. I know that, Ayamonn.

Ayamonn [*indicating document—to 1st Railwayman*]. What are th' Committee going to do with this?

1st Railwayman. What would you do with it, Ayamonn?

Ayamonn [*setting it alight at the fire and waiting till it falls to ashes*]. That!

2nd Railwayman [*gleefully*]. Exactly what we said you'd do!

Sheila [*haughtily*]. It's not what any sensible body would think he'd do.

1st Railwayman [*ignoring her*]. Further still, Ayamonn, me son, we want you to be one of the speakers on the platform at the meeting.

Sheila [*bursting forward and confronting the railwaymen*]. He'll do nothing of the kind—hear me? Nothing of the kind. Cinder-tongued moaners, who's to make any bones about what you suffer, or how you die? Ayamonn's his reading and his painting to do, and his mother to mind, more than lipping your complaints in front of gun muzzles, ready to sing a short and sudden death-song!

1st Railwayman [*a little awed*]. To see Ayamonn we came, an' not you, Miss.

2nd Railwayman [*roughly*]. Let th' man speak for himself.

Ayamonn [*catching Sheila's arm and drawing her back*]. It's my answer they're seeking. [*To railwaymen*] Tell the Committee, Bill, I'll be there; and that they honour me when they set me in front of my brothers. The Minstrel Show must be forgotten.

Sheila [*vehemently—to the Rector*]. You talk to him; you're his friend. You can influence him. Get him to stay away, man!

Rector. It's right for me to warn you, Ayamonn, and you, men, that the Authorities are determined to prevent the meeting; and that you run a grave risk in defying them.

2nd Railwayman [*growling*]. We'll chance it. We've barked long enough, sir; it's time to bite a bit now.

Sheila [*to Rector*]. Warning's no good; that's not enough—forbid him to go. Show him God's against it!

Rector [*standing up*]. Who am I to say that God's against it? You are too young by a thousand years to know the mind of God. If they be his brothers, he does well among them.

Sheila [*wildly*]. I'll get his mother to bar his way. She'll do more than murmur grand excuses.

[*She runs to the door of the other room, opens it, and goes in. After a few moments, she comes out slowly, goes to the chair left idle by the Rector, sits down on it, leans her arms on the table, and lets her head rest on them.*

Ayamonn.   Well?

Sheila [*brokenly*].   She's stretched out, worn and wan, fast asleep, and I hadn't the heart to awaken her.

Rector [*holding out a hand to Ayamonn*].   Come to see me before you go, Ayamonn. Be sure, wherever you may be, whatever you may do, a blessing deep from my breast is all around you. Goodbye. [*To the railwaymen*] Goodbye, my friends.

Railwaymen.   Goodbye, sir.

[*The Rector glances at Sheila, decides to say nothing, and goes towards the door; Ayamonn opens it for him, and he goes out through the semicircle of men and women, still softly singing before the Statue of the Queen of Eblana's poor. Sheila's quiet crying heard as a minor note through the singing.*

Oh, Queen of Eblana's poor children,
Bear swiftly our woe away,
An' give us a chance to live lightly
An hour of our life's dark day!

CURTAIN

ACT III

A part of Dublin City flowering into a street and a bridge across the river Liffey. The parapets are seen to the right and left so that the bridge fills most of the scene before the onlooker. The distant end of the bridge leads to a street flowing on to a point in the far distance; and to the right and left of this street are tall gaunt houses, mottled with dubious activities, with crowds of all sorts of men and women burrowing in them in a pathetic search for a home. These houses stand along another street running parallel with the river. In the distance, where the street, leading from the bridge, ends in a point of space, to the right, soars the tapering silver spire of a church; and to the left, Nelson's Pillar, a deep red, pierces the sky, with Nelson, a deep black, on its top, looking over everything that goes on around him. A gloomy grey sky is over all, so that the colours of the scene are made up of the dark houses, the brown parapets of the bridge, the grey sky, the silver spire, the red pillar, and Nelson's black figure.

On one of the bridge parapets a number of the men seen in the previous scenes are gathered together, their expressionless faces hidden by being bent down towards their breasts. Some sit on the parapets, some lounge against the gaunt houses at the corner of the street leading from the bridge, and, in one corner, a man stands wearily against the parapet, head bent, an unlit pipe dropping from his mouth, apparently forgotten. The sun shines on pillar and church spire, but there is no sign of sun where these people are.

On the pavement, opposite to where the men sit, nearer to this end of the bridge, sit Eeada, Dympna, and Finnoola, dressed so in black that they appear to be enveloped in the blackness of a dark night. In front of Eeada is a drab-coloured basket in which cakes and apples are spending an idle and uneasy time. Dympna has a shallower basket holding decadent blossoms, and a drooping bunch of violets hangs from a listless hand.

Eeada [*drowsily*].   This spongy leaden sky's Dublin; those tomby houses is Dublin too—Dublin's scurvy body; an' we're Dublin's silver soul. [*She spits vigorously into the street.*] An' that's what Eeada thinks of th' city's soul an' body!

Dympna.   You're more than right, Eeada, but I wouldn't be too harsh. [*Calling out in a sing-song way*] Violets, here, on'y tuppence a bunch; tuppence a bunch, th' fresh violets!

Eeada [*calling out in a sing-song voice*].   Apples an' cakes, on'y tuppence a head here for th' cakes; ripe apples a penny apiece!

Dympna.   Th' sun is always at a distance, an' th' chill grey is always here.

Finnoola.   Half-mournin' skies for ever over us, frownin' out any chance of merriment that came staggerin' to us for a little support.

Eeada.   That's Dublin, Finnoola, an' th' sky over it. Sorrow's a slush under our feet, up to our ankles, an' th' deep drip of it constant overhead.

Dympna.   A graveyard where th' dead are all above th' ground.

Eeada.   Without a blessed blink of rest to give them hope. An' she cockin' herself up that she stands among other cities as a queen o' counsel, laden with knowledge, afire with th' song of great men, enough to overawe all livin' beyond th' salty sea, undher another sun be day, an' undher a different moon be night.   [*They drowse, with heads bent lower.*

1st Man [*leaning wearily against the parapet*]. Golden Gander'll do it, if I'm e'er a thrue prophet. [*Raising his voice a little*] He'll flash past th' winnin' post like an arra from th' bow, in the five hundhred guinea West's Awake Steeplechase Championship.

2nd Man [*drowsily contradicting*]. In me neck he will! He'd have a chance if it was a ramble. Copper Goose'll leave him standin', if I'm e'er a thrue prophet.

Eeada [*waking up slightly*]. Prophets? Do me ears deceive me, or am I afther hearin' somebody say prophets?

Dympna. You heard a murmur of it, Eeada, an' it's a bad word to hear, remindin' us of our low estate at th' present juncture. Th' prophets we once had are well hidden behind God be now, an' no wondher, for we put small pass on them, an' God in His generous anger's showin' us what it is to be saddled with Johnnies-come-marchin'-home, all song an' shirt an' no surety.

Finnoola [*shaking her head sadly*]. A gold-speckled candle, white as snow, was Dublin once; yellowish now, leanin' sideways, an' guttherin' down to a last shaky glimmer in th' wind o' life.

Eeada. Well, we've got Guinness's Brewery still, givin' us a needy glimpse of a betther life an hour or so on a Saturday night, though I hold me hand at praisin' th' puttin' of Brian Boru's golden harp on every black porther bottle, destined to give outsiders a false impression of our pride in th' tendher an' dauntless memories of th' past.

> [*The Rector and the Inspector appear at the farther end of the bridge, and come over it towards where the men and women are. The Rector is dressed in immaculate black, wears a glossy tall hat, and carries a walking-stick. He has shed his topcoat, but wears his green scarf round his neck. The Inspector is clad in a blue uniform, slashed with silver epaulettes on the shoulders, and silver braid on collar and cuffs. He wears a big blue helmet, back and front peaks silver-bordered, and from a long silver spike on the top flows a graceful plume of crimson hair. On the front is a great silver crown throned on a circle of red velvet. A sword, in a silver scabbard, hangs by his side. He is wearing highly-polished top-boots. They both pause on the bridge, the Rector looking pensively down over the parapet at the flowing river.*]

Inspector. It was a great wedding, sir. A beautiful bride and an elegant bridegroom; a distinguished congregation, and the Primate in his fine sermon did justice to the grand occasion, sir. Fittingly ended, too, by the organ with *The Voice that Breathed o'er Eden.*

Rector [*apparently not very interested*].   Oh yes, yes; quite.

Inspector.   Historic disthrict, this, round here: headquarters of a Volunteer Corp in Grattan's time—not, of course, that I agree with Grattan. A great-great-grandfather of mine was one of the officers.

Rector.   Oh yes; was he?

Inspector.   Yes. Strange uniform he wore: richly black, with sky-blue facings, a yellow breast-piece, ribbed with red braid, and, capping all, a huge silver helmet having a yellow plume soaring over it from the right-hand side.

Rector [*smiling*].   Your own's not too bad, Mr. Churchwarden.

Inspector.   Smart; but a bit too sombre, I think, sir.

Eeada [*whining towards them*].   On'y a penny each, th' rosy apples, lovely for th' chiselurs—Jasus! what am I sayin'? Lovely for th' little masters an' little misthresses, stately, in their chandeliered an' carpeted dwellin'-houses; or a cake—on'y tuppence a piece—daintily spiced, an' tastin' splendid.

Dympna [*whining towards them*].   Tuppence, here, th' bunch o' violets, fit for to go with th' white an' spotless cashmere gown of our radiant Lady o' Fair Dealin'.

Eeada [*deprecatingly*].   What are you sayin', woman? That's a Protestan' ministher, indeed, gentleman, Dympna!

Dympna.   Me mind slipped for a poor minute; but it's pity he'll have on us, an' regulate our lives with what'll bring a sudden cup o' tea within fair reach of our hands.

Eeada.   Apples, here, penny each, rosy apples, picked hardly an hour ago from a laden three; cakes tuppence on'y, baked over scented turf as th' dawn stepped over th' blue-gowned backs o' th' Dublin Mountains.

Dympna.   Tuppence a bunch, th' violets, shy an' dhrunk with th' dew o' th' mornin'; fain to lie in the white bosom of a high-born lady, or fit into th' lapel of a genuine gentleman's Sunday courtin' coat.

[*The Rector takes a few coins from his pocket and throws them to the women, who pick them up and sink into silence again.*]

Inspector.   Swift, too, must have walked about here with the thorny crown of madness pressing ever deeper into his brain.

Rector [*indicating the men and women*].   Who are these?

Inspector [*indifferent*].   Those? Oh, flotsam and jetsam. A few of them dangerous at night, maybe; but harmless during the day.

Rector. I've read that tens of thousands of such as those followed Swift to the grave.

Inspector. Indeed, sir? A queer man, the poor demented Dean; a right queer man.

> [*A sleepy lounger suddenly gives a cough, gives his throat a hawk, and sends a big spit on to one of the Inspector's polished boots, then sinks back into sleep again.*

Inspector [*springing back with an angry exclamation*]. What th' hell are you after doing, you rotten lizard! Looka what you've done, you mangy rat!   [*He takes hold of the lounger and shakes him sharply.*

2nd Man [*sleepily resentful*]. Eh, there! Wha' th' hell?

Inspector [*furiously*]. You spat on my boots, you tousled toad—my boots, boots, boots!

2nd Man [*frightened and bewildered*]. Boots, sir? Is it me, sir? Not me sir. Musta been someone else, sir.

Inspector [*shaking him furiously*]. You, you, you!

2nd Man. Me, sir? Never spit in public in me life, sir. Makin' a mistake, sir. Musta been someone else.

Rector. Inspector Finglas! Remember you wear the King's uniform! Quiet, quiet, man!

Inspector [*subsiding*]. Pardon me. I lost my temper. I'm more used to a blow from a stone than a dirty spit on my boot.

Rector [*shuddering a little*]. Let us go from here. Things here frighten me, for they seem to look with wonder on our ease and comfort.

Inspector. Frighten you? Nonsense—and with me!

Rector. Things here are of a substance I dare not think about, much less see and handle. Here, I can hardly bear to look upon the same thing twice.

Inspector. There you are, and as I've said so often, Breydon's but a neat slab of a similar slime.

Rector. You wrong yourself to say so: Ayamonn Breydon has within him the Kingdom of Heaven. [*He pauses.*] And so, indeed, may these sad things we turn away from.   [*They pass out,*

Eeada [*thinking of the coins given*]. Two tiny sixpences—fourpence a head. Oh, well, beggars can't be choosers. But isn't it a hard life to be grindin' our poor bums to powder, for ever squattin' on the heartless pavements of th' Dublin streets!

Dympna. Ah, what is it all to us but a deep-written testament o' gloom: grey sky over our heads, brown an' dusty streets undher our feet, with th' black an' bitther Liffey flowin' through it all.

Eeada [*mournfully*]. We've dhrifted down to where there's nothin'. Younger I was when every quiet-clad evenin' carried a jaunty jewel in her bosom. Tormented with joy I was then as to whether I'd parade th' thronged sthreets on th' arm of a 16th Lancer, his black-breasted crimson coat a sight to see, an' a black plume droopin' from his haughty helmet; or lay claim to a red-breasted Prince o' Wales's Own, th' red plume in his hat a flame over his head.

Dympna. It was a 15th King's Own Hussar for me, Eeada, with his rich blue coat an' its fairyland o' yellow braid, two yellow sthripes down his trousers, an' a red bag an' plume dancin' on his busby.

Eeada. Lancers for me, Dympna.

Dympna. Hussars for me, Eeada.

Eeada. An' what for you, Finnoola?

Finnoola. What would a girl, born in a wild Cork valley, among the mountains, brought up to sing the songs of her fathers, what would she choose but the patched coat, shaky shoes, an' white hungry face of th' Irish rebel? But their shabbiness was threaded with th' colours from the garments of Finn Mac Cool of th' golden hair, Goll Mac Morna of th' big blows, Caoilte of th' flyin' feet, an' Oscar of th' invincible spear.

Eeada [*nudging Dympna*]. That was some time ago, if y'ask me.

> [*Brennan comes slowly over the bridge from the far side. His melodeon is hanging on his back. He looks around for a likely place to play. He leans against a parapet, some distance off, and unslings his melodeon from his back.*]

Eeada. Here's that oul' miser creepin' after coppers, an' some bank bulgin' with what he has in it already.

2nd Man [*waking suddenly, spitting out vigorously, and speaking venomously*]. Rowlin' in th' coin o' th' realm—bastard!

> [*He sinks into a coma again.*]

Brennan [*giving himself confidence*]. Evenin', ladies an' gentlemen. Good thing to be alive when th' sun's kind. [*They take no heed of what he says. Brennan sighs; then plays a few preliminary notes on the melodeon to make sure it is in tune. He begins to sing in a voice that was once a mellow baritone, but now is a little husky with age, now and again quavering a little on the higher notes in the song. Singing:*]

I stroll'd with a fine maid far out in th' counthry,

Th' blossoms around us all cryin' for dew;
On a violet-clad bench, sure, I sat down beside her,
An' tuck'd up my sleeves for to tie up her shoe.
An' what's that to anyone whether or no
If I came to th' fore when she gave me th' cue?
She clos'd her eyes tight as she murmur'd full low,
Be good enough, dear, for to tie up my shoe.

Eeada [*with muttered indignation*]. Isn't that outrageous, now; on a day like this, too, an' in a sober mood!

Dympna. In front o' decent women as well!

1st Man [*waking up suddenly*]. Disturbin' me dhreams of Golden Gandher gallopin' home to win in a canther!

Brennan [*singing*]:

Th' hawthorn shook all her perfume upon us,
Red poppies saluted, wherever they grew,
Th' joyous exertion that flaunted before me,
When I tuck'd up my sleeves for to fasten her shoe.
An' what's it to anyone, whether or no
I learn'd in that moment far more than I knew,
As she lifted her petticoat, shyly an' slow,
An' I tuck'd up my sleeves for to fasten her shoe?

The heathery hills were all dancin' around us,
False things in th' world turn'd out to be thrue,
When she put her arms round me, an' kiss'd me an' murmur'd,
You've neatly an' tenderly tied up my shoe.
An' what's that to anyone whether or no,
I ventur'd quite gamely to see th' thing through,
When she lifted her petticoat, silent an' slow,
An' I tuck'd up my sleeves for to tie up her shoe?

> [*Some pennies have been thrown from the windows of the houses. Brennan picks them up, and taking off a shabby, wide-brimmed hat, bestows a sweeping bow on the houses. During the singing of the last verse of the song, Ayamonn and Roory have strolled in, and have listened to the old man singing while they leant against the balustrade of the bridge. The scene has grown darker as the old man is singing his song, for the sun is setting.*]

2nd Man [*waking up suddenly*]. Off with you, old man, thinkin' to turn our thoughts aside from th' way we are, an' th' worn-out hope in front of us.

1st Man [*waking up—wrathfully*]. Get to hell outa that, with your sootherin' songs o' gaudy idleness!

Eeada. Makin' his soul, at his age, he ought to be, instead o' chantin' ditties th' way you'd fear what would come upon you in th' darkness o' th' night, an' ne'er a sword be your side either.

3rd Man. Away with you an' your heathen songs to parts renowned for ignorance an' shame!

Finnoola. Away to where light women are plenty, an' free to open purple purses to throw you glitterin' coins!

[*Brennan slings his melodeon on to his back, puts his hat back on his head, and wends his way across the bridge.*

Roory [*as he passes*]. Isn't it a wondher, now, you wouldn't sing an Irish song, free o' blemish, instead o' one thickly speckled with th' lure of foreign enthertainment?

[*Brennan heeds him not, but crosses the bridge and goes out. The men and women begin to sink into drowsiness again.*

Ayamonn. Let him be, man; he sang a merry song well, and should have got a fairer greeting.

Roory [*taking no notice of Ayamonn's remark—to the men and women*]. Why didn't yous stop him before he began? *Pearl of th' White Breasts*, now, or *Battle Song o' Munster* that would pour into yous Conn's battle-fire of th' hundhred fights. Watchman o' Tara he was, his arm reachin' over deep rivers an' high hills, to dhrag out a host o' sthrong enemies shiverin' in shelthers. Leadher of Magh Femon's Host he was, Guardian of Moinmoy, an' Vetheran of our river Liffey, flowin' through a city whose dhrinkin' goblets once were made of gold, ere wise men carried it with frankincense an' myrrh to star-lit Bethlehem.

Eeada [*full of sleep—murmuring low*]. Away you, too, with your spangled memories of battle-mad warriors buried too deep for words to find them. Penny, here, each, th' ripe apples.

Dympna [*sleepily—in a low murmur*]. Away, an' leave us to saunter in sleep, an' crave out a crust in the grey kingdom of quietness. Tuppence a bunch the fresh violets.

Finnoola [*sleepily*]. Run away, son, to where bright eyes can see no fear, an' white hands, idle, are willin' to buckle a sword on a young man's thigh.

1st Man [*with a sleepy growl*]. Get to hell where gay life has room to move, an' hours to waste, an' white praise is sung to coloured shadows. Time is precious here.

2nd and 3rd Men [*together—murmuringly*]. Time is precious here.

Ayamonn.   Rouse yourselves; we hold a city in our hands!

Eeada [*in a very low, but bitter voice*].   It's a bitther city.

Dympna [*murmuring the same way*].   It's a black an' bitther city.

Finnoola [*speaking the same way*].   It's a bleak, black, an' bitther city.

1st Man.   Like a batthered, tatthered whore, bullied by too long a life.

2nd Man.   An' her three gates are castles of poverty, penance, an' pain.

Ayamonn.   She's what our hands have made her. We pray too much and work too little. Meanness, spite, and common pattherns are woven thick through all her glory; but her glory's there for open eyes to see.

Eeada [*bitterly—in a low voice*].   Take your fill of her glory, then; for it won't last long with your headin' against them who hold the kingdom an' who wield th' power.

Dympna [*reprovingly*].   He means well, Eeada, an' he knows things hid from us; an' we know his poor oul' mother's poor feet has worn out a pathway to most of our tumbling doorways, seekin' out ways o' comfort for us she sadly needs herself.

Eeada [*in a slightly livelier manner*].   Don't I know that well! A shabby sisther of ceaseless help she is, blind to herself for seein' so far into th' needs of others. May th' Lord be restless when He loses sight of her!

Finnoola.   For all her tired look an' wrinked face, a pure white candle she is, blessed this minute by St. Colmkille of th' gentle manner, or be Aidan, steeped in th' lore o' Heaven, or be Lausereena of th' silver voice an' snowy vestments—th' blue cloak o' Brigid be a banner over her head for ever!

The Other Two Women [*together*].   Amen.

Roory [*impatiently*].   We waste our time here—come on!

Ayamoon.   Be still, man; it was dark when th' spirit of God first moved on th' face of th' waters.

Roory.   There's nothin' movin' here but misery. Gun peal an' slogan cry are th' only things to startle them. We're useless here. I'm off, if you're not.

Ayamonn.   Wait a moment, Roory. No-one knows what a word may bring forth. Th' leaves an' blossoms have fallen, but th' three isn't dead.

Roory [*hotly*].   An' d'ye think talkin' to these tatthered second-hand ghosts'll bring back Heaven's grace an' Heaven's beauty to Kaithleen ni Houlihan?

Ayamonn.   Roory, Roory, your Kaithleen ni Houlihan has th' bent back of an oul' woman as well a th' walk of a queen. We love th' ideal Kaithleen ni Houlihan, not because she is false, but because she is beautiful; we hate th' real Kaithleen ni Houlihan, not because she is true, but because she is ugly.

Roory [*disgusted*]. Aw, for God's sake, man! [*He hurries off angrily.*

Eeada [*calling scornfully after him*]. God speed you, scut!

Ayamonn [*placing a hand softly on Eeada's head*]. Forget him, an' remember ourselves, and think of what we can do to pull down th' banner from dusty bygones, an' fix it up in th' needs an' desires of today.

> [*The scene has now become so dark that things are but dimly seen, save the silver spire and the crimson pillar in the distance; and Ayamonn's head set in a streak of sunlight, looking like the severed head of Dunn-Bo speaking out of the darkness.*

Finnoola. Songs of Osheen and Sword of Oscar could do nothing to tire this city of its shame.

Ayamonn. Friend, we would that you should live a greater life; we will that all of us shall live a greater life. Our sthrike is yours. A step ahead for us today; another one for you tomorrow. We who have known, and know, the emptiness of life shall know its fullness. All men and women quick with life are fain to venture forward. [*To Eeada*] The apple grows for you to eat. [*To Dympna*] The violet grows for you to wear. [*To Finnoola*] Young maiden, another world is in your womb.

Eeada [*still a little gloomily.*] Th' soldiers will be chasin' us with gunfire; th' polis hoppin' batons off our heads; our sons an' husbands hurried off to prison, to sigh away th' time in gloomier places than those they live in now.

Ayamonn. Don't flinch in th' first flare of a fight. [*He looks away from them and gazes meditatively down the river.*] Take heart of grace from your city's hidden splendour. [*He points with an outstretched hand.*] Oh, look! Look there! Th' sky has thrown a gleaming green mantle over her bare shoulders, bordhered with crimson, an' with a hood of gentle magenta over her handsome head—look!

> [*The scene has brightened, and bright and lovely colours are being brought to them by the caress of the setting sun. The houses on the far side of the river now bow to the visible world, decked in mauve and burnished bronze; and the men that have been lounging against them now stand stalwart, looking like fine bronze statues, slashed with scarlet.*

Ayamonn. Look! Th' vans an' lorries rattling down th' quays, turned to bronze an' purple by th' sun, look like chariots forging forward to th' battle-front.

[*Eeada, rising into the light, now shows a fresh and virile face, and she is garbed in a dark-green robe, with a silvery mantle over her shoulders.*

Eeada [*gazing intently before her*]. Shy an' lovely, as well as battle-minded!

[*Dympna rises now to look where Ayamonn is pointing. She is dressed like Eeada, and her face is aglow. The men have slid from the parapets of the bridge, turning, too, to look where Ayamonn is pointing. Their faces are aglow, like the women's, and they look like bronze statues, slashed with a vivid green. Finnoola rises, last, and stands a little behind the others, to look at the city showing her melody of colours. Finnoola is dressed in a skirt of a brighter green than the other two women, a white bodice slashed with black, and a flowing silvery scarf is round her waist.*

Finnoola. She's glowin' like a song sung be Osheen himself, with th' golden melody of his own harp helpin'!

1st Man [*puzzled*]. Something funny musta happened, for, 'clare to God, I never noticed her shinin' that way before.

2nd Man. Looka the loungers opposite have changed to sturdy men of bronze, and th' houses themselves are gay in purple an' silver!

3rd Man. Our tired heads have always haunted far too low a level.

Ayamonn. There's th' great dome o' th' Four Courts lookin' like a golden rose in a great bronze bowl! An' th' river flowin' below it, a purple flood, marbled with ripples o' scarlet; watch the seagulls glidin' over it—like restless white pearls astir on a royal breast. Our city's in th' grip o' God!

1st Man [*emotionally*]. Oh, hell, it's grand!

Eeada. Blessed be our city for ever an' ever.

Ayamonn [*lifting his right hand high*]. Home of th' Ostmen, of th' Norman, an' th' Gael, we greet you! Greet you as you catch a passing hour of loveliness, an' hold it tightly to your panting breast! [*He sings:*]
Fair city, I tell thee our souls shall not slumber
Within th' warm beds of ambition or gain;
Our hands shall stretch out to th' fullness of labour,
Till wondher an' beauty within thee shall reign.

The Rest [*singing together*]:
We vow to release thee from anger an' envy,
To dhrive th' fierce wolf an' sly fox from thy gate,
Till wise men an' matrons an' virgins shall murmur
O city of splendour, right fair is thy fate!

Ayamonn [*singing*]:
> Fair city, I tell thee that children's white laughter,
> An' all th' red joy of grave youth goin' gay,
> Shall make of thy streets a wild harp ever sounding,
> Touch'd by th' swift fingers of young ones at play!

The Rest [*singing*]:
> We swear to release thee from hunger an' hardship,
> From things that are ugly an' common an' mean;
> Thy people together shall build a brave city,
> Th' fairest an' finest that ever was seen!

> [*Finnoola has been swaying her body to the rhythm of the song, and now, just as the last part is ending, she swings out on to the centre of the bridge in a dance. The tune, played on a flute by someone, somewhere, is that of a Gavotte, or an air of some dignified and joyous dance, and, for a while, it is played in fairly slow time. After some time it gets quicker, and Ayamonn dances out to meet her. They dance opposite each other, the people around clapping their hands to the tap of the dancers' feet. The two move around in this spontaneous dance, she in a golden pool of light, he in a violet-coloured shadow, now and again changing their movements so that she is in the violet-coloured shadow, and he in the golden pool.*

Eeada [*loudly*]. The finest colours God has to give are all around us now.

Finnoola [*as she dances*]. The Sword of Light is shining!

1st Man [*exultantly*]. Sons an' daughters of princes are we all, an' one with th' race of Milesius!

> [*The dance comes to an end with Ayamonn and Finnoola having their arms round each other.*

Eeada. Praise God for th' urge of jubilation in th' heart of th' young.

1st Man. An' for th' swiftness of leg an' foot in th' heart of a dance.

2nd Man. An' for th' dhream that God's right hand still holds all things firmly.

> [*The scene darkens slightly. Ayamonn loosens his hold on Finnoola and raises his head to listen to something. In the distance can be heard the sound of many feet marching in unison.*

Finnoola [*a little anxiously*]. What is it you're listenin' to?

Ayamonn. I must go; goodbye, fair maid, goodbye.

Finnoola. Is it goin' to go you are, away from the fine things shinin' around us? Amn't I good enough for you?

Ayamonn [*earnestly*].   You're lovely stayin' still, an' brimmin' over with a wilder beauty when you're dancin'; but I must go. May you marry well, an' rear up children fair as Emer was, an' fine as Oscar's son; an' may they be young when Spanish ale foams high on every hand, an' wine from th' royal Pope's a common dhrink! Goodbye.

> [*He kisses her, and goes across the bridge, passing out of sight on the farther bank of the river. The figures left behind have shrunk a little; the colours have faded a good deal, and all look a little puzzled and bewildered. The loungers have fallen back to the walls of the houses, and, though they do not lie against them, they stand close to them, as if seeking their shelter. There is a fairly long pause before anyone speaks. They stand apart, as if shy of each other's company.*]

Eeada [*murmuringly*].   Penny each, th' ripe apples. Who was it that spoke that time? Jasus! I musta been dhreamin'.

Dympna [*in a bewildered voice*].   So must I, th' way I thought I was lost in a storm of joy, an' many colours, with gay clothes adornin' me.

Finnoola [*puzzled and dreamy*].   Dhreamin' I musta been when I heard strange words in a city nearly smothered be stars, with God guidin' us along th' banks of a purple river, all of us clad in fresh garments, fit to make Osheen mad to sing a song of the revelry dancin' in an' out of God's own vision.

Eeada [*murmuringly, but a little peevishly*].   For God's sake give over dwellin' on oul' songs sung by Osheen, th' way you'd be kindlin' a fire o' glory round some poor bog-warbler chantin' hoarse ditties in a sheltered corner of a windy street. [*Very sleepily*] Th' dewy violets, here, on'y tuppence a bunch—Jasus, apples I mean!

> [*Now the tramp-tramp of marching men is heard more plainly.*]

Dympna [*a little more awake*].   Tuppence each, the bunch of vio—— What can that be, now?

1st Man [*gloomily, but with a note of defiance in his voice*].   Th' thramp of marchin' soldiers out to prevent our meetin' an' to stop our sthrike.

2nd Man [*in a burst of resolution*].   We'll have both, in spite of them!

> [*The scene darkens deeply now. In the pause following the 2nd Man's remark, nothing is heard but the sound of the tramping feet; then through this threatening sound comes the sound of voices singing quietly, voices that may be of those on and around the bridge, or of those singing some little distance away.*]

Voices [*singing quietly*]:
We swear to release thee from hunger and hardship,

From things that are ugly and common and mean;
Thy people together shall build a great city,
The finest and fairest that ever was seen.

CURTAIN

ACT IV

Part of the grounds surrounding the Protestant church of St. Burnupus. The grounds aren't very beautiful, for they are in the midst of a poor and smoky district; but they are trim, and, considering the surroundings, they make a fair show. An iron railing running along the back is almost hidden by a green and golden hedge, except where, towards the centre, a fairly wide wooden gate gives admittance to the grounds. Beyond this gateway, on the pathway outside, is a street lamp. Shrubs grow here and there, and in the left corner, close to the hedge, are lilac and laburnum trees in bloom. To the right is the porch of the church, and part of the south wall, holding a long, rather narrow window, showing, in coloured glass, the figures of SS. Peter and Paul. Some distance away from the porch is a rowan tree, also in blossom, its white flowers contrasting richly with the gay yellow of the laburnum and the royal purple of the lilac. The rest of the grounds are laid out in grass, except for the path leading from the gateway to the entrance of the church. It is a warm, sunny evening, the Vigil of Easter, and the Rector is sitting on a deck-chair, before a table, on which are some books and papers. He is evidently considering the services that are to be held in the church on the following day.

The Rector is wearing a thick black cassock lined with red cloth, and at the moment is humming a verse of a hymn softly to himself, as he marks down notes on a slip of paper before him. A square black skull-cap covers his head.

Rector [*singing to himself, softly*]:
  As Thou didst rise from Thy grim grave,
  So may we rise and stand to brave

Th' power bestow'd on fool or knave;
We beseech Thee!

[*The verger comes out from the porch and walks towards the Rector. He is bald as an egg, and his yellowish face is parched and
woebegone-looking. He is a man of sixty, and shows it. His ordinary
clothes are covered with a long black mantle of thin stuff, with a
small cape-like addition or insertion of crimson velvet on the shoulders.*

Rector [*noticing the verger beside him*].   Hymn 625: we must have that
as our opening hymn, Samuel.

Samuel.   It's got to go in, sir.

Rector.   As you say—it's got to go in. Did you want to speak to me, Samuel?

Samuel.   Excuse me, sir, for what I'm agoin' to say.

Rector [*encouragingly*].   Yes, yes, Samuel, go on.

Samuel [*mysteriously*].   Somethin's afther happenin', sir, that I don't
like.

Rector [*turning a little in his chair*].   Oh! What's that, Sam?

Samuel.   Mr. Fosther was here this mornin' runnin' a hand through th'
daffodils sent for Easther, an' found somethin' he didn't like.

Rector.   Yes?

Samuel.   It's not for me to remark on anything that manœuvres out in
front o' me, or to slip in a sly word on things done, said, or thought on, be
th' pastors, masthers, or higher individuals of th' congregation; but, sometimes, sir, there comes a time when a true man should, must speak out.

Rector [*with a sigh*].   And the time has come to say something now—
what is it, Sam?

Samuel [*in a part whisper*].   This mornin', sir, and th' dear spring sun
shinin' through th' yellow robes of Pether an' th' purple robes o' Paul, an'
me arrangin' th' books in the pews, who comes stealin' in, but lo and
behold you, Fosther an' Dowzard to have a squint round. Seein' they're
Select Vesthrymen, I couldn't ask them why they were nosin' about in
th' silence of th' church on an ordinary week-day mornin'.

Rector [*patiently*].   Yes; but a long time ago, you said something about
daffodils.

Samuel.   I'm comin' at a gallop to them, sir.

Rector.   Good; well, let's hear about the daffodils.

Samuel. Aha, says I, when I seen th' two prowlers with their heads close together, whisperin', aha, says I, there's somethin' on th' carpet.

Rector. Is what you have to tell me something to do with Dowzard and Foster, or the daffodils?

Samuel. Wait till you hear; sometimes Fosther an' Dowzard'll be to th' fore, an' sometimes th' daffodils. What can these two oul' codgers be up to? says I, sidlin' up to where they were, hummin' a hymn.

Rector. Humming a hymn? I'm glad to hear it; for I'd be surprised to hear either of them humming a hymn.

Samuel. Me it was, sir, who was hummin' th' hymn; for in a church, I like me thoughts to go with th' work I'm doin', if you know what I mean.

Rector [*impatiently*]. It'll be nightfall before you get to the daffodils, man.

Samuel. Wait till you hear, sir. There I was gettin' close to them be degrees, when, all of a sudden, didn't Fosther turn on me, shoutin' "Are you goin' to be a party to th' plastherin' of Popish emblems over a Protestan' church?"

Rector. Popish emblems?

Samuel. Th' daffodils, sir.

Rector. The daffodils? But they simply signify the new life that Spring gives; and we connect them in a symbolic way, quite innocently, with our Blessed Lord's Rising. And a beautiful symbol they are: daffodils that come before the swallow dares, and take the winds of March with beauty. Shakespeare, Sam.

Samuel [*lifting his eyes skywards and pointing upwards*]. Altogether too high up for poor me, sir. [*He bends down close to the Rector's ear.*] When he seen the cross o' daffodils made by Breydon, he near went daft. [*A pause, as if Samuel expected the Rector to speak, but he stays silent.*] God knows what'll be th' upshot if it's fixed to the Communion Table, sir. [*Another slight pause.*] Is it really to go there, sir? Wouldn't it look a little more innocent on th' pulpit, sir?

Rector [*in a final voice*]. I will place it myself in front of the Communion Table, and, if Mr. Foster or Mr. Dowzard ask anything more about it, say that it has been placed there by me. And, remember, when you say Mr. Foster and Mr. Dowzard, it's to be Mr. Breydon too. [*He hands some leaflets to Samuel.*] Distribute these through the pews, Sam, please. The arranging of the flowers is finished, is it?

Samuel. Yessir; all but the cross.

Rector. I will see to that myself. Thanks, Sam.

[*Samuel goes off into the church, and the Rector, leaning back in his chair with a book in his hand, chants softly.*

Rector [*chanting*]:
May wonders cease when we grow tame,
Or worship greatness in a name;
May love for man be all our fame,
We beseech Thee!

[*As he pauses to meditate for a moment, Mrs. Breydon is seen coming along, outside the hedge. She enters by the gate, and comes over to the Rector. Sheila has come with her, but lags a little behind when they enter the grounds. The Rector rises quickly from his chair to greet Mrs. Breydon.*

Rector [*warmly*]. My dear Mrs. Breydon! Hasn't it been a lovely day? The weather promises well for Easter.

Mrs. Breydon. It would be good if other things promised as well as the weather, sir.

Rector. We must be patient, and more hopeful, my friend. From the clash of life new life is born.

Mrs. Breydon. An' often new life dies in th' clash too. Ah, when he comes, sir, speak th' word that will keep my boy safe at home, or here.

Rector [*laying a gentle hand on her arm*]. I wish I could, dear friend; I wish I could.

Mrs. Breydon. His mind, like his poor father's, hates what he sees as a sham; an' shams are powerful things, mustherin' at their broad backs guns that shoot, big jails that hide their foes, and high gallows to choke th' young cryin' out against them when th' stones are silent.

Rector. Let those safely sheltered under the lawn of the bishop, the miniver of the noble, the scarlet and ermine of the judge, say unto him, this thing you must not do; I won't, for sometimes out of the mouths of even babes and sucklings cometh wisdom.

Sheila. If what's against him be so powerful, he is helpless; so let this power go on its way of darkened grandeur, and let Ayamonn sit safe by his own fireside.

[*To the left, on the path outside the hedge, the Inspector, in full uniform, appears, evidently coming to see the Rector; on the right, followed by the men and women of the previous scenes, appears Ayamonn. He and the Inspector meet at the gate. The Inspector and he halt. The Inspector indicates he will wait for Ayamonn to pass, and Ayamonn comes into the grounds towards the Rector. The Inspector follows, but, in the grounds, stands a little apart, nearer the hedge. The men and women spread along the path outside, and stay still watching those in the grounds from over the hedge. They hold themselves erect, now; their faces are still pale, but are set with seams of resolution. Each is wearing in the bosom a golden-rayed sun. Brennan comes in and, crossing the grass, sidles over to sit down on the step of the porch.*

Rector [*shaking Ayamonn's hand*].   Ah, I'm so glad you've come; I hope you'll stay.

Ayamonn [*hastily*].   I come but to go. You got the cross of daffodils?

Rector.   Your mother brought it to us; it will hang in front of our church's greatest promise. Come and place it there with your own loyal hands, Ayamonn.

Inspector.   Loyal hands engaged in rough rending of the law and the rumpling-up of decency and order; and all for what? For what would but buy blacking for a pair of boots, or a sheet of glass to mend a broken window!

Brennan [*from his seat on the porch's step*].   He's right, Ayamonn, me son, he's right: money's the root of all evil.

Ayamonn [*to the Inspector*].   A shilling's little to you, and less to many; to us it is our Shechinah, showing us God's light is near; showing us the way in which our feet must go; a sun-ray on our face; the first step taken in the march of a thousand miles.

Inspector [*threateningly*].   I register a lonely warning here that the people of power today will teach a lesson many will remember for ever; though some fools may not live long enough to learn it.

Mrs. Breydon.   Stay here, my son, where safety is a green tree with a kindly growth.

Men and Women [*in chorus—above*].   He comes with us!

Sheila.   Stay here where time goes by in sandals soft, where days fall gently as petals from a flower, where dark hair, growing grey, is never noticed.

Men and Woman [*above*].   He comes with us!

Ayamonn [*turning towards them*].   I go with you!

Inspector [*vehemently*].   Before you go to carry out all your heated mind is set to do, I warn you for the last time that today swift horses will be galloping, and swords will be out of their scabbards!

Rector [*reprovingly—to Inspector.*] I hope you, at least, will find no reason to set your horses moving.

Inspector [*stiffly*]. I'll do my duty, sir; and it would be a good thing if someone we all know did his in that state of life unto which it has pleased God to call him.

Rector [*losing his temper*]. Oh, damn it, man, when you repeat the Church's counsel, repeat it right! Not *unto which it has pleased God to call him, but unto which it shall please God to call him.*

Inspector [*losing his temper too*]. Damn it, man, do you believe that what the fellow's doing now is the state of life unto which it has pleased God to call him?

Rector [*hotly*]. I have neither the authority nor the knowledge to deny it, though I have more of both than you, sir!

[*The Inspector is about to answer angrily, but Sheila catches his arm.*

Sheila. Oh, cancel from your mind the harder things you want to say, an' do your best to save us from another sorrow!

Inspector [*shaking off Sheila's hand roughly, and going to the gateway, where he turns to speak again*]. Remember, all! When swords are drawn and horses charge, the kindly Law, so fat with hesitation, swoons away, and sees not, hears not, cares not what may happen.

Mrs. Breydon [*angrily—up to the Inspector*]. Look at th' round world, man, an' all its wondhers, God made, flaming in it, an' what are you among them, standing here, or on a charging horse, but just a braided an' a tasselled dot!

[*The Inspector hurries off, to pause, and stands outside the hedge, to the right, the men and women shrinking back a little in awe to give him a passage.*

Mrs. Breydon [*to Ayamonn*]. Go on your way, my son, an' win. We'll welcome another inch of the world's welfare.

Rector [*shaking his hand*]. Go, and may the Lord direct you! [*He smiles.*] The Inspector's bark is louder than his bite is deep.

Ayamonn. For the present—goodbye!

[*Ayamonn hurries away through the gate, pausing, outside the hedge to the left, turning to give a last look at the Inspector.*

Inspector. Bear back, my boy, when you see the horsemen charging!

[*He goes out by the right, and Ayamonn goes out left, followed by the men and the women. There is a slight pause.*

Rector [*briskly—to banish a gloomy feeling*]. Now, Mrs. Breydon, you run along to the vestry, and make us a good cup of tea—I'm dying for one. [*To Sheila*] You'll join us, Miss Moorneen, won't you?

Sheila [*immediately anxious*]. Oh no, thanks. I . . . I shouldn't even be here. I'm a Catholic, you know.

Rector. I know, and I'd be the last to ask you do anything you shouldn't; but rest assured there's no canonical law against taking tea made by a Protestant. Off you go, and help Mrs. Breydon. I'll join you in a moment.

[*Sheila and Mrs. Breydon go off by the south wall of the church.*

Brennan [*as the Rector is gathering his books and papers from the table*]. Hey, sir; hey there, sir! It won't shatther th' community at large this disturbance, will it, eh?

Rector. I hope not.

Brennan [*with a forced laugh*]. No, no, of course not. Bank of Ireland'll still stand, eh? Ay. Ravenous to break in, some of them are, eh? Ay, ay. Iron doors, iron doors are hard to open, eh?

Rector [*going off to get his tea*]. I suppose so.

Brennan. Ay, are they. He supposes so; only supposes—there's a responsible man for you!

[*The verger comes into the porch and bends over Brennan.*

Samuel [*in a hoarse whisper*]. Come in an' have a decko at our grand cross.

Brennan. Cross? What cross?

Samuel. One o' daffodils for Easther, to be put in front of th' Communion Table.

Brennan. Popery, be God!

[*Booing is heard a little distance away, followed by the rattling fall of a shower of stones.*

Brennan. What's that; what's happenin'?

Samuel [*going to back, and looking down the street*]. A crowd flingin' stones; flingin' them at two men runnin' for their life.

Brennan [*nervously*]. Let's get into the church, quick. Throuble's beginnin' already.

[*They both go into the church, and Samuel closes the door. A crowd can be heard booing. Men and women, among them Eeada, Finnoola, Dympna, the Railwaymen, and the Lurchers who were on the bridge, pass across outside the hedge. The Leader carries a red flag, and all march with determination. They are all singing the following song:*

Leaders [*singing*]:
    If we can't fire a gun, we can fire a hard stone,
    Till th' life of a scab shrivels into a moan;

Crowd [*chorusing*]:
    Let it sink in what I say,
    Let me say it again—
    Though the Lord made an odd scab, sure, He also made men!

Leaders [*singing*]:
    Th' one honour he'll get is a dusty black plume,
    On th' head of th' nag taking him to the tomb;

Crowd [*chorusing*]:
    Let it sink in what I say,
    Let me say it again:
    Th' scab's curs'd be th' workers, book, candle an' bell!

> [*They cross over and disappear. After a pause, Dowzard and Foster come running in; they hurry through the gateway, and dash over to the church's porch.*

> [*Dowzard is a big, beefy, red-faced man, rolls of flesh pouring out over the collar of his coat. His head is massive and bald, with jet-black tufts behind his ear, and a tiny fringe of it combed across high over his forehead. Foster is small and scraggy, with aggression for ever lurking in his cranky face, ready to leap into full view at the slightest opportunity. His cheeks and lips are shaven, but spikes of yellowish whiskers point defiantly out from under his chin. His voice is squeaky and, when it is strengthened in anger, it rises into a thin piping scream. Both are dressed in the uniforms of railway foremen, blue cloth, with silver buttons, and silver braid on Dowzard's peaked hat and coat-sleeves, and gold braid on those of Foster. Both have their coats tightly buttoned up on them. They take off their peaked caps and wipe sweat from their foreheads. Dowzard pushes the door.*

Dowzard. We're safe here in th' grounds; Church grounds sacred. Unguarded, verminous villains—Papists, th' lot o' them!

Foster [*venomously*]. On' one o' their leaders a Select Vestryman. On' thot domned Rector stondin' by him. Steeped in Popery: sign o' th' cross; turnin' eastward sayin' th' Creed; sung Communion—be Gud, it's a public scondal!

Dowzard.   Some o' them stones scorched me ear passin' by. We shouldn't have worn our uniforms. Gave us away. I knew we were in for it when they called us scabs.

Foster.   Scobs themselves! Smoky, vonomous bastards! I tull you I'd wear me uniform in th' Vutican. [*He unbuttons his coat and shows that he is wearing a vivid orange sash, bordered with blue.*] Thor's me sash for all tae see. You should ha' stud with me, mon; stud like th' heroes o' Dully's Brae!

Dowzard [*shouting and knocking at door*].   Ey, there, in there, come out, open th' blasted door an' help a half-dead man!

> [*The church door is opened, and the Rector, followed by the verger and Brennan, comes out into the grounds.*

Rector.   What's wrong; what has happened?

Dowzard.   Th' Pope's bullies with hard stones have smitten us sore. Honest men, virtuous an' upright, loyal to th' law an' constitution, have this day been smitten sore with Popish stones—oh, me poor head!

Foster.   St. Bartholomew's Day's dawnin' again, I'm tullin' yous, an' dismumbered Protestants'll lie on all th' sthreets!

Rector.   You can't be badly hurt when you complain so grandly.

Foster.   Stand up for th' ruffians be makin' luttle of our hurts, so do, ay, do. [*Noticing Brennan who has edged towards the gate and is about to go away*] Eh, you, aren't you goin' to stay an' put tustimony to the fullness o' th' Protestan' feth?

Brennan [*with slight mockery*].   Ay, I would, an' welcome, if I hodn't to go, forbye, at this hour of on uvery day, I mak' ut a rule tae be sturdy in th' readin' of a chapther o' God's word so's I won't hold on tae wordly things too strongly.   [*He goes out.*

Foster [*fiercely*].   A jully-fush Protestant! [*To the Rector*] Look see, I tull you th' fires o' Smithfield 'ull be blazin' round Protestant bodies again, an' coloured lights 'ull be shown in th' Vatican windows soon!

Dowzard.   An' we'll be th' first to go up in the flames.

Rector [*laughing contemptuously*].   Nonsense, oh, nonsense.

Foster [*almost screaming*].   It's not nonsense, mon! Every sable-robed Jesuit's goin' about chucklin', his honds twitchin' to pounce out on men like me here, an' Eddie Dowzard there, tae manacle us, head, hond, and fut, for th' wheel, th' thumbscrew, an' th' rack, an' then finish us up at th' stake in a hoppy Romish auto-dey-fey! The Loyola boyos are out to fight another buttle with th' men o' King Bully!

Rector [*amused*]. Well, let the Loyola boyos and King Bully fight it out between them. I'm too busy to join either side. Goodbye.

Foster [*catching his arm as he is going—viciously*]. You're no' goin' tae be lut slide off like thot, now, with your guilty conscience, mon. There's things to be done, and things tae be ondone in yon church, there; ey, ey.

Rector [*quietly*]. Indeed?

Foster [*angrily—to Dowzard*]. Uh, speak, speak a word, mon, on' don't leave ut all tae me.

Dowzard. First, sir, we want you to get rid o' Breydon from the Vesthry an' from th' church.

Rector. Oh, indeed?

Foster [*almost screaming*]. It's no' oh, indeed; answer th' question—plain yes or no!

Rector [*coldly*]. Gentlemen, Mr. Breydon stays in the Vestry till the parishioners elect someone else; as for the church, God has seen fit to make him a member of Christ, and it is not for me, or even for you, gentlemen, to say that God did wrong.

Dowzard [*sneeringly*]. An' when did that wondherful thing hoppen?

Rector. At his baptism, as you yourself should know.

Foster [*with an agonised squeal*]. Popery, Popery, nothin' but Popery! Th' whole place's infusted with it!

> [*The verger appears at the porch door with the cross of daffodils in his hand. It has a Keltic shape, the shafts made of the flowers, and the circle of vivid green moss. The verger shows it to Dowzard, behind the Rector's back, and Dowzard, sidling over, takes it from him, the verger returning into the church again.*

Rector. And now be good enough, Mr. Foster, to let my arm go.

> [*In the distance, a bugle-call sounding the charge is heard. Foster lets go of the Rector's arm; and they all listen.*

Foster [*gleefully*]. Aha, there's the bugle soundin' th' charge, an' soon the King's horses an' th' King's men'll be poundin' the riothers undher their feet! Law an ordher in the State an' law an' ordher in th' Church we must have. An' we're fightin' here as they're fightin' there—for th' Crown an' ceevil and releegious liberty!

> [*The sound of galloping horses is heard, followed by several volleys of rifle-fire. They all listen intently for a few moments.*

Foster [*gleefully*]. Hear that now? Your Breydon fullow'll soon be doshin' in here for th' church to hide him.

Rector. The cross of Christ be between him and all harm!

Dowzard [*dancing out in front of the Rector, holding out the cross—with exultant glee*]. The cross—a Popish symbol! There y'urre, see? A Popish symbol flourished in th' faces o' Protestant people! [*With a yell*] Ichabod!

Foster [*venomously*]. I'll no' stick it, no; I'll no' stick it. Look-see, th' rage kindlin' godly Luther is kindlin' me! Here, go, gimme a holt of thot. [*He snatches the cross of flowers from Dowzard, flings it on the ground and dances on it.*] Th' bible on' th' crown! The twa on' a half, th' orange on' blue; on' th' Dagon of Popery undher our Protestant feet!

Dowzard [*wildly*]. Th' dhrum, th' dhrum, th' Protestant dhrum!

> [*While Foster and Dowzard have been dancing about and shouting their last few words, the men and women have run frightened along the path, behind the hedge. Those running from the right, turn, and run back to the left; those running from the left, turn, and run back to the left again, passing each other as they run. They suddenly see the men and women running about behind the hedge, and at once plunge into the porch, almost knocking the Rector down.*

Foster [*as they fly—to the Rector*]. Out uh th' way, mon, out uh th' way!

> [*After a pause Eeada comes running through the gate, into the garden, over to the Rector.*

Eeada [*beseechingly*]. Oh, sir, please let me into the church, till all th' sthrife is over—no place's safe with the soldiers firin' an' th' police runnin' mad in a flourish o' batons!

Rector [*reassuringly*]. Be calm, be quiet, they won't touch a woman. They remain men, however furious they may be for the moment.

Eeada. Arra, God help your innocence! You should ha' seen them sthrikin' at men, women, an' childher. An' me own friend, Dympna, in hospital gettin' her face laced with stitches, th' way you'd lace a shoe! An' all along of followin' that mad fool, Breydon!

Rector. Go in, then. [*To the verger, who has come to the entrance*] See her safe.

> [*Eeada and the verger go into the church. Finnoola comes slowly along the path outside the hedge, holding on to the railings as she moves, step by step. When she comes to the gateway, she sinks down to the ground and turns a white and distorted face towards those in the grounds.*

Finnoola [*painfully*].   For th' love o' God, one of you tell me if th' Reverend something Clinton's here, or have I to crawl a long way further?

Rector [*hurrying over to her*].   He's here; I'm he, my good woman. What is it you want of me?

Finnoola.   I've a message for you from Ayamonn Breydon.

Rector [*eagerly*].   Yes, yes; where is he?

Finnoola.   He's gone.

Rector.   Gone? Gone where?

Finnoola.   Gone to God, I hope.   [*A rather long pause.*

Rector [*in a low voice*].   May he rest in peace! And the message?

Finnoola.   Yes. He whispered it in me ear as his life fled through a bullet-hole in his chest—th' soldiers, th' soldiers. He said this day's but a day's work done, an' it'll be begun again tomorrow. You're to keep an eye on th' oul' woman. He wants to lie in th' church tonight, sir. Me hip's hurt; th' fut of a plungin' horse caught me, an' I flat on th' ground. He sent a quick and a long farewell to you. Oh, for Christ's sake get's a dhrink o' wather! [*The verger runs for a drink.*] We stood our groun' well, though. [*The verger comes back with the water, and she drinks.*] Now I can have a thrickle of rest at last.

                    [*She stretches herself out on the ground.*

Rector.   Where did you leave him? Where is he lying now? [*She lies there, and makes no answer. He picks up the broken cross of flowers and is silent for a few moments. With head bent low—sorrowfully*] Oh, Ayamonn, Ayamonn, my dear, dear friend. Oh Lord, open Thou mine eyes that I may see Thee, even as in a glass, darkly, in all this mischief and all this woe!

[*The curtain comes down to indicate the passing of some hours. When it rises again, it is evening. The lamp over the porch door is lighted, and so is the church, the light shining through the yellow robe of St. Peter and the purple robe of St. Paul from the window in the church's wall. The church organ is playing, very softly, a dead march. The lamp on the path, outside the hedge, isn't yet lighted. The dark figures of men and women can be faintly seen lining themselves along the hedge. Mrs. Breydon is standing in the grounds, near to the gateway. Foster and Dowzard stand on the steps of the porch. A little in front, with his back turned towards them, stands the Rector, now with white surplice over his cassock, his stole around his neck, and the crimson-lined hood of a Doctor of Divinity on his shoulders. Sheila, holding a bunch of crimson roses in her*]

hand, stands under the rowan tree. Partly behind the tree, the In-
spector is standing alone. A lamplighter comes along the path, carry-
ing his pole with the little flower of light in the brass top. He lights
the lamp on the path, then comes over to peer across the hedge.

Lamplighter. What's up? What's on? What's happenin' here? What's
they all doin' now?

1st Man. Bringin' th' body o' Breydon to th' church.

Lamplighter. Aw, is that it? Guessed somethin' was goin' on.

1st Man. He died for us.

Lamplighter. Looka that, now! An' they're all accouthered in their best to
welcome him home, wha'? Aw, well, th' world's got to keep movin', so I
must be off; so long! [*He goes.*

Dowzard [*speaking to the Rector's back*]. For th' last time, sir, I tell you
half of the Vestry's against him comin' here; they don't want our church
mixed up with this venomous disturbance.

Rector [*without moving, and keeping his eyes looking towards the gate-*
way]. All things in life, the evil and the good, the orderly and disor-
derly, are mixed with the life of the Church Militant here on earth. We
honour our brother, not for what may have been an error in him, but for
the truth for ever before his face. We dare not grudge him God's forgive-
ness and rest eternal because he held no banner above a man-made custom.

Foster [*savagely*]. Aw, looksee, I'm no' a mon to sut down on' listen to a
tumblin' blether o' words—wull ye, or wull ye not, give intil us?

[*In the distance a bagpipe is heard playing* Flowers of the Forest.
Mrs. Breydon's body stiffens, and Sheila's head bends lower on her
breast.

Rector. It is a small thing that you weary me, but you weary my God also.
Stand aside, and go your way of smoky ignorance, leaving me to welcome
him whose turbulence has sunken into a deep sleep, and who cometh
now as the waters of Shiloah that go softly, and sing sadly of peace.

[*As he is speaking, the lament ceases, and a moment after, a*
stretcher bier, bearing the covered-up body of Ayamonn, appears at
the gateway. It is carried down towards the church, and the Rector
goes to meet it.

Rector [*intoning*]. Lord, Thou hast been our refuge from one generation
to another. For a thousand years in Thy sight are but as yesterday. [*He*
chants:]
　　All our brother's mordant strife

Fought for more abundant life;
For this, and more—oh, hold him dear.
Jesu, Son of Mary, hear!

Gather to Thy loving breast
Ev'ry laughing thoughtful jest,
Gemm'd with many a thoughtful tear.
Jesu, Son of Mary, hear!

When Charon rows him nigh to shore,
To see a land ne'er seen before,
Him to rest eternal steer.
Jesu, Son of Mary, hear!

[*The bier is carried into the church, and, as it passes, Sheila lays the bunch of crimson roses on the body's breast.*

Sheila. Ayamonn, Ayamonn, my own poor Ayamonn!

[*The Rector precedes the bier, and Mrs. Breydon walks beside it, into the church, the rest staying where they are. There is a slight pause.*

Dowzard. We'd betther be goin'. Th' man's a malignant Romaniser. Keep your eye on th' rabble goin' out.

Foster [*contemptuously*]. There's little fight left in thom, th' now. I'll no' forgive thot Inspector fur refusin' to back our demond.

[*They swagger out through the gateway and disappear along the path outside the hedge, as those who carried the bier come out of the church.*

2nd Man. That's the last, th' very last of him—a core o' darkness stretched out in a dim church.

3rd Man. It was a noble an' a mighty death.

Inspector [*from where he is near the tree.*] It wasn't a very noble thing to die for a single shilling.

Sheila. Maybe he saw the shilling in th' shape of a new world.

[*The 2nd and 3rd Men go out by the gateway and mingle with the rest gathered there. The Inspector comes closer to Sheila.*

Inspector. Oughtn't you to go from this gloom, Sheila? Believe me, I did my best. I thought the charge would send them flying, but they wouldn't budge; wouldn't budge, till the soldiers fired, and he was hit. Believe me, I did my best. I tried to force my horse between them and him.

Sheila [*calmly*].   I believe you, Inspector Finglas.

Inspector [*gently catching her by the arm*].   Tom to you, dear. Come, Sheila, come, and let us put these things away from us as we saunter slowly home.

Sheila [*with a quiver in her voice*].   Oh, not now; oh, not tonight! Go your own way, and let me go mine, alone tonight.

Inspector [*taking her hand in his*].   Sheila, Sheila, be sparing in your thought for death, and let life smile before you. Be sparing in thought of death on one who spent his life too rashly and lost it all too soon. Ill-gotten wealth of life, ill-gone for ever!

Sheila [*withdrawing her hand from his gently*].   Oh, Tom, I hope you're right; you are right, you must be right.

> [*They have walked to the gateway, and now stand there together, the men and women along the hedge eyeing them, though pretending to take no notice.*

Inspector.   You'll see it clearer, dear, when busy Time in space has set another scene of summer's glory, and new-born spring's loud voice of hope hushes to silence th' intolerant dead.

Sheila [*musingly*].   He said that roses red were never meant for me; before I left him last, that's what he said. Dear loneliness tonight must help me think it out, for that's just what he said. [*Suddenly—with violence*] Oh, you dusky-minded killer of more worthy men!

> [*She runs violently away from him, and goes out, leaving him with the men and women, who stand idly by as if noticing nothing.*

Inspector [*after a pause*].   What are ye doing here? Get home! Home with you, you lean rats, to your holes and haunts! D'ye think th' like o' you alone are decked with th' dark honour of trouble? [*Men and women scatter, slowly and sullenly, till only Brennan, with his melodeon on his back, is left, leaning by the gate. To Brennan*] Heard what I said? Are you deaf, or what?

Brennan [*calmly*].   I'm a Protestant, an' a worshipper in this church.

Inspector.   One of the elect! So was Breydon. Well, keep clear of unruly crowds—my men don't wait to ask the way you worship when they raise their arms to strike.

> [*He goes slowly away down the path. A few moments pass, then the Rector and Mrs. Breydon come out of the church. He arranges a shawl round her shoulders.*

Rector.   There; that's better! My wife insists you stay the night with us, so there's no getting out of it.

Mrs. Breydon. She's kind. [*She pauses to look at the rowan tree.*] There's th' three he loved, bare, or dhrenched with blossom. Like himself, for fine things grew thick in his nature: an' lather come the berries, th' red berries, like the blood that flowed today out of his white body. [*Suddenly—turning to face the church.*] Is it puttin' out th' lights he is?

Rector. Yes, before he goes home for the night.

Mrs. Breydon. Isn't it a sad thing for him to be lyin' lonesome in th' cheerless darkness of th' livelong night!

Rector [*going to the porch and calling out*]. Sam, leave the lights on tonight. [*The church, which had dimmed, lights up again.*]

Rector. He's not so lonesome as you think, dear friend, but alive and laughing in the midst of God's gay welcome. Come.

> [*They slowly go through the gate and pass out. The verger comes from the church and swings the outer door to, to lock up for the night. Brennan comes down into the grounds.*

Samuel [*grumbling.*] Light on all night—more of his Romanisin' manœuvres.

Brennan. Eh, eh, there; houl' on a second!

Samuel. What th' hell do you want?

Brennan. Just to sing a little song he liked as a sign of respect an' affection; an' as a finisher-off to a last farewell.

Samuel [*locking the door*]. An what d'ye take me for? You an' your song an' your last farewell!

Brennan [*giving him a coin.*] For a bare few minutes, an' leave th' door open so's th' sound'll have a fair chance to go in to him. [*The verger opens the door.*] That's it. You're a kind man, really. [*Brennan stands facing into the porch, the verger leaning against the side of it. Brennan unslings his melodeon, plays a few preliminary notes on it, and then sings softly:*
> A sober black shawl hides her body entirely,
> Touch'd be th' sun an' th' salt spray of th' sea;
> But down in th' darkness a slim hand, so lovely,
> Carries a rich bunch of red roses for me!
> [*The rest of the song is cut off by the ending of the play.*

CURTAIN

COCK-A-DOODLE DANDY
(1949)

TO

JAMES STEPHENS

the jesting poet
with a radiant star
in's coxcomb

✿ ✿ ✿

CHARACTERS IN THE PLAY

THE COCK

MICHAEL MARTHRAUN, *a small farmer, now the owner of a lucrative bog*

SAILOR MAHAN, *once a sailor, now the owner of a fleet of lorries carrying turf from bog to town*

LORNA, *second young wife of Marthraun*

LORELEEN, *Marthraun's daughter by his first young wife*

MARION, *helper in Lorna's house*

SHANAAR, *a "very wise old crawthumper", really a dangerous old cod*

1ST ROUGH FELLOW ⎱ *peasants working on the bog*
2ND ROUGH FELLOW ⎰

FATHER DOMINEER, *the parish priest of Nyadnanave*

THE SERGEANT, *of the Civic Guard*

JACK, *Mahan's foreman lorry driver*

JULIA, *Lorna's sister, a paralytic on a visit to Lourdes*

HER FATHER

ONE-EYED LARRY, *a peasant lad and potential sacristan*

A MAYOR

A MACE-BEARER

THE MESSENGER, *in love with Marion*

THE BELLMAN, *a kind of town crier*

A PORTER, *of a general store in the near-by town*

SCENE

SCENE I · The front garden outside Michael Marthraun's house, in Nyadnanave. Morning.

SCENE II · The same. Midday.

SCENE III · The same. Dusk.

SCENE I

Part of the garden outside the house of Michael Marthraun. It is rough and uncared-for, with tough grass everywhere, sprinkled with buttercups and daisies. It is surrounded by a stone wall, three to four feet high, which is pierced by a wooden gate to the right of any visitor entering the garden. To the left, a little way from the gate, a clump of sunflowers, in full bloom, stand stiff and stately, their blossoms big as shields, the petals raying out widely and sharply, like rays from an angry sun. Glancing farther to the left, a visitor would see the gable-end of the house, with a porch jutting from it, and a window above the porch. The porch is supported by twisted pillars of wood, looking like snakes, which are connected with lattice-work shaped like noughts and crosses. These are painted a dazzling white. The framework of the window above is a little on the skew, and the sash-work holding the glass is twisted into irregular lines. A little way from the porch, towards the wall, is a dignified-looking bronze urn holding a stand-offish, cynical-looking evergreen. Farther up, near the wall, the Irish Tricolour flutters from a flagpole. The house itself is black in colour, the sash and frame of the window in it is a brilliant red.

It is a brilliantly fine day in summer, and as there is nothing in the garden to provide a shade, the place is a deep pool of heat, which, seemingly, has lasted for some time, for the grass has turned to a deep yellow hue, save where the house and porch throw a rich black shadow. Stretching away in the distance, beyond the wall, is a bog of a rich purple colour, dabbed here and there with black patches. The sky above it is a silvery grey, glittering like an oriental canopy.

Some little distance away, an accordion is heard playing a dance tune, and, a few moments after, the Cock comes dancing in around the gable of the house, circles the dignified urn, and disappears round the farther end of the gable-end as the music ceases.

He is of a deep black plumage, fitted to his agile and slender body like a glove on a lady's hand; yellow feet and ankles, bright-green flaps like wings, and a stiff cloak falling like a tail behind him. A big crimson crest flowers over his head, and crimson flaps hang from his jaws. His face has the look of a cynical jester.

Michael Marthraun, followed by Sailor Mahan, comes into the garden by the porch. Each carries a kitchen chair, which they set down some way from the house. Michael is a man who is well over sixty years of age, clean-shaven, lean, and grim-looking. His lips twitch nervously whenever he forgets to keep his mouth tightly closed. He is dressed in a blackish tweed suit, and his legs are encased in black leggings. A heavy gold chain stretches across his waistcoat, and he wears a wide-leafed collar, under which a prim black bow is tied.

Sailor Mahan is a little over fifty, stouter than his companion, and of a more serene countenance. He has a short, pointed beard, just beginning to show signs of greyness. His face is of a ruddier hue, and shows that the wind and the stress of many storms have made it rugged, but in no way unpleasant. There is, maybe, a touch of the sea-breeze in his way of talking and his way of walking. He is wearing light-grey flannel trousers, a double-breasted royal blue coat, and has a white scarf round his neck, over a light-blue shirt. They come to the two chairs, and stand there facing each other.

Michael. Come out here, come on out here, where a body can talk free. There's whispers an' whispers in that house, upsettin' a man's mind.

Mahan [puzzled]. Whispers? What kinda whispers?

Michael. Sthrange kinds; whispers good for neither soul nor body.

Mahan. But there's no-one in the house but your wife, Lorna, Marion the maid, and your own girl Loreleen?

Michael. Ay, so you think; but I know different.

Mahan [breezily]. Nonsense, Mick; you're haulin' on a rope that isn't there!

Michael [raising his voice]. You don't live in th' house, do you? [*Mahan is silent.*] You don't live in th' house, do you?

Mahan [raising his voice too.] I know I don't live in it, an' if it's like what you say, I don't want to live in it!

Michael. Well, then, keep quiet when a man speaks of what he knows.

Mahan. I know as much about a whisper as you do.

Michael. You know about th' whispers of wind an' wave, harmless an' innocent things; but I'm talkin' about whispers ebbin' an' flowin' about th' house, with an edge of evil on them, since that painted one, that godless an' laughin' little bitch left London to come here for a long an' leering holiday.

Mahan. Loreleen? Why, man, she's your own daughter by your first young wife!

Michael. So it was said at th' time, an' so it's believed still; but I had me doubts then, and I've more doubts now. I dhread meetin' her, dhread it, dhread it. [*With a frightened laugh*] Michael Marthraun's daughter! [*Gripping Mahan's arm*] Is she anyone's daughter, man?

Mahan [impatiently]. She must be somebody's daughter, man!

Michael [impatiently.] Why must she be, man? Remember what th' Missioner said last night: Sthrange things are foisted by the powers of evil into th' life o' man. Since that one come back from England, where evil things abound, there's sinisther signs appearin' everywhere, evil evocations floatin' through every room.

Mahan [*puzzled*].　What kinda evocation an' significality is there?

Michael [*looking suspiciously at the porch, then at the window above it, and drawing Mahan farther away from the house*].　Looka, Sailor Mahan [*he speaks furtively*], there's always a stern commotion among th' holy objects of th' house, when that one, Loreleen, goes sailin' by; an invisible wind blows th' pictures out, an' turns their frenzied faces to th' wall; once I seen the statue of St. Crankarius standin' on his head to circumvent th' lurin' quality of her presence; an' another time, I seen th' image of our own St. Pathrick makin' a skelp at her with his crozier; fallin' flat on his face, stunned, when he missed!

Mahan [*doubtful, but a little impressed*].　Good God, them's serious things, Michael Marthraun! [*A pause.*] Are you sure, now, Mick, you're not deludin' yourself?

Michael.　Have sense, man! An' me own wife, Lorna Marthraun, is mixin' herself with th' disordher, fondlin' herself with all sorts o' dismayin' decorations. Th' other day, I caught her gapin' into a lookin'-glass, an' when I looked meself, I seen gay-coloured horns branchin' from her head!

Mahan.　No! Oh, Mick, you're fancyin' things. Lorna's a fine, upstandin' woman, an' should be respected.

Michael.　Are you gone on her, too? I tell you, I seen the way th' eyes of young men stare at her face, an' follow th' movements of her lurin' legs— there's evil in that woman!

Mahan.　But there's nothin' evil in a pretty face, or in a pair of lurin' legs.

Michael.　Oh, man, your religion should tell you th' biggest fight th' holy saints ever had was with temptations from good-lookin' women.

Mahan [*getting nervous, and eager to change the subject*].　Looka, let's sit down, an' thry to settle about what you're willin' to pay for th' cartage of th' turf.

Michael [*ignoring Mahan's attempt to change the tide of talk*].　Up there in that room [*he points to the window above the porch*] she often dances be herself, but dancin' in her mind with hefty lads, plum'd with youth, an' spurred with looser thoughts of love. [*As he speaks, the sounds of a gentle waltz are heard, played by harp, lute, or violin, or by all three, the sounds coming, apparently, from the room whose window is above the porch. Bitterly*] There, d'ye hear that, man! Mockin' me. She'll hurt her soul, if she isn't careful.

Mahan.　She's young enough yet to nourish th' need o' dancin'. An' anyway, why did you insist on marryin' her, an' she so young; an' she so gay? She was all again' it herself.

Michael. She consented to it, at last, didn't she?

Mahan. Ay, when you, her father, an' th' priest had badgered th' girl's mind into disordered attention over th' catch she was gettin'.

Michael. Oh, well you know, Sailor Mahan, that she had her blue eye on th' fat little farm undher me feet; th' taut roof over me head; an' th' kind cushion I had in th' bank, against a hard day.

Mahan. I seen you meself throtting afther her from starboard to port, from poop to quarther-deck, hoistin' before her th' fancy of ribbon an' lace, silver-buckled shoes, an' a silk dhress for Sunday.

Michael. An' what had she but a patched petticoat, a worn look, an' broken brogues to wear to Mass on Sundays? An' didn't I give her oul' fella fifty solid pounds so that her ailin' sisther could thravel to Lourdes to get undher th' aegis of th' Blessed Virgin? An' what did I get for them but a scraggy oul' bog of two hundhred acres?

Mahan. An' you're makin' a good thing out of it since turf came into its own. It's made you a Councillor, a Justice of th' Peace, an' th' fair-haired boy of th' clergy.

Michael. As you mentioned turf, we'd betther settle this question of you demandin', for carting it, an exthra amount I couldn't possibly pay.

Mahan [*stiffness coming into his voice*]. You'll have to, Michael Marthraun, for it can't be done now for a cent less.

Michael. We'll have a drink while we're discussin'. I have a bottle of th' best, ten years maturin', inside. Sit down there till I get it. [*He goes into the porch and, after a few moments, comes quickly out again, his mouth twitching, his voice toned to fear and hate.*] That one, Loreleen's comin' down th' stairs, an' I don't want to come too near her. We'll wait till she goes. Let's talk of our affairs, quietly, while she passes by. Th' thing to do, as Shanaar would tell you, when you hear a sound or see a shape of anything evil, is to take no notice of it. [*Whispering impatiently*] Sit down, man!

Mahan [*sitting down—dubiously*]. Are you sure, Mick, you have a close-hauled comprehension of th' way you're thinkin'?

Michael. Ay, am I sure; as sure as I am that a cock crows!

[*A cock suddenly crows lustily as Loreleen appears in the doorway of the porch. She is a very attractive young woman with an air of her own. A jaunty air it is, indicating that it is the sign of a handsome, gay, and intelligent woman. She is dressed in a darkish green* dress, with dark-red flashes on bodice and side of skirt. A saucy hat of a brighter green than the dress sports a scarlet ornament, its shape suggestive of a cock's crimson crest. Her legs—very charming ones— are clad in brown silk stockings; brown that flashes a golden sheen.

[*Michael, who has sat down, jumps startled to his feet at the sudden sound of the cock's crow and, stretching over the table, grips Mahan by the shoulder.*

Michael. What's that, what's that?

Mahan [*startled by Michael's frightened movement*]. What's what, man?

Michael [*trying to recover himself*]. Nothin', I heard nothin'. What was it you were sayin'? [*In a whisper*] Get goin' on th' turf, man.

Mahan [*mystified, but doing his best*]. You'll have to grant th' two shil- lin's additional on each load, Mick. I'd work me lorries at a loss if I took less. [*Placing an affectionate hand on Michael's shoulder*] An' you know well, you're such an oul' an' valued friend, I'd do it for affection's sake, if I only could.

Michael [*forgetting about Loreleen*]. Don't I know that well, Sailor Mahan; an' I'd do th' same, an' more, be you; but if I surrendhered two shillin's, I might as well give you th' bog as well. I have to live, Sailor Mahan.

Mahan. Damn it, man, haven't I to live too? How th' hell am I goin' to give th' men a shillin' more without th' exthra two shillin's from you? Pray to th' saints to let them fall like rain from heaven, eh?

Michael [*putting his face closer to Mahan's, hotly*]. Looka here, Sailor Mahan, you're not goin' to magicfy me into th' dhream of believin' you're not addin', every hurryin' week, a fine bundle o' notes to th' jubilant store you've there already, forcing overtime on th' poor men o' th' bank, flickin' th' notes into imperial ordher.

Mahan [*as fiercely—standing up to say it, his face close to the face of Michael*]. An' you yourself, Michael Marthraun, aren't worn away with th' punishment of poverty! Puttin' on a poor mouth, an' if you set out to count graciously all you have in hidlins, you'd be workin' many a long, glad day, without supper or sleep, be day-light an' candle-light, till your mind centhred on th' sum dominated be th' last note flutherin' from your fingers!

Loreleen [*who has strolled slowly over to the gate, listening to the talk the while, turning at the gate to watch as well as listen*]. Lay not up for yourselves treasures upon earth, where moth and rust doth corrupt, and where thieves break through and steal!

Michael [*in a frightened whisper*]. Don't turn your head; take no notice. Don't pretend to hear her lyin' hallucinations!

[*A young, rough-looking Fellow, well-set and strong, comes running along the pathway to the gate. He is wearing dark-brown corduroy trousers, belted at waist, grey shirt, and scarf of bright green, with yellow dots. He pushes Loreleen aside.*

1st Rough Fellow [*pushing Loreleen out of his way*]. Outa me way, woman! [*He sees how charming she is as he swings her aside.*] Be God, but you're th' good-lookin' lass! What are you doin' in this hole?

Loreleen. Seeking happiness, an' failing to find it.

1st Rough Fellow. It isn't here you should be, lost among th' rough stones, th' twisty grass, an' th' moody misery of th' brown bog; but it's lyin' laughin' you should be where th' palms are tall, and wherever a foot is planted, a scarlet flower is crushed; where there's levity living its life, an' not loneliness dyin' as it is here.

Loreleen [*dropping him a deep curtsy*]. Thank you, sir knight, for th' silken compliments to your handmaiden.

[*She turns to go out, and the Rough Fellow hurries in through the gate, down to the two men.*

1st Rough Fellow [*going through the gate down to where the two men are, and turning to speak up to Loreleen, still standing at the gate*]. If you wait till I'm done with these fellas [*he indicates Michael and Mahan*] I could go to th' bend o' th' road with you, for it's meself would surrendher a long spell of heaven's ease to go a long day's journey with a lass like you!

[*Another Rough Fellow hurries in along the pathway outside to the gate, pulling Loreleen aside when he finds her in his way. He wears light-brown corduroy trousers, check shirt, and has a scarf of light yellow, with green stripes, round his neck.*

2nd Rough Fellow [*pulling Loreleen out of his way*]. Eh, there, woman —outa me way! [*He sees, as she swings around, how charming she is.*] Arra, what winsome wind blew such a flower into this dread, dhried-up desert? Deirdre come to life again, not to sorrow, but to dance! If Eve was as you are, no wondher Adam fell, for a lass like you could shutther th' world away with a kiss!

[*He goes through the gate, and down to the other men, pausing to look up at Loreleen again.*

2nd Rough Fellow [*to Loreleen*]. Wait, lass, till I'm done with these fellas, an' I'll go with you till youth's a shadow a long way left behind!

Loreleen [*down to the two Rough Fellows*]. I'm not for you, friends, for I'm not good for decent men. The two old cronies will tell you a kiss from me must be taken undher a canopy of dangerous darkness. [*She kisses a hand to them.*] Goodbye!   [*She goes out.*

Michael ⎫ [*together*]. What d'ye th' two of yous want here?
Mahan ⎭   Why aren't yous at work?

1st Rough Fellow [*laying a hand sternly on the shoulder of Mahan*]. Looka, you; you give us th' exthra shillin', or we leave your lorries standin', helpless an' naked on th' roads!

2nd Rough Fellow [*laying a hand sternly on Michael's shoulder*]. Looka, you; looka that! [*He throws a cheque contemptuously on to the table.*] D'ye think a good week's wages is in a cheque for tuppence?

Michael. You didn't work a week, because of th' rain, an' canteen contribution an' insurance brought your wage for the week to tuppence.

2nd Rough Fellow. Tell me how I'm goin' to live a week on tuppence?

1st Rough Fellow. Seein' th' both of them's Knights o' Columbanus, they should be able to say.

Michael. That's a social question to be solved by th' Rerum Novarum.

2nd Rough Fellow. Fifty years old; not worth much when it was born, an' not worth a damn now. You give a guaranteed week, or th' men come off your bog!   [*He goes off towards the gate.*

1st Rough Fellow [*going to the gate—to Mahan*]. Take our demand serious, or your lorries stand still on th' highways!

2nd Rough Fellow [*impatiently*]. Looka, there she is! [*He points a finger in front.*] Let's hurry, an' we'll ketch up on th' fine, fair lady.
             [*They hurry along the path, but suddenly stop to stare ahead.*

1st Rough Fellow [*with awe in his voice.*] What's happenin' to her? A cloud closin' in on her, flashes like lightning whirlin' round her head, an' her whole figure ripplin'!

2nd Rough Fellow [*frightened*]. Jasus, she's changin' into th' look of a fancy-bred fowl! It's turnin' to face us; it's openin' its bake as big as a bayonet!   [*The crow of a cock is heard in the distance.*

1st Rough Fellow [*frightened*]. Here, man, th' other way for us! It's an omen, a warnin', a reminder of what th' Missioner said last night that young men should think of good-lookin' things in skirts only in th' presence of, an' undher th' guidance of, old and pious people.
             [*The two of them hurry away in the opposite direction.*

🌳

Michael [*to Mahan*]. Did you hear that? I'm askin' you, Sailor Mahan, did you hear what them two graspin' rascals said?

Mahan. I heard, but I can see no significality in it, unless th' two of them had dhrink taken.

Michael [*warningly*]. Looka, Sailor Mahan, if you aren't careful, your wilful disbelief in things'll lead you asthray! Loreleen isn't me daughter; she isn't even a woman: she's either undher a spell, or she's a possessed person.

Mahan [*with contempt*]. Aw, for God's sake, Mick, have sense, an' get that bottle o' whiskey out to put a spell on us.

Michael [*almost shouting*]. Have you forgotten already th' case of th' Widow Malone who could turn, twinklin', into a dog or a hare, when she wanted to hide herself? An' how, one day, th' dogs followed what they thought was a hare that made for th' widow's cottage, an' dived through an open window, one o' th' dogs snappin' a leg off before it could get through. An' when th' door was burst open, there was th' oul' witch-widow screamin' on her oul' bed, one leg gone, with blood spoutin' from th' stump, so that all th' people heard her last screechin' as she went sliddherin' down to hell!

Mahan. I heard tell of it months after, when I come back from Valparaiso.

Michael. Well, if you heard of it, you know it must have happened. An' here you are, thinkin' only of whiskey, and showin' how ready you are to ruin me be askin' more than I'm able to give. You, a good Christian, a Knight of St. Columbanus, a student in th' Circle studyin' th' Rerum Novarum, you should show a sign of charity an' justice, recognisin' th' needs of th' people rather than your own. [*Suddenly*] Here, I'll add thruppence, an' make th' offer ninepence. Hold out th' hand, an' clinch th' bargain.

Mahan. I'll be scuppered if I will! You'll not use me like th' oul' father of th' good woman within, who sold you th' bog when he thought it was derelict, though you're makin' thousands out of it now.

Michael. You forget I gave th' oul' cod enough to bring his other daughter to Lourdes for a cure!

Mahan. You know th' way th' men are actin' now—goin' slow, an' doin' two journeys where they used to do three.

Michael. An' aren't my men threatenin' to come off th' bog altogether? It's this materialism's doin' it—edgin' into revolt against Christian conduct. If they'd only judge o' things in th' proper Christian way, as we do, there'd be no disputes. Now let's be good sons of Columbanus—you thinkin' of my difficulties, an' me thinkin' of yours.

Mahan.   Make your offer one an' sixpence, an' I'll hoist th' pennant of agreement?

Michael.   I couldn't. Looka, Sailor Mahan, it would ruin me.

Mahan [*viciously*].   You'd rather throw th' money after a tall-hat so that you could controvert yourself into a dapper disturbance th' time the president comes to view th' workin' of th' turf. Talk about Loreleen castin' a spell! Th' whole disthrict'll be paralysed in a spell when your top-hat comes out to meet the president's top-hat, th' two poor things tryin' to keep people from noticin' what's undher them! Two shillin's, now, or nothin'.   [*He sits down in disgust.*

> [*Behind the wall, Shanaar is seen coming along the road; he opens the gate, and comes slowly down to where the two men are. He is a very, very old man, wrinkled like a walnut, bent at the shoulders, with longish white hair, and a white beard—a bit dirty—reaching to his belly. He is dressed peasant-wise, thin, threadbare frieze coat, patched blackish corduroy trousers, thick boots, good and strong, a vivid blue muffler round his neck, and a sackcloth waistcoat, on which hangs a brass cross, suspended round his neck by twine. A round, wide-brimmed, black hat is on his head.*

Shanaar [*lifting his hat as he comes in by the gate*].   God save all here! God save all that may be in th' house, barrin' th' cat an' th' dog!

Michael [*with great respect*].   An' you, too, Shanaar, old, old man, full of wisdom an' th' knowledge of deeper things.

Shanaar.   Old is it? Ever so old, thousands of years, thousands of years if all were told.

Michael.   Me an' Sailor Mahan here were talkin' some time ago, about th' sthrange dodges of unseen powers, an' of what the Missioner said about them last night, but th' easiness of his mind hasn't been hindhered.

Shanaar bending lower, and shoving his bearded face between the two men].   If it doesn't hindher th' easiness of his mind now, it will one day! Maybe this very day in this very place.

Michael [*to Mahan*].   What d'ye say to that, now?

Mahan [*trying to be firm, but a little uneasy*.   Nothin', nothin'.

Shanaar [*shoving his face closer to Mahan's*].   Ah, me friend, for years an' years I've thravelled over hollow lands an' hilly lands, an' I know. Big powers of evil, with their little powers, an' them with their littler ones, an' them with their littlest ones, are everywhere. You might meet a bee that wasn't a bee; a bird that wasn't a bird; or a beautiful woman who wasn't a woman at all.

Michael [*excitedly*].   I'm tellin' him that, I'm tellin' him that all along!

Mahan [*a little doubtfully—to Shanaar*].   An' how's a poor body to know them?

Shanaar [*looking round cautiously, then speaking in a tense whisper*].   A sure sign, if only you can get an all-round glimpse of them. [*He looks round him again.*] Daemones posteriora non habent—they have no behinds!

Michael [*frightened a lot*].   My God, what an awe-inspiring, expiring experience!

Mahan [*frightened too, but trying to appear brave*].   That may be, but I wouldn't put innocent birds or bees in that category.

Shanaar [*full of pitying scorn for ignorance*].   You wouldn't! Innocent birds! Listen all: There was a cuckoo once that led a holy brother to damnation. Th' cuckoo's call enticed the' brother to a silent glade where th' poor man saw a lovely woman, near naked, bathin' her legs in a pool, an' in an instant th' holy man was taken with desire. Lost! She told him he was handsome, but he must have money if he wanted to get her. Th' brother entered a noble's house, an' demanded a hundhred crowns for his convent; but the noble was a wise old bird, an' said he'd have to see the prior first. Thereupon, th' brother up with an axe, hidden undher his gown, an' cleft th' noble from skull to chin; robbed th' noble, dhressed himself in rare velvets, an' searched out all th' rosy rottenness of sin with th' damsel till th' money was gone. Then they caught him. Then they hanged him, an', mind you [*the three heads come closer together*], while this poor brother sobbed on the scaffold, everyone heard th' mocking laughter of a girl and th' calling of a cuckoo!

> [*As Shanaar is speaking the three last things, the mocking laughter of a girl is heard, the call of a cuckoo, and a young man's sobbing, one after the other, at first, then they blend together for a few moments, and cease. Shanaar stands as stiff as his bent back will allow, and the other two rise slowly from their chairs, stiff, too, and frightened.*

Shanaar [*in a tense whisper*].   Say nothing; take no notice. Sit down. Thry to continue as if yous hadn't heard!

Mahan [*after a pause*].   Ay, a cuckoo, maybe; but that's a foreign bird: no set harbour or home. No genuine decent Irish bird would do a thing like that on a man.

Michael. Looka here, Sailor Mahan, when th' powers of evil get goin, I wouldn't put anything past an ordinary hen!

Shanaar. An' you'd be right, Mr. Marthraun, though, as a rule, hens is always undher th' eye an' comprehension of a Christian. Innocent-looking things are often th' most dangerous. Looka th' lad whose mother had set her heart on him bein' a priest, an' one day, at home, he suddenly saw a corncrake flyin' into a house be an open window. Climbin' in afther it, he spied a glittherin' brooch on a table, an' couldn't resist th' temptation o' thievin' it. That lad spent th' next ten years in a reformatory; his mother died of a broken heart, and his father took to dhrink.

[*During the recital of Shanaar's story, the "crek crek, crek crek" of a corncrake is heard.*

Michael [*in a tense whisper—to Mahan*]. D'ye hear that, Sailor Mahan?

Shanaar [*warningly*]. Hush! Take no vocal notice. When yous hear anything or see anything suspicious, give it no notice, unless you know how to deal with it.

Michael [*solemnly*]. A warnin' we'll remember. But supposin' a hen goes wrong, what are we to do?

Shanaar [*thoughtfully*]. It isn't aysey to say, an' you have to go cautious. The one thing to do, if yous have the knowledge, is to parley with th' hens in a Latin dissertation. If among th' fowl there's an illusion of a hen from Gehenna, it won't endure th' Latin. She can't face th' Latin. Th' Latin downs her. She tangles herself in a helluva disordher. She busts asundher, an' disappears in a quick column of black an' blue smoke, a thrue ear ketchin' a screech of agony from its centre!

Michael [*tremendously impressed*]. Looka that now. See what it is to know! [*A commotion is heard within the house: a loud cackling, mingled with a short, sharpened crow of a cock; the breaking of delf; the half-angry, half-frightened cries of women. A cup, followed by a saucer, flies out through the open window, over the porch, past the heads of the three men, who duck violently, and then crouch, amazed, and a little frightened.*] What th' hell's happenin' now?

[*Marion rushes to the door of the porch, frightened and alarmed. She is a young girl of twenty or so, and very good-looking. Her skirts come just to her knees, for they are nice legs, and she likes to show them—and why shouldn't she? And when she does so, she can add the spice of a saucy look to her bright blue eyes. Instead of the usual maid's cap, she wears a scarf-bandeau round her head, ornamented with silver strips, joined in the centre above her forehead, with an enamelled stone, each strip extending along the bandeau as* far as either ear. *She wears a dark-green uniform, flashed with a brighter green on the sleeves and neck, and the buttons of the bodice are of the same colour. Her stockings and shoes are black. A small, neat, white apron, piped with green, protects her uniform.*

Marion [*excitedly—to the men*].   It's flyin' about th' house, an' behavin' outrageous! I guessed that that Loreleen's cluck, cluck, cluckin' would upset th' bird's respectable way of livin'!

Michael [*frightened*].   What's wrong with you, girl; what's up?

Marion.   Will one of yous come in, an' ketch it, for God's sake, before it ruins th' house?

Mahan [*shouting*].   Ketch what, ketch what, woman?

Marion.   A wild goose! It's sent th' althar light flyin'; it's clawed the holy pictures; an' now it's peckin' at th' tall-hat!

Michael.   A wild goose? Are you sure it was a wild one?

Marion [*in great distress*].   I dunno, I dunno—maybe it's a wild duck. It's some flyin' thing tearin' th' house asundher.

Michael [*trembling—to Shanaar*].   D'ye think it might be what you know?

Shanaar [*his knees shaking a little*].   It might be, Mr. Marthraun! It might be, God help us!

Mahan [*nervous himself*].   Keep your heads, keep your heads! It's nothin'.

Michael [*beside himself with anxiety and dread—shaking Marion roughly by the shoulders*].   Conthrol yourself, girl, an' speak sensibly. Is it a goose or a duck or a hen, or what is it?

Marion [*wildly*].   It's a goose—no, it's a hen, it must be a hen! We thried to dhrive it out with flyin' cups and flyin' saucers, but it didn't notice them. Oh, someone should go in, or it'll peck th' place to pieces!

Shanaar [*prayerfully*].   So long as it's not transmuted, so long as it's not been transmuted!

Michael [*shaking Marion again*].   Where's Lorna, where's Lorna?

Marion [*responding to the shaking listlessly*].   Last I seen of her, she was barricadin' herself undher th' banisters!

Michael [*pleadingly—to Mahan*].   You've been free with whales an' dolphins an' octopususas, Sailor Mahan—you run in, like a good man, an' enthrone yourself on top of th' thing!

Mahan [*indignant*].   Is it me? I'm not goin' to squandher meself conthrollin' live land-fowl!

Michael [*to Shanaar—half-commandingly*].   In case it's what we're afraid of, you pop in, Shanaar, an' liquidate whatever it is with your Latin.

Shanaar [*backing towards the wall*].   No good in th' house: it's effective only in th' open air.

Michael [*in a fury—to Marion—pushing her violently towards the gate*].   You go, you gapin', frightened fool, an' bring Father Domineer quick!

> [*All this time, intermittent cackling has been heard, cackling with a note of satisfaction, or even victory in it, interspersed with the whirring sound of wings.*

> [*As Marion rushes out through the gate, she runs into the arms of the Messenger, who carries a telegram in his hand. He clasps Marion tight in his arms, and kisses her. He wears a silvery-grey coat, buttoned over his breast, and trousers. On the right side of the coat is a flash of a pair of scarlet wings. A bright-green beret is set jauntily on his head and he is wearing green-coloured sandals.*

> [*Michael and Mahan have moved farther from the house, and Shanaar has edged to the gateway, where he stares at the house, ready to run if anything happens. His hands are piously folded in front of him, and his lips move as if he prayed.*

Messenger [*to Marion*].   Ah, lovely one of grace an' gladness, whose kiss is like a honied flame, where are you rushin' to in such a hurry?

Michael [*angrily—up to the Messenger*].   Let her go, you—she's runnin' for th' priest!

Messenger.   Th' priest—why?

> [*The cackling breaks into intensity, the whirring of wings becomes louder, and a plate flies out through the window, followed by a squeal from Lorna.*

Messenger [*astonished, but not startled*].   What's goin' on in th' house?

Michael.   There's a wild goose, or somethin', asthray in th' house, an' it's sent th' althar bowl flyin'!

Marion.   An' it's peckin' th' holy pictures hangin' on th' walls.

Mahan.   Some think it's a wild duck.

Shanaar.   It may be a hen, only a hen.

Messenger [*releasing Marion, and handing the telegram to Michael*].   Here's a telegram for you. [*Michael takes it mechanically, and stuffs it in a pocket.*] Is it losin' your senses yous are to be afraid of a hen? [*He goes towards the porch.*] I'll soon settle it!

Shanaar [*who is now outside, behind the wall*].   If you value your mortal life, lad, don't go in, for th' hen in there isn't a hen at all!

Messenger. If th' hen, that isn't a hen, in there, isn't a hen, then it must be a cock. I'll settle it! [*He rushes into the house.*

Michael [*in agony*]. If it's a cock, we're done!

Shanaar [*fervently*]. Oh, rowelum randee, horrida aidus, sed spero spiro specialii spam!

> [*The head of the Cock, with its huge, handsome crimson comb, is suddenly thrust through the window above the porch, and lets out a violent and triumphant crow. Shanaar disappears behind the wall, and Mahan and Michael fall flat in the garden, as if in a dead faint.*

Michael [*as he is falling*]. Holy saints preserve us—it's th' Cock!

Shanaar [*from behind the wall*]. Oh, dana eirebus, heniba et galli scatterum in multus parvum avic ashorum!

> [*The Cock's head is as suddenly withdrawn, and a louder commotion is heard to be going on in the house; the Messenger shouting, a Woman's squeal. Then silence for a few moments as puffs of blue-black smoke jet out through the window. When the smoke has gone, the Messenger comes from the house into the garden. His cap is awry on his head, his face is a little flushed, and his mouth is smiling. He carries in his right hand what might have been a broomstick, but is now a silver staff, topped with a rosette of green and red ribbons. He is followed out by the Cock whom he is leading by a green ribbon, the other end circling the Cock's neck. The Cock follows the Messenger meekly, stopping when he stops, and moving when the Messenger moves.*

Shanaar [*peeping over the wall*]. Boys an' girls, take no notice of it, or you're done! Talk only of th' first thing entherin' your minds.

Messenger [*looking with astonishment at the two men sitting up now on the ground, as far as possible from the house, and moving away when the Cock comes nearer*]. What's th' matther with yous? Why are yous dodgin' about on your bums? Get up, get up, an' be sensible.

> [*Michael and Mahan scramble to their feet, hurry out through the gate, and stand, warily, beside Shanaar. Lorna's head appears at the window above the porch, and it is at once evident that she is much younger than her husband, very good-looking still, but the bright and graceful contours of her face are somewhat troubled by a vague aspect of worry and inward timidity. Her face shows signs of excitement, and she speaks rather loudly down to the Messenger.*

Lorna [*to the Messenger*]. Robin Adair, take that bird away at once. Hand him over to th' Civic Guard, or someone fit to take charge of him.

Messenger [*up to Lorna*].   Looka, lovely lady, there's no danger, an' there never was. He was lonely, an' was only goin' about in quest o' company. Instead of shyin' cups an' saucers at him, if only you'd given him your lily-white hand, he'd have led you through a wistful an' wondherful dance. But you frightened th' poor thing!

Lorna.   Frightened him, is it? It was me was frightened when I seen him tossin' down delf, clawin' holy pictures, and peckin' to pieces th' brand new tall-hat that Mr. Marthraun bought to wear, goin' with the Mayor to greet His Brightness, th' President of Eire, comin' to inaugerate th' new canteen for th' turf workers.

Michael [*enraged*].   Is it me new hat he's desthroyed?

Shanaar [*pulling Michael's arm in warning*].   Damnit, man, take no notice!

Michael [*turning indignantly on Shanaar*].   How'd you like your sumptuous, silken hat to be mangled into a monstrosity!

Shanaar [*with concentrated venom*].   Hush, man, hush!

Marion [*who has been looking at the Cock with admiration*].   Sure, he's harmless when you know him.

Messenger [*stroking its back*].   'Course he is! Just a gay bird, that's all. A bit unruly at times, but conthrollable be th' right persons. [*To the Cock*] Go on, comrade, lift up th' head an' clap th' wings, black cock, an' crow!

[*The Cock lifts up his head, claps his wings, and lets out a mighty crow, which is immediately followed by a rumbling roll of thunder.*

Michael [*almost in a state of collapse*].   Aw, we're done for!

Shanaar [*violently*].   No notice, no notice!

Lorna [*from the window*].   God bless us, what's that? [*Down to the Messenger*] Robin, will you take that damned animal away, before things happen that God won't know about!

Messenger [*reassuringly—up to Lorna*].   Lovely lady, you can let your little hands lie with idle quietness in your lap, for there's no harm in him beyond gaiety an' fine feelin'. [*To the Cock*] You know th' goose-step done be the Irish Militia in th' city of Cork more'n a hundhred years ago? Well, we'll go home doin' it, to show there's nothing undher th' sun Ireland didn't know, before th' world sensed it. Ready? One, two—quick march!

[*The Messenger and the Cock march off doing the goose-step. Marion follows them, imitating the step, as far as the end of the garden; then she stands looking after them, waving them farewell. Michael and Mahan come slowly and stealthily into the garden as the Cock goes out. They go to the chairs, on which they sit, exhausted, wiping their foreheads with their handkerchiefs. Shanaar comes towards them more slowly, keeping an eye in the direction taken by the Cock and the Messenger. When the place is clear, he anchors himself behind the table.*

Lorna [*down to Marion*]. Marion, dear, come on in, an' help me to straighten things up a little. [*She goes away from the window.*

Marion [*going slowly towards the house, after having given a last farewell —gleefully*]. Wasn't it a saucy bird! An' th' stately way he done th' goose-step! [*She playfully shakes Michael's shoulder.*] Did you see it, sir? [*Michael takes no notice.*] God forgive me, but it gave us all an hilarious time—didn't it, sir?

Michael [*coldly*]. Your misthress called you.

Marion. I heard her, sir. What a clatther it all made! An' yous all quakin', an' even Sailor Mahan there, shakin' in his shoes, sure it was somethin' sinisther!

Mahan [*angrily*]. You go in to your misthress, girl!

Marion [*giggling*]. Th' bould sailor lad! An' he gettin' rocked in th' cradle of th' deep! Me faltherin' tongue can't impart th' fun I felt at seein' yous all thinkin' th' anchor was bein' weighed for th' next world!

Michael [*loudly*]. Go to your misthress when you're told.

Marion [*giggling more than ever*]. An' oul' dodderin' Shanaar, there, concoctin' his Latin, an' puttin' th' wall between himself an' th' blast! Well, while yous sit all alone there in th' gloamin', yous won't be in heart for singin'. [*She chants*] "Only to see his face again, only to hear him crow!" [*She runs merrily in.*

Shanaar [*warily—in a warning whisper*]. Watch that one!

Michael. Th' ignorant, mockin', saucy face of her afther us bein' in danger of thransportation to where we couldn't know ourselves with agony an' consternation!

Shanaar [*fervently*]. Sweet airs of heaven be round us all! Watch that one, Mr. Marthraun. Women is more flexible towards th' ungodly than us men, an' well th' old saints knew it. I'd recommend you to compel her, for a start, to lift her bodice higher up, an' pull her skirt lower down; for th' circumnambulatory nature of a woman's form often has a detonatin' effect on a man's idle thoughts.

Michael [*pensively*]. How thrue, how thrue that is!

Shanaar. What we have to do now, is to keep thought from dwellin' on th' things seen an' heard this day; for dwellin' on it may bring th' evil back again. So don't let any thought of it, *ab initio extensio*, remain in your minds, though, as a precaution, when I'm passin' th' barracks, I'll acquaint the Civic Guard. Now I must be off, for I've a long way to thravel. [*He goes as far as the gate, and returns.*] Mr. Marthraun, don't forget to have th' room, where th' commotion was manifested, *turbulenta concursio cockolorum,* purified an' surified be an understandin' clergyman. Goodbye. [*Again he goes as far as the gate, and returns.*] Be on your guard against any unfamiliar motion or peculiar conspicuosity or quasimodical addendum, perceivable in any familiar thing or creature common to your general recognisances. A cat barkin' at a dog, or a dog miaouin' be a fire would atthract your attention, give you a shock, but don't, for th' love of God, notice it! It's this scourge of materialism sweepin' th' world, that's incantatin' these evils to our senses and our doorsteps.

Mahan [*pensively*]. That's th' way th' compass is pointin', Shanaar—everyone only thinkin', thinkin' of himself.

Shanaar. An' women's wily exhilarations are abettin' it, so that a man's measure of virtue is now made with money, used to buy ornaments, bestowed on girls to give a gaudy outside to the ugliness of hell.

Michael [*fervently*]. Oh, how thrue, how thrue that is!

Shanaar. An' th' coruscatin' conduct in th' dance-halls is completin' th' ruin.

Mahan [*solemnly*]. Wise words from a wiser man! Afther a night in one of them, there isn't an ounce of energy left in a worker!

Shanaar [*whispering*]. A last warnin'—Don't forget that six thousand six hundhred an' sixty-six evil spirits can find ready lodgin's undher th' skin of a single man!

Michael [*horrified*]. What an appallin' thought!

Shanaar. So be on your guard. Well, goodbye.

Michael [*offering him a note*]. Here's a pound to help you on your way.

Shanaar [*setting the note aside*]. No, thanks. If I took it, I couldn't fuse th' inner with th' outher vision; I'd lose th' power of spiritual scansion. If you've a shillin' for a meal in th' town till I get to the counthry, where I'm always welcome, I'll take it, an' thank you.

[*Michael gives him a shilling.*

Shanaar. Thank you kindly. [*He goes out through the gate, and along the pathway outside. Just as he is about to disappear, he faces towards the two men, and stretches out a hand in a gesture of blessing. Fervently] Ab tormentum sed absolvo, non revolvo, cockalorum credulum hibernica!*

Michael [*with emotion*].   You too, Shanaar, oul' son; you too!

[*Shanaar goes off.*

Mahan [*after a pause—viciously*].   That Latin-lustrous oul' cod of a prayer-blower is a positive danger goin' about th' counthry!

Michael [*startled and offended*].   Eh? I wouldn't go callin' him a cod, Sailor Mahan. A little asthray in a way, now an' again, but no cod. You should be th' last to call th' man a cod, for if it wasn't for his holy Latin aspirations, you mightn't be here now.

Mahan [*with exasperation*].   Aw, th' oul' fool, pipin' a gale into every breeze that blows! I don't believe there was ever anything engenderogically evil in that cock as a cock, or denounceable either! Lardin' a man's mind with his killakee Latin! An' looka th' way he slights th' women. I seen him lookin' at Lorna an' Marion as if they'd horns on their heads!

Michael [*doubtfully*].   Maybe he's too down on th' women, though you have to allow women is temptin'.

Mahan.   They wouldn't tempt man if they didn't damn well know he wanted to be tempted!

Michael.   Yes, yes; but we must suffer th' temptation accordin' to the cognisances of th' canon law. But let's have a dhrink, for I'm near dead with th' drouth, an' we can sensify our discussion about th' increased price you're demandin' for carryin' th' turf; though, honest to God, Sailor Mahan, I can't add a ha'penny more to what I'm givin'.

Mahan.   A dhrink would be welcome, an' we can talk over th' matter, though, honest to God, Michael Marthraun, blast th' penny less I'll take than what I'm askin'.

Michael [*going to the porch, and shouting into the house*].   Marion, bring th' bottle of ten years' maturin', an' two glasses! [*He returns.*] It's th' principle I'm thinkin' of.

Mahan.   That's what's throublin' me, too. [*Marion comes in with the bottle of whiskey and the two glasses. She places them on the table, getting between the two men to do so. Reading the label*] Flanagan's First! Nyav na Nyale—th' heaven of th' clouds! An' brought be a lass who's a Flanagan's first too!

Marion [*in a jovial mood*].   G'long with you—you an' your blarney!

Michael [*enthusiastically*].   Had you lived long ago, Emer would have been jealous of you!   [*He playfully pinches her bottom.*

Marion [*squealing.*]   Ouch! [*She breaks away, and makes for the porch.*] A pair o' naughty men!   [*She goes into the house.*

Michael [*calling after her*].   I forgot th' soda, Marion; bring th' siphon, lass.

Mahan [*complacently*].   I could hold that one in me arms for a long time, Mick.

Michael.   Th' man would want to be dead who couldn't.

Mahan [*enthusiastically*].   I'd welcome her, even if I seen her through th' vision of oul' Shanaar—with horns growin' out of her head!

> [*Marion returns with the siphon which she places on the table. The Two Men, looking in front of them, have silly, sly grins on their faces.*
>
> [*The ornament, which Marion wears round her head, has separated into two parts, each of which has risen over her head, forming two branching horns, apparently sprouting from her forehead. The Two Men, shyly gazing in front, or at the table, do not see the change. Marion's face has changed too, and now seems to wear a mocking, cynical look, fitting the aspect of her face to the horns.*

Marion [*joking*].   Two wild men—it's afraid I am to come near yous.

> [*Michael puts his right arm round her waist, and Mahan his left one.*

Mahan [*slyly*].   What about a kiss on your rosy mouth, darlin', to give a honied tang to th' whiskey?

Michael.   An' one for me, too?

Marion [*with pretended demureness*].   A thrue gentleman'll rise up an' never expect a thrue lady to bend down for a kiss. [*With vigour*] Up an' take it, before yous grow cold!

> [*They rise from their chairs, foolish grins on their faces, settle themselves for a kiss, and then perceive the change that has taken place. They flop back on to the chairs, fright and dismay sweeping over their faces.*

Michael }
Mahan }   *together*].   Good God!

> [*They slump in the chairs, overcome, their hands folded in front of their chests, palm to palm, as if in prayer. Marion looks at them in some astonishment.*

Marion.   What ails yous? Was th' excitement too much for yous, or what?

Michael [*plaintively*].   Saints in heaven help us now!

Marion. What's come over yous? Th' way yous slumped so sudden down, you'd think I'd horns on me, or somethin'!

Michael [*hoarsely*]. G'way, g'way! Shanaar, Shanaar, where are you now!

Marion [*going over to Mahan, and putting an arm round his neck*]. What about you, gay one?

Mahan [*gurgling with fright*]. You're sthranglin' me! G'way, g'way, girl!

Marion. Looka, a kiss would do yous good. Yous think too much of th' world!

Mahan [*chokingly*]. St. Christopher, mainstay of mariners, be with me now!

> [*Lorna thrusts her head out from the window over the porch.*

Lorna [*down to Marion*]. Let them two oul' life-frighteners fend for themselves, an' come in. From th' back window, I can see th' crowd gathered to give Julia a send-off to Lourdes, so come in to tidy if you want to join them with me.

Marion [*half to herself—as she runs into the house*]. God forgive me—I near forgot! Here we are followin' laughter, instead of seekin' succour from prayer!

> [*She runs in, and Lorna takes her head back into the room again.*

Michael [*frightened and very angry*]. Now, maybe, you'll quit your jeerin' at oul' Shanaar! Now, maybe, you'll let your mind concentrate on higher things! Now, maybe, you won't be runnin' loose afther girls!

Mahan [*indignantly*]. Damnit, man, you were as eager for a cuddle as I was!

Michael [*lifting his eyes skywards*]. Oh, d'ye hear that! I was only tolerā́tin' your queer declivity, like a fool. An' afther all th' warnin's given be wise oul' Shanaar! Looka, Sailor Mahan, you'll have to be more on your guard!

Mahan [*trying to defend himself*]. How could any man suspect such a thing? We'll have to think this thing out.

Michael [*with exasperation*]. Think it out! Oh, man, Sailor Mahan, have you nothin' more sensible to say than that we'll have to think it out?

Mahan. Let's have a dhrink, for God's sake, to steady us down!

Michael [*hurriedly putting bottle and glasses under the table*]. What're you thinkin' of, Sailor Mahan? We can't dispense ourselves through a scene of jollification an' poor Julia passin' on her way to Lourdes!

[*Along the path, on a stretcher, carried by the two Rough Fellows, comes Julia, followed by her father. The stretcher is borne to the gate, and there laid down, so that the head of it is flush with the gate-posts, and the rest of it within the garden. The framework of the gate makes a frame for Julia, who is half sitting up, her head supported by a high pillow. Her face is a sad yellowish mask, pierced by wide eyes, surrounded by dark circles. Her father is a sturdy fellow of fifty, a scraggly greyish beard struggling from his chin. He is roughly dressed as a poorer peasant might be, and his clothes are patched in places. He wears a brown muffler, and a faded black trilby-hat is on his head. All the time, he looks straight in front with a passive and stony stare.*

[*Before the stretcher walks the Mayor, rather stout, clean-shaven, wearing a red robe over rough clothing; he has a very wide three-cornered hat, laced with gold, on his head. Behind him walks the Mace-bearer, a big silver and black mace on his shoulder. He is tall, and wears a bright blue robe, trimmed with silver, on his head is a huge cocked hat, laced, too, with silver. These two do not enter the garden, but walk on, and stand waiting near the house, beside the flag-pole, but without the wall.*

[*Lorna, followed by Marion, comes out of the house. Instead of the bright headgear worn before, they have black kerchiefs, worn peasant-wise on their heads—that is, they have been folded triangularly, draped over their heads, with the ends tied beneath their chins.*

[*Lorna runs over to the stretcher, kneels down beside it, and kisses Julia.*

Lorna [*affectionately*]. My sister, my little Julia, oh, how sorry I am that you have to go on this long, sad journey!

Julia [*her voice is low, but there is a hectic note of hope in it*]. A long journey, Lorna darlin', but not a sad one; oh, no, not a sad one. Hope, Lorna, will have me be the hand all the long way. I go to kneel at the feet of the ever Blessed Virgin.

Lorna. Oh, she will comfort you, me darlin'.

Julia. Yes, she will comfort me, Lorna [*after a pause*]; an' cure me too. Lorna, say she will cure me too.

Lorna [*stifling a sob*]. An' cure you, too.

Julia [*to Michael*]. Give me your good wishes, Mr. Marthraun.

Michael [*with genuine emotion*]. Julia, me best wishes go with you, an' me best prayers'll follow all th' long way!

Julia [*to Mahan*]. An' you, Sailor Mahan—have you no good wish for the poor voyager?

Mahan [*fervently*]. Young lass, may you go through healin' wathers, an' come back a clipper, with ne'er a spar, a sail, or a rope asthray!

> *Father Domineer comes quickly in on the path outside. He is a tall, rather heavily built man of forty. He has a breezy manner now, heading the forlorn hope. He is trying to smile now, but crack his mouth as he will, the tight, surly lines of his face refuse to furnish one. He is dressed in the usual clerical, outdoor garb, and his hard head is covered with a soft, rather widely brimmed black hat.*

Father Domineer [*as happily as he can*]. Now, now, no halts on th' road, little daughter! The train won't wait, an' we must have a few minutes to spare to make you comfortable. Bring her along, Brancardiers! Forward, in th' name o' God and of Mary, ever Virgin, ever blessed, always bending to help poor, banished children of Eve!

> [*The two Rough Men take up the stretcher and carry it along the pathway outside, the Mayor, followed by his Mace-bearer, leading it on. Father Domineer follows immediately behind; then come Lorna and Marion, followed by Michael and Mahan.*

> [*As the stretcher moves along the pathway outside, a band in the distance is heard playing "Star of the Sea", to which is added the voice of a crowd singing the words:*

Hail, Queen of Heaven, the ocean Star!
Guide of the wand'rer here below!
Thrown on life's surge, we claim thy care—
Save us from peril and from woe.

Mother of Christ, Star of the Sea,
Pray for the wanderer, pray for me.

Father Domineer [*enthusiastically*]. Julia will bring us back a miracle, a glorious miracle! To Lourdes!

END OF SCENE I

SCENE II

The Scene is the same as before, though the sunshine isn't quite so bright and determined. The Irish Tricolour flies breezily from its flag-pole; the table and chairs stand where they were, and the bottle and glasses are still under it.

No-one is in the garden, all, apparently, having gone to see Julia away on her long, long journey. Away in the distance the band is playing "Star of the Sea", and the tune can be softly heard from the garden.

After a few moments, Lorna and Marion come along the path outside, enter by the gate, and cross over into the house.

Marion [*anxiously*]. What d'ye think of th' chance of a cure?

Lorna. I'm afraid th' chance is a poor one; but we won't talk about it.

Marion [*piously*]. Well, it was a grand send-off, an' God is good.

Lorna [*coldly*]. An' th' devil's not a bad fella either.

> [*They both go into the house, and, a few moments later, Michael and Mahan stroll along the path, come into the garden, and go to where the table and chairs are.*

Mahan. Well, th' anchor's weighed.

Michael. It was an edifyin' spectacle, Sailor Mahan, thrustin' us outa this world for th' time bein'. Julia's asked for a sign, Sailor Mahan, an', believe me, she'll get it.

Mahan. She will, she will, though I wouldn't like to bet on it.

Michael. She'll get what she's afther—a complete cure. Me own generous gift of fifty pounds for th' oul' bog'll be rewarded; an' th' spate o' prayin' goin' on, from th' Mayor to the Bellman, is bound to get th' higher saints goin', persuadin' them to furnish a suitable answer to all we're askin'.

Mahan [*impatiently*]. Arra, man alive, d'ye think th' skipper aloft an' his glitterin' crew is goin' to bother their heads about a call from a tiny town an' disthrict thryin' hard to thrive on turf?

Michael [*indignantly*]. Looka, if you were only versed in th' endurin' promulgacity of th' gospels, you'd know th' man above's concerned as much about Nyadnanave as he is about a place where a swarm of cardinals saunter secure, decoratin' th' air with all their purple an' gold!

Mahan [*as indignantly*]. Are you goin' to tell me that th' skipper aloft an' his hierarchilogical crew are concerned about th' Mayor, the Messenger, Marion, me, an' you as much as they are about them who've been promoted to th' quarter-deck o' th' world's fame? Are you goin' to pit our palthry penances an' haltin' hummin' o' hymns against th' piercin' pipin' of th' rosary be Bing Bang Crosby an' other great film stars, who side-stepped from published greatness for a holy minute or two to send a blessed blast over th' wireless, callin' all Catholics to perpetuatin' prayer!

Michael [*sitting down on a chair*].   Sailor Mahan, I ask you to thry to get your thoughts ship-shaped in your mind.

> [*While they have been talking, the Messenger has come running along the path outside, and is now leaning on the gate, listening to the two men, unnoticed by them.*

Mahan [*plumping down on the other chair—indignantly*].   D'ye remember who you're talkin' to, man? Ship-shape in me mind! Isn't a man bound to have his mind fitted together in a ship-shape way, who, forced out of his thrue course be a nautical cathastrope, to wit, videliket, an act o' God, ploughed a way through th' Sargasso Sea, reachin' open wathers, long afther hope had troubled him no longer?

Michael [*wearily*].   Aw, Sailor Mahan, what's them things got to do with th' things tantamount to heaven?

Messenger [*over to them*].   Mick's right—them things can't be tantamount to anything bar themselves.

Mahan [*turning fiercely on the Messenger*].   What do you want? What're you doin' here? Your coalition of ignorant knowledge can't comprehend th' things we talk about!

Messenger [*with some excitement*].   Listen, boys—I've a question to ask yous.

Michael [*with a gesture signifying this isn't the time to ask it*].   Ask it some time more convenient. An' don't refer to us as 'boys'—we're gentlemen to you!

Mahan [*to Michael*].   Looka, Mick, if you only listened to Bing Crosby, th' mighty film star, croonin' his Irish lullaby, [*he chants*] "Tooral ooral ooral, tooral ooral ay", you'd have th' visuality to see th' amazin' response he'd have from millions of admirers, if he crooned a hymn!

Messenger.   I was never sthruck be Bing Crosby's croonin'.

Michael [*wrathfully—to Messenger*].   You were never sthruck! An' who th' hell are you to be consulted? Please don't stand there interferin' with the earnest colloquy of betther men. [*To Mahan*] Looka, Sailor Mahan, any priest'll tell you that in th' eyes of heaven all men are equal an' must be held in respect an' reverence.

Mahan [*mockingly*].   Ay, they'll say that to me an' you, but will they say it to Bing Crosby, or any other famous film star?

Messenger.   Will they hell! Honour be th' clergy's regulated by how much a man can give!

Michael [*furiously—to the Messenger*].   Get to hell outa here! With that kinda talk, we won't be able soon to sit steady on our chairs. Oh!

[*The chair he is sitting on collapses, and he comes down to the ground on his arse.*

Mahan [*astonished*].   Holy saints, what's happened?

Michael [*in a fierce whisper—to Mahan*].   Take no notice of it, fool. Go on talkin'!

Mahan [*a little confused*].   I'll say you're right, Mick; th' way things are goin' we won't be able much longer to sit serene on our chairs. Oh!

[*The chair collapses under Mahan, and he, too, comes down to the ground.*

Michael [*in a fierce whisper*].   Don't notice it; go on's if nothin' happened!

Messenger [*amused*].   Well, yous have settled down now, anyhow! Will I get yous chairs sturdy enough to uphold th' wisdom of your talkin'?

Michael [*angrily—to Messenger*].   There's nothin' wrong with th' chairs we have! You get outa here! Nothin's wrong with th' chairs at all. Get outa here—I don't trust you either!

Messenger.   I've somethin' important to ask yous.

Michael.   Well, ask it at some more convenient time. [*To Mahan*] It's a blessin' that so many lively-livin' oul' holy spots are still in th' land to help us an' keep us wary.

Messenger [*scornfully*].   An' where are th' lively holy spots still to be found? Sure, man, they're all gone west long ago, an' the whole face o' th' land is pock-marked with their ruins!

Michael [*shouting at the Messenger*].   Where are th' lost an' ruined holy places? We've always cared for, an' honoured, our holy spots! Mention one of them, either lost or ruined!

Messenger [*shouting back*].   There are thousands of them, man; places founded be Finian, Finbarr, an' th' rest; places that are now only an oul' ruined wall, blighted be nettle an' dock, their only glory th' crimson berries of th' bright arbutus! Where's th' Seven Churches of Glendalough? Where's Durrow of Offally, founded be Columkille himself? Known now only be the name of the Book of Durrow!

Michael [*ferociously*]. Book o' Durrow! It's books that have us half th' woeful way we are, fillin' broody minds with loose scholasticality, infringin' th' holy beliefs an' thried impositions that our fathers' fathers' fathers gave our fathers' fathers, who gave our fathers what our fathers gave to us!

Messenger. Faith, your fathers' faith is fear, an' now fear is your only fun.

Mahan [*impatiently*]. Let him go, Mick, an' let's have that dhrink you mentioned a year ago.

> *Marion's head appears at the window, looking down at the Messenger. The decorations on her head have now declined to their first place.*

Marion [*down to the Messenger*]. Hallo, Robin Adair! [*He looks up.*] Where are th' two oul' woeful wondhers? [*He points to where they are.*] Oh, they've brought the unsteady chairs out, and now they've broken them up! [*To Michael—angrily*] You knew well th' chairs in the hall were there only to present an appearance.

Messenger [*up to her*]. Oh, Marion, Marion, sweet Marion, come down till I give you a kiss havin' in it all the life an' longin' of th' greater lovers of th' past!

Marion [*leaving the window*]. Now, now, naughty boy!

Michael [*sourly*]. You'd do well to remember, lad, the month in jail you got for kissin' Marion, an' the forty-shillin' fine on Marion, for kissing you in a public place at th' cross-roads.

> [*Marion comes from the house, goes toward the Messenger, who seizes her in his arms and kisses her.*

Messenger. I'd do a year an' a day in a cold cell of pressed-in loneliness, an' come out singin' a song, for a kiss from a lass like Marion!

Marion. Don't think too much of me, Robin Adair, for I've some of th' devil in me, an' th' two fostherers of fear, there, think I wear horns on holy days.

Michael [*impressively*]. See—she's warnin' you, herself, young man!

Marion [*to the Messenger*]. An' what has you here arguin' with them two oul' fools?

Messenger. I came to ask a question of them, but they were buried in their prayers. Did you see him? Did he come this way?

Michael [*suddenly alarmed*].   Come where?

Mahan [*alarmed*].   See who?

Messenger.   Th' Cock.

Mahan ⎱
Michael ⎰ [*together*].   Th' Cock!

> [*They carefully creep away from the broken chairs, and stand up when they are some distance from them.*

Messenger.   Ay. I thought he'd make for here first.

Michael [*echoing the Messenger*].   Make for here first!
> [*In the distance, the loud, exultant crow of the Cock is heard.*

Messenger [*excitedly*].   There he is! Away in the direction east of th' bog! I'll go get him, an' fetch him home.

Marion [*kissing the Messenger.*]   Bring him here first, Robin, an' I'll have a wreath of roses ready to hang round his neck.

Messenger [*rushing away*].   I will, I will, fair one!
> [*He goes off. She takes the broken chairs into the house.*

Marion [*carrying in the chairs*].   Next time, you boyos, take out two steady ones.

Michael [*horrified*].   Did you hear what she said, Sailor Mahan? Hang a wreath of roses round his neck! Well, I'll have th' gun ready! Ay, now!

> [*He goes over to the porch, but Mahan lays a restraining hand on his arm.*

Mahan.   What good would th' gun be? Have you forgot what Shanaar told us? Your bullet would go clean through him, an' leave him untouched. Now that we're in peace here, let's have th' dhrink we were to have, an' which we both need.

Michael [*halting*].   You're right, Sailor Mahan. If he comes here, what we have to do is to take no notice. Look through him, past him, over him, but never at him. [*He prepares the bottle of whiskey and the glasses.*] There's sinister enchantments all around us. God between us an' all harm! We'll have to be for ever on our guard.

Mahan [*impatiently*].   Yis, yis; fill out th' dhrink for God's sake!

Michael.   May it give us courage. [*He tilts the bottle over the glass, but none of it spills out.*] Good God, th' bottle's bewitched too!

Mahan.   Bottle bewitched? How could a bottle be bewitched? Steady your nerves, man. Thry givin' it a shake.

Michael [*who has left the bottle back on the table—retreating away from it*]. Thry givin' it a shake yourself, since you're so darin'.

> [*Mahan goes over to the table with a forced swagger, and reaches out a cautious hand for the bottle. As he touches it, its colour changes to a glowing red.*]

Mahan [*fervent and frightened*]. St. Christopher, pathron of all mariners, defend us—th' bottle's changed its colour!

Michael. There's evil things cantherin' an' crawlin' about this place! You saw th' seal on th' bottle showin' it was untouched since it left th' store. Flanagan's finest, Jamieson's best, ten years maturin'—an' look at it now.

Mahan. How are we goin' to prevent ourselves from bein' the victims of sorcery an' ruin? You'd think good whiskey would be exempt from injury even be th' lowest of th' low.

Michael. It's th' women who're always intherceptin' our good intentions. Evil things is threatenin' us everywhere. Th' one safe method of turnin' our back to a power like this is to go forward an' meet it half-way. [*He comes close to Mahan, and whispers hoarsely*] Selah!

Mahan [*mystified and frightened at what he thinks may be something sinister*]. Selah?

Michael [*emphatically*]. Selah!

Mahan [*agonisingly*]. Good God!

Michael. Now, maybe, you'll believe what th' Missioner said last night.

Mahan [*a little dubiously*]. He might have been exaggeratin' a bit, Mick.

Michael. Look at th' bottle, man! Demons can hide in th' froth of th' beer a man's dhrinkin'. An' all th' time, my turf-workers an' your lorry drivers are screwin' all they can out of us so that they'll have more to spend on pictures an' in th' dance halls, leavin' us to face th' foe alone.

Mahan [*abjectly*]. What's a poor, good-livin', virtuous man to do then?

Michael. He must always be thinkin' of th' four last things—hell, heaven, death, an' th' judgement.

Mahan [*pitifully*]. But that would sthrain a man's nerves, an' make life hardly worth livin'.

Michael. It's plain, Sailor Mahan, you're still hankerin' afther th' things o' th' world, an' the soft, stimulatin' touch of th' flesh. You're puttin' th' two of us in peril, Sailor Mahan.

Mahan [*protesting*]. You're exaggeratin' now.

Michael. I am not. I seen your eyes followin' that Loreleen when she's about, hurtin' th' tendher muscles of your eye squintin' down at her legs. You'll have to curb your conthradictions, for you're puttin' us both in dire peril, Sailor Mahan. Looka what I've lost already! Me fine silk hat torn to shreds, so that Lorna's had to telephone th' Firm for another, that I may suitably show meself when I meet his Brightness, the President; an' looka th' whiskey there—forced into a misundherstandin' of itself be some minor demon devisin' a spell on it! Guess how much good money I surrendhered to get that bottle, Sailor Mahan?

Mahan. I've no idea of what whiskey is a gallon now.

Michael [*impatiently*]. What whiskey is a gallon now? Is there some kinda spell on you, too, Sailor Mahan? You can't think of whiskey in gallons now; you have to think of it in terms of sips; an' sips spaced out from each other like th' holy days of obligation.

Mahan. An' how are we goin' to get rid of it? We're in some danger while it's standin' there.

Michael. How th' hell do I know how we'll get rid of it? We'll have to get Shanaar to deal with it, an', mind you, don't go too near it.

[*The Porter appears on the sidewalk outside the wall. He is a middle-aged man with an obstinate face, the chin hidden by a grizzled beard. He is wearing a pair of old brown trousers, an older grey coat, and an old blue shirt. On his head is a big cap, with a long, wide peak jutting out in front of it. The crown of the cap is a high one, and around the crown is a wide band of dazzling scarlet. He is carrying a parcel wrapped in brown paper, either side of which is a little torn. He looks north, south, west, and then, turning east, he sees the two men in the garden.*]

Porter [*to the two men*]. Isn't it handy now that I've clapped eyes on two human bein's in this god-forsaken hole! I've been trudghin' about for hours thryin' to find th' one that'll claim what's in this parcel I'm bearin', an', maybe, th' two of yous, or maybe, one of yous, can tell me where I'll find him. I'm on th' thrack of an oul' fella callin' himself a Councillor an' a Jay Pee.

Michael. What's his name?

Porter. That's more than I can say, for th' chit of th' girl in th' shop, who took th' ordher, forgot to write down th' name, an' then forgot th' name itself when she started to write it down. All I know is that in this disthrict I'm seekin' a Mr. Councillor So-an'-so; one havin' Councillor at his head an' Jay Pee at his tail.

Michael [*with importance*]. I'm a Councillor and a Jay Pee.

Porter [*with some scorn*].   D'ye tell me that now? [*He bends over the wall to come closer to Michael.*] Listen, me good man, me journey's been too long an' too dangerous for me to glorify any cod-actin'! It would be a quare place if you were a councillor. You'll have to grow a few more grey hairs before you can take a rise outa me!

Michael [*indignantly*].   Tell us what you've got there, fella, an', if it's not for us, be off about your business!

Porter [*angrily*].   Fella yourself! An' mend your manners, please! It's hardly th' like of you would be standin' in need of a silky, shinin' tall-hat.

Michael.   If it's a tall-hat, it's for me! I'm Mr. Councillor Marthraun, Jay Pee—ordhered to be sent express by th' firm of Buckley's.

Porter [*with a quick conciliatory change*].   That's th' firm. I guessed you was th' man at once, at once. That man's a leadher in th' locality, I said, as soon as I clapped me eye on you. A fine, clever, upstandin' individual, I says to meself.

Michael [*shortly*].   Hand over th' hat, and you can go.

Porter.   Hould on a minute, sir; wait till I tell you: I'm sorry, but th' hat's been slightly damaged in thransit.
                    [*He begins to take the hat from the paper.*]

Michael.   Damaged? How th' hell did you damage it?

Porter.   Me, is it? No, not me, sir. [*He stretches over the wall towards them.*] When I was bringin' it here, someone shot a bullet through it, east be west!

Michael.   Nonsense, man, who'd be shootin' bullets round here?

Porter.   Who indeed? That's th' mystery. Bullet it was. People told me the Civic Guards were out thryin' to shoot down an evil spirit flyin' th' air in th' shape of a bird.

Michael [*alarmed*].   Th' Cock!

Porter [*placing the tall-hat on the wall carefully*].   An' seein' how things are, an' th' fright I got, it's welcome a dhrink would be from th' handsome bottle I see paradin' on th' table.

Michael [*in a loud whisper*].   To touch it is to go in danger of your life —th' bottle's bewitched!

Porter.   Th' bottle bewitched? What sort of a place have me poor, wandherin' feet sthrayed into at all? Before I ventured to come here at all, I should have stayed at home. I'm already as uneasy as th' place itself!

[*A shot is heard, and the tall-hat is knocked from the wall on to the road.*] Saints in glory, there's another one!

Mahan [*excitedly*].   It's your hat, man, th' red band on your hat!

Porter [*to Michael—speaking rapidly, picking the tall-hat from the road and offering it to Michael*].   Here, take your hat, sir, an' keep it safe, an' I'll be goin'.

Michael [*frightened and angry*].   Take it back; it's damaged; take it back, fella!

Porter [*loudly and with anger*].   Fella yourself! Is it takin' th' risk I'd be of a bullet rushin' through me instead of th' oul' hat? [*He flings it towards the two men.*] Here, take your oul' hat an' th' risk along with it! Do what you want with it; do what you like with it; do what you can with it—I'm off!

[*He runs off in the direction he came from, while the two men gaze doubtfully at the hat lying in the garden.*

Michael [*tremulously*].   The cowards that are in this counthry—leavin' a poor man alone in his dilemma! I'd be afraid to wear it now.

Mahan.   Aw, give yourself a shake, Mick. You're not afraid of a poor tall-hat. An' throw away ten good pounds.

[*He goes toward where the hat is, but Michael holds him by the arm.*

Michael [*with warning and appeal*].   No, don't touch it till we see further.

[*The Sergeant appears on the pathway outside. He has a rifle in his hands; he leans against the wall looking towards the two. He is obviously anxious, and in a state of fear.*

Sergeant.   Yous didn't see it? It didn't come here, did it?

Michael [*breathless with the tension of fear*].   No, no; not yet. [*With doleful appeal*] Oh, don't be prowlin' round here—you'll only be at-tractin' it to th' place!

Sergeant [*ignoring appeal*].   Three times I shot at it; three times th' bul-lets went right through it; and twice th' thing flew away crowing.

Michael [*excitedly*].   Did you get it th' third time, did you get it then?

Sergeant.   Wait till I tell yous: sthrange things an' unruly are happenin' in this holy land of ours this day! Will I ever forget what happened th' third time I hot it! Never, never. Isn't it a wondher an' a mercy of God that I'm left alive afther th' reverberatin' fright I got!

Michael [*eagerly*].   Well, what happened when you hot it then?

Mahan [*eagerly*].   When you hot it for th' third time?

Sergeant.   Yous could never guess?

Michael [*impatiently*].   Oh, we know we'd never guess; no-one can go guessin' about demonological disturbances.

Mahan.   Tell us, will you, without any more of your sthructural suggestions!

Sergeant.   As sure as I'm standin' here; as sure as sure as this gun is in me left hand [*he is holding it in his right one*]; as sure as we're all poor, identified sinners; when I hot him for th' third time, I seen him changin' into a——

Michael }
Mahan   } [*together*].   What?

Sergeant [*whisperingly*].   What d'ye think?

Mahan [*explosively*].   Oh, we're not thinkin'; we can't think; we're beyond thinkin'! We're waitin' for you to tell us!

Sergeant.   Th' soul well-nigh left me body when I seen th' unholy novelty happenin': th' thing that couldn't be, yet th' thing that was. If I never prayed before, I prayed then—for hope; for holy considheration in th' quandary; for power to be usual an' spry again when th' thing was gone.

Michael.   What thing, what thing, man?

Mahan [*despairingly*].   Thry to tell us, Sergeant, what you said you said you seen.

Sergeant.   I'm comin' to it; since what I seen was seen by no man never before, it's not easy for a man to describe with evidential accuracy th' consequential thoughts fluttherin' through me amazed mind at what was, an' what couldn't be, demonstrated there, or there, or anywhere else, where mortals congregate in ones or twos or crowds astoundin'.

Michael [*imploringly*].   Looka, Sergeant, we're languishin' for th' information that may keep us from spendin' th' rest of our lives in constant consternation.

Sergeant.   As I was tellin' you, there was th' crimson crest of th' Cock, enhancin' th' head lifted up to give a crow, an' when I riz th' gun to me shouldher, an' let bang, th' whole place went dead dark; a flash of red lightning near blinded me; an' when it got light again, a second afther, there was the demonised Cock changin' himself in a silken glossified tall-hat!

Michael [*horrified*].   A silken tall-hat!

Mahan. A glossified tall-hat!

Michael [*to Mahan—viciously*]. Now you'll quit undherestimatin' what th' holy Missioner said last night about th' desperate an' deranging thrickeries of evil things loose an' loungin' among us! Now can you see the significality of things?

Mahan [*going away as far as he can from the tall-hat lying in the garden*]. Steer clear of it; get as far away from it as we can! Keep well abaft of it!

Sergeant [*puzzled*]. Keep clear from what?

Mahan [*pointing to the hat*]. Th' hat, man, th' hat!

Sergeant [*seeing the hat beside him, and jumping away from it*]. I was near touchin' th' brim of it! Jasus! yous should have warned me!

Michael [*close to the Sergeant—in a whisper*]. Does it look anything like th' thing you shot?

Sergeant [*laying a shaking hand on Michael's arm*]. It's th' dead spit of what I seen him changin' into durin' th' flash of lightning! I just riz th' gun to me shouldher—like this [*he raises the gun to his shoulder*] to let bang.

> [*The garden is suddenly enveloped in darkness for a few moments. A fierce flash of lightning shoots through the darkness; the hat has disappeared, and where it stood now stands the Cock. While the lightning flashes, the Cock crows lustily. Then the light as suddenly comes back to the garden, and shows that the Cock and the hat have gone. Michael and Mahan are seen to be lying on the ground, and the Sergeant is on his knees, as if in prayer.*]

Sergeant. Holy St. Custodius, pathron of th' police, protect me!

Michael [*in a whisper*]. Are you there, Sailor Mahan?

Mahan [*in a whisper*]. Are you there, Michael Marthraun?

Michael. I'm done for.

Mahan. We're both done for.

Sergeant. We're all done for.

Mahan. Th' smell of th' sulphur an' brimstone's burnin' me.

Michael. Now you'll give up mockin' Shanaar, if it's not too late. You seen how Marion's head was ornamented, an' it'll not be long till Lorna has them too.

Sergeant [*now sitting down, so that he is to the left of Michael, while Mahan sits to the right of him, so frightened that he must blame someone*]. We'll have to curtail th' gallivantin' of th' women afther th' men. Th' house is their province, as th' clergy's tired tellin' them. They'll have to realise that th' home's their only proper place.

Michael. An' demolish th' minds that babble about books.

Sergeant [*raising his voice*]. Th' biggest curse of all! Books no decent mortal should touch, should never even see th' cover of one!

Michael [*warningly*]. Hush! Don't speak so loud, or th' lesser boyo'll hear you!

Sergeant [*startled*]. Lesser boyo? What lesser boyo?

Mahan [*whispering and pointing*]. Th' boyo in th' bottle there.

Sergeant [*noticing it for the first time*]. Why, what's in it?

Michael. Th' best of whiskey was in it till some evil spirit put a spell on it, desthroyin' its legitimate use.

Sergeant [*unbelievingly*]. I don't believe it. Nothin' could translate good dhrink into anything but what it was made to be. We could do with a dhrink now.   [*He advances cautiously towards the table.*

Michael [*excitedly*]. Don't meddle with it, man; don't stimulate him!

      [*The Sergeant tiptoes over to the table, stretches his hand out, and touches the bottle. He immediately lets out a yelp, and jumps back.*

Sergeant. Oh! Be God, it's red-hot!

Mahan [*angrily*]. You were told not to touch it! You're addin' to our dangers.

Michael [*shouting*]. Good God, man, couldn't you do what you're told! Now you've added anger to its impositional qualities!

Sergeant [*nursing his hand*]. Aren't we in a nice quandary when an evil thing can insconce itself in a bottle!

Michael. Th' whole place's seethin' with them. You, Sergeant, watch th' road north; you, Sailor Mahan, watch it south; an' I'll keep an eye on th' house. [*Mahan goes to one end of the wall, the Sergeant to the other, and both stretch over it to look different ways along the road. During the next discussion, whenever they leave where they are, they move cautiously, crouching a little, as if they were afraid to be seen; keeping as low as possible for security.*] One of us'll have to take th' risk, an' go for Father Domineer at once. [*He waits for a few moments, but no-one answers.*] Did yous hear me, or are yous lettin' on to be deaf? I said one of us'll have to go for Father Domineer. [*There is no reply.*] Are you listenin' to me be any chance, Sailor Mahan?

Mahan. I heard you, I heard you.

Michael. An' why don't you go, then?

Mahan [*coming down towards Michael—crouching low*]. Nice thing if I met th' Cock barrin' me way? Why don't you go yourself?

Michael. What about th' possibility of me meetin' him? I'm more conspicuous in this disthrict than you, an' th' thing would take immediate recognisance of me.

Sergeant [*coming down towards them—crouching too*]. Me an' Sailor Mahan'll go together.

Michael [*indignantly*]. An' leave me to grapple with *mysteriosa Daemones* alone? [*He turns his face skywards*] Oh, in this disthrict there's not a sign of one willin' to do unto another what another would do to him!

Mahan [*fiercely*]. That's a lie: there isn't a one who isn't eager to do to others what others would do to him!

The Bellman, dressed as a fireman, comes in, and walks along on the path outside. He has a huge brass fireman's helmet on his head, and is wearing a red shirt and blue trousers. He has a bell in his hand which he rings loudly before he shouts his orders. The three men cease their discussion, and give him their full attention.

Bellman [*shouting*]. Into your houses all! Bar th' doors, shut th' windows! Th' Cock's comin'! In the shape of a woman! Gallus, Le Coq, an' Kyleloch, th' Cock's comin' in th' shape of a woman! Into your houses, shut to th' windows, bar th' doors!

[*He goes out in the opposite direction, shouting his orders and ringing his bell, leaving the three men agitated and more frightened than ever.*

Sergeant [*frantically*]. Into the house with us all—quick!

Michael [*hindering him—ferociously*]. Not in there, you fool! Th' house is full o' them. You seen what happened to the whiskey? If he or she comes, th' thing to do is to take no notice; if he or she talks, not to answer; and take no notice of whatever questionable shape it takes. Sit down, quiet, th' three of us.

[*The three men sit down on the ground—Michael to the right, the Sergeant to the left, and Mahan in the center.*

Michael [*trembling*]. Now, let th' two of yous pull yourselves together. An' you, Mahan, sing that favourite of yours, quietly, as if we were passing th' time pleasantly. [*As Mahan hesitates*] Go on, man, for God's sake!

Mahan [*agitated*]. I can't see how I'll do it justice undher these conditions. I'll thry. [*He sings, but his voice quavers occasionally:*]
  Long time ago when men was men
  An' ships not ships that sail'd just to an' fro-o-o,
  We hoisted sail an' sail'd, an' then sail'd on an' on to Jericho-o-o;
  With silks an' spice came back again because we'd nowhere else to go!

Michael
Sergeant } [*together*]. Go, go!

Mahan [*singing*]:
  Th' captain says, says he, we'll make
  Th' pirates where th' palm trees wave an' grow-o-o,
  Haul down their sable flag, an' pray, before we hang them all, heave yo-ho-ho;
  Then fling their bodies in th' sea to feed th' fishes down below!

Michael
Sergeant } [*together*]. Low, low!

  [*A golden shaft of light streams in from the left of the road, and, a moment afterwards, Loreleen appears in the midst of it. She stands in the gateway staring at the three men squatted on the ground.*

Loreleen [*puzzled*]. What th' hell's wrong here?

Michael [*in a whisper—motioning Mahan to continue*]. Go on, man.

Mahan [*singing—with more quavers in his voice*]:
  An' when we've swabb'd th' blood away,
  We'll take their hundhred-ton gunn'd ship in tow-o-o;
  Their precious jewels'll go to deck th' breasts of women, white as snow-o-o;
  So hoist all sail an' make for home through waves that lash an' winds that blow!

Michael
Sergeant } [*together*]. Blow, blow!

  [*Loreleen comes into the garden, and approaches the men. The golden light follows her, and partly shines on the three singers.*

Loreleen [*brightly*]. Singin' is it the three of you are? Practisin' for the fancy-dress ball tonight, eh? Ye do well to bring a spray of light, now and again, into a dark place. The Sergeant's eyes, too, whenever Lorna or me passes by, are lit with a light that never was on sea or land. An' th' bould Sailor Mahan is smiling too; only dad is dour. [*She glances at the bottle on the table.*] The song is heard, th' wine is seen, only th' women wanting. [*She runs over to the porchway, and shouts into the house.*]

Lorna, Marion, come on down, come out here, an' join th' enthertainment!

[*Lorna and Marion come trotting out of the house into the garden. They are both clad in what would be called fancy dress. Lorna is supposed to be a gypsy, and is wearing a short black skirt, low-cut green bodice, with a gay sash round her waist, sparkling with sequins. Her fair arms are bare. Her head is bound with a silver and black ornament, similar in shape to that already worn by Marion. Her legs are encased in black stockings, and dark-red shoes cover her feet. Marion is dressed as a Nippy, a gay one. She has on a short, bright-green skirt, below which a black petticoat peeps; a low-cut bodice of a darker green, and sports a tiny black apron to protect her costume. She wears light-brown silk stockings and brown shoes. Outside the white bandeau round her head she wears the ornament worn before. The two women stare at the three men.*]

Lorna [*vexatiously*].   Dhrunk is it? To get in that state just when we were practisin' a few steps for tonight's fancy-dress dance! [*She notices the bottle.*] Looka th' dhrink left out in th' sun an' air to dhry! [*She whips up the bottle, and places it inside on the floor of the porch.*] An' even th' Sailor Mahan is moody too! [*She goes over to the Sergeant, stands behind him, and lays a hand on his head. She is now in the golden light which shines down on the Sergeant too.*]

I saw a ship a-sailing, a-sailing on th' sea;
An' among its spicy cargo was a bonny lad for me!

[*The Sergeant rises slowly, as if enchanted, with a foolish look of devotion on his face, till he stands upright beside Lorna, glancing at her face, now and again, very shy and uncertain. While this has been happening, Loreleen has gone to Sailor Mahan, and now stands behind him with a hand on his head.*]

Loreleen [*down to Sailor Mahan*]:
I saw a man come running, come running o'er th' lea, sir,
And, lo, he carried silken gowns
That couldn't hide a knee
That he had bought in saucy towns;
An' jewels he'd bought beyond th' bounds
Of Asia's furthest sea.
And all were lovely, all were fine,
An' all were meant for me!

[*Sailor Mahan rises, as if enchanted, till he stands upright beside Loreleen, slyly looking at her now and again.*]

Marion. Aw, let's be sensible. [*She sees the gun.*] What's th' gun doin'? Who owns th' gun?

Sergeant. It's mine. I'm on pathrol lookin' to shoot down th' demon-bird loose among innocent people.

Marion. Demon-bird loose among innocent people! Yous must be mad.

Sergeant [*indignantly*]. We're not mad! It's only that we were startled when th' darkness came, th' lightning flashed, an' we saw Mr. Marthraun's tall-hat turnin' itself into th' demon-bird!

Lorna [*mystified*]. Th' darkness came, th' lightning flashed? A tall-hat changin' into a demon-bird!

Michael [*springing to his feet*]. Ay, an' this isn't th' time for gay disturbance! So go in, an' sthrip off them gaudy things, an' bend your mind to silent prayer an' long fastin'! Fall prostrate before God, admittin' your dire disthress, an' you may be admitted to a new dispensation!

Lorna [*to Michael*]. Nonsense! Your new tall-hat was delivered an hour ago, an' is upstairs now, waitin' for you to put it on. [*To Marion*] Take that gun in, dear, outa th' way, an' bring down th' tall-hat to show him he's dhreamin'.

> [*Marion takes up the gun, and goes into the house with it, as Michael, in a great rage, shoves Mahan aside to face Lorna fiercely.*

Michael [*loudly*]. Who are you, you jade, to set yourself up against th' inner sight an' outer sight of genuine Christian men? [*He shouts*] We seen this thing, I tell you! If you knew what you ought to know, you'd acknowledge th' thrained tenacity of evil things. Betther had I left you soakin' in poverty, with your rags coverin' your thin legs, an' your cheeks hollow from mean feedin'. Through our bulgin' eyes, didn't we see th' horrification of me tall-hat turnin' into th' demonised cock? Me tall-hat, you bitch, me own tall-hat is roamin' round th' counthry, temptin' souls to desthroy themselves with dancin' an' desultory pleasures!

Mahan [*gripping Michael's arm*]. Aw, draw it mild, Mick!

Michael [*flinging off Mahan's hold*]. Go in, an' take them things, showy with sin, off you, an' dhress decent! [*He points to Loreleen.*] It's you who's brought this blast from th' undherworld, England, with you! It's easy seen what you learned while you worked there—a place where no God is; where pride and lust an' money are the brightest liveries of life! [*He advances as if to strike her, but Mahan bars his way.*] You painted slug! [*Marion comes from the house, carrying a fresh, dignified tall-hat, noble in its silken glossiness. She offers it to Michael who jumps away from it.*] No, no, take it away; don't let it touch me.

[*Marion puts the hat on the table, and the three men stare at it, as if expecting something to happen.*

Lorna [*darting into the porch, and returning with the bottle. It has gone back to its former colour*]. Let's have a dhrink to give us courage to fight our dangers. Fetch another glass, Marion.

[*Marion goes in, and returns with a glass. Lorna uncorks the bottle, and takes up a glass to fill it.*

Michael [*warningly*]. Don't meddle with that dhrink, or harm may come to us all!

Lorna [*recklessly*]. If I can't wrap myself in th' arms of a man, I'll wrap myself in a cordial. [*She fills the glass, then she fills another one, and gives it to Loreleen; then she fills a third, and gives it to Marion.*] Here, Loreleen, [*Loreleen takes the glass.*] Here, Marion.

[*Marion takes the glass from her.*

Mahan [*doubtfully, and with some fear*]. I wouldn't, Lorna, I wouldn't dhrink it—there's some kind of a spell on it.

Lorna. Is there, now? I hope to God it's a strong one! [*Raising her glass*] Th' Cock-a-doodle Dandy!

Marion ⎱
Loreleen ⎰ [*raising their glasses—together*]. Th' Cock-a-doodle Dandy!

[*The three women empty their glasses together. Lorna fills her glass again, and goes over to the Sergeant.*

Lorna [*offering the glass to the Sergeant*]. Dhrink hearty, man, an' praise th' good things life can give. [*As he hesitates*] Dhrink from th' glass touched by th' lips of a very fair lady!

Sergeant [*impulsively*]. Death an' bedamnit, ma'am, it's a fair lady you are. [*He takes the glass from her.*] I'm not th' one to be short in salutin' loveliness!

[*He drinks, and a look of delightful animation gradually comes on to his face.*

Loreleen [*who has filled her glass again—going over to Sailor Mahan, and offering him the drink*]. Here, Sailor Mahan, man of th' wider waters, an' th' seven seas, dhrink! [*As he hesitates*] Dhrink from th' glass touched by th' lips of a very fair lady!

Mahan [*taking the glass—impulsively*]. Here's a one who always yelled ahoy to a lovely face an' charmin' figure whenever they went sailin' by— salud!

[*He drinks, and the look of animation gradually comes on to his face too.*

Marion [*who has filled her glass the second time—going over to Michael and offering him the drink*]. Dark man, let th' light come to you be dhrinkin' from a glass touched be th' red lips of a fair young maiden!

Michael [*who has been watching the others enviously—taking the glass from her*]. Gimme it! I won't be one odd. Yous can't best me! [*He drinks it down greedily. A reckless look steals over his face.*]

> [*During the last few moments, Lorna has been humming a tune, which has been taken up by an accordion, very softly. Then the Messenger appears on the pathway outside, and it can be seen that he is the player. He sits sideways on the wall, still playing softly a kind of a dance tune.*

Michael [*to Marion*]. In our heart of hearts, maid Marion, we care nothin' about th' world of men. Do we now, Sailor Mahan?

Mahan [*cautiously—though a reckless gleam is appearing in his eyes too*]. We all have to think about th' world o' men at times.

Michael. Not with our hearts, Sailor Mahan; oh, not with our hearts. You're thinkin' now of th' exthra money you want off me, Sailor Mahan. Take it, man, an' welcome! [*Enthusiastically*] An' more! You can have double what you're askin', without a whimper, without a grudge!

Mahan [*enthusiastically*]. No, damnit, Michael, not a penny from you! We're as good as bein' brothers! Looka th' lilies of th' field, an' ask yourself what th' hell's money!

Michael [*excitedly*]. Dhross, be God! Dhross, an' nothin' else! [*To Marion*] Gimme that hat there!

> [*She gives it to him. He puts it on, puts an arm round her waist, and they begin to move with the beat of the music. As Michael puts his arm around her waist, the ornament on her head rises into a graceful, curving horn, but he does not notice it.*

> [*At the same time, the Sergeant, having put an arm round Lorna, moves in the dance, too. As he does so, the ornament on her head, too, becomes a curving horn, but he does not notice it. Then Mahan goes over stealthily to Loreleen, who is watching the others, and stabs her shyly in the ribs with a finger. She turns, smiles, takes hold of his arm, and puts it round her waist. Then the two of them join the others in moving round to the beat of the music, the cock-like crest in Loreleen's hat rising higher as she begins to move in the dance.*

> [*After a few moments, the dance quickens, the excitement grows, and the men stamp out the measure of the music fiercely, while*

the three women begin to whirl round them with ardour and abandon. While the excitement is at its height, a loud, long peal of thunder is heard, and in the midst of it, with a sliding, rushing pace, Father Domineer appears in the gateway, a green glow enveloping him as he glares down at the swinging dancers, and as a loud, lusty crow from the Cock rings out through the garden.

[*The dancers, excepting Loreleen, suddenly stand stock still, then fall on one knee, facing the priest, their heads bent in shame and some dismay. Loreleen dances on for some few moments longer, the music becoming softer, then she slowly ends her dance to face forward towards the priest, the Messenger continuing to play the tune very softly, very faintly now.*

Father Domineer [*down to those in the garden—with vicious intensity*]. Stop that devil's dance! How often have yous been warned that th' avowed enemies of Christianity are on th' march everywhere! An' I find yous dancin'! How often have yous been told that pagan poison is floodin' th' world, an' that Ireland is dhrinkin' in generous doses through films, plays, an' books! An' yet I come here to find yous dancin'! Dancin', an' with th' Kyleloch, Le Coq, Gallus, th' Cock rampant in th' disthrict, desthroyin' desire for prayer, desire for work, an' weakenin' th' authority of th' pastors an' masters of your souls! Th' empire of Satan's pushin' out its foundations everywhere, an' I find yous dancin', *ubique ululanti cockalorum ochone, ululo!*

Messenger [*through his soft playing of the accordion*]. Th' devil was as often in th' street, an' as intimate in th' home when there was nor film nor play nor book.

Father Domineer. There was singin' then, an' there's singin' now; there was dancin' then, an' there's dancin' now, leadin' innocent souls to perjure their perfection. [*To Loreleen*] Kneel down, as th' others do, you proud an' dartin' cheat, an' beg a pardon!

Loreleen [*obstinately*]. I seek no pardon for th' dance that's done.

Father Domineer [*turning away from her*]. Seek for it then when pardon hides away.

Michael. Oh, what have I done! I've bethrayed meself into a sudden misdoin'!

Mahan. *Mea culpa*, me, too, Father!

Father Domineer. Oh, Michael Marthraun, an' you, Sailor Mahan, Knights of Columbanus, I come to help yous, an' I catch yous in th' act of prancin' about with shameless women, dhressed to stun th' virtue out of all beholders!

Michael. It was them, right enough, Father, helped be th' wine, that done poor me an' poor Sailor Mahan in! I should have remembered that a Columbanian knight told me a brother Columbanian knight told him another brother has said that St. Jerome told a brother once that woman was th' gate of hell! An' it's thrue—they stab a man with a knife wreathed with roses!

Father Domineer. Get up, get up, an' stand away from me; an' let ye never be loungers again in th' fight for good against evil. [*They all rise up humbly, the women to one side, the men to the other, and go back some way, as the Priest comes into the garden. Loreleen strolls defiantly over to the table, and sits sideways upon it. To Mahan*] An' now, Sailor Mahan, a special word for you. On my way here, I passed that man of yours who's livin' in sin with a lost an' wretched woman. He dodged down a lane to give me th' slip. I warned you, if he didn't leave her, to dismiss him—did you do so? [*Mahan is silent.*] I have asked you, Mahan, if you've dismissed him?

Mahan [*obstinately*]. I see no reason why I should dismiss me best lorry driver.

Father Domineer [*coldly*]. You don't see a reason? An' who are you to have any need of a reason in a question of this kind? [*Loudly*] I have a reason, an' that's enough for you!

Mahan [*defensively.*] He's a fine worker, Father, an' th' nation needs such as him.

Father Domineer [*loudly*]. We're above all nations. Nationality is mystical, maundering nonsense! It's a heresy! I'm the custodian of higher interests. [*Shouting*] Do as you're told—get rid of him!

Michael [*wheedling.*] It's all right, Father—he'll do what your reverence tells him. Sailor Mahan's a thrue Columbanian.

Mahan [*angrily—to Michael*]. He won't do what his reverence tells him!

[*Down the path outside comes the Lorry Driver, a man of thirty years of age. He doesn't look a giant, but there is an air of independence and sturdiness about him. He is wearing a leather jacket, a pair of soldier's khaki trousers, and an oily-looking peaked cap. His face is tanned by the weather, and his upper lip is hidden by a well-trimmed moustache. He hesitates for a moment when he sees Father Domineer; but, stiffening a little, he continues his walk to the gateway, into the garden. He stands a little way from Mahan, looking at him, evidently having something to say to him.*]

Father Domineer [*sneeringly*]. Ah, the gentleman himself has arrived.

[*To the man*] We were just talking of you, my man. I have told Mr. Mahan to dismiss you. You know why. You're a scandal to th' whole place; you're a shame to us all. Either leave this woman you're living with, or go to where that sort of thing's permitted. [*Loudly*] You heard me?

Lorry Driver [*surlily*].   I heard you.

Father Domineer [*impatiently*].   Well?

Lorry Driver.   I come to speak with Mr. Mahan, Father.

Mahan [*quickly*].   Me, Jack! Oh, yes; what's the throuble now?

Lorry Driver.   Plenty, sir. The turf-workers have left th' bog, an' we've no turf to load. Th' delegate says he sent a telegram to Mr. Marthraun, sayin' th' men would leave th' bog, if no answer came within an hour.

Messenger.   He did, an' I delivered it.

Michael.   Damnit, but I forgot about it! The tension here put it out of me mind!

Father Domineer [*catching the Lorry Driver by an arm*].   Never mind turf or tension now. Are you going to go from here?

Lorry Driver [*obstinately*].   I'll go, if Mr. Mahan tells me to go.

Father Domineer [*in a fury*].   Isn't it a wondher God doesn't strike you dead! I tell you to give the wretched woman up, or go, an' that's enough for either Sailor Mahan or you. [*He shakes the Lorry Driver's arm.*] Will you give that wretched woman up; will you send that woman of yours away?

Lorry Driver [*resentfully*].   Eh, don't be pullin' th' arm outa me!

Father Domineer [*his fury growing*].   Did you send that woman away; are you going to do it?

Lorry Driver [*shaking his arm free, and stepping back*].   Aw, let go! I didn't an' I won't!

Father Domineer [*in an ungovernable burst of fury*].   You wretch, would you dare to outface your priest? Get out of me sight!

[*He lunges forward, and strikes the Lorry Driver swiftly and savagely on the side of the head. The man falls heavily; lies still for a moment; tries feebly to rise; falls down again, and lies quite still.*

Mahan [*frightened*].   He's hurted, Father; you hot him far too hard.

Father Domineer [*frightened too—with a forced laugh*].   Nonsense! I just touched him. [*He touches the fallen man with his foot.*] Get up, get up—you're not that much hurt.

Mahan [*bending over the Lorry Driver, and placing a hand on his breast*]. I'm afraid he's either dyin' or dead, Father!

> [*Father Domineer runs over agitatedly to the fallen man, kneels down beside him, and murmurs in his ear. Then he raises his head to face the others.*

Father Domineer [*to the others*]. Yous all saw what happened. I just touched him, an' he fell. I'd no intention of hurting him—only to administer a rebuke.

Sergeant [*consolingly*]. Sure, we know that, Father—it was a pure accident.

Father Domineer. I murmured an act of contrition into th' poor man's ear.

Messenger [*playing very softly*]. It would have been far fitther, Father, if you'd murmured one into your own.

END OF SCENE II

SCENE III

It is towards dusk in the garden now. The sun is setting, and the sky shows it. The rich blue of the sky has given place to a rich yellow, slashed with green and purple. The flag-pole stands black against the green and yellow of the sky, and the flag, now, has the same sombre hue.

The big sunflowers against the wall have turned into a solemn black, too; the house has a dark look, save where a falling shaft from the sun turns the window above the porch into a golden eye of light. Far away, in the depths of the sky, the evening star can be faintly seen.

In the distance, for some time, the sounds of drumming, occasionally pierced by the shrill notes of a fife, can be heard.

Mahan is sitting at the table, busy totting up figures on papers spread out before him, his face knotted into creases of anxiety and doubt.

Lorna and Marion are leaning against the wall, away from the gateway, and near the house. Their gay garments are covered with dark hooded cloaks to temper the coolness of the evening air.

Lorna. They all seem to be out on th' hunt—police an' soldiers, with th' bands to give them courage. Th' fools!

Marion. D'ye think they'll get him? Th' place'll lose its brightness if th' Cock's killed.

Lorna. How can they desthroy a thing they say themselves is not of this world? [*She goes over to Mahan, and stares at him for a moment.*] It's cooler. The sun's settin'.

Mahan [*hardly noticing*]. Is it? I didn't notice. I'm busy. Everything thrust through everything else, since that damned Cock got loose. Th' drouth now dhryin' everything to dust; the turf-workers refusin' to work, th' women thinkin' only of dancin' an' dhress. But we'll lay him low, an' bury him deep enough to forget he ever came here!

Lorna. Th' men on th' bog work hard; they should get all you've got to give them.

Mahan [*resentfully*]. An' why th' hell shouldn't they work hard? Who'd keep th' fires of th' nation burning, if they didn't?

Lorna. They work for you, too; an' for Michael. He's got a pile in th' bank, an' rumour says you've got one too.

Mahan [*whining*]. Michael may; I never had, an' I'm losin' th' little I had since I lost me best lorry dhriver—blast th' hand that hot him! [*The Cock suddenly glides in, weaving a way between Mahan at the table, and Lorna, circling the garden, and finally disappearing round the gable-end of the house; the dance tune softly keeps time with his movements. Jumping to his feet*] What was that? I thought I saw him prancin' by me!

Lorna [*startled too*]. What was what?

Mahan. Th' Cock in his black plumage, yellow legs, an' crimson crest!

Marion [*who has gone tense*]. You put th' heart across me! I thought you meant th' poor dead man.

[*She turns to look along the road again.*]

Lorna [*to Mahan*]. There's a little use worryin' over figures till you settle with th' men.

Mahan [*irritably*]. That's Mick's business, that's Mick's business!

Marion [*running over to whisper excitedly to Lorna*]. Here they are— Father Domineer an' Mr. Marthraun comin' along th' road!

Mahan [*irascibly*]. Aw, what does that Father Domineer want comin' here when we've so much to think about! Delayin' things! I want to get away from here before it gets dark.

Lorna. Didn't you know they're goin' to purge th' poor house of its evil influences?

Mahan [*irritably*]. Oh, can't they do first things first?

[*Along the pathway outside come Father Domineer and Michael, followed by a lad. The lad is One-eyed Larry. His face is one alternately showing stupidity or cunning, according to whomsoever may be speaking to him. Where his left eye was is a black cavity, giving him a somewhat sinister look. He is lanky and rather awkward-looking. He is wearing a black cassock or soutane, piped with red braid, and is bare-headed. He is carrying a small bell, a book, and an unlighted candle. He shuffles along after the two men, and follows them into the garden.*

Father Domineer. We'll banish them, never fear, Michael, before I have to leave th' parish because of that unhappy accident. I've faced worse. Be staunch. Th' bell is powerful, so is th' book, an' th' blessed candle, too. [*He glances at the women.*] Let yous women keep to th' farther end of th' garden. [*He glances at Mahan.*] We won't be long, Sailor Mahan. [*Suddenly, as he, Michael, and One-eyed Larry reach the porch*] Where's that other one?

Michael. Is it Loreleen, me daughter, Father?

Father Domineer. She's no daughter of yours, Michael. [*Bending down to whisper warningly*] Get rid of her, get rid of her—she's dangerous!

Michael. How get rid of her, Father?

Father Domineer. Pack her off to America!

Michael [*respectfully—as they are about to go into the house*]. I'll go first, Father.

Father Domineer [*setting him gently aside*]. No, no; mine th' gap of danger.

[*The three of them go in, the Priest first, then Michael, and, lastly, One-eyed Larry. Marion and Lorna move over to the farther side of the garden.*

Lorna. It's all damn nonsense, though Michael has me nerves in such a way that I'm near ready to believe in anything.

Mahan. Waste of time, too. It'll take a betther man than Father Domineer to dhrive evil things outa Eire.

Marion. Messenger says he's only addin' to their number, an' soon a noddin' daffodil, when it dies, 'll know its own way to hell. [*The roll of a drum is heard and a great boo-ing. Marion runs to the wall to look over it, and up the road. Excitedly*] A girl runnin' this way, hell for leather. My God, it's Loreleen!

> [*After a few moments, Loreleen runs along the pathway outside, and dashes in through the gateway to Lorna, who catches her in her arms. Clumps of grass and sods of turf, and a few stones follow Loreleen in her rush along the road.*

Loreleen [*out of breath*]. God damn th' dastards of this vile disthrict! They pelted me with whatever they could lay hands on—th' women because they couldn't stand beside me; th' men because there was ne'er a hope of usin' me as they'd like to! Is it any wondher that th' girls are fleein' in their tens of thousands from this bewildhered land? Blast them! I'll still be gay an' good-lookin'. Let them draw me as I am not, an' sketch in a devil where a maiden stands!

Lorna [*soothingly*]. Be calm, child! We can't go in, for Father Domineer's inside puttin' things in ordher. [*Releasing Loreleen*] I'll run along th' road to them disturbers, an' give them a bit o' me mind! [*She catches hold of Marion's arm.*] Come on, Marion!

> [*She and Marion rush out along the road, and pass out of sight.*

Loreleen [*staring at the house*]. He's inside, is he? That's not where th' evil is, th' gaum, if he wants to know.

Mahan [*seriously*]. Come here, Loreleen; nearer, for I've something to say to you. [*As she does not stir, he grips her arm, and draws her farther from the house.*] We might be heard.

Loreleen [*suspiciously*]. What do you want, Sailor Mahan? You're not of one mind with them who chased me?

Mahan [*a little embarrassed*]. Aw, God, no! Me sails of love are reefed at last, an' I lie quiet, restin' in a lonely harbour now. I'm too old to be flusthered with that kinda folly. I just want to warn you to get outa this disthrict.

Loreleen [*bitterly*]. Why must I go? Is it because I'm good-lookin' an' gay?

> [*But the bold Mahan isn't indifferent to the charms of Loreleen. So he goes on to show Loreleen the youthfulness of his old age; that his muscles are still strong, his fibres flexible. He becomes restless, and walks about, occasionally glancing at the house, nervous at what may be happening inside. When he comes to a chair, he nonchalantly swings a leg over the back of it, turning on the*

foot of the same leg to swing the other one back again. These actions, like the conversation, though not done in a hurry, are done quickly, as if he wanted to say all he had to say before any interruption.

Mahan [*swinging a leg over a chair*].   Partly because you're good-lookin' an' partly because of th' reckless way you talk. Remember what happened to poor Jack. I'd clear out if I were you.

[*He vaults on to the table, swings round it on his backside, and vaults from it on the opposite side, a little stiffly.*

Loreleen.   How'm I to clear out? I've no money left. Th' forty pounds I had, Dad put into his bank for me, an' now won't give me a penny of it, because he says if I got it, I'd go to England; an' if I went to England, I'd lose me soul, th' shaky, venomous lout! An' I keep quiet because of Lorna. [*Hurriedly, as Mahan is stiffly climbing a few feet up the flag-pole*] Oh, don't be doin' th' monkey on a stick! Maybe you could help me? Could you, would you?

Mahan [*sliddering from the pole, swinging a leg over a chair, and coming closer to her*].   Now that's what I'd hoped you'd say. This is th' first time I've caught you alone. I'll give you what you need, an' you can weigh anchor, an' be off outa this damned place. Listen, darlin': you steal out tonight to th' Red Barn, west of th' Holy Cross, an' I'll dhrive there with what'll get you as far as you want to go. [*He suddenly puts an arm round her in a kind of clutch.*] Jasus, you have lovely eyes!

Loreleen [*trying to pull his arm away*].   Oh, Sailor Mahan, don't do that! Let me go—someone may see us!

Mahan [*recklessly*].   You deserve to be ruffled a bit! Well, will you come to th' Red Barn, while th' rest are goin' to th' dance, an' save yourself? Yes or no!

Loreleen.   Maybe, maybe; yes, yes, I'll go. Let go your clutch!

[*The house shakes; a sound of things moving and crockery breaking comes from it; several flashes of lightning spear out through the window over the porch; and the flag-pole wags drunkenly from side to side.*

[*Marion and Lorna appear on the pathway outside the wall, and hurry along into the garden just as One-eyed Larry comes running out of the house, his face beset with fear. His one eye takes in the picture of Loreleen breaking away from Mahan. Loreleen turns aside from One-eyed Larry, while Mahan, embarrassed, turns to face him.*

One-eyed Larry [*excitedly*]. It's startin' in earnest! There's a death-sthruggle goin' on in there! Poor Father Domineer's got a bad black eye, an' Micky Marthraun's coat is torn to tatthers!

Lorna [*hurrying into the garden*].   What's happened, what's happenin'?

Mahan [*with dignity—to One-eyed Larry*].   Misther Marthraun in your mouth, me lad.

Loreleen [*mischievously*].   Let th' lad tell his funny story.

One-eyed Larry [*turning on Loreleen*].   It's funny to you because you're in league with th' evil ones! [*To the others*] One o' Father Domineer's feet is all burned be a touch from one o' them, an' one o' Micky's is frozen stiff be a touch from another. [*To Mahan*] Maybe you'd ha' liked me to have lost me other eye while you were warmin' yourself in that one's arms!   [*He points to Loreleen.*

Mahan [*furiously*].   You one-eyed gett, if you had two, I'd cyclonise you with a box!

Loreleen [*unmoved—a little mockingly*].   An' how did th' poor lamb lose his eye?

Mahan [*indifferently*].   Oh, when he was a kid, he was hammerin' a bottle, an' a flyin' piece cut it out of his head.

One-eyed Larry [*venomously*].   You're a liar, that wasn't th' way! It was th' Demon Cock who done it to me. Only certain eyes can see him, an' I had one that could. He caught me once when I was spyin' on him, put a claw over me left eye, askin' if I could see him then; an' on me sayin' no, put th' claw over th' other one, an' when I said I could see him clear now, says he, that eye sees too well, an' on that, he pushed an' pushed till it was crushed into me head.

Loreleen [*mockingly*].   What a sad thing to happen!

[*The house shakes worse than before, and seems to lurch over to one side. The flag-pole wags from side to side merrily; there is a rumble of thunder, and blue lightning flashes from the window. All, except Loreleen, cower together at the far end of the garden. She stands over by the wall partly framed by the sable sunflowers.*

Marion [*full of fright*].   Sacred Heart! Th' house'll fall asundher!

Loreleen [*gleefully*].   Let it! It's th' finest thing that could happen to it!

One-eyed Larry [*trembling violently*].   It's now or never for them an' for us. They're terrible powerful spirits. Knocked th' bell outa me hand, blew out th' candle, an' tore th' book to threads! Thousands of them there are, led be th' bigger ones—Kissalass, Velvethighs, Reedabuck,

Dancesolong, an' Sameagain. Keep close. Don't run. They might want help. [*Screeches like those of barn owls are heard from the house, with the "too-whit too-whoo" of other kinds, the cackling of hens, and the loud cawing of crows. Frantically pushing his way to the back of the others*] Ooh! Let me get back, get back!

> [*The house shakes again; the flag-pole totters and falls flat; blue and red lightning flashes from the window, and a great peal of thunder drums through the garden. Then all becomes suddenly silent. They all hang on to each other, shivering with fear, except Loreleen, who lights a cigarette, puts a foot on a chair, leans on its back, looks at the house, and smokes away serenely.*

Lorna [*tremulously*].   Why has th' house gone so silent suddenly?

One-eyed Larry [*from the rear.*]   They've either killed th' demons, or th' demons has killed them.

Marion.   God save us, they must be dead!

Loreleen [*with quiet mockery*].   Welcome be th' will o' God.

Lorna [*suddenly—with great agitation*].   Get back, get back! Run! There's something comin' out!

> [*She, Marion, and One-eyed Larry race for the gateway, rush on to the sidewalk, and bend down, so that only their heads can be seen peeping over the wall. Mahan shrinks back to the far end of the garden, and Loreleen remains where she is.*

> [*From the house, sideways, through the now lurching porch, come Father Domineer and Michael. Both are limping, Father Domineer on his left foot, Michael on his right one. Domineer has a big black eye, his coat is awry on his back, and his hair is wildly tossed. Michael's coat hangs in tatters on him. Father Domineer's face is begrimed with the smudges of smoke, and both look tired, but elated.*

> [*One-eyed Larry at once runs out, and takes his place reverently behind them, standing with his hands folded piously in front of his breast, his eyes bent towards the ground. Mahan straightens up, and Lorna and Marion return to the garden. Loreleen remains as she was.*

Father Domineer [*as he enters with Michael*].   Be assured, good people, all's well, now. The house is safe for all. The evil things have been banished from the dwelling. Most of the myrmidons of Anticlericus, Secularius, an' Odeonius have been destroyed. The Civic Guard and the soldiers of Feehanna Fawl will see to the few who escaped. We can think quietly again of our Irish Sweep. Now I must go to my car to go home, and have a wash an' brush up. [*To Marion and Lorna*] Off you go into the house, good women. Th' place, th' proper place, th' only place for th' woman. Straighten it out, and take pride in doing it. [*He shoves Marion towards the porch*] Go on, woman, when you're told! [*To Michael*] You'll have to exert your authority more as head of the house.

Michael [*asserting it at once—to Lorna*].   You heard what Father Domineer said. Go on; in you go, an' show yourself a decent, God-fearin' woman.

Father Domineer [*trying to be gracious—to Lorna*].   Th' queen of th' household as th' husband is th' king.

> [*Marion has gone into the house with a sour-looking face, and Lorna now follows her example, looking anything but charmed.*

Father Domineer [*turning to Loreleen*].   And you—aren't you going in to help?

Loreleen [*quietly*].   No, thanks; I prefer to stay on in the garden.

Father Domineer [*thunderously*].   Then learn to stand on the earth in a more modest and suitable way, woman! [*Pointing to ornaments on crest of hat and breast of bodice*] An' do you mind that th' ornaments ye have on of brooch an' bangle were invented be th' fallen angels, now condemned to everlastin' death for worshippin' beauty that faded before it could be clearly seen? [*Angrily*] Oh, woman, *de cultus feminarum malifico eradicum!*

Michael.   That one's mind is always mustherin' dangerous thoughts plundered outa evil books!

Father Domineer [*startled*].   Books? What kinda books? Where are they?

Michael.   She has some o' them in th' house this minute.

Father Domineer [*roaring*].   Bring them out, bring them out! How often have I to warn you against books! Hell's bells tolling people away from th' thruth! Bring them out, *in annem fiat ecclesiam nonsensio,* before th' demoneens we've banished flood back into th' house again!

> [*Michael and One-eyed Larry jostle together into the porch and into the house to do Father Domineer's bidding.*

Loreleen [*taking her leg down from the chair, and striding over to Father Domineer*].   You fool, d'ye know what you're thryin' to do? You're thryin' to keep God from talkin'!

Father Domineer.   You're speakin' blasphemy, woman!

Mahan. What do people want with books? I don't remember readin' a book in me life.

[*Michael comes back carrying a book, followed by One-eyed Larry carrying another. Father Domineer takes the book from Michael, and glances at the title-page.*

Father Domineer [*explosively*]. A book about Voltaire! [*To Loreleen*] This book has been banned, woman.

Loreleen [*innocently*]. Has it now? If so, I must read it over again.

Father Domineer [*to One-eyed Larry*]. What's th' name of that one?

One-eyed Larry [*squinting at the title*]. Ullisississies, or something.

Father Domineer. Worse than th' other one. [*He hands his to One-eyed Larry.*] Bring th' two o' them down to th' Presbytery, an' we'll destroy them. [*Loreleen snatches the two books from One-eyed Larry. One-eyed Larry tries to prevent her, but a sharp push from her sends him toppling over. Loreleen, with great speed, darts out of the gateway, runs along the pathway, and disappears. Standing as if stuck to the ground*] After her, after her!

Michael [*astonished*]. Me legs won't move!

Mahan
One-eyed Larry } [*together*]. Nor mine, neither.

[*As Loreleen disappears, the Cock suddenly springs over the wall, and pirouettes in and out between them as they stand stuck to the ground.*

[*Cute ears may hear the quick tune, played softly, of an accordion, as the Cock weaves his way about. The Sergeant appears running outside, stops when he sees the Cock, leans over the wall, and presents a gun at Michael.*

Michael [*frantically—to Sergeant*]. Not me, man, not me!

[*Terribly excited, the Sergeant swings the gun till it is pointing at Mahan.*

Mahan [*frantically*]. Eh, not me, man!

After the Cock has pirouetted round for some moments, while they all remain transfixed, the scene suddenly goes dark, though the music continues to sound through it. Then two squib-like shots are heard, followed by a clash of thunder, and, when the garden enjoys the light of early dusk again, which comes immediately after the clap of thunder, the music as suddenly ceases.

[*The returning light shows that Father Domineer is not there; that*

> *Michael and Mahan are stretched out on the ground; and that*
> *One-eyed Larry is half over the wall, his belly on it, his legs trailing*
> *into the garden, his head and shoulders protruding into the road.*

Michael [*moaning*].   Shot through the soft flesh an' th' hard bone!

Mahan [*groaning*].   Shot through th' hard bone an' th' soft flesh!

One-eyed Larry [*shouting*].   Mrs. Marthraun, Marion, we're all killed be th' Cock an' th' Sergeant!

> [*Lorna and Marion come running out of the house over to the*
> *two prostrate men.*

Lorna.   What's happened? Where's th' Sergeant?

One-eyed Larry [*sliddering over the wall, frantic with fear*].   I seen him runnin' off when he'd shot us all! I'm goin' home, I'm goin' home! Father Domineer's been carried off be th' Demon Cock—I'm off!

> [*He runs swiftly down the road, and disappears.*

Lorna [*bending over Michael*].   Where were you hit? D'ye think there's a chance of you dyin'?

Michael [*despairingly*].   I'm riddled!

Lorna [*feeling his body over*].   I can't see a speck of damage on you anywhere, you fool.

Marion [*who has been examining Mahan*].   No, nor on this fella either.

Michael.   I tell you th' bullet careened through me breast an' came out be me back!

Mahan.   An' then tore through me back an' came out be me breast!

Lorna.   What darkness was One-eyed Larry talkin' about? An' Father Domineer carried off be the Cock! Me nerves are all gettin' shattered. It's all very thryin'. [*She pokes Michael roughly with her foot.*]   Here, get up, th' both of yous. There isn't a thing wrong with either of you.

Mahan [*sitting up cautiously, and feeling in his breast pocket*].   What th' hell's this? [*He pulls out a bullet bigger than a cigar.*] Looka, Michael Marthraun, th' size of th' bullet that went tearin' through you an' then through me! [*Very devoutly*] Good angels musta gone along with it, healin' all at th' same time that it tore our vitals.

Michael [*as devoutly*].   Some higher an' special power musta been watchin' over us, Sailor Mahan. Sharin' a miracle, now, Sailor Mahan, we're more than brothers.

Mahan [*fervently*].   We are that, now; we are indeed. I'll keep this bullet till th' day I die as a momento of a mementous occasion!

Lorna [*impatiently*]. Get up, get up. An' don't disturb us again while we're practisin' for the fancy-dhress dance tonight in th' hope of winning a spot prize.

Michael [*furiously to her*]. You'll win no spot prize, an' there'll be no dance till that Demon Cock's laid low! [*To Mahan—piously*] Thrue men we are, workin' in a thruly brotherly way for th' good of th' entire community—aren't we, Sailor Mahan? That's what saved us!

Mahan [*as piously*]. We are that, Michael; we are indeed; especially now that we've settled th' question finally so long disputed between us.

Michael [*suspiciously, a note of sharpness in his voice*]. How settled it?

Mahan. Be you arrangin' to give me, not only what I was askin', but twice as much.

Michael [*sarcastically*]. Oh, did I now? That was damned good of me! [*Angrily*] No, nor what you were askin' either. D'ye want me to ruin meself to glorify you? An' didn't I hear a certain man promisin', nearly on his oath, he'd give his lorries for next to nothin' to serve th' community?

Mahan [*shouting*]. When I was undher a spell, fosthered on me here! I'm goin', I'm goin'. I'll argue no more! [*He goes out by the gate and along the road, pausing as he is about to disappear.*] For th' last time, Michael Marthraun, are you goin' to do do th' decent for th' sake of the nation, an' give me what I'm askin'?

Michael [*with decision—quietly*]. No, Sailor Mahan, I'm not. [*He shouts*] I'd see you in hell first!

Mahan [*as he goes*]. A sweet goodbye to you, an' take a dhrug to keep from stayin' awake o' nights thinkin' of the nation's needs!

Lorna [*persuasively*]. Be reasonable, Michael. You're makin' enough now to be well able to give him all he asks.

Michael [*savagely seizing her arm*]. Listen, you: even though you keep th' accounts for me, it's a law of nature an' a law of God that a wife must be silent about her husband's secrets! D'ye hear me, you costumed slut?

Lorna [*freeing herself with an effort*]. Don't tear th' arm out of me! If you want to embalm yourself in money, you won't get me to do it!

> [*The sound of the wind rising is heard now—a long, sudden gust-like sound, causing Michael to do a sudden rush towards the gate, pressing himself back all the time, and gripping the wall when he gets to it. The two women do not notice the wind.*]

Michael.   Jasus! that was a sudden blast!

Lorna [*wondering*].   Blast? I felt no blast.

Marion [*shaking her head*].   He's undher a spell again.

> [*One-eyed Larry comes running along the road outside, excited and shouting. He is holding on tensely to the waist-band of his trousers.*

One-eyed Larry [*without the wall*].   A miracle, a miracle! Father Domineer, outa th' darkness, was snatched from th' claws of the Demon Cock, an' carried home safe on th' back of a white duck!

Lorna [*amazed*].   On th' back of a white duck? When will wondhers cease! They're all goin' mad!

Michael [*clapping his hands*].   Grand news! Was it a wild duck, now, or merely a domestic one?

One-eyed Larry.   Wild or tame, what does it matther? It carried him cheerily through th' sky, an' deposited him dacently down on his own doorstep!

Michael [*with deep thought*].   It might well have been one of me own sensible ducks that done it.

One-eyed Larry [*coming to the gate*].   Wait till I tell yous. Th' Demon Cock's furious at his escape, an' he's causin' consthernation. He's raised a fierce wind be th' beat of his wings, an' it's tossin' cattle on to their backs; whippin' th' guns from th' hands of Civic Guard an' soldier, so that th' guns go sailin' through th' sky like cranes; an' th' wind's tearin' at the clothes of th' people. It's only be hard holdin' that I can keep me own trousers on!

Michael [*eagerly*].   Th' wind near whipped me on to th' road a minute ago.

> [*The Bellman enters on the pathway outside, and meets One-eyed Larry at the gateway, so that the two of them stand there, the one on the left, the other to the right of it.*

> [*The collar and one arm are all that are left of the Bellman's coat, and his shirt has been blown outside of his trousers. He is still wearing the brass hat. His right hand is gripping his waist-band, and his left carries the bell that he is ringing.*

Bellman [*shouting*].   Get out, get in! Th' Demon Cock's scourin' th' skies again, mettlesome, menacin', molestifyin' monsther! Fly to your houses, fall upon your knees, shut th' doors, close th' windows! In a tearin' rage, he's rippin' th' clouds outa th' sky, because Father Domineer was snatched away from him, an' carried home, fit an' well, on th' back of a speckled duck!

One-eyed Larry [*startled into anger*]. You're a liar, it wasn't a speckled duck! What are you sayin', fella? It was a pure white duck that carried th' Father home!

Bellman [*angrily—to One-eyed Larry*]. Liar yourself, an' you're wrong! It was a speckled duck that done it; speckled in black, brown, an' green spots. I seen it with me own two eyes doin' th' thrick.

One-eyed Larry [*vehemently*]. I seen it with me one eye in concentration, an' it was a duck white as th' dhriven snow that brought him to his domiceel.

Lorna. I'd say white's a sensible colour, an' more apter for th' job.

Michael. I'd say a speckled duck would look more handsome landin' on a doorstep than a white fowl.

Marion [*thoughtfully*]. I wondher, now, could it have been Mr. McGilligan's tame barnacle goose?

Michael [*explosively*]. No, it couldn't have been Mr. McGilligan's tame barnacle goose! Don't be thryin' to scatther confusion over a miracle happenin' before our very eyes!

[*The Sergeant comes rushing in along the pathway outside the wall, and runs into the garden through the gateway, roughly shoving the Bellman and One-eyed Larry out of his way. His cap is gone, a piece of rope is tied round his chest to keep his coat on; and, when he reaches the gate, all can see that he wears no trousers, leaving him in a long shirt over short pants. He is excited, and his face is almost convulsed with fear and shame.*]

Sergeant [*shoving One-eyed Larry and Bellman aside*]. Outa me way, you fools! [*Rushing into the garden—to Michael*] Give me one of your oul' trousers, Mick, for th' love o' God! Whipped off me be a blast of th' wind me own were. When I seen them goin', me entire nature was galvanised into alarmin' anxiety as to what might happen next.

Michael. A terrible experience! What's to come of us, at all!

Sergeant [*tearfully*]. Why isn't Father Domineer here to help? He doesn't care a damn now, since he was carried home, safe an' sound on th' back of a barnacle goose!

One-eyed Larry [*dumbfounded and angry*]. A barnacle goose? What are you sayin', man? It was a dazzlin' white duck that brought him home.

Bellman [*to One-eyed Larry*]. I'm tellin' you it was a specially speckled duck that done it.

Sergeant [*emphatically*]. It was a goose, I'm sayin'. Th' Inspector seen it through a field-glass, an' identified it as a goose, a goose!

Lorna [*amused—laying a hand on Marion's shoulder*]. Look at him, Marion. All dollied up for th' fancy-dhress dance!

Marion [*hilariously*]. It's lookin' like th' blue bonnets are over th' bordher!

Michael [*angrily—to the Sergeant*]. Get into th' house, man, an' don't be standin' there in that style of half-naked finality! You'll find some oul' trousers upstairs. [*Turning on Lorna and Marion as the Sergeant trots timidly into the house*] You two hussies, have yous no semblance of sense of things past an' things to come? Here's a sweet miracle only afther happenin', an' there yous are, gigglin' an' gloatin' at an aspect in a man that should send th' two of yous screamin' away! Yous are as bad as that one possessed, th' people call me daughter.

[*The sound of the wind now rises, swifter, shriller, and stronger, carrying in it an occasional moan, as in a gale, and with this stronger wind comes the Messenger, sauntering along outside the wall, sitting down on it when he reaches the end farthest from the house. Nothing in the garden is moved by the wind's whistling violence, except Michael, the Bellman, and One-eyed Larry (who have been suddenly hustled into the garden by the wind). These three now grip their waist-bands, and begin to make sudden movements to and fro, as if dragged by an invisible force; each of them trying to hold back as the wind pushes them forward. The Messenger is coaxing a soft tune from his accordion; while Marion and Lorna are unaffected by the wind, and stand staring at the men, amused by their antics.*]

Michael [*a little frantic*]. Listen to th' risin' evil of th' wind! Oh, th' beat of it, oh, th' beat of it! We know where it comes from—red wind on our backs, black wind on our breasts, thryin' to blow us to hell!

Bellman [*gliding about, pushed by the wind; holding on to his trousers with one hand, while he rings his bell with the other one*]. Fly into th' houses, close th' windows, shut th' doors!

One-eyed Larry [*gliding in opposite direction*]. We can't, we can't—we go where th' wind blows us!

Messenger. What ails yous? I feel only th' brisk breeze carryin' the smell of pinewoods, or th' softer one carryin' th' scent of th' ripenin' apples.

Michael [*to the women, while he holds fast to his waist-band*]. Get in, an' sthrip off them coloured deceits, smellin' of th' sly violet an' th' richer rose, sequestherin' a lure in every petal! Off with them, I say, an' put on a cautious grey, or th' stated humbleness of a coal-black gown! [*The Sergeant comes from the house wearing Michael's best black Sunday trousers. He comes from the porch shyly, but the moment he steps into the garden, his face flashes into a grim look, and he grabs hold of the waist-band, and glides about as the others do. Michael, seeing the trousers—with a squeal of indignation*] Me best Sunday black ones! Couldn't your damned plundherin' paws pounce on something a little lowlier to wear?

Bellman. Get into th' houses, shut to th' doors, close th' windows!

    [*Father Domineer suddenly appears on the pathway outside, and stands at the gateway looking into the garden. A gust of wind, fierce and shrill, that preceded him, declines in a sad wail, and ceases altogether, leaving a sombre silence behind it. Father Domineer's hair is tossed about; he has a wild look in his eyes, and he carries a walking-stick to help him surmount the limp from the hurt he got when warring with the evil spirits.*]

Father Domineer [*stormily*]. Stop where yous are! No hidin' from the enemy! Back to hell with all bad books, bad plays, bad pictures, and bad thoughts! Cock o' th' north, or cock o' th' south, we'll down derry doh down him yet. Shoulder to shoulder, an' step together against th' onward rush of paganism! Boldly tread, firm each foot, erect each head!

One-eyed Larry
Michael
Bellman   } [*together—very feebly*]. Hurraah!
Sergeant

Father Domineer. Fixed in front be every glance, forward at th' word advance!

One-eyed Larry
Michael
Bellman   } [*together—very feebly*]. Advance!
Sergeant

Father Domineer. We know where we're goin', an' we know who's goin' with us.

Michael. The minsthrel boy with th' dear harp of his country, an' Brian O'Lynn.

Bellman. Danny Boy an' th' man who sthruck O'Hara.

One-eyed Larry. Not forgettin' Mick McGilligan's daughter, Maryann!

[*Sounds of fifing and drumming are heard, mingled with the sound of boo-ing, a little distance away.*

Father Domineer [*jubilantly*].   Listen to th' band! We're closin' in; we're winnin'! [*He puts a hand up to shade his eyes, and peers forward.*] They've collared one of them! Aha, a woman again! [*A pause.*] A fine, familiar one too. [*He shouts*] Lead th' slut here, Shanaar, right here in front of me!

[*He goes through the gateway, and waits in the garden for things to come.*

[*Shanaar appears on the pathway, followed by the two Rough Fellows dragging Loreleen along. She is in a sad way. Her hair is tumbled about; her clothes are disarranged; her bodice unbuttoned, and her skirt reefed half-way up, showing a slim leg, with the nylon stocking torn. One of the Rough Fellows is carrying her hat with its cock-like crest in his hand. A blood-stained streak stretches from a corner of an eye half-way down a cheek. Her face is very pale, and intense fright is vividly mirrored in it. She is dragged by the arms along the ground by the men, led by Shanaar, to where the Priest is standing. When she is nicely placed before him, she hangs her head, ashamed of her dishevelled state, and of the way she has been pulled before him. Other men and women follow them in, but are checked from crowding the pathway by an order from the Priest. The Messenger rises from his seat on the wall, and comes near to where the men are holding Loreleen. He has placed the carrying straps of his accordion over his shoulders, and now bears the instrument on his back. Michael, the Bellman, and One-eyed Larry stand some way behind the Priest. Marion and Lorna have started to come to Loreleen's assistance, but have been imperiously waved back by Father Domineer, and have retreated back towards the house, where they stand to stare at what happens. Shanaar stands at the gateway, gloating over the woeful condition of Loreleen.*

Father Domineer [*to those following the men dragging in Loreleen*]. Go back; keep back there! Give th' honied harlot plenty of space to show herself off in.

Shanaar [*down to Father Domineer*].   Tell her off, Father; speak to her in th' name of holy Ireland!

Father Domineer [*to Sergeant*].   You go, Sergeant, an' keep them from coming too close; [*to Shanaar*] an' you, Shanaar, stand at the opposite end to keep any others from pressing in on us. [*To the men holding Loreleen*]   Bring her a little closer.   [*The men drag her closer.*

Father Domineer. Now, jerk her to her feet. [*The men jerk her up-right.*] Well, me painted paramour, you're not looking quite so gay now; your impudent confidence has left you to yourself. Your jest with heaven is over, me lass! [*To the men*] How did you ketch her?

1st Rough Fellow [*with pride*]. We've been on her tail, Father, for some time. We ketched her in a grand car with a married man; with a married man, Father, an' he thryin' to put an arm round her.

2nd Rough Fellow [*butting in to share the pride of capture*]. So we hauled her outa th' car, and hustled her here to you.

Lorna [*running over to the man nearest to her, and catching his arm*]. Let th' poor lass go, you cowardly lout! I know you: your whole nature's a tuft of villainies! Lust inflames your flimsy eyes whenever a skirt passes you by. If God had given you a tusk, you'd rend asundher every woman of th' disthrict!

Father Domineer [*angrily—to Lorna*]. Get back to your place woman! [*Shouting, as she hesitates*] Get back when I tell you!

[*Lorna moves slowly away from Loreleen's side and goes into the house.*

Marion [*as she follows Lorna into the house*]. Dastard Knights of Colum-banus, do noble work, an' do it well!

Loreleen [*to Father Domineer—appealingly*]. Make them let me go, Father, an' let me get into th' house! It was Sailor Mahan promised me enough to take me away from here that made me go to him. I shouldn't have gone, but I wanted to get away; [*brokenly*] get away, away! Five pounds he gave me, an' they took them off me, with th' last two pounds of me own I had left.

Father Domineer [*savagely*]. Sailor Mahan's a decent, honest soul, woman! A man fresh for th' faith, full of good works for clergy an' his neighbours. [*He bends down to hiss in her ears*] An' this is th' man, you sinful slut, this is th' man you would pet an' probe into a scarlet sin!

Loreleen. I only wanted to get away. I wanted to get away from Sailor Mahan as much as I wanted to get away from all here.

Father Domineer [*to the two Rough Fellows*]. Where's Sailor Mahan?

1st Rough Fellow. Th' people pelted him back to his home an' proper wife, Father, an' he's there now, in bed, an' sorry for what he thried to do.

Loreleen [*plaintively*]. Make them give me back th' last few pounds I had.

Father Domineer [*to the Rough Fellows*]. You shouldn't have handled Sailor Mahan so roughly. Where's the money?

2nd Rough Fellow. We tore it up, Father, thinkin' it wasn't fit to be handled be anyone of decent discernment.

Loreleen [*emphatically*]. They didn't; they kept it. [*Stifling a scream*] Oh, they're twisting me arms!

Father Domineer [*cynically*]. Don't be timid of a little twinge of pain, woman, for, afther th' life you've lived, you'll welther in it later. [*To the two Rough Fellows*] Yous should have kept th' money to be given to th' poor.

Messenger [*coming over to the Rough Fellow on Loreleen's right—calmly*]. Let that fair arm go, me man, for, if you don't, there's a live arm here'll twist your neck instead. [*With a shout*] Let it go! [*After a nod from the Priest, the 1st Rough Fellow lets Loreleen's arm go. The Messenger goes quietly round to the 2nd Rough Fellow.*] Let that fair arm go, me man, or another arm may twist your own neck! Let it go! [*The 2nd Rough Fellow sullenly does so.*] Now stand a little away, an' give th' girl room to breathe. [*The two Rough Fellows move a little away from Loreleen*]. Thank you. [*To the Priest*] Now, Father, so full of pity an' loving-kindness, jet out your bitther blessin', an' let th' girl go. An' thry to mingle undherstandin' with your pride, so as to ease th' tangle God has suffered to be flung around us all.

Father Domineer [*fiercely—to the Messenger*]. Keep farther away, you, for th' crowd is angry and their arms are sthrong! We know you— enemy to th' glow of tradition's thruth, enemy to righteous reprobation, whose rowdy livery is but dyed in rust from th' gates of hell! [*To Loreleen*] An' you, you'd hook your unholy reputation to a decent man's life. A man, like Sailor Mahan, diligent in his duty, th' echo of whose last prayer can ever be heard when another worshipper enters th' church. You'd sentence him to stand beside you, you shuttle-cock of sin!

Loreleen [*roused to indignation*]. Oh, end it, will you! You fail in honesty when you won't make them give me back what they robbed from me. When you condemn a fair face, you sneer at God's good handi- work. You are layin' your curse, sir, not upon a sin, but on a joy. Take care a divil doesn't climb up your own cassock into your own belfry!

Father Domineer [*furiously*]. You'll dhribble th' blackness of sin no no longer over our virtuous bordhers! [*He hisses the words out*] *Stipendium peccati mors est!* Get away from here quicker than you came, or it's in your coffin you'll be—in your coffin, your coffin!

Shanaar [*from the gateway*]. A merciful sentence, an aysey one, for a one like her!

Loreleen [*half defiantly*]. How am I to go where I'd like to go, when they took all I had off me? How am I to go for miles with me clothes near rent from me back, an' frail shoes on me feet?

Father Domineer [*putting his face closer to hers*]. Thrudge it; thrudge on your two feet; an' when these burn an' blister, go on your knees; an' when your knees are broken an' bruised, go on your belly; crawl in th' dust, as did th' snake in th' Garden of Eden, for dust is th' right cushion for th' like of you! [*He raises himself erect, and commands in a loud voice*] Go now!

> [*Loreleen turns away, goes slowly through the gateway, and along the road outside. As Loreleen reaches the gate, Lorna runs out of the house. She is wearing a dark-red cloak, and carries a green one over her arm. She has a fairly large rucksack strapped on her back.*

Lorna [*calling as she runs out of the house*]. Loreleen! [*Loreleen halts but does not turn her head.*] Loreleen, I go with you! [*Lorna shoves Father Domineer aside at the gateway, nearly knocks Shanaar over, and hurries to Loreleen. Draping the green cloak over Loreleen's shoulders*] I go with you, love. I've got a sthrong pair of shoes in the sack you can put on when we're free from th' Priest an' his rabble. Lift up your heart, lass: we go not towards an evil, but leave an evil behind us!

> [*They go out slowly together.*

Father Domineer [*taking the Sergeant by the arm*]. Let her go quietly to her own. We'll follow some of the way to prevent anyone from harming her. [*Down to Michael*] Be of good cheer, Michael; th' demon is conquered—you can live peaceful an' happy in your own home now.

> [*He goes out with the Sergeant, followed by all who may be there, except Michael, the Messenger, and Shanaar.*

> [*The Messenger goes back to the wall, sits on it sideways, takes the accordion from his back, and begins to play, very softly, the air of "Oh, Woman Gracious". Shanaar leans on the wall from the outside, looking down at Michael, who is now seated gloomily on a chair beside the table, an elbow resting on it, his head resting on the hand.*

Shanaar [*down to Michael*]. His reverence never spoke a thruer word, Mick, than that of you'd have happiness an' peace now. You were a long time without them, but you have them now.

Michael [*doubtfully*]. Maybe I have, Shanaar, an', God knows, I need them. [*He pauses for a moment, thinking*] I wondher will Lorna come back?

Shanaar [*emphatically*].   Oh, devil a come back! You need have no fear o' that, man. An' fortunate you are, for a woman's always a menace to a man's soul. Woman is th' passionate path to hell!

Messenger [*playing softly on his accordion and singing*]:
    Oh, woman gracious, in golden garments,
    Through life's dark places, all glintin' go;
    Bring man, in search of th' thruth tremendous,
    Th' joy that ev'ry young lad should know.
    Then come out, darlin', in reckless raiment,
    We'll dance along through Ireland gay,
    An' clip from life life's rich enjoyments,
    An' never want for a word to say.

    [*Marion has come into the porch, and now stands at the door, watching the Messenger. She is covered to her knees by a bright-blue cloak.*

    Cling close to youth with your arms enthrancin',
    For youth is restless, an' loth to stay;
    So take your share of th' kisses goin',
    Ere sly youth, tirin', can slink away!
    [*Marion crosses the garden towards the gate, and is about to go through it when the Messenger catches her by the arm.*

Would you leave me here, alone, without a lass to love me?

Marion [*gently removing the hold of his hand on her arm*].   Your voice is dear to me; your arm around me near seals me to you; an' I'd love to have——

Messenger [*quickly*].   Your lips on mine!

Marion.   But not here, Robin Adair, oh, not here; for a whisper of love in this place bites away some of th' soul! [*She goes out by the gateway, and along the road taken by Lorna and Loreleen. The Messenger stays where he is, wistful and still. Just before she goes*] Come, if you want to, Robin Adair; stay, if you will.

Shanaar [*to the Messenger*].   Stay, Messenger. Take a warnin' from a wise oul' man, a very wise oul' one, too. [*He turns his head to look peeringly to the left along the road.*] What's this I see comin'? If it isn't Julia, back from Lourdes, an' she on her stretcher still! I'd best be off, for I've no inclination to thry a chatter with a one who's come back as bad as she was when she went.

[*He bends down nearly double, so as not to be seen, and slyly and quietly steals away.*

[*After a pause, Julia comes in on her stretcher, carried by the two Rough Fellows as before, her father, silent and stony-faced, walking beside her. The stretcher is laid down in the garden just inside the gate. Julia is covered with a rug, black as a winter's sky, and its sombre hue is enlivened only by the chalk-white face of the dying girl. The Messenger has gone from the gateway, and now stands in a half-to-attention, military way, a little distance from the stretcher, looking down at Julia. Julia's father stands, as before, behind her head. Michael sits, unnoticing, elbow on table, his head resting on his hand.*

Julia [*in a toneless voice—to no-one in particular*]. Lorna, I want Lorna.

Messenger [*gently*]. She's gone, Julia.

Julia. Gone? Gone where?

Messenger. To a place where life resembles life more than it does here.

Julia. She's a long way to go, then. It's th' same everywhere. In Lourdes as here, with all its crowds an' all its candles. I want Loreleen.

Messenger. She's gone with Lorna, an' Marion's followed them both.

Julia. Then there's no voice left to offer even th' taunting comfort of asking if I feel better.

Messenger. 'There's Michael Marthraun there.

Julia [*after a long look at Michael*]. He, poor man, is dyin' too. No-one left, an' th' stir there was when I was goin'—th' mayor there, with all his accouthered helpers; th' band playin'; Father Domineer spoutin' his blessin'; an' oul' Shanaar busy sayin' somersaultin' prayers; because they all thought I would bring a sweet miracle back. [*She pauses.*] There was no miracle, Robin; she didn't cure me, she didn't cure me, Robin. I've come back, without even a gloamin' thought of hope. [*She pauses again; with a wan smile*] I can see your whole soul wishin' you could cure me. Touch me with your questionable blessin' before I go.

Messenger [*very softly*]. Be brave.

Julia. Nothin' else, Robin Adair?

Messenger. Evermore be brave.

Julia [*after a pause*]. Dad, take me home.

[*The Rough Fellows take up the stretcher and carry it out, the stony-faced father following in the rear without a word.*

Michael [*raising his head from his hand to look at the Messenger*]. Maybe Lorna might come back. Maybe I mightn't have been so down on her fancy dhressin'.

Messenger [*tonelessly*].   Maybe she will; maybe you mightn't.

Michael [*tonelessly too*].   It'll be very lonely for me now. All have left me. [*He takes a set of rosary beads from his pocket, and fingers them.*] I've no one left to me but th' Son o' God. [*He notices the Messenger settling the accordion comfortably on his back, and watches him going to the gate.*] Are you goin' too?

Messenger [*shortly*].   Ay.

Michael.   Where?

Messenger.   To a place where life resembles life more than it does here.

Michael [*after a pause*].   What, messenger, would you advise me to do?

Messenger [*turning at the gate to reply*].   Die. There is little else left useful for the likes of you to do.

    [*He swings his accordion comfortably before him, and plays a few preliminary notes. Then he starts to sing softly as he goes away along the pathway outside; while Michael leans forward on to the table, and buries his head in his arms.*

Messenger [*singing and accompanying himself on the accordion—as he is going off*]:
    She's just like a young star out taking the air—
    Let others be good or be clever—

    With Marion gay, a gay flower in her hair,
    Life becomes but a pleasant endeavour.

    When building a city or making the hay,
    I'll follow her close as night follows day,

    Or lads follow lasses out nutting in May,
    For ever and ever and ever!

THE END

BEDTIME STORY

An Anatole Burlesque in One Act

(1951)

✿ ✿ ✿

CHARACTERS IN THE PLAY

JOHN JO MULLIGAN, *a clerk*
ANGELA NIGHTINGALE, *a gay lass*
DANIEL HALIBUT, *a clerk—friend to Mulligan*
MISS MOSSIE, *a very respectable lodging-house keeper*
A POLICEMAN
A DOCTOR
A NURSE

SCENE

A bachelor-flat in Dublin.

TIME · The present.

The sitting-room of the bachelor-flat rented by John Jo Mulligan from Miss Mossie, owner of one of the old houses of Dublin, decayed a little, but still sternly respectable, and kept presentable by her rigid attention to it. She has divided it into lodgings for respectable young gentlemen. A rather dull though lofty room. To the right is an ordinary gas fire; over it a mantelpiece on which is a clock, flanked on either side by a coloured vase; over these, on the wall, a square, gilt-framed mirror. Further up, towards back, is a door leading to Mulligan's bedroom. By the back wall, near this door, is a small bookcase with a few books sprawled out on its shelves; and on top is a pale-green vase holding a bunch of white pampas grass. To the left of this is a window, now heavily curtained with dull, brown hangings. In the window's centre is a stand holding a coloured flower-pot containing some kind of a palm plant. Further on is a picture of a whitewashed cottage, well thatched with straw, a brown pathway before the door, with purple heather growing in tufts on its edges, and, in the distance, the dark-blue peaks of hills, all surmounted by a bright blue sky. In the side wall on the left is the door leading to the rest of the house. On this door several overcoats are hanging. To the left of it is an umbrella-stand in which are a walking-stick and two umbrellas, one newer than the other. Close to the fireplace is an armchair clad in dark-green leather, and further away, at any angle, is a settee to hold two, clad in the same colour. In the room's centre is a round table covered with a red table-cloth. On the table are a photograph or two, a vase of chrysanthemums, and a book, open, with its face turned down, so that the place might not be lost when the reader left it aside. The room is lighted from a bulb hanging from the centre of the ceiling; the light is softened by being covered with a yellow parchment shade. A standard lamp stands on the floor a little way from the sitting-room door, towards the window, its light mollified by a deeply-fringed red silk shade. A key is sticking in the keyhole of the sitting-room door. A pair of Mulligan's tan shoes are beside the fireplace. It is three or four of a cold, sleety January morning.

The fire is unlit, the room in darkness, when, presently, the bedroom door opens, and Mulligan comes into the sitting-room, showing the way to himself by the light of an electric torch. He is but half dressed, in blue shirt, bright-checked, baggy plus-fours, and coloured-top stockings. He is a young man of twenty-four or -five; tall, but not thin. His hair is almost blond, and he wears it brushed back from his forehead, which is too high for the rather stolid face, giving him, at times, the look of a clown having a holiday. His upper lip has a close-cropped moustache. He is a constitution-ally frightened chap, never able to take the gayer needs of life in his stride —though he would be glad to do it, if he could; but he can never become convalescent from a futile sense of sin. His clean-shaven face shows a very worried look. He comes into the room cautiously, waving the light over the floor, the table, the chairs, as if looking for something—as a matter of fact, he is; then returns to the door to peep into the bedroom.

Mulligan [*sticking his head into the room—in a cautious whisper*]. I can't see the thing anywhere. Sure you left it out here? [*There is no reply to the question.*] I say I can't find it anywhere out here. [*There is no reply. He mutters to himself as if half in prayer*] I shouldn't have done it; I shouldn't have done it! I musta been mad. Oh, forgive me! [*He clicks his tongue, and peeps into the room again.*] Dtch dtch! Gone asleep again! [*Whispering*] Angela! Angela! [*In a louder whisper*] Are you awake? Eh, Angela?

Angela [*within the room—sleepily*]. Wha'?

Mulligan [*echoing her*]. Wha', wha'! [*To himself*] Oh, it was a mad thing to do. Miserere mei. [*Speaking into room with irritation*] Have you forgotten what you sent me out to get? [*Appealingly*] Please try to arouse yourself, Angela!

Angela [*within*]. Wha'?

> [*Silence again for a few moments while Mulligan flashes the light on to the clock.*

Mulligan. It's going to four o'clock in the morning, Angela.

Angela [*within*]. Didja get the lipstick?

Mulligan [*testily*]. I've told you I can't see it anywhere.

Angela [*sleepily*]. Have another look—there's a dear. I know I left it out there somewhere.

Mulligan [*shivering a little*]. It's nothing like a tropical climate out here, you know.

Angela [*sleepily*]. It's easy to li' the fire, isn't it?

> [*Mulligan crosses to the fireplace, turns the gas tap, and sees that the meter wants another shilling. He irritatedly turns the tap off, and, crossing quickly back to the bedroom, knocks over the vase of flowers on the table, sending the water spilling over the table and on to the floor.*

Mulligan [*half to himself and half to Angela—with annoyance*]. There's the vase down! Wather into me shoes and all over the floor! [*Putting his head into the bedroom again*] I've knocked the vase down now! The place is flooded! And I can't light the fire—the meter needs another shilling.

Angela [*sleepily*]. Look in me han'bag, somewhere about. Maybe there's a bob in it.

[*In desperation, Mulligan goes to the cupboard, opens it, takes out a wallet from which he takes a shilling, goes back to fireplace, puts it in the slot, and lights the fire. Then he returns to the bedroom door.*

Mulligan [*putting his head into the bedroom again*].   Angela, are you up yet? The whole place is flooded. [*He gets no answer.*] You're not going asleep again, are you? Angela!

Angela [*within—sleepily*].   What time is it?

Mulligan [*in a loud and impatient whisper*].   I told you long ago. It's going to four o'clock in the morning. That friend of mine I told you of, will be back any minute from his all-night dance, before you slip away, if you don't hurry.

Angela [*from within*].   And what if he is? If he knew what had been going on in here, he'd be sorry he ever went to the dance.

Mulligan.   Looka, Angela, I don't feel a bit funny about it. We should never have done it. Please get up, and face the situation. Remember your solemn promise to slip off when things were still.

[*Angela appears at the door. She is a girl of twenty-five to twenty-seven, tall, trimly-formed, and not without dignity. Her hair is auburn, inclining towards redness. She is something of a pagan.*

[*At present, she is dressed in her cami-knickers, covered by Mulligan's brown dressing-gown, and her bare feet are thrust into Mulligan's slippers. Far and away too good a companion of an hour, a year, or a life, for a fellow like Mulligan.*

Angela [*from the doorway*].   D'ye like the dark because your deeds are evil, or what? Switch on the light for God's sake, man, and let's have a look at each other before you banish your poor Eve from her Mulligan paradise.

Mulligan [*as he switches on the light*].   I was afraid someone outside might see it, stay to look, might hear our voices, and wonder.

Angela.   Wonder at what?

Mulligan.   At hearing a girl's voice in my room at this time of night or morning.

Angela [*mockingly*].   And isn't it a sweet thing for a girl's voice to be heard in a man's room at this time o' the night or morning?

Mulligan [*almost tearfully*].   You know it's not; not as we're situated. You know you did wrong to practise on a body who didn't know enough. Situated as we are, without divine warrant, it's not proper. We're in the midst of a violent sin, and you should be ashamed and sorry, instead of feeling sinfully gay about it. It's necessary to feel sorry for a sin of this kind.

Angela. You were quite gay when we were coming in, boy, weren't you? You've had your few bright moments, and you've given a sparkle to your life, so don't spoil it all. It may well be more serious for me than it is for you. [*She shivers.*] Burrr! It's cold here! I'll come back when the room's warmer, and make myself ready to meet the respectable world.

> [*She goes back into the bedroom, while he stands at the bedroom door for a few moments, not knowing what to do.*

Mulligan [*eyes raised appealing to the ceiling*]. Oh, that one'll be well punished for her gaiety and carelessness in sin! Oh, when will I forget this night's doings? Shattering fall! The very next day after me Novena too! [*He peeps into the bedroom.*] Don't get too cosy there, or you won't want to move. Move we must, and soon. [*He goes to the cupboard, relocks it, and puts the key in his pocket; then he goes to the armchair, sits down in it, and starts to put on his shoes. Putting on a shoe—in a half-prayer*] Sweet Saint Panteemalaria, get me outa this without exposure. [*He clicks his tongue*] Dtch dtch! Soaking wet! and I'll be a cautious goer from this out—I promise. [*He goes over to bedroom door again with but one shoe on, and peeps in.*] Angela, room's warm now; quite warm. The time's flying, mind you. [*There is no reply.*] Aw, God, have you gone to sleep again! Please, Miss Nightingale, please have some regard for others!

Angela [*from within—sleepily*]. Did you find it?

Mulligan. Find what, find what?

Angela. Me lipstick you were looking for?

Mulligan. No, no, I didn't; must be in there somewhere.

Angela. I remember I had it when you had me perched on your lap. Remember?

Mulligan [*as if to someone in sitting-room*]. Oh, don't be reminding me of things! [*Into the bedroom*] No, I don't remember. Oh, for goodness' sake, get up!

Angela. All right, all right. Put out a glass of wine, and I'll be out in a minute.

> [*Mulligan goes to the cupboard, unlocks it, and takes out a bottle of wine and a glass. He locks the cupboard again, leaving the key in the keyhole. He goes to the table, fills out a glass of wine, and leaves it, with the bottle, on the table, in readiness for Angela.*

> [*He sits down in the armchair, puts on the other shoe, then winds a*

woollen muffler round his neck, puts on a pullover and coat that have been hanging over the back of a chair, and finally places a trilby hat on his head. As he does these things, he occasionally mutters to himself.

Mulligan [*busy with the wine for Angela*].   Not a single thought has she for what might happen to me if discovery came. Utterly abandoned to her own intherests. [*As he sits in chair putting on the second shoe—in a full-blown prayer*] Oh, gentle Saint Camisolinus, guardianess of all good young people, get between me and this petticoated demonsthrator of sinful delusion, and I'll be O.K. for evermore. I will, I promise!

> [*Angela comes into the room at last, and makes quick for the fire. She has put on her stockings—silk ones—and skirt, a short, well-tailored one of darkish green, with broad belt of dark red and black buckle. She carries a brown jersey over her arm, and her shoes in her hand.*

Angela [*throwing her shoes on to the armchair, and stretching her hands to the fire*].   Burrr! It's cold out here still! I thought you said the room was warm? [*She notices how he's dressed.*] All ready for the journey, eh? Soon we'll be skiing down the stairs, wha'? Praying to all the saints you know to see me out, eh?

> [*She puts the jersey on over her head before the mirror over the fireplace, and pats it down smoothly over her breast and shoulders.*

Angela.   We have to face the hard, cold facts now, haven't we, dear?

Mulligan.   We've got to think now of what would become of me if you were discovered here.

Angela [*mockingly*].   Really? Of course, when one thinks of it, that becomes the one important problem.

Mulligan [*not noticing the mockery*].   It is, actually. You see, Angela, the head of my department's a grand Knight of Columbanus, an uncompromising Catholic, strict in his thought of life, and if he heard of anything like this, I'd—I'd be out in the bleaker air, quick; the little gilt I have on life would be gone; I'd run to ruin! God help me!

Angela [*prompting him*].   And then there's Father Demsey?

Mulligan.   Then there's Father Demsey whose right-hand man I am in the Confraternity and at all Saint Vincent de Paul meetings, with his "We can safely leave that matter with Mr. Mulligan", or "John Jo will do this for us". You see, it's a matter of importance to more than me. So, come on—we betther get off at once.

Angela [*rising from the chair, and drinking the glass of wine*].   Angela's bright eyes, her scarlet lip, fine foot, straight leg, and quivering thigh have lost their charm for Mr. Mulligan. He's all for go-ahead godliness now! [*She pours out another glass of wine and drinks it.*] And what is to become of me? You don't care, and I don't care either.

> [*She moves about the room in a slow, semi-reckless rhythm as she lilts—Mulligan following her trying to get her quiet again.*

Angela [*lilting and moving about*]:
> I don't care what becomes of me,
> I don't care what becomes of me.

Mulligan [*shuffling after her as she moves as well as he can—in a low, anguished voice*].   Angela, please! Sit down, do!

Angela [*lilting*]:
> I don't care if I'm out till two,
> I don't care for the man in blue.

Mulligan [*following her*].   Please, Miss Nightingale, be serious! The landlady'll hear you, and then we'll be done!

Angela [*lilting*]:
> I don't care what the people say,
> Here, there, and everywhere;

Mulligan [*appealing to the ceiling*].   Saint Curberisco, help me!

Angela [*in a final burst*]:
> For I'm going to be married in the morning,
> So tonight, boys, I don't care!

[*Facing towards Mulligan.*] Sometime or other, we have to face out of all we get into: face out of getting into bed with a woman no less than face out into silence from the glamour of prayer; face out of summer into winter; face out of life into death!

Mulligan [*crossing himself*].   Your talk's near blasphemy, Angela! Now you're going where you shouldn't venture. You'll bring a curse down on me, if you're not careful! Please be more discreet.

Angela.   They're facts.

Mulligan.   We're not fit for facts now.

Angela [*facing him fiercely*].   You stand there mustering up moans for yourself, and never once realise that you've ruined me! Yes, ruined me!

Mulligan [*startled*].   Oh, God, d'ye hear her! Ruined you? Oh, come, now, don't thry to act the innocent.

Angela.   It's you who's acting the innocent, but it won't work. I was only an innocent kid till I met you. You led me on and destroyed all confidence in the goodness of me own nature! You never, never ceased from persuasion till you got me here. I wasn't even to take off my hat, if I was the least bit suspicious. We were just to sit quiet discussing Yeats's poems. You were to sit ice-bound in your chair.

Mulligan [*indignantly*].   I led you on! Angela Nightingale, you're inventing things. It was you insisted on coming, because you didn't like restaurants. A sorry thing for me I ever listened to you!

Angela [*ignoring his remarks*].   It's me's the sorry soul for listening to you. You promised a quiet hour of poetry, but we were hardly here when you began to move. Yeats's poems soon flew out of your head and hand. You got as far as "I will arise and go now, and go to Innisfree"; then before the echo of the line was hushed, you had me clapped down on your knee. [*She becomes tearful.*] That was the start of my undoing. What am I going to do!

Mulligan [*lifting his eyes to the ceiling*].   There's lies! [*Facing her*] Astounded I was, when without a word of warning, I found you fitting into me lap! [*Coming closer to her—fervently*] The thruth is, if you want to know, that all the way to here, I was silently praying to a bevy of saints that you'd stay torpid in any and every emergency of look or motion!

Angela.   You took care to leave our saints out on the doorstep; ay, and shut the door in their faces, too. You gave your solemn word, before I'd take one step to this place, that you'd be as harmless as an image in a looking-glass. I trusted you. I had heard you were a good boy. I thought you were a gentleman.

Mulligan.   What about your uplifting can-can round the table while I was reading Yeats's poem?

Angela [*going her own way*].   You made me believe you'd keep the width of a world between us while we were together, so's to avoid accidents. You said anyone who knew you would tell me you had a profound respect for girls; that you were slow in love-making.

Mulligan [*with insistence*].   The can-can; what about the can-can around the table?

Angela [*with a great wail in her voice*].   And then you stunned me with your speed!

Mulligan [*with greater insistence*].   I'm asking you what about the can-can you danced around the table while I was thrying to read "I will arise and go now, and go to Innisfree"?

Angela [*acting the innocent*].   What can-can? What are you talking about? I don't know what you mean by can-can.

Mulligan. I mean the dance that uplifted your skirt out of the way of your movements and juggled a vision of spiritual desolation into a mirage of palpitating enjoyments.

Angela [*appealing to the world at large*]. Oh, d'ye hear the like o 'that! Meanness is most of you to try to put the cloak of your own dark way round my poor shoulders! The dance I did could be done by an innocent figure in a nursery rhyme. You were bent on this awful mischief from the first. I sensed it when I walked with you—something evil hovering near. Oh, why didn't I follow me intuition! [*She begins to be hysterical.*] And I thought you such a nice man; and now, after fencing me in with shame, you're making out I gave you the stuff to make the fence around me. Oh, the infamy of it! [*She moves rapidly up and down the room, clasping and unclasping her hands.*] Oh, what shall I do, where shall I go, what shall I say!

Mulligan [*getting very frightened*]. Angela, calm yourself. Speak lower, or you'll wake Miss Mossie, and we'll be ruined. Sit down; do, please!

Angela [*fluttering about and staggering a little.*] I'm undone, undone completely. I won't be able to look any honest woman in the face; I won't be able to shake the hand of any honest man I meet; my future's devastated! [*She presses a hand to her heart.*] I'm not feeling well; not at all well; you'd better get Miss Mossie.

Mulligan [*horrified and very agitated.*] Angela!

Angela [*staggering towards the chair*]. Not well at all. I feel I'm going to faint! No, no; yes, yes—I am going to faint!
          [*She sinks down on the chair, stretches out, and closes her eyes.*

Mulligan [*falling on a knee before her—well frightened now*]. Angela, don't! Angela, dear, wake up! [*Lifting his eyes to the ceiling*] Saint Correlliolanus, come on, and deliver us from utther desthruction!

Angela [*plaintively and faintly*]. Wather!

Mulligan [*panic-stricken*]. No, wine! [*He rises from his knee, pours out a glass of wine, and brings it to her.*] Oh, Angela, why did you let yourself get into such a state? Here, take it quietly in sips. [*As she drinks it*] Sip, sip, sip. That should do you good. Hope no one heard you. Miss Mossie sleeps with one ear cocked. [*He strokes her hand.*] You'll soon be all right, and able to slip away in a few minutes.

Angela [*noticing the ring on the hand stroking hers*]. Pretty ring; garnet set in gold; precious garnet didn't you say?

Mulligan [*none too sure of what he should say*]. Yep. Not much value though.

Angela. Why's it on the little finger?

Mulligan. Knuckle's too big on the right one; won't go over it.

Angela [*fingering it*]. Let me see it in me hand. [*He hesitates, then takes it off, and gives it to her with reluctance. Putting it on the engagement finger*] Fits me to a nicety. How did you come by it?

Mulligan. An uncle left it in my care when he went on a job to Hong Kong. He never came back, and as no one asked about it, I made it my own.

Angela. Oh? Lucky one. [*She looks up into his face, smiling archly, displaying the finger with the ring on it.*] Looks like we were an engaged couple John Jo, dear, wha'?

Mulligan. An engaged couple? [*With an uneasy and constrained laugh*] Yis! Funny thought, that; quite. Feeling betther?

Angela. Seem to; hope it won't come over me again.

Mulligan [*fervently*]. God forbid! What about taking off our shoes, and making a start?   [*He takes off his.*

Angela [*taking off her shoes*]. I suppose we must go sometime.

Mulligan [*trying to speak carelessly*]. Let's have the ring back, dear.

Angela [*as if she'd forgotten it*]. The ring? Oh, yes; I near forgot. [*She fiddles with it; then suddenly straightens herself to listen.*] Is that the sound of someone at the door below?

Mulligan [*agitated again*]. Oh God, if it's Halibut home from the dance we'll have to wait till he settles down! I wish you'd gone when the going was good!

Angela [*who has taken off her shoes—rising from the chair*]. Come on, we'll chance it!

Mulligan [*pushing her back*]. Chance it! We can't afford to chance it. [*Going over to the door leading to rest of the house*] I'll reconnoitre down, and make sure the way's clear, before we chance it.

[*He goes out of the room, is absent for a few moments, while Angela swallows another glass of wine; then he returns hastily, a hand held up warningly for silence.*

Mulligan [*in a frightened whisper*]. Near ran into him on the stairs. Thank God it was so dark. Just had time to turn back. We'll have to wait now till he settles in. [*He listens at the door, shuts it suddenly, and glides over to Angela.*] Quick! He's gone by his own place, and is coming up here! [*He catches her by the arm, hurries her across the room, and shoves her into the bedroom.*] Get in, and keep silent for God's sake!

[*As he shoves her in, a knock is heard at the sitting-room door. Mulligan shuts the bedroom door, slides over to the chair, sits down, takes the book from the table, and pretends to be reading.*

[*Another knock is heard at the door, then it opens, and Mr. Daniel Halibut is seen standing there. He is a man of twenty-five, a little below medium height, inclining to be plump. His hair is reddish, and a thick moustache flowing from his upper lip hides his mouth. Sometimes his hand tries to brush it aside, but the moment the hand is removed, it falls back into its old place at once. A fawn-coloured overcoat covers an informal evening-suit—dinner-jacket and black tie. A black homburg hat is on his head. He comes in as one who is full of himself as if he had done himself well at the dance, and as one who feels himself a man of the world above the cautious and timorous Mulligan. His hat and coat are damp.*

Halibut [*coming into the room*]. Ha, there you are, me son, rotten night out; sleet. Coming up, I could have sworn I seen you coming down the stairs.

Mulligan [*in pretended surprise*]. Me coming down the stairs? At this time of the morning? What would I be doing on the stairs at this hour?

Halibut. Well, what are you doing up at this time of the morning?

Mulligan. I found it impossible to sleep, so got up to see if a bit of Yeats's poetry would make me drowsy.

Halibut. Is it Yeats, is it? God, man, he wouldn't let you sleep; drive you nuts! All people liking Yeats are all queer. He's all questions. What am I? Why am I? What is it? How did it come? Where will it go? All bubbles. Stuck up in the top of his ould tower, he sent the bubbles sailing out through a little loophole to attract the world outside. And all the little writers copied them, and blew bubbles of their own, till you could see them glistening among the things of the althar, or shining in the hair of the girl you were courting.

Mulligan [*with an obvious yawn*]. Well, Yeats has made me sleepy, anyway. [*He flings the book on the table, and goes to get out of the chair.*] I'll be off to bed again.

Halibut [*shoving him back into the chair*]. Wait till I tell you. You should ha' been at the dance. There never was a grander occasion; divel a grander ever! The place was fair gushing with girls. And only a few who'd make you shut your eyes if they were sitting on your knee. A hilariously hopeful whirlwind of skirt and petticoat, John Jo, when a waltz was on!

Mulligan [*getting up and edging Halibut towards the sitting-room door*]. Go to bed, now, like a good fellow. I'm tired. We'll talk about it tomorrow. Goodnight.

Halibut [*edging Mulligan back towards the fireplace*]. Wait till I tell you. You are a boyo. You'd never guess who was there? Your old flame of a week—Jessie! She told me things! When will you wake up? When he asked me out for the first time, says she, I expected a hilarious night at a dance or a music-hall, says she; I near fainted, says she, when, instead, he asked me to go with him to Benediction! Mulligan's management of maidens! Oh, John Jo, when will you wake up?

Mulligan [*annoyed, pushing Halibut towards the door.*] If I elect to keep from danger, that's my affair. Looka, Dan, I've got to get up early to go to Mass on my way to the office, so be a good fellow, and go. I'm not concerned with girls.

Halibut. Betther if you were. [*He pushes Mulligan back toward the fireplace again.*] You'd sleep betther at night for one thing. [*He puts an arm around Mulligan, and forces him into being a partner.*] Roamin' in th' gloamin', eh? Oh, boy! [*Lilting*] With a lassie by yeer side. Oh, it's lovely to go roamin' in th' gloamin'!

Mulligan [*angrily—struggling from Halibut's hold, and rather roughly forcing him to the door*]. Aw, lay off it, damn it, Dan! I'm in no mood for a Highland fling! Please go to your own room, and leave me in peace —I'm done in!   [*He shoves him out and closes the sitting-room door.*

Halibut [*as he's being shoved out*]. All right, if that's the way you feel. It'd be a good thing to put your hand on a girl's knee, and chance it.

[*Mulligan listens at the door for a few moments. Then he gets down on his knees, and puts an ear to the floor. He rises, goes to the bedroom door, opens it, and calls Angela out.*

Mulligan. Now, Angela; now's our time. No delay, please.

Angela [*going behind the curtains on the windows*]. What kind of a night or morning is it? [*From behind the curtains*] Christ! It's snowing or something! [*She comes from behind them, goes to the door, and takes one of Mulligan's coats hanging there.*] I must have a coat.
                                    [*Angela puts the coat on.*

Mulligan [*in a faint protest*]. Eh, Angela, that's me best one.

Angela [*taking an umbrella from the stand*]. And an umbrella, too.

Mulligan. That's me best umbrella.

Angela.   Never mind, dear. I'll let you have it back when you hand me into the taxi on the all-night rank. Let's hurry now, boy. [*Mulligan opens the door cautiously, listens a moment; takes a torch from a pocket, and shines it forth, then leads the way from the room, shutting the door gently behind him. Both of them are in their stockinged feet. After a few moments have passed, the door suddenly flies open, and Angela hurries in, followed by Mulligan wearing a look of agony on his face. They carry their shoes under their arms. As she comes in*] You louser, you'd have let me go off without it! Didn't care a damn once you were rid of me. And all I have for another fortnight is in that handbag!

Mulligan [*appealingly*].   Speak lower, Angela, or you'll have the Mossie one down on top of us! I just can't remember you having a handbag when you first came in.

Angela [*angrily*].   You can't remember! Well, I had one, and a good one, too, and I've got to get it—see! D'ye mean to hint I'm making it up?

Mulligan [*in agony*].   No, no; but for God's sake, speak easy; please, Angela!

Angela [*leaving her shoes down, and pulling the cushions off the settee and throwing them on the floor*].   Well, then, find it for me. Mind you, had I been down the street when I missed it, I'd have banged the door down to get in to get it!

Mulligan [*leaving his shoes down, and pulling the table about, pulling the chairs from the wall, and pulling the umbrella-stand away, to look behind them*].   This is terrible! I'll be ruined if I'm discovered. What colour was it? Where had you it last? Where d'ye think you could have put it?

Angela.   I don't know, fool. It was a dark-green one I bought last week, and gave five pounds for. I got confused and forgot about everything when you started to pull me on to your knee.

Mulligan.   But we can't stay to look for it. Miss Mossie'll soon be going about with her candle in her hand.

Angela.   I'm not going without it! I think I remember you snatching it outa me hand when you started to pull me on to your lap.

Mulligan.   Oh, give over about me pulling you on to me lap, and give us a hand to look for it! [*He runs into the bedroom, and starts to search there, flinging the bedclothes about. In bedroom*] I can't see it anywhere here, so I can't.

Angela [*tearfully*].   And I was to come here only for a quiet glass of wine and a biscuit. That's what you said, and kept repeating; and I believed you, oh, I believed you!

Mulligan [*coming out of bedroom*].   No sign of it there.

Angela [*marching up and down the room, clasping and unclasping her hands*].   Oh, isn't this a nice end to a quiet glass of wine and a biscuit!

Mulligan.   Get a hold of yourself. What sort was it?

Angela.   A pure morocco leather one, dark green, with initials on it filigreed in mother o' pearl.

Mulligan [*impatiently*.]   Yis, yis; [*anxiously*] but how much was in it altogether?

Angela.   Fifteen pounds odd.

Mulligan [*ahast*].   Good Lord!

Angela.   And the lipstick you couldn't find musta been in it too; silvercased and all; and a lovely bracelet watch waiting to be mended. Oh, what will I do! Oh, yes, and a silver brooch I wanted to get a pin for. What will I do, what will I do?

Mulligan.   You slip off, and when I come back, I'll search high and low for it.

Angela [*with rising nervous tension*].   And how am I to fare till you find it? You wouldn't turn a hair if I was willing to go in my shift! John Jo Mulligan, you're a dasthard! It would be the price of you to let Miss Mossie and the whole house know the sort you are!

Mulligan.   For God's sake, Angela! What d'ye want me to do; only tell me what you want me to do?

Angela [*moving about distracted*].   And to think I thought I was safe with you! [*Her glance falls on the cupboard, and she makes a bee-line for it.*] Could it have got in here?

Mulligan [*hastily*].   No, no; it couldn't have got in there.

Angela [*drawing out a leather wallet*].   What's this?

Mulligan [*going over to take wallet from her*].   Nothing there but a few private letters, and a lot of bills.

> [*But before he can reach her to get it away, she has whisked a bundle of notes from it.*

Angela [*giggling—a little hysterical*].   John Jo's hidden treasure. [*She counts them rapidly.*] Eighteen pounds ten. All fresh ones too. Nice to handle.

Mulligan.   They're not mine. I'm minding them for a friend. You can put them back.

Angela [*mockingly*].   At once, dear. I'll mind them for you, dear. [*She takes a cheque-book out of the wallet.*] A cheque-book, too. [*As he comes closer*] Keep your distance, keep your distance, or I'll claw the gob off you!

Mulligan. I was only going to give you a few of them to tide you over, dear.

Angela [*fiercely*]. You were? How sweet of you! I'll have them all, you primly-born yahoo. And more. [*She raises her voice*] And more!

Mulligan [*whisperingly*]. All right, all right, only keep calm; keep quiet.

Angela [*indicating the cheque-book*]. Make me out a cheque for five pounds like a decent, honest man.

Mulligan [*taking a fountain pen from his pocket, and settling down to write*]. All right; anything to pacify you.

Angela [*patronisingly patting his head*]. You're not the worst, John Jo. You're really a pleasant chap when you get going. Make a cheque out for ten, darling, to compensate for the goods in the handbag. Ten, dear; that's all now. Well, we've had a right good time together. Pity I can't stay longer. See you again soon, when you're feeling frisky, eh? Naughty boy! [*She has taken the cheque from the dazed Mulligan, put it in his wallet, and now straightens herself to go, taking her shoes off the floor, and putting them under an arm. At the door*] I know my way down, so don't you stir. I'll steal away like a maid of Araby. I'll be seeing you. Be good.

> [*Dazed and stunned, Mulligan sits still for a few seconds; then he gets up from the chair to look around him.*]

Mulligan [*rising from the chair*]. Fully-fledged for hell, that one, and you never noticed it! Oh, John Jo, John Jo! [*He suddenly stiffens.*] She had no handbag! She never had a handbag! Oh, Christ, she's codded me! [*He looks in the cupboard, then looks over the table.*] She's taken away me wallet, too! Me umbrella!

> [*He runs out of the room to follow her, so agitated that he leaves door wide open behind him. There are a few moments of silence; then Miss Mossie appears at the open door with a lighted candle in a candlestick in her hand. She is a short, stout woman of thirty-five or so. She is dressed in a brown skirt reaching to her ankles, and we get a glimpse of black stockings sinking into a pair of stout black shoes. Her dark hair is gathered into a knob, and made to lie quiet on the nape of her neck. She wears a yellow jumper, and a brown Jaeger topcoat is flung over her shoulders. She wears spectacles. She looks into the room for a moment, a look of perplexed anxiety on her face, then turns aside to call to Halibut.*]

Miss Mossie. Mr. Halibut, Mr. Halibut, come up, come up quick! [*Halibut appears at the door. He is now wearing a pair of blue pyjamas, covered by a dressing-gown of dark red, and his bare feet are slippered.*] Oh, Mr. Halibut, what can the matter be? Oh, dear, what can the matter be?

Halibut [*agog with excitement*]. What's up, Miss Mossie?

Miss Mossie [*coming into the sitting-room, followed by Halibut*]. Looka the state of the room; and Mr. Mulligan's just run out into the street in his stockinged feet!

Halibut [*astonished*]. No? How d'ye know he went out into the street?

Miss Mossie. I seen him go. I heard something stirring when I was putting on me jumper, so I looked out, and there was Mr. Mulligan scuttling down the stairs. Walking in his sleep, he musta been. He had an air on him as if he was enraptured within himself; a look as if he was measuring life and death together to see which was tallest.

Halibut. Is that right? Coming back from the dance, I thought I saw him on the stairs, too, but when I came up, he was sitting reading Yeats's poems. Said he couldn't sleep. I warned him against the poems.

Miss Mossie [*coming over to the bedroom door, and opening it*]. Oh, looka the state of this room, too! Everything flung about.

Halibut [*awed*]. Looks like he had a wild fit, or something!

Miss Mossie. Something terrific! This isn't just disarray, Mr. Halibut— it's an upheaval! You don't think it could be that something suddenly went wrong in him?

Halibut [*startled by a thought*]. Wrong in him, Miss Mossie? What could go wrong in him?

Miss Mossie. A quietly-disposed man like Mr. Mulligan doesn't do this [*indicating disorder of rooms*] without something whizzing within him.

Halibut [*frightened*]. You mean in his mind?

Miss Mossie [*firmly*]. We must act. We can't let him roam the streets or do any harm here. I'll phone the police and a doctor, and I'll slip out for the constable that usually stands at the street corner. [*They move to the sitting-room door.*] I'll go now. You stay on the lobby here in the dark, and watch over him if he comes back.

Halibut [*dubiously*]. I'm not a strong man, Miss Mossie.

Miss Mossie. After all, Mr. Halibut, we don't want to be murdhered in our beds.

Halibut [*crossing himself*]. God forbid, Miss Mossie!

Miss Mossie.   And the odd thing is, he'd be doing it with the best intentions. If he comes back, he may still be asleep, so don't shout at him and wake him too suddenly. Just humour him, unless he gets violent.

Halibut [*picturing in his mind all that might happen*].   Ay, violent—that's the danger!

Miss Mossie.   Then you'll just have to close with him, and hold him till the constable comes.

Halibut [*panic-stricken*].   Close with him? Hold him till the constable comes? But, woman alive, I'm not gifted that way!

Miss Mossie.   You'll do your best, I know; if he overcomes you, it won't be your fault.

Halibut.   Don't you think it would be only prudent to have a poker handy?

Miss Mossie.   Too violent-looking. [*Indicating a corner of the lobby*] There's the bit of curtain-pole I use to push the window up—you can keep that handy; but don't let him guess why you have it. [*She takes the key from the inside and puts it in the keyhole on the outside of the door.*] There now, if the worst comes, you can fly out and lock him safely within the room.

Halibut.   It sounds easy, but it's really a desperate situation.

Miss Mossie.   Don't let him see you're frightened. Keep him under command. That's what me sisther did with me when I used to walk in my sleep a few years ago.

Halibut [*stricken with confused anxiety*].   What, you used to sleep-walk, too?

Miss Mossie.   That's why I dhread the habit coming back to me, for then you never know whether you're always asleep and never awake, or always awake and never asleep. I'll be off now. You'll be quite safe if you only keep your wits about you.

> [*She goes off with her candle, leaving a world of darkness to poor Halibut. There is a silence for a few moments, then the watcher in the darkness, and any who are listening, hear a patter of feet on stairs outside, and the voice of Mulligan calling out loudly the name of Miss Mossie several times. Then a great bang of a closing door; dead silence for a moment, till Mulligan is heard calling again.*]

Mulligan [*outside*].   Dan, Dan, are you awake? Dan Halibut, are you awake, man? [*Mulligan appears on the lobby just outside the sitting-room door. He is talking to himself, a haggard, lost, and anxious look on his face, and he is a little out of breath. His coat and hat are damped by the falling sleet outside; his feet wet. He pauses on the lobby, and waves his electric torch about till its beam falls on the silent and semi-crouching Halibut.*] Oh, it's here you are? Thought you were in bed fast asleep. Called you, but got no answer. What a night! Twenty-eight pounds ten gone with the wind! [*He lifts a cushion from the floor to look under it.*] It's not there! [*He flings it viciously away. To Halibut*] What has you here in the dark and the cold?

Halibut. Just shutting the window to keep it from rattling.

Mulligan [*going into the sitting-room*]. We must do something. Miss Mossie's gone rushing hatless out into the darkness and the sleet. Hatless, mind you! Looked as if she was sleep-walking again. A one-time habit of hers, did you know? You'll have to go after her.

Halibut [*coming a little way into the room, but staying close to the door, holding the sprig of curtain-pole behind his back*]. I know, I know; but what were you doing out in the sleet and the darkness *yourself*? And in your stockinged feet, too, look at them!

Mulligan. Me? Couldn't sleep; felt stifled; went out for some fresh air. Didn't think of shoes. Something whizzing in me mind. [*A little impatiently*] But you dress and go after Mossie. See what's wrong with her. Several times, before you came, she came into my room, fast asleep, at dead of the night, with a loving look on her face. We can't afford to let ourselves be murdhered in our sleep, Dan. [*He flops into chair.*] Saint Fairdooshius, succour me this night.

Halibut [*bewildered with anxiety, eyes lifted to ceiling in a low appeal*]. Oh, sweet Saint Slumbersnorius, come to me help now! [*To Mulligan*] All right; yes. I'll settle you in first. You go to bed, John Jo, quiet. Go to bed, go to bed, and go asleep, and go asleep!

Mulligan [*looking at Halibut curiously—a little impatiently*]. I've told you I can't sleep. Twenty-eight pounds ten, and my fine leather wallet gone forever!

Halibut [*in a commandingly sing-song way.*] Never mind. Put them out of your thoughts, and go to bed, go to bed, and go to sleep, and go to sleep—I command!

Mulligan [*half rising from his chair so that Halibut backs towards the door—staring at Halibut in wonderment*]. What's wrong with you, Halibut? [*He sinks back into the chair again, and Halibut returns into the room.*] Me best coat and best umbrella, too! Gone.

[*His glance happens to fall on his hand, and he springs out of the chair with a jump, sending Halibut backing swiftly from the room again.*

Mulligan. Me ring! I never got it back!

Halibut [*straying cautiously back into the room again*]. Money, best coat, best umbrella, wallet, and ring! When did you lose all these things, man?

Mulligan. A minute or so ago; no, no, an hour ago; two hours ago; more. [*He leans his arms dejectedly on the table, and buries his head on them*]. I di'n't lost them, Dan; I gave them away, flung them all away!

Halibut. In an excess of charity of having too many possessions, or what? You know, I've warned you, John Jo; often warned you.

Mulligan [*raising his head from his arms—resentfully and suspiciously*]. Warned me? How warned me?

Halibut. I warned you that running out to devotions morning and night, and too much valuable time spent on your knees, would upset you one day or another. And, now, you'll have to admit that these things couldn't have happened to you if you had had a girl with you tonight.

Mullgian [*with a wail of resentment*]. Oooh! Don't be a blasted fool! [*He notices that Halibut has something behind his back.*] What's that you have behind you?

Halibut [*trying to be carelessly funny.*] Me tail. Didn't you know? I'm a wild animal. [*He wags the piece of curtain-pole.*] Now, the wild animal says you're to go to bed, go to bed, and go to sleep, and go to sleep. Obey the wild animal at once!

Mulligan [*slowly rising from the chair, staring anxiously and suspiciously at Halibut*]. What's amiss with you, Halibut? Are you sleep-walking, too? Leave down that curtain-pole. Don't be acting the goat, man. [*Coaxingly—as Halibut brings the piece of curtain-pole to his front*] Go on, Dan, oul' son, leave the thing down!

Halibut. As soon as you're safely settled in bed, John Jo. Then I'll pop out after Mossie. To bed; to bed; and go to sleep, go to sleep—I command!

Mulligan [*fear having come on him—suddenly seizes the wine-bottle by the neck, and holds it as a club, running to window, swinging back the curtains, and trying to open it*]. God Almighty, I'm alone with a lunatic! [*Shouting—as he tries to open the window*] Help!

Halibut. I'll not let you destroy yourself—come away from that window, or I'll flatten you!

Mulligan [*wheeling round, still holding bottle by the neck to use it as a club, and facing towards Halibut.*] Looka, Halibut, leave that club down. [*Coaxingly*] Now, be sensible, Dan, like a good chap, and drop that club.

Halibut. Drop that bottle first, I say; drop that bottle first!

Mulligan. Drop that club, I tell you. [*Fiercely*] Drop that club!

Halibut [*dancing up and down—panic-stricken*]. Put that bottle down! Put it down, and go to bed, I tell you!

Mulligan [*dodging about*]. Drop that club at once, Halibut!

Halibut. Put that bottle down immediately!

Mulligan. I command you!

Halibut. I command you!

> [*They have been dodging about without coming near to each other; Halibut swinging the piece of curtain-pole to and fro in front of him for protection. In one of the blind swings, the pole slips from his hand, and sails out through the window, causing a great sound of falling glass. They both stare at the window—dumbfounded for a few moments.*

Mulligan [*exultingly*]. Aha, I've got you now!

> [*But Halibut has fled from the room, banged the door after him, and locked it from the outside. Mulligan hurries to the door and presses his back to it. Then Miss Mossie's voice is heard outside.*

Miss Mossie [*outside*]. Oh, what's happened? I feared it would end in violence! Mr. Halibut, Mr. Halibut, are you much hurted?

Mulligan [*shouting through the door to Miss Mossie*]. Miss Mossie; here, Miss Mossie!

Miss Mossie [*from outside*]. Oh, Mr. Mulligan, what have you done to poor, innocent Mr. Halibut? We've found him lying in a dead faint out here on the lobby.

Mulligan [*indignantly—shouting outwards*]. Poor, innocent Mr. Halibut! What has he not tried to do to me! He rushed in here, lunacy looking out of his eyes, and tried to shatther me with a club, with a club; tried to murdher me! Now he's locked me in.

Miss Mossie [*soothingly*]. Now isn't that a shame! What a naughty man he is! Never mind now. You go to your chair and sit down by the fire, and I'll get the key to open your door. Everything will be all right, Mr. Mulligan.

Mulligan [*indignantly*]. Everything isn't all right now! I'll live no longer in the same house with Halibut!

Miss Mossie [*coaxingly*]. Do go and sit down by the fire, Mr. Mulligan, there's a dear. I'll bring you a hot drink, and we'll talk about things; do, now, like a good man. [*Mulligan goes to the fireplace, and sits down in the armchair. He lights a cigarette and puffs it indignantly. After a few moments, the door opens, and Miss Mossie lets into the room a big, top-coated and helmeted policeman, the doctor with his case, wearing an anxious look on his face, and a nurse, enveloped with a dark-blue cloak on the left side of which is a white circle surrounding a large red cross. She carries the usual nursing-suitcase in her hand. Miss Mossie is in the midst of them, and Halibut, in the rear, with a ghastly pale face, rises on his tiptoes to gaze over their shoulders. All but Halibut form a semicircle round Mulligan's back, who puffs away, unconscious of the entrance of the crowd. Bending sidewise from behind the policeman to speak to the sitting Mulligan*] Now, Mr. Mulligan, we'll see what all this little disturbance was about, and what was the cause of it, and then we'll be all—er—O.K., eh? And I've brought in few kind friends to help me.

Mulligan [*rising from his chair in blank surprise, and almost echoing Miss Mossie*]. A few friends to help you? [*He turns around to face Miss Mossie, but is confronted by the big, helmeted policeman, the doctor, and the nurse. He slides back into the chair almost in a dead faint. Falling back into the chair*] Good God!

CURTAIN

THE DRUMS OF FATHER NED

(1959)

NOTE

The Drum Roll heard in the play at stated times should be of the kind used by Haydn in the Symphony No. 103, (Salamon No. 8) in E Flat Major, as given in Decca Record LX 3018.

> This comedy's but an idle, laughing play
> About the things encumbering Ireland's way;
> A flag shoved from a window, and a cry
> To wake up drowsy girl and drowsier boy,
> To snatch from Erin's back the sable shawl,
> And clothe her as she was before her fall;
> In cloak of green as bright as spring's young call;
> Beside her Tara's harp from off a time-stain'd wall,
> To play new dandy airs; holding high the poet's hazel rod,
> String tied to tip, hook-holding a crimson berry,
> With myrtle and with laurel wove, deep-dipp'd in wine,
> Champagne or sherry;
> That mobled minds may all new courage grow,
> And miser'd hearts be merry.

CHARACTERS IN THE PRERUMBLE

OFFICER OF THE BLACK AND TANS

1ST BLACK AND TAN   2ND BLACK AND TAN

3RD BLACK AND TAN   4TH BLACK AND TAN

McGILLIGAN   BINNINGTON

CHORUS OF VOICES IN THE DISTANCE

SCENE · The Main Street in the Town of Doonavale thirty-four years or so ago.

CHARACTERS IN THE PLAY

ALDERMAN ALOYSIUS BINNINGTON, *Mayor of Doonavale, a solicitor and owner of General Store*

ELENA BINNINGTON, *his wife*

MICHAEL BINNINGTON, *their son*

COUNCILLOR McGILLIGAN, *Deputy Mayor, a building contractor and builders' provider*

MRS. MEEDA McGILLIGAN, *his wife*

NORA McGILLIGAN, *their daughter*

BERNADETTE SHILLAYLEY, *maid to the Binningtons on three days a week: to the McGilligans on the other three days*

TOM KILLSALLIGHAN, *a carpenter, Foreman of Works for McGilligan*

OSCAR McGUNTY ⎫
MAN OF THE MUSKET ⎬ *Doonavale workers helping with Tostal Play and Pageant*
MAN OF THE PIKE ⎭

REV. D. FILLIFOGUE, *Parish Priest of Doonavale*
ALEC SKERIGHAN, *Ulsterman from Portadown, down in Doonavale on business*
MR. MURRAY, *Father Fillifogue's organist for the Church of Our Lady Help of Christians, Doonavale*
ECHO

SCENE

ACT I · The drawing-room of the Binningtons.

ACT II · The drawing-room of the McGilligans.

ACT III · The same as in Act I.

TIME · The present day.

PRERUMBLE

Some time after midnight, we see a street in an Irish country town, shadowy, outlined only in a dream-like way, giving vague shapes of houses and shops, and vaguer outlines of others farther away. Among them, behind them, and from windows and doors, come vivid streams of red and yellow flames, for the town is burning. Behind all, beyond the pale of the burning, the spire of a church sticks up, silver in the midst of the black night and the red flame. In front of the houses, almost in the street's centre, but towards the sidewalk, a Keltic Cross, dazzling in its whiteness, stands quietly, but a little crookedly, its symbol silent now, and near forgotten. It is winter, snow has fallen, which has hardened from the touch of frost, and the street-way sparkles. Three Black and Tans, one an Officer, are standing like statues in the street. One is holding a hand-torch, and where the light falls from it, the frost sparkles more gaily. Each holds a revolver in his right hand, the weapons made by the shadows of the night into a size much larger than a gun of a normal look.

One Black and Tan is dressed in a black tunic and vivid yellow trousers, the second in a vivid yellow tunic and black trousers, the Officer is all in black; all are wearing black berets, except the Officer, who wears a vivid yellow one. Their faces are blackened so that they stand out vaguely as blacked-out humanity against the red glow of the burning town. The figures stand stiffly, motionless, but for their heads which turn right, left, back and forward—watchful, wary.

A chant of voices, a chant of misery and defiance, is heard from behind the burning town. It is low, as from a distance, but clearly heard.

> The Black and Tans are blasting now
> Ireland's living into the dead;
> Her homes and shops in flames fall down
> In red ashes on her bonny head.

> May God leave none of th' Tans alive,
> May His big fist destroy them all!
> Each curse of the Holy Book of th' Psalms
> An' the Prophets upon them fall!

The scene looks like a sudden vision of an experience long past conjured up within the mind of one who had gone through it.

Officer. How slow the damn town burns! As if to deny us the right to see its ending.

1st Tan [exulting, but still wary]. When the fire's done, they can cram what's left of the town inta a jar!

Officer. We'll never get them far enough into fear till we turn a town into a cinder for a bruised finger.

2nd Tan. Ay, sir; topple all their blasted towns down into big an' little cinders.

Officer [*to Tan holding the torch*]. Keep that torch covered, man, or some skulking sniper may make a cinder of one of us.

1st Tan [*musingly*]. Everything quiet as a grave a generation old.

Officer [*bitterly*] Quiet graves in this country have a habit sometimes of spitting out bullets.

2nd Tan. Here's Tutnal, sir, comin' with the two blokes who, livin' on opposite sides of the same street, never speak to each other; never as much as hullo to one another for years.

> [*The 3rd Tan comes in driving before him two men, perhaps in their thirties, at the point of his revolver. They have their hands raised over their heads. They are dressed in shirt and trousers only, and are in their bare feet. They keep their heads turned away from one another; the one to the right looking right, the one to the left looking left; a set, determined, yet frightened look on their faces. Their trousers and shirts are grey, so are their faces with anxiety, so that they look vague and ghost-like beside the black and yellow figures of the Tans.*]

3rd Tan [*as he drives the two men in*]. March! left, right . . . left, right . . . left . . . left—lift yer feet! [*As they come near the centre*] Halt! 'shun! Chins up, chins up! [*To the Officer*] Th' two prisoners, sir.

Officer [*indicating McGilligan*]. You halt where you are. [*To Binnington*] You—two paces forward—march!

3rd Tan [*prodding Binnington forward*]. Go on—march!

> [*Binnington steps forward two paces, so that he and McGilligan are in file, two paces apart, McGilligan facing Binnington's back.*]

Officer [*to Binnington*]. Right about turn! [*He makes no movement.*]

2nd Tan [*violently*]. Ri' about turn! [*Binnington stays put.*] Turn! [*He whirls Binnington around so that he faces McGilligan.*] 'Shun!

> [*The two, when they find themselves facing each other, turn their faces aside, one to the right, the other to the left.*]

Officer. Eyes front! [*They remain as they are.*]

2nd Tan [*angrily*]. Eyes front, yeh bastards!

> [*They make no move. 1st Tan twists McGilligan's head to face*]

front; 3rd Tan does the same for Binnington, while the Officer stands a little apart so that he can see and speak to either.

3rd Tan [as he twists Binnington's head facing front]. Eyes front, an' keep lookin' at each other's ugly Irish mugs, yeh curs!

Officer [quietly—interested]. I'm told you two hate each other; that you haven't spoken for ten years or so—true? [*The two make no answer.*] Dumb, eh?

1st Tan. Th' two of 'em need a good dustin' with th' butt-end of a gun, they do. [*To the Officer*] A bad ruddy lot, sir. Shows what we are up against, it does. Terrifyin' thugs they are.

Officer [quietly]. You'd better answer my questions, you two. I'm going to ask a few more, and you'd better answer. We don't like mutes—hear me?

2nd Tan. Answer, or we'll leave you so's you'll never be able to answer no more, see!

Officer. Now, you two, I want some information, and you've heard what may happen if you don't give it.

1st Tan [ominously]. An' we don't ask twice neither.

McGilligan [finding his voice]. You'll get no information from me.

Officer [patiently—to Binnington]. You then?

Binnington. I'm no informer, but a true-born Irishman.

McGilligan [with a wail of contempt]. A true-born Irishman! D'ye hear that? [*He hangs his head as if in shame—pathetically.*] Poor Paudrig Pearse!

Binnington [bitterly]. Oh, may th' man who uses th' holy names of our dear dead heroes for his own purposes be hemmed in be a clusther of his children's headstones!

Officer [amused]. You certainly have an astonishing respect for each other. Quite natural, for I'm told you were born in the same year, in the same town, in the same street on opposite sides of the road.

1st Tan. An' th' blighters are courtin' sisters.

Officer. Good God! [*To Binnington*] What school did you go to?

Binnington. Th' parochial school attached to th' church.

Officer [to McGilligan]. And you?

McGilligan [sullenly]. Th' same one, if you want to know.

2nd Tan [tapping him on the shoulder]. Sir, sir; add sir to your lingo, see!

Officer [*to Binnington*].   In what church do you worship?

Binnington.   Church of Our Lady Help of Christians, sir.

Officer [*to McGilligan*].   You?   [*McGilligan doesn't answer.*

3rd Tan [*rarping McGilligan on the back with the revolver*].   Go on, you ripened ruffian—what church do you go to?

McGilligan.   To th' church of Our Lady Help of Christians, sir.

Officer.   Mass in the morning and murder at night. Well, you can have a good look at what it has done for your town. [*To Binnington*] What trade do you follow? Labourer of some kind?

Binnington [*somewhat indignant*].   Nothing of the kind! I'm a professional man, a solicitor, owning the General Store in th' town.

McGilligan.   An' town coroner, too; secretary to the Rural Council an' Commissioner for Oaths—oh, some parties I know have done well outa their love for Ireland.

Officer [*to McGilligan*].   Is he [*indicating Binnington*] your boss, you like him so much?

McGilligan [*most indignant*].   My boss? No, by God, he's not! I'd have you know I'm a merchant, an' a most important citizen of this town. I'm a Building Contractor, an' as well, provide other builders in th' Disthrict with any materials they need.

Binnington [*mockingly*].   A builder of houses shaken be th' sound of the sea fifty miles away from where they're standin'!

McGilligan [*to Officer*].   Oh, do whatever you're goin' to do, an' put us outa th' agony of lookin' into each other's face!

Officer [*amused*].   Now, now, don't be too ready to go. Time to end this ridiculous feud. Shake hands and be friends, like when you were kids.

Binnington [*vehemently*].   Never!

McGilligan [*as vehemently*].   I'll die first!

Officer.   You'll die if you don't. [*With a shout*] Shake hands, I tell you!

McGilligan.   Not while there's foam on a river, or a leaf in a forest.

Binnington.   Let me flop into me grave first.

Officer.   All that's left of your town's the church and round tower. We'll dynamite that, but if you shake hands, we'll leave it standing. So shake hands.

McGilligan.   Not for a hundhred round towers.

Binnington.   Not for a hundhred more.

Officer [*fiercely—turning the pair to face right, and pushing them side by side*]. I'll test you, you stubborn bastards! [*He points right.*] Run side by side to that lamp-post there; we'll fire to either side of you, so keep close, for if either of you move a foot from the other, he'll run into a bullet—see? [*With a shout*] Go!

[*The two men run off and out while the Tans fire after them.*

1st Tan. Shockin' show-down of hatred, sir.   [*He fires to the left.*

2nd Tan. Flyin' in God's face it is.   [*He fires to the right.*

3rd Tan. Wonder if they ever went to Sunday School when they was kids?   [*He fires to the left.*

[*As the two men run, the flames of the town take on a more vivid red, and rise higher into the sky.*

Officer. Hold your fire—here they come back.

[*The two men trot in together again, close to one another, but turning their heads away the one from the other as much as possible, till they come to where the Tans are standing.*

Officer [*to the two men*]. Well?

McGilligan. Me feet's bleedin', sir.

Binnington. So's mine.

Officer. Listen, you fools: I understand, in spite of this animosity, you do business together. Do you do business together?

1st Tan [*prodding McGilligan's back with his gun*]. Do you do business together!

2nd Tan [*doing the same to Binnington*]. Answer!

Binnington. That's different, for business is business.

McGilligan. Yis, business is business.

Echo. Business is business.

Officer [*startled into alertness*]. What's that?

1st Tan [*startled too*]. Sounds like an echo, sir.

McGilligan. 'Tis an echo. When th' winds is right, th' higher hills round th' town sometimes give an echo.

Officer [*relieved*]. Oh? [*Roughly*] Now, shake hands. [*The men stay silent.*] Well, off you go again, you poor blighters, and keep close, or a bullet'll plough a way into one of you!

[*The two men start off again, while the Tans fire after them as before.*

3rd Tan [*stupefied with amazement*]. Never seen such coves. [*He fires.*] Hatin' each other more'n they hates us.

2nd Tan [*very puzzled*]. Not a ruddy quiver outa them, an' them knockin' at death's door. I don't savvy. [*He fires.*]

Officer. Perfect hate casts out fear.

1st Tan. Goin' to church reg'lar an' behavin' as such, beats me. Not natural. [*He fires.*]

> [*After a short pause, the two men reappear, staggering in, breathless, but close together, each turning his head away from the other. They totter to the centre, and sink down on the street from exhaustion between the group of bewildered Tans.*

Officer [*looking down at them*]. Well, have you come to your damned senses? Shake hands, and be pals in the centre of your burning town.

1st Tan [*derisively*]. Go on; be pals. Jolly old pals, clingin' together in all kinds of weather, shake hands, you blighted buggers!

Officer. Are you going to shake hands, or shall we plug the two of you?

McGilligan. Shoot if you want to. [*Crossing himself.*

Binnington [*crossing himself*]. Plug away.

> [*The Officer stands over them, mystified at this example of inveterate hatred.*

2nd Tan [*pointing his gun*]. Shall we, sir?

> [*The Officer makes a gesture of denial, and the Tan lowers his gun.*

Officer [*thoughtful and bewildered*]. They must be mad. [*He looks around.*] The town's burning well now. This'll send the rats to their hovels, and we'll have things our own way for a long time.

3rd Tan [*gleefully*]. We've got 'em on th' run!

> [*4th Tan hurries in from the end of the town, breathless; excitement and anxiety flush from his looks.*

4th Tan [*saluting—rapidly*]. Lieutenant Barrow's lorry's been ambushed, sir, on the way here. Better get our men together—they're out in force.

Officer [*alert at once*]. Who are out in force?

4th Tan. Sinn Feiners, sir; Sergeant got through, shot in th' arm.

Officer [*rapidly*]. The other six?

4th Tan. Wiped out, sir.

2nd Tan [*savagely*]. Then, by God, we'll settle these two bastards!

[*He points his revolver at the two men, but the Officer shoves it aside.*

Officer [*to 2nd Tan*]. No, you fool! Can't you see that these two rats will do more harm to Ireland living than they'll ever do to Ireland dead? —Keep your gun down.

2nd Tan [*thrusting his gun into its holster—surlily*]. You know best, sir.

Officer [*angrily*]. Take that gun from the holster and keep it in your hand—at the ready. [*The Tan takes it from its holster.*] Break it, break it! [*The Tan breaks it, and the Officer glances into the chamber.*] Empty, by God! Keep your wits alive, man. Keep your gun full [*as the Tan reloads*]. Our lives shelter in its chamber. A fraction of a second's delay in the handling of a gun may mean one life gone; may mean more; may even mean all.

1st Tan. My oath, it may!

Officer [*to 4th Tan*]. How many were in the attacking column? Quick —answer!

4th Tan [*hurriedly*]. Shots came from everywhere, sir; I'd say a hundred of them. Enough to be dangerous.

Officer. Probably twenty-five, or, maybe, thirty. [*To 3rd Tan*] Where are our lorries?

3rd Tan. Parked in th' Market Square, sir.

Officer [*sarcastically*]. Packed tight together. One grenade might easily make half of them hopeless. [*To the Tan with the torch*] Put out that torch. We must get to the lorries quick, and get going. By God, we'll make Irish towns pay in huge heaps of ashes for th' loss of our comrades! I'll court-martial any man who hits arm or leg of these Sinn Fein murderers. Hit head, hit belly, and hit heart! [*Sharply*] Form file! Each man three yards behind the other. Number 1, watch forward; Number 2, to the right; Number 3, to the left; I'll watch behind. March!

> [*They march out as the Officer commands, leaving the two men lying near to the cross. Glancing around, Binnington sees McGilligan near to him, and, with a spit of disgust, crawls on hands and knees to the back of the cross, leaning his back against the shaft. McGilligan crawls to the front of it, and squats there.*

Binnington [*after a pause—crawling away to the right*]. God could never put me far enough away from a cunnin' dodger.

McGilligan [*crawling away in the opposite direction*]. Phew! A fume from hell's comin' from somewhere near me.

[*A number of shots are heard from the direction in which the Tans have marched. It is distant, and though the sounds are faint, they can be heard distinctly.*

Binnington [*halting in his crawl and cocking an ear—exultingly*].   Aha, our boys are givin' it to them! God direct their aim!

McGilligan [*halting in his crawl, cocking an ear the same moment as Binnington has cocked his—with disgust at Binnington's last remark*]. Is there anything worse than a pious prayer from an impious party red with th' rust of roguery? [*He turns in his crawl to face towards Binnington.*] You muddy ditch-worm!

Binnington [*who has turned in his crawl to face towards McGilligan*]. You dung-beetle!

[*The two of them reverse to face away, and they crawl off in opposite directions. As they crawl away, the red flames rise higher than ever, and again is heard the mourning chant of the people, faintly in the distance.*

The Black and Tans are blasting now
Ireland's living into the dead;

Her homes and shops in flames fall down
In red ashes on her bonny head.
[*A very faint, distant roll of drums mingles with the chant.*

END OF PRERUMBLE

ACT I

The drawing-room and parlour of Alderman Binnington, Mayor of the town of Doonavale. It is a large, long room, furnished with an attempt at Irish middle-class pomp and circumstance. Everything in the room is new and polished, to be displayed rather than used. A large round mahogany table stands in the centre of the room, with large stiff armchairs at either end, both upholstered in emerald green. On the table, right in its centre, *is a tall gilded vase, ornamented with embossed, highly-coloured flower-patterns. At one end is an album, at the other a photo of the Alderman in a wide and brightly gilded frame. A heavy brown-coloured door on the right leads to the rest of the house, opposite another smaller door leading to the Mayor's office. At the back is a large oblong window looking out over the front lawn, beyond which are a few trees, and beyond these the tops of the town's houses, and the spire of the town's church. This window is ornamented by thick curtains of green plush, tied back by heavy gold cords with gold and silver tassels. To the right of the window is a picture of Michael Collins; on the opposite side, a picture of St. Anthony of Padua. A pompous mahogany sideboard stands to the right of the window; on it are wine-glasses, a decanter, a bottle of whiskey, and some heavy silver-ware, a coffee-pot, silver cups and saucers, silver tray and a silver salver—all for show. At the back of the sideboard, to its centre, stands another gaudily-gilt vase. In front of the window are a number of small chairs, green upholstered, so stiff that they look as if they dared anyone to stir them. The fireplace—aglow with heavy brass fender and fire-irons—is to the left, and a sofa stretches itself out diagonally, the head nearer the fire, the foot towards the window. On the mantelshelf are bronze figures, a man in eighteenth-century costume at one end, a lady at the other; and beside these figures, at either end, stand vases thick with colour and with gilt; while in the mantelshelf's centre is a big golden clock decorated with gilt leaves and blossoms. To the left of the brown door is an upright piano, agleam, with a silver candlestick at either end, with more vases standing between them. In the right corner of the back wall stands a big pink delft flower-pot containing a palm about six feet high, with long, lance-like vivid blue leaves and vivid yellow trunk. The floor is covered with a beige carpet covered with a gay flower pattern. Leaning against one end of the piano is an object tied around with white linen, showing the shape of a cross clearly.*

The lower part of the window is open, and the ends of a ladder are seen sticking up beyond the sill. The time is about 12 noon. It is early spring, and sky is a virgin blue.

If one was to enter the room now, Bernadette would be seen trying with a finger or two to coax out the notes of the hymn, 'Adeste Fideles'. She has an intense look on her face as she fingers the notes out slowly and carefully. She is a girl of nineteen or twenty, pretty in a simple way, with dark clustering hair—a little untidy now, a face that is pleasing, though a little plump, a finely-formed mouth that gives an easy-going glance to the face, a slightly snub nose, firm cheeks, and a lovely pair of deep blue eyes which flash forth, now and again, a sly shrewd look. She wears ordinary clothes, black skirt, deep yellow jersey, faded a little in patches, most of which are covered by a large blue apron. Her skirt is short enough to show that she is wearing a first-class pair of nylons. In the disengaged hand she is carelessly clutching a duster.

Far away in the distance, as she is playing, we hear the faint sound of a roll of drums. She stops playing to listen intently and somewhat dreamily.

Bernadette.   Th' dhrums again. Father Ned is busy. Practisin'.

> [*The drum-roll and drum-beat fade away, and she resumes her playing.*
>
> [*The door opens swiftly, and Elena Binnington runs into the room, followed some time later by Aloysius Binnington, the Mayor. Mrs. Binnington is a middle-aged woman who must have been a handsome lass in her earlier age; her face still carries many traces of good looks, but it is rather a tired one now, but still trying to keep calm and gay. She is dressed for going out—a greenish tweed skirt, a white blouse, and she is wearing her hat and a light tweed coat of grey with green facings. Binnington is tall, thin, and wiry. He is older than his wife; his hair, moustache, and close-cropped beard are greying. He is dressed in good, richly-brown tweeds; but over all is a red Mayoral robe, ornamented at cuff and collar with rich green velvet. Around his neck his Mayoral Chain, at the end of which hang a cross and harp, cross in gold, harp in silver. He wears a rather high, stiff white collar, and a brown, yellow-spotted tie. A thick gold watch-chain stretches across his belly from one waistcoat pocket to the other. Business-man, patriot, and pietist, he loves himself more than anything else living or dead, though he isn't really a bad chap. He carries an attaché-case, which he now opens, spreading a few papers out on the table.*

Mrs. Binnington [*running over to piano, pulling Bernadette away, and banging the lid down*].   What're you doin'? That piano was bought for good money, an' not brought here for you to go tantalisin' it with your fingerin' ding ding, ding ding!

Bernadette.   I was only thryin' to give it a warmin'.

Mrs. Binnington.   It doesn't need a warmin'. That insthrument is only to be touched be an edifyin' finger.

> [*Mrs. Binnington is practising deportment and balance of body, so she circles herself on one foot as Bernadette speaks, facing her when the circling movement is completed, which she does very awkwardly.*

Bernadette.   It was 'Adeste Fideles' I was playin', an' there's no ding-ding-dingin' about the hymn.

Mrs. Binnington. Don't argue. Knowin' I have to go out to practise deportment an' dancin' for the Reception our President's givin' for important persons in Dublin Castle, you take advantage, when me back's turned, an' go ding-ding-dingin' on our new piano. [*Mrs. Binnington does a half-heel, half-toe pirouette, arms extended from her sides, asunder, suddenly dropping with a flop to the floor.*] God damn it! [*To Bernadette*] Do go on with th' cleaning of th' window, and stop gapin'! [*She gets up.*] Where's th' laddo who was paintin' th' window? [*She looks out of it.*] Gone!

Bernadette. He had to go to practise his part in the pageant.

Mrs. Binnington [*grumblingly*]. This Tosthal's goin' to cost us something. [*To Bernadette*] I'm goin' now, an' don't disturb the Mayor; an' don't you lay a finger on that piano again.

Bernadette [*sullenly*]. Someone, some time or other, will have to give it a rattle.

> [*Binnington comes in, goes to the table, sits down, and spreads his papers out on it.*

Mrs. Binnington [*suddenly stopping awkwardly in a pirouette—indignantly*]. A rattle! No somebody or other's goin' to give that piano a rattle! A piano isn't made for a rattle! A rattle indeed!! Whoever sits before that piano'll give it something more genteel than a rattle!

Binnington. A piano's a dignified insthrument, me girl, an' you can't put its music into any conformity of a rattle.

Bernadette [*angrily and sullenly*]. Yous wouldn't have a piano if it wasn't for the dead who died for Ireland!

Mrs. Binnington [*quietly but positively*]. Maybe not. But all that's well over now. [*Murmuring to herself*] Before sittin' down, do a graceful wheel on th' left toe, swingin' right leg round, with th' body lax, then sink into th' chair, he said. [*Wheeling round, she doesn't do it right, misses the chair, and slidders to the floor.*] Oh, God damn it! [*Recovering her breath—to Bernadette—while still sitting on the floor*] All over now. We've done our best for our glorious dead with murmurin' of thousands of Rosaries, hundhreds of volleys fired over where they lie, an' th' soundin' of hundhreds more of Last Posts. All that can be done for a dead hero is to put a headstone over his grave, an' leave him there.

Bernadette [*bitterly*]. An' forget all he said an' all he ever done.

Echo. All he ever done.

Mrs. Binnington. God's will.   [*She gets up stiffly.*

Binnington [*with irritation*]. That's enough of arguin'. Our work now is to sort ourselves out into our proper an' propounded places.

Bernadette [*maliciously*]. Th' McGilligans'll best yous at it. Theirs is a bigger piano than yours, an' yestherday they got in a palm three half as tall [*indicating the tree*] again as that one. They're the ones thuddin' their way up in th' world!

Binnington [*severely*]. That's enough, I tell you. It's just a sorryful sight to see th' McGilligans thryin' to ape their betthers. They'll never be anything above th' etcetheraras of th' Doonavale community. [*To Mrs. Binnington*] Ah, look, Michael is goin' about too much with McGilligan's daughter. It'll have to stop.

Mrs. Binnington. They're workin' for th' Tosthal, and th' Tosthal is above th' laws of gentility.

Binnington. I'll not have it, Tosthal or no Tosthal! A waste of sacred time! with their French an' Italian films dancin' our simple minds into delirium; music, too, that no one can get undher or over; when the minute a tune starts it stops, an' is off into a thousand tootles no mind can folly, makin' a body want to run out into a summer breeze or a wintry wind for a chance of survival.

Mrs. Binnington [*irascibly*]. Don't be lettin' your ignorance loose! [*Admonishingly*]. We just have to let it come, an' get it over. We can't afford to go against the Tosthal, for it's a National Festival now; fixed an' famous.

Binnington [*furiously*]. It's never over, woman! Soon as one is ended, they're startin' on th' next! An' I'll go against it! McGilligan's again' it, Father Fillifogue's again' it, all men with a stake in the townland's again' it. Losin' money instead of makin' it— With their Shumman an' Shubbert, an' that other fella, what's his name—makin' us wondher where we are. An' that wild fool, Father Ned!—shoutin' that he wouldn't be satisfied till the people of Doonavale would sit enthranced listenin' to music from—what's his name?—what's this it is?— Back, yis, Back, mind you, whoever he is. Shumman, Shubbert, an' now Back—what names! [*Shouting*] When I hear music goin' an' words with it, I want to see th' mountains o' Mourne comin' down to the sea; and with other music an' other words sayin' there's not in this wide world a valley so sweet, I see the Vale of Avoca, an' I go queer all over.

Bernadette. Father Ned says that through music, good books, an' good pictures, we may get to know more about th' mysthery of life.

Binnington [*furiously*]. Oh, doesn't this stuff make a body yell! Mysthery of life! There's no mysthery in it, girl. There's nothin' more in it than gettin' all you can, holdin' what you have, doin' justice to your religious duties, and actin' decent to a neighbour.

Mrs. Binnington [*to Bernadette*]. Run down, Bernadette, an' make a few sandwiches, for me dancin' lessons won't let me have the usual lunch today.

Bernadette. This Tosthal will make some I know dance in more ways than one! [*She goes out.*

Mrs. Binnington [*to Binnington, indignantly*]. Why do you go spoutin' outa you in front of Bernadette? The Tosthal's here, an' we must put up with it. Now she'll gab out all you said to everyone in Doonavale, addin' her own inventions to it, till you'll stand out as an enemy to Ireland's newest passion to take cognisance of the cultures of th' world.

Binnington [*frenziedly*]. We've our own culture, woman! We've our own dances, our own music, our own games, our own language, an' our own way of propoundin' out a preparation for the life to come. We want nothin'; an' we're all proud of what we have.

Mrs. Binnington. I'm sure you are, though I never knew you to play any Irish game; I never seen you in an Irish dance; an' all you know of Irish is a greetin', an' even when you use one, you've to hurry in its sayin' for fear you'd lose it. That robe an' cocked hat of yours weren't fosthered from any concept creepin' outa Tara Hill.

Binnington. Me hand goes into me poor pocket often enough to keep them all goin', doesn't it?

Mrs. Binnington [*sarcastically*]. Ay, a shillin' for Ireland comin' outa one pocket, an' a pound from Ireland slippin' into th' other!

Binnington [*impatiently*]. Listen, woman! I've no time to waste repudiatin', see? I expect McGilligan here on business any minute now.

Mrs. Binnington [*stupent*]. What! McGilligan here? McGilligan here in th' Binnington drawing-room?

Binnington. Yis, yis, amn't I afther sayin'! Here, here! There's no other place. Me office an' everywhere else is swarmin' with Tosthal workers, an' this is th' one private place left. It's business that can't be put off.

Mrs. Binnington. What kinda business? Is it th' ship fulla timber comin' into——

Binnington [*sharply*]. Oh, never mind what business! Just business. Another thing—there's a business man, an Orangeman from th' North, comin' to Doonavale too.

Mrs. Binnington. What? An Orangeman from th' North!

Binnington. Yis, yis, amn't I afther sayin' it! An' we have to take dinner with him tonight.

Mrs. Binnington. With an Orangeman from th' North?

Binnington. Yis, yis; we're takin' dinner with him tonight.

Mrs. Binnington. Where?

Binnington [*testily*]. We'll be takin' dinner with him at th' McGilligans'.

Mrs. Binnington. At th' McGilligans'! [*She remains silent in astonishment for a few moments.*] Sacred Heart! Are we gettin' a little civilised at last! [*Looking anxiously at Binnington*] Or is it, Aloysius dear, that you're wandherin' in your mind?

Binnington [*impatiently*]. Ah, have sense, woman! I'm tellin' you it's only pure business we're doin', uncontaminated with any smidereen of friendliness.

Mrs. Binnington. Well, for th' love o' God, put a little contamination into our meetin', an' let the quarrel of a generation end! I'm sick of it.

Binnington [*shouting*]. Well, I amn't! Me soul's not a pebble on th' beach for McGilligan to pick up an' pocket!

Mrs. Binnington. Well, I love Nora, an' I'm Meeda McGilligan's friend, even though th' McGilligans aren't as good or refined as th' Binningtons.

Binnington. Looka, Elena, go an' get your dancin' lesson. I've to think how to do this business with McGilligan, an' still keep me soul safe. An' send that one up to finish th' winda before McGilligan comes.

Mrs. Binnington [*dropping a curtsy awkwardly*]. Goodbye, sir.

Binnington. An' tell Bernadette to bring an oul' kitchen chair up with her. [*Mrs. Binnington goes out. He goes to the table and starts calculating figures set down on the documents he is examining. Bernadette comes in with the kitchen chair.*] There—[*pointing to the side of the door*] put it there. [*She does so, and then goes to the window to resume its cleaning.. Muttering*] 20 stannards, be 12 foot at 9 be 3 . . . 20. 14 be 9 be 1½; 10 at £183 per stannard—10 183's is—is—is——

Bernadette [*singing softly, half to herself, and half to an unlistening world*]:
Mellow the moonlight to shine is beginning,
Close to th' window young Eileen is spinning,
Bent o'er the fire her blind grandmother's sitting,
Is crooning and moaning and drowsily knitting.

'Eileen, a chara, I hear someone tapping.'
''Tis the ivy, dear mother, against the glass flapping.'

'Eily, I surely hear somebody sighing.'
''Tis the sound, mother dear, of the summer winds dying.'

Merrily, cheerily, noisily whirring,
Swings the wheel, spins the wheel, while the foot's stirring;
Sprightly and brightly and airily ringing,
Thrills the sweet voice of the young maiden singing.

Binnington [*muttering*]. That's enough, girl. How'm I goin' to get figures circumspect through that chantin'? 10 at 183 per stannard is—is—let me see. Eh, is—[*his voice goes away into a low murmur*].

Bernadette. I'm just doin' a murmurin' practice for th' Tosthal Concert.

Binnington [*tossing his head back in a scornful movement*]. Oh, th' Tosthal again! [*He goes on murmuring the figures.*] 10 at 183 is—700 an'—an', let me see now.

[*Bernadette rubs the window for a moment, then leans dreamily on the sill, then begins to sing softly again, while Binnington goes on with his figures.*

Bernadette.
There's a form at the casement, the form of her true love,
And he whispers with face bent, 'I'm waitin' for you, love.
Get up on the stool, through the lattice step lightly,
We'll rove in the grove while the moon's shining brightly.'

Binnington [*with irritation.*] I told you that was enough, didn't I? Rove in the grove! Thinkin' of your own pleasure always. This appalling materialism's spreadin' everywhere. [*He goes on muttering.*] An' ten an' ten each stannard is four tons is twenty stannards, which is—is——

Bernadette [*a little mockingly*]. Why don't you count them on your fingers? Or get one of them machines that puts the figures down before you can guess what they are?

Binnington [*loudly—protestingly*]. You get th' winda done an' go!

Bernadette [*again dropping into her dream*]:
The maid shakes her head, on her lips lays her fingers,
Steals up from her seat, longs to go, and yet lingers.

[*Suddenly a door-bell rings long and sharply from below. Binnington starts, and jumps up from his chair.*

Binnington. That must be that dung-beetle, McGilligan. [*To Bernadette*] Let him in, an' bring him up here.

Bernadette [*shocked*]. Up here—McGilligan? Into th' drawing-room?

Binnington [*catching her by the arm, and forcing her to the door*]. Do what you're told!

[*He opens the door, and pushes her out, then lifts a small chair to the far side of the room; placing it so that it is opposite the kitchen chair standing by the side of the door. He brings the papers he has been examining in his hand and sits down on the chair farthest from the door.*

[*In a moment or two, Bernadette enters again.*

Bernadette [*mockingly.*]   The Deputy Mayor, Councillor Mr. McGilligan.   [*She goes out.*

[*McGilligan comes in after her. He, too, is wearing his municipal robe, red like Binnington's, but with a deeper cape and cuffs of green, bordered with gold braid; a richer and more pompous robe than the Mayor's. He is a stoutish man, half bald, with tightly-clipped greyish-black hair from the skull's centre to the neck's nape. His suit is a dark-grey one, brown shoes, a high stiff collar, and green tie. Across his belly, too, stretches a gold watch-chain, from one waistcoat pocket to the other. Binnington stares at him, fixing his eyes on the robe, while McGilligan stands like a statue, with a dead-pan face, beside the door. Binnington gives a modified snort of disdain as he stares at McGilligan's robe.*

McGilligan [*with bitter dignity*].   What are you snortin' outa you for, you cunnin' bloated cockroach!

Binnington [*with quiet but aggressive dignity*].   I suggest you should know—if you know anything—that it is a dereliction of good taste for a Deputy Mayor to wear a more gorgeous gown than the Mayor.

McGilligan.   I am a McGilligan as well as a Deputy Mayor.

Binnington.   A Gael who betrayed the dead when he took th' threaty, gave away Ulsther, an' took an oath of allegiance to an English King.

McGilligan.   An' when you and your gang found yous would lose th' pay if yous didn't enther th' Dail, yous ran to th' registherin' Officer, an' all Ireland heard your mouth smackin' th' Testament takin' th' oath!

Binnington [*raging*].   We took no oath, yeh red-robed renager! I took no oath, I'm tellin' you, no, nor wouldn't with th' Ulsther Rifles proddin' me at one side, an' th' Iniskillen Fusiliers proddin' me on th' other!

McGilligan.   Faithful to th' English King an' his successors forever; ay, forever, be God!

Binnington.   A mottled lie! I'll take no oath, says I to th' officer attendin'; no oath, sorra one, says I, or any words that might fashion a similarity to any oath either, says I. You can take it or leave it, says he, for all I care, says he; right, says I, so sign here, says he, an' fit yourself to take your seat.

McGilligan. Deny as you like, all Ireland heard the thunderclaps of your kisses hoppin' off th' holy Testament!

Binnington. I'll deal with you at the comin' Election afther th' Tosthal's come an' gone. [*The sound of a ship's siren is heard in the distance.*] There, you heard that! You can guess what it is.

McGilligan. The ship.

Binnington. With its cargo of timber on its way up th' channel to the wharf of Doonavale. She'll dock any minute now.

McGilligan [*all alive, rising from his chair*]. I'll get the men and lorries out at once, for I'll never be easy in my mind till the timber's safe in the yard.

Binnington. An' beyond the yard, hidden in the roofs, doors, an' windas of th' new houses. It's a big risk, McGilligan.

McGilligan. We took th' risk before.

Binnington. An' will again, please God, though me conscience is against it.

McGilligan. Our people must have houses.

Binnington. An' we need timber to build them.

McGilligan. An' business is business.

Binnington. Yes, business is business.

Echo. Business is business.

Binnington. Skerighan's comin' today to collect his cheque from you.

McGilligan. Quick on the mark! Well, I'll have it waitin' for him.

Binnington. God help us if anyone guesses!

McGilligan. They're too busy with this damned Tosthal to bother about anything else.

Binnington [*irritably*]. There's ne'er a caw from a crow within fifty miles but someone hears it; there's ne'er a swalla flyin' swift over our roofs, but someone sees it, an' then the world is told. Busy with th' Tosthal—so they are, be day; but there's th' night, man, an' in Doonavale th' night is always whisperin'!

McGilligan. There's no livin' soul hates atheistic Communism more'n I do.

Binnington. That goes for me too.

McGilligan [*sarcastically*]. Goes for you! You wouldn't care a musty damn if the timber came from Hell, much less from the Red Port of——

Binnington [*interrupting him*]. For God's sake, man! Are you ready to send th' hidden word drummin' through the air of th' day, an' have it murmured again be th' whisperin' breezes of th' night? What is done was done only to help th' people to homes they need.

McGilligan. You're right. It was done in a good cause, a good cause.

Binnington. An' business is business.

McGilligan. An' business is business.

Echo. Business is business.

Binnington [*indicating the linen-covered cross*]. Th' Crucifix is back again. [*He takes the linen cover off and shows the figure of Jesus on the cross.*] All newly painted and varnished, ready for th' factory wall again.

McGilligan. They'll hardly notice it any more now than they did when it was dull and shabby. They soon get used to it, and eyes fixed on th' clock haven't time for a glance at th' cross.

Binnington [*replacing linen cover over the Crucifix*]. Prayers before work starts, an' the Rosary when work ends, an' they aren't satisfied, wantin' both to be said in th' factory's time, an' not in theirs; an' gettin' it, too.

McGilligan. Poor Father Fillifogue is hoarse teachin' them th' right way to look at th' Pope's social teachin's, but it's no go; with their Yis, Father, when he's facin' them, but they're off to th' plan of doin' little as you can for as much as you can get, when th' poor man's back is turned.

Binnington. Will he ever get them to realise that when they work for us they're workin' for God?

McGilligan. Never.

Binnington. Never.

Echo. Never.

McGilligan. Ten more are leavin' the factory within a month's time.

Binnington. My God, ten of them! Leavin' for where?

McGilligan. For England, soon as they get th' Tosthal over.

Binnington. This Tosthal'll ruin us! Gave twenty-five of th' best for th' damned thing. Then a subscription to the hurling club, one to the choir—a choir, mind you, in Doonavale—to send them to singin' instead of to work; one, too, for th' debatin' society—a debatin' society, mind you, in Doonavale—an' now, if you please, they're afther me for one for a drama club—a drama club, mind you, for Doonavale, an' th' whole of th' town play-actors in their own right!

McGilligan. Ah, an' your own son leadin' them on!

Binnington. Ay, an' your own daughter holdin' his hand.

McGilligan. It'll end when th' Tosthal's done.

Binnington. Ay, will it, for my son wasn't meant for a McGilligan's daughter.

McGilligan. Me daughter was reared a lady, see, an' isn't to be wasted on a boundher of a Binnington boy.

Binnington. Me bould man didn't say so when he was workin' to get me boy made Medical Officer of Health in Doonavale disthrict.

McGilligan. Nor you of McGilligan's daughter when you worked to get her made teacher an' librarian of th' town an' counthry.

Binnington. God forbid either event would bring us even one false step closer.

McGilligan [*fervently*]. Amen!

Binnington. What we done was just a quid pro quo.

McGilligan. Just a quid pro quo.

Echo. Quid pro quo.

[*The door opens suddenly and a whole bunch of young excited people flood into the room. Michael Binnington leads the group. He is a young man of twenty-four or so, tall, slim, with a handsome look, shaped to the lines of a well-faced fox, his grey eyes lit by the gleam of an enthusiast. He is dressed in the garb of a gentleman leader of the Ninety-eight insurgents—dark-green tailed coat, white shirt with white-frilled stock, white knee-breeches, and polished top-boots. A light-green shoulder-sash carries a sword hanging on his left hip.*

[*Tom Killsallighan, carpenter, is a sturdy lad of twenty or so, not as tall as Michael, but stouter, and of a more muscular build. He is dark-haired, a pleasant face, with protruding upper lip and humorous black eyes. He is dressed in the uniform of an English captain of the eighteenth century—crimson cutaway coat, the frock-flaps turned back, showing a blue lining; he wears white buckskin breeches and top-boots, and the cuffs of his red coat are blue, ornamented with gold braid; his shoulders are decorated with gold epaulettes. He wears a dark-crimson sash round his waist, and carries a sword by his left side.*

[*The girls, including Nora, daughter of McGilligan, are dressed in the peasant dress of the time—red, brown, or striped petticoat, bodices of calico or linen brown or dark green, and black, with brightly-coloured kerchiefs round their necks, or worn peasant-wise round their heads. Nora is dressed more neatly than the others, with finer shoes, white frilled bodice, and blue skirt, with a finer scarf around her neck. She is a pretty girl of nineteen or twenty, slim, with brown hair, a nose that is slightly snubbed, oval face, rather pale, with full mouth, neatly shaped, and bright blue eyes that have at times a very firm look in them, but most of the time look out steadily and humorously upon all things and people around her.*

[The men, too, are clad in the peasant dress of the period—corduroy or tweed knee-breeches, grey worsted stockings, cutaway cloth coats, and old half-tall hats, narrowing towards the top, or squashed soft cabeens; waistcoats of various coloured tweeds, all a little the worse for wear. Two carry pikes, and one carries a musket, and wears a belt passing over the right shoulder to the left hip; and from this belt hang two pouches, one for powder, the other for ball.

Binnington [as they surge into the room]. What's this? Who brought yous here? What do yous think yous are doin' here? What d'yous want?

Man of the Pike. When we hadn't enough space, Father Ned says, go to Binnington's place, he says; shift the furniture outa th' way, says Father Ned, an' yous'll have all th' space yous want, he says; wide an' truly commodious; with no one, says he, to disturb your improvin' an' positive exertions.

Binnington. Get outa here—all of yous! This room is only for them that know how to walk with threpidation! *[To a man who has gone close to the palm]* Eh, you, come away from th' palm! A touch'll bruise it.

Michael. Now, Father; now, Dad, learn to take new things easy.

Man of the Musket [shoving Binnington aside]. Mind th' way, mind th' way! We're in a hurry.

Binnington [shoving man away—furiously]. How dare you, man, shove the Mayor about in his own house!

Man of the Musket [shouting]. We have to get on with th' Tosthal! We're in a hurry!

Binnington. Why don't yous pick out McGilligan's house for your anthrimartins?

Nora. There's another group workin' for the Tosthal in me father's house, Mr. Binnington.

McGilligan. Good God! I won't stand for this, Nora.

Man of the Pike [*pushing him aside*]. Mind th' way, get outa th' way! We have to get on with th' work of resuscitatin' Ireland.

Binnington. Resuscitatin' Ireland! It's a waste of time!

McGilligan. An' a waste of money. You won't resuscitate us be bringin' back shaddas o' men who done an' said things in a tormented time of long ago that have no bearin' on th' life we live today.

Nora. The things said be Ireland's old leaders are livin' still, and are needed as much today as when they were first spoken.

McGilligan. Our needs'll be well satisfied if we listen to, an' act on, what our pastor says.

Michael. Do you mean Father Ned?

Binnington [*viciously*]. No, he doesn't mean Father Ned! He means th' parish priest. Your Father Ned's a menace to th' town an' th' whole counthryside.

McGilligan. Fitther for yous to be doin' useful work, such as a hammer knockin' a nail into timber to help fix a house together, or send a sickle swishin' down corn to give th' people bread.

Michael. To you the hammer knockin' nails into timber and th' sickle swishin' down corn are noble because they bring you money to widen the walls of a bank.

Nora. Our Blessed Lord often held the hammer an' He knew well the use of the sickle, but He also heard the rose of Sharon singin' her song, an' He saw the lilies of the field dancin' to the tune of a whistlin' wind, or doin' a floral minuet to a whisperin' one.

Man of the Musket. Ay, an' He musta remembered the song of Sharon's rose 'n seen the lilies dance again, even in His deepest sorra, within th' whisperin' of the night.

Tom. If a song doesn't encircle the hammer and sickle, or a song silence them, at times, when a man's longing goes gay, then they become, not the tools of men, but the tools of a slave.

Binnington. Our Blessed Lord never joined in a dance, never halted in His work to sing a song.

Man of the Musket. How d'ye know He didn't?

Nora. If He didn't dance Himself, He must have watched the people at it, and, maybe, clapped His hands when they did it well. He must have often listened to the people singin', and been caught up with the rhythm of the gentle harp and psaltery, and His feet may have tapped the ground along with the gayer sthrokes of the tabor and the sound of the cymbals tinkling.

Man of the Pike. Aysey, aysey, there, with that kinda talk that might send some misfortune sparklin' in on us unawares! Let's only remember th' Tosthal, an' all it means, to bring us out of our idle dhreamin'. Murray, our singin'-teacher, 'll be in on us before we have our part practised. [*He pushes Binnington out of his path.*] Mind th' way, mind outa th' way.

[*Just then, three sharp hoots of a steamer's siren are heard clearly, though still at a distance.*

McGilligan [*starting to excited life*]. There she is, moored fast! [*He runs over to Tom, and grips him by the shoulder.*] Tom, the ship with the timber! Get the men out, get the men out, unload the timber into lorries for the yard!

Binnington. An' look sharp! Th' damned Tosthal can wait.

Tom [*shaking himself free*]. Th' timber can wait; the Tosthal can't. [*He pushes McGilligan towards the door.*] Mind th' way.

McGilligan [*furiously*]. I'm your boss, you're th' foreman of me buildin' jobs, an' I ordher you to get goin' with th' timber! [*The Pikeman and Man of the Musket push them out gently but firmly, and close the door. As he is pushed out*] This is certainly a nice hand-out to God's goodness!

Michael. Now, lads. You've the script, Nora—follow us and see we don't miss anything. Your start, Tom.

[*They place themselves properly; Tom facing Michael in the centre; the Pikeman to one side, Man of the Musket on the other; Nora standing back in the centre, script in hand; the other men and girls in a semicircle around her, a little behind.*

Nora [*to Michael and Tom*]. A little farther back from each other so's to give a chance to come nearer when you get excited. Now, Tom.

Tom [*a little nervous*]. I tell you, Mr. Forsyth, that you gravely err in thinking discontent can bring either safety or peace.

Michael. The time has come to strike for liberty!

The Rest [*shouting*]. For liberty!

Michael. We have stood quiet in our fields, on our hills, in our valleys; we have sat quiet in our homes, trusting the power that held us down would show justice; but we have found neither security nor peace in submission; so we must strike for the liberty we all need, the liberty we must have to live.

The Rest [*shouting*].   The liberty we must have to live!

Tom.   Liberty? And pray, sir, what right have the Irish people to liberty other than that God-ordained liberty, sanctioned by your holy bishops, of faithful submission and true loyalty to His Majesty the King of England and Ireland as well?

Michael.   We deny and repudiate, sir Captain, the right or the rule that would put any government over our people other than he or them selected by the people's choice; the united Irish people; we avow the right and rule only that we, Catholic, Protestant, and Presbyterian, have to choose our own governors, the power to dismiss them when we think them unfaithful or incompetent; and we avow the God-given right to have the power and to be within the condition of framing a government and law by ourselves and for ourselves; and, if need be, this right and this rule we are determined to maintain by every means within our power.

Tom [*mockingly*].   Maintain them with a few thousand pikes and half a dozen ageing muskets?

Michael.   We are young, and God has given us strength and courage and counsel. May He give us the victory!

Tom [*indignantly*].   This, sir, is high treason!

Michael.   That is our stand; that is our story; and that is our resolution. It is high time for a change, for the Republican principle that all men are equal, that they should have the right to declare who shall govern them, and that the law should be beneficial, not to the few, but to the many. Your peace, Captain, within the life we live, is but quiet decay.

Tom [*furiously*].   I arrest you, Michael Binnington, for high treason against this realm and the realm's law; I arrest you in the King's name! Hand me your sword!

Michael [*slapping his hand on the hilt of his sword*].   Come and take it!

Man [*from the back running forward and shouting*].   Our chapel's on fire! The Yeomanry are settin' it ablaze!

Michael [*to Man of the Musket*].   Gather the men together, Pat, by the risin' of th' moon, and we shall march.

Tom [*drawing his sword*].   Defend yourself, you traitor!

Nora.   Now the duel! You begin, Tom, and I'll call out.

[*The duel begins, Nora calling out the strokes to be given, in the method of the old melodrama. The swordsmen's movements are rather slow, and show they need a lot of practice.*

Nora [*calling out.*]   Head, right shoulder . . . left shoulder . . . right leg, left leg. Now, Michael—head . . . right shoulder . . . left shoulder . . . right leg . . . left leg . . . now, you again, Tom. . . . And try to make the duel a little more fierce.

[*The duel goes on a little more fiercely, but still very warily, when suddenly the door opens to allow the swift entrance of Mr. Murray, followed by some additional boys and girls, all seemingly in a hurry and all excited.*

[*Murray is a man of middle height, plump, and easily agitated. He carries his head a little thrust forward from his shoulders, as if he were about to rush at whomsoever he happened to be speaking to; a clipped grey moustache covers his upper lip. He speaks with a kind of lisp, pronouncing words like 'this' and 'that', as 'dish' and 'dat', and gives a liquid sound to some of his words—perhaps Limerick fashion. He is dressed in a black frock coat, waistcoat, and trousers, the waistcoat cut rather low, showing a full white front, winged collar, stiff, and underneath the wings a large flowing black tie. He wears a black soft hat with a wide brim. He has a habit of brushing his moustache aside occasionally while he is speaking excitedly, as if he were wiping froth away. He is carrying a walking-stick in his right hand, gripping it tightly by its centre. He is in a state of excitement.*

Murray [*pushing a way towards the piano through the duellers and the others*].   Outa dee way, all of yous! Where were dee whole of yous? I've been after you for monts. How we goin' to sing dee Tosthal song widout practice? And dee Bossman, Father Fillifogue, afther me to stop id. All he wants is hymns, hymns! Det todether, det todether! [*He whips up the lid of the piano.*] If we want th' Tosthal song to go, we must det down to id, det up to id, go round about id. Gusto! That's what we must have—[*with a shout*] Gusto! Led every singin' mout' be one big round O! [*He opens his own mouth far and wide.*] Let dee sound of dee voice out into dee room, out into dee street, out into dee world. Gusto! When I count tree—go. One two tree—now! [*He hammers the tune on the piano, one or two of the impromptu singers make a straggling start, stop, and all is silent. Sarcastically*] Dat was too loud; too much gusto; derrible, derrible! [*Angrily*] Oh, for Dod's sake, dive dee world a whisper! Dee bossman'll be here any minute, an' den we'll be drownin' in hymns. Again: one two tree—now!

All [*singing fairly well*]:

Put out th' flags an' raise
Th' voice in happy numbers O!

Shake th' lazy, fire th' tame,
An' rouse up all th' sleepers O!
      Chorus
Hurrah for th' Tostal O,
That tempts us from our sleeping O,
When Erin sings and laughs and shouts,
Instead of always weeping O!

Murray [*very excited*].   Put gizz into it, for Dod's sake. Louder an' wid
vigour. Now!

All.

Eire stands with arms outspread
To welcome here all comers O;
To hear us sing, to see us dance,
An' watch our merry mummers O!

Murray [*waving his stick furiously*].   Let her rip, lads an' lasses; let
her rip!

With laurel, bay, an' myrtle, weave
Yeats' hazel rod an' berry O.
Dip all in wine of vintage fine,
To make them bright an' merry O.
      Chorus
Hurrah for th' Tostal O!
Th' dawn o' day is peepin' O;
An' Eire laughs an' sings an' shouts,
Instead of always weepin' O!

Murray [*excited*].   Chorus again—louder, louder! Gusto, gusto!

[*In the midst of the hubbub, the shouting of the song, the head
and shoulders of Father Fillifogue appear above the window-still.
He listens to the din for a few moments. If he could be seen
wholly, we would be looking at a stout man of middle age,
baldish, with tufts of grey hair protruding from beneath a soft
black hat. His head is very round and broad, a thick nose, and a
mouth seemingly forever compressed, the lips tight together in a
mood of resigned annoyance with the world around him. He is
dressed in conventional clerical garb, but his trousers are baggy,
and a little too short even for his short legs. He carries an umbrella
in his right hand, uses it to emphasise whatever he may be saying
when he gets excited, as he sometimes does, though he speaks
usually in a calm and sarcastic manner. His voice seems to be a
trifle husky, or maybe it comes from the back of his mouth; anyway, it has in it the suggestion of a purr, a sarcastic one, as if he*

were making a great effort to remain within the bounds of charity.
He now wears a look of blended annoyance and scorn as he
stretches head and neck into the room, the umbrella gripped
fiercely in his right hand.

Father F. [*softly, but trying to make himself heard*]. Mr. Murray! Boys,
boys; girls, girls! A minute, please. [*But the singing goes on, so he
speaks louder.*] Mr. Murray! [*He waves and bangs the umbrella on the
window-sill—with a purring shout*] Mister Murray!

[*The song stops dead suddenly. The boys and girls slide to the
left and right, trying to hide themselves, some of them getting half
behind the curtains. Michael and Nora stand where they are, gazing
somewhat amusedly at the Parish Priest. Murray stiffens on his
seat at the piano, sitting there motionless and a little shaken.*

Father F. [*quiet and sarcastic*]. Busy bees—buzz buzz buzz! Too busy
to bother about my knockin' at the door. [*Calmly*] Knock knock knock.
[*Loud and sharp*] Knock knock! So your play babbles about the rights
of man. [*He chuckles mockingly.*] What with your rights of women,
rights of children, rights of trades unions, rights of th' laity, an' civil
rights—[*shouting angrily*] yous are paralysin' life! [*He raps the window-sill with his umbrella. Loudly and impatiently*] Isn't somebody goin'
to open the door an' let me in? [*No one speaks, but Bernadette moves
slowly out of the room to let him in, and after a few moments Father
Fillifogue comes in, his face full of annoyance, his lips pressed tightly
together.*] Dabblin' in, an' babblin' about, things you don't understand.
[*He notices that Bernadette hasn't come in; he runs back to the door
and calls out*] Come back, you! Don't run away, don't run away! [*As
she comes in again*] Slip away, slip away! Prowl into church, an' slip
away before th' sermon. I know you all!

Nora [*to Michael*]. Come along, Michael, to th' Dance Hall, an' see how
Father Ned's gettin' on with th' decorations. We're no use here now.

[*They go out. The rest—except Murray, who seems to be chained
to the piano—try to follow, but Father Fillifogue is too quick for
them. He glides to the door, shuts it and faces the rest who retreat
shamefacedly.*

Father F. Slip away, slip away! You'd all rather be watchin' your Father
Ned in th' Dance Hall. Father Ned, indeed! [*He pushes one of the
crowd farther away up the room.*] Farther away from th' door, my child,
farther away. Ah, then, when I meet Father Ned, I'll have something
to say to him. I'll show your Father Ned that th' Church comes before th'
Tosthal. [*With impatient scorn*] Th' Tosthal, huh! [*On guard near
the door, he stretches out his arm holding the umbrella, and pokes*

Murray in the back with the ferrule]. Take that hump off your back, Mr. Murray, an' buck up! We must get that hymn to our Blessed Mother right, Tosthal or no Tosthal. [*Appealingly*] Oh, children, take that look of misery from your gobs, an' try to look cheerful! Mr. Murray, if he is alive, will give th' note. Now, remember what I've so often said about singing 'Oh Mother!—[*pause*] I could weep for mirth', and don't bellow it. [*Prodding Murray with the umbrella*] Mr. Murray, Mr. Murray! Note!

> [*Murray gives the note too suddenly, and the crowd start the hymn, but in a ragged manner, behind the time of tune.*

Crowd [*singing*].   Oh Mother I——

Father F. [*tapping the ferrule of umbrella smartly on the ground*].   No, no, no! It is not Oh Mother I! This is the way it must be sung. [*He sings huskily*] Oh Mother! Pause! I could weep for mirth.

Murray [*echoing Father Fillifogue*].   Oh Mother . . . Pause . . . I could weep for mirth.

Father F. [*impatiently—prodding Murray*].   The note, Mr. Murray; the note!   [*Mr. Murray gives the note.*

Crowd [*singing*].   Oh Mother I——

Father F. [*frantically*].   Stop, stop! The pause, the pause! You see, Mr. Murray; you hear, Mr. Murray?

Murray [*shouting*].   Dee pause, dee pause, boys; dee pause, girls!

Father F. [*to Murray*].   Don't bellow, Mr. Murray! You can make a statement clear better quietly. [*To the crowd*] Now, children, look at me, listen to me; when I raise my umbrella so [*he raises the umbrella in the manner of a bandmaster's staff*] you are to pause, to pause! Mr. Murray will give us the note. Mr. Murray, the note, the note.
    [*Murray gives the note.*

Crowd [*singing as before*].   Oh Mother I——

> [*At the word Mother, Father Fillifogue has frantically raised the umbrella, but the Crowd has taken no notice of the signal.*

Father F. [*banging his umbrella on the floor*].   Stop! [*A silent pause*] Who is Mother I? [*With anguish*] Oh, who is Mother I?

Murray [*swinging round on the piano-stool to face the singers*].   Hear Fader Fillifogue's question! [*Emphatically*] Who is Mudder I?

Father F. [*gesticulating towards Murray for silence*].   Mr. Murray, Mr. Murray!

Murray [*carried away*].   It is nod Mudder I, or Mudder me, or Mudder you!

Father F. [*loudly and protestingly, moving away from the door to be closer to Murray*].   Mr. Murray, Mr. Murr—ay! They don't know because they are not told; not told by you how to sing it properly. You're so wrapped in your tinkling Tosthal song that you never think of the hymns, Mr. Murray; the hymns, the hymns.

Murray [*beginning to lose his temper*].   Oh, yes, dee hymns! Dee hymns, dee hymns! Dee hymns an' dee prayer till Ireland sinks into a deep freeze of frosty piety an' sham. We are nod in heaven; we are nod on the earth—we're nowhere. So where are we?

> [*The Man of the Musket, the Man of the Pike, and several others have stolen away by the door, and shortly afterwards the others go, slinking out till Father Fillifogue and Mr. Murray are left alone to carry on the vehement argument without any audience.*]

Father F. [*who is losing his temper too*].   We are in Doonavale, Mr. Murray, and you are the Organist of Our Lady Help of Christians; and I'm your Parish Priest. Now listen to me.

Murray.   You listen to me!

Father F. [*gripping umbrella by the stem, and banging the handle on the table*].   Listen to me, Mr. Murray! You're not going to play on me the way you do on the piano—[*banging the keys over Murray's shoulders*] thump thump; or on the organ, battering the pedals. [*He stamps violently on the floor.*] Stamp stamp!

Murray.   When dee moosic says fortissimo, I press dee pedals.

Father F.   I'll nail them down, I'll nail them down, Mr. Murray.

Murray.   I'll pull dem out, I'll pull dem out, Fader Fillifogue.

Father F.   I'll see that you'll think more of our sacred church music than you do of Mozart. There's nothing apostolic or evangelical in the riddle-me-randy music of Mozart. Pah!

Murray [*shouting back*].   Pah, you! [*Madly sweeping his hands over the piano keys, producing a shrieking medley of notes*] Listen, you! When we worship Mozart, we worship God; yes, God, Fader Fillifogue! Mozart's moosic can be as dee murmur of a river's first flow among dee forget-me-nots an' dee meadow-sweet; as gay as a dance of boys an' girls at a fair, an' no priest present!

Father F. [*furiously banging his umbrella on the table*].   Be silent, sir; be silent!

Murray [*beside himself with anger*].   Riddle-me-randy moosic! I tell you, Fader Fillifogue, dat his moosic is both evangelical an' apostolic! It can be as tender as a lily resting on dee bosom of dee Blessed Virgin; as indignant as tunder from any Hill of Horeb; it can be as dee sound of a mighty wind shakin' dee biggest beech an' pine of dee biggest forests, an', Fader Fillifogue, dee most of it would fit wid grandeur many songs dat Dod Himself might like to sing!

Father F. I'm going, Mr. Murray, till you come to your senses. [*He turns and notices that the room is empty of its audience.*] Ah! Your wonderful pupils have done a flit! Gone to work for that Tosthal. [*He wheels round to face Murray—angrily*] Oh, this Tosthal in lifting us up is getting us down! [*He bangs his umbrella on the table.*] I won't have my organist doing for this Tosthal what he should do for the Choir! The millennium, the millenium! With their flowers in coloured boxes on their window-sills; their flags flying from their windas; painting their doors red, yellow, blue, green, an' orange, till they have our respectable, modest town looking like a grinning, gaudy whore!

Murray. It's but dee beginnin', Fader Fillifogue! The painting of dee doors orange, green, blue, yellow an' red, an' dee puttin' out of flowers in coloured boxes on dee winda-sills, is but dee beginnin'! Dee day of small tings we do not despise.

Father F. [*stretching his head towards Murray—mockingly*]. Dee beginning! is often very near dee end! [*He goes to the door and halts there.*] A last word: are you listening? [*Turning as he speaks. Murray turns his back. Father Fillifogue pokes him in the back with his umbrella—impatiently.*] Are you listening!

Murray [*turning and grasping end of the umbrella, and holding on to it*]. Fader Fillifogue, I do not permit myself to be poked!

Father F. Take care you're not poked out of th' Parish! [*Essaying to pull the umbrella from Murray's hold, but the chuck only brings Murray closer*] Get it into your mind—your Mozart will not come hiking into this parish; never!

[*He pulls his umbrella again, but Murray holds fast.*

Murray [*chucking the umbrella so that Father Fillifogue is pulled nearer to him—Father Fillifogue has backed a little when he gave his pull*]. He is on his way here, Fader, and dee people will give him a laurel wreath of deir delight.

Father F. Deir delight! [*He pulls at his umbrella.*] Let go my umbrella, Mr. Murray! [*He backs away.*] Mozart, did you say?

Murray [*pulling Father Fillifogue towards him again—loudly*]. And Bach!

Father F. [*with a mocking chuckle*]. Chuh! Bach, too! Let go my umbrella, Mister Murray!

Murray [*exultantly*]. An' Angus, too.

Father F. [*stiffening in puzzlement*]. Angus, too? Angus who?

Murray. An' all dee great ones chosen by God to give moosic an' joy to His people.

Father F. [*losing all patience, and giving a violent chuck to the umbrella*]. Let go, man! [*The violent chuck makes Murray let go of the umbrella suddenly, and Father Fillifogue staggers back—caught off guard—so that he nearly falls. As he goes out of the room*] Mozart, Bach, an'—an' Angus! [*He turns for the last shot.*] We'll see about that, Mr. Murray, we'll see.   [*He goes out chuckling in a mocking manner.*

Murray [*running to the door, and shouting after Father Fillifogue*]. All dee great ones, Father Fillifogue; all dee great ones! [*He runs to the window, bends out over it, and shouts down to the street.*] Mozart, Bach, Beethoven, Haydn an' Handel, too!

Echo. Haydn an' Handel, too.

> [*Through this last phrase the roll of the side-drums, faint and far away, is heard.*

END OF ACT I

ACT II

Evening. McGilligan's drawing-room, looking almost exactly like the one in Binnington's except that the curtains and sashes are of reverse colours—the curtains yellow, the hold-back sashes green; and the palm tree has long yellow leaves with blue stems and trunk, the reverse of the palm in Binnington's. However, on the table, same kind as Binnington's, are a number of coloured window-sill boxes having patterns on them in colours varying from the general one of the box, all of which are filled with flowers—geraniums, wallflowers, celandines, bluebells, cuckoopint, etc., all

much larger than life, and fashioned in a stylised way. McGilligan's piano is placed exactly as is the one in Binnington's drawing-room. Half over the picture of the Pope hangs a home-painted poster, gayly coloured, with announcements about the Tostal; those in large print plainly visible. They are TOSTAL IN DOONAVALE . . . HURLING MATCH . . . BAND . . . CONCERT . . . OPERA . . . PLAY . . . DANCE . . . FAIR . . .
WE *were* DEAD *and are* ALIVE AGAIN!

There are a number of flags leaning against the walls, and large streams of coloured stuffs for festoons which are draped over the chairs. A pile of well-planed planks, for making window-boxes, and for use in the decorations, form a pile on the floor. Against another wall, a number of pikes are leaning, their tin spears agleam, and the whole room presents the appearance of a busy workshop, contrasting oddly with the stiff furniture, the curtains, palm and other objects indicating a most respectable and rather pompous drawing-room of a middle-class family.

It is dusk, the sky a delicate mauve and yellow.

In through the open door comes Tom carrying yet another gaily-painted box of flowers for a window-sill. He planks it on the table beside the others.

Bernadette's Voice [*outside*].   How many's that we have now, Tom?

Tom [*glancing over the table*].   Four before, an' this one makes five, so that's a hundhred and eighty-two we've made up to now.

Bernadette's Voice [*outside*].   We're gettin' on. [*She comes in.*] But there's still a hundhred to be made; so get a move on, lad, an' don't dally.

Tom.   Dunno if we'll ever get through; an' y'know, after all our throuble, we mayn't have many visitors to see our work.

Bernadette.   What if we won't aself? Ourselves'll be lookin' at an' enjoyin' ourselves, won't we? [*He is silent.*] Won't we?
                              [*She lays an appealing hand on his arm.*

Tom [*dubiously*].   We'll be lookin' at each other, right enough; but I don't know about enjoyin' it.

Bernadette.   'Course we'll enjoy it. Listen more to Father Ned.

Tom.   Things here have aged too long for us to try to make them young again.

Bernadette.   Old fields can still bring forth new corn, says Father Ned, my Tom; an' wintry minds give place to thinking born of spring. Doonavale'll know, says he, something about the liveliness of colour; an' Doonavale'll hear music—great music, a little, good music, a lot, says he; an' near the end the setting sun, with music at the close, says he, that sometimes fills the heart with the burden of beauty.

Tom. Burden of beauty: an odd, sthrange thing to say.

Bernadette. He does be dhreamin' times. He means, maybe, that then we bear within us things greater than ourselves. He said another thing I won't forget in a hurry.

Tom. What was that then?

Bernadette [*shy now and uncertain*]. Somethin' he shouldn't have said, maybe.

Tom [*very curious*]. What was that now? [*As she hesitates—putting his hand on her shoulder*] Come on—tell us.

Bernadette. He said that within th' timid stir of this dim town would come laughter and a song or two; that girls who hurried off from boys, an' boys from girls, would linger close together now.

Tom [*taking his hand slowly from her shoulder*]. A dangerous thing to say.

Bernadette [*vehemently*]. Oh, here, in Doonavale, near everything said or done is dangerous. We're tired out at feelin' afraid of a word or a look bringin' courage or affection into our lonely souls!

Tom. You're right, Bernadette; an' so is Father Ned.

[*He puts a hand on her shoulder again.*

Bernadette. An' then, he said, 'I shouldn't wondher', says Father Ned, 'if th' slight acquaintance swung many a longin' for a kiss to life'.

Tom [*his arm slipping down from her shoulder goes under her right arm, his hand on her body below her breast*]. Father Ned said that, did he now?

Bernadette. An', oh, Tom—[*she hesitates*].

Tom. Yis?

Bernadette. He said that he wouldn't wondher either if undher th' stars, th' night would be full of whispers.

Tom. Mine, maybe. My whispers an' your whispers, Bernadette.

Bernadette [*pulling some faded leaves from the flowers in a box*]. We mustn't leave a fadin' flower or a witherin' leaf on one of th' plants.

Tom [*ignoring the change of subject—bending his head to be close to hers*]. Yours, too. Yours an' mine—two of the sweet whispers of th' night: yours an' mine: mingling together.

[*He moves to kiss her, but she shyly and swiftly turns her face aside.*

Bernadette. Not one fadin' blosssom; not one witherin' leaf.

Tom [*softly*]. Bernadette!

Bernadette [*turning to look at him*]. Well?

Tom [*kissing her swiftly as she turns her face to his*]. Th' first whisper before th' night falls!

Bernadette. Every flower in its fullness of colour an' scent; every leaf as fresh an' green, veined without spot or blemish, as the sun an' itself can make it—Oh, Tom, what a garden we might have!

Tom. The ageing rose must fade an' th' tiring leaf must fall. As we, one day, sweet Bernadette, must fade an' fall, too.

Bernadette. Yes, yes, when all that could be done is done; not be a wild grab at life, but a sturdy, steady livin' of it; when all our deeds an' joys'll be as many as the leaves on an ash or th' blossoms on a three of hawthorn. Then we can fade in quietness, and fall with the carelessness of satisfaction.

[*Father Fillifogue comes running, half stumbling into the room. He is out of breath, and makes a beeline puffing for a chair; face flushed, and sweat-beads on his brow.*

Father F. [*after he has fumbled into a chair—puffing*]. Who is this Father Ned? Where is he, an' who is he? Me breath's gone! Where's that Father Ned of yours? At the Tosthal flag-pole; at the Town Hall; in the main street watchin' the window-boxes go up; yet I found him nowhere! Where is he?

Tom. Father Ned? He was here some time ago, I was told, but went runnin' off to see afther the decoration of th' lamp-posts.

Father F. Went runnin' off! An' I'll have to go runnin' afther him! Decoratin' th' lamp-posts! Oh, an' if I lay a hand on him, he'll be runnin' off somewhere else! [*He stamps with his umbrella on the floor.*] Where's Deputy-Mayor McGilligan?

Bernadette. Him an' Mrs. McGilligan are down in the Dance Hall, practisin' dancin' an' deportment.

Father F. [*sarcastically*]. Dancin' an' deportment for the Tosthal Ball! Splendid! An' your Father Ned dancin' around the lamp-posts! Splendid! An' poor Father Fillifogue dancin' afther them all! Would yous call that splendid? [*The boy and girl remain silent.*] Wouldn't yous?

Tom. I dunno.

Father F. Of course you dunno. [*With a sudden shout*] It's monstrous! When I was told that Father Ned was here, I near killed myself runnin' to ketch up with him; riskin' a heart attack, but soon as I got here, I'm told he's dancin' round our lamp-posts.

Tom. They're paintin' th' ordinary ones black, an' gildin' them that are on the corners.

Father F. [*wrathful and mystified*]. Th' ordinary ones black an' the corner ones gilded—what are you sayin', fool? What corners, what ones is gettin' gilded?

Tom. Th' lamp-posts, Father.

Bernadette. Black as mournin' for our dead heroes, an' a gildin' for th' glorious things they done.

Father F. [*savagely*]. If th' heroes runnin' round Doonavale would only die, we'd gild them all, we'd gild them all! [*To Tom and Bernadette*] What are th' two of you doin' here alone? Up to no good, I'll go bail.

Tom [*ignoring the remark—to Bernadette*]. How many more boxes is this we have to do?

Bernadette. A little more'n a hundhred more.

Father F. [*sarcastically*]. Only a hundred, eh? That's nothin'.

Tom [*ignoring Father Fillifogue*]. Oh, well, there's ten of us makin' them, an' two more doin' th' painting, so we should be shut of them in a few more hours.

> [*He takes up some of the timber to carry it away for the making of the boxes.*

Father F. [*sarcastically*]. Only a few more hours; only a hundred more boxes; sure, that's nothin'; nothin' at all! [*He suddenly leaps up from the chair with a shout.*] I'll stick it no longer! If I do, I'll be as mad as th' rest of them! [*To Tom*] D'ye know the Mayor an' his Deputy haven't yet handed in their Nomination Papers for the Election, and the Office shuts in a few hours?

Tom [*soothingly*]. Don't worry, Father; Father Ned says we'll see about that business lather.

Bernadette [*as Father Fillifogue sits speechless down on the chair again—to Tom*]. You go on hurrying up th' boxes, an' don't waste time gossipin' to Father Fillifogue!

Father F. [*indignantly*]. Gossipin'! Since when has it become a mortal sin to answer your Parish Priest's question, girl?

Bernadette [*ignoring the remark—going to Tom, and laying a hand affectionately on his shoulder*]. Do hurry, dear, or Father Ned'll be very annoyed.

[*Father Fillifogue rises swiftly from the chair, runs over to the couple, and roughly switches Bernadette's arm from Tom's shoulder.*

Father F. Don't you remember th' kinda girl you are? D'ye want to folla in th' mad manner of your dead mother?

Bernadette [*with a shrill artificial laugh*]. Maybe I do; maybe I am.

Tom [*looking at the priest balefully, then at Bernadette sympathetically*]. Come on with me, Bernadette; come with me, lass.

Bernadette [*sullenly*]. I can't; you know how I divide my time—three days with the McGilligans an' three here; an' this is a Binnington day.

Tom. Oh, all right.

[*He lifts several planks of the slenderer ones, places them under an arm, and settles himself to go. As he moves to the door, Skerighan enters with half a rush, excited and loud-voiced.*

Skerighan. Where's McGillighan, eh? [*Turning to Bernadette*] Where's McGillighan, you? [*As Tom and Bernadette don't answer, he turns to Father Fillifogue.*] Are ye duff? Can ye no hear a question?

[*Skerighan is a man of forty or so, with the look of a Jersey bull. He has thick-jowled cheeks and a fattish roll under his chin; his eyes are small, but dark and piercing, in an argument intense. He has an air of dominance, and his clothes show a semi-prosperity, but maintained by constant application to work. He is dressed mostly in a dark suit, bowler hat, stiff collar and dark tie, with a white silk scarf round his neck, wound so that it doesn't hide the collar and tie. His hair is dark, but flecked with grey tufts.*

Father F. [*astonished*]. An' who may you be, sir; an' what has you in such a flutther?

Skerighan [*indignantly*]. I'm no' in no flutther! I'm Alec Skerighan, a business-mon fra' Portadoon, an' McGillighan was tae meet me hours ago ut hus office, but thur's naethin' thur but a mod crowd o' girls on' boys in th' get-up of th' long sin', on' no McGillighan.

Father F. Indeed?

Skerighan. Ay; on', with thom sayin' find Feyther Nud, on' he'll find McGillighan. [*He sees bottles on sideboard, runs over, pours out a stiff whiskey, and lowers it.*] On' down on th' wharf, expectin' tae find the shup half unloaded, I find her stull full tae th' brim with tumber. I tull ye, I'll no' pay captain on' crew just tae hove a looksee over this skuttle-alley town o' yours!

Father F. [*indignantly*].   Our town, sir, is Christian an' cultured; it is a borough, sending two members to the Dail; and no skuttle-alley, as you call it!

Skerighan.   Oh, I'm no' in th' vein for argument. [*He lowers another stiff glass of whiskey.*] Ut's a grond town. I just want th' tumber outa th' shup.

Tom [*as he goes out*].   Don't worry—Father Ned knows all about it, an' we'll push into work under th' early eye o' th' morning.

Skerighan.   The urly eye o' the murnin'! [*To Bernadette, sinking wearily into a chair*] Whaur is this Feyther Ned?

Bernadette.   Here; but he might be anywhere, though some may think he's nowhere; again he may be everywhere; but he's always with th' dhrums.

Skerighan.   Th' dhrums? What dhrums? [*In despair, to Father Filli-fogue*] Who is this Feyther Nud?

Father F. [*turning as he goes out; going close to Skerighan, and bending over him*]. The wizard of the town—here tomorrow; gone today!

[*He goes off.*

Skerighan [*to Bernadette*].   Ye're no' McGillighan's daughter, urre ye?

Bernadette.   I'm his maid.

Skerighan.   Oh, his maid. What's makkin' th' toon mod? There's a gay lot o' loddies, some on their lone, some togither, gangin' about in th' rud coats of th' English Ormy of th' long sin'!

Bernadette.   It's gettin' ready they are for the play of th' Tosthal.

Skerighan.   Th' Tosthall? I asked a gay wheen o' people what th' word means, on' all th' onswer I got was thot everyone in th' world knew what th' turm meant. Is it a buttle of some kind they're goin' tae do?

Bernadette.   Ay, it is so, th' time when we skelped th' English outa th' towns of Wexford.

Skerighan [*with amused mockery*].   Aw, lass, ye con do a gay lot in your dhreamin'.

Bernadette.   We have our history, misther.

Skerighan.   Wouldn't it be a lut wiser if ye med your bacon butther on' brought your formin' up till date, like us in Ulsther?

Bernadette [*dreamily*].   An' what about th' winds that blew, an' th' waves that lifted Colmcille away from Ireland; an' him writing his holy poems be th' light of candles till they gave out, an' then writin' on from th' eager light comin' from th' five fingers on his opposite hand!

Skerighan. Oy, on' all th' time ye get what ye can for your bacon, without knowin' how to go about it to get more.

Bernadette [*still dreaming*]. Or of holy Deeusk sittin' in a sulthry desert, addin' coloured spirals to a written psalm, an' he dhryin' up with th' dint o' thirst, when green grass grew round him, an' in th' grass a well of ice-cold wather, a little bush suddenly fruitin' full of barley loaves, fresh-baked, an' flavoured with honey made be th' wilder bees from heather an' th' wild-rose of a land hidden well from th' desert's heat.

Skerighan [*bewildered, but sceptical*]. Be God, if your Tosthal strengthens yon dhreamin' of yours, odd things'll hoppen here!

Bernadette [*waking up*]. Oh, th' Tosthal? That's different. Then there'll be games, music, shoals of songs, plays, an' gay girls with boys who are gayer still!

Skerighan. That's more like it—gay girls dancin' with boys gayer than th' girls.

Bernadette [*suddenly going gay*]. Like this, bo; like this!

[*She dances about in a half-waltz, half-folk-dance, shaking her hips, whirling her skirt in a swift turning movement, and jutting her bottom out in an exciting way, smiling and nodding at Skerighan as she dances.*

Skerighan [*enthusiastically*]. Now you're no' dhreamin', lass; bonny in your movements as ye are in your looks!

Bernadette [*extending her hands towards him*]. Come on, an' join us!

[*He rushes to the door, and shuts it; he rushes to the window, and shuts it; then he joins her, holding her in a way that is a quarter hold and three-quarters of an embrace, as they dance round together; she lightly and he in rather a clumsy way.*

Skerighan [*after a little dancing*]. A kiss wud go down well th' now!

Bernadette [*coyly*]. Don't grip me so tight—maybe it's a kiss you want!

Skerighan. Just as a fine beginnin'.

[*He suddenly tightens his embrace, and seeks to kiss her.*

Bernadette [*resisting, but still coyly*]. You mustn't, you bad man!

Skerighan [*tightening his hold, forcing her face towards his and kissing her*]. Mustn't I! [*As he kisses her*] There!

Bernadette [*struggling to get away*]. Let me go! [*She lets out a rasping scream.*] Let me go!

Skerighan [*releasing her, in fright, so suddenly that she falls on to the floor*]. Ye little fool—I was only jokin'!

> [*She looks astonished for a moment, then rises and staggers around the table, finally reaching the sofa, and subsiding there, half on it and half off.*

Bernadette [*staggering around*]. Me head, my head! I'm goin' to faint! [*As she subsides on to the sofa*] I'm passin' out! [*She gives a squeal out of her.*] Passin' out!

Skerighan [*annoyed, but frightened*]. You'll be all right in a monnit.

Bernadette [*she is struggling into a sitting pose on the sofa*]. Me heart! [*She catches her breath, and gulps, as if she is choking.*] I'm in a bad way. D'ye hear that gaspin'? I'm goin' out on th' gaspin'! [*She screams again.*] I'm goin' fast!

Skerighan [*in a sad way with fear of discovery*]. For God's sake, quit your howlin', or th' whole town'll come runnin' tae see what's up!

Bernadette [*with what is meant to be a convulsive movement*]. I'm stiflin'! Open th' winda, open th' winda—I'm stiflin'! Oh, help me! Don't yeh know something about artificial respiration!

Skerighan. I dinna know onythin' aboot it, on' if I dud, I'd no' thry it on you! [*Running to the window and opening it a little*] There, now! You'll be awright in a monnit.

Bernadette. What'll you do if I die here gaspin'?

Skerighan. Ye'll no die, I'm tullin' you. Stay stull, on' you'll be leppin' 'bout, gay as ever. Domn it, you weren't in me arrms f'r more'n a monnit, girrl, on' I thinkin' you were one who wouldn't wondher away from a wee kiss!

Bernadette [*with a squealing moan*]. A wee kiss! Only a monnit! An' me arrm bruised, me legs twisted, me shouldher dislocated—you've tangled one part of me body with another!

Skerighan [*anger overcoming fear at last*]. Domn it, girrl, it was yoursel' led me intil it! Everything was innocent on' firm, till ye pranc'd round swingin' your skirt, twirlin' your legs, on' sailin' ahead twuttering your luddle bum!

Bernadette [*prostrate on the sofa—horrified*]. Twitherin' me luddle bum! Oh, blessed saints above, d'ye hear that! Oh, the villainous thought worse nor the villainous action! Twittherin' me luddle bum!

Me that never heard th' word utthered before, an' guess only dimly at its meanin'! An' Father Fillifogue dhrivin' th' poor innocent Tom away, to thrust me into the throe of a desthroyer.

Skerighan [*imploringly*]. Can't ye thry to pull yourself taeguther before someone arrives tae mak a song about it? [*He puts some notes on end of table nearer her.*] There's a few pounds 'ull hulp ye tae come tae your senses.

Bernadette. Bribin 'me now, maybe in me last few moments! Money didn't get me into this state, an' money can't get me out of it. [*As if to herself*] Oh, won't someone bring Mrs. Binnington or Nora to me till I sthrive to mutther a few last words?

Skerighan [*appealingly*]. Aw, do, like a gude girrl, have sense. You're no' so bad. Keep quiet and forget about it.

Bernadette [*thoughtfully*]. If I only could keep quiet; till I got some of th' terrible shock outa me scatthered system. Th' blessed ones an' th' sanctified ones'll help me over this sore calamity. If anyone questions, I'll just murmur it was a sudden spasm brought on be overdoin' it for the Tosthal. I'll just have to strive all I can to piece some of me parts together again. [*She gives a long sad sigh.*] I must be careful how I move. [*She presses a hand to her heart.*] Now get over from me far as you can, for fear of another hot seizure takin' you when I get up on to me quivering feet.

[*Skerighan goes over to the farthest end of the room, and presses his back to the wall.*

Skerighan [*viciously*]. Thot's as far as I can go; on' I wush me own quuverin' feet was crossin' th' blessed Bordher this monnit of space on' time.

Bernadette [*rising slowly and painfully to her feet, standing still for a moment doubtfully*]. A safe journey over th' Bordher, poor sinful man; for I forgive you th' dhreadful harrm you have done to a poor innocent counthry girrl. [*She staggers to the table, takes up the notes lying on the table's edge, as if in a dream, and then moves to the door, pressing her hand to her heart, breathing heavily and with difficulty.*] Mornin' an' night, I'll pray for you. [*Pause while she gets back her breath.*] Shut th' door afther me. I have to keep the little energy I have to get down. If you hear me fallin' down th' stairs, don't move; take no notice.

[*She goes. Skerighan waits a moment or two, then crosses the room slowly to the door, peeps out, and then slowly closes it. He stays a moment listening there, then goes swiftly to the sofa, flops*

*down on it, takes a large pocket-handkerchief from a pocket, and
wipes his brow. Then he takes his wallet from his breast pocket,
peeps into it, gives a long, deep sigh, and replaces it in his pocket
again. He again wipes his brow; rises, goes to the window, and
looks out into the street. As he is looking out, the door opens, and
Father Fillifogue hurries into the room, his face red, his breath
coming in gasps.*

Father F. Oh, McGilligan is not here yet! An' that one, Bernadette
Shillayley, gone down th' sthreet, gallopin' like a goat! Afther the boys
again, I'll bet.

Skerighan. Who, sir?

Father F. [*irascibly*]. Who, sir? [*Impatiently*] That giddy, impudent
sthreel who was here to tidy an' polish th' room; an' looka th' way she's
done it! [*He flops down on a chair.*] Oh, I'm near done in!

Skerighan [*confused about the news of Bernadette galloping off*]. Are
you sure, sir, about the young girrl gallupin'? She didna look well; she
didna feel well; she didna look fut for a gallup.

Father F. Ah, didn't she? That's all you know. That sly little vixen
schatthers occasions of sin everywhere she goes. [*Suspiciously*] What
did she say to you?

Skerighan. Me? Th' girrl hardly opened her mouth tae me, mon. Me? I
was gay busy wud me own thochts about th' business I have wud Mr.
McGillighan on' Mayor Binnington. I mind, now, she remarked thot
th' Tosthal was fair gettin' her doon.

Father F. She's gone gallopin' off for th' Tosthal to get her down further.
Gettin' her down! This Tosthal's gettin' the poor Mayor down; it's gettin' Councillor McGilligan down, an' [*he hammers the floor with the
ferrule end of his umbrella*] it's gettin' me down too! An' that Organist
of mine, Murray, worse than th' most of them. I was told if I came here
quick, I'd ketch McGilligan. I come here at a fast throt, exhausted;
exhausted, sir, an' then found here nothin' save empty air an' yourself.

[*The door opens and in comes the Man of the Pike followed by
the Man of the Musket, the former with a slip of paper in his
hand.*

Man of the Musket. What wan is it, Terry?

Man of the Pike [*looking at the slip of paper*]. Yella one. Mrs. Gerathy;
red door, red windas, so a yella winda-box.

Man of the Musket [*going to the table, and lifting up a yellow-painted
window-box*]. This'll be th' fiftieth one we've done. I'm tellin' you,

Aidaun, when th' whole street's done, th' night itself'll be whisperin' of th' gay look comin' over Doonavale!

[*During this talk, and all through, the two men have taken no notice whatever of Father Fillifogue or Skerighan. Skerighan, standing back, watches with some bewilderment; Father Fillifogue sits stiff and upright on his chair, a baleful look of resigned annoyance on his face.*

[*The Man of the Musket lifts up the window-box and carries it out, followed by the Man of the Pike, in silence; the latter closing the door behind him as he goes out.*

Father F. [*looking towards Skerighan as Skerighan looks towards him*]. See? Oh, all done so nice and slick! [*With pent-up anger*] Th' night whisperin' of th' gay look on Doonavale! When all is still an' the' sky grows dark, th' night'll be whisperin' to me of madness, madness!

Skerighan [*bewildered*]. I canna ken aw this tupsoteerie business. Why the hull canna ye no' put your fut down?

Father F. Put me poor fut down? Th' Bishop himself daren't raise his little finger against th' Tosthal! Neither Binnington nor McGilligan has put in his Nomination Papers, and the Returning Officer is very anxious, for the night is near.

Skerighan [*suddenly jumping to his feet out of his chair, agitated and excited*]. Whishst! Thot was hom, ut musta been! [*He runs to the sideboard, pours out a stiff whiskey, and lowers it at a gulp.*] It was hom I seen!

Father F. [*startled*]. Seen who?

Skerighan. Feyther Nud, whon th' car was taken from in ondher me!

Father F. [*half rising from his chair—mystified*]. Your car? Father Ned?

Skerighan [*taking more whiskey*]. Stondin' in a lorry, naked tae th' world.

Father F. [*shocked*]. On a lorry—Father Ned—naked!

Skerighan. Not thot way, mon, for there wasna claithin' on a body that wasna there, but fierce green eyes shinin' lak umeralds on fire in a white face thot was careerin' aboot though stayin' stull as an evenin' star, starin' up tae me frum doon in th' valley below.

Father F. [*mystified*]. Like an umerald afire, careerin' aboot, yet still as th' evenin' star, starin' up from doon in th' valley below.

Skerighan. Aw'y, on' a wild flop of ruddy hair, flamin' lak a burnin' bush; one long white hond pointin' up, th' ither one pointin' doon, forbye th' sound of a clear voice sayin' naethin' on' meanin' all, all surrounded by a michty clerical collar round a neck I couldna see; all th' time, th' green eyes starin' doon at me frae th top o' th 'hill, on' up at me frae th' valley below that werena there.

Father F. [*fascinated*].   Ane white hond pointin' up on' anither pointin' doon; a voice from a high hull on' frae a valley below, on' a michty clerical collar fencin' a neck thot wasna there; up on' doon, on' your car taken from in ondher you. [*Checking himself with sudden reflection*] I'm mimicking him! Thot's odd! [*He laughs.*] Ha ha ha ha! [*Suddenly checking himself*] Is it gangin' mod I am, or wha'? Your car taken from in ondher you!   [*He sits staring before him.*

Skerighan.   Takken from in ondher me tae fetch tumber, paint, flowers, coloured bulbs for coloured lights from th' station; a lorry with thom, two of your constables in it holdin' a flag with an odd horp in its muddle; but I canna ken richt if I seen thom, or didna see, for ut was sudden-like, on' I seen or didna see yin, on' a'w through a gay green mist; thon a' through a gay golden light, on' yin on' a' buzzin' off in a purple glow!

Father F. [*anxiously*].   Sit doon, Mr. Skerighan; oh, sit doon, like a good man.

Skerighan [*sitting down, and wiping his face*].   Ut shhook me, ut dud! This Tosthal's gruppen' me, on' I'm no' me ainsel' I was afore!

Father F. [*soothingly*].   Sit quiet, friend; close your eyes, an' forget. [*Warningly*] An' no more dhrink!

> [*The horn of a motor is heard in the near distance, surrounded with cheers, and the sound of a pipe band playing the Tostal Song. These sounds go on merrily for a few moments, and then fade away in the distance. Father Fillifogue and Skerighan straighten up in their chairs, stiffen, and stare, listening, out in front of them.*
>
> [*Skerighan jumps out of his chair, runs to the window, sticks his head out, watching the stir till it fades away.*

Skerighan.   Thur's me car goin' by, leadin' th' lorries, packed up with flags, tumber, shrubs, floors, on' a'! [*He leans out further.*] On' th' folk sprattlin' on' bickerin' a owre th' whole toon! Sic a sight! [*A loud cheer rings out: 'Hurrah!' He turns back from the window towards Father Fillifogue.*] I tull ye th' Tosthal's gruppen' me, too. [*He stops, frightened.*] What om I saying! No, no; ut's no' gruppen' me! I'll no' sell me sawl tae Feyther Nud; I'm no' sae saft!

> [*Father Fillifogue has subsided into his chair, shocked into semi-insensibility, his eyes half closed in weary and resentful resignation.*
>
> [*When the tumult fades, the door opens, and Murray hurries in, his*

face radiant; his stick held in his hand as if it were a sword, walking with a strut that is half a dance.

Murray [*excitedly*]. Where's McGilligan, where's McGilligan? We want his piano down in dee Parochial Hall at once, pronto, now! To practise for dee Tosthal Concert. Binnington's piano's gone to dee Dance Hall already. [*He notices Father Fillifogue.*] An', oh, Fader Fillifogue, we're goin' ahead with gusto, with gusto! What do you tink, what do you tink, Fader Fillifogue, of dee news? Dee Hermacadian String Quartette are comin' here; here, to Doonavale, with Mozart's works in D Major, in C and F. Just tink! Mozart, my Mozart, here in the Parochial Hall. [*He runs over to the piano, lifts the lid, and rattles his fingers over the keys.*] Ah, not a bad tone. [*He plays a few bars from a Mozartian piece, then shuts down the lid.*] Aah, my Mozart! Welcome to Doonavale! [*Suddenly to the others*] An' who gets dee Quartette to come, eh? Who?

Father F.　⎱　[*Together; faintly,*　⎰　Father Ned!
Skerighan　⎰　*with resignation*].　⎱　Feyther Nud!

Murray [*jubilant*]. Fader Ned it is! [*Coming closer to Father Fillifogue*] Dee night is whisperin', Fader Fillifogue, an' dee day will shout out soon!

> [*Again the door opens, and the Man of the Pike and the Man of the Musket come in, the Man of the Pike as before with a slip in his hand.*

Man of the Musket. Which one this time?

Man of the Pike [*reading from slip*]. Mrs. Kinnegan; crimson door an' windas; white winda-box, picked out with black, an' filled with bronze-coloured an' blood-coloured wallflowers.

Man of the Musket [*selecting the box from the table*]. Here 'tis. Very nice, too.

Murray [*tapping Man of the Musket on the shoulder*]. Leave dat. I want dis piano taken to dee Parochial Hall.

Man of the Musket. We're not stoppin' you.

Murray [*authoritatively*]. You leave dat [*indicating boxes*] an' do dis. [*Indicating piano.*]

Man of the Pike. Our job's to beflower th' winda-sills of th' houses. Let nobody coax or ordher yous away from it till it's done. Father Ned's sthrict ordhers.

Man of the Musket [*shoving Murray aside*]. Outa th' way!

Murray [*as they are going out with the window-box*]. An' where's Fader Ned now?

Man of the Pike. Superintendin' hoistin' th' Tosthal flag on th' big flag-pole.

Murray. Over dee Parochial Hall?

Man of the Musket. Nix: over th' Presbytery.

Father F. [*bounding from the chair*]. The Presbytery! My Presbytery! [*Sinking back into chair*] Oh, this goes beyond the beyonds!

Murray [*as the men are going out*]. I must see him. Is he dere now?

Man of the Pike. Dunno. Father Ned'll be where he's wanted.

Man of the Musket. Father Ned's everywhere; he may be anywhere; he may be nowhere to a seeker who gets in his way.
                    [*The two men go off carrying the window-box.*

Father F. [*getting quickly out of chair as Murray makes to follow the Men*]. And where are you off to, Mr. Murray?

Murray. To Fader Ned—where else?

Father F. [*gripping his arm*]. You come with me. I'll keep hold of you, at least! The Latin hymns, Mr. Murray; the Latin hymns.

Murray [*fiercely*] Dee Tosthal Song, Fader Fillifogue; dee Tosthal Song! An' Mozart.

Father F. [*holding Murray fast by the arm*]. Dee *Tantum Ergo*, Mr. Murray, dee *Tantum Ergo*.

Murray [*as they go out*]. Dee Tosthal song, Father Fillifogue.

Father F. [*halfway outside*]. Dee *Tantum Ergo*, MISTER MURRAY!

            [*Skerighan tries to wipe desperate mystification from his brow with his fingers, sits still for a moment, then rises, and shakes himself.*

Skerighan. Mod, th' lut of thom; mod! Yin on' all of thom! [*He goes to the piano, and looks at it, touches it with a finger.*] Huh! I've seen but-ther insthruments, so I hove, but ut's bron' new. [*He lifts the lid and plays a few notes.*] Heard ones with a butther tone, so I hove. [*He plays the tune of 'Lillibulero', singing the words in a low voice, getting louder as he goes on.*]

            Though, be my soul, de English do prate,
            Lillibulero bullen a law;
            De Law's on der side on' de divil know what,
            Lillibulero bullen a law.

        Lero lero—

            [*The door opens, McGilligan runs in, excited and angry, but trying to keep calm and look it. He is followed by Oscar McGunty dressed*

as a sergeant of the British Army of the eighteenth century; red coat,
caught back at the ends showing blue lining; crossed white belts over
breast, with black pouches at either end; blue cuffs and epaulettes,
with three wide white stripes on left arm—chevrons. He is wearing
a shako, ornamented with a red, or red and white woollen ball.

McGilligan [*as he runs in*].   What'r' you doin', Skerighan; what th' hell
are you doin'?

Skerighan [*gayly*].   I'm just thryin' tae bring a wee but of ceevilisation
intil Doonavale.

McGilligan.   Give over lettin' your rough fingers batther down me new
piano! An' a Protestant tune's no fit thing to be played on a Catholic
piano.

McGunty [*indignantly*].   No pounds, shillin's, an' pence Protestant tunes
here; an' no Orange uttherance in song or story, either. That's the sound
an' that's th' climmax of Oscar McGunty's instigation!

McGilligan [*irritatedly*].   Oh, shut up, you!

McGunty [*angrily*].   Shut up yourself! You're not in your blasted factory now; you're out in th' open, an' this is a national question!

McGilligan [*to Skerighan*].   If you had any decency, you'd know it was
most unmannerly to go an' play a Protestant tune on a Catholic piano.

Skerighan [*growing angry*].   I'll no' be called onmannerly be ony Doonavale ill-wullie bummler! [*Indignantly*] A grand greetin' for a mon ticklin' oot a wee sthrain of music tae enthertain his silent sulf! On', looksee,
I'll play a Protestant tune on onny piano, onnywhere, onnytime, no'
carin' a feg for your fearfu' animosity!

McGilligan [*fiercely*].   You'll tickle out no Protestant tune in a Catholic
house, on a Catholic piano!

McGunty.   No, nor in no Catholic town, or on a Catholic street!

McGilligan [*fiercely turning on McGunty*].   You shut that big gob of
yours, will you!

McGunty [*tapping McGilligan on the shoulder—seriously*].   Looka, careful what you say to McGunty, an' how yeh say it. You're only a pathetic
hangover, dismantlin' yourself thro' ignorance be day an' be night!

McGilligan [*shouting*].   Gather the pikes an' get the flag, an' go about
your business, for I'm well fitted meself [*indicating Skerighan*] to deal
with this fella!

Skerighan [*shouting louder than McGilligan*].   Y'or, or you? Looksee,
you there on' you yon, I'll chont when I like on' play a Protestant dutty

on onny insthrument ondher me hond, be it piccolo, cornet, or on an aul' banjo; ay, or on a dhrum, offhond, ay wull I, onnytime, onnywhere, before ony bletherin' batch o' Papish bigots!

McGilligan [*hysterically shouting*]. You will, will you? No, not here, you won't! Never!

McGunty [*shouting*]. Never; no, never, now nor any day after!

> [*Mrs. McGilligan comes in with an anxious, half-frightened look on her face. She is a middle-aged woman, who must have been a handsome lass in her younger days. Her face carries traces of good looks still, but it is rather a tired one now, trying to keep calm and gay, like her sister Mrs. Binnington. She is dressed in semi-evening dress, dark-blue gown, cut decorously at the bosom; the dress is picked out with white, and she wears blue shoes to go with the gown. Dolled up now, she looks handsome.*]

Mrs. McGilligan. What's all these goin's-on, Mick, an' we about to go to the Binningtons' for dinner? What's this unholy shoutin' mean?

McGilligan. Down below, I heard the piano goin' up above, an' when I come up, here was th' laddo hummin' a Protestant song, an' thumpin' th' tune of it out on our piano.

> [*Throughout her chat, Mrs. McGilligan, between phrases, or during their expression, pirouettes round herself on the ball and toe of either foot; or drops a curtsy to the air as a practice in deportment for the coming Tostal Ball.*]

Mrs. McGilligan. Oh? Th' Protestant tune didn't dinge th' piano, did it?

McGilligan. Not th' piano, woman—th' tune that dinged us! A Protestant tune bein' played on a Catholic piano in a Catholic home!

Mrs. McGilligan. Oh? What a naughty man! But I'm sure Mr. Skerighan meant no harm. [*To Skerighan*] What tune an' song was it?

Skerighan. A gay Protestant tune, mo'om, thot dings th' ears of thom not hovin' th' thrue licht.

McGunty [*indignant*]. D'ye hear that? He calls his oul' Protestant will-o'-th'-wisp a thrue light!

Mrs. McGilligan [*shoving McGunty aside*]. Shut up, Oscar! [*To Skerighan*] What way does th' song go, Mr. Skerighan? I'm sure we can hear it without wincing.

Skerighan. Aw'll do me best, mo'om, but it needs the roar of a dozen dhrums—thon it's no tune, but th' duvestatin' rumblin' of thrutenin' thundher through th' nearby hulls! [*He sings a verse and chorus a little shyly, but with pride and some defiance:*]

Ho, brother Teig, dost hear dee decree,
Lillibulero bullen a la;
Dot we sholl hove a new debitee?
Lillibulero bullen a la.

Lero lero lero lero, lillibulero bullen a la,
Lillibulero lero lero, lillibulero bullen a la!

[*When he has sung the verse and the chorus, there is a short silence.*

Mrs. McGilligan [*clapping her hands*]. Well sung, Mr. Skerighan; but what do th' words all mean?

Skerighan. Mean, mo'om? It's just a gay Protestant song.

Mrs. McGilligan [*briskly*]. Now sit down, th' three of you, an' tell me what it all means. [*They don't sit down, but stand where they are, looking sheepish and confused.*] Well, go on, Mr. Skerighan; who's Teig, what is dee decree, and who is dee debitee? Well, Mr. Skerighan?

Skerighan [*nonplussed at being challenged*]. It's a plain on' outspoken Protestant song, mo'om, meanin' only what it says.

McGunty. There y're—everyone knows its meanin'. Th' North's vibratin' with it! [*Passionately*] Every note o' th' tune's stitched tight to hathred of everythin' we hold dear! Even to dhream of it is a big bethrayal of Ireland. Dhrive it away; send it scomperin' back over the Bordher!

Mrs. McGilligan. I haven't an idea what it means. [*To Skerighan*] What on earth does Lillibulero bullen a la mean? It must have some meanin'.

Skerighan [*confused*]. Th' dhrums give it its meanin', mo'om; th' dhrums, th' dhrums!   [*He waves his arms as if he were beating one.*

McGunty [*scornfully*]. Your oul' dhrums. You wait, me Northern bucko, till your ears clang to th' dhrums of Father Ned!

Mrs. McGilligan [*bewildered*]. Which dhrums, what dhrums? You, Oscar McGunty—you tell me what 'Lillibulero bullen a la' means.

McGunty [*flabbergasted*]. Me, ma'am? Sure, I could never make head or tail of it! [*Defiantly*] All I know is there's no room here for a cock o' th' north! Lillibulero's not goin' to be let loose down in Doonavale!! That's McGinty's climmax.

Skerighan [*still excitedly beating an imaginary drum*]. Th' dhrums! Puttin' a spurt tae th' spurit of th' Ulsthermon, on' raisin' th' dondher of his onemies!

McGilligan [*angrily*]. There he goes—threatenin' us all!

Mrs. McGilligan [*firmly*]. He said the Ulstherman's enemies, Mick. An Ulstherman has no enemies here, nor anywhere else in Ireland; so don't be actin' th' goat, th' three of yous. [*To McGunty*] You go an' get th' Tosthal Flag in the dining-room. You'll see it in front of your nose, an' bring it at once to someone who'll give it straight to Father Ned. [*McGunty goes into the dining-room by the door at back, and returns with the Flag. Catching McGunty by the arm, and standing him in the centre, so that the rest form a rough circle round him and the Flag*] Here we all are now, undher the Green Flag with its Golden Harp; th' harp that can play an Orange tune in Belfast an' a National tune in Cork, an' yet remains a thrue Harp; an' th' green grass that fattens th' cattle of Ulsther as well as it fattens the cattle on the plains of Meath, still remainin' th' thrue grass of our Irish pastures. [*A motor horn toots outside the house. Flutteringly*] There's the Binningtons; that must be th' Binningtons! [*She shoves McGunty and the Flag out of her way, catches McGilligan by the arm, and runs to the far end of the room, shoving Skerighan aside as she pulls McGilligan along with her. To McGilligan, who is on her left*] Th' other side, man, she's sure to be on his left. [*She pulls him to her right side, and they arrange themselves, facing the door.*] Now, Aloysius, don't dhroop, for God's sake; stand stately.

[*The door opens, and Bernadette enters, wearing a maid's cap and apron.*

Bernadette. The Lord Mayor and Lady Mayoress.

[*The Binningtons come in, both in evening dress—he in tails. When they have stepped into the room, McGilligan and Mrs. Mc-Gilligan advance towards them—she smiling, he with a set and somewhat tortured-looking face. They come so close that when Mrs. McGilligan makes her curtsy, she can but bend her knees awkwardly, and Binnington is prevented from making a proper bow; while Mrs. Binnington, trying to make her curtsy, loses her balance, and clutches the legs of McGilligan.*

Binnington [*impatiently*]. Yous came too damn close!

McGilligan [*with irritation—to Binnington*]. Yous stood there with your kissers set, never givin' us a beck to halt.

McGunty [*ominously*]. Yous are hopeless. Yous'll never get it right. It's terrible!

McGilligan [*angrily turning on McGunty*]. Maybe you could do it betther.

McGunty. 'Course I could! [*To Bernadette*] Here, Bernadette, let's show them how to do it. [*Bernadette goes and stands just inside the door;*

McGunty goes to the opposite end of room, then advances steadily and elegantly to Bernadette. He gives an elegant bow; she a graceful curtsy; he then finely offers her his arm, she takes it graciously, and both walk in a quiet and graceful way to the opposite side of the room.] That's th' way to do it. Yous thry again now. The men bow, th' women curtsy, way we did; then take arms, way we did, an' then walk off outa th' room to your dinner. Take it quiet. Here, I'll play an air slow to help yous. [*He runs to the piano.*] Ready? Well, go! [*The men bow, Binnington to Mrs. McGilligan, McGilligan to Mrs. Binnington; the women curtsy, but all do it as awkwardly as ever—all to the tune of 'Lillibulero', played slow; Skerighan staring bewilderedly and fixedly at the pianist. Resignedly*] Aah! I wouldn't thry to do too much of that when yous go places. It's not in yous, it's not in yous.

Skerighan [*coming close to McGunty and bending over him*].   D'ye no' ken th' tune you were playin', mon?

McGunty [*impatiently*].   Yes, yes; 'course I did—[*casually*] 'Lillibulero'. [*Skerighan is dazed.*] Mind th' way. [*To the others*] Now, thry to walk outa th' room, anyway, without rumplin' yourselves—way we did. Here, do it to th' chimes of a church clock—slow an' steady.

> [*He plays the notes of the chimes, lilting them himself as he plays, and the couples parade self-consciously across the room, and go out by the door; Bernadette holding a hand over her mouth to conceal her amusement.*

Skerighan [*following them, and lifting his eyes to the ceiling as if appealing to heaven*].   Th' sooner I'm back over th' Bordher th' butther!

Bernadette.   The night is whisperin' that their day is endin'.

McGunty.   It's their climmax! [*Lilting and playing*] Th' chimes of time is playin' them out. La la la la; la la la la.

Echo.   La la la la; la la la la.

END OF ACT II

ACT III

The scene is the same as the first Act—the drawing-room of the Binning-
tons. There is, however, a definite change in its look, for neatness and pol-
ish are greatly qualified by the activity of the Tostal. The piano has been
taken away, and the stately palm tree no longer stands in its corner. The
table has been cleared of all objects, the chairs are no longer in a neat line,
and the sofa has been hustled away against one of the walls. A number of
flags and pennons stand about; large varicoloured shields, some of them
bearing the faces of old-time gods and heroes, stand on the chair-seats, and
lean against their backs. A few pots of paint stand in a bunch by the door,
and Tostal posters are draped over the pictures, hiding them from view.
The curtains are pulled together.

Tom, in his shirt-sleeves, is busy planing a thin plank stretched out on
the table; the Man of the Pike is colouring and gilding a shield showing the
face of Angus the Young caught among the golden strings of his harp, a
thin, poetic face, long black hair flowing behind his head, while at the butt-
end of the harp is a gayly-plumaged bird—green breast, black satiny head,
wings tipped with crimson and gold.

Man of the Pike.   The stars are big tonight. [*He comes away. A pause.*] I
    wonder why Father Ned, or Michael either, wanted to show th' world th'
    kissers of th' old Irish gods an' heroes? Conn of th' Hundhred Fights,
    with a red face to denote battle; Brian Boru—a golden face to denote th'
    Thributes; Columcille, with a white face and gold hair, to denote holi-
    ness; a Pillar holdin' up th' head of young Dunbo—whoever he was—a
    harp at th' pillar's butt, played be shadowy hands, th' thin sthrings
    showin' through th' white twinklin' fingers; an' this one I'm doin' now:
    I've heard of th' others, save Dunbo, of Cuchullain, of Brian Boru, of
    Columcille, an' Th' Man from God Knows Where; but who was this kid
    Angus, anyhow?

Tom.   He was th' Keltic god of youth an' loveliness.

Man of the Pike.   Th' laddie musta flown to England with his bird, for a
    lot of th' loveliness and all th' youth is hurryin' over there!

Tom.   Maybe this Tosthal'll steady us a little to stand where we are.

Man of the Pike.   If it doesn't, Tom, here's another'll folla afther Angus
    an' his bird. Some hop out of Ireland, some just step out of it, and some
    take a lep away; but they all go.

> [*Previously, the sound of hurrying feet has been heard in the street,*
> *several times the sound of trotting horses going by, and a motor-horn*
> *hoots; now the sound is heightened into a run.*]

Man of the Pike. Th' Tosthal's makin' th' town move fast. [*The sound of a horse trotting by*] That's Gerachty's nag—his rear hooves sthrike the sets more lightly than the fore ones.

Tom. You must have a damn keen ear.

Man of the Pike. No more'n others. I know all th' sounds. [*A man's footsteps, walking fast, are heard going by.*] That's Jack the Cantherer, Doonavale's postman: walkin' or runnin', he always breaks the regular beat of run or walk every tenth step or so.

Tom [*musingly*]. The little sounds we make on this earth, an' then we go: we whistle an' sing, we hammer an' saw, talk in anger an' talk in love, say a few prayers in a hurry; then we go, an' the little sounds cease.

Man of the Pike. I'd say th' sounds'll soon cease for Father Fillifogue, th' way he's runnin' round wild, fair gorged with anger, yet afraid to say much against th' Tosthal. I seen him miss his footin' comin' down th' Presbytery steps, afther closin' his eyes, th' way he couldn't see th' flag flyin' in th' little front garden. When he sees some of these pictures hangin' on his railin's, he'll finish up in a fury.

Tom. An' bid th' world farewell!

Man of the Pike [*going to the door, looking out, closing it again, and coming over cautiously to Tom*]. D'ye think, Tom; d'ye think, now, there's anything in th' rumour about th' timber on th' wharf bein' Red wood?

Tom. When I work timber, avic, I don't ask th' wood if it's Christian or Communist.

Man of the Pike. I dunno; you have to be on th' alert, Tom. There's ne'er a one I know here would sleep easy, knowin' th' roof over them came from a Communist counthry. [*The sound of feet running along on the sidewalk is heard, and Man of the Pike stiffens to listen.*]Whisht! That's th' step of Father Fillifogue quickened into a run. Comin' here, likely; lookin' for someone. Curious sudden stop, that. Right outside.

    [*They listen for a few moments. The sounds suddenly stop.*]

Tom [*resuming his work*]. Not comin' here, anyway.

Man of the Pike. Th' poor oul' man should go off till th' Tosthal's over. Goes about everywhere now, with his umbrella up, thryin' to hide away from all that's goin' on, poor man.

    [*The door opens, and Murray comes tottering in, his hands pressed over his ears, a look of torment on his face. He goes to the sideboard, seizes a decanter and tumbler, pours out a whiskey and soda for himself, drinks a slug, then subsides into a chair, the glass in his hand, from which he drinks occasionally as he is speaking. His stick is held under the left arm.*]

Murray [*agonisingly*].   Dod help me! Dat McGunty'll be dee death of me. He will never get it. Dee brain, dee brain is too tick! I lead him up dee hill—bad; I bring him down to dee valley—worse. I say blow soft, an' he blows hard; I say blow hard, an' he blows soft. Oh, it was derrible! Now he has followed me here; but, no; never again! [*From below comes the tune 'Boot and Saddle' played on a cornet or a horn. They all listen, Murray slowly taking his hands from his ears. The tune is played correctly; wonder first, then delight spreading over Murray's face. Leaping from his chair—delighted*] He's dot it, he's dot it! [*Banging his stick on the table*] A miracle, gentlemen!

> [*Man of the Musket runs into the room, over to the sideboard, pours out a drink into a glass, swallows it, and pours out another.*

Man of the Musket [*said in a buzz, pouring out a drink*].   He's got it, but at a price. [*He drinks it himself, and pours out another, then makes for the door.*] When he found he'd done it, he just filthered off into a dead faint! A sad sight. [*He suddenly drinks what is in the glass, hurries back to sideboard, gets another drink, and sallies again to the door.*] The two of yous Dance Hall . . . at once . . . practise . . . last stand on slopes of . . . Barnabweel . . . band playin' . . . if McGunty survives . . . Mick, Nora . . . below . . . gettin' him into life . . . again.   [*He hurries off.*

Tom.   Betther hurry.

Man of the Musket [*running in again over to the sideboard, and seizing the bottle from which he has poured the drinks*].   Might want th' bottle!

> [*He runs off. Tom and the Man of the Pike are gathering their things together—Tom the planks he's planed, Man of the Pike his pictures, when Nora followed by Michael comes in, looking happy, but a little tired. Michael has the bottle taken by Man of the Musket, which he restores to the sideboard.*

Michael.   Keep an eye on that laddie, boys; we must have no hitch in play or pageant. An' Tom, we'll go through th' play when the meeting's over.

Tom [*as he and the Man of the Pike go out*].   Righto; we'll tail the Pike Man till th' Tosthal's over.   [*They hurry away.*

Michael.   Well, the Pageant is in good shape at last. We deserve a drink. [*He goes to sideboard and fills out two drinks, giving Nora one of them.*] Guh mwarry on Thosthal slaun!   [*They clink glasses, and drink.*

Nora.   Go mwarry guh feer woon éy!

Michael.   An odd fight: I against your father and you against mine.

Nora.   Oh, not against our fathers! We're fighting what is old and stale and vicious: the hate, the meanness their policies preach; and to make a way for th' young and thrusting.

Michael.   Easier said than done, Nora.

Nora.   Everything said, Michael, is easier than anything done. It is a fine fancy to say brave things; better to do them.

Michael.   Look at the shock McGunty got when he found he'd won a tune from a trumpet.

Nora.   Well, he won one. Now, he can't hide himself in a fog of failure, as so many do, sneering out of it at others who are trying. Having done one thing well, McGunty must go on to do many things better.

Michael [*pouring out another drink for Nora and himself*].   Guh mwarry on Thosthal slaun!

Nora [*clinking glasses with him*].   Guh muh mar sin guh minick éy! [*She goes to the window, and looks out, musingly.*] The sky of Doona-vale is a casket of stars. Look, Michael, that glittering glow there to the west—is it the west? I wonder what stars stay here?

Michael [*looking out*].   I don't know. Maybe the Pleiades. [*Musingly*] What's this I read about them once?—Many a night, I saw the Pleiades —Oh, I've forgotten the poem, and the poet, too.

Nora.   Tennyson, I think, dear:
Many a night I saw the Pleiads, rising thro' the mellow shade,
Glitter like a swarm of fire-flies tangled in a silver braid.

Michael [*moodily*].   My God, an' we're tangled, too, in life's great glittering braid! To know the stars only through the song of a poet; then to forget the poet and the song he sang! [*He suddenly clasps Nora in his arms.*] All the stars of heaven are close to me when you are near. Angus the Young is by our side; we hear his harp-music, and his brilliant birds are perching on our shoulders.

Nora.   For a brief while, my Michael. The purple tint of love must fade, and its passion becomes a whisper from a night that's gone. May our love pass quietly into companionship, for that is the one consummation of united life.

Michael.   Yes, the Bard and his harp, with his birds, must go one day, leaving us to live in our own light, and make our own music. So we shall; then take a kiss for what it's worth, and let the dream go by.
[*The door opens, and Bernadette thrusts her head beyond it.*

Bernadette.   They're comin', th' whole crowd of them.

[*In a moment they do come in, Bernadette holding the door open for them—Mrs. Binnington with McGilligan; Mrs. McGilligan* with Binnington; Skerighan alone between the couples, as if they were his bodyguard. They have left their coats below, and are dressed as they were, formally, during the dinner at McGilligan's, though the Mayor and the Deputy Mayor wear their respective chains of office. They are all full of food, mixed with wine, look satisfied, and act with restrained gaiety, though Skerighan's face is one of grimness, half hidden by a half smile.

Mrs. Binnington [*doing one of her pirouettes, and losing her balance in the effort*]. Spread yourselves out, an' make yourselves comfortable, boys an' girls. Room a bit desolate, but there's a Tosthal on.

Binnington [*ejaculating with anger*]. My God, th' palm tree's gone now!

Mrs. Binnington [*with irritation*]. Oh, never mind th' blessed palm tree, man!

Michael. Gone to decorate the Parish Hall. [*To McGilligan*] By now, yours has gone, too.

Mrs. Binnington. We can do without palm trees. Sit down all. [*To Skerighan*] In this armchair, Mr. Skerighan, with a cushion undher you. [*As he sits, she does a curtsy to him, clumsily as ever.*] Your servant, ma'am—sir, I mean.

Mrs. Binnington [*to Mrs. McGilligan*]. Here, dear; this chair.

Mrs. McGilligan [*doing her own pirouette as she goes to the chair*]. Thank you.

Mrs. Binnington [*doing a curtsy to her*]. Your servant, ma'am.

Mrs. McGilligan [*reciprocating with another as she sits down*]. You're welcome, ma'am.

Mrs. Binnington [*to Bernadette*]. Go, girl, an' get th' coffee, an' don't stay there gapin'.

Bernadette [*to Nora*]. Come along, Nora, an' give us a hand to bring it in.

Mrs. Binnington [*shocked—sharply*]. Nora'll do no such thing! Your helper, indeed! I'd have you remember that my daughter is a lady!

Nora [*laughingly indignant*]. Mother—for God's sake! A lady is as a lady does, not as a lady doesn't. [*She puts an arm round Bernadette.*] We'll bring th' coffee in together, dear.   [*They go out to get the coffee.*

Mrs. Binnington. It's fine how us of th' South an' a clever man from th' North can get together, an' enjoy themselves without a hard word.

Mrs. McGilligan. Yis; without a single hard word.

Echo. A single hard word.

Skerighan [*gratified*]. It's no' so wondherful. Ye are a' richt, yin on' a' of ye, so ye are. Ceevility is deep dune in a' our hearts, on' North on' South: this day hae shown thot our dufference in politics on' releegion is a' fasht with delusion. [*He bangs his hand on the arm of his chair.*] On', this day, Alec Skerighan says 'Tae hull with purtition!'

Echo [*very faintly*]. Tae hull with purtition.

Mrs. McGilligan [*effusively*]. It is delightful——

Mrs. Binnington [*effusively*]. An' stimulatin' to hear——

Mrs. McGilligan. Such sensible talk——

Mrs. Binnington. From an Ulstherman.

Skerighan [*suspiciously*]. I'd lak ye tae know thot it's no' an uncommon occurrence for on Ulsthermon tae speak sunsible. The worrld kens thot Ulsther's th' one sunsible on' foreseein' pruvence left in Ireland.

Binnington [*good-humouredly*]. I don't know that you are altogether right in your big claim for Ulsther, Alec.

Skerighan. Dinna ye, now? Wull, I ken it wull, looksee; on' th' worrld kens it too. Thot's why England luks tae Ulsther for wusdom on' plain dealin'.

McGilligan. We know th' North has her good points, but we have a few here in th' South, too.

Skerighan [*with a dismissal-wave of a hand*]. Feth, mon, there's no' much doon here tae brag aboot, while th' worrld wondhers at th' luvel-headed North, whaur th' steady din-ding of industhry goes hond in hond with th' Northerner quittin' himself lak a mon, forbye always aboundin' in th' works of th' Lord.

    [*Nora and Bernadette bring the coffee in on a trolley.*]

Mrs. Binnington [*to Skerighan*]. Now, a cup of coffee, Mr. Skerighan; nice an' hot an' fresh.   [*Nora, she and Bernadette hand it around.*]

Skerighan [*taking it from her*]. Thank ye, mo'om.

Mrs. Binnington [*curtsying*]. Your servant, sir.
    [*She pirouettes back to her chair.*]

Skerighan [*resuming*]. No, th' Ulsthermon doesna thrang th' air with talk of what Ulsther does. He doesna haver aboot his linen mills, his shipyards, his rope-walks, his tobacco factory—th' greatest in th' worrld, mind ye; on' th' worrld kens it.

Mrs. Binnington [*getting out of her chair, and doing a pirouette*]. Indeed, we can learn a lot from Ulsther, we can that, Mr. Skerighan. It's grand to be together in a spirit of good-will an' companionship, however we may differ in one way or another.

Mrs. McGilligan [*crooning murmuringly*]:
    So let th' Orange Lily be
    Thy badge, my patriot brother;

Mrs. Binnington [*chiming in murmuringly*]:
    Th' everlastin' green for me,

McGilligan
Binnington } [*chiming in on last line*]:   An' we for one another.

Skerighan [*cautiously*].   Mind ye, I'm fast tae th' Crown an' Constitution, but ma Ulsther heart longs tae see th' Republic of Ireland goin' strang; but watchin' on' lussenin', suttin' aside this mod Tosthal, most of your festeevities seem tae be around some grave here, or round anither grave yon.

Michael.   You're right there, Ulsther; our hearts beat best to th' music of a dirge; our marching feet too often point th' way to a grave. But with Father Ned, th' young will let th' dead bury their dead, an' give their thought an' energy to th' revelry of life!

Bernadette.   An' near time, too!

Skerighan.   A grond ombeetion, lad; but somewhere ye'll floundher on' fall. Howe'er far ye gae, ye'll ever be afeart on' feckless, sae lang as ye suffer—[*He hesitates.*]

Michael [*prompting*].   Suffer what?

Skerighan.   So lang as ye suffer th' inseedious dumination of your Church, on' th' waefu' intherfurence of your clergy in what ye thry tae do.

Binnington [*trying to be conciliatory*].   Now, Alec, that's a matter of diversified opinion. The Catholic Faith is never an obstacle to any man's advancement.

Skerighan [*somewhat warmly*].   I'm tullin' you dufferent, Mr. Binnington, on' wull ye know yoursel' it's thrue. There's one thing stuppin' ye doon here: th' clingin' tae what has no wurrant from the mind o' mon, or th' plain ravelations of Holy Scrupture.

Mrs. McGilligan.   Shishto, oh, whish.

Binnington [*a little less conciliatory*].   That's a debatable question, Mr. Skerighan; a highly debatable question.

Skerighan [*warmly*].   It's no' a debatable question, I'm tullin' you! It's th' pure on' prime thruth! What ye call your releegion has put your thochts aswither, on' turned ye all intil tuttherah toddlem duves!

McGilligan [*explosively*].   I strongly resent being called a tuttherah toddlem dove!

Mrs. McGilligan [*soothingly*].   Mr. Skerighan, I'm sure, is jokin', but he should ha' left th' tatterah out.

Bernadette [*patting Binnington on the head*].   Elena's own little tattherah toddlem dove!

Mrs. Binnington [*anxiously*].   Oh, let's change th' subject, do. [*To Binnington*] What's this that story was about the poet Yeats an' Gogarty goin' down some street or other?

Binnington [*seizing on his chance*].   Oh, yes, Elena, that one! I remember one day, in Dublin, when th' poet Yeats an' Gogarty were goin' down Sackville Sthreet—

Skerighan [*stifling Binnington's effort*].   Wait a munnit, you; wait a munnit, tull we suttle this question of releegion once for all; then we can lussen to your blether aboot Yeats on' Gogarty goin' down Suckville Sthreet. This question concurns thruth on' mon's future, on' canna be compurred with Yeats on' Gogarty goin' down Suckville Sthreet. What has God's own thruth got tae do with Yeats on' Gogarty goin' down or comin' up Suckville Sthreet? Naething! Th' question we have to suttle, on' that we're goin' tae suttle, is God's own question, I'm tullin' ye.

McGilligan [*half rising from his chair, leaning for support by his hands on the chair's arms, and stretching himself forward to better meet Skerighan's outburst*].   It's all settled already! St. Pether, an' afther him St. Pathrick, is our man, th' Rock on which our Church stands. What's yours piled up on? On a disgraceful, indecent attachment of a despicable English king for a loose woman!

Skerighan [*trying to overthrow McGilligan*].   Lussen, mon, lussen tae me!

McGilligan [*furiously*].   I've lussened to you long enough—Henry the Eighth I am an' his harlot! Th' two saints of your Church—Henry the Eighth an' a harlot! Oh, it makes me laugh—ha ha ha ha!

Mrs. Binnington [*doing a pirouette and trying to practise a curtsy in front of McGilligan*].   Now, now, lads! [*To McGilligan*] Wasn't that movement fine?

Bernadette.   Lovely, ma'am; lovely.

McGilligan [*rising from his chair, and pushing her from before him*].   Oh, outa th' way, woman! [*He goes to the end of the table opposite to where Skerighan now stands, and thrusting his face forward, recites defiantly:*]

In God's all-important an' armament plan,
There's no room at all for th' Protestant man,
Except it be out in th' wind an' th' rain!
We walk a broad road, yous in a dark lane,
Naked an' cold, an' all flusthered with pain—
Weeping souls lost in th' wind an' th' rain!

[*He moves back a little.*]   An' it makes me laugh—ha ha ha!

Bernadette [*mocking*].   Me, too—ha ha hee!

Mrs. Binnington [*to Bernadette*].   Clear away the coffee cups, dear—ah, these arguments.

Mrs. McGilligan [*doing a pirouette before Skerighan in a childlike attempt to smother a reply*].   Now, now, now!

Skerighan [*shoving her from the way*].   A', gang awa', woman! [*He turns to McGilligan.*] Ye can laugh th' now, but whon ye gets tae th' pearly gate—gin ye go sae high—your St. Pether'll lakly say till ye

Come, Roman lad, on' meet your fate—
Aha, th' ruein' o't;
Ye didna hulp th' sauls in need,
Na ken th' real plant frae th' weed;
I scorn th' blether of your creed—
Gang off frae here, on' gang wi' speed—
Aha, th' ruein' o't!

Nora [*lively*].   What say if we all go down to the dance hall for a spot of rock 'n roll?

Bernadette [*enthusiastically*].   Yes, let's!

Skerighan [*shocked*].   This is no time for idle acteevities, girrls! [*To Michael—appealingly*] What for dae you say? Go on, say oot th' richt thing lak a mon. You are on enlightened mon, as I om.
[*Nora and Bernadette have gathered the delft and go off.*

Michael.   A fella would want to be within the wide-open spaces when a row starts between Wittenberg and Knox, on the one hand, and Bellarmine and Maynooth, on th' other. In these desperate disputes we are but frightened birds jostling together in the dark.

Skerighan [*indignantly*].   We're no' birds, on' we're no' frightened! We huv' our intullects, on' we're wull abune th' birds. If ye know the Scriptures, thon quote them, on' ye'll be nearer th' murk.

Michael.   If God be what He ought to be, must be, if He be God, then He has no time to bother about the Anglican Thirty-nine Articles, the Westminster Confession, or the Creed from the Council of Thrent.

Binnington [*explosively*].   I'll not have such a thing said about th' Council of Thrent undher my roof, sir; not undher my roof!

Michael [*quietly*].   Your roof, Da? What is it but a few wisps of straw, a few clods of clay, mixed together to keep th' rain out an' keep th' wind away. Put out th' lights and hide th' roof of man and let us look at God's.

Echo.   Look at God's.

> [*Michael pulls the curtains aside, as the scene gets dark, and reveals a sky filled with vast stars, one red, one green, one golden, with smaller stars between them, all aglow with gentle but amazing animation in a purple sky.*]

Michael.   Our real roof, ladies and gentlemen, th' royal roof over Doonavale, over th' world—the stars. God's great nightcap. There they are—half th' host of them. And ne'er a man, save Father Ned, can pick them out by the names man has given them.

Skerighan [*impatiently*].   We're talkin' no' aboot th' affairs of mon, Michael Binnington, but of God. What I want tae know is whether God is ipso a Protestant or a Roman Catholic.

Michael [*laughingly*].   He's neither; but He is all, and above noticin' th' tinkle of an opinion. He may be more than He is even claimed to be; He may be but a shout in th' street.

McGilligan.   A shout in a street! Blasphemy!

Skerighan.   A lumentable remark. Tull us what kind of a shout God could be?

Mrs. McGilligan.   It must be a shout of something for a person to believe in, Michael; of a Church for all an' God's world for us all until the end.

Michael.   It might be a shout for freedom, like th' shout of men on Bunker Hill; shout of th' people for bread in th' streets, as in th' French-Revolution; or for th' world's ownership by th' people, as in th' Soviet Revolution; or it might just be a drunken man, unsteadily meandhering his way home, shouting out Verdi's [*he lilts the words*] 'Oh, Le-on-or-a'.

Mrs. Binnington [*a little frightened*].   Michael, Michael, you foolish boy, thryin' to reduce God to a common shout or a common song in a sthreet!

Michael [*gently*].   No, not a common shout, mother; not a common song either.

Mrs. McGilligan [*wailingly*].   Where's our good-will gone?

Mrs. Binnington.   An' sweet harmony?

Skerighan [*impatiently—to the ladies*].   We're no' afther haurmony—we're afther th' absolute thruth! I want no guessin'. [*To Michael*] I'm tired o' lussenin' tae th' blether of Binnington on' McGilligan. I want th' absolute thruth—you tull us, lak a mon, which of th' two does God love tae see—th' yella on' white of th' Vutican, or th' orange on' blue of Nassau!

> [*As he ends speaking the sounds of pattering feet are heard, and while they all listen the door flies open, and Father Fillifogue staggers in, his open umbrella held over his head, flushed, a little dishevelled, and panting for breath. He leans over the table, his head in his arms, half buried, recovering from the flutter of his running; one hand still holding the umbrella over himself as he half lies over the table.*

Father F. [*rising a little to let his voice go forth, but leaning heavily on the table*].   Oh, where is your pride, Councillor McGilligan and Mayor Binnington? D'ye realise tha' th' town is tumbling down? What is this I hear; what is this th' people are sayin'?

Binnington [*anxiously*].   What dudya hear? What'r' they sayin'?

Father F.   Are we goin' to be out in th' dear, dead days beyond recall? Me an' me boys of the old brigade. [*Suddenly to Binnington and McGilligan*] What's all this talk I hear in th' town 'bout the wood on th' wharf bein' evil timber?

Skerighan [*impatiently to Binnington and McGilligan*].   On th' whurf—haven't ye hod it lorried to your yard?

McGilligan [*a little wildly*].   Th' Tosthal, man; couldn't do anything with th' damned Tosthal!

Skerighan [*furiously*].   Would ye make a worrld's feckless fash o't? Wull ye no' tak' th' tumber awa' frae th' wharf tull th' muckle Lammas moon is glintin' on ye!

Father F. [*raising his head, lowering it, raising and lowering it*].   I've other things to tell you; not here, not here: to th' Vestry, to th' Vestry.

> [*McGunty comes hastily into the room, excited, taking no notice of anyone, but staggering over to Father Fillifogue, whom he touches gently and reverently on the back. His bugle hangs by his side.*

McGunty.   I seen you runnin', Father, an' I tried to ketch up with you, but couldn't. You should go an' see th' door.

Father F. [*faintly*].   The door? A door, now. What door?

McGunty.   Instead of bein' white, with yella panels, as a body would expect, it's a flamin' red; redder than th' reddest sun a frosty sunset ever seen.

Father F. [*dreading the answer*]. Oh, no, no; not th' door of th'——

McGunty. Yis! Your own door, Father; door of the Presbytery—a crimson portico.

> [*Father Fillifogue sinks down on the table, his head in his arms, one hand still holding the umbrella up. The sounds of a busy buzz in the street are heard, and the patter of feet on the sidewalk, later, on the stairs outside.*

McGunty. Whisht, they're comin'! They're out to burn th' Red timber.

McGilligan [*tapping Father Fillifogue on the back*]. Please, help us to face them.

Binnington [*doing the same*]. Lead us, Father, against th' mob.

Skerighan. Ay, on' pull yoursel' taegether.

Father F. You rascals, how can I let my people live under roofs of atheistical timber?

Binnington. For the sake of your church, Father.

Father F. God's church, you fool, not mine. Would you like the roof of His church to be made of Red timber?

Michael. Yes, why not?

Father F. [*with a moan*]. Why not! You hear—why not?

McGunty. Don' know where I am. Th' night's wide lips are movin'-mad with whisperin' into th' wider ears of the comin' open-mouthed day! St. Anthony guide!

> [*In through the door come Nora and Bernadette, both dressed in the modern style of Irish costume; the Man of the Pike, carrying the weapon; the Man of the Musket, carrying his gun; Tom, and others who group at the room's threshold.*

Nora [*gayly*]. Here's the whole town currying a question to be answered, not with a whimper, but with a bang!

Man of the Musket. What's this whisper about Red timber on th' wharf of Doonavale?

Man of the Pike. Communist timber.

Girl at the Door. Atheist timber.

Michael. Speak, McGilligan.

Nora. Speak, Binnington.

Man of the Musket ⎫
Man of the Pike ⎬ [*together*]. Speak, you bastards!

Father F. [*planting his open umbrella before him like a shield, while Binnington and McGilligan stand behind him*]. Get back there, with your musket an' your pike! This Tosthal ree-raw is makin' yous all too randy.

Man of the Musket. You're wrong, Father. Go ahead, says Father Ned, an' think. [*Jauntily*] Thractor runnin' round aul' Castle ruins, says he.

Man of the Pike. Go ahead, an' say things, he said. [*Jauntily*] The pylon, says he, as well as th' Round Tower.

Man of the Musket. Go ahead, says Father Ned, an' do things.

Father F. I'll do th' thinking for yous; I'll say th' things that should be said; an' yous'll do th' things I'll tell yous to do. Now go ahead, an' burn th' atheistical timber, or something may happen to our town.

Man of the Pike [*hesitant*]. I dunno, Father, about burnin' it. We handled it outa th' ship, an' nothin' has happened to us.

Father F. [*angrily*]. Burn it as a reparation to God for landing atheistical timber on th' holy wharf of Doonavale.

Nora [*indignantly*]. They'll do no such thing! [*To the men*] To burn it would be to burn th' homes of the people.

Michael [*quietly and somewhat musingly*]. It is good an' healthy timber, with th' scent of pine in its drying sap, born within it when the saplings sprouted first in the forests of Red Siberia.

Skerighan [*approvingly*]. A sunsible sayin' frae a sunsible mon!

Michael. It is the very wood we need to make fine sturdy window-frames an' fine doors for our homes; to put a sturdy an' sensible roof over our heads, and a safe an' pleasant floor undher our feet. What's more, Father Ned has said Take it, and be thankful.

Skerighan [*enthusiastically*]. Anither sunsible sayin' frae th' same sunsible mon!

Tom. There's other things need burnin' more than th' timber on th' wharf. Th' things of th' earth that God helps us to grow can't be bad, let them come from Catholic Italy, Protestant Sweden, or Communist Russia. I say take what God gives us by the labourin' hands of other men.

Skerighan [*solemnly*]. Sound, sunsible Christian docthrine!

Father F. [*exasperated—despairingly*]. Listen to him—the know-all from th' North. [*To Skerighan*] Leave Christian doctrine to me, you dangerous fool. [*To Michael and Nora*] We have had peace here till yous came back from Dublin with your design to use the Tosthal for your own ends; but I won't allow your idle impudence to molest our pure peace. [*To Nora*] You, young lady, daughter of the Deputy Mayor and all as you are, you have been dismissed from the post of Librarian, and the books chosen by you have been cleaned away from th' Library shelves; taken to the Town Clerk to be burned.

Nora [*smilingly*]. Th' books have been retaken from him, replaced on the shelves, and most of them have already been borrowed.

Michael. With the Library Committee's agreement.

Father F. What are you talking about? What Committee, sir?

Michael [*to Father Fillifogue*]. Bernadette Shillayley's one of them.

Nora. With Tom Killsallighan, meself as Secretary, and Michael, son of the Mayor; and our Chairman is——

Man of the Musket } [*bringing butt of gun and butt of pike down with a*
Man of the Pike } *bang on the floor—together*]. Father Ned!

> [*Father Fillifogue subsides wearily into a chair, leaning forward, his elbows on his knees, his head in his hands. Binnington goes to one side of the chair, McGilligan to the other, each laying an encouraging hand on the priest's shoulders.*]

Binnington. Come, come, Father, keep smiling.

McGilligan. Horsey, keep your tail up!

Nora. You see, Father, we're fed up bein' afraid our shaddas'll tell what we're thinkin'. One fool, or a few, rules th' family life; rules th' school, rules th' dance hall, rules th' library, rules the ways of a man with a maid, rules th' mode of a girl's dhress, rules th' worker in fields and factory, rules th' choice of our politicians, rules th' very words we try to speak, so that everything said cheats th' thruth; an' Doonavale has become th' town of th' shut mouth.

Father F. [*sitting up a little, holding his arms out despairingly*]. Yous see, yous hear? This is all along of th' College lettin' th' students wear jeans. I warned th' Chancellor that allowing the students to dress like manual labourers would have a Communistic tendency and influence. My warning went unneeded an' unheeded, and [*indicating Michael and Nora*] this is one result.

Binnington [*to Michael—violently*]. When this damned Tosthal's over, you'll see no more of that girl there!

McGilligan [*to Nora—violently*]. Ay, an' you'll see no more of that fella there!

Michael [*laughingly*]. A bit late now to give th' ordher.

Binnington [*angrily*]. How's it too late?

Nora. Well, we studied at the same College.

Michael. An' lived in the same flat.

Nora. An' slept in th' same bed o' Sundays.

> [*Binnington, McGilligan, and their wives sink down into chair or sofa so amazed that they are silent, wearing woebegone faces.*

Father F. [*with his despairing gesture*]. Yous see, yous hear! The jeans, jeans, jeans!

> [*Mr. Murray comes hurrying in, stick and all, excited and rejoicing, waving his stick on high.*

Murray. Where's dat McGunty? [*He sees him.*] Dere you are. Where's your trumpet?

McGunty. Here, hangin' on me side.

Murray. Off you go, den; dey are all waitin' for you. Dee trumpet is sounding. [*He lifts his stick like a sword.*] Blow dee Forward! Boot an' saddle! [*He pushes McGunty out of the room.*] Dey wait, dey wait. [*To the others*] To dee meetin'! Dee trumpets blow, dee banners wave—to dee meetin'!

McGilligan [*restless with animosity and anxiety—from his chair*]. Is th' fella gone mad? What meetin', you fool?

Father F. [*furiously, but despairingly*]. What meetin'! Yous are asleep! [*He tries to rise from his chair, but sinks back again.*] I wanted to meet yous be moonlight alone, to tell yous they were out to pull away th' roses growin' round your doors. If yous don't stir yourselves, yous'll be outlaws in a land forlorn.

McGilligan. Outlaws? Is everyone demented, or what?

Father F. [*to McGilligan*]. Mayor Binnington's son, Michael, is standin' against you in th' Elections of th' comin' month. [*To Binnington*] McGilligan's daughter Nora's standin' against you. If ye don't move, they'll be Doonavale's new members of the Erin's Dail!

McGilligan [*to Nora*]. You hussy! You'll make a show of yourself, for you won't get ten votes!

Binnington [*to Michael*]. You want to do your Da down, do you? You damned fool, you won't get ten votes either!

Man of the Musket. We'll soon see. Th' meetin' tonight'll start us all listenin' to th' whisperin' of th' night.

Man of the Pike. Down, derry, down; right down from th' stars, said Father Ned, givin' some of their glitther to the turf an 'th' sthreet.

Father F. [*to McGilligan and Binnington*].   You hear? Where do we go from here?

McGilligan [*testily*].   Ah, pull yourself into yourself again, Father! I'll fight, anyway.

Binnington [*getting heavily out of his chair*].   An' me, too. [*To Mrs. Binnington*] Me robe!

McGilligan [*getting heavily out of his chair—to Mrs. McGilligan*].   Me robe, too!

Binnington.   Me cocked hat an' me chain!

McGilligan.   Mine, mine, too!

> [*Mrs. McGilligan and Mrs. Binnington have run out, and now run in again with the Mayor's and Deputy Mayor's official garments. They hurriedly help the two men to put them on, but the robes seem to have become too big for them, the chains dangle down too far, and the cocked hats fall down to their eyes.*]

Binnington [*feebly*].   Bring me me bow of burnished gold!

McGilligan [*attempting to be bolder*].   Bring me me arras of desire! Now, where's your damned meetin' to be?

Man of the Pike.   Folly th' crowd, an' yous won't lose your way, for people are on their way from th' Glen of the Light, from th' Meadow of Knowledge, an' from th' Gap of Courage; all assemblin' on th' fringe of th' town to march to th' Hill of th' Three Shouts.

McGilligan.   Go, but we'll go, too.

Binnington.   Ay, an' outface yous on your own platform.

Father F. [*rising from his chair with a great effort*].   I'll help yous. I'll assert meself, an' end th' irreverence creepin' out of th' Tosthal. Th' Macebearer will walk before yous; th' Town Clerk'll go between yous; an' I'll lead th' way; I'll lead th' way. [*He suddenly stiffens, as do McGilligan and Binnington, when, at a distance, the first few bars of 'The Dead March in Saul', are heard accompanied by a bell, sounding faintly at a farther distance, tolling for the dead. Or Chopin's 'Funeral March', going on till just before Binnington asks 'Who gave dee shout?'*] What's that?

McGilligan.   Who th' hell's dead now?

Murray.   Didn't ye know? Th' two of dem, one afther dee oder—plonk plonk—just like dat!

McGilligan [*mystified*].   Plonk? Who went plonk?

Father F. [*staring before him as in a half dream*].   Plonk, plonk!

Murray.   While th' Town Clerk was gapin' at Fader Fillifogue's scarlet door, he heard a shout in dee sthreet, an' went plonk! Dead as a door-nail. Dee Macebearer followin' him heard dee shout too, took a look at dee sky, an' went down plonk! Plonk plonk, dee two of dem—just like dat! At dee shout!

   The 'Funeral March' and tolling bell have faded, and cease now.

Binnington [*wildly*].   Who gave dee shout? Where did dee shout come from?

Murray.   Dey're sayin' dee shout came from Fader Ned.

Skerighan [*ominously*].   Aw dongerous mon, this, mind ye!

   [*The bugle-notes of the 'Boot and Saddle' ring out clearly from a near spot in the town; Binnington, McGilligan, and Father Filli-fogue listen limply; Skerighan alert, with cocked ear, and a look of inquiry on his face; the rest stand in a semi-attitude of attention.*

Michael.   Lasses an' lads, it's time to go, for more life, more laughter; a sturdier spirit and a stronger heart. Father Ned is on the march!

Tom [*triumphantly*].   An' we go with Father Ned—March!

Michael [*to Mrs. McGilligan*].   Come, come and join us.

Nora [*to Mrs. Binnington*].   You, too, dear; come with us.

Mrs. McGilligan [*to Mrs. Binnington*].   Let's go, Elena.

   [*Binnington and McGilligan make violent efforts to rise out of their chairs in a semi-stupefied way. Father Fillifogue, too, makes an ef-fort to get up, but it is no more than a rocking back and forward, up and down.*

Binnington [*muttering and bewildered*].   I'll fight yous; fight yous!

McGilligan [*mumbling*].   Me, too, me, too; me——

Father F. [*dreamily*].   I'll lead yous. Minsthrel boys, minsthrel boys, harps an' swords, swords an' harps.

   [*The rest file out of the room—Man of the Pike and Man of the Musket leading; followed by Tom hand in hand with Bernadette; then Mrs. Binnington and Mrs. McGilligan, followed by Michael hand in hand with Nora; Murray lingering for a moment at the door.*

Murray [*gayly—to Father Fillifogue*].   My Mozart will be soon in dee Parish Hall, Fader Fillifogue, an' in dee church. My feet will press dee pedals.

Father F. [*mumbling.*]   I'll nail them down.

Murray [*fiercely*].   I'll tear dee nails out!

> [*The Mayor is now slumped down on the sofa, the Deputy Mayor lolls in a chair, and Father Fillifogue sits back limply in another, staring vacantly out in front of himself. Skerighan gazes in some bewilderment and confusion at the three prostrate men.*

Skerighan [*gently shaking Father Fillifogue's shoulder*].   Are ye no' gaein' tae put your fut doon? What's scaurin' ye?

Murray [*loudly*].   Dee moosic of life is scarin' him!

Father F. [*chanting in a very low and dazed way*]:
  Oh, dear, what can the matter be?

McGilligan [*chanting in the same way—a little later than Father Fillifogue*]:
  Oh, dear, what can the matter be?

Binnington [*chanting in the same way—a little later still*]:
  Oh, dear, what can the matter be?

The Three together.   Ireland has gone to the fair!

Binnington [*making a feeble effort to rise*].   We will arise and go!

McGilligan [*feebly*].   Firm each foot, erect each head, an' step together.

Father F. [*feebly*].   Like the deer on mountain heather.

Skerighan [*despairingly and pityingly*].   They're a' in a lumentable con-deetion, so they are. [*He goes over and shakes the other two by the shoulders roughly. To McGilligan*] Wauk up! Are ye no' gangin' tae make a ficht o' it? If ye dinna, oor business'll be no comfort in th' future. Is it deid dune ye all are, or what? I'd no' give in. [*He shakes Binnington.*] Awauk, mon, on' dinna lut your dondher dee! [*He shakes Father Fillifogue.*] Are ye no' gangin' tae ootface yon Feyther Nud? [*He thinks for a moment. He pulls an orange sash from a pocket, and puts it around him.*] I'll thry a rousin' spell of a Protestant hommer song tae wauk th' bigots, on' put a butt o' Northern iron intil thom. [*He whips the um-brella out of Father Fillofogue's hand, grips it by the stem, and uses it as a drumstick, beating time lustily on the table as he sings defiantly to-wards the recumbent men. Bizet's March from 'Suite, Maid of Perth' begins.*]
  Lero lero lero lero, Lillibulero bullen a law,
  Lillibulero lero lero, Lillibuero bullen a law!

[*Despairingly*] I'm nae gude withoot th' dhrums! Oh, hod I but a fife in ma hond, on' a hundhred big dhrums behint me!

[*He is about to start again when the bugle-call, 'Forward', sounds, mingling with the music of the March. He listens, statue-like, the umbrella held high as he was about to bring it down on the table, his mouth half open, spell-bound.*

Murray [*whipping the umbrella from Skerighan, and waving it excitedly*]. Come on out, man, an' let th' orange sash join dee green ones!

[*A roll of drums in the distance.*

Skerighan. Th' thondher of th' dhrums! A murracle, be God! [*He listens for a moment.*] Now, is thot th' thonder of th' dhrums of th' North, or th' thonder of th' dhrums of Feyther Nud?

Murray [*shouting triumphantly*]. Dee drums of Fader Ned!

Echo [*very quietly but very positively*]. Dee dhrums of Fader Nud.

[*The music of the March goes on.*

THE PLAY ENDS

AUTOBIOGRAPHIES

A CHILD IS BORN

(FROM "I KNOCK AT THE DOOR", 1939)

✲ ✲ ✲

In Dublin, sometime in the early eighties, on the last day of the month of March, a mother in child-pain clenched her teeth, dug her knees home into the bed, sweated and panted and grunted, became a tense living mass of agony and effort, groaned and pressed and groaned and pressed and pressed a little boy out of her womb into a world where white horses and black horses and brown horses and white and black horses and brown and white horses trotted tap-tap-tap tap-tap-tappety-tap over cobble stones, conceitedly, in front of landau, brougham, or vis-à-vis; lumberingly in front of tramcar; pantingly and patiently in front of laden lorry, dray, or float; and gaily in front of the merry and irresponsible jaunting-car:

Where soldiers paraded, like figures taken out of a toy-box, wearing their red coats with yellow breastpieces; blue jackets with white breastpieces; and tight trousers with red stripes or white stripes or yellow stripes down the whole length of each leg; marching out on each royal birthday of the Queen to the Phoenix Park for a Review and Sham Battle, with guns and lances and swords and cannons; going by the Saluting Point at a quick march, or at a trot, and lastly, at a gallop, with a thunder of hoofs and a rattle of shaking cannon, that made all hearts quiver with hope for a new war; while the soldiers having got back to barracks when the fun was all over, rubbed down their sweating horses or cleaned their rifles, murmuring all the time against the birthdays of queens that gave them all so much mucking about for nothing:

Where a great poet named Tennyson, anticipating Hollywood, had built up in the Studio of his mind, his Come into the garden, Maud, the black bat night has flown; and had sent his cardboard kings and warriors and uncompromising virgins out into the highways and byways that sprinkled the lawns of the welltodo, men bowing low to the knights as they went galloping by like the wind in a hurry; and the maidens smiled and beckoned and sighed as the knights careered about among the roses and the hollyhocks, gathering on the points of their lances lovely little bunches of rosemary and rue:

Where energy was poured out in Bibles and tracts and hymns; and sweet little stories, swinging little boys and girls up to heaven or down to hell; where the hosts of heaven, embattled, assembled for the fray on a croquet lawn; and all the passion, frightfulness, laughter, strife, tears, peace, defeat, victory, agony, and bloody sweat of heaven's war with hell sank into a delicately scented, gently moving, sweet conversing, pink and mauve and cream-coloured garden party:

Where it was believed that when children died of croup or consumption or fever, they were simply not, for God took them:

Where Ruskin, with his delicate mind and Christianly crafted hands, modelled his figures of speech with mud and tinsel; and Mr. Poynter, president of the Royal Academy, summoning up all his powers of imagination, and summing all that ever had been or would be in art, painted the *tour de force* and cul-de-sac of a visit to Æsculapius:

Where almost all found all in all in God on Sundays; and the rest of the week found all in all in bustles, Bibles, and bassinets; preaching, prisons, and puseyism; valentines, victoria crosses, and vaccination; tea fights, tennis, and transubstantiation; magic lanterns, minstrel shows, and mioramas; music-halls, melodramas, and melodeons; antimacassars, moonlighting, and midwives; fashions, fenians, and fancy-fairs; musk, money, and monarchy:

Where every shrubbery in every pet-of-heaven house held a monkey, stuck there by Darwin, a monkey that stretched out a sudden paw to rip a bit of fragrant lace from the petticoat of any lady stooping down to pull a sprig of lavender, sending the ladies flying with fear into the churches to pull and pull the bells, making all the clergy run like hell into the pulpits to yell Peace, be still, for there is nothing revealed that cannot be hidden away; and so queen and consort, peers, clergy, commons, and people buried deep this monkey bone of our bone and flesh of our flesh, thick edge of the wedge, whereby millions of years were thrust between themselves and other people and God, jerking away a sense of nearness so obliging that it put a latch-key into the pocket of every catholic and protestant for a private gateway into the kingdom of heaven.

And the woman in child-pain clenched her teeth, dug her knees home into the bed, became a tense living mass of agony and effort, sweated and panted, pressed and groaned, and pressed and pressed till a man child dropped from her womb down into the world; down into a world that was filled up with the needs, ambitions, desires, and ignorances of others, to be shoved aside, pressed back, beaten down by privileges carrying godwarrants of superiority because they had dropped down into the world a couple of hours earlier. The privileges were angry and irritable; but the round-bellied, waggle-headed, lanky-legged newborn latecomer kicked against the ambitions, needs, and desires of the others, cleared a patch of room for itself from the trampling feet and snapping hands around it; was washed, napkined, and fed; added on three, four, or five ounces of weight every week, taking most of it from its mother and a little from the life around it; and so grew gradually, and gathered to itself the power, the ignorance, the desire, and the ambition of man.

Forty years of age the woman was when the boy was three, with hair still raven black, parted particularly down the middle of the head, gathered behind in a simple coil, and kept together by a couple of hairpins; a small nose spreading a little at the bottom; deeply set, softly gleaming brown eyes that sparkled when she laughed and hardened to a steady glow through any sorrow, deep and irremediable; eyes that, when steadily watched, seemed to hide in their deeps an intense glow of many dreams, veiled by the nearer vision of things that were husband and children and home. But it was the mouth that arrested attention most, for here was shown the chief character- istic of the woman: it quivered with fighting perseverance, firmness, human humour, and the gentle, lovable fullness of her nature. Small strong hands, hands that could slyly bathe a festered wound or scour a floor—wet cloth first, then the brush soap-foamed, tearing the dirt out, then wet cloth again and, finally, the dry cloth finishing the patch in back and forward strokes and twisting circles of rhythmic motions. A sturdy figure carried gracefully and with resolution; flexible, at peace in its simple gown of black serge, with its tiny white frill round the neck that was fair and unwrinkled still. A laugh that began in a ripple of humour, and ended in a musical torrent of full-toned mirth which shook those who listened into an irresistible com- panionship.

And all this was seen, not then, but after many years when the dancing charm and pulsing vigour of youthful life had passed her by, and left her moving a little stiffly, but still with charm and still with vigour, among those whose view of the light of life had dimmed and were mingling more and more with a spreading darkness; and vividly again, and with an ago- nised power, when she was calmly listening to the last few age-worn beats of her own dying heart.

This had been the shake of the bag, and she knew that she would never have another child. She had had seven before—three boys and one girl living, and one girl and two boys dead. Each of the two dead boys had been called John, and her husband said that this last boy's name was to be John, too. She thought for a long time. It seemed to be a challenge to God to do that, to give the name of John to this new child. He was undoubtedly her last child, and she wanted him to live. The two born before that had been called John had died, died of the same thing, died of croup.

She remembered how the first had died, died before she knew he was dying, died of croup. Then after another two years, another boy had come, and they had called him John. Her husband had said we must have a boy called John. Her husband with doggedness and she with misgiving had called him John. He had been vigorous enough, and had sprawled and kicked a twelve-month way into the world, when suddenly he seemed to get a feverish cold, a little cough and a watering from the eyes. Then one evening on her way to his bedside she stopped frightened by the sound of a hard choking cough. Prompted, at first, by fear to go away and refuse to hear, she went slowly to the room over to the bed, and found him struggling from under the clothes, his arms moving wildly, his eyes staring, his face bluish, and his breath coming in short and cluttering gulps. She remembered that, in a panic, she had slapped a bonnet on her head and a shawl round her shoulders, had gathered the little body into a blanket, rushed out of the house, down the street, climbed into a passing cab, calling on the driver for God's sake to drive fast, fast, fast to the Abercorn Hospital.

—He can do it, if He wants to, she murmured in the cab all the way to the hospital, He can save the child; the other died, but this won't, this won't, won't, won't die. With a thought, God can take this choking lump from the little child's throat, and give him back his healthy happy breathing.

And the child got it harder and harder to get its breath, and the choking effort of the child to breathe whistled agony into her brain. She tore up the steps of the hospital, rang and rang and rang the bell, pushed past into the hall when the door was opened.

—Get the doctor, she said, pantingly, to the porter, get the doctor, get him quick to look at this child of mine quick, to treat this little child of mine, quick please, for he's dying, but can easily be saved if the doctor comes quick, bring me quick to the doctor or let him come quick to me here, there's no time to be lost, for it's the croup he has, and he's dying fast and will be dead if the doctor doesn't come quick, go and get him, go and get him, go, go and get him quick.

And she had walked up and down, down and up the hall, waiting, waiting for the porter to bring the doctor, afraid to look at the convulsed little face hidden under the shawl, and trying to hear less clearly the choking cadences of the shivering cough shaking the little figure sheltering in her arms.

The porter came back and told her that the doctor was attending a patient, and would be with her in a brace of shakes.

—This child can't wait, she answered threateningly; and he must be treated at once, the other patient must wait, but this child is choking and may die any moment, man; where's the doctor, and I'll bring the child to him myself?

She ran over to a passing nurse, held the child firmly to her bosom with one hand, and caught the nurse's arm tightly with the other.

—A doctor for this child, nurse, before it's too late, she pleaded, for this child that's dying with the croup. See, his face is getting black with the choking; nurse, quick, please, for he's getting less and less able to breathe, and I'll hold the hospital responsible for anything that happens to him; for I've been left here waiting too long, too long, and the child choking, without any attention; for it's the croup he has, and I'm afraid he's dying.

The nurse led her gently over to a side of the hall, and pressed her gently down on a seat.

—Sit down, on the bench there, sit down, she said softly, and I'll get the doctor to see the child. She had shouted after the departing nurse, This'll be my second Johnny that'll have died of the croup, if you don't hurry.

And again she had asked God to help and hurry the doctor so that her child wouldn't die in her arms.

Suddenly she held her breath as she heard a curious rasping sigh, and her bosom shuddered as she felt the little body in her arms give a mighty straining stretch; then she knew that what she wanted to keep away had come to her; and she pressed to her breast a dear possession that had emptied itself of life. She had sat, stricken dumb, motionless for some moments, then she had laid the little form down on the bench, and looked at the rigid little face tinged with purple; she had closed the shades of the staring eyes, placed two pennies on the lids, and bound them there with her handkerchief.

Some time after, the doctor, followed by the nurse, came up the corridor, and she had called out to them, You came too slow, for God came quicker and took the child away. The doctor had come over to her, put his hand over the child's little heart, murmuring, Yes, he's gone; but no skill of ours could have saved him. And she had answered bitterly, None of you broke your heart trying.

She had taken up the dead form in her arms, and said to the nurse and to the doctor, Open the door, now, that I may pass out, and leave you all in peace.

The doctor had laid his hand on her arm to say, You can't carry the dead child home with you like that; better leave him in the deadhouse for the present.

She had answered hotly, I will bring him home, and lay him out at home, and bury him from the home where he lived and played out his little life, and let whosoever will try to stop me.

They had opened the door, and as she passed out the nurse whispered, Have you got your cab fare? but she passed out without giving the thanks of an answer.

She nodded to a cab on the rank opposite; when it came over, she got in carefully, hugged the body to her breast for a few moments, then laid it down on the seat opposite, stretched the little legs straight, placed the arms tightly down the body, instead of folding them over the breast in the form of a cross as the Roman Catholics were in the habit of doing. She kept her hand with a loving pressure on the breast of the child, for the jolting of the cab over the stones of the street made the body lie uneasy on the seat. She hadn't cried, but she pressed her lips tightly together, and with the fingers of one hand, dressed the fair hair neatly back from the dead-cold forehead. This would be another painful halting place in her own and her husband's life. All usual things would stand still till this was over. Had she come in a victoria, a brougham, or a landau, all the bells in the hospital would have been ringing attendance on her. Even the food eaten by her and her husband would taste of sorrow till his body had been buried, and they felt that their little boy's soul was getting accustomed to God.

In the agitated state of her mind she tried to think of a portion of the Bible that would soften a little the hardness of her trouble. She could think only of the widow, the widow's little son, and of Elijah. But there was no Elijah now to take this little son out of her arms, and stretch himself upon the boy, call three times upon the name of the Lord, and bring the living soul back again to the dead body—only a doctor who had delayed his coming, and a deadhouse.

Such a bright little youngster as he was too. Everybody admitted that he was far ahead of most children of his age. Peculiar look in his eyes that showed intelligence. Curious quick and alert manner he had. Not much movement in him now. In her heart she was glad that he had been baptised, though the Roman Catholic idea of original sin was ridiculous and laughable. Imagine that little child stretched there consigned to hell, or limbo, or whatever they called it, because he hadn't had a drop of water sprinkled over him. Terrible religion to believe in a thing like that.

She heard, subconsciously, the playing of a band and the sound of many voices, and the steady regular sound of many marching feet. Then the cab stood still. The sound of the band got louder, and the sound of the voices and the marching feet came close. The driver got down from his seat, and stood beside the window of the cab.

—We'll have to go a roundabout way, he said, or wait here till God knows when, for a fly couldn't get through a crowd like this, much less an animal like a horse. They're bringing Charlie Stewart Parnell to the Rotunda with bands and banners, where he's to speak on the furtherance of Home Rule for Ireland. That band knows how to rattle out The Green Above the Red, I'm telling you. They've the best belly-drummer in the whole bloody counthry. My God Almighty, looka the way that fella's twirlin' the sticks! He's nothin' short of a genius at it.

Then she heard a rolling roar of cheers breaking out that held on for many minutes, the cab-driver waving his hat, and yelling out a fierce and excited approbation.

—That's Parnell himself that's passed, he said, when the cheering had subsided, Ireland's greatest son. I'd sell me hat, I'd sell me horse an' cab, I'd sell meself for him, be Jasus, I'd nearly sell me soul, if he beckoned me to do it. He's the boyo'll make her ladyship, Victoria, sit up on her bloody throne, an' look round a little, an' wondher what's happenin'.

She shrank back into the shadow of the cab, and looked at her dead child lying stiff on the seat-cushions, stained with spots of tobacco and smeared with spilled beer. She waited dumbly for the crowds to pass, longing to get home so that she might bring her husband within the compass of her sorrow.

—The soldiers are all confined to barracks, went on the cab-driver; an' it's just as well, for we're in no humour to be lookin' calmly on at the redcoats on their backs and the crowns an' roses in their caps, noddin' misrule and persecution to the whole of us. Parnell has taken from England's strength so that his name stands big in Ireland, an' that God'll keep him sthrong's a prayer that keeps on in an echo dying away to begin in a powerful prayer again.

—I happen to be a loyal woman, she had said, with all my hopes gathered round the person and the throne, though, she thought, it hasn't rendered me much, it hasn't rendered me much. God Almighty, heavenly Father, you might have spared this little son of mine.

She had been a good woman; she had done her daily round and common task, tainted with only a little grumbling; she had worshipped Him in spirit and in truth; she had held fast to the faith once delivered to the saints; her husband knew his Bible well, most of it in the letter and all of it in the spirit; always arguing and proving popery was dangerous and repugnant to the plain word of scripture; that the sinner could always go straight to God without passing round saints or angels, there being only one mediator between man and God, the man, Jesus Christ. After all, He might have let this occasion of the chastening of those whom He loveth slide aside from the smiting of her harmless innocent baby.

Or, even if He had taken the little boy when the boy was at home with his father and mother; or in the hospital with the doctor striving to help him, and the nurse watching the failure of the doctor's skill; it would have been more bearable and better than to have wriggled into death in her arms, and go off, with no-one she knew near enough to give her the pity of relationship or friendly company.

—Now, suddenly said the cab-driver, the procession's endin', an' we can follow on, crawlin' cautiously at the tail-end of it.

He jumped up on his seat again, said yep to the horse, and went on slowly, halting now and halting again whenever anything intervened to interfere with the progress of the crowd who marched with pride and defiance, carrying in their midst the Leader who symbolised the body, spirit, and soul of the marching people. On crept the cab following hundreds of flaming torches reddening the excited faces of the marchers, the glow forming a huge smoky golden halo above the heads of the crowd. On crept the cab after the mighty yellow and green banners that each section of the crowd carried, the bands playing with a reckless crash and blare that, for many, fashioned drab thoughts of risk into a vision of men gathering to the trumpet call of God.

Slipping, at last, down a side turning, the cab passed through several streets, and then stopped outside her door. Stepping out of the cab, she bent down and in, lifted the little stiff shawled figure in her arms, and asked the driver the fare. One an' a tanner, he said, and added that he hoped there wasn't much wrong with the child, ma'am. Then as he caught sight of the little face as it slid from the fold of the shawl, he ejaculated, Jasus Christ, the kid's dead!

He took the one and sixpence silently, lifted his hat, mounted to his seat, gathered the reins in his hands, and quickly cantered away.

She brought the body in, laid it down on the bed, then went out to her husband. He had looked at her, and murmured, Oh, is he worse, then? They had gone into the room together; she had pulled off the handkerchief tied over the face of the little child, and the two of them had gazed at the rigid little face silently and long.

—He has stretched a lot, she said.

—When did he go? he asked.

—In the hospital, lying in my arms, before one came to look at him, she answered.

She felt his arm round her, pressing tenderly.

—Dear Sue, he said, my poor dear Sue.

She had quivered a little, and murmured brokenly, He is the second Johnny that has been taken from us. Perhaps we didn't do well, when the first died, to call the second one John.

The circling arm tightened round her. She looked up at him, and saw his face form into a fresh and firmer tightness.

—Sue, he answered, we may yet have another child; that other child may be a boy; if we should have another child, and that other child should be a boy, we shall call his name John.

FIRST THE GREEN BLADE

✤ ✤ ✤

The third Johnny, passing by the doggedness of his father and the superstitious anxiety of his mother, crawled a little further into life. Delicately and physically undecided, he crept along. He has a stout heart, said his mother, the first five years are the worst, and, if he can get over them, God is good. With ever verdant care, she watched him. She gave him his full share in the attention she had to pay to others, and the little leisure she snapped now and again from her household work was crowded with thoughts for Johnny's fuller and firmer settlement in the world. She had nursed him viciously through an attack of bronchitis when he had made but a six months' journey into the world; but no cough had lingered, and he ran about and laughed like other children; so where there was life there was hope, and God was good. The others murmured, it's Johnny here and Johnny there; but she reminded them that they were well into the thick of the world, while Johnny had only started. But God had not forgotten, and the trial was sent at last.

When he was five, his mother noticed a look of torment in his eyes. They harboured a hot and torturing pain that made him rub them vigorously, and cry long and wonderingly in the sunny hours of the day and through the long dark hours of the night. Small, hardy, shiny, pearly specks appeared on the balls of his eyes. He began to dread the light; to keep his eyes closed; to sit and moan restlessly in the darkest places he could find. For many weeks life became a place of gloom, streaked with constant flashes of pain. They folded a big white heavy handkerchief into a bandage, and wound it round his head, like a turban, to guard his eyes from the touch of whatever sunlight tottered in through the little windows of the little house.

Johnny had no sense of danger, no fear of any possible loss, no idea that something was happening which would mean agony for many years, and be a persistent and inscrutable handicap to him throughout the rest of his life. He felt only a curious resentment that he wasn't as others of his age were, and as he himself had been, able to run, to shout, to rejoice when the sun shone; to go to bed tired and full of sleep when the sun went down, getting strength for another and another chance to run, to laugh, and to rejoice in the middle of the sun's encouragement towards merriment and play. It was a time when eye troubles were thought little about, nor any weakness of the body when the weakness didn't pin the body to the bed. Pennyworths of golden ointment, zinc ointment, zinc and rosewater were the eye remedies of the people, except when an eye was cut asunder by an accident.

Such things as smallpox, typhoid fever, diphtheria, and scarlet fever were the only blights that stimulated the doctors to rush about, hair-tossed and coatless, to blow, blow on the bugles of alarm, forcing the people to close up their houses, seal themselves away from the fresh air, and burn sulphur in their rooms, filling the place with fumes, like incense rising from an altar in hell.

It was a time when every infant on some day in each passing week had to be filled with castor-oil, and dosed with syrup of squills, first having their chafed buttocks rubbed with stuff that had the grittiness of powdered steel. A time when only a few brave men separated themselves from this dung-like heap of ignorance, and, in a few bare corners of the world, sought to learn more about the mysteries of life, disease, and death, rather than seek safety with the crowd that ambled and arsed its way easily and nicely about through the hours of life; life under cocked hats, red gowns, and black gowns, droning out the laws of men; life under snowy surplices droning out the laws of God; and life under silk-scented gowns droning out the laws of love.

So his eyes grew worse and the pain waxed sharper. His mother, from an eggcupful of zinc and rosewater, with a tiny piece of rag, bathed them three times a day, and at night smeared the lids heavily with golden ointment taken from a penny box; but no strength crept into the weakness and no softness into the pain. The others, irritated by his crying, warned his mother than the habit of crying would only make them worse, and told the boy that his eyes were beginning to look like two burnt holes in a blanket. His mother, recommended to it by a neighbour, applied a poultice of sodden tea-leaves, a remedy that had once cured the neighbour's child of a horrid redness of the lids; but no strength crept into the weakness, nor did any softness creep into the pain.

Then a friend of one of his brothers said that if the boy's head was plunged into a bucket of cold water and the eyes held open beneath the water for five minutes or so at a time, several times a day, this would bring hardiness to the most stubborn weakness any eye ever had. Johnny was seized and, screaming protests, his head was pushed down into a bucket of dead cold water till the eyes were underneath; and he was vehemently called upon to open his eyes, open his eyes, damn it, couldn't he open his eyes, and let the water get at them. When he struggled, cold and frightened, they pushed him further down till the water flowing through his nostrils gurgled down his throat, almost choking him, leaving him panting for breath, shivering and wet, in the centre of reproaches and abuse because he had kept his eyes fiercely closed underneath the water. Threats, thumps on the back, failed to make him promise that he would open his eyes under the water; and all round him despaired of the remedy, saying it was waste of time if he wasn't made to open his eyes under the water, not worth a curse so long as he keeps his eyes shut; if he goes blind, it'll be his own fault; while Johnny stood there obstinately, with his head bent down on his breast, shocked and shaken, the water from his saturated hair trickling, by way of his neck, steadily down his back, and by way of his cheeks, dripping down to his belly; crying over and over again, The bandage, the bandage, put the bandage over me eyes again, they're paining me terribly. And so no strength crept into the weakness, neither did softness creep into the pain.

Then they all forsook him, saying, Leave him to the pain, then, since he won't do the one thing that will do him good; he has been pampered too much for anyone to pity him. Only his mother harassed her mind for help; only she, with deep pity and unbreakable patience, stood between him and the chance that his sight might go, leaving him helpless in the hands of man and no nearer to God; only she raised the banner of fear for him in the face of everyone she met, and pried everywhere for assistance to save him from the evil of perpetual darkness.

One day his mother suddenly remembered that she had heard a sister make mention of a kid having sore eyes going to some place or another, getting treatment, and getting well again. So out she set with the bandaged Johnny to see her sister, going a third of the way by tram and the rest by foot, to a low-roofed white-washed cottage stuck in a place by the back o' beyond in the Tenters' Fields, where they used to bleach the linen, over by Dolphin's Barn. There she and Johnny had a nice tea with homemade scones well warmed in the oven, melting in your mouth before you'd time to sink your teeth in them.

—Johnny's a case for a doctor, said the sister. You cart him off to St. Mark's Ophthalmic Hospital for Treatment of Diseases of the Eye and Ear, that's in Lincoln Place, just beside the back enthrance of Trinity College. Everyone who isn't a pauper pays sixpence for a ticket, lasting for a month, with attendances three days in each week. Go on Monday, or Wednesday, or Friday, for on any one of these days you're sure to see Mr. Story, who's the greatest of living men, knowing how, when and where to fiddle with the eyes. It's safer to go early at nine if you want to get away quick, for it's getting more and more crowded every day, an' everyone has to take his turn; an' sometimes the doctors take a long time over a case, especially if it is an ear; and you can do nothing better than to bring Johnny there to hear what they say and to see what they can do for him.

And Johnny's mother got up, and thanked her sister, and said she'd have to be goin', but she'd bring Johnny to the hospital the first thing on Monday morning. And Johnny's mother's sister kissed him, and put a new penny quietly into his pocket, and said God wouldn't let him lose the sight of his eyes.

Then they departed, and, going through The Liberties, came to where Meath Street meets Thomas Street. There Johnny and his mother took a tram which sailed along merrily as far as the top of Cork Hill, and was there stopped by a crowd.

—It's the Ball, said the conductor, the Vice-Regal Ball with all the gulls o' Dublin gawkin' at the notabenebilities flockin' in to a fine feed an' a gay night in Dublin Castle.

—An' we'll be stuck here for ages, said a woman in the corner.

—We might as well have a decko at the grandeur that's keeping the country going, before Mister Parnell and his poverty-stricken dupes reduce us all again to a state of nature, said a genteel-looking man, with a watery mouth and a drooping moustache, sitting in the centre of the car, as he got up from his seat, and climbed down nicely on to the street.

—The day isn't far distant, said the conductor, when that gent that's just gone out'll doff his hat to another tune, or hang as high as Gilderoy; and leaning against the entrance to the tram, he hummed:

> Oh, black's your heart, Clan Oliver, and coulder than the clay!
> Oh, high's your head, Clan Sassenach, since Sarsfield's gone away!
> It's little love you bear us, for sake of long ago,
> But hould your hand, for Ireland still can strike a deadly blow.

Johnny's mother got up, climbed down, and helped Johnny off the tram.

—Little protestant boys should never listen to Fenian songs, she said to him; whenever you hear one, you must always murmur God Save the King to yourself.

Mingling with the crowd, they couldn't get out of it, and were carried along to a spot almost beside the entrance to the Castle where they found Ella and Archie gleefully watching the glory passing in to the fine feed and the gay-grand night of dancing.

—Come here, in front of me, said Ella, pulling Johnny beside her, and stay quiet and stand still and don't stir, till we see all the lovely lords and ladies tripping and trotting into the Castle.

—I'm bringing Johnny to a special hospital for the eyes and ears only, on Monday morning, said Johnny's mother to Archie.

—He ought to be brought somewhere, said Archie, for his crying by day and his crying by night is becoming more than most of us can stick.

—When I was on me way along, said Ella, the carriages stretched from the Castle Yard, down Dame Street, Westmoreland Street, through Sackville Street, and right into Cavendish Row. Oh, look at the oul' fogey in blazing blue, with a pile of gold braid on his chest, and a slip of a girl nearly on his knee, in that brougham just gone by us.

—Stuck fast in the arms of a pleasure he'll never feel, murmured Archie.

—I'll get Johnny up early on Monday, said the mother, and bring him to the hospital, whatever happens.

—Th' oul' fogey, said Ella, had a jewelled star hanging be a blue ribbon in the middle of the pile of gold braid—Order of the Garter, I suppose.

—Not the Garter, said Archie, for only a few, outside of princes of the Royal Blood, get the Garter. Mantles of purple velvet lined with silk the knights wear. Musta been the Order of St. Patrick you seen, for it has a blue ribbon an' the motto, *Quis Separabit;* but if they'd only known the right way to do things here they'd have gone the whole hog an' made the ribbon green.

—I wish I hada known about this hospital before, said the mother, for Johnny might have been saved a lot of pain by gettin' attention in time.

—Looka' the kids over there, ejaculated Ella, all in their bare feet an' without a flitther on them. Shame for their mothers to let them look on at a sight like this.

—The whole thing gives a great amount of employment, said Archie encouragingly. Even the photographers benefit, for the whole crowd get their photos taken after the ball is over, after the break of morn, after the dancers leaving, after the stars are gone, to be able to look back at themselves in their old age in their gala get-up.

—Sixpence a month, with three visits a week, isn't a lot to charge, if they can do anything at all for Johnny, murmured the mother.

—Some of the dresses of the duchesses cost hundreds an' hundreds of pounds, said Ella.

—And sweet goodbye to the kingdom, the power, and the glory, if we get Home Rule, added Archie.

—Well, we'll see what they can do for Johnny on Monday, said his mother, putting her hand protectingly on his head.

—Here's a crowd of them coming, said Ella excitedly, here's great crowd of them coming quick and fast, thuick and last, comin' thro' the rye, comin' thro' the streets, comin' to the castle ball.

* * *

Two more nights of misery limped slowly by for Johnny, sitting up in bed, squirming his body and grinding his teeth; while his mother, with an old topcoat round her shoulders, stood over him in the shadowy light of a candle, holding old cloths saturated with cold water to his eyes, trying to mollify the pain, her face white with suppressed sympathy whenever he implored her to do something to take the pain away, murmuring that the hospital would do all that and more for him, and that he had only to stick it for two more short days; and when many hours had crept slowly and ashamed away, exhaustion lulled the pain, the saturated head of the boy sank more deeply into the drenched pillow, his mother put an arm around him, and hummed a hymn, There's a Friend for little children above the bright blue sky, a Friend who never changes, whose love will never die; our earthly friends may fail us, and change with changing years, this Friend is always worthy of that dear name he bears; and the two of them slumbered together.

THE HILL OF HEALING

At half-past eight in the morning, washed and dressed, with a thick hand-kerchief over his eyes, Johnny, helped by his mother, ate sparingly of his bread and tea, for he was soon to be given over to a power that could do many things to hurt and frighten him, and force him to suffer a fuller measure of pain.

He went down the street, holding his mother's hand, as slowly as he could, so that what was going to come to pass might not come too quickly. Opposite the end of the street, he heard a tram stop, and felt his mother lifting him inside and helping him on to a seat, and saying, if he was good and gave the doctor no trouble, she'd buy him a sponge cake, and they'd take the tram home again. The tram, pulled by patient, muscle-wrenched horses, jingled along, stopping now and again to take passengers on and let passengers off, each pull, to get the tram restarted, giving the horses a terri-ble strain. The conductor came along, with his money-bag and gleaming silver punch, and gathered the fares, tuppence for his mother and a half fare of a penny for him. He heard the punch ring with a clear shrillness as the conductor holed the tickets which were given to Johnny by his mother to hold, a red one for her, she said, and a yellow one for him; an' maybe you'll be able to look at them when we're comin' back, for the doctors may do you so much good that you may be able to fling the bandage off when we leave the hospital.

They got out at Westland Row, and his mother led him down Lincoln Place till they came to the hospital, a timid shabby-looking place, having a concrete path, with a few beds dotted with geraniums, before the entrance which wasn't any bigger than the two windows that would form the front of a grocer's shop. Over the big shop-like windows, in big letters, were the words, St. Mark's Ophthalmic Hospital for Diseases of the Eye and Ear. Going inside, they found themselves in a long narrow hall, divided in two by a barrier of polished pine. At the upper end were two doors, one to let the patients in to the doctors, and the other to let them out when the doctors had finished with them for the time being. The hall was furnished with long, highly-polished, golden-coloured pitch-pine benches on which a number of men, women, and children were sitting, slowly moving up to the door leading to the room where the doctors were. Near the entrance was a huge stove, and near this stove was a table on which, like an offering on an altar, was a big book enshrining the details of the patients' names, homes, and occupations. At this table sat a big, heavy, stout man of sixty-five with a white beard, a short bulgy neck, an incessant cough, a huge head, the skull of which was bald and hard and pink and polished like the pine benches. He was called Francis.

Johnny's mother gave the details asked for—his age, where he lived, and that he suffered from a disease of the eyes; and when Francis was told that the boy's father was dead, he shoved the word orphan into the space required to denote the father's occupation. The sixpence was handed over, and they were given a ticket of admission which would also be used by the doctor to write down the prescribed remedies to be applied to the diseased eyes. These were made up and handed out to the patients at the dispensary, a little closed-in booth-like space with a sliding panel, stuck in a corner of the hall. They got, too, a large sheet fixed in a cardboard protector, having on it diagrams of the eye, so that the doctor could record the origin, nature, and progress of the ailment, to be filed and retained by the hospital for future reference. They sat down on the bench among the patients, and waited for their turn. The people were being admitted in batches of five or six at a time, the rest moving up nearer as the others went in. As they waited and moved up and waited, his mother read what was written on the ticket:

St. Mark's Ophthalmic Hospital for Accidents
and Diseases of the Eye and Ear

Out-patients attending this Institution, under the care of
MR. STORY
are to attend on
Mondays, Wednesdays, and Fridays
before ten o'clock
Each person (not a pauper) will pay sixpence for a ticket
which will last for one month from date of issue. This
Ticket must be kept clean, and presented open at each
visit, and preserved when the attendance ceases.

Johnny heard the people round him talking of their complaints, their pain, and their hopes of improvement.

—I have to go months yet, he heard a voice say, before there'll be any improvement. Steel chips in a foundry flew into me eye, an' they had to get them out with a magnet. They made me jump when they were doin' it, I can tell you.

—He had to cut the sthring, said a voice a little nearer, to separate the bad blind eye from the good one, an' now he's breakin' his arse to cut the blind one out altogether, sayin' that it's no use havin' a dead eye in your head; but I have me own opinion about that, for the dead one isn't so disfigurin', if you don't examine it too closely, so it 'tisn't.

—It's wonderful, murmured another voice, what a lot of things a man can do without, accordin' to the doctors.

—Some o' the buggers would give up the spendin' of the first night with a lovely woman he was after marryin' for a half-hour's hackin' at a man, said the first voice.

—The first real touch o' spring is comin' into the air at last, said a soft voice, a little lower down; in the people's park yesterday the main beds were a mass o' yellow daffodils. The whole time I was gettin' a mug o' tea an' a chunk o' bread down me, I was lookin' at them.

—Geraniums, red geraniums for me, said an answering voice, every time, every time.

—I don't know, I don't rightly know, answered the soft voice; to me, red geraniums or geraniums of any other colour seem to have a stand-offish look, always, while daffodils seem to welcome you to come in and walk about in the midst of them.

—There was a moment's silence, then Johnny heard the second voice saying, maybe you're right, but I still hold to the red geraniums.

—See that man sittin' opposite, said a woman to his mother, have a glance at his ticket, and you'll see it's printed in red—don't look over too sudden—see?

—Yes, he heard his mother say, I see it's printed in red, while ours is printed in black. Why is that, now?

—Because he's a pauper, and doesn't, as we do, pay for his treatment.

Johnny felt a glow of pride. He wasn't a pauper, and he held the card of admission out so that all could see it was printed in black.

Suddenly they found themselves in the doctor's room, and a nurse made them sit down on a special bench to wait for Mr. Story. It was a room full of a frightening light, for the whole north wall was a window from side to side, and from floor to ceiling. There was a ceaseless sound of instruments being taken from trays and being put back again. Tinkle, tinkle, tinkle, they went, and cold sweat formed on Johnny's brow. All round the wall terrible pictures of diseases of the eye and ear were hanging. A nurse, in a blue calico dress, with narrow white stripes, was hurrying here and there, attending to the doctors; and everywhere there was a feeling of quiet, broken by a man's moan, or by a child's cry, that made Johnny tense his body with resentment and resistance.

At last, Mr. Story, a tall thin man, with a sharp face and an elegantly-pointed reddish beard, came over to them, and said shortly, bring the boy over to the window. Johnny was led over to the window, and the bandage taken from his eyes: the light, the light, the cursed, blasted, blinding light! He was seated on a chair; he was fixed between the doctor's legs; his head was bent back as far as a head can go; he could feel the doctor's fingers pressing into his cheek just below his eyes: the light, the light, the cursed, blasted, blinding light!

Open your eyes, said Story, and look out of the window; go on, open your eyes, like a good little boy.

—Open your eyes for the doctor, Johnny, said his mother.

—Open your eyes, said Story, sharply, open your eyes, at once, sir.

But the cursed, blasted, blinding light flooded pain in through the lids, and he kept them tightly closed. His mother nervously shook his arm.

—Open your eyes, you young rascal, she said.

But he sat, stiff, firm, and silent, and kept them closed.

—Story beckoned to two students. One of them held his head from behind the chair, the other held his arms, but still, firm, and silent, he kept them closed. His obstinacy forced them into fierceness; they took him out of the chair, while his mother, embarrassed, threatened him with all sorts of violence when she got him home. They stretched him, on his back, froglike, on the floor, students holding his legs, nurses holding his arms, while Story, kneeling beside him, pressed his fingers under his eyes firmly and gently, till with an exasperated yell, Johnny was forced to open them, and Story, from a tiny glass container, instantly injected into his eyes a tiny stream of what looked like cold water, which spread like a cooling balm over the burning ulcerated surface of his eyeballs.

Silently, then, he submitted to a fuller examination in a pitch-dark room, filled with little cubicles, in each of which a gas-jet flared; and from a mirror-like instrument strapped on the doctor's head, Story searched his inner eye for a fuller indication of the disease that took from his life the sense of sight in agony and sweat. After two hours of examination and treatment, Story returned to his desk, and beckoned to Johnny's mother to come over to him. She came, slowly and anxiously, and listened to what the doctor had to say.

—The boy will not be blind, he said, writing rapidly on the case-sheet, but getting him well's going to be a long job. Bathe the eyes regularly in water as hot as he can bear it, afterwards with a lotion they will give you at the dispensary. Most important of all, some of the ointment, as much as will fit on the top of your finger, is to be inserted underneath the lids—not on, mind you, but underneath the lids—every night and every morning; and the boy will have to wear a bandage for a long time. He is to be given nourishing food, and he is to take a teaspoonful of Parrish's Food, after each meal.

—Can he go to school, doctor? asked the mother.

—No, no school, he said snappily. His eyes must be given absolute rest. No school for a long, long time.

—If he doesn't go to school, sir, he'll grow up to be a dunce.

—Better to be a dunce than to be a blind man, said the doctor. The boy must be brought here on each Monday, Wednesday, and Friday till an improvement removes the necessity for attendance oftener than once a week. Get these remedies at the dispensary, he added, giving her the prescription, do all that I've told you, be patient, and don't let the boy go to school; and Mr. Story, with his elegant white hands, his red pointed beard and his morning coat, hurried away, followed by a flock of students, to attend to another patient.

—Me eyes must be pretty bad, said Johnny to his mother, as she was being fitted out with ointment, lotion, syrup, and bandage, at the dispensary, when he won't let me go to school.

Not to have to go to school—that was a thought full of a sweet savour. No schoolmaster, no lessons, no wear and tear of the mind with reading, writing, and arithmetic. He was saved from being one of the little slaves of the slate and satchel.

—It won't be nice, he murmured to his mother, if, when I grow up, I amn't able to read and write, will it ma?

—No, said she, it would be terrible; but, please God, you'll soon be well enough to go, for it might easily be as well to be blind as not to be able to read or write.

Then a nurse heavily bandaged his eyes, and his mother led him forth from the hospital, having finished his first day with an Institution that was to know him so well in the future that the doors nearly opened of their own accord when they saw him coming.

* * *

HIS DA, HIS POOR DA

❦ ❦ ❦

And all this time and for many months before, he who was called Michael, the old man, his mother's husband, the father that begot him, was lying in a big horsehair-covered armchair, shrinking from something that everybody thought of, but nobody ever mentioned.

Out of Limerick he had come, walking the roads to find a job, and settle down in Dublin. Down in Limerick, a catholic man had married a protestant maid; all the children had been reared up in the thick of the catholic religion; but the catholic father had died when Michael was an infant, so his mother had taken the chance to bring up her last-born in the true protestant faith once for all and once for ever delivered to the saints. When Michael had grown up into a young man, his mother had been taken up to heaven. Then his catholic brothers and sisters began to quarrel bitterly with Michael over the things that Jesus said and the things that Jesus did and the meanings that were hidden in the things that Jesus did and Jesus said, and by all accounts, Michael had a pretty tough time of it. So one fine day, without as much as a goodbye or a kiss me arse to the rest of them, he set his face towards Dublin, and turned his back on the city of Limerick forever and ever, amen.

> *Brandenburgh the ditch has crossed*
> *And gained our flank at little cost,*
> *The bastion's gone—the town is lost;*
> *Oh! poor city of Luimneach linn-ghlas.*
> *Out, with a roar, the Irish sprung,*
> *And back the beaten English flung,*
> *Till William fled, his lords among,*
> *From the city of Luimneach linn-ghlas.*
>
> *'Twas thus was fought that glorious fight,*
> *By Irishmen, for Ireland's right—*
> *May all such days have such a night*
> *As the battle of Luimneach linn-ghlas.*

Up he came to Dublin, and married Susanna, who became the mother of his children, with Johnny as the shake of the bag. He was known to the neighbours for many years in his simple suit, half-tall hat, and black-thorn stick, bringing home his two pounds, weekly, to his wife, like clockwork; liked by many, a little feared by all who knew him, having a sometime gentle, sometime fierce habit of criticism; and famed by all as one who spat out his thoughts into the middle of a body's face. A scholar he was to all, who was for ever poring over deep books, with a fine knowledge of Latin, and a keen desire that others should love learning for its own sake, as he did.

And here he was now reclining in a big horsehair-covered armchair, shrinking from something that everyone thought of, but no-one ever mentioned.

A ladder on which he stood, it was said, had slipped from under him, and, in falling, his back had struck a chair, and his spine had been injured. Doctors came in by the door, examined him, asked him what was wrong; and he annoyed the doctors by replying that the doctor had been sent for to find out. The doctor ordered that the patient should be rubbed all over with fine lard, and then left as wise as he was when he first came in. So the delicate sensitive face, fringed by a soft brown beard, grew paler and thinner day by day, the white shapely hands moved more restlessly over the rests on the chair, and the reading of his beloved books became a burden too heavy to bear. He wanted Ella to read Shakespeare to him, for Sue, his wife, wasn't much good at anything above Dickens (though she knew all about Falstaff); but Ella wouldn't, for Ella, studying to be a teacher, was too busy, and the dad, anyhow, had crept a little too close to the grave to be pleasant or interesting. And death was death and life was life and Ella was Ella.

There was a little more give and take in life, too, since his dominance had been confined to the armchair. The boys could stay out a little later; return, too, with a whiff of drink off their breath, and stand square-shouldered and proud-mannered in front of their mother, knowing that the probing eyes were dimming in the other room, and were trying to see through a darkness that buried in its silent blackness the coming call of God; and that lips that might have framed a message of scorn were now sadly forming messages claiming kinship with Jesus, son of man, and son of God, who came into the world to save sinners.

There was one comfort that, if he died, he would die in the midst of his books. There they were in the big bookcase, snug in a recess to the side of the fireplace. Marshalled tightly together, there they were, the books he used to read, pore, and ponder over: a regiment of theological controversial books, officered by d'Aubigne's *History of the Reformation*, Milner's *End of Controversy*, Chillingworth's *Protestantism*, holding forth that the Bible, and the Bible alone, is the religion of protestants, with an engraving of the fat face of the old cod stuck in the front of it; Foxe's *Book of Martyrs*, full of fire and blood and brimstone, *Popery Practical Paganism, Was St. Peter Ever in Rome?* having in it a picture of divines battering each other with books, and SS. Peter and Paul, in the clouds of heaven, looking down and laughing at the fighters, actually saying, if pictures could speak, Go it, boys, give each other socks. Like inspection officers, the English Bible, the Latin Vulgate, and the Douai Testament stood pompously together, and, to the right, *Cruden's Concordance* acting as orderly officer; a neatly uniformed company of Dickens', Scott's, George Eliot's, Meredith's, and Thackeray's novels; Shakespeare's Works; Burns', Keats', Milton's, Gray's, and Pope's poetry; on the top shelf, six or seven huge volumes, like podgy generals, of *The Decline and Fall of the Roman Empire*; and leaning idly by their side was Locke's *Essay on the Human Understanding*; and a whole crowd of school books that had been used by the boys and Ella, with a number of camp followers consisting of prizes they had won at Sunday school, such as *I and Jesus with the Zulus; Little Crowns and How to Win Them; Boys and Girls of the Bible; Gospel Garlands for Little Girls; The Sieges of Gibraltar; From Crécy to Tel-el Kebir;* while in the corner was a shy little book calling itself *Creation's Testimony to its God*; and locked away in a drawer, forbidden to be touched by anyone save the head of the house, lay a mysterious book which the father said confined the dangerous teaching of a Bishop Berkeley; and, mother added, was all about nothing being real, and that all things we saw were only images of our own ideas, and that such books were only to be read and thought of by minds big enough to understand that they were rubbish.

Her husband had spent most of his life among his books, and though it was nice to know that the whole neighbourhood respected your father as a great scholar, and at home with the Latin, said Ella, yet what use was it all when the time came for you to hand in your gun? Locke's *Essay on the Human Understanding* was all balls, said Mick, for the very look of the thing was enough to start you praying to God that the human mind would never become anything like what it was represented to be in the book.

Several times only, Johnny had come into touch with his father. When he was old enough to know about things, his father was ill, and he was bad with his eyes; and his father hated the thought that, because of his eyes, Johnny would grow up to be a dunce, a thing that was an abomination in the sight of the lord, his father, so the two seldom came together. Once when nobody was in the house, save his mother, and she busy in the sick room, he had been sent out to buy an ounce of Cavendish cut plug.

—The dunce will forget what he's been sent for before he's half-way there, his da had said, as his mother carefully fixed his cap on his head while his little body vibrated with anxiety and importance.

—No, he won't forget, said the mother, for he isn't quite the dunce you think he is, and bending down, she had whispered in his ear, now, remember, say it to yourself all the way to the shop, ounce of Cavendish cut plug, ounce of Cavendish cut plug.

And he had run swiftly and anxiously to the little shop three streets away, gripping closely the money in his little fist, murmuring rapidly, constantly, and breathlessly, ounce of Cavendish cut plug, ounce of Cavendish cut plug, ounce of Cavendish cut plug. Then he had run back as rapidly, anxiously, and breathlessly to his mother, who examined the little parcel carefully, and pronounced it to be good. She brought him in to his father so that he might deliver it himself, and his father took it from him silently and wearily, as he sat in his chair. Johnny stood with his head bent down, looking at the bony knees giving angles to the black trousers, and the small firm feet, thrust into slippers, nestling together on a small red and black rug stretched before the fire.

—Now, his mother said, expectantly, now you see, father, he didn't make any mistake after all.

Then the wasted sensitive hand left the arm of the chair, and Johnny felt it resting on his head, as his father said softly and sadly, No, he is a brave little fellow, and his father's son.

Shy, without the power to raise his head to look at his father, Johnny left the room, joyous and triumphant, murmuring, ounce of Cavendish cut plug, ounce of Cavendish cut plug.

Once again, when the parlour door had been left open, Johnny, passing by, had ventured to peep into the room. There he was sitting stilly in the large gorse-hair horse-hair armchair, rimmed with mahogany, the armchair that, after his father had died, had fallen asunder. All that Johnny could see was a thin white wasted hand resting grimly on the arm of the chair, and a patch of intensely black hair beneath a cricket-cap made of red, white, and blue segments. There was his poor da, or, his father, as Johnny's mother spoke of him to his brothers and sister, sitting facing the fire, with the little coloured mermaid in a glass bowl on a little table to his right, and a picture of Queen Victoria in her coronation robes on the wall to his left.

He must have sensed the boy peering in at him, for the head in the cricket-cap suddenly turned, and the boy caught a frightening glimpse of a white, wasted agony-lined face, jewelled with deep-set eyes now gleaming with appealing anger at the boy who was looking in at him. Johnny saw the blue veins swell in the delicate hand that rested on the chair, and his ears were shocked by the sound of the low weak voice trying to shout at him, Go away, go away, you, and shut the door at once—this is no place for little boys.

Johnny had closed the door quick, had run for his life through the hall out into the street, full of the fear of something strange, leaving his da, his poor da, shrinking from something that everyone thought of, but nobody ever mentioned.

HIS FATHER'S WAKE

☘ ☘ ☘

One very cold morning Johnny's mother wakened him up, saying, Get up, Johnny, get up, me poor boy; there are many things to be done, and you must be washed, and take your breakfast a little earlier than usual.

He rubbed away some of the matter that clung to his eyes, and shivered in his thin shirt.

—Ugh, he muttered, it's cold, it's very cold.

—There'll be many a cold morning to face from this out, said his mother, as she helped him on with his trousers, and rearranged the crumpled bandage on his forehead. Tell Ella, she went on, to give you a clean bandage.

—Not Ella, he said, you, mother: Ella's rough, and Ella doesn't care.

—Ella will have to do it this morning, she said, for I have to stay with your poor father.

He groped his way to the kitchen, and Ella caught him by the arm, saying, Come on here, till I bathe your eyes and wash your face. She sponged the caked matter from the lids of his eyes in water as hot as he could bear, grumbling most of the time she was doing it.

—It won't be long now till you'll have no servants to be dancing attendance on you. Cuddling's over, now, and you'll have to fend for yourself.

She washed his face and neck with particular vigour, combed his hair determinedly, twisted and bound a fresh bandage round his left eye, buttoned a collar round his neck, fixed his coat on, and brushed it briskly.

—Now, she said, sit down, take your breakfast, and give God thanks you have it.

He sat down by the deal kitchen table, the top worn thin by continual scouring, which had a white loaf in the centre, a drop of butter in the middle of a plate, seemingly miles from the rim, a cup and saucer, and, on the hob, a brown teapot that sparkled with the reflection of the flames that shot up every second from a warm coal fire. Tom was standing moodily by the fire, with one elbow leaning on the mantelpiece; Archie was drumming softly with his fingers on the window that looked out into the backyard; and there seemed to be a curious silence in the house; a silence that flooded in and flooded out whenever a door was opened; a silence that made the whole house feel silent and solemn.

—Four minutes past three, this morning, said Archie, just said to the mother, put your arms round me, Sue, and before she had time to call anyone, he was gone.

—I'm glad, murmured Ella, that mother has decided in having a closed-in hearse, for people that are anything at all always use a closed-in hearse.

—We've got the ground in perpetuity, said Archie, and no-one, bar ourselves, can ever be buried in it.

Something had run up against them, and had jolted them from one uncertainty into another. Not knowing exactly how to take it, they took it in silence; for the few words they said were invisible fingers pointing out the silence. They were harnessing, in ritual of word and manner, the disturbance and silence on to God, though His name was not mentioned. God would be present to help as long as they had to think of these things, for He was a very present help in time of trouble: Come in the evening, come in the morning, come when you're called, or come without warning.

The thing that had jolted them lay in the parlour, the little parlour, kept perpetually swept and garnished for visitors that demanded some ceremony, and were entitled to see all the best that the family had. The room with the horsehair-covered furniture, the polished mahogany cabinet, dainty little brackets, supported by little pillars, decorated with mirrors, that was called an overmantel; ecru lace curtains, girded in the middle with crimson knitted cords, on the windows. On a little table, by the window, a large glass bowl filled with clean water in which floated a coloured glass mermaid, with yellow hair, black spots for eyes, big breasts, with scarlet nipples on them, and a blue, yellow, and green tail, shaped like the tail of a fish. The mermaid had a golden comb in her hand, and she stared out of her glass bowl at all who came into the room and at all who went out of the room. Now her little black spots óf eyes were staring at something that lay very still in a bed at the opposite side of the room. On the wall over the bed was a big picture of Lord Nelson Bound for Trafalgar's Bay, all his orders aglitter on his breast, and he stepping out like a whole man for his last scrap in this world. Beside him walked a man in a white beaver hat, green cutaway coat, and brown plush knee-breeches. He was looking up into Nelson's face with a look of worship for the great one who had inspired The boy stood on the burning deck whence all but he had fled, the flame that lit the battle's wreck shone round him o'er the dead; while with one hand the same man in the cutaway coat and the brown plush knee-breeches, in the same picture, pushed aside a stout enthusiastic fishwoman who was trying to get close to the sailor hero, well away, and lack-a-day on his last road to do battle for his England, home, and beauty. Facing Nelson on the opposite wall was a picture of Queen Victoria, all decked out in her coronation robes, with none of the fun and all of the pomp, power, wealth, and parade of her colonial and Indian empire peering out of her bulgy blue eyes.

Here in the same room, under the stare from the paper faces of Lord Nelson and Queen Victoria, protected by the rear-guard of his beloved books, lay Michael O'Casside from Limerick. Stretched out he lay, his firmly-closed eyes staring backwards, arms and hands lying straight down by his sides, his dark beard so neatly trimmed that there wasn't a hair astray, nicely folded up for heaven beneath a snowy sheet, a sharply cut outline of stiffening flesh and bone: thought, education, toil, laughter, tears, sex, turned into dust and ashes.

Cold, stiff, and quiet the thing lay, while life outside hurried about settling everything for it, rushing to the registrar of deaths; going to leave an order for an open grave; selecting the coffin, heavy oak, with heavy brass plate and handles; hiring a four-horsed hearse; telling the clergyman the time of burial so that he would be on the spot to spread the rumour of the resurrection; letting people out who had seen the body and letting people in who hadn't; listening to and answering the murmur of questions.

—Hardly althered a bit although he was twelve and more months lying, but thank God that gave him a peaceful end to the end of it all, for he was a good man and quite happy now wherever he may be, sayin' that it was nothing short of hypocrisy to blame the romanists for veneratin' the relics of the saints when we ourselves snatched handkerchiefs an' tore them into shreds as sacred souvenirs because Moody and Sankey had wiped their brows and their noses in them after gassy speeches and holy serenades in the Rotunda or Christian Union building filled with souls packed like sardines together busy beseechin' that their sins bein' red like crimson might be made as white as snow, an' now when I look at him the nose seems a little thinner, no, yes just a shade, though you'd hardly notice it if you didn't look close from where I'm standin'; he simply put his arms round Sue's neck she says, says Dear Sue, dear dear Sue, sighed and stretched and stretched and sighed again a little, and went away where the good niggers go a little pale an' haggard-lookin', but she's bearin' up wonderfully under it all, was a cruel blow but God will lessen the knock in it in His own good time an' in His own peculiar way, for I nearly dropped when I heard her sayin' such a thing to a woman still weak with the first impressions after losin' her husband only a few moments before holdin' Sue's hand in a vicey way, out of place an' terribly ignorant, underminin' the sympathy simmerin' in your soul for the sorrow starin' you in the face with her folds shall be full of sheep and the valleys shall stand so thick with corn that they shall laugh and sing, makin' a conundrum of the connection between what she was sayin' and the mystery of the stiffness that's stretched out undher the snowiness of the death linen, unheeding Sue telling her of the sore that spread over the butt of his spine and the doctors looking anxiously couldn't make it out having come quietly after he lay down on the bed he's dead in now, following the giving under him of his legs getting thinner an' thinner every day that passed by with Sue his wife never ending tending to him, larding his limbs every night regular in the hope of some movement coming into them out of a doctor saying that you couldn't tell what would happen if you tried hard enough, thinking of what she'd do if he died with an unreared child clinging to her, and the gameness of him refusing to have any clergyman near him in his last moments, holding on to the fact there's no mediator between God and man save only the man Jesus Christ, messing about trying to twist the thoughts of a man to things of no account, slipping soft and slow into the arms of Jesus like the winds that blow from the south sighing so soft and low, whisper their secrets sweet, whisper and I shall know that he never missed sending his children as regular as clockwork to church, Bible class, and Sunday school, keeping them from spoiling the sabbath by singing hymns in the twilight when the lights were low and the flickerin' shadows softly come and go whenever the weather stopped them from going to worship God in His holy temple, showing that he was in favour of worshipping in spirit and in truth wherever two or three are gathered together in His name, hardening infancy into the ways of the Lord who is the rock himself an' not Peter, at all, who forgot himself whenever anything crossed the confidence and quietness of his mind by a torrent of curses that must have made the hair of the other apostles who weren't use to it stand on its end, listening to the crowing of the cock as he warmed himself at the fire and hearkening to the little maid saying that his voice showed plainly he must have come from Galilee, hiding himself frantically away from what he was, which is as bad as shoving on to show yourself forth for what you're not, like that Katie Johnston over there, trying to plunder attention from everyone round her with her bustle so pronounced as to form a swell altogether too lavishly extended over her behind, disturbing the gaunt and sober decency of the forms and signs gathered together in a house that has a stiff dead man lying in one of the rooms giving a species of serenity even to the pictures of Nelson and Queen Victoria hanging on the walls, who came up from Ballina only a couple of years ago wearing the airs and graces of having lived in Dublin all her life, though a city-cut skirt on a pair of country hips only helps to accentuate the difference between them, with the dry cough and the red-glazed cheeks tellin' of a comin' dissolution that'll happen vividly in the full knowledge of the present generation which should recommend to her, if anything ought, the marrying of the lunatic asylum attendant who's a bit queer himself, coming into constant contact with the mad people, and her mother making much of him in season an' out of season an' Katie keeping him at arm's length when she finds him thrilled and panting with the saucy delusion of getting him to tie her shoe beneath a skirt lifted to show a leg fading deliciously up under a cloud of white fancy flounces, or fastenin' a brooch slyly sliding out of her breast, purposely done to let him fiddle longingly with her diddies, an' after a little while when he was hot an' full of a choky sensation, puttin' the pin back in its place herself an' tellin' him an' thankin' him that would do nicely, gigglin' up in his face when she saw that he had gone far enough to try an' tear off every stitch she was wearing and fling her flat on the floor in front of the eyes of all in the room, shy at the sight of fifty-four years of experience gesturin' in frantic emotions that were only the resuscitation of a withered imitation of youth's spring, and go for a woman young enough to be a daughter as old as possible for the man to have, though it's not easy to blame a supple-legged lassie of twenty-three for thinking twice before takin' on the dhry, unlively, lack-pressure embraces of an old cod controlled by his years from doing anything desperate in the way of fanciful lovemaking which are unsuitable considerations for the occasion here present with us, sitting as we now are pressing the hard seats of chairs with tender bottoms burnin' for something soft under them while we are waiting for the men to come with the coffin so that the dead man may be made snug and ready before he goeth to his long home far away from this one where he'll nevermore have a portion, nor in anything that is done under the sun we all hope'll be shining when the poor body's taking its last tour through the streets, following the horses wearin' a resigned and determined look on their faces of no turning back while they're pulling their little cargo of what was once a man like meself, though I'm really a woman an' different in every way after gettin' down me a dollop of tea, I'll thry to forge to the front in the rush at the end of getting close to the clergyman doing the needful at the rim of the grave makin' the best of a bad bargain with God, tellin' Him of the words spoken by the mouth of His own apostle that appearances didn't matter a damn and that death had lost its sting and that the grave has been swallowed up in victory.

* * *

THE STREET SINGS

Golden and joyous were the days for Johnny when he was free from pain; when he could lift the bandage from his eye, and find the light that hurt him, hurt no longer; that the shining sun was as good today as it was when the Lord first made it; glorifying the dusty streets, and putting a new robe, like the wedding garment of the redeemed, on the dingy-fronted houses. Now he could jump into the sunlight, laugh, sing, shout, dance, and make merry in his heart, with no eye to see what he was doing, save only the eye of God, far away behind the blue sky in the daytime, and farther away still behind the golden stars of the night-time.

The pain was gone, and life was good and brave and honest and whole-some and true. No sitting down, cramped in every arm and leg at school. No whining out, now, of numbers and of words; no reading that gave no hope, or put no new thing in front for him to see; no maps that made the living world a thing of shreds an' patches; no longing for the day to hasten its slow march forward; no wearying talk of God and His davyjack, the giantkiller;—nothing but the blue sky with its white clouds by day, and the black sky with its silver stars by night; no thought but his own—and God's warning against joy a long way off from him.

Sitting on a window-sill, he could watch the women scouring their door-steps; or, possibly, one with a little more money, painting it a bright red or a fair blue; or, in old skirts and blouses, cleaning their windows with rags and paraffin, sometimes exchanging gossip from opposite sides of the street, both busy at the windows, and never once turning to look at one another.

He loved to see the bakers' carts trotting into the street, Johnston, Moo-ney, and O'Brien's cart at one end, and Boland's at the other, one coloured green and the other coloured a reddish brown. The carts were big and box-like, filled with double rows of shallow trays on which rested row after row of steaming loaves, tuppence or tuppence-farthing each. Underneath a deep deep drawer, going the whole length of the cart, filled with lovely white an' brown squares, soda squares, currant squares, and crown loaves, covered with their shining golden crust, ruggedly tapering at the top, like the upper part of a king's crown. He loved, too, to watch the milkcarts come jingling into the street, filled with shining churns, having big brass taps sticking out through holes in the tailboard, all polished up to the nines; though, as Johnny's mother often said, if they were as particular with the insides as they were with the outsides, the milk'd be safer to dhrink. From these big churns the milkman filled a can with a long snout on which rattled the half-pint and pint measures used to dish out the milk as it was required to the women waiting at the doors with jugs and mugs in their hands, to buy just enough milk that would temper the bitterness of the tea they so often made for themselves, their husbands, and their children. Whenever he was fit, Johnny used to help the milkman, running around with the long-snouted can, filling half-pints and pints of milk into outstretched jugs; the women constantly grumbling that Mr. Divene always gave them a betther tilly, so he did; Johnny defending himself by saying that he had to be careful with other people's property, so he had; and then, when the work was done, with the milkman sitting on the seat, he'd stand up in the cart, gather the reins in his hands, sing out a gee-gee-up, suit his balance cutely to the jig-jog of the cart, and drive the jennet back to the dairy.

Sometimes with other kids he'd stand stiff staring hard and listening curiously to a German band, foreigners—fleecing their pennies from the poor, so Archie said—wearing their blue uniforms braided with red or green, blowing their best into their big brass bugles; while the big drummer kept time, one two, one one, one two, to the tune of a song about a German soldier on his way with his regiment to the war:

> *They marched along down the village street,*
> *Their banners floating gay;*
> *The children cheered to the tramping feet,*
> *As they marched to the war away;*
> *But one of them turned around*
> *To look back once again,*
> *Although his lips gave forth no sound,*
> *His heart sang this refrain:*

> *Oh, love, dear love, be true,*
> *My heart is only thine;*
> *When the war is o'er, we'll part no more*
> *From Ehren on the Rhine.*
> *Oh, love, dear love, be true,*
> *My heart is only thine;*
> *When the war is o'er, we'll part no more*
> *From Ehren on the Rhine!*

On special nights, Johnny would hurry off to the back gate of the grocery store; would watch and wait for his opportunity to run over to the boxes that were piled against the wall, and swiftly pilfer all the lovely coloured sheets and slips of paper that had lined or bordered the boxes, gathering, like lightning, the blue, black, crimson, yellow, and green treasures to make crimson chevrons for his sleeves or yellow epaulettes for his shoulders; a green sash to go across his breast; blue belt round his waist; and many coloured strips waving gaily from his cap. Then armed with a home-made wooden sword, he turned himself into a warrior, a conqueror of many, bent on battle, free from terror, ready to strike at the first enemy that came near, as he strode along streaming with coloured orders persented to him by Her Majesty Queen Victoria. Whenever a chance came, he would share his treasures with a group of catholic boys, just home from school, decorating them with minor-coloured strips, changing them into soldiers, sergeants, with an ensign carrying a many-hued paper flag, and a drummer bearing on his hip a tin, veiled in strips of yellow and blue, rallying away for dear life, while the boys sang at the top of their voices,

We are ready for to fight,
We are the rovers;
We are all brave Parnell's men,
We are his gallant soldiers!

a song Johnny didn't like, for he was afraid that, in some way or another, it had a connection with the Fenians; though his mother had told him his father had said that Parnell was a great protestant, a great Irishman, and a grand man; and it was a good thing there was someone, anyway, fit to hinder the English from walking over the Irish people. When all the battles had been won; every country conquered; the army safely home again; the decorations carefully removed, collected, and put away again, till the army was needed again, it was grand to stand in the sunny street to wonder and argue about what would be the next best thing to do.

—Let's have a go at Duck on the Grawnshee, Touhy would say, an' I'm first.

—That me neck! Kelly would cry. Let's have Fox in the Den—a far betther game.

—Ball in the Decker, would be O'Halloran's choice; the daddy of them all, he'd add, an' I'm first.

—Count me out, if it's goin' to be Ball in the Decker, said Touhy.

—An' me, if it's goin' to be Duck on the Grawnshee, grumbled Kelly.

—Let Casside choose, then, said O'Halloran; an' for the sake o' the game, we'll fall in with whatever he chooses. Hands over your hearts, an' promise yeh'll abide be whatever he says.

The catholic boys got a thrill in playing with a protestant. All the things promised by the Church to them were far away from him. They stared with interest at the look of fear and wonder that came into his face whenever he saw them crossing themselves, or heard them muttering a Hail Mary to the chime of the Angelus. And Johnny, though he liked them, thought them strange and to be pitied; for it is written, idolators shall not inherit the kingdom of God; and these comrades of his worshipped images, said prayers for the dead, which is contrary to the plain word of Scripture wherein it is written, God is not the God of the dead, but of the livin'; and again, Blessed are the dead who die in the Lord; showin' as plain as a pikestaff that if you are good, and die, you go straight up; and, if you're bad, and die, you go straight down; so that when you're once dead, prayers availeth nothin'. Then, too, they had a mortal dread of the protestant Bible, the plain word of God, easy understood, even be kidgers; if you only have faith, and don't forget to ask God to open your eyes, you'll see all you want to see, an' hear all you want to hear, and understand all you want to understand of the truth as it is in Christ Jesus. Then they thought it a great sin to miss what they called Mass on Sundays an' holy days of obligation; and they had a curious custom of sprinkling themselves with holy water to keep the devil at a safe distance. Still, they laughed the same way as he laughed; and played the same way as he played; and shared what could be bought for a penny, whenever they had a penny to spend. So here he was in the midst of his catholic comrades, singing and shouting and playing and making merry in his heart; with no eye to see, save only the eye of God that never closed, now far away beyond the bright blue sky; and farther away at night, hidden behind the shine of the silver stars.

—Let's have Ball in the Decker, first, said Johnny, an' afterwards, Duck on the Grawnshee; an' I'll be last in both for the sake of the game.

Then they all laid their caps in a row at an angle against the wall of a house. They took turns, Touhy first and Johnny last, trying to roll a ball into one of the caps, the player doing his best to avoid rolling it into his own. When the ball rolled into a cap, the owner ran over to his cap, the rest scattering in flight, caught the ball up, and flung it at a boy nearest and easiest to hit. If he missed, a pebble was put in his cap, but if he hit a boy, then a pebble was put in the cap of the boy the ball had struck. The game went on till a boy had six pebbles or more (the number being decided at the beginning of the game). Then the boy with the six pebbles in his cap had to stand by the wall, and stretch out his arm, and press the back of his hand firm against the bricks. Then each boy, with a hard half-solid ball, had six shots at the outstretched hand; each aiming at hitting it as hard as he could, and enjoying the start of pain appearing on a boy's face whenever the hard ball crashed into the palm of his hand. Each boy had to go through the ordeal, the number of blows being the same as the number of pebbles in his cap. Johnny liked the ordeal; his hands were small and firm and hard, and the impact of the ball stung his hand far less than it stung the softer and larger hands of his comrades. So the game went on till they were tired, and many eyes were blinking back the tears from the smart of hands that were red, and stung fiercely.

Then followed Duck on the Grawnshee in which a marble was placed on a slight depression making it look like a squatting duck. Round the resting marble, a chalk circle was drawn. The boy who owned the duck on the grawnshee stood, with one foot within the chalk circle, watching the other boys who shot their marbles from the kerb, trying to knock the duck off the grawnshee. If a boy failed to knock it off, he had to gather up his marble again without letting himself be touched by the boy who was doing the duck on the grawnshee; if he was touched by the duck, with a foot in the circle, after lifting or touching his marble, then the touched boy became the duck, and the other joined the rest who were trying to knock the duck from the grawnshee. When the marbles thrown had stopped so near the duck that the outstretched hand of the boy who guarded the grawnshee could easily touch any who ventured to pick up a marble, the owners had to stand still, and depend on one who was a good shot to send the duck flying from the grawnshee, for when the duck was off the grawnshee the touch lost its magic, and the boys could seize their marbles and run off without danger, till the owner of the duck had replaced it on the grawnshee. So Johnny shot his marble at the duck on the grawnshee, or stood, watchful and alert, with one foot in the ring, ready to touch any boy within reach who made to get his marble lying motionless on the ground near the grawnshee; shouting, laughing as he did so, for hunger was forgotten, time had stopped, and his joy was full.

Often in the evening when the stars were still pale in the sky, the boys would see the girls skipping at the other end of the street, as many as ten or fifteen of them jumping gracefully over a regularly turning rope. The boys would slink up nearer and nearer to the skipping girls; the girls would occasionally glance disdainfully at the boys, but in their hearts they wished them to come closer. With a defiant shout, weakened with the tone of a shy shame in it, a boy, bolder than the rest, would jump in merrily; the rest would follow him, and joyous faces of boys and girls would shine out of thin dusty clouds raised out of the road by the beating of the skippers' feet dancing in the way of peace.

Tired of skipping, someone would suggest a ring; and boys and girls, their shyness gone, would join hands in a great ring, a girl, pretending to be weeping with her hands over her eyes, standing in the centre. Older people, the men smoking, the women knitting or gossiping, would stand at the doors, and watch the circling ring, singing as it circled,

> *Poor Jennie is a aweeping, aweeping, aweeping,*
> *Poor Jennie's aweeping on a bright Summer day.*
> *Pray tell us what you're weeping for, aweeping for, aweeping for,*
> *Pray tell us what you're weeping for on a bright Summer day.*

> *I'm weeping for my lover, my lover, my lover,*
> *I'm weeping for my lover on a bright Summer day,*

the girl in the center of the ring would answer.

Or the ring would stand still with arms held high while a player would dart in and out of the ring under the upraised arms as the circle of boys and girls sang in a metre livelier than the first tune,

> *In and out the window, in and out the window, in and out the*
> *window,*
> *As you have done before.*

Stand and face your lover, stand and face your lover, stand and face your lover,
As you have done before.

Shy, grey-eyed Jennie Clitheroe, with her curly head hanging, stood before Johnny. He wished she hadn't picked on him, for a lot in the ring knew he was gone on her, and had seen his uncovered eye often seeking her out as she sat on the seat opposite in the Sunday school; and his face went scarlet as he heard the titters of the ring.

Chase him all round Dublin, chase him all round Dublin, chase him all round Dublin,
As you have done before.

Johnny made off round the circle of players, dodging in and out under the upraised arms, with Jennie hotfoot after him. For a while he kept well in front, then slowed down so that she could catch him, but dodging her at the last moment so that she had to fling an arm round him. Pretending to struggle, he managed to give her girlish body a sudden and affectionate pressure, releasing her at once when the ring shouted Oh, Johnny, fie for shame!

So, in a cute and gentle way, this play and these songs touched the time when the girl would long to let him kiss her with the kisses of his mouth and his banner over her would be love.

Or, best of all, when the boys had come back from school; when they had done their home lessons, and had come out into the street to get what fun they could: some of them, with suitable sticks, would start a game of hurley; others would rush away, to return with old legs of chairs, ashplants with crooked ends, walking-sticks, or a rib of a big box, pared at one end to give a grip. Opposing sides would be chosen, and the real game would start—one group striking the ball up, the other group striking the ball down the street—pushing and cursing when the game went against them; and shouting and cheering when a goal was scored. And Johnny, with his long hair growing into his eyes; his bandage thrust like a wad into his pocket; his face flushed and wet with sweat, rushed here, rushed there, swinging Archie's ashplant, cursing, shouting, cheering with the best of them, pucking the ball viciously when it came his way, slashing at any shin that came too near the ball, his own legs trickling with blood from blows received from others, feeling no pain; for alive with energy, hunger was forgotten, time had stopped, and his voice rang loud in the chorus of the song of the street.

* * *

CRIME AND PUNISHMENT

✤ ✤ ✤

Without his usual cut of bread for lunch that day Johnny sat on a mangy clump of grass watching, with his good eye, Georgie Middleton and a group of cronies sitting between two church buttresses, playing cards, smoking fags, and arguing vigorously. He looked, came nearer; and Middleton lifted his head, and smiled.

—Come over here, and stand near me for luck, he said to Johnny.

Johnny came nearer, a little shyly, leaned a hand on Georgie's shoulder, and watched the play. They were playing twenty-fives for a penny a game and a ha'penny for the best trump out each deal. After every sixth game a boy took his turn for the following six games to stand aside and keep watch in case they should be suddenly surprised by oul' Slogan coming upon them unawares. Massey was now watching, and impatiently waiting for the six games to pass so that he could get back to the sport again. The cards were dealt, the tricks played and gathered, and Middleton won. Again the cards were dealt, given out, the tricks played and gathered, and again Middleton won.

—That's the third game for me, hand-runnin', said Middleton delightedly. Look alive, Ecret, and deal while the luck's my way.

—I'll deal, ejaculated Massey. That's the sixth game, now, and it's Ecret's turn to stand and keep nix.

—It's only the fifth, responded Ecret, there's another game to go yet.

—Sixth, I tell you, persisted Massey; didn't I count them carefully? So up with you off your hunkers, and take my place here.

—I tell you it's only the fifth game, growled Ecret, as he shuffled the cards.

—Sixth, sixth, sixth, repeated Massey impatiently, and he stretched over to take the pack of cards from Ecret's hands.

—No blasted bickerin', now, while I'm winnin', said Middleton testily.

—But fair's fair, grumbled Massey. I've watched here through the six games; and, accordin' to rules, it's Ecret's turn to take my place and keep nix for the crowd.

—Sit down then, snapped Middleton, eager to get another penny in the pool while he was winning; sit down, if you want a hand so badly, and Johnny, here, will keep nix for us all. He looked up at Johnny, and added, Make yourself useful, Johnny, be keepin' your good eye well peeled, an' if you see oul' balls Slogan turning the corner, give us the tip so that we'll all be talkin' about David watchin' Bathsheba havin' her bath, before he comes close.

Johnny became almost ill with fear that he wouldn't see Slogan quick enough, if he came round the corner. He hadn't the courage to say that his eye wasn't good enough; so he strained this one eye open, and stared fixedly at the corner round which Slogan would probably come, if he came at all. He prayed that he would not come, and that the bell would shortly be heard proclaiming that the time for cards was past, and that all must return to the song of the spelling and the sums.

—Somebody shy in the pool, said Middleton; only ninepence in it, so there's a wing missin'—who's shy?

—I am, said Massey, who was dealing the cards. When he had given them out, he added a penny to the pool. Ecret's lead, and spades is trumps, he added, peering expectantly into his hand.

They led and trumped and took their tricks; shuffled and cut and led and trumped and took their tricks, while Johnny stared and stared at the corner round which danger might come, and longed and longed for the warning bell to ring.

Suddenly there shot into his eyes a pain like the piercing of many needles, flooding into an agony that shocked his brain and flashed a glare of crimson light before him that made him clench his teeth and press his lids tight together till a stream of scalding evil tears forced their way between them, and ran hotly down his cheeks. Then he felt himself jerked back by the shoulders, and heard the sound of scrambling feet. When the pain subsided, he opened the good eye, and saw Slogan taking up the money in the pool, and gathering the cards, with a scowl on his face; while the group of boys looked on, embarrassed and silent. When Slogan had gathered up all the money and the cards, without speaking a word, he left them standing there, awkward and resentful.

Middleton turned savagely on Johnny.

—How the hell did you manage to let him sail down on the top of us like that? he snarled, but Johnny, burning with shame and shaking with sensitive fear, gave out no answer.

—Caught us all, like a lot of shaggy sheep, muttered Massey.

Middleton turned and struck Johnny sharply across the mouth with the back of his hand, making the boy's lip bleed, as he shouted, You half-blind, sappy-lidded, dead-in-the-head dummy, you couldn't keep your eyes skinned for a minute or two an' save the few bob we were bettin' from buyin' Bibles for the heathen buggers of Bengal!

—Caught us all, like a lot of shaggy sheep, muttered Massey.

Middleton gave Johnny a vicious shove that sent him reeling.

—Away, for Christ's sake outa me sight, you hand-gropin' pig's-eye-in-a-bottle, you!

The others laughed loud, crowded round Johnny, pushed and pinched him, as he turned and walked slowly away from them.

Turning the corner, he heard Slogan belling the end of the play-hour; and, passing the master, he entered the schoolroom, sat down in his place, and screwed his good eye into a lesson book, while his heart thumped in his breast. The boys poured into the school, and his classmates sat down beside him, whispering excitedly about all that had happened.

Suddenly the hum of the school was hushed, for Slogan, standing at his desk at the upper end of the room, was ringing his bell, and all the boys, save Johnny, knew that when the bell was rung from that place some very important thing was about to be said by the master. All that were in the school heard the master's voice coming out of the stillness, with a dull tone of joy in it, like the quavering notes of a sickening bird.

—As I was walking about the playground today—prowling about, I think you all call it—I caught a number of our more respectable boys deep in a very sinful pastime, a pastime that we can safely associate only with papist corner-boys; to-wit too-whoo videlicet, card-playing, and gambling like good ones in this game with the devil's prayer book, forgetful that they were protestant boys baptised in the brine of the Boyne water giving them a great responsibility to behave blameless before God and man and roman catholics, who are always on the alert to exaggerate any little indiscretion that respectable protestant boys may commit. In the first feeling of righteous indignation that came over me, I was going to make an example of every boy connected with this sin by giving each a sound and thorough whaling; but instead of that, I will leave it to their conscience to punish them more than a firm application of the cane could. But there is a certain boy mixed up with it whom no-one would think, at the first go, could be connected with the card-gambling, and this boy must be punished; and I am going to punish this boy now, and punish him well. I am going to punish him in such a way that he will think twice before he indulges in the vice again. This brave little fellow, on whom I'm going to test the valour of my cane, was on the *qui vive* so that the card-school wouldn't be disturbed by the bold bad teacher, but this brave little boy didn't watch well enough. He fell asleep at his post, and in a few minutes he is going to feel very sorry that he didn't keep a better Spartan watch and ward. That little boy's mother is a widow, so he has no father to take care of him; and it is meet, right, and my bounden duty to do everything possible to make sure that no bad tendencies are allowed to creep into the nature of the widow's little son. And when I have reddened his backside with this cane, I'm sure he'll be a better and more careful little boy for a long time to come, and run a mile away from a card whenever he sees one. He swished the cane through the air, and grinningly asked the school, Who was he who said, spare the rod and spoil the child, boys?

—Solomon, sir, Solomon, sir, shouted a dozen of the boys.

—And in what part of the Bible do we read that counsel?

—Proverbs, chapter thirteen, verse twenty-four, shouted a dozen of the boys.

—And what are the exact words, boys?

There was a dead silence, and only one boy held up his hand.

—Well, Ecret, my boy, tell the dunces the exact words used by the wise man, Solomon, when he advises us to deal in a bright way with bold boys.

—He that spareth his rod hateth his son, sang out Ecret, with his head up.

—And wasn't Solomon inspired of God? asked Slogan.

—Yessir, responded the school.

—How do we prove that? questioned the master.

The school was silent.

—All Holy Scripture is inspired of God, said Slogan, and the Book of Proverbs is part of Holy Scripture, and chapter thirteen and verse twenty-four is part of the Book of Proverbs; *ergo,* the counsel in the verse, he that spareth his rod hateth his son, is holy and inspired of God without a possible doubt. So, boys, wouldn't it be very sinful of me to neglect or despise the teaching inspired of God, seeing that I stand *in loco parentis* to you all, and particularly to the widow's little son, brave little Johnny Casside?

—Yessir, Yessir, responded the whole school, all save only Georgie Middleton, for Johnny saw that his head hung down, and that he took no part in what was going on between the boys and their master.

—The ayes have it, said Slogan, nodding brightly towards the boys; so come along, Johnny, come along up here to me, my son, till I pay you the attention counselled of God, which will be painful, but which will, ultimately, add a lot to your moral and, I hope, spiritual progress.

—Slogan's callin' y'up, whispered a boy on Johnny's right; wants to biff you for playin' cards durin' play-hour, so he does. But Johnny cowered his head down to the desk, and made no offer to stir.

—Eh, there, said a boy to his left, nudging him in the side, d'ye hear? He's callin' you. Y'are to g'up to him—d'ye hear?

—Come along, boy, said Slogan, down to Johnny; come along, and get it over. But Johnny hung his head towards the desk, and made no offer to stir.

—He hesitates, said Slogan. Thus conscience doth make cowards of us all; and thus the native hue of resolution is sicklied o'er with the pale cast of thought. Come on, come up here.

—He's not makin' a single move to stir, sir, said the boy on Johnny's left.

—Come on, come up, come up, come on, chirruped the master. Remember what your godfathers and godmothers promised for you—to submit yourself lowly and reverently to all your governors, teachers, spiritual pastors, and masters; so up you come; and in later years you'll rejoice when you remember the caning a good master gave you. Then he looked down at Johnny, and went on in a voice of quiet and steady sternness: Are you going to come up quietly, boy, to take your medicine, or must I go down, and wallop you up to me?

Johnny slowly and fearfully climbed out of the desk, and taking as many steps as possible, came towards Slogan, his heart thumping hard, and the sweat breaking out all over his forehead. He felt that Slogan wanted to beat away on him the fear that made him afraid to lay a hand on the other and bigger boys; for he had heard Middleton, Massey, and Ecret say that if Slogan ever tried any thrick of caning them, they'd open his bald skull with a slate. He halted a little distance away from the master, just out of reach of the cane.

—A little nearer, a little nearer, boy, purred Slogan; you've got to get it, so make up your mind to take it like a little Spartan. Tell me, boy, what's a Spartan? He doesn't know what a Spartan is, grinned Slogan, turning towards the school. Well, Spartans lived a long time ago in Greece, and were famous for bearing pain without a murmur. In Sparta every little boy, whether good or bad, was continually caned to make him hardy. So just shut your mouth, close your eyes, take your caning calmly, and all the school will look upon you as a little Spartan. I see your britches are a little threadbare, but that will make it all the more exciting for you. Now all we want are two strong and willing boys to come up here and stand ready to hold you down, if you squirm too much, so that you can get the full benefit of a kindly, if stern, Christian castigation. Whom shall I choose for the honour? And Slogan looked slowly and lovingly at the tense figures sitting in bunched-up lines in the yellow wooden desks.

—Will I do, sir? called out Massey, popping up his hand to attract the master's attention.

—You, Massey, said the master, will do nicely for one. You're pretty strong; and, if the need arises, I'm sure you will do your duty. Now, just one more. The biggest boy in the school ought to have the honour of holding the bold boy down—you, Georgie, come along here, and help.

Middleton's face reddened as he bent his head down to the desk and muttered, I'd rather not, sir.

Slogan put a hand behind a less-deaf ear, bent forward sideways, and said, Eh?

Middleton, keeping his head bent, raised his voice and said doggedly, I'd rather not, sir. I want no hand in any boy's batterin'; an' besides, the kid's too delicate to touch.

Slogan went white to the gills.

—Middleton, he said, with quiet bitterness, you had better learn to give an opinion only when your master asks for one.

Middleton suddenly stood up, and a dirty, dog-like scowl lined his harsh face as he pressed his soiled hands on the top of the desk so hard that the knuckles whitened.

—The kid had nothing to do with it, he rasped out; it was me and the others. He didn' play, an' doesn't know how, an' he kep' nix because we made him.

A deep silence spread over the whole school.

—Georgie Middleton, said Slogan, in a dead level voice, glancing over the whole school with his shallow eyes, will be leaving us all in a month or two to go out and fight his way in the world, and I'm sure we all wish him the best of luck. He is to try for a job in a big store where the manager wishes to give a start to a boy who has just left school. Mr. Middleton has asked our rector to give Georgie a character, and the rector has asked me for a general report of his conduct here. If Georgie wants to get on in the world with the help of a good start, I'd advise him to be careful to make his master think well of him. Am I right, Georgie Middleton? asked Slogan, now fixing his eyes on the head-bent boy.

Middleton fought his fear for a moment, then the whole school heard him murmur, Yessir, as he sank into his seat, shocked into the feeling that dangers flooded the way of an open courage.

—And don't you think, Georgie, that this boy here should be punished for his own sake? went on the master. There was a pause, and then the whole school heard the murmur of Yessir from the mouth of Middleton.

—Come along up here, then, said Slogan, and stand ready to help as soon as I need you. And Middleton, pale, and a little sick with shame, slouched up; and, sullen and bitterminded, stood near the radiant, iron-bowelled, ratty-hearted master, who put his hand out and patted Georgie's shoulder.

—You're a good boy, Georgie, he said, for you have had the manliness to acknowledge an error which many of us might very well hesitate to do; and there is more joy in heaven over one sinner that repenteth than over ninety and nine that need no repentance. And now, he went on, gripping Johnny by the collar of his coat, we start to cane a little conscience and a lot of caution into the soul of a wilful little boy.

Johnny shook when he felt the grip on his shoulder, and his stomach went a little sick with the foreknowledge of the pain that was to come upon him.

—Me mother said I wasn't to be touched because me eyes are bad, he said hurriedly and imploringly. Don't beat me, and I'll promise I'll never do the like again. Then he felt the searing sting of the cane across his thighs, and he screamed and tore at the master with his little hands, twisted his body and lashed out with his feet at the master's shins. Some of the kicks got home, the master gave a dog's yelp, and a burning glare of cruelty shot into his paly eyes.

—Here, Massey, and you, Middleton, he yelled, hold his arms stretched out over the desk till I knock the devil of resistance out of him!

The two boys caught hold of Johnny's arms and pulled him over the desk, leaving him at the mercy of the smiter, while the panting boy pleaded please, sir, don't. I didn't mean to watch for the card-playin', really I didn' —oh, you're cuttin' the skin off me!

But the bastard, sweating and puffing, with rigid snarling face and shining eyes, panted and sliced and cut and cut again and again. Johnny felt Massey twisting his arm, pretending that he was hard to hold. Slogan, at last easing off, gave a few more vicious strokes, then stopped to wipe his face in his handkerchief.

—Up on the chair with you, now, beside the desk, he said to the quivering boy, and let the school have a good look at you. A slice across the legs sent Johnny, with a suppressed cry, to leap quick on to the chair, chorused by a titter from the school at his haste to get there. Ashamed to rub the maddening sting in his backside and legs before the school, he balanced himself on the chair, with the eye-bandage that had loosened in the struggle, hanging round his neck, his eyes torturing him with the ache of the disease and the tears that had poured out of them, and his whole nature shaken with the confused wonder at what people were doing to him and what people were thinking of him; there he stood balancing on the chair, doing his best to check the sobs that tossed about the very beating of his heart.

Slogan looked at him for a minute, and then shook his head, and there was contempt in the shake.

—He wasn't much of a Spartan, after all, he said, turning to the school, with a grin, and the opinion I have of him now is less than the one I had before. Well, we'll have to be careful of him, for one sickly sheep infects the flock, and poisons all the rest. He glanced again at Johnny. We'll give him a minute or two to pull himself together and try to be a man, but if he goes on annoying the school with his baby blubbering, we'll have to cane him quiet—isn't that so?

—Yessir, chorused the school.

A bell rang for change of positions; those who had been seated in desks, formed into standing classes, and those who had been standing, sat themselves down in the desks. Johnny still shook a little with gentle crying till Slogan stood before him, angry, threatening, cane in hand.

—Finish the whinging, finish the whinging, boy, quick, or—and he shook the arm of Johnny. The boy tried to check the sobbing, tried to look calm, and sobbed again.

—Stop it at once. D'ye hear? Are you finished?

—Yessir, murmured Johnny.

—Finished, quite, quite finished, are you?

—Yessir.

—Well, let's hear no more of it. Not a squeak out of you, or the cane'll be twisting round your legs again.

With a steady effort of will, Johnny kept quiet, stood sullen on the chair, and waited and watched Slogan return to his desk, and bend over it to correct exercises. He looked at the thin stream of sunlight flowing in by the door, left open to give air to a room hot with the breath of children and teacher.

Then the bell rang again, and all that were standing filed into the desks. The Regulations of the Board of Education were turned with their face to the wall, and an oblong strip of millboard having written on it, Religious Education, was turned to face the school. Rapping on his desk with a heavy, glossy ebony ruler, Slogan silenced the murmur of the school. He put down the ruler on the desk beside him, and bent his hoary oul' head, saying softly, Let us pray.

There was a clatter of moving bodies as all got down on to their knees. Slogan knelt down, too, resting his hoary oul' head on his arms that rested on the seat of the chair from which he had risen to pray. The ebony ruler lay motionless on the desk beside him. O Lord, open Thou our eyes that we may behold wonderful things out of Thy law. The ebony ruler lay quiet on the desk beside him. Our Father which art in heaven. Hallowed be Thy Name. Johnny could see the pink baldy head of him, with its hoary edging, as Slogan bent down over the seat of the chair on which his arms rested.

Johnny suddenly slipped down from the chair he stood on, a flood of mighty rage swept through him; he whipped up the heavy ebony ruler, and with all the hate in all his heart, in all his mind, in all his soul, and in all his strength, and a swift upward swing of his arm, he brought the ebony ruler down on the pink, baldy, hoary oul' head of hoary oul' Slogan, feeling a desperate throb of joy when he heard the agonising yell that Slogan let out of him when the ebony ruler fell.

Still gripping the ebony ruler, he made for the open door and the sun. He saw Georgie Middleton grip Ecret's shoulder as Ecret made a movement to rise and stop his flight. He saw, as he flew past, the hand of Massey stretched out to hinder, and he heard the blasting curse of Massey in his ears as the ebony ruler came down on the outstretched hand. Away out through the door he dashed, across the road, down the narrow mucky Brady's Lane, shinned speedily up the rough-cut stone wall of the railway embankment, dropping the ruler as he climbed, heard in a clitter-clatter way the rush of an oncoming train, cleft by a sudden frightened, piercing whistle, plunged over the rails, checked for a second or two by the rush of the wind carried by the train as it went thundering by, saw dimly as in a mist a white-faced driver's mouth opening and shutting frantically; but pulling violently out of the intaking wind of the passing train, he sliddered down the other side of the embankment, ripping his trousers and tearing a rent in his leg with the jagged end of a jutting stone; rushed up the street opposite, turned down the next on the left, pushed open the hall-door of the house, burst into the room, and fell, exhausted and fainting, at his frightened mother's feet.

When he came to himself, his mother was bathing his body with water soothing and warm. The sting in his legs had ceased, for his mother had softened them with vaseline. He stretched his hand out, and gripped his mother's bodice.

—Don't let oul' Hunter or oul' Slogan come near me, Ma, he pleaded.

—They won't be let within an ace of you, she answered; but why did you come dashing in, and why did they beat you till your poor legs were covered with bunches of weals?

—Oul' Slogan bet an' bet me because he said I watched an' kep' nix for boys playin' cards behind the buttresses of the church at playtime. I couldn't get out of it for they were biggern me; an', besides, me eyes 'ud be in the way of me seein' how to use me mits in a fight; 'n I didn't want to, but they made me, 'n oul' Slogan came on top of us; 'n because all the boys were biggern me, he bet 'n bet me till he was tired.

His mother softly fixed the bandage round his bad eye, snuggled him gently under the bed-clothes, bent down and kissed him.

—Rest and sleep sound, she said, and forget all about it till the morning.

And he lay down safe with her who would watch over him, and wended his way into a deep sleep.

* * *

COMIN' OF AGE

(from "Pictures in the Hallway", 1942)

✤ ✤ ✤

Johnny was getting on in years now, growing old with the world and all who were in it. Lean and lanky he grew, with masses of hair growing low down in front, that his mother laboured to brush back from his forehead, saying he'd look as if he knew nothing if he hadn't a high brow. A few days before his fourteenth birthday, he could manage to read, skipping the biggest words, the stories in *The Boys of London and New York,* and the various coloured-cover penny adventure books, and *Ally Sloper,* a weekly comic, whenever he had the penny to spare for one of them. So, if you ask me, he knew nearly as much as there was to be known, and fit he was to take his place in the world, paddle his own canoe, and fill a job with the best boy going, as soon as he could get one. Every day Archie carefully scanned the "Situations Vacant" columns of the *Daily Express,* on the lookout for a suitable chance for Johnny.

Early on one fair morning in April, Johnny was wakened by having his shoulder shaken by his mother.

—Get up, she said, get up, like a good boy, for Archie has just come across the very thing for you.

Johnny slowly opened his sleep-dim eyes and murmured, Let him speak, for I can hear as well lyin' down as I can sittin' up.

—Get up, get up, man, said Archie impatiently; and when you've washed your face you'll be better able to take in what I've got to say to you.

Johnny got up, dressed, and washed his face, wondering how he could be able to understand better when all this had been done. Then he sat down by the fire to listen to what the one and only Archie had to say.

Archie opened out the *Daily Express* and looked earnestly into it. Then, in a stately and dignified voice, he read, A smart, respectable, and honest boy wanted. One just finished school preferred. Apply by letter to Hymdim, Leadem & Co., Henry Street, Dublin. There y'are, he added, the chance of a lifetime.

—Maybe a godsend, said his mother.

—A fine big Firm, said Archie, one o' th' biggest in th' whole city, an' protestant to the backbone.

—Johnny'll never know what he'll rise to, in a Firm like that, murmured the mother.

—Let him run down, now, to Ella, an' get her to write out a letther for him, applyin' for the job; an' another of her own as a schoolmisthress, sayin' Johnny was a good boy, an' most attentive to his studies, instructed Archie. Let her just sign it E. Benson, so as to show no sign that it was written by a woman.

—An' I'll ask Mrs. Middleton for the loan of her boy's new topcoat, said Mrs. Casside, for Johnny to have a betther chance of lookin' the boy the job was meant for; an', if he gets the job, we can get one for himself at a bob a week from oul' Greenberg. Hurry off, now, she said to Johnny, to your sisther, an' get her to write the two letthers; on your way there, buyin' a pennorth o' notepaper an' envelopes, a penny bottle of ink, an' a ha'penny pen, in case Ella 'ud be empty-handed. Then hurry back; I'll have th' coat waitin' for you, an' you can go at once and see if they'll give you th' job.

Johnny girded up his loins and set off at a quick walk to his sister's place in Summerhill, popping into a shop on the way and buying all he needed; quickening the walk to a quicker trot, then to the quickest gallop; sliding down, after a while, to a trot, then to a quick walk for a rest; then breaking into a gallop again, going on like Paul Revere to tell the town the enemy was on the way, till he came panting to his sister, showed her the news his mother had cut from the paper, and telling her what she had to do.

In a hurry, she washed her hands for fear of soiling the letter, and saying that when it was written he'd have to copy what she had written, for they'd know her neat hand was hardly the hand of a schoolboy. So when she had written, Jonnny, with his face screwed up, and with much labour and care, wrote in a large-lettered hand, the following:

Dear Sirs,
 I have observed by an advertisement appearing in the *Daily Express* of this morning's issue, that your Firm is in need of an honest, smart, and respectable boy, and that you prefer to employ one who has just finished school. I venture to say that I have all the qualities required, and, as I have just left school, I beg to offer myself as a candidate for the position.
 Very respectfully yours,
 JOHN CASSIDE

Messrs. Hymdim & Leadem.

Ella then wrote on another sheet of notepaper:

St. Mary's National School,
Lr. Dominick Street.

The Bearer, JOHN CASSIDE, has been a pupil in the above school, during which period I have always found him a truthful, honest, and obedient boy, and, at all times, most attentive to his studies. I feel sure he will give perfect satisfaction to any employer good enough to use his services.

E. BENSON,
School Teacher

Johnny hurried home with the letters; dressed himself in all his faded finery, putting the almost new blue Melton coat, loaned to his mother by Mrs. Middleton, over the lot, and hastened off to join those who were busy battling with the world.

When he came to Sackville Street, he felt hot and a little out of breath. He felt the sweat oozing out between his thighs, making his trousers feel a little damp. He had gone too quickly, he thought. His stomach felt as full as if he had just eaten a great meal, but he had had only a cup of tea and a cut of dry bread. Tight it felt as a tightly laced drum. If he could only pop into the job, without having to see anyone about it. Still, he was here, and in he'd have to go, and finish what he had begun. But better wait till he had cooled down a little; never do to show you were in a sweat to get it. Go in, cool and collected, and appear as if you didn't care whether you got it or not: and had just dropped in because you had nothing else to do, and the day was long. He'd sit here for a few seconds, till his heart got down to a quieter beat, and then go on: forward—the Buffs! He sat down on one of the pedestals of one of the General Post Office's great pillars, listening to the tram timekeeper, a brown-bearded man, wearing a half-tall hat, calling out for the trams to make a start: Sandymount, and away would go that tram; Palmerston Park, and away would go that tram too, with a tinkle from the bell the conductor pulled. All aboard for Palmerston Park, where the gentry lived. Most of them were moving to where the gentry lived, passing through the poorer quarters, out to where there were trees, air, and sunshine, where the gentry lived.

For the tenth time, Johnny took the letters from his pocket and read them, before he finally sealed them up for ever. Not so bad, he said, as he licked the flaps and closed them down, for if they want a genuinely honest, truthful, and willing boy, they needn't look over my shoulder for one.

He watched for a few more moments the soldiers streaming past him: Hussars, in their gorgeous crimson trousers; Army Service Corps, with their sober blue-and-white uniforms; Lancers, white-breasted, red-breasted, or yellow-breasted; Guards, in their tight little trousers, tight little white pea-jackets, tight little caps; Highlanders, with their kilts swinging—all on the hunt for girls; always strolling on the same side of the street, the west side, never on the other, where all the respectable people walked who didn't like to make a contact with a common soldier; from the corner of Great Britain Street, principally, to the Royal Bank of Ireland, back and forward, stopping when they made a catch, restlessly moving backwards and forwards, on the hunt for girls.

> *While up the street, each girl they meet,*
> *Will look so shy, then cry, my eye!*
> *Och! Isn't he a darling,*
> *Me bould sodger boy!*

He felt quite cool, now, so he licked three of his fingers, and smoothed his hair back from his forehead as far as it would go. He dusted the seat of his trousers, felt that his Eton collar sat still and safe, pulled the lapels of his blue Melton coat forward, and sallied up Henry Street, threading his way through the crowds of people coming out and going into the shops. Right into the big stores he dived, asking where he could deliver a letter that answered an advertisement wanting a truthful, honest, and willing boy. The far end of the great shop was pointed out to him, and he was told that when he passed through a door there, he would find a Mr. Anthony who would deal with the matter contained in the letter applying for the post. So Johnny went on a long journey by steep mountains of chandlery, terraces of lamps of every sort, table lamps, tiny lamps, bracket, hanging, hall, and reading lamps; small wick, wide wick, single wick, and double wick lamps; forests of brushes, hair, fibre, and twig; valleys of curtains, cloth, beads, and bamboo; huge rockeries of ironmongery; while overhead was a great gallery, circling the whole of the ground floor, filled with all kinds of delft and chinaware, beetling over all as if eager to look at all the other wonders piled in the valley below. Through all these he wended his way to a glass-panelled door leading to the packing and despatch departments. Pushing this open, he came into a long dark store, holding all the future supplies for the shop inside, and divided into heavy benches on which goods were piled, to be parcelled and packed and sent to various parts of the city and suburbs. On one side of this store, near the glass-panelled door, was a boxed-in office, full of windows, so that everything everywhere could be seen by a tiny lift of the head of anyone who might happen to be in it. In this office was a tall lean man, with a head like a fairly thin egg, whose hair began to sprout in the middle of his head, giving him the look of a waning scholar, who glanced up and looked at Johnny with a keen look in a pair of watery eyes that were thinly blue in colour.

Johnny, with his cap held respectfully under his arm, handed the two letters to this man, who was Anthony Dovergull, one of two brothers, owners of this big Firm of Messrs. Hymdim, Leadem & Company; the other brother (Johnny found out afterwards) was as jet-black as this one was fair, with a heavy moustache losing itself in a heavy coal-black beard (his brother was clean-shaven), with brilliant black eyes that never knew how to soften. He was as tall as his fair brother, but had thick legs, massive shoulders, like a bull's, that gathered together and bent, when he was angry, like a bull about to charge; and his only smile, seen when the House was doing good business, was like a wintry sunbeam finding a home in an icicle. The dark fellow watched over the front of the Firm, standing on a bridge stretching from one side of the chinaware gallery to the other, stood all the day like a skipper on the bridge of a ship.

Mr. Anthony Dovergull took the letters from Johnny, read them silently, and looked Johnny all over. Johnny was glad that he had Middleton's Melton overcoat on him. Then Mr. Anthony read the letters again, thought for a moment or two; then looked at Johnny again.

—You are a protestant, young man, are you not? he asked.

—Oh, yes, of course, sir, answered Johnny, feeling that he had a close kinship with the mighty man in the boxed-in office.

—Well, we'll try you, said Mr. Anthony. You can start tomorrow morning. Hours, eight till six; wages, three shillings and sixpence a week; rising, of course, annually, if your services are found to be satisfactory. And he dismissed Johnny by turning to resume the work he had been doing when Johnny handed him the letters.

So here he was standing in the street again, a child of fortune, a member of Hymdim, Leadem & Company, and an inheritor of three shillings and sixpence a week. He had made a flying start. He would begin life at eight o'clock the following morning. In the morning his life would break into bud. Aaron's rod all over again; it would bud and blossom. He was a child no longer. He had put childish things far from him. He was a worker. Henceforth he would earn his bread in the sweat of his face. The earth was his, and the fulness thereof. Glory be to God. Out of the darkness had come a saving light.

And Johnny felt that it was good; and the morning and the evening were the fair'st day.

BRING FORTH THE BEST ROBE

✢ ✢ ✢

Johnny was up betimes, gay and fussy, in the morning. He took no notice of his mother advising him to get down as much bread as he could, for he'd have a long fast; but hurried over his breakfast, and, excited and nervous, got into the new array, brown coat, long trousers, grey cap, and new black boots, got from Mr. Greenberg the previous day.

Mr. Greenberg was a Jew; not an ordinary Jew, Johnny's mother said, but a most respectable one. He had never carried a pack, but had turned the front room of a little house in a terrace off the Drumcondra Road into a shop. There clients came quietly to be satisfied, after a bargain made in their own houses. He had come to Johnny's house the evening before, and had promised to fit out Johnny from top to toe for five shillings down, and the rest of two pounds ten to be paid at one shilling a week; the instalments to be paid on the first day of every month. Mrs. Casside had paid the five shillings deposit, and he had entered it in a little blue-covered pass-book below the articles bought: A brown suit, one pound; a navy-blue topcoat, one pound; pair of boots, ten shillings; and the grey cap, Mr. Greenberg said, because of the boy making a start in life, would be thrown in free. Thrown in free, he murmured again, with a sigh. He glanced round the room, saw its scanty furniture, and sighed again. Didn't look like a very promising customer. His eyes roved over the collection of books that remained out of all that Johnny's Da had loved. His eyes took on a look of surprise. He went over to where they were, and took one of them into his hand, a thick, heavy, purple-covered one. It was *The Wars of the Jews,* and he opened it, and began to read.

—One of my poor husband's books, murmured Mrs. Casside.

—Ah! said Mr. Greenberg, Josephus, Josephus; a great writer; a great man. Our people, our poor people. Have you rread it, Mrs. Casside?

—No, indeed, I'm sorry to say, she answered. But my poor husband knew it near by heart. Everyone regarded him as a great scholar. Nothing was beyond him.

—Ah! said Mr. Greenberg murmuringly, zee gruel, derreeble, veeked Romans! Ven they took Jerusalem and destroyed dee ceety, they crucified us in dousandts, dousandts, and dousandts. Zey could not get enough vood to make zee crosses they needed; dousandts and dousandts.

—What, the Holy Romans? asked Johnny.

Mr. Greenberg turned towards Johnny, with a puzzled look on his face.

—He means the roman catholics, explained Mrs. Casside.

—Not zee catolics, not zee roman catolics, said, Mr. Greenberg. Zee old Romans, zee ancient vones, years and years ago, hunderts and hunderts of years before you or I vos born. But eet is all ofer now, he added; all ofer now. It ees lif, and—vot you say? he asked of Mrs. Casside.

—Live an' let live, she said.

—Live, and let live, he repeated. Ve are—vot you call it?—ceevilised now. He put the book back where he got it, and settled his half-tall hat on his head, and stroked his beard thoughtfully.

—Goodbye, he said, shaking hands with Johnny; you vill find zee goods vot you want: a vonderful bargain. And read zee vars of zee Jews, my boy, ven you haf dime, ven you haf dime. It ees goot to read books; zey dell you zings, and it is goot to know zings; zee more zee better. Goodbye, my boy, and goot luck.

—Rather a nice old boy, for a Jew, said Johnny when he had gone.

—He's all right, replied his mother, but he knows how to charge, all the same. Had I had the ready money, I'd have got all he's given for half the cost, an' less.

Here he was now, dressed in the new garments, at a quarter-past seven in the morning, with his mother putting the last touches to them; pulling down his dark-blue topcoat behind him, fixing his cap straight on his carefully brushed hair; going to the door with him, advising him not to be nervous, and bidding him godspeed.

Johnny hurried along the almost empty streets and passed the closed-up shops, opening his topcoat wide so that the few who passed at this early hour could see that he was wearing long trousers. What a swell he looked, and what a man he felt as he trudged gaily and swiftly along. A few trams, with nobody in them, hung around Nelson's Pillar, looking higher and statelier for the want of a crowd. Only the pubs were beginning to open as he went by, grocers' porters slashing buckets of water in front of the brightly-painted fronts to take away the raucous smells and smudges of the night before. Johnny got to the Firm nearly half an hour before the time of opening; and he leaned against the sombre revolving shutters, waiting for whomsoever came to open up the shop for the work of the day. There was nothing but a dog wandering up the street; and even the great General Post Office looked surly and sad. Opposite him loomed up the great drapery firm of Sir John Arnott & Co., another firm, he knew, stocked with good protestants as tightly as it was stocked with good goods. There wasn't a doubt about it; we were, in some way or other, a goodlier run of people than the poor roman catholics.

At five minutes to eight he noticed that men and boys began to gather, and lean against the sombre shutters, just as he was doing, some of them glancing at him, curiously, as they settled their backs into a comfortable position. Eight o'clock struck from the big clock outside Arnott's, and still no-one came to open the shop. He edged a little nearer to the waiting crowd so that he might catch a word or two of what was being said.

—Musta slept it out this morning, he heard one man say, when the clock showed it was five minutes past the hour.

—He's given us time for a longer smoke before dinnertime, responded another; but you'll soon see him come gallopin' round the corner. Didn't I tell you, he added, for here he comes fallin' over himself with the dint of hurry.

Johnny saw the long lank figure of him who had given him his job hurrying up the street, black suit, black bowler hat, black gloves, and black umbrella, like a thin black bat fluttering in a hurry along to get in out of the daylight. Anthony came up, and, without as much as a good-morning to a soul, opened the black wicket-gate in the centre of the shutters, and hurried in, the crowd of clerks and boy assistants pouring in, one by one, after him. And Johnny, last of all, went in too, and found himself in the lonely darkened shop full of the smell of soda, soap, candles, and beeswax.

They all streamed away to where they left their coats and hats, leaving Johnny standing alone, alone in a darkened world, with the hundreds of lamps hanging overhead looking like stars that had died down, had lost their light, and shone in the firmament no longer.

Presently, he saw a man at the far end of the shop beckoning to him. He went down and stood in front of a man with a pale, handsome, Jewish-like face, who looked him all over, smiled rather sarcastically, and said, Mr. Anthony tells me you're the new boy assistant, and you're to come with me so that I can show you what to do, and generally show you the way about the Firm. This man was Mr. Prowle, an Orangeman, it was said, who was over the despatch of all things going away by rail or sea; a silent man, who spoke to no-one, and no-one spoke to him; always looking like a juvenile mariner, waiting on a painted ship upon a painted ocean.

He went before Johnny through the door leading to the despatch store, and, showing Johnny a huge pile of waste paper, said, Sort that, smooth the sheets out in their different sizes, put holes through them when the heaps are big enough, and string them up for use in parcelling up the goods we send away. When that's done, tie up all those clothes-pegs into dozens, and pile them neatly on the shelf behind you.

While he was working away at the waste paper, Johnny saw two messengers carry a small bench over into a corner of the stores, and cover it with a bright-green cloth, on which they placed a big white vase filled with red and yellow artificial flowers, making it look, for all the world, like a clumsy-looking altar. Then they carried two big parcels and placed them on the bench covered with a green cloth. Each parcel was backed by a big label, bearing on one the words, For Good Boy, Number One; and on the other, For Good Boy, Number Two. Stuck jauntily into the first parcel was a little paper Union Jack, with a bronze shaft as thick as a knitting needle, and a gilded paper point; on the other parcel, a little Royal Standard of the same kind. In front of each parcel stood a rather faded bowler hat, one lined with white silk and the other with crimson. And everyone who passed by wore a wide fat grin, holding tight to it, and not suffering it to depart when they had gone by. Johnny noticed, too, that Mr. Anthony, in his desk above at the top of the store, wore a grin too; a quieter and more subdued one, as if he just done something good and pleasant and quietly noble.

Johnny was working like a good one, tying the pegs into dozens, when Prowle called him, handed him a slip, and told him to get the things mentioned on it and parcel them up for him.

Johnny stared at the pencilled slip, and couldn't make head or tail of it. Six lbs.—that was clear enough, but what did S *Sp* mean? Or *B w cls,* or *Bwx* mean? He looked and stared and looked again for a long time, till Prowle snatched the slip out of his hand.

—Can't you read? he asked sharply. What school did you go to?

—He went to college, said a packer at the other side of the bench, eager to fall in with Prowle; none o' your common schools for him.

—Six pounds of Sunlight soap, two of British wax candles and a pound of beeswax—could anything be plainer? You'll have to brighten yourself, me boy, if you want to stay here. We don't want duffers. They're all on the shelves behind you; open your eyes and you'll find them, said Mr. Prowle.

Johnny strayed up and down the long avenue of shelves, looking for what was on the slip. Probing the spaces, he came near to the desk where Nearus, the head clerk of the stores, was writing. Nearus was a big fellow, over six foot, and broad-shouldered; good and kind of heart he was, as Johnny soon discovered; but he was rotten at the core, for, on the top of each cheek, he wore the rosy cross of consumption, and a cough told the tale of a tomb.

—What are you looking for, what are you looking for? he asked, in a rough-and-ready way, when Johnny came close to him; but there was a soft note in the bark of his voice. There you are, he added, pointing to some shelves; candles there; soap here; and the beeswax over your little head. He took down the things himself as he spoke, and laid them on the counter for Johnny. If you're in any fix at any time, come to me, and don't fret if I shout the answer at you.

So the long day wore on, with Johnny, under the firmament of heaven, tying up pegs into dozens, sorting out paper, running all sorts of errands, finding out how puzzling little words could be when they were written down on paper, discovering, like an explorer, the new regions of the big Firm, and learning where the multitude of differing stores were packed away in their various places; all the time glancing frequently at the bench covered with the green cloth, and wondering what was in the parcels, and why everyone smiled as they passed the parcels by.

Coming back five minutes before the time at lunch hour, he found Nearus alone, bending over his desk, busy with an army of figures. He glanced up when he saw Johnny signing on in the book that lay, like a warrior taking his rest, beside the big desk of Nearus.

—Eh, kid, he said, is that a new suit of clothes you've on you, or is it only an old one varnished?

—New one, sir, said Johnny; bought only yesterday.

—Well, it won't be worth a wax in a week here, man. No one wears a new suit working. Bring an old coat with you tomorrow, and hide it under the bench to wear when you're working. It's enough to look a toff when you're coming in to start, or going out when you're finished.

Thank you, said Johnny. I'll tell my Ma when I get home.

—Well, kid, he said, how do you think you'll like your job?

—I'm sure to like it well, said Johnny; all the people here seem so happy and smiling.

He beckoned to Johnny to come a little nearer, and bent over till his mouth was close to Johnny's ear.

—Keep your mouth shut and your ears open, and you won't see much, he said. They're all a gang of superior hangmen here. They're smiling today because they have to, for today is the great day of atonement. Know what atonement means?

Being at one with someone who has had a row with you, said Johnny.

—If you din't knock it down, you staggered it, said Nearus. Well, we're all, for this one day of the year, at one with Mr. Anthony and Mr. Hewson, and that's why we're all smiling, my boy. The master is at one with the man, and the man is at one with the master. He stretched a big and thinning hand towards the bench covered with the green cloth. And that's the altar of friendship, he said.

—An' what's in th' parcels? asked Johnny.

—Goodly threasures for two goodly men, answered Nearus. An old suit that Anthony's tired wearing, and another that Hewson's tired wearing, for Enthrews, the packer here, and O'Reilly, the porter in the front shop.

—They must be two good men, murmured Johnny, for he wist not what to say rightly.

—Too good for God, said Nearus. He leaned over closer to Johnny, and whispered in his ear: Don't ever say anything to either of them; don't let them hear you saying anything to anyone else; don't even let them hear you saying your prayers.

Others began to come back from lunch. Nearus got close to his desk to fight the army of figures again, and Johnny went his way behind the great counter to his tying of pegs, sorting of paper, or any extra thing he might be called upon to do.

The long day wore on, and the quiet evening came, and the work slackened when it was but an half-hour before the time to quit.

And all the house was smiling, all except Nearus; for Johnny thought it would be a good thing to smile too.

Suddenly the big black Hewson came in from the front shop, and, joining the skinny, fair-eyed Anthony, both of them, smiling, sauntered down to where the bench, covered with the green cloth, was standing, looking like a clumsy altar bearing on it outward and visible signs of an inward and spiritual grace. Shortly afterwards O'Reilly came in from the front shop, and stood, smiling, at the north end of the store, while the packer Enthrews stood smiling, at the other end, gently tapping straw into a case he was packing for the country. The vanmen, messengers, and other packers stood in a grinning group near the big gateway; and the clerks from the various despatch rooms, and the assistants from the front shop, came hurrying in and stood in a smiling row along the length of the warehouse, their eyes staring at the bench covered with the bright-green cloth. Then, after a fit pause, Mr. Hewson beckoned to Enthrews, and Mr. Anthony beckoned to O'Reilly; and the two came, each from the other end of the earth, trusting, not in their own righteousness, but in the manifold and great goodness of their two Masters, who were ready to bestow upon them some of the crumbs that would soon fall from the table covered with the green cloth.

And when they drew near, Hewson stretched out his hand and took a parcel, and handed it to Enthrews, at the same time that Anthony stretched out his hand and took a parcel, and handed it to O'Reilly. Then Hewson placed a bowler hat on the head of O'Reilly, and Anthony placed a bowler hat on the head of Enthrews, and lo! both were crowned, and a fine glory shone round about them; and a lowly murmur of praise went up from the clerks, assistants, vanmen, and messengers, as they saw this good thing done, and the murmur testified to the goodwill among men.

And Enthrews opened his mouth, saying unto Anthony, Thanks be unto thee, O sir; your kindness was unexpected, and your goodness endureth for ever.

And O'Reilly opened his mouth, saying unto Hewson, Thanks be unto thee, O sir; your goodness was unexpected, and your kindness endureth for ever.

Then the two men who had been so favoured went into a secret place to take off their old clothes and put on the new garments that had been given them; while Hewson and Anthony, smiling and chatting together in amity and peace, waited leaning against the bench that was covered with the bright-green cloth.

And Johnny, looking on, fancied he heard a voice from heaven saying, Let your light so shine before men that they may see your good works, and glorify your Father which is in heaven.

By and by the two came back rejoicing, clad in their new raiment, walking the one after the other, sellovish pride irrigating both their hearts, lifting their eyes to the hills, passing backwards through a lane-way of smiles; Enthrews with the little Union Jack sticking up from the band on his bowler hat, and O'Reilly with the little Royal Standard sticking up from the band in his.

And all hands were admonished by this display to behave better and to serve honestly the two men who, now and again, deigned to think of common men, and to look down from the ownership of might and mercy in the centre of Dublin City, hard by the protestant church on the one hand and the catholic church on the other.

A low, lorn murmur of satisfaction rose from the assembled clerks, assistants, vanmen, and messengers; and in the midst of the murmur Mr. Anthony and Mr. Hewson moved away from the bench that was covered with the bright-green cloth, and walked slowly towards the glass-panelled door leading to the front shop. Then Mr. Prowle lifted up his fine voice a little, in a respectable manner, and sang, and all except Nearus, who coughed and leant over his desk with his head bent down, joined in, singing softly, soberly and slyly, for very fear that God might hear them:

> *An' here's a hand, my trusty fiere,*
> *An' gie's a hand o' thine;*
> *An' we'll tak' a right guid-willie waught,*
> *For auld lang syne!*
> *For auld lang syne, my dear,*
> *For auld lang syne,*
> *We'll tak' a cup o' kindness yet,*
> *For auld lang syne!*

Then it was time to go and all slunk their several ways home for the night, to eat, to whore, to sleep, perchance to dream. And Johnny went with them. Peace and fellowship were everywhere; but Johnny felt uneasy, and saw that it was not good; and the morning and the evening were the sicken'd day.

* * *

THE SHAME IS A THIEF AND A ROBBER

✠ ✠ ✠

Johnny, working away, had grown in wisdom, if he hadn't grown in grace. Although there was nothing against him, he knew the heads of the house didn't like him. Many whispers had dribbled into his ear, asking him to come to the meetings in Merrion Hall, but Johnny, saying that he felt it was all very nice and comfortable and godly, didn't ever go; and once, in a fit of recklessness, said to one of the evangelical whisperers that he'd rather open a girl's bodice than open a prayer-book, making the whisperer turn pale and turn tail and hurry away in a hot quick trot. But, still an' all, he had learned a few things. He could make out, without any bother, the differing handwriting of assistants and vanmen; count money quick and correctly; balance three hundredweight on a truck nicely, and push it safely; lay out orders swiftly, and parcel up goods; pack chinaware with any packer in the shop; stand on a high ladder, and catch, with a cunning hand, packages thrown up to him for packing away on to high shelves; cleverly handle casks of oil; tip over heavy cases towards him, and edge them from where they were to where they ought to be; carry six-stone loads on his back through long distances for hours, without feeling faint at the end of the day; and fight his corner with the best or worst of those who worked around him.

The vanmen and messengers had fought shy of him for a long time, ever suspicious of a member of the staff; but one time, when a messenger happened to be in his way and delayed to get out of it, Johnny had given the fellow a hasty kick in the backside; and had suddenly found himself on his back in the straw from a puck in the snout the angry messenger had given him. He, thinking he had hit another messenger, got the fright of his life when his rage let him see it had been Johnny, one of the staff, hurrying to help Johnny up, and murmuring, for fear of losing his job, that he hadn't meant it, hadn't known it was Casside, thought it was only another messenger, and begging Johnny, with tears in his eyes, to say nothing about it. Johnny had shaken hands with him, saying, never fear, for a Casside was never known to be an informer; and, after that, Johnny was the heart of the rowl with vanmen and messengers, especially when they found out he could curse with the worst of them.

Johnny was feeling very cocky, and now marched about with a long-handled pen stuck behind his right ear. He had been promoted to the bright position of despatch clerk, over the Sandymount and Ringsend delivery, at a salary of six shillings a week. Every Friday he handed his mother four and six out of his wages, for he let on he'd only five, which was fair and square, for wasn't it him who earned the money, an' hadn't she only to sthretch out her hand to take it? An' looka all he gave her besides. He had now a free hand in getting goods for the customers his vanmen served, so why couldn't he get a few goods for himself? No sooner asked than answered. Johnny in his heart decided that it was neither godly nor wise to muzzle the ox that treadeth out the corn. So, on principle, he never went home without bringing something with him; and, after a while, his mother, with a few frightened warnings to him to take care, made a few special pockets in his coat, deep and wide so that things could be spread out without bulging. So he carried home tiny cargoes of matches, soap, candles,

borax, ink, blacking, ketchup, tins of enamel. Hudson's extract of soap and
Monkey Brand that wouldn't wash clothes, an odd knife and fork, now and
again, a spoon occasionally, combs and hairbrushes, chamois leather, egg-
cups—though they were more ornamental than useful—salt-cellars, night-
lights, knife polish, with a picture of Wellington on the tin, shoebrushes,
clothes-brushes, floor-cloths—particularly prized by his mother—small
scrubbing-brushes, Goddard's Plate Powder that went to Tom and Mick to
clean their buttons and badges, at tuppence a tin, little white-headed mops
for cleaning lamp chimneys, among other things, with various little toys at
Christmas for Ella's kids, and, any over, for the kids in the neighbourhood,
Johnny getting the blessing of the mothers for his kind thought of bringing
to the poor kids a real ray of Christmas kinsolation.

It was quite an innocent practice, thought Johnny; not like the heavy-
handed foolishness of poor Botolph, the young clerk over the Rathmines
delivery, who had landed himself in a raw plight with his picking and
stealing; and was turned out of the Firm for ever one day as soon as he had
come back from his lunch. Through a customer sending back goods paid for
to the vanman at the door, Anthony found that no record existed of the
payment in the vanman's book or in Botolph's ledger; and growing suspicious, they had watched for a week, and found that the bold Botolph
entered up no bill that had to be paid, nor did any of them appear in the
vanman's book. The vanman, pressed to explain, stammered that it must be
a mistake; threatened with the police, he blurted out that this thing had
been going on for some weeks; that the money received had been divided,
two-thirds to Botolph and one-third to him; yessir, months, maybe, I can't
well remember when I was led into it; it was Botolph who had enticed him
to thievery, for he was naturally a very honest man, very, as all the world
knew; Botolph had kept on appealing, persuading, nagging him, till he gave
in for the sake of peace; he often an' often made up his mind to tell Mr.
Anthony all 'bout it, but, somehow or other, it went out of his mind; an'
wasn't it a poor thing that a decent, honest, sober, steady, and most respectable workman an' vanman should have been thrapped into thievery by a
vicious, dangerous, eely gougher.

Botolph standing beside him, pale as the twin brother of death, mois-
tened his cracking lips and biting his hot nails, backing, backing till his
back felt the prop of a bench, for he was frightened and getting faint.

And Anthony, stern and stiff and tight-lipped, listened, and said, in a
voice loud enough to be heard by the hard o' hearing, while all listened so
as not to miss a word of it:

—You have been a vanman here in a Firm that any common man would
be proud to work for; you have answered that honour by turning out to be a
vagabond, a mean thief, a perverse reprobate, a ragged rogue. Leave my
sight, you ruffian!

And the vanman, with tears trickling down his cheeks, departed from the sight of his master, Dyke giving him a vicious kick in the arse, followed by one from Enthrews, and one each from the messengers, while, finally, Johnny got one home on him as he passed out by the gate; but he suffered them all gladly, in return for the sad things he had done, and never putting a single sign of quickness into his steps as he went slowly down the passage.

They had brought down Botolph's sister to be in at the death. In she came between Hewson and Sorrasaint, a plump, reddish-haired youngster with grey eyes and a face full of freckles. Not a one to want to put yoor arms around, thought Johnny, unless your sight was failin'. She had been told of what had happened, and had been given her walking papers, everyone concurring in the impossibility of her staying in a Firm her brother had robbed.

She stood there, dressed in black, with a white frill on her neck, tight white-starched bands round her wrists, a black felt hat with a green bird's wing in the band, and a brooch of an ivory deer, running hard, in an oval brass-rimmed case, rising and falling on her bosom.

She stood there, a step away from her brother, two away from Anthony, a little handkerchief sheltering her face, crying softly into it, waiting to hear what Anthony had to say to her brother.

Anthony, when he had seen the stricken vanman fade away round the gateway, slowly turned his head, and gazed on Botolph slinking against the bench behind him, rigid, staring, and seemingly unable even to bend his head away from Anthony's snaky stare.

—Come nearer, sir, come a little nearer, said Anthony.

Botolph shoved himself away from the propping bench, and took a few paltry, shuffling steps nearer to Anthony.

—Were it not that we don't wish to make it known that our Firm could possibly graft a thief on to its staff, said Anthony, you'd be leaving my presence now tucked into the arms of two policemen. Though the sun may shine on the evil and the good, the sun will not be allowed to shine on the evil here. You have been given the privilege of working for a Firm with a reputation as high as any Firm could hold; you had a fine future in front of you; but you elected to become perverse and dishonest; and have brought shame upon your family and ruin to your sister. Had you not wickedly chosen a froward life, you would today have been receiving your wages instead of your dismissal. Instead of being a trusted servant, you are now but a low-minded rascal and a decently clad thief. We are all very glad to be rid of you. Get out of my sight, you laundered vagabond!

And Botolph, moistening his stiff lips, trying to keep his twitching legs steady, stumbled away from the face of his master, Dyke giving him a vicious kick as he passed by, followed by one from Enthrews, and one each from the messengers who happened to be within range, Johnny finally getting one home on him as he shuffled out by the gateway into the lane. Botolph bore them all well, sighing for the sad things he had done, and feeling that these things were but a small penalty to suffer for his mischievous behaviour.

—Phew! said Dyke, with his nose in the air, and loud enough for Anthony, Hewson, and Sorrasaint to hear him, thank God that stink is gone! The air already feels a lot fresher without it.

Hewson and Sorrasaint turned and went back to their haunts in the front shop, and Anthony withdrew into his shell of an office, leaving the freckle-faced, red-haired girl, in black, standing against the desk of Nearus, with her face sheltered in her little handkerchief, and the brooch of an ivory deer, running hard, within the oval of the brass circle, rising and falling on her bosom.

After a few minutes of quiet crying, Nearus bent over his desk and touched her on the shoulder.

—Steal away home, girl, he said softly, and lie away as far as you can from everything that has happened to you today.

The touch startled her into movement. She moved away from the desk, keeping the little handkerchief pressed to her face; and the black figure, the felt hat, with the bird's green wing in it, and the ivory deer, running hard, went down the passage, out of the gateway, and passed out of the sight and scene of the shop for ever.

All this had happened yesterday, and Johnny was picturing it in his mind all over again as he walked along Sackville Street, glancing at the fireman sitting outside his sentry-box, smoking his pipe under the stars that filled the sky, and ready at a second's warning to unlock the fire-escape chained through the spokes of a wheel to a stone post, and hasten, with a crowd of eager civilians, to push it wherever the fire might be.

Johnny was hurrying on to meet his vanman, Dorin, at Dooney's pub in Great Britain Street, thinking all the time of the kicks, Botolph, and the ivory deer, running hard, on the bosom of a crying red-haired girl. Dorin, a day or two ago, had seen the heap of cracked delft and ironmongery that Anthony sold at a bargain price to Biddy, a street hawker who went round with a donkey and cart reselling the broken ware to the poorest people cast away into the slums. He had asked Johnny for a cracked teapot, and Johnny had given him a new one, adding that, if cautious arrangements could be made, he could give him many more things. Then had come the exposure of Botolph, and Johnny had arranged to hold a council meeting between himself and Dorin in Dooney's pub to arrange the business in a safe way.

* * *

He crossed over Sackville Street, turned down Great Britain Street, and came to Dooney's pub where Dorin was waiting for him, under the clock, with his eyes on the hands. They went inside, moved to a quiet corner, and Johnny took a small port on Dorin's invitation while Dorin's eyes beamed over the creamy top of a pint of porter.

—Now, said Johnny, when he had taken half of the port, and Dorin had golloped down half of the beer, to business: After what happened to Botolph, we'll have to keep our weather-eye open.

—It was a lousy thing for him to go and dip his hand into the money, said Dorin; why couldn't he ha' played fair, an' stuck to simple goods, like us?

—An', then, added Johnny, to go scattherin' it around so that everyone knew he was diggin' up buried threasure somewhere.

—Th' white-collared get, said Dorin.

—You've got a boy nearly fourteen years old, have you?

—Ay, have I, said Dorin, an' though it's his father sayin' it, a well-up kidger for any fair dodge goin'.

—Well, said Johnny warningly, when I give you anything, you must never—never, mind you—dhrive up to your own hall-door to deliver it. It's soon the tongues of th' neighbours 'ud get goin', blow on us, an' I'd begin and you'd end your further days in jail. So I'll never give you anything on any delivery, except your last one, so that you'll never be sure that I won't be dodgin' about the sthreet you live in, an', if I once see your van anywhere near it, you'll never get another thing outa me.

—Be Jasus! swore Dorin, I'd never do a thing like that. I'm not the one to frighten away th' goose layin' th' golden eggs. I'm no gaum. I'll work th' delivery in such a wise way that neither of the boyos'll fall into the suspicion they had lost as much as a burnt-out match.

—What we have to do is this, instructed Johnny. You get your eldest boy to meet you a good way from where you live. Give him whatever you have to give, an' dhrive on, so that he can carry th' things home as if they had been bought in a shop in th' usual way. D'ye understand?

—Entirely, said Dorin; but Jack, wouldn't th' missus be betther than th' boy?

—Oh, no, no; not th' missus, said Johnny impatiently. On no account, or at any time, let th' missus come to collect th' goods. If a policeman happened to be knocking about, an' saw you givin' it to th' missus, he might be suspicious, an' start askin' questions. No, th' missus won't do. Th' boy'll look more innocent; he'll look as if he were your vanboy, an' a policeman passin' 'll take no notice.

—Be God, I never once thought o' that! ejaculated Dorin, draining a last drop from his tumbler of beer.

—Well I did. We can't be too careful. He took a slip of paper and a pencil from his pocket. Now, he said, tell us what you're most in need of, for a start?

Dorin tightened his lips, and shut his eyes for a moment, taking a long swig from a new pint he had just ordered, opening his eyes for a second to put the tumbler back on the counter, and then closing them again, so that the darkness might be an aid to deeper thought.

—We need a helluva lot, he murmured, for all we had at th' start's bid us goodbye years ago. Th' missus washes a lot, aways thryin' to keep things clean—soap, matches, starch, an' blue, f'rinstance.

—Righto, said Johnny, making some notes. I'll make up a fine parcel o' chandlery for you tomorrow evenin'. Now, anything else—saucepans, brushes, or things like that?

—Aw, Jasus, said Dorin, I wouldn't like t'ask you to get me things like that—we must be fair.

—Fair? queried Johnny.

—Well, I ought to give you something every time you make me a present.

—No, no; that won't do, said Johnny swiftly; none o' that for me. It would make you careless, as if you were payin' for them, an' th' money might make me careless, too. I mightn't watch to make sure you were cautious, an' th' two of us would be landed. No; the minute you don't do what we have arranged for you to do, the bargain ends, an' it will never be begun again.

Dorin seized Johnny's hand and shook it, again and again.

—I understand, he said heartily, an' your way's th' way it'll be done. You're a decent lad, a real decent lad, heart o' th' rowl, he said; th' real Annie Daly, he said, one in a thousand, a trusty mate, a lad of a good breed, he said; not like th' rest o' them, nose-rags, toe-rags, flittin' afther Mr. Anthony here, an' Mr. Hewson there, sucks who would sell their mothers for a smile from a boss, he said; but you're a change from all those, a dear change an' a genuine change; an' standin' out as a sowl man, a solid man, hindherin' th' rich to give help to the poor, sound an' thrue in all your dealin's with your fellow-man.

Johnny's face flushed with pride, and he shook hands heartily with Dorin. Then they left the pub, and parted at the corner of Sackville Street.

—Safe home, Jack, said Dorin, again shaking hands with Johnny. Rest assured, he went on, that th' missus'll never fail, come what may, to inthercede for you whenever she goes to Mass, with an occasional blessed candle for company before the shrine o' Saint Anthony quietly beggin' help in our endayvours to knock a little reason outa life.

The sickle moon fair followed Johnny home when he parted from Dorin. He walked faster, and the moon moved quick in the heavens; he walked slow, and the moon mended her pace to keep him company. Slitting the heavens, she seemed like a sly shy face peeping through the curtained stage to see how the house looked. Of all the brightness of heaven, the moon was by far the nearest to him. Where was the sun, now? Somewhere to the east; or, as the old story went, speeding along the bitter waters of the north in Vulcan's golden goblet, on its way to where the sun was to rise again, the first thing in the morning. Strange belief. Ignorance of the early ages. Poor man.

What's this he was to get for Dorin? Dozen of matches, pound o' soap, two packages of Hudson's Extract, one o' candles, some blue an' blacking, a sweeping brush, and a three-pint saucepan. A fair start, anyway.

The heaven and the earth. Look up, and they don't seem to be so far away from each other. Anyhow, they were made together. In the beginning, God created the heaven and the earth; pretty close, what? Yet, sometimes it seemed that they were a hell of a way asunder.

When he came to the door of his house, he looked up before he went in. The moon was right in front of his face. Reminding him of something. What? Oh, yes: the brassy circle enclosing the ivory deer, running hard, rising and falling on the sobbing breast of a red-headed girl.

Oh, well.

He went in; and the morning and evening were the froward day.

* * *

ALICE, WHERE ART THOU?

🌳 🌳 🌳

Johnny didn't feel comfortable on his way to work the following morning. He was almost sure to get his docket. Well, if he did, aself, he'd stick it out like a man, and tell them they could go to hell for Johnny. That was the only way to meet the situation.

Still he felt uncomfortable and cold, and shivered a little. He hadn't said anything to his mother. Why should he, anyhow? She wouldn't say much, if he was sacked—that was the worst of it; if she'd only burst out an' bark at him, he'd find it easier to fight; but, no; she'd just sigh, an' that was hard to counter. Seven an' six a week wasn't a fortune, but it went a fair way to keep things from fallin' over; so, when it was lost, you couldn't really blame her for sighin'—when you thought of it. Ah, anyhow, another sigh or two won't take much out of a woman who has had a thousand an' two sighs in a lifetime.

An' he had to stick up for poor Dorin forcin' a man to walk, an' his thigh ripped open. Job or no job, he couldn't stand for that. Be God, there she was, walkin' right in front of him—Alice Boyd, the presbyterian. Yes, a pretty mot, right enough, with her mop o' curly red hair, her glittering green eyes, and her jib as jaunty as the jib o' Jenny.

He hastened till he fell shyly in beside the girl, setting his pace to keep time with the shorter and quicker steps of her little feet, while she carried her head high, for she had dropped into long skirts just a week ago, and felt all the world realised that she was a genuine woman, now.

—Why'r you goin' to work at this early hour o' the morning? he asked her.

—I have to make ready for the comin' of a special consignment of china-ware, she answered.

His tongue felt dry and his voice sounded husky as he said, I wish I was beside you all the time, givin' you a hand; but I'm a clerk, now! an' besides, I'm expectin' to get the push out of the job today.

—Oh! she ejaculated.

—Ay, indeed. I was kept over me time, yesterday, an' I gave oul' Anthony and Hewson what for, so I did. Just you watch, when he comes to open the shop, an' says anything to me; just you watch, an' see what I'll say about him an' his job.

She marched on, and was silent. He looked sideways at her, but his boasting hadn't prompted her to any admiration of him—he could see that; afraid to agree with anyone up against Hewson and Anthony; thinking of her own job. He was in the battle alone.

Passing by Nagle's pub, the porter, who was washing away from the front of the shop the filthy turmoil of the night before, suddenly slashed a bucket of water towards them, sending it streaming under their feet. Alice, with a little scream, caught up her skirt and jumped clear into the street, so as to save her dress from the slush that spread over the sidewalk. Johnny felt that he should have gone for the unruly porter, but his thoughts were all on the slim leg that Alice was showing in her search for any mark of the water or the slush. Still looking, and tucking her skirt towards the front in an effort to see the back of it, she showed her black-stockinged leg nearly up to the thigh, making Johnny's heart to beat and his face to flush.

—There's no actual damage done, is there? he asked, making over to her.

—I hope not, she answered. Can you see any?

He handled her skirt tenderly and lingeringly, tucking it up still higher, till a rim of white lace appeared, looking white and lovely against the black stocking that disappeared up under it. His hand moved along her stocking, feelingly, shaking a little as it felt the vibrant life running along the leg of the girl.

—You're all right, he said slowly, no damage done; only a tiny splash or two on the stocking. His hand began to sneak up under the rim of white lace, but she suddenly shoved it away and let her skirt fall down to her feet.

—That'll do, she said; I don't like that sort of thing.

They walked on, Johnny keeping as close to her as he could, occasionally giving her arm a saucy pressure with his fingers. About to cross Sackville Street, Alice stopped, looking undecided for a moment.

—You'd better walk one side o' the Pillar, she said, and me the other, to keep the shop from talking; and she stepped from the sidewalk to cross the street.

—Eh, wait a minute, will you? he said, catching her arm. I'll see you this evenin', comin' home.

—No you won't, for that would be as bad as them seein' us together now.

—After, then, he said huskily, pulling her towards him, and pressing his knee against her leg; sometime, somewhere, tonight?

—I don't know. Maybe I will, maybe I won't, she said.

—Tonight at Binn's Bridge at eight o'clock, certain, sure? We can saunter along the canal, and one arm was going around her, and a hand was trying to lift her skirt.

—Let me go! she cried, goin' on, and everyone looking. She jerked his arm away from her and hurried across the street.

—Don't forget, he called out after her; tonight, Binn's Bridge, eight o'clock—I'll be there!

But she went on, never heeding him. He, on his own side of the street, walked more slowly, past the fireman guarding the fire-escape, and smoking his pipe at the door of his wooden hut; past the flower-sellers, piling up their old boxes into counters, laying out apples, oranges, and flowers of every hue in rising ranks for the coming day's sale; over into Henry Street, where troops of assistants were on their way to the several stores; and seeing the bony form of Anthony hurrying to open the shop with the speed of a man eager to marry the loveliest girl in the world, or to be at the funeral of his bitterest enemy.

Glancing over, he saw his little Alice hovering near Harrison's, the elegant pastrycooks, where Anthony took his lunch, waiting for the men to go in before her. He felt a tremor of fear when he came to the shop, just as Anthony was opening the little wicket-gate in the revolving shutter. He'd wait till Anthony was well in, before he'd go; but, when the door was open, oul' Anthony stood back and waited for all the rest to go before him, a thing he'd never done before. So Johnny, making the best of it, had to go up, stoop down, with the cold eyes of Anthony staring down at him, and go in, with the cold eyes watching him behind, and the soft steps following his, follow, follow, I will follow Jesus; anywhere, everywhere, I will follow on; follow, follow, I will follow Jesus, everywhere He leads me, I will follow on, but the followed J. C. this time's Johnny Casside, for when he signed his name in the time-book, the cold eyes were staring down at the moving hand that wrote; and when he was at his desk, gathering together the postal orders that had come in from the customers in his district, there were the cold eyes of Anthony watching him, like a careless cat watching a mouse.

—Get them done quick, said Anthony, for you're wanted for another job this morning.

Setting out the goods required, making them into parcels, labelling them, entering names and addresses on the delivery sheet, were all watched over by Anthony. He was joined by Hewson before the delivery was half ready, and the two of them stood, side by side, watching the work of Johnny. Not a word was said to him of what had happened the evening before; but Johnny knew that they were taking it out of him for the affront he had given them the night previous.

—Want to make me nervous, thought Johnny, and so make a muddle to give a ripe cause for a growl; but Johnny was on his mettle, going about his work methodically, softly lilting Me Lodgins on the Cold, Cold Ground do' in all the parcelling and clerical work with deliberately grand precision, while the boyos over the other deliveries in the store watched furtively, and wantonly wondhered; glad that a comrade was going through a tough time; all of them putting on an airy look of righteousness, as if to sing slow and soft, behold I am not as Casside is, but truly, ruly, schooly, pewly, fooly, dooly, humble servants, doggedly faithful in all things appertaining to their *simper feedielus,* and they praying all the while that Anthony or Hewson would blaze forth into a hunting reprimand at something that Johnny had done before, or that he was doing now; but, to their discomfort, everything was done fair and well, and Johnny stood beside the delivery, all packed, and waiting for the van to come.

—Now, said Anthony, out you go, and help carry up the new chinaware that the storeman is already unpacking.

* * *

He climbed up to the very top of the house, stopped before a door, opened it, and went in to a big attic kind of a room.

Such a sight you never saw, such a sight as he saw, when he opened the door and went in:

> *There she was:*
> *Sweet and glowing, fair and sweet; flushed and fair,*
> *flushed and comely,*
> *like a healthy hawthorn in a smoky street.*

There she was, with her little hands moving about in a grimy bin; sorting out the dusty china, there she was.

> *Rise up, my fair one, and come away, my love,*
> *The time of singing of birds is come;*
> *The praties are dug, an' th' frost is all over!*

There she was, with one little foot on the second highest step of a ladder, and the other resting on the edge of a bin, her skirt so crinkled by the stretched-out limb that an ankle and calf of one fine leg was there for all to see, shining high over the hem of her white petticoat:

> *There she was, like a lily squandered in a murky pool;*
> *Alice!*

She turned her head, and her eyes lit up when she saw Johnny. He stood there gaping.

—I was sent up, he said shyly, to give you a hand.

—Well, she said with a pout, you'll have to come a little nearer, won't you, if you're to be of any use?

He went swiftly over to where she was, and stood there beside her with a beating heart.

—You heard what happened to Suresaint? she asked.

—I saw him driven forth, an' I guessed the reason.

—Mr. Hewson caught him interferin' with Miss Vaughan an' Miss Grice, she said. They let out on him in a note th' day before to Mr. Hewson; couldn't stand it any longer. His sisther's gone with him too, thank God!

—Horrible thing for him to do, commented Johnny. No one with a decent mind 'ud thry to do that sort of thing on a poor girl.

—Well, he done it, she said. It's not a nice thing to think of, much less to talk about.

There was silence between them for some time, while she handed down to him the china that remained in the bin.

—It was grand, she said, th' way you spoke up to that fellow Dyke, an' to that oul' Anthony!

—Didya hear me? he asked, swelling with pride. It's only th' beginnin', for Johnny Casside's not to be walked on—not even be th' lordly queen herself.

—I have to sthretch further in, now, she remarked, so don't forget to keep a steady hold o' th' ladder.

He drew closer in to the ladder, his eyes sparkling, his heart beating, and his hand timidly edging as near as it could get to the pretty, lace-fringed leg of the girl. She went on arranging the chinaware in the bin, but, stretching over a little more, the ladder wobbled a bit, and she let a quiet little squeal out of her.

—Steady, steady, Alice, dear!

—You're not holdin' it right, she said complainingly.

—Let me up there—I'm used to laddhers.

—You wouldn't know how to sort th' china, she answered, giving a graceful toss to her head that shook her wavy hair back from her forehead. No good, just holdin' th' ladder, however tight; hold me, instead, an' I'll feel safer. Oh, that's not any betther either, she said peevishly, when Johnny's right arm had firmly encircled her skirt; you're only making it now so's I can't move at all!

—Well, how'm I goin' to hold you so's you can move about th' way you want to?

—If you can't think of a betther way of holdin' than th' way you're holdin', then don't hold me at all!

He took his arm from around her skirt and again got a grip of the ladder, a tighter one this time.

—What d'ye think, Alice, he said, after a long pause, neither oul' Anthony nor Dyke knew nor wanted to know a single thing about th' plays of Shakespeare. Funny, isn't it?

—I see nothing funny in it, she responded snappily; for Alice Norris doesn't want to know anything about them either!

Johnny was puzzled. It was hard to know what to say to a girl. You never knew when you had them. No use of venturing to put a hand on her knee while she was in this cross mood. He'd chance a remark, anyhow.

—Nice stockings you're wearin', Alice; how far do they go up on your leg?

She glanced down at him with a mischievous light in her eyes, and gave her head a saucy toss.

—That's hardly part of your business, she said.

—I'm goin' to have a look, he threatened.

—You'll make me wriggle if you do, an' knock me off. I'm powerless up here. Help me to keep steady, or we'll never get finished. She smoothed her skirt with rapid, clever strokes of her hand, and pulled it a little higher on her leg. Just rest your hand on my ankle, an' then I'll feel safe.

He placed a hand on her neat little ankle, and slyly slid it up as high as her knee. Then something fierce and lovely shot through Johnny's blood. The rustiness of life fled from him, and a world of blossom circled him round about. The stir of Spring, the flush of Summer, the fruitful burden of Autumn, and the rushing of water in the Winter-time moved, flowed, and jostled together in his being; and God's love and care were here, full measure pressed down, and overflowing were here in the form of a pretty face and a quivering slim leg.

—Your skirt's a lot in th' way, he said, as he tucked it tighter behind her, up, up to the lacy halo of her drawers, half-way up her thigh.

—Fancy now, said Alice, beaming down at him, Anthony an' Dyke knowin' nothin' about Shakespeare! Hardly believable, is it? You'd imagine they'd be ashamed to show their ignorance, wouldn't you?

—Pretended to be proud of it, so they did, said Johnny; but I could easily see a shadow of shame in their eyes. Woa, careful! he added as Alice seemed to give a little slip, and his hand slid over her garter, over the rim of her long black stocking, to hold and fondle her firm white thigh.

—Nearly down that time, she said laughingly, an' would have been if you hadn't been there to hold me. She took her foot off the rim of the bin, brought her leg back to the ladder beside the other one, and Johnny felt his hand being tightly pressed between her two thighs.

The ladder shook, and she half climbed, half slid down into his arms; he pressed her to him till she was panting for breath, he frantically searching to cover her mouth with his own, while she pantingly twisted her bonny head this way and that to avoid the contact.

—You mustn't, you mustn't, she cried; 'tisn't fair on me!

Suddenly the little head stopped twisting, the red mouth brushed his and rested there, her arms went round his neck, her luminous eyes closed happily, and her slim body answered back every venomous pressure given by Johnny.

He was clawing at her skirt when her eyes opened again, with a start; she tore his hands away, panting and pressing herself out of his grasp, till she stood, breathless and flushed, beside the little dusty window looking down to the distant street. Whimperingly she stood there, trying to smooth down her frightened dress and hanging stocking, patting back into order her rowdy locks of wavy hair, pressing her lips to keep them from quivering, and keeping her eyes well away from Johnny's hungry looks.

—You're a bad boy, she murmured cryingly, a bad boy to take me unawares, like that! To tumble me about as if I wasn't a good girl, such a sudden pounce that I couldn't even get breath to tell you to stop, fixin' on me before I knew where I was, seizin' on me like a savage, windin' me into a fear of a wicked thing impendin', ravellin' every stitch on me into an untidy tangle, plain to anyone careful enough to give a hasty glance at me! There, now, she went on, glancing out of the little window, there's Arnott's gettin' ready to put their shutters up, an' closin' time'll be here on top of us before I'll get anything like a quiet look into th' disturbance that's pictured all over me.

She made for the door with quick steps, keeping her face turned away from Johnny. He grabbed her by the arm as she passed, holding her at arm's length while she struggled to make him let her go.

—Oh, let me go! she said vehemently, let me go, you! I must tidy meself before I'm put to shame be wonderin' glances at the troubled look of my appearance.

—Give's a kiss before you go, Alice!

—Maybe it's a kiss you want, after th' way you've surprised me with your disregard for a good girl's feelin's. Let me go, she added, whipping her arm from his loosening grip, and never again thry to hurt a young girl when she's helpless.

She turned round when she got to the door, hesitated, and looked a little tearfully at Johnny.

—If you thought a lot of a kiss, you'd take it, and be done with it; an', if you're genuine and want to, you can meet me tonight where you said, an' when we come to some grassy nook, you can tell me more about your Shakespeare; but you mustn't try to pull me asunder when you feel you'd like a little kiss. There, she said, coming back into the room, and looking brightly into his darkened face, I know you didn't mean to be so rough, an' we'll make it all up in th' quietness of th' night when we reach th' lanes o' Whitehall.

When she lifted her sweet face for a kiss, he hesitated, then he bent down and pressed his mouth to hers. She turned away and went swiftly from the room. He waited for some time, then went down the stairs into the shop, now darkened by the shuttered windows, where he saw Hewson and Anthony with their gobs together, and the assistants waiting for the signal to go. When he reached his desk, he took off his old coat and put on his good one, went with the rest out of the shop, and hurried home, thinking of the hour when he'd be close beside his Alice, fondling her, and pressing sturdy kisses on her mouth.

He lilted softly to himself as he went along, never minding a soul:

> *The birds sleeping gently,*
> *Sweet Lyra gleaming bright;*
> *Her rays tinge the forest,*
> *And all seems glad tonight,*
> *The wind sighing by me,*
> *Cooling my fevered brow,*
> *The stream flows as ever,*
> *Yet, Alice, where art thou?*

And the morning and evening were the sexth day.

* * *

TO HIM THAT HATH SHALL BE GIVEN

* * *

☙ ☙ ☙

He had put by thruppence a week till he had one and six, an' today, even if he didn't get the expected rise, he'd spare the other shillin', come weal or woe, and buy it! And when the day of rest came, he'd spend the whole of it with Johnny Milton.

Anyway, if things happened as they have happened so far, he was sure of a rise of a shilling today. So, then, he'd get the book without the actual loss of a make. For weeks he'd watched the lovely book in its blue and gilt binding in the little bookcase at the back of the open-air bookstall at Hanna's shop; for ever fearing that by the time he got the money; the book would be gone. Every evening, going home from work, he'd gone out of his way to make sure the book was still there. It was there yesterday, and it was bound to be there today. He hadn't done badly so far—he had three of Dickens' and four of Scott's; two of Balzac's and one of Hugo's; Ruskin's *Seven Lamps of Architecture, Sesame and Lilies, Ethics of the Dust, The Crown of Wild Olives,* and *Unto This Last;* Darwin's *Origin of Species and Descent of Man,* to be read when he knew more about things in general; two by Fenimore Cooper and three by Dumas; Tacitus' *Germania* and the *Life of Agricola* with *Plutarch's Lives* to keep them company; Reade's *Cloister and the Hearth;* Carlyle's *French Revolution* and Mignet's, too; Bunyan's *Pilgrim's Progress* and Sheridan's *Plays;* Taylor's translation of *The Aeneid* and a *Classical Geography;* Ball's *Story of the Heavens;* and, in poetry, the works of Byron, Shelley, Keats, Goldsmith, Crabbe, Tennyson, Eliza Cook—a terrible waste of sixpence—Gray, and the Golden Treasury, with the glorious Globe Edition of Shakespeare falling to bits; all backed up with Chambers's Dictionary, a stiff purchase, costing three shillings, bought after an old one, left behind by his father, had faded away in fragments. All these, with the old religious controversial works of his father, looked grand, and already made a fine show, above the delft, on the top shelf of the old dresser.

He'd add another fine volume to the stock today, *Milton's Works,* a blind man seeing more than a man with many eyes—that is, if he got the rise he expected. Well, it was next to certain, for everyone was talking about the rises that were due, and someone in the know had said that it was coming today for all who deserved it.

In passing to and fro about his work, Johnny had tried to search for a sign in the fixed look on the gob of Anthony, but there was only there the shuttered look that hid everything behind it.

Everyone was working with a will today. All smiles, too. Manna was expected to fall from heaven. Each looked as if he liked his job, and was in love with Anthony. Perhaps they were—for that one day, anyhow. It was an anxious time, waiting, especially for Johnny.

—D'ye know how much you're down for, Jack? asked Carey, a cunning look on his foxy face, and he caught Johnny by the arm as he was passing by.

—Is it th' rise you mean? No; a shillin', I expect.

—One an' six, me boy, said Carey knowingly.

Johnny thrilled, but doubted. Too good to be true. If he got a shillin', he'd be well satisfied. Another sixpence would be too much to look for, afther his row with Anthony too. Still one never knew: no use o' bein' a man of little faith.

—No, no, Carey, he replied, catch Anthony givin' too much. You can't lure me into that fancy. Who told you? Where'd you get that news?

—Ah! said Carey, with a cunning leer, that 'ud be tellin' you. Then as Johnny moved away, he came nearer, and whispered over Johnny's shoulder into his ear: Dyke it was; he knows—don't say I said anything about it.

Passing by Dyke, Johnny got a punch in the chest that staggered him and made him catch his breath. Dyke's face as he saw the pain he caused moved from a keenly pointed smile to a snarling laugh. Johnny, smiling eagerly, put a hand over his breast in mock defence.

—Huh, grumbled Dyke, following up the one blow with a rain of them, why you're picked for a favour, God knows! What Mr. Anthony sees in you it would be hard to say. Get away, you lost an' lumberin' looney! and Johnny thought he felt the force of good humour in the blows he ran from.

The rumour was right then—Dyke's manner showed it. He'd say nothing to his mother for a few weeks so that he could add some more books to his store. He had so few, and needed so many. His row with Anthony had left no ill-feeling. Maybe the reverse. You see, a fellow loses nothing by standing up for his rights: to thine own self be true, and it must follow as the night the day, you cannot then be false to any man. Good old Shakespeare—he knew more than most. Of course, he'd let Dyke thump him, without saying a word, but Dyke hadn't really meant to be rough. Just his way o' goin' on. At bottom, he was really a decent fellow. Dyke had told him of the rise in a rough way, but it was decent not to keep the knowledge to himself. Perhaps, even oul' Anthony wasn't quite so bad as he thought. Anyhow, he'd got to be a little stiff with those who worked for him, or he wouldn't get anything done.

He'd get another book next week. Ay, but what? Dickens? Carlyle? A new Shakespeare? No; th' old one would do grand for a little while longer. He'd not decide; betther prowl round th' stands an' see what was goin'; buyin' a book was a serious thing.

Good God, didn't the time go slow! *Tempus Fugit* me arse! An hour dawdles into an age when you want it to hurry. There's oul' Anthony fillin' th' pay envelopes now, his long bony hands sortin' th' silver, slippin' th' coins into th' tiny envelopes, an' closin' th' flaps with a sly lick o' th' tongue an' a swift pressure of th' slender fingers.

While Johnny was writing a label for a parcel, Hyland halted beside him, his black eyes showing a good-humoured light.

—So Casside's down for a big rise, eh? Nine bob a week now, eh? Let's hope he deserves it. How'r you feelin' about it?

—Oh, all right, said Johnny, wearing an air of indifference; if it hadn't come, I'd have known what to do.

—What? asked Hyland.

—Fling th' job to hell! said Johnny carelessly.

—Really?

—Yea, verily, an' by my own help so I would.

—Talkin' big, jeered Hyland.

—Go to th' devil an' shake yourself! said Johnny.

He saw all the clerks, who had been paid, counting and recounting their gains, sorting the coins out, folding them together, and dropping them back again, gracefully, into their little envelopes, finally placing the envelope, with a kingdom of God look on their faces, into their favourite pockets. He hadn't been called in yet. He hoped he'd be sent for before he had to go to his dinner. He hoped to God he wouldn't have to go up and ask Anthony for what was coming to him. Like th' oul' bugger to make me, thought Johnny.

He heard a tapping on one of the windows of the counting-house, and, looking round, saw that Anthony was beckoning to him.

—There y'are, there's th' signal, Casside, said a number of the clerks.

Johnny, settling his hair on the way and giving a tug to his coat to make it sit straight, hurried to Anthony's little counting-house. The bony hand placed Johnny's little envelope on the ledge of the desk, without a word. Johnny took it with a Thank-you, sir, and hurried back to his own little desk, his heart beating and his joy full. He waited till he saw that the clerks were busy bending over their desks; then he opened the envelope and spilled the gleaming coins on to his desk that he might have the full feeling of handling the one and sixpence extra.

Good God, th' oul' fool had made a blunder! There was only five and six in the envelope—two two-shilling pieces, a shilling, and a sixpence. How well the blunder was made with his wages! Now he'd have to go back and argue it with Anthony, a hateful thing to have to do. He fancied he heard some titters over against him. With a flushed face and a disturbed heart-beat, Johnny hurried back to the counting-house.

—Excuse me, Mr. Anthony, he said, I'm afraid you've made a little mistake, and he smiled forgivingly; there's only five an' six in th' envelope, instead of seven an' six, sir.

Anthony looked up from a letter he was slowly typing, and fixed a cold grave gaze on Johnny's excited face.

—How much did you say? he asked.

—Only five an' six in it, sir.

—That is the correct amount for this week, said Anthony calmly, and went on with his typing.

—Oh, no, no, sir, said Johnny, seven an' six, sir—what I've been gettin' for a year.

—If you'd taken the trouble to look at your envelope, Casside, you'd have seen that we've fined you two shillings, making five and sixpence the amount due to you.

—Fined, echoed Johnny, fined for what, sir?

—For impudence and disobedience, Casside. Next week we hope we may be able to give you the seven and six as usual, and the bony hands went on uncertainly, clumsily, gropingly, at the typing.

Sick and stunned, Johnny was thinking, and not able to think; getting back to his desk, blindly; fullness of rage making him feel tight and breathless, his thoughts broken and confused, mixed up in a medley of anger that this thing had been done to him so slyly, so quietly, without a wind of the word reaching him, cool and calculated villainy—th' bony scoundrel, th' dead-fac'd whore's melt! Silently and steadily the money had been taken from him—may th' guts in his narrow belly corrode and swell and rise and burst out of the slit of his mouth! They all had known of it, and stayed their work to laugh at him, with Dyke leading them on, and cheerin' in their throats, in honour of Casside's hardship—may their ill-got lives be lost in a sludge of woe; may their hearts be cakes o' rust; and a tangle of rotting fibres burn in every twist and crook of their bodies, hieing them yelpin' to a bitther grave!

—How much of a rise did you get? whispered Hyland over his shoulder.

Without the power of answering, he was so stuffed with anger and dismay, Johnny crushed his cap on to his head, took his lunch from under his desk, and walked away out of the shop, down Henry Street, into Sackville Street, mechanically turning up Bachelor's Walk, the ringing of the hand-bells, announcing second-hand auctions all along the way, sounding as if they were coming from a far distance. He walked on, deep curses burning in his heart; walked on till he came to a stop before Hanna's benches filled with books of all kinds, many of which he would love to have, and bitter with the one thought that he had lost the power to buy even the poorest of them. For a while he managed to keep his eyes off the corner where Milton should be; but his eyes got there at last; and, sure enough, the book dazzled him, gleaming like a precious stone from a heap of rubbish, almost asking him, for God's sake, to come and take it.

Take it? For nix? Steal the damned thing? Good God, no; too dangerous. The youngster keeping an eye on the books outside wasn't there; strange, that. Must ha' gone to his dinner.

He peered through the dusty window: oul' Hanna was at the far end of the shop. Sorting out a new selection. Johnny's hand stretched towards the book; his fingers went round the upper end of the spine, and, gently and cleverly, he pulled the book out, handling it lovingly.

An old man came up and began rooting among the volumes, an old man with a hooky nose and a spreading beard, rooting with piercing eyes among the volumes. Johnny put the book under an arm and took up another, looking at it with eyes that didn't see, for there was a trembling mist before them. He dimly saw the man with the hooky nose, piercing eyes, and spreading beard take a book to his bosom, turn away from the strand, and enter the shop to pay for it.

Johnny then put down the book he was looking at, turned, and, with his heart beating like the heart of a bird caught in a squeezing hand, and his feet feeling as if they were trying to drag him back again, he sauntered away with Milton under an arm, expecting every second to hear a wolfish shout from Hanna calling for a policeman to come and catch a felon. He went on slowly, wheeling into Liffey Street, then tore along as fast as a rapid walk could take him. Excited, panting, and thoughtless, he turned into Upper Abbey Street, then into Jervis Street, not stopping even to glance at a casualty case getting taken into the hospital; into Britain Street, up Sackville Street, into Henry Street again, to bolt into the Henry Street Stores, flushed, covered with sweat, but with the sweet book cuddled under his arm.

He had risked a lot to gain a lot, and he had succeeded. He had a half-crown book in his hand and his week's pay in his pocket. God was good. No, not his week's pay, for two bob of it was snug in Anthony's pocket. A Robin Hood outa hell who robbed the poor to pay the rich. Was he goin' to let himself be robbed? Afther givin' a hard-earned shillin', too, to help buy him a clock? An' without a fight, either? He was in the right: no-one need tell him God would put a hand into the pocket of a poor man. He'd argue it out with Anthony. He'd get what was be right comin' to him, or go! Hyland, Dyke, an' th' rest weren't goin' to have it all their own way.

His file was packed with orders, but Johnny put no pass on them. And wouldn't, till he got what was rightly due to him. Then, he might; anyway, he'd see. There was Anthony, now, back from his haughty lunch, pegging away, in his clumsy manner, with his typewriter. Bony and slender as his hands were, they were slow and awkward at typing, Johnny could see that. All were back at their work, now, all busy, all but Johnny, who hung over his desk, trying to think of what to say to Anthony. He couldn't think, so he'd depend on God to put the right words into his mouth.

Several times he started for the counting-house, and several times he found himself back at the desk again, uncertain and afraid. Once he went as far as the entrance, but his heart failed him and he came back to his desk. He felt a little sick. He should have gone when he was roused, when the anger was on him.

Screw your courage to the sticking point, said Shakespeare.

—Oh, to hell with it! he said, roughly to himself, here goes!

Straightening himself stiffly, he marched to the counting-house and stood near Anthony, waiting to be noticed. After a long interval, Anthony raised his head from his typewriter and looked at Johnny.

—Well, Casside, he said, what's the trouble?

Before he could answer, the dark form and dusky face of Hewson edged its way forward from the background, and Johnny found himself loosely hemmed in between the two God-belauding brothers.

—Well, said Anthony again, what is it, Casside?

—I just came to say a word about the fine, sir.

—All that ought to have been said has already been said, said Anthony shortly.

Johnny conjured up all the new strength that had begun to come into his speech. He had written as many letters as he could to his brothers, trying to put into them all the things he had learned the week before, and choosing the most elegant words he could think of to describe what had happened in the locality. He had done it so well that Tom had praised him for the brightness and skill shown in the letters written to him. So with a little trembling in his mind, he settled himself down here to do what he could in his own defence.

—I don't think so, sir, he said; you, yourself have said but little, and I have said nothing at all.

—Oh! said Anthony in an astonished voice, and what have you to say about it?

Although, now and again, there was a slight quiver in it, Johnny's voice was firm and clear; and he felt that Dyke, Nearus, and the rest of them listened and were wondering.

—Well, sir, said Johnny, I'd like to know, first, what was the impudence and disobedience complained of, where it happened, for which I have been fined what is, to me, a very large sum of money?

—I see we have a lawyer amongst us! said Hewson, with a dark grin.

—It is recent enough for you to remember it well, said Anthony, and I've neither the time nor intention to go over it again with you. You have been fined, and there is nothing more to be said about it.

—That's all very well, sir, but I think I have the right to say something in my own defence. The occasion that brought about what you are pleased to call disobedience and impudence was really my own time; and it was you, sir, who were unjust in keeping me beyond the stipulated hour for leaving work.

Anthony had resumed his typing, pretending not to listen to Johnny, and there was a pause, broken by the jerky rattle of the keys clicking clumsily because of the unsteady movement of Anthony's fingers.

—Besides, sir, went on Johnny, had what you allege against me happened even in the rightful time of the Firm, the amount of the fine, if you weigh it with the weekly wage I get, is altogether too large and unnecessarily severe.

Hewson roughly pushed in past Johnny, anchoring himself beside his brother; and the two of them bent over an invoice of goods, taking as much notice of Johnny as they would of a fly on a distant star.

—I have saved up hard to buy a book I want badly, said Johnny in a louder voice, and the fine has made my well-nourished plan go all agley.

—Book! snorted Hewson; maybe it's a book he wants!

—Casside, said Anthony, with a tinge of a smile on his bony face, attend to your work, and you'll have little need of books.

—I have attended to it well, responded Johnny vigorously, and for the past year not a single complaint has been made against me by a single customer. My need of books is my own need, an' that need's my own business, an' no-one else's.

—Casside, said Hewson viciously, it's plain that a fine is the one thing you can understand. Go back to your work or you may have a bigger fine to face this day week!

—I have no fear of a fine next week, for I refuse to be fined now; and what I am refusing today, I will refuse tomorrow.

—Go back to your work, Casside, said Anthony, a little more softly, in an effort to be kind, before you go too far.

—I'll go back when the two shillings taken from me are given to me again.

—Casside, said Anthony solemnly, you will have to submit to the fine imposed upon you, or—and he paused to make what he was about to say more impressive—or leave our employment. You must make your choice.

—I have already made it, said Johnny.

—What is it, then?

—To leave.

After a moment's hesitation, Anthony opened a drawer, rooted in it, took out some silver, and flung two shillings on the desk beside Johnny.

—It is plain, he said, that you are wholly unsuitable to us.

—That's possibly something to be unashamed of, said Johnny bitterly. And let me tell you there's another shilling of mine embedded in the clock you have at home! I could ill afford it. I gave it unwillingly. I thought joining in the gift would make things safer here. I need a book more'n you need a clock; but keep it; it will remind you of me when the clock strikes!

Anthony's face went a flaming red. He bent down over his desk and remained silent. But Johnny stood there, as pale as Anthony was flushed.

—Get out! said Hewson furiously. How dare you mention such a sacred thing? Get out, or get kicked out!

Johnny sensed that the whole staff was disturbed, and he glimpsed a worried look defiling Dyke's foxy face. He had made them sit up. Whenever Anthony looked at the clock, he'd remember what Johnny had said to him.

—No-one will kick me out, said Johnny. I'm going. God rest you merry, gentlemen. I'm due a rest, anyway. Farewell, a long farewell to all your greatness.

The fleshy hand of the dusky-faced Hewson sought his shoulder, giving him a push that sent Johnny colliding with the desk of Nearus.

—Get out! he said angrily; this Firm has no room for a vulgar corner-boy!

Dyke snatched the precious book from under Johnny's arm and flung it far down the passage-way into the dirty straw, a messenger meeting it with a kick that sent it away beyond into the dirtier lane.

—Follow your book, said Dyke, to your rightful place in the dirt of the street!

—There he'll find his happiness and his hope, said Hyland.

Nearus looked on and sighed and said nothing.

With his face pale as a lily lying in a dark corner, his mind a smarting hate, and rage rough in him, Johnny gathered himself together straight again, faced the two signalmen of God, saying savagely, in half a chant:

> *I leave th' pair of you with your godliness and go;*
> *And when th' ending day comes, day of wrath, I hope*
> *You two may catch a glimpse of heaven's glory;*
> *Then sink down, sudden, down, deep down to hell,*
> *Amazed and sightless!*

Half blind himself with rage, he left them, picked up his precious book out of the gutter, wiped with a handkerchief the specks of cow-shit from the cover, and wended his way homewards.

And the morning and evening were the seheaventh day.

TOUCHED BY THE THEATRE

☙ ☙ ☙

Archie was now completely gone on the stage, and Johnny was following close behind. Archie lived and fought and died and lived again in the toils of the great persons treading out their glorious lives, gorgeous before the footlights. The Theatre housed the quick, the rest of the world encased the dead. Some time before, they had formed the Townshend Dramatic Society, had rented some unused stables in Hill Street for a shilling a week. These they had gutted of all partitions, had whitewashed the walls, putting a deep yellow border round the top of them, with a harp in one corner, a wolf-dog in the second, a round tower in the third, and a huge shamrock in the fourth so as to show decidedly the true nature of the work. From old timber taken from the loft they had made a stage at one end, and benches from what was over. Ould lanterns, bought second-hand, shaded with cardboard, coloured yellow and black, did well as footlights; and a turkey-red twill curtain went up or came down at the ringing of a handbell. The stage was fitted with lovely parlour, hall, and landscape sets, provided from the better parts of old canvas cut away from old cloth thrown away by the Queen's Theatre. Here sketches were given to audiences of forty or fifty, who paid tuppence a head to get in, to see Archie playing the Duke of Gloucester to Johnny's Henry the Sixth; or to see Johnny playing Brutus in the Forum scene, followed by Archie as Mark Antony, friends in the audience shouting the exclamations of the crowd for them; or the scene between Wolsey and the nobles, sorted out to be one, played by Johnny in dark-blue tights, yellow buskins, black trunks, brown velvet coat, and rich green silk cape, lent by Tommie Talton for the bright occasion; while Archie strutted as the Cardinal, in a red gown, topped with a low-crowned, wide-brimmed jerry hat that had been soaked for days in soda to remove the black colour, then dyed in crimson, with red curtain cords laced round the crown, the heavy tassels hanging down over his left shoulder. Johnny had to hurry out after the sly blow at the Cardinal,

> *An' so I'll leave you to your meditation*
> *How to live betther. For your stubborn answer,*
> *About the giving back the great seal to me,*
> *The king shall know it, and, no doubt, shall thank you.*
> *So fare you well, my little good lord cardinal,*

to come back in a long black cloak and wide-brimmed black hat to play the part of Cromwell to give Archie his chance in the cardinal's great renunciation. As well, they played scenes from *The Octoroon*, especially that between Jacob McClusky and Salem Scudder, Johnny doing McClusky and Archie doing Scudder; and the scene between Corry Kinchella and Harvey Duff in *The Shaughraun*, with lots of others in Dick's little orange-coloured books of *Standard Plays*; though Johnny didn't like the rowdy arguments that went on afterwards, for a lot didn't want to praise Archie, being main jealous of his natural gifts and acting vigour; doing all they could in cold water to disparage everything they'd seen him do, making Archie hot and irritable, threatening to tear down the curtain that his money had paid for, all the time asseverating that without him there wouldn't be much of a Dramatic Society left. Indeed, once during an interval in the performance given by the Anna Liffey Minstrel Troupe, playing in the Coffee Palace, Townshend Street, they had played the quarrel scene between Brutus and Cassius, Johnny doing Cassius, both of them crimson-cloaked, and wearing greaves and breastplates, made from stereotype paper, silvered over, that Archie had pinched from the *Daily Express*. But the whole thing was taken silently by the audience, neither hiss nor clap was heard, and Archie got gloomy, and for long after he was content to play one of the corner men, making a bigger noise with the bones than he did with Shakespeare.

Better times had come. Now Archie was a friend of Tommie Talton's brother-in-law, Charlie Sullivan, who did things of great magnitude when the theatre was the theatre, to an audience who knew what acting was; when he played the great Conn the Shaughraun, the great Shaun the Post, in *Arrah na Pogue*, and the greatest Miles na Coppaleen the world, or even Ireland, had ever, ever seen; filling the playhouses throughout the civilised world with laughter, softening it with sad and sympathetic tears, and making them thunderous with cheers, the way you'd like to shoulder him high, and carry him through the world's laudation.

But now, with the world's people fading into ignorance and low regards, he had to do the best he could for the drama by playing in the Mechanics' Theatre, in Abbey Street, strutting the stage there before a rough-and-randy crowd who came to while away the time, but who put great pass on the suffering and rollicking that shivered and shone on the stage; with the lights dim when the tears were falling, and the lights high when bravery took the branch, or when fun gambolled its way from the stage into the hearts of the laughing people watching from the darkness. Here Charlie played all the Irish plays, mixing them with *The Octoroon*, *The Corsican Brothers*, or *Saved From the Sea*, Johnny enjoying them on a free pass from a front bench in the pit, his brother Archie having a small part in each of them, training himself for a fuller future.

A kidger had brought a letter to Johnny from Tommie Talton, marked

Urgent, asking to come to see him at once, without a minute's delay, on business; and here was Johnny, with his heart athrob, hurrying on to answer it. He turned swift into Temple Street, went past George's Church, dived into The Pocket, and knocked at a genteel door, a little parched for want of paint, with a white plaster horse, for ever on its hind legs, prancing, in the fanlight. This was a token that those who lived there, though a little down in the world, held fast to the fancy of living a select and lofty life among ordinary people. Every fanlight in the place exhibited a plaster horse, standing still, trotting neatly, or dancing sadly on its hind legs, like a tired animal rehearsing for a turn in a circus. These were carried about in baskets, by Italians, mixed with images of St. Francis, St. Patrick, and Madonnas with their children. Johnny had often watched them being sold; had often wished that his mother had had enough to be able to put one in the fanlight. Sometimes staring at the seller speaking to a housewife at her door, a look in the Italian's eyes motioning him to get away, he'd say, How much do they cost, sir? And the seller would ask, Weech—the holy ones, or the seemple horses? And Johnny, answering, the horses, would be told that the leetle ones were two sheelings, and the beeg ones four; the seller turning to the woman to say, once in zee vanlight, ladie, zay breeng a change, oh, so beeg, that no-one knows eet anymore vor zee same house; for zee leetle horse or zee beeg horse een zee vanlight leeft, leeft zee house up, up so high, ladie, zat zee house ees not zee same no more, oh, no, for eet has been leefted, leefted up, up; for zee horses geeves zee house, oh, deegneety, much, much beeg, what you call a lot. Often the ladie would buy, Johnny envying her the horse, now taken so gently from the basket, though he knew well it was a sin to covet his neighbour's goods. But he'd go on coveting while there was anything left to covet.

These houses were let in floors to genteel persons; had oilcloth on the halls, a stand, where hats and coats were hanged, a big gilt-framed picture on a side wall, variegated carpets with brass rods on the stairs, and an air that seemed to tell you to knock at the door softly. This was the first fine house he'd entered since he stood in Dovergull's, when they were presenting the clock; and though it wasn't as imposing as the other, it was grand enough to make him nervous; for patched boots and threadbare clothes didn't go well with the white horse in the fanlight or the cream curtains on the windows. He dared say they wanted him to earn a few pence by placing bills in some of the shops, telling all that *The Shaughraun* was in full swing at the Mechanics' Theatre.

He raised his hand to the knocker—a lily growing out of a bunch of grass—and knocked softly at the genteel door. Hardly had the sound died away in the nearness, when the door was opened by a little woman with a shawl over her shoulders whose hair was gray, who peered out at him through soft, dark eyes, fixed, sorrowful, in a pale troubled face.

—Is that Johnny Casside? she asked. Oh, come in, my son. I've been listening for your knock this hour or more.

She brought him into a room that was neither big nor small, with much furniture scattered about. There were big black and blue vases, swelling into wide bowls at the top, standing on the mantelpiece; from tiny brass hooks embedded in the wide bowls hung crystal glasses cut to catch the light, and a bright fire, burning lustily, threw dancing gleams of lovely colours into the glasses hanging from the vases. Right in the centre stood a large square mahogany clock, with a coloured pictured panel on it of two white swans swimming on a blue lake, fringed with dainty yellow and green palm trees. Over all was a huge coloured picture of Charlie Sullivan as Conn the Shaughraun, a roguish smile on his ruddy face, a fiddle strapped to his back, dressed in his tattered crimson hunting-coat, and the terrier, Tatters, at his heels. Dispersed round were pictures of him again as Miles na Coppaleen, with the keg of poteen on his shoulder; as Salem Scudder, paring a stick with a long yankee knife; and Shaun the Post, standing, well fettered, in a prison cell. Besides, there were smaller photographs of Tommie Talton as Corry Kinchella, as Captain Molyneux, and as the military O'Grady in *Arrah na Pogue*. A faded red carpet covered the floor, dotted with tiny fur rugs to hide the parts that had trembled into threads. In the middle of the room, a little nearer to the fire, stood a table covered with a white cloth, and having on it breakfast things for one.

—Give me your cap, she said, an' sit down be the fire. You'll have a cup of tea when Tom comes down. Isn't what you're looking at fine? Charlie himself, taken in his heyday, costing no end of money, just afther Charlie had shaken hands with kings an' all kinds o' monarchs, elevated be the way he played his parts before them; an' God be with the old days, an' that's herself, she went on, pointing to a picture of an angelic-looking young girl that Johnny hadn't noticed before, me own daughter, me Mary, in the part o' Moya, who could hold a lily to one cheek an' a rose to the other without makin' either feel outa place, fitted be God with a smile that simply made an audience thrance itself into a feeling of kindliness for the world at large, before she gave a sigh an' took a soarin' lep to heaven outa the throes of thryin' to bring a new child into the world. I hear Tom's bed movin', the signal for me to put his egg on, for he's a changed boy, now, that used to have his breakfast sprawlin' in bed, and the first tint of the night comin' into the sky; now not lettin' me do a hand's-turn, dustin' and sweepin' his own room, makin' his own bed to save his old mother any exertion, lockin' the door, even, for fear I'd sneak up when he's gone to lay a hand over things. Here he is, now, an' here's Johnny Casside waiting for your lordship, dying for a cup of tea before he harbours a thought of doing the thing you're going to set before him.

The long lanky figure of Tom came strutting into the room, dressed in faded black broadcloth trousers and a dazzling white shirt, spliced in many places, the cuffs frayed sharply, but still brave and challenging. His pale pitted face was merry with a grin; his hair a mass of golden curls, parted impudently by a curling-over quiff, cascading down elegantly over his pock-marked brow.

—Well, Johnny, me lad o' gold, he said intimately, as he slid into a chair beside the fire, and began on the egg, while Johnny munched a junk of buttered toast and sipped from a cup of tea, you know that tonight's Charlie's benefit performance? Well, Cleggett, who plays Father Dolan, 's gone and got ill; none o' the rest know the part, so we're in the devil of a hole. We want you to fill the part for us, me lad.

—An' well he'll fill it, too, murmured Mrs. Talton.

—Aw, no, no; indeed I couldn't, exclaimed Johnny excitedly; but the thrill of a cheering audience went through his beating heart.

—You're goin' to do it, said Tom emphatically. Haven't I seen you doin' the parlour scene to Archie's Conn, an' the one in Ballyragget House to Archie's Kinchella, to the manner born, too? Besides, you know the whole part, don't you?

—Yes, I know it all, said Johnny; the whole play, I know it nearly all.

Tommie jumped up, wiping bits of crumbs from his mouth, his eyes ashine, showing a problem solved.

—Me sowl man, he said heartily; now, mother, turning to Mrs. Talton, measure him so that you can stitch enough tucks in Father Dolan's togs to fit him fair.

The breakfast things were swept from the table. The sombre garments of Father Dolan were spread out, Mrs. Talton measuring the length of Johnny's arm and legs and the width of his waist, making chalk lines on the black cloth as she measured, murmuring, Tucks won't be many, long legs, long arms, and fairly wide round the waist; but what about the hat? I can't put e'er a tuck in that.

—He wears it only a couple o' times, commented Tom; so he can carry it in his hand. Now for the theatre, me laddo, to run over the words, and give you the feel of the stage.

Johnny, all of a glow, hurried out with Tom, and they got a tram going to Nelson's Pillar.

—I heard th' oul' one muttering out of her, an' I tidyin' me room, said Tom. What was she blatherin' about? Tellin' you what a white-haired boy I'd become, eh?

—Yes, answered Johnny, how you did everything for yourself, makin' your bed an' all, even lockin' the door so as she wouldn't be able to tire herself doin' things.

—If she only knew, and he laughed loudly, pushing his jerry hat to a rakier angle on his curly head. I was at a low ebb a few weeks ago, and I pawned the blankets off the bed, so I do for myself, an' keep the door locked to prevent her finding out. It was all right then, for the nights were warm; but, Jasus, now I'm perished, an' have to bury myself undher old clothes from the baskets!

They got to the theatre, and found two men setting the first scene for the play. Part of a house appeared at the left corner, with steps going up to the door; and Johnny rehearsed the going up and coming down of these steps, till Tom was satisfied that some of the priest's dignity appeared in his walk. Then they went over the more important scenes in the play, several times; then every part of the play where the priest appeared; and Tom's face was a beam of enthusiasm at the end of it all.

—Bravo! he shouted, running over and clasping Johnny's hand. Did yous see him, did yous hear him? he added, turning to the two men who had set the scene.

—Ay, we did, said one of them, an betther it 'ud be hard to get, if you et an' slept in Drury Lane, itself, for a month o' Sundays!

—Henry Irving's a great man, there's no denyin', said the other; but if some I know keeps goin' th' way he's shapin' now, Irving'll be devulged only as an I roved out kind of an acthor!

Tom plunged a hand into a pocket, took out some coppers, and tossed four of them to the two men.

—Out for a dhrink! he shouted.

Then there was great haste in hurrying over to a pub, for bread and cheese and a bottle of stout for Tom, and one of ginger beer with a ham sandwich for Johnny; then back to Tom's, where he fitted on Father Dolan's clothes, more tucks being added here and there, till all was said to be well; then home, with his head spinning, Tom's advice to lie down and forget it all till the time came, ringing in his ears; with Johnny's mother, when she heard it, saying, that even were the stage what it should be, there wasn't much to be got out of it by any respectable person; everyone knew what the people there were like, livin' languidly a low life of gay an' coloured divilment; a lure of envy to them who had to stay in the straight road; wastin' away a boy's life, sightseein' the chamberin' of light men with fast women; when you should remember that neither your father nor mother was ever in a theatre, except to see the wondhers of Shakespeare's plays, done be God-fearin' men, full of honest laughter, dimmin' with tears whenever the occasion called for them; adding, as Johnny was going out, well, since you've committed yourself, do your best, and don't, for goodness' sake, make a show of the Cassides by givin' a bad performance.

Johnny raced all the way to the theatre, finding it dark and deserted, so that he had to edge away, come back, and edge away again for upwards of an hour, till he saw one of the men go in. Him he followed, and was told he'd come too soon, but could go to Mr. Talton's dressing-room and wait there till the time came for him to dress and be made up for his part.

A tiny room it was, made of thin board partitions, with a table scattered over with all kinds of face-paints and powder. The green coat and buckskin breeches of Kinchella were hanging from a hook, next to his own black ones; a little cracked looking-glass was on the table, propped up against a tin box; and on the walls a score or more of photographs and coloured pictures of lovely ladies in lovely dresses; dresses so disarranged by the pose of the girls, or the saucy pull of their dainty hands, that lovely legs were peeping at him from all sides and corners, and swelling white breasts all but out of the fair bodices the charming girls were wearing.

> *My bodice, neat an' modest, oh, is slippin', sir—*
> *Be careful, sir, be careful, please;*
> *The silken thread that holds it up is rippin', sir—*
> *Oh, do be careful!*
> *There now! It's down about me waist,*
> *My pearly goods are all uncased,*
> *I hope they're temper'd to your taste—*
> *St. Patrick's Day in the morning!*

> *My skirts are up above me knees, I'm dancin', sir—*
> *Be careful, sir, be careful, please;*
> *Your eyes are like twin stars o' fire, advancin', sir—*
> *Oh, do be careful!*
> *Good sir, you gave me quite a scare,*
> *I hope you'll find your huntin' fair—*
> *Yes, yes, you're bound to find it there—*
> *St. Patrick's Day in the morning!*

Tommie Talton came bustling in, and Johnny jumped away from the pictures. Tom's hat had a hastier rake on his head than ever; his face was flushed; and some of the smallpox holes in his cheeks seemed to fill up and empty again as he breathed.

—There's every sign of it, Johnny, every sign of it; we've done it, I think, at last.

—Yes? questioned Johnny.

—There's a queue forming already, me son. We're going to have a full house; and no paper, no paper, me laddie. Now sling yourself into your priestly duds, and I'll make you up. We've more'n half an hour, before the curtain rises.

Johnny got into the sober clothes of Father Dolan, and felt a bit astray in them. The tucks, ironed out, were still visible, and the trousers looked a bit wide, though the stiff white paper band, stitched to the coat, made a fine Roman collar. A yellowish-grey paint was thinly smeared over his face to take away the bloom of youth; thin streaks of brown across his forehead and under his eyes added a few wrinkles, and made him look thoughtful and serious. Flour scattered over his brown hair made it grey, and finally, a book, representing, Tom said, a Breviary, was put into his hand, and he was all ready for the fray.

—Don't forget not to take the book from your left hand, said Tom. Always keep the right one free for your gestures. He cocked his head to one side and stared at Johnny. You'll do. Look the part to the life. Perfect.

Tom was dressed for his part of Corry Kinchella, buckskin breeches, top-boots, green cut-away coat, white waist-coat, and grey tall hat. He dabbed some red paint on his cheeks, put short thick lines of black paint, to represent sideboards, before his ears, and a thick streak across his upper lip to represent a moustache. With his hunting-crop in his hand, he stood smiling, waiting the time to go on to the stage.

—We'd betther be goin' down, he said, for me bones tell me the time's gettin' short. Remember, he said warningly, to keep your head well up while you're speakin', so that the gallery can hear; never stand in front of anyone an' spoil the picture; and don't forget a priest always walks with dignity on the stage, an' speaks slow an' sure.

They went downstairs, Johnny's heart swelling so that his chest felt tight and his stomach felt queer. Passing through an iron door, splashed with the word SILENCE, they came on to the stage.

What with the lights and the curiously dressed people standing about, silent and still, and the murmuring that floated up from the audience, the dirty stage and the dusty scenery turned into a golden world.

—Do like you done today, an' you'll do grand, whispered Tom, as he slid softly by to take his place where he was to make his first entrance.

Several people who passed patted Johnny gently on the shoulder; and he knew, if he failed, he'd for ever be undone; but he wouldn't fail, for he'd live the part for the time being.

There on the stage, behind the lights, in front of his eyes, stood the cottage of Arte O'Neill, in Suil-a-beg, with the ruins of Suil-a-more Castle a few feet away, and the Atlantic Ocean near enough to let the sound of its waves be heard; an' there was Captain Molyneux, of the 49th Foot, come to the place to capture the escaped Fenian, Robert Ffolliott, a convicted felon because he wasn't afraid to speak of Ninety-eight; and the green-coated Squirren Kinchella, striking his top-boots with his elegant whip, striding before the cottage, a villain, doing his friend, Ffolliott, out of his property, coming between the Fenian and his own beloved fiancée, pretending friendship all the time, but conniving with the grey-coated police spy Harvey Duff, to nail Ffolliott again, so's he'd be out of the way; with the black-coated Father Dolan, frantic, knowin' all, but darin' to say nothing conceived in the confessional.

Johnny stepped through the door into the glare, the white light, the dazzling place of play, sensing, though he didn't see, the vast gathering of watchers hidden in the gloom, waiting, wondering, pitching their tents of thought with the players in the pool of light that showed another world of good and bad, gay and glum; knowing and simple people, in silks and friezes, in crimson and green garments, and weather-worn grey, aligned together for good or evil, with God on the alert above to ensure that to the true, out of many tribulations, would come an exceeding weight of glory.

There he stood, now, outside the cottage door, his glance resting on the agitated Kinchella asking himself who was it had sent money to Ffolliott in Australia to keep him from starving; with Johnny's answer sounding loud and clear and strange, I am the man, Mr. Kinchella; the play flowing on with Johnny stressing the villainy of the Squireen, answering him when Kinchella pleads for Father Dolan's help in persuading Arte O'Neill to become his wife, I'd rather rade the burial service over her grave, an' hear the sods fallin' on her coffin, than say the holy words that would make her your wife; for now I know, Corry Kinchella, that it was by your means, and to serve this end, my darling boy—her lover—was denounced and convicted; and Kinchella's snarling denial, 'Tis false! cut be Johnny's 'Tis true; but the truth is locked in my soul, and heaven keeps the key! with the vindictive Kinchella threatening venomously, Then out of this house these girls shall go, homeless, ay, an' beggars, followed be Johnny's declaration with a force in it, like God's hidden thunder, rivin' a villain's last hope, Not homeless while I have a roof to shelter them; not beggars, I thank God who gives me a crust to share with them! going in slowly, leavin' Kinchella gnashin' his teeth in the midst of a storm of hand-clapping and cheers from the audience, incensing him with the feeling that his playing of the part was safe, while the main characters silently shook his hand, and the minor ones touched him respectfully on the shoulder; while the play went on to show the sisther of the Fenian fallin' madly in love with the English Captain; tellin' how Conn poached the Felon home out of Australia, and brought him safe to Father Dolan's house where, in the midst of their jollity, the redcoats come, informed of Ffolliott's whereabouts by Harvey Duff; the Fenian runnin' to hide in the kitchen clock, with Captain Molyneux questionin', an' Father Dolan stutterin' that he was, was here, but had, had—, an' Conn chimin' in with, Yissir, he wint away before he came here at all; then the Captain sayin' solemn, Have I your word as a priest, sir, that Robert Ffolliott is not under this roof? showin' Father Dolan strugglin' with his conscience, saved from a lie be the brave Fenian rushin' in to shout, No, sir; Robert Ffolliott is here; Conn consolin' the priest be sayin' that Robert would rather have the irons on his hand than the sin of a lie upon your soul; endin' with the grand tableau of the handcuffed prisoner embracin' his beloved, the poor priest, convulsed with grief, leaning his head on the table, the Captain pointin' the way out with his naked sword, an' Conn prevented be the claspin' arms of his Moya from flingin' a heavy bottle at the Captain's head, with a long, lone, sad sigh goin' up from the watchin' people. So it flowed on to the last scene where Kinchella, abductin' Arte and Moya, is shot be Conn, where Arte throws down the ladder from the cliff, preventin' any of the villains goin' to the waitin' lugger, on to Harvey Duff's flight from the furious people, beggin' mercy from Conn who flings aside the crouchin' Informer, sayin', Ay, as you spared me, as you spared the men at whose side you knelt before the althar, as you spared them whose salt you ate but whose blood you drank. There's death comin' down on you from the cliff above, there's death waitin' for you on the rocks below— Now, Informer, take your choice! And Robert, freely pardoned, no longer needin' to fly to America where Irishmen were held in honour and threated right, and made welcome, and given power, and shown favour, where no information was sworn against them, where no narrow walls were built to hold them tight, where no ropes were woven to hang them high, where no iron was forged to mar them manacled; but could stay at home, and marry his loved one, and Captain Molyneux, too, Englishman and all, as he was; and Conn, happy at last, with his own Moya, and the priest's blessing at long last given.

And Johnny bowed his head with the rest, standing in the midst of a huge, coloured bubble of applause, Johnny watching some of the people mooching out, wading through a drift of orange peel and crumpled programmes, with the curtain coming slowly, slowly down for the last time.

All of them, nearly, hurried away then, patting him on the back as they passed; but Johnny lingered a little, looking at the stage wistfully as the lights began to dim, and the fairy feelin' faded. Behind a wing he heard the voices of two men who played the minor parts of Kinchella's henchmen. He listened, for he had heard his name mentioned.

—Didja ever see the like before? said one voice. Whenever I met the cocky kid strollin' about, like a god who knew nothin', I'd ha' liked to have given him a wholesome paste in the snot!

—Father Dolan, how are you! I've a pain in me arse, lookin' at him. A sad sight I hope I'll never see again. Disasthrous, disasthrous! If you'd done it now—Oh, I'll say nothin'.

—Or you, Jem, but mum, though, not a word. The cocky kid done it; an', oh, Jasus, help the poor Theatre!

Johnny hurried up to the dressing-room, where he took off his stage clothes silently, only half listening to Tommie's praise, for a good deal of the glory was gone.

—You were really fine, said Archie, when they were on their way home. Even Sullivan said that only once before had he seen a better Father Dolan —the time he once played it himself. Splendid he said you were.

—I heard him saying everyone was splendid, answered Johnny moodily.

—Ay, in an offhand way; but he didn't harp on anyone as he did on you. I got Harvey Duff over betther than ever before—they hissed like hell!

But the goodness was out of it, and the glory was gone for Johnny. To forget what he had heard the two bastards saying of him, he broke softly into a gay Dublin ditty:

> *A sober black shawl hides her body, entirely,*
> *Touch'd be the sun and the salt spray of the sea;*
> *And safe in the darkness her slim hand, so lovely,*
> *Carries a rich bunch of red roses for me!*
>
> *Her petticoat's simple, her feet are but bare,*
> *An' all that she has is but neat and scantie;*
> *But stars in the deeps of her eyes are exclaiming,*
> *She carries a rich bunch of red roses for me!*
>
> *No arrogant gem sits enthron'd on her forehead,*
> *Or swings from a white ear for all men to see;*
> *But jewell'd desire in her bosom most pearly,*
> *Carries a rich bunch of red roses for me!*

—If I was you, said Archie, as they walked along Sherriff Street, I wouldn't go an' get a swelled head.

* * *

I STRIKE A BLOW FOR YOU, DEAR LAND

❦ ❦ ❦

Johnny's whole world was divided against itself. England was at war with the Boer Republics. His brother Tom, who had had a job of temporary postman at twelve shillings a week and was on the Reserve, had been called up; had been dressed in khaki, helmet and all; had marched, with a contingent of his regiment, the Dublin Fusiliers, through the city, Johnny by his side, carrying his rifle, and had gone long ago to the front, after promising Johnny he'd bring home a bunch of hair from Kruger's whiskers. He had gone up to Natal under General Sir Redvers Buller, and nothing had been heard of him for weeks. Johnny was troubled that he might have perished in the battle of Tugela; for Johnny and Tom had a real affection for each other. Thousands of Irishmen were out there on the veldt, risking all for England; for her honour, and, Johnny thought bitterly, for the gold and diamond mines of Johannesburg. She had been fortified in her attack on the Boers by testimonials from the Basutonians, Zululonians, Matabelians, Bechuanalandians, Bulawayonians, Mashonians, and the Kalomonians, who had all in a great chorus sung hail hallelujah to the great white queen mother, Victoria.

All civilisation, save alone the Irish. Ireland had become a place of stormy argument, with Dublin as its centre. Every man, woman, and child fought battles hour by hour, either for the British or the Boers. Transvaal flags were in everyone's house, in everyone's window, or in everyone's hand. At times spontaneous processions formed in the streets, marched through the city, booing every redcoat that passed, and often coming into collision with the irritated police. All fancy goods shops and newsagents were filled with Boer symbols; streams of ribbons flashing the colours of England's enemies flowed through every street and sparkled in every second window. Every patriot carried in the lapel of his coat a buttoned picture of Kruger, Steyn, Botha, Joubert, or De Wet; and a story went everywhere that De Wet was really Parnell come·to life again, and up in arms against the English. Day and night the office of the *Irish Independent* flashed on a screen the latest news, a red light burning for a British victory and a green one for a Boer success, thousands gathering to cheer when the green light shone, and to groan and hiss when the red light was shown. A Transvaal Committee had been formed, with Arthur Griffith and some Irish Members of Parliament, to help the brave Boers to an Irish ambulance. A meeting had been called, but the Castle had proclaimed it; and Dublin tossed her head and clenched her teeth.

Today Johnny and Ayamonn were standing in the crowd watching the lights, when the news was flashed on the screen that the British had lost ten guns, and a great cheer, thundering defiance, made the street tremble in an agony of joy. Ayamonn, hoarse with mad emotion, whipped his hat from his heavily-haired head and waved it round in circles, as he shouted with the crowd.

We should ha' gone to where th' meetin' was to be, he said, proclaimed or no.

—We're better here, said Johnny; for he didn't relish the chance of a tussle with the police; and here he knew that wasn't likely to happen.

In the crowd, right in front of Johnny, stood a lissome young woman dressed in a gay dark-green dress suit, the skirt barely reaching to her ankles; a black bolero jacket, trimmed with flounced epaulettes which were rimmed with a brighter green than the green of the suit, and flecked with scarlet. She wore high-laced boots that disappeared up under her skirt, which, whenever it was swung by a lively movement of the girl's, showed the fringe of a white lace petticoat. Perched daintily on a curly roll of reddish hair was a dark-green felt hat sporting a black-and-white wing of a bird in its side. Several times Johnny's knee had touched her thigh, timidly at first, then with steadier resolution; and now, with a beating heart, Johnny found that the girl hadn't taken her leg away from his touch.

Ayamonn, full of himself, was gently swaying to and fro, as far as the crowd's pressure would permit, and singing, half to himself and half to the crowd, his eyes filled with a far-away look:

> "My boyish ear still clung to hear
>   Of Ey-eyrin's pri-ide of yore,
> Ere Norman foot did dare pollute
>   Her in-independent shore;
> Of chiefs, long dead, who rose to head
>   Some gallant pathriot few;
> Till all my aim on earth became
> To strike one blow for you, dear land,
>   To strike one blow for you,
> To stri-ike one blow for you, dear land,
>   To stri-ike one blo-ow for youooo!"

A woman striding towards middle age, wearing a disorganised straw hat on her tousled head, patched boots, one brown, one black, the brown one darkened with blacking to make it feel more at home with the other. She wore a black and white check skirt, the white square making up to the black ones by the grime gathered in street and house, the whole scalloped by wear and tear along the edges. She wore a large brown shawl flowing down to beyond her hips. Suddenly, she darted out from the crowd to a vacant place on the sidewalk, flung her shawl open with a sweeping flip and tucked it more closely round her body, as if she were clothing herself in armour.

—I don't care who hears me, she shouted, for we're full of life today, an'—puff—we're gone tomorra. To every man an' woman their own opinion, square or round or crooked or cornered, which is only right an' proper, an' a fair division. Sayin' nothin' calculated to hurt a soul, I'll say yous are a lot o' starin' fools, watchin' an' waitin' for somethin' yous'll never be spared to see. I wondher, she went on, raising her voice to a screaming pitch, I wondher what all of yous, what any of yous 'ud do, if England went undher!

—Die with joy! a man's voice shouted from the crowd, and a great cheer added an amen to the declaration.

The protesting woman flapped her shawl like a bird flapping its wings, gave a clumsy little lep from the pathway into the air, flapping open her shawl again, and closing it tighter as she did a nervous defiant dance on the pathway.

—There's ne'er an element of surety in your shoutin', she yelled, or the pourin' out of your poor white ignorance an' coloured venom. It 'ud be fitther for yous to work to help yourselves than to set yourselves dhreamin' of help for the Boers; for listen to me—in about as much time as it 'ud take a clever hand an' a sharp knife to peel an apple, England'll put the sign o' death on Kruger an' his gang!

The lissome young lassie standing in front of Johnny, with her leg touching his knee, moved angrily, and turned her pretty head to stare at the yelling woman; and Johnny cursed the oul' one for an ignorant, meddling bitch. Then with a handsome wriggle of her young body, the girl slid from the crowd and stood, red-faced and defiant, before the ill-dressed, blustering woman yelling out for England.

—Will you go home, for God's sake, woman, she said fiercely, an' clap yourself in bed, since you can't help yourself to a suitable understanding! We're serious people here, in no way wishin' to confuse our decency with the dirty tournament of England's attack on inoffensive peoples.

—General Roberts, General French, an' General Kitchener, three Irishmen—remember that! shouted the blustering woman. They'll soon put the lonesome sign of death on Kruger an' his gang!

—Will they now? asked the young woman. You know all about it, don't you? Well, if I read the news right, Gatacre didn't do it at Colesberg, or your great Lord Methuen at Magersfontein, where he led thousands of th' poor bewildered Scots o' th' Highland Brigade to leave an everlastin' farewell to their wives, sisthers, an' sweethearts. And your Buller hasn't done it at Colenso, has he?

A policeman, big and brave, for he knew there were hundreds of his brothers less than half a street away, came up, and eyed the pretty lass with an evil look, his mouth, thought Johnny, wathering for an excuse to haul her to the station, so that he might handle her hidden loveliness while he was doing his duty.

—Eh, you, he said to the lissome lassie, draw it mild an' let the woman have her say. The law allows free expression of opinion to all.

—Come on back here, sweet lass, whispered Johnny, going over slyly, and timidly touching the girl's arms, and never mind that ignorant and insignificant woman; but she brushed his enticing hand away, and he went back to the crowd abashed.

—Irishmen all! yelled the older woman, flapping her shawl, doing her little lep up from the pavement after every sentence, Kitchener, Roberts, Kelly-Kenny, French, Mahon, fightin' for England. Five o' th' best, an' Irishmen all—remember that, now!

—Maybe you've forgotten how th' English went clattherin' down Nicholson's Nek, so's you couldn't see their heels for dust, went on the young lassie, an' thousands now of their best are floatin' fast dead an' down th' Tugela river, headin' out for the sea!

—Irishmen all—you can't get over that, now! screamed the oul' one. Whenever oul' England's in a quandary, up comes th' Irishman, tearin' up he comes, an' turbulent to pull her out of it—ah! me faithful, darlin' Dublin Fusiliers!

A surge of many people cheering came from some distance away, like the first rolling billows of a tidal wave. Ayamonn sniffed, tossed up his head, and listened.

—Somethin's goin' on below, he said; come on, me boy!

—We're all right here, said Johnny, pulling back, and it's safer to stay where we are.

—We don't want to be safe, cried Ayamonn, making off for the wider vista of Dame Street, followed by the pretty red-haired girl; and the crowd, turning from the lights, swept down, carrying Johnny with them close to the girl, knocking over the boisterous oul' one just as she was doing her little lep from the pathway, and flattening the burly constable against the wall of a building. When they streamed into Dame Street, they mingled with a tremendous crowd, cheering fiercely, and waving hundreds of Boer, Irish, French, and American flags. Some way after the head of the crowd was a brake, a long car, benched on both sides, drawn by two frightened hearse horses. A stout, short, stocky man, whose face was hidden by a wide-awake hat, was driving them. Several other men, pale-faced and tight-lipped, sat on the seats, facing each other; and with them was a young woman with long lovely yellow hair, smiling happily, like a child out on her first excursion.

—Look, Sean, me boy, look! shouted Ayamonn, didn't I tell you we wouldn't take things lying down much longer! That's James Connolly dhrivin', and that little man with the square jaw's Arthur Griffith; an' th' lovely lady's Maud Gonne—help us, Jasus! an' we'll win our freedom yet! Come on!

The horses were moving along at a steady trot, the crowd were keeping up a trot in unison, and after the brake a large mass of heavy-coated, helmeted policemen trotted sullenly, and as nimbly as their bulky bodies would allow. That part of the crowd nearest to the police were laughing animatedly and jeering into their red and sweaty faces, goading them with cries of Shake a leg, there, bring your knees up; take id aysey, me poor men; hay foot, straw foot; keep your chests in an' your bellies well out; it's a damned shame to have th' poor men runnin' their guts out—cruelty t' animals, so 'tis; at th' double, min—quick march; eh, keep back there, an' give th' min breathin' room.

—Keep as close to th' brake as you can, said Ayamonn, pulling at Johnny's arm, while Johnny kept fast hold of the girl's hand, who twined her dainty fingers round his. Pushing hard, they were soon but a few steps behind to one side of the brake, near the great persons who were sitting, tense and tight-lipped, there. In high good-humour they all were, with the police helpless, jammed in the crowd, looking ridiculous as they lumbered along stiffly in an unsteady trot.

Now brakes filled with police forced their way through part of the crowd and followed those trotting along on foot. Passing by the gates of the Castle, there, snug in that deep gash of the city's body, were drawn up all the squadrons of the Horse Police. There they sat their horses, darkly seen for a few moments by those marching by, in the shine of silver on helmet and tunic; gloomily they sat there, a frozen frieze on the façade of the Castle, motionless; not a jingle from stirrup, bridle, or bit, not a hair of a helmet-plume stirring. As they passed and saw, the murmuring, chattering people grew silent, and nothing was heard but the trotting fall of the feet of the crowd; nothing seen but the dark forms, silent, behind the shine of the silver. And Johnny remembered when he last saw such a sight he was safe on the top of a tram, warm and confident, close to his mighty mother's side.

The procession swung into Parliament Street, everyone tense, silent, expectant, waiting. Johnny heard the sound of a sharp order, saw the dark figures coming to life; heard another sharp order, and saw many flashes of light as swords were drawn; saw the plumes stirring as the horsemen moved; heard another shouted order, and the squadrons came galloping down on the crowd. Johnny tried to push a way towards a side street, holding on to the hand of the girl, but they were wedged fast in the crowd, and they were swept beyond it. He saw the people in the brake stand up to watch the charging police, and the driver checked the horses to half turn round and look back over the heads of the swaying crowd. The flashes of steel light were rising high and falling on the heads of the people. The air was deaf with shouts and screams and curses. Those nearest the edges began to seek safety in the side streets; the manly jog-trot of the procession was now but a medley of scuffling feet; the clack of iron hooves on the stone sets, mingled with the cries of those who hadn't yet felt the fall of a sword, and the sombre silence of the Horse Police, trotting here, trotting there, prancing their horses against the tumbling breasts of the people, lifting their heavy sabres as if drilling to the musical notes of a murderous tune, to let them fall on frantic heads trying swiftly to wag aside from each glitter-ing blow.

The people were resisting now. Poles, sticks, bars of iron, and bare fists were contesting the fight with the police.

The horsemen had made a mistake by coming down on them too quickly, giving them no time to scatter, so that wedged together, cut off from a way of escape, the sabre-stormed people were forced to fight back. The Dubliners were angry, and, caught like this, they became a troublesome mass of fighters. Stones snapped asunder some of the chin-chains, and police were riding about bareheaded, with blood trickling down their faces. Some of them had been pulled from their horses, and were struggling on the ground beneath a mass of pummelling fists. Their batons were being used by men in the crowd, and a few had swords which they gripped tensely, but didn't like to use.

—We're caught in a thrap! said Ayamonn hoarsely, grinding his teeth, caught in a thrap!

Johnny put his arms across his chest, pushing out as strong as he could, to keep his ribs from cracking, the sweat rolling down his face and his breath coming out in bitter panting gasps. The girl, flattened beside him, had closed her eyes, and her little red mouth was gaping open. Many dark figures were writhing curiously on the road, dotted here and there with a helmeted body, crouching down on hands and knees, blood dripping on to the sets from some hidden wound. A horseman, well in advance of his comrades, was forcing a way towards Johnny and his two friends, kneeing his horse through the crowd, hacking away with a sabre gleaming sourly in the grey air. Johnny saw a gleam fall on the face of an elderly man, saw a bloody cheek suddenly separate itself from the face and fall away from it, to be frantically clapped back to its place, with a yell, by the stricken man, who suddenly sat down on the road, moaning, pressing his two twitching hands to the horribly gashed face with all his power. Still Johnny stood staring at the slashing horseman, coming closer; still Ayamonn crouched, his arms held high, sheltering head and face; still the pretty girl stood with her eyes closed and her little red mouth gaping. Back, inch by inch, came the crowd, melting before Johnny as the horseman advanced to where but a few yards separated them from the slash of his sabre. A man in front of them, carrying a gaudy Boer flag, screamed when he saw the gleam circle over him, and then sank down without a murmur when the flash fell, let-ting the flag go from his grip, and as it toppled backwards, the staff came to rest on Johnny's shoulder. Now the horseman curveted round to where they stood, and Johnny saw a pair of eyes, like flaming carbuncles, fixed on him from under the helmet's peak; saw the thick mouth of the half-mad man opening and shutting nervously, the heavy yellow teeth clashing together as he roughly swung his horse round to where they stood. In the madness of fear, Johnny gripped the pole of the flag with both hands and blindly thrust it forward at the rider with all his might as the horse came prancing round on his hind legs. The hard, sharp, wooden spearhead of the flagpole caught the rider on the side of the neck under an ear, and Johnny caught a glimpse of an angry red tear where the spear had struck, as he tumbled off his horse with a sliding crash on to the hard ground, letting a smothered grunt out of him before he lay stunned and still there. Johnny felt a horse's hoof grazing his leg, splitting a trouser-leg from knee to ankle; he saw Ayamonn running furiously over to the fallen rider; saw him stamp his heavy boot on the horseman's face, and though the hard rim of the helmet saved the face from being caved in, Johnny plainly saw that the iron heel had left a horrible bloody blob on the rider's chin; he felt Ayamonn pulling him madly by the arm, and shouting at him, This way; up this street, for Jasus' sake, or we're for it when the others come!

Then they ran; the three of them ran up a side street, ran through the streets before them till they had utterly lost the sound of the tumult in the place they'd left behind them.

Diving into a pub, Ayamonn called for three halves of malt, hot, to get them sober, he said, and to take away the chill that follows the brazen heat of a battle. Johnny smiled, tried to look indifferent, then hurried out to lean against a lamp-post and be sick on the road, Ayamonn watching him anxiously from the doorway.

—All right? he questioned. It's the terrible pressure of the crowd that's upset your stomach. Come in an' get th' ball o' malt down you, an' you'll be right as rain.

—Yes, said Johnny, the pressure of the crowd—that was it; but in his heart he knew that it was fright and the things he had seen. He was no soldier. Never would be—he felt it. There was no use trying; but he'd say nothing before the girl. He went back into the pub.

—That was a glorious prod you gave th' helmeted bowsey, said Ayamonn —right undher th' lug! Save us, you did. He'd ha' sliced us as you'd slice a salmon. God, I did laugh when I seen him hurtlin' off his horse! Well, we stood up to them today. Our dhreams are comin' thrue. Eh, he said suddenly to the barman who had put three whole balls of malt on the counter, I said halves; and Johnny knew that he hadn't enough to pay for the whole ones.

—That's all right, whispered the barman, leaning over the counter, th' drinks are on me, see? I guess what you've been doin'—standin' be th' Poor Oul' Woman, wha'?

They all shook hands with the barman, murmured good health, and lowered the steaming amber whiskey. Johnny felt the cold leaden pain in his belly change into a delightful glow of comfort, and his face flushed with a new contentment. He saw the colour creeping back into the girl's face, the sparkle leaping into her dulled eyes, and he saw, with a thrill, her two pointed breasts falling and rising deliciously behind the sweet shelter of her bodice. He caught her arm in his hand and squeezed it, pressing it tighter when she smiled happily back at him.

—Look at his leg, she said, indicating to the barman Johnny's torn trousers; a prancin' horse done it. A wondher he wasn't desthroyed! And the scared face of the falling horseman again came before Johnny's eyes.

—Now, we'd better scatther, said Ayamonn, when they'd come out of the pub: I this way, yous that. Slan libh till we meet again; and off he went, while Johnny and the girl, in a roundabout way, walked to Ballybough, she with her arm in his, and he pressing it close to his side. He felt lovely thoughts singing her beauty straying through his head, but his heart beat so fast, and his chest felt so tight, that he could hardly say a word.

—You're limping a little, she said, when they were passing over the Tolka.

—The leg's hurting a little, he said.

—Here we are, she said, stopping before a cottage in a little avenue. You'll have to come in for a second an' let's have a look at it. I can put a stitch in your trousers at the same time.

—No, no; I couldn't he said shyly; thanks all the same, though he longed to go in and seek out a chance to fondle her; I'd betther leave you now, really.

—You're a shy fellow, she said, laughing. There'll only be th' two of us, so you needn't worry, and she opened the door with a latchkey. She gave him a pull towards her, saying sharply, Ah, go in, man, or you'll give the neighbours another chance for a fancy-born story.

They went into a little room to the right off a narrow hall, furnished with a table on which was a white cloth and the stuff for a meal, some ham, bread, and an egg in a cup waiting to be boiled, while a shining tin saucepan sat itself within the fender before a brightly burning fire. Along the wall, under the window, ran a sofa with two big crimson and darkgreen covered cushions on it; two rather stiff upright chairs, leather-bound; against the wall opposite, a mahogany cupboard, having on it a gilded vase and many photos of the girl in various positions, with a parasol on the seashore, sitting on a carved stone bench, with a book in her hand, leaning against a fat and fluted pillar; and one, that made Johnny's eyes linger there, of her in low bodice and tights, and a saucy smile on her wide and neatly curved little mouth. A warm brown carpet, sprinkled with large blue blossoms, covered the floor, and yellow curtains prettily draped the window. The wallpaper was cream-coloured, with trellises of yellow and pink rosebuds everywhere your eye went. Pictures from the Christmas number of

Holly Leaves covered some of them, and a few were hidden safely by a green-coated Robert Emmet waving a plumed hat over the mantelpiece. Johnny's eyes gave a swift glance at all these bright things, but came back to linger on the photo of her little ladyship wearing the low-cut bodice and the charming tights.

That's a good one, she remarked, noticing where his eyes had strayed. I'm a good dancer, and whenever there's a panto or anything on with a chorus, I get a job in th' front rank. An uncle of mine lets me have a couple of quid a week, so I don't do too badly. An' how d'ye like me, she added roguishly, in a fie-for-shame costume?

—You look lovely, he said earnestly; you look lovely as you are; and you would blossom forth fair in anything.

—I see, she said, her face flushing pleasantly, you can put a silvery sound into your words when you want to deludher a poor girl. But sit down there till I see to your leg, an' we can talk afterwards.

She put a kettle on the fire, and fetched a basin and a towel from another room. When the water was hot, she poured some into the basin and gently bathed his leg with an old clean linen rag.

—There's a bruise there, she said, an' it has bled a little. When the wound was clean, she smeared some vaseline on a white handkerchief and tied it firmly round his leg.

—There, that should feel easier now, she said. When we've had some tea, I'll do your trousers. Me name's Daisy, she added, Daisy Battles. She went on chatting while she made tea and boiled two eggs. She cut some ham, and placed an egg before him. Eat, she said; you must be nearly starving.

He felt too full and excited and expectant to eat, but he swallowed the egg and drank a cup of tea, watching her making a tidy meal of it.

—Me skirt an' petticoat an' what I wouldn't like to mention are all creased an' twisted with the crush of the crowd. I'll have a job to get them into a proper shape again. Well, it's all for oul' Ireland anyway.

When they'd finished eating, she pulled the table back with a swift movement to the far end of the room, and placed the sofa lengthwise in front of the fire.

—That's much nicer, she said. Sit you down here, an' take off your trousers while I get a needle and thread. Go on, she added, laughing, seeing him hesitate, don't be so shy—I won't look at you, I promise; and she hurried out of the room. Flushed and agitated, he took them off, sat down on the sofa, took off his jacket and draped it over his bare legs. When she came back, he saw she had a dark-green shawl swung from her shoulders down to her hips, fastened over her bosom by a large oval brooch framed in dull gold, having on it a naked girl in ivory standing daringly out from a black velvet background. She sat down beside him, took up his trousers, and began to mend the rent in the leg. He guessed now that there was nothing beneath the dark-green shawl but a thin chemise or something. Frightened, he turned his gaze to the fire, and saw there a glance of agony on a twisted face, a blazing red mark under an ear, and a chin smashed into a bloody blob. He turned his face to watch her stitching.

—God, she said, looking down at his feet sticking out from under his jacket, what tiny feet you've got! An' hands, too! patting one of them; lady's hands an' lady's feet. But you've lost your tongue. Haven't you ever talked to a girl before?

—Of course I have—in Irish, too.

—In Irish, eh? You know Irish then?

—Of course I do.

—What's tabhair dham póg, then?

—Give me a kiss, of course.

—Well, give me one, can't you? Well, you take care not to hurt yourself when you're kind to a girl, she said, after he had bent shyly over and kissed her lightly on the cheek. What body would believe you bowled a policeman from his horse? There now, that looks a little better, and she held up the trousers with the long rent neatly sewed together. No one'll know you were in a fight, an' you goin' home; and she flung them over the back of a chair behind the sofa.

—That's a nice brooch you're wearing, he said, pressing closer to her now.

—Isn't it? A present from the oul' uncle, taking it out of the shawl, and handing it to him. Supposed to be Vaynus. Naughty girl in the altogether. She shook her shoulders, and the shawl fell from her, leaving her in chemise and stockings. You'll scorch your jacket, and she whipped it off his legs, and flung it on the chair behind. My goodness, I can hear your heart thumping from here!

—Isn't yours thumping too? he asked. Let me feel; and he pulled loose the bow-ends of the ribbons, opening her chemise halfway down so that her taut white breasts with their rosy nipples appeared bare before him; and he pressed his hot hands over them. Then he tugged at her chemise to raise it higher on her legs, and she half-rose from the sofa to let him do it properly, before she stretched down on it to wait for his coming.

Some hours afterward she was lying on the sofa, the shawl around her, the brooch, with its dull gold rim framing the naked lady, fastening it together over her bosom; but the naked lady was naked no longer, nor did his hands ache to tear away the dark-green shawl hiding again her many buoyant beauties.

—You're in a great hurry, she said, looking at him through half-closed eyes. Can't you stay a little longer?

—I can't, he said. I have a lot of work to do.

—Work! she echoed. Work on a day like this? What kinda work?

—I have a lot of things to learn, Daisy.

—Well, she said, giggling, you've learned a lot with me today, haven't you? You'll be a knowin' fellow from this out. Won't you come to see me soon again?

—Yes, of course I will. Goodbye for the present—I must be going.

—Well go, she said, sharply; no one's keepin' you. You're a good boy, she said in a softer tone, holding out her hand. There, as he pressed it hard, don't break it. You have me half dead, she added roguishly, an' poor me thinkin' you too shy to do anything dangerous! Shut the door softly afther you; and closing her eyes, she lay back on the sofa with a happy long-drawn sigh as he left her.

* * *

AT THE SIGN OF THE PICK AND SHOVEL

(FROM "DRUMS UNDER THE WINDOWS", 1946)

✼ ✼ ✼

Pug-faced, pleasant-hearted Georgie Middleton had pulled him to the job, hearing he was idle; big gang at work on a railway siding, more wanted; make a man of you. He brought Sean straight to the Foreman, had whispered into his ear, One of ourselves, and the Foreman, a modified true-blue, had decided to give him a start. A big man was the Foreman, over six feet and broad-shouldered. A handsome face, spoiled by a big crooked clumsy chin, falling away from a large mouth, well shaped; deep clefts from each corner of a handsome nose furrowed the cheeks to the frame of the chin, looking like taut ropes keeping the heavy chin from falling away altogether; but he'd taken him on, and that was a decent thing to do.

The ganger, Christy Mahon, looked doubtfully at Sean when he came to the job with a navvy shovel on his shoulder. Mahon was another big and powerful man of fifty or so, wide-shouldered and deep-chested; lazy as sin, and as ignorant as a kish of brogues. Doesn't know the name of his own religion, couldn't recognise the number on his own hall-door, and hardly make out a bee from a bull's balls, one of the workmen whispered to Sean, a few days later. He had a rugged, rather distinguished face, a heavy grizzled moustache, a bush of the same sort of hair, tousled as if it had never come within sight of a comb, and his chin, hardy and strong, was covered with a week's growth of hair. There was one remarkable thing about him— he had a very small arse for such a big man, and the part of his trousers there looked like the drooping mainsail of a ship in a fitful wind when he walked. Too much beer, whispered another workman to Sean, a few days later. This ganger mostly remained torpid, but was under the habit of sudden fits of passion for an hour's occasional work to show the others how it was done; and would seize a shovel or a pick to work like a nigger for a spell, the effort gradually declining till the tool dropped from his hand, and he sank into torpidity again. He spoke through his nose in a querulous way, and got good-humoured only when he was half-seas-over by drinking the bullage from empty whiskey barrels, made by steeping the damper ones with boiling water till the whiskey still in the wood had soaked its way into the water. He lived in Yellow Walls, near Malahide, the stronghold of the Talbots, where he had a whitewashed cottage with clay floors, a wife, two children, less than an acre of ground, and an animal that he said was a cow. He was the richest man in the hamlet. All life centred round the cow. Up every night he had to be when she was calving, squatting on the bare earthen floor of the byre, a huge, shaking, shadowy figure in a dim pool of light from a storm-lantern, watching every twist and turn of the cow, sensing her condition in every moaning bellow she gave, echoing each moan in his own aching, wondering heart; with his wife at home in bed on her back, ears cocked to hear a possible yell from her husband to come and give her fellow a hand with the suffering animal; while the few houses round hers sank into the night's silence, for they had not on them the care of a cow calving. There he sat in the darkness and dirt, cooped in with the cow, the heat from her body and the steam from her nostrils enfolding them both and making them one, a thick needle threaded with a thick cord near by, ready to stitch her belly up if it got torn during the delivery. His life, literature, art, and leisure were all embedded in the cow calving.

Every morning at four o'clock, this ganger forced himself from bed to catch the four-fifteen coming from the black north, nodding in the cold carriage with three comrades till it was five-to-six, and time to climb from the carriage resting in a Dublin siding, when they heard the bell calling them all to begin a day's work. He got home again, with his comrades, at eight o'clock, so doing sixteen hours a day at his everyday job with a few hours added to till his patch of ground and care for the cow; yet withal, he had plenty of leisure to go to Mass on all the Sundays.

This shaggy, lumbering, dim-minded man looked at Sean doubtfully, shrugged his shoulders, and grumbled to his gang, God in heaven! What kind of a scrawl am I gettin'? For Sean stood mute before him, a blink of fear in his eyes as if he expected to be set to move a mountain. Didja never ever have ne'er a shovel in your hand before in your life? he asked.

—Ay, said Sean; but not this sort of a one.

—An' which would you liefer start with—pick or shovel?

—Don't mind, said Sean carelessly; it's all the same to me.

—Ay, it's all th' same because you don't know how to use nather.

—Give him a shovel, said a stocky, red-bearded man anxiously, for he'll be penethratin' one of us if he thries to use a pick.

Sean thrust the shovel feverishly into the earth already hacked out of the little hill that was to make way for the new siding. It was a hard push to the broad-bladed shovel, with a short handle, and a crook like a crutch on the end of it, a push given by all the strength in his forearm only, unaided by the thrust of the knee the navvy gives whenever he forces the shovel home. He emptied what was on the shovel into a waiting cart, and thrust the blade into the hacked-out heap again. By the time a crawling half-hour had passed his hands were smarting; the veins in his forearm seemed to be knotting themselves together; salt sweat was trickling down his forehead and cheeks, oozing into his eyes, making them burn and veiling their vision with a salt smart. Now his chest was getting so tight that he could breathe only in short intermittent gasps. The first quarter of this work would do him in; he could never come back to this ordeal by sweat, pain, and breathlessness. He was flabby, soft, inalert, and useless. Through a reddish mist he saw the rest of the gang working away easily as if they were made of well-oiled steel. He sensed that they were enjoying themselves watching him, grimly glad to see his staring eyes, groggy legs, and hear his gasping breath.

—Not worth a damn to me, he heard the ganger mutter as he turned away to miss the new man's agony; lifts up as much on his shovel as a new-hatched hen 'ud lift up in her bake.

A low lot, thought Sean, a low lot to have to work with, and all rejoicing at the poor show I'm making. The less I'm able, the more hilarious and comfortable they'll feel. Oh, if Georgie was only here, but he's a tradesman, and above this crowd.

A tall, dark, raven-haired man edged close to him, saying softly out of the corner of his mouth, Go easy, take your time, draw it mild; watch me. You'll kill yourself the way you're goin'. Lower the shovel, bend quietly, don't jerk; now, the knee against the crutch of the handle—shove! Lift gently, don't jerk, and fling with a slight swing of both arms—see? Don't be afraid to straighten your back when you feel a sthrain, so's to keep yourself from gettin' too stiff. It'll all come to you in a few weeks, and you'll be as good as the best.

Try as he would, it only grew worse in spite of Bob Harvey's attempt at tutoring, and through the mist Sean saw the ganger shaking his head with annoyance, though he had kept his back turned on Sean's agony. His arms had grown into things torturing his body, and his gasping breath seemed to cling to where it was in his lungs, stifling him, rather than to tear a way through his gaping mouth. Sweat was hiding the blue sky above him; the sky itself was damp with sweat, the whole earth was tired and aching, all save only those dim figures working by his side, laughing silently at him for thinking he could become a navvy; but it was for food, for security, for freedom from want, and stick it he must. Now things at a distance seemed to be swinging about, as if they had suddenly gone tipsy, and the earth shook like a thing infirm. Every shovelful now pulled a bigger strain out of his taut, rebelling muscles; put a sharper ache into his creaking back. He was going slower; he could barely get the heavy shovel from the ground. He got reckless, gave a mighty lift and a jerking throw, sending a shovelful of earth and stones clattering against the neck and over the head of the startled ganger, knocking a pipe from his big mouth so that it fell to the ground and smashed itself into many pieces.

—What th' hell! he roared. What d'ye think ye're throwin'—thunderclaps, or wha'? Is it buryin' poor men alive yeh want to be? He looked down at the shattered pipe. A year's hard work seasonin' her gone for nothin'! Here, get a hold of a pick instead, th' way we won't have to be diggin' people outa what you've buried them in!

But the pick in Sean's lacerated hands was worse than the shovel, for he didn't know how to swing it neatly back over his shoulder within a small space, but swung it clumsily and widely so that those who worked next to him hurried away to give him room, and stood bunched together, watching in wonder the wild swing of the pick, effective in his hands as it would be in the hands of a child of twelve.

—Oh, Lord, what am I goin' to do with the boyo at all! burst out of Christy Mahon; keepin' three men from work to let him do a little. You're only ticklin' it, man. You'll kill somebody, so you will; that waypon's deadly in your dangerous hands; you'll dhrive it deep into the broad of somebody's back before you're done. You'll never do on this job. It's not fair to me. *Christy Mahon, is this all you've done for the day?* the Foreman'll say when he sthruts up; an' he after sendin' me a man that's burnin' to hamsthring half th' men workin' with him; an' afterwards their mothers or widows comin' in black blamin' me for permittin' murdher to be done in all innocence be a fella fortified be not knowin' what he was thryin' to do! Go on, an' get into it! he roared to the others, for it's a risk yous have to take, dependin' for safety on a smart lep outa th' way when yous see the point of the pick comin'.

So it was, too, carrying sleepers, slippy, hot, and pungent with the soak of creosote, he at one end, and a man at the other. They fought shy of joining him for fear he'd let his end go before the right moment, jabbing their end into their bodies, or nipping a finger by failing to give the heavy baulk of timber a tuneful swing before casting it from the permanent-way wagon. Bob Harvey, the tall, raven-haired ex-Guardsman, was the only one ready to man the end opposite to him, giving him slow sage counsel, showing him how to keep a proper poise, forward or backward counting the swings quietly, one, two—go! and in a little more than no-time Sean swung sleepers out of a wagon, or on the ground, and on to the ordered piles in perfect tune with his partner's help. Carrying the twenty-five-foot rails, six or eight men at one end, and the same number at the other, he was always opposite the ex-Guardsman, and his and Sean's shoulders and hands were always interlocked; and though he went home, night after night, a clumsy-moving mass of aching stiffness, seeing when he got home an anxious look in his mother's eyes, and heard her murmur, when she saw the raw red on the palms of his hands, Maybe the job's too much for your strength, he stood up to it, silent, with no shadow of a song near his lips, and no sigh either, grim and grand; mouth-clenched resolution his armour, and the determination to become as good as the next, his shield and buckler. His first fortnight's pay opened the heart of the dirty little grocer, purveyor of the workers' district, so that for the first time for a year and more he and his mother fed well. He went on wringing power and confidence from the passing hours, till the aches gradually left him, and the stiffness was gone. His body now became flexible, his arms strong, his legs firm in tackling shovel, pick, crowbar, rope, scaffolding-pole, wheelbarrow, hod, or sledge with the best of them, beating the ex-Guardsman who got pale, and whimpered when asked to mount higher than the sixth rung of a ladder; and, at last, found himself the one man in the gang who could mount a ladder with a hod carrying near eight stone in it, balancing it with equal ease on right shoulder or on left.

God, he felt proud all right. Felt as proud as he did when he first fell into step with Shakespeare. His body was now in fine alignment with his mind. *Mentis sano in corpore sanis*, that's how it went, he thought; and, if the words were curious, the sense was sane. He often inflated his chest now, forty-four inches round normally; often felt the sturdy muscles in arm and thigh; and as he swung pick or sledge-hammer, thrust in shovel, hung on a rope, or swarmed up a ladder with a hod on his shoulder, song once more bubbled brightly from his lips. And to him, most of the songs were new; songs of an Ireland astir, awake, and eager; an Ireland forging fresh thought out of bygone history, and present hopes to create a glowing, passionate, and permanent chapter from which a great nation would be born. Oh, silver trumpets be ye lifted up, and call to the great race that is to come! cried Yeats, and Sean cried the call with him too. The sword was being polished, the rifle cleaned, and a new banner of green, white, and orange was being attached to the old staff, and was nearly ready to be broken out to fly in the four winds of Eirinn. Dr. Douglas de Hyde was rushing round, shouting in at the Dublin Castle Gates, It's a Gael I am without shame to meself or danger to you; in at the windows of Trinity College, A country without a language is a country without a tongue; on every hill in the country, Waken up your courage, O Ireland; and in at the doorway of Maynooth College, in rather a quiet way, Irish in the New University—or else . . . !

Gaelic Leaguers were pulling reluctant and timorous native speakers from the darkness of their little grey homes in the west, hardly waiting, when they laid hands on one, for him to get his coat on, shoving him where he didn't want to go, amid the clapping of white hands; mixing his tatters with the elegant array of tweed suits, high white collars, and poplin ties of civil servants, doctors, chemists, revenue officers, and teachers, hauling the frightened fellow into the midst of garrulous emotion, declaring that the native speaker was all in all to Ireland, was Ireland, all Ireland, the whole Ireland, and nothing else but Ireland, so help us God; the long-hidden Ireland, chidden Ireland, forbidden Ireland by the Ascendancy gang that ruled the land. The native Irish speaker was forced to walk upright through a fierce white light beating on him everywhere, and he seeking often in his heart a kindlier darkness so that he could slink into the friendliness of gloom again; but they placed him to the forefront of every meeting, applauded every word that came out of his mouth, assuring him that the day of shame for the native speaker had gone forever; for now whenever two or three were gathered together in the name of Ireland, there was the native speaker in the midst of them.

And while all these respectable, white-collared, trim-suited Gaelic Leaguers, snug in their selected branches, living rosily in Whitehall, Drumcondra, Rathgar, Donnybrook, and all the other nicer habitations of the city, nuzzled round the bewildered native speaker, away went, without money, with often an empty belly, on rusty bicycles, under scorching suns or pelting rain, eyes gleaming, backs bent, hands blenched by the tight grip on the handlebars, unmindful of the hawthorn in June, changing the hedges into never-ending miles of nuns' veiling, or the sparkle of frost on the twisting roads, or of mountains towering up around them to threaten or protect, or of the gentle lap-lap of the waves on a summer sea, or of their battering on to the beach when the winds of winter blew, went the travelling teacher; backs bent, eyes gleaming, hands asweat or frozen on the handlebar, their feet going round endlessly on a glorious treadmill, went the travelling teacher, rushing here, dashing there, to teach a class, to help found a new branch, spreading the Irish as a tree sends forth its pollen, seeking neither to gain a reward nor to pay a penance, but for thee, only for thee, dear land, and for thy language that it may come back to us, be brought back to us by persuasion or by force; snatching time reluctantly to take a meal, spending a few restless hours in jaded sleep, exposed to sun and rain and wind and frost and snow and black sleet, hot and cold by turns, many of them sliding with a wan sigh into a grave by the wayside where they went, worn and worried, into a quiet end from the warm fight and the hope that flickered wanly in most hearts save their own fiery ones; others seizing their bicycles ere they had flattened in their fall, to bend their backs, evoke a gleam in their eyes, to grip the handlebars till the knuckles whitened, and dash off, too, through shower and shine and storm, wet with summer's dew, or soaked in wintry sleet; on, on endlessly, endlessly, reckless and frenzied, endlessly cycling on through country road, through village street, by hilly paths, lifting the heads of grazing mountain-sheep to glance and wonder, skirting mountains alive with their loneliness, a goat, browsing rapidly, lifting a bearded chin to cast a sudden look at the stir that marred his solitude, unawake to the need of the fevered man's hurry to keep a step ahead of time; to bring their lovely language back to the Gael, he hastened on, endlessly, hastening on, the muinteor taisdal, the travelling teacher; Caitlin ni Houlihan busy in the woods near by searching for leaves to weave a garland, but finding naught but bramble and coarse gorse, thistledown and thorns, jagging her bare feet, but searching still, and silence everywhere.

Here and there, in one or another hole or corner, Tim Healy was mocking Dillon, while down south William O'Brien was trying to fight everyone in his All For Ireland League, unaware, the fools, that when they killed Parnell they killed themselves too; while their followers sauntered in and out of the House draping their souls with all the moods and manners of their masters, carrying in occasionally a stuffed wolf-dog to give a mechanical bark to show that Ireland still lived through joy and through tears, while Johnny Redmond smilingly waved a bright-green flag smelling sweetly of the fragrant English rose.

Far away from it all, a tiny group of men followed Jim Connolly through the streets to the cul-de-sac curving round the circular side of the Royal Bank of Ireland, a large slouch hat covering Connolly's head, a large round head, fronted by a rather commonplace face, its heaviness lightened by fine, soft, luminous eyes; the heavy jaws were jewelled with a thick-lipped, sensuous mouth, mobile, and a little sarcastic, bannered peacefully by a thick and neatly-trimmed moustache. His ears were well set to the head, the nose was a little too thick, and gave an obstinate cast to the bright eyes, and a firm fleshy neck bulged out over a perfectly white hard collar. The head and neck rested solidly on a broad sturdy trunk of a body, and all were carried forward on two short pillar-like legs, slightly bowed, causing him to waddle a little in his walk, as if his legs were, in the way of a joke, trying faintly and fearfully to throw him off his balance. Silent, he walked on, looking grim and a little surly, followed by the tiny dribble of followers, one of them carrying a box so that, when Connolly spoke, he might be lifted up before the people as he preached the gospel of discontent smoking faintly in the hearts of most men. Up on the box, the soft slouch hat came off, and the hard, sparsely-covered head turned this way and that, the mobile mouth flickered with words, red with the woe of the common people, words that circled noisily over the heads of the forty or fifty persons hunched clumsily together to oppose the chill of the wind that whipped around the corner of the curving, graceful, classical hip of the Bank, murmuring in the mellowed, matronly, plump loveliness of its lines and curves, *Here in my ample and elegant belly lies safe the golden life of Ireland, fructifying warmly there, fulfilling the Jehovahian command to multiply and replenish the earth.*

A step aside, within the counter-spoiled building, lay the dead ashes of the last fire lit in the Assembly Room of the Irish House of Lords; a fire that had warmed the backsides of the Lords in their crimson-plush coats and black-satin breeches, or black-satin coats and crimson-plush trousers; or of them that strutted in a bright-blue Volunteer military coat, gleaming yellow trousers, all bedecked with crimson braid and the richest of gold embroidery, that voted for the Act of Union with England, side by side with the Maynooth catholic bishops; or against the Act, side by side with the Orange Lodges of Dublin and Belfast.

Here was Up Griffith's seed of life for Ireland, needing but her King, Lords, and Commons to form a coloured trinity that would forge a terrifying power in Ireland of the Wise Welcomes, darken the seven seas with Irish shipping, deaden the songs of birds with the hum and whirr of machinery, and flood the quays, the streets, the homes of the two gigantic Atlantic ports of Galway and Sligo and the one-way street town of Blacksod Bay with corn and wine and wool, oil and amber, mahogany, teak, and rosewood to build houses for the Irish to live in; juniper gin and jars of spices; Indian muslin, cashmere shawls of crimson and white, or green and turquoise for every Irish snowy-breasted pearl, each colleen dyas, for every girl milking her cow, each dark rosaleen, every dark woman of the glen, and every red-haired man's wife; tobacco the rarest the sun could season, peculiar birds for all the parks, bales of shimmering silks from China, and snowy ivory, too, for beads; luscious figs and pomegranates in curious coloured wickerwork baskets, lying in down of the Tibetan ducks, all gums and perfumes of Arabia; and dainty leather for ladies' shoes, all tooled for style in a Persian garden; sherbet rich in crystal vases for a ploughman's drink through the pull of the harvest. Jasus Christ, the vision was lovely!

It was all written in the book of *Resurgamise Upsadaiseum Hungarius*, a huge tome five feet long, three feet wide, and two feet deep, containing in itself all the lore that is or ever was, all laws, licenses, customs, pardons, punishments, perquisites, genealogies, constitutions, magna chartas, social contracts, books of rights, das kapitals, origins of species, tallboy talmuds, speeches from the dock, carried about everywhere on the back of Up Griffith Up Davis, as a pedlar carries his pack, compiled from the original sources by the sage himself, deep in a corner under a secret rowan-tree, in the dim cloisters of the old Abbey of St. Fownes, the Soggart Aroon acting as secretary, assisted by Kelly and Burke and Shea all in their jackets green, with the Bard of Armagh stringing the harp to *He's the Man You Don't See Every Day* to give their minds a lift.

Here Sean was now, free for the moment from the pick and shovel, for it was Sunday, of a January, on his way home after playing centre-field in a hurling match, and having had tea with a comrade hurler, stopping for a few seconds to listen to this man, Connolly, who was trying to destroy the fine work being done by Up Griffith, and make a medley of his cut-and-dried Hungarian Gospel. A thin, haggard, lugubrious young fellow, wear-

ing a red tie, moved aimlessly through the little crowd, droning out the
titles of a bunch of colour-covered pamphlets that he carried in his hand, a
drone that was half a whisper and half a threat, *Socialism Made Easy*, a
penny a copy, only a penny the copy; tuppence each, *Can a Catholic be a
Socialist?* only tuppence each; the truth for tuppence; Hubert Bland's great
work, *Can a Catholic be a Socialist?* The gaunt young man, whose name
was Tom Egan, was the most cheerless sight ever seen by Sean. Everything
about him had a downward drag; his jaws sagged down to the edge of his
chin; his long nose seemed to be bent on pulling itself out of his face; his
eyes were mirrors of energetic despondency; his lips were twisted into lines
of deeply-cut complaints; but in the midst of all this misery his red tie
blazed in his shallow bosom.

—Who's th' big-bodied man gettin' up to speak? asked a man of him as
he passed displaying the pamphlets.

—That's James Connolly, our secretary, an' if you knew all you should
know, you'd know without askin'.

—Secretary of what? asked Sean.

—Aw, God, th' ignorance here's devastatin'! said Egan, giving a wryer
twist to his melancholy mouth; Secretary of the Irish Socialist Republican
Party, an' if you knew all you should know, you wouldn't have t' ask.
Penny each, *Socialism Made Easy*, be the renowned Socialist leadher,
James Connolly.

—It doesn't look to be a mighty force of a party, murmured Sean.

—Aw, you count be numbers, d'ye? and he looked with pitiful tolerance
at Sean.

—There's certainly something in them, said Sean; God fights on the side
of the big battalions, you know—or so Napoleon said.

—We aren't concerned with Napoleon, an' God has nothin' to say in this
meetin'.

—Jasus, don't we know it! burst from the man who had asked the first
question.

—An' if you were with us, comrade, said the gaunt one, laying a hand on
Sean's shoulder, and ignoring the ignorant remark of the ignorant man,
you'd make one more.

—I thought you said you didn't put any pass on numbers?

—With a hurley stick under your arm, a gay blue-and-green jersey on
your chest, and, I suppose, a cushy job, you can well afford to mock the woe
of th' world!

—I am a labourer, and that's not quite a cushy job; I have no desire to
mock anything, and there's more things than woe in the world.

—What more is there, comrade?

—There's joy and a song or two: the people sang as they went their way
to tear the Bastille down.

—You're too oul'-fashioned for me, mate, said the gaunt one. Look! there's your proper leadher there, and he gestured to the fringe of the crowd, a little way from where they stood; Arthur Griffith, who's stopped to have a little quiet silent laugh. Well, he'll wake one day before he knows the night is gone to find himself and his gang swept away by what he's scornin' now.

Right enough, there was Up Griffith Up Thomas a Davis, hunched close inside his thick dark Irish coat, a dark-green velour hat on his head, a thick slice of leather nailed to his heels to lift him a little nearer the stars, for he was somewhat sensitive about the lowness of his stature. His great protruding jaws were thrust forward like a bull's stretched-out muzzle; jaws that all his admirers spoke of, or wrote about, laying it down as an obvious law that in those magnificent jaws sat the God-given sign of a great man. And Arthur Up Griffith, to give him his due, did all he could to give the fiction substance and fact. As plain as a shut mouth could say, he said he was Erin's strong, silent man.

What was he thinking of as he stood there, grim and scornful? Tormenting himself with the fading vision of a most lovely lady whose golden hair was hanging down her back, so full of fire that a tress of it would give light to a group threshing corn in a black barn on a dark night. Maybe stroking the right hand, oh! worthy right hand, that had laid a whip on the back of a little tittle-tattle Dublin editor of a gossip journal when he whispered *spy* about the Helen of Eireann who had the loveliness to launch a battle and go through it with the walk of a queen. He hid his hatred of a rival in the wrapping of Erin's noble emblem, boys, the green flag, around him; he composed gnarled remarks in his weekly paper against him who embroidered lovely cloths to put beneath the feet of the fair one, to shelter their grace and whiteness from the dust of the street; and sang songs that made a flame of her fair ear and sent a swell into her bosom with the pride of what a singer can say out of a purple-and-white love. Art Up Griffith Up Thomas a Davis's cold eyes saw the black-maned head of Yeats in the clouds, saw it on the earth beneath, looking at him from the *Book of Kells,* and staring down from the ceiling of the simple room wherein he slept. So he began to mock at the phantoms, saying that the fashioner of the play *Caitlin ni Houlihan* had become a king's pensioner; that he had walked away from her four beautiful green fields into an English paved court; Ochone, widda Malone, d'ye hear me talkin'? And widda Malone said she'd heard right enough, and th' name that was once a jewel in Erin's girdle had dwindled into a dull stone; and Willie Reilly and his dear colleen bawn said, He was never much; he is nothin' now; and the Rose of Tralee said that he was just a lonely gateway now, where no-one enthered; and Mary sitting on the stile murmured it was all very shocking; the minstrel boy went about saying that Yeats now was no more than the seams on the grass showing where a house once stood; while Nora Creena closed her eyes, nodded her pretty head sagely, and murmured the less said about it all the better. A pensioner of an English king—pooh! bah!

Instinctively Sean stood by Yeats, in spite of the little he could guess then, and the less he knew. We have too few, too few such men to spare a one like Yeats the poet, and the Gaelic Leaguers who heard him grew silent. Devil a much you fellows do to keep a few shillings jingling in the poet's pocket. What about the Israelites who took gold, silver, and jewels from the Egyptians before they left them? If England pays the man's rent, then let it be counted unto righteousness for her. None of you know a single poem by Yeats. Not even *The Ballad of Father Gilligan.* And the poor oul' gaum, Cardinal Logue, condemning *Countess Cathleen* though he hadn't read a line of it. We were paying a deep price for that sort of thing since Parnell went away from us. He himself had read the ballad only.

There the little squat figure of Griffith stood, no tremor stirring the spectacles on his nose. Probably thinking more of Yeats than of Connolly, thought Sean. It wasn't Connolly's face Griffith saw, but Yeats's, and the evening was full of the poet's verses. Well, the golden tresses would gleam no more for Yeats, at any rate. The small white feet would seek another pathway, one of thorns rather than of broidered cloths or dreams. Oh, Cathleen ni Houlihan, your way's a thorny way! And Ireland's rock of ages, Griffith, stiffened with elation, firm in his Irish woven tweed, armoured with the stamp of Deunta in Eirinn on its collar and on the seat of the pants. And wasn't Up Griffith a poet himself? You bet he was. What about the one written to give Major McBride a lift in the Mayo election?

> God bless you, John McBride, aroon,
> God bless your Irish corps!
> With courage of the Keltic race you've gone to help the Boers.
> True friends by Bann and Liffey banks,
> By Suir and Shannon side,
> Send you their hearts' best sympathy—
> God bless you, John McBride!

Let Yeats arise now and go to Inisfree, and stay and hide himself well there in his strict cabin of clay and wattles made—though, if y' asked me, thought Griffith, he wouldn't know what wattles were,—and let him sow and hoe and crow over his nine bean rows, and live on them, with honey from the hive of the honey bees, and his evening full of the linnet's wings, regardless of the fact that no-one in Eirinn wants an evening full of a linnet's wings. Far more profitable for them to go to hear me lecture on how Hungary hitch-hiked herself into independence; or to listen enthralled to

the gallant deeds done by the wild swans of Coole—whatthehellamisaying
—of the wild geese in far foreign fields from Dunkirk to Belgrade, the
O'Haras, Maguires, Reillys, McGauleys, O'Briens and O'Brady's, with
hosts of other leaders, and men of many clans, fighting for anyone that
would furnish them with a sword, a good word to go on, and a glass of malt
at the end of a battle.

Sean edged nearer to where the great man, Griffith, stood surrounded by
the gaunt one, now behind, now to his left, to his right a moment later, and
then circling in front of him, murmuring balefully in Griffith's direction,
Socialism Made Easy, by the renowned James Connolly, only a penny
each. But the great man with the brain of ice, in the greatcoat, underneath
the green velour, never moved. The widely-lensed spectacles and the thick
moustache and the thrust-out chin listened in cold silence to Connolly's
words; and Sean remembered how, at meetings in the rooms of the Sinn
Fein Central Branch, Up Griffith had often called on Sean to speak, and he
had spoken eloquently in Irish and English, amused that Connolly, Pike,
Ling, and a few other Irish Republican Socialists had to listen silent and
respectful to the flow of the Gaedhilge, understanding not a word of what
was being said; with Up Griffith sitting bolt-upright and grim in the chair,
huge jaws forced forward, ears cocked, though he understood no more than
he'd understand the sad songs sung by the Children of Lir tossed about on
the foam of the Swanee river. So he edged nearer till his elbow gently
touched the stiff frame standing in the greatcoat.

—It's cold it is the night that's in it, he said in Irish.

The widely-lensed spectacles, velour hat, and intrusive moustache turned
towards him, the rocky road to Dublin jaws thrust themselves farther out
over the turned-up collar of the greatcoat, but the clenched mouth
remained shut; then all turned, and, without a word, went their way.

—Little bourgious bastard! growled the gaunt one, glaring after the little
conceited figure. Not enough banks in the counthry but he must start another—him and his Sinn Fein Bank! The dumb yahoo! Curse o' God on
the bit he is above an ordinary little bourgious bastard!

Thinking, most likely, of what Connolly has been saying, thought Sean
as he followed the great man slowly. *Cheek of those fellows stating the
English were brothers. Connolly should know better. But my icy brain can
never be deceived. A capitalist government would never destroy capitalist
property. Bah! As if an English government cared a damn about Irish property. Dog won't eat dog, says Connolly. Nonsense! Besides the Irish aren't
dogs, even if the English are.*

Griffith doesn't understand Ireland, thought Sean; no, in no way. He is
simply delighted to dream as he walks through Ireland's junk-shop of all the
tawdry paraphernalia of 1882. He hasn't the slimmest connection with a

Gaedhilge proverb or a Gaedhilge song. He has no inkling of what burns in the breast of him who looks back on, and lives with, the

> Outlawed man in a land forlorn,
> He scorned to turn and fly;
> But he kept the cause of freedom safe
> On the mountains of Pomeroy.

He never even walks with the shade of Swift, for if I brought him tomorrow to be with them who work with me; among Christy Mahon, Bob Harvey, Bob Jones who'd sell the King of Ireland's son for a pint, Ned Smith who'd steal a cross off an ass's back, and all the rest, he'd be lost. His highest vision is no higher than the counter in his Sinn Fein Bank. He strikes a match, and thinks it the torch of freedom. A lighter of little gas-lamps to show the Irish where to walk. The sword of light would turn him to ashes if ever he tried to hold it. Ah! he's thinking of Trinity College; for he saw the green velour turning to look at the austere façade of the memorable building, sighing, probably, that the young man inside didn't hear ear to ear with him. More inclined to Yeats's poetic bombast than to me. One of England's strongest bastions. Here was a group of them coming along now, singing *Daisy, Daisy, Give Me Your Answer, Do,* shouting it out with vengeance and vim. Oh! the vulgarity of the anglicised Irish mind! To think that Thomas a Davis had once gone in and out of those gates. Hardly believable. They surged uncivilly around him, jostling him out into the gutter. Oh, Cathleen ni Houlihan, your way's a thorny way!

—God, it's Arthur Griffith! shouted one of them.

—*Alumna licentiae, quam stulti libertatem vocabunt,* bawled another, waving his cap over his head, shouldering Up Griffith with a sly sliding movement, making the man nearly lose his balance; but he recovered, walked slantwise back to the side-walk, bypassing the students, and marched on without either a word or a gesture.

Sean felt angry, for Griffith was something of a leader, deserving jail from the point of view of the conquerors, but deserving respect as well. Strange, he thought, swinging his hurley into a poise that could swiftly jab the ribs of anyone likely to try to jostle him from the pathway. Strange and curious, he thought, that one able to speak Latin, who got a golden education denied to Griffith or himself, having a fine home in the country or in Rathmines, son, maybe, of a clergyman, a doctor, or a judge, strange he didn't know what decent manners were. He could calmly understand them hotly cracking skulls in the emotional medley of a royal visit, when the Dubliners were out with the battle-cries and their green flags; but in the cold of a quiet wintry night when citizens moved about intent on business, recreation, or love, indifferent to their national submission for the moment, to spout abuse on a citizen without warrant even of English law, or the gallant provocation of opposing tirades, was, to Sean, a thing that couldn't be understood of common sense or tangible decency. Let them look to it if they pushed him a hair-breadth away from where he was walking. But they didn't; they passed by and took not the slightest notice of him as he followed Arthur marching on sturdily ahead as if nothing had happened.

The next day of a dark cold morning, Sean in the forge blowing the bellows to make the fire roar so that the smith might repoint his pick blunted by the work of the day before, for the soil of the deep trench navvies dig, to sow great iron pipes to carry a main supply of water, is hard and stony, and the point of a pick is soon deprived of its eagerness to bite: here in the yellow and red gleam of the flame of the fire, watching the smith, Dick Bagnal's lanky form waiting for the pick to redden, one sooty hand on the butt of the pick, its point in the heart of the fire, Sean saw again the meeting of the night before, the squat, swaying form of Connolly speaking from his box, and the cold staring lens-covered eyes of Griffith watching, the big mouth beneath the great moustache grim and clenched and silent. Both of them out for Ireland, all for Ireland, yet neither of them could understand her. Both were a wide way from the real Ireland, and it was not in either of them to come closer. One man alone, of that time, had in him all that prophesied of the Ireland yet to come; the Ireland that would blossom into herself many, many years from now. This man alone had the hand to hold the sword of light. He held it now, and its rays were sparkling all over the valley of the Boyne. There were visions of handicrafts, of furniture, of woven garments, new, yet full of the scent of the days gone by; of pottery decked with the coloured glory of Keltic spirals and intricate, waving, twisting patterns, new too, but touched with the grandeur of the *Book of Kells* and the gaiety of the *Book of MacDurnan;* here, whereof old time protestant men for King William wrestled to the death with catholic men for King James, falling with the arms of hatred round each other by the borders of the Boyne, was seen again the sway of the scarlet, green, grey, or saffron kilt; here was heard the musical scream of the war-pipes; here were heard the countless stories of Eireann, long in thrall, with the scent of freedom clinging round them still; and song burst out, and filled the valley with hope; and the plough and the cross shone on the biggest of banners; and *The Irish Peasant,* one of the finest papers Ireland ever had, told all about them; while among all this gay-coloured energy and excitement walked the dark-eyed, black-haired W. P. O'Ryan, shy, sensitive, one with the peasant, the worker, and the scholar. All aglow he was, and firm set to make the Pope's green island a busy place and beautiful. Half a step behind came a Man, a bacon-curer, the surety of the paper, and a helper with money for the things they thought of doing, whose heart was warm with the coloured resolution all around him. All was fine till the clergy came to murmur against it, and Cardinal Log lashed out to yell that it was a shame to undermine the Holy Faith! And the Man's wife said to her husband, You've got to hearken to what these holy men witness against them and thee. Have nothing thou to do with this bad bold man, O'Ryan, but cast him off, and come thou into the house, lest an evil thing befall us here, and lest worse befall us when we pass away to Purgatory. And he hearkened unto his wife, and shut himself up in his own house, condemning certain things written by O'Ryan, already condemned by the Cardinal, though never read by him; for the Cardinal had the power to see a hole through an iron pot; and so O'Ryan was left alone to fight a host of snarling clergy who silenced song and story, drove away the marching, kilted men, hunted O'Ryan from the Boyne to the Liffey, then to the Dublin Quay, and finally from the last spot where his clinging feet still stood, away, away with you, from Ireland altogether, away from her for ever and a day! And Sean wondered that Hyde said nothing, that the Gaelic League made no moan, and Griffith, indifferent to a greater man, shook no angry fist, but let him go, and so he went for ever. And Sean was sad, for it was O'Ryan who first gave his written words a value, and spaced his thoughts over a fine column of The Irish Nation; words, under the name of Sound the Loud Trumpets, that struck at the educational system Augustus Birrell was hanging around Ireland's neck. Over the grave of this brave man, this cultured man, a silent hurrah; a big, broad, and scornful spit on the grave of the Cardinal.

Down in the deep trench, shored up with planks and cross-pieces, a long way from Ireland's four beautiful green fields, side by side with the huge glossy black cylinders, Sean watched the broad backs of the navvies bending, rising, and bending again, as they worked on, making way for another length of the monster black pipe, looking like a prehistoric ebony worm that men were uncovering now after a rest of a million years; while far above their heads a dim damp dawn crept slowly over the sky. Not one of these brawny boys had ever even heard of Griffith or of Yeats. They lived their hard and boisterous life without a wish to hear their names. A good many of them had done seven years' service in the British Army, and now served on the Reserve, for sixpence a day wasn't to be sneezed at. What to them were the three Gaelic candles that light up every darkness: truth, nature, and knowledge. Three pints of porter, one after the other, would light up the world for them. If he preached the Gaelic League to any one of them, the reply would probably be, Aw, Irish Ireland me arse, Jack, not makin' you an ill answer, oul' son. What would the nicely-suited, white-collared respectable members of the refined Gaelic League branches of Dublin do if they found themselves in the company of these men? Toiling, drinking, whoring, they lived everywhere and anywhere they could find a ready-made lodging or room. They didn't remember the glories of Brian the Brave. Beyond knowing him as an oul' king of Ireland in God's time, they knew nothing and cared less. Their upper life was a hurried farewell to the *News of the World* on Sunday morning, and a dash to what was called short twelve Mass in the Pro-Cathedral, the shortest Mass said in the land; and then a slow parade to the various pubs, and a wearisome wait till the pubs unveiled themselves by sliding the shutters down, and let the mass of men crowd in for refreshment. And yet Sean felt in his heart that these men were all-important in anything to be done for Ireland. Well, there was no sound of a linnet's wings here; nothing but the thud of the pick, the tearing sound of the shovel thrust into the gravel, the loud steady pulse of the pump sucking away the surface water, and the cries of the men handling the derrick from which the huge pipes swung, and the irritating squelch of the men's boots as they sunk into, and were pulled out of, the thick and sticky yellow clay. While he swung the sledge-hammer down on the hardy head of the bright steel wedge imprisoned in a gad held by a comrade, to break through a harder crust the pick couldn't penetrate, he cursed himself that he couldn't afford to spend a month, a fortnight, or even a week in a summer school at peace in an Irish-speaking district. Three or four visits, and he would be as fluent a speaker of the Gaelic as any in Ireland. Even now, with all their chances, all their means providing them with the best of books, there were few of them could speak as well and as rapidly as he; and none of them with such a fire of eloquence. Few of them hadn't heard him speak at one time or another, yet never a one of them had even asked why he didn't go to Rinn or Tourmakeady when the summer sun shone, and share with them the joy of living with their very own. If he went up to a meeting of the Coiste Gnotha, the Head Executive of the Gaelic League, and, leaning over the table they sat around keeping time in their talk to the snores of Edward Martyn, asleep in an easy-chair, said, Look here, boys, I love the Irish; I've learned a lot; I want to spend a holiday in an Irish district, Connemara for preference, but I've no money; couldn't you people fork out enough to fix me there for a week or two, so that my Irish may be as the rain falling on the earth, or the lightning splitting the black clouds? What would happen? The tidy-minded, uninspirable secretary, Paddy O'Daly, would come over, grip his arm, lead him to the door, and say, Now, now, we're engaged in very important business. The like of them would hurry by Whitman spitting out of him as he leaned by a corner of the Bowery. And doing so, they'll die, for whoever walks a furlong without sympathy walks to his own funeral dressed in his shroud. Ah, to hell with them!

—Eh, there; look out, Jack! warned his mate: the sledge near missed the wedge that time!

* * *

PROMETHEUS HIBERNICA

✤ ✤ ✤

It was a bitter day. Winds, cold and nipping, deeply swept up from the bay, curling crossly round into Beresford Place, trying to snarl its way through to the heat in the dense crowd packing with warm life the square that stretched out in front of the King's elegant Custom House. Here, too, had Parnell stood, defiant, speaking from the building's wide steps, like a flame-pointed spear on the people's altar, endurance and patient might in his beautiful wine-coloured eyes. The rascals, cleric and lay, out-talked thee, hissed thee, tore at Ireland to get at thee, and God remembered for many a long year, silencing their voice till He grew sorry for the work-worn people, and sent another man into their midst whose name was Larkin.

Through the streets he strode, shouting into every dark and evil-smelling hallway. The great day of a change has come; Circe's swine had a better time than you have; come from your vomit; out into the sun. Larkin is calling you all!

And many were afraid, and hid themselves in corners. Some ventured as far as the drear and dusky doorway to peer out, and to say, Mr. Larkin, please excuse us, for we have many things to do and to suffer; we must care for cancerous and tubercular sick, and we must stay to bury our dead. But he caught them by the sleeve, by the coat collar, and shouted, Come forth, and fight with the son of Amos who has come to walk among the men and women of Ireland. Let the sick look after the sick, and let the dead bury the dead. Come ye out to fight those who maketh the ephah small and the shekel great; come out that we may smite the winter house with the summer house; till the houses of ivory shall perish and the great houses shall have an end. And Sean had joined the Union.

Following afar off for a while, Sean had come at last to hear Larkin speak, to stand under a red flag rather than the green banner. On this day the Liffey's ruffled waters were roughly lapping the granite walls of the quays; the dark-brown tide was high, and above it, the big white gulls, squealing, went circling round, tensing their wide wings whenever they went against the wind that made them turn to cut it sideways. Brown and yellow leaves, drifting from the little trees along the paths, curled restlessly along the streets, rustling against the legs of the people as if eager to find shelter and safety there from the peevish and vexing wind. A grey, sulky sky overhead was the one banner flown, but all eyes were on the brave new sign in golden letters on a green field, running along the length of the building, telling all that here was the rallying camp of *The Irish Transport and General Workers Union,* while over the massive doorway the name *Liberty Hall* gave a welcome and twenty to all who came to fight for a life something higher than the toiling oxen and the bleating sheep. Here were the sons of the Gael, men of the Pale, brought up, lugged up, in the mire of Dublin's poverty, their children slung about at school, while those a little more adventurous than the rest were carted away to the reformatories of Artane and Glencree.

Aha, here now was the unfolding of the final word from the evolving words of the ages, the word of the modern, the word En-Masse, and a mighty cheer gave it welcome. From a window in the building, leaning well forth, he talked to the workers, spoke as only Jim Larkin could speak, not for an assignation with peace, dark obedience, or placid resignation; but trumpet-tongued of resistance to wrong, discontent with leering poverty, and defiance of any power strutting out to stand in the way of their march onward. His was a handsome tense face, the forehead swept by deep black hair, the upper lip of the generous, mobile mouth hardened into fierceness by a thick moustache, the voice, deep, dark, and husky, carrying to the extreme corners of the square, and reaching, Sean thought, to the uttermost ends of the earth. Here was the word En-Masse, not handed down from Heaven, but handed up from a man. In his voice was the march of Wat Tyler's men, the yells and grunts of those who took the Bastille, the sigh of the famine-stricken, the last shout from those, all bloodied over, who fell in Ninety-eight on the corn slopes of Royal Meath; here were nursery rhyme and battle song, the silvery pleasing of a lute with the trumpet-call to come out and carry their ragged banners through the gayer streets of the city, so that unskilled labour might become the vanguard, the cavaliers and can-noniers of labour's thought and purpose.

The voice of mingled gold and bronze went on picturing the men to themselves—as they were, as they ought to be; showing them that they hadn't been denied the gift of a holy fire from God; this man in the drab garments of a drink-sodden nature; that man whose key of Heaven was a racing record; yonder fellow fearing to be above a black-leg, refusing to join his comrades out on strike; and, worst of all, the unsightly scab taking the job of a comrade out in a fight for better conditions for all. The voice called for the rejection of the timid one who led them, who hid in an armchair and let their men be ruled by the strength in a policeman's baton.

—Who will stand, who will fight, for the right of men to live and die like men? he called out, the large, strong hand stretched out of the window gesturing over the head of the crowd.

—We will! came back in a serried shout that echoed along the restless river, making the gliding gulls pause, turn away, and wonder, as a cloud of chapped and gnarled and grimy hands were lifted high in the air; strong hands and daring, hands that could drive a pile, handle a plough, sail a ship, stoke a furnace, or build a city.

—Gifts of the Almighty, went on the voice, labour—a gift, not a curse—poetry, dancing, and principles; and Sean could see that here was a man who would put a flower in a vase on a table as well as a loaf on a plate. Here, Sean thought, is the beginning of the broad and busy day, the leisurely evening, the calmer night; an evening full of poetry, dancing, and the linnet's wings; these on their way to the music of the accordion, those to that of a philharmonic orchestra; and after all, to sleep, perchance to dream; but never to be conscious of a doubt about tomorrow's bread, certain that, while the earth remaineth, summer and winter should not cease, seedtime and harvest never fail:

> *The bell branch of Ireland may chime again,*
> *To charm away the merchant from his guile,*
> *And turn the farmer's memory from his cattle,*
> *And hush to sleep the roaring ranks of battle,*
> *And all grow friendly for a little while.*

No; for ever. Battles of war changed for battles of peace. Labour in all its phases the supreme honour of life, broadening the smile on the world's creased face daily.

The workers of Dublin, Wexford, Cork, Galway, Waterford, Limerick, and many towns, rallied to Larkin's side. Out of jail he had come into their arms. Starting in Belfast, Larkin brought orange and green together as they had never been together before. On to Derry, city of Columkille and the brave Apprentice Boys. Down to Cork, then, where the employers marshalled their first phalanx of bitter opposition. There he was charged with a conspiracy of trying to defraud the workers of their hard-earned money by a witness who had to be sent home because he was drunk; and a Crown and Anchor solicitor who was also the solicitor to the Employers' Federation, harmonising in himself the glory of God and the honour of Ireland; though one of the two magistrates trying the case, Sir Edward Fitzgerald, had the temerity to declare that every fair-minded man in Cork had the idea in his head that if there was a conspiracy at all, it was a conspiracy of Dublin Castle and the Cork employers to prevent the working men of the city from uniting for their self-defence in the future. But, all the same, for this reason Jim got a sweet little sentence of twelve months with hard labour by the other magistrate on the bench, justifying the righteousness of the Lion and Unicorn over the magistrate's head. But the grin came off their faces when the King, after some months had passed, had the common sense and graciousness to grant a free pardon to a fine man who was dragging images of

God from a condition worse than that of the beasts in the field of the poorest Irish farmer.

So Jim came out of jail, and in a room of a tenement in Townshend Street, with a candle in a bottle for a torch and a billycan of tea, with a few buns for a banquet, the Church militant here on earth of the Irish workers, called the Irish Transport and General Workers Union, was founded, a tiny speck of flame now, but soon to become a pillar of fire into which a brand was flung by Yeats, the great poet; Orpen, the painter; A.E., who saw gods in every bush and bramble; Corkery, the story-teller, James Stephens, the poet and graceful satirical jester; Dudley Fletcher, the Rector of Coolbanagher, and even Patrick Pearse, wandering softly under the Hermitage elms, thinking, maybe, of Robert Emmet, the darlin' of Erin, and his low response to the executioner's *Are you ready, sir?*, of *Not yet, not yet;* even he was to lift a pensive head to the strange new shouting soon to be heard in Dublin streets, loosening the restraining hands of St. Patrick and St. Laurence O'Toole, holding his girdle, to say, *No private right to property is good as against the public right of the people.*

The tramway workers, the worst slaves Ireland ever knew, grew restless, and were trying to key themselves up to make a fight of it. They had no settled job, no settled hours, no settled pay even, for every journey they made was crammed with trivial excuses for a fine that made their wages undergo a weekly shrivel, so that they deprived themselves of what they needed when they gave a penny to Jesus at Mass on Sundays. At midnight, when the last tram had been bedded for the night, to win courage from Larkin's faith they came to Liberty Hall in trains of wagonettes, caravans of toil, playing melodeons, concertinas, mouth-organs, and singing an old Irish ballad, or a music-hall song, as the horses plodded along from the depots of Inchicore, Clontarf, and Ringsend. As the crowded cars pulled up outside Liberty Hall, they were cheered by crowds gathered there, for each arrival was hailed as a reinforcement for an army about to march to battle. The tramwaymen crowded into a hot and stuffy hall, already nearly packed to the doors, the sweat often dripping from the foreheads of the speakers, all of them wiping it convulsively away as they went on speaking; Jim Larkin alone carelessly brushing the bigger drops aside with a sudden impatient movement of his hand, too full of fiery thought to bar the salty moisture from entering into his gleaming eyes.

The employers gathered their forces together too, to harass the workers and stamp their menace out. William Martin Murphy, their leader, who owned the Dublin tramways, Clery's huge stores, and God knows what else besides, determined to get the employers to refuse to give work to any man who was a member of Larkin's Union. Let them submit, or starve. Jacob's the biscuit-makers, Shackelton's the millers, Eason's the newspaper and magazine distributors, along with coal factors, timber merchants, and steamship owners, came along to Martin Murphy and said, We're with you, old boy. What thou doest, we will do; what thou sayest, we will say; thy profits shall be our profits; and thy gods, ours too. And so it was. Catholic, Protestant, Quaker, and pagan employer joined hand and foot, flung their money into one bag, and with bishop and priest, viceroy and council, infantryman and cavalry trooper, and bludgeon-belted policeman, formed a square, circle, triangle, and crescent to down the workers.

A foreman came slowly to Sean, a paper stretched out in his right hand, and said, Sign this, you. It was headed by a skull and cross bones, with a tiny cross in a corner, above the motto of *Per ardua add fastra*. The document went on to say:

> Under the holy and undivided patronage of St. Ellessdee, I, M or N, do solemnly swear, without any reservation whatsoever (cross your heart, and say, I hope to die), that from this day forthwith I shall cease to be a member of Larkin's Union, and will forswear his company, give him no aid, in thought, word, or deed, cross to the other side of the street when I see him coming, inasmuch as he has persuaded me to try to bite the hand that doesn't feed me; and I further promise and undertake and expressively swear that I will faithfully serve my employers, assisted by whatsoever Union they may form, or allow me to join; and so I shall incur the beloved and much sought-after brazen benediction of the holy Saint Ellessdee, and the goodwill of bishop, priest, and deacon, till the act of God, in old age or through an accident, shoves me from the job I'm no longer fit to fill: all this I swear for the third time grinning. Aman. Inscribed with solem derision on the twelfth day of the eighth month in the year of our Lord, William Martin Murphy.—T. Gomarawl.

—What's all this mean? asked Sean.

—It means, said the foreman, winking an eye, that Mr. Martin Murphy knows what's good for you betther than yourself; so be a good boy an' sign.

—Tell your ignorant lout of a Murphy and his jackal, Bimberton, that I'd see him in Hell first!

—Don't be a fool, Jack, said the foreman smoothly, to do in a second what you may regret for a year. Sign, man, an' then go when the pressure gets too sthrong—there's no law again' you signin' the thing, an' breakin' it when you have to.

—Look, Bill, said Sean, a great poet once wrote,

> *A knight there was, and that a worthy man,*
> *That from the time that he first bigan*
> *To ryden out, he loved chivalrye,*
> *Truth and honour, fredom and curteisye;*

and were I to sign this thing, all these things would turn aside and walk no more with me.

—I dunno, said the foreman, and scorn touched his tongue, that e'er a one of those things ever did, or could, walk with any of us. It's only poethry talkin' big. The ten commandments are enough for a working man to go on with—too much, if y'ask me! An' more—you may be a worthy man, but you're hardly a knight.

—Well, I'd be less than a man if I signed, Bill.

—Have it your own way, Jack, but you're no betther than others who will; and raising his voice, he said, If you can't sign, get off th' premises— we want no Larkinism here! And, seeing that Sean hesitated, he added, An' if you try to cut up rough, there's police within call to come an' shuffle you out!

—I'm off, said Sean; but tell your boss, Gomarawl, and let him tell Martin Murphy that I said that they'd auction off the coat of Christ; they'd coin the stars into copper coins; make a till out of the wood of the holy cross; they'd line their hats with the silken sounds of Shakespeare's sonnets; they'd haggle with Helen of Troy about the price of a night in bed with her; and force the sons of the morning, were they hungry, to be satisfied with a penny dinner from St. Anthony's Fund: there's nothing they wouldn't do to damn themselves with God, with angels, and with men.

On a bright and sunny day, while all Dublin was harnessing itself into its best for the Horse Show, the trams suddenly stopped. Drivers and conductors left them standing wherever they happened to be at a given time in the day when the strike commenced, to be brought to their sheds by frightened inspectors and the few scabs and black-legs who saw in Martin Murphy another God incarnate. And the employers kept on locking out all who refused to abandon their Union, mill men, men and women from the factories, from the docks, from the railways, and from the wholesale and retail warehouses of the cities and towns. They came out bravely, marching steadily towards hunger, harm, and hostility, just to give an answer for the hope that was burning in them.

The dust and mire in which the people lived and died were being sprinkled everywhere through the gallant, aristocratic streets; it drifted on to the crimson or blue gold-braided tunics of the officer; on to the sleek morning coat and glossy top-hat of the merchant and professional man; on to the sober black gown and grey-curled wig of the barrister and judge; on to the rich rochet of immaculate surplice and cocky biretta; on to the burnished silk and lacquer-like satin frocks and delicate petticoats of dame and damsel.

Those who lived where lilacs bloomed in the doorway, where the dangling beauty of laburnum draped itself over the walls, where many a lovely, youthful rose crinkled into age, and died at last in peace, where three parts of the year was a floral honeymoon—here the dust and the mire came too, and quiet minds knew ease no longer. Magic casements were opened cautiously, and handsome or dominating eyes gazed out on a newer fairyland, a Keltic twilight growing into smoky tumult, enveloping rough and ugly figures twisting about in a rigadoon of power and resolution.

Standing to arms, the soldiers were confined to barracks; town and country police began to go about in companies; and the horsemen came trotting down this street and up that one. And the clergy, if they weren't denouncing strike organisers, kept fast together in a secret silence. And at the wall of an end house in every tottering street stood groups of mingled black and blue police as if the rotting building had suddenly thrown out a frieze of dark and sinister growth. There they stood, never moving, though every eye turned slow in its socket to follow the figure of every passing man. And every passing man tried to pretend he hadn't seen them; or, if he had, that they were no concern of his, for he was on the Lord's side, out to serve the King, and loyal to William Martin Murphy. Sean, whenever he passed them, shuddered, for in his mind's eye he could see the swiftly rising arm, the snarling face, and feel the broad bone of his skull caving in on his brain, with the darkness of death beside him.

Sean wondered why the clergy didn't stand with the men for their right of choosing their own leader and their own Union. He remembered the Polish poet, Mickiewicz's enthusiasm for the haughty, desperate rising of the French Communards, after he had hurried to Rome to form a legion to strike at Austria for the freedom of Italy; how mad he was at the difficulties so civilly thrust in the way of all he wanted to do by crafty, timid, crimson-clothed cardinals. Were he, Sean, able to pick the lock of the massive gate in the grounds of the Primate's palace, or climb in the dead of night over its high, cold, ashlar-moulded walls; creep through shrubbery and gaudy flower-bed, creep through window thoughtlessly left open; pass by secretary and usher, unbeknownst, right into the presence of the right reverend gentleman, reading his breviary, he would catch him by the arm, as the Polish poet caught the arm of the Pope, and say to the Primate what the poet said to the Pope, Good God, man, know that the spirit of God is under the jackets of the Dublin workers!

With six constables sitting on it, six mounted men leading, six following behind, a lorry driven by a scab came slowly down the quays. Suddenly a crowd of dockers were between the leading horsemen and the lorry; another between the lorry and the horsemen following; while a third attacked the foot police, and pulled the scab from the cart, the mounted men trying to shelter their faces and control their frightened horses in the midst of a shower of stones and jagged ends of broken bottles. Before they could recover, the scab was splashing in the river, and then like lightning, many hands scurried the horse from the cart, dragged the lorry to the river wall, where, with a shout of All together—up! the lorry was raised and sent hurtling down into the river on top of the screaming scab.

The dust and savage creak of this bloody scuffle had no benison of feeling for Sean, so he turned away to go from the place as quick as he dared to move; for, if he met a police patrol, speed would tell them he had been doing something, and a baton might crunch in his skull. So he walked on as carelessly as he could, and oh, Christ! a staggering tatter-clad figure, clasping a jaw with both hands, caught up with him. From a side glance, Sean saw that the figure's jaw had been slashed down by a sabre-cut, and it kept calling out, A handkerchief, a handkerchief, someone! Jasus! is there ne'er a one rich enough among the millions o' Dublin's city to spare a poor bleedin' bugger a handkerchief!

Sean's one handkerchief was safe at home, thank God, and the bit of rag he was using, and always used, except on very special occasions, was too precious to be given away; for there was no way of getting another, for with them rags were as scarce as purple cloth or linen fine; so he kept walking on with the wounded man following. A jarvey driving slowly down the street stopped, jumped down, had a look, and said hastily, and with horror, Here, man alive, climb up, an' I'll dhrive yeh to Jervis Street Hospital before half of your dial is missin'; an' you, he added to Sean, jump up, an' hold him on.

Sean hadn't the courage to persist in going on his way; so he climbed on to the side-car, putting an arm round the stricken man to keep him steady, who kept muttering tensely, If I only hadda had a handkerchief, I'd ha' stayed on in the fight. Only let me get a few stitches in it, an' I'm back for the bastard who done it!

Turning into another street, they came on a police patrol, led by a sergeant, who stopped them, asked where they'd been and where they were going.

—Oh, I'm only doin' th' good Samaritan, said the jarvey jollily; jus' picked him up to bring him to Jervis Street, havin' nothin' betther to do, sergeant.

—Yous gang o' goughers! snarled the sergeant. I know yous of old. Here you, seizing the wounded man by the arm and pulling him headlong from the car, walkin's good enough for you, instead of plankin' your bum on a car in your Larkinistic idea of proper an' proverbial comfort an' calm. In this war, me bucko, th' wounded'll have to be their own sthretcher-bearers, an' carry themselves to hospital! And he gave him a woeful kick in the backside, shaking him so that he drew his hand from his face, letting the cloven cheek fall like a bloody flap over his chin, giving a howl as his hand caught it again and fingered it back to its proper place; his other hand rubbing his under backbone, as he shambled away moaning.

—And don't be so quick an' ready with your grand charity the next time, you! he said, turning on the jarvey.

—I don't know, sergeant, murmured the jarvey. Me an' this good man here helped him, thinking he'd met with a purely innocent accident.

—What a pair o' gaums yous are! roared the sergeant sarcastically. Be off with you before I bring you, horse, car, an' all, to the station! An' what are you gawkin' at? he wheeled round on Sean, who was afraid to go or stay. You're another of them that want to change th' world, eh? Well, go an' change it somewhere else, yeh miserable remaindher of some mother's bad dhream! An' here's a hand to help you there; and before Sean knew enough, a heavy hand swung swiftly to his ear, sending him spinning down the street, his vision a blaze of shooting lights, his knees shaking under him as he staggered away, never waiting to give a groan till he was out of sight and sound of the savage group, glad in his heart that it had been a hand, and not a baton, that had clipt him on the head.

The meeting of the locked-out workers, arranged for the following Sunday, had been proclaimed by Dublin Castle. The night the proclamation had come to Liberty Hall, a vast crowd gathered to hear what was to be done. The meeting would be held; Jim Larkin would be there in O'Connell Street. The darkness was falling, a dim quietness was spreading over the troubled city. Even the gulls muted their complaining cries; and the great throng was silent; silent, listening to the dark voice speaking from the window. To Sean, the long arm seemed to move about in the sky, directing the courses of the stars over Dublin; then the moving hand held up the proclamation, the other sturdy hand held a lighted match to it; it suddenly flared up like a minor meteor; in a dead silence it flamed, to fall at last in flakes of dark and film ashes down upon the heads of the workers below, fluttering here and there, uncertainly, by the wind from the mighty cheer of agreed defiance that rose to the sky, and glided away to rattle the windows and shake the brazen nails and knobs on the thick doors of Dublin Castle. Resolute and firm, thought Sean; but they have no arms, they have no arms.

Oh! O'Connell Street was a sight of people on that Sunday morning! From under the clock swinging pedantically outside of the *Irish Times* offices, across the bridge over the river, to well away behind the Pillar, topped by Nelson, the wide street was black with them; all waiting for Jim to appear somewhere when the first tick of the clock tolled the hour of twelve.

In this very street, not so very long ago, the gentle Shelley had stood, handing out to the staring, passing people his Declaration of Rights. From one of the windows of the restaurant, almost facing Sean, he tossed his leaflets of hope and stormy encouragement to the gibing Dublin citizens. Shelley who sang,

What is freedom? Ye can tell that which slavery is too well,
For its very name has grown to an echo of your own.
Rise like lions after slumber. . . .
Shake your chains to earth like dew. . . . Ye are many—they
are few.

Maybe he is looking down upon this very crowd now, seeing, and applauding, the change that has come to the mind of the Irish workers. Oh! If they only had arms!

—Lo, Jim is there! a voice would say, and the crowd, like a cornfield under a rough wind, would sway towards the bridge; lo, he is here! another voice would say, and the crowd swayed back towards the Pillar.

—There's a funeral to come along, said a voice at Sean's elbow, an' when th' hearse gets to the middle o' th' crowd, Jim'll pop up outa th' coffin an' say his say.

—No, no, another voice replied; as a matther of fact, he's stealin' up th' river in a boat.

—Couldn't be that way, answered still a third, for the quays are crawlin' with polis.

Sean shivered, for he was not a hero, and he felt it was unwise to have come here. He felt in his pocket: yes, the strip of rag and his one handkerchief were safe there. It was well to have something to use for a bandage, for a body never could tell where or how a sudden wound would rise. Although the police were instructed to hit the shoulders of the people, they always struck at the top or the base of the skull. He turned to look back so as to assure himself that he hadn't got too far into the crowd. No; with a quick wheel of his body, a few swift sweeps of his arms, and he'd be out of it, and a few paces only from the side streets opposite the Pillar: so far so good. Maybe the police were out just to fulfil regulations. They had to be wherever there was a crowd; it was customary, and of little significance. If they hadn't wanted the people here, they could have prevented them from gathering by cordoning the street off; and the people around looked quite at ease, and would be very peaceable. They were intent on seeing where Jim would appear, and heads were constantly twisting in every direction. A little way down, on a narrow ledge of a doorway, holding a column to keep steady, Sean saw the figure of a man whose head and face were heavily bound in bandages; and from what he saw of the cap, the coat, and the bit of the face visible, he'd swear it was the man whose cheek hung over his chin but a few days ago. A wicked thing for a man in his condition to come to a place like this, he thought.

—There he is! suddenly shouted a dozen voices near Sean. Goin' to speak from the window of the very hotel owned be Martin Murphy himself! and there right enough, framed in an upper window, was a tall man in clerical garb, and when he swept the beard from his chin, the crowd saw their own beloved leader, Jim Larkin.

A tremendous cheer shook its way through the wide street, and Sean raised his right arm, and opened his mouth to join it, but his mouth was snapped shut by a terrific surge back from the crowd in front, while another section of it, on the outskirts, surged forward to get a better view, though now the cheer had been silenced by a steady scream in the near distance, by the frantic scuffling of many feet, and loud curses from frightened men. Twelve rows or so ahead of him, Sean saw a distended face, with bulging eyes, while a gaping mouth kept shouting. The police—they're chargin'; get back, get back there! Let me out, let me out; make a way there for a man has a bad heart! They're batonin' everyone to death—make a way out for a poor, sick man, can't yous!

Sean made a desperate try to turn, but the jam became so close that he was penned tight to his struggling neighbour. He felt himself rising, but fought savagely to keep his feet on the ground; and try as he might, he couldn't get his lifted arm down to fend off the pressure on his chest that was choking him. He could neither get his right arm down nor his left arm up to loosen the collar of his shirt, to get more air, a little more air; he could only sway back and forward as the crowd moved. The breathing of the suffocating crowd sounded like the thick, steamy breathing of a herd of frightened cattle in a cattle-boat tossed about in a storm; and over all, as he tried to struggle, he heard the voices of the police shouting, Give it to the bastards! Drive the rats home to their holes! Let them have it, the Larkin bousys!

—Jesus, Mary, an' Joseph be with us now! burst from the voice beside Sean as two sickening sounds told of two skulls crunched not very far away; and Sean closed his eyes, waiting for a blow. The ache in the pit of his belly was agonising, and the heat of the pressure against him was sending the sweat running in rivulets down his chest and spine.

—We should never ha' listened to Larkin, wailed the voice beside him. Our clergy were always warnin' us, an' we should ha' gone be them! Jesus, Mary, an' Joseph be with us in this hour o' need! If I ever get outa this, I'll light half a dozen candles to St. Nocnoc of Duennadurban.

Sean felt he couldn't stick it much longer. Carried along by the ebbing and flowing mass of people, he saw dimly that they had gone beyond Nelson's Pillar; while, topping the crowd, he could see police helmets darting hither and thither, batoning and blustering, batoning, batoning everyone. A minute later his toe struck something soft, and a moment after his feet were trampling a body that never made a move. Now he couldn't get his feet to the ground again, and in a spasmodic effort to do it, he only managed to rise higher so that his head and shoulders looked over the struggling mass of men. He could see no women, though he had heard a woman's screaming several times. Yes, there was one, a well-dressed lass too, lying alone beside the chemist's shop at the corner of Henry Street. The part of the crowd in which he was jammed now took a half-wheel, and he saw they were battling furiously among themselves to be the first to force a way into the narrow lane that led to the Pro-Cathedral. In the pause that came while he waited to be carried to the narrow neck of safety, Sean looked ahead and saw Jim Larkin pulled, pushed, and shoved along by four constables, a crowd of others keeping guard around their comrades, their batons in hand, ready for any head that came within circling range of it. And following some distance away, there, by God! was his friend of the cleft cheek, a sleeve torn from his coat, the bandages hanging wildly round his neck, forced along by three policemen, making things worse by shouting, Up the Dublin workers! Up Jim Larkin! and making Sean shudder at the thought of what they'd make him look like when they got him to the cell and no-one was there to see.

Now with an angry surge and a pressure that cracked his ribs, Sean was borne into the narrow way that led unto life; the pressure, pressing in, eased, and his feet touched the ground. A pale paladin of the people, he stood there, his escort fleeing on ahead to crowd into the church and fill themselves with its peace and promise of security. An inward pressure pressing out assailed him now; his breathing could barely keep in time with the frantic flutter of his heart; his head ached, and the church railings seemed to move this way and that before him. He felt as if he must fall to feel safe. Each time he took a step towards the side-walk, his foot made a half-circle, and the road seemed to rise and slap the sole of it. Getting there at last, he leaned against the railing, slid down to sit on the pavement and wait for his heart to slow down and his breath to order itself into a quieter commotion. God! it had been a day and a half!

* * *

Along a wide lane of littered bodies, amid the tinkling of busy ambulances picking them up, one by one, pushed, shoved, and kicked by constables, the man with the cleft jaw trudged to jail, the wide stitches in his wounded face showing raw against his livid skin, the torn bandages flapping round his neck; shouting, he trudged on, Up Jim Larkin! Nor baton, bayonet, nor bishop can ever down us now—the Irish workers are loose at last!

MRS. CASSIDE TAKES A HOLIDAY

(from "Inishfallen, Fare Thee Well", 1949)

✤ ✤ ✤

Sean had at last written something for money. It was a tiny booklet called *The Story of the Irish Citizen Army*, and Dublin publishers, Maunsel & Son, had promised to print it, provided it passed the British Censor. He was to get Fifteen Pounds on its day of publication, and all the energy left to him became a curse as day after day, week after week, passed without showing any sign of the censored manuscript. Beyond an occasional day of scrappy work they were living on Mrs. Casside's old-age pension, which, when four shillings rent was paid, left six to provide them with all the bad things of life. When the manuscript did come back, it was a creased and tangled mass, with Sean's small, cramped longhand heavily underscored on every page with red, green, and blue pencil lines. With his eyes the way they were, it took him a week to get the sheets into orderly rotation. They were curious-looking documents now: the first Censor had encircled with red anything he thought to be dangerous to the British Government, peace, and God's truth; the second Censor, mind superior, went over what had been marked in red, and confirmed whatever he thought damaging by adding a green circle to the red one; and the third, mind *superiorum*, decided, finally, what was indeed dangerous, by encircling the red and green attempts with a lofty blue one of his own. After what seemed to be ages of labour, Sean filled the gaps in, the Censors, with a few more alterations, passed it, and Sean found himself waiting for fifteen pounds.

Fifteen pounds! Enough, with the pension, to keep them for seven months; for five, if they bought lavishly to give themselves the clothes they needed so badly. The sun became by day a golden sovereign, the stars by night turned into glittering silver shillings. Though the walk was a long one, every second day, or so, Sean tramped up to Baggot Street to stare at the humble façade of the publishers who were to give to the world his book. One day he went in to ask for the cheque, or a portion of it, but was told it wasn't due yet. Next week, he returned, to be told the Manager was away. The golden sovereign in the sky began to dim, and the shimmer of the stars at night began to tarnish. At last, he was told if he came in a week's time, the cheque would be waiting for him.

A few days before he was to call, he heard his mother coughing, and asking what was wrong, received the usual reply that it was but a bit of a cold. He persuaded her into bed, and gave her a hot cup of tea; all that he had to give; all that remained in the house to give its head. If he only had enough of the promised fee to buy a little brandy. He heard her coughing through the night, and grew frightened, for he dreaded her death. He had lived so long beside her, from the day she had brushed his brown childish hair from his forehead to the one that found grey hairs tingeing his temple. She had been his comforter, his rod and his staff, his ever-present help in time of trouble. She had been so understanding, too; never crossing him. Ever silent when she saw him thinking out things in a reverie; breaking into the quiet crooning of some favorite song when she saw the reverie was over. Night after night, when he had been stretched on the old sofa, dreading the onset of paralysis, to screw up his courage he had sung, full-voiced, almost every song he knew, and hymns when the songs gave out; and she had joined in discreetly, adding her sincere and quavering tone to the more militant sound of his voice. Tired of singing, he had read to her from Scott and Dickens, stopping often to listen to her young, fresh, and gleaming laughter, so strange from one who had gone through so hard, bitter, and thankless a life for nearly eighty years; fifty of them little less than terrible; years that had withheld joy, raiment, food, and even hope; for she never had a hope that she could ever be better than she was. But she was always a proud woman, hating charity as an enemy, and never welcoming it, so that all these bitter years had never mastered her, never diminished the sturdiness of her fine nature. Tom's death had silenced her for awhile; Ella's pitiable end had been a battering blow, but she recovered enough to sing a swan-song: a confident, patient, lovely folk-version of the Nunc Dimittis. She went jauntily to her death; whether to another life or no, death scored no victory over her; she never felt its sting. God or Nature, had, at least, given her that reward.

On the day he was to go for the fifteen pounds he bent over the sofa, a little fearful of leaving her alone.

—I'm off now, he said, trying to speak cheerily as he put his hand on her hot forehead, and I won't be long.

—You never watered the poor flowers last night, she complained, for I had to get up in the night to do it myself. I don't know what they'd do without me.

—You're not to get up, he said earnestly; and as she stayed silent, d'ye hear me? You're not to stir from where y'are.

—I'm really a lot bether, Jack, she smiled up at him, and wouldn't hurt if I got up for a little. There's a few things to be washed, and hung out to dhry.

—I'll wash them when I come back, he said irritably, and put them out to dhry. I've already left them soaking.

—You're not to get up. Promise me, mother, he added appealingly, that you'll stay comfortably where you are; for he knew the quick urge in all women like his mother to be forever useful in illness or in health. He was afraid, too, of the epidemic of influenza raging everywhere, killing hundreds of the young and vigorous weekly, so that street after street had dark convoys of funerals passing through them daily. If she got that in her low state she was done. Mother, he repeated, you're not to get up.

—If you go on pamperin' me this way, she said, her deep eyes a bonny twinkle, you'll spoil me forever from doin' anything again.

Pampering her! There she was, feverish, cough-ridden lying on a hard, flea-infested sofa, a few scraps of blanket covering her—and she thought she was being pampered! She who hadn't had for years a sound boot on her foot, a solid meal in her belly, or a warm stitch on her back. The Christian iron of resignation had entered her soul!

—An' don't worry she called out as he reached the door, if you don't manage to get th' money today—we'll manage somehow.

He went out thinking of her. She had had a quiver full of children—some said thirteen; and but five of them had reached an adult age. Two went in their infancy from croup, and a third—a lively little girl, by all accounts, called Susan, after her mother, from the same complaint at the age of six. She had never mentioned the little lass; but Michael and Ella had spoken of her to him. Of the two Johnnies, she had spoken, because he, the third, had managed to live. Ella had told him her mother had spoken about Susan several times. When Susan died, she seemed to have crept into her mother's heart, for, Ella said, tears had always decked her eyes whenever the little one's name had been mentioned.

All who had survived were clever, each in his own way: Archie, clever-handed, could do almost anything with wood and a few tools, and could model astonishing things from papier mâché; Tom, with method and order in his slower cleverness, would have made a grand soldier; Michael had been a superb hand with pencil and crayon, and would, if chances had been good, have made a fine artist; while Ella, graceful and retentive, with her white hands at home on the keys of a piano, reading music easily at first sight, full of Scott's poetry, familiar with Shakespeare and Milton, might have become a gleam from the beauty of Beethoven and Bach. But they were all four failures: no-one was there to point a way further on from where they found themselves when they entered into personal and responsible life. Social surrounding and the Idylls of Religion persuaded, or shoved, them back to where they had started from; the colours of life gradually faded, and they groped boastfully and defiantly about in the gloom again. Social privilege and Christian conduct took their talents away from them, and buried them in a wasteland.

It lay in his pocket at last with his good right hand surrounding it—the cheque for fifteen pounds. Pay to Sean O'Casside, on Order, the sum of fifteen pounds sterling; so he started homewards, face flushed, heart panting, lips murmuring thanks to God. He'd buy a hot-water bottle to keep his mother's feet cosy; oranges to cool her hot tongue; some meat to make beef-tea to renew her strength, and some sugar, tea, and a few eggs—for a start. Oh, yes, and he'd call in on his way, and get Dr. Delany to see her; a five-shilling fee, and she was worth it. But first, he'd have to get this cheque turned into money.

Here was the Bank named on the cheque. Here was the Bank. A heavy door against which he had to push his full weight to open it. A place rich in polished mahogany and the shining of brass grilles. A solemn, subdued air, like what you'd feel in a church. A glass-panelled door, well behind the mahogany barricades, with the title of *Manager* written across it in letters of purest gold. Wise-looking heads, some old, some young, bent down, battling over big books. Sean felt awed, and a feverish feeling swept over him so that his hand trembled when he held out the cheque. Cash for that, please, he had asked with a dry tongue that made his voice husky. He got it back again. Couldn't cash it, oh, no. It was crossed or something. Find one with an account, and, maybe, he'd do it. Sorry; no, couldn't oblige him. He hastened out, and hurried into another. Sorry; they couldn't possibly do it for him either. Where did he get it? What did he get it for? Where did he live? No; they couldn't cash it for him: rules were rules. He hurried out frightened, and ran back to Maunsel's. Mr. the Manager was out. Oh, no; they never paid in money. Rules were rules; but anyone would cash it for him.

He hurried homewards again, excited and afraid. Now his way was blocked by a crowd staring towards Trinity College; blocked his way, and held him there, fuming, and cursing silently. A hell-blast blight them all! His mother might well be in her last moments, might be calling for him, and he stuck there among these gapers! A stream of coloured pennons fluttered over the College entrance. He could hear his mother calling faintly, Jack, Jack; where's Jack? He tried to push into the crowd to get by, but he was stopped by a policeman. Can't I pass? I have important business to do. No; have to wait now till he goes in. Wait till who goes in? The Lord Lieutenant. Why, what's on? Cricket match, or something. Jasus! hold up a finger, and you'll get a Dublin crowd. How often had his mother said that to him! Here they were hard at it. Supposing she wanted anything, and he wasn't there to get it! Here comes the gent now; Life Guards round the carriage drawn by snow-white animals flecked with golden-brown patches, and a squadron of arrogant hussars to follow. Trit trot, trit trot goes Dublin's dearest toy into trit trot Trinity College. Six hundred pounds a week for going about all plumes and pleasures. Wonder what would happen if I went in and asked him to cash the cheque for me? In duty done in a state of life, God sorted men out in a comical way; here am I with fifteen pounds in my pocket that are no good to me; there he goes trit trotting into a temple of learning with more money than he can inconveniently spend. If his mother was ill, there'd be nurses sitting on every chair in the house, doctors coming in by every door and trying to climb in by every window, with chemists in every store compounding medicines. There'd be silk sheets under and over her on a bed as cosy as a well-built bird's nest in the heart of a sunny tree; while silky white magnolias and crimson rhododendrons nodded anxiety outside a window discreetly curtained with brocade. And if she died, no less a protestant than an archbishop, no less a catholic than a cardinal, would be robing themselves in a chasuble and stole, afire with embroidery, to go trit trot to where the coffin lay, and there waft her upward with a first-class testimonial to the reception saints and angels waiting to set her down among heaven's best people.

—Wait a minute, he thought as he went on when the crowd had scattered—a skirt and a warm petticoat for the mother—say a pound; trousers, boots, and a cap for himself—say another one; five weeks' rent owed—a third; and near two more for tea, sugar, coal, bread, and milk. They go quick, one after another—five of them vanished already at one swoop!

He went into McCartan's hardware and crockery shop; asked to see some hot-water jars; chose one, and presented the cheque. The girl assistant took it into an inner part of the shop and came back with the boss who stared at Sean as he returned the cheque.

—We don't do business this way here, he said. We'd soon be out on the street if we done that. Put that hot-wather jar back in its place, Sarah; and he watched her till she did it, then came to the door to stare after Sean as he hurried down the street. A curse seemed to doom the coloured bit of paper in his pocket. Where was he to get the beef, the jar, the fruit, and other things he needed for the sick woman? He made towards home, the sweat running down him with the dint of hurrying from place to place, the cheque getting crumpled from the nervous fingering of his hand: a moment ago, a treasure; now a drop of poisoned anxiety in the core of his mind.

Taking a last gamble, he burst into Murphy's, to whom he was indebted for goods, easing up to stroll jauntily into the store that was but too ordinary houses knocked into one, but which was stacked with everything from milk and coal and oil to bacon, tobacco, sweets, and fruit. He stretched the cheque over the counter to Murphy, who stared at it wonderingly, wiping hands, smeared with the grease of bacon, before taking it gingerly between his fingers with a murmured Wha's this?

—Just come to pay what I owe, Sean said, carelessly; that's a cheque, Mr. Murphy—just want you to cash it for me.

—Ah, said Murphy, I daren't do that, now, for how do I know it's genuine?

—Oh, it's genuine all right, said Sean gaily; you can tell by the weight of it.

—We have to be on our guard. I'll let th' bank see it, an' if they say it's a good one, I'll get you th' money.

—I want the damned money now! said Sean tersely.

—Well, you can't have it; even was I willin', I haven't got such a quantity o' money in th' house.

—Well, let's have half of it then.

—I couldn't, so I couldn't—it mightn't be passed.

—How it mightn't be passed?

—The payer mightn't have a thing in the bank to meet it; I got caught wanst that way before.

Here was another anxiety for Sean! Something new he had never heard of before. Thieves and tricksters—the world was crawling with them! The whole thing mightn't be worth the half of an honest-to-god ten-shilling note! May the flaming weirdness of hell envelope them all!

—How long will it take to get passed? asked Sean.

—Aw, not more'n a week or so.

—I want some money now, said Sean fiercely; the mother's ill, and there isn't a thing in the house!

—Well, I tell you wha', said Murphy sympathetically, I'll let you have credit to another five shillings—that's as fair as I can do.

—That's no use! said Sean furiously, I want to get a hot-water jar for her feet.

—Oh, that? Wait now; th' missus's got one she'll lend you. He ran off to come back with an old white jar in his hand. There y'are, and he handed it over to Sean. A half a crown for it, if it doesn't come back. If th' cheque's passed, you can have what's comin' when I take what's owed.

—Give me five shillings, damn you, said Sean, or hand back the cheque and you can whistle for what's owed to you.

—I make it a rule never to lend money, grumbled Murphy, as he slowly counted five shillings into Sean's eager, outstretched hand.

He hurriedly bought a pound of beef, a few eggs, some cornflower, and several oranges, fancying all the time he heard her calling him, though very faintly the shrivelled lips moved in the crinkled, pallid face in the midst of the fuchsia, geranium, and the musk. He ran back, softly mounted the stairs, and crept into the room. She appeared to be sleeping quiet. Good! He got a small sack, went to Murphy's, and carried back two stone of coal, bread, sugar, tea, and a small jug of milk. Soon he had a good fire going, and when the kettle boiled, he filled the jar, wrapped it in an old torn shift, and carefully shoved it under the old bedclothes to her feet which to his touch felt icily cold. He sensed her feet stretching towards the jar, and heard her lips giving a purring murmur of pleasure. He put the beef into a saucepan to stew; peeled the oranges; squeezed with the pressure of his hands as much juice as he could from them into a tumbler, adding some sugar and hot water. He brought it to her, and she swallowed it in a few quick gulps, though her forehead, when he felt it, seemed now to be as cold as her feet. He noticed that she never asked him about the cheque, and seemed to have forgotten all about it. Too sleepy, maybe, he thought, pushing away the dread that cheques even of the highest value wouldn't interest her any longer now. A tap at the door. Christ! he'd forgotten the doctor, and here he was now without the money to pay his fee! With steady and gentle hands the doctor examined her while she stared at him with a vacancy Sean didn't like.

—A great old woman, said Sean, trying to be bright after the examination was over. Had a hard life, but can stand anything. She'll be all right in a few days; and as the doctor remained silent, added, think so, sir?

—She's a very old woman, the doctor remarked, very old; and tired, too. The pulse is weak; very weak; and he stood, staring at the still figure stretched on the sofa—waiting for the fee, Sean thought bitterly.

—I can't give you the five shillings just now, he said aloud, flushing crimson, for a cheque I got hasn't been cashed yet.

—Cheque? The doctor was startled. What cheque would you have? and he set his soft hat firmly on his head, looking searingly into Sean's face.

—One I got for writing a book, said Sean; it's to be published soon.

—A book? Indeed? Well, the next time you haven't a fee handy, get the Dispensary doctor, please; that's what he's for—to attend to you people. And without another word, he left the room, leaving the house without telling Sean what was to be done for his mother.

He went to the fire, stirred the beef-tea, and tasted it. It was good, better than any medicine for her, he thought. When it had cooled a little, and hearing her stir, he touched her gently into noticing it. Sitting on the old red-covered box, he fed her from a spoon till half of it was gone. Then with a murmured, Grand; that was grand, Jack, she sank back on the hard horsehair pillow that Sean had covered with an old towel to try to keep the bristles from annoying her neck and shoulders.

—Everything's grand to her, he thought; she has accepted anything given to her without a murmur of complaint. A cup of tea; a glass of beer; a sip of orange juice; and now a few drops of beef-tea—all grand, and welcome gifts from the giver of all.

Going down to the yard to fill a kettle to make himself some tea, he was greeted by a neighbour hanging out some ragged clothes on to a rope line.

—Your mother was in great fettle this morning, she said thickly, for she held a clothes-peg crossways in her mouth; she'll live to be a hundhred.

—Why! Were you up to see her?

—Up? No; but wasn't she down here early on puttin' out her few old things to dhry, after washin' them out, an' she laughin' an' jokin' with any that happened to come into th' yard. You could hear her a mile off!

Now he knew why her heart had gone weak and her pulse slow. She had risen while he was away, had washed the clothes, and had hung them out to dry. There they were, hanging limp on the line, a last testimony to a brave and resolute woman. In his mind's flurry over the cheque, he hadn't noticed them before. She had used up her last spark of energy keeping useful in life. It was done now. He might have known that she couldn't keep a promise to lie still and stay in bed.

He went back to the room, and looked steadfastly down at the dear, wrinkled face; and his heart sank to see how worn it was, how pale it seemed to be growing. There were the humorously-curving mouth, now tightly, almost grimly closed; the strongly-made nose, and the firm, resolute chin; the sleek hair, still with many dark hairs threading a pattern through the grey locks, that he had combed and brushed every morning for a week now. Life would be chill for him when that warm heart had ceased to beat.

He shook himself violently. It was neither honest nor manly of him to wish her to live longer. If ever a woman in this world had earned a rest from her labours, this was the one. He didn't wish her to live because of any pleasure death might take away from her. He wished it simply because she seemed to make life easier for him. Nay, not seemed; she did. To wish her to live was a great weakness that he couldn't shake aside. He was the one of her children who had been with her all the time. Thirty-five years or so she had cared for, and defended, him. Her works would follow her. What works? Attending to him! That wouldn't fetch her even a good-conduct medal from a local G.H.Q., of heaven! This woman's spiritual hardihood, her unshakable energy, her fine intelligence had all been burned to unusable ashes in the tedious smokiness of a hapless life. Life had wasted all her fine possessions. None, save he, could recognise her for what she was; and he was powerless to yield her any words of praise, for if he spoke them, there were none to hear. She would die alone—unhonoured and unsung. Unwept, too? Almost, indeed; for who was there to weep for her going? The poor had precious little time or chance to weep. She seemed to expect these things from no-one. She was far above any praise that could be given for anything she had done. Silence was the highest praise that could be given her. And the resolve that he, too, would become as she had been—indifferent to the phases of fortune; indifferent, if possible, to what the world regarded as praise, peace, and prosperity; to bear all things—while fighting them fiercely—pain, poverty, and wretchedness with dignity and silence; and, finally, to meet death with a careless nod of greeting, to suffer his cold clasp with a calm closing of the eyes, and a silent hail and farewell to a world left living.

His beginning of bravery wasn't too good. Grief was tightening his breast, and his breath came too quick at the thought of losing her. Self-pity had ambushed his hardy designs, and before he knew it, tears had welled from his eyes, and had splashed down on to the pale face so full of settled peace. The black eyes of her suddenly opened, and, startled, stared up at his anxious face. His tears had roused her from a graceful quietness, just as she was about to round off life with a little sleep.

—Ah! Jack, she murmured pitifully, her lips quivering, her worn and gnarled old hand stroking his, resting on the edge of the old sofa; ah! Jack, Jack, Jack!

He bent down, and kissed her warmly, and the black eyes, still agleam with pity, closed slowly, and her head sank on to the hard old pillow, as she murmured, I'll be up and about again soon. With another shake of his body, he calmed his emotion, rearranged the old clothes over her as comfortably as he could, glad to see her sliding into her quiet sleep again.

He felt a little more hopeful now. She hadn't coughed for quite a time. He listened; she seemed to be breathing more easily. She might get over it. She had, so far, escaped the plague that had darkened every Dublin street with mourning, hanging crêpe from the knocker of every door, white ribbons for the young, black for the old; the heavenly slogan of R.I.P. on every one of them. He'd disturb her no more: he'd let her come out of it her own way, or quietly go her own way out of the world.

He went over to the fire, and set the kettle on it for a cup of tea. He pulled over the little table, set pen, ink, and paper on it, stiffening himself to go on writing his *Three Shouts on a Hill*—a shout at the Gaelic League, a shout at Sinn Fein, and a shout at Labour. Most of it had already been written, and he was now working at the epilogic chapter called Descending the Hill. When it was done, maybe, he'd send it to Shaw, and ask him to write a preface praising it. He wouldn't part with this new work for less than twenty-five pounds. With cunning, that would keep him going for a year, and give him time to think of something else to do.

He went to the window, and looked out at the sky. It was stridently lovely in green and purple and crimson. Like a fat, fully-robed cardinal giving a blessing to the world. Curious that Oscar Wilde hurried to pull down the blind whenever a sunset reddened his room, calling it old fashioned, belonging to the time when Turner was the last note in art. A lilylike, drooping sky murmured to him in delicate phrases, but this red-faced, impudent lass, arrayed in crimson taffeta was too much for him. It was too familiar, and came too close. And yet the pearly chasteness of the evening star swung in its folds, soothing the rowdy showiness of the vaunting heavens. Sean gave welcome to its manly warmth; bawdy it might be, and rough-toned, too; but it had life, and shared it lavishly with the earth beneath. When the sky was thoughtful in its pale and dreamy colours, let the lute be vocal; when the sun flared red and purple, let the trumpet sound.

How quiet the house had grown. Not a mouse stirring. He had never sensed the house so still before, as if life had gone, and left it breathless. Quieter than a nun, breathless with adoration; as still as death itself. He shivered as if a creepy silent wind had entered the room; cold, as cold could be. As cold as heaven would be if God cast a cold look on a well-loved saint.

He went back to the little table to resume his work, but strive as he might, no thought allowed itself to enter his mind. The curious silence remained as if some virtue, some warmth had gone from the little room forever. He glanced over at his mother, and saw her face calmly lying still in a deep sleep. She was just asleep. This curious feeling was but imagination, gone fretful and cold; yet a great dread crept over every beat of his quickening heart. He got up slowly, and walked over firmly to the sofa. He bent down low over her, listening, listening; and then he knew that she was dead. He felt her forehead—it was turning into the coldness of marble. She had gone from him when the silent wind had crept into the room. She had died without one murmur for attention; unbreakable, tireless, and quite confident. Indomitable woman. She had stretched out only when all usefulness had left her body, possessing nothing but the sweet peace that gave courage to her fine, gay heart. She had taken a holiday from life at last. She had come very close to her Michael now; he had won her away from the world at last. She had died divested of decoration, even of one glittering word of praise. No matter. No earthly diadem would be brilliant enough to wear well on that seamed and fearless brow. All the perfumes of Arabia could add no further beauty to those worn and gnarled hands. Only such a gem as the evening star on that forehead could safely set off that hardy, gentle, patient face. He bent down, and kissed her. Her lips were very cold now. Careless, he let the tears fall on the wrinkled cheeks, but no lids fluttered open to let the bright, dark eyes stare hope and courage into his own now; nor did the cracked lips give as much as a quiver. Ah! Jack, Jack, she is dead indeed!

Through a gay, warm, golden haze, curtained with a magenta sky, Sean moved to the business of his mother's burial. But no summer sun could gild the streets with hope, or make them genial for him. Each street was a paved courtyard to a tomb. Although he hurried about, getting three pounds advance from the Agent on his mother's five pounds life insurance, registering her death, seeking a coffin, he scarcely seemed to move. Under the magenta sky, through the shimmering golden haze, everything seemed to come towards him, passing by ere he could see the shapes plain, or mind comment on what he saw, as they flowed by him under the magenta sky, through the quivering golden haze. Streams of funerals came moving towards him, black plumes for the old, now and again, nodded a timely farewell from the horses' heads; but white plumes for the young never seemed to cease nodding a sad greeting from the golden haze enlivening their last hour among the living; the bold, black hearses moving with glossy impudence, the brown coffins aglitter with brass, their lids bearing up a burden of blossoms trying to smile away the silent grief that lay beneath them.

Throughout the golden haze, he saw neither bird nor bee; yes, a butterfly; just one, a tiny white one, lost, knowing not whether to come or go, seeking, maybe, a sad sip of nectar from flowers decking the top of a coffin. Out of the enveloping haze a girl's hand wrapped up for him in tissue paper, tied it with black tape, a snowy shroud and soft pillow; the finest shift his mother had ever worn, the softest pillow her head had ever touched; while dimly he realised that a pound of his had gone into the sunny hilarity around him. Then the hand of another girl, in some faintly sketched-in shop, gave him half a dozen crimson gladiolas, that they might shine a torch of defiance beside the grey head of the brave, dead woman.

Out of the dancing shimmer came the thin voice of a drowsy clerk in the cemetery office droning out the order for the opening of the grave, purchased in perpetuity by the deceased years and years ago for the family, the one piece of property she ever had possessed, and proving to be a sound investment now; and again he felt that another pound had vanished into the bright-blue and gorgeous haze from his store of three.

Then from the satisfied splendour of the sun, crept the rectory garden with the sensitive face of Mr. Griffin, white and worn from a recent illness, quietly looking at Sean, his shoulders heavily shawled, murmuring comfortable words towards Sean's dull ear, words that were coloured soberly with sympathy, that one of God's dear children had come closer to Him to be calmly received into a quiet order of sainthood, with all heaven watching her stepping shyly into the joy of her Lord; for her heavy afflictions had been but for a moment, and had worked for her an exceeding weight of eternal glory; who, having had nothing, now possesses all things; bringing no thrill to Sean's heart, for he welcomed words like these no longer; and through all the sunnied harmony of the day, a dark path led him everywhere, and crêpe bordered the zenith and nadir of all he saw.

Hard he found it to get a coffin—the last gift he was to give her; for, in the shimmer, piles of coffins shone outside the doors of them who made them, and within were towering barricades of them, already sold, yet many more were needed for those who had died in the epidemic. Busy and sweating hands, raised above the coffins, impatiently motioned him away; and hammers thudded ceaselessly, day and night, down on elm and oak and pine to meet the needs of those eager to bury their dead.

At last when he found a merciful dealer, he was satisfied and tired; his legs so numb that no feeling came to them when he moved. He was glad when he passed out from under the magenta canopy, out of the golden haze, into the house, into the cooler room, where Mrs. Casside, dressed in her spotless wedding-garment, lay still, something of a smile on her face, maybe because she had quietly prevented any further discouraging interference with the beginnings of her long journey from where she had secretly crept silently away from life.

Over the white shroud, over the coffin, he draped the red cloth that had covered the box on which she had so often sat. It would be her red flag, ignorant as she was of all things political, and seemingly indifferent to the truth that the great only appear great because the workers were on their knees; but she was, in her bravery, her irreducible and quiet endurance, her fearless and cheery battle with a hard, and often brutal, life, the soul of Socialism; and the red symbol, draping her coffin, honoured itself in warming the dead-cold breast of an indomitable woman.

He was glad, after waiting five days, when the morning of the funeral came. Strive as he might, he couldn't force himself to realise that all life had left the frail body lying so safe and still in its faintly-polished box. He would have been shocked, but not surprised, if he had heard her voice crooning quietly some old, sweet song; or saw her suddenly lean out of the window to send a greeting down to a passing neighbour. Perhaps, a young, black-haired miss once more, she was with her Michael again; he with his white brow and bronze beard, looking down at her, stroking her hand, and murmuring, You took a long time to come to me, Sue; a long, long time. And she would say, I came quick as I could, Michael; and when I found the way, I hurried.

Sean broke off a sprig of fuchsia, another of musk, and a crimson disk from the geranium, and carefully arranged them under a fold of the shroud, near her right hand. They would be her gold, her frankincense, and myrrh; her credentials to show to the first guardian saint she'd meet. I cared for these, she'd say, and honoured them, for they were of the gifts that the good God gave me. Then, maybe, with a dim smile, he'd ask her what favours she expected to get in return for these trivial things; she'd answer, permission to sing a few old songs, some useful work to do in the daytime, and a chance to walk with Michael under the evening stars.

He knew well that what he saw in his mind's eye was but a fantastic remembrance of one, now gone; one whom he thought he loved because she had been very useful to him. He knew that this hurly-burly of thought and confused vision would gradually resolve itself into a newly-ordered life; a life broken sharply from the more immediate past; and that his new life would go on striding ever further away from the geranium, the fuchsia, and the musk. She had come the way all had come, and had gone the way all had gone; as he would go. The rest was silence. Death wasn't a lonely thing. Here, before him, with all outside lively and quick, death looked sad and separated; but great multitudes had died as she had, in the same way, at the same moment. Never morning wore to evening, but some heart did break. Leaves of grass, all, which today is, and tomorrow is cast into the oven. *In memoriam ad gloriam sed asthoriam non nomoreum,* amen. Leaves of grass, all; that the dews spangled, the frosts bit, the sun burned. It was passing strange—set beside the supercilious contempt some had for mass production; or the passionate, almost idolatrous honour paid by so many to the individual—that the biggest mass production known to man came from the mind of God! Or, if no god lived, then, from the indifferent energy of nature. God imitated his creations, not in two or thousands, but in millions; they were poured out in crowds, from dread and useful viruses, through the leaves of grass up to the innumerable flaming suns. Mass production, mass order, and mass community life seemed to be the fullest and happiest manifestation of heaven's many laws. It wouldn't do to say that each differed from each in some trivial, imperceptible way, blade of grass from blade of grass; leaf of tree from leaf of tree; human face from human face. Who is he who having examined each blade of grass, every leaf of every tree, would say no one of them was like its like? And though human faces might differ, and did, the darkness of hatred, the light of love, the glint of fear, the lightning flash of courage shone the same from every human eye, and the thoughts surrounding them were, in essence, the same in every human heart.

He went to the window, and looked out. A few cabs had gathered to carry a few neighbours to help in the carrying of Mrs. Casside to the grave. Carry me back to old Virginny; back to where she came from, back to ashes and back to dust. All for the forbidden bite of an apple. A benevolent sentence from a benevolent god. Nonsense. Death is but change, and change has been with us, in us, through us, since the world began. We are frightened at the thought of ceasing to be, because the thought implies that consciousness of annihilation persists. But we shall never know that we are dead.

Here came the hearse, crawling along like a polished black beetle under the vivid blue sky, through the golden haze. He felt for coins in his pocket, and slid them through his fingers, counting; just enough to pay his cab-fare, tip the hearseman and the grave-diggers. She'd soon be buried now out of the world's way. Heavy steps came up the stairs, and when he said, Come in, to a knock on the door, two hearsemen entered, clad in the blue-black suits of their kind, their heads furnished with high top-hats, their faces firmly set in seriousness. They were followed by some neighbours who came to help to carry the coffin down.

—We'll miss her, Sean, said one of them; and the kids will too—badly. A great oul' woman gone west—th' light o' heaven to her!

—There y'are, said the leading hearseman, handing an envelope to Sean; that's for you—th' bill.

—The bill? Oh, righto, said Sean carelessly, thrusting the envelope into his pocket. You can start to screw her down now.

—There'll be no screwin' down, nor no effin' funeral here till th' money's paid, said the hearseman harshly. Right, Bill? he added, turning to his mate.

—The bill'll be paid, said Sean, as soon as a cheque I have is cashed—your manager knows about it.

—I'm tellin' you no funeral'll leave here till th' money's paid, repeated the hearsemen fiercely; we want no thricks with cheques.

—Aw, murmured one of the neighbours, you couldn't leave th' poor woman sthranded like that; th' money'll be paid.

—Sthranded or no, said the hearseman, if th' money owed, four pound nineteen shillings, an' sixpence, isn't in them two hands—stretching them out—in ten minutes' time, we sail off, an' you can do what you like with th' stiff; an' them's th' last words!

Sean jumped down the stairs, rushed along the road, darted into a side street, and burst into Murphy's to splutter out the way things were, pleading for God's sake to let him have enough to pay the bill for coffin and hearse.

—Wait, now, said Murphy slowly; for it never does to rush money matters. Cheque passed awright, couple o' days ago; so we're all serene. Had I known you were in a hurry, I'd a had things ready. I don't know there's as much as you want in the till—th' day's young yet. He stuck a hand into the till, raking forward some coins, and fingering gently a few pound notes. Wait till I see. One, two, three, four—there's four o' them, anyway for a start; an' five, ten, fifteen shillins in half-crowns—for a funeral you should ha' warned me beforehand—sixteen, seventeen, eighteen—if I hadda known, I'd ha' had everything ready—nineteen; now which'll you have—two thrupenny bits, or six coppers?

—When'll I get the rest due to me? asked Sean, swiftly gathering up the notes and coin as they were handed out to him.

—Aw, sometime at th' end o' the week, when I've taken what's mine, an' when th' till's flush. If I hadda known you were in a hurry, I'd ha' had things ready; but Sean heard only the beginning of the sentence, for he was racing back, breathless, to where his mother patiently lay, waiting to be laid to rest. He handed the money to the hearseman who signed the receipt, the lid of the coffin was screwed down, and then the hearseman gestured to the neighbours to bear the box below.

—The burial docket? he asked of Sean, and carefully put it into a breast pocket. We'll have t'hurry, Bill, he said to his mate, if we're to get to th' cemetery in time to settle th' old lady properly.

Sean heard them hurrying down the stairs, heard the coffin bumping against the corners, and, with a bitter heart stood watching at the top, tense with shame at the scene about the money that had been played before the neighbours. He'd wait till the coffin had been rolled into the hearse, till the neighbours had climbed into their cabs, then he'd run down, and jump quietly into his own. Hearing a half-threatening, half-coaxing mutter of gee-up gee-up, there, he glanced from a window, and saw the funeral moving off at a quick trot without him, while the driver of his own cab, standing on the footboard, was trying to flick the window with his whip to draw Sean's attention to the departure. He rushed hither and thither looking for his cap, and finally tore down bareheaded, opened the door of the cab, and sprang headlong into it.

—Where'r all the others? came from the head of the driver which had suddenly thrust itself in at the window.

—T' others? What others?

—What others! testily—why them's acomin' with you.

—There's no others coming with me, and Sean saw a look of dazed dismay spreading over the driver's face.

—Wha'—ne'er a one?

—No, ne'er a one. It doesn't matter.

—It matthers a helluva lot to me! he half shouted. A cab at a funeral with only a single one in it was never known before in th' world's histhory! If the cab carried you there on your own, I'd never be able to lift me head again in th' light o' day!

—Please go on, said Sean, plaintively, or I'll not be in time to take a part in the burial. I'll let you have five shillings for your pains.

—Five shillins, an' a funeral a gala occasion? With a load o' four, now, I'd look complete, an' be in ten shillings; with a full cab o' six, I'd look complete, an' feel complete, an' be fifteen shillins to th' good. Is there ne'er a one o' yous, he shouted to a sniggering group near by, ne'er a one o' yous man enough to lep into a cab beside a neighbour, near suicide with loneliness an' sorra, an' cheer him up with a glowin' pipe an' a warm word from t'other seat opposite? Ara, this is a poor place for a poor soul to set out on its last journey to meet its God.

Sean was about to jump from the cab, and overwhelm the driver with a burst of curses, but, thinking better of it, he sank back on the seat, and sighed. History was repeating itself; something like this had happened at his sister's funeral. What did it matter in the end? He had seen the last of her long ago. It was an empty world, an empty world for him.

—I tell you wha', said the driver, sticking his head in again at the window; I'll take you fifty foot from th' gate, where I won't be seen, an' dhrop you there, if you pay me six shillins, an' say no more about it, for fair's fair.

—Yes, yes; agreed, said Sean, after he had slid the coins in his pocket through his fingers to make sure he had enough to meet the demand.

Sean heard the driver flinging curses at his mare, heard the swish of a whip, and felt the animal surging forward at a clumsy gallop; so maybe he'd be in time to see the coffin lowered, when Mrs. Casside, baptized Susan, would be committed to the ground amid the trumpet obligato of the Christian faith, sendings its notes, boastful and satisfying, into every present ear, save that of the dead woman, and his own. Fearful consciences would believe the proclamation, that, at the last day, at the sound of the trump, the dead would rise, and each individual body would be reunited to its individual soul; when the natural would be changed for the spiritual, the corrupt for the incorruptible; that which was mortal for amazing immortality. A tall order. A mystery. That is Paul's only explanation. But what is the soul? Where is it when the body is present, and where does it go when the body is but dust? A substantial form of the body? But how can that be? If I cease to be myself, how can I persist as myself? If, when I die, I become a disembodied spirit, then I am no longer what I once knew myself to be, and so how can it be said that I am what I once was and now am not? The being which is I gets all my joy, exhilaration, feels all my pain, sees things lovely and things evil, hears all soft and harsh sounds through the senses, through the nerves, all in delicate and delightful union with the coarser parts of the body; but when I die, all these die, too, and I that was am then no more: nothing left but a fading memory among a few. No; say what they like, there's nothing above but the blue air, or the soft, grey cloud taking the gay sun's gilding; or the black one hoarding a storm for our heads. No; the banner waving over every grave is silence.

But let them say out their jewelled words over Susan's body, to the last word; unto this last; for they were part of her strange and happy dream, and dear to all her secret thoughts; though Sean knew that, unattended, though the mind was lovely and the body pure, the clay of the grave would bring forth coarse grass that would soon hide it from the sight of man forever.

* * *

THE RAID

The cold beauty of frost glittered everywhere outside, unseen, unfelt, for the slum was asleep. An uneasy silence echoed over the house, for awake or asleep, everyone knew that death with his comrade, the inflictor of wounds, roamed the darkened streets. Stretched out in a truckle bed in a tenement room, its murky window facing on to the street, Sean thought of the tapestry of the day. He could see the street stretching along outside, its roughly cobbled roadway beset with empty match-boxes, tattered straws, tattered papers, scattered mounds of horse-dung, and sprinkled deep with slumbering dust waiting for an idle wind to come and raise it to irritating life again. Lean-looking gas-lamps stood at regular intervals on the foot-paths, many of them deformed from the play of swinging children, bending over like old men standing to gasp, and wait for a pain in the back to go. The melancholy pathway meandered along by the side of the tall houses, leading everywhere to tarnishing labour, to consumption's cough, to the writhings of fever, to bitter mutterings against life, and frantic calls on St. Anthony, The Little Flower, and Bernadette of Missabielle to be absent helps in time of trouble. Upon these stones, I will build my church.

There were the houses, too— a long, lurching row of discontented incurables, smirched with the age-long marks of ague, fevers, cancer, and consumption, the soured tears of little children, and the sighs of disappointed newly-married girls. The doors were scarred with time's spit and anger's hasty knocking; the pillars by their sides were shaky, their stuccoed bloom long since peeled away, and they looked like crutches keeping the trembling doors standing on their palsied feet. The gummy-eyed windows blinked dimly out, lacquered by a year's tired dust from the troubled street below. Dirt and disease were the big sacraments here—outward and visible signs of an inward and spiritual disgrace. The people bought the cheapest things in food they could find in order to live, to work, to worship: the cheapest spuds, the cheapest tea, the cheapest meat, the cheapest fat; and waited for unsold bread to grow stale that they might buy that cheaper, too. Here they gathered up the fragments so that nothing would be lost. The streets were long haggard corridors of rottenness and ruin. What wonderful mind of memory could link this shrinking wretchedness with the flaunting gorgeousness of silk and satin; with bloom of rose and scent of lavender? A thousand years must have passed since the last lavender lady was carried out feet first from the last surviving one of them. Even the sun shudders now when she touches a roof, for she feels some evil has chilled the glow of her garment. The flower that here once bloomed is dead forever. No wallflower here has crept into a favoured cranny; sight and sign of the primrose were far away; no room here for a dance of daffodils; no swallow twittering under a shady eave; and it was sad to see an odd sparrow seeking a yellow grain from the mocking dust; not even a spiky-headed thistle, purple mitred, could find a corner here for a sturdy life. No Wordsworth here wandered about as lonely as a cloud.

> The decent dead provoke no blood-congealing fear,
> Like the dread death that lives to fester here.
> Here children, lost to every sense but life,
> Indulge in play that mimics social strife;
> And learn from strenuous practice that they may
> Act well their part at home some future day:
> The girl trains her lungs to scream and shout,
> The boy his arms to knock a wife about.

And yet this riddled horridness had given root to the passion flower. What had been lost was found; what had been dead came to life again. The spirit beneath the coat brocaded, with slender sword quivering, had come into being again, not in brocade, but in rags; not with sword or dainty phrases, elegant in comedy and satire; but with bitter curses, blows as hard as an arm can give, and a rank, savage spit into a master's face. Fought these frantic fools did, led by Larkin and by Connolly; fought till the daystar arose in their shivering hearts, the new and glorious light, the red evangel, the light of the knowledge of the glory of God, manifested in the active mind and vital bodies of men and women and little children. And now something stronger than bare hands were in the battle. Many a spearpoint flame from a gun frightened a dark corner or a shadowy street, making armed men in khaki or black crouch low in their rushing lorries, firing rapidly back at the street grown shadowy again, or the corner now darker than ever before.

Now the old house was still. Comely Bessie Ballynoy, on her way up, had knocked; but finding Sean in bed, had bid goodnight, and gone. Lazy sleep had crawled in by the dark hallway to soothe restlessness and to hush the clamour from the attic above to the basement below. A lousy sleep, dreary-eyed, in loosely slippered feet, torn and muddy, calling in a shoddy whisper for quietness; creeping in yawning, leaving no-one on watch, though every night now was a perilous night for Dublin. In all the rooms, all the cheap crockery stood quiet on the shelves; the chairs leaned against the shaky walls; rosy-faced fires had all gone pale; the patter of children's feet had long since ceased; only dreams crept slyly in to fill the ugly rooms with sparkling peace for a few dark moments, clothing the sleepers with a cautious splendour; setting them, maybe, to sip rare wines from bulging bottles, or led them to yellow sands bordering a playful sea. A younger lass, perhaps, dreamed of scanty night attire between snowy sheets, with a colour-robed prince by the bedroom door in haste to come in, and bid her a choice goodnight; while the younger men saw themselves, sword in hand, driving the khaki cut-throats out of Eire's five beautiful fields.

Every guardian angel relaxed now, and nodded sleepily by tattered counterpane and ragged sheet, for sin usually curled up like a dog to sleep at their feet, waiting for the tenement life to go on again in the morning. So after Curfew the silent tenement slept, unconscious even that every whining wail of every passing motor sang a song of death to someone; for in sleep the slimy roof above them had slid aside, and left the stars but a hand's breadth out of reach.

When will the day break in Eirinn; when will her daystar arise? How often had he heard these words sung in a languishing voice after an eight-hand reel or a high-cauled cap at *ceilidh* or *sgoruidheacht*! Well, no day would ever break here, nor would the shadows ever flee away. Sean's eyes were closing, and dimming thoughts swooned faintly from his mind into the humming whine of motor-engines coming quick along the road outside. Up on his elbow he shot as he heard the sound of braking, telling him that the lorries were outside of his house, or of those on either side. Then he shot down again to hide as a blinding beam from a searchlight poured through the window, skimming the cream of the darkness out of the room. It silvered the old walls for a few moments, then withdrew like a receding tide to send its beam on another part of the house. Then there was a volley of battering blows on the obstinate wooden door, mingled with the crash of falling glass that told Sean the panels on each side of it had been shattered by hammer or rifle-butt.

A raid! All the winsome dreams of the house had vanished; sleep had gone; and children dug arms and legs into the tensing bodies of their mothers.

Which were they—the Tommies or the Tans? Tans, thought Sean, for the Tommies would not shout so soullessly, nor smash the glass panels so suddenly; they would hammer on the door with a rifle-butt, and wait for it to be opened. No; these were the Tans.

He heard the quick pit-put, pit-put of stockinged feet, faint as it was, coming down the stairs, turning left at the bottom of them, and hurrying along the hall towards the back-yard. His ears were so cocked that he heard the soft, silky pad of the hurrying feet plainly through the storm of blows falling on the street door; then he thought he heard the back door open softly and gently close again.

—Who could that be? he thought. Might be anyone of the men. Those who didn't take part in ambushes often carried ammunition to those who did; and the dockers and seamen gave a ready hand to the smuggling in of arms. If it wasn't for his own poor sight, he'd probably be doing it himself. All were friendly, save the thin and delicate husband of Mrs. Ballynoy, who cared for no manner of politics. Someone, anyway, slipping into the back to dodge over the wall into the dark lanes, with fear but without fuss. The Dublin slums at war with the British Empire; all the power of an army, flanked by gangs of ruthless ruffians; all the ordered honour of a regal cabinet and the mighty-moneyed banks fighting the ragged tits of the tenements. An unequal fight, by God, but the slums would win! There goes the door!

A great crash shook the old house and shook the heart of Sean, for well he knew the ordeal that might be in front of him once the light from a Tan's torch smote the darkness of the room. A mad rush of heavy feet went past his door, to spread over the stilly house; for no-one had come from a room to risk sudden death in the dark and draughty hallway. He remembered the two boys brought bound from Dublin Castle to a dump-field on the edge of the city by two Auxie-Tan officers, who set them sitting against an old stone wall, extinguishing each young head under an old bucket picked from a rubbish heap. Then going away forty paces or so, they fired away at the buckets till they were full of holes, leaving what they had done behind them to put the fear of the Tans into the hearts of the surviving I.R.A. men. He thought, too, of Clancy, Clune, and McKee, caught and brought to the Castle, where the Tans interviewed them with the stimulant of bayonets, prodding them gamely till none of the three could sigh any longer, for each at last was dead. Now he could hear neither sound nor murmur—all had gone quiet after the crashing fall of the door. No sound even of a child's protest, though that wasn't surprising, for all of them would be too frightened to squeal till a gun exploded somewhere: all was quiet—the sad silence of a sleeping slum. Yet Sean knew that the house must be alive with crawling men, slinking up and down the stairs, hovering outside this door or that one, each with a gun tensed to the last hair, with a ready finger touching the trigger. He guessed that a part of them were the Auxies, the classic members of sibilant and sinister raiders. The Tans alone would make more noise, slamming themselves into a room, shouting to shake off the fear that slashed many of their faces. The Auxies were too proud to show a sign of it. The Tommies would be warm, always hesitant at knocking a woman's room about; they would even be jocular in their funny English way, encouraging the women and even the children to grumble at being taken away from their proper sleep.

All Sean could do was to try to lie dead still, digging down deeper without a sound into the hard mattress of his truckle bed; stifling any desire to steal to the door to listen; to try to modify his breathing till it became unnoticed by himself; for a profound silence might make the Tans disinclined to probe a way in to find out the cause of it; though the Auxies cared nothing for silence, but would lift a corpse from a coffin to search for a gun. He always left his door unlocked now, for past experience had shown him that the slightest obstacle to a swift entrance to a room always irritated them.

From the corner of an eye he could see through the window the searchlight gliding, now up, now down the street, and once for a few moments it blinded him by flooding the room. Then he heard sullen, but loud, thuds of heavy iron falling on heavy wood, coming from the back, and he guessed they were breaking in the entrance to the large shed that was said to be used as a carpenter's shop, and in which Mrs. Ballynoy's husband sometimes worked. Now he heard soft, sly steps going down the hallway to the back. After whomsoever had crept away while the door was being broken down. He had climbed the wall, thought Sean, and somewhere—maybe just behind it—crouched silently in the darkest corner of the narrow lane, a revolver tight in his hand, his shoes slung round his neck, so that, if he had to run, no sound of running feet would give an enemy a cue of a direction through which to send a hail of bullets: a bitter night for a pair of bare feet.

Sean could sense the women, and, maybe, the men, praying while the hammering lasted, to cease at once when silence came again, for it wouldn't serve them to let the Auxies hear them trying to talk to God. These silences were the worst: during the hammering one knew where they were; throughout the silences one didn't. Then they might be anywhere; might be opening his very own door snakily, softly, now; some of them might be even in the room, for their black uniforms fitted the darkness they loved, and black juices, smeared over their cheeks and brows, mixed them cosily with the darker shadows of the night. Any moment a brilliant torch might blind his slatted eyes, and a string of shouted questions blast his ear; a pressed-in, cold pistol barrel make a tiny livid rim on his naked chest. He tried to forget thought, making his mind one with the darkness, losing his fear in the vastness of space; but it was no use, for thought never got farther than that the Tans were there, and his mind came back to think of how it would feel to have a bullet burning a swift channel through the middle of his belly.

Azrael, Azrael, gentle, dignified being of spirit, graceful spirit of death, come, and minister unto us, and save us merry gentlemen!

> *Come lovely and soothing death,*
> *Undulate round the world, serenely arriving,*
> *Arriving*

In the day, in the night, to all, to each,
Sooner or later, delicate death.

Ah! Whitman, Walt Whitman, you never knew the Tans! Death doesn't arrive serenely here, his hands are desperate, and neither is delicately formed. Here the angel of death is a biting bitch!

The silence was startled by the sound of a motor-engine warming up, getting ready to go. He heard steps now in the hall, and the sound of *bravura* jests from a few voices. They were going. They mightn't be, though: they pretended that at times, driving the lorries away a bit, but leaving the men behind, to come with a rush into the house again among foolish people hurrying in their nightclothes out of their rooms to ask questins of each other. Stay still; don't move; not a stir; some of them still might be just beyond the door.

He lay there for what seemed a long time, the sweat of fear damping his body, and making him shiver. Stay still; don't move—someone was beside the door. He heard the handle giving a faint, brassy murmur. Soon, a black-clothed arm would thrust itself within, and a shot might go off that he would never hear. He silently squirmed deeper into the bed, and left the rest to God.

—Eh! he heard the voice of Mrs. Ballynoy whisper from the darkness, Are you there, or did they take you? Are you gone, or are you asleep, or wha'?

—That woman again! he thought resentfully—what a fright she gave me! Awake, Mrs. Ballynoy, he whispered back.

—Well, she said softly, you can take your ayse now, an' sleep tranquil, or get up, an' talk about th' queer things done in a Christian age.

—Wait till I light a candle, he said, making a great creak as he heaved himself out of the bed's hollow.

—You'll light no candle while I'm here, young man, said her voice, dressed in a titter, for a slip of overall's th' only shelter between me and a piercin' look from a young man's eyes; an' it wouldn't be good to go from one extreme to another on an identical night.

—Did they discover anything? asked Sean.

—Not a thing, though they took two o' th' men away with them. A sudden end to them all, an' a short fall to th' hottest hob that hell can heat! Don't light that candle yet, she added, for minds that have safely passed a danger near them are often reckless in their dealin' with an innocent female; though you're not that kind of a man, I know.

He heard the door softly closing and her hand fumbling with the lock. He hoped she wasn't going to stay. Ah! here's the key, for it's safer to put a locked door between eyes that pry into other people's affairs day an' night, tintin' everything with the colour of their own minds.

—Hadn't you better go back to your room, Mrs. Ballynoy, he warned. You need all the sleep you can get these days. We all do; and someone might be prowlin' round an' see an' think th' worst.

—Ay, she said; bad minds, th' lot o' them—that's why I've locked th' door. An' call me Nellie, for you know me well enough be now. Light th' candle now you can, but leave it on th' far side of where I'll be, for it's only a flimsy apron-overall I have between me an' all harm; and she tittered gaily as Sean very slowly lighted a candle on a box beside his bed.

She was a fine-looking heifer, right enough: long reddish hair coiled up into a bunch that rested neatly on the nape of a white neck; a well-chiselled, pale face, with large grey innocent eyes that seemed to be shrouded in a mist from the valley of the Missabielle; a fine figure set these charms off, and when she slyly waved this sweet figure in front of a man, he no longer saw, or wanted to see, the mist of Missabielle. A rose of Tralee, without the flower's serenity, maybe; but certainly a lovely rose of the tenements. But Sean was in no mood now to enjoy the charm of her fine figure and face. Once let a soul see she had been in his room and the whole house would be declaring that he was carrying on with Mrs. Ballynoy. He should have had the courage to get up and push her out. He almost wished now that the Auxies had stayed a little longer.

In the sober light of the candle he saw that she had just decorated her delightful body in a pair of brown slippers and a flowered overall reaching only half-way down her thighs, and showing a wide part of her white swelling bosom; a show that was very charming, but damned uncomfortable to one who was determined to take no notice of it.

—Oh! There y'are, she said, when the candle-light got steady, nice an' snug an' all alone. She came over and sat down on the edge of the bed beside him. I'm askin' meself why a land, overflowin' with prayer an' devotion, should be so often plunged into dhread in the dead o' night for nothin'? An' they tellin' me it's for Ireland's sake. Them politics'll be the death of us some day. I feel terrible shy in this get-up she said suddenly. Afther washin' the one good nightgown I have, I was sleepin' in me skin, an' this overall was th' first thing I laid hands on when the Tans came thundherin' at the door. Pansies on it, she said, giggling, pulling it a little from her thigh, pansies for thought! and she poked Sean in the breast, playfully, with a hand reddened by the soda she used in the washing of clothes.

—Isn't Mr. Ballynoy at home, said Sean, trying to get her mind away from the overall, while he thought of a way to get rid of her.

—Didn't I tell you this mornin', on the stairs, that he was on a counthry job! He would be when the Tans come; though it's little good he'd be in any emergency, bein' born timid, with a daisy in his mouth. So I'm a poor lone lassie now, and she gave him another poke—this time in the thigh.

Don't you think you ought to get back, he warned; the Tans might come again.

—Ay, indeed, they might; a body can never know what them fellas'll do. An' it only a little way from Christmas, too. Ah! she said suddenly, looking away into a dream distance; it's good to be near one of your own: th' only two protestants in th' house, not countin' me husband. Of the crowd, not countin' him, only two who have th' proper way o' worshippin' an' are able to foresee th' genuine meanin' of th' holy text.

—There's me for you, said Sean, thinking neither you nor your husband bothered about religion, one way or another.

—Then you're sadly mistaken. I can't remember a year we missed feelin' the curious chantin' glow in th' air of a Christmas mornin', an' us on our way to church. In a proper mood, an' that was often, I could see what you'd think's th' star, ashine on the tip of the spire's top; an' me ears can hear th' dull plod of the three camels' feet in th' deep sand, bearin' th' three kings with th' three rich gifts from Persia, or some other place in th' wilds of a faraway world; an' all th' time an anxious man seekin' shelter for his good woman, with the valleys levelled an' th' hills hidden be th' fallin' snow, dyein' her rich hair grey with its fallin' flakes, a sly soft carpet for her sandalled feet, an' sore they were from th' sting in its frosty tendherness; while th' tired Joseph thrudged demented behind, wondherin' if they'd find their lodgins only on the cowld, cowld ground. But God was good, an' found the shelther of a stable for the bewildhered, half-perished man, with his thin gown sodden, his toil-marked hands a hot ache, an' his poor feet blue with the bitther penetration of th' clingin' snow; an' afther Joseph had shooed th' puzzled animals to a safe an' ordherly distance, th' little fella was soon snug in a manger on top o' warm heaps of sainfoin, thyme, rosemary, an' lavender.

You're wrong there, said Sean; for how in such a bitther season could anyone come on spring and summer plants like those?

—I dunno, she murmured, unless God turned th' hay an' th' sthraw into th' sweet-savourin' herbs. But it's far betther not to thry to go into them things. Are you afraid to look at me, or what? she ejaculated, turning away from her dream; for Sean had turned his head away to escape the charm of the white bosom and soft thighs. As long as you don't make too free, I don't mind, though I feel a little shy in this scarce get-up.

A shoulder-band of the overall had slipped down, and she had saucily drawn an arm out of it altogether so that near half of her body to the waist was bare, and he saw a breast, rather lovely in the light of the candle, looking like a golden cup with a misty ruby in its centre. If he only had her in a shady corner of the Phoenix Park, or in a room of his own in a house where she wasn't known, the world would be well lost for a period of ecstasy. But not here.

—Your husband's a good fellow, he said trying to keep his mind off her, and would rejoice to see you as you are now. He thinks a lot of you.

—He oughtn't, she said sarcastically; where'd he get another like me? He means well, poor man, but honest, it's pathetic when we're alone, an' he thries to get goin'. Askin' me to tell him when he's hurtin' me! She went into a soft, gay, gurgling laugh, putting a hand over her mouth to quench the merry sound of it. It's funny to talk of it here, but maddenin' when I'm with him. I'm often near worn out thryin', thryin' to coax a little flesh of endeavour outa him. He does his best, but the little sting he once had's gone with the wind—joy go with it! She now laughed venomously and loud, making Sean fearful of someone hearing her. Wait till I tell you, she went on—you'll die laughin'! You should see Charlie when he's at the he-man business—are you sure you won't get faint, Nellie? Don't forget to say if I'm hurtin' you, dearie! One night, when he was—you know—I jerked him clean outa th' bed on to th' floor—th' bump shook th' house! D'ye know, honest t'God, he just lay stunned there. Put th' heart across me. Ever afther, d'ye know, I've had to handle him like a delicate piece of china! No; poor Charlie's style's too shy for me. Not like Jim Achree's. J'ever hear o' his?

She slid down till she was half lying over him, and sang sedulously beside his ear:

> Jim Achree's style has a wondherful way with it,
> All th' girls' minds are in sad disarray with it;
> Whenever they venture to have a short play with it,
> Good girls want to stay with it, ever an' aye.
> Oh, Jimmy Achree, shure your style is your own,
> Amazin' th' way it has flourished an' grown,
> With lovely threats shakin', tense with mischief makin',
> Knockin' poor women flat like a gorgeous cyclone!

—Looka, she said breathlessly, th' least bit o' fondlin' now, an' I'd swoon away, helpless an' benighted.

—In the midst of death we are in life, thought Sean. He tried to turn his head away so that he wouldn't be prompted by the white breast that was like a golden cup with a misty ruby in its centre; but his head refused to stir. Instead, he found his hand sliding over her fair bosom. He felt her arm pushing a way under his head till it was firmly round his neck, while the other pushed the clothes from covering him. He was lost, unless he yelled for help, and that he couldn't do.

—You're a good young man, he heard her whispering, an' would never take advantage of a woman alone in your room in th' dead o' night, with but a loose slip between you an' a swift lie-down on a bed o' meadow-sweet.

Don't sthruggle, man, or you'll upset things! Why'r you thryin' to keep me from gettin' the clothes down? You've far too many on you; a little cool air'll do you good. Take th' good things while they're goin'. She whipped the clothes down with a fierce jerk, and lying beside him, pressed her mouth to his. Her big innocent eyes looked frantic now.

—G'won, she muttered, panting, be as rough as you like with me—it's what I'm longin' for for weeks! And half mad himself now, he gripped her like a vice, and sank his fingers into her flesh.

Then they suddenly went still as death, listening; listening to the whine of a motor-engine cruising down the road outside. Then another whine followed that, and another, the last, till they mingled into one shrill, threatening whine that went echoing round the walls of the old house.

—Out in strength tonight, thought Sean; more'n three of them; each of them crooning a song of death to someone. Ireland's modern, senseless Tanshee!

Suddenly the shrill whine lifted into a shrill, quavering scream, the scream fading into the throb, throb of active engines as the lorries stopped outside, or very near, the house.

—They've stopped at this house, or th' next one! said Nellie, loosening her arm from around his neck, and sliding swift from the bed to the door. Who' ha' thought th' bastards would bother to come twice th' same night? Christ! It's this house they're makin' for! And swiftly came a great hammering on the door again. Nellie frantically twisted and turned at the key, but she couldn't get the door of the room open.

—In they'll come, she squealed softly, an' I'll be exposed to th' world as a fast woman. She tugged and writhed till the slip fell from her shoulders, leaving her naked, fuming, at the door. You it was, she half shouted, turning a red bitter face towards Sean, that lured me into this predicament, never able to let any decent woman pass without thryin' to meddle her!

Sean, as eager as she was herself that she should go unseen, leaped out of bed, hurried over, and with a hard twist, turned the key. Snatching up her flowered overall, she whipped the door open, rushed out, and up the stairs, without another word. Shutting the door again, he fled back to bed, digging himself down deep into it once again, listening to hear if it was Tan or Tommy who had entered the house.

The door spun open, and a torchlight shot terror into his eyes. Silently he waited for a blow or a shot, but neither came. He opened his eyes, and saw a young khaki-clad officer just inside the door, a torch in one hand, a revolver in the other. Behind him were two soldiers with rifles at ready. The officer stared at Sean, then slowly returned the gun to a holster, and the soldiers, at this sign, stood at ease, and rested the butts of the rifles on the dirty floor.

—Get up; dress; go out to the street, said the officer tersely; this house has to be searched room by room. Don't try to go farther than the wire cordon ringing the district: orders are to fire on any who do. He watched Sean dressing, and when he saw him clap a cap on his head, asked, Haven't you an overcoat?

—A sort of a one, said Sean.

—Better than nothing; you'd better put it on—it's damned cold outside.

—Decent man, thought Sean, putting on his old coat; has an occasional thought for others. Thank God, the Tans are absent!

He went out into the dark hall, and near bumped into a Tan standing there, fingering a heavy revolver. A cold shiver trickled down his spine.

—Where are you going? he asked.

—Outside to street—officer's orders, said Sean.

—What officer? asked the Tan.

—Military officer, sir.

—Oh! Military officer, eh? Well, we give the orders here—understand?

—Yessir, said Sean promptly.

—Are you a Sinn Feiner? he questioned, twisting the gun in his hand.

—A Sinn Feiner? Me? No fear.

—You were one, then.

—No; never, said Sean emphatically. Thank God, thought Sean, he didn't ask if I had ever been a Republican. The ignorant English bastard doesn't know the difference.

—Well, you're an Irishman, anyway—you can't deny that!

—No, sir, I can't deny that: I'm an Irishman, right enough.

—Well, shout To Hell with Ireland, and you can go—no mutter, but a shout the house can hear. Now!

But Sean fell silent. God damn him if he'd do that! He knew his face was white; he felt his legs tremble; but he fell silent, with a stubborn look on his face.

—Go on, you Sinn Fein rat, shout it!

A streak of light fell on them, and Sean saw the young officer coming to them. He stopped, looked at Sean, then looked at the Tan.

—What's wrong here? he asked. Let that man go into the street.

—You mind your own damned business, snarled the Tan.

—I am minding it, said the young officer. I happen to be an Irishman, too. Have you any objection to it?

—I don't take orders from you! said the Tan roughly.

—I'm not sorry for that, the officer said; but this man does—didn't I give you an order to go into the street? he asked, turning to Sean.

—Yessir.

—Carry it out, then, he said sharply; and Sean, turning swiftly, made a quick march through the hall, out by the door, into the street.

It was very cold, and from the timid gleams from a waning moon, Sean saw that path and road were white with a covering of rich rime frost. Groups of people were standing, huddled up against the railings of the houses, while more were oozing sleepily out of the remaining ones, shepherded into bunches by armed soldiers. The women were trying to coax warmth into their tearful and shivering children by wrapping flimsy rags round their shoulders, and tucking the little ones under them into their arms.

Several searchlights wandered through the street, flashing over the groups of people, or tinselling along the walls of the houses. At one end stood an armoured car, the lids raised, showing the heads of several Tommies who were quietly chanting an advice to the shivering people to pack up their troubles in their old kit-bags. Along the road, over the calm, quiet chastity of the white frost, slid a diamond-shaped tank, looking like a dirty, dangerous crawling slug, machine-guns sticking out from slits, like ugly protruding eyes staring at the cowering people.

He saw a commotion round the door of the house he lived in. He mooched over till he was beside the steps to look over the shoulders of a rank of soldiers. A prisoner! Who could it be? He whisperingly asked the soldier in front of him what had happened.

—An awrsenal! whispered the soldier hoarsely. Rear of th' ouse, an awrsenal discovered! 'Nough gelignite to blow up 'ole neighbourhood. A blighter there drew a gun, but was shot through hand afore 'ee could pull trigger. 'Ere's the bawstard coming!

Amid a group of soldiers with rifles at the ready marched a thin forlorn figure, but the lips in the pale face were tight together, and the small head was held high. Peering closer, Sean saw that handcuffs kept the two small hands locked together, and that from one of them red blobs were dripping on to the white frost on the path, leaving little spots behind like crimson berries that had fallen on to snow. In the hall he heard the voice of Nellie shouting.

—That's me husband! he heard her shout; a good man an' a brave one! Yous'll never shoot the life outa Ireland, you gang o' armed ruffians! Here, take me, too, if yous aren't afraid. Keep your pecker up, Charlie—Ireland's with you!

Sean peered closer. Good God—the prisoner was the timid, insignificant Charlie Ballynoy who took no interest in politics! A lorry, full of soldiers, swirled into the kerb. The handcuffed prisoner was pushed and lifted into it. Standing there in the middle of the soldiers, with the searchlight covering him with glory, he held up his iron-locked hands from which clouts of blood still dripped.

—Up th' Republic! he shouted with the full force of his voice.

The lorry drove off, and the red specks in the rime turned brown and lonely. Heads that had lifted bent again, and all was quiet once more. A bleak dawn at last began to peel the deeper darkness from the sky, and the scene crept into a ghostly glamour, brightened by the pale faces of the waiting people; the pale moon sinking deeper into a surly sky, and the rimy frost on pathway, road, and roof grew whiter. Dirty-yellow-clad figures moved into the whiteness from one dark doorway, to move out of it again into another blacker still; while the brown, slug-like tank crept up and down the road, charring the dainty rime with its grinding treads—the new leviathan that God could ne'er control.

* * *

BLESSED BRIDGET O'COOLE

✠ ✠ ✠

There she was before him. The lean, wand-like arm of Lennox Robinson had waved her out of her chair in a dark corner of the Abbey Theatre office; waved her out to meet Sean, whose play, at last, had been accepted for production. There she was, a sturdy, stout, little figure soberly clad in solemn black, made gay with a touch of something white under a long, soft, black silk veil that covered her grey hair, and flowed gracefully behind halfway down her back. A simple brooch shyly glistened under her throat, like a bejewelled lady making her first retreat, feeling a little ashamed of it. Her face was a rugged one, hardy as that of a peasant, curiously lit with an odd dignity, and softened with a careless touch of humour in the bright eyes and the curving wrinkles crowding around the corners of the firm little mouth. She looked like an old, elegant nun of a new order, a blend of the Lord Jesus Christ and of Puck, an order that Ireland had never known before, and wasn't likely to know again for a long time to come.

The first night was very disappointing, for few came, and only thirteen pounds worth of tickets were bought; the second night was much better for it was more than half-full; and the third capped the previous two, for the house was packed. Going to the theatre early, Sean enjoyed a look of ecstasy on the Old Lady's face as she stood to watch the people gathering round her little theatre. She ran to him when she saw him, caught his hand in hers, and led him out to see the queues forming a long, long trail right round the famous building. Well, he had done what he had set himself to do seven or more years ago: he had mounted a play of his on the Abbey stage. Odd, he felt no great elation; no more than he would have felt in the middle, or at the end, of a speech in Irish delivered before a crowd of Gaels. He felt, though, as he stood quiet in the vestibule, that he had crossed the border of a little, but a great, new kingdom of life, and so another illusion was born in his poor susceptible soul. He didn't know enough then that it was no great thing to be an Abbey playwright; and, afterwards, when he knew a lot more, he was glad he had suffered himself to feel no jubilation to mar his future by thinking too much of a tiny success: life remained a mystery to him. He thought, not of what he had done, but of what he had to do in the form and substance of his second play; realising, though unaware of it at the time, that to be a great playwright was a very different thing from merely being one who had had one, two, or even three, plays produced by the Abbey Theatre. Coming out of the theatre, however, he shook himself, thinking in himself that sufficient for the day is the good thing thereof. Some time after, he sent in two one-act plays, *Cathleen Listens In* and *The Cooing of Doves*; the first a skit on the Irish politics of the day, the second full of wild discussions and rows in a public-house. The first play was taken by the Abbey, the other returned, and later was used to form the second act of a later play. This was the first shock given to Sean by the selective committee of the theatre, for the second work was definitely better as a play than the first. This was the first jolt he got, but he was to get many more before he was much older, and from the same source, too.

The third play was the biggest success of all, for the theatre was booked out in a few days for the whole week. Lady Gregory began to get young again, for all the weight of her seventy years and more. Hands everywhere were shaking Sean's. After his first play, during the recess, the Abbey Company had engaged the theatre to produce a play of their own selection, to keep themselves from the sin of idleness. The play they chose was Ervine's *Mary, Mary, Quite Contrary*; and Sean went to it as a token of his thanks for what they had done for him in the performance of his two works. He was damned glad he did. There he saw, for the first time, an actor, Barry Fitzgerald, glorifying comedy on the Abbey stage. He had never met the man, and no-one had ever mentioned his name to him. Seething with excitement, when the play ended, Sean ran behind the stage to pour out his enthusiasm into the unwilling ears of the others actors. Fitzgerald's not bad, he was told, when he gets a part that exactly suits him. Not bad? echoed Sean; why he's a born clown! And, when he went with his third play, he had a suggestion for the cast: Fitzgerald was to play the chief comedy part in it. Mr. Robinson demurred, and mentioned the name of another fine actor, F. J. McCormick, for the part; but Sean held firm for Fitzgerald, knowing in his heart that he, and he alone, could get the arrogant, boozy humour from the character. Fitzgerald, himself, was very hesitant about taking it on, and Sean, with another member of the Company,

Gaby Fallon, who had a very fine understanding of acting, stage and production, spent a long time arguing, demonstrating, and cursing, before Fitzgerald finally could be convinced he would do well in the part. The first night showed Dublin that Fitzgerald stood in the front rank of comedy actors, and Sean and Lady Gregory were delighted.

Letters came asking for his autograph; he was stopped in the street by levelled fountain-pens and pencils held firm by persons demanding his signature on scraps of paper; notes, bearing dignified addresses on their summits, came from others, announcing that They would be At Home on a certain day, at a precise hour, with a hope, in letters of purest gold, that he would be found among the number knocking nicely at Their big hall doors; and, lastly, a letter from Mr. Robinson inviting him to a monthly dinner furnished by a Thirteen Club (or some name of that kind), with a gilded addendum that W. B. Yeats would be there. The ritual was held in a well-known Dublin restaurant bearing a sturdy poetical name. This invitation couldn't be set aside, for it was one conferring real honour; so, trimly dressed and neat as he could make himself, Sean hurried off to mingle with the elect people of Ireland in a ceremonial meal.

Hiding his nervousness, Sean quietly greeted Mr. Robinson and Arthur Shields, brother to Barry Fitzgerald, who gently led him, the first before, the second behind, to a table for three, hedged safely in a corner of the room. Away in the dim distance, a far larger table served a number of persons whom Sean did not know yet, though, through a murmur of submissive conversation, he heard the booming voice of Yeats chatting in a lordly lilt about Utumara, Brahmin Mohini, birds born out of the fire, the two inflows to man's nature—the one common to him and all animals which is natural; and the second, which is intellectual, coming from the fire. Yeats murmured about coming through the fire as if it were but coming through the rye, going on from that to chatter about *anima hominis* and *anima mundi* and spirits that walked only once on a Sunday, while his listeners cocked their ears and bowed their heads, murmuring, *Lord, Lord, thou hast the words of infernal life.*

It was all very mysterious to Sean, and he realised that he had not yet entered within the veil of the temple, but still was allowed to but stand reverent on the doorstep. So he did what he could to ingratiate himself with his hosts, eating what he thought was a badly-cooked meal as delightfully as he could; answering questions put to him as wisely as possible; but discovering that he knew nothing about writers that were common names in the mouths of those who sat beside him. No, he had never seen or read *The Life of Man,* by Andreiev, or *Falling Leaves,* by Giacosa, or *Monna Vanna* and *Joyzelle,* by Maeterlinck; no, nor Benavente's *Passion Flower,* or Pirandello's *Right You Are (If You Think So);* while Sean whispered the names of Shaw and Strindberg, which they didn't seem to catch, though he instinctively kept firm silence about Dion Boucicault, whose works he knew as well as Shakespeare's; afterwards provoking an agonised My Gawd! from Mr. Robinson, when he stammered the names of Webster, Forde, and Massinger. So Sean hunched his shoulders, and sat silent, while the other two went in and came out with arguments about them and about the works of playwrights whose names Sean had never heard of, much more read. He shut an ear to the talk nearby, and cocked the other to the voice of Yeats blossoming into a fuller booming about Megarithma who had told him he must live by bread and water and avoid woods, because the woods concentrated the solar rays; afterwards asking himself why woods concentrated the solar rays, and deciding to reject that part of the counsel as an error (Petrushka deciding to fight rather than to run away); though Sean wondered if he didn't know why the solar rays did, or did not, concentrate in woods, how he could decide what Megarithma said must be an error; but the voice went on booming about the divine spirit of the path Samekh, the golden heart that was the central point of the cabbalistic Tree of Life, corresponding to the Sephiroth Tippereth. The rest round the round table bowed their minor heads, murmuring *This same is a voice that is more than the wind among the reeds.*

Sean was awakened out of the booming by the voice of Mr. Robinson asking him if he had enjoyed the dinner, Sean dazedly and innocently replying with The Rhubarb and Custard were Fine, thanks, but the rest of the things were badly cooked; to be startled by Mr. Robinson ejaculating What a Terrible man you are to bring to Dinner! Another shock for Sean, and he felt his face go red. What was there terrible in saying food was badly cooked? He based his remark on his mother's skill. Whenever she and he had anything worthwhile, steak, mutton, liver, or fish, garnished with vegetables, they were always sure to be handed up in simple, but first-class style of cooking. And all done on a plain open coal fire. Seldom it happened, but when it did, there was always the next thing to perfection. To this day, he remembered the soiled, sloppy look of the greens and the tattered dry look of the meat, served in the poetically-named restaurant. A ceremonial meal to Megarithma, or any other deity, wasn't going to make him say what he felt to be badly-cooked food was good and appetising. There was make-believe here, he thought, in spite of the solid aura of Keltic twilight that envelopes the group.

* * *

He [Sean] had entered places unfamiliar; he had done things he did not yet fully understand; and he was quietly excited about it all. Anyway, he was quite at ease with the Old Lady. They got on grand together. They had many things in common besides the theatre. He loved pictures, and she was brimful of what her nephew, Hugh Lane, had done to diamond-clothe the walls of precious buildings with fair paintings of the men of the day, and with those done by their fathers in the old time before. She loved good books, and Sean felt that he was a little ahead of her there. She saw humour sparkle from things thought to be dead, or dull, and so did he; and they often talked and laughed together over tea in a hotel that overlooked the fair form of Stephen's Green; Sean trying to look at home in the posh place, and succeeding in a way; she eating bun after bun, murmuring that she was very, very hungry; and saying that their talk was lovely; though, best of all, she rejoiced that his plays were forcing queues to stand outside her little theatre, ringing a chime of cheeriness into all their chat. So here was Sean, sober and thoughtful, reading a warm invitation to come and spend a week or two in Coole Park, in Galway; eager to go, but a little nervous at the thought of setting out to visit foreign parts.

The Galway Express left Dublin at 8 A.M. He was to get out at Athenry, the King's Ford, where she would be there to meet him so that they could go together to Gort, and on to Coole Park on her own side-car—she had carefully planned it all out in a previous letter to him.

* * *

WHERE WILD SWANS NEST

♆ ♆ ♆

A long, sweeping drive, left and right, gave a ceremonial pathway to Coole House, which shone out, here and there in hand-broad patches from between majestic trees, ripe in age, and kingly in their branchiness. The House was a long, yellowish-white Georgian building, simply made, with many windows, while a manly-looking entrance—tightly shut now for a long time—faced what was once a curving expanse of lawn, smooth as green enamel in a rajah's brooch; but was now a rougher, but gayer, gathering of primrose and violet, making themselves at home where once prime minister, statesman, and governor, with their silk-gowned and parasoled women, strolled over the velvety green, their grace, charm, and power manœuvring the poor world about to their own sweet liking.

Lady Gregory was a Connachtwoman, knowing every foot of the province; every story told by every bush and stone in the counties of Galway and Clare; and she showed her Connacht rearing by compelling her seventy-odd years to climb down, like a stiff gazelle, from the high seat of the side-car, running to the threshold of the house, turning, and stretching out her two hands to say, with a beaming smile, One and twenty welcomes, Sean, to the House of Coole!

Mistress of a grand house, dying reluctantly, filled a little too full with things brought from all quarters of the known world; some of them bringing into his fancy the ghosts of a Victorian age, and others, more modern, that would send these ghosts away again, moaning; a huge gleaming marble figure of Andromeda in the drawing-room, brought in from the terrace when it had shocked the finer feelings of the people with its clean, cold, nakedness; the really glorious library, walled with precious books in calf and vellum, forgotten, the most of them; unheeded, too, though they still murmured in Sanscrit, Greek, and Latin, against the changing tempo of the reading world. Here was a house that for a century and more had entertained great people as well as tinkers and tailors, for every old or young fiddler, passing through south Galway, came to patronise Coole, receiving praise and largesse after playing, maybe, *Blue Butterfly Dancin'*, *The Soft Deal Board*, or, *Pulse of the Bards, Awaken*: and as he went up the stairs (the walls covered with engraving and mezzotint so that you passed by, without knowing it, half of England's history), he fancied he heard the dancing notes of *The Red-capped Connachtman* flowing from an old fiddle, mingling with the sonorous voice of Yeats chanting out of him about the wild swans of Coole.

In the Library o' nights, heavy curtains pulled taut, a blazing fire in a huge open grate, Sean stretched out cosy in a deep settee, while she, from the gentle aura of soft candle-light, read him Hardy's Epic-Drama of the war with Napoleon, in three parts, nineteen acts, and one hundred and thirty scenes; read and read till he found himself battling sleepily for dear life to keep himself awake, and be polite to the Spirit of the Years, the Spirit of Pity, the Spirit of Rumour, the Spirits Ironic and Sinister. The poem seemed to have been begun in the dark ages, and he felt that it would roll on till the light of the sun gave out; though he murmured it was all lovely when she paused for breath, cutely conjuring her not to tire herself too much with the dint of the direful reading. But, night after night, she pegged away at it, till the very last word was spoken, and she could murmur, half exhausted, Dat's de end! Two great achievements: one for her—that she survived the reading; the other for him—that he kept awake, though feeling old and grey and full of sleep when she was finished. But later on, Hardy came to him a far, far greater man than Sean had thought him then.

However, the gentle lady made up for the strain by reading him *Moby Dick* and Hudson's fine *The Purple Land*. Once only did he burst out into protesting: when she, full of enthusiasm, and certain of pleasing him, read a Labour play called *Singing Jail Birds;* to Sean, then, to Sean now, the worst play ever written signifying its sympathy with the workers.

Oh, stop, woman, for God's sake! he had bawled, forgetful of where he was, rising, and pacing to the far end of the room: the Labour Movement isn't a mourning march to a jail-house! We are climbing a high hill, a desperately steep, high hill through fire and venomous opposition. All of those who were highest up have dropped to death; lower down, most of the climbers have dropped to death; lower still, many will drop to death; but just beneath these is the invincible vast crowd that will climb to the top by the ways made out by their dear dead comrades!

Perhaps you're right, Sean, she had said, hurriedly putting the book away, something ashamed at having so delightedly praised such an insignificant work.

One evening she came in, aglow with a surprise for Sean—a new petrol lamp into which air was pumped so that, she said, we'll have a light that makes the night even as the day of a sunny summer morning. She stood the lamp on a stand on a high table; and a lovely thing it looked with its silver-like stem and opalescent shade. Lady Gregory's maid, Bridget, hovered round while her ladyship pumped air into the petrol bowl, anxiously watching, and murmuring, Let me handle that, leave it to me, now, me lady, to be answered with the angry and impatient retort of Doh away doh away, woman; it's twite simple, and I tan handle it myself. Turning to Sean, she added, and now you'll soon see a light dat never was on sea or land.

She was right, too, for as soon as she put a light to it, the thing gave out a mighty hiss that was half a scream, a bluish-white flame shot up high as the ceiling, the old lady's face, panic in her eyes, became as opalescent as the lampshade, and her wildly-puckered little mouth began to send frantic and harmless puffs of air towards the soaring, hissing flame, the agitated mouth suddenly opening wide, between the puffs, to shout at Bridget, Bring a blanket, bring a blanket, Bridget, before de house does up in fire! Sean whipped up a rug from the settee, and placed it between their faces and the flame for fear it might explode; and behind this safety-curtain the three of them juggled, blew, and smothered the thing till the fire died down; standing round it on guard till it cooled, and Bridget could safely carry the soiled silver bowl and cracked opalescent bowl out of our sight into the kitchen.

—Oh! murmured her ladyship, sinking down to the softness of the settee, a bunishment for my banity; tinking I could do it alone; tinking I knew too much. Back to de tandles dat bring peace and surety to men of dood will.

It was strange to see that white, frightened look flash across the face of a brave soul; that fine firm face shrinking from physical fire, though she walked calm through the ordeal of spiritual and mental fire when she fought the good fight for the freedom of the theatre against priest, peasant, and politician, howling loud and long for the putting down of Synge. Against them all she stood, fighting it all out victoriously in Ireland's heart, and dipping deep into the battle again throughout the mighty cities of America, choosing strife that was good rather than the loneliness of a false peace. Again, later on, she defended *The Showing-up of Blanco Posnet* against Dublin Castle, its robed Lord Lieutenant, its pursuivant, its equerries, men-at-arms, scrolls, parchments, laws and crests, archer Shaw beside her, shooting many a broadcloth stinging arrow of wit into the squirming enemy, making them fall back, and yelp, and lower their banners, and seek shelter in the hollows of the hills of silence.

Again her banner of courage (a gay one, too) had gone up on a day that brought Yeats, Florence Farr, Arthur Symons, and others, to take dinner with her in London. Seeing a letter from home on the table, she took it to another room to read it quiet, finding that every line told of a new disaster, caused by the Big Wind of that year—great lime trees laid flat, oaks, elms, pine, and larch, the calm growth of near a century, had come tumbling down, shattering demesne walls, impeding the public roads; and a tremendous and lovely ilex, the pride of the place, had fallen, given up the ghost, and was no more. But not a word did she say of all this to her guests, but sedately read the play, *Riders to the Sea,* that they had come to hear.

When she got home again, she didn't sit down to wail, but set out on a journey seeking a sawmill, and picked up a second-hand one somewhere; found suitable and unsuitable men to get it going, making all sorts of things for the comfort and convenience of the local people; selling them at cost prices, so cleverly turning an evil into a good thing; the good stretching far, for when Sean came to Coole, the sawmill was still working hoarsely and jerkily, turning out things from the remnants of the fallen timber. And so this brave old Commissar of Galway turned the *Keening of Kilcash* into a busy, surging song of work, though still retaining some of its sadness for the loss of so much upright elegance.

He hadn't been ten minutes at the table before he felt he had often been there, to eat soberly, and talk merrily of books and theatre, and of the being of Ireland; she in simple and most gracious ways showing how things were handled; pointing out that dese things were done, not because of any desire for ceremony, but because dey made one more comfortable, and made things easier to eat. So he was soon at rest, she, when she wanted something from the kitchen, snapping a finger against a tiny Burmese gong that gave a soft, pensive, penetrating note, holding in its quivering sound the muted song and sadness of Burma. Once, after such a meal, they passed through a room where the blue mountains of the Barony of Loughrea nodded in at the great bow-windows; and halting his steps, Sean paused in front of a picture of a young, broad-shouldered man with an open and courageous face.

—My dear son, she murmured softly, my dear, dear son, lost leading his air-squadron over de Italian battlefield. For months and months I had dreaded it, for I knew de German planes were well ahead of ours in design and swiftness.

He wished he hadn't paused before the picture. What the hell could he say to her. He gave a quick glance, and saw that holy tears were racing down the wrinkled channels of her cheeks. He touched her old arm softly.

—Dear lady, dear friend, he said, a little savagely, the falling into death of a young, hearty man is a common thing, and may be a more common thing in days to come. The death of youth has been glorified in the damnable beauty of the belief that They will not grow old as we grow old. That is the heresy of age comforting its conscience in its own comfort and continued security. I am, and always will be, against the death of the young. It is for us who are still standing to fight for the deliverance of the young from a youthful death; from the cruel and wasteful banishment of our younger life, with all its lovely and daring visions barely outlined, becoming, when they go, a tinted breath of memory. To the old, death comes as a fair visitor; to the young, death is a savage intruder.

—We must be brave, she said, forcing her head higher; we must fence our sorrow away so that no shadow falls on those left singing and dancing around us. Come, let us doh for a walk in de woods.

The Seven Woods of Coole with their many winding-paths, so many that it behooved a rambler to go warily that he be not lost in the mazes among the trees. These were among the beloved walks of Yeats, though Sean never cottoned to them, disliking their gloom, with the weight of gorgeous foliage drooping down, sombre, full of sighs and uneasy rustling, as if God had made them plaintive. Sometimes, what Lady Gregory called a badger, cut across their path, and red squirrels shot up the trees at their coming, moving on to the ones nearer the orchard so that they might be close to the fruit when the workers went home by the evening star. In her working overalls, which were an old black dress, an older, wide-brimmed, black straw hat, leather gauntlets over her able, wrinkled hands, one of which clutched a keen, chisel-edged stick, the Old Lady walked beside him, or a little before when the going got bad. Here, in the Wood of the Nuts, right in their way, callous and impudent, rose a mighty thistle, fully eight feet high, thrusting out its savage barbs towards their breasts, daring them to come on. Then, with the fire of defiance in her eyes, her ladyship charged down on the foe, hissing angrily, one gauntleted hand seizing a spiked branch, while the other stabbed the main butt of the thistle with the chisel-end of the stick, till the branchy spikes tottered, bent back, and fell to the ground, the victory celebrated by an uplifted stick and fierce muttering of So perish all de king's enemies!

Occasionally, through the lusty leafage of hazel and ash, they caught a silver glimpse of Coole river flowing by, a river that bubbled up suddenly from the earth in a glade, a lonely corner, alive and gay and luminous with a host of pinkish-blue and deeply-blue and proud forget-me-nots; a secret corner that Lady Gregory had challenged Sean to find, and which had suddenly surrounded him on his third day of searching; a place so lovely in its blossoming loneliness that he felt he should be there. Not a note from a bird disturbed its quietness; no lover and his lass, even, had passed through this glade; no breeze brought the faint lowing of far off cattle to his ears; the blue of a serene sky overhead mantling the blue of the flowers at his feet; no sound save the musical gurgling whisper of the water calmly gushing out of the earth; so still, so quiet, so breathless, that Sean thought God Himself might well ponder here in perfect peace; and the merry Mab, in her mimic wagon, might journey home there through the tangled forest of forget-me-nots, without disturbing thoughts of things remembered in tranquillity. This was the river, which, after leaving the quietness of God, ran swiftly to widen out into a lovely lake on whose soft bosom wild swans settled and wild swans rose, lifting up the noble head of Yeats to watch them,

> Scatter wheeling in great broken rings
> Upon their clamorous wings,

possibly a little envious of them, and wishing, faintly, he was one, because

> Their hearts have not grown old;
> Passion or conquest, wander where they will,
> Attend upon them still.

But Yeats grew old, and cursed the dread handicap of age; but passion lingered with him to the last, and conquest went before him till he laid himself down in rest to leave us.

Books and trees were Lady Gregory's chief charmers: the one nearest her mind, the other nearest her heart. She laboured long and lovingly in the woods of Coole. She hated rabbits and squirrels only when they nibbled the bark from her young saplings. It was she who first taught Sean to distinguish between the oak—the first dree dat Dod made,—beech, elm, hazel, larch, and pine. She marched along telling their names, the way an eager young nun would tell her beads. Away in a sacred spot of the garden, a magnificent copper beech swept the ground with its ruddy branches, forming within them a tiny dingle of its own. This was the sacred tree of Coole. On its trunk were carved the initials of famous men who had come to visit Coole, so that they might be remembered forever. The initials of Augustus John were there, and those of Bernard Shaw and Yeats were cut deep into the bark that looked like hardened dark-red velvet.

With all her bowing down before the mystery of poetry and painting, she never left the sober paths trod into roughness by the feet of the common people. One very wet day, she was busy helping to make what was called a Gort Cake. When she and Sean returned in a day or so to Dublin, the cake was to be the centre of a tea given in the Green Room of the Abbey Theatre. She usually brought one up for the actors when she visited Dublin. A lot of the actors and actresses elected to regard the cake with contempt; but they ate it all right, and when the tea was done, though the cake would feed a regiment, he had noticed that there was little left behind. The cake was a rich thing of spice, raisins, and currants, but rarest thing in its make-up was a noggin of brandy to help to damp the dough.

Sean was standing before one of the great bow-windows, watching the rain slashing down in silvery sheets over the saturated lawn, and listening to the sighs of the big lime tree bending discontentedly before the sharp and bitter wind blowing its branches to and fro. Suddenly, through the mist of the rain, he saw a dark figure, crouching to fight the wind and the rain, battling his way up the circling drive to reach the Big House.

—Derrible day, Sean, said Lady Gregory coming in to have a look out of the window; derrible day!

—Whoever's coming up the drive, Lady Gregory, must feel what you say to be true.

Oh! It's Sammy Mogan toming to det pension papers signed, she said, staring gloomily at the figure struggling onwards. De foolish man to tome on a day like this; de foolish man!

She was gone in a second. He heard the bell of the side-door ring; heard someone entering the hall, and then a long silence came. Tired of watching the rain, he strolled about staring at the pictures hanging on the stairway wall. Out comes an old man to the hall, muffled up in a big coat, eyes and ears only apparent, a bundle of soppy clothes under an arm, and he bidding her ladyship goodbye at every step.

—You must never tome out on a day like dis aden, Sam, murmured her ladyship.

—What signifies it, me Lady? What's in it for a day but a harmless sup o' rain? Goodbye, now, me Lady. Penethratin' though th' rain is, it treats th' skin quietly, like th' tendher touch of a mother bird's wing reachin' over th' nest of her young ones. Well, me Lady, goodbye now. An' isn't th' cordial you've just given me afther liftin' me into thinkin' th' heaviest rain on the cowldest day to be no more than the tired leaves fallin' from the high-born branchy threes. Goodbye, me Lady, for with the form signed safe in me pocket, it's whistlin' I'll be all th' way home, intherspersed with prayers for seven blessin's seven times a day on you and all your house. Goodbye, me Lady.

—Whisper, Sean, said Lady Gregory, as they went back to the fire in the library, de Gort cake will lack its warm life dis time. Sam Mogan was so perished wid the wet and cold that I poured the naggin of brandy into him to bring him back to life.

Sitting in the long and handsome garden, he saw the sun going down behind the grey garden wall and beyond the Hills of Burren, giving Coole a crimson and gold salute before it went. He realised that Lady Gregory, in the midst of her merriment and mourning, was ever running round, a sturdy little figure in her suit of solemn black, enlivened by gleaming eyes and dancing smile; ever running in and out of Yeats's Keltic Twilight, which she could never fully understand; turning his Rose Alchemica into a homely herb; and turning the wildness of his Red O'Hanrahan into the serious steady dancing of a hornpipe on the Abbey stage. In her humorous and critical moods, swinging a critical lantern, she trespassed into A.E.'s amethystine no-man's land where A.E. became delirious with quivering peacock-tinted visions, seeing things innumerable and unmentionable, beings plumed, from pituitary gland to backside, with red, white, green, blue, and orange flames. There he sat, with notebook in hand, taking down divine orders of the day from brother-selfs, master-souls, ancient-beauties, elfs and faeries, madly dancing a rigadoon a dad a derry o. Here she'd trot forward impudently, pulling aside A.E.'s twilight curtains, half hiding the Pleroma, gone today and here tomorrow; disturbing the dusky grandeur of the Great Breath's breathing, and frightening away the dim moths of twilight trees, twilight hills, twilight men, and twilight women, by crying out in her quiet, determined way, through all the mumbo jamboree of twilight thought that there were things to cook, sheets to sew, pans and kettles to mend.

It was hard for Sean to single out the best work done by this old woman, flitting through life like a robin with the eye of a hawk; for she had as much to do with what she did not do as she had with what she did; whether it was the writing of plays, or the lofty encouragement (not forgetting the blue curtains for the windows of his little flat) given to Yeats, making the poet at home in the dignity, comfort, and quiet of a fine house; soothing him with a sunny seat under a spreading catalpa tree in a flower-lit garden, where a summer evening was full of the linnet's wings; whether it was the warm determined will that gave her little theatre a local habitation and a world-wide name; for not Yeats, nor Martyn, nor Miss Horniman gave the Abbey Theatre its enduring life, but this woman only, with the rugged cheeks, high upper lip, twinkling eyes, pricked with a dot of steel in their centres; this woman, only, who, in the midst of venomous opposition, served as a general run-about in sensible pride and lofty humility, crushing time out of odd moments to write play after play that kept life passing to and fro on the Abbey stage.

On a stone wall surrounding what was once, maybe, a meadow, Sean sat one day simmering in the sun. All over the heath, the crowds of wild waste plants were covered with wide mantles of brilliant-blue butterflies. Never had he imagined such a host of blue evanescent divinity. In the formal garden, here and there, one, or maybe a pair, flew about from this flower to that one, but here they were in tens of thousands. As they settled and rose, they looked like a multitude of tiny blue banners carried by an invisible army. Or the bright blue mantle of St. Brighid down from the sky, fluttering near the half-remembered things of earth. How delightful the sturdy black figure of her ladyship would look doing a slow, graceful, if a little stiff, minuet among the brilliant-blue fluttering things. Sean wondered if Yeats had never set eyes on these. Hardly, for they were off the beaten, formal track of his strolling: garden, lake, woods were as far as he got; and so the gurgling rise of the river, and these brilliant-blue angels of an hour were denied the lyric their loveliness commended.

She loosened the tautness of her own work by taking too much time helping others, Sean thought as he sat on the wall, encircled with the cloud of blue butterflies. She became foster-mother to some plays of Yeats, weaving in dialogue for *Caitlin ni Houlihan* and his *Pot of Broth;* helping in the construction of *The King's Threshold* and *Where There Is Nothing,* throwing in, for good measure, scenarios from which Douglas Hyde made *The Poorhouse* and *The Marriage.* In the theatre, among the poets and playwrights, herself a better playwright than most of them, she acted the part of a charwoman, but one with a star on her breast. Ay, indeed, this serving eagerness of hers was a weakness in her nature. She thought too much of the work of others, foaming with their own importance, leaving her but little time to think of her own. So signs on it, a good deal of what she did shows hurry, hinting in its haste that no matter if mine be not good so long as that of others be better.

Once troubled with the pushful realism of the younger writers, she started to write a romantic play around Brian Boru, called *Kincora*. She made many false starts, but kept hammering away, in spite of Yeats's advice to give it up; and, though the play got its share of applause, it wasn't in itself, she says, the success it might have been, and so hindered a welcome from critic and audience. Give it up! No wonder it wasn't the success it might have been. Why didn't Yeats mind his own business! A pity the woman was so near to Yeats while she was writing the play: he had a bad effect on her confidence in her own creation. She was concerned with him and her play; he concerned only with himself. He had no right to tell her to give up writing the play; but she served so frequently in so many common ways that Yeats easily dismissed from his mind her natural vigour in the creation of imaginative drama. It was a shame that the modelling of the play should have been chilled by a scornful wave of a delicate hand from a poetical mind that so often dismissed everything save what was dissolving in the wonder of his own thought.

Lady Gregory had her own Three Sorrows of Storytelling; three sorrows that were rifling her heart when Sean first came across her, and founded a friendship with Coole. The tumbling, burning death of her son Major Robert Gregory, on the battlefield of Italy, was but being softened slowly by her transferred devotion to his three young children. His death, too, was a loss to Ireland, for to his many qualities, he added that of a fine and sensitive designer for the theatre. In the play, *Kincora*, the king's Great Hall was shown by the hanging of vivid green curtains; there were shields, embossed with designs of gold upon the walls, and heavy mouldings over the doors. For Brian's tent at Clontarf, a great orange curtain filled the background, with figures standing out against it in green, red, and grey. In *The Shadowy Waters*, he made the whole stage the sloping deck of a galley, blue and dim, the sails and dresses were green, and the ornaments all of copper. When Robert Gregory fell on the hilly soil of Italy, Ireland may have lost an Irish, and more colourful, Gordon Craig.

The Second Sorrow was the Atlantic weaving with her waves a winding-sheet for Sir Hugh Lane, her nephew, when he went down in the *Lusitania*, almost within view of his birthplace in the county of Cork. He it was, who through heavy opposition, gave many gems of painting to many galleries, scattering these lovely things all over Dublin, as another would scatter rose-petals about in the heat of a carnival. A loss he was, a great loss to his people, though only a very few felt it, besides the lonely woman in her home at Coole. To Sean, then, he was none; he felt it not; knew it not; but he knew it well now.

The Third Sorrow was the taking away of the Lane pictures from Dublin by the then British Authorities. A scurvy trick, one of the many done by British authority on Ireland. The lousiest and meanest of robberies ever perpetrated by one country or another. To her last breath, she followed after them, seeking them, seeking them, and often Sean had gone with her. They are still exiled from their native land; but they will be brought back. Though many in Ireland were blind to their beauty, so were others, better placed than the Irish to recognise their loveliness; for one of them, Renoir's *Umbrellas,* lay for a long time deep in the cellar of the National Gallery, too trivial, as the big shots thought, for a hanging on a respectable wall. A scurvy trick, England!

What shall we bring to the place where she now lies asleep forever? Easy enough to answer; easy enough: A promise not to forget the Lane pictures; some of the shining forget-me-nots from the glade where the fresh river rises; a branch from the copper beech that bore the initials of those who had sat at her table and walked in her garden; an old fiddler to play *The Blackberry Blossom;* a butterfly from the gorgeous blue swarm that clouded the heath, like the blue mantle of Brighid, behind the House of Coole; a vine leaf, or two, in token of her gay heart; since she elected to live and die a Christian, a cross; and the voice of her poet friend chanting:

> *Here, traveller, scholar, poet, take your stand*
> *When all those rooms and passages are gone,*
> *When nettles wave upon a shapeless mound*
> *And saplings root among the broken stone;*
> *And dedicate—eyes bent upon the ground,*
> *Back turned upon the brightness of the sun*
> *And all the sensuality of the shade—*
> *A moment's memory to that laurelled head.*

All the rooms and passages are gone, and saplings root among the broken stone, for an elevated Irish Government has broken down the House and levelled it smooth for nettles to grow upon a shapeless mound. Oh! a scurvy act for an Irish Government to do on the memory of one who was greater than the whole bunch of them put together and tied with string. The goddamned Philistines!

* * *

THE TEMPLE ENTERED

The bells were ringing an old year out and a new year in for Sean: he was on his way to the temple of drama, the Abbey Theatre, where he was an acolyte now, in full canonical costume. Among his thoughts was none of either success or failure. He knew nothing about these things. What he thought of was how much money he would get from the performances. He would soon be in a position to buy many books, and live comfortably reading them, for a considerable time. He found himself going through the streets without noticing the people passing, or the shops, hearing but faintly even the chatter from the public-houses as he passed them by. It was as if he was on his way to meet a girl. Well, this was Marlborough Street, and further down was the Abbey Theatre, renowned, people said, the world over. There opposite was the Pro-Cathedral, the Church of the Immaculate

Conception. An ugly sight. A dowdy, squat-looking imitation of some Italian church, done up in a back-handed Greco style; a cheaply-fashioned souvenir of Rome. No indication that this was Dublin, and that an Irish church, except the stiff statue of St. Laurence O'Toole, standing grim and uneasy-looking on a corner of the entablature. Inside of the church, not a sign of the Book of Kells, nor that of Lismore; or ever a peal from St. Patrick's Bell; or even a painted symbol of the Cross of Cong. All of it imitation, silly, slavish; pompous imitation of the Latin, Italian order of the Vatican. A cheap home for Our Lady of Eblana, a cheap and distressing vase for the madonna lily of the slums.

Here is the church, thought Sean, stopping to look at its brawny and vulgar façade, this is the church that refused to shelter the body of a dead Fenian for a night. St. Laurence O'Toole refuses to allow a ray from the smallest of holy candles to reach as far as the body of a dead Fenian. Here the top-hatted, holy ones streamed sterilely in, on ceremonial occasions, to pay their sweet respects to Jesus. Here at this church, Matt Talbot, a Dublin labourer, full-up of sanctity, stretched himself flat on the pavement to say preliminary prayers, then crawled up the steps on his belly to the big door closed against him, waiting prone on the stones till it opened to let him join in the first Mass, so that he might go merry to work; dropping dead one day as he hurried to another church in an effort to fulfil the obligation he put upon himself to pray without ceasing. But he hurried too fast this time, for his heart gave out before he got there, and he fell down dead. But he died with harness on his belly. Afterwards, in the mortuary, it was found that he was wearing a cart chain round the middle of his body, with another round one of his legs, while a rope was tied tightly round the other one, and all were spangled with holy medals. *A model workman and a model catholic,* the courtly knight, Sir Joseph Glynn, calls him, *and his life points out the only path to true peace for all who labour, a life of self-discipline lived in perfect agreement with the law of God and His church. Ecce hobo sapiens.* Blow, crumpeter, blow! So workers of Dublin, and the world, you know now what you have to do. Follow Matt Talbot up to heaven. You've nothing to lose but the world, and you've the holy chains to gain. Read this Glynn's *Life of Matt Talbot,* then read Stalin's *Life of Lenin;* and take your choice. Make the world safe for the bosses. If you do, you're sure to get to heaven when you die.

Think deep on these things, working-men. Why do you waste time demanding a living wage? Think of eternity, and remember there may be none there. Why do you want to bother about the health and vigour of your children? Pain and woe and disease may help them upwards. Why do you look for a comfortable home, with light and heat and colour in it? You fools! Consider Mutt Talbot, and you'll realise that these poor things are but vanity. Worse than vanity—burdens, clogs, stumbling-blocks, impeding your precious way to heaven. Listen, you dockers and labourers of Dublin! When a boat has to be unloaded in quick time so that she may catch a tide, and you get an extra two shillings for the hurried job, don't take them. Refuse this bonus as Mutt Talbot did, feeling with him that idle moments waiting for lorries to come to be unloaded should be set against the extra work. That was Mutt Talbot, that was! This refusal of extra money, says the knight of Glynn, *was due to the high sense of justice this man Talbot possessed*. Oh, how far short do we come of this man's high sense of justice! Mutt always thought of his poor boss. Look at all the boss had to do with his money—keep a big house going, a carriage and pair, a well-dressed wife, and high education for his little ones. If indifferent workers could but see the truth hidden in time and eternity, they'd refuse any extra reward of wage or bonus. They'd advance through life on white bread and black tea to the glory of God and rich benefit of their own souls, and so allow the bosses to enjoy their chicken and wine in peace. Do these things, workers, and you'll all be lifted up to heaven with sparkling cords made out of the gold of the rich men. And the sight entrancing you'll all see there—Mutt Talbot and the knight of Glynn shaking hands among the gallant and glittering angels.

—To hell with Mutt Talbot! muttered Sean, glancing up at the cold statue of St. Laurence O' Toole, without the chime of a word from him; we won't give in to the bosses as you, St. Laurence, gave in to the Normans. If any saint is to be preferred, I choose St. Joan, who, at least, prayed with a sword at her girdle. She was a fighter who disturbed great cleric and great lord, and so signs on it, she was burned before she was blessed.

This church was nicely set down, for it was but a minute's walk from Dublin's fairest thoroughfare—O'Connell Street; a minute's walk from fine business and great banking; and it was but another minute's walk from the street, where, in tumbling houses, fat-breasted, big-thighed women, clad in brilliantly-coloured calico gowns of crimson or green, sat at twisted windows, calmly drinking down tumblers of luscious stout, frothing over the rim of the glasses. A gentle shake of these gaudy gowns would show bare shoulders and barer breasts, signalling seduction down to any likely man passing by beneath; and many a wayward and unstable Mutt Talbot would lift a wavering but flaming eye to the visions at the windows.

Here was the Abbey Theatre—a red flower in the slum; but a minute's walk from the church, too, so that judgement, heaven, and hell were but a short way from each other. Sean had entered the temple. He had passed under the glass-roofed awning, its iron standards and framework gilded discreetly, showing that, though austerity couldn't suitably don a golden shawl, she could decently wear a golden brooch in a black one. He remembered the first time he had stood in the tiled foyer through which so many fine souls had passed to watch Ireland finding at last her soul in literature and the drama. Sean had come in by the front way, and was now among the gods. To the left were the stairs going down to the stalls where Sean would sit now, to watch the play of another, and to see and help to guide the evolution, through acting and design, of his own. To the right was a door leading to the Manager's office and the stage, and in between these two entrances stood the tabernacle of all theatres—the box-office. Opposite, parallel with a stained-glass window, was a little narrow counter where the audience from the stalls drank coffee, ate biscuits, and discussed the play. Beside this counter, high up on the wall, hung Dermod O'Brien's painting of Barry Fitzgerald in the part of the King from Lady Gregory's *The Dragon*. A poster on another wall told in French when Synge's *Playboy of the Western World* was first performed in Paris.

Inside, Sean saw how small the theatre was, holding only half a thousand. It, somehow, looked smaller now than when he knew it so well as The Mechanics Theatre. The freshness, the red-leather upholstered seats, the shields, bearing on them the armorial signs of Ireland's Four Beautiful Fields, and the black curtain with its gold stripes, showed up the points of the building, and brought them closer together. Again Sean was treading the poor, narrow stage, its expansion backwards forever prohibited by a slum laneway running from Marlborough Street, where stood the Abbey Theatre itself, to Beresford Place, where stood the Liberty Hall, made so famous by the eloquence and flame of Jim Larkin, the Labour Leader.

He told no-one that he had known this old stage well, that he had even played a part on it; that one of his brothers had often done so; that he had watched, from the pit below, men, with hands tied behind their back, struggling to swallow boiling-hot suet puddings; in their haste, knocking them from the table to floor, and so forcing themselves to stretch there, eating with voracity; for ten shillings reward was to be given to him who finished his pudding first. He remembered the drop-curtain, showing, in fading colours, the lovely Lakes of Killarney; now displaced by the dignified one of sable and gold, but showing signs of fading too. He had drunk glasses of diluted claret, sweet with sugar, with those who had played the principal parts in Boucicault's *The Shaughraun*, in a pub opposite the theatre; in a private room, too, for the pub proprietor had something to do with the venture. All changed now, changed utterly; and here he was now with plays of his own showing themselves off on the very same stage that he himself had trod as a growing youngster so long, so long ago. His brother, Archie, had played the part of Harvey Duff. Archie was a good black and white man with pencil or pen, a splendid carpenter, and a brilliant accountant, but there he was now, up in Liverpool, sweeping the floors of a Dunlop rubber factory. The lad's will hadn't been guided rightly into a fighting, fuller life when he left school; his talents had been left to perish.

The first night of his first play [the Shadow of a Gunman] had gone very well indeed, and Sean had been congratulated by all the actors. But he was troubled with vexation of spirit when he was told that the play was to run for three nights only, and this vexation was sharpened when the Secretary of the theatre added the information that there was but thirteen pounds received for the night. However, the second night's receipts jumped to thirty pounds, and the last night to over fifty which meant the first full house for the Abbey Theatre for many a long night. Sean smiled benignly at the Secretary, when he was told the theatre would have no money in the bank till the guarantors sent in their guarantees; but, if Sean so desired, he could be paid from the cash received at the door, instead of in the usual way, by cheque. Full of shy vanity, with a grand wave of the hand, Sean told the Secretary he wasn't to bother, and that he'd willingly wait for the cheque.

When it came, it was less than four pounds. Less than four pounds! And he had bargained in his mind for twenty, at the least. And, if the receipts hadn't jumped up at the end, he'd have had but half of that amount. Dimly he began to realise that the Abbey Theatre would never provide a living. It was a blow, a bitter disappointment. The black stripes in the theatre's curtain were far wider than the gold stripes. Less than four pounds wouldn't even pay his passage to England for a chat about the Soviet Union with Raissa Lomonovska. It looked as if things would allow his talent to perish too. What he had got wouldn't even pay what he owed. The amount didn't extend even to the purchase of a book. What was he to do? One thing, and one thing only—go forward. He had put his hand to the plough, and he wasn't the one to look back. He would start a new play that very night.

So he had, and he called it *Cathleen Listens In,* a jovial sardonic sketch on the various parties in conflict over Irish politics—Sinn Fein, Free State, and Labour. It was a short one-act work, and was performed after a major play had ended. Another experience for Sean! The audience received the little play in dead silence, in a silence that seemed to have a point of shock in its centre. Not even a cold clap of a hand anywhere. They all got up from their seats, and silently filed out of the theatre. He was the one and only playwright to have had a play received in silence by an Abbey audience; the only one to be deprived of even a single timid hand-clap. Indeed, it did look as if his talent, too, would have to perish in silence and with malice of afterthought. What would he do, for he was vexed, and a sense of humiliation discouraged him; what would he do? Go on, go on! Forever he would go on seeing through his own eyes, hearing with his own ears, speaking with his own tongue. No power of influence, no seduction of wealth, no affection for friend, nor would any love for woman draw him away from his own integrity. Let that integrity be right or wrong, it would be a true reflection of what he felt in his nature from the things he saw and the things he heard around him.

*   *   *

The third work, [Juno and the Paycock] a full-length play, was, from the Abbey Theatre point of view, an emphatic success, and Yeats halted in his meditations to tell Sean that he had given new hope and new life to the theatre. The house had been booked out for the first week, and the run of the play was extended for a week longer. Sean had come into his fortune of twenty-five pounds, after waiting more than a year for it.

Books, books, more books! And a step nearer to a trip over the waters to England. His choice of Barry Fitzgerald for one of the two chief parts had been more than justified. When Sean had mentioned his name, Mr. Robinson had demurred, had murmured the name of F. J. McCormick as a better selection for Boyle; but Sean had insisted on the selection of Fitzgerald, and the choice had been triumphant. After the Abbey season had ended a year ago, to give place to a long holiday, the Abbey actors had taken the theatre, and put on Ervine's *Mary, Mary, Quite Contrary* so as to furnish themselves with something more in the way of money to tide the holiday over, and Sean had gone to see it, in a spirit of loyalty to those who had so generously helped him by their fine acting. He had known all who had played in it; all save one whom he had never heard of, whom he had never seen. This newcomer filled the part of the Anglican clergyman. The play began, and Sean sat easy wondering who was the new fellow that had joined the company. Sean soon sat up. This new fellow could act. This fellow was a great comedian. This fellow was an artist. Sean never looked at a programme in a theatre because of his bad sight, so he did not know the fellow's name. He would go behind, and find out. This fellow was the man for him. He had never seen him before; none of the actors had ever mentioned his name. Well, if they didn't, Sean would, and out loud, too.

When the play ended, he rushed round to tell all of his discovery. It was an unwise thing to do; a foolish thing, a stupid thing to do. But Sean was altogether ignorant of jealousies behind the curtain. He rushed across the foyer, through the doorway at the back, up the stairs, down the corridors where the dressing-rooms were, yelling, Who's the fellow that played the clergyman? Where's the chap that played the clergyman? Michael Dolan's dressing-room door was open, for it was a warm night, and the actor was busy taking the grease-paint from his face. He listened without a flicker of an eyelid to Sean's excited demand to know who and where was the fellow who played the part of the clergyman. A great actor, said Sean vehemently; a grand comedian; an artist born suddenly for the theatre.

—He's not bad, murmured Mr. Michael Dolan, rubbing quietly away at his face—when he happens to get a part that suits him.

—Good God, man, said Sean, it's long since the theatre's seen the like of him! And then there was silence, for Sean began to realise that such things spoken loudly were not wise or welcome. For the future, if circumstances called for it, he would praise what he thought was bad, and censure what he felt to be good—he would, like hell! But his ardent acclaim of what he thought was fine raised the first breeze of coolness between him and the Abbey actors.

Passing by his third play, a one-act work called *Nannie's Night Out,* a play no-one liked, except A.E., otherwise known as George Russell, who thought it O'Casey's best work; an opinion that didn't bother Sean, for he knew A.E. knew nothing about the drama, and felt it a little less; Sean, at length, found himself attending the rehearsals of his fourth one, a full-length drama. [The Plough and the Stars.] He was now taking an active part in a rehearsal for the first time. He had stayed silent and passive during these of his first two plays, and during those of his third play, he had been in hospital with a sharp attack of bronchitis most of the time, finding the play well set when he came out, so that he had very little to learn to do, except to persuade the timid Barry Fitzgerald that he could, and must, play the part.

But Sean's persuasion laboured on, for he saw before him clearly now a fine library and a visit to England where his second play was doing well in the West End of London. He was buying furniture bit by bit, and still had a lot to get before he could be decently comfortable. He wanted to move somewhere else to a place in which he would find fairer comfort, greater space, and a steady quietness. He could do all this in England, but the expense would be great, and he hesitated. If the plays brought in double of what he had now, he would go. If the play on in London really settled down, and if this new play went well in the Abbey, he would hoist his sail, and go. A short farewell to Ireland; a hasty look round the places he had known for so long; a last thought of Irish gods and fighting men, and then he would go.

But he was anxious about the present play. He had fancied that when he had fought his way to the Abbey stage, all his troubles would end. Poor, guileless innocent! He had left old troubles to embrace new ones. He had noticed an odd coldness and an irritant nervousness in the manner of the Caste. He sensed that something was going wrong. A number of the actors were doing their parts lazily, as if the play held no interest for them. Mr. Robinson, the Producer, was inclined to be irritable, and he was at times abrupt when Sean ventured to make a suggestion. Then a whisper in Sean's ear told him that Miss Crowe had decided not to play the part of Mrs. Gogan. Sean went to her, and asked if what he heard was true. She said it was. He asked why she wouldn't play the part, and was told that *The part was not genteel.* Oh, Jesus! A Miss May Craig, an actress little thought of, but very good, was got to fill the part, and filled it to perfection. Miss Ria Mooney, chosen for the part of the prostitute, was bombarded with barbed beseeching to rise out of the part; for, if she didn't, she might no longer be thought respectable, and might risk her future in this world and even the next. Fortunately for the play, she held on, and put more fire into the part because of the opposition. F. J. McCormick was hesitant, and seemed to be responding reluctantly to his part. Then, in the midst of the anxiety, Gabriel Fallon, whom Sean had selected to play the part of Peter Flynn, came stealing up to beg this part be taken from him, and the part of Captain Brennan given in its stead. All this made Fitzgerald more nervous than ever, for he had none of the arrogant courage, and none of the jovial determination, which, under different conditions, might have made a great man of Fluther. And, finally, when Sean had ventured to suggest the kind of instrument needed to simulate a band leading the Dublin Fusiliers to the boat, Mr. Robinson's outburst of Oh, shut up, for Christ's sake, man! I've got enough to do to deal with the Caste! settled Sean into a wondering silence. To this day, Sean isn't sure—for no word ever came to him—that the Caste, or any members of it, had heard of the vigorous opposition the play was to meet with when it came to the stage.

While he had been writing the play, Liam O'Flaherty had brought David Garnett to the tenement house to see Sean, and had persuaded Sean to tell of the play he was writing; so, round a blazing fire, Sean had a vigorous chat with this clever and most amiable writer. Both Garnett and O'Flaherty, probably out of politeness and goodwill, had agreed that the play would be a work to be remembered. Afterwards, O'Flaherty's letter to the *Irish Statesman,* definitely and emphatically condemning the work as a bad play, shoved Sean into taking a vow that never again would he reveal to anyone what he was trying to do; never again, except under curious circumstances, would he speak of work in progress. If he spoke at all, he would talk of something he but faintly intended to do. He would think it quietly out, do it the best way he could, and then send it out in the name of God and of O'Casey.

Coming close to the first night, Sean's eyes filled with inflammation, and in-growing eyelashes made the inflammation worse. Dr. J. D. Cummins, now an intimate friend, did all he could to lessen the searching pain; but on the night of the first performance, Sean found it hard and painful to keep his eyes fixed on the bright zone of the stage. The theatre was packed to the doors; the curtain went up; the play began. Though some of the actors didn't seem to strive very earnestly to swing themselves into the drama, most things went well, and the audience sat still, intensely interested in what they saw before them—the mimic, but by no means unimportant portrayal of a part of Dublin's life and feeling. When the end came, the audience clapped tumultuously, and shouted applause. They shouted for the author, and Sean went on to the stage, quietly glad that the play had succeeded. He took the appreciation of those there nicely, though the flame of pain in his eyes pricked like red-hot needles. But all was pleasant, and the loud applause flowed from the serenity of agreement with, and appreciation of, the play. Tightening the belt of his rubber trench-coat tight around him, he went home settled in mind, happy in heart: the worst was over. He was very much the innocent gaum.

The next night he sauntered into a storm. Holy Murther had come again on a visit to the Abbey Theatre. When he entered the foyer, he was hurried up to the Secretary's Office where W. B. Yeats was waiting for him. Listen to my tale of woe. There he was told that the theatre was in an uproar, and that the play could not go on, if something definite wasn't done; that missiles were being flung at the actors, and that it looked as if the stage would be stormed.

—We think it necessary that the police should be sent for immediately, so that the mob may be kept from preventing us carrying on the work we have set our hands to do, said Yeats. We want your consent, O'Casey, to send for the police, as you happen to be the author of the play.

The police! Sean to agree to send for the police—never! His Irish soul revolted from the idea; though Yeats and others reminded him that the police were no longer in a foreign service, but were now in Ireland's own. That the tricolour waved over their barracks, and that it even graced the big drum of their band. Even so, Sean couldn't see his way to ask them to come. No, no; never! But a wild roar heard in the theatre, seeming to shake the room where they all stood, told him to make up his mind quick; and swearing he could ne'er consent, consented.

The police were summoned, and the play began again—two, in fact: one on the stage and the other in the auditorium. Yeats tore down the stairs, and rushed on to the stage to hold the fort till the constables came. The whole place became a mass of moving, roaring people, and Yeats roared louder than any of them. Rowdy, clenching, but well-groomed hands reached up to drag down the fading black and gold front curtain; others, snarling curiously, tried to tug up the very chairs from their roots in the auditorium; while some, in frenzy, pushed at the stout walls to force them down. Steamy fumes ascended here and there in the theatre, and a sickly stench crept all over the place, turning healthy-looking faces pale. The high, hysterical, distorted voices of women kept squealing that Irish girls were noted over the whole world for their modesty, and that Ireland's name was holy; that the Republican flag had never seen the inside of a public-house; that this slander of the Irish race would mean the end of the Abbey Theatre; and that Ireland was Ireland through joy and through tears. Up in the balcony, a section was busily bawling out *The Soldier's Song*, while a tall fellow frantically beat time on the balcony-rail with a walking-stick.

Barry Fitzgerald became a genuine Fluther Good, and fought as Fluther himself would fight, sending an enemy, who had climbed on to the stage, flying into the stalls with a flutherian punch on the jaw. And in the midst of the fume, the fighting, the stench, the shouting, Yeats, as mad as the maddest there, pranced on the stage, shouting out his scorn, his contempt; his anger making him like unto an aged Cuchullin in his hero-rage; his long hair waving, he stormed in utter disregard of all around him, confronting all those who cursed and cried out shame and vengeance on the theatre, as he conjured up a vision for them of O'Casey on a cloud, with Fluther on his right hand and Rosie Redmond on his left, rising upwards to Olympus to get from the waiting gods and goddesses a triumphant apotheosis for a work well down in the name of Ireland and of art.

Then the constables flooded into the theatre, just in time. Rough and ready, lusty guardians of the peace. They filed into the theatre as Irish constables for the first time in their life; mystified, maybe, at anyone kicking up a row over a mere play. They pulled the disturbers out, they pushed them out, and, in one or two instances, carried them out, shedding them like peas from the pod of the theatre, leaving them in the cold street outside to tell their troubles to their neighbours or to the stars. Then the play went on, halting often, and agitated to its end. For the first time in his life, Sean felt a surge of hatred for Cathleen ni Houlihan sweeping over him. He saw now that the one who had the walk of a queen could be a bitch at times. She galled the hearts of her children who dared to be above the ordinary, and she often slew her best ones. She had hounded Parnell to death; she had yelled and torn at Yeats, at Synge, and now she was doing the same to him. What an old snarly gob she could be at times; an ignorant one too.

He left the auditorium where the people were watching the play, subdued and nervous, hedged in by the silver-plated helmets of the police, and strayed out into the foyer, right into the midst of a group of women squealers, members of Cumann na mBan—the Society of Women. They shot remarks at him from where they stood or lounged. They said he was a renegade, a friend to England, and that he would soon have a government pension. They said he had held up Ireland's sacred name to ridicule for the sake of the money he'd get for doing it; that it was he who, sooner or later, would feel the shame, and not Ireland. They said he was one now with those who had always hated Ireland, and that the Union Jack was his flag now, and not the Irish tricolour that he had defamed.

—Yes, said one, leaning against the wall, an' I'd like you to know that there isn't a prostitute in Ireland from one end of it to th' other.

Cathleen ni Houlihan was talking. Drawing her patched and fading skirt close around her, she was talking big. Through these women, she was talking. There wasn't a comely damsel among them. Sean noticed this with some surprise. They were all plain, provoking no desire in him to parley words with them, as a pretty face would have done, had one been among them. So after listening for awhile, and saying a few words, he left them to go up to the office to see how things were going. Yeats was shaking hands with an Inspector of Police who was introducing Sergeant Bantry Bay to the poet. The sergeant had developed into a mood of hilarious nervousness. He bowed to the poet, took off his hat, offered his hand, and when Yeats offered his, shook it vehemently, bending Yeats forward with the power of his hand's pull, blurting out a greeting that he must have been practising all the way to the theatre: *It is to be greatly regretted sir, that I have had the honour and pleasure of meeting you for the first time undher such disthress-ing circumstances!* The Inspector looked silly to hear this greeting, and its unexpected eloquence stunned Yeats out of his senses for a few moments, so that he stared at the sergeant till he summoned enough thought to mutter confusedly, Yes, yes; quite. It is, it is.

Sean went home feeling no way exalted by his famous apotheosis. He was bewildered, and felt sick rather than hilarious. Slandered the people! He had slandered his class no more than Chekhov had slandered his. Did these bawling fools think that their shouting would make him docile? He would leave them to their green hills of holy Ireland. His play was doing well in London, and the Producer, J. B. Fagan, had written several times to him, asking him to come over. Why didn't he go, and leave the lot of them? The land of Nelson and of Clive was beckoning to him more clearly than ever before; and he was near ready to leave the land of Patrick and of Tone.

A few days after he received a letter from Frank Ryan of the National University telling him that Mrs. Sheehy-Skeffington challenged him to a debate about the play. Would he take up the challenge, or would he not? He would; and he wrote to Frank Ryan telling him so. It was foolish to bother, but Sean felt that if he didn't take it up, it would be thought he was afraid, and his pride, stupid pride, couldn't allow that to be thought by anyone. He hadn't learned enough yet. He was still a gaum. When he got to the hall, he found it packed to the door, so crowded that those in the front were almost on top of him; so crowded that the air was gone, and a damp heat everywhere. That was one of the things he was never able to bear—a crowded, airless room always made him sick. And now that his eyes were full of pain, the sense of breathlessness would be worse, and thinking would be hard to do. He listened to Mrs. Sheehy-Skeffington speaking against what she called realism in the drama, and pleading very cleverly for the continuance of romanticism on the stage, especially in an Ireland fighting against many odds for her finest national conceptions.

But Sean knew well that those who had fought against the British had no interest in, no knowledge whatever of, the battling difference between romanticism and realism. What concerned them was the implication of fear showing itself in the manner and speech of the fighting characters of the play; and in the critical way their patriotism was ignored, or opposed by Dublin's poor. Mrs. Sheehy-Skeffington, a very clever and a very upright woman, saw it the other way, or thought she saw it so, and turned the dispute into an academic question, because—Sean often thought afterwards—she wished him to do the same, and so lift the question on to a higher plane that that of roars, fights with fists, savage abuse, and the tearing down of a theatre. But Sean couldn't, and wouldn't, get away from the everyday words and conduct of the common people, and what they thought of the things that had happened among them, adding to these things the thoughts which afflicted him about these same things too.

Ill as he fell with the heat and the thickened air, coupled with the neuralgic pain pressing on his eyeballs, forcing his thoughts into the confusing fear that he would speak badly, Sean watched the figure of Madame Gonne-McBride, seated, like a quiet stone image this side of Mrs. Sheehy-Skeffington, and but a little distance from himself. She was clad in a classical way, with a veil of dark blue over her head, the ends flowing down over her shoulders. She turned slowly, only once, to glance at him; and Sean saw, not her who was beautiful, and had the walk of a queen, but the poor old woman, whose voice was querulous, from whom came many words that were bitter, and but few kind. This was she of whom it had been said that men could thrash out, on a dark night, a full barn of corn by the light from one tress of her hair. This was she for whom Yeats had woven so many beautiful cloths of embroidered poetry. She, too, was changed, changed utterly, for no ring of glory now surrounded that crinkled, querulous face. Shadows now were all its marking, shadows where the flesh had swelled or where the flesh had sagged. This is she, who, as Yeats declared,

Hurled the little streets upon the great.

She had never done that, for her knowledge of the ways of little streets was scanty, interesting her only when they issued from their dim places headed by a green flag. She never seemed to have understood Yeats, the poet. Indeed, she could not, having little of the poet in herself, so that she never felt the lure of melody. She forever sat within the folds of, or stood talking before, a velvet green curtain, and never thought to take a peep behind. Here she sat now, silent, stony; waiting her turn to say more bitter words against the one who refused to make her dying dream his own. There she sits stonily silent, once a sibyl of patriotism from whom no oracle ever came; now silent and aged; her deep-set eyes now sad, agleam with disappointment; never quite at ease with the crowd, whose cheers she loved; the colonel's daughter still.

The sickness, suffocating, seized Sean when he got up to speak after Mrs. Sheehy-Skeffington had ended, and he was forced to sit down to wait till the pain in his head steadied into a droning discomfort; till the giddiness lost its power over his thoughts. He did not know, till more than twenty years after, that silicosis had, in shrivelling a lung, pulled his heart out of its place. Some said, go home, and do not stay, for you look ill, and should be careful. But Sean barely listened to them, for he had come there to speak, and speak he would; and speak he did. But it was a hard fight to get going, and his whole being was strained with the effort, and in his heart he despised, more bitterly than ever, the ones who made it necessary for a writer to defend a work so many hated and so few admired. Weary and scornful at the end of it all, Sean went home to his tenement in the little car of Frank Hugh O'Donnell. He felt very tired, and very sad. He lit the lamp, thanked Frank for giving him a lift, looked round, and saw a telegram that had been thrust under his room door. Must have come while he was out. Write to please the Mary MacSwineys, the Countesses Markievicz, the Madame Gonne-McBrides! Jasus Christ, the very thought was laughable! He stooped, picked up the telegram, tore open the envelope, and read the message. It was from Fagan telling him that his play was coming off at one theatre, but another had been engaged, and the play would go on there; but there wasn't much of a chance of a new success, unless Sean came over for the first night, and so created a little publicity for the newer effort.

—I'll go, he said to Frank O'Donnell. I'll go over to help the play's entrance into a new theatre, and leave the wrack behind me.

When the shouting had died down, and the rowdier captains had departed, the turn of the intellectuals came to cheat Sean from any success he might be expecting. Sean saw another side of Ireland's enterprising malice and envy. He was learning more in a few weeks than he had learned in a lifetime. The intellectuals began to send letters to the Press, and to A.E.'s journal, *The Irish Statesman,* condemning and upbraiding the plays. Some of them were influenced to do this, Sean thought, because he had definitely refused to join them in a Club or Society which was to be organised to put the arrogant Yeats in his place. He would argue with Yeats, oppose him manfully, but personally, on any question of religion, politics, and even literature, if he happened to differ from the poet; but he wouldn't join any clique to do it, because he thought this opposition was born of envy of the great fame the poet enjoyed as the leading man of Irish Letters. He had never mentioned the matter to Yeats, for, having done, or refused to do, what was right, or what he thought was right; he was satisfied in his own soul, and nothing else mattered.

Sean's plays were stoned with many criticisms from the intellectuals, so that he passed from one bewilderment to another. *The plays,* said one, *are naught but a series of Tableau Vivants; O'Casey is purely a photographic artist. He is striving after a literary quality of speech which is entirely alien to the Dublin slum-dwellers; the plays have the structure of the cinema and the revue. They are a series of scenes rather than a play. The career of O'Casey induces fear for the future.* All this came from the bracing brain of Dublin's then first critic—Andrew E. Malone. Again, as if he felt he hadn't said enough, he goes on to add, *His plays are phases of Dublin life as abnormal as they are transient. O'Casey's humour is the humour of the music-hall without the skill of the music-hall or the sharpened point of its wit. Is O'Casey a dramatist, or is he but a combination of the cinema and the dictaphone?* That was written more than twenty years ago, and the Irish critics haven't been able to answer the question yet.

Following O'Flaherty's direct announcement (as pompous as anything Yeats could have said) that *The Plough and the Stars was a bad play,* came the young poet Fred O'Higgins's remonstrance and criticism, saying, *A new political quality approved by the arrogance of the Anglo-Irish is the only quality for which O'Casey is offered applause. His is a technique based on the revue structure, in the quintessence of an all-Abbey burlesque, intensified by "diversions" and Handy Andy incidents, with somewhat more original settings. O'Casey in his new play entirely lacks the sincerity of the artist.*

Another coloured bullet-bead was added to the string by a letter from Austen Clarke, another poet, who said with poise and gentle dignity, that *Several writers of the New Irish School* (himself included of course) *believed that Mr. O'Casey's work was a crude exploitation of our poorer people in the Anglo-Irish tradition that is now moribund.* Still another writer, R. M. Fox, referred to the plays as *The Drama of the Dregs,* adding that *The peasant plays have been followed by slum plays, but their reign will not be long, though as entertainment these slum dramas are permissible. But truth is wanted as well as entertainment.*

So Sean, at first bewildered by the riot, was now puzzled by the Irish critics, for, innocent gaum that he was, he didn't realise then that these fellows didn't know what they were talking about.

He wondered how he could have built on the revue structure, for he had never seen a revue in his life. He knew nothing about the cinema. If any of them had only mentioned melodrama, he would have cocked an ear, for he had seen many of these, and had enjoyed them all. They saw in Sean that of which they themselves were full—the cinema and the revue. Then first began Sean's distrust of, and contempt for, the Irish critics. Knowing all, they knew nothing. Two critics now began to shine on his thoughts—one Irish, curiously enough, and the other American. They were George Jean Nathan and George Bernard Shaw—the two Georges. He had got Shaw's two books of *Dramatic Criticisms* from America, paying twenty-five shillings for them—a big sum for Sean to hand out those days; but he found them to be worth the sacrifice. The books formed a gorgeous episode in

Sean's life. Shaw's comments were on plays which—bar Shakespeare, Wilde, and Ibsen—he had neither seen nor read, and which, now, he would never see nor read, for they were all dead, never to rise again; but the criticisms lived on, and gave Sean a candle-light view of the theatre dead, and an arc-lamp view of the theatre living. Another book, Nathan's *The Critic and the Drama,* was a book of revelations to Sean. He was becoming less of the innocent gaum every page he passed. Here was a live man of the drama. As deep in what he wrote as he was gay. A wise philosopher, an undaunted critic, a lover of the theatre with cothurnus and sock attached to the glittering costume of the harlequin who carried a torch in his right hand instead of a lath. The Irish drama critics, even those who were poets, could now go to hell for Sean!

But, soberly, while he was here, he'd have to deal with the critics at home. How? By going his own way. That was the one thing to do, for there wasn't even a hint of guidance in what they said. They were no good. He would have to go a long way from the cliques of Dublin. But how could he escape? By living in the country or by crossing over to England. It was time he saw newer streets than those of Dublin. If he went to the country, he'd still be confined within the ken and den of Cosgravian and De Valerian politics, and well within the sphere of influence set up by Irish rosaries, Anthony's Annals, and all the crowding rolipoli-holiness of the Pope's green island; with Church of Ireland stained-glass windows shining timidly through the mist that does be on the bog. No, not that way. His future connection with Ireland must be somewhat similar to that of De Valera's association with the British Commonwealth—neither in it nor out of it. For him, the land of Nelson, Clive, and Canning in place of the land of Patrick, Tone, and Parnell. Not quite—Tone and Parnell would be forever very near to him.

Some little time after, the Abbey selected Shaw's *Man and Superman* for performance, and gave the play, in Sean's vision, a very bad production indeed. It had its comic side, for all the actors were subdued by the relentless enthusiasm of F. J. McCormick who played Tanner, who seemed to be always hustling them off the stage. Barry Fitzgerald, who played the part of Roebuck Ramsden, could only timidly stare, and sputter out his part in an apologetic and bewildered way, like a man asking questions in a crowd speaking another language. It was a helter-skelter performance, and one would have felt no wonder if the characters had suddenly broken up, and joined together again, in a song and dance assemble. Ignorant and innocent gaum that he was, Sean, thinking now that he was among old friends, ran round when the play ended to tell the artists what he thought of it all. They were all shocked, and murmured Hush hush hush. Sean thought they would all roar out laughter with him over the production, but they refused. They kept silent, except to say Hush hush hush. F. J. McCormick

came close to him, and said, "I hear you've been criticising our rendering of
Shaw's play. You've got a bit of a name now, and you must not say these
things about an Abbey production. If you do, we'll have to report it to the
Directors; so," he added a little crudely, "so try to keep your mouth shut."

Bewilderment again afflicted Sean. Just fancy that now! After all Sean
had gone through; after all his mouth had dared to say, it was to be kept
closed at an Abbey actor's order. Sean went home, sat down, wrote a long
letter, pointing out the bad parts of the production; why and how he
thought them to be bad; added a note to Mr. M. J. Dolan, the then Manager, saying that the letter held his views of what had happened, and that
he was at liberty, if he wished, to read the letter out loud to the Abbey
Directors, have it printed in papers, and show it to the world at large. This
letter was shown to Mr. Lennox Robinson, who, in an ethereal voice murmured, "It's just like Sean!" The letter was then pinned up on the notice-
board for all to read. Some nights following, Sean was on his way over the
Abbey stage to join the actors in the Green Room for a chat, when he was
stopped by Sean Barlow, a scene painter, in an old-fashioned way; a maker
of properties, again in another old-fashioned way, who asked what he was
doing on the stage. On my way to the Green Room, replied Sean. There's
none but the actors and officials allowed on the stage, said the bold Barlow,
with a dominant note in his voice; and we'd be glad if you came this way no
more.

No more? Quote the raven, Nevermore. Never again. Nevermore. Ordered from the stage he had trod so many years ago and he a kidger, ay,
mouthed the part of Father Dolan in *The Shaughraun* from its boards, ere
ever the Abbey Theater had entered its beginning; the stage on which his
brother, Archie, had played Harvey Duff in the same play, and others in
Peep o' Day Boys, The Unknown, Green Bushes, and *The Colleen Bawn.*
Never again; nevermore. He turned away, leaving the other Sean victor on
the field, and never after set a foot either on the Abbey stage or in the
Abbey Green Room.

He'd hoist his sail and go to England,

> *Neptune's park, ribbed and paled in*
> *With rocks unscalable and roaring waters.*

* * *

INISHFALLEN, FARE THEE WELL

⚜ ⚜ ⚜

Sean felt that if he stayed in Dublin, life would become embarrassing to meet. Dublin was too close to everyone. All its streets led into the one square where everyone met, where hands were shaken, shoulders clapped, and drinks taken to every other person's health. Sound and happy association, with one reservation—that when one was on the way to a good creation, he might be waylaid, left by the wayside, to die there, unfortified by the rites of the church. He remembered what he had gone through with his last play: Mr. Robinson agitated during rehearsals; silent sullenness stiffening the dialogue spoken by the actors; Lady Gregory anxious, and talking to Yeats about what might happen; and gigantic whispers wandering from one room to another in the Abbey Theatre, making the sullen more sullen still. "I refuse to say the word Snotty," said F. J. McCormick, while someone, in the background, murmured For righteous men must make our land a nation once again; "and I," said Miss Eileen Crowe—having first asked her priest about it—"refuse to say the words, 'Ne'er a one o' Jennie Gogan's kids was born outside of th' bordhers of the Ten Commandments'." A chorus in the background chanting,

> *Oh, sure you're right, allanna, for decent people know*
> *That every girl in Ireland, as things at present go,*
> *Is the soul of truth and of melting ruth,*
> *With a smile like a summer at dawn;*
> *Like the colleens that trip up and the colleens that trip down*
> *The sweet valley of Slieve na Man, amen.*

O Yes, O Yes, and there was Mr. O'Brien, the Abbey Director, running round moaning, "The Song, The Song! That'll have to come out; Yeats, you've got to be careful." And the lights in the pubs went higher and higher, and everything in them were agog and aglow. And Mr. Michael Dolan, the Theatre's Manager, writing to Lady Gregory beseeching her, with tears in his eyes, beseeching her, of her charity, now that the theatre was booming, to have nothing to do with this play; for the language, oh, the language in it goes beyond the beyonds; and the song at the end of the second act, oh, the song at the end of the second act, sung by the girl of the streets, is, is unpardonable; and we don't want to give any enemy of the theatre Anything To Grasp At. And Mr. Michael Dolan, eaten up with his zeal for the good name of the theatre, went on assuring Lady Gregory that there would be real difficulty in getting the Company to play in it, so he begged her ladyship to have a care. He had had a hot argument with O'Casey over the recent performance of *Man and Superman,* when O'Casey called the production a very bad one, and then added a letter to prove he was right; but this, of course, had nothing whatever to do with Dolan's dislike of, and fear of, this new play of O'Casey's, which, in his opinion, would do harm to the dear little, sweet little theatre of Ireland.

And all this time Mr. O'Brien, the one and only catholic Director on the Theatre's Board, was going here and going there, asking all whom he met, "Would the Song be cut out? You know, the song at the end of the second act, the one which tells about the woman's objectionable preference for a sailor—will it go; will it tarry; will Yeats do the right thing, and have it removed?" And the whispers of the pubs quivered like things infirm when they touched on the beyond the beyond language of the play; and some said this, and others said that if the play was allowed to go on the public stage as it was, it would have been just as well if St. Patrick hadn't come to Ireland at all. The song in it was bound to slip over the seas, and destroy the reputation of the Irish Race. Now, just imagine it! After five hundred years of work here and intercession in heaven, just imagine St. Patrick (I won't mention the name of Bridget in the circumstances) hearing that song for the first time in London or in New York; and then, when St. Patrick rebuked the English or the American saints for allowing this song of bawdry, to hear that it was first sung in holy Dublin, See of St. Laurence O'Toole; and that a catholic actor had sung it out loud, and shamelessly! So even a blind man could see clearly that something must be done.

All the time, in the foyer, a Mr. Holloway, who had superintended the architectural change in the theatre, under Miss Horniman, spluttering spit over anyone stopping to listen to him, kept saying, "This play was an abominable one, for there never was a street-walker in Ireland since reliable history began to be written; and, if the truth had to be told, he'd say every girl in Ireland was an angel's whisper. Look at poor O'Brien, there, going by, his honest heart sore troubled with the echoing in his mind of that song at the end of the second act in O'Casey's play! The implicity of that song is appalling, and it'll go down the ages against us, if it's allowed to be sung."

Sean looked around the room at all the furniture he had. All of them would fit into a small container—settee, desk, chair, filing-cabinets, and books; and he could get them over to England a day or two after his own arrival. He would leave all the rest—the linoleum, curtains, bed, saucepans, crockery, and oddments—to the lady below him. Then his customary footfall would never again be heard in a Dublin street. And the lamp—he'd leave that too; for he felt that, in England, there'd be electric light wherever he chose to live. A tip of a switch, and the room would flood with light. That in itself would be a great step forward. Lead kindly light, amid the encircling gloom—electricity now one of his gods. More light, murmured Goethe with his dying breath. Let there be light! said Faraday; and there was light. How much richer, how much more like a god, than the bishop in his gaudy dalmatic, does Faraday look in his dalmatic of light.

Sean realised now that the theatre, called the Abbey, as a whole, was against him, and that it would be a good thing to put a greater distance between them and him (though it was very ironical to look back to see that some of these very actors, who had so strongly protested against the play, afterwards—when the tumult had died down—carried it all over the United States to their own advantage, bringing back many dollars which happily made their future a little less uncertain for them than it had been). At present there wasn't even the width of the Liffey between the theatre and him; soon the expanse of the Irish Sea would separate them. To go a fair distance away was the best way to check a developing difference. An' seas betune us braid hae roared, sin auld lang syne.

He packed his few last personal things into his one suitcase; the suitcase that had gone with him to Coole, and was now to shepherd the things that would allow him to strut respectably through the streets of London. There was nothing to keep him here: he had no part in Cosgrave's party, or in De Valera's policy; nor had he any in the Labour Movement bossed by William O'Brien; no, nor any part in the Protestant Church of Ireland, or that of the Roman Catholic Mission here; though each and all of them had had a part in making his life as it was now, and in streaking it with many colours. He would soon be crossing the border of his own life. To London! To art galleries and picture shows. He would learn a lot more about painting. He would see something of what Van Gogh, Cézanne, Renoir, and Manet had done, for, as yet, they were but glittering names to him. London! He wouldn't have to listen to A. E. any longer, who couldn't comment on a painting unless it had a label. And Augustus John's *Galway*—he had seen it pictured in a magazine; but now he'd see it as John had done it—life-sized and magnificent. This magnificent man as well as magnificent painter had come into the Abbey Green Room once, fleeing from Count McCormick who was beseeching John to paint him; and Sean had asked the artist why he didn't do it, to be answered, brusquely, Because there is nothing to paint!

Yes, London would mould him into a more fully-developed mind and man. The booming of Big Ben would deafen his new-listening ears to any echo from the bells of Shandon. Though he felt curious, and a little anxious, about meeting things he did not know, he felt relief at leaving behind the things he knew too well. The Easter Rising had pulled down a dark curtain of eternal separation between him and his best friends; and the few that had remained alive and delightful, now lay deep, with their convivial virtues, under the smoking rubblement of the Civil War. It was getting very dark in Ireland, so his flight to London would be a leap in the light.

He strapped the suitcase tight. Any minute now the jaunting-car would come to take him to the station where he was to take the train for the boat. He went to the window, and looked out—a cold, windy, harsh March morning. Early on a wild March morning. An old song strayed into his mind:

> And as I stood upon the quay, a tear fell from my eye,
> For divil a blessed soul was there to say, old friend, goodbye;
> They were glad to see me sail, far away from Inisfail,
> Early on that wild March morning!

The weather meant a rough passage, but he'd stick it calmly, however roguishly rough it might be. His day in Ireland had been a long one, but the long day was over at last; a long day over; long day over; over at last.

He would leave Yeats on his Island of Inisfree, standing pensively at the door of his small cabin of clay and wattles made; or moving, slow and moody, between his nine bean rows, thinking of peace where there was no peace; for Ireland's red-rose-bordered hem was muddy now, and ragged. There was no making love to Kathleen, daughter of Houlihan now, untidy termagant, brawling out her prayers. He would leave Lady Gregory in her Seven Woods of Coole; and the lesser writers, too, conceiving little things of verse chipped from the touch of little things timidly seen and carefully handled; and his brother, Mick, with his dream of an endless queue of pints waiting to be swallowed.

Here comes the car. Sean swung his suitcase up on it, and climbed into a side-seat; and away they went on the first trotting steps to England. England? Well, Sean was going into a land enslaved to ill-doing and left alone by God, according to Father O'Reilly, who, at a meeting of Maynooth Union, whose members were priests, is reported to have said but fifteen years ago: "The character of the English mind ought to be understood in Ireland. It is a fleshy spirit, bent towards earth; a mind unmannerly, vulgar, insolent, bigoted; a mind whose belly is its god, yet which cannot endure the word belly; a mind to which pride and lust and mammon are the matter-of-course aims of life; a mind where every absurd device, from grossest Darwinism to most preposterous spiritualism is resorted to, and hoped in, to choke the voice of eternity in the conscience; a mind to which the idea of a churchman possessing real, efficient, and spiritual authority over his flock would be unspeakably ludicrous."

A bad place to be going to, certainly. But while this reverend cleric was speaking, down south a farmer had become certain that his handsome young wife was possessed of a witch, and got the local reverend cleric to say Mass in the house to deliver her. But the intention failed, and the farmer, with the help of neighbours, set about it himself, burning her with a red-hot poker, forcing her to drink things made from herbs gathered over the mountains; and when these sensible and holy acts didn't do, carried her down in her shift, and held her over the fire till she was roasted alive; and then buried her away in a lonely place of gorse and thorny briars. A week later she was dug up, displaying purple marks round her throat, and with the muscles of her spine burned away. And, after the inquest, neither lay nor clerical would give a hand to bury her; so the police had to do it by the light of lanterns, and in the dead of the sympathetic night.

The outside-car swung along down Dorset Street, where Sean had first seen the peep of day; past George's church, in the pocket of which had lived the Dalton family with whom he had trod, as a youngster, the stage of the old Mechanics Theatre, now known the world over as The Abbey; down Cavendish Row where the Dispensary had been from which the gentle Dr. Oulton had come to cure Sean of a fever; down Sackville-O'Connell Street, catching a good glimpse of the Post Office, where Padraic Pearse had sounded the horn that roused Ireland out of her sleeping. In this very street, on the top of a horse-drawn tram, when a little boy safe beside his mother, he had swept into the galaxy of illuminations, lit to honour an English queen; and, years after, had been almost suffocated in this very street by the surging crowd escaping from the batons of the police. In this very street.

The car turned down Abbey Street, and swung into Beresford Place, trotting past Liberty Hall, once the sweltering, weltering University of the Dublin workers, now a dead tomb held by an enemy, with Ichabod written all over it, for Larkin had gone, and its glory had departed; down Tara Street, surely the drabbest and dirtiest street in Dublin, looking as desolate as Tara itself; wheeling into Brunswick Street, passing the Queen's Theatre where Sean had seen his first play, *The Shaughraun;* past the Ancient Concert Rooms, where the National Theatre performed some of its early plays, before it had a habitation or even a name. It was this street that had been Sean's via dolorosa, through which he had passed, three times a week, year after year, for fifteen or more of them, with his mother first, then on his own, to the Ophthalmic Hospital to seek ease for aching eyeballs. Ah, here was Westland Row Station—the last spot of Dublin that would feel his footfall. It was from this sad site that the coffin holding Parnell came slowly out, borne by strenuous, tearful men, hesitating to part even with the dead body of their persecuted Chieftain. Oh, God Almighty, the life he was living now had almost all been spun from what he had felt, had seen, had touched in these few Dublin streets!

He was on the deck of the mail-boat, feeling her sway and shyly throb beneath his feet; watching the landing-stage drift afar away, getting his last glimpse of Eireann—separated for the first time from her, and never likely to stand settled on her soil again. It was bitterly cold, with a fierce, keen wind blowing, and soon it was sending sharp sleety hail and salty spray into his face, stinging it deeply—Ireland, spitting a last, venomous, contemptuous farewell to him.

Well, everything of any value he was carrying away with him: the moral courage and critical faculties of his father, and his love of good books; the gay humour and dogged resolution of his mother, and her love for, and understanding of, the bright colours among dead, drab things; the remembrance of the warm clasp from the Reverend Mr. Griffin's firm, white, delicately-shaped hands; the love of his comrade workers, catholic and protestant, with whom he had fought and starved and fought again; all the fair things he had learned during his sojourn with the Gaelic League; the affection and goodwill of Lady Gregory; the reluctant godspeed from Dr. Cummins; a fond recollection of brother Tom; pity for his sister Ella, and a little less of it for Mick; and, above all, a strict and determined confidence in himself. Jewels he could never sell; jewels that no thief, however cute, could take out of his hands.

> *Sail on, sail on, thou fearless bark,*
> *Wherever blows the welcome wind,*
> *It cannot lead to scenes more dark,*
> *More sad, than those we leave behind.*

The ship turned giddily to right, to left, plunged with upturned bows, dipping them again as quick, for there was more than a half-gale blowing. Sean had been anxious about sea-sickness, but he felt no discomfort. He was a good sailor. He faced resolutely towards where the ship was going. Sweet Inishfallen, fare thee well! Forever!

LONDON APPRENTICE

(FROM "ROSE AND CROWN", 1952)

☘ ☘ ☘

Here he was now, planting a foot for the first time on the pavement of London; planting it firmly, with a confident air and a fluttering heart. Sliding with the hiss of steam and the throb of pistons into the heart of the

> *Great flower that opens but at night,*
> *Great city of the midnight sun,*
> *Whose day begins when day is done.*

A London apprentice now. Listen!

> *Oranges and lemons, say the bells of St. Clements.*
> *When will you pay me? say the bells at Old Bailey.*
> *When I grow rich, say the bells at Shoreditch.*

How different was the view now from that of the lovely coast of Wales, lacing the land's edge from Holyhead to Chester. Coming within the grip of the city, he had been wondering through miles of the journey at the dismal wretchedness of the houses, apparently trotting away from him as the train ambled to the end of its journey; trotting away from him so that he mightn't fully see the abject royalty of their miserable appearance. The train had run through a long, drab gauntlet of houses, some of them fat with filth. The magnificent, wealthy city of London, with her gilded Mayor and red-robed Aldermen, was entered through long kennels of struggling poverty and disordered want. Sisters to the houses he had so often seen, slinky with shame, in the shabbiest streets of Dublin. There were the lacerated walls, the windows impudent with dirt, the poor, shrinking clothing, reluctant to be washed, hanging from poles thrust through the windows, fixed to the sills. Just like the hidden parts of Dublin. 'Faith, her privates we. One didn't land in London through a lane of roses.

Euston! Alight here as many Irish had done before him; a short visit so often extended to take the emigrant's rest of life. England; Sasana! Euston; a sprawling untidy place, dim and dark; tormented with many sounds—the clatter of trucks, the patter of hurrying, fussy feet; babble and squeak of passengers not sure of the right train or the proper platform; the sibilant hiss of steam; the sturdy smell of smoke; the soothing, sickly scent of oil; porters hurrying, guards sauntering amid the rustle of paper and magazine, bought by people who would never read the half of them; women sitting semi-alert on benches, waiting for the hands of a big clock to tell them when to move; streams of men, women, and children, dropping from the train that had just stopped, pouring along under the grimy roof like an underground river towards an open sluice-gate, to divide into rivulets and trickles, spreading fanwise to different parts of the mammoth city. Each one an individual, a soul-body; something separate from each so like itself, conceit concealing that each one is a simulacrum of the other;

> Albert Johnson is my nayem,
> England is my nation;
> London is my dwelling-place,
> And heaven my destination.

Heaven! Meanwhile, we must be satisfied with the smoke and the grime of Euston. "Seen at night, or through a mist, Euston Station is one of the most impressive sights in London," said Aubrey Beardsley. Well, seen by night, or through a mist, there may be many things appearing impressive, be it either man or dog or eunuch; and the picturer of his own horrible delusions added, "Euston Station has made it unnecessary to visit Egypt." The slimy, fruitful Nile, sun, sand, date-palm, and bedouin—none are needed. Pharaoh porters about here.

To Sean, who stared at the building before he hid himself away in a taxi, the entrance looked surlily bewildered, as if it had been set down in the wrong place, as indeed it had, for ancient Egyptian architecture does not wed itself with English life. Though it forced itself into the appearance of a temple, here was no shrine at which to pray for a safe journey from one place to another. The ponderous pillars holding up its tremendous back looked like a monster's heavy feet standing in a jungle clearance, the whole brute staring in front of itself, not knowing which way to turn.

There was James B. Fagan hurrying towards him, having caught sight of the red muffler encircling Sean's neck, the insignia Sean had written to say would reveal his advent to London. Sean's play had been transferred from the Royalty to the Fortune, a little theatre directly opposite the towering, bully-like Royal Theatre in Drury Lane—Falstaff and the little page. The play was to open itself out in the new theatre two nights from now, and Sean was to be kept hidden till then so that familiarity with others should not mar the appearance of the slum dramatist on the first night in the Fortune; enhancing publicity by standing on the stage, grinning, bowing, and saying a few sweet words to the applauding audience that had filled the house for the first performance.

Embedded in a taxi, he was bowled off to the Kenilworth Hotel, Bloomsbury; hustled up in a lift to his room, while Fagan waited below, like a warder, till Sean had freshened himself with a wash, and was ready for Fagan to take him off silently. He was to be kept like a peril in an oyster till the first night of the play had passed into time that neither he nor Fagan would ever touch again. After a light meal in Fagan's flat in Great Russell Street, Sean was again embedded into a taxi, and taken, like a prisoner out for an hour's amusement, to the Duke of York's Theatre to see Jean Forbes-Robertson playing in Chekhov's *Uncle Vanya*. The theatre he was in was no different from the big ones of Dublin. That was all he learned from this outing. Things were so different with him now, so new, so far from what he had been used to; his future was so uncertain, his mind so buoyant with jostling thoughts; and he was hushed so deeply back to the rear of the box, with Mary Grey and James Fagan in front of him, that to this day he cannot remember a single thing about the play, the acting, or the production. The one memory remaining is the name of the play and the name of the leading actress, and these were fixed in his mind by the lovely coloured lights of red, yellow, and white, flashing over the entrance of the theatre, telling out her name and the name of the Russian play she acted in. The first London play he had seen, he hadn't seen at all. A long wait in the box when the play was over to ensure that the crowd had gone, in fear anyone among it should have recognised Sean, and have shouted out the hot news that O'Casey was here. Then a quick retreat into a taxi again, and so to bed.

* * *

THE SILVER TASSIE

Sean stood in the office of a business-man in whose fancy the sombre blackness of coal glittered more than the onyx, jasper, and chrysolite of heaven's architecture. It was a big, dull, thoughtless room, deprecating any emotion other than one connected with the sale of coal.

Hush! This room is sacred to the transubstantiation of coal into the shimmer of money. In front of a big, dusty window stood a wide table-desk of the dullest brown Sean had ever seen. It stood where it was, like a rock of ages, steadfast, and, apparently, immovable. No wisp of poetry, no wistful tinkle of a folk-song had ever entertained its lonely bulk. Inks, pens, blotting-paper, a ruler, and office writing-paper, each in its proper place, were piled on its pompous top, as if invoking animation out of the stillness, saying silently, Use us, and make the big desk hum. To tinge the common hue of business with the colour of art, two pictures of a costermonger and a costerwoman, by Jack Morrow, had been hung on the wall; badly done, they went on withering, colourless and cold, pictures that must have been dying while they were being painted. In a glass-doored bookcase, handy to the great desk, were two books on the value and quality of coal, flanked on one side by a huge brass-bound, brass-buckled family bible, intimating that with the things that belong to Caesar, the things belonging to God may be very near and very dear to the business-man. Under all, a red and blue rubber carpet covered the floor, the red dull, the blue duller.

There the boss sat at his desk in a wide, leather-seated swivel-chair, a portly man as firm in his seat as the desk was on the floor. A large head, bald on the top, but sprayed at the sides and back with sturdy tufts of iron-grey hair. A broad, ruddy face like a big cheese turning rusty, with small, shrewd, beady eyes; eyes that were never dimmed for more than a moment or two by any thought of worry. A thick soft nose, and under it, a broad, thick-lipped mouth which laughed or shouted vehemently, any reason for laughing or shouting, invariably equalling the others in futility.

Knowing little of art, literature, or science; self-centred, not only in the earth, but in the very universe, he sat there, humming; yet possessing a charm and forcible personality that seemed clouded with a knowledge of all things; a friend of artists, with a charm that was irresistible in a restaurant at a luncheon, or sitting, sprawled before an intimate fire with a friend or two, or persuading a doubtful business-man that his way was the best way; a volatile mind that could gather coloured thoughts round trivial things, and present them to any company ordered into the frame of a confused and hilarious picture: a molten mass of brazen energy without a hope of taking an ordered form. A great soul lost in the flood of its own hilarity.

There he sat idle in his swivel-chair, a wide-brimmed black hat slung carelessly on the desk beside him; there he sat, a big, hooked pipe dangling from his red, fleshy lips, his stout, short fingers tapping out some inconstant, uneasy tune on the top of the hardwood desk.

He had nothing to do; the miners were on strike, and no coal crept up the river in big-bottomed barges to herald the income of heartening cheques in return for the toil of writing a letter after breakfast, one after lunch, and another before the office closed for the evening. The fires of the nation were going out: the big-topped desk could do no more.

Idly, the strong, fat fingers tapped the desk-top, and the thick, fleshy lips moved moodily to the humming of an air. Then the hum changed to a whistle, then words began to trickle through it to an air Sean had never heard before. He cocked an ear to listen; the words came huskily to his ear, uttered thoughtlessly, unemotionally by the moody crooner:

> *Gae fetch to me a pint o' wine,*
> *An' full it in a sulver tossie;*
> *That I may drink before I gae*
> *A service tae my bonnie lossie.*

—Ay, Sean, me lad, it's a woefu' state o' things: th' flooers o' th' forest are a' wede awa'. There isn't as much as a bean in th' locker, th' day.

> *But it's no' the roar of sea or shore*
> *Wad mak' me langer wish tae tarry;*
> *Nor shout o' war that's heard afar—*
> *It's leavin' thee, my bonnie lossie.*

Sean was startled. Aaron's rod had budded. A riotous and romantic song had drifted up from the solid rancour of the big, impassive desk, that was to hum in his mind for many months to come. He hummed it in his tiny flat in South Kensington; he hummed it in the dead of night, strolling down the Cromwell Road. He would give the title of the song to his next play. He would set down without malice or portly platitude the shattered enterprise of life to be endured by many of those who, not understanding the bloodied melody of war, went forth to fight, to die, or to return again with tarnished bodies and complaining minds. He would show a wide expanse of war in the midst of timorous hope and overweening fear; amidst a galaxy of guns; silently show the garlanded horror of war. However bright and haughty be the burning of a town; however majestic be the snapping thunder of the cannonfire, the consummation is the ruin of an ordered, sheltering city, with the odious figure of war astride the tumbled buildings, sniffing up the evil smell of the burning ashes. The ruin, the squeal of the mangled, the softening moan of the badly rended are horrible, be the battle just or unjust; be the fighters striving for the good or manifesting faith in evil.

And he would do it in a new way. There was no importance in trying to do the same thing again, letting the second play imitate the first, and the third the second. He wanted a change from what the Irish critics had called burlesque, photographic realism, or slices of life, though the manner and method of two of the plays were as realistic as the scents stealing from a gaudy bunch of blossoms.

He was working on the last act when Mr. Lennox Robinson suddenly paid a visit to his flat in South Kensington. Not to linger, he said, but just to ask about the new play. There were rumours in Dublin that the play wouldn't be given to the Abbey Theatre. The rumours aren't true? You will give the play? Oh, that will be joyful! Yeats and I were sure the rumours were false. No, I can't stay for a cup of tea. Just called because of the silly rumours in Dublin that your play would not be given to the Abbey. Mr. Robinson held out an aesthetic, tentative hand. Goodbye, Sean. Sorry I can't stay; so glad you'll give your play to us; and off he went to the air, it seemed to Sean, of *Danny Boy*.

Rumours? Sean couldn't believe it. If there were, surely he would have got letters asking if they were true, and he hadn't received a line. He was puzzled. The Abbey seemed to be eager to get the play; he was eager to give it, and so all was peace. He calculated the play would run in the Abbey for at least three weeks, maybe four, and the royalties he'd get would about cover the expenses of the birth of their child. Oh, that would be joyful, too! [O'Casey's marriage to Eileen Carey is referred to on page 800.]

Later on, while a play of his was running in the London Court Theatre, and Sean was in the office chatting about the poor houses, the Commissionaire came in to say that there was a bloke called Yeats outside who wanted to see him. Before he had ended the sentence, the stately figure of the poet stepped in as if it was marching to the tune of *Old Comrades*. He would sit down only for a moment. No, wouldn't take a whiskey and soda—doctor's orders. The company in the play were good, very good. He came to ask O'Casey if he intended to give his new play to the Abbey. Rumours in Dublin said O'Casey had decided to ignore the Abbey, which would be a pity. O'Casey had come to the Theatre when he had been most needed, and a refusal of the new play would cause irritation. The rumours untrue? O'Casey will give the new play? Oh, that will be joyful! He could assure the other Directors that the Theatre would get the play. No, he couldn't stay longer. Friends were waiting. Goodbye; and the great man stepped out as if marching to the tune of *Your Tiny Hand is Frozen*.

Sean had promised the first glimpse of the play to Sir Barry Jackson, had sent him the manuscript, and had forgotten about it. Then one day Sir Barry came bustling into the house when he and Eileen were busy trying to make the debts they owed meet and marry the money they had in hand. Sir Barry was in a hurry, a panting hurry; he sat down on a chair in a hurry, first setting down a burnished bowler hat on the table in a hurry, and arranging a pompous-looking umbrella to a stately stand in a corner in a hurry too.

—You've written a fine play, he said; a terrible play! An impossible play for me. I dare not put it on—an English audience couldn't stand it. There's the script. I'm grateful to you for letting me read it. His hand shot out for the burnished bowler hat. I must go now. The play would lacerate our feelings; it would be unbearable. Goodbye; and he hurried out to his waiting car, and vanished: a plain man in a plain van rushing from life. The next morning, the plain van slid up to the door, and the plain man slid into the house, and hurried to the stately umbrella still standing in the corner. My umbrella—I forgot it yesterday; and the plain man vanished into the plain van again, and Sean saw him no more.

With, in some ways, a difficult cast, Raymond Massey, the Producer, had a hard task with a most difficult play. He had never seen in the theatre before a scene like the second act; neither had Sean, so he could be of no help to the Producer. But Massey's strange patience, his skill and experience, came to his aid, so that the second act, helped hugely by Augustus John's serenely coloured church window and sinister, savage gun, stood out oddly, eerily, and effectively, throwing confusion and some panic into the minds of most of London's drama critics. Over all and through all, went C. B. Cochran's quiet, strange, and mysterious influence. So dapper; so pompously simple in his way of walking; so unassuming in his way of talking that few would say There goes a man of the Theatre. But there he was, a man of the Theatre from the sole of his small foot to the dignified crown of his bowler hat. Every glance of his discerning eye; every sound in his eager ear; every word from his firm mouth; every gesture of his hand, had something to do with the Theatre; the greatest supervisor, most imaginative and courageous man, of things low and things high in the English Theatre. An England consciously thinking the Theatre more than the life or death of a sparrow, would have made Cochran independent of the Backer. Had this man had a theatre and no necessity to coax the coming of coins into the box-office, out of a few mistakes, would have risen pride, elegance, and fun, making the English Theatre of today share the glory and gusto of the Theatre in the generous days of Shakespeare and his comrades. The Clowns were always on one side of Cochran, the Tragedians on the other, and he had the imaginative eye and cunning hand to weave lovely patterns round the pair of them.

On account of the child's size, the doctor in charge of Sean's wife decided, after consultation with a colleague, by an operation to make the birth immediate; so, to be out of the way, Sean was packed off to spend the night with a friend. The next morning, a telephone call told him a big boy had been born, and that Eileen was eager to show it to him. He hurried off, opened the door of the house in Woronzow Road, entered the hall, and saw a large envelope from the Abbey Theatre lying *solus* on a table; too big to hold an advisal of a coming production. He opened it, and read the letter from Lady Gregory and the letter of condemnation, peppered with pompous advice, from Yeats. Curse o' God on them! His anger grew at every line he read.

He went upstairs, saw his wife, congratulated her on the birth of her big boy, looked at the laddo, touched his cheek, and said nothing about the play's rejection. He would have to wait till she was safe; till she was up and about; and then he would send a salvo of words that would shake the doors of the Abbey and rattle the windows.

He read the letters again: the one from Yeats was the one to be answered. Sean could not but believe that the play's rejection had been decided upon before the play had been sent. To answer Yeats would be a dangerous thing to do. Yeats in his greatness had influence everywhere, and the world of literature bowed before him. But answered he must be, and answered he would be, even though the strife meant the end of Sean. His mind tore through the letter again.

The most considerate thing for us to do is to suggest that he withdraw the play. My letter gives an opinion, doesn't absolutely reject. He could withdraw the play "for revision" and let that be known to the Press. He should say that he himself had become dissatisfied and had written to ask it back. If he disagrees with our opinions as to its merits, he can wait a little, and offer it to some London Manager. If the London Manager accepts, then our opinion of the play won't matter to him at all. Or, on the other hand, if no Manager accepts, or if he doesn't offer it there, he can keep it by him, revising, or not revising, as he pleases. I want to get out of the difficulty of the paragraphs in the Press saying that the play has been offered to us (and hard both you and Mr. Lennox Robinson asked that it should be offered to you. S. O'C.). *I have not told anyone what I think of the play, and I will get Lennox not to give his opinion. You have, perhaps, already written to Casey* [sic], *but even if you have, I should like you to write making this suggestion.*

This to Lady Gregory and then to Sean. Obviously, Yeats was sure Sean would shake at the knees when he got this opinion; would hasten to sit down and write for the play back; would light a fire with it the first thing the following morning. Would he? He thought and thought it out: He was fenced in with money anxieties; he had now a wife and a child to guard and keep, and a rented house which needed many things more before it could become a home. Indeed, but for what his wife had brought into it from her own flat, there would have been barely enough in it to suit himself. Before they were married, she had sublet her flat; had got no rent from the tenants; and only by last-minute efforts did she manage to get her belongings back again. When he and she had come to the house they were in now, the sitting-room had had but a carpet on the centre of the floor, with a broad border around it varnished by Eileen herself; one chair, John's pictures, one of a Gitana, the other of Sean himself; a coal-scuttle and fire-irons; so that, while he sat on the floor before the fire, she sat on the chair, and wept. But not for long: they soon saw the grim humour of it, and laughed merrily over the barren way the room looked. The little they had was oozing away; now, since the child had come, what was left would depart in a steady stream; and, if *The Silver Tassie* didn't bring in enough for a further year's life, then the nights would be full of anxiety's light and the days would be gloomy and glum. Still, he had been in worse circumstances before, and had come out of them. But then he had been alone—his mother didn't count, for she had the faculty of being able to live on air, and laugh. Yeats's rejection of the play was a blow on the heart.

Casey could write for the play, and say he wanted it for revision—that was the meanest moment in the letter of Yeats. It was a bitter suggestion, and made him live with anger for a long time to come. A fight was the one honest way out of it. Almost all the literary grandees would, naturally, be on the side of Yeats, and most of the Press that mattered would, directly or indirectly, make a bow to his decision. This was inevitable because of Yeats's reputation as a literary genius; and what made it harder for Sean was that the reputation was a suitable crown for the man's achievement. But fight he should; and fight he would.

Well, here he was surrounded by Yeats's opinions. *You are not interested in the Great War; you never stood on its battlefields, never walked its hospitals, and so write out of your opinions. You illustrate those opinions by a series of almost unrelated scenes, as you might in a leading article.* Oh, God, here was a man who had never spoken to a Tommy in his life—bar Major Gregory; and to him only because he was an artist as well as a soldier—chattering about soldiers to one who had talked to them all; infantry, cavalry, and artillery; who knew most of the regimental marches; who, when a kid, had listened to them telling, in their halting way, stories about Canada, Hong Kong, India, Gibraltar, Malta, and the wilds of Shorncliffe Camp and Salisbury Plain. One who had known soldiers since he was a kid of six; whose uncle had been wounded on the field of Balaclava; whose brother had gone through the Boer War in the Dublin Fusiliers; whose elder brother had worn the khaki in the first World War; who had walked with the Tommies, and chatted with them, had sung songs with them in the hospitals of St. Vincent and of Richmond; who had followed the Great War from its first declaration, through the Russian Revolution to its final end by the surrender of Germany. And now he was being told by one who wouldn't know a Life Guard red from a Horse Guard blue, that he wasn't interested, directly or indirectly, in the Great War! *Not interested* to one who had talked and walked and smoked and sung with the blue-suited, wounded men fresh from the front; to one who had been among the armless, the legless, the blind, the gassed, and the shell-shocked!

Among the things that dramatic action must burn up are the author's opinions. Do you suppose for one moment that Shakespeare educated Hamlet and Lear by telling them what he thought and believed? As I see it, Hamlet and Lear educated Shakespeare, and I have no doubt that in the process of that education he found out that he was altogether a different man to what he thought himself, and had altogether different beliefs. D'ye tell me that, now, Mr. Yeats? Well, I don't know; but one thing's certain, and that is if Shakespeare became a more educated man while writing *Hamlet,* then it wasn't Hamlet who educated him, but Shakespeare who educated himself. But what proof—beyond an opinion—has Yeats that what he says was so? As he sees it—of course; but it doesn't necessarily follow that everyone, or anyone, will see it the same way. A man altogether different, with altogether different beliefs when he'd finished the play from what he had been before he started! Here, the poet is suggesting, or trumpeting, the opinion that he was as intimate with Shakespeare as he was with the number of his own hall-door. There are as many opinions about the character of Hamlet as there are lines in the play. Even Shakespeare wasn't sure himself, for we are told: "The variations of an early copy from the play of *Hamlet* in its improved state, are too numerous and striking to admit a doubt of the play having been subsequently revised, amplified, and altered by the poet." Of one thing we can be certain, namely that what Shakespeare makes Hamlet say was not what the living Prince would, or could, have said, but what Shakespeare wanted him to say; that the play is largely a biography of Shakespeare's thoughts.

Sean carried the letters of Yeats to Macmillan's. He presented them to Mr. Daniel Macmillan, remarking that if the Firm wished, after reading them, he would allow the contract to be withdrawn. Mr. Daniel read the correspondence through. He handed it back to Sean, saying, This is, of course, a matter between Mr. Yeats and you. It does not concern us. We do not agree with the criticism. We think the play worth publication, and we will publish it. We make our own decisions, and this controversy cannot alter our intentions.

Very kind, very manly, and very encouraging to Sean, for he had had a half fear that the criticism from Yeats might check, might even prevent, the play's publication. This was his first victory over the potent, almost impregnable, influence of Yeats. So he hied himself off to C. B. Cochran, and put the correspondence before him. Beyond saying to Sean that he should never have given another party the option of a production while the play was under consideration by a London Manager, Cochran was undisturbed. Sean was taken aback by Cochran's indifference to the denunciation of the play by Yeats; for denunciation it was rather than a criticism. But the two decisions—Macmillan's to publish the play, Cochran's to produce it, defended the flanks of Sean's effort. Had Macmillan's withdrawn from their promise of publication; had Cochran decided to abandon production, then Sean's defence of the dramatist's right to experiment would have been a hard one indeed. It was very curious, this rejection of the new play, for Yeats had known it wouldn't be done in the old way. In the Court Theatre, Sean had told him it would be different from what had gone before; that the second act would be an impression of the World War, and that the play would be written in a new manner; but Yeats had made no comments on Sean's rapid and excited account of the new idea: he sat silent there, listening. Yet during his stay in London, at that very time, Yeats, speaking before the Irish Literary Society, had enthusiastically mentioned the receipt of a play from a young dramatist which contained the promise of a new idea in Irish drama. The first act showed a group of young men making bombs in an underground cellar. They had been confined to this work and to this room for a long time, Yeats said, and the act was an expressionistic effort to show the psychological reaction of these young men to their peculiar circumstances. He went on to say that this act foreshadowed a new direction in Irish drama, and regretted that the rest of the play had been very bad; adding that O'Casey had built the bridge across which the coming Irish dramatists would pass to a new technique and a new art. But the poet had, apparently, waxed faint and furious to find that the first dramatist to cross the bridge was the dramatist who had, according to Mr. Yeats, built the bridge himself. It was very curious. Though the play might not be what Sean thought it, it was far above three-fourths of the plays appearing on the Abbey stage, and it stood up, fearless and steady, to the higher standard of the Theatre.

Sean sent the letters written by Yeats with his own replies to St. John Ervine, who sent them to *The Observer*; and to A. E. for publication in his *The Irish Statesman*. The first journal published them; but a letter came sailing over the sea from the lordly A. E. saying that he wouldn't, couldn't, and shouldn't publish the correspondence in his journal for fear of a possible action for breach of copyright. Brother Yeats taking an action for breach of copyright against Brother A. E.! It didn't make sense. The man who had sung about "the golden heresy of truth" was hedging. A few days later the Irish Press informed the world and Sean that Dr. Yeats declared a serious breach of copyright had been committed by the publication of the correspondence, and he was about to take legal action through the Society of Authors. So Sean got another letter from A. E. saying, Aha, I told you so! All Sean could do was to write to the Press to say that he was indifferent to the threat, even if Dr. Yeats decided to lay the dispute before the League of Nations.

The dispute, fostered delightedly by most of the Irish Press, jumped over to the English Press, wafted itself across the Atlantic, and spread excitedly over American papers, big and small; while many European journals carried the story further, and tossed the names of Yeats and O'Casey into minds which had never bothered about them before, and would hardly ever bother about them again, many of the comments showing Sean that the name and reputation of Yeats were much more important than his arguments.

One dignified Irish paper opposed the coloured clamour. Spraying itself with the hood of literature over one shoulder, and that of civil law over the other, the *Irish Times,* accompanied by the Borris-in Ossory Thing at Arms, hastened first to the pinnacle of Christ Church Cathedral, and then to the entablature of the Bank of Ireland, where, after the Thing at Arms had blown a funfare, she proclaimed to the listening ears of Ireland, the following proclamation: Whereas the essential feature of the correspondence about O'Casey's play is its portentous gravity; whereas Yeats and O'Casey discuss the play as if its goodness or badness really were a matter of vast importance, showing that they are unable to grasp two facts: Nobody in this generation—certainly not O'Casey—has written, nor is likely to write, immortal literature. O'Casey's two acted plays are good and striking plays, but no better than a thousand that have been forgotten. If they survive for fifty years, they will survive not as plays but as historical documents.

So the manicured hand, in a kid glove, of the *Irish Times,* tossed the controversy in her waste-paper basket, and turned to better things—the church services, the racing lists for the Derby, the differences between De Valera and Cosgrave, and the price of fat cattle.

It was very important to Sean, touching the security of his life, his wife's, and the kid in the cradle in the room beyond him. They were all depending on what the play would bring in to allow them to live decently for one more year. The first honest home he had ever had, simple as it was, stood silent and shaking. The previous ones had been dens to eat in, to sleep in agitation, tormented with flea and bug; raucously restive, dark, menacing, and ugly, save where the glow from his mother's life made them bearable and good. His life pressed more heavily on him than ever, for his anxiety was threefold now—for himself, for his wife, newly fledged with motherhood, and the babe, newly fledged with life. The play was very important to him.

Some months ago Lady Gregory had written to say how glad she was to hear he had a little house and little garden of his own; and how pleasant it would be for him there, to sit in the sun among the flowers. The flowers! Sean hopping and happy among the hollyhocks. The syringa tree was wearing its bridal-robe of snowy blossoms, and the lilac her purple gown of modest royalty; the pansies were tumbling out in groups, brown and blue, white and speckled; and the little lawn—about as big as the floor-space of his last tenement room—looked green and buoyant. But there was no peace among them for him. Even the rose of Sharon or the lily of the valley would be no solace to him now. He could eat no pleasant bread amid their scents, among their coloured blossoms. Their ways were ways of pleasantness no longer.

While clenching his spirit into the fight against the Abbey Theatre's determination to stereotype a writer's manner and style, and, through them, to fight the wider literary influence of those who believed that at the name of Yeats every knee should bow, Sean received unexpected reinforcement from the mind of Bernard Shaw. Out of Passfield, where the great man was staying with the Webbs, came a fiery letter, saying: *My dear Sean, what a hell of a play! I wonder how it will hit the public. Of course the Abbey should have produced it, as Starkie rightly says—whether it liked it or not. But the people who knew your uncle when you were a child (so to speak) always want to correct your exercises; and this was what disabled the usually competent Yeats and Lady Gregory. Still it is surprising they fired so very wide, considering their marksmanship. . . .*

If Yeats had said "It's too savage; I can't stand it", he would have been in order. . . . Yeats himself, with all his extraordinary cleverness and subtlety, which comes out when you give him up as a hopeless fool, and (in this case) deserts him when you expect him to be equal to the occasion, is not a man of this world; and when you hurl an enormous chunk of it at him, he dodges it, small blame to him. However we can talk over it when we meet. Cheerio, Titan.—G.B.S.

But although Bernard Shaw stood by his side, Mrs. Shaw tried to prevail upon him to restore the sword to the scabbard. On her pressing invitation, Sean and Eileen went to Whitehall Court on the 21st of June 1928 to have lunch with her and her husband, so that, Mrs. Shaw wrote, "they might talk freely (about our friends?—No—about the play!)". Over a charming lunch Sean soon discovered that the ray of support from G. B. S. was being deflected away from his conception of the scurvy way the Abbey had handled his work to the ending of the dispute; towards the silencing of Sean; and towards soft persuasion to be used on Yeats to induce him to change his mind, and allow a production of the play in the Abbey. From doctor and saint he heard great argument about it and about: but evermore came out by the same door as in he went. Through the delicate fume of the conversation, Eileen's silvery voice suggested the compromise of Sean submitting any further letters to Shaw, who, if he disapproved of a paragraph or sentence, could edit it into a more suitable and tactful expression. Mrs. Shaw vigorously applauded the idea, G. B. S. approved, and Sean sat silent. Mrs. Shaw and her husband would come to lunch with the O'Caseys in a couple of days to push the plan further ahead. Some days after, a letter came from Mrs. Shaw to Eileen to say they couldn't come to the O'Caseys because they were *Just starting off abroad for a holiday and have got so terribly tied up with all the silly odds and ends we have to get done before we go. We have taken our sleepers for Sunday, and are remaining in Passfield till Thursday. Then there will be an orgy of business and packing!*

I am the more sorry for this as I do feel Sean wants a lot of looking after just now. He is going to be very naughty and fierce and resentful—and he is a terribly hard hitter!

That idea of getting G. B. S. to see his letters to his "friends" is a grand one. Do keep him up to it. Any letters addressed to 4 Whitehall Court will be forwarded at once, and I will send you an address the moment we are settled, and Sean must write about all he is doing, and G. B. S. will answer quickly, and try to act as a lightning conductor! Directly we come back, we will go to lunch with you, and see Breon, if you will ask us again. Yeats didn't come to see us about the play, but about the Irish Literary Academy they are trying to get up. He never mentioned The Silver Tassie. It was I who insisted on talking about it, and he was rattled, self-conscious, and reluctant! Our very kindest and most friendly thoughts to you both.—C. F. Shaw.

Well, so near, so bad. Sean couldn't welcome this kind of help. He had no wish to have his letters edited, even by such a man as Shaw. Yeats had hit as hard as he could, and Sean wasn't inclined to hold his punches. He had refused the counsel of Uncle Yeats, and he had no intention of taking the counsel of Auntie Shaw. He would fight alone; one alone and not a second. He would fence in his own sour way, thrust, parry, and cut with his own blade of argument, in his own way, not according to rules perfumed with the stale musk of custom; but according to the measure of his own heart, the rhythm of his own mind, logical now, savage and sudden a moment after: in this fight, he would face any opponent, and thrust straight at the side where the heart lay.

But Mrs. Shaw, in her heart, resented Sean's independent critical outcry, and remembered it against him.

THE FRIGGIN FROGS

✿ ✿ ✿

Watched by Mrs. Yeats, helped by the sun of South Europe, Yeats was spared for another spell with Time. Mrs. Yeats still held death away from him; and the summer saw him again in Dublin; heard his voice in the Senate; and his hand, less vigorous now, still held the Abbey Theatre back from falling flat before the cleric and the clown. Sunning himself in his charming little house in Rathfarnham, in the midst of wife and children, the poet lingered in a quietness he had rarely known before; for even in the stilly nooks of Coole's gardens, roused only with rustling of linnets' wings, Yeats had always been agitated in the explanation of mysteries his own ruffling mind imagined, shaping them into living shadows following where he went.

Coming to Ireland for a brief visit on money gained out of New York's production of *Within the Gates,* Sean had got a kindly letter asking him to come to lunch and spend afternoon and evening with Yeats in Riversdale. He crossed a plankway, forming a bridge over a little brook, and came to the house to be received with a quiet, gracious welcome from Mrs. Yeats, who left him to chat with the poet for a few minutes before lunch. Again they talked of the Abbey: how tiresome the customary Abbey play was becoming; how the Theatre needed new life through a newer type of play; and how several new Directors had been added to the Board to create a richer variety of opinion; but Sean's grouping of thoughts about the Theatre, past and present, were rudely scattered by a vehement and sudden remark from Yeats.

—O'Casey, he said, bending towards him, you've succeeded in your last play, *Within the Gates.* The coordination of mood, dialogue, and technique there is a success, where, I think, it is a failure in your *The Silver Tassie.*

Oh, thought Sean, forcing his thoughts onto what Yeats had said so suddenly, *The Silver Tassie is still in his mind.* He's excusing the rejection of one play by his praise of another. Aloud, he said, Do you really believe, Mr. Yeats, that *Within the Gates* is a successful achievement?

—I do, he said, emphatically; I believe it to be a most successful achievement in your newer manner.

—I wish to God I could believe it too! came from Sean in a burst of frank fervency; and he was amused at the signs of hesitation, surprise, and doubt that flooded into the poet's expressive face. Sean learned then that Yeats wanted the Abbey to do *Within the Gates.* He objected. He wouldn't refuse, but set out the difficulties of production by the Abbey company, and showed the poet that the Abbey stage would never accommodate the play's action. Besides, the play was clumsy in parts, and, some day, he would try to amend it. He made it clear that never again would he send a play to the Abbey; but that the Abbey was always welcome to do any play of his they wished to do. He suggested *The Silver Tassie,* a play far easier to put on the Abbey stage; that Yeats could have the other, if he insisted; but that *The Silver Tassie* was a far easier venture. The poet was silent for a few moments, and then said he would put the question before the Directorate.

After lunch, a young and vigorous man, Captain McManus, of the Free State Army, came on an evening visit. Yeats at once proposed a game of croquet. Yeats, by far the best player, his daughter, next best player, on one side; McManus, a fair player, and Sean, no damn good at all, since he had never seen a croquet ground, much more played a match, on the other. Sean heard Yeats murmuring to McManus that he could show O'Casey how to play as the game went on; but, in spite of efforts towards tuition, O'Casey did very badly, and the poet and Anne won by a very large margin. Yeats was elated, McManus a little crestfallen, O'Casey glad to get in out of the sharp wind blowing from the Dublin Mountains, but a few feet away from the croquet pitch; though, when she had seen him shiver, Mrs. Yeats had thoughtfully made him wear his overcoat. His first and last game of croquet. A game in which Yeats played like a champion. The only game of croquet Sean had ever played; the only one he would ever play, played with the poet Yeats.

Sean noticed how stiffly Yeats slid into the comfortable chair by the cosy fire. He was bright, though, and aimed at gaiety; had he nested sooner here and longer, letting restlessness ooze out of him, he'd have had a chance of a longer life. He couldn't, for there was in Yeats an irresistible leaven of childlike desire for glitter in imagination and masqued activity. He loved to *pace upon the battlements and stare on the foundations of a house*. The battlements, the battlements of a tower; the winding stair to the same battlements, with Sato's gift, a changeless sword on a table, forged before Chaucer saw the light o' day; and the poet's crook o' th' knee to an old and gallant ancestry. There he was, ailing, but in his insight still declaiming:

> *I declare this tower is my symbol; I declare*
> *This winding, gyring, spiring treadmill of a stair is my ancestral*
> *stair;*
> *That Goldsmith and the Dean, Berkeley and Burke have travelled*
> *there,*
> *Swift beating on his breast in sibylline frenzy wild.*

Signs and symbols! Seeking substance from shadows, shining or shrieking. The poet had played with his toys too long. Aristocratic toys, self-fashioned; a few coloured with a wild philosophy, all tinged with beauty, some even with a gracious grandeur; but he had played with them all too long. More than half of life had passed him by while he was unsheathing and sheathing Sato's sword, staring over decaying battlements, or restamping out a dim impression of a long-forgotten ancestral crest. Young mortality. Ancestry had long since lost its handfast hold of man's mind. Man was no longer bothering to claim big house or battlemented castle, but was claiming the whole earth for his ancestry. Yeats was tired, and so the morioned head, the sword at hip, the spurred heel, had given place to the soft slipper, the comfortable chair, and the cosy fire.

But the poet, when he wished, with a light spring, could jump down from the battlements to the earth again. The bold Yeats! Here he was now, talking laughingly about the censorship. In the beginning when Yeats and the intellectuals saw censorship was bound to come, they planned how to make it ineffective. Before a book could be banned, the Censorship Board had to come to a unanimous decision that the bloody book deserved it. The cunning mind of Yeats moved that a protestant clergyman be included on the Board, Yeats and the intellectuals feeling certain that a protestant divine would, *pro natura antagonisticeomnibus,* oppose any opinion expressed by the catholic members of the Board. They were wrong: any incautious mention of a girl's gown, or any whisper of a crack in the concrete solidarity of a creed, caused the reverend gent to close his eyes, tap the table, and cry hem! He was worse than any of the others.

—An odd man, thought Sean. No; let Yeats try ever so hard, he could never have been an aristocrat. With his castle, his crested spoons, his sword of Sato, he was no more an ancestral aristocrat than James Joyce; or even than Fluther Good when Fluther was singing his song about *The Wedding of Glencree.* The poet was too passionate. Too dispersed in thought. The bigger weakness of Yeats was that he could never hammer his thoughts into any harmony of unity. Joyce did; Yeats couldn't. Image after image did a ballet-dance in his mind; when he chose one as perfection, he lost it among the other dancing images, and when he found it again, he saw that it had changed into another form and a different fantasy. And yet he could stamp on the earth as firmly and as rudely as any Joyce could. He was one who could sail for a year and a day in an argosy, and then go for a voyage of a week in a tramp steamer. Born into the proletariat, Yeats would have made a magnificent docker.

When the evening had dwindled into a darkening dusk, Sean bade farewell to the poet; an affectionate farewell, with a tight grip of clasped hands.

Some time after Sean's return to London, the Abbey Theatre produced his *The Silver Tassie,* seven years after it had seen the lights o' London. When it appeared, Joyce's terrible clap of thunder, that frightened the primitive man into frenzy, shot into the startled ears of Eireann; and all Eire's sacred frogs began to croak, Brékkek Kékkek Kékkek Kékkek Kóax Kóax Kóax! A reverend member of the Dominican Order had issued a premature warning in a semi-canonical proclamation, saying: *There have been tentative announcements in the Press recently of the forthcoming production of The Silver Tassie by the Abbey Theatre. The Abbey once rejected this play to which it now offers the hospitality of its boards. Dublin is to have the opportunity of drinking deep* (Drinking, drinking, drinkinkin, ing, inking!) *from The Silver Tassie. I fancy Dublin is a little too wise in nineteen hundred and thirty-five to put its lips to a cup that possibly may have been filled from a sewer.* (Guinness is good for you.) *The Play has been published, and is in our hands for cold inspection. It defies analysis. It is a vigorous medley of lust and hatred and vulgarity. I have no hope of conveying any adequate idea of its deliberate indecency and its mean mocking challenge to the Christian Faith. The fracas over The Playboy was but a flash in the pan, a child's cracker, in comparison with the hostility with which the Abbey is confronted if it persists in defying Catholic principle and flouting that reticence which is characteristic of our people. Plain etiquette will not tolerate horror, indecency, or blasphemy, on or off the stage.*

Sublime is the warning, so, quick! we have but a second! Here's a hot inspection for you, from a truly, ruly, reverend gentleman too. Here's one destined to drive out the indecency of poverty, the blasphemy of disease, the dull despair of dirt, the horror of war, with the midget-magical sword of Plain Etiquette. Stainless steel. Drive these things from the Abbey stage as a preliminary, and then drive them hellter-skelter out of the world: One, two, three—go! Hearsemen, pass by!

But the heated hostility, desired by the cleric and sedulously prophesied by him, made no appearance to disturb the production. The Reverend Gentleman had a quiet guard; not a mouse stirring. But there was a commotion within the theatre, behind the scenes. One of the Directors got the shock of his life. He came rushing out of the theatre, horrified that such a thing could be. The ripe ribaldry of O'Casey's play was a severe shock to his finer feeling. He exclaimed to all that he felt an outrage had been committed. Two of them now fierce in the fight: the cleric and the Theatre Director, layman,—to God and Ireland true. Two true now. The Director, in a burst of holy indignation, told O'Casey where to get off, for he was keen and tempered to uphold *Catholic cleanliness and wholesome entertainment in a theatre which our Catholic Government is subsidising. Insane admiration here, and the half-witted culture of New York and London's admiration for O'Casey's vulgar and worthless plays, where they are always failures, filling O'Casey full of a fantastic opinion of his own importance, though he is best at his gutter level in controversy with Mr. Yeats, who has replied, after silently enduring years of the foulest abuse, with this gesture which forces our audience to endure The Silver Tassie, even though it was only for a week.* He sought out those in authority, and demanded that all the impudent, naughty words be cut out of the play, for as he says, *The onus lay upon the other Directors and the Producer to respect the suggestion I had made about the cutting of the play, and act accordingly. Their duty was clear, and I did not wish to be unduly insistent in pointing it out to them further. At the same time, I did not altogether leave out of consideration what I felt must be the reactions of the players to the offensive portions of the play; but since the publication of my statement, Mr. F. J. McCormick has made an explanation on behalf of the players that these reactions were such as might have been expected, and that he, himself, were he a free agent, would not, as a Catholic, have appeared in the play. On Friday last, I expressed my regrets to the players that my statement should have involved them, and I now take the opportunity of saying that I wholeheartedly accept Mr. McCormick's explanation. I felt it necessary to explain that some steps had been taken to mitigate the offence of the production so that it might not be taken as a lasting disgrace to the Abbey Theatre.*

Get out the harp, Pat, and play. The catholic Harp, man. We're all pupae in the Papal flag. Let me alone, though I know you won't, I know you won't; let me alone, though I know you won't, impudent Jimmy O'Dea!

But, whisper again, boys and girls, whisper: While eager to cut things out of O'Casey's play, he didn't like the same thing happening to his own. Oh, no, boys and girls. Earlier on, he had complained to the Abbey Directorate that actors were leaving out words from authors' plays, as was explained by the Theatre's Secretary reporting to the Press that "Owing to representations made by the Director at a Board meeting, instructions were issued to the Company that no word must be left out, no sentence changed during a performance." It is usual when cuts are thought to be desirable, to ask the author about them; but here was the lad bouncing about demanding cuts without even letting O'Casey know that such a thing was in his mind.

Reinforcements were hurried up to the Director. The Irish Press, secular and sacerdotal, bawled a blast on the play. *The Cross,* magazine of the Passionists, hands on hips, declared, *It is a poisonous draught from a dirty cup. There was a time when the Dublin men had the courage of their convictions, and were not afraid to make effective protest against anything that outraged their feelings. In these good old days, as anyone familiar with the history of the Abbey Theatre can recall* (out in the dear, dead days beyond recall!), *there was a famous week when riots took place every night during an offensive performance, and five hundred police were needed to keep order in the Theatre and its vicinity. But times have changed, and O'Casey's The Silver Tassie, with its dreary monotony of blasphemy, vulgarity, and filth, passed off quietly without the need to call in one single officer of the law to preserve order. We have no hope of arousing the decadent Directorate of the Abbey Theatre to a sense of its public duty. But the Abbey audience that could contentedly sit through such a performance is certainly worthy of examination. What witless fools are in our midst, that could sit, open-mouthed and empty-headed, and gape at the guttersnipe's rhapsody presented on the stage for their delectation! The people that could applaud such blatant blasphemy had not even enough intelligence to see that they were throwing bouquets at one who was dragging them down with him to wallow in the mire.*

Well, boys and girls, what do you think of that delectable denunciation by a Father of the Passionist Order, a Brother of St. Paul of the Cross? And a Scholar too, for he is the Editor of the magnificent magazine; a learned man; a Doniel come to judgement. How genteel and reticent the comments are. Sparkling with the divine courtliness of the St. Paul of the Cross community. Deeply disappointed, too, that disorders hadn't afflicted the performances. Delicate detonations of phrase worthy to be framed and placed on the white walls of the Marian League of Art.

Here is the report from *The Irish Catholic,* full of a pure and holy purpose: *If The Silver Tassie withstands the test of fire to which it has been subjected within the last ten days* (ten days that shook the world), *then, though it would not thereby be proved genuine silver, the base metal of which it is composed is at least equivalent to asbestos. Personally we believe that the effect of the flood of correspondence will be the exclusion for all time from the boards of any Irish theatre of Mr. O'Casey's precious production. Galway and the Catholic Young Men's Societies have been in the forefront in bringing about this highly desirable result. The bitterness of the atheist heart is seen by the judicious in all that Mr. O'Casey has got put upon the boards—it gives its repulsive and morbid tang to whatever comes from his dramatic pen. Those who relish the rank sort of fare that Mr. O'Casey provides ought to be denied by law the opportunity of indulging their debased tastes.*

Let us take a thimbleful of stimulant now as a sursum cordial against the effects of these blows from Balaam, by quoting the famous American drama critic, George Jean Nathan: *If The Silver Tassie with all its admitted deficiencies is not one of the most honorable experiments, then I am not the man to have been engaged to write this foreword.*

Another holy snarler, *The Standard,* otherwise *The Eagle,* came out like this: *It was a revolting production in which the Church was mocked, the name of God insulted, immorality flaunted as a matter of course, and the foulest language of the gutter used before audiences overwhelmingly Catholic. As a play—though this seems beside the point now—the production is mere trash. Nothing even remotely approaching the dirtiness and stupidity of this wretched attempt at drama would be permitted to be shown on the screen. This play gives us a golden opportunity of improving our stage, and of reconsidering the value of our literary heroes who have been set up for our admiration. Mr. W. B. Yeats is no literary leader for a Catholic country.* (Remember Parnell!). *No matter to what poetic heights he may soar, he will never lift us to the heights to which we aspire.* The eagle's whistle! Excelsior!

Cu Uladh, President of the Gaelic League (the one who when the Treaty was signed, rushed out to hang a notice on the railings outside his office thanking God, in pitiable Irish, for the sake of freedom; then, when De Valera disavowed the Treaty, rushed out to bring his blessing in again), came out with *The Abbey Theatre at its worst, which seems to be at the present moment, is intolerable and must be swept aside. I have not seen, thank God, this latest horror, but I remember some years ago going to see The Plough and the Stars, and having to leave before the second act from a fit of nausea.* And this *item indignatio* adorned himself with the title of Ulster's Hound, the title of Cuchulann, greatest hero of the Red Branch Knights. Sean could only murmur, as big Joe Brady, the Irish Invincible, murmured on his way to the scaffold, Poor oul' Ireland, poor oul' Ireland!

The crinolined, Roman Catholic *Tablet* ventured out with no direct opinion about the play. Sitting safe among her cushions, perfume on one side of her, smelling-salts on the other, she gracefully fluttered her fin, snowy-white, streaked with yellow, and simpered, in reply to a question put by a reader. *To this inquiry we cannot make an answer worth having; because we have neither seen O'Casey's play nor read it in print. The Silver Tassie is known to us only by what we have heard and read about it. While refusing to give a critical opinion of our own, we are at least entitled to say that Irish Catholics, both priests and laymen, for whose honesty and intelligence we have deep respect, deplore O'Casey's play, not only in itself, but as a very blatant sign of a very evil tendency in Irish dramatic circles. Mr. Louis J. Walsh has a strong article about this tendency in the October number of the Irish Rosary. He thinks that the temptation for an author to write down to what he regards as Abbey standards is tremendous for a poor or overambitious man; and he believes that there is a definite malignity in the whole Abbey outlook.*

Louis J. Walsh! Well, he wasn't poor, but he was ambitious. A competent solicitor, but an incredibly bad playwright. The title of one of his plays alone sounds his requiem: *The Pope in Killybuck.* Walsh had sent it to Sean for commendation, with a letter gleefully adding that he had modified it when it went north so that it might meet a welcome in protestant Ulster. The play was too bad to bother about, so Sean sent it back, but kept the letter, which frightened Walsh because of what he had said in it, so that he demanded it back. Give me back, give me back what I wrote unto you, for what I have written I have not written. A nest of frightened people. Fear and a sly expediency are the immoral fibres spreading viciously through Ireland's soul.

A roman catholic secular paper, *The Evening Herald,* had a leading article about the production. The article was headed by the notification of The Feast of the Day—the Beheading of John the Baptist. Holy humbug hanging on to God. It said, *It is strange that the severe criticisms which appeared in the Dublin Press (before production) of this play were not sufficient to satisfy the producers of the utter unsuitability of this blasphemous and sordid play. It is time a check was put to such productions that appeal to morbid minds.*

Brékkek Kékkek Kékkek Kékkek Kóax Kóax Kóax. Croak away!

In the midst of the frogs, one blackbird whistled a melody for Sean. One Roman Catholic, Robert Speaight, the prominent English actor, in a letter to the Press, denounced the attack saying, *The play is an outcry from a passionate and embittered mind. But it is much nearer to Christianity, because it is nearer to life, than the complacent criticisms levelled against it. The soul of the bourgeoisie has betrayed itself. This surely is the essence of the bourgeois mind—that it cannot look tragedy in the face; for O'Casey has seen into the heart of the horror of war, and wrenched out its dreadful secret; that the co-heirs with Christ destroy one another in the sight of the Son of Man.*

Sean sauntered away from the frogs, getting away from their croaking to busy himself with other work. He would forget them for a time—the journals, the bawling priests, the shouting members of the Catholic Young Men's Societies, the very wise and stout-hearted defender of decent literature, including Shakespeare, of course, Dr. J. Murphy, representing the University of Galway grey (representing the same community, oddly enough, long after and later on, when the poet Yeats was finally laid to rest within the reach of the strong arms of famed Ben Bulben). Let them all alone for the present. Like Graham Greene's Father Rank in *The Heart of the Matter,* they didn't quite like observant men. They saw too much, and what they saw, they saw too clearly; and when they saw, they said. And that doesn't please the papal priest or the papal bishop, as Dr. McDonald saw so clear and said so promptly. The day of blinkered blessedness was nearly over. God is numbering them off on the rosary of the years. The light of other days is light no longer.

Twelve years later, *The Silver Tassie* was performed for two crowded weeks in the Gaiety Theatre, the largest one Dublin has in her pocket; and, throughout the performances, not a word was spoken, not a drum hit, not an ecclesiastical curse was uttered by sunray, lampglow, or candlelight. The holy hibernians were hibernating. The play could rest in peace now.

But no! Nearly two years later, Sean gets a letter from Mr. Ward Costello, an airman in the last World War, now a student of drama at Yale University, Connecticut. He wrote to say that he had defended O'Casey during an attack made upon him in a lecture given by Mr. Lennox Robinson to the University's students of drama, with Marc Connelly in the Chair. The young student asked Mr. Robinson "if *The Silver Tassie,* since it had not been produced by Yeats because of his prejudice, had been produced, or considered for production, since his death?" And "Mr. Robinson had answered with a flat 'No,' adding that it was a bad play; even though Lady Gregory had changed her mind about it." The old lady had said Yes, when the Hundingdons brought her to see the London production of the play.

Perhaps this was the last stroke of the bell tolling for the demise of the play. But no: *The Silver Tassie* is dead, but the damned thing won't lie down. This very month of October, nineteen hundred and fifty-one, a revival of the play in the Queen's Theatre by the Abbey brought on more thunderclaps of resentment. Miles na gCopaleen, in *The Irish Times,* quotes the critic of *The Evening Herald* as saying, "It's a poor play. The second act, set in the trenches [by the way, the scene is Not set in the trenches, but behind them; the trenches are out on the horizon as the script plainly says: but this is but a minor part of an Irish critic's splendid critical equipment], finds O'Casey having a shot at expressionism—and in the process being weird, vague and lamentably wide of the mark. For the majority of playgoers this act is in exceeding bad taste. The litany to the gun is the crowning piece of offensiveness." Bring out the hackbut and battle-brand! Miles na gCopaleen, after the sermon, gives the priestly curse: "In the Queen's Theatre, the Abbey makes its début with as loathsome and offensive a 'play' that has ever disgraced the Dublin boards. The second act is a perfectly plain, straightforward travesty of Catholic Church ritual. The rest is bunkum and drool." The toll has changed into a tocsin!

The Irish critics have made all the use they could of the Abbey's first rejection of the play, and have pursued it with curious and persistent hatred; but it still refuses to lie down. Peace, be still, heart of O'Casey: It is only Ireland that abuses the play now. Everywhere else, the play has been accepted as a fine and courageous experiment in modern drama, and only the other day the drama critic of *The Times Literary Supplement* said of this very play, this very act, "If the voluble rapscallions of Dublin tenement life are unforgettable, so, too, is the pre-presentment in universal terms of the horror of war in the expressionistic act of *The Silver Tassie*"; an opinion oddly different from that of J. J. F. of *The Evening Herald.* For reasons too short to explain, Sean preferred to embrace the opinion of the English *Literary Supplement* rather than that of the Irish journal.

But Yeats was stretched out, alone and motionless, in a grave, thrust away in a farther corner of France. The battler was gone from the field. His bow was broken, and the scattered arrows lay where they had fallen; but

> *Here, perhaps, a hundred years away,*
> *Some hunter in day dreams or half asleep*
> *Will hear his arrows whizzing overhead,*
> *And catch the winding of a phantom horn.*

And, now, his young shield-bearer, F. R. Higgins, has followed him: the riverside is lonely, and the street where the Abbey is; the plains of Meath and the fields of Connacht lack a lover.

Cold, cold!
Cold tonight is broad Moyburg.
Higher the snow than the mountain-range,
The deer cannot get at their food.

The frogs were happier now; louder: Brékkek Kékkek Kékkek Kékkek Kóax Kóax Kóax.

FEATHERING HIS NEST

✤ ✤ ✤

The General Strike in 1926 had emptied the Fortune Theatre. The packed houses had given way to audiences of ten and eleven nightly; so Sean's first play was taken off, and the second one, *The Plough and the Stars*, was put into rehearsal, its first night to be given in the New Theatre. A few days before this, the young girl playing the part of Nora fell ill, and Fagan got another young Irish lass named Eileen Carey, who had been in the cast of *Rose Marie*, to take on the part. She came to settle the arrangement while Sean was in the Theatre's office, talking to Fagan. In she came, neatly and delightfully dressed, and a lovely lass she was; a very lovely lass. Sean's Irish eye was as keen in the choice of a pretty lass as the American eye of George Jean Nathan, so he stood staring at her for a long time. He had rarely seen a lovelier face or figure anywhere in this world, and didn't expect to find anything better in the delectable world to come. She was nervous; Sean saw she was sensitive, for the talk about wages embarrassed her, so he helped by demanding that she get the same as had been given to the girl whose place she had taken—for Fagan had offered her five pounds a week less, reproaching Sean when she had gone for adding to the expenses of the production. But Sean was well pleased to be of service to such a delightful girl whose voice was clear and musical and whose bright eyes betrayed a natural but hidden intelligence.

The poor girl accepted an almost impossible job, for the rest of the company were now perfect in part, movement, and position, while she had to begin, teasing them and silently asking them to show her the way through the play. And scant sympathy and little help she got from them in her efforts to come level with their knowledge and experience of the play. Had Sean had then the knowledge he acquired afterwards, he would never have allowed the young lass to undertake the uncongenial and thankless task; but she bore it all patiently and doggedly, and played the part till the other young actress was fit enough to take it on again. There was, too, an affinity of race between Sean and her, for she was as Irish as the heather on Howth Hill. But there was nothing in her of Harry Lauder's Scotch Bluebell, and, indeed, Sean didn't believe there was such a lass in Scotland either, down in the Lowlands or up in the Highlands. He could see that she had many undeveloped gifts; that she was a fighter, that she was of the earth, knowing that there was a deep blue sky over it; that, though she was nervous now, and a little shyly hesitant, she had courage and a determined spirit, mingling with a true kindliness—gifts that can form, and be, only what we call the kingdom of heaven within us. And time has proved that he made a good guess. Emerson has said that a pretty face is a great gift to a woman, an attractive figure a greater one, and a charming manner the greatest of all; and when one gets these in a *trio juncta in uno,* then one has been promoted in life by the gods themselves; especially when their grandeur is subdued by a gloriously human sense of humour. There's nothing lovelier in life than a lively laugh. Eileen had faults; a lot less than he had himself, for these were many; but faults are trivial things in a nature worthy of all men to be accepted.

During a lot of this time the General Strike had spread itself all over England, and Sean had been amazed at its quietness. At first, he had thought, Now is the accepted time, now is the day of salvation; but no voice spoke, and quietness seemed to brood all over England. Three million of men out on a militant strike, and it looked as if they had all gone to bed. He couldn't help comparing the dense quietude of this effort with the exhilarating uproar and daring intensity engendered in Dublin by the Lock-out of nineteen hundred and thirteen, when every worker was a warrior and any who blenched were banished from the fighting tribe. Everyone was in the struggle, from the Viceroy of Ireland to the raggedest urchin of the slums who had reached the years of talk and a prentice understanding of events. Then every vantage point had its machine-gun, and the Viceroy was praying to God for help.

The excitement, as far as Sean could see, was all on the side of those who wished to maim the strike; with those who had more than they needed, with those who depended on those who had more than they needed, and with those who depended on those who depended on those who had more than they needed. The Two Nations of England were lined up for war, the one against the other. *Two Nations: between whom there was no intercourse and no sympathy; who were as ignorant of each other's habits,*

thoughts, and feelings, as if they were dwellers in different zones, or inhab-
itants of different planets; who are formed by a different breeding, are fed
by a different food, are ordered by different manners, and are not governed
by the same laws—THE RICH AND THE POOR; and Sean wondered if Disraeli
had meant this when he set it down, and, if he were here now, would he
get a Vavasour to lead his baronets, with their coronets of two gold balls,
against this menace of men out to fight for the right to live; to fight the men
wearing the Mons Star who were threatening the safety of the unearned
incomes.

Those who had more than they needed suddenly displayed and paraded a
remarkable burst of Christian charity and kindliness. They had cars, and
they insisted in placing them at the services of those who preferred to walk.
They slung placards on their windscreens saying, Ask me for a Lift, and
were much upset and annoyed when a lift was refused. Young aristocrats
and university men, oil-spattered and smoke-grimed, helped by soldiers,
stood on the footplates of engines and tried to drive them hither and
thither; and rushed here, rushed there, rushed everywhere to keep the essential services going; even the younger sons, who, as Disraeli says, *Should*
be the natural friends of the people, though they are generally enlisted
against them. The more fools they; to devote their energies to the mainte-
nance of a system which is founded on selfishness and which leads to fraud;
and of which they are the first victims. So the eldest sons stood with the
fathers and the young sons stood with their elders to oppose the menacing
workers who had spread a pall of quietude very like death over the whole
land; revealing to all but themselves that without labour there can be no
life.

All the Unions had been called out by the Labour Leaders in support of
the miners; for by coming out to help a comrade, they had but come out to
help themselves, and Jim Larkin's slogan flashed through Sean's mind, An
injury to One is the concern of All. They silenced England that their voice
might be heard and the needs of their wives and children known. As it had
been, so it was still:

> *The golf links lie so near the mill,*
> *That almost every day*
> *The labouring children can look out*
> *And see the men at play.*

The strike began on May the 4th and ended on May the 13th, a nine
days' wonder. The Trades Union leaders found fright in their hearts when
the stillness began to brood over the land; they feared for the fat salaries
their jobs gave them; they feared to lose the happy assimilation of friendship with those who had more than they needed; their wives had cast off

the hodden grey and had put on fine linen and silk, and they had no desire to go back to the hodden grey again; and Sir John Simon, after a search through many old books of parchment, discovered that the strike was illegal. Parchment, sacramented with sealing wax, declared against the workers. The leaders called the strike off; the men, all but the miners, went back beaten, and Sir John Simon put the precious parchment back into the safe again. So the homes fit for heroes to live in that had been bobbing up and down on the waves all round the coast, disappeared over the horizon; for it was all a mirage; and there never will be any houses fit for heroes or humans to live in till the heroes and humans build the houses themselves. The hour had not struck.

The miners held out, and Sean sent a subscription to their funds, with a message of a comrade's support of their fight, adding another to the man for Labour who stood for the workers' cause in the by-election of Leith. It was this support that first showed Sean that free thought didn't altogether go unchallenged, even in England. He received a rather indignant and advisory letter from William Blackwood, the great friend of Harry Lauder. William Blackwood was a prominent man in the Northcliffe publications, editor of *Answers,* and he had used every possible appeal to induce Sean to write an article for the periodical, but Sean wasn't interested enough in the publication to do it. An election took place in Leith, and Sean had sent a letter of courage and good hope to the Labour candidate. Some time after a letter came from Fleetway House, signed by Billy Blackwood, saying:

"What is this I hear about you? Namely that you have been putting your name to election literature of the most seditious kind.

"I happen to mention the other day to a well-known literateur that I had the honour and pleasure of your friendship. He thereupon went off the deep end, cursing you loudly and bitterly for taking part in the recent Leith by-election, and allowing your name to go on some pamphlets which were distributed by the tens of thousands all over that section of my beloved land affected by the election. This morning he sends me a copy of the document, along with a note urging me in impassioned language to ask you to refrain in future from lending so distinguished a name as yours to the Anti-christs and Bolsheviks of Britain!!

"Joking apart, my own idea is that probably you never saw the document in question, and, in any event, I am not sufficient of a politician to be concerned by it either way. But I think seeing your name on such a virulent Red pamphlet has been rather a jolt to some of your literary and dramatic admirers."

And Sean, thinking over it once only, sent something like the following:

"A leterateur, a literateur—what the hell's a literateur? How does it look? What does it eat? Where does it live? I know some of these 'Literateurs'—nancy boys in art whose hands will never stretch to pluck bright honour from the pale-faced moon. . . . And they can go to hell, and tell them that from me. I know very little about politics, but enough to save me from the stupidities of the H. of Commons. As there are 'tied houses' so there are tied men, and your literateur is probably one of them: a one whose humanity is as broad as the cheques he gets for the work he does. And he can go to hell, and tell him that from me. And I will probably go on jolting my literary and dramatic admirers; let them wash their own feet and comb their own hair, for they won't get me to do it."

He had offended Fagan too. Fagan had given him the typescript of his play, *And So To Bed* to read, and so Sean had, and had flung it aside on to a table, forgetting about it in the excitement of his lady's loveliness and the roar of London, blazoned with business; for he had become one more among the city's crowds rushing hither and thither, waiting at the crossings till the mighty surge of oncoming traffic, bullied by the big red buses, was suddenly stayed by the upraised hand, white-gloved, of a big policeman, who stood, or moved right and left, with a calmness astonishing in the midst of so many impatient, panting, go-ahead, on-ahead vehicles, crouching in alertness, waiting for the stately, white-gloved hand to come down, to shoot forward. So Sean watched, waited for the hand to go up, and, when it did, shot forward in the midst of the crowd to the other side of the street, separating to this side, or that, to allow an opposing crowd forging forward to get to the side of the street he had just abandoned. So he forgot the play.

The telephone rang at his flat, and Fagan's voice, a note of reproach in it, begged him to take a taxi, and bring down the play to his office at once. So Sean did, hurrying down with it, slapping it into Fagan's hand, and saying, jaunty with the sights and sounds pressing on him everywhere, and buoyant with ignorance, There it is, Jim, and don't waste my time any more by making me read such trivial plays. Fagan said nothing; silently told a stout, smiling man beside him who this excited fellow was; gave the play to him, and bid him a smiling goodbye. Then Fagan said quietly, You might have waited to say what you thought of the play till my friend had gone: that was Edmund Gwenn who is to play the part of Pepys in my play, that was. Sean was thoughtless still. He had plagued Fagan in other ways, for Fagan had insisted on becoming his father and friend, watching over him, telling him what to do, where to go, whom to meet, till Sean was angry and resistant. He got a blank invoice from a Bond Street tailor, and, disguising his handwriting, had entered thereon a bill for a plum-coloured velvet jacket, black satin trousers, a yellow-flowered waistcoat, the lot costing seventy-five guineas, which he told Fagan he wanted to wear when he was going to answer evening invitations by personal presence, making the producer shake with nervousness that Sean would put him, with his ignorant, exhibitionist ways, to an open and a shut shame. Again, Sean bought a gaudy little watch for three shillings, got a plush case for it, and telling

Fagan the price was twenty-five pounds, asked him very seriously to lock it in the theatre safe till he made up his mind as to whether or no he'd buy it. A few days later a bill for the amount came to the theatre demanding the twenty-five pounds without delay, or the immediate return of the watch. This Fagan had read, for the bill came unsealed, and he, immediately, without Sean's knowledge, returned the watch. When Sean learned of this, he became artificially angry, and demanded that Fagan should never interfere with his affairs again. Afterwards, the papers recorded that the dramatist, O'Casey, had bought a baby elephant, and was taking him out for walks in Hyde Park; so Fagan got frightened, and left Sean alone, asking him no more to meet particular friends, or to come to his flat for a meal. So now Sean could sit on his own chair, and eat at his own table, and look about for a friend or two of his own choice. Yet Jim Fagan meant well; he was gentle—a little too gentle—and he had a very kind nature.

So, surrounded by these things and many more, Eileen and Sean went on building a nest. They entered a little three-storied house, including a basement, used as a dining-room because it was near to the kitchen, when the streets were knee-deep in snow. It was a simple Georgian house, one of a long terrace, with two decent rooms, a tiny bathroom, and a huge kitchen, with an old-fashioned range in it big enough to do as an altar for Stonehenge. And, by God, it burned the coal as fast as one could shovel it in, but took its time to heat the water. There was an oven in it would roast half an ox, my ox, your ox, his ox, her ox; but you would have to put a turkey into it on the very first of January if you wanted it cooked for Christmas. Going down the basement stairs, one had to hold tight and pray fervently to prevent a broken neck. After a short time in residence it was found that the tank holding the household water leaked badly, and, when examined, it was seen that the tank had been stuffed in many places with rags to keep the bulk of the water from flooding the whole locality. But these things took time to discover, and, first, the home had to be furnished. They were, he and Eileen, full of the necessity to make the home comfortable, bright, and original. It was delightful and easy to picture it as they thought it should be. They would search for cretonne, for prints, for chinaware, for curtainstuff, for chairs, tables, and divans till they saw what their hearts desired and their minds understood to be suitable. Life was singing a song in their hearts. They spent days in Heal's and holidays in the print shops of Charing Cross Road. They were for ever handling things they couldn't buy. Lifting lovely things, then hurrying away when told the price of them. The house had been taken on a lease which swallowed nine-tenths of what they had had. Now they were discovering that the house demanded more, for a new tank had to be bought, the roof had to be repaired, a man had to be employed, according to the lease, to keep the little garden in order, the house had to be kept insured; again, by order of the lease, old pipes had to be stripped from the outer walls, and new ones put in their place; and Sean began to wonder if he would have enough money left even to buy spoons for the two of them. Jasus, it wasn't half as easy as it had looked!

But they had to do something; so they hurried off, hurried to Harrod's, buying there a fender, fire-irons, a polished-steel bucket in which to put coal, an oak chest for linen, and a hearth-brush with a brass back. Leaving the chest behind, they carried all the other treasures back in a taxi. When they had settled the things in the big front room, they looked around, and saw on the floor a square of brown carpet, meeting a wide frame of stained flooring, for their money didn't allow them to carpet the room to the walls, the stained margins and the empty room making the carpet shrink to a smaller size; a single armchair by the fire and curtains on the big window, and that was all—a bare room, looking like a native, naked but for a loin-cloth; a room declaring an imminent departure rather than a hurried entry; and Eileen after a glance around, plumped into the chair, and wept. But not for long: shortly after, the room's repellent glare changed to a comic look of an appeal for help, and Eileen and he laughed loud and long, saving themselves from the folly of self-pity.

Eileen had let her flat before meeting Sean, and they were now waiting for her furniture to set the home fair for living in, for he had but a few things, mostly books, which wouldn't even furnish a decent room for his own use. She had got no rent from the tenants, and couldn't get any reply from them when she asked them to return the furniture she needed herself so badly now. By a lucky chance, she managed to get the key as they were about to flit to another place; but she found the furniture in a woeful state, for they had planked hot saucepans on divans, carpets, and chairs; the carpets were torn and stained, and the kitchen-ware had never been cleaned from the day Eileen had handed over to them. It was all very vexatious and discouraging, but a great many things were salvaged, lovely things in mahogany, fine cutlery, much linen, and a beautiful Bechstein piano; so Sean, in the end, found himself in intimate touch with a few of the elegant things of life. To this very day, he doesn't know what they'd have done had not Eileen brought as her dowry the furniture of her four-roomed flat. With all my worldly goods I thee endow; an easy endowment, indeed, for all he had were two pictures, a chair, a desk, kept together by the mercy of God, a cheap divan, a crowd of books, a spoon, knife and fork, a kettle, teapot, and a few articles of delfware. But they were kept going to supply the bare essentials, ekeing out payments with the few royalties he got now and again for performances of his plays. None of the fitments of either flat, his or hers, would suit the requirements of the house they now had. To supplement the hot-water system, they installed a gas geyser to help the panting, gurgling pipes coming from the range which were choked, and now almost useless. The geyser was easy to work (so it was said), a thing that a child could use;

foolproof (so it was said). Eileen strolled to the sparkling copper geyser to sample its first bath, while Sean chatted by the fire with a friend, Billy McElroy, roguish, bombastic, laughable, and a wonderful personality. The two of them heard things hissing, the hissing changing to a dull thump at times; but they put no pass on it. Then Eileen came in to say she couldn't get the geyser to work. Sean looked it over, tried to light the jets, but, after a long effort, gave it up. He told Eileen that she must forgo the bath for that night, and returned to his friend by the fire. Suddenly, the whole house rocked to a foul explosion, fretted by the mocking tinkle of breaking glass, and from the noise's centre came a frightened scream from Eileen. She had managed to get the geyser to work. Sean ran to the bathroom—Eileen was staggering about, moaning that the child within her had been killed. The bathroom window, frame and all, had been lifted clean out of the wall, and now lay shattered down in the street below. Sean got Eileen stretched out on the bed, and, rushing to the telephone to summon a doctor, he saw his friend tip-toeing down the stairs, saw him placing his big-brimmed black hat quickly on his head; saw him open the door softly and close it quietly after him as he hurried away home. But Eileen was none the worse for the accident, beyond a few weeks of anxiety about her baby and unpleasant buzzing in her head; but the restoration of the window made quite a hole in the little pile of money remaining, for neither Eileen nor he even guessed that they might have claimed the cost of replacement and of the doctor's fee against the incompetent, and even dangerous, fixing of the geyser. Eileen had come out of it unhurt, and what claim could thankfulness have against anyone?

The little house was one of two stuck together, as if the one couldn't stand alone; so were they all on their side of the road, each a clump of two joined together with a space of little more than four feet between each clump, the back gardens hemmed into their own privacy by low walls. A small garden, its length three times that of its width; in the centre a narrow strip of grass that residents called a lawn, surrounded by a border holding flowers, dominated by a graceful white syringa, a fragrant lilac bush, and a delightful laburnum. Eileen and he had bought prints of pictures by Van Gogh, Utrillo, Renoir, Manet, and Segonzac. Eileen had framed the pictures in her own way, refusing to make use of the conventional gilt frames. She had narrow frames made to tone with the chief colours in the prints so that, when the pictures had been hung on the walls, they looked like coloured panels which formed decorative parts of the walls themselves. And she dispersed them in a new way. She didn't hang them so that a big one took the centre flanked by smaller ones at either side. A big one might be closer to one side than the other, and a smaller one would flank it far away on the opposite side, but not on the same level. Between them, not in the centre, but nearer the smaller one, would be a vase of blossoms; and well the gay simplicity looked, forming an added picture of harmony and divided lines to the coloured dignity of the pictures.

The only gilt frame in any room was the dark gold one surrounding John's beautiful *Head of a Gitana,* one of the loveliest expressions of graceful delight in paint Sean had ever seen. Taking lunch with Augustus John in a restaurant in Chelsea while the artist's exhibition was on in a gallery opposite, Sean had shyly and timidly offered John a tenth of what he had for a picture, for all of them as marked were wildly above anything Sean dare chance. Without a word, Augustus John had written a note to the manager of the exhibition directing him to give Mr. O'Casey any picture he might choose; so Sean had run straight over to the gallery, had made his choice, and had been rewarded by John saying, when he saw it, You made a good choice, Sean. So he had, and the picture is still the O'Casey centred jewel hanging upon the wall. Supplementing this treasure was the royal portrait that John did of Sean himself, in blue-green coat, silver-grey sweater, with a gayer note given by an orange handkerchief flowing from the breast-pocket of the coat; the face set determinedly in contemplation of things seen and heard, the body shrinking back tight to the back of the chair, as if to get farther away to see and hear more clearly; a sensitive and severe countenance with incisive lines of humour braiding the tightly-closed mouth—a princely gift from a great artist and a most generous man.

But when all had been done, when the simple, little house had begun to look fine, like a quakeress wearing a bright bandeau round her head and a daring locket on her bosom, they discovered that the district was a very expensive one to live in. They knew nothing, or next to nothing, about marketing or about the domestic ways of life, and had to learn by rough and punishing experience. Piously and vehemently, Eileen and he, now and again, hurried off to do the marketing in Kilburn, but the strain of the journey and the burden of hiking back all they bought, impaired their ardour, and so they plunged again into the dearer market of their own district, and the flabby little bag of money at the bank became far flabbier still. Then their first baby's birth had been a costly affair, the doctor taking fifty pounds, plus the cost of a nurse who stayed with them for six weeks. When he remembered what it cost a woman to have a kid in the tenements, he realised more fully than ever the terrible difference between one birth and another. And the Income Tax Collector, a kindly man, was coming to the house on the track of fifty pounds owed to the Revenue, which sum Sean hadn't got, but which the Collector thought must be found somewhere. Sean had tried to interest the kindly man in the bees in the garden, but the Collector didn't care about bees. He said he didn't know a thing about bees; how they lived, or how they were brought up, or a ha'porth. He knew a bee could sting a man, but that was about all. He was glad to hear that they were so useful to man in the pollination of flowers, a thing he hadn't known before. He knew, of course, that bees were thrifty things, laying up a store for a rainy day, and so a lesson to us all. He had other calls to make, but hoped he'd get the fifty pounds before the week-end, for he couldn't wait indefinitely, and went his way.

He got a letter from Lady Gregory saying how glad she was to hear he had a home of his own, with a garden too, a thing he would very much enjoy. Well, though he got in this home the rejection of *The Silver Tassie*, and all the anxiety and trouble that went with it, he had spent many enjoyable hours with the bees and the flowers, the only ones, bar those enjoyed during his days in Coole, he had ever been able to handle and watch without feeling they were not for him to pluck. He had had many still and happy hours with the spiders too, covering shrubs and bushes in the autumn with their beautifully balanced webs. He had wondered at the spider's speed, at its patience, waiting, sphinxlike, for the prey to come; at its frenzied haste, whenever a huge insect like a bee became enmeshed, to envelop it completely with silken threads, lest its frantic struggles should tear the web to pieces. Sean could never understand why some hated the spider. He knew one man who hated them so that he hunted them out, plucked them from their webs, and gloatingly plunged them into water to drown, or, if he could conveniently manage it, into hot water to be boiled; and, oddly enough, this man was a rabid pacifist; a conchie who had served a long time in jail rather than stick a needle into another man. He remembered how he himself had felt grieved in his heart when September's heavy rain ruined many of the lovely webs. Now he would have to go. He'd leave these things behind him. They'd have to sell the remainder of the lease, and live on what they got for another year. Looking at his bank book, he found that expenditure was two hundred and seventy-three pounds, against three hundred and twenty-nine pounds on the credit side, so that he had fifty-six pounds left to face the roll-call of payments which would be advancing on him soon. He'd have to sell out and go.

Yeats's denunciation of *The Silver Tassie* had done Sean's name a lot of violence. The Nobel Prize winner, the Leader of English literature was a judge against whom there was no appeal for the time being. Sean's flying start had been rudely curtailed of its fair proportions, and he would have to start over again, and fight the battle anew. He would have to hand over his little grey house in the north-west to another. The sale to a Film Company of one of his plays had stayed the inevitable away for a few years. He had got a thousand pounds for it—six hundred down and four hundred in six months' time. One night of fierce wind and heavy snow, when the house shivered in the midst of the glow from all the fires they could afford to light, a Mr. Mycroft came driving up from Elstree to offer the money for the making of the film. Out of his speedy little car came Mycroft, covered with thick flaky snow, a genuine *deus ex machina* when funds were gone and hope was waning. Pressed to stay the night because of the fierce wind and the falling snow, Mycroft refused, anxious to get back to report that consent had been given, and that the Company could go on with its terrifying plunge into experimental art; so out and on Mycroft went through the fierce wind, under the falling snow, fervent as a dashing courier carrying home the news of a gallant victory against heavy odds. Hysterical vanity of film production, hasty excitement in the production of the theatre, like hungry hens rushing headlong for a handful of scattered corn. Hysteria in the production of a mediocre film, clownish excitement in the production of a mediocre play; the more mediocre the play, the greater the excitement; the more mediocre the film, the greater the hysteria.

But Sean found that a lot of the film money would have to go into preserving the sanctity of an original peppercorn lease, and keep the house merry and bright for the present landlord. The Estate Surveyor, a Sir Someone or other, with his clerk, and the heir to the estate came to check up on the state of the properties, and, in due time, came to where Eileen and Sean were finding it hard to live. Outside, round about, with a man to examine the roof, like druids in modern dress, the three of them circled, the clerk jotting down items at a whisper from Sir Someone; through room after room, the three of them marched, halted, looking up, looking down, looking round, the clerk again jotting down items in a notebook at a whisper from Sir Someone. When they came to Sean's room, they gave but a faint echo to his lusty good-morning; Sir Someone was quiet; the clerk quiet and deferential; the heir excited, thrusting his face forward towards Sir Someone to say, Quite a nice little property, sir, which caused the Sir Someone to quietly leave the room, possibly having caught a glimpse of Sean's sardonic grin as he watched the ritual.

Property is theft, said Proudhon, but he must have been doting. Property must add to righteousness, for it is supported and sanctified by bishops, priest, and deacon. Some talk of morality, and some talk of religion; but give me a snug little property, sang Maria Edgeworth; and she was right. This lad had a snug little property, and he was beaming. And Tennyson chorused:

> Dosn't thou 'ear my 'erse's legs,
> As they canters awaäy?
> Proputty, proputty, proputty—that's what
> I 'ears 'em saäy.

Even horses know the importance of property, so who was Sean to question the demand to fork out what he needed for himself and family, to plaster ceilings, pipe walls, repair roofs so that a nice little property of another might remain a nice little property still. But nice and all as it was, it would soon have to see the last of Sean and of those who were his.

From this nice little nest of property, so beloved by the heir who owned it, which had filched a lot from Sean's limited means, he had flown to two organised meals only: one, an Annual Dinner of the Critics Circle; the other, a lunch given to Jim Brady, the celebrated New York Theatre man, by C. B. Cochran. And these two were quite enough for a lifetime. He had been selected by the critics to respond to the Toast of the Drama, and before the date fixed for the event he had had three different reminders not to forget to be in his place to respond when the toast was given. He was there all right, and, when the time came, spoke too damn wisely and too damn well. He criticised the critics for their jaunty adulation of trivial plays, the actors for their devotion to, and admiration of, their insignificant parts in these trivial plays, and the playwrights for writing down to the leading actors and actresses by scorching out of their work any good or important element in the secondary characters so that the part of leading lady or leading gentleman might add perceptibly to their own importance by the lessening of the importance given originally to the other characters circling around them. The speech didn't go down well, though it was politely honoured by a timid and hesitant handclap. But Sean was bucked up afterwards by the distinguished guest of the evening, Lord Cromer, telling him that it was easily The best speech of the evening. But the critics weren't at all pleased at having their colours lowered, even for a time, to a half-mast flutter; and so, signs on it, Sean has never had, for over twenty years, a whisper of an invitation to come within talking range of any annual gathering of these gentlemen: they didn't like the flash of criticism within the orbit of their own united circle of comment. Had Sean been less ignorant and innocent then than he became afterwards, he wouldn't have given "the best speech of the evening".

There was a big crowd of chaps only at the theatrical lunch given by that great man of the theatre, Cochran—St. John Ervine, Noel Coward, Archie Selwyn of New York, old Jim Brady, Branker, afterwards lost in a flaming dirigible, and many others. Sean never cared for stag parties, and it wasn't long till he was longing for the sight of a pretty face and the swish of a woman's skirt. Never to him could a place be comfortable or fully human without a woman. But here the stags, the men, felt free, and let themselves go. The silent censorship of delicate-minded woman was absent, and unfettered language flowed free from some of the mouths. It was romantic nonsense to imagine that women couldn't swear as well as a man. There was no docker of the tenements, no labourer of the slums, proficient in what is called vile talk, who couldn't find a woman his equal in the same tenement or the same slum. Old Brady made a speech that was lurid with the lightning of bad language. But it was stage lightning badly lit. The words were forced out of a pretended intimacy with profanity. They were not natural. The poor man didn't know how to use them, and so they sounded horrible in their deformed obscenity. There was no health in them. He should, before using them, have taken a long course of lessons from some lusty seaman, some ignorant navvy, some lowly docker. For the first time in his life Sean felt uncomfortable at the sound of bad language because it was unsound. The difference between it and that of a woman of the slums was that the old man's language made his blood go hot, while the language of a woman of the slums would have made his blood run cold. Neither was it the profanity which, in general circumstances, often gave off a glow, or a great humour. Cochran made a speech as neat, as orderly, and as respectable as his own appearance. A very good speech. A quiet man, Cochran. Under the neat quietness a deep well of artistic emotion. What a will he had for the Theatre! But his way was blocked, turn him how he might. Had he had the way as well as the will, the last forty years of the English Theatre would have been fretted with many stars. Well, these two feasts were a long way off now. The last glimpse of the luncheon which lingered in his memory was of Archie Selwyn, the New York producer, impressed mightily by the thought of Jack Buchanan and Evelyn Laye strutting majestically on a New York stage in *Bitter Sweet,* pacing up and down the room feverishly, exclaiming *Jack Buchanan and Evelyn Laye together; in the one show. My God, what a sensation!* He seemed to think that the combination would be so tremendous that God Himself would leave heaven to make a personal appearance among the audience.

Sean tried heavens hard to imagine *Bitter Sweet* to be a good and charming musical play, principally because his wife was acting a part in it, so presenting an importance to him another play of its kind could not have. The first night cost him thirty-four pounds, for Eileen sent tickets to many friends, anxious, of course, that the show would be received well, if not tumultuously. Sean went a second time with the doctor, Harold Waller, who had brought their first-born into the world, and who had become a great friend of the family. (Sean seemed to get on well with doctors. There was Dr. Cummins, of course, whose friendship he would remember to his dying day; again, Dr. McGuinness, who had attended him for bronchitis, and whom he met in London; Dr. Waller, who gave up a West End practice to be chief of a maternity hospital in Poplar, a son of the clergyman, Waller, who had been the friend of Livingstone; and Dr. Varian, of Totnes, a Dublin man and a fine fellow.) Dr. Waller, who knew a lot about it, thought the music bad, and Sean, try how he might to think the contrary, thought the wording worse. There seemed to be nothing in the first week's glow to predicate a success, but wizard Cochran worked a miracle, and by lusty nursing made of this poor thing a tremendous success for himself and for Mr. Coward.

They put off the day of decision, but they knew that the day was coming when they would have to leave the pleasant little house. He remembered how many good hours he had had with his boy, Breon, watching him begin to crawl on the grass, then make primitive and violent efforts to get to his feet, enacting over again man's first painful evolution from a four-footed animal; then the thrill of seeing the tiny boy plunge forward recklessly into the steps betokening the coming man who must stand alone and walk his own way through life; who had had his own birth, and would have his own development, his own sorrow and joy, his own wife and children, his own old age, and, finally, round it all off with a sleep. Many good hours had been spent in Regent's Park, but half an hour's stroll from the house, one side of the Park running round the Zoo, where wild horses could be seen in their paddock (though they looked very much like tame ones), and the wild goats jumping about on their rocky heights. At times, the air was made uneasy by the scream of a tiger or the roar of a lion.

Occasionally, half-way on to the Park, he turned into the churchyard of the parish church of St. John's Wood, opposite Lord's Cricket Ground, and sat him down to watch the nurses and nannies—too tired to go the further way to the Park—airing their bottoms on benches, a pram holding a baby beside them, and older charges, eminent in being fit to run, tearing about on scooters, or riding sedately on tricycles along the paths bordered by grass and measured by decaying tombstones that were frantically trying to keep their heads from sinking under the ground. Some of the sturdier youngsters, risking the fire of adventure, careered away on their tricycles to the uttermost ends of the churchyard, and, with toy pistol in a hand, shot all who passed without the railings, and a few that ventured nearer within, returning to their nannies breathless with the risks they had taken and the difficulties they had overcome. Voyaging further into life among the dead. Here, indeed, were the quick and the dead. Near to each other, yet wide apart, but near enough. The graves had no meaning for the youngsters within, or for the hurrying citizens without. The ardent young ones blew their toy trumpets, shot their toy guns, careless of the rebuke of the silent dead. The living dust was vivid, asparkle, bounding about; the dead dust had ceased to shine, even in the memory of man. The dead thrust down here had been forgotten: they had died too far away in time for men to bother about them, for even the dead grow old. No stone should show where the deep dead lie.

Did Yeats ever chronicle himself as sitting and sounding out thoughts in a churchyard? Sean failed to think of any reference to such a crowded isolation. Death would have been too like death to him in a graveyard. And yet the explanation of it was here and it is that there is none; except that that one who has died ends his importance, while this one newly born begins it. If Yeats were passing by here now, even as those citizens hurrying along the street outside, he would act as they do, never turning a head to look within. They leave the buried dead to take care of themselves and answer their own questions. Not among the dead, but among the living, Yeats sought an answer to the riddle of death. Old mortality had no interest for the poet; he sought out the newer mortality within a room, having heavy curtains on the windows, making himself a part of a circle of clasped hands; the lights extinguished, the hymn sung, and a diamond-tipped pencil scratching out words upon a window-pane. But all he could gather from his quivering search as an answer was the echo of his own thoughts.

Sean's own sturdy lad was gallivanting about among the graves. He and his companions were making fun of death; playing tag around him; hide-and-seek between his legs; tiring him with their tireless movements, their present laughter, and their noisy cries. Death is helpless to prevent them; unable to force the sombreness of the scene before them. Life is too busy, too gay, to be bothering about bones hidden beneath the soil. *Weep, for ye are but mortal,* Death tries to say, but he stands there mute. He is silenced by life. He is disregarded, pushed about, dishonoured in his own domain. He is as powerless as his own dead battalions. The little bugles blow the call of life, the little drums beat the march of life, and Death has to stand still and listen.

Yet for a little while longer, till sense and regard for life come creeping into the mind of the common man, Death, getting savage and resentful, may choke a little child with croup here; sling another under a swiftly moving car there; or thrust another little one, astray from her place of safety, under the slimy waters of a city canal; but young life in street, park, and playground laugh and mock him into quietness again. So there they go dodging in and out among the dead, their tombstones thrusting themselves despairingly up to insinuate their importance to the notice of the passer-by, an identity and presence that have long since ceased to be. No name of a chimney-sweeper on any tomb: all seemed to have lived and died in good circumstances: golden lads and lasses all. Vanity of death, for even the name-remembering stones are crumbling too. The dead disappear from view; they fade from the memory of them who knew them; from the memory of them who loved them; and when these die too, the dead, who went from life before them, go from life altogether.

What does the hurrying sun think of Yeats's eight and twenty phases of the moon, the great Yeats, with some majesty even in his medley? What do the dead here and the living beyond think of Yeats's grouping and groping of life through various incarnations? The poet, so restive against discipline concerning his own art and thinking, would bring the whole universe within a discipline of his own. He points a finger at the dead and shouts Come forth! But not a mouse stirs. The laughing secular sun, the superstition-breeding moon, the evening star, the bright and early morning star, and all the graces and the airs within the universe, declare the monstrous insignificance of the dead.

What did this old church here think of them? The old church of either St. John who baptised towards repentance in the river Jordan, or St. John who saw in Patmos a rabble of sights surmounting all that Yeats himself saw in the room of the Golden Dawn. The church probably never thought at all; it was beyond thinking, and it looked to be ageing. It was trying to stand up and look important, but there was an air of deep decline about it. Time and thought had made it shabby. What did it stand for; what was it for; what did it do? It seemed to be a sentry guarding the dead, but looked like a sentry asleep at his post. Custom kept it standing; custom kept its door open. It looked lonely, and seemed to be aware of its loneliness. Am I nothing to all ye who pass by? Not much.

The day is long gone when what you wearily symbolise now was the power of the city, of the whole land, of the whole known world: faith unquestioned and power unchallenged were yours. When the monks were masters. Monastery, nunnery, church, college, chantry, and chapel watched over the land, and rooked it of all it had. The Pope was Lord Mayor of every city and town in merrie England. To please the people the Grey Friars came over in rags, and, on Cornhill, built themselves homes of clay and wattles made. They were living as the followers of Christ should live, and the people were delighted; but not for long: they soon moved into a monastery in Newgate Street whose church was made of dressed stone, with a nave three hundred feet long and sixty-four feet high, the friars sitting down to tables of polished pine from which they took the best the land could give, adding wine of the better vintage from the lands where the good grapes grow; while Dick Whittington filled out a fine library for them of fine books, which a few of them read. Pile the weight of wealth and power and mighty buildings on top of the grave of Jesus, driving him deeper down. All gone now, and young lads of the Blue Coat School used to run and step and leap over where the Grey Friars sleep as do the golden lads and girls in this very churchyard of St. John's Wood.

England was made merrier with Austin Friars, Black Friars, Canons Minor and Canons Regular, so that a buzzing swarm of busy bedesmen turned the land into a realm of litanies and lice. And the bells tuned them into time and authority. The bells bullied the people about from the cradle to the grave. They belled the baby into the world and belled the dying man out of it; they belled the bride to her bed; they belled the workers to field and workshop, and belled the time for him to straighten his back and give over for the day, charging fees most of the time, according to the bigness of the bell and the time he took in tolling.

This old church in St. John's Wood, this spare relic of a powerful, busy past—how lonely it looked, and how shamefacedly it seemed to be aware of its unlamented loneliness. Ichabod. Am I nothing to all ye who pass by? Not much now. The Christians who have more than they need, with those who depend on them, gathering crumbs, have crucified Christ afresh, and have buried him down with the dead men. You do not mean much to us now. We are busy with other things. You have no bearing on our thoughts today. You rarely had, except to frighten us with myth and legend. A meagre myth by now. We know the herald angels didn't sing, and we are not sure that Christ was born in Bethlehem. Some say he was. They say: What is there for the man of today? Let us go even unto the little town of Bethlehem. Who goes there? And what shall we find when we get there, and how many want to go? Bethlehem is little more than a little toy for Christmas now; brought into play for a little hour, and put away again. Butlin's holiday camp is the popular rendezvous now. Yeats would sail the seas to come to the holy city of Byzantium. His holy city. Flecker would go the golden road to Samarkand. His holy city. Eileen's is New York. And what was Sean's? Moscow. Not a holy city, but an able one, a flame to light the way of all men towards the people's ownership of the world; where revolution stands in man's holy fire, as in the rich mosaic of a red wall. But he would not soon forget the lot he owed to London, or the warmth and good-fellowship of New York.

Well, for the moment, he'd have to bid goodbye to the vision of Yeats rushing round Ireland's market-place; his quick mounting of the political pulpit and the quicker dismounting of it; his divining the accurate way in which the Abbey Theatre ought to go; and his sudden rushes away from all to put an eye and an ear to the keyhole of the ivory door of death, to try to catch a glimpse and hear an odd sound of what was going on behind it. He'd have to leave his spiders, some of which he nearly knew by name, his charming little garden, and the pleasant district of St. John's Wood for some place they couldn't think of yet; not Rapallo or Capri or the Riviera; just some place out of London that might soften the worry of what they were going to do to make both ends meet. All the gallant recreation they had cadged from what they had had, were a few weeks' stay in a boarding-house at Margate.

Came a friend of theirs, whose daughter and her husband had held a cottage in Buckingham, and who had now abandoned it, to tell Eileen and Sean that they could have this wee house for as long as they liked to live in it. Another grand myth, lifting up his heart for a day, then sending it down deeper than ever for a year.

* * *

BLACK OXEN PASSING BY

✤ ✤ ✤

After the threat of an action for breach of copyright, which was never carried out, Yeats fell silent. He returned to the attack no more; no longer stood on the defensive. Perhaps the comments made by Mrs. Shaw when they lunched together persuaded the silence; maybe it was the letter written by Bernard Shaw to Lady Gregory, criticising the conduct of the Abbey, shamed him into it; or a decision to ignore Casey as a contemptible item in his life. Perhaps, like Aeschylus who delighted to begin a play with an awful silence, Yeats liked to end a discussion with another awful silence. Whatever the reason, the poet decided to stay in his room with the blinds down. To Sean it seemed that the great man was determined to be interested in, to listen to, to dispute with, those only who were content to be so many coloured buttons on the poet's dinner-jacket.

Up went the London curtain on *The Silver Tassie*, and, in spite of the fact that Laughton was badly miscast, and had a bad cold, that a few others were as bad as he, in spite of a few mishaps, the play was a hit; not at all in the conventional sense, but in a moral and a complex sense: using a Joxerian expression, the play gave the patient, wondering public a terrible belt in the kisser. It caused many of the critical minds to turn their usually serene and complacent comments into a shout; for comments were so many, so angry, and so conflicting, that only a bawl of an opinion could be heard through the din; an opinion, though heard, was not listened to, for each who saw it, wanted to yell out his own. They didn't want such a play; they didn't wish for it. They wanted war with the flame died down in it, and the screaming silent. This thing was so different from the false effrontery of Sherriff's *Journey's End,* which made of war a pleasant thing to see and feel; a strife put spiritually at a great distance; a demure echo, told under candlelight, at a gentle fireside, of a fight informal; a discreet accompaniment to a strident song, done on a lute, played low; the stench of blood hid in a mist of soft-sprayed perfume; the yells of agony modulated down to a sweet pianissimo of pain; surly death, or death exultant, fashioned into a smiling courtier, bringing himself in with a bow; a balmy breath of blood and guts; all the mighty, bloodied vulgarity of war foreshortened into a petty, pleasing picture. Here is shown, according to the famous G. J. Nathan, "a ladies' war. A second view of *Journey's End,* widely acclaimed as a masterpiece, emphasises my original conviction that there is a humorously falsetto note to the exhibit, and that the late war, as the author sees it, apparently needed only a butler to convert it into a polite drawing-room comedy."

But this play of Sean's was a very different thing. It tried to go into the heart of war, and, to many people whom it blasted with dismay, it succeeded. The curtain fell on the last scene amid a chorus of boos. The critics were confused, one saying this, and another saying that about the play, failing to analyse it faithfully or well, which was no wonder; for, if the author had been asked to analyse it himself, he would have failed as badly. One kind and effective thing the critics did for him: Almost unanimously, their criticisms implicitly declared that the play, with all its faults, was a work well worth producing by the Abbey Theatre; and that the play, far from taking away its high fame, would have added another spot of honour to the Theatre's reputation. And Sean knew that their comments had, unintentionally, delivered him from the thickest of the dangers that had come upon him through the contemptuous rejection of the play by the Abbey Directorate. He had but to wait a few years longer.

Sean O'Faolain ran home to tell Da Russell that "it was to be feared that before he had exhausted the possibilities of the technique he knew, O'Casey turned to technique that proved beyond his powers. Showed in other words that this play is not good theatre as we understand the term in these islands. O'Casey and the producer found the result of this experiment in a new technique a little beyond the capacities of the modern stage. The second act suggests that Mr. O'Casey finds the conventions of the modern stage insufficient for his purpose; though, as I suggest, he has written far too little to say so with any authority. The producer was clearly at a loss. The second act he must have found easy game; that sort of stuff has been done more than once before. Augustus John designed the scene, the chanting was handed over to a special man, and, anyway, there wasn't enough sensible core to the rigmarole for anything much to be obviously wrong. It was clear that neither money nor trouble was spared to fashion Mr. O'Casey's noveletta into a stage play. O'Casey must not be angry with us because we do not flatter him, as his easy English critics do. His talents are undeniable, but, so far, as all agree, they have not produced a play without the stamp of the workshop on it, and this one as much as any." The Wild Irish boy soothing O'Casey's last moments.

In the quiet domestic turmoil of living from week to week, Sean got a letter from Lady Gregory saying she was in London, and would like to come to see him, his wife, and their baby. He was greatly troubled, and wished that Lady Gregory had forgotten him. He would not let her come. He would say hard things about Yeats and Robinson that would hurt her. His wife begged him to let Lady Gregory come, for she was eager to get to know the woman of whom he had so often spoken affectionately and well. No; he would not let her come. Eileen begged him again to change his mind, saying his refusal to see her would hurt Lady Gregory more than anything he might say. But, no; he would not let her come. So Lady Gregory went back to Ireland without a word with him; without a last affectionate handshake, for he never laid eyes on her again. This refusal was one of his silly sins. He still thinks angrily of himself when he thinks of her, or hears the name of the gracious, gallant woman. He should have listened to Eileen.

SHIP IN FULL SAIL

Bound for New York, for the Manhattan of Whitman! A huge ship, unwieldy-looking, seeming too massive to move, rising up from the Mersey like a futuristic town, with her short masts—really derricks—her big-bellied funnels, wider than many of the English roads to take buses and lorries along, her sides peppered with portholes; the whole aspect of her shouted to all who looked that she had a mighty confidence in herself, her broad sides and sturdy bow asking what wave on God's ocean could topple her over. Like the world at large, she was divided into classes—steerage, tourist-class, and cabin-passengers. The last—which shall be first—had two decks to themselves on which to promenade and play; the tourist-class had more than half of a deck below, and the steerage had the bit that remained. Yet the steerage travellers numbered a huddled hundred to each of the others' ten; so, even here, passengers were divided into the nice sheep, rougher sheep, and the goats. The white-coated stewards, dashing about with the smoothing-iron, were running up and down the gangways, silent, in rubber-soled feet, settling the passengers into their cabins, thinking out the tips they'd get at the journey's end. Sean had been warned that the chief steward must get two guineas, his own steward a pound, the waiter at his table another one, with other tips, suiting the amount of work done, to him who provided a deck-chair, to him who handed out books from the library, to the barman who served the drinks, and to the quarter-master supervising the deck-sports. It seemed to Sean that he should have taken the fifteen pounds and left the five with Eileen. No deck-chair, no book, no drink for him; nothing beyond the bare necessaries bringing him safe to New York City. He must have been the poorest cabin-passenger that had ever set foot on a

White Star liner. A record established, never to be broken. He was amazed at the quantity of luggage brought aboard by the passengers; some had a ton of it. The men dressed differently six times in a day, and the women seven times, or more. A friendly steward showed him a cabin of a couple when they were rushing around in shorts on the sports-deck, playing deck-tennis: clothes were flung about everywhere, across chairs, on the floor, over the beds; good clothes, too, much of them costly, flung about like litter left behind on a camping-field. Enough of it to clothe a slum family for years. These self-busy ones never asked a single question about the stuff in the steerage; never once thought of them. Occasionally, a few cabin-passengers stared down at the deck where the tourist-class paraded the limited space provided, but none gave the tribute of a look to where the steerage mammals prowled about their closely caged-in quarters: they were but part of the cargo.

The stewards slipped along the corridors in their snow-white jackets and black trousers, half ghosts, half men, hiding themselves under the passengers' orders, rarely giving themselves a glimpse of the sea, inhaling the testy smell of the cabins from port to port, answering all questions, asking none, linked to the bodies of the passengers but not to their souls; their whole life upon the ship the waiting upon a wish. Once only had Sean caught a steward looking over the ship's side at the swell of a subsiding gale, and heard him say, with a shudder, Deep troughs, sir; must be thirty feet down; seem to want to coax a man down to them; and shuddering again, slid through a doorway back into the ship to be safe with the will of the passengers. The friendly steward brought Sean stealthily down to their quarters, down very low in the ship's belly, where the top of the ocean was but a foot or two below the lower rim of the port-hole, so that, even in a light swell, the port-hole had to be closed, or the sea would come pouring in on top of them; almost airless, too, with tiers of bunks leaving but a head's space in which to preen themselves into the natty, white-coated figures one saw gliding around the ship.

The liner made a curving cut up Cork Harbour, going slow, for there were shallow banks on either side that might ground the big ship. Sean looked about for Spike Island where John Mitchel had been as a treason-felony prisoner on his way to the convict settlement of Bermuda, and where he had met the gentle, scholarly Edward Walsh who taught the convicts. Walsh was a harper and a Gaelic scholar wasting his sensitive life away teaching the convicts how to add two and two together, his golden hair grey, his beloved harp dusty, his heart hanging hazily on to life, working that he might have bread and water with a taste of meat on Sunday. Out came the tender carrying another crowd away from the western holy land to The New Island as the United States was called by the Gaelic speakers.

They streamed into the ship, and but two, who were priests, came to the cabin-class passengers; the rest were lost, a few to the tourist-class and a crowd to the steerage. Away round the cliffs of Kerry to Galway for another crowd, a "great port" which the people had made with their own hands out of their pipe dreams. It was dark night now, and the tender came with a green light and red light sparkling on port and starboard. Again the gangway fell; Galway passengers came aboard, three priests, a bishop, and a solicitor to join the cabin-passengers, a few others joining the tourists, and the crowd again pouring into the steerage. All the descendants of the clans were streaming like silent sheep into the steerage of the White Star liner.

> Goodbye, acushla, goodbye, me darlin',
> I can no longer stay.
> The good ship she is waitin',
>   Grief must be abatin';
> Goodbye, me darlin',
> I'm off for Amerikay!

American soil is rich with the dust of the descendants of Irish king, chief, tanist, poet, bard, and artificer. Many and many a son of Conn, and many a blue eye of Clan Colman lie deep in the earth of New York, of Indiana, Butte of Montana, and Texas in the deeper south; forgotten. And more go freely. Let the singers who stay chant how they may about the lure of Ireland, the brown of the bog, purple of heather, blue of lake, red of fuchsia, white of lily, the gold of the whins; the goers will go timidly or go galloping to where they think the corn to be nearer to the groping hand. The few among the tourist-class, the fewer among the cabin-passengers, may return; but the ones in the steerage have muttered a kiss-me-arse goodbye to Banba of the Streams.

Flying from history, too; from fine history lapping Ireland round in greatness, with many a remembrance giving glory even to that which has none; glory not needed with Burren of the kings, Tir Fhiachrach Aidhne; Gaura in Meath, where Oscar fell and the Fianna were broken; the cromlech covering Aideen's grave, Oscar's sweetheart, on the head of Howth; Tara and Emain Macha, and Cong where Ireland's last king lies stretched;

> Peace and holy gloom possess him,
> Last of Gaelic monarchs of the Gael,
> Slumbering by the young, eternal
> River-voices of the western vale.

And what is Rury O'Connor, dead these many hundred years, to those hurrying into the steerage, or to the better places of the ship; what is he to them, or they to him? Nothing.

Clear as air, the western waters
Evermore their sweet, unchanging song
Murmur in their stony channels
Round O'Connor's sepulchre in Cong.

Galway itself, while stout William of Orange, helped by his stouter officers, was shoving Ireland into England's bag, sheltered the Irish Tirconnell and the French Lauzun who had fled from Limerick, laughing at Sarsfield when he said he would hold the town; Lauzun telling him the town walls could be battered down with roasted apples. There, shrunken into saviours of themselves, glittering in their rich uniforms, they paddled in the sea when the sun shone, and played bagatelle when the rain fell; while Sarsfield fought with the men, the women, and the children of Limerick; fought so heartily that William was thrust back, who, disillusioned, packed his troubles in his new kit-bag, and returned to England, leaving General Ginkel to carry on, which he did, right worthily, by packing up too, and getting as far away as he could from Limerick, while Lauzun and Tirconnell paddled away in the sea round Galway. So, signs of Irish regard for Sarsfield's gallantry, Patrick became a common name for the boys born in Ireland from that day forth. But Churchill, later Marlborough, greatest grandfather of the present one, battered down the walls of Cork, and took the city, forcing the Irish to abandon the fight for the Stuart King, who left them to recover from the war in the worst way they could. Christ, Ireland has had a rough time with God and Man!

The big ship swung round, and set her course for Boston, in a calm sea, with the Aran Islands fading away into dark dots, then vanishing from ken, leaving the men of Aran behind among their tiny homes, their patient cattle, their pitiful potato patches made from handfuls of earth pilfered from grasping crevices in the brine-soaked rocks and from kelp gathered dripping from the sea, and carried home on their backs to fertilise futility—a suitable life of austerity for the workers in the heaven-loved Aran of the saints.

The passengers settled down, some to play shuffleboard, some deck-tennis, others parading round the promenade deck and around, at a great pace, while the crowd stretched themselves stiff on to deck-couches, covering themselves with thick rugs, so that the ship seemed to be on the way to Lourdes:

There they lay all the day
On the broad Atlantic low;

Long they pray—keep thy sway
Gentle, mighty ocean O!

On the first evening of the voyage, the Chief Steward had asked Sean if he would like to have his meals at a table presided over by an officer, or would he prefer a place less conspicuous, and Sean had bewildered the Steward by asking him if he could have them with the crew. Less than a hundred miles from the Irish coast, the sky darkened and the wind blew, setting the ship to a jauntier motion on the sea's surface. Sean noticed the crew taking things from the main deck, tarpauling the hatches, and fastening loose things firmly. There was a scurrying among the ones reclining, who flung their rugs away, and hurried off to their cabins, and the hardier promenaders walked the deck no more. Sean found that but he, a priest, and a ship's officer remained on deck watching the rise of the sea and listening to the gathering howl of the wind. The deck he stood on was forty feet above the sea, and was surrounded by thick glass so that the wind gave no feeling of its strength, the breaking sea not strong enough to smash the glass, so he could face it all, and enjoy it all, with acclamation at the wonder of its fierceness. As far as the eye could reach, wave after wave, in close battalions, came rushing towards the ship, the waves following those about to strike her pushing the ones in front, as if in a desperate hurry to strike the ship themselves. The cleaving prow of the huge vessel cut through the surge of the piled-up mass of agitated waters, which, after a ponderous pause, roared over the deck, everything on it disappearing under the swell of the green and white tumble of waters, so that Sean seemed to be standing in a glass-house tossed about in a surging greenery of waves, the tops of them shattering asunder to slash viciously against the thick glass through which Sean looked, often now but a screen of streaming water between him and the tumult outside. Then as the stream rushed its hasty way down the glass, and vision came again, he saw the deck below buried under a passionate surge of wave for a few moments, till the ship rose out of the trough, and the waters poured away through the scuppers down to the leaping sea again.

Hour after hour, Sean watched the waves and listened to the wind, feeling a thrill whenever a mountainous wave rose up level with the upper deck, poised itself for a moment, and then fell, like fronds of a horrifying fern, in a downfall on the main-deck, hiding everything below from all watching eyes under a tumbling millrace of wriggling, rushing greenwide waters.

What crowds of glimmering ghosts floated aimlessly about underneath all these waters, from the years of the famine to years of the first World War! How many of the Irish fleeing the famine in the coffin-ships, fell into their keen, cold, undulating grip, and found their never-ending silence there!

Swing him over the gunnel—one, two, three, while some storm-a-long tried to mutter a prayer he couldn't remember. Now! And down went McGinty to the bottom of the sea. Many an old man, old woman, chattering child; many a lusty youth, handsome maiden went down engulfed in the proud, pouring toss of the billows. Billows? Somewhere in a letter, the fine poet, W. B. Yeats, rebukes a poet for calling a wave a billow, adding the news that another fine poet, T. S. Eliot, wouldn't permit the word billow to enter *The Criterion* for fear of smearing its odorous and austere integrity. But these seething masses of waters, rearing up, with menace in their aspect, before they came tumbling down on the quivering ship, were more than mere waves. These bulging breasts of sea, gigantic and fierce, as the eye searched into their smothering depths, made the nerves thrill and the body shudder, for in them was no rest, even for the tossed-down dead. Each oncoming mass had in itself its own half-hidden tempest. It was within these sly, green billows that many a soul went tumbling, scrambling down through the fierce ebb and flow and sway of the deep green sea. Many a lass whose name was Mary; many a blue-eyed Irish boy; many a Nora creena, many a larboard watch ahoy. Many a frantic lad saw, for the last time, his true-love's gasping, last farewell: Adieu! she cried, and waved her lily hand. Sean could see sweet faces, fair forms lunging round, helpless in the swelling sway of the tumbling sea: Propertius's Cynthia; Yeats's Dectora, sadly mingling with the common ones outside the longing, lasting memory of verse.

> I'm coming, quite fast, on a ship sailing south,
> To print all my love with a kiss on your mouth,
> She murmur'd; I heard her, and waited in glee;
> But the ship and my true love sank in the green sea.
>
> She lies fathoms down, lapp'd in mother-o'-pearl,
> Lies quiet that once was my high-hearted girl;
> And over her all the wide, green billows roll
> Chanting a green keen for her sea-shrouded soul.

Sean noticed a heavy iron door, grimly bolted and locked, in one of the lobbies. A door leading to the steerage through which cabin-passengers weren't allowed to pass, though Sean saw none making an effort to try. He did; a steward left it open for him, and down he went, like another Dante touring Inferno, with the circles growing hotter as he descended. Down to the steerage. The corridors were crowded, the little lounge was packed. The throb of the engines here was palpable, pant pant pant, and the place quivered with their movements. No privacy here, no room to stretch away a bit of boredom. Here was Galway, Mayo, Roscommon, Cork, and Tipperary, standing, squatting in the stairs, crouching on the floors, wedged together, while Sean, crouched on the floor, too, talked to some of them. Sean surmised the many miseries that must have fruited here while the storm was on; and no priest from the cabin-passengers came here to share the discomforts of this part of their flock. No; comfort was the priests' guardian angel, poker their amusement. Squeeze people closer, cram them together, make a herd of them, so that neither soul nor body has room, and then bellow about the sacred rights of the individual!

Along the coast of Newfoundland through a thick fog the ship crawled, with Sean on the deck all night, listening to a sailor calling out the soundings, while an officer took them down in a log-book, the siren shrilling shudders through Sean at regular intervals. The passengers, paralysed by the storm, slept peacefully through the dangers of the fog, unafraid of a greater danger. Sean, chilled to the bone, remained throughout the night ready to leap for his life-belt if any crash came; for he could see the officer was anxious, even telling him that a captain sleeps neither long nor well when there's a fog round his ship. Slow, slow, through the fog, the ship crawled, breaking out at last into a dreamy sky of slowly-drifting clouds, and the steady set was dotted with boats, some puffing steam from them, others spreading a wide sail. The passengers came pouring out from the saloon, hurrying over to the gunnels to peer away into the misty distance.

—There she is, said a puffed-out man, staring through a pair of binoculars; there she is, at last, stout and taut as ever.

—What is it? ventured Sean; what do you see?

—Statue of Liberty, said the puffed-out man.

America's Lady of the Lamp. He couldn't see her, but he knew the golden words she nourished on her lap:

> *Give me your tired, your poor,*
> *Your huddled masses yearning to breathe free*
> *The wretched refuse of your teeming shore.*
> *Send these, the homeless, tempest-tossed to me:*
> *I lift my lamp beside the golden door.*

Little sparkle in the words now; well worn and nearly rubbed away; the refugees musta worn their welcome out. America now had huddled masses and homeless of her own, and there were a lot more than a hundred most deserving cases of poverty in the United States; thousands of very poor, unhappy souls. The words on Miss Liberty's apron had lost their meaning. But wait a minute, think a little, boy. Wasn't he, in a lot of ways, a refugee himself, coming to the United States out of necessity rather than out of love? He was already half-homeless, and would be homeless altogether, if he didn't succeed in getting American dollars to carry home with him.

There was no denying of it. Like a budding hero, he carried a drama with him as a banner, hoping to astonish the Americans with a work of art; but down in his heart he knew he was here to collect funds. He was a refugee, for Ireland had cast him forth, England couldn't afford to keep him, so he depended on America now to provide him with a sufficiency to keep him and his family for another year or two. An unpleasant fact, but a solid, sober one.

Sweet Miss Liberty, Belle of New York, and Man of Manhattan, hear my prayer, and let my cry come unto ye!

A new land, honoured nowhere with a Greek temple or a Roman road; no medieval monastery showing itself off as a tasty heap of ruins; no Norman castle to let us fancy seeing bowmen from the walls shooting arrows into the bowels of people living round it; no Ides of March, or anything else like them, to remember. Here, instead, were the cloisters of Emerson, the limitless habitat of Walt Whitman, the battlefields of Washington, and the rush and rendezvous of modern mechanics; all the lure of freshness and of power. They were enough, and had in them many miracles for the future.

He would meet new people, and see new things. He would see the Hudson River, Grant's tomb, Bunker Hill, maybe, and Brooklyn, the camp of the dead brigade; for the first time he would set a foot on foreign soil, though, for him no land was a foreign one, since all were peopled by the same human family. But it was like the squirrel meeting the mountain, and having words with him. Well, if a squirrel couldn't carry forests on his back, neither could the mountain crack a nut.

* * *

WITHIN THE GATES

❦ ❦ ❦

There is nothing in life so dusty and dismal as a curtainless, gaping stage yawning out at those sitting down in front of it, and to those treading about within the poverty of its boastful emptiness, during the harassing transports of a rehearsal. In one of these dark places within a first-class New York theatre, the rehearsal of *Within the Gates* went on under the guidance of Melvyn Douglas, a stalwart chap, handsome and able, and, after many struggles, began to show itself off from among the dusty shadows. These times are very harassing to all, but most so to a dramatist whose conscience ranges a little outside of himself and his own interest. He has to think (though he tries not to) of the actors who work so hard for weeks, and yet may walk about idle again, after performing for a few nights, even, maybe, for one night only; and of him who furnishes the money for the play's production, however wealthy the man may be; but especially if the producer be one who has just managed to scrape enough dollars together to lift the play to the stage. Grey hairs grow fast during the rehearsal of a play, brazen with imagination and experiment, on the commercial, or any other kind of stage. And the finer the production the greater the anxiety, for, in a bad production, the dramatist is almost assured from the start that the play will be a failure. So Lillian Gish, Moffat Johnston, and Bramwell Fletcher, with many others, were busy on the play's behalf; went on gaining ground over difficulties, till, at the dress rehearsal, it broke out into an unsteady but glowing cascade of speech, movement, colour, and song. Sean was glad; let it succeed, let it fail; at least the play would justify its full and defiant appearance.

During the whole period between emptiness and dusty posturing, in dull working-kit, to the breaking out of the play into colour and song, there was but one disturbing incident. One day, Moffat Johnston, who was playing the bishop, came to Sean, very worried, to say that the designer had arranged the crucifix he was to wear so that it would dangle, not upon his breast, but at the base of his belly. The amiable actor was very uncomfortable, and many others of the company were distressed, too. Sean assured him that the symbol was meant to hang on the bishop's chest, and there and nowhere else it would be worn. He went to the designer, Irish by descent, and, by all accounts, a roman catholic, and told him so. The designer angrily said he had so designed the symbol to hang between the legs, and there it was to hang, or he'd have nothing more to do with the production. Sean said the symbol would hang in the place where the script had placed it, but he was told that the design was more important than the play; Sean, responding to the angry face glaring at him, said, The play was the living body and soul and the clothes that covered them, while the designing added coloured buttons, braid on the sleeves, and, maybe, epaulettes on the shoulders; but however important and lovely these things might be, and often were, without the play they couldn't be summoned even into existence. The script says the symbol is to hang on the bishop's breast, and there it will lie till the play comes off; and, in a high rage, the designer ran from the theatre, and they saw him no more.

At intervals, or whenever he could sneak away from rehearsals, Sean sauntered the New York streets, trying, in a once-over, to get some idea of what New York was like. The great city is indeed an animated place; a glittering go-boy, with a grace and dignified strength that makes the go-boy grand. Many have said that the city is a place of confounding noise, and some have said that its clatter kept them from even one decent night's sleep during their stay in it. Sean slept there as serenely, more serenely, than he sleeps now among the quiet hills and valleys of Devon. The road to Plymouth running outside his house, with the sounds of its passing lorries, vans, private cars, varied three times a day by the more musical tumult of noisy children just let loose from school, makes more noise than any Sean heard, even adding the siren calls of the rushing police-cars, in the abiding places of New York city. Then, in summer, all the day, and on into the evening, ears are entangled in the ceaseless calls of the cuckoo cuckoo; and, later on, when the cuckoo has got tired, there's the bark of a dog here, there, and over yon, crow after crow from many a cock; and, in the night, the eerie squeal of the screech-owl out on the prowl for prey. Again, in the first freshness of morning, when all but the farmers sleep on, the chant of competitive birds shrills out as soon as the sun sends his first finger of light into the low sky; and sleep, except for the hardy, becomes a contest in a restive bed. A countryman soon gets used to a town; a townsman finds it harder to get used to the country.

The first natural thing Sean enjoyed in New York was the sparkling blue sky overhead, giving a clear and buoyant air in which to breathe alertly. The desecration came along some of the Avenues, from the sombre, crudely woven steel and timber of the Elevated Railway, running from one end of Manhattan to the other. The trolley-cars came swift behind it. Sean watched for well over an hour one night these strange-looking cars swinging around Fortieth Street, or one near by; watched them clanking along, clod-like on their iron rails, bringing home to his ears sounds common on the quayside of Dublin's docks. Long and low, solidly framed, doorway and body, dull-coloured, borne heavily along on cumbersome swivel and wheel. It might almost be that, out of this one, clumsily clanking around the corner, Walt Whitman would step down jauntily, lilting one of his many songs of Manhattan.

The New York Subway in harmony of structure, comfort of use, or brightness of aspect, limps a long way behind the London Underground, and a longer way behind its remarkable cousin in Moscow; and the pale, mauve lights, indicating a station, show all the apologetic timidity of a poor relation to the prouder and more opulent activities of the city. So, too, are the buses running along Fifth Avenue, looking like expanded perambulators carrying the family as well as the baby. It is the taxi which commands the streets of New York; fleets of them, like gay-plumaged swallow flocks, red, yellow, green, brown, white, and black, ground-bound birds skimming along the road's surface as if swiftness were all; a thrust-forward tension in each of them, even when they come to rest; a sway upward and forward as the lights suddenly call a halt to the swift going, an agitated purr of an engine delayed; and, as the shadow of green appears in the lights, a slim, sliding spring ahead, and the eager bird is on the swift wing again. It seemed to Sean that the American taxi, in its indolently slim form, is a daughter of the gondola transfigured into the muse of energy, while the English taxi, in its stiff, box-like stand, is the son of the sedan chair.

One day, he sped in one of these swift cars to a great synagogue, the Temple of Rodeph Sholem, if he remembered right, whose pastor was Rabbi Newman, a young man with a pretty wife, three children, and a passionate love for plays and literature. He had invited Sean to come to speak to his people when they had gathered together for a Sabbath Service in a building so long and wide that a microphone stood by the rails of what Sean thought to be the chancel. After the chanting of psalms, led by the Cantor (identical with Caintaire in Gaelic, signifying a singer or chanter), the Rabbi spoke a few words of introduction, and Sean, greatly harassed by shyness, found himself speaking to a great crowd of Jewish people. There was no conceit in his stand, for he would far rather have been down among them, speaking to this man, that woman, as time and strength allowed. Conceit is a mother of many evils. Oh, Jesus, Oh, Buddha, Oh, Krishna, let a core of humility be in every conceit of energy necessary to life or dear to the heart of man!

Sean spoke about the curious resemblances existing between the Jews and the Irish—apart from the wild legends of the Irish being the descendants of the lost Ten Tribes, or that the first to land on an uninhabited Ireland were a granddaughter of Noah, her husband, Fintan, who lived for five thousand years, and fifty companions, who came there to try to escape death from the flood. The Irish were always eager to make themselves out to be as old a race as the Jews. Maybe they are, too. But, apart from these, there are many points in which the two resemble each other. There is a likeness between the old Gaelic poetry, in rhythm, emotion, and manner, and the poetic literature of the Jews; the Irish country people like bright, even gaudy, colours (Sean had a gradh for them himself); the one power of the Irish was their wit and nimbleness of mind, like the Jews; and, like the Jews again, the Irish were a scattered race, and had suffered great persecutions in their time. Spenser, the Elizabethan poet, gives an appalling picture of Ireland in his day; and, later on, in 1846–47, famine swept millions into the grave and millions more to the kindlier shore of America. So Sean went on, probably the first Irishman who had publicly spoken in a synagogue.

When the service ended, Rabbi Newman told him there were many Irish men and Irish women there who wished to go by Sean, shaking his hand as they passed him; so for a long time Sean stood astonished, shaking hands with an Irish woman married a Jewish man, or an Irish man married to a Jewish woman. He heard the name of almost every county Ireland had, including Connemara and his own Dublin, so that by the time his hand began to ache, all Ireland had paraded before him. Greatly—perhaps foolishly—moved, Sean had to murmur in his heart that the world's best blessings would swarm round the Shield of David and the Harp of Eireann.

The play was presented to a large audience, went well, though reviews the following morning were sharply divided; some were hot in their praise, others cold and caustic. It was a beautiful production in every way, and any fault shown on the stage was in the play itself. No voice, clerical or lay, was raised against its mood or its manner, and after a number of weeks' run, a tour of the play was planned, beginning at Boston. While the play was on in New York, coming up to Christmas, Sean left New York for home to be with his wife who was soon to have the other child. Two children now for them, but the tour was almost bound to bring Sean enough to make one more year reliable. Hurrah! Silence for a while, then the news that the Bostonian clerics were out in force against the play, and that the Mayor had banned it. Sean was being tossed about once more in the old sturm of style. Oh, God, here it is again! Wesleyan and Jesuit had joined hands to down the play.

"While I was in Maine," said the Wesleyan bishop, Charles Wesley Burns, "my preachers in Boston held a meeting, and, when I got back, I was told they had voted to protest against the play because of what they had been told by Father Sullivan; and so I added my name to the protest." The coo of the Wesleyan pigeon was aligned with the croak of the Jesuit raven. Point counter Point. Keep the kingdom of heaven respectable, please. So a bishop of a big church, eminent in the great city of Boston, decided a question of art and morals, not on first-hand news, not even on second-hand news, but on third-hand evidence: he decided to protest because of what his preachers told him of what Father Sullivan had said. Father Sullivan, S.J., representing the Boston College of Roman Catholic Organisations and Head of the Legion of Decency, followed the bishop with, "any religious affiliations [curious phrase—religious affiliations] would protest against the sympathetic portrayal of immorality, and all right-minded citizens, too, would protest against these things described in the play, and even more so the setting forth of the utter futility of religion as an effective force in meeting the problems of the world." Sweet Jesus, will you listen to this! He thinks the futility of bishop or priest is equal to futility of religion. Do not the thoughts of this Jesuit themselves show how ineffective his part in religion is, anyhow, in meeting the problems of the world? Is it immoral for a young woman to desire motherhood? Or to want to earn a living without having to prostitute herself to her boss? Or even to go away with a young man who loves her, and who was the one who showed understanding and regard for charm and vivacity? Isn't the whole play a cry for courage, decency, and vitality in life? Is it any more an act of immorality for a man and a woman to come together without a permissive chit from a priest than to make golden corn a flaming martyr before the eyes of hungry people that profits may be kept steady and sincere? Bum priests blathering.

Sullivan was joined by a brother Jesuit, the Rev. Terence Connelly, S.J., the "noted dramatic critic." Worse and worse. Here he is starting—he's off: "The whole play is drenched with sex. The love song in the play is but a lyric of lust and a symbol of death. O'Casey has written on immoral subjects frequently in the past, but in art, as in life, the end does not justify the means. There are degenerates who delight in looking at raw human flesh, and in art there are those who demand life in the raw. But normal human beings swoon at the sight of human flesh exposed. They require the silken curtain of the skin to tone down the sight, and give the human flesh the normal colour that is the symbol of life. O'Casey has often written on immoral subjects. It appears first in the incident of the betrayal of Mary Boyle in *Juno and the Paycock*". Even Juno; even she! Never a word, never a public word about the well-known and very able roman catholic writer, Graham Greene's *Brighton Rock,* in which Brighton becomes a city of darkest night and darkest morn, too; in which everything and everyone seems to be on the road of evil. Talk of James Joyce! Joyce had humour, Greene has none; and in the darkest parts of Joyce there are always bright flashes of light; here the very light itself is rotten. Even the blessed sun "slid off the sea and like a cuttlefish shot into the sky with the stain of agonies and endurance". Here the roman catholic girl of sixteen and the boy of seventeen, respectively, are the most stupid and evil mortals a man's mind could imagine. One more quotation, and, if the clerics want to stick their noses deeper, let them get the book: "She was good, but he'd got her like you got God in the Eucharist—in the guts. God couldn't escape the evil mouth which chose to eat its own damnation".

Stand up there, now, Terence Connelly, stole and all on, if you want to wear it, till O'Casey has a word with you; a word he wanted to say when the row was on, but couldn't, because influences were used to prevent its printing. Isn't it amazing that such things should be said but a few years after a war had flung millions of men out of life and had so mangled millions more that they had just enough life left in them to hang on to it for a few years longer! Just as they did in the middle ages, so they do now, like this lord high admirable crichton of morals and art, going about to damn any who see and hear better than they; damning all as if they were bosses of the universe, cosmopolitans of the cosmos, dukes of divinity, and blights of the world, with the right to decide what man shall think, say, do, and imagine at all times, even to the time and the manner in which and by which any man or woman whatsoever shall proceed in slow motion to the hymeneal bed, or, in perversity, shall, on the other hand, fling themselves, as it were suddenly, with ravening speed, on to a couch without prim and purposeful preparation for the roister-doistering deed of love. It's funny, when one thinks of it, that a permissive chit from a cleric makes all the difference in the world, presenting those who get it with what Bernard Shaw said was "the maximum amount of temptation with the maximum amount of opportunity". Aw, let them blather! Neither life nor art cares in its creations a damn about them. Look at the God-laurelled ghosts in literature hovering about and laughing at these black-clad figures spitting on the musky petals of the rose—Tristan and Iseult, Abelard and Heloïse, Romeo and Juliet, Paolo and Francesa, Parnell and Kitty O'Shea, Jennifer and Dubedat. Let them rave: the musk of love will ever cling to the rose of life.

"The curtain of the skin has been put there by God to tone down the horrors beneath"—as another cleric said: By God, it hasn't! It has been said that the skin—far from being there to save man's feelings—is there to protect the delicate and vital tissues beneath it; not one, but two of them to make assurance double sure. Whoever created the human skin (or any other kind), or however it came to be evolved, it didn't come into existence to save man an emotional shock, but to save him from a physical one; to protect the amazing network of vein and artery and tissue beneath it, which the poet Osbert Sitwell so poetically (and so rationally, too) calls *The Scarlet Tree*.

And here's a frill to the stupid remarks of the learned Jesuit: "Normal people swoon at the sight of human flesh exposed". Wouldn't it indeed be a hapless thing when man was plunged into an accident on rail or road, in factory or in mine, or in the deliberate mangling of the battlefield, if normal fellow-beings, running to help and deliver, swooned down dead at the sight of flowing blood or human flesh exposed by the lacerating infliction of an accident, or the deliberately imposed injuries of the battlefield! Or, again, wouldn't it be frightening if a surgeon about to separate flesh from quivering flesh so as to take away some poisonous interference with healthy life, fell flat in a swoon when he caught sight of what he was doing! Salute to Florence Nightingale and all true nursing sisters who nurse men out of plague and fever, and bind up wounds with courage and with skill. Silliest idea of all is that of God plastering silken skin over a body to enable normal people to live in harmony away from the sight of all that throbs beneath it. A comical association of a theological aspect of the biological reason of protection. And, anyway, who are Fathers Sullivan and Connelly to denounce the body when God Himself found it good enoughsky? D'ye call dis religion? No, no. D'ye call dis religion? No, no. D'ye call dis religion? No, No-o! What is it, then? Dope? Is it any wonder Bernard Shaw wrote down that he had " never yet met an intelligent Jesuit"?

But the Wesleyan bishop and the Jesuit priests didn't quite get it all their own way. The students of Harvard stood by the play, as did those of Radcliffe, Wellesley, and Tufts Colleges. A letter to Sean from Richard C.

Boys of Lowell House E-42, Cambridge, Massachusetts, said: "We are in the midst of the furor created by the banning of your play in Boston by Mayor Mansfield. Realising the stupidity of such an action, we have circulated petitions to the prominent colleges of the Boston area, and the response has been great, and in two hours last night four hundred signatures were obtained in Harvard alone [Atta Boys!]. Part of the Petition runs, 'We protest that the action of Mayor Mansfield in banning *Within the Gates* on grounds of immorality and irreligion is not warranted . . . and we urge a reconsideration of the Mayor's decision. If religion today has not developed in its many adherents a moral and religious attitude capable of withstanding the "insidious attack" allegedly made in this play, it is a criticism, not of the play, but of the religion, which should be able to stand against the gates of hell. It would appear, furthermore, that the play does not attack the essence of religion, but only those external and ossified fripperies, which, in the play, as so often in life, are presented to the communicant as true religion'." (Atta Boys, again!) But the Jesuit janissaries had their way, and the play was banned. The lads and lassies from Harvard, Radcliffe, Wellesley, and Tufts Colleges came in special trains to see the play performed in New York City. Other places, frightened, followed Boston, banning the play, disrupting the plan of the tour so that it had to be abandoned, and so Sean's additional reliable year went vanishing into the stuff that dreams are made on. Abandoning the crackling fire around the figure tied to the stake, the clerics do things now in a more refined way. Cunning boys!

Apart from the Wesleyan bishop Burns, and Fathers Sullivan and Connelly, who are most honourable, very learned, and fit to stand, heads up, among first-rate men; let us look at the average and a half of the roman catholic clerics who walk the world, teach in the seminaries (as described by their own Dr. McDonald, for forty years Professor of Theology in Maynooth College, Eire), or sitting by their fireside in their presbyteries as parish priests or catholic curates; those who set themselves up as anointed authorities on what should be read in a book, or what should be seen and heard in the activity of the Theatre. Looka that chap walking along before us—just like ourselves. As a young fellow, he has gone (probably) to Maynooth where he has read "a bulk of books—à la tra la Cardinal McRory—listened to lectures, tried to crook himself away from the touch of any passing skirt; till, finally, he has said certain things in front of a bishop and the bishop has said certain things in front of him; then with many gestures, touches, and genuflections, he receives the authority to serve the sacraments to the faithful, which, even in the rigidity of his own limited community, doesn't give him the authority or the education to be an authority on the art of the Theatre. Thousands of these laddos swarm the world, having gone through a systemised ceremony, filled their minds with a smattering of

Latin (and in the matter of Latin, not only parish priests and their curates, but the starlit cardinals of Rome; for, as Dr. McDonald, so long Professor of Theology in Maynooth, tells us, when a petition or document in Latin goes to Rome, the first thing done is to translate it into decent Italian so as to make it easy for the Curia to read); and then scatter over the world, to settle down and inflict their infallible awethority on men concerning literature, art, drama, science, morals, height of bodice, length of skirt, politics, and God wot else; if there weren't spirits near enough and capable enough to keep them in their small corners. It's a big beneficium clergicorum they are after; and not only that, but curselorum, too, ay, and rato-lorum as well. They had them all once; but man's wiser now; and the venomous denunciation of *Within the Gates* brought no restoration nearer.

What splashed from the play over the Jesuits wasn't filth in any form, but hyssop, purifying hyssop, though the clerics didn't like the sting of its cleansing criticism. There is no more of venomous vice in the young woman of the play than there was in the young woman, Katerína Maslova, of Tolstoy's *Resurrection;* a book which, probably, the Jesuits never read, though a reading of it would do them more good than the reading of their Breviariums. But to a lot of clerics, as Tolstoy said, "What they consider sacred and important were their own devices for wielding power over their fellowmen". They tried to wield this power over Sean by making it more difficult for him to live; but dark difficulties have often proved to be brighter angels, and, in this instance, he doesn't grudge the throe, for their enmity towards the play has made them, not more, but less, and him it has made, not less, but more.

* * *

CHILDERNESS

(FROM "SUNSET AND EVENING STAR", 1954)

✣ ✣ ✣

Another child was on its way into the world. A world weird and wonderful.
Well, it wouldn't know what was being forged in front of it. Here was the
new life pushing a way out into smoke, into fire, into shouting; woven
within the walk of Ribbentrop among the roses of England and the lilies of
France; within the hearing of the cocksparrow chirrup of Chamberlain
charming away war, and the distant humming of waiting panzers, impatiently ready to make a rush at life. But new life is careless of what may
front it, and so a new life was pulsing its way out of a peaceful darkness
into a marring and menacing light. A difficult time for man and woman;
difficult in the way of doing the right thing by life and making both ends
meet. It is an expensive thing to bring a life from the womb into the world.
Was then; worse now. The middle-class now die and are born beyond their
means. Unto us a child is born, unto us a son is given, is an alarming
announcement today, giving to the tenor of the joy-bell the ugly minor note
of the knell.

Through the stir of middle-class emotion, and by a middle-class doctor's
advice, Eileen had booked a berth in a London wist-not nursing-home,
many miles from the Monument, the fee being twelve guineas a week, not
counting extras of course. Adding the doctor's fee of fifty guineas, Sean saw
in his mind the mighty sum of a hundred pounds demanded of him, with
other costs lurking in dark corners ready to come out when the bigger bill
was paid. The uncertainty of how the common claims of life are to be
managed is the laocoon with which man is forever struggling.

Sean had no respect whatever for London nursing-homes, nor for the
middle-class emotion that kept the contemptible things going. The knights
and dames of low degree had to have their tiny honours. Sean had visited
three of these places to see sick friends, and had been stabbed by amazement at their drabness and dirt; how unsuitable they were for the needs of
the sick. On entering, he had run his fingers along the ledge of the dado,
and had shown them covered with thick dirt to the friend that was with

him. The rooms were heavy with old air, and wore a weak look, as if they, too, were sick; and all he saw seemed to whisper cynically of uncleanliness and of clumsy, uncomely methods of management and care. He was to have his surmises habited by proof. Eileen entered, and became a patient. Sean went to see her settled there. As in the others, here in this nursing-home, the glamour was gloom. Rowland to the dark tower came: The hall rimmed with dust; no sign of surgical cleanliness or of that quiet alertness felt where doctors and nurses are. The Home was joined on to a crowd of similar buildings so that there was little air in the room, and whatever air crept in was immediately swallowed up by the dusty-thick curtains blotting the window, and the dustier and thicker carpet smothering the floor. Brown curtains, a browner carpet, brown dado, sovereign effects to hide the clinging dangerous dust. A grey-green bedspread covered the couch which was soon to see the birth of a new life. In a glumly-grey jug on a bedside table, a massive spike of crimson gladioluses flamed a challenge to the bum-pomp of all the room's pattern; a present from a friend, and no indication by the nursing-home of any desire to brighten and sanctify the room.

Various kinds of ailments were tethered to this place; there was a patient down with double pneumonia, a lady trying to wriggle out of mental dementia through having nothing to do and taking too much drink to pass away God's good time, a duodenal ulcer case, and another of appendicitis— not a merry or a wholesome throng to greet a new-born babe. Britannia, mother of jellabies, stretching out her generous hand to teach children of Africa, Asia, and the West Indies, shoves her own children behind her, and squanders the priming force of her people. The thought given to the mind and body of the English child is the thought, not of a cultured leadership, but one as low as that given by a rude council pow-wowing under a cowhide wigwam. Childless with all her children. The middle-class are to blame. Caught in the glare of their snobbery, they strain, not after knowledge, but after Eton; not after human development, but after a nameless name; suffering indignity and danger, rather than give up a few pieces of silver, a good address on their notepaper, and a badged blazer for a son or a daughter. Ad ardua sed disastra.

The two housemaids seemed to have the minds of backward ten-year-olds; they were untidily dressed, clumsy, and incoherent when asked a question; giggling rather than answering, mouths sloppily open; a grin without a gusto. Cheap labour out of some Institution, thought Sean. Besides the matron, whom Sean never saw, there were two nurses—one for day, one for the night; each, from what was said, eager to find another place. Won't find it easy, thought Sean, for they didn't soothe his idea of what efficiency and carefulness should be. Clearly the place was being run for profit; not clean or competent profit, but profit grimed with a corpulent greed. Eileen agreed with him, but hushed him whenever a protest in his

mind rushed forward to the tip of his tongue. Many a time he had sat at
Eileen's bedside, fuming at the way things were being done—the wobbling
walk of the housemaids, the dirty tray of slopped-over tea, the dirty window, the whole aspect of continual carelessness; fuming so plainly that
Eileen stretched out a hand to touch his arm, and whisper—quiet, Sean,
you will only make bad things worse with a temper. Then he would close
his eyes, sever the tension by a great effort, and sigh for the cowardice of his
human heart. Children brought to birth in a dust-bowl. The Little Johns
and Maid Marions whose people had enough to pay for decent attention,
were getting the worst in the world. No complaints. The middle-class
would stick anything to preserve the wan and wasteful manner of their
status, burying under it the best of their intelligence, energy, and sense.
They chloroform themselves with snobscent. The moment a boy shapes
himself into the world, while he is giving his first cry, his parents dwell in
Etonsville; if a girl and an anglican, then Roedean—Roedean, oh, girl! If a
roman catholic, then a posh school of the Sacred Heart or the Ursulines to
learn all she needeth to know of how and when to ape the gentility. Cease
to be human, learn to be swell. They shove aside even the sacred name of
hospital and hang out that of nursing-home, so that they may feel themselves of a loftier mien than the mass of men, even in sickness and in pain.
Sheltering a stranger, entertaining a guest—so hangs the holy name of hospital; and to the Christians all sick persons should be guests of Jesus. He is
on His way to visit a sick woman—no, a lady. What hospital? No hospital,
man; a nursing-home. Does Jesus, then, turn his nose, too, up at a hospital?
Oh, no, not exactly that; but the sick lady's a lady and thinks herself something of a nob snob, and must stretch herself higher than the ordinary
commonality of the country.

> *When I was a lady, a lady, a lady,*
> *When I was a lady, a lady was I.*

The sacrifice of children on the altars of Eton and Harrow to a will-o'-the-
wisp conception of grandeur is as superstitious as, and sillier and much
more subtly dangerous than, the sacrifices offered at Stonehenge to the
Sun.

Eileen and he went for walks in the afternoon to give her exercise, waiting, waiting for the event to happen; all along the streets nearby, fearful to
go too far lest the thing might come upon them in the twinkling of an eye.
Down and up a bit of Knightsbridge, glimpsing Hyde Park, but never venturing in; in and out by Lowndes Square, out on to Cadogan Square and
Cadogan Gardens, till they knew every number on every hall door. Round
and round the village, round and round the village, as they had done before. Down the opposite way for a change; slow march down Sloane Street

and around Sloane Square, and around again, bringing back to him memories of his first fast days in London, his memory helped by the desire to creep away from the fear that was with him now, walking with Eileen. She was silent, dwelling in her condition, and so helped him to slip away from the fear of a too sudden birth.

* * *

The two of them, Eileen and he, now were concerned most nearly with the strange energies of the body, and with the life a body was soon to bring forth to the world they knew. More children, with little thought for them, and less room. Round and round the two of them travelled, past the Court Theatre, where she had acted in a play of his, and where both of them had first seen Shaw's *Back to Methuselah;* fainting memories just now, for they had new events to record, bringing hope and not a little fear. Up and down again, past a school where, in a tiny closed-up yard, the children could but ape the action and spirit of play; down and up, Eileen's steps growing slower, an odd spasm of pain smiting her, sending them back at a quickened rate to the nursing home. Half-way there, Eileen would say with a laugh, False alarm, and round and round they would go again.

One day in the hall of the home, about to go out, he saw a look of disquiet on her face, and, answering an inquiry, she said she didn't feel too good; then suddenly bent down in a violent spasm of pain.

—I won't go out, she said; I feel it may come on me any minute now.

I will greatly multiply thy sorrow and thy conception; in sorrow thou shalt bring forth children; thy desire shall be unto thy husband, and he shall rule over thee. A fine Dadlantic Charter! The king put into the parlour, the queen put into the kitchen. Woman has brought forth children with pain, and her husband has ruled over her for twice a thousand years; but things are changing, and, and now only, the church is busy bouncing this bonnie law about. The pain, subjection, and sorrow have declined with the years, and will be entirely banished in some year to come. The agony and sweat were still with the woman, but not so dangerously now, though shouts were still needed to prevent a woman being forced to go through this furnace of pain and danger too often. There must be a good rest between one ordeal and another. He for one would oppose the celibate clerics who frightened woman into having a child year by year till she was battered into dumb agreement with her devitalised life and the ghastly problems of attending to a horde of children. One of the ghastliest pictures he ever saw was one in a roman catholic journal showing the Pope with a father and mother and their twenty children; and another of Cardinal Spellman, a grin on his face, standing before a kneeling Pole, surrounded by his wife and fifteen children, who had travelled to New York by air, though the journal said they were utterly penniless. It was said that the Cardinal had emptied his wallet of a wad of notes, and had given them all to the old Polish ram;

the journal adding that the Cardinal had entered New York without a penny. Left himself without a dime! Your need is greater than mine. And how! Now what sarcastic voice whispers that it wouldn't be long till the Cardinal's wallet would be as full as ever with the finest and fairest of dollar notes? Since then the Cardinal has given ten thousand pounds to Ireland's St. Vincent de Paul Society; Dublin's Archbishop has given a thousand; and Cardinal Griffin two thousand towards the rebuilding of Southwark Cathedral; three plates in the trim hands of three prelates, one carrying a thousand, the second, two thousand, and the third, ten thousand. Pie from the sky. God's Episcopate is doing very nicely, thank you. Gold and silver have I none—it's all in notes, crisp and fresh from the bankery. There's more, lads, where these came from. Do they work overtime?

Sean would like to see a celibate cleric stay with a pregnant woman day after day, hour after hour, during the last three months of her trial; to try to help her along, entertain her with chat, go for walks with her, bring change of thought through a game of cards: it would learn the cleric a little; teach him that birth wasn't just a thing to make a joke about from a pulpit. It's easy for them to rant to women about their duties to their husbands or to praise the big families. Some day the clerics will get their answer: like the woman coming out from a Mission to women, conducted by a friar of orders while boosting bigger catholic families, shouting at them to reproduce catholic life quicker and oftener; the flushed and angry woman coming out from it all with an angry ejaculation of—Jasus! I wish I knew as little about it as he does!

A houseful of children! No glory left in that boast now. We have begun to realise that children need not only life, but liberty too. For too long the children have been buried alive in church, in school, in the home. As Bernard Shaw has said, 'The most grotesque, wild, and costly absurdity in our social order is the strictly enforced reservation of large tracts of country as deer forests and breeding grounds for pheasants whilst there is so little provision of the kind made for children'. Sean knew himself of a discussion about a playing-field for the young in a country town lasting for twenty-five years; and, today, the field isn't yet ready for the newer young born into the locality. The child is surrounded with enemies who imprison it in a corner called a school, or a corner called a church; it is a great concession when it is let loose on the playing-field. One great blessing enjoyed by the kids of the poor is that they spend a great part of their lives on the streets; the parents have to let them, for there is no room in the house for them. They get many a blow, but a blow is nothing to the stealing of curiosity and conscience from the mind of the child: those, says Shaw, 'who devote themselves to the very mischievous and cruel sort of abortion which is called bringing up a child in the way it should go; perverting that precious and sacred thing the child's conscience into an instrument of our own convenience, and to use that wonderful and terrible power called Shame to grind our own axe'. How conceited we all are to wish our children to be like ourselves! She's very like her mother; he's the dead spit of his father! Put into the same kind of schools, made to read the same kind of books, pray the same way, think the same way, and make it a custom, instead of a religion, to honour the God of Abraham, Isaac, and Jacob. And such schools and such books! The books are getting better now, most of the schools getting worse. Hundreds and hundreds of them in Ireland and England, packed with children, though fit only as the dwelling-place of the rat, the cockroach, and the woodlouse. No; children, as Bernard Shaw says, 'should look up to their parents, not as an example, but as a warning'.

> *Childer, beware, childer, take care!*
> *They're eager to make*
> *You waddle through life like a duck, like a drake;*
> *To turn each new soul to a shivering fake,*
> *Forever too frail just to open its bake;*
> *Quack-quacking consent to men and to movements well out on*
> *the make.*

Bent down in a spasm of pain, Eileen stretched out a hand to touch Sean, and say, Don't get frightened. It will be all right; don't worry.

He hurried back into the hall to shout up the stairs, Nurse, nurse! The only nurse there came slowly down the stairs, an impatient look on her face as she asked, Well, what's wrong now?

—The woman's in her labour! said he, fearfully; bring the matron.

—The matron's out, and won't be back till night-time.

—Phone her, then; phone her, woman!

—She didn't leave word where she was going; I don't know where to phone. You are both too anxious. Try to be a little braver. It won't happen today, or tomorrow either. She took Eileen by the arm. Go off, now, for a nice walk with your husband; and saying so, she turned back, and went up the stairs again.

They stood hesitant in the gloomy hall, then began to cross it to go out; but she bent again in a greater spasm of pain than before.

—Go home, she said to him, go home. Go home—I'll manage all right; and she ran from the hall and made for the room, with its dull bed, duller curtains, and dullest of carpets; while he running up the stairs caught the retreating nurse harshly by the arm.

—Get the doctor, woman, he said, fiercely, if you can't get the matron; and go to her yourself till the careless and negligent bitch comes back!

A look of alarm flooded the nurse's face, and she rushed from him into the room of delivery. She was of little use, and Eileen had to bear the most of it alone; the frantic rush in the stripping of herself; the flinging of herself on the bed, the deep crescendo of ascending pain that seemed to be engendering death entering through a riving body, with ne'er a drop of chloroform to modify the biting torment of the struggle, and ne'er a voice near to say a word to cheer her on; for the air-tight box of bandages and drugs was away in a cupboard in the housetop, so that by the time it was hurried down and opened for use, by the time hot water and towels had been gathered, the courageous woman had delivered a boy herself. A young girl inexperienced, just beginning to realise and comprehend the seriousness of her own life and the lives budding from her; so sensitive that she shuddered at the thought of any child in pain; a lass who had had her first-born in her own home, a clever, sympathetic doctor beside her, a capable nurse at his right hand to help; now having her second one alone, surrounded by hasty confusion, with nothing ready, and with those who were, perhaps, competent to help, away in other places doing other things. Fortunately, she was vigorous and healthy, and had a curious quietness in serious circumstances and time of stress; so throughout all the pain that stormed over and through her, she kept her alert mind set on a determination to deliver the boy safely: a brave girl fought incompetence and carelessness to a standstill, and gave successful birth to a big and healthy boy.

Their one idea now was to get away from the nursing-home as soon as possible, for she had discovered that the babe, when taken from her after a feed, was often in the charge of a maid with a thickened mind, and that the child was set to sleep in the operating theatre, reeking with the smell of ether; added to the suspicion that the ether was helped by an opiate whenever the mite happened to be restless enough to disturb the nurses.

They fled from the curse-home on a cold, grey day in January, the strong tail of an east wind teasing their faces, tilting at the dust in the kennels, and chiding the scraps of paper thrown carelessly aside by passers-by; grey and cold, with a sky of a deeper and heavier grey hanging down overhead; no comfort without, but joy within that they were getting away from a place that was a menace to the health, and so to the life, of their child.

* * *

So, well within the borders of Battersea, Eileen and he went on with their life, now widening out into a family; receiving friends from Ireland, from Manhattan, Massachusetts, Pennsylvania, Minnesota, and California farther away, to say a few words, and to let the great Republic shake hands with the little one, standing unsteady yet on one foot only; old comrades from Dublin who had gone with him through the great Lock-Out of nineteen hundred and thirteen, grey now, and wrinkled, like himself, but eager to go over again the scenes of battles long ago, filling the room with their own husky laughter, mixing with the slender, silvery laughs of Eileen, when they told Dublin stories of man's ridiculous conceit, or woman's comic frailty. Souls so different from the jodhpurred souls of Battersea's middle-class, so different from the soul of Tay Pay O'Connor, M.P., yet no different from his own or Eileen's, and very little from the soul of Lady Gregory or soul of W. B. Yeats.

All mingled with the growth of their two sons, Breon and Niall, Eileen smiling and delightful with all comers against the background of a vanishing bank account; and, through all these friendly and human activities, the casting of bread upon the waters in the writing of a first biographical book—*I Knock at the Door*. Those who came, came, and in their going, went not, but left impressions clinging to the life of those to whom they came; came, and went not, the time T. S. Eliot was passing through his *Ash Wednesday* in prayer and meditation within the desert in the garden and the garden in the desert, in and out between the blue rocks, going in white and blue, colours of Mary's mantle and Mary's frock, hoping to hear and hear not, to care and care not, to be still among a thousand whispers from a yew tree; they came, and were distrained to waver between loss and gain, for this was God's disposal, saying, The land thou tillest shall be plundered with thistle and with thorn, and in the sweat of thy face shalt thou eat bread. Sweat-stained bread. Tommy Tucker must sing for his supper. The life God gave cannot be silent, cannot be still; it has too much to say, too much to do to live; and he who runs away to hide, deserts the life that God gave. God has decreed the whole earth to be a forced labour camp, and so we must work before we eat. He has not put wings to time, and so we can build from toil and time but a little corner in a little room for a little thought. To sit still and care not in desert or garden, is a vain thing, and may but ripen a soul into drying dust that cannot be spat out like withered apple seed. The blue isn't always bright, and the white must at times be blemished in the cares of life and the keeping of a household going; the slender hands grow rough in time with the washing and the work. In the voice of many speaking, in the whirl of the world's changing, the word is heard; and the whirl of the world's changing is the word, and the noise of men is the word growing louder. Among all who come and go, who is there fit to say that in men's anxiety, their bargaining, their lovemaking, their laughter, there is no sign of the blue of Mary's mantle, the white of Mary's frock, or the red-like crimson of Jesu's jacket?

Sweat-stained comrades of building-site, railway-line, and ship-lined dock, you did what you could to make on-coming life safer and sounder, in bitter strike and vengeful lock-out. Coarse you were, but never common. Yes, we have all done something to change the childermess to a Childermas of security, health, and a bonnie-looking life. You, Promethean Jim Larkin, with the voice born of the bugle and the drum, Barney Conway and Paddy Walsh of the docks, Paddy Mooney of the horses, Shawn Shelly of the workshop, O'Casey of the pick and shovel; you, W. B. Yeats of the lovely lyrics, Augusta Gregory of the little, the larger, laughing plays and the wisdom of guidance, Shaw of the drama and the prophecies, and Joyce of the sad heart and the divine comic mind, touselling and destroying our mean conceits and our meaner vanities. We all ate of the great sacrament of life together.

> *Yes, we had some bread and wine,*
> *We were the Rovers;*
> *Yes, we had some bread and wine,*
> *For we were the gallant Soldiers.*
>
> *What car'd we for the red-coat men?*
> *We were the Rovers;*
> *What car'd we for the blue-coat men?*
> *For we were the gallant Soldiers.*
> > *Nothing, comrades.*
> > > * * *

DEEP IN DEVON

✤ ✤ ✤

There is an immense amount of activity, of anxiety, of care, and of thought, in the bringing up of children. It is a harder job than that of any prime minister, of any archbishop, of any general on a horse, or any admiral on a quarterdeck. A mother is busy the livelong day and the deadlong night. She has been left alone too long at the wearing job, and now the man must join in with a sensible helping hand. In spite of all the scientific and mechanical equipment surrounding us, and the colleges and schools, we know next to nothing about the strangest equipment of all—the child, the greatest, the loveliest, and the most delicate equipment we have for the development of life's future. We know more about the child than we did even twenty-five years ago, yet there are still millions of ageing minds who think that the best way to fit a child for happiness and resolution in life is to stuff his delicate mind with a creed, Christian or Communist. For Christ's sake, let the child laugh, let the child play, let the child sing, let the child learn, let the child alone.

A deep talk about schools. Prospectuses fluttering in from various places, all very fine and large and damned expensive. Two boys to be educated now, and another child on the way. Eileen, asking all the questions and answering them herself, wanted a school where the boys would be welcomed as day-pupils, for G.B.S. had advised against boarding the children, saying that a mother's affectionate regard and care should remain breast to breast with children till they had reached an age that allowed them to go forward gay and strong without them. Eileen sought a school where a child's nature would be neither checked nor ridiculed by customs stale; one where no fantasia of pietistic chanting would deafen a child's mind away from its own thoughts; where a child would see trees, herbs, and animals living a natural life, and not as they appeared woven into a nursery-rug, or emblazoned on a nursery-plate or pie-dish.

—Dartington Hall is the place for your boys, said Shaw.

—It's going to cost a lot, murmured Sean, anxiously.

—No more than the others, said Shaw, shutting up Sean. Give the children the good things and the fine things, and, when they grow up, they'll refuse to do without them; and that is what we need, he added emphatically, the refusal to do without the finer things of life.

Eileen thought the world of Shaw, and loved his magnificent, laughing austerity; so it was decided that the two lads should go to Dartington Hall School. Another upheaval for Sean! A change from the city's busy life and colour for the wider and quieter ways of the green country. He feared the country, for it robbed him of much, his eyes there losing a lot of the little power they had. In a city the view was a short one, and his eyes hadn't to travel far to see things; all was at his elbow. The great sky was always a narrow strip, hugged by the city's skyline. In the country the way was wide open, and all around was a great carousel of sky, forcing him to keep his cap well down over his eyes so as to cut most of the sky away, and keep a workable focus in front of him. In a city, on a sunny day, one side of a street was usually shaded, so he could stride along in comfort; in the country, the sun spread everywhere, so he would have to march, head bent, and slowly. In a city, at night, the street-lamps and lighted shop windows were a wide lantern to his feet, so that he could go anywhere safely; but all through the winter, in the country, he would be blind at night, and every step he took from the house then would have to be arranged by some guiding hand. Night-time would take away his independence; and he hated any hand trying to guide him in the way he should go.

Down they went to Devon for the children's sake, carrying all their wealth of worldly goods with them, settling in the busy little town of Totnes, and, once more, going through the arduous orgy of fitting into a new home—a big, clumsy house, full of pretension only, the only one they could get; a one that even a miracle couldn't make comfortable. Totnes is set out so that its main street slinks slowly up a slender hill in the valley of the Dart, Devon's beautiful *Anna Livia Plurabelle*. Half-way up the hill of the main street stood the church, its spire rising over all, and higher up on a spur of the hill on the church's flank, stood the circular stone keep of a Saxon castle. The castle and the church—the two *sine qua nons* of the long ago. The guardians of God's Truth in the town are plentiful, for we have in this town the anglican church of the priory and St. Mary, the roman catholic one of St. George and St. Mary, the wesleyan church, the baptist church, the congregational church, the gospel hall, with sundry amateur evangelists, a couple of salvationists, and visits from jehovah's witnesses knocking at our doors to hand in tracts, sell books, and give a quick word or two about the surest way to get to God. A little way off, if we happen to stray, in a beautiful part of the Dart's flow, we knock up against the Benedictine monastery of Buckfastleigh, a simpering silhouette now of what was in the Middle Ages when the Abbey owned many fine fat smiles of the shire. It has its languishing pipe-dream that England again will be managed by monasteries and pickled in priorities. Help, help! Help to build up Fountains Abbey! Help to build up Prinknash Abbey! Names entered in the Golden Book of Remembrance for a guinea a time. Buy away, buy away, fond hearts and true, and open up heaven for England, their England. A guinea for God. Guineas are good for us. Send them twinkling in; invest in monahysterical consoles, Jerusalem the golden with milk and honey blest.

Here, in Devon, they were anchored on the real red earth, rich earth, and very fruitful. Here, maybe, Adam was made, for in a bible Sean had had when a kid, he remembered a marginal note telling the world that Adam meant red earth; so here, maybe, Adam was needed into life. Adam filled a vacuum. All he had to do was to keep his feet, and all would have been well, and all would have gone on living. God, what a grand world it would have been! The brontosaurus would have been a pet, and pterodactyls would have been flying in and out of our windows, chirruping just like robins! But the man had to fall down. The woman done it, sir—pushed me down; caught me off guard. Couldn't keep his feet for all our sakes; fell, and ruined the whole caboosh.

Here, now, in a house in Devon, he was looking over the page-proofs of his first biographical book; for, while writing plays and thinking about the Theatre, his mind had become flushed with the idea of setting down some of the things that had happened to himself; the thoughts that had darkened or lightened the roads along which he had travelled; the things that had woven his life into strange patterns; with the words of a song weaving a way through a ragged coat, or a shroud, maybe, that had missed him and covered another. His own beginning would be the first word, a little logos born into the world to speak, to sigh, laugh, dance, work, and sing his way about for a day, for tomorrow he would die. First weave in a sable tapestry would be the colourful form of her whose name was Susan, ragged dame of dames, so quietly, so desperately courageous. Life couldn't get rid of her till she died. She went on going forward to the end, ignoring every jar, every misfortune, looking ahead as if she saw a great hope in the distance. A dame of dames, a patient, laughing stoic. Always forward, with her gleaming black eyes, her set mouth, forever smitten with a smile; ragged and broken-booted, still looking forward as if she saw freedom and everlasting truth beside her. A dauntless feminine brennan on the moor of life. Thirteen children, and only five surviving. Next door to a Niobe. Apollo shooting: bring me my bow of burnished gold; and he shot eight of them. Whizz! Thinned out now; safe; go ahead. Eight little O'Caseys planted safe in God's acre. *Confiteor meum.* She never mentioned but three of them—Susan and the two Johns. Maybe she had forgotten the others. Maybe she thought there wouldn't have been room in the world for so many; or room in her own deep heart for so many. She had certainly fought death away from him. Here he was, deep in Devon, surrounded by his wife and two children (soon to be three), and the savage grace of a day that is dead cannot come back to him. Only in sleep might he dream it back; never again, except in sleep.

Here in his little garden, as the year branched into the month of August, two rows of runner-beans were gaily climbing up their tapering bean-poles —called string-beans in America, and scarlet runners in Ireland. The twining stems have topped the poles, and hundreds of vivid scarlet flowers hang pensively among their handsome greenery, like rubies resting from their fuller glow. They bring to his mind the scarlet runner, planted by his mother, that grew up around the framework of the tenement window. Somewhere, from someone, she had got a bean, had shown it to him, remarking on its odd colouring of blackish purple, mottled with pink blotches. She had coaxed him into getting enough fresh clay from an old dump-field to fill a small box, and had carefully sown the bean in its centre, gently tickling it into exhilaration with some rotting dung gathered by her from the street outside. She had watched the first leafing of the scarlet runner with delight, feeling sure that a bright jewel would one day hang from it. When she saw the twisting stem, she knew it was a climber, so she wove threads in and out along the window's side to help it up. Then came the crimson flower, just like the flower of a sweet-pea, and all red, and she rejoiced with a quiet joy, her hand touching it gently; and, at times, Sean saw her pouring over the clay the sup of milk she needed for her own tea, flushed with the idea that since the milk nourished her, it would nourish the plant as well; and it seemed she was right, for when the plant was in its prime, the scarlet runner was hanging out its gently-vivid, red flowers all round the side of the window's edge. In the later autumn, the flowers shrivelled and fell off, the leafage grew dry and wrinkled, and long pods dangled down where the crimson flowers before had fashioned their own beauty. Waiting till the pods seemed to be ripe, she took a number of beans from the pods, and sowed them in the cold clay; but no leaf appeared when the summer came again, nor did any thrust itself up from the clay in the summer of the following year, though she watched for it day by day, evening by evening for the sign of a rising leaf. Her fuchsia, her musk, her geranium, came up steadily year after year, never failing her; but the scarlet runner never came again. Neither he nor she had known that the pods could be eaten, had ever tasted one. Though they had been put before him at dinner while staying at Coole Park with Lady Gregory, he had never connected the succulent green strips with the scarlet runner that had draped with red and green glory the framework around the tenement's miserable window-frame; and it wasn't till they had grown some themselves while they lived in Buckinghamshire, and he saw the blossoms, that he realised he was looking at the red flower which had delighted his mother, that had withered away in the autumn, and had never come again.

Now he was handling *I Knock at the Door*, his first biographical book, which would give her life for an hour again; but some other book soon would shut away the story of her days. The lover of the scarlet runner would be gone forever; gone after her fuchsia, her musk, her geranium, and her scarlet flower. Fuchsias are still here, hedges of them; geraniums bloom again in countless gardens; musk grows in many places; and his own wee garden here, deep in Devon, is alight with the scarlet stitching of the runner-bean. But not hers. They are gone as she is gone. Thoughts in the memories of the living alone ruffle the dead into living again: the muffled drums of the dead beating a faint roll of remembrance; so faint that the memory ceases to hear it before it ends.

* * *

There is nothing sham about Totnes. Next to London, it is the oldest borough in England. All its 'shoppes' are genuine examples of Tudor or Jacobean housing; not in any way so splendid as those found in Conway or Shrewsbury, but as genuine all the same. Neither is there anything 'arty-crafty' about from the bottom to the top of its hill. The housewives who stand in the queues are far from 'gloomy'; they haven't time to be, for they are too busy with the things of life. And there are many Irish incidentals about Totnes: the caretaker of the Drill Hall was a Tipperary woman; the owner of a café was another, but now has one in Stoke Gabriel, a few short miles away; the plasterer who pasted up new ceilings in the O'Casey house, brought down by bomb concussion, came from Roscommon; the parish priest and the O'Casey family doctor are Dublinmen. The one postwoman Totnes had, during the war, came from Tipperary, too. A few miles away, in Brixham, a statue of King Billy stands on the quay, and like Dublin's old figure, has twice been given a contemptuous coat of football coloured paint. O'Casey is as relevant in Totnes as he would be in Navan or Kells, and more so than in Dublin now; and Johnston's article is pertly and partly proof of it.

Totnes is about the size of Mullingar, but busier, wealthier, and much more lively. Apart from the quiet hurry of market day, gentleness is the first quality to give to it; gentleness in its buildings, and in the coming and going of its people; and in the slow, winding, winding of the River Dart from the moor to the sea. Oh, Lord, the natural lie of it is lovely. Except when visitors pour in during the brief summer, the town is so quiet that it looks like a grey-haired lady, with a young face, sitting calm, hands in lap, unmindful of time, in an orchard of ageing trees, drowsy with the scent of ripened apples about to fall, but which never do; hearing echoes of her own voice in the laughing play of children; or in the whispers of that lover and his lass seeking out some corner of the drowsing orchard that is free from any entanglement of time, care, thought, or casual interference.

Though getting some ready money from summer visitors, the town, like so many Irish ones, depends mainly on the farming communities surrounding it. So the eyes of all often scan the sky—not to see the reality of the sensuous enjoyment of its beauty shown by a Constable, a Ruisdael, or a Turner; but to judge the coming weather, for their livelihood depends on it. In a rainy season, they look for a sign of the sun; in times of undue heat, to catch sight of a hidden cloud. Cattle, sheep, poultry, and crops depend largely on what the sky gives; so, when the sun wears his welcome out, or the rain falls too fulsomely on the land, all eyes search the sky for the chance of a coming change.

An old town stretching out from Lugh of the Long Hand to Winston Churchill and Clement Attlee, a coming together of a strange god and odd men. Years later, it is said that the Romans came clanking along with spear, short sword, and pilum, the time Julius Caesar was mapping out the way the world should go; but it is doubtful if the Romans pierced farther than Exeter, and, held back by the fighting Kelts, ever had a chance to cool their tired and sweating bodies in the waters of the Dart. Fact or fancy, Totnes is a very ancient borough, stuffed with potent parchments signed by kings and princes, giving it a gorgeous right to live. Ancient, too, are its narrow streets, once fitting well the knight's charger, the lady's palfrey, the abbot's mule, and the peasant's cart; now altogether too lean to enclose comfortably the fleet of horning motor-cars and the clattering lorries that shove and push a stammering way through them. Ancient with its old butterwalk, its guild-hall, its Saxon castle, its redstone church, so commingling with the past that a reminiscent mind might see again an abbot on a mule, padding up the street to a priory, an armoured knight on his war-horse, followed by a squire, the knight carrying on his shield the red rose of Lancaster or the

White Hart of the Hollands; or a velvet-skirted damsel or dame on a palfrey trotting through the old archway that was once a town-gate. But no more shall be seen the casqued horseman clattering up the slope to the mouldering castle, a blood-red cross on his surcoat, the head of a poor paynim at his saddle-bow, slain before the walls of Jerusalem, the golden; the knight chaunting a merry strain in a merry-hearted mood:

> *Where I did slay of Saracens*
> *And Haythin pagans many a man;*
> *And slewe the Souldan's cousin deere,*
> *Who had the name doughty Couldran.*

The pageantry of banner, banneret, and trumpet, appears suddenly on occasion in a new way, as when band and banner heralded Victory Day, and at night, from the Market, began a torchlight procession of excited relief and thanks, a gathering of the Devon clans, and a truly moving picture as the procession wended a flaming way down the hill of the town to the level of a green field. In this array of light, the O'Casey little girl of six carried a torch, innocently honouring the gallant dead who had died that she might live and sleep unharmed, and grow confidently into a fuller knowledge of life, with all her other thousand sisters and brothers of Devon's red soil and tor and moorland; the gallant dead who had put our feet into the way of peace again.

In Devon, many of the women and men never seem to grow old; they keep going till they skip off forever. They skip through the hours till the very last hour of all; though in the hour of middle-age, they skip more cautiously. The West Country people are human, talkative, and tolerant; seeming slow to city people, but they work harder and quicker than any city artisan or labourer. Many work far too hard and far too long; for like country people in Ireland, they are too anxious to lay up for themselves treasure, not in heaven, but, more safely, in the banks; reminding one of Joyce's sleepy remark in *Finnegans Wake*:

> *Anno Domini Nostri Sancti Jesu Christi.*
> *Nine hundred and ninety-nine million pounds sterling in the*
> *blue-black bowels of the Bank of Ulster.*

Standing on the top of the hill that carries Totnes so lightly on its back and shoulders, a lot of what is fine can be seen in the county of Devon. Overhead, often, a rich blue sky, touched with leisurely clouds reluctant to leave the silky splendour of their blue bed, though in winter that same sky can glower grey or glitter with the threat of a piercing frost. Occasionally, higher than the white clouds, the dark shadow of a buzzard sails across the sky on wings that never seem to fly, satisfied with his own rare company. Hidden to the east lies Torquay, stretching herself languorously, letting herself be fondled by a soothing sea; a dwelling-place where many who are old and well-off live, some sick and resentful, trying to imagine they hear in the sad notes of the Last Post the stirring call of a new Revelle. Away to the west is Plymouth, a fair part of it bloodily scooped away by war; but definite still and as alive as ever; where Drake set foot on his rocking ship to sail out to shatter the bombastic shadow and substance of Spain's Armada, and so disperse the glowing dream of John of Austria, after the Duke himself withdrew from the coloured shadow-play of life. Newly-ploughed fields of red earth, spreading out in a view as wide as the eye can cover, aglow with their differing hues, from reddish-purple, reddish-brown, to what seems to be a vivid crimson, separated here and there by squares and diagonals of a green as rich and velvety as the red, a sight to be wondered at and loved. Oh, the Devon people have a beautiful carpet under their feet. Through the crimson, maroon, golden-brown, and green goes the River Dart, binding the colours together with a ribbon of silvery loveliness, awakening in the sightseer the desire to wait, to linger, and to look on the common clay, and feel how wonderful common things may be.

Though few of the farmers, shopkeepers, or labourers bother about literature or art, rarely thinking of them, or even dreaming about them, Devon is never without a sign that the body and its needs are not all. The other day a farmer visited Sean; he was in a lather of sweat, for he had just helped a brother to gather in the hay from a ten-acre field while the sun shone hot; and, while he talked of the hay and its value, he also talked of his lovely rows of purple, yellow, white, and scarlet sweet peas that were worth nothing beyond the beauty of their bloom and fragrance of their perfume. Though every garden be set aside to grow the things the body needs, there is always a spot there dedicated to a creamy rose or a crimson one. There they are by the fence, beside the door, the creamy and the scarlet roses, showing that Devon, however mindful of the needs of the body, never forgets the beauty of the rose of sharon and the lilies of the valley.

* * *

RED LAUGH OF WAR

♣ ♣ ♣

The shout of war had become more than an echo; it was close to every ear now, a bellow. Hitler's heil was hurrying for honour everywhere. Soon the battle would close in, thick and bloody. The waste land wondered at its own scurrying to defend itself. Everyone was out preparing; all were one. Corporal Nym lived by Pistol, telling winds and walls what he would not do if the Nazis came his way; and Pistol lived by Nym. Pickwick side by side with a Weller learned to hold a hose; and Prufrock was fitting on a steel helmet, reconciling himself to a sharp and stinging death in the midst of what he called his duty. The threat of death was bringing the waste land to life again. Oh, Mr. Prufrock, what shall I do? Our home's become my husband's grave, and my babes are buried, too. The Englishman, so clever in his foolishness, was fighting for his life, and the Irishman, so foolish in his cleverness, was fighting with him. It was more than touch and go now; it was all touch and little go, for England was nearly naked. Not much else save the symbolic trident remained in her hand. A few lonely-looking tanks, a few guns, and a few ageing aeroplanes were all she had to call her own. Oh, Mr. Prufrock, what shall we do? God has turn'd away, and left the most of it to you. We have a few guns, a few tanks, a few old aeroplanes, and we have the spirit of a brave people. All of what she once had, had been left scattered along the way to the coast of Dunkirk. All her treasures of destruction had been abandoned to the Nazis. Prufrock and his friends could be armed only with a pike and the courage to use it. He had a splitting headache from the pressure of the steel helmet on his head; his legs ached in every joint from the dint of drill; his hands were torn by barbed wire learning how to make a prickly barricade. The ageing Churchill stood by the wireless to promise the British people a succession of gala years of blood, sweat, and tears; Prufrock beside him, murmuring Get us the tools, sir, and we'll do the job. Prufrock, you have busy days before you. He took off his collar and tie, put a muffler round his thin neck, raw with the sun, the wind, and the rain; he covered his thinning hair, thin legs, thin arms with steel helmet and battle-dress. More clearly than ever before, he saw the Eternal Footman holding his coat, heard him snicker, and was not afraid. Things were too active, too terrible to let fear get in the way. Home they brought her warrior dead. Who is it? Some bloke named Prufrock.

Lonely men, leaning out of windows, in their shirt sleeves, were lonely no longer; things were too terrible, too active for them to be lonely. In carpeted rooms, with pictured walls, and cushions on the settee, women no longer come and go, talking of Michael Angelo. They were buzzy fixing helmets on curls, natural or permed, cutting them down a lot to let the helmet cover the nape of the neck; flitting out of their rooms to join the Waacs, the Wrens, or to fix Red Cross armlets on a sleeve of their coats. Men and women were measuring out life now, not with coffee spoons, but with rifle, tommy-gun, sling, splint, and bandage. A bitter change, but not all evil. Common life had to go on, but with a very different rhythm. Things were changed, changed utterly. Church worship in any sense of thought towards a Prince of Peace or a Father of Love was demolished in the fire and detonation of the struggle. All political diversions ran from the stage as the curtain rose upon war. Fee fum family reunion. A whole people massed communistically for such a war as had never been known before; no peace, no sign of peace, till one side or the other lay dead. The chastisement of Hitler was upon us all. Invasion! Well, fight! Than to be subjects of Hitler's herrenfolk, better to be

> *A pair of ragged claws,*
> *Scuttling across the floors of silent seas.*

The gentle town of Totnes, cuddling itself in its quietness, jumped out of its gentleness, and jumped into action. All classes strained themselves into activity, ready to fight in streets, in the fields, on the hills, against the Nazi. Invasion! They meant it, too, nearly killing themselves with the preparation. Fellows of well over fifty ran and jumped about, climbed walls, and flung themselves down to the field on the opposite side, unmindful of a broken leg or a cracked skull; old codgers did bayonet drill and turned somersaults till one's eyes grew blurred and one's head grew dizzy looking at them. Sprained arms and ankles, pulled muscles, and black eyes sprouted out everywhere. In every corner, one heard the crack crack of rifles going and the explosions of hand-grenades, till it seemed that England was blowing herself to pieces. Busy people were getting ready for their own burial. For a long time, the Home Guards were very excited, and did everything at a bound. A driver of a car, or a passenger in one, had to be wary, and keep an open ear for the cry of Halt! A heedless driver, or a scornful one, would hear a bullet whistling past an ear, or, maybe, feel one tearing through his back. All were on the watch, for no one knew how soon, or where, the Nazis might show themselves in the London thoroughfares or in the Devon lanes. That they would come, and soon, was certain. Hitler had set the whole world the job of wasting energy, time, and thought.

Eileen was never so busy in her life. Minding the latest infant, she forced time to let her gain a first-class certificate in the science of first-aid; she practised how to deal with an incendiary bomb, creeping, done out in dungarees, on her belly into a hut filled with old furniture, set ablaze with magnesium. Within smoke and fume, and heat of the blaze, she worked the hose of a stirrup-pump—first the spray to gradually coax the flaming venom from the home-made bomb, the spray from the nozzle was turned to the jet till the flames died, and curling smoke round the charred furniture showed that danger was over. Then, each day, she hurried up to Dartington to help with the midday meal for the refugee children, watching warily and brightly over her own flock in her spare time; for she and he often spent anxious times till their two lads were safely home from school, having passed through the sullen black-out of the bitter wintry evening. So many women had been called to the colours that housewives with children had now more work than three of them would be expected to do normally. Then there were the lectures given to teach us all how to deal with injury from poison gas, that turned the flesh into a green cindery rot; how to deal with burns from an incendiary bomb, or from fire caused by one; how to deal with shock, with splintered bones, with severed arteries: Everyone was learning anew and in a fresh way that God was Love.

All road sign-posts were swiftly taken down, all names of places blotted out from railway stations, so that all England quick became a land without a name. The district was segmented by geometrical design into sections, subsections, and semi-sub-sections, each having it own letter and number as well as its warden, sub-warden, and semi-sub-warden, with messengers, callers, and couriers added to them, topped by a head-warden over all. There were those who wore khaki-coloured helmets, those who wore black ones, those who wore whites ones; first-aid wardens, ambulance wardens, rescue-squad wardens, and church-wardens—the land bristled with wardens. No one was left out, grandsires and old women forming part of England's guard. The men pulled up their socks, the women their skirts. Cut your here up to your ere, your kirtle to the knee. Barriers were put up to check tanks at various parts of the roads, and one stood on the road directly in front of the O'Casey garden gate—thick portly pillars of concrete so placed that passing cars had to wriggle in and out through them. But convoys of heavy guns and tanks couldn't go through, so the portly ones had to come down, to be replaced by V-shaped angle irons, set into sockets of concrete, which were left on the sides of the road, ready to be thrust into the concrete sockets as soon as the rumble of the Nazi tanks shook the English roads, and tightened the hearts of the Devon people; the military experts seemingly unaware that the invading tanks had but to sidestep the barriers to make their way through the gardens fronting the houses, and go on their way, gay with the prospect of goring out England's vitals, belching fire and smoke, as if the dragon, killed by George, had come to life, had bred a host of his kind, and had gathered them together to destroy altogether the cocky consequence of the tarnishing legend.

One day, suddenly, the local park, the town, and the district flooded up with American troops, white, chocolate, and black. Men from almost all the States were represented by those who sat, who sang, and slept in the tents that formed line after line in the grounds; men from the borders of the Great Lakes, men from the West, from New York, and from Texas, too. All in for fight. Sean often sauntered round the camp, for there were few restrictions, and the Americans were comradely, and ready to talk. Even the lonelier sentries meandering around the fringe of the camp were glad to halt for a few moments to say Hallo, guy. How different these sentries from those around Buckingham Palace or those who had once kept watch over Dublin's Bank of Ireland! The American sentry had his rifle right enough, so many rounds of ammunition, and his greyish-green helmet was pressed down on his head, but there the military formality ended. No sane person would think of entering into conversation with a sentry around Buckingham Palace; it would be low treason. He had ceased to be a human being for the time being, and must comport himself as if he were a changed man. Puppet passes; major movements by strings.

The American sentry carried his rifle sloping across his arm, the barrel resting in the socket of an elbow. He sauntered round, stopping, maybe, to look at the scratch baseball match his comrades were playing; or gazed after a girl that happened to pass by, calling to a comrade within earshot that there was a good-looking dame. One of them Sean spoke to was from Kansas City, a lorry-driver in a store there, he told Sean. He wasn't a big fellow; rather one of the smaller men of the detachment; thin, too, but wiry and firm in his stand. His face was thin, made to look thinner by the enveloping steel helmet. His nose stretched down, thin and long, coming down more than half-way over his upper lip. The biggest mark in his face were the big, brown, wide-open eyes that gently and quietly stared out from the long thin face; eyes that saw little outside what they had already seen at home. The big, brown, wide-open eyes always carried about in them an image of Kansas City. Back in Kansas, he would forget the faint impressions, not only of Totnes, but of England. The Yeomen of the Guard in their scarlet and gold, the Horse Guards Blue on their nobly-formed horses, found no nest in his thoughts: Kansas men, Kansas women, and Kansas town were all the world to him. He was satisfied with the streets of his city, its life, and the roads of Kansas and Missouri.

—Don't get this place, he said to Sean. What's its name?

—Totnes, the oldest town in England, bar London, and it's near the coast of a county called Devon.

—Ay, Devon, he echoed tonelessly. A long way from my home town, he added, after a pause; a long way; yessir.

—You'd like to be back in Kansas City? Sean queried.

—I sure would! he said quickly, a gleam of interest coming into the big, brown, wide-open eyes. Kansas suits me, suits me fine. Yessir. I'd like to be back in Kansas. Guess I will, one day.

—Devon's a very lovely county, said Sean, hoping to interest him into asking questions.

—It sure is, buddy, he responded, again tonelessly. Kansas suits me better. I'm Kansas born an' Kansas bred an' I jus' can't get goin' anywhere else; I really can't.

—Well, I hope Kansas City will like Totnes Town, murmured Sean.

—It sure will, murmured the sentry; it sure does. It's a small hang-out, though, ain't it, buddy? Guess it could be dumped down in Kansas City's smallest street, and not be in the way. You could carry all that's goin' round here under one arm. But the people are swell; gotta give them their due; swell, yessir.

—Where do you go from here? asked Sean.

—Dunno, buddy. That's only our second hop. Wonder what the next hop's gonna be like? The eyes went dead again, hiding any sign of an image of Kansas. Well, so long; be seeing you. Gotta get goin' the round; and he turned away to continue his sauntering parade, slow and mechanical, round the camp, seeking silence and solitude to bring the image of Kansas into the big, brown, wide-open eyes again; and a red laugh of war stung the ear of Sean.

Each was homeless near a thousand homes. Oh, to be home again, home again, home again, under the apple-boughs down by the mill. Throughout the camp there was an air of gay, almost reckless, bewilderment, mild, but bitter, as if the G.I.'s silently thought it unwise to be here. The innocents abroad. Far away from Jelly Roll and from Lead Belly, from their racing simple songs, their wisecracks. Where is now the merry party I remember long ago! Laughing round the Christmas fire, laden by its ruddy glow. Or in summer's balmly evenings, in the fields among the hay? They have all dispersed and wandered far away, far away. Some have gone from us forever; longer here they could not stay—Oh, change it, buddy; don't make gloom gloomier. Who was it, what bastard laughed in that harsh, red way?

One or two of the tents had a ukulele-player, who could be heard strumming out lively notes, with, maybe, some comrade singing some jazz-song or hot ditty: singing sorrow and fear away. Away, away! A hard thing to do, buddies. It didn't sound merry. If one came from Chicago, another from Texas, they were all, all lonely and all far from home; from things familiar, from a sweetheart's kiss, from a mother's fussy care, from a wife's companionship, from all things settled. They had been hunted from the serene monotony of peace to the savage, purposeless monotony of war. Privacy was gone and all lived an alice-in-blunderland life, with death, maybe, round the corner of the next hop. Some of these men, many of them, perhaps, may be phantoms already, gay as so many of them pretended to be. The Spirit of Pity no longer hovers over, no longer probes, the heart of war; the Spirit of Irony only gets where war is waged.

The Stars and Stripes flying from a tall pole at the camp's entrance made the place American territory, but it refused to make the place a home. The kindly and talkative Devon folk made things as easy and as natural as they could for the soldiers, but the Americans, white and black, carried but an image of home in all their eyes. The life in camp was dirty, dull, and boring. Besides, the guns were being stuffed now with something more than wadding and powder. There was more of death than of pageantry in their booming. None here sought death at the cannon's mouth. The next camp might be a camp of a dead brigade, and far away from Brooklyn. Gay as they might be, they all knew that they faced towards the front where the graveyards were. Many comrades were already under ground in the Philippines and other isles of the Pacific, never again to return to Dixie Land, to the cornfields of Kansas, or hear the patter of their own feet on the pavements of Broadway. It was all dreadful; yet here in the recreation grounds of the little town of Totnes, hundreds more were waiting to join the dead. However they might hang out the colours of motley, however they might play their ukuleles, however they might shout their wisecracking comments on an improvised baseball game, the camp had around it a deep black border.

The Panzers were racing over Russia! Totnes was busy presenting things, making toys, holding concerts and dances to provide funds for Mrs. Churchill's Russian Red Cross Fund. In the window of the Anglo-Soviet Headquarters stood three huge photographs, four feet tall and three feet wide, of Churchill to the right, Stalin to the left, with Franklin D. Roosevelt in the centre. The Soviet Flag was seen for the first time in Totnes, and hundreds wore a little Red Star in the breasts of blouses or in the lapels of their coats; for the fight of the Red Army had modified the fear, and had removed the very present danger of invasion; while through all the hurrying activities moved the American soldiers, attending concert and dance, their convoys of great guns and tanks rumbling along the street of the town, often to the gentle accompaniment of a tinkle tinkle from a ukulele playing somewhere from a tent in the camp.

The Panzers were racing over Russia! We're owre the border, and awa'! Russia first; England next, and within a year the Wehrmacht will be doing the Lambeth Walk along Piccadilly and the Mile End Road. Race on, my brave warriors, invincible and hitlarious! Let the united drums of a united herrenfolk beat a united roll when Hitler enters Moscow! Henceforth, the world would form its life to the beat of Hitler's heart. Race on, my men! This is the way that Hitler rides, a gallop, a gallop, a gallop! Another day or two will see the Russians parking their cannon, garaging their tanks, and the Red Army dropping their rifles to lift their hands, and cry for peace. But the cannons went on blazing, the Russian tanks split the German tanks in two; and at Stalingrad, Germany's woe began. Oh, weep for the German dead; the young and sprightly ones lie still forever! Red laughter of war echoing over the graves. And Hitler heard it; yes, Hitler heard it. It would soon be louder.

The work for England and for the Soviet Union went forward in the little town of Totnes. The rose and crown looked fine beside the hammer and the sickle. Sean helped as well as he could, addressing envelopes and delivering circulars, for one thing. He tapped at the door of a Totnes bungalow to deliver a circular notifying a meeting. The door half opened, and he saw half of a middle-aged woman standing there, crying silently, crying deeply. Mechanically, Sean extended the letter; she made no movement to take it; she didn't look at it; just looked aimlessly before her, crying silent.

—Notice of a meeting, he mumbled, trying to think how he could get away quietly.

—I don't want it, she said, tonelessly; don't want anything now. Just got a telegram telling me son's killed; killed, an' us doesn't know how or where. No grave of his own even, for us heard they are buryin' 'em in bundles now, an' us doesn't know where; doesn't know where. Crying silently and deeply, she slowly and silently shut the door.

She hadn't had the comfort of hearing her son's last moan, hadn't had the joy of committing his body to the grave. She had been denied the mystery of sorrow in stroking her loved one's body for the last time, like Gilderoy's sweetheart, who, at least, had had that gaunt privilege:

> *Wi' tears that trickled for his death,*
> *I washt his comely clay;*
> *An' sicker in a grave sae deep,*
> *I layed the dear-loved boy.*

Not even that; not even that much elation for the mother.

It was everywhere: it followed Hitler about; it sounded soft, ironic, murderous, in the ears of the Nazis racing across Russia; it trickled through the fancies of the Americans digging trenches by the side of their camp, offset by deep pits for ack ack guns; it circled round the British depriving England of a name, the hurried medical inspection of youth, the drill-donned gas-masks, the call for identity cards, heard in the sound of the siren's wail, gurgled through the curses misspent fixing black-outs over the windows, its derision blurs blasphemously the gasps of a deep-wounded, dying lad, and here a gust of it had swept through a humble Devon bungalow, soft, ironic, murderous—the red laugh of war.

* * *

SHAW'S CORNER

✿ ✿ ✿

A letter came when stars were paling, came from Charlotte Shaw; a letter that was kind and homely; a letter that was law; written in that style of handwriting so oddly like that of her great pard; the confident manner of its phrasing sending out the idea that the invitation was a minor command to come when you're called; inviting Eileen and him to lunch in Whitehall Court. Indeed, an invitation connecting itself with a visit to G.B.S. was a command that few would like to disobey or ignore. A visit to him always made Eileen's heart and his own beat a little faster. Mrs. Shaw liked Sean, but seemed to like him in a bitter way; a shrill kind of attachment. She looked upon him as a somewhat refractory fellow, and was too anxious about him. She had resented his silent refusal to accept the offer of her husband's mediation in the contest with the Abbey Theatre over the rejection of his *The Silver Tassie*. She seemed to think that Sean's choice to fight it on his lone was something of a snub to her great husband. She was eager to direct him in the way he should go, through literature, through art, through drama, through life. She had an earnest admiration and deep respect for some things that Sean wouldn't stop to look at twice; and she vehemently resented his demolishing regard for George Russell's works, for she placed Russell firmly before Yeats, taking him to her bosom as Ireland's most brilliant, spiritual, and powerful avastar. Avast! Her cheeks glowed whenever she muttered the magic symbol of AE, as if this diphthong had within it the whole kind kingdom of heaven. To Sean, he was Ireland's brazen Buddha. One sentence criticising anything said or done by Russell would tense the curiously soft face into a flint-look, cold anger sparking from its flushed compression. Numerous times, she had commanded Sean to honour and obey the genius of AE, but Sean had smiled and registered a refusal in solid silence.

Another writer she had tried to force into his esteem and affection was the scholarly Miss Helen Waddell, a fellow-adorer of George Russell. Mrs.

Shaw sent him Miss Waddell's *The Wandering Scholars* and *Mediaeval Latin Lyrics,* calmly commanding him to give direct attention and whole-hearted admiration to the works. They were the works. But Sean side-stepped away from Mrs. Shaw's peppermint-explosions of You Must read and re-read them till you Understand them, and so gradually get to realise how fine they are, and get to Love Them. Come with me and be my love. But Sean hadn't the time. Or the scholarship. Anon, sweet wag; anon, anon!

Later on, she tried to make the philosophy of Gerald Heard a pulse-beat in his mind, but he slipped away from Heard without even hearing him speak. Mrs. Shaw used every call to lunch to mention something he should do or not do, or name a book he should read which would wave him along some one-way road of spiritual life and mental wisdom; her great husband gazing at her all the time, silently, with a patient, quizzical face. He had such an affection for her, and she was so necessary to him in his going out and his coming in, that he rarely tried to cross her; or, maybe he thought it best to let the advice given be left or taken, according to the nature of him or her to whom it had been offered.

Once at a lunch, with Charlotte at one end of the table, Shaw at the other, Eileen at one side, Sean facing her at the other, the group looking like a four-leaved shamrock, Mrs. Shaw, grim-faced, waiting for the lunch to be served, and the maid to go, Shaw chatting about the sharp spring air that tingled the cheek and nipped the ear. Sean had long noticed that Charlotte ate heavily, a great pile on her plate, thickly covered with what-ever sauce went with the main dish; that she leant forward determinedly to swallow whenever she filled a forkful, using a sluggish energy to bring it to her mouth and get it down quickly, quietly rebuking him because he ate sparingly, never allowing a heap on his plate; for, however hungry he might be, a piled plate shoved away any desire to eat. Mrs. Shaw felt the cold keenly, and she sat over her plate, hunched up, a shawl round her shoulders, and an electric fire beside her chair—symptoms, probably, of the dread disease that, later on, shoved her into the grave. Shaw sat erect in his high-backed chair, eating his baked eggs and vegetables, and drinking his milk with graceful ease; chatting away, evoking a burst of laughter from Sean, a rippling one from Eileen at some witty comment given about some former incident, startling Mrs. Shaw away from her attention to her plate, and delighting the great man himself, who leant farther back on his stately chair to give a musical laugh himself. While Sean was eating his share of apple-tart, Mrs. Shaw suddenly asked him what he was doing now.

—Nothing at all, at the moment, he said; for he had no wish to undergo a catechism of what it was about, how it was growing, and when it would end; he added: Nothing at the moment; I'm afraid I am an idle man just now.

—Too busy quarrelling, she said, rather viciously. I hear you have quarrelled with Agate now. You will have to learn a better way of conducting yourself. You will get nowhere by these senseless disputes.

—Not even into heaven? queried Sean, not knowing what to say to this sudden assault, and trying to put it aside with a hasty laugh.

—It's no light matter, she said. Quarrelling with people this way, you will have enemies everywhere. Why do you do it?

This was unexpected, and damnably embarrassing to him. Eileen, more embarrassed even than Sean, lifted her head, smiling uncomfortably; bent her head, lifted it again, hoping that Sean wouldn't burst out in resentment at Mrs. Shaw's rebukes. He had, apparently, been led into a trap: brought to a private, personal lunch so that Mrs. Shaw could go at him to her heart's content. She didn't seem to realise that she was doing now what she was condemning him for, with the advantage of being the hostess, and so making it hard for Sean to reply. Silent for a moment, he then said, If a critic judges a writer by what a writer may say to him or even about him; if he denies merit in a work because of dislike for the author, then he's not a critic, but a dastard.

—There you go again! she said, angrily. You must learn to be more agreeable to critics. You mustn't go on disturbing important people in this reckless way; you must be made to check this reckless urge towards opposition. You must control him, she added, turning suddenly on Eileen; you must advise him, and modify what he is inclined to say; while Shaw sat straight up in his chair, listening; silent.

—Sean is too honest, ventured Eileen. He says things in a very blunt way. It seems unpleasant, I know, but I think he is right.

—He isn't right! said Mrs. Shaw, emphatically. He's too peevish, too peevish altogether. You shouldn't encourage him. She turned swiftly towards Sean again. Why do you do it?

—Why do I do it? echoed Sean, trying to think out what he ought to say to such an attack by such a woman. Somehow or other, I am made to do it. Your own husband did it, and does it still, Mrs. Shaw.

—There you go again! she said, and the too soft face crinkled with vexation. You quarrelled with Yeats, you quarrelled with AE, as great a man as Yeats, and, in some respects, a greater one—no, you don't think so, I know, she said quickly, sensing Sean's rejection of her claim; and now you've quarrelled with James Agate.

—I didn't quarrel with Yeats, said Sean, quietly; I differed from him on a question of drama; so, too, with Agate: I withstood him to his face because I thought he was to be blamed—if he doesn't like it, he can lump it.

—You see, you stay obstinate! No one will have a good word for you if you go on in this irritating way. Why do you do it?

—I have to, said Sean; I can no else. Something within me speaks before I am aware of it, and the harm is done. Sean was trying to be good-humoured. Maybe it's the prompting of what some venture to call the holy ghost.

—What do you exactly mean by the holy ghost? The voice was sharper than before, and the soft face was flushed and even quivering a little with anger. You must learn to define your words before you use them. Just what do you mean?

—He means, said Shaw, in a calm, even voice, never moving the white, clinging hands from the back railings of the high chair; he simply means, Charlotte, that he has got something and I've got something that you haven't got.

Sean had been several times to lunch with them when they had lived in Adelphi Terrace; and he had wandered round the district, remembering how many great men had lodged and dodged about the streets: Garrick, Pepys, Turner, and even Peter the Great. Dust of time was everywhere, and mustiness clung to hall, stairway, and room. Streets crowding after each other's heels everywhere; houses pressed so close together that few found space to breathe in. How we cling to old and dying things! To things Doric, Corinthian, and Ionic, as if these were to be the everlasting architectural for all ages; as if no new thought of building could infuse human imagination with forms as fine, and far more suitable. And for family worship no finer forms of furniture than those of Sheraton, Chippendale, and Hepplewhite; lost now with the fop, the dandy, the curtsy, the low bow, and the jewelled snuff-box. All gone; gathered up and taken away by the groping hand of time. The hardier things about them stayed, table, chair, and ceiling; snuff-box, necklace, and sword; stuffed into a museum, and set out in ritual tier and row; the men and women themselves no more than the scintillating dust of England.

Sean entered by the wide-open doorway, climbed the stairs, fumbled a long time with the chevaux-de-frise, spears against uninvited probers. He got it open at last, passed through, and was guided by a maid into the presence of the great man and his wife. A vast experience to the shy and inexperienced Sean; but the genial twinkle in the sage's questioning eyes, and the soft, motherly welcome of Charlotte dissolved the nervousness, and Sean's nature fused pleasantly with the Shaw household. At a lot of these lunches, curious customers gathered to meet the Shaws. Only on a few occasions did Sean see sweet feminine face and form and hear elegant or sturdy talk from visitors. Looking like human goofies, Sean himself among them; for once Shaw had asked John Dulanty, Eire's Ambassador, How lovely Eileen Carey had come to marry such an ugly fellow as Sean. (Although it was little known, and few thought it, Shaw, like every intelligent Irishman, had a keen eye for a good-looking woman.) 'Mostly, Mrs. Shaw's cronies', a handsome young visitor once whispered to Sean. How singular, Sean thought, Eileen and a handsome young Russian named Duiska looked, caged among so many gnarled and uncouth guests, gabbing away importantly to Mrs. Shaw and her white-bearded sage. Shaw alone put brightness and daring into the current remarks, though they forced him to give opinions of persons and things, long ago dead, and never before the eyes of the present generation. The faded puppets of long-dead dramas, Balfour, Bonar Law, Bannerman, were marched about and handled, by this one, by that, as they munched and munched meat and swallowed wine round the round table.

At one of the lunches, there were a man and his wife who were crooked as cods in a pot. Both were lame, and each carried a stick to help them over a stile, one veering to the right, the other to the left, as they toddled along. The man's voice sounded like the sound of a saw going through a rusty nail embedded in wood the saw was cutting, and whatever humanity was left in a sourpuss was evicted by a black patch over one eye. His wife sang the praises of some osteopath, who, she said, had straightened her into what she was now, Mrs. Shaw nodding in agreement, and mentioning that her own bones had been put into a smart conception of what they were originally meant to be by another osteopath. The husband assailed Shaw with some old history of something that had sucked from political life and usefulness a man named Sir Charles Dilke in the days of Gladstone, forcing Shaw to prod his mind back to a reconception of, and to comment upon, an event that had died, and lay like a log, deep buried under the loam of time. Shaw was plagued with persons insisting on hearing his opinions past and gone, who came with pick and spade to disinter the near forgotten dead, and make them look lively again: the encumbrance of the remembrance of things past.

At a lunch given by Lady Lavery (whose face appeared on the first issue of Ireland's national pound note), wife of the painter, Shaw entertained everyone present with racy accounts of incident after incident, while Lady Londonderry, Mrs. James McNeill, wife of Ireland's High Commissioner, and others enjoyed themselves; the magnificent head of Augustus John, moving slowly on his broad shoulders, gazing at the company, the brilliant, piercing eyes seeing all in anything worth seeing, noticing nothing where there was nothing to notice. Afterwards, when most had gone, and Mrs. Shaw with Mrs. McNeil was upstairs looking at a recent painting, by Sir John, of a prelate—Archbishop Mannix—if he remembered right—he who had led the hostility to Dr. O'Hickey, in Maynooth, the time Mannix was President of the College, Shaw walked firmly up and down the dining-room, pausing for a moment to say to Sean, Great strain on one this necessity to keep talking during the time of a luncheon.

—Why the hell do you do it? asked Sean. Is it vanity, his mind asked, silently; is it just trying to shine? Shine out, fair sun! We're all doing it, doing it, doing it.

—They all expect it of me, Shaw said; and one can't sit in silence, staring at the others.

—Why not? queried Sean. If the others can stick it, you can; and, if they can't stick it, they'll talk themselves, and save you some of the strain. Augustus John talks only when he feels like it. Unless talk comes spontaneously to me, I'm dumb. I don't make conversation at lunch a question of conscience.

—That's sound advice, said Shaw, halting in his patrol, slanting back his remarkable head, and letting out a musical laugh. Shaw stops talking— what would the world say!

Sean wondered if Shaw really took all this in so as to sit more silent sitting at a foreign table, reserving his queer, salient talk for the time he would be at his ease sitting at his own. Under those bristling eyebrows, behind those brilliant Irish eyes, over that thick-ended nose, under that frosty pow, thinning thickly now, the alert, witty, and peerless mind peered out at the present, peered into the future; almost faultless, utterly unafraid. Oh, Shaw, there is not your equal now! When shall we see your like again!

*   *   *

Shaw's *pied-à-terre* in London was a roomy and comfortable one, and for all that it must have heard, many times, many great arguments about it and about, the whole impression it gave out was one of commonplace serenity; a cushioned recess for the mighty mind. Here was nothing vulgar, nothing modern either, in furniture, picture, or stone, except the painting of Shaw himself by Augustus John, hung so high that the eyes of Shaw or of his wife never met it during their sitting down or standing up in the room. The head had to be thrown back on the shoulders to see it, and Shaw never, far as Sean knew, pointed it out to a visitor. Let it hang there quietly out o' the way. Eileen's eye caught sight of it the moment she entered the room, and halting to stare, she cried out, happily, A John!

It was amusing to see the half-startled way Shaw turned up his head to squint at the picture, turning his head down again, to wait patiently till Eileen and Sean had ended their look at it. Perhaps it was too lyrical, too far away from the cloudy emphasis of a photograph, too sensuous, though the sensuousness was a gentle mingling of lovely silvery greys and gentle blues, giving it a look of gay loneliness; and from these lyrical greys and gentle blues, peeped impudently the wise and humorous face of the dramatist and the fighter. A suggestion from Eileen that it should be placed where the eye could see it comfortably evoked no comment from Shaw and but the short statement from Charlotte that G.B.S. didn't like it well enough to change it from where it was. Ricketts was about the furthest that Shaw got towards the enjoyment of the painter's art. He preferred the ghastly picture of himself done by John Collier to the lyrical impression of himself done by John. It would seem that he had gunned the art of painting away from him by a multitude of shots from his camera. What a great loss this lack in the Shaws was to Ireland. With their wealth how many fine pictures they could have gathered to be presented, sometime, to Eire's National Gallery, or to the Municipal Collection housed in Parnell Square. His friends didn't help him any, for few, if any, cared a damn about Raphael or Renoir. Few of those pictured beside him had shown any desire to mingle their souls with the old painters or the new; indeed, some of them—like the Webbs— were as deaf as the mole is blind to all art and all literature. They spent their working-hours and leisure sorting men and things out in tier and row. They never sought out a second for a song and a dance. What would the Webbs have thought had they seen Joyce suddenly indulging in his mad, amazing, wild-man dance on a bridge of the Seine? Shaw would have wondered, and laughed; the Webbs would have hurried away, for it wouldn't have been either possible or seemly to have tucked away such an item into a pyramid of statistics. Dublin workers, had there been any there to see it, would have remained hushed for a few moments, and then they'd have hilariously joined in—hoosh the cat from under the table! Joyce for all his devotion to his art, terrible in its austerity, was a lad born with a song on one side of him, a dance on the other—two gay guardian angels every human ought to have. And what is the universe but a dance of orbs? Brooks Atkinson in his *Once Around the Sun* tells us that Canis Minor's Procyon is rushing towards us at the rate of two and a half miles a second; and many other stars are rushing away; this way, that way, in the expanding universe: so if we go wild at times, as Joyce did, we are errant in magnificent company. Life will be on a high plane when life becomes a song and a dance and a serious thing.

Music. A harpsichord. Shaw's crest and arms. A lovely one, encased in polished yellow wood, standing in a prominent part of the room. Shaw's heart was here. He was blessed with a deep love for, and a deep understanding of, the melody, intricate, rippling and majestic, that flowed from, and thundered out of, the magic weaving of sounds by Beethoven, Brahms, Wagner, and Mozart. These were his God be praised. These glories balanced safely his lack of feeling for the glories of painting in the past and the present outspread of its experimental valour. Shaw had deeply what Sean lacked altogether. Not altogether, maybe, for he could, at least, love the melodic bars in opera, oratorio, and symphony. But Shaw had the knowledge of music in brilliant abundance, and this, maybe, gave him his serenity, as it, maybe, did to Joyce, too. The lullaby to irritation and anger in David's harp still sang through the music of the day. It wasn't, of course, that Shaw was always serene. He very often felt the flame of indignation alight within him; he felt anger at stupid things said and cruel things done;

and he felt the sick heart when fools assailed him. He could calmly set down hard things without a quiver in a bristling eyebrow when writing of revolutions; but he was always damnably reasonable: 'Even in the first flush of the Soviet Revolution, the Soviet was more tolerant than we were when our hour came to revolt. We frankly robbed the church of all it possessed, and gave the plunder to the landlords (a lot of them catholic, by the way). Long after that, we deliberately cut off our archbishop's head. Certainly, the Soviet made it quite clear to the Russian archbishop that if he didn't make up his mind to accept the fact of the Revolution, and give to the Soviet the allegiance he had formerly given to the Tsar, he would be shot. But when he very sensibly and properly made up his mind accordingly, he was released, and is now, presumably, pontificating, much more freely than the Archbishop of Canterbury'.

Music helped to keep Shaw calm, and made a fine dramatist of him, for music sings in most of his plays. Oh, lackaday, that Sean had so little of its solace! One had to be a constant practiser, or a constant listener, to know or feel anything right about the form and style of beautiful sounds which we call music. How is the ordinary man to enter into an intelligently emotional enjoyment of music? Sean could think of but one way: listening. Listen to the band, for that was what an assembly of eminent musicians really was, though given the lordly, and deserved, name of an Orchestra. Now that their three children were constant listeners to Beethoven, Mozart, Bach, and the rest, flowing from the wireless, the gramophone, and, more simply, from the stately piano they had in their best room, he was often sprayed with beautiful sounds. But it was but a lovely baptism. Too late, now; too late. He would never be able to go further than the porch of the temple; never see the lights gleaming on the altar; never hear the full hymn sung.

Had Mrs. Shaw lived longer, Shaw would have lived longer, too. She cushioned away a lot of the hardness of life for him. She was his woeman of the guard. She travelled a lot, following the sun for warmth, and he went with her; for boat-decks, cabins, and foreign lands with her were better than Ayot St. Lawrence without her. Constant comfort and companionship departed from him with Charlotte. He tried to take it cheerily, but he was just an old boy whistling in the dark. In a letter to Sean, he said he was all right, but damnably lonely. A lone one at last. The state of a lone star; and to remain damnably lonely till he departed too. Though they had their differences. Once sitting pleasantly by the fire, just four of them, Shaw, Charlotte, Eileen and Sean, chatting generally about the drama, Mrs. Shaw suddenly asked Sean which did he think was G.B.S.'s best play; Sean replying, immediately, that it was *Heartbreak House*. Shaw's face lit up instantly, and he took his elbow from the mantelshelf to give fuller attention to what Sean had said; but a cloudy look settled on the face of Charlotte.

—Do you? said Shaw, delightedly. That's odd. Few do, though I think myself that it is my best play. Charlotte doesn't like it.

—Nonsense, said Mrs. Shaw to Sean; *Saint Joan* is the best play G.B.S. has written.

—No, no, said Sean, innocently and fervently. *Saint Joan* is his most popular play, maybe. It is a lovely play, but a compiled one. *Heartbreak House* is deeper, far more original, and nearer to life. It is as a fine symphony with flaws in it, to a perfectly-modelled folk-air. There is no heartbreak in *Saint Joan;* she burns too triumphantly. G.B.S. knew this, and so he added the Epilogue.

—It cannot compare with *Saint Joan,* said Mrs. Shaw—a note of finality in her voice. I don't like *Heartbreak House.*

Shaw saw that there was disorder in poverty, and he liked order, said to be 'heaven's first law'; he saw that there was disease in poverty, and he liked health; he saw that there was death in poverty, and he loved life. He was the first saint to declare that God no longer liked to look upon the face of the poor, so different from the Jesuit, Vaughan, who, well-fed, well-clothed himself, said that the poor were God's own aristocracy. What voice has shouted Dope! Banish poverty from our midst and from our ken, and with it her foul breed of deformed men, deformed women, deformed children. Force the Christians to seek divine election through their own efforts and development, and suffer them no longer to feel they are jolly good fellows by doling out to others what they never miss themselves. Take the wine away from them, and let them drink a little water for their stomach's sake. To the Lyons with the Christian rich! Shaw is the workers' War-cry!

There is sense for everyone in Shaw's corner who hates the ulcerous misery of poverty. He was one of those who never hesitated to say into the ears of the man isolated by wealth, and in the ears of the multitude, that what are called man's petty and insignificant needs are related to the stars. 'Men honoured Christ', he said, 'so long as he remained a charming picture in a golden frame, or hung helpless on a varnished cross; but men begin to yell with alarm when the picture leaves the frame, or when the figure comes down from the cross to become a moving, terrible force in the world'. The picture is out of the frame now, the figure is off the cross, and Christ now marches in the surge forward of the masse-men. Blok saw him march through Leningrad at the head of the Red Guards, and he has appeared in China amid cheers; today, too, his shadow falls on Africa: Lo, I am with you always—March! Left, left, left!

Some critics say Shaw was no poet (indeed, Sean remembers arguing against this precious aversion of men and women to others, having greater gifts than their own, in Dublin, thirty years ago, with Sarah Purser, a notable lass of the city of that day); that he was one almost incapable of emotion. Hens cackling, cocks crowing, at the eagle's whistle. There is poetry in a lot of his plays, emotion in some of them, and laughter and thought in all of them. A fine synopsis of active and poetic life—tears, laughter, thought, and song. He will live in the life following his own for his jewelled courage, his grand plays, his penetrating wisdom, his social sense, his delightful, effective criticism of the theatre of his day, his fight for Ibsen, Wagner, Brahms, his uncanny knowledge of children, his battles for womanhood, and for his brilliant leadership in the thought of man.

A great man, but not great enough for the closed shop of saintship in the Christian church. Indeed, a name to be mentioned with great caution; and so the churchmen slip down to the hell of mediocrity. No, no; not Shaw. What a scandal it would have aroused had Shaw been allowed to climb into a pulpit! Bernard Shaw in the pulpit of Westmonaster Cathedral. Monastrous! Do stop him from playing such fantastic tricks before high heaven as make the angels laugh. Church in danger! The gates of hello are prevailing against her! Even the figures in the stained-glass windows are climbing out to go. Mention a more suitable name. Here's the Prefect of the Sacred Congregation of Rites, and there's the Reverend President of the Anglican Convocation; so, mention a more suitable name—we're listening. Johnny Appleseed, sirs. Who's he, and what did he do? Done millions of miracles, sirs; scattered appleseeds wherever he went. Appleseeds? You don't know your catechism, son. Don't you know what the read is safe reading, and that is our only need. We must have virtue at all costs; and no inquiries, no questions. D'ye hear me talking? No inquiries, none at all, I'm saying!

No, no, it wouldn't do. Unsettling saint; never do for us. Let St. Peter go back to his sedia astoria in Rome, and Patrick to his stone stand on Tara's Hill or Croagh Patrick. The names mentioned aren't quarter good enough to be thought of by the roman catholic church, or even good enough to win a thought from an anglican pulpit. They are man's saints; our saints, registered in the wide church of humanity; if not for social service, then for heroic virtue in the integrity of their art; the people's choice.

Yeats got a large medal from a Swedish artist, and was so dazzled with the design that he decided to form an Irish Academy of Letters. A circular, signed by some prominent Irish writers, was sent out, appealing to others to become founder Academicians or associate members. The circular came to Sean signed personally by Bernard Shaw. Shaw was asking a favour from Sean; the first favour ever asked, and Sean saw himself threatened with the hardest refusal he had ever had to face. Shaw had fought by his side in the Abbey Theatre controversy over *The Silver Tassie,* and now Sean had to refuse the one favour the great man asked of him. He didn't know what to say, though he knew what he would do—refuse to join. Indeed, he had sent a laughing, critical article about the scheme to *The American Spectator,* and its Editor, George Jean Nathan, had replied, saying it would appear in the next number. Sean didn't like institutions powered to decide what was good literature and what was not good: they had made too many mistakes before. They were inclined to look kindly on those who flattered their own work. He spent a long, long time thinking out a loving letter in whose core was a firm and final refusal. The letter of refusal was sent to the sage, but no answer came back. It was but an incident in a busy life. No malice touched Shaw's nature; he was the most forgiving man Sean had ever met. Nothing mean ever peeped out of his thought or his manner; the noblest Irishman of all Irishmen. Sean and he met many times again, but neither of them ever once mentioned the Irish Academy of Letters.

Later on, when the O'Casey family shifted down to Devon to be near the school Eileen had chosen, on Shaw's emphatic recommendation, for the children, they rented a house that was the only one vacant for miles around that could shelter them in a partially suitable way; a pretentious place, originally built by some lower middle-class snob who feinted towards being an ape of his betters. The landlord didn't like the look of Sean, or mistrusted anyone trying to make a living by writing (small blame to him for that), and demurred about agreeing to the tenancy, demanding credentials as to the prospective tenant's character and good repute. As to his character, Sean told him he would ask no one to trust it, for he couldn't trust it himself. Though he knew many who would readily give him a bad name, he knew no one who would give him a good one. This made the landlord more dubious, but he brightened up when he was promised a guarantor who'd pay the rent, if Sean didn't. The landlord agreed to allow the tenancy if the name Sean gave proved to be satisfactory. Not wishing to bother G.B.S., Sean wrote to Mrs. Shaw, and asked her to do him this favour. Almost immediately, a letter came back asking them to lunch in Whitehall Court to talk about the matter. After lunch, before a fine fire, Mrs. Shaw started questioning; asking how much a year the house would be, including rates, if Sean was working at anything; if a play, had it any prospect of production; while G.B.S. leaned over the back of the chintz-covered sofa, listening to all that was said by Mrs. Shaw sitting on the sofa's centre. Sean was put through a means test, his face flushing, his nerves urging him to walk out of the room, out of the house, his necessity riveting him to where he stood listening.

—Oh, give it to him! suddenly ejaculated Shaw from the cloud of the questioning. He has told you all you need to know. Mrs. Shaw stopped dead, and immediately changed into a gracious readiness to do all she was asked to do.

But all for nothing. When Sean handed out the news that Mrs. Shaw would stand as guarantor, the landlord let a snort out of him, jumped from his chair, ran to the farther end of the room, and almost shouted. It's no

good; I'll not take any woman's guarantee! I won't let you into the house on
any woman's name. I'll let no woman meddle in my affairs!

Oh, Jesus! First Mrs. Shaw's hesitation and distrust; now this old-fashioned fool's rejection of a name Sean had gone to so much trouble to get!
So Sean had to write to Mrs. Shaw telling her that her signature would
not do. G.B.S. then took over the guarantee, first indulging in a spicy correspondence with the landlord's solicitors, and a subsequent letter told Sean
that the business had been carried through:

> 4 WHITEHALL COURT, LONDON. S.W.1.
> *17th October*, 1938.
>
> MY DEAR SEAN,
>
> Your landlord, being a dentist, has developed an extraction complex.
> He proposed a lease in which I was not only to guarantee all your cov-
> enants, but indemnify him for all the consequences. I said I did not know
> his character, but I knew enough of yours to know that the consequences
> might include anything from murder to a European war; so I re-drafted
> the agreement. The lawyers, knowing that their man was only too lucky
> to get a gilt-edged (as they thought) security, and that his demands were
> absurd, made no resistance. I mention it as you had better watch your
> step, not to say his, with the gentleman. Anyhow I had a bit of fun with
> him. I seem to have picked up completely. The anaemia was not really
> pernicious. I am glad to learn that the two miniature O'Caseys are happy
> among the young criminals at Dartington and that their mother is now
> one of the Beauties of Devon. Charlotte sends all sorts of affectionate
> messages.
>
> G. B. S.

The fun Shaw had cost Sean guineas he could ill afford to spare, for the
lawyers charged for all the letters. But the great-hearted G.B.S., Sean
thought, imagined he'd have to pay, not only the costs, but the rent as well,
and so he thought he might as well have a good laugh out of the loss. Sean
thanks heaven, feasting, that G.B.S. never had to pay a red either of costs
or of rent. The Agreement is with T. Cannon Brookes of Cannon Brookes
and Odgers, London, who cried out that he wouldn't part with it for anything. T. Cannon Brookes is a direct descendant of Napper Tandy (the one
who Met with poor old Ireland, and shook her be the Hand, according to
the famous ballad of *The Wearin' o' the Green*. Napper Tandy afterwards
became a general of France's Grande Armée, and lies buried in Bordeaux),
with the Napper Tandy nose which he has handed on to his tall son, and
whose little son is sprouting the same nose too.

Then came the long, sad shock of Charlotte's illness; the gradual distor-
tion of the stout body, the sinking away from association with the companion she had loved and guarded so long. The great and sensitive man had to
watch the life of his wife declining day by day; the flag of companionship

slipping down the staff. She is very much deformed, he wrote to Eileen. Though the day ends the same way for us all, there is infinite variety in the place, time, and manner of its ending. There was a great deal of goodness dying side by side with Charlotte Shaw; and the greatest good was the care she gave to the people's champion. Still she was there while the shadow of herself lingered in the home; there beside him. But shrink from it as he might, he had to let her go at last. She is dead, G.B.S.; ay, indeed, she is dead right enough. Shaw's Corner suddenly expanded into a wide and desolate world. One was taken and the other left. Put a brave face on it, man. I will, I will; but icy death that has taken Charlotte has touched me, too, as he passed. My wife is dead. She was called Charlotte; a good woman, a very good woman; and, now, she's gone. Alone, at last. Oh, Charlotte, where art thou, and why art thou silent, thou pulse of my heart? The place is full of shadow, even when the cuckoo calls. The summer is acumin in, but it will always be winter, now. Life is like a withered tree; what is all the world to me; life and light were all in thee. I am very busy trying to answer the thousands of letters of sympathy coming from four quarters of the earth. It will take months; I am very busy. Ah, my heart is sair, I darena' tell, my heart is sair for somebody. Busy, yes, busy. A fistful of dust about the garden blows. I said to the rose, the brief day goes. Silence everywhere. The housekeeper talks, the maid talks, the visitors talk; but there is silence everywhere. Silence in my own heart. I wander lonely as a cloud, a lone, lorn critter. The brief day goes. She was old; she had her day; the day soon goes. The evening star is gone, the shine has faded from the morning star.

> I'm here alone, I'm there alone;
> All that was here is here, yet all is gone;
> The star that glittered, the sun that shone.

> Visitors come and go,
> To laugh, murmur, and crow;
>   All has been said and done.
> Death faces a friendly foe;
> Tho' there's still things I'd like to know.

> I'm withered to creaking bone,
> And I potter round here alone.

> A few more years shall roll,
> A few more seasons fade;
> This mind of mine if it shall last
> Behind death's lone façade,

Shall question many things mismade:
Shall question unafraid.
Oh, Charlotte, well-beloved, I hear you
calling me.

Eileen and Sean sent several letters to him to assure him that he was far from being forgotten, but no reply came to the letters, and both were troubled. Sean wondered if they had been kept from him (afterwards, Shaw seemed to confirm this, for when, on a visit to Ayot Saint Lawrence, Eileen told him she had written some time ago, the old man said she must be mistaken, for he got no letter). Then Sean thought Shaw might be too tired or too busy to be bothered with him. Later on, a letter from George Jean Nathan, the American drama-critic, told him that he had written to G.B.S., enclosing one of his books, but had got no acknowledgement. They all puzzled over the reason why Shaw could be so silent. Later, Sean forwarded to Shaw a letter from a Dublin friend, Peadar O'Donnell, Editor of *The Bell,* pleading for a preface to a book written by an ex-soldier of the Irish Republican Army. This brought an affectionate reply from G.B.S., saying he had written to Peadar pointing out why he couldn't write the Preface, adding that Peadar couldn't have had a better introduction that one from Sean. Then came word from George Jean Nathan, saying Shaw had acknowledged the book, and had written 'Attaboy! Write a thousand of them. I like your stuff, and rank you as Intelligent Playgoer Number One!' So all smiled again, George Jean in New York, the O'Caseys in Devon, for all was well with the glorious sage of Ayot Saint Lawrence.

After they had sent him, at his request, a portrait of the family, Eileen on his invitation went, with John Dulanty, Eire's Ambassador, to have tea with him, caged now in his own home, where they had a fine time, John Dulanty brimming over with stories, Shaw commenting on them with many a musical laugh, Eileen adding her own merry laugh and good humour to the party. But the day soon goes. Some time later came the news of the accident; he had fallen while pruning a plum- or a pear-tree, and had broken a thigh. And he was ninety-four; there was small hope now, said Eileen, he is so old. No, no, said Sean, though, in his heart, he feared that Shaw, at last, was on the way to the land o' the leal. Carry him off to the hospital, where, it was said, the great man was quite chirrupy. It is odd to think of so many unable to see that this manner was assumed by Shaw to veil his shyness, to conceal his hatred of having to be helped by others; and strangers, too. To be helpless and dependent on others was a taste of horror for Shaw. Meagrely patched up, Shaw returns to his home, and soon after, hearing that she is in London, Shaw asks Eileen to come to see him. She goes, and that night her voice from London comes down to Devon over the telephone to say, Sean, Shaw is dying! Can you hear? G.B.S. is dying.

—Nonsense! went the voice of Sean from Devon up to London. You're imagining things. He's no more dying than I am.

—If you saw him, Sean, you'd know he was dying.

—He'll rally out of it. He'd rally out of anything.

—Not out of this, Sean; not out of this. When he looks at you, death looks at you, too.

Some days after, Eileen heard from John Dulanty that Shaw would like to see her again, but she put it off, having to give a lot of time to two of her children who are with her in London. But the thought that she should go down again to Ayot Saint Lawrence keeps coming into her mind. She should go, she shouldn't go, she couldn't go. She would ask John Dulanty as to whether she should or should not go; for she feared to disturb Shaw, or receive a snub from those who had charge of him. She journeyed down to the Ambassador's Office, but he was out. That settled it: she would not go. The secretary asked her to come the following day, and Eileen, murmuring that she would, decided that she wouldn't. Anyway, it was hardly likely that Shaw really wanted to see her. He had always liked her greatly, wondered sometimes why she had married such a one as Sean, at times gently teasing her about it. He liked her intelligence, not only of her mind, but also of her heart; so natural, vivid with friends; so real and generous with children. She understood as many didn't the odd, sparkling mind in the weakening body of Shaw; the mind still gay and as unpredictable as ever under the shawl of age. But she wouldn't go to John Dulanty's Office tomorrow, and so would never see the bold G.B.S. again. But in some strange way, the thought that she should go never left her mind, and, on the morrow, she went down to the Ambassador's Office, and met him as he was going out for the biggest part of the day. He came forward, saying Ah! I want you! He told her Shaw would very much like to see her, adding that, if she hadn't come, he would have written to her. Like Sean himself, John didn't believe that Shaw was dying, saying so to Eileen, and adding that when he was in Ayot Saint Lawrence a week or so ago, the old man was in fine fettle; but Eileen still fears that she is right, and that Greatheart, Captain Valiant, is dying; that the last moments of this battler, this lover of laughter, are saying farewell to the world and us all.

The Ambassador tells her to ring up to see if a visit would be all right at the moment. The housekeeper answers Eileen, goes away to ask Shaw, and comes back to say that Eileen is to come at once, for Mr. Shaw would very much like to see her. So Eileen goes down to stay for a few minutes, but remains for a long, long time with the departing Titan. He is slowly leaving the ken of the world, chatting in whispers so low that Eileen has to bend down close to the gentle face to hear what he says, sinking into a doze occasionally that was the shadow of coming unconsciousness.

He was lying in a sloping position in a bed against a wall, in a ground-floor room; dying there, waxen-faced, calm and patient; his eyes, bright as ever, shaded by the bushy brows, common sense alert in them, humour still aglow in them: living to the last. Another bed, narrower, lay alongside a wide window, looking out into the garden, sanctified now with the dust of his Charlotte; the flowers and walks he loved hidden away from him forever. Looking round while he dozed, Eileen saw on the wall a big photograph of the upright Stalin, full face, handsome and jovial, and, near by, one of Gandhi—both fine fighters, like Shaw himself, fighters in different ways; equals in ideal and outlook, fundamentally three in one: the world's peoples have spoken by and through the three of them. Eileen panted a little, very quietly, so as not to disturb the dozing Shaw, for the room was very hot, vainly assailing the coldness of death creeping over the life of the losing leader. The young woman and the old man; the one in life's centre, the other about to slide away from its oldest circle. The keen eyes slowly opened again, and she bent low to catch his whispering chat.

—I'm going, at last, Eileen; and I'm glad of it.

—Nonsense, G.B.S. You'll rally out of it, and live for us all a long time yet.

—No, no, Eileen; no longer. I want to die. What good would it be going from this bed here to that bed there; and all the time to be handled by those I don't know; by strangers? No, it is time for me to go; and he slid into a stilly doze.

—Are you there, Eileen? Are you still there? he whispered, coming back to the world again for a few moments.

—Yes, I'm still here, Eileen whispered back. Tell me if I bore you, or if you wish me to go away.

—No, no, he said, in a hasty whisper; stay till I sink into a deeper sleep.

—A sleep will do you good, she said; you'll be better then—not rightly knowing what to say.

—No, I'll never be better, he whispered back. Then the bright eyes closed again, and the long, lean figure lay still, the handsome hands, transparent now, lying quiet on the quilt. Eileen waited till the eyes opened again, the wan but still powerful face turned towards her, and a gentle smile creased the whitening lips; I have no desire to live longer. Could you stroke my forehead for a little while?—it seems to soothe the pain; and she stroked the high forehead gently, feeling that Shaw imagined himself back in his childhood with his mother watching over him.

—It is very pleasant to feel the touch of a soft Irish hand, and to hear the sound of a soft Irish voice. He was going from the world with his comrade-fighters, Gandhi and Stalin, watching from the wall. A quizzical smile flickered over his face. It will be interesting anyhow, Eileen, to meet the Almighty.

—I'm sure, G.B.S., that He and you will get on well together.

—I'll have a helluva lot of questions to ask Him, and the old humorous look lighted the wasted face again.

—Wait for Sean, she whispered; wait till he joins you, for he is a bit of a fighter.

—I'm a fighter, too, and the whisper became emphatic; but here my fighting is finished. It's up to Sean, now.

—Sean is too old, said Eileen quickly; he's seventy, now.

—Well, then, it's up to one, or both, of the boys, if their lives aren't wasted in another war.

Quietly and softly, he stole away into a sleep, and quietly and softly Eileen tiptoed out of the room, leaving him looking as if he were already dead. Outside, she talked for some time to the nurse. Then, suddenly, the bell, fastened to Shaw's shoulder, rang to bring attention. When the young nurse went in, he asked her if Eileen had gone, and was told she had not, but was about to go. He said he'd like to say goodbye to her. She went back, sat down by the bedside, and with a lovely smile that flashed back into his face the younger Shaw to view again, he said, Goodbye, Eileen, goodbye; give my love to all the O'Caseys. She lingered there over the goodbye till the great, tired soul sank into sleep again, a deeper sleep than before; then she stole from the room, and left Shaw's Corner, and left the great householder in sleep, that he might be free to go forth to meet death, to give death welcome, and see death bow before his greatness.

He died two days later. These were his last words: That youth might not be wasted in another war. Kind man, brave man, wise soul, indomitable spirit of the indomitable Irishry.

* * *

AND EVENING STAR

☙ ☙ ☙

Old, oh, so old! Yet he couldn't see the logic of the calendar or give ear to the ticking of the clock. He knew that the bit of life-tapestry he was weaving would come to an end before long. Soon the loom he was at would go clack clack clacking no more; nevermore. He had to go to make room for the young; recognise as Tennyson did that 'old men must die, or the world would grow mouldy, would only breed the past again'.

Well, the clack of his loom had always gone with the louder clack of life. The loom worked slower now, but there was no rust on it. It was a little tired, a little worn, for it had never rested, and never would. The young are knocking at the door. The old must decrease, the young increase. He hoped his children would throw a wider chest than his own. Down below, the elder lad hammered a frame together for a picture he was painting, the younger lad, laying aside biology for a spell, was blasting out music from a fine second-hand trombone, the young girl was merrily tapping out a Mozartian minuet from the piano—all indifferent—all careless of the tumult of mind afflicting the old codger up above, labouring over finding words for his wonderful work. Heartless youth; didn't give a damn how they distracted him. Thinking of themselves only. And who else should they be thinking of, in God's name?

> *When the rain raineth and the goose winketh,*
> *Little wots the gosling what the goose thinketh.*

And why the hell should it? It is only the young who possess the world.

Past achievements, failures, experiences, were echoes in his ear now; all echoes under the sunset and the evening star; echoes of places where he had lived and moved and had his being; echoes all echoing around everywhere, in the strength of the day, in the still deep of the night.

> *Echo, I will not talk with thee,*
> *For thou art a dead thing.*

He couldn't linger long among a crowd of echoes, however charming they might be; there were too many things to think of, too many things to do: things to think about, things to do in the home, in the wider community of the nation, in the widest community of the world. The world now was like a jig-saw puzzle; though some had fitted the pieces well and securely together, others, in conference, committee, assembly, and what not had jumbled the pieces so confusedly that few knew even where to look for the most of them. The nations of Europe have fallen into a screaming coma. A lot of them are yelling out for help. America's feet are worn away running from one to the other. Oh, there's another one down! Prop him up, buddies! But before this guy is properly propped, two more are down on their backs; and soon there's a queue lying, dead to the world, waiting to be lifted to their feet again. The coma conquers them. Neither dollars nor machinery are worth a damn if the people haven't the will to do. A nation though immersed in wealth and cluttered with machinery, but without a will, would surely, if slowly, die.

Ireland's idea of safety with her roads adance with jeeps was neither a

will nor a way. He had just read in an Irish journal that a roman catholic
dignitary, preaching in an Irish town, had condemned Communists, their
friends, and their friends' friends, adding, as a sorrowful affix, that for the
whole year there had been but one marriage in the town. Ha ha ha! Looks
like Ireland was becoming like heaven itself, where they neither marry nor
are given in marriage. Ha ha ha! Last May, the Blessed Virgin's month,
before the bloom was on the rye, a letter came to Eileen from a woman
living in a Dublin cottage slum, with eight children to keep. The last baby
had come six years after the seventh, and had left the mother prostrate for
months. Ever after she was to feel the effects of the strain. She wrote,

'My dear Mrs. O'Casey, Thank you for your letter. We all had flu. Una
got it Bad and I have her in Bed with Pluresy at the Moment. She is not
quite as bad as she was she is a bad fighter and lets everything in on her lets
hope she wont be long till she is well again. You know I am a Bad letter
writer cant think of what to say when I sit down to write. Ill say goodbye
for now Ill get this off to you and get the kids to bed love to Shivaun
Sincerely Chris.'

A bad fighter, letting everything in on her! A bad character for a slum-
child. Written, probably, in the irritation of a great weariness, or written
out of a vague reason for the child's lack of toughness; for the woman,
Chris, was a fine mother and a very kind one; but she had too many kids to
keep and care for, and, now, with all things dearer, it wouldn't be long till
thousands of other kids would cease to be fighters, and would let everything
in on them. Anyway, it was far more urgent for the defence of the country
to have jeeps prancing along the roads than to fill the bellies of the nation's
children with the food they urgently needed. Let the kids go—we need
jeeps; we do, be jeepers!

Same here, same in England. All was needed for the arms, and little
needed for the man. Even in the wealthy and imperative United States,
many a still, small voice cried out in solitary places. Writes an American
mother to him:

'Not knowing a mother, I was brought up by a grim, hard-working father, who, bending over a noisy sewing-machine, six days a week (doing
that still today at sixty six). We were never hungry, but there were many
things daily to remind us that it happened to the best of working-class
families; that our furniture as well as next family's could be put out into the
street; that Santa Claus wasn't abroad at Christmas time, or sitting in the
grocer's shop; that the landlord was a force to be reckoned with almost on
the lofty level of the Government and the Lord above. Today, they gave my
little girl a bit of metal on a chain to wear around her neck. It's called a Dog-
Tag (der Tag!). United States soldiers wear it in Korea and wherever they
are. That's if Russia bombs us we'll be able to identify the pint-sized remains. The stamped letters with the child's and father's names are supposed

to be especially durable. Flame-tested, I guess. Neither I nor my child will ever wear one.'

There is no need to wear them, O little girl and grown-up woman. Soviet bombs will never fall on New York City, unless New York bombs fall on Moscow first. There would be no gain to either city if each destroyed the other, for both would be gone, and the world would miss them. There is no danger, no danger, for though man be foolish, men are not fools. Each great city will go on living; living in its own vigorous, beautiful way.

He was writing now in the Fall of the Year, while the leaves of the trees were taking a last flutter through the air, whispering a goodbye to life as they fell. Sere and yellow, they were useless now to the tree; they had done their work, and the newer buds beneath were busy pushing them off; pushing them away from life, never to return again. Sere and yellow leaf, fall fluttering, and fade from all you knew, carrying to earth with you some tender fragment of the summer's dream. So are many now, so was he— waiting for that gentle but insistent push that would detach his clinging desire, and send him, like the tumbling autumn leaf, sinking from life's busy tree to the dull flavour of death in the kingly dust where all men mingle in a sleep unending.

Outside, in the tiny garden, the few flowers have faded, or have been shoved from life by the sharp frost of the night before. The tall hollyhocks have toppled, leaving a few lingering rose-like forms on one dismantled stalk nuzzling itself into the chilly clay. Only the michaelmas daisies are topped with fading stars of crimson and mauve, and in the sullen hedge, hacked into rough-arrayed order, a few golden-brown blossoms still peer out from the prickly barberry bush. A spreading bloom of a purple dahlia and the crimson disk of a single one have slunk heavily to the ground, oozy with a brownish slime that almost hides the memory of their bygone brilliancy. A short time ago, he had watched two big, handsome bees, delicately furred and red-banded, in the yellow centre of the crimson dahlia disk, one bee in its core, the other on its fringe. Honey-drunk and half dead they seemed to be. After a long time, the furry fellow on the fringe sleepily began to press himself deeper into the yellow core of the crimson disk, his twitching legs moving about to get a firmer grip, touching the other fellow's legs in the centre, who, with the tiniest show of irritation, shoved them twitchingly aside, just as a woman in the honey-hush of sleep might sleepily shove away from her body the wandering legs of a husband. Dead the blossoms, half-dead the bees, and the leaves all round fluttering down. A beautiful sadness everywhere. But in a few days, the crimson disk will be there again, the purple-spreading dahlia will flaunt its pomp in the world's face, and the bees will buzz and hum and buzz again, as if the sun shone always and the frost was all over forever. Even the winter has her many beauties, even for the old who shiver; the crisper air; the cold mists of morning, the fretted framework of the trees against the sky, the diamantling frost biting a harsh beauty into the earth's soft bosom; the stillness of the earth herself under it all, waiting for the spring. Ah, yes; to the old, spring and its budding bring a welcome as well as to the young. Sweet spring, full of sweet days and roses.

Even here, even now, when the sun had set and the evening star was chastely touching the bosom of the night, there were things to say, things to do. A drink first! What would he drink to—the past, the present, the future? To all of them! He would drink to the life that embraced the three of them! Here, with whitened hair, desires failing, strength ebbing out of him, with the sun gone down, and with only the serenity and the calm warning of the evening star left to him, he drank to Life, to all it had been, to what it was, to what it would be. Hurrah!

OPINIONS
ALSO, A SHORT STORY

UNDER A GREENWOOD TREE HE DIED

(FROM "UNDER A COLORED CAP", 1963)

To all mothers and fathers
mourning loved ones who died too young.

☘ ☘ ☘

That is all he is now: a hand of greeting falls for ever upon a sad sweet shadow.

He had come down from London bringing his sister, Shivaun, with him, in the little red Ford van, to spend Christmas and the holidays at home. He looked somewhat tired, but there was a good reason, more than one, why he should look a little pale, and feel a little weary. A week before, he had come down in the red van, bringing some friends with him, to attend a party given by the Bursar of Dartington Hall School for his daughter's coming of age; and had driven back to London the next morning, taking the friends with him, so that all could end college or school term before the bells rang for the festival, before the holly was carried in to hang on a wall or crown a picture. Before that, he had rushed into busy activity, with Shivaun, preparing for the great meeting in Trafalgar Square, carrying a banner in the procession, while Shivaun at his side carried another; all to show, and all to prove, that peace rather than war and aggression was the present and the future ideal of the young. So Eileen and I whispered together that what with his running around and his biological studies at London University, he had overdone it, had wearied himself, and what he needed was a good long rest. God knows, he has gotten it. Never again will he shout in a demonstration for peace; never carry a banner. But, for the moment, he was just a little tired. We little knew, nor did he know, that he had already drunken a deep glass of Mr. Weston's Good Wine.

The next day, fifteenth of December, he went with Eileen to Dr. Doran, who said he had a very acute attack of anaemia, and that he would know its depth and extent when a sample of the lad's blood had been tested in the laboratory. On the eighteenth the disease was declared to be leukaemia, and Niall knew that he had been sentenced to death with a scant chance of any reprieve; a chance in ten that he might survive for a month or two longer. The ambulance would come in half an hour to take him away, away to hospital; the second time the ambulance came here—first for me exactly a year ago; now it came for Niall, our darling boy; came to bring him on his way to death; not here shalt thou die, but in London where thou wast born. I went in to him while we waited for the ambulance to come. He looked up at me, no tear in his eye, but a wistful look asking me something silently. I took his hand in mine, and felt the pressure of his, a pressure that was wistfully asking me something, something I felt to be Why and Whither? I pressed his dear hand as lovingly and as encouraging as I could; again, he returned the pressure.

'It's hellish', he murmured, very lowly. He said no more, so we stayed together, hand in hand, he in bed, I sitting on the bed's side, close to him as I could get; leaving him but for a few moments to see the specialist, Dr. Haddon, who had come down to examine him, and who was to follow him to Exeter Hospital to do all science could do to soften a disease science knew very little about. He told us that he dared not give any comfort; that the most science could do, with its present knowledge, was to try to keep the boy with us for a month or two longer. Only another month or two—oh, Jesus, and our boy would be no more with us; never come in, never go out, never sit at table, never lead us in a bright and reckless laugh, never inquire what I thought of a book I, or he, had just read, never drive or ride in the red van again, never drive his mother about in her Minx car, never wear the bright blue jersey we had gotten him for Christmas. In another month or so he would be gone, and already he heard the rushing of the dark river across which he would soon have to go, leaving the rest of us on the farther bank; away from our sight for ever. But there was hope: those doomed by doctors did not always die. He was a vital lad; he had an intense desire to go on living; he would fight against death to the end; so there was still hope in our hearts, but hope herself was ever murmuring within our minds, there is no hope.

The ambulance-men came into the room and gently lifted Niall from the bed on to the stretcher to take him from the home he loved, the home he would never see again. I bent down to kiss him, and his lips clung longingly to mine, as if he would gather back again from my poor breathing the life he was losing. 'My young darling boy', I murmured, as I kissed him again, 'May God go with you'; and, oh, I could not guess the agony that was in his mind as he could not guess the agony that was in mine. The evil bud of an anxious dread was alive and growing in the heart of mother, father, brother, and sister, and growing, too, in the beating heart of our sick boy.

For Niall, the active and delightful communion with family and with friend would be lost for ever: never again would he play treble on the piano to Shivaun's or Breon's bass of some piece by Beethoven or Mozart; when I mentioned the great lizards' failure to survive, never again would he tell me that they were far from a failure, that they had roamed this earth for a hundred million years, and, if man could live so long, it would be well;

never again would he put on cricket-pads to go out to bat, or don shorts and crimson jersey for a football game; never again would I hear his merry and prolonged laugh in the next room, so hilarious that it made me join in alone in my own chair in my own room; never go out again, alone with him, or between him and Breon, to stroll along Dartington Drive, by the river Dart, through a summer evening, returning in the deeper dusk, the gentle evening star aglow within the colors of an opal and amethystine sky; walking together while it was yet light before the darkness came upon him, came upon our young and darling boy; a few brief moments in the garden of life, going where the primroses go, and then the night came, and we lost him, lost our boy in the midst of the darkness. As he entered the darkness, the little subdued cry of 'I must confess, I feel a little frightened"; and then the quiet resignation, and, last, the rambling, broken by clear periods, and then the rambling again, and lastly, the quiet, calm disappearance. Our darling boy, our dear, darling boy was gone. But this last had not come yet: he was lifted into the ambulance, Eileen, dry-eyed and cheerful, a bruising ache in her heart, went with him, holding his hand, ready with a loving pressure to help him on his wan way, while I sought the solitude of thought to will with all the nerve-power, all the vitality left in me after just seventy-seven years of life, that our boy would not bow before the doctors' judgement, but would be able to mingle his young life with the life of the family and the life of the world again; my mind following the ambulance to Exeter, looking at the boy stretched in it, his mother lovingly holding one hand, death grimly gripping the other.

For the next few days, Eileen stayed close to Niall, her shadow falling on the hospital walls, her saucy presence, pressing down an aching heart, strolling into the ward where he lay, his finely-formed hand fluttering out to warm itself within her enclosing clasp, his eyes alight, for the bed for a while checked its growth into a tomb. Silently, the boy's eyes said Mother, and, as silently, hers said My darling son. For the next few days, Breon and Shivaun went to Exeter to keep in touch with Eileen, and on the eve of Christmas Eve I set out with them, watching the blurred forms of tree and house hurrying by as the car journeyed through the fog and the misty rainfall. He had had a number of blood transfusions, the blood coming from a vessel above through a tube and then a needle into a vein in the arm, tightly bandaged so that no movement might upset the slow and silent drip, a young lad being buoyed up with the richer blood of another, someone, a brother or sister unknown, who had thought 'Silver and gold have I none, but what I have, that I give unto thee'; the blood flowed into the waiting vein, drop by drop, slowly, taking hours to spill out its last drop of healing virtue, Eileen holding the boy's free hand during the buzzing discomfort to vein and feeling from the blessed intrusion of a comrade's blood, till the restlessness eased, till the boy grew drowsy, till the drowsiness strengthened into a painless sleep, and the finely-formed hand of the lad no longer sought a contact with the mother's. Oh, the sad shadow of a coming event when no contact could be sought, no contact could be given. Lulla, lulla, lulla, lullaby; the restlessness of body and of thought is hushed in sleep, but it is a hush more dead than any sleep, unwilling sleep for one so young, so active, and yesterday, but yesterday, his mind was so quietly thronged with ideas of what the future would bring him forth to do.

So within the car I swung into Exeter for the first time, an old city knowing many names from the time of William the Conqueror and King Alfred, still a little rueful from the bombs that shook its walls during the last big war, known to most for its cathedral, to me for its hospital; a city that will for ever now give an ache to my memory, for here our son made his first stop on his way to death. A huge building where many find healing and many find the end. Visitors went in two at a time, and Breon and Shivaun were the first to go, Eileen and I waiting till their allowance of time had ended. Anxious to see Niall, we moved slowly to the doorway, entered, going slowly down the corridor towards the ward where our son lay.

By the door of the ward where he lay we waited; still we stood, silently waiting for Breon and Shivaun to come out so that we might go in to stand where our young son lay dying. Motionless we waited to go in and stand beside where he lay, our hearts aching, minds thoughtless, refusing to believe that our boy was bound to die. At that time there was but one life worth saving—the life of our dear boy. Nurses flitted by us, efficient, unsparing of themselves. Doctors, white-coated, strode by, cool, sure, for ever facing pain and death, fighting to remove the pain, fighting to keep back death from coming too soon. Two of these were giving our Niall ever and never-tiring attention; but Eileen knew in her heart, and Sean did too, that their urgent and constant skill would not do: it wasn't good enough. No doctor the world over could save boy or girl stricken down with acute leukaemia. It was just a question of time, and a very short time, too. We waited between the clean white walls of the corridor, so calm, so dignified, that it was hard to imagine Death would disturb so precise and passionless a place. But Death was there; Death was near, right between the mother and the father of the young lad, almost ready now to take his hand and go.

We met Breon and Shivaun coming out, and were warned not to be shocked to find Niall talking oddly, and finding it impossible to say a full sentence. We hurried into the ward, to the bedside, and found him calm and quiet as ever, but worried that he had to be mute, and could not talk or tell his thoughts to those who had come to hear them. 'Pencil', he murmured; 'I . . . write'. Eileen gave him one, and he wrote down how he felt, how his throat seemed to lock itself away from speech, suggesting that Eileen should ask the Sister why. Eileen hurried away, returning to tell us that the

Sister said Niall being in a low condition had caught some slight infection; that it wasn't to worry him, and that it had nothing to do with the prime disease. So Eileen and I convinced ourselves, convinced Niall, that he had no need to worry; but out of kindness, the Sister had deceived us, for the locked throat was indeed another grip the disease was tightening on the bodily life of our boy.

The bed where our boy lay was up at the farther end of a long ward. There was no complacency here, all doctors and nurses were for ever busy healing; discharging those who had gotten better, receiving fresh cases immediately, and quietly removing anyone who had died on them. The younger doctors and most nurses were busy, too, rehearsing songs and carols so that patients might be helped to enjoy themselves at Christmas, to dawn upon the Christian faith within a few days now. A great Christmas tree, its top branch almost touching the high ceiling, had been dressed and shone with glittering balls and segments of all colors and shapes, the sprays sprinkled with frost, some of the tree's long side branches stretching out almost over the bed where our boy lay along alone with death.

A few moments later, a look from Eileen and a murmur that she would like to be alone for a little with Niall, told me to go, for it was clear that Niall wanted Eileen to be near him more than anyone else in the world. Poor brave Eileen who had had such a long vigil over me a few months ago, but from which there was a fair return, would now have a shorter but a much more bitter vigil from which she alone would return, leaving her beloved boy for ever behind. The boy could not have made a finer choice of a companion for his ending, so I pressed his hand that I had been holding, looked down on the sharp intelligent face with its penetrating blue eyes, its delicate nose, its shock of hair, the firm and humorous mouth; bent down and kissed the lips, a warm touch which he eagerly returned, and murmured that I would be with him again very soon, very, very soon, pressed the dear hand once more, and again as he smiled up at me, and left him alone with his mother. No troubling thought struck me then that this was the last time I should ever look upon that intelligent and delightful young face, smiling up at me from under a greenwood tree.

So we came back home to prepare for Christmas, to wrap up the books and the bright blue jersey to be presented to Niall when we gathered round his bedside, so that, even in his torment, he might catch a glimpse of the goodness-custom of Christmas Day, an excitement that had been banished from our own anxious hearts; while Eileen remained behind to minister to him, telling us that night she had soothed him into drinking fruit juice and inducing him to swallow a quantity of chicken-jelly; fighting for him, and helping him to fight for himself; adding hopefully that he was much better and very cheerful. So Breon and Shivaun wrapped up what we wanted to take with us the next day to Exeter—fruit, wine, sweets, and Niall's bright blue jersey, a record, and two books on biology that he had asked for, little thinking that a white shroud would be worn by our boy instead of the bright blue jersey, while I sat by the fire filled with my own thoughts that draped a mourning badge round every thought of Christmas; filled with the thoughts of what Niall had been, and of what we hoped he would have been when a time came to do things.

Alone with my own thoughts? nay, rather alone with what I thought to be his, wondering what they were now. Before, his boy's way was the wind's way, and his young thoughts were long, long thoughts; but now? My own thoughts had all gone into a will; a will as strong, as determined, as the nerve and vitality left in me after seventy-seven years of life could make it, that my boy should live and return to the glow and murmur of our family life. My thoughts were all of him. Looking idly through an old black-covered, blue-lined day-book in which I had written scraps of thoughts for biography, or jottings for plays, I came across a dated reference to our Niall. It read: On the twenty-second of January, nineteen hundred and forty-nine, Niall arrayed himself in a brilliant crimson football-jersey, blue shorts, and black stockings, barred with vivid red stripes, for a match on Dartington Hall's home ground. Solomon in all his glory wasn't arrayed like this young lad, minding me of the day when I donned a jersey of blue, barred with green hoops, white shorts, and running shoes, to go forth to play my first fast hurling match, and to play well and play fast for the honour of the club. Eileen had marched through many streets, had visited many shops, had searched high and low, before she had managed to pounce on the jersey and the stockings that alone would fit our Niall for the fight in defence of his club and his school; then he was fourteen years old, and it was but seven years ago that he had first worn the crimson jersey, and now it was very likely that he would never, never wear the blue one.

Two years later, another casual note in the same old book tells me To-night, October the twenty-second, Niall spoke enthusiastically about his partnership with the Dartington Hall Choir who are to sing Handel's version of Milton's *L' Allegro* and *Il Penseroso*. He read the libretto from the score first, read it splendidly and enjoyably so that it was plain that he knew and understood all he recited, though he had to guess what a Rebeck was meant to be. Then we got out Milton's works, and read and re-read the two poems, discovering the parts and phrases that Handel had left aside; reciting them together, I finding beauties in them, marked out by Niall, that I had never noticed before. I was surprised and gladdened that Milton could appeal so delightfully to such a young mind. A little later, he acted Mark Antony, and we plunged into *Julius Caesar,* he and I acting the bigger scenes with all the energy we had within us, and it was a lot; later still, just before he entered the army, he played his last role (but one)— that of General Burgoyne in Shaw's *The Devil's Disciple.* Oh, had I known, had I but guessed, how I should have lingered over all this singing, these recitings, fondling every phrase he tried to sing, every line he spoke from Shakespeare and from Milton! Now, he was playing his last role, silently singing a swan song, under a greenwood tree.

A wide-mannered lad who ranged in sound from Jazz to Beethoven, from Dickens to James Joyce, from biology to football. He was a fine cook, hardy and active at family gatherings with our guests, his mother's right hand at birthday festivals, or the bigger and more blatant one of Christmas; could play the trombone, and often did, in any amateur dance band; knew all the families of all the plants of Europe; used some of his last hours studying algae and fungi in Smith's book on *Cryptogams* (botany was a wonderful link in the unity of our children, for they were almost three in one and one in three); was gifted with a fine sense of fairness to all outside of himself; the penetrating blue eyes peered into all sides of life, peered fearlessly, with sometimes a deep sigh, and often a rollicking laugh. Oh, my darling lad, when you went, we lost a lot, but life lost more. Perhaps he would pull through; he was so vital; he had been busy to the last, rushing round, pushing tiredness away from him so that his doctor said he must have done it all on his abounding nerve strength. There was hope still.

So we parcelled the few presents, hoping Niall would be better, and looking forward to spending an hour or so beside his bed, trying intangibly and gropingly to graft a little of our own assurance of life into a young mind that was soon to sigh out its ending. So Breon, Shivaun, and I set out in the Hillman Minx that Niall loved so much and drove so well; to Exeter, to join Eileen at her hotel right in front of the Cathedral, and then go with her to spend what we could of Christmas Day with the dying boy. It was a shocking day, the wind blowing fierce and the rain slashing down with vicious insistence, and the wind was a bitter one. A lone road, with scarce a car passing; big pools through which the car plunged sending spray over the bonnet; the trees bending before the wind, and every house passed seeming to huddle itself closer to its own walls. Fear no more the heat of the sun, nor the furious winter's rages. Cold comfort: Niall feared neither. He revelled in the summer sun and the snows of a wild-cat winter. Oh, the changes of the seasons are a joy to a young mind within a healthy body. There's no voice or even whisper in rain, wind, frost, or snow that says 'die' to a young heart. Let the greenwood tree be bare and bony, or lush with leaf and blossom, the young heart sings beneath it.

The Minx slid into the Cathedral Close and halted outside the hotel. We were close to him now, and soon would be beside him, be beside him. A few lonely cars jutting from the pavement's edge, and the Cathedral lifting its bulky towers up to a sky so dark and lowering that it seemed to touch their tops, were the only signs of life standing silent beneath the pelting rain, and against the panting, pushing wind; an unlit Christmas tree beside the Cathedral's wall heralded no happiness to a soul, but dripped disconsolate where it stood. A lonely crib with the hulking Cathedral in its centre, the wind's fierce blast and the rain a-pelting: little Jesus wouldn't like a day like this. We hurried into the hotel's hall, away, away from the cold wind, to seek Eileen, and to set out to carry good cheer to our stricken boy; but Eileen had left word that she was with Niall, and she would be back as soon as she could; that we were to go to her room, to light the fire there, and to wait for her coming.

Waiting! We had a lot of waiting to do: Waiting now for Eileen's news; waiting to go to the bedside of our Niall; waiting till he had gathered enough strength to go from Exeter Hospital to St. Bartholomew's in London; waiting for a possible smile from a dour hope that our boy might be able to be with us again for a year, for a few months even; while the boy himself had to bear the most agonising wait of us all. In Eileen's little bedroom, with its little gas fire trying to cheer away the yell of the wind and the whip of the lashing rain on the window-panes; Eileen's bits of things scattered over the bed, hanging on the chair, and a few in the wash-basin soaking there till she had a minute to wash them clean; our few parcelled presents placed among Eileen's things on the bed, looking as if they too were on the way out of the world of Christmas merriment and good cheer. Then Eileen came in, her fawn mack black as a mourning gown with the slash of the rain. She was in a hurry. Her face was pale, and lines of anxiety had been strengthened into lines of determination, her blue eyes had a soft light of battle in them. She had to go back at once to Niall; she had just run over to tell us that he wasn't too well, and that the Christmas gathering couldn't gather to his bed. He wasn't able again to speak more than a few words, and each word meant an effort of nerve and will. The best thing we could do was to have some tea, and then go back home, leaving the chance of seeing him for another day. She would just have a glass of wine, and then run back to the bedside. 'We can't bother him with presents just now. He knows the danger he runs, but he is very brave. I have to wash out his mouth every so often, and when the doctor comes to give him the drug that relaxes his throat, I have to be ready with the fruit juice and the beef essence, so that he may swallow as much as possible before his throat stiffens again'. So she drank the glass of wine and hurried down to the car for Breon to drive her to the bedside of her boy. Kind, indomitable Eileen battling for her boy's life; the pelican opening her breasts to give life to her young, careless of the life she needs herself. Oh, mother, mother, mak' my bed, to lay me down with sorrow; and we all felt that the bleakness and cold of the merry day was making a deep home in our hearts.

There was no use, Eileen said, of us waiting there longer. The hope of Christmas Day was gone. Breon would bring us home, and would come back to stay with her. So we went into the foul evening again, into the car, and away, the wind as strong and harsh as ever, the rain heavier, leaving our boy with the knowledge that death was nearer, but welcoming the thought that he would have Eileen beside him till the last sigh came. Through deep pools the car plunged, and through the headlights full-on we saw the sheets of rain falling on road, hedge, house, and field. Ten miles on we came to a car halted on the roadside, blinking its lights as a signal for us to stop. The driver warned us not to go on, for, he said, he had just managed to come through, with the waters over the bonnet. We pushed on, however, but soon found we were plunging into swirling waters, rising higher as we went, and the wind shook the car when a gust came sideways, with a sight of roughly dancing waters fronting us as far as the eye could see. We turned back towards Exeter, crawling down the hills, for the waters had loosened the soil of the roads, and the inclines were dangerous and slippy. We were glad to get back to Eileen's hotel where we got rooms for the night; and later on, when Niall had slipped into a sleep, Eileen managed a hurried dinner with us, before she fled away again to the hospital. Niall's home now, and her home too, to stay with him till the drugs made him drowsy and indifferent; then creeping out, ashamed to leave him for fear he would awake and seek to look into her eyes or grope for the soft and encouraging touch of her hand. She, too, needed sleep, a wan sleep, a sleep that but helped to make her fit for another day of helping her son on his sad way; rising from bed every third hour or so to hurry to where he lay, staying there, if he were awake, till he sank to sleep again. I went to bed at two of the clock, but turned and twisted, wide awake, till after I had heard some bell chime the hour of four, and then the sleep was fitful and full of foreboding. The next day, St. Stephen's, Eileen was early at the hospital, coming back to tell us that Niall seemed a little better, but wasn't fit to see us yet, but was looking forward to a visit when he became stronger; and that his mind now leaned to the hope of being well enough to make the journey to Bart's Hospital in London tomorrow; tomorrow, if he were well enough, he would go; and Dr. Haddon was doing all that science could do to make the journey possible.

Leaving Breon with Eileen, Shivaun and I came back home by train through a flooded country to wait for news; Shivaun and I to wait for news. Yes, he could make it: he had gone on the journey the next morning, travelling with a nurse and Eileen in a special compartment, the long journey to London and Bart's, through a thick fog that delayed the arrival for over an hour; cheerful, he went, with renewed hope that science there might preserve him to the world for some time longer. The Lord God had been good to him. He had arrived. Breon hurries back in the car to garage it, and let it wait too, like us all; snatches a quick meal, and away with him again to catch a train to London to be at Eileen's side; to be her guide, her prop and stay, a very present help in her present day of trouble: a gallant lad who rarely left her side since Niall fell; while Shivaun and I went on with living at home, I getting the breakfast, she cooking the other meals, I washing things up, she drying them as they were washed; at night, seeking in the stupid face of Television a way out from anxious fear, but seeing there only the young face of my boy, her brother, and within the young face the sad pain of having to go away from life so soon.

All that could be done was being done for him, said Eileen. He has had drugs which allow him to talk more freely, and he is as vital as ever in his thoughts for things outside of himself; of the sad happening in Hungary which distresses him; of his belief in the future; and of Eileen herself, vehemently counselling to be always true to herself, always; she was a great woman, and he begged her to be always true to herself; that she mustn't let more prosperous times shift her from where she stood; that nothing within her must be lost, but all things, all her fine qualities must be strengthened by her sense of honour for them; that she must never fear to hold her own opinions, never fear to be herself: she must never lose sight of herself. His searching mind was still searching; the crusader's spirit was still vital within him. 'Dear Eileen', he said, 'I love you deeply, we all love you, and you should hold fast your ideal for ever'.

Dear kid, in a rationalist form and fancy, he preached the kingdom of heaven to Eileen and to Breon; declaring to them in his human mystic, that the kingdom of heaven is within us; he was using his last moments to mould a world nearer to his heart's desire; a ray from a spirit moving over to the face of the darker waters. Dying old men in the same ward had called for priest or parson, had cried out loud that they didn't want to die; bawling that they were afraid of hell, while the priest tried to calm them; but the young one had held his peace, though God knows, he didn't want to die either. He held silent about his fear, except once in the darkness, an hour or so before the end, with Eileen and Breon beside him, he had murmured, 'I must confess that I feel a little frightened'. Dear, dear boy, there is no dishonour in feeling a little frightened; but when Eileen put the light on, and pressed his hand, the boy was calm again. Unaware of them in a credal form, he had within him the cardinal virtues of justice, prudence, temperance, and fortitude, bearing the lost loveliness of life without a moan. Oh, my lovely boy, woe is ours that you were taken away so soon! Once only had he seemed to show how bitter the loss was: when he saw Breon distressed, and tears in his soft eyes, he said, 'There is no cause for you to worry, Breon, for it is I who have to die, and not you'. It was hard to resign himself away for ever from the many things he longed to do; to go from the companionship of young friends who thought so much of him, and looked up to him for advice in any problem; for even in the midst of dancing, he had a mind ready to comment wisely on a problem presented by a young friend.

So Eileen kept close to her younger son, anointing him with her calmness and her courage; washing out his hot mouth every few minutes, giving him a little less discomfort; changing his pyjamas when they got wet with sweat, and helping him to put on fresh and warm ones; while Shivaun and I waited at home for whatever news grim time might bring. Niall had gone to Bart's on the twenty-seventh of December, and doctors were busy doing all they could for him, distressed that one so intelligent and so gallant should die so young; though there was fine hope that he would live for some time, maybe for three months or longer. Breon rings up on the evening of the twenty-eighth to say that Niall is not so well, but he is cheerful, and the doctors have relieved his throat so effectively that he has been talking away, and still had much to say; he has taken a cup of tea, the first for weeks, and has eaten an orange, given carefully in tiny fragments, Eileen, foreknowing in some curious way that he might like one, has brought some with her, and is able to hand him one when he asks for it. Perhaps he may live longer. The next evening, we are told that Niall is cheerful, and even a little gay, but hardly ever lets his eyes stray from his mother's face. And Breon is rarely more than a foot or two away from Eileen ministering to her son. Poor, gallant boy with his poor, gallant mother.

On Sunday morning, the thirtieth, Eileen rings up, and tells Shivaun, first at the phone, some news, I waiting impatiently beside her. Shivaun hands me the receiver, saying, 'I have terrible news, the most terrible news in the world', and hurries to her room crying. It is indeed terrible news, that Niall died at nine o'clock the night before; died quietly, swiftly, and bravely. Up to the last, nearly, he had talked seriously, and had spoken about us all during the day, a painful one, a day of battle indeed, for at times his body went cold, his teeth chattered, and blankets had to be piled over him; while, later on, his poor body burned so that Eileen had to strip all off, to let him lie beneath a sheet only, and kept going to the kitchen for ice-cubes to put over his eyes to soothe away the burning of his brow; but in between, he talked to her about herself, about Shivaun, making shrewd remarks, and giving that advice that was so characteristic of his great, gay, and prudent nature. Eileen hadn't rung up the night he died to tell Shivaun and me that he had gone away from us, that we had lost him for ever, so that we might sleep quietly unaware of our Niall's end. He had slept soundly, God knows, slept more deeply than he had ever desired or intended to sleep; slept more soundly than we had ever wanted him to do: a sleep from which he would never awake.

That evening, that very evening, Niall had seemed to be decidedly better; more restful and settled. The doctors said so and the nurses thought so too. Doctor and nurse advised Eileen that she could safely go, have a quiet meal, and rest for the best part of the night. Eileen had felt doubtful, and she hesitated. Didn't they think she should send for his young friends? Not just now, they had replied; no need for haste; it will be quite safe to wait till

Monday. So Eileen left Niall sleeping calmly under the glittering green-wood tree, for there was a great Christmas tree in the ward at Bart's, taller, more wide-spreading branches, and with a greater glitter, than the tree in the ward at Exeter Hospital, and left with Breon to get a quiet meal which both badly needed. She was still doubtful; some odd feeling within her urged to go to where her boy lay. She told Breon, but he assured her it was but imagination. It lingered, and she had hardly begun the meal when she told Breon that she must go. In a taxi she hurried away, urging the driver to go quick, for her boy was dying. He did his best, and his fare had to be pressed upon him at the journey's end. She ran into the hospital, up the corridor where the ward was, meeting the Sister, who hurried her along, saying how glad she was Eileen had come, for Niall was on his way from the world; on a swift way from all he had loved.

He had had moments of delirium during the last hour, and strangely his thoughts crossed to America, calling out gayly that we must get the Minx car, and get to America to see Sean's play, and where he could hear the genuine jazz played. At the last, he had asked for his young friends, and was told they were on the way to him; he had flung his legs from the bed to be on the way to America, and it took Breon some effort to get him back again, for Niall had never lost his swiftness and strength of limb, and his vitality still surged through his soul. He had called for Shivaun and for me, and Eileen told him we were just around the corner waiting to come in to him; while the young nurse was visibly affected that such a gallant lad should have to go, and the doctor who had attended to him was distressed that his greatest skill and knowledge could keep him alive no longer, for the swift end was rare, but it occurred occasionally, and it came to Niall. The fight was over for him, but the fight was not over for poor, brave Eileen.

At home here, with me the struggle began to try to forget that Niall had ever lived. I set my mind down and up to it: I help Shivaun about the house, keeping my eyes off her face, for its occasional quivering upsets me; I try to work, tear up letters I don't wish to keep; tidy up the table I work at; but the effort at relief is a dull bubble that swiftly vanishes, and Niall is the fullness of my mind again. I find myself, against all my forcing will, crying out, Oh, Niall, my Niall, my darling son. Let it be called unmanly to show and voice the quivering of the heart. I cannot help my grief, and, God knows, I know no shame in feeling it, or of letting the lips quiver, the heart shake, the voice cry out against the darkness of the hour. Every now and again, when I have imagined I have forced myself into quietness, a convulsive sob shakes me; Niall's loveliness and youth fills my mind, and I cry out against the darkness of the time, on the eve of a New Year that will remain for ever an old one for Eileen and for me. We go about the flat, Shivaun and I, trying to hide our feelings from one another. From here, he went to his death; in this room, where he had been first told of his probable end, I had given him the first kiss of my agonised love for him, in Exeter Hospital I gave him the last kiss, till, maybe, if there be such a thing as a second life, I may give him the third kiss when I meet him, after I, too, have gone the way of all flesh.

My bitterest pain of remembrance is not of our loss, not of mine, but of his: it must have been hard and agonising to suffer the thought, the knowledge, that he would have to go; go from life just as he had fully entered into its rich vigour and its youthful beauty; so hard to be always thinking that he would have to go. Oh, my darling boy, so lithe, so jovial, so full of humour, so thoughtful in the midst of his enjoyment; you knew you had to go away from all these things gave you; away from life, and for ever. My boy, my heart-loved boy, death came to you like a damned thief in the daytime, when all was young and everything was bright and brave, and life was dancing.

So poor Shivaun and I waited for Eileen and Breon to come home; waited, trying to forget Niall and ever remembering him, and all our little world went slow. Dr. Varian, who had been our family doctor for near twenty years in Totnes, came today to give us his sympathy. He had known Niall well, but he had little to say, though he cursed and exclaimed most bitterly that this damned leukaemia was one of the few things about which medical science knew little or nothing. Little or nothing, yet the young are dying from it every day of the year, and science is checked in its studies by the legal insanity of those who care more for mobile missiles than they do for life. Dr. Varian, dear man, and I embraced and parted, for there was little to say.

Eileen had loaned Niall's body to the doctors to be examined and explored in the hope that they might see something to guide them in the treatment of future sufferers, while she arranged to have it cremated the day after they had found whatever was to be found within it. That night, she told me, by some curious and irresistible impulse, she had gone alone to where he lay to have her last look at him, a long last look at the dear, dear young face. He had looked, she said, strangely like me as I surely looked when I was young, peaceful, very peaceful as if asleep, and she had laid a bunch of flowers beside his fair young cheek, the last token of her deep love for her dear young son. My poor darling Eileen, you have had a wondering woe encircling you. Her pilgrimage of pain stretched out a long way before her still. She had gone all along with her boy to the gateway of death, where they had to part, and parting was such bitter sorrow. Farther, she could not go; he had to go alone the rest of the way. His was indeed a short journey into night: a few swift days, with the sun of life going farther and farther away from him till the darkness was reached. Goodbye, my darling mother: Life was but a swift hail and farewell to me. The sunset came too soon for me, and I never saw the evening star. My lovely rose of youth faded when it promised to be full-blown; the petals all fell away together, fell to the chilly earth, and the bloom was gone. Goodbye, dear mother; the music I hear now no longer tells of youth and home.

He had been sorely distressed by the tragedy in Hungary, by all its desolate confusion, and couldn't understand the Soviet Army's methods in quelling the semi-popular, semi-fascist revolt. He had come down from London to talk with me about it, for he had a great regard for my review of things political. We had talked long about the upheaval, he from his viewpoint, I from mine; he very vehemently, I very gently, for I loved the boy's intense sincerity, and grieved at his agitation. But we couldn't agree with what had happened, which to him was a blunt and clumsy interference, and to me a sad necessity. I got up out of my deep armchair and stepped to the austere and simple one in which I sat when I wrote or typed, and in which he sat then; I put my arm around him and pressed him warmly to my side, saying, 'You must cling to your own opinions, and not be influenced by mine, for your intelligence is, at least, equal to mine'. Then I pressed him to my side again, and, bending down, kissed his bushy head of hair as he smiled up at me. How glad I am now that I didn't get testy—as I occasionally do when what seems plain to me seems obscure to others— How sadly glad I am now that I had caressed him then, for within a few more bare days, my boy was dead; he had gone, and had left the distress of Hungary far behind him.

Why do I write like this? Before God, I don't know. The impulse moves me; a proud urge to silence guards the impulse, but the guarded impulse overcomes the guard, and the moving finger writes. As I write, I hear the swift wind shaking the crowded line of cypress trees along the margin of what is called the drive. Kinder their greeny gloom, softer the rasping of their sighing, than the cynical silence and the glittering bauble-clad greenwood tree that houseled the last hours of our beloved lad. The wind blows strongly as it often does here, and I hear it loudly. This wind is not the wind in the willows, but a dark wind and a brazen one, filling the room with sharp, violent sighs. The wind bloweth where it listeth, but we know not whence it cometh or whither it goeth. I stand for a few moments on the balcony outside the front door watching the cypress trees bend back from the wind, each a rustling black smudge beneath the lesser darkness of a starless sky; the rain gentle when the wind falls for a moment, then slashing the face sharply when a gust of wind whips by strongly. So I write as the wind goes, knowing not whence the impulse cometh or whither it goeth; but strive as I may, the guarded impulse overcomes the guard, and the moving finger writes the words pressing down agony within them. Life's day is a short one, but Niall had but a dawn, a false one, for the dawn faded before he knew it was there.

Niall's body was cremated today, the third of January, two days following the first one of the New Year: his merry Christmas and his happy New Year are over and done with; at two o'clock, he passes through the midst of a fiery furnace, and is utterly consumed. There are no miracles these days: Meshach, Shadrach, and Abednego have ceased to live. He had gone the way he had lived—as a flame of serious vitality, gaiety, and glee. He is now a handful of dust scattered over a Garden of Remembrance; a handful of purple dust—good God, the irony of it. No, no; golden dust, for he was a grand lad, serious when it was time to be so, gay when it was time to be gay. However hard I try to quench remembrance, a flash of agony sweeps through me, the tears fall, and I hear myself crying, My boy, my darling, gallant lad. However hard I press my lips together, the cry comes; but only when I am alone; maybe, occasionally when Eileen is present, but almost always when I'm alone. Surely nothing dies but something mourns.

The calendar is useless, and the clock's tick has lost significance: no more shall I mark a calendar-day as one more through which my son liveth; no more watch the hands of the clock moving, waiting for Eileen or Breon to tell me of hope or a deeper despondency: no need to be anxious now, for all signs of a living Niall have gone from the world, from the family who loved him; our eyes shall see him no more, no hand of ours shall ever touch his again, neither shall any hear his eager animated voice in a room or by the laburnum tree in the little garden. As I write this, our boy will have been a week dead. A fortnight or so ago, he was dancing and delightful; now all that was dancing and delightful has been a week dead.

A little Ford car, an Anglia, had been a great family treasure for ten years, bought when our income from America increased; but, like all simpler and poorer things, it had been often over-burdened with work. So when income from America increased again, when I returned home from hospital, the family decided to buy a new car. After many talks, it was decided to get a Hillman Minx. There was pride in the heart and joy on the face when the car came—thro' the valley and over the hill in the Minx! Happiness in all hearts, but indifference in mine, for I always felt better and more important getting out of a car than getting into one. I enjoyed a drive only when I had to pay a visit to a doctor, and illness made me disinclined to bear the burden of going to his surgery in a bus. Eileen decided to give the little Ford to the boys, who were fine drivers, and they at once swopped it for a light blue-black van which they got painted a brilliant orange-red instead, typical of their bright feeling for life. I felt that way, too, and I looked with more liking at the cocky gay orange-red van than was in any glance I gave to the more elegant and dignified Minx in its sober silver-grey coat. It was owned equally by the boys, and they made much use of it, bringing Breon's material to the room he used as a studio, carrying their lunches and swimming-gear to the sea when the summer came, returning old books and bringing back new ones from the local library, Shivaun delighting in the journeys as much as the boys did. A gay time for the three of them, and well it was, for none of us had an inkling that though two would be left, the third would be taken. But they lived and laughed as if death did not exist, and indeed, death didn't exist for them. They had heard of it, but the very idea of it was always enveloped and lost in the gay glow of life. The boys had gone to Cornwall in the orange-red van with tent and food in September. Niall had driven in it to London, carrying a few things for the room he had there; he had brought Eileen once to a London theatre in it; he had carried friends down to Dartington that they might have a good time at a party there, and had taken them back to London again in the little orange van, the little orange van. Then came the London University Christmas recess, and Niall took his last voyage home, carrying his sister, Shivaun, with him in the little orange-red van; he stepped out of it in the evening with his sister and never set foot into it again, for a fortnight later he began to be but a memory: the one who took life, not only with eagerness, but with glee, was gone; he who took life as daffodils take the winds of March was dead.

How well I remember him even before he came, for this was the boy Eileen was having when I was in New York, and he came forth to the world less than a month after I had returned. I had followed his whole growth, as his mother had, remembering how when he was two or so showing him with hands and fingers the miracle of

> *This is the lady's knives and forks,*
> *This is the lady's table,*
> *This is the lady's looking-glass,*
> *And this the baby's cradle.*

The times I played with him in Battersea Park, the time we first saw the Dart together when we went to Devon; the times I met him, or Eileen and I met him, coming home from school along the Dartington Hall Drive or along the Plymouth Road, the times I played hurley with him outside of the house of Tingrith, or cricket, or football, on the lawn; or golf with him and Breon on the lawns by the sea in Goodrington, near Paignton; the questions he had asked me about the Soviet Union, about plays, books, and politicians; about the queer ways of Ireland, the tinsel chatter of the many, the mighty thoughts of the few; but silence sits now where once an eager voice spoke, and I shall never be puzzled by a question from him again. I remember how nervous he became when the bombs fell near, and how I held his shaking little body close to my own, and kissed him warmly, though I, too, was sore afraid, while the calmer Eileen looked after the baby Shivaun, and the calmer Breon looked after himself. How Eileen taught him to read—as she taught them all, Breon before him, and Shivaun afterwards—quietly coaxing him into effort through an infant school-book or an infant comic, leading him to the way wherein he found the joy of Shakespeare, Dickens, Milton, Shaw, and many others; sowing within his mind the seed that developed into the keen, questioning mind that later on had to reject the myths of Christianity, and made it hateful of Christian hypocrisy and humbug that were ramping and ruining the world.

Remembrance—all the joy that is left to us now; a poor joy, but our own.

How, later on, he had forgotten his fear of the bombs, and had handled the guns as a gunner, doing his National Service in the Field Artillery. How on account of his knowledge of books, he had been made librarian of the camp up in North Shropshire; how, for no specific reason, he had been taken away from the library, and sent to Germany; how there, the Adjutant of the regiment had liked him, and had needed the sharp and accurate mind of the lad to help in the work the Adjutant had to do; how it was necessary, before he could do so, for him to have a stripe, and how puzzled the Adjutant became because of objections that came from higher quarters; how the officer had had a private chat with him, and Niall had told him frankly about his father's left-wing views; how the officer had said that it was the son he wanted, and not the father, that it was all very farcical, and that he needed Niall's steady and accurate intelligence, and made a Lance-Bombardier of him, in spite of the objections from the gold-braided amadauns of the British Army. I remember how he shuddered telling me about a visit to Belsen Camp while the regiment was on manœuvres, a place where thousands of bearded Jews, wrinkled women, handsome young Jewesses and vigorous lads, and crowds of little Jewish children died; destroyed so exclusively and terribly that even remembrance died with them: nothing there now but the wind to tell of the sorrow and the gloomy silence to cover the dead.

I remember how he visited me stretched out in Torbay Hospital, and the anxiety that welled up in him when he saw the thinning body and haggard face of the old man, praying that I would rally back into life, never once having a thought that within nine months he himself would be dead; going himself where he hoped his old father would not go. Oh, my Niall, my darling boy, I am ashamed that it was not I but you who had first to make the journey into night. Now I and Eileen have nothing but remembrance with which to touch an absent hand, to hear the sad echo of a silent voice, a brief and a bitter consolation. Never again will Niall tell me how many runs he made at cricket, never ask me if I think the weather will stand that the match might go on; never; never tell me of his search in Dawlish Warren for some rare herb or some uncommon grass. Useless now is the Pelican book on *Grasses* by C. E. Hubbard that I made Shivaun get me in London for the Christmas just gone, that I might be able the better to talk to him about this widespread and life-essential plant. Never again will he show me the fossil shells and worms embedded in the granite forming the two piers to the gateway of our home; fossils that lived sixty million years ago; never again will he pounce on the *Scientific American* coming from New York, and delivered by a Devon postman; or finger the letters lying on my table and comment on what some of them said; never listen again with me to a Mozart, a Beethoven, or a Haydn symphony; he will never rest a hand on my shoulder again, watching something showing on the television; neither I nor Eileen will ever speak to our boy again, nor shall he ever speak to us.

Ah, Niall, amhic, never again shall you stand with Eileen and me beneath the awesome trilithons of Stonehenge, or pause beside the stretched-out stone where poor Tess of the D'Urbervilles slept her last sleep of freedom in this world; never again walk along the Avon with us, or stand under the mulberry tree in Shakespeare's garden; never come into my room again to talk about a beetle or about a bird. To go so young, and life so much within you and around you. Oh, where was the Lord's deliverance?

> *He delivered Daniel from de lion's den,*
> *Jonah from de belly of de whale,*
> *The Hebrew chillun from de fiery furnace;*

but he never delivered you. God wanted him, and it pleased him to take the boy, says a voice from Ireland. Oh, God, oh, Ireland! We wanted him to stay far more than God wanted him to go. He was needed and so God called him away, said another voice—from Ireland. God must be hoarse calling to heaven all the young lads and girls who die far before their time. Hear what comfortable cancerous words these canting Christians speak unto the sorrowful; God called the lad up to heaven though the lad was more than content to stay pat on the earth; sweet poison doping us against any effort to keep death away before a life's ending is due, and Science alone can, like Hercules, stand between death and the dying young. It is Science alone which can mend God's image, when the image is hurt; and when Science fails in its mending, then God's image falls away into dust. It is Science we must try to help, Science we must encourage, if golden lads and girls are to safely claim the heritage of life, and pass through the allotted span of threescore years and ten.

His worldly wealth he left behind him wasn't much: a good gramophone, a few pounds in the Post Office Savings Bank; a wristlet-watch which he wore for the last few days, his last present; a bright blue jersey he never saw; a fine collection of records—classic and jazz; a three-speed record player; and a much-loved trombone; and a number of books, one of which,

Story of Living Things, presented to him when he was fourteen years of
age by his sister, Shivaun, was a gorgeous gateway to the knowledge of how
life had come, how life had grown all the world over. They are very dear to
us, but the dearest of all is the memory of a beloved boy with a warm heart,
a penetrating mind, a gay long laughing sense of humour; a lad who was as
brave when death came for him as he had been when life was brimming in
him, so that Breon said, 'I always loved him, but I will revere him now'.

I cry a caoine for my Niall, for though I may bear it like a man, I must
also feel it like a man, and cannot feel ashamed that my sigh will be in the
winds that blow where'er his dear ashes blow, for he had very gentle,
loving ways within him; but the caoine, as he would wish, goes out for all
the golden lads and girls whose lovely rose of youth hath perished in its
bud. The bell that tolled for him, when he was going, tolled for others too,
and will toll for many more of darling young ones departing before their
due season, till Science teaches fools that a breaking heart above a young
and silent body is more sacred than a bursting bomb set to kill ten thousand
old and young and children, too; till Science comes to deliver the young
from danger, and takes the victory from the grave and the sting from death.
Science has done wonderous things for the young, but at times Science still
has to stand helpless by while young and lovely ones go from life for ever—
like you, my lovely darling lad.

And all the thought I had, the plans I made, to try to live a few more
years at least till Shivaun would be sweet and twenty, till you had ended
your college course, and were facing the world, then I could lead the way
for the family into darkness after a long, rugged, and exciting journey, a
natural scheme for the oldest mind to fashion, but

> *The best-laid schemes o' mice an' men*
> *Gang aft a-gley,*
> *An' lea'e us nought but grief an' pain*
> *For promis'd joy.*

As mine did, my darling boy, as mine did; we were close together in love
and understanding, and when you were wrenched away from me, your
young life took away with it a great part of the pride and joy of my own old
withering one.

Death cut down the vigorous young sapling, and left the gnarled old tree
standing, left the gnarled, old, withering tree standing.

Clearly, I can hear what she said, what Eileen said, what she said brokenly, when she came back from committing her darling son's young body to
the flames: when she put her arms round me, she said, 'Oh, Sean, Sean,
what a terrible thing has happened to us'.

Yes, a terrible thing to us, and terrible to our dear Niall, too, taken away in the fair spring of his youth as he was opening the gateway to the sweet meadow of summer. The broken cry of Eileen will ever be an echo in the home. His voice too; the voice that tried so bravely to tell his thoughts, his last brave thoughts, spoken while he lay dying under a greenwood tree.

BONFIRE UNDER A BLACK SUN

(from "The Green Crow", 1956)

✼ ✼ ✼

Fire, Fire, Fire! Where? Who Done It? Who do you think done it? O'Casey done it. After thirty years of strenuous strain to keep him out, the agile interloper slidders in and kindles a fire, hot and hard to smother; kindles it right in the middle of our alley of sacred silent solus bolus. While we slept, little dreaming of what was to bee. Stung again! Stung again! Are we drama critics or are we not? Are we men or are we mice? Look out! Mind yourselves, or you'll be crumpled with these senseless droves of mental destitutes running to warn and warm themselves at O'Casey's bonfire!

The fire was blazing, the papers were full of it, the police were there, and the people flocking. The misery, *miserere mei*, of it all. Says one paper, 'a queue began forming early at two p.m. outside the theatre entrance. It grew and grew till it stretched down South King Street into South William Street, and an hour before the play began, the Civic Guards had a busy time keeping the streets free for traffic'. Says another paper: 'It was quite an occasion, this O'Casey first night. Seats weren't to be had for love or money. Even members of the Diplomatic Corps weren't able to get tickets. From Britain, America, and all over Ireland, the rich and titled, ministers of state, and theatre critics fought their way through the crowds to see O'Casey's new play.' What was it like? Well, a critic of the *Daily Mail* said: 'O'Casey has exploded a stick of dramatic dynamite. An ugly play, beautifully written'. Trumpeter, sound! The Irish paper goes on: 'The critic of the *Times* said: "O'Casey's best play for the last twenty-six years. Sean's best since *The Silver Tassie*. A little mellower, with a new kind of tenderness". The *Daily Telegraph* said: "I think it a much better play than anything O'Casey has written since his early masterpieces". And now for our own *Irish Press* critic, who says, "Each attempt at an eagle soar was brief and always ended in that swamp of prejudices and bitterness which have kept O'Casey so long in the dramatic wilderness. A grievous disappointment. In fairness to himself as a creative writer, he should return to Ireland without delay [next boat, lad]. At present he is completely out of touch with modern Irish life and thought. It seems to me that he was writing about the Ireland of fifty years ago. It had that old-fashioned air. Even the funniest scene in the play had the echo of the music hall".'

> *Heigh ho! Fifty years ago,*
> *We stroll'd along together, you and I, me old shako;*
> *Faith, we didn't care a button if the odds were on the foe,*
> *Ten, twenty, thirty, forty, fifty years ago!*

And don't care now, either. But imagine condemning 'the funniest scene in the play' because it had an 'echo of the music hall'! Another of the silk-stockinged chaps. But, later on, we'll bring this toff near to the Ireland, not of fifty years ago, but the Ireland of today, and hold his lofty, snifty nose close down to the cracked mirror showing Ireland's figure and Ireland's face as it appears sad and shining in the play called THE BISHOP'S BONFIRE.

How mortified the Irish drama critics were to find that English and American critics happened to be interested in the new O'Casey play! It made them very resentful, for these foreign critics impeded and impaired the aim of the Irish ones so that their darts went wide away from what they aimed at; the foreign critics were damnably in the way. They were not only there, but there before them. So angry were they that they wouldn't let the sun go down upon their wrath.

Says one—a tip-top chap—says he, 'When we went to the theater, we found before us such an intimidating array of the critical faculty of London and New York that we might well have questioned our right to be there at all. This was clearly an occasion. Thanks to Mr. Cusack's acumen the mountain was coming to Mohamet. It is true, of course, that the most notable applauders of the master's barren years were conspicuously absent (or if present, not publicly listed), the Cornish J. C. Trewin, and the redoubtable man-of-the-world, George Jean Nathan. (Perhaps, like the master, they have arranged to come over should the weather be favorable.)'

Not content with criticising the play, this critic must attack 'the master'; not only the master, but also those who think that 'O'Casey's barren years' have borne some fruit, bitter fruit to this critic, setting his teeth on edge; for everything O'Casey has written for the last twenty-five years has been to this critic fruit from a forbidden tree, forbidden by the critic himself: in the day thou dost eat of the fruit of this tree, thou shalt surely die. A hot-war chappie, this, among the many Irish ones carrying on a cold war against O'Casey and all his works, the pomps and vanities of his wicked nature, and all the sinful lusts of his laughter at hypocrisy and humbug.

Of the play, this critic says, 'Dramatically, it is a series of not too bright music hall sketches [exactly what was said of the 'masterpieces' in the old time before him], strung on an outlandish string and laced with the extraordinary encyclical pronouncements of Mr. O'Casey himself. A sad evening in the theater if ever there was one'.

Three columns of this, and, boxed in the center, in towering type, the encyclical announcement that 'Our critic will have more to say about *THE BISHOP'S BONFIRE* in his usual Saturday column'.

No more, I pray thee! Oh yes, a lot more. Three more columns in the evening edition, but not enough yet. What, more? The critic has to sit down and set down four more columns as 'An Open Letter to O'Casey', plus angry replies to correspondents who had written to oppose things he had said in his previous criticism. The 'Open Letter' opens with a bang and ends with a simper. Now for it: 'What in the name of good fortune is the matter with you?'

> *O'Casey, what ails you?*
> *Is the question that tails you;*
> *For years you have gone to the fair.*
> *To pose as a playwright*
> *Is to burn good daylight,*
> *And your books are but blasts of hot air.*
> *So we say and we shout out, beware!*
> *Beware!*
> *Take care!*
> *Are you there?*
> *To prevent you goin' quite quare,*
> *Our critics will flail you,*
> *Assoil and assail you,*
> *Till they bring you back whole from the fair.*

After quoting some good things about O'Casey said by Brooks Atkinson, George Jean Nathan, and others, which so agitate the angry lad that he shouts the question, 'What's wrong with you, man? Why can't you count your blessings and keep your mouth shut?' I don't really know, buttie; mine is a wide mouth, and hard to keep shut. I do count my blessings, though, and count your curse in as one of the best; for (whisper) I've gotten tired of counting blessings, so tired that a curse—especially if the curse be a comic one—is a new joy, always remembering blessed Blake's 'damn braces; bless relaxes'.

This critic has a pretty wide mouth himself, for he goes on—get back a little, reader; there's a bit of an explosion here—'I'll tell you what's wrong with you, Sean O'Casey; in the first place it is because your overweening vanity is severely hurt. You don't like criticism, Sean O'Casey; you only like praise'.

Recovering speech after hours of unconsciousness from this blast, I faintly answer: Every man likes praise, and a fine thing, too, when it comes from those qualified to give it. This critic, who is something of a devotee, should know that to like praise isn't a mortal sin, or, far as I know, a venial one either. Christ Himself sanctions it with His hearty 'Well done!' to His good and faithful servants. God likes it too, as this critic may discover if he reads almost any of the books of the Bible. The saints like it, though, according to accounts, they don't live for it, but relish their share of it when the Church puts them into the Gerontion elevator, and sends them up beyond the clouds; and can't I see Saint Patrick cocking his ears whenever he hears a Limerick Confraternity bawling out his praise! Another thing— however I may dislike criticism, I have to put up with it; even with this criticism which isn't criticism at all. 'It is easy to confute, but impossible to silence', said Jefferson; so, since criticism, however stupid, can't be silenced, it must be borne. Though I have to put up with it, I'm not going to be put down with it, for that is a matter of salvation. We mustn't live for praise, neither must we work to gain praise; but, if it comes, there is no declension in giving it a welcome.

As a matter of fact, criticism is a part of my best-loved literature. I have read as much of it as I have of story, poem, or play. A big amount—Atkinson, Nathan, Watts, Gassner, Emerson, Matthiessen, Coulton, Coleridge, Dryden, Shaw, Yeats, Shelley, Read, Eliot—to mention a worthy few; criticism of philosophy, religion, of story, poem, and play; from Shakespeare's comments on life and love in the Sonnets to Yeats's sad comment on a young man's foolishness in his *Down in the Salley Gardens;* for every poem, play and story enshrines its own comment. Criticism at its best is like well-chosen blossoms in a vase, showing off, adding to, and honoring, whatever grace and colour the vase may have. Good criticism is at times mistaken, but it is invariably interesting, and always leaves us to follow our own judgement. 'Take it or leave it' is always written on the brow of her bright face. To me, literature in its obscurity and reserve seems to be trying to hide from criticism; but succeeds only in getting deluged with more and more of it.

We must get back to our penance and the shouted rebuke of the Irish drama critic into the ears of the trembling O'Casey. So here we go again: 'You choke with rage, O'Casey, because an insignificant handful of Irish drama critics find that they cannot see eye to eye with the world's view of you, and more particularly with your world view of yourself. . . . The British stage, for all its current guff, saw fit to neglect you for years; and Broadway, in spite of Nathan's panegyrics, turned its back on you'.

Looks like he is using this neglect for years by the British stage, and the turning of its back by Broadway, as a full and triumphant justification for his previous statement that the last thirty years have been 'barren years' for O'Casey. But for many years, the British stage turned its back on Shakespeare, but that doesn't say that Shakespeare's years were barren ones. Only now are the British drama critics beginning to discover something of the grace, the fantasy, and the deep feeling in the plays of Giraudoux. Broadway turned her back on him; but this dramatist throughout the time of this neglect was the first-class fellow that he is now when they are taking him out to have a look at him, and give him the bow he always deserved, though Nathan sang his praises many a time, many a year ago. No, buttie, you don't prove anything that way. To play this tune of shoving a dramatist away from life because Broadway turns her back, and the British stage ignores him, is just to show that The Strings, My Lord, Are False. Be sure, buttie, that though the British stage neglected the dramatist, the dramatist didn't neglect the British stage; though Broadway turned her back on him, the dramatist didn't, hasn't, won't turn his back on Broadway. You have me, have you not?—as Polonius says to Reynaldo.

The same drama critic (or is it another? They all write alike in thought and phrase; so many of them parade their criticisms before the saluting point of an initial, or another name) says, 'Mr. Cusack's curtain speech made it only too clear that Mr. O'Casey had his support and blessing'. Well, since Mr. Cusack took the play, put his money into the production, managed it, liked the part he played, liked the part his wife played; since the production was a great success, far exceeding expectations, it would have been hardly decent on the part of Mr. Cusack to refuse his support, or send a curse hurtling at O'Casey's head, instead of balancing a blessing over it.

To show the rapid run of his cordiality, this chap speeds from play to book, saying in another place, 'Milton's Samson, "eyeless in Gaza", was tortured by the knowledge of his having misused the power with which he had been endowed. But there is a grim gaiety in the irascible, quirky authorship of the fifth of O'Casey's adventures in autobiography which suggests that he is now contented to labor "at the mill with slaves".' When, where, and how did this glittering simile come into his mind, I wonder? I wonder, is it a subconscious effort to transfer the torture of his own lot, of his own labor at the mill with slaves, to the wished-for picture of O'Casey doing it instead? Is the 'mill' that part of Dublin which John Mitchel declared to be a city of 'bellowing slaves and genteel dastards'? He knows and God knows, does this free and fetterless thing. I'm giving this lad's wise criticism a world-wide view so that he may reveal himself to the many rather than to the few:

> For to have a thing is nothing
> If you've not the chance to show it,

> *And to know a thing is nothing,*
> *Unless others know you know it.*

Another note from the eagle's whistle: 'Deep down in you nags the possibility that the Irish critics may be right. Time was when you acknowledged one of them as your 'first friend in literature and drama', when you claimed that 'his friendship and talent was, and is, a wonderful gift to his friend and buttie, Sean O'Casey'. Isn't there an awful possibility that such a fellow may not have lost his wits completely and that with a sparkle of that talent left he may, like his colleagues, be visionary enough to see what pride and willfulness can do to a greatly gifted writer'?

Hold me up, constable, hold me up! Wait till I get my breath back. Let me think, now, let me think. Tell this critic from me that I don't believe either this or those to be right, and I greatly doubt the honesty of some. Why? Well, the early O'Casey plays which present critics call 'masterpieces' (not because they believe them to be such, but because it serves their purpose so to do), were condemned by critics past—a much more competent group than critics present—in similar phrases, almost identical in word, which critics present apply to the later O'Casey plays. Which be right? Critics present have been challenged on this question before, more than once, but have ever remained silent. They have never ventured to even whisper that the critics past were wrong. Again, if critics present were lads of judgement and sense, they would never have criticized the play, *THE BISHOP'S BONFIRE,* by comparing it with the earlier plays; for this play is of another method and manner, a different genre. They should have compared it with the play that went before which is of the same method, manner, and the same genre: the play called *Cockadoodle Dandy.* Instead of coming close to this play, they spurred away from it. They knew the play was there; they had read it; one of them saw it done; and it had been reviewed in the Irish papers; but they deliberately and dishonestly ignored it. The American drama critics, 'venal' as some of the Irish critics think them to be, had the critical faculty of knowing what ought to be done, and immediately and inevitably compared the last play—not with the earlier ones—but with the play that had gone before it.

As for the time when time was I acknowledged this bird as 'first friend in literature'—well, that's

> *A very long time ago, a very long time ago:*
> *Just let me see, just let me see,*
> *It's thirty years or so:*
> *When bells began to chime,*
> *And I began to go,*

I knew this bird, and so,
It's a very long time, a very long time, a very long time ago!

As for his wail of 'Isn't there an awful possibility that such a fellow may not have lost his wits completely?': there remains, too, the awful possibility that he has.

Another Irish critic, a tufted toff this time—Hush! Open your ear softly. This one is of the Committee, Cultural Conference, or Arts Commission which aims at making Ireland's finer ways of life known upon earth, her quaint and jewelled arts and crafts among all nations. So this drama critic is a most important person, for the Cultural Committee, of which he is an honoured member, is part of Ireland's Department for External Affairs. This critic is one of Ireland's silver cops. We just must listen to him as he flicks a glove or makes a moue at any vulgarity that comes between the wind and his nobility. Are you all in a state of respectful repose and artistic grace?

He tells us in the *New Statesman and Nation* that on the first night of *THE BISHOP'S BONFIRE,* 'The audience was crackling with excitement, delighted at the sense of a big occasion, ready to laugh or cry and, above all, ready to shout down the interruptions that were expected from militant pietists, maddened by the muezzins of a local paper. No other living dramatist could have created such an audience, ready to do half his work for him before ever the curtain went up. When the curtain went down on the last act there was a round of polite applause, matched by a little timid booing from the shock troops of the Right. Mr. Cusack made his curtain speech with the air of Ajax defying a damp Monday evening, and the great audience sagged sadly homewards. To achieve this effect [the sagging sadly homewards?], in such conditions, it took the exile of Totnes three maundering hours, twelve ventriloquists' [sic] dummies, and the kind of prose he puts into his autobiographies. Nothing less could have done it'.

'Done it'—there's an echo here: Done it, dunnit, Donat O'Donnell abu! No disrespect; it isn't the critic's right name; only a num mum de plume, a kind of alter ego, as if 'twere one yet a different person, a concealment within a revelation. But brave, for so many veil themselves under initials that it is a stern one who pushes forward into a full name other than his own.

A little gnarled nut of ignorance peeps out among the leaves of this chap's critical cornucopay. He says, 'We never see the Bishop, and we hear nothing about him except that he is of peasant origin, a fact which Mr. O'Casey—wobbling surely from the Party Line?—appears to consider regretable'.

Now a Bishop can make himself felt without showing himself, as Dunnit should know. And when O'Casey sits down to try to write a play, he doesn't allow himself to bother about any Line—Party Line, Mason and Dixon Line, Protestant or Papal Line, or even the line of least resistance, or the Line taken up by any member of the Cultural Staff in Ireland's Department for External Affairs. But in point of fact, there doesn't happen to be any 'wobble' in the play. There are haves and have-nots among the peasants, and the peasant farmers—from whom almost all the priests come—look down upon the peasant laborers. I met it myself a year or two ago when on a visit to a farm some miles from Athlone (Ireland's center). There, when I suggested that the peasant taxi-driver who had brought us should receive some refreshment, I was met with the remark, 'What, him? He's of no account. Such as us have no truck with him'. Let this Donat read what Professor McDonald says about the class of peasant from which the priest comes. He himself was one, poor and struggling, carrying a basket of grub with him when he walked to boarding-school; poor but property owners, therefore not peasants in any common application of the term, but the gentry of the Irish countryside. Out of his scholarly enrichment surely this Donat should have read, in *John Bull's Other Island,* the contempt that Haffigan, the peasant-farmer, had for Patsy Farrell, the peasant-laborer.

Speaking as a critic over Radio Eireann, this same lad told his listeners what torments his delicate senses suffered, sitting out a performance of a dreadful shoddy vulgar play called *The End of the Beginning,* stirred and starred with slapstick! Oh, the beginning of it even was nearly the end of him. Oh, the shameful time for Ireland and for me! Shut your ears, and don't look; close your eyes, and don't listen. This sort of thing stretches out and deepens the natural agony of a silken soul. Oh, what a passionate relief it was when the curtain blotted it out—and the creatures round me laughing.

Oh, learned son of agony, this little boisterous, knock-about one-acter was born out of a folk-tale, known to children all over the world. Nearer home, too, it is known in Dublin and in the country places where the plough speeds and the corn is green or yellow. Bring it nearer still to the cultured member of the Irish Culture Committee of the Irish Department for External Affairs, for it is to be found clad in the merriest Gaelic in the book called *An Baile Seo 'gainne (In Our Townland),* among a crowd of other comics compiled by the well-known native speaker, An Seabhac; the whole was edited by Seosamh Laoide, M.R.I.A., a scholar and leader of the Irish movement in the earlier nineties. These comics compiled by An Seabhac are redolent—not of Dublin or the music hall—but of Corca Dhuibhne. Oh, Donat, Donat, you've dunnit, you dunno everything!

Isn't it a wonder, now, that these great Irish eagles won't suffer a little bird to sing? These chaps are always seeking to cage O'Casey, spreading nets of advice behind and before him. One of them, at frequent intervals, tries to lead O'Casey back to where he was more than thirty years ago, urging him to say again what he then said to the Grand Old Dame of Coole, when he went, all dollied up, to see her for the first time: 'I owe a great deal to you, Lady Gregory, to Mr. Yeats, and to Mr. Robinson, but to you above all. It was you said to me, "Mr. O'Casey, your gift is characterization"; and so I threw away my theories, worked at characters, and *The Shadow of a Gunman* is the result'.

The timid drama-postulant knocking at the temple door, ready to wear any habit offered to him, and take any vow required. The habit to be thrown off when it got too tight; the vow abandoned when it grew too narrow; a vow vain-glorious as Jethro's vow that lost him his daughter. Both abandoned: the vow before it had been fully uttered, the habit before it had settled round the body. Certainly, Lady Gregory's importance to him had been nicely balanced by his importance to her; for, since she looked upon the Abbey as her 'liddle theatre', she was obliged to O'Casey who came to the theatre when things were so bad that his plays saved the theatre from closing (for so Yeats publicly declared). So he saved Lady Gregory from a bad heart-pain, and those who loved the theatre from the shock of a bang from the closing door. The Irish drama critics, out of pure love only, are always chanting 'Remember the advice of Yeats, remember the advice of Lady Gregory, and, oh, remember ours!' I remember, boys, only to forget. I remember the advice given by a lad named Bernard Shaw, and it shall be remembered forever. Bernard Shaw, when commenting on a book, *Advice to Young Musicians,* written by Schumann, said, 'Decidedly, if I ever write a book of advice to young musicians, the first precept in it will be Don't Take Schumann's. Indeed, the beginning and end of it will be, Don't Take Anybody's'. I stand beneath the shelter of the Prophet's beard.

More odd than these critics' strife to lead one into the wasteland of self-derivative art is the odder effort to lime his soul as well; for, incredible as it may appear, Ireland is dotted generously with leading and unkindly lights. One day, years ago, sitting chatting to two literary chaps, I vaguely became suspicious when I found that I was answering twenty questions about things that (it was hinted) belonged to my peace. The two friends discussed, even argued, between themselves as to what books I should be given to read: A poor thief between two saviours! 'Most suitable, not suitable at all; I think so, I don't think so', and such murmurings were bandied about between them. One of the friends, wiser no doubt, left it there; but the other persevered, for there was a spiritual war on; and a few days after, a book (I've forgotten the name), written by a Kuhnelt-Leddihn, came to me, a calmly-hysterical tale of a devoted layman's surreptitious journey through the U.S.S.R. to get in touch with the underground movement there for the Preservation of the Faith. I was to turn again, turn twice, and make for the twilight kingdom where I might hide from the Big Bad Wolf, to become a spiritual effigy widely away from the world of man. No, sir, the big bad wolf was no more than a Big Good Brother. Totality of being doesn't begin with baptism, or with art; it begins in life when a babe sucks its first food from its mother's breast; and is confirmed each time we sit down at table to eat. For however man may soar, like Yeats, like Eliot, he has to come down to have a bite and sup when hunger takes him.

The suspicion of being followed deepened and strengthened as days went by; the shadow was at his heels; the voice whispered

> '*I will show you something different from either*
> *Your shadow at morning striding behind you*
> *Or your shadow at evening rising to meet you;*
> *I will show you fear in a handful of dust*'.

But O'Casey goes on puddling and muddling through the winsome ways of the flesh, eating, drinking, and singing an occasional song; gratified at Wexford winning the All-Ireland Hurling Final, because when he was a young fellow he knew Wexford lads in a club called The Blues and Whites, and had played hurling with them many a time in the Phoenix Park; going about grieving for a while because Dublin had lost the All-Ireland Football Final to Kerry, but consoled somewhat by the happy fact that Dublin had made a grand fight of it.

Some time after, he got a new hint of solicitude from him who knoweth which is which in those things that pertaineth to the body's correctness and the soul's security in the world that is and in the world which is to come; a man: amen. A stimulating thought for a new focus of living came in the shape of a slender copy of the play *Everyman*, which O'Casey foolishly takes to be one of the dullest plays ever written; and later on still, came a copy of the poem, *The Hound of Heaven*, and to Sean a poem of one, who, to the sound of his own toy trumpet and drum, ran from heaven's pursuer through valley low and hill high, through verseays and the fooleries, till he was caught, and brought to where there was peace, a safe bed, and something to eat first thing in the morning.

Later still, came the flotsam and jetsam of a medal, a moony picture of Virgin and Child, backed by a sentimental prayer, and a Catholic Truth booklet, sent to the critic by a simple soul with a request that they be forwarded to Mr. O'Casey, with a prayer for his spiritual advancement; a request that the critic couldn't conscientiously refuse. Still O'Casey sauntered on among the coloured lights, singing, even now in the evening of life when his shadow is always rising to meet him; watching many of the young leaning from magic casements, opening on the foam of perilous seas; for the poem was one which had never appealed to him, and the trinkets were but ephemeral wisps of emotion, in no way able to turn a sinner from his ways, even were he so declined; or, if it went to the push, wasn't he able to see for himself the words in green on the red streak of the rainbow, 'I've got the cinch on you this time, amhic'.

So shines forth some of the background to the comments made by Irish critics on O'Casey's biographies and his plays, up to and including *THE BISHOP'S BONFIRE*. One thing these critics shared in common: they were insistent that O'Casey had 'lost touch with Ireland', that his play 'was old-fashioned, representing things that lived fifty years ago, but were all dead now'. Old things had passed away and all things had become new. Ha, ha, aha, let us see then; let us brood a bit.

'The priest is no longer a power in the land'. A dead letter? Only yesterday, October the thirty-first, 1955, a Holy Ghost Father, speaking at a meeting of Regnum Christi, said, 'Some well-educated Catholics think it fashionable to question and contradict in private—and even in public— the teaching and decisions of the Bishops, which clearly showed how ill-instructed many Catholics were in the elementary Christian duty—obedi-ence. . . . To the Bishops alone it belongs to decide both where the limits of their authority extend, and when and in what measure to exercise it'.

That's pretty sure going, and what makes it secure is the fact that it would be a brave laddie of any Irish Clan who would stand on any political platform to deny that this Holy Ghost Father hadn't spoken as he was moved by the Holy Ghost when he gave his listeners this mouthful of ipse-dixit dogma. Last week only, the Irish Football Association had arranged for an International Match between Ireland and Yugoslavia, and there were Great Expectations of a thrilling day. The President was to be there; the Army Band was to shake the Irish Air with melody, the Match was to be broadcast by Radio Eireann, and many distinguished personages were to be there. They didn't go. No? Divil a one of them. The Chancellor to the Roman Catholic Archbishop of Dublin spoke unto the children forming the Council of Ireland's Football Association, saying, 'The Most Reverend Dr. McQuaid had heard with regret that the match had been arranged'. Dub-lin's fat was in the fire. Take it out, take it out! The President will not attend; the Army Band will not be present. The head of the Army Athletic Association said, 'He was in an awkward position. Without saying more, he must oppose the proposal to go on with the Match'. The Radio Eireann Broadcaster said he wouldn't go near the microphone; and there were hot and hasty runnings around by many to get away from even the thought of it all. Here is a quotation from a letter in the *Irish Times*: 'The saddest thing about the whole business was the spectacle of those who last week thought a match with the Yugo-Slavs all right, scurrying back to give the impression that this week they thought it all wrong. No doubt their excuse would be "the Bishop said", but that is simply not good enough. There is nothing in Catholicism that makes it necessary for the laity to retreat violently from reason whenever a Bishop expresses an opinion'. A hardy little skiff launching out on a perilous sea, flanked by the Scylla of Regnum Christi on the one hand, and by the Charybdis of Duce Maria on the other; for has it not been reported that Dr. Lucey, Bishop of Cork, declared (not fifty years ago, but in nineteen hundred and fifty-five) that 'the Hierarchy of Ireland were the final arbiters of right and wrong even in political matters'? Ay, and in football matters and mutters, too, apparently. Bona fide finis. What goes for Bishop, goes for the Monsignor, goes for the Canon, goes for the Parish Priest; and the ordinary ones of the Order of Saint Peter, the Boheroes, have little chance of standing on their toes; as little as had Dr. O'Hickey, Fathers Sullivan, Flanagan, Dr. McDonald, and his old class-mate, Father Sheedy, exiled for giving evidence on behalf of a priest against a bishop. Twenty years ago, I myself chatted with Father Flanagan, desperately trying to hold on to a life of thought while prisoned in a Convalescent Home for Sisters of Charity within the lonely wilds of Wicklow; and no voice from Irish Ireland—which he had served, like Dr. O'Hickey, so well—raised itself even to a whisper to help him out, or give him hope.

More than thirty years ago, I caused a semi-ignorant character in *The Shadow of a Gunman* to say of a young girl, 'All she thinks of is dancin', picture theaters, an' dhress'. Today we hear its echo in what a Holy Ghost Father, Rev. Reginald Walker, said at a meeting of the Catholic Women's Federation of Secondary Schools: 'The world has gone crooked. In the case of many Catholic women there was little or no difference between their standards of judgement and those of non-Catholics. They went to the same films, and followed the same fashions in dress, many of which emanated from non- and anti-Catholic salons'. 'Emanated' is good. Catholic girls dollying up in fancy dress; clerics dollying up in fancy words. But the clerics are butting their tonsured heads against a wall when they try to frighten football fans or threaten pretty girls away from the desire to dress in what the latest fashion may happen to be. Lawus Deo!

From a Gaelic article in the *Irish Press,* called *Going to School:* 'In September, they flock back to the boarding-schools on bus and by train. Forty of them sleep together in a long room, and eat a meal in the company of two hundred others. Newcomers asking those who might know if the priests beat them as the teacher had in the local school at home; and told that the priest's blow was twice as heavy as that of the old schoolmaster. Fog and drizzle throughout seven weeks till Christmas; the dead chill of the morning drowsiness at seven o'clock, the towel hard as a blackboard with frost. But don't let on; pretend not to notice it all'.

Don't let on; cry of the school-kids, cry of the Irish critics: don't let on.

From the same daily, same time: 'The gentle glare of the green covered with the yellow of the ragwort—orange and green, the national colors blended together gracefully, a lovely sight till it is realized that ragwort is a poisonous plant, harming the grassy turf wherever it may be. It spreads rapidly and sets itself deep in the farm meadows and pastures through the seasons. It isn't seldom that a cow or a horse eats of this plant, and goes off in death from their owners forever'. One can hear The Codger talking! From the same writer: 'And our ruins, oh, our ruins! There they are, a source of shame to us: monasteries, castles and chapels, now covered with filth, mighty weeds boring into them, creeping over them, and burying within them forever the pavements once beaten by feet unafraid, sometimes holy, and always prominent in the world by knowledge, of battle, or of cunning creations in illuminated print. The weeds of the farm colliding with the weeds in the ruins of the old-time sacred places. All so stridently and impudently active that it is perilous for any to make an effort to go to see them [see *Time to Go*]'.

Again, one month earlier, in the same Journal, an Agricultural Correspondent writes, 'The amount of food matter produced by the average Irish pasture is very much lower than it should be. There is too high a proportion of our grazing land on what are called permanent pastures. Many of these are so old that they have not been ploughed within living memory'. Listen to The Codger talking about Reiligan's grass and Reiligan's hay!

There are many things said about the sucker-hold fastened on the young by the old up to forty, fifty, and even sixty years of age. Wherever one goes, the withering man without a wife and the withering woman without a husband can be found, threatening many districts with the condition of being without chick or child within a generation or two. And all these things stated and quoted appeared in the papers years after THE BISHOP'S BONFIRE had been written. One Gaelic writer mocks at those wailing about the low marriage rate; for, says he, it will soon be in Ireland that there won't be any women to marry.

How did I know these things before these things were said? I know the red wind that comes from the east, the brown wind that comes from the west, the white wind that comes from the south, and the black wind that comes from the north; I know the mind of Ireland because I am within it; I know the heart of Ireland because I am one of its corners; I know the five senses of Ireland because I am within them and they are within me; they bid me look, and when I look, I see; they bid me listen, and when I listen, I hear. Tell us what you see, says Ireland, and tell us what you hear; you speak out, son, and break the silence; for so many of the others are so afraid of their damned souls that they can but mutter prayers no good to God.

Here's a limelight flash from the mouth of another Irish drama critic: 'The Ireland of the young O'Casey is dead. The priest no longer is a power in the land, and the O'Casey tirades against him no longer provoke the "heretics" to rebellion or the angels to anger. As Joseph Tomelty is currently pointing out in the Abbey, the people are no longer priest-ridden— it is the priest who is people-ridden'!

This in spite of the incidents that whirled round the Students' Debating Society only the other day; the ecclesiastical hand (bishop's ring on a finger) that stretched out from Maynooth, and tore the Mother and Child Bill straight in two; in spite of the fact that the children of elementary schools are not allowed to sit down to a hot meal in the middle of the day—for fear, the clerics say, it would mean the intrusion of the thick wedge of Communism into Irish common life; in spite of the censorship of books, of films— even though almost all films coming to Ireland have already been sifted and sorted and screened by the Production Code Authority of Hollywood, the American Catholic Legion of Decency, and the British Film Censorship, they have to get another look-over and rub down by the holier Censors of Ireland, heads tufted with fairy-lights symbolical of the Pentecostal fire; in spite of the hundreds of instances of clerical control given in *The Irish and Catholic Power,* three hundred pages of them all documented, and indisputable; in spite of a single Member of the Dail, who had written to the press questioning a declaration made by the Bishop of Cork, saying at his letter's end, that he didn't sign his name to it because he had 'no wish to end his political career before he had well begun it'.

In his play *Is the Priest at Home?* Mr. Tomelty is a safe rider, and sits the saddle well. But then, the steed is a rocking horse that goes gaily forward and as gaily backward, though always remaining in the same spot, to the tinkle of little tin bells attached to the bridle holding the wooden charger from bolting, preventing any foolish prance or dangerous caracol. Ironically, the playwright reveals a tiny community 'in the back of beyond', unintentionally, of course, that hasn't yet come out of a primitive time earlier than even fifty years ago, what with splicing the name of Communist to anyone seeking piped water in the home and flush closets to go with it; and a young priest reminding his parishioners of the fine men and women that were once raised in Ireland on spuds and buttermilk. Even the 'death offerings', according to the play, are flourishing still in this parish 'in the back of beyond'. This is the cultural custom of collecting money to show respect to a dead neighbor. At the ceremony, the priest, or the official collector, sings out the name of the donor and the amount given as the tribute is put in the plate resting on or beside the coffin; all making desperate assaults on themselves to give as much as they can so as to preserve a high standing within the community. In my young days, it was known as 'canting the corpse', from the Irish word *cantail,* selling by auction. The playwright makes the young priest say, 'That's another thing I'd like to put a stop to'; but behind Father Malan is the Canon—and what would he say! It brings in money, and money is always needed to deepen and outstretch the kingdom of God. The playwright passes this civilising custom by with a pat on the back as a sensible and amiable Catholic practise; for, of course, it goes into the cleric's pocket. The question that is there and yet that is not there, is the genial practise throughout the whole play. The small souls here haven't even a chance of 'curling up in a window seat behind the *Encyclopaedia Britannica*'.

The placid assertion of the Irish drama critic that the clergy have little say in Ireland now, and the waving of Mr. Tomelty's play before the world as a proof, is barriered back by the quiet statement in the Introduction to *The Irish and Catholic Power*: 'Although I am deeply grateful to the many Catholic and non-Catholic friends who helped me, I shall not thank them by name'. Why not, why not? 'Under the circumstances it is best to respect and preserve their anonymity. Ireland is not a place where men can express frank and unorthodox opinions on Church and State without penalty. Many of the men who gave me the most significant information are Catholics or non-Catholics living in an atmosphere approximating genteel terror in which any association with an outspoken critic of the hierarchy's policies might lead to the end of their professional careers'.

A writer in the *Irish Times,* commenting on life in an Irish-speaking district, says: 'Needless to say, there are no theatres, no race courses, virtually no cinemas, and there is a great shortage of dance halls. The latter is probably the greatest privation in the recreational life of the Irish-speaking districts, and also is most surprising. Formerly, there were dances on the crossroads and in private houses. It appears, however, that the clergy consider such functions to be "occasions of sin", and, in the majority of cases, have succeeded in ending them. There is no chance whatever of a dance hall controlled by a layman being allowed to remain in existence. In Rosmuc the Parish Priest used to run ceilidhes in the former Gaelic League College, but twelve years ago, he decided they were a danger to morals, and closed the hall. Since then, never a dance in the parish'.

Bang! What's that? The door closing. What's that lightning-like flash crossing and re-crossing the way before the door? That's God's Angel with his sword of fire keeping the people from dancing. In one of my books, I gave an account of Gaels dancing on a crossroads four miles from Dublin; and how on the second evening the priest calmly came along, ordered all who were there to go home; and like children, home they went. Fifty years ago, and yet they're doing it still. The Ireland of the young O'Casey dead? It must have suffered a recent resurrection, and a perfect one, too. No; Mr. Tomelty's people-ridden-priest play (and Mr. Tomelty is an honourable man) is but a lipso facto; and the drama critic's (and he, too, is a most honourable man) belief that the Ireland of the young O'Casey is dead must be in the nature of a die-dream. It is worse than it was fifty years ago. Is there a single member of Ireland's Government, Dail, or Senate, any one member of the Irish Drama Critics' Circle, who would dare to stand up today, and say to the Bishop of Cork as Michael Davitt said fifty years or so ago to the Bishop of Limerick: 'Make no mistake about it, my Lord Bishop of Limerick. Democracy is going to rule in these countries'? Come on, now, give us a shout, Comrades of the Great Scare!

But all this is little but here and there, and written only to show that even in common things, the Irish critics are ignorant of (they don't, apparently, read what is written in Gaelic; if they did, they would know more about Ireland than they do), indifferent to the things happening around them; or they deliberately falsify their knowledge of things so that they may (as they think) injure what O'Casey tries to do and silence what he tries to say. It may be that they haven't the courage to look at anything other than what is shown in their own little cracked pocket looking-glasses.

It is a pleasant experience and a pleasanter sight, on another day, and at another hour, to look out of a window and watch the Irish drama critics on their way to enjoy and report upon the tick and chime of Lady Longford's *Stop the Clock,* produced by the Lord Longford Productions in the building known as The Gate Theatre.

> *Look at them, look at them—there they go,*
> *Hidden away in their Sunday best;*
> *Peruke on head and cane in hand,*
> *Black soutane and plum-colored vest,*
> *Humming a Me So Do;*
> *Knowledge their armour, caution their crest;*
> *Profound, but bland, as born to command;*
> *Peruke on head and cane in hand,*
> *In soutane black and plum-colored vest,*
> *They go—a Jest.*

Then come the reviews, each a low bow and a kiss blown from the fingertips. Madame, I am pleased with you. I protest, 'twas fine, it was, really. Like all mortals, some of the Irish drama critics are Called, and but a few are Chosen. One of the Chosen speaks first: 'To the unitiated it ought to be sufficient to say that Christine Longford has done it again; working in her happiest vein she has produced yet another of her sparkling comedies. *Stop the Clock* may easily prove to be the best of them . . . What is it all about? Well what is any laughter-provoking life-rooted whimsy all about? . . . If the characters have touches of caricature, the fact is proper to her purpose. Is there anything more to it than that? I think there is. But you must go and find that out for yourself'. Thanks, sir. Very nicely said. One of the Called speaks now: 'Christine Longford again proved her mastery of witty dialogue. She skimmed lightly over the political and social antagonisms of an Irish village and handled them in a spirit of gay burlesque [singing willow, titwillow, titwillow]. . . . Lady Longford winds her characters up and sets them going and then lays them back in the box to the general satisfaction'. Very nice and very proper. Thank you, too, sir. Let one more of the Chosen speak: 'Christine Longford may be congratulated once more for her shrewd eye on what goes on in the country, and the comedy that offers in two of its three acts a laugh a line—and that is as much as one can reasonably be expected of any comedy nowadays'.

Glory for Christine, glory for her! O Lord, give me a glory and a workman's pride; for you've got to get a glory, or you're dead inside.

Let us read quickly and then slip away from a few remarks made in a general way about the drama by our Irish critics. One: 'Incalculable harm can be done to competitions and young writers by an adjudicator making a wrong selection or giving uninformed criticism'. 'Uninformed criticism' is good, but he leaves out the selections given and the selections made by him and his critic-comrades. Another, writing of Irish drama of the future, says, 'Irish drama should have some amalgam of the fundamentals of Greek, Mediaeval, and Elizabethan theatre'. Well, 'amalgam of the fundamentals' is better even than 'uninformed criticism'. It's just lovely. One more: 'Abbey plays dealt in general with superficial things that did not set any deep thinking process moving in the public mind'. Would it be good for Ireland and her Theatre if some miracle would set this 'deep thinking process' moving in the private minds of the Irish critics themselves! For all the glory of Christine's comedies doing it over again, there is no vision in the Irish Theatre of today. This year no prize was awarded for a three-act play in Gaelic, and last year—though prompted by a prize of two hundred and fifty pounds— forty-seven plays were sent into the Abbey, but not a single one of them, it was said, was good enough to be produced. The gap of brightness has darkened since Yeats followed Lady Gregory to the grave, and Fred O'Higgins, Yeats's hope, followed after, far, far too soon. The theatre-sense in Ireland today wouldn't stitch enough things together to make a shift for young and pretty Miss Mary Hynes. Indeed, there is no vision in Ireland herself, bar the one of 'Who is to have the power and so hold the jobs', with Fianna Fail in one group, Fine Gaedheal in the other, and Labor sucking a thumb to try to decide on which side the jobs shine for the Union Bosses, prologued by hurried visits to the altar to light a candle and shove up a prayer for their holy intentions: a low state of social morality for the highest Christian State in all the world. In spite of the Radio Eireann Orchestra, Music as an Art is a one-eyed lass in a gloomy room, with a tiny skylight in the roof as a hope and a way to get out (more than thirty years ago, Dr. Larchet—then Leader of the Abbey Orchestra—started a Fund to build a Concert Hall in Dublin; I subscribed to the Fund, but some months later got the money back, because the response to the appeal had been negligible. The Concert Hall isn't there yet; though, to be fair, it does appear occasionally in a dream); Sculpture—bar, as it is connected with architecture, the Bus Station in Dublin, the Air Ports, a few factories, fewer hospitals, and a lonely

Catholic church in County Cork—hasn't moved a step aside away from
Victorian leaves and lollipops. The other day, Dublin wouldn't touch a
sculpture by Henry Moore, and thrust a *Reclining Woman* out in the cold;
though before that, they had taken with tears of joy an atrocity of a *Pietà*,
weighing a hundred tons or so, from Italy, and carefully set it down in the
National Museum—'the Musey Room', as Joyce called it—without a single
word of protest from artist, cleric, or layman. A picture by the Catholic
painter, Rouault, was boohpoohed out of Dublin's Gallery, too, because of
its blasphemous aspect, for the muddy eyes of ignorance couldn't see the
penetrating pathos peering out from the stained-glass effects of this painter's
art. The clergy, thank God, weren't to blame here, for the Authorities of
Maynooth welcomed it, and, I understand, there it hangs today; but low
and all as the meaning and enjoyment of these arts be in Ireland, the state
of the Drama is lower than them all. The drama is hobbled here by fear of
the clergy watching what is being done from the valleys below and from the
hills above; by the Catholic Press who employ the angels to beat away the
lovers who are coming thro' the rye; by the Abbey in a panic whenever
the box-office shows a pound less than the week before; by the Maria Duce
with her broom sweeping the cobwebs of contraperception off the Irish
skies; and, worst of all, the drama critics hobbled fast to where they were
before they listed; with a brilliant member of the group exploding the brilliant dictum, 'Only a dramatist of ideas can offer any hope of leading the
theatre, astray in the commercial labyrinth, out into the light again. When
he appears, all lovers of the theatre ought to stand up and applaud him. But
they should first be sure that he is the right man and has the right ideas'.
The right man with the right ideas—see the conquering hero comes! They
also serve who only stand and prate.

No hope then for Ireland? A lot of it, for hope springs infernal in the
Irish breast. There are brave ones, thinking bravely, in Ireland's three Universities; there are brave men, thinking bravely, among the workers; all isn't
a sing-song acceptance among the younger clerics; the Friends of our National Galleries stand by the artists who express new ideas in a right way or
a wrong way with the medium wherein they work; there is a hospital ward
to be named in honour of Nurse Quinn, who stood to the death beside her
patients when big bombs fell on London; there are the gallant boatmen of
Ballycotton who bullied their way out through fearful seas to save the lives
of comrade sailors; there are those who had the courage to go to Moscow,
turning a laughing back-o'-me-hand to the yelling yahoos of Maria Duce;
there is the cheeky and gallant town of Wexford, a little less in size than
Littlehampton in Sussex, holding its annual Festival of the Arts, with opera
flourishing, the finest of film shows, chamber music, and an art exhibition,
with Trinity College students flaunting themselves in the poetic plays of
Yeats, Continental eminence present, and Glyndebourne giving the town a

bow. The Boys (and Girls) of Wexford are beginning another Rising: and there are still young writers bending over the maze of making a drama; there is Molloy, there is Burns, with others, and that is good, for it is more than something. One day, the poor old woman will dance again.

And where's and how's O'Casey, after the flarum harum scarum of *THE BISHOP'S BONFIRE?* At home, thank ye, and safe. A bit broody, trying to think out if he be the right man with the wrong ideas, or the wrong man with the right ideas, in the hope that, taking thought, he may assume the right proportions, add a cupid to his stature, and so be able to come before the Irish drama critics with a right reverend song. Diverted he often is by the buzz of bees and the sound of the wind in the trees; and watching the strut of the blackbird or the thrush on the lawn-patch, or admiring the coloured lights strung along the promenade from one end to the other by Babbacombe Beach. He does not weep for himself as the Irish critics say they weep for him. He laughs, lads, he laughs. Laughs as Cuchulainn did, even when his shadow rises up to meet him, showing that the day is far spent, and the night is at hand. It is the right thing to do, for it is part of man's right and part of God's pleasure.

Laugh, for the time is brief, a thread the length of a span.

Laugh, and be proud to belong to the old proud pageant of man.

SHAKESPEARE AMONG THE FLAGS (1964)
(FROM "BLASTS AND BENEDICTIONS", 1967)

🌴 🌴 🌴

At last all the flags are out, all the pipes of the great organ play, and the commemorative postage stamps are out. The four-hundred-year-old grudge against the acknowledgement of Shakespeare has given way to a national acclamation. The dramatist has made a wonderful fight of it. He began within the torment of an inferior education, separating him from the more fortunate writers of his time. His father had failed in business, so he was poor, possessing nothing but the urge of the genius within him. The university wits more or less despised him, though they couldn't altogether shake his confidence out of him. One of these wits, even when he was dying, cursed Shakespeare as an upstart, and warned his fellow-wits against this impudent, ignorant interferer. So, alone and warming his five wits, the young grammar-school lad sat down to begin the work that was to sweep the others aside, and make the lonely one the greatest poet and dramatist of them all. Fortunately he was helped by the Earl of Southampton, about whom Shakespeare wrote many of his sonnets; and by the time that patronage began to be transferred to a dangerous rival, Marlowe, Shakespeare was independent, and able to whistle 'Merrily, merrily, shall I live now, under the blossom that hangs on the bough'. He was a freelance, able to probe and prod anyone, anywhere he liked.

What a different tale today to the tale of thirty years ago! Then Shakespeare was as quiet as a mouse, for the theatre then was the theatre of Pinero, Lonsdale, Barrie and Coward. One playwright of that time whose play[1] employed six or more companies surging through the English cities and towns was a lad who was then regarded as England's herald and hope in drama. He had neither seen, nor heard, nor read a Shakespeare play, an experience then suffered or enjoyed by millions of English people. A sin of

An article written to commemorate Shakespeare's anniversary, published in *The New York Times Magazine* on Apr. 19, 1964, under the title 'Ode to an "Impudent Upstart".' The conclusion to the manuscript, published here, is slightly different from that of the version printed in the *N.Y.T.*

[1] R. C. Sherriff's *Journey's End*.

omission, a grave sin of omission! So he was hurried off to see *Hamlet,* and as he and his friends homeward plodded their weary way, he was asked what he thought of it! The play would be better without the Ghost, he murmured. Was he moved? Well not half as much as he had been moved by a performance of *Young Woodley.* That was just the temper of the times.

An Irishman in England at the time came seeking out Shakespeare; he had received from the then President of the Soviet Union of Writers a gorgeous golden book, with a frontispiece of the poet, and a host of illustrations showing the designs and characters of the plays that were being performed in Moscow, Leningrad, Kiev, and other towns in honour of England's genius. Pinned to the cover was a letter asking him to write an account of the many productions reeling through the English theatres, giving their bow and obeisance to the Elizabethan literary giant.

The Irishman sought in vain. Shakespeare was in the land of Erewhon— the Stratford Theatre was shut and no play was on from Penzance to John O'Groats. He had become a mere neglected English antiquity. Some day, maybe a literary archaeologist would ferret him out, and critics would lazily wonder if the find was a genuine one. The Bright Young Things of the period found him heavy going, and kept him at a safe distance; while the sombre group, the Angry Young Men, blew themselves up into a tappertit revolt against capital and convention, and so had no time to pick a leaf from Sheakspeare's laurels for a badge, or pluck a rose from his great bush of blossoms for awearing in their coats.

There is wonder in it that one said to have been dead for so long can still prance and pirouette about as if in the virile and idyllic year of his youth. Why is it that the great Marlowe and the equally great Ben Jonson are so relatively stiff in their stride to-day compared with the gay and supple agility of Shakespeare? Chiefly, I think, because the two loved so little and loved so few, and the third loved so much and loved so many.

Yet Shakespeare could be terrible in his bitterness about the things of life: of man's ingratitude, of friends remembered not, that most love was mere folly, most friendship mere feigning. But in all, and through all, ran the pulsing vein of compassion and love for all things. He loved all things; he missed nothing, for nothing was too lowly for him to touch with a beautiful phrase. He looked up at a lofty tree and looked down at the speckled cowslip; rosemary, rue, wild thyme, and the pansy grew by his doorway, or scented the ways he walked in, and he often saw the morning dew shine for a moment before it slid off like a blessing from God. There was nothing of the literary popinjay in Shakespeare as there was in Marlowe, or of the literary swashbuckler as there was in the rare Ben Jonson. Bottom, Falstaff, Dogberry, Feste, and even the humour-obsessed Nym, were his companions as well as King Richard, Hamlet, Anthony, and Cleopatra. He seemed to know Bible and prayerbook like the palm of his hand, and used both to add point and flavour to the dialogue in his plays. Marlowe, Jonson, and the other University men wove most of what they wrote out of themselves as spiders weave silk threads from their own bellies; but Shakespeare gathered a lot of material for his miracles from the talk, the mannerisms, and eccentricities of those with whom he mixed and had his being. They stood still in the centre of learning; he walked, talked, and ran around in the centre of life.

The world of life was Shakespeare's oyster, and, unlike Auden who found it empty, Shakespeare found it packed tight with good and grand things. He saw all, heard all, tasted many things, felt all the emotions, and he scented the sweet perfumes coming from the hearts of flowers and shrank from the rotten smell that came from war. The great Marlowe, too, had his five wits that clubbed together in a mind keener, possibly, than Shakespeare's, but they never seemed to warm towards anyone outside of himself and confined him to a reckless importance alone among his university companions. He was cold and had little sense of humour. Whenever he tried to raise a laugh, it was clumsy, and dull, falling on the ear like clay falling on a coffin's lid. Shakespeare's sense of humour was heart-felt and full-bosomed, for he loved liveliness and his feet tapped out many a dance, for he would foot it featly here and there on yellow sands or in a candle-lighted room. For these reasons, Shakespeare has lived on, forever young, forever the supreme playwright of his time, of yesterday, today, and will be supreme tomorrow too. This is why when Marlowe, or even Jonson enters our home, we meet him with a deferential bow; but when Shakespeare comes, we cry welcome, and shake his hand, and set him down in the cosiest seat by the fire.

But Shakespeare isn't all smiles by any means. In his plays, he can be a man of sorrow and acquainted with grief. He has no delusions about life; he knows that man, born of woman, has but a short time to live; that he cometh up, and is cut down like a flower; he fleeth as it were a shadow, and never continueth in one stay. He was able to see change and decay all around him, as he showed in a sonnet to the young and handsome Earl of Southampton. He counted the clock that struck the time, saw the brave day lost in the night, noticed the fading violet past its prime, lofty trees barren of leaves, summer's green gathered into sheaves and borne on a bier with white and grizzly beard, saw sable curls turned white with age; then questioned the beauty of the Earl that in the waste of time must go:

> *Since sweets and beauty do themselves forsake,*
> *And die as fast as they see others grow.*

He saw change and decay as keenly, and felt it far more deeply than we present-day dramatists do, but he saw new growth as well. He knew that man cometh up and dieth as a flower in the field; but beside every fading flower, he saw a fresh blossom rising. A brief candle blown out gave place to another: *lux mundi* never goes out, never grows less. There is always someone in the house with Dinah playing on the oul' banjo.

I usually listen to the B.B.C. Schools Broadcasts, junior school as well as sixth form. I enjoy all the programmes, especially the one called 'Time and Tune', for it teaches me something about music, of which I know very little. One item recently was a gay, simple song, most enjoyable, which went like this:

> *We are dancing as we sing,*
> *Gaily, gaily are we singing,*
> *We are dancing in a ring,*
> *Come and join us dancing.*

Were he here to listen to this simple song and see the fun, the great poet who knew well that man's life fleeth as it were a shadow, would have been within this ring, this round O of hilarity, in the twinkling of an eye.

As long as Shakespearean flags fly, bugles blow, drums beat; as long as his glorious and graceful words sound in our ears, we need care little about the wolf-howl of the Avaunt Garde, or, in any way, be afraid of *Who's Afraid of Virginia Woolf?* The dance and the song no less than the requiem and the funeral march is Shakespeare's way with life.

THE BALD PRIMAQUEERA (1964)

(FROM "BLASTS AND BENEDICTIONS", 1967)

✣ ✣ ✣

Oh, don't tarnish the memory of the marvellous play we've just seen. Let not your heart be troubled, nothing ridiculous can linger longer so. Let us steep and seep our souls in the gospel, the last gospel according to Artaud.

> *Artaud! Artaud!*
> *Pounding a play to a wordless thesis,*
> *Beating up life into bloody pieces,*
> *An' the birds of Swan Lake to a gaggle of geeses.*
> *Artaud!*
> *Cut down the ivy, hack down the holly,*
> *Life is sure gruesome, death is most jolly,*
> *Keep the axe poised over Pineapple Polly.*
> *Artaud!*
> *Rape, murder, and suicide for brave British writers,*
> *And a kicking to hell for the song-singing blighters.*
> *Artaud! Artaud!*
> *For man is a louse and woman's a folly,*
> *An' the way to the grave's the way that is jolly,*
> *So hack down the ivy and burn up the holly,*
> *Into black urns with each Mick and his Molly,*
> *An' keep the axe poised over Pineapple Polly.*
> *Artaud!*

There are mild Mabels among the axe men, those of calmer and more civilized propulsions, who rarely go farther than marauding invasions into bedroom curiosities, and spectroscope probing into the mysteries of the toilet, the lavatory, or the water closet, according to the more or less refinement of the several writers of the several plays.

This essay on the Theatre of Cruelty, completed on Aug. 21, 1964, was the last article written by Sean O'Casey.

There was a play[1] done on B.B.C. Television in which a man and woman, visiting a couple, met in the hall, came up together and exchanged remarks when they had settled down on chairs, one making himself known to the lady, explaining that he lived in a certain road, to be surprised by the lady saying that she lived there too, adding that it was 'a remarkable coincidence' followed by the coincidence of living in the same house, the same floor of the house, the same flat on the same floor, the same bedroom in the same flat, the same bed in the same room. All just coincidence, variously called 'Marvellous, Amazing, Extraordinary, Astonishing, and Tremendous'. Seeing that though they came so close together in so many ways, even to him, presumably, mounting her while they were in bed together, yet could never become acquainted, they were persons of very poor powers of observation. Then in the midst of the coincidences came the climax—a maidservant slipped forward to tell the audience that she had bought a chamber-pot, and in the production of this play, as a suitable coat of arms for it, a chamber-pot was planted in the stage centre, plumb and ferocious, in plain view of the audience, their rosy faces trying to keep calm, and look ahead as if they had seen nothing. It was the consecration of the house.

Apart from being old-fashioned, the chamber-pot is almost non-existent now. It used to be the third piece in a set of three for a bedroom. The ewer, the basin, and the pot, in the upperclass and middle-class homes in the day of my youth, but times and new dispositions displaced them from favour, and now it would be hard to spot them, even in an old-fashioned junk shop. Apart from this, these peering, leering playwrights have no natural or supernatural licence to jeer at these essential bodily practices. None of them is the mental and physical outcome of an immaculate conception. Each has a mortal button on his belly.

These are the pacifist Freudians of the theatre who see sex in a raincloud, the way a spoon is used, and the way one holds a knife and fork. These, too, are half-brothers with the dare-devil Horrorhawks of the theatre of murder, rape, and cruelty and all are arm in arm with the Theatre of the Absurd. As Minerva is said to have sprung from the head of Jupiter, so these playwrights seem to claim they have jumped from the head of Freud, a shocking mishap to happen to anyone. They dibble and dabble in their plays with the Freudian faculties, turning them into neurotic fixatives and erotic fribbles and frabbles of their own. There must be some Freudian reason for their frequent leering, sneering among the lower depths of the human body. To them a body is a vile body, and it is nothing more. The Christian Church nourished and nursed this idea, aiming at getting out of the body to be present with the Lord. The idea didn't work and it doesn't

---

[1] *The Bald Prima Donna* by Eugène Ionesco; entitled *The Bald Soprano* in the U.S. translation.

work now—except among a lot of playwrights, busy making the mind worse than the body. The comic thing is that their plays declare that they know little or nothing about either. Psychology and psycho-analysis are sciences, life studies, and cannot be acquired by just reading a book at bedtime. Freud spent his life studying the human mind, yet, at the end, admitted he had learned little about it.

Yet a lot of these boyos sit in the minds of their characters like a spider in a web's centre, noting every vibration and agitation in their characters, as if, like the spider, they themselves had woven the mysterious and multi-multiple web of the human brain. Freud knew the first thing about it, but these know the first and last about it. Each is in his own swollen ego, the Alpha and Omega in the know-how of the whole psychological nature of man, the peak of mammals, yet scientists are now studying the psychology of captive animals, in relation to their food and habits, and they aren't finding it as easy as kiss hands.

Do they know much more about the body which they so often abuse by sneer and snarl in their plays? It is odd that the body from the waist down should be used as a gibe in the plays of so many present-day playwrights. It would seem that they resent being endowed with a belly. They seem to regard it as an unnatural and unwarranted degradation. They don't relish the idea of having to carry a basement department with them, they refuse to admit that the lower storey is just as wonderful as the upper one, that there can be no *apartheid* here, for the upper, lower, and middle body, brain, and mind, are one unified whole.

It is the middle parts of fortune which hold the golden issues of life. All our wealth of great minds through the ages, in art, science, literature, music, and great and small buildings, all have to make their first passage to life through the belly, and the clash together of complementary bellies has given the world a bewildering mass of wonderful animation in hand and head, with many more to come, all giving problems that keep hands and heads busy trying to keep things steady, shipshape, and cheerful.

It was Artaud—the latest trumpeter of the Primaqueeri—or one of his brethren, who gave us a picture of a beautiful girl, naked, with a malignant tarantula spider between her lovely thighs. An ugly guardian for the seat of life, a vision that could only be seen by a savage Primaqueera—one who is thinking he is looking through a lens which reflects back into the mind of the onlooker, showing that this tarantula spider is squatting, not between the lovely thighs of a woman, but in the searcher's skull, weaving its tendrils in and out of the web of his brain. It is an opposite vision seen by Peter Keegan [in Shaw's *John Bull's Other Island*], but is, too, the vision of a madman. All the greatness of man in wealth of science, art, literature, human healing, the fire of vision, the urge of effort, have all come in a little life from between the thighs of a woman. Such writers blaspheme against humanity, for even the tarantula spider has its place in nature, and in its own haunts is harmless to man.

These fellows rarely mention animals, and when they do they make them as horrible as they make men and women. The tarantula has been shown by Artaud ensconced secure, ready to pounce and poison, between the soft thighs of a young woman. None of these Primaqueera playwrights seem to like either beast or blossom. When they do mention any, they seem to give them a sinister or savage symbolism. A travesty on the old and charming tale of *Androcles and the Lion* told us that when the lion and his master had gone through their romance in the arena of Rome, and they were returning home at night in the dark, with the busy streets empty and still, the lion turned on Androcles, rent him to pieces, and ate the poor bugger up, leaving not a wrack behind. Another story tells us of a fellow absorbing the nature of a dog; not a gay dog, but one apparently on the way to madness. Now a mad one is no more a true dog than a poor demented person is a true human being. Soon there will be no necessity for a da to buy his daughter a bow-wow, bow-wow, for with little effort, apparently, he can become one, and a fierce one, too. Ionesco, the playwright, tries to show us men and women turning into rhinoceroses, with but one man left opposing the Muttamorphosis. Funny, this, for while there is no fear of the rhinoceros exterminating man, man has to engage in a feverish fight to keep a few of these strange and remarkable animals alive. There is no fear of us turning into rhinoceroses, but there is a possible chance, if these playwrights get their way, of us all turning into Ionescos, a more terrible fate still.

Hitchcock is the latest champion in the fray, but he, in a film, gives the venom and the violence to the birds. Our feathered friends become our spear-beaked enemies, according to the talk I've heard around me. The birds (very different from those imagined by Aristophanes) set themselves to overthrow the dominance of the human family; to pierce and rend them as the frenzied women of Thebes tore their king, Pentheus, to pieces for ignoring and mocking the power and divinity of the god Bacchus. Euripides was bad enough, but he rent but one man, and him for blasphemy against a god. The present literary group, in their work in drama, novel, poem, and film, seem to revel in the rending of all men, mentally and physically, to act like Shakespeare's wanton boys with flies. They get sport out of it all. They want to be the *avant-garde* gods. They are a kinda requiem get-together group, and there dare not be any sing-along Saturday in their poem or play.

The most recent addition to the dark stars that have swum into the sky of English dramatic literature is the play *Afore Night Come*.[1]

1 *Afore Night Come* by David Rudkin, produced by the Royal Shakespeare Company at the New Arts in June 1962 and revived at the Aldwych in June 1964.

world, should have gone home in the darkness, having called upon the robin red-breast and the wren.

Mr. Harold Pinter is more of a gentleman; you could never see him going about with a hayfork. Yet all critics admit, nay, agree, that he is a sinister fellow as far as his work is concerned. Not only every sentence, but almost every word, is sinister in its menace; hidden, but none the less visible in emotional penetration. Rudkin works barehanded; Pinter wears gloves so that not even a finger-print is deposited in the writing. Rudkin roars like any sucking dove. Prim Pinter is genteel, he rarely shouts, but uses the voice like the sibilant purr of a Siamese cat, ready to change to the danger-ous hiss of a snake at any minute. His quicker dialogue, as in that of the mother in *A Night Out*, is like the hammering of a woodpecker's beak against the trunk of a tree! His slower tense is like the tap tap tap of the stick of Tiresias. Pinter doesn't behead his *personae non gratae* with a hay-fork! He pulls them to pieces in his pauses; the one kills with a shout, the other in a silence. His silence is like that of a cemetery, menacing and creepy, making each individual hair upon one's head stand up like quills upon the fretful perkypine. In these plays we know not the why or the wherefore. No one knows whence the persons come or whither they goeth. Hecuba doesn't know where she stands. Pinter and Rudkin keep their mouths shut. To any questions they answer not. No names, no packdrill.

They must be meant for NO plays. Neither Pinter nor Rudkin likes people. Indeed, Mr. Rudkin declares with a flourish that he despises audi-ences. Perhaps he means only that he despises them as audiences but really loves for themselves alone. He dislikes them only when they get in his way. They certainly are a nuisance to all playwrights when they don't come. Mr Pinter's play *The Birthday Party* is a tour de farce of the menace in the common word, the cliché, and the menace in the pause. It seems to frighten the critics. One of the radiant members of the Sunday School of radio critics referred to a pause as a 'bumbinating vacuum'. I imagine that the characters as well as the pauses are other kinds of bumbinating vacuums. These are the woman of the house, her husband, a chair attendant, and a lodger named Stanley. There is a young girl, too, and, later on, two visitors who turn out to be megatonic, bumbinating vacuums, who, towards the play's end, take away poor Stanley. The play opens with an overture on the theme of cornflakes and fried bread for breakfast! A brilliant line of chatter which is apparently meant to make a heart stand still. It is Stanley's birth-day, so a boy's drum is bought and presented to him, apparently for his amusement, or to encourage his musical tastes, for he was once a pianist in some kinda show or pub. He fixes the drum round his neck, beats a simple stepping tap tap, and parades around the table to the delight of the woman of the house—left—right—left. He increases the beat quicker and quicker, he walks faster, then beats a frantic roll on the toy drum, facing the woman!

His whole aspect changes; he looks terrible so that the lady collapses away from him in abject terror. The dolldrum! The dolldrum! The Congo is strongo, the Congo will how do hoo do voodo you! Coming events cast their shudders before, the gods arrive in the shape of the two visitors, Goldberg, an effusive Jew, and a surly brutish Irishman, members of the two races which have given a lot of trouble to a too-complacent world. They have no trouble here. Goldberg, when he hears it is Stanley's birthday, calls for a party, the woman of the house says she'll wear her party dress, and hopes she'll look well, Goldberg replying that 'she'll look like a tulip'. In the end Stan is taken away by the visitors for God knows what to God knows where.

As far as the mind can go, this is the one instance in the plays of the *avant-garde* where a flower is mentioned. The tulip suddenly flowers, but only in mockery, and is swiftly sheared from the mind of any who noticed it. A flowering plant would be an obnoxious intruder into any *avant-garde* play. If one was brought in it would be a festering lily, for we are told 'Lilies that fester smell far worse than weeds'. I wonder if any of the *avant-garde* playwrights has a garden, and if he has, do flowers grow in them, and if flowers grow there, does he notice them in his goings out and his comings in? If he doesn't, then he is contemptuous of a larger part of the loveliness around him, and so is contemptuous of life, for plants are living things as he is a partly living thing; they spring from seed as he does, and germinate in the earth's womb as he does in the womb of a woman. They eat and drink as he does, they are attacked by enemies under the earth and above it, as man is by bacilli and virus, but in spite of these distresses they express themselves in beauty of colour and scent. They are useful, too, for man could not go on living on this earth without them.

One play belonging to what we are told is 'Theatre of the Absurd', *A Resounding Tinkle*,[1] mentions a garden, but no herb or shrub grows there, but an elephant romps around in it. Small chance for a plant or shrub where an elephant is, for an elephant in a garden is as damaging as a bull in a china shop. In the mind's eye one might see a lovely woman in a garden, like Maud among the musk roses, or see the beautiful lady Handel saw walking in a garden shady, bathed with the evening air, with a glory of golden hair. Or a simple farmworker on seeing a daisy might say:

> *Wee, modest, crimson-tippèd flow'r,*
> *Thou's met me in an evil hour;*
> *For I maun crush amang the stoure*
> > *Thy slender stem.*
> *To spare thee now is past my pow'r,*
> > *Thou bonie gem.*

[1] By N. F. Simpson.

But not they. Tree, shrub, or herb grow nowhere near them. They may have glimpsed a tree as they raced past, but their eyes never seem to have rested on the graceful beech, the sturdy oak, the immemorial elm, or the tender ash. They live in a silent spring. Of course we know that this elephant was put into the garden as an item of assurance that this play belonged to the Theatre of the Absurd. For the life of me I can't find anything humanly absurd in any of them. These playwrights seem to be vying with each other as to which can be more absurd than the other. A kinda 'what you can do well, I can do better' slogan. Shouldn't be surprised if one day we had a hippopotamus, not in a garden, but in the cage of a canary, and he singing away like any nightingale. They see none of the wonder of animals. They don't even take a passing interest in them. All kinship is lost between animals and them. If they be mentioned, they are but mentioned in mockery, like the rhinoceros trotting through the town and the elephant in the garden. A Pinter play mentions a slug, and that is all, as far as I have read or can remember.

Arden, of course, writes about a workhouse donkey, but he isn't one of the *avant-garde* and doesn't deal only with nonsense and savagery. Indeed, it seems to me that Arden's *Serjeant Musgrave's Dance* is far and away the finest play of the present day, full of power, protest, and frantic compassion, notwithstanding that, on its first presentation, it was scowled and scooted from the theatre by most of our intelligent and unintelligent drama critics. I wonder why! What dazzling Freudian id or idiom swept this rejection into them, making them reject the denunciation of war's horrors, and led them to embrace the plays which despise and hate life. They take all they can get out of life, like the most of us, enjoy its sweets and recreations, pilfer its pleasures, and dial 999 as soon as they feel a chill in body or in bone.

There was one lone but grand exception—Mr. Harold Hobson, drama critic of the *Sunday Times*. He told his many readers, without any qualification, how much he regretted the cold reception he gave to such a fine play. He had been greatly mistaken in his first opinion of the work and went on to give the play the fullest and most eloquent praise any intelligent critic could give to any fine and powerful work. It is naturally hard for a critic to proclaim a mistake in the first estimation of a play, and so Mr. Hobson's handsome admission of one was a very courageous thing to do, and it shall be counted unto him as righteousness.

PESTSCRIPT

The newest example of the theatre's condition of mind is a play now appearing in London, called *Entertaining Mr Sloane*.[1] The author gave an

[1] *Entertaining Mr Sloane* by Joe Orton, published in *New English Dramatists 8*, 1965.

interview on the B.B.C. network recently. The interviewer asked him to explain the plot, the meaning of the play, or to say something about it. The author responded as readily as any of Chaucer's storytellers wending their way to Canterbury. No, he wasn't influenced by either Oedipus Rex, or Oedipus Rix. It was a gathering together of many phases and psychologically disturbed characters, woven in and out into a simple dramatic pattern. Shakespeare did the same kind of thing. The play told of a house where dwelt a father with his two adult children, a man and a woman. The woman met a man in a public library who happened to be looking for a lodging. She invited him home to see if a room would please him. He went with her, was very pleased, and decided to dwell in the tent of the scarabs. Within the space of eight pages of typescript—say five minutes—she succeeds in getting his trousers off—the outer barbican stormed. Then the brother of the woman enters, and he too, immediately desires to take the young man's trousers off. Yet no homosexual he. The author gives us a plump assurance that he is bisexual, so, while remaining a man, he can, at a drop of the trousers, become a perfect woman-impersonator. Another trivial point—the newcomer, before he arrived, had murdered an old man, and the other old man upstairs knew of it. Someway, the brother and sister become aware of it too, and she blackmails the lodger into her bed with a hey nonny o. Afterwards, the brother succeeds in blackmailing him into his bed in rare counterpoint style, and to brighten the borders, the newcomer kills the old fella upstairs.

Here we have a theatrical gallimaufry of murder, odd sexual surges, a kinda incestuous indulgence on the part of brother and sister, with a man lodger in between, and a variegated assortment of psychiatric phases. A play to make a man pull his trousers up. The future is to have the inheritance of the theatre of the ridiculous, of the absurd, of rape, of murder and sudden death, of incest, of futility, of violence, and of a basilisk pot of sexual distortions; the land of Hope and Glory will disappear beneath the mud of a dull inferno.

Alfred Hitchcock has added an addendum crescendo to all these by his many films of mystery and horror. In a recent interview over the wireless he recounted with opulent satisfaction all he had done, and all he might yet do. Without seeming to see any difference between fear and fright, he told us that people like to be frightened, that they came to the cinema to be absolved from some kind of psychic fear. They joined their emotions with those shown in the picture, leaving the cinema chastened, and easier in mind and stronger in body—the film director adding with a beaming and patronizing air that all this fear and need to be frightened, sprang from the nursery tale of Little Red Riding Hood. Does the child really carry this tale in his or her mind from the cradle to the grave? There was a wise man who said, long, long ago that 'When I was a child I thought as a child, but now, having become a man, I put childish things from me', but maybe he didn't know what he was talking about. There are many more nursery rhymes than one, and any one of them might become a psychic influence as the one quoted by Hitchcock. I would shove aside his for this:

> *Ride a cock-horse to Banbury Cross,*
> *To see a fine lady upon a white horse;*
> *Rings on her fingers and bells on her toes,*
> *And she shall have a music wherever she goes.*

Today I heard on the wireless of a fifteen-year-old lass diving into the sea to save a boy of ten. The boy was saved, she was lost. And of a policewoman who risked her life on a roof-ridge to save a baby which a half-mad father had in his arms, ready to jump off the roof, baby and all, had the brave woman not snatched it from the frantic father. Brave woman, brave teen-ager lass. Ah, to hell with the loutish lust of Primaqueera. There are still many red threads of courage, many golden threads of nobility woven into the tingling fibres of our common humanity. No one passes through life scatheless. The world has many sour noises, the body is an open target for many invisible enemies, all hurtful, some venomous, like the accursed virus which can bite deeply into flesh and mind. It is full of disappointments, and too many of us have to suffer the loss of a beloved child, a wound that aches bitterly till our time here ends. Yet, even so, each of us, one time or another, can ride a white horse, can have rings on our fingers and bells on our toes, and, if we keep our senses open to the scents, sounds, and sights all around us, we shall have music wherever we go.

CRABBED AGE AND YOUTH (1957)

(FROM "BLASTS AND BENEDICTIONS", 1967)

🌲 🌲 🌲

Crabbed age and youth cannot live together, says Shakespeare, and he was no fool. On the whole, this is very true, so what are we going to do with the old, even though they be not necessarily crabbed? What are we to do with them? In other words, how best can we get rid of them? To me the main question is, what are the old going to do for themselves? If they don't help themselves, assistance from the younger is of little use. But of this again.

Does creativity decline with age? No. Activity is bound to be less, but the creativity of an active mind goes on. In age many ills unknown to healthy youth slow down the aged; give him or her less time in which to work, for in times of [in] disposition, the aged have to rest and try to nurse themselves away from illness's worse pains, with the help of science; so the little time left with the old is lessened still more by age's infirmities. But even these [difficulties] can be conquered by the determined will. Beethoven wrote his greatest symphony when he was deaf; Prescott wrote his monumental works on the *Conquest of Mexico* when he was half-blind; and Renoir painted on when he had to tie a brush to a rheumatic hand.

What advice shall I give to the millions of men and women who are to retire in another five years? None, if they don't know what to do with themselves, I or no one else can tell them. Certainly, I say they shouldn't retire from life till life herself says go. To retire from a job doesn't mean the end; it means but another beginning; not such a long time, maybe, as before, but long enough to learn and practise a different, but useful and enjoyable, way of living. In a few more months, if I be spared that long, I shall be seventy-eight, and, if I be alive, I shall be still on the go. I have just finished a new play; I am working on a new book; I write many letters, and here, now, I am telling those who may be a little younger, or as old as

This article is based on the answers to five questions put to O'Casey by Thomas C. Desmond, chairman of the U.S. Senate Committee on Affairs of Cities; it was intended to be read at a public hearing of the New York State Joint Legislative Committee on Problems of the Ageing held on Dec. 18, 1957.

myself, to go on too. Another thing—there must be still a tremendous amount of energy left within this crowd of millions about to retire, and, if the State be as wise as the State should be, then this energy should be organised and a chance given to this energy and intelligence to go on doing useful work, not only for those who have it, but for the whole community, so that they may not be wholly dependent upon the productivity of the young. To leave energy idle, is, to me, a woeful fault in the social system of a nation.

I can hear a murmur saying, 'Easy enough, when you're a writer, to go on with the job', and, maybe, the murmur is right. Here, though, are two examples of carrying on by old ones who hardly ever wrote a letter and probably never read a book in their lives. With our little flat goes a small garden which we have to take care of; a task which we, young and old, found beyond us. It was in a wild state when we took over, but our efforts at improvement, if they didn't make it worse, made it no better. Finally, we managed to get a man on pension, who knew something about the work. He was seventy-one, blind of one eye, with the good one not so keen as in his younger days. After a few months of quiet work, he brought tidiness and order out of its wildness, and when the summer came, it shone with a bright glow of colour from plants his cunning hand had set out for our enjoyment. Many an American has sat in that little garden, enjoying the blossoms and the finches, blackbirds, and thrushes hopping about in and out of them—all the work of the hands of my friend Harry, of the one eye and the bright heart. Another friend of mine, Charlie, an old lad of seventy-two, who went through the horrors of Mesopotamia during the First World War, living with his wife on the old-age pension, got hold of an old taxi that couldn't go, worked on it till it did, and now is very useful to us and other neighbours doing shopping and bringing the goods back, taking people to the station, and, in many other ways adding to the security of his own life and the comfort of the lives of others. Our son, Breon, knew two women in London, one ninety years old, the other but two years younger. The older one, when she sat in a chair for a while, found it difficult to rise, and the younger one had to come to help her out of it; but the glorious thing about these two very old women was that they were both busy learning Greek! They would never say die till death came. Remember, too, that Bernard Shaw didn't kill himself writing, but by manual labour, for he was on a ladder pruning a plum tree when he fell, broke his thigh, and never really recovered from the injury; but this warrior of ninety-four used his hands as well as his head during the last years of his life.

What is my daily regime in my later years? Work with hands and head, too, though the hands don't handle heavy things, and the head has to take an odd rest not needed in far younger days. When I was seventy and over, my favourite work was swinging a heavy axe, breaking up blocks of trees for the fires when winter made us need them, but this work became dangerous, and I had to give it up. I do the washing up, peel potatoes for a meal, at times get the breakfast in the morning, carry down the pail of rubbish to the ashcan, lay the table, and help my busy wife in any way I can. I take walks when the weather is not too bad, and find that even the same road changes its look during the different days and the differing seasons. I read a little, and am interested in painting and music, and science, too, reading *The New Scientist,* published in London every week, and *The Scientific American,* published in America every month; so I find each day, not too long, but far too short to do all that my heart and mind so eagerly wish to do.

Do [I] have a 'formula' for long life? No. There is no formula that can make a life last a day longer. Life has lengthened over the years, but not through the force or inwit of any formula. It has become longer by the greater knowledge of health and by the great discoveries of medical and surgical science. Life owes a lot to the brave searchers in the world of science.

In my opinion the chief problems the old have to face are three: social, economic, and the young. From the viewpoint of corporal livelihood, they don't get enough to keep them safe and satisfied. They should receive enough in pension, that is in money, and in kind, to allow them to live within a very moderate independence. In kind, they should be provided with a fair-sized room, or even a one- or two-roomed cottage, if they be active enough to be able to care for themselves; and now, with the advance of the science of health, the far greater part of the ageing will retain their activity to a very late year; so this problem of provision is really for the Muncipal authorities, the architect, and the engineer, with, of course, the advice of the social worker who has had an experience of the old in this respect.

The social problem is one more nearly concerning the old people themselves. Many of them find it hard to get along with their neighbours, and little envies, rivalries start up here and there when they live in communities, causing quarrels and unpleasantness, though this, I think, will not be so prevalent in the present generation that is growing old as it was in the one preceding. But many of the old are inclined to be too querulous, and make themselves a nuisance and something of a burden to those who try to help them.

One fierce problem for the old is to keep their minds occupied so as to fix their attention on something outside of themselves; for the old have a tendency to think too much upon the conditions that age brings to them. They can't keep up with the young, and it is useless and distressing to try to do so, for the young can't be bothered with them—they have their own problems, and can't give too much time trying to lift the old out of theirs. The old must depend on themselves, using all the power left to them to do so. We old people try too much to get comfort and stimulation from sources outside of ourselves, from the younger ones, from television, from the wireless and from the cinema. These are good in their way, but they tire sooner or later. We who are old should try to get more entertainment out of ourselves than out of others ·who are busy with other things. Good reading from good books is one fine way to do it; but this needs practice, and is hardly possible for those who have not had some experience of good reading while they were young. These can enjoy lighter reading, and God knows there is enough of this to be found in all the libraries. Good music on the wireless, good painting—through looking at and enjoying the many art books to be had full of reproductions of the old and present masters of painting; but these again need practice, but once acquired, the enjoyment of mind and emotion in these arts will never allow one to feel that he or she is alone in the world, for they will link those who enjoy them with the mighty past and the busy present, with the everlasting communion of beauty and truth.

Then there are games for those who have never encouraged the habit of enjoyment in literature and art; cards, backgammon, draughts, and chess, each of which require but two players. Alone, there are a hundred ways of playing patience with cards. It is not difficult to get a simple idea of the game of chess, and many a delightful game can be played between two people who could never become masters of the game. The pity is that so many old people have always depended upon others for amusement when they were young, and never thought of creating within themselves the gift of providing their own interesting activities, the one thing that can really allow themselves to enjoy their own companionship.

The more important thing, to me, is the looking after of the old of tomorrow rather than the old of today, so that tomorrow's old people will be more adapted to take care of themselves, and serve themselves out of their own thought and emotion with pleasant and profitable entertainment when old age settles down upon them. We must begin with the young. Indeed, a beginning has been made, and today, in the schools, music, literature, art, and handicrafts are practised as they never were in my young days. The young of today who become old tomorrow will have a far better background, giving them a richer chance to enjoy themselves when youth has left them, going its own way in the eager activities of others.

One thing more—most important of all—the old must realise that they are old and not venture upon any activity that will distress them physically, making them an anxiety to the young; they must remember that their life is behind them, and that every evening is eternally drawing to a close. So they must look back with satisfaction, and be thankful that they have lasted so long. Of course, once in a while, we may regret our lost youth, but this must be quickly set aside, for we have had our day, and we must leave the world to the young, as Shaw and Tennyson so aptly tell us to do. We must not resent the young, their seeming thoughtlessness, for they are, as we were once, full of themselves; and must be if they are to become useful and sensible citizens of their nation. We must decrease, and they must increase, so we should be glad and rejoice in their energy and their eagerness. It is good to be alone in one's thoughts at times, to think of the end, to face it bravely, and go calmly and quietly when the time comes to go.

THE DAY THE WORKER BLOWS A BUGLE (1958)

(FROM "BLASTS AND BENEDICTIONS", 1967)

🌱 🌱 🌱

The First of May! The Anniversary, the great day, when the workers parade themselves to take pride in what they have done, and what they are determined to do in the days to come. The day when the banners are unfolded, freshened up to take the air with colour and with gaiety; the day when the workers march in column of companies, trade following trade, each with its own symbol of what the trade does, all blending together in unity of achievement and harmony of endeavour; the day when the workers remember their strength, and renew their youth like the eagles; the day when the workers show that work, far from being a curse, is the activity that blesses all men; the day when all workers, those of the skilled hands and those of the clever minds, join together in parade and party to cheer as partners, and to cheer as one; the day when sounds of revelry by night tell of the joy, in song, in dance, and in story, of how blessed a thing it is to work together for the good of all.

These demonstrations, in the U.S.S.R. on the first day of the month, in other countries, not yet socialist, on the Sunday before or after the first day, show the importance and the power that Labour has achieved in many countries. Labour is now, thanks to the people of the Soviet Union's tremendous revolution, well on the road to a sensible and progressive socialism. The communist countries have reached the top, and face now towards the peak of communism; other lands are but half-way up, but climbing; others still are but planting their feet on the foothills of the higher ranges; but all face forward, and all look up to where they are determined to reach. It has become now but a question of time till the lowest in the climb join their comrades higher up, for now they can clearly hear the cheering of the peoples who have reached the higher or the highest parts, and their longing eyes can see them weaving a coloured pattern of life bringing into being a safer, a more comfortable, and more colourful and joyous civilisation. All have now heard the battle-cry of Workers of all Lands, Unite! And all are

Article written for *New Times* (Moscow), May 1958.

echoing it, or singing it, as they climb upwards. Victory is certain now, and, even in the lowliest states, reactionary forces are kept on the defensive, presaging their final defeat.

To get where the workers are now was a bitter, long, testing, and a bloody climb; a long road first to the climb, then a rough and often perilous ascent. When did the climb begin? When and where was the first effort made to find the road on which the fight forward could be made to reach the place whereon to climb? God only knows. All we know—all I know, anyway—is that it began a very, very long time ago; thousands of years, thousands of years, if all were told. We do not know what stirrings went on in the hearts of the herdsmen who tended the flocks of their patriarchal masters; or of the discontent smouldering in the breasts of those who toiled in the building of the pyramids; who silently resented the crack of the foreman's whip around their shoulders, or the hatred for the scorn of those who flung away to die those who could no longer do the work demanded of them. We cannot tell how many mute-tongued rebels are now but deep dust in the plains of old Mesopotamia, or deeper still in the sands of the Egyptian deserts. We can surely guess that they were many, and, perhaps, spoke their resentment and their hatred in whispered words to their toiling comrades, or enshrined their feeling in a simple song, as so many workers did in the years that were to follow. We do not know when first the mills of man's mind began to grind out thoughts of resentment, or think of ways by which to loosen the hold their masters held over them. All we can be sure of is that these thoughts must have been there, and that those who thought of them were braver than the many, and that they were few. But there they were, and a few seeds must have been sown before the life of [recorded] history began.

We know that there were artists among them by the way in which they decorated their primitive pots and pans, and the lively, and often beautiful, way in which they painted the walls of their caves. We know the story of Spartacus, the great gladiator, who hated the Roman grandees, those who used the toil of the slaves to produce their wealth, and those who used the stronger ones to provide their sport. This gallant Thracian slave organised his comrades into an army that defeated again and again the well-trained Roman Legions sent against him; but the time was not yet, the rest of the workers remained bewildered, for there had been no previous theory to guide them into co-ordinated thought, and Spartacus and his army was finally defeated, and the gallant leader slain. All fought and many died, becoming, perhaps, the first fine bugle-call for the workers of the world to hear and stand up for the freedom of all downtrodden men. No memorial yet marks the graves of these heroes who fell on the slopes of Vesuvius, but the time is coming when the name of the brave Spartacus will suddenly appear on the banner of Italy.

Afterwards the revolutionary ethical turmoil of Christianity, its tenets and teaching falling like the gentle dew from heaven upon the poor and the oppressed. However poor and miserable one might be, he and she now became, not only sons and daughters of men, but also daughters and sons of God. It was an hilarious thought! Do unto others as ye would that others should do unto you, promised a new life and a fine freedom from want and care. The life of the Christians set an example; goods were held in common, and, for a while a new earth seemed to be within the process of a great birth; a new dawn had come to all men, so all those who suffered, who were weary, all who laboured and were heavy-laden, flocked to the new idea. The workers had only to believe, and all would be well. It didn't turn out that way. It felt fine for a few years; many suffered death for their belief, and those who survived were strengthened in their hope that freedom was at their door. As soon as it was seen that Christianity could not be over-thrown; as soon as it became powerful, the rich and powerful got busy. The then Emperor, Constantine, blessed the new creed, and made it official, and struck it dead, as far as the poor, the needy, and the workers were con-cerned. They remained as poor, as needy, and as miserable as ever; the grandees, the rich, and their lick-spittle followers became the governors, not only of the Church, but of the State, too; and the lot of the workers became worse than ever; they could have heaven if they wished, but the rich and the privileged continued to inherit the earth. The workers lived in the earth's worst room; they still had a world to win. The poor workers! They had had the rich on their backs before, now they had the prelate and the priest there as well.

During the centuries following, we are only now beginning to forage out records of how the common people lived; they are few, but we know that life for them was both miserable and uncertain and short. They must have muttered together about their hard lot; maybe made rhymes in their own way, and chanted them softly as they toiled in the fields; but, by and large, the workers were poor dumb mouths; bearing all too patiently, depending on the talismanic benefits from Catholic sacrament and Catholic relic, fear-ful now not only of their earthly master, but of their heavenly one too. Obedience to their masters was what they had to keep in mind, in pain of punishment in this world and eternal penalties in the next. The workers most certainly rejoiced in the legend of bold Robin Hood, the outlaw who made the woods unsafe for the travelling rich, and who often raided them in their manors, exacting from them much money and goods for the better provision of those who needed those things more than they who had too much. The toiling people must have longed for a Robin Hood on every estate, close to the walls of every monastery, and among the clusters of filthy mud huts where the common people lived and died.

These people became children of God when they were born (so it was said), and were confirmed in this happy connection when they died, and became ashes, no longer of any use to those who had employed them; but throughout the long or short journey of life between birth and death, they toiled for eighteen hours a day, fed on the coarsest food, lived in a verminous mud hut, slept on a pallet of straw, owning a rough bench at which to eat, a stool or two, and a few pots to boil their porridge in. If they were of the more fortunate few, having two cows and a plough, a reaping-hook or scythe, when the possessor died, the lord of the manor took the better cow, the better agricultural tool, and the priest of the parish took what was left, leaving the weeping widow with her mud hut, her pot and her pan, and her pallet of dirty straw. It was taking a long time and many terrible lessons to teach the common people that they had no aid to hope for in anyone, or anything, but their own unity and organisation to compel the privileged and powerful to recognise their right to live decently, and to enjoy the fruits of their labour.

The workers were eternal, and development of thought went on in their minds, and each attempt for freedom brought fuller confidence, fuller knowledge, even in defeat. The peasants rose in France, and showed their power for a time, shaking the nobles with not a little fear. The peasants rose in Germany, and the masters saw the fire and felt the blows of the risen workers; and the peasants in England, galled into desperation by the poll-tax, rose in revolt under Wat Tyler, swarmed from Kent and Essex towards London, and took the city, but they were so destitute of a preparatory plan that, with the king and government of nobles in their power, one dagger-blow ruined them and turned a triumphant army into a fleeing rabble, followed by a merciless slaughter of the peasants by the very nobles who a moment before had promised them every reform they had demanded.

The old slavery came back on them, but the echo of what they had done lingered on, thought grew, and man, slowly and unconsciously, went forward. The workers worked for their masters, fought the wars for their masters, amassed new wealth for them and went unrewarded; toiled till they could toil no longer, and then died wherever they happened to be; but the worker crept nearer and nearer his vindication.

A rifle-shot! from Bunker Hill, and colonialism, with all its evils, suffered its first defeat; a rifle-shot that proclaimed the birth of some of the world's grandest democrats—Jefferson, Lincoln, Whitman, and Roosevelt; and the flag of the world's first wide Republic was born; to be followed by the tremendous French Revolution that shook Europe, put a cap of death on absolute monarchy, and the Third Estate came to political life, and the workers defeated the trained armies of Europe. Social evolution was quickening its stir. The Industrial Revolution came racing in on the scene, and the peasant now had a powerful comrade in the proletarian. Organisation began, and the self-educated miner, Keir Hardie, with his cloth cap, appeared among the tall silk ones in the British House of Commons. The workers were climbing the hill. The spearhead of revolution was being fashioned by Trade Unions all over Europe, and political Labour movements fashioned the workers' shield. Labour leaders appeared out of corners into public places, and voiced a revolt against the filthy and slavish conditions under which the workers lived; while Lenin, bent over the works of Karl Marx, gathered into his wide-ranging mind the visions of the poets, thinkers, and scientists of the centuries, and forged them, with gigantic skill, into an amazing plan of offensive and constructive action to convert the upheaval of a revolution into a thriving and invincible socialist republic. The workers were half-way up the hill.

We honour those who fell in the many defeats suffered by the struggling workers; honour them as much as we honour those who rejoiced within the glory of victory, for those who fell went down willingly for a cause they knew could never find defeat final. Labour never suffered a defeat, for each defeat meant another step on the way to the hill; and so we honour the numberless unknown heroes equal to the greatest heroes known. The Red Flag, respected now the world over, waves for them as it waves for us; for the dead as well as the living. It was a long, long fight, and those who carried it on in the earlier days of desperate odds mingle with the dust of many places, Chicago, Detriot, Moscow, Pekin, Dublin, Manchester, and many lesser places, laurelled with no less of a glory. When Keir Hardie, the ex-miner, became the first Labour leader to enter the English Parliament, I was a young man of twenty years, and now, during my own lifetime, I have seen the workers become the great power of more than half of the world, with the other half beginning the climb of the hill; I have seen the workers, peasants and proletariat, widen their ranks to welcome home as workers, too, the poet, the artist, the scientist, the doctor, the teacher, and the thinker, who in their labour in their differing ways are all one, proving the truth of the old slogan of Each for All, and All for Each. There are many countries still within whose borders the workers still struggle; whose lives are unhappy and whose chances are few to enjoy a fuller and more harmonious life. But they are learning from those others who have done so much, and these undeveloped peoples are hearing now the Voice that said many years ago: 'The strongest bond of human sympathy, outside of the family relation, should be one uniting all working people of all nations, tongues, and kindreds'.

So, we the workers blow a bugle on May Day morning; blow long, blow loud for all to hear: a merry, merry sound. In the old days, the serfs used to dance on this day around the maypole. The grandees danced in their castles or their manors, and the peasants danced beside the graveyard holding their dead; danced to depart for a moment from their hard life, and to colour their imagination with hope. So we dance now, not to forget our unhappy life, but in loud rejoicing that we have done so much, and that the worker now is a power, a great and eternal power in the world of life.

On this first day of May, under the birch tree or the oak; under the cedar of Lebanon or the palm; in the sandy places, the cold snows, or where the rich grapes grow, the worker blows a bugle; a moment for a dance and a song, a kiss from a girl, and a merry meal, for all of us who are 'too busy with the crowded hour to fear to live or fear to die'.

NOT WAITING FOR GODOT (1956)

(FROM "BLASTS AND BENEDICTIONS", 1967)

❦ ❦ ❦

If your magazine [*Encore*] be seen and *read* by five hundred students, then you have a very important audience, for I hope none of them is a greybeard. What would my old raucous voice be doing among your young, shrill, eager ones? It is you who have, or ought to have, the say in the world now. My world is gone, gone in the winds of yesterday, and I don't intend to run back after it, like a man running after his hat. You will have to write for yourselves—a Magazine of the Students, by the Students, for the Students.

Beckett? I have nothing to do with Beckett. He isn't in me; nor am I in him. I am not waiting for Godot to bring me life; I am out after life myself, even at the age I've reached. What have any of you to do with Godot? There is more life than Godot can give in the life of the least of us. That Beckett is a clever writer, and that he has written a rotting and remarkable play, there is no doubt; but his philosophy isn't my philosophy, for within him there is no hazard of hope; no desire for it; nothing in it but a lust for despair, and a crying of woe, not in a wilderness, but in a garden.

The earth isn't either a grave-yard or a roaring camp—save in a war, when it is both; but today war is a *non est,* for with the new nuclear explosive power, all are within range of death; the rich and the poor, the ones who go out to fight, the ones who remain at home; the Catholic pope and the Catholic peasant share its shivers, and so aren't ready to nod the head in favour of strife. And there is life and energy even in decay (not Beckett's, but nature's), for dead leaves turn to loam, and dry bones to phosphates.

What witnesses does this Beckett call? A dowdy and doleful few: Camus, Kafka, Orwell, Graham Greene, Huxley, with T.S. Eliot a wan follower, cross on breast and hands clenched in an obscure prayer. And what witness have we? A cloud of them: Copernicus, Newton, Beethoven, Angelo, Shelley, Whitman, Balzac, Faraday, Titian, and, yes, by God, and Shakespeare, too, with ten thousand others close up to the greatest!

Published in *Encore: A quarterly review for students of the theatre,* Easter 1956.

As for the English theatre, it is but a ghostly memory, with the Irish theatre a runner-up. There is, of course, Joan Littlewood's Theatre Workshop in East London—a cinderella without a fairy godot-mother; a theatre that should get what is given to the Old Vic, for it is as adventurous as the other is timid and tired and lazy. There's the People's Theatre in Newcastle, a venture that is spreading into what may become a sanctuary for the drama, the film, and chamber quartet. A nest of amateurs who have kept the rose of Lancaster, rose of York, and Tudor rose in a state worthy of wearing: colour and scent are in them still. But what are these among so many? The rest is silence; or a mutter and a *moue*, hurting a silence that would be a finer honour. Today, bar the musicals, *Waiting for Godot* and *The Wild Duck*, there isn't a play worth a penny on the London stage; and these are by an Irishman and a Norwegian. No, sir, English drama is the bird in the golden cage, and it is safe in the vaults of the Bank of England.

I WANNA WOMAN

A Short Story

(from "Windfalls", 1934)

✵ ✵ ✵

Jack Avreen was waiting for a girl to come and have a light little supper with him in his flat. Between half-past eight and nine she was to arrive, and it was now a quarter to nine. Any minute she might be here now, tossing all his emotions into a hot and exquisite whirl of uncertain anticipations. The packed bud of anticipation might burst into a rich-coloured realisation to-night if he was careful enough. It wanted a little careful handling, that was all. A girl didn't come along to a man's flat for nothing. Sit down calmly together and sing hymns? Not damn well likely. He would have to move cannily tonight, though. Bring her along gradually. A hasty movement might frighten her and spoil everything. It would be maddening if she fought shy of it again. Like the night a week ago when she was with him here, and he hurried the pace on too suddenly. Everything was going grand, and if he only had had the patience to spread the final fuss over another half-hour or so, he'd have got her sure—but no, he must try to rush things, and in ten minutes she had her hat on saying she'd have to go, and biding him an agitated good-night. Then for a week he had to bring her to a theatre, to meals in public restaurants, and to walk respectfully and respectably with her till he had subdued her timidity into coming again to his flat for a light supper and an hour or so of secluded companionship. She was a Catholic and that made it more difficult, though it shouldn't, for plenty of Catholics were hot stuff. But Catholic or no Catholic, if he couldn't get her going this time, he'd just shunt her off finally about her business. She went too far altogether without going far enough. It was a bit thick to applaud desire till it was a passion ready to overthrow everything, and then to expect a sudden thought of shyness or fear to trim it down to a cool-centred flame of torturing self-control. Pandering to passion, playing with passion, and then asking passion to behave itself. She wouldn't get him to stop so easily this time. When he saw that passion had filled her with a wild, throbbing, and delicious confusion he would go on determinedly and exact a full and perfect satisfaction out of her. She could even do a faint if she liked; that wouldn't lure him into any frightened, pitiful, or conscientious withdrawal. In fact a faintness would make the job easier. When she weakened with emotion, that was the time to hammer a job on her. So long as she didn't start to yell. That would make everything impossible. He remembered the last time she was with him here how she started to yell when he tried to show her how nice she'd look lying down stretched out on the divan. The roars of her . . . let me up . . . let me up . . . let me up! Pretence, the whole of it. Imagine a girl, even a Catholic, living in London all her life not knowing her way about. The idea was stillborn. He would carry on this time if only she didn't start to yell. Then he'd have to put the brake on, for he couldn't afford to let the people in the other flats hear a girl yelling in his room. He didn't want to have a cloud of witnesses to the thing he wanted to do. But he didn't think there was any real risk of a yell tonight. Even though she did yell the last time there were signs that she was beginning to get into her stride. She came, if she came at all, expecting things to happen, and she had no reason to grumble if she wasn't disappointed. Besides there was the present he had bought for her nestling up on the mantel-shelf in its satin-lined casket: a twenty-guinea gold and jewelled wristlet watch which was worth something more than a kiss. A big expense, he thought, but she was worth it. . . . Oh, she was fairer than the evening air clad in the beauty of a thousand stars. . . . Not quite so wonderful as that, but she was fair, and he was mad for her.

Everything was ready, and everything was waiting for her. The room was aglow with the heat from a blazing fire. Everything whispered encouragement to, and tolerance of, the solace of sex enjoyment. Food, fruit, and flowers; light glowing softly through amber shades; the bottle of wine offering exhilaration; cushions coyly clamouring for the vivid conclusion of passion. And all would contribute to, and form, a happy harmony, hiding in softness and colour the savageness and sadness born in the energy and ecstasy of the sex encounter.

After they had taken supper they could sit down courageously and cozily on the divan. He wouldn't force or even press her to take any wine, but if she would take a glass or two, all the better. After a little while he would place the watch around her wrist . . . and listen to her cries of admiration . . . he would kiss and kiss her while he was looking quietly to see how her things were fastened . . . then fondle some of them open here and there . . . so that when the right moment paused in front of him, a little struggle, sweet and rapid, would be a sweet beginning of a sweeter end.

He glanced around the room to see that everything was in order. To see that there was nothing that could even delicately interfere with the plans or the excited emotions of the evening. There now; look at it, look at it, look at it! He had overlooked the print of Lochner's picture of the Crucifixion, hanging on the wall so that when she was lying on the divan, it would be staring her in the face . . . that gruesome, beautiful, tranquil, primitive expression of the last terrible act of the Passion. . . . To the right on the Cross the stark, wasted figure of Jesus with the look of pre-destined, agonising resignation on His tortured, peaceful face. . . . Three wondering, funny-looking angels, fluttering like little birds in the air, each with a tiny chalice in tiny hands; two of them catching in the tiny cups the blood that trickled from the nailwounds in His hands; the third gathering in the cup the blood that streamed from His wounded side. . . . Mary Magdalene, dressed in brown and modified purple, kneeling at the foot of the Cross, the train of her gown sweeping around a bare skull and a bare bone. . . . To the left of the picture, the rich purple-mantled St. John sup-porting the fainting, black-gowned figure of the Saviour's Mother. . . . Behind, the peaceful features of a valley, with a narrow, curving, swift-flowing brook in its bosom. . . . And high up in the background, to the left, on a tiny indication of a road, the little figure of a soldier marching up and down on guard.

That picture would have to come down and be hidden away for a while. It was bound to be a disturbing element. Once let it catch her eye, and superstitious fear would make her briskly button up all her secrets, and fend her back into a condition of agitated and implacable primness. Besides he wouldn't feel perfectly comfortable himself, now that his attention had hovered around it. Something strange and sorrowful would be there con-testing silently everything they said, everything they did. It must come down and be set aside. Perhaps that very picture was the influence that stood in the way on previous occasions when she was here, and was ready apparently to go the whole hog, and then suddenly became hard and deny-ing. . . . Curious that it never occurred to him before. He extended his hand to take it from the wall, and withdrew it again. He wished the picture had never been where it was. . . . He felt a chill thrill at the thought of removing it. Was he getting superstitious too? He laughed softly and deridingly at the thought. . . . It was pitiful that this silly feeling of nerv-ousness should dart through him. . . . He wasn't a Catholic or even a Christian, so down, down you come. He turned his head a little aside, and pressing his lips together, he lifted the picture from the wall, smiling, to rebuke his infirmity of sudden fear, went into another room quietly and deliberately, and placed the picture behind a bookcase there. Returning, he sat down, lighted a cigarette, and puffed and puffed, and waited tremu-lously. She was twenty minutes behind her time now, and that wasn't promising. She really was a provoking little bitch. Between eight-thirty and nine—that was what she had written to him, and have a nice little supper ready for his little darling. Well, the supper was here, but where was the little darling? And at the end of the letter that she wouldn't be later than nine-fifteen, so if she wasn't with him by nine-twenty, he needn't wait, for she wouldn't be coming. . . . Nine-twenty now, and she wasn't here. . . . One thing certain—if she didn't come tonight, she had seen the last of him. He toyed with the flowers in the vase on the table; he read the label on the bottle of wine; he put some more coal on the fire; he crossed to the window, pulled the curtains aside and looked out on to the street; he pulled the curtains back, returned to his seat by the fire and smoked furiously. . . . A quarter to ten, by God, and she hadn't come. If she wasn't coming, couldn't she phone, and not keep him waiting this way for her? Or if she was afraid of reproaches if she phoned, couldn't she at least send a telegram? He took a little book mechanically, opened it and began to read a few lines. . . . 'Critics have referred to Monet as being of Norman birth, when as a fact his mother was of a Lyons family, and the artist was born in Paris. . . .' Happy Paris, happy Monet. . . . Lucky fellows these artists who could make a high hill of dainty, fragrant garments stripped from pretty women. . . . If he were a sculptor or a painter or something of that kind, this jade wouldn't be keeping him waiting like this, time nipping into his anticipations of delight with uncertainty and misgiving. . . . Still she might come yet. . . . Many things in London might delay her. . . . The traffic . . . a bad jam. . . . Ticking of the clock getting on his nerves. . . . He'd just wait patiently a little longer, then if she didn't come he'd seek a compensation down in Piccadilly. . . . Ten times the little clock on the mantelpiece struck. . . . He sat like a stone listening, puffed up with rage and disappointment. The clock stopped striking and resumed its laughing tick, tick, tick. He sat there still as a stone. . . . He saw his maid come in, leave a small tray of things on the table beside him, and heard her say 'Cup of tea' while he was 'wyting' . . . 'didn't look as if she'd come tonight . . . wot a shime, and things so nice and comfy. . . .' He sat there still as a stone, sick and hot with rage and disappointment. . . . His mind went forth savagely and sought her out; his hands went round her throat and he shook her and shook her. Perhaps it was just as well. . . . What fools men were to lacerate their senses with these delicious and dangerous emotions. . . . He sipped his tea with a stiff, set face, and nibbled his toast, while his hands in imagination circled her throat and shook and shook and shook her. . . . He would go out and take a long walk, a swift walk, a furious walk, and sweat all his longing and disappointment out of him. . . . He put on his heavy coat and wrapped a muffler round his neck. . . . His eye fell on the little blue box on the mantelpiece, and snapping it open he fixed the gold and jewelled watch round his wrist. . . . She had missed something, anyhow, by not coming to him. . . . Then he descended the stairs and passed out into the street. She could come now if she liked. . . . Hoped she would. Price of her to come and find him out. . . .

Here was a taxi coming up the street. . . . No, but she might be in it. . . . He'd peep as it passed. Damn fellows allowed to drive too quickly.

Couldn't snatch a glimpse of whoever was in it, he flashed past so fast. . . . Dangerous speed altogether. He'd go back a little just to see if it stopped at his place. . . . Wouldn't go back though if she was in it. . . . No demeaning himself that way. Damned taxi had flown past his place. Might have known it couldn't have been she.

He tightened again his loosened emotions, and walked swiftly, never lowering the quickness of his pace till he came into sight of a glow in the near distance that told him he was coming into the colour-lighted sprightliness of Piccadilly Circus. Pausing at the corner by Swan and Edgar's, he looked on at the streaming, hurrying, pleasure-seeking, prettily dressed, neatly dressed, snappily dressed hordes that surged along and around, that crossed and passed and crossed again in all the curious, bewildering, merging and rejecting jugglery of human life and movement. The circle of life streamed round and round, moving off the Circle down Shaftesbury Avenue, towards Leicester Square, or up Regent Street. Long, lithe limousines, purring confidently, joining in the orgy of movement, slipped by with a majestic glide, passing superciliously the perky little two-seaters that raced vehemently alongside for a while, then shamedly dropped behind and followed afar off with a cringe in their perkiness. Bull-bodied taxis, graceless, assertive, self-absorbed, facing forward, ignoring all the wheels around them, nosing boldly up to the front of a traffic jam, standing still or rushing along, ever determinedly minding their own particular business. Buses, big and red-faced, abrim with strength, bullying their rumbling way through the traffic, trumpeted around corners with engine-whir and horn-hoot. And all this streamed in, rushed round, and poured out within a blazing halo of lights, rich blue, light blue, purple, bright red, pale red, rich green, light green, mauve, yellow, and orange, flashing, dimming, vanishing, moving slowly, whirling fast, rippling down yellow, rippling up green, gliding across to the left red, gliding purple across to the right, making an endless flow and ebb of animated colour. Over opposite, a steady, dignified, silvery yellow glow told that a Cochran Revue had a home there. The name of an actress that carried a terrible load of loveliness about with her blazed imperiously in golden lights on the breast of Shaftesbury Avenue. Over to the right, on a great broad space, a shower of red, yellow, and green stars, flanked by zig-zagging, curving lines of red and green, merged into a huge, gorgeously flamed announcement of an unction of beer in flashing yellow, changing in a moment to half green and half yellow; then all yellow again, with a crimson strip in the centre of each letter; then the upper half became red and the lower half remained yellow; then it was entirely red; then all green; then the upper half red and the lower half green, then it became all yellow again, to vanish in darkness and give place again in a few moments to the shower of red, yellow, and green stars that recommenced its cycle of announcement. On the wall of a restaurant in brilliant colours were the orange sunbright blue sea and emerald-green trees of some resort in Southern Europe. The whole place flamed with the gaudy gusto of advertisement.

But he hadn't come here to look at the lights, he hadn't come here to look at the lights. He came to get a woman. But the woman must be something worth while to compensate him for what he had missed. He hummed softly to himself:

> *I wanna woman, oh, bo, I wanna woman,*
> *With wavy hair and time to spare to banish care,*
> *I wanna woman, I wanna wanna woman, wanna woman.*
> *That's always gay, doesn't pray; for last hours o' night, first hours*
>   *o' day;*
> *I wanna woman, I wanna woman.*
> *That'll say, oh gee, my guy, you know the way; now my clothes*
> *are astray, you know the way, my guy; oh gee,*
> *I wanna woman, I wanna wanna woman . . . today!*

He watched a man coming towards him with a placard hanging over his breast looped over his shoulders to another hanging down his back. He read the one in front, 'The wages of Sin is Death'. He looked at the face of the man passing and saw there a sign of severe, sodden, and enviously imagined sanctity. He watched him, moving quietly and obstinately onward, mingling with the crowd, looking to neither the right nor the left, carrying his holy placard glorified with the reflected glow of the vanishing, reappearing, gleaming, twisting, rippling, coloured lights of the Circus. Nobody took the slightest notice of this wandering herald of heaven. He wondered—oh that wasn't a bad little bird that passed; face just a little bit too coarse though— at the curious sensations different people sought to bring them pleasure. Churches were old-fashioned. Hanging on still to pulpits and placards. No novelty in them now; what was wanted were Stations of the Cross in coloured electric lights. Ireland's one-up there, for, in Dublin, he remembered seeing a statue of the Blessed Virgin with a ring of coloured electric bulbs around her head for a halo. Unbecoming thoughts for a man on a mission like his, so he crossed the Circus and wandered down Piccadilly towards Leicester Square, humming softly to himself:

> *I wanna woman, I wanna woman,*
> *For first hours o' day, last hours o' night,*
> *I wanna, wanna, wanna woman.*

He kept watching out keenly for a suitable bit of skirt. They were streaming past him, many giving him an inquiring and desirous glance as they went by. No, thank you, he wouldn't have any of those. They were all so common, so coarse, and so obvious. He wanted just a little elegance of manner and a saucy reticence that surrendered with a sad, sham charm what it was paid for and had to give. These were rare among birds, for their life muddied their manners as well as their bodies.

He passed into a bright patch of coloured light on the pavement flowing from a window display of green, black, crimson, and yellow dresses. Glancing casually at the richer light and colour in the window, he saw a woman leaving it and walking off in the opposite direction. Pretty, dressed in a smartly-made tailored suit, covered by a fur coat that reached to the hem of the skirt, short enough to show the full knee when she took a step forward; a delicious helmet hat of modest red made a sweet frame for her face. His indifference flaming into excited interest, he swung round, said 'Sorry' to a man he bumped into, and hurriedly walked after her. Was she one? Hard to say. She seemed to have an elegance and taste in dress, and a gracefulness in walk that few tarts had, but there still seemed to be something about her that suggested the possibility of hire. He'd walk on quickly, get in front of her, stop at a shop window, and eye her as she passed. He went by her rapidly, walked on in front for a few moments, stopped at a shop window, watching her sideways as she came along. His heart beat a little faster as he saw first the right, then the left leg from the knee down issuing out of the narrow sweep of her neatly-tailored frock. Trim, and he loved them trim, and with this bird everything else seemed to be in coy conformity with the pretty legs. He wheeled around as she came level with him, and looked longingly and inquiringly at her, but she apparently took no notice and walked on. This was disappointing, and made things doubtful. Was she one, or was she not? She was worth following for a while, and if she only would turn down one of the quieter streets, he'd tighten up to her, and ask her how she felt towards the world. Wouldn't be nice to get a choke-off in a crowd, so he'd wait a quieter chance to find out if her clothes came off easily. He hadn't the courage yet to go up and say 'Good evening' and chance it. She might be waiting for some man to do the clicking quietly. Some birds were like that—only out occasionally to add a little week-end tail to their wages; or, those that were a little new at the game, still frightened and shy. If he wasn't quick some johnny was bound to nip in and she'd be snapped up before his eyes just because he hadn't enough of the pure stuff in him to Charleston up to her and whisper, 'Say, kid, you'd look nicer with a little less on; oh, you'd look a lot nicer with a lot less on. . . .' Damn this leisurely moving crowd that was hindering his efforts to keep close to her. He could see in the distance the little soft red hat dodging forward, in and out through the people, apparently with ease and certainty, while every man and every woman that came toward him seemed to plonk themselves right in front of his face, and then begin to dodge the wrong way to get by. He hurried and twisted as cleverly as he could. She was a lovely bird, and he'd willingly bury four or even five quid under the world-forgetting trickeries of a night with her. There was the soft little red hat crossing Wardour Street. He'd hurry, reach her, walk side by side and get it over before his halting hesitation lost her. . . .

Now he was caught in a crowd gathered at the edge of the path gaping greedily at something that probably wasn't worth a flickering thought, coming up Wardour Street. . . . Oh, procession of people singing something like a hymn. . . . Church Parade. Leader carrying a cross. . . . Lift the cross higher, brother. . . . Choir in white surplices and black cassocks with heads reverently bent over their hymn-books. Jammed here now for at least three minutes and the soft little red hat getting farther and farther away. . . . Why do the authorities shut their eyes to this sort of wandering, maundering, philandering missionary mania holding up regular and necessary traffic? My God, listen to them:

> *Lord in this Thy Mercy's day, ere it pass for aye away*
> *On our knees we fall and pray.*

No use, gentlemen; no one in Piccadilly has the slightest intention of falling on his knees. . . . She'd be miles away before he'd get himself out of this mess. . . . Hurry up, hurry up; get along, please. . . .

> *Holy Jesus grant us tears, fill us with heart-searching fears*
> *Ere that awful doom appears.*

Soft, sloppy, winding, creeping, crawling, snaily, snobby, snarling bastards dividing him from all the heart-quickening gifts beneath the red hat, the tailored suit, and the silk stockings. . . . Oh, if he were a savage how he'd like to jump in and spear a hundred per cent of them. . . . Not a sign of her now. That procession had crossed the hunt and saved the quarry. He breathed deeply in disappointment and rancour. And they did this sort of thing out of their love for men. Annoying thing to come up against and mingle with his present mood. Even if he did manage to get into touch with her again, things wouldn't feel so comfortable, for he knew the hymn by heart, and here it was maliciously humming in his mind, blunting the innocence of his eagerness. She might be anywhere now. . . . Grant us tears . . . fill us with heart-searching fears. . . . No use of looking any longer. . . . To go home is best. . . . Nothing in skirts could interest him now till he'd forgotten a little about the girl in the soft red hat. A peach. . . . No doubt about it, he'd missed a peach. . . . Lord in this Thy Mercy's day, ere it pass for aye away. . . . Bakerloo, from Piccadilly to Baker

Street, and then a bus to Swiss Cottage. . . . On our knees we fall and pray. . . . It was just twelve anyhow, and only the 'Pros' that time has tossed a lot paraded now. . . . Strange, determinedly sliding movement of the escalators. . . . Wonder how the procession would look coming up or going down one of them. . . . Keep time and step off together, please. . . . Trains going west . . . that was his platform . . . empty carriage . . . drowse to Baker Street. . . . When eyes are closed curious feeling runs through body with the gentle, rumbling shake in the movement of a tube train. . . . Feeling of motion and of rest . . . Oxford Circus. . . . Two more stations. . . . Somebody coming in . . . sitting opposite him. . . . Woman . . . see so by shoes. Some uninteresting looking old cow or young heifer not worth noticing. . . . Keep his eyes closed. . . . Regent's Park. . . . Next stop. . . . Nothing exciting in the night after all his hope. . . . Procession spoilt everything. . . . Procession spoilt sport. . . . Perhaps it was just as well to get a check now and again. Thoughtless compliance with the complaints of sex was bound to overbalance his nervous system, and that wouldn't do at all. He was almost glad now that the procession had poked its way between him and his desire to make a fool of himself. He wouldn't feel that seething sense of remorse that invariably followed a night with a new woman; the dead, revolting dissatisfaction of deliriously misspent energy and passion; the miserable surge of emptiness that followed the feat of giving too much for a short enjoyment. He could rest and go to sleep without the soul-nagging sense of sex weariness. Perhaps this would be the first step towards a stronger self-directed life, of decided and persistent effort towards self-control. Back to a virtuous bed. . . . Good bed; better bed; best bed.

Baker Street . . . oh hell, don't stir. . . . Fur coat, tailored suit, and soft red hat sitting opposite. Damn fool keep eyes closed. Where's she getting. . . . Passing Marylebone. Oh, that was a cute glance. . . . Measuring up his naughtiness. Opening her fur coat. Too hot in here, dearie. Good sign; wants to show her legs. . . . Passing Warwick Avenue. . . . She's a peach, boys, she's a peach. . . . A sense of uncomfortable fullness made his heart beat faster. . . . He lighted a cigarette, and his hand shook. . . . His nerves were tingling again. . . . Oh, gee, my guy, you know the way, now my clothes are astray, you know the way, my guy, oh gee, you wanna wannna wanna woman. . . . Getting out at Maida Vale. . . . So was he, you bet. . . . Along the passages to the lift. . . . He feverishly paid his excess fare from Baker Street to Maida Vale to the attendant, watching her from the other end of the lift. Anyhow, she knew that he was interested in her. She had seen him look at her with suggestion in his eyes, and had shown no annoyance. Indeed, she had sent him glances that seemed to venture an invitation. The lift doggedly moved upwards, came to the road-level, the gates crashed open, and they passed out into the street. If she hopped off quickly now, all was over, but if she went on slowly the thing promised fruit. The street was quiet and restful, animated only by an odd taxi cruising past. Up in the sky, in the northwest shone The Plow and in the northeast sparkled The Lyra. . . . She went along slowly. His mouth that had dried twitched a little, and his heart beat unpleasantly as he hurried on and walked by her side. . . . 'Good evening', he murmured nervously. She gave a slow, careless glance at him, and continued to walk on slowly. . . . 'The air is very clear tonight', he went on, 'and the stars are remarkably plain. . . .'

She turned her head to him, smiled and said, 'What are you doing with yourself at this time of night?'

He stammered a little as he murmured, 'Oh, just taking a stroll round about thoughtlessly'.

'You passed me in Piccadilly', she asked, 'didn't you?'

'Yes', he said, 'I think that I did see you somewhere in Piccadilly'.

She's very cool about it all, he thought; she must be a bird after all.

'Well, now that you've seen me again', she said, 'do you fancy me as much as ever?'

She was a Pro then, so he'd have to be carefully indifferent, for the more desire he showed, the higher would be the fee. So he kept silent.

'You'd like to come up to my flat and have a drink or a cup of tea, wouldn't you?' she asked.

'Yes, I wouldn't mind', he answered.

'I'm afraid if I let you come you might want to be naughty, would you, my dear?' she asked smilingly.

'I might, you never know', he answered.

'If I let you come, and was very nice to you, you'd give me a little present, darling?'

'Oh, of course', he replied.

'How much?'

'Two pounds', he murmured.

'You're not out to spend much!' she said disdainfully, hastening away from him. 'Cheerio, darling!'

He hurried after her and said, 'Don't run away, dear; let's talk together for a minute or two. There's no necessity to rush off in a rage'.

'I'm not in a rage, dear', she said, 'but I don't let myself be man-mauled for two quid. Go back to Piccadilly and you'll get lots of girls ready to accommodate themselves to your idea of generosity'.

He was fascinated; she was a rare bird, and he didn't want to lose her, but he wanted to get his pleasure as cheaply as possible.

'How much do you want then, to let me go home and make a fuss of you?' he asked.

'Five pounds, at least', she said.

'That's a lot of money for a few hours. I'll give you four', he bargained.

'Five, dear, or there's nothing doing. If you fancied me so much, and followed me so long, I'm worth a fiver'.

He walked beside her pondering, fingering in his pocket one note from another and counting thoughtfully. . . . One . . . two . . . three . . . four . . . five . . . six . . . seven . . . and a ten-bob note.

'Oh, be a sport', she said encouragingly, 'and I'll give you a right good time'.

'All right', he answered. 'I'll give the fiver'.

Stopping at a house of flats, she took a key from her bag, opened the hall door, ascended to the first floor, where she rang a bell; the door of the flat was opened by a maid who gave him a quick, furtive look as they entered. She brought him into a sitting-room, quietly and comfortably furnished with easy-chairs and lounges. Some ordinary landscapes were on the walls, and on the mantelpiece were two large photographs of pretty women pictured in a state of saucy and semi-nudity. She pulled brilliantly green curtains that were on the window closer together as she said to him: 'Take off your coat, dear, and make yourself at home'.

To the right of the fireplace were six shelves filled with books. Spicy, naughty, and nonsensical, the lot of them, he thought.

'Tilly', she called to the maid, 'bring me and my gentleman friend some tea and biscuits'.

She took off her fur coat and soft red hat, and sat down in one of the easy-chairs before the fire, crossing one leg over the other. 'Nice to be sitting before a fire on a cold night like this', she said as she sipped her tea.

'Nothing better', he said, 'with a pretty girl waiting to be nice to you'.

'And with a man that wants to be naughty', she added.

'I see', he said, 'you're interested in books'.

'Just a little', she answered, glancing at the shelves. 'They pass in a pleasant way many a dull hour'.

'Who's your favorite writer?' he asked.

'I've none', she said. 'I like Hardy, France, and Dostoevsky a lot'.

'Dostoevsky's one of the Russian fellows', he said; 'don't know how anyone could be interested in such a writer, though I haven't read him myself'.

'If you haven't, how do you know?' she asked.

'I know from those that tried to read him', he said, 'that he's a terrible writer'.

'Yes', she admitted, 'he is, sometimes . . . terrible'.

'Who's the johnny that wrote all the books you have covered in green?'

'Balzac', she said. 'Wonderful writer. Never read his *Poor Relations?* *Madame Marneffe, Baron Hulot,* and *Cousin Pons* —far greater than his better known *Père Goriot.* Powerful realism, and pathetic, remorseless imagination'.

'Come over here', he said, 'and sit beside me; I don't want to be bothered about Balzac just now'.

She got up out of the chair, smiled, lifted her skirt a little, danced over to him, and sat down by his side on the settee. She put an arm round his neck, kissed him quick and cooed into his face, the suggestive look in her eyes hardening a little.

'Now, darling', she whispered, 'what about my little present? Not nice to talk about it, but it's best to get all the nasty things over at once'.

'Oh, I'll give it to you all right', he said.

'I know, but I might as well have it now'.

'You won't trust me?' he asked peevishly.

'I know you're a sport', she said, 'but it's just as well to get it over and done with before we begin to amuse ourselves'.

He took the notes from his pocket with a serious, half-timid sigh, and handed her five, saying, 'Here you are, five of the best and brightest'.

She quickly and gently caught hold of his hand, and with a confident smile said, 'The ten-bob note as a little present for the maid, dear'.

'Oh, now you've had enough out of me', he protested.

'I always get a present for the maid', she insisted; 'she's a dear woman, and I never forget to ask for a little tip for her. . . . Go on, don't spoil things now by a mean refusal of such a small thing; we're getting on so nicely together'.

And the ten-shilling note was pulled gently from his hand, added to the five, and all were locked away in a drawer of a cabinet that stood quietly and expectantly close to the window. Then she removed her skirt, coat, and blouse, pulled loose the ribbons threading the shoulders of her caminickers, showing her breasts, animatedly sat beside him, put her arm round him, and murmured, 'Now, darling, don't you like me a lot better with a little less on?'

He abandoned himself to the surge of desire that swept through him. He caught her in his arms and tried to bend her back on the settee. With a sour laugh she freed herself, crossed the room, and opened a door opposite.

'Come into the bedroom, dear', she said, 'where we'll have plenty of room'.

What a fool he had been to stop so long with her. It was maddening to have to stay on here in bed beside her, after having got all that he wanted. She had fallen asleep, while he was still awake listening to the ticking of the little clock at the other end of the room, thinking and cursing deeply in his mind about the weariness and waste of affection, energy, and money that made this honeycomb a bitterness and a loathing to him. He sat up in bed and winked his eyes several times to press the heaviness out of them. The first glimpse of a cold dawn was trickling in through the green curtains that covered the window. The room that had looked so full of nimbly dancing promises of pleasure was now filled with a sickly sense of weariness, and seemed to be stuffy with the breath of dead things. He moved as far away as possible from his companion, and looked down at her sleeping there with her bare breasts, tossed hair, and partly open mouth. Attractiveness had ceased to meddle with her now. He felt a wish to beat till he bruised the breasts that he had fiercely fondled only a few hours ago. Tear and rend them for the ruin of tiredness and silent agony of remorse that they had helped to bring upon him. Lying here for three hours he had been trying to deafen himself to his thoughts, and put away the memories that had stormed his mind before he had bargained with this unashamed whore that now lay asleep and naked beside him. ..... The procession that had cut across his path and the hymn they had been singing. . . . 'Holy Jesus grant us tears, fill us with heart-searching fears. . . . .' Keep it out, keep it out. . . . I wanna woman, I wanna woman, with wavy hair, to banish care, I wanna woman . . . keep it out, keep it out. . . . .

She had felt him moving and was murmuring drowsily, 'Lie down, sweetie; cold coming in under clothes, and I've nothing on . . . lie down, sweetie'.

He plunged down into the bed again, and roughly pushed away a leg of hers that had wandered over near him. 'Not so rough, dear', she murmured.

What vice-armored souls these women had. But perhaps it was better if one wanted to be anything, to be that thing right out. Wallowing grandly in her own shame. Let the light of dawn but mount a little higher up and he'd slide from bed, and dress and leave this place of poisoned satisfaction.

Her eyes opened a little and a peculiar, spiteful smile darkened them, and her hand began to fondle him. 'Keep that damned hand quiet', he said, as he jerked it away with a savage and resentful movement.

'Sweetie doesn't want pretty Alice any more', she murmured, giving his cheek a malicious caress.

'I'm going out of this', he said surlily, getting out of bed and beginning to creep shiveringly into his clothes. Glancing in the glass he saw himself hollow-eyed, hair-tossed, with his chin darkened where his beard was beginning to show strongly.

She sat up sleepily, resting on her elbow, took a card from a drawer in a bedside table, held it out to him and said, 'Card, dear, double ten double nine Berkeley. You might like to ring me up some evening'.

Paying no attention to her, he tugged on his heavy coat, pulled on his hat, wrapped his muffler round his neck, glanced at the cabinet where his five pounds ten were stored, and said, 'I'm off now, good-bye'.

She snuggled down in the bed, pulled the clothes warmly round her shoulders and under her chin, and murmured, 'Don't make a noise, dear, to wake the maid . . . she's such a dear woman, and I'm very fond of her

. . . close the street door after you as gently as you can. . . . Cheerio, darling'.

It was cold and damp coming into the air of the street. Leaving that whore warmly nested in her bed, too. He was done with women for a long time. He kept his head bent as he slouched sleepily homewards. The exhaustion of the night was letting this dampness into his marrow. Ding, dong, ding, dong, dell. . . . Some damn church bell ringing for some damn service. Waste of time. . . . Never keep people from making fools of themselves. . . . Ding, dong, dell, sinners sent to hell, to clothe their pain in an everlasting yell; so cease to do evil, learn to do well; ding, dong, ding, dong, ding, dong, dell. . . . Palpitating nonsense, these bells.

He opened the door of his flat, and let himself shivering in. He would sleep till about five in the evening, then he would have a warm bath, a brandy and soda, a good dinner, and he would feel a lot better. He stripped to his shirt, and let his clothes slide from him in a heap on the floor. He slipped his pajamas on over his shirt. Must be getting on for eight, now. . . . He bent his arm to look at his wrist. . . . Jesus, he had left the wristlet watch in the house of the whore! He didn't—he couldn't—have stuck it in one of his pockets. . . . He rummaged fiercely in the pockets of his trousers. . . . No, and he flung them savagely back on the floor. . . . His coat? He rummaged through the pockets of the coat . . . no, and flung it down again on the floor. . . . He remembered . . . he had put it down on the little table beside the bed, and had forgotten it was there in his eagerness to get away from the place. . . . Oh, the idiot, the fool, the ape, to forget to take it up and put it on when he was leaving. Oh, what a stinkingly stupid thing to do. . . . What did he want to bring it out with him for? And he had no idea of the street or the house, only that they were somewhere in Maida Vale. . . . He had hurried away noticing nothing. . . . Wouldn't take her card even. . . . Hadn't the least idea of her telephone number. . . . A big-brained idiot, that's what he was. . . . She had been well paid for her favors—five pounds ten and a wristlet watch and bangle worth twenty guineas. . . . She was laughing at him now . . . and fitting it on. . . . Pity it couldn't turn to steel and stop the circulation of her blood. . . . He turned down the clothes and stormed into bed. As he lay down his eye caught sight of Lochner's Crucifixion hanging again on the wall over his bed. . . . That blasted maid of his couldn't keep from ferreting around. . . . Fished it out from behind the bookcase and replaced it on the wall. . . . Frantic to meddle with everything. . . . Mocking him there with its tale of tragedy. . . . Take him weeks now to recover from the shock of his stupidity. He pressed himself down on the bed in a rush of rage. His head throbbed with the nerve-rack of his loss. Forget it and sleep. . . . That's all he could do . . . sleep and forget it. . . . He lay silent. . . . The telephone bell rang, rang . . . rang. He snapped down the receiver and bellowed, 'Hello? yes, this is Mr. Avreen. . . . Yes, it's Jack. . . . No, you can't come tonight. . . . I'll be engaged till long after midnight. . . . If you long to see me, why didn't you come last night? Explain . . . yes it will need some explanation. . . . Angry? why of course I'm angry. No, I won't post the watch to you, or see you tonight either. . . . Must go now to keep an appointment'. And he firmly and angrily replaced the receiver. . . . Then he gathered the clothes tightly around him, closed his eyes, and quivered in a mad medley of thoughts. This was the crowning of his foolishness. He stiffened with repressed and remorseful rage. . . . The telephone bell rang . . . and rang . . . and rang. . . . Ringing me again, he thought; well, let her ring.

A faint trickling beam of light from a timid rising sun crept in through the window and spread over the picture of the Crucifixion, showing wanly to the right the figure of Christ hanging on the Cross, the three funny little black-robed angels with tiny chalices in tiny hands catching the blood that dripped from hands and side; Mary Magdalene, in her brown and purple robes, kneeling at the foot of the Cross; to the left the crimson-mantled St. John supporting the fainting Mother; the brook swiftly flowing through the peaceful valley, and away in the dim distance, the little figure of a careless soldier marching up and down on guard.

And he tightened his teeth together, cursed deeply and lay still, as the telephone bell rang . . . rang . . . rang.

PURPLE DUST IN THEIR EYES

(FROM "UNDER A COLORED CAP", 1963)

♣ ♣ ♣

An eminent London drama critic, reviewing the play *Purple Dust* in the
Sunday Times of 19th August 1962, says 'Sean O'Casey likes men and
women. It is an uncomfortable combination for a dramatist who believes in
revolution. How can one condemn to destruction, ruin, and spoliation, people in whom eccentricities are delightful?'

I don't feel in the least uncomfortable within the combination of revolutionist and a drama-maker. A dramatist is one thing, a revolutionist is quite
another; one looking at life in the form of individuals, the other is part of
the collective urge and forward thrust of man. In my mind I think, not of
the revolution born in cannonpeal and riflefire, such as that which swept
away colonialism in the United States, the one that swept away feu-
dalism in France, or the last mighty revolutionary throe giving power to the
Russian People to take over and control the wealth their labor produced,
and use it for the general good of all. No: what is in my mind is the
revolution brought about by Time and the slow-moving or swift-moving
winds of change. The play, written in 1937–38, saw the disappearance of
what was called the Empire, and so it happened, and with its departure
from India, what was for long but a breeze became a fierce and destructive
wind blowing over Asia, from Cochin China to the great expanse of land
and people ruled over by the then invincible Chiang Kai-Shek, who failed
to see or feel the tremendous changes the winds of thought were bringing.
The winds of change come, and no one feels them till they become strong
enough to sweep things away, carrying men and women (however comic
and enjoyable), bearing off their old customs, manners, and morals with
them. So in the decline and fall of the British Empire (she seems to be in
danger now of losing her Commonwealth) many picturesque things, some
even lovely, fell with it, and are now but a little heap of purple dust. A few
album mementoes survive, such as the Yeomen of the Guard and the cui-
rassed horseman standing under the archway of the Horse Guards centre,
and the bearskin of the Household Regiments; quaint things now, and but

–

part of an open-air museum. There are those who clutch at things that are departing, and try to hold them back. So do Stoke and Poges, digging up old bones, and trying to glue them together again.

They try to shelter from the winds of change but Time wears away the roof, and Time's river eventually sweeps the purple dust away. Fifty years ago one thought that Viceroys, Governors-General, with a host of lesser lights, would be always with us, but Time took them off while they yet lived; and even the mighty men of war, the generals, with the garden of colored ribbons on their chests, are passing into creeping, ghostly forms, for the true generals now are the scientists in the laboratory, or those standing by the launching pad. There were probably eccentrics among the generals, likeable, even lovable, characters among them, but revolutionary change didn't give a damn, but ruined, despoiled and destroyed them. As a man the revolutionist playwright is much the same as the drama critic: he has to get better from an illness by sending for a doctor; his personal problems cannot be solved by a constant reading of the Communist Manifesto; so when he's writing a play, the dramatist is neither Tory nor Communist, but only a playwright, setting down his characters as he knew them, giving, if he can, an added depth, height, and lilt to the words he makes them speak.

Besides, these characters, these eccentrics, loved by the drama critic (loved by me, too, so long as I am independent of them, and amn't forced to live with them) are always a nuisance to those who live with them, at times a menace, despoiling and ruining the lives of others (as per Captain Boyle), hindering and thwarting sense and sensibility; so when Time and Change go too slow, life takes a hand herself, and shoves them out of her way.

The drama critic thinks that 'the prophecies of doom spring from an old national jealousy and dislike'. This is a mistake, I think, due to so many critics reading old hatreds and jealousies into every O'Casey remark, even into a farewell of 'so long', sensing every common saying with nonsense and deceit—the critic deceiving himself, then through his statements deceiving his readers. The critics now see a Freud in every bush and a Jung squatting on every doorstep. Better to leave subconscious as expression to those who have studied psychology and psychiatry most of their lives, and know something of what they write or talk about.

As for me, I abandoned the romantic cult of Nationalism sixty years ago, and saw the real Ireland when I read the cheap edition of Shaw's *John Bull's Other Island*; hating only poverty, hunger, and disease. For nowadays Jung and Freud seem to peer over every playwright, and appear as actors, as designer, director, even as stage manager, in many ways, almost all of them in fact. It looks as if this habit were becoming a fixation, not only within the nature of a playwright, but also within the nature of a critic too.

The critic says: 'At the end of the play, words scowl and mutter, and this would have been in order had not the playwright, in the course of the evening, so clearly fallen in love with the two characters to whose destruction they are addressed'. Quite so. The characters are foolish, inept, pompous; but they are comic, at times pathetic, and all through likeable, if not exactly lovable. But Time and Change do not care a damn for these lovable things, neither can the playwright care either. All that they are, and all they represent, must go; Time and Change will sweep them off, however hard they try to cling to the tinsel and brocade of a past life. A new age is not only knocking at the door, it has broken into the house, and taken it over. And in the course of the change, many a David will lose a Jonathan, many a Tennyson will lose a Hallam.

The other symbol in the play is of course the working class; they are realists, regarding the two gadabouts as fools, getting all they can out of them, before the two poor guys are borne off by the coming change of wind. All workers, including the Communists, give all the help they can to Nationalists in subject countries, though Communists look far ahead in thought and theory beyond all nationalist hopes; knowing that when national freedom is won, national unity tends to break up; new groups are formed, opinions differ, and the battle of the dialectics begins. Drama critics aren't interested in this kind of thought or action, indifferent, apparently, to the fact that these activities weave different strands of life round themselves, for better or for worse. Indeed, indifference to most world affairs seems to afflict many of them with blind eyes and deaf ears, inspired often by a scornful shrug of the shoulders. They don't even turn to glance at these faces peering in through the windows of England, gawking at all that goes on inside, many of them, indeed, within the English home taking a part in trying to keep the house in order. I remember once when James Agate was reviewing some Australian play, he said among other things, that he didn't know anything about Australia, and certainly didn't want to know either; the remark striking me as an odd one for a loyal Englishman to make about one of the more important Members of the Commonwealth.

The eminent critic's review of *Purple Dust* was bannered by the title of 'Doom without a Profit'; but there is no doom in a change except for those who refuse, or who cannot accept, the change—those like Stoke and Poges who tried to live in the past till the present overthrew them. A change invariably brings a profit, never a doom. The Irish peasants of the play, less comic, less picturesque, less lovable maybe (though I wouldn't agree to this), survive the winds and the rising flood because they are more adaptable, and so of the two contraries, the fitter to survive: life—not O'Casey—chooses these and destroys the others. It is true that while O'Killigain is a realist, O'Dempsey is a romanticist, but as the play shows, O'Killigain can understand, and further, the romanticism of his friend, and O'Dempsey can understand, and aid, the realism of O'Killigain. The change that came to the farmer's field didn't bring doom to the farmer. I can remember as a young man the handsome sight of a team of horses pulling a plough, the plough-man cheering on the animals while he drove a straight furrow from one end of a field to the other, the shrilling flock of birds boisterously picking up worm and grub from the tumbling rich soil on a hardy spring day; or, later, in the autumn, the sturdy row of mowers, advancing together, step by step, each in his own measured-out avenue, rhythmically swinging their scythes while the rich corn sank aside before them as they cut it down in a mass, beautiful movement of arm and instrument. Who sees that now? Millions of youngsters growing up today will never see a scythe in action, never hear the sharp, pleasant sound of honestone on a blade; never see the straining horses pull a plough, never see 'the ploughman homeward plod his weary way', for all have gone, and we have now the much more effective tractor and combine-harvester. The chimney-sweeper, mentioned by the drama critic in his review, is gone too; no more do we see the sooty-faced figure, black as a crow, a bundle of long, socketed rods on his shoulder, one of them topped by a circular brush, plodding a way through streets of city and town, crying out, shrill as a curlew, 'Swee . . . eep, swee . . . eep!' Electricity and gas have downed him, and he has been gathered to his fathers like the muffin man and the fish vendor, or the lavender lady crying her bunches of tiny mauve flowers that carried a melody of perfume into every home that bought one. No doom, but many profits came to the farmer when farming machinery invaded his fields; and no doom, but many profits came to the housewife when electricity and gas flowed into her home. I surmise that the drama critic takes these things for granted, for he probably never knew the spirit of evil irritation and dirt that lurked within the smoky kerosene lamp and the sputtery candle. Things outworn, drama critics and playwrights too, must, sooner or later, give ground to make way for the new, this being old in its time, must yield to the newer, and, again, the newer must shrink from the newest; and men or things that cannot pass from the old to the new, from the new to the newer, the newer to the newest, will be flung away, far away from the sight, mind, and sound of man. So Stoke and Poges, however comic and lovable, encumber the ground, and will inevitably be destroyed by those who are ready and eager to build better than the others knew. Often and often, we don't like this, but we've got to lump it.

Another eminent drama critic, Mr. Kenneth Tynan, in the *Observer* of 19th August 1962, dismisses the play, *Purple Dust*, as 'a tenuous [Why not thin?] one-joke jape'. This verdict, pronouncement, or dictum, is disappointing, for the labor used, the thought given, and the time spent in the creation of this 'one-joke jape' were far longer, deeper, and harder, than those energies in action would take Mr. Tynan to write a year's worth of his world drama reviews. However, time, labor, and thought do not prove the play to be more than what the critic thinks it to be; time alone can tell, so I record his decision in a more permanent form than that of a hurried and a brief-lived notice in a weekly newspaper. The critic makes some blimpish remarks: he says, 'What bores one about the English upper classes is not, as Mr. O'Casey insists, that they are ignorant of country life, but that they know it inside out and never stop talking about it'. O'Casey doesn't insist on any such thing: first, the Blimps aren't the 'upper classes', and if the critic thinks they are, he knows very little about them. Realistically, they are of the many who do well in business or on the stock market, and then come down to a country house because they think it's the thing to do, and this is made plain in the play. Mr. Tynan should know that everyone who has a big title, who may fish, shoot, or ride, isn't a member of the 'upper class', and never can be one. He should know that aristocracy is a closed shop; that no one is admitted without a genealogical passport; and that no member of this rigid class would, for a moment, recognise himself in either the comic frenzy of foolishness shown by Stoke on the one hand, or by Poges on the other. I have never tried to write about the 'upper classes', for I know too little about them, but I do know something about their apers. The upper classes were no fools, and in spite of their gorgeous robes, their stars and garters, their plumes and pennons, they were ruthless realists, grabbing for themselves nine-tenths of the wealth the workers produced, grabbing the best education the times could give, denying any to the 'lower classes'; and so they developed a power within their families that made them the governing class for many, many centuries; but now things are altering, the working class have whipped the pennons from them, have seized part of the education, some of the wealth, so that what was a power in the land is sinking down, here and there, into little heaps of purple dust. (Tynan puzzles me. In his review of *Red Roses*, he refers to the character, Ayamonn Breydon, as an 'Orangeman', though the play shows explicitly that, not only is he no such thing, but is firmly against all their gaudy bigotries. Yes. Tynan puzzles me.)

Mr. Tynan says that 'what bores us about the English upper classes is not . . . that they are ignorant of country life but that they know it inside out, and never stop talking about it.' Well, well! Though this is irrelevant, since I was not depicting the 'upper classes' in the figures of Stoke and Poges, the critic's remark tells us he knows as much about the country as he knows about the U. classes. It looks like he was thinking of those who gave a lot of time to fishing, hunting, and shooting, but these things don't make a country life, except an amusing or leisurely one for the few. Country life is a vastly bigger way of living than these three things, even were they carried on night, noon, and morning. The life of the country is the market town, the village, and the farm. Then there are the many things surrounding these—the roads, the birds and beasts, the bees and butterflies, the trees, the winds, the rain, snow, ice, and frost; parched lands and flooded lands; skies clear or cloudy; the landscape with its trees filigreed in a morning mist—as Corot so often saw them—and yet, and yet Mr. Tynan tells us with a yawn that talk of these things by 'the upper classes' bores him; 'bores us', he says, leaving us all to guess if he means all the others, or if he means only that this talk bores the critics. Artists and writers have revelled in all these things, but they bore Tynan. All of us at one time or another have talked about them; they are eternal matter, not only for talk, but for constant and anxious study, for they affect the life of every man, woman, and child, including— though he doesn't know it—the life of the critic himself. When things go contrary in the country, we all do badly; when things go smoothly there, we all do well. There are hundreds of scientists working in universities trying to solve the multitude of problems that outface the farmer in his never- ending work to produce the food of the nation; but Mr. Tynan says it is boring, and Mr. Tynan is an honorable man. I wonder why? Perhaps he knows the country only as a summer day's day-dream, unaware of the frosts of winter there, the fall-fall of life and leaf in the autumn, the sharpness in the hope of spring, and the push of all life among the kindly fruits of the earth when the sun is in his prime.

Frankly, from what the critic says about the 'upper classes' and the 'coun- try', I'm afraid the critic doesn't quite know what he's talking about, though I'm sure he could tell a bee from a butterfly. But could he see the difference between an Aberdeen Angus, a Hereford, and a Devon Red? Does he really believe that the amusements of fishing, shooting, and hunting are the coun- try? This is something like the belief of the many who see the country as a sea b ·ch; that out of the cities all England is a wide and lengthy beach, a sight of warm sands and gentle wavelets, blue as the blue of a tourist poster. But there goes Mr. Tynan in swim-suit and sandals with stage hayseeds in his hair. Looks like he never peered over the gateway into Philip's farm, or even glanced at the brook bickering by to join the brimming river, itself on its way to join the sea. Some of the upper classes own large tracts of the country, and let out portions of it for others to till; but even so they do not deal directly with those who farm the land; they employ an agent, who deals with the tenant farmers, so that the agent knows more about the land, the country, then the upper-class landlord who owns it. I suggest to Mr. Tynan that he listens to *The Farmer,* broadcast every week by the B.B.C., and then during an idle hour or two of a winter's evening he should read Spenser's *The Shepheards Calendar,* so that he might come to know a little more about the country before he mentions it in his critic's bulletin.

Then there is the airy dismissal of 'Ireland's past glories' as 'four-fifths in- comprehensible'. Yet take one, 'The Sword of Light': there is the sword of the Lord and of Gideon; it was on the sword's hilt that the knights took their vows before they set sail to deliver the Holy Land from the infidel; there was Excalibur—this was the flash, I believe, that was worn on the jacket sleeve of those who were on General Eisenhower's staff during the last World War; and the Sword of the Spirit—enough to show the sword as a well-known symbol, but not, apparently, to Mr. Tynan. A number of the figures in the play are mentioned by Yeats in his poems, by Synge in his play about the Sons of Usna; by Lady Gregory in her *Gods and Fighting Men*, but maybe Mr. Tynan hasn't read any of these: he would know more if he had.

Why is it that this critic seems to dismiss a play that laughs and makes merry, or one that hangs out a banner on an outer wall? Is it that he sees nothing, regards nothing save what occurs on the farther side of the 'Straight-Edged Stage', the form of stage that he prefers to all others, according to his article. The round O could do a lot, but it couldn't put a world on the stage, and Shakespeare, as far as I know, never said it could; but though he didn't say the stage is all the world, he did say 'All the world's a stage'. A critic should know more about this world.

Mr. Tynan should occasionally squirm out of the round O, not only for his own advantage, but also for his own pleasure (as should other critics too), and saunter here or loaf there, in England and Ireland, giving a handshake over the Border to a Scot or two, not only when the sun shone, but also when the rain fell, the winds blew, and when frost lay thick upon valley, hill, and farm field; then he might know more about 'country life', finding out, as he would, that the farming population was a vast army, spending little or no time in shooting, fishing, or hunting. The land, the country, Mr. Tynan, employs three-quarters of a million persons, and of all these, though an odd farmer may join in an occasional hunt, the rest of them don't hunt, or shoot, or fish, preferring football any time to a rod and line. These, Mr. Tynan, are the 'country life' you obviously know nothing about; these are they who talk of country things, of everlasting things; talk that began when hunting, nomadic man halted to sow a first harvest and settle in one place; talk that goes on still, and will go on for ever; talk that bores no one, for it concerns the life, all life living in England, boring no one save only Mr. Kenneth Tynan.

Stoke and Poges were not pictured in the play as members of the 'upper classes', but as business men, or plutocrats who were aiming at being what they never could become; they were aping the 'upper classes', and Mr. Tynan should have known that the 'upper classes' never try to ape themselves, for they have been born into that condition of life, living it without needing to act what they naturally are. They might try to imitate the working class —'pigging it', as one of them told me and he on his way for a holiday to one of the Hebridean Isles, but never so ridiculous as to aim at imitating themselves. Have you me, Mr. Tynan? As for 'the country', he will have to live longer, know more, before he can sit on a bank where the wild thyme grows, talking easily to Bill Brewer, Jan Stewer, Peter Gurney, Peter Davy,

Dan'l Whiddon, 'Arry Hawk, old uncle Tom Cobbley and all; or be able honestly to whistle even a bar of *The Farmer's Boy.*

Is Sir Kenneth Tynan right about this play, *Purple Dust?* Does he see clear, does he hear well, does he understand it at all? It's not that he dislikes the play; he simply despises it as 'a boring one-joke jape'. But is he right? He thinks he is, so he lets out a piping 'Yes, Sean, Yes!' I call friendly drama knights to my aid, who come cantering up, and let out a bellowing cry of 'No, Ken, No!' I name them now: they are Brooks Atkinson—for many years drama critic of the *New York Times;* Richard Watts of the *New York Evening Post,* backed by the shade of George Jean Nathan of many a journal and magazine. All have highly praised on papyrus and parchment the play Tynan calls 'a boring one-joke jape'. Were all these wrong and only Tynan right?

Just listen now, Mr. Tynan, to what comfortable words George Jean Nathan hath said about this very 'one-joke jape'. Here we go: '*Purple Dust* is a ringing moving melody, orchestrated with a resounding slapstick'; recorded in the Random House edition of *Five Great Irish Plays.* Another knightly defender came trotting to my side only the other day; this help came from John Gassner, Sterling Professor of Dramatic Literature at Yale University, a writer of many fine books about the drama of the western world. In a letter to me from New York, dated 2nd September 1962, he writes about this very play, saying: 'I very much hope that the Mermaid Theatre will do you more justice with the remaining productions of the O'Casey Festival. I was truly astonished that an English cast should have spoken so poorly—so indistinctly. Still, I found the play once more singularly funny [Does Tynan object to a play being funny?], tender, passionate, and poetic. It is no accident of the stage that the long poetic passages should have won spontaneous applause for the actor in the midst of slack acting that a tour in the provinces could have greatly improved.' Funny, tender, passionate, and poetic! J.C. Trewin, the Cornish drama critic, is of one mind with the four American critics. Each of these is as eminent a critic as Tynan; they have given a large share of their lives to the theatre; and each has a far longer experience of drama than has Kenneth Tynan; and they chorus 'Yes' when Tynan shouts 'No'. These have taken the ball from Tynan's toes, and left him kicking viciously at the air. It is natural, and I think fair, that I should gratefully accept the opinions of these five critics, and cast Tynan's into the waste-paper basket; but, instead, I have argued his opinions out, have tried to justify O'Casey's ways to the cause of drama, and, incidentally, have helped Kenneth Tynan to become immortal.

Of course it is quite possible that these five drama critics may be wrong, and Mr. Tynan be right; but since each of these five is as eminent a critic as he, and each has a longer and wider experience of the world's stage than he has so far; and since the playwright himself has a love for the drama equal at least to Tynan's, it seems to be very unlikely, and so a work of his deserves a kindlier regard than the insult of having this play dismissed as 'a one-joke jape'.

The London drama critics, with a few honourable exceptions (deviationists!), seem to have an edge on the Mermaid Theatre and on everything the theatre tries to do in the way of drama or play. When a new play is done there, they flock in and they pour out, the clumsy points in play or production burning the tips of their tongues, the good points in play and production hidden away in the darkest limbo of their minds. The idea began in the persevering and buoyant mind of Bernard Miles, but it took a very, very long time to bring the idea to a practical pass; for he had to buy it brick by brick, plank by plank, and seat by seat before it stood where it stands now; and this great feat alone deserves, not a spiteful dislike of the great adventure, but praise and encouragement, for where there was no drama, there is drama now.

Of course, the productions at the Mermaid cannot be what they ought to be, for the theatre has a very lean purse. The theatre at Stratford was already there for the gay producers, and few first-class actors would refuse the play there; the theatre has an artist snob value that excuses a reduced weekly wage. The big commercial theatres can fling out ten-pound notes without blinking an eyelid; the one at Stratford and its subsidiary, the Aldwych, can dispense pound notes without heart-throbs; but the poor Mermaid has to count the pennies pulled out of a lean and hungry purse. Even the Royal Court Theatre does not seem to shiver when it hands out a pound note; but the Mermaid has always to be penny cautious. Yet it has gone on now for three years and to my knowledge still flourishes, as results from my own plays show, facing out the almost unanimous objections of the London critics to the plays and the productions.

Mr. Tynan, dismissing the first play as 'a one-joke jape', the second one as sentimental nonsense, goes for the third play, *The Plough and the Stars*, because of its long speeches. He quotes the late critic, James Agate, to prove his point, for this critic scorned speeches that were longer than a few lines, which for James Agate was a bellringer for Pinero whose plays are as dead now as the dodo; and Agate with his coadjutor critic, Archer, disliked the great Elizabethans (except Shakespeare whom they didn't dare despise). Probably Mr. Tynan shares Agate's dislike of these great dramatists, too, with their long speeches, and wouldn't say of one of them with Herrick,

> *Candles I will give thee,*
> *And a new altar,*
> *And thy name, Saint Ben, shall be*
> *Writ in my psalter.*

So Mr. Tynan's guesses are, at least, quite as good as Mr. Agate's. Tynan listens, but he doesn't seem to hear; he looks, but he doesn't seem to see; and the value of his review of *The Plough and the Stars* can be shown in his statement about the Easter Rising, when he says 'the brave were stupidly slaughtered while the cowards went out looting and came home gambling'. Now the looters gambled before they went looting, and to go looting was a brave thing to do, for the streets sang songs of menace from bullets flying about everywhere; and the play explicitly states and shows the courage of Bessie Burgess who risked her life for her neighbour, as did the bold Fluther, too; more, the sons, fathers, and husbands of thousands of these 'cowards', thousands of them, were fighting in Flanders, Mesopotamia, and on the death-swept Gallipoli peninsula. Mr. Tynan, too, should remember that the progenitors of these tenement people everywhere fought for, and created, the powerful Labour Unions which made the Labour Movement possible, of which, I believe, Mr. Tynan is himself a member; and these great Unions still form the spearhead of Labour. I can tell him, too, that more civilians than combatants were killed and wounded in the general fighting of the famous week. Roses don't grow around tenement doors; pianos are rare in rooms; but brave people are there, and many have wider visions and more original chatter than others who come from dignified college or glossier high school.

A Sean O'Casey Bibliography

The following bibliography, complied by Charles A. Carpenter, appeared in *Modern Drama* for May 1967 under the heading: "Sean O'Casey Studies Through 1964." Mr. Carpenter has defined the scope of his bibliography in the following preliminary note:

> A reasonably comprehensive list of biographical, critical, and other scholarly studies of Sean O'Casey has been needed for a long time. Otto Brandstädter's (see below) is out of date and by no means readily available for many scholars; besides, it neither covers the ground adequately nor distinguishes between the useful and the trivial, the "solid" and the ephemeral. It even refers to a few books which do not have O'Casey material at all. The following list is at once more exhaustive and more selective than Brandstädter's. I have omitted most reviews and all apparent trivia, and have checked as many bibliographical references as possible against the books and articles themselves. (Items not examined, and thus not verified, are marked "nv.") For practical reasons, I have not listed material published after the year of O'Casey's death.—C.A.C.

Abirached, Robert, "Deux Pièces de Sean O'Casey," *Études*, CCCIX (1961), 382–387.

Adamov, Arthur, " 'La Femme Avenir de l'Homme' dans l'Oeuvre de Sean O'Casey," *Lettres Francaises*, No. 1028 (1964). nv

Armstrong, William A., "History, Autobiography, and *The Shadow of a Gunman*," *Modern Drama*, II (1960), 417–424.

———, "The Irish Point of View: The Plays of Sean O'Casey, Brendan Behan, and Thomas Murphy," in *Experimental Drama*, by Armstrong et al. (London, 1963), pp. 79–93.

———, "The Sources and Themes of *The Plough and the Stars*," *Modern Drama*, IV (1961), 234–242.

Ayling, Ronald, "Feathers Finely Aflutther," *Modern Drama*, VII (1964), 135–147.

———, "Feathers Flying: Politics in the Early Life and Thought of Sean O'Casey," *Dubliner*, III (Spring 1964), 54–67.

———, " 'Nannie's Night Out,' " *Modern Drama*, V (1962), 154–163.

———, "The Poetic Drama of T. S. Eliot," *English Studies in Africa*, II (1959), 247–250. (O'Casey's possible influence on Eliot's technique)

———, "Sean O'Casey: The Writer Behind His Critics," *Kilkenny Magazine*, No. 11 (Spring/Summer 1964), 69–82.

Bachmann, C. H., "Das Spiel als Zuflucht: Notizen zu Stücken von Schéhadé, Jeffers, O'Casey und Barrie," *Anregung* (Köln), XII (1960), 246–247. nv

Baggett, Patricia, "Sean O'Casey's Development of a Basic Theme," *Dublin Magazine*, XXXI (October–December 1956), 25–34.

Barzun, Jacques, "O'Casey at Your Bedside," *Tulane Drama Review*, II (February 1958), 57–61. (First published in *Griffin*)

Bellak, George, "Tea with Sean," *Theatre Arts Monthly*, XXXVII (September 1953), 70–71, 91–92.

Benstock, Bernard, "A Covey of Clerics in Joyce and O'Casey," *James Joyce Quarterly*, II (1964), 18–32. nv

Bentley, Eric, *The Playwright as Thinker* (New York, 1946), passim.

Bergholz, Harry, *Die Neugestaltung des Modernen Englischen Theaters 1870 bis 1930* (Berlin, 1933). nv

——, "Sean O'Casey," *Englische Studien*, LXV (1930), 49–67.

Blöcker, Günter, "O'Casey oder das Heilsame Chaos," *Tagesspiegel*, XXIX (September 1950), 3. nv

Blyth, Ernest, *Trasna na Boinne* (Dublin, 1957). nv

Boas, Guy, "The Drama of Sean O'Casey," *College English*, X (1948), 80–86.

Boyd, Alice K., *The Interchange of Plays Between London and New York, 1910–1939: A Study in Relative Audience Response* (New York, 1948), passim.

Brandstädter, Otto, "Eine O'Casey-Bibliographie," *Zeitschrift für Anglistik und Amerikanistik*, II (1954), 240–254.

Brandt, G. W., "Realism and Parables (from Brecht to Arden)," in *Contemporary Theatre*, Stratford-upon-Avon Studies, IV (New York, 1962), pp. 36–40.

Bromage, Mary C., "The Yeats-O'Casey Quarrel," *Michigan Alumnus Quarterly Review*, LXIV (1958), 135–144.

Brugère, Raymond, "Sean O'Casey et le Théâtre Irlandais," *Revue Anglo-Américaine*, III (1926), 206–221.

Brulé, A., "Sean O'Casey et le Théâtre Moderne," *Revue Anglo-Américaine*, VI (1928), 53–57.

Burton, Philip, "Something to Crow About: An Approach to 'Cock-a-Doodle Dandy,'" *Theatre Arts*, XLII (November 1958), 22–24.

Byrne, Dawson, *The Story of Ireland's National Theatre: The Abbey Theatre, Dublin* (Dublin, 1929), pp. 125–133.

C., W. M., "'The Plough and the Stars,' By Sean O'Casey," *Queens Quarterly*, XXXIV (1927), 420–429.

Caswell, R. W., "Sean O'Casey as a Poetic Dramatist," unpubl. diss. (Trinity College, 1959 or 1960). nv

Colum, Padraic, "The Narrative Writings of Sean O'Casey," *Irish Writing*, No. 6 (1948), 60–69. See also O'Casey's reply, a letter of November, 1948, *Irish Writing*, No. 7 (1949), 87.

——, *The Road Round Ireland* (New York, 1926), pp. 262–271.

Corbolan, Pablo, "Sean O'Casey," *El Noticiero Universal*, September 25, 1964. nv

Coston, Herbert H., "The Idea of Courage in the Works of Sean O'Casey," unpubl. diss. (Columbia), *Dissertation Abstracts*, XXI (1960), 619–620.

——, "Sean O'Casey: Prelude to Playwriting," *Tulane Drama Review*, V (September 1960), 102–112.

Cowasjee, Saros, *Sean O'Casey; The Man Behind the Plays*, New York, 1964. (Derives from a diss.)

Coxhead, Elizabeth, *Lady Gregory, a Literary Portrait* (London, 1961), pp. 196–206.

Cubeta, Paul, *Modern Drama for Analysis*, rev. ed. (New York, 1955), pp. 617–621. (Commentary on *Juno and the Paycock*; not in 3rd ed.)

Cunliffe, John W., *English Literature in the Twentieth Century* (New York, 1933), pp. 114–121.

——, *Modern English Playwrights* (New York, 1927), pp. 231–250.

Daniel, Walter C., "Patterns of Greek Comedy in O'Casey's *Purple Dust*," *Bulletin of the New York Public Library*, LXVI (1962), 603–612.

DeBaun, Vincent C., "Sean O'Casey and the Road to Expressionism," *Modern Drama*, IV (1961), 254–259.

Druzina, M., "O Scenicnosti Dramaturgii Sona O'Kejsi," *Teatr*, XXIII, No. 11 (1962), 180–184.

Duranteau, Josane, "Notes sur le Théâtre de Sean O'Casey," *Critique* (Paris), XVI (1960), 935–940.

Eaton, Walter P., *The Drama in English* (New York, 1930). nv

Elistratova, A., "Sean O'Casey," *Soviet Literature*, November, 1952, 164–169. (Reprinted in *Neues Deutschland*, XXX [June 1953])

Ellis-Fermor, Una, *The Irish Dramatic Movement*, 2nd ed. (London, 1954), pp. 196-200.

Esslinger, Patricia M., "The Dublin *Materia Poetica* of Sean O'Casey," unpubl. diss. (Tulane), *Dissertation Abstracts*, XXI (1961), 2291-92.

———, "Sean O'Casey and the Lockout of 1913: *Materia Poetica* of the Two Red Plays," *Modern Drama*, VI (1963), 53-63.

Fallon, Gabriel, "The House on the North Circular Road: Fragments from a Biography," *Modern Drama*, IV (1961), 223-233. (Talks with O'Casey)

———, "Pathway of a Dramatist," *Theatre Arts Monthly*, XXXIV (January 1950), 36-39.

Farragher, Bernard, "Brendan Behan's Unarranged Realism," *Drama Critique*, IV (February 1961), 38-39. nv (*The Hostage* apparently exploits O'Casey's method)

Fay, Gerard, *The Abbey Theatre* (London, 1958), passim.

———, "The Irish Theatre; A Decline and Perhaps, in the End, a Fall," in *Theatre in Review*, ed. Frederick Lumley (Edinburgh, 1956), pp. 80-89.

Fechter, Paul, *Das Europäische Drama*, Vol. III (Mannheim, 1958), 378-380.

Fehr, Bernhard, *Die Englische Literatur der Gegenwart und die Kulturfragen Unserer Zeit*, Vol. III (Leipzig, 1930). nv

Findlater, Richard, *The Unholy Trade* (London, 1952), pp. 170-184.

Firth, John M., "O'Casey and Autobiography," unpubl. diss. (Virginia, 1964).

Fraser, George Sutherland, *The Modern Writer and His World* (London, 1953), pp. 160-161 and passim.

Fréchet, René, "Sean O'Casey: Un Épisode de la Vie du Théâtre Irlandais," in *Le Théâtre Moderne; Hommes et Tendances*, ed. Jean Jacquot (Paris, 1958), pp. 321-336.

Freedley, George, "England and Ireland," in *A History of Modern Drama*, ed. Barrett H. Clark and Freedley (New York, 1947), pp. 226-229.

Freedman, Morris, "The Modern Tragicomedy of Wilde and O'Casey," *College English*, XXV (1964), 518-522, 527.

Freundlich, Elisabeth, "Der Dramatiker Sean O'Casey," *Theater und Zeit*, III (July 1955), 181-183. nv

Fricker, Robert, "Sean O'Casey: *Juno and the Paycock*," in *Das Moderne Englische Drama; Interpretationen*, ed. Horst Oppel (Berlin, 1963), pp. 183-202.

Garrison, Emery C., "The Structure of Sean O'Casey's Plays," unpubl. diss. (Stanford), *Dissertation Abstracts*, XVII (1957), 186.

Gassner, John, *Form and Idea in Modern Theatre* (New York, 1956), passim.

———, "Genius Without Fetters," in *Selected Plays of Sean O'Casey* (New York, 1954), v-xxi.

———, *Masters of the Drama*, 3rd ed. (New York, 1954), pp. 566-571, 728-729.

———, "The Prodigality of Sean O'Casey," in his *The Theatre in Our Times* (New York, 1954), pp. 240-248.

Gelb, Arthur and Barbara, *O'Neill* (New York, 1962), pp. 787-790.

Greany, Helen T., "Some Interesting Parallels," *Notes and Queries*, CCIII, n.s. V (1958), 253. ("Pope and the Paycock")

Gregory, Lady Augusta, *Journals, 1916-1930*, ed. Lennox Robinson (Dublin, 1946), pp. 71-79, 86-91, 93-100 and passim.

Griffin, Gerald, *Wild Geese; Pen Portraits of Famous Irish Exiles* (London, 1938). nv.

Guthrie, Tyrone, *A Life in the Theatre* (New York, 1959), pp. 297-299.

Gwynn, Stephen L., *Irish Literature and Drama in the English Language* (London, 1936), pp. 209-212.

Habart, Michel, "De Charrues et de Drapeaux," *Lettres Francaises*, No. 926 (1962). nv

———, "Introduction à Sean O'Casey," *Théâtre Populaire*, XXXIV (1959). nv

———, et al., "O'Casey, Roses Rouges pour Lui," *Lettres Francaises*, No. 1047 (1964). nv

————, "Sean O'Casey," *Avant-Scène*, No. 230 (1960). nv
————, "Le Théâtre Irlandais et Sean O'Casey," *Bref*, XLIII (1961). nv
————, "Une Mère et Deux Fils," *Cahiers de la Compagnie Madeleine Renaud-Jean-Louis Barrault*, XXXVII (1962). nv (O'Casey and Shaw)
Henn, T. R., *The Harvest of Tragedy* (London, 1956), pp. 212–214.
Hethmon, Robert, "Great Hatred, Little Room," *Tulane Drama Review*, V (June 1961), 51–55. (On *Kathleen Listens In*)
Hodson, James L., *No Phantoms Here* (London, 1932), pp. 147–156. (Interview)
Hogan, Robert G., *The Experiments of Sean O'Casey*, New York, 1960. (Derives from a diss.)
————, "The Experiments of Sean O'Casey," *Dublin Magazine*, XXXIII (January–March 1958), 4–12.
————, ed., *Feathers from the Green Crow: Sean O'Casey, 1905–1925* (Columbia, Mo., 1962), Introduction and notes, esp. pp. 269–277 and 300–302.
————, "O'Casey's Dramatic Apprenticeship," *Modern Drama*, IV (1961), 243–253.
Hone, Joseph, *W. B. Yeats, 1865–1939*, 2nd ed. (New York, 1962), pp. 387–389.
Huscher, Herbert, "Das Anglo-Irische und Seine Bedeutung als Sprachkünstlerisches Ausdrucksmittel," in *Englische Kultur in Sprachwissenschaftlicher Deutung; Festschrift für Max Deutschbein* (Leipzig, 1936), pp. 40–59. (Passim on O'Casey)
Igoe, W. J., "Sean O'Casey, Tragic Jester," *Critic*, XIX (June–July 1961), 15–16, 67–69. nv
Jacquot, Jean, "La Tragédie et l'Espoir," in *Le Théâtre Tragique*, by Jacquot et al. (Paris, 1962), pp. 518–519.
Johnston, Denis, "Joxer in Totnes: A Study in Sean O'Casey," *Irish Writing*, No. 13 (December 1950), 50–53.
————, "Sean O'Casey," in *Living Writers*, ed. Gilbert Phelps (London, 1947), pp. 28–38.
————, "Sean O'Casey: A Biography and an Appraisal," *Modern Drama*, IV (1961), 324–328. (On the books by Hogan and Krause)
————, "Sean O'Casey: An Appreciation," *Living Age*, CCCXXIX (1926), 161–163. (Reprinted from the *Daily Telegraph*, March 11, 1926)
Jordan, John, "The Indignation of Sean O'Casey," *Irish Writing*, No. 29 (December 1954), 57–63.
————, "The Irish Theatre: Retrospect and Premonition," in *Contemporary Theatre*, Stratford-upon-Avon Studies, IV (New York, 1962), pp. 164–183.
Kavanagh, Peter, *The Irish Theatre* (Tralee, 1946). nv
————, *The Story of the Abbey Theatre* (New York, 1950), passim.
Kellerson, Ph., "Sean O'Casey," *Courrier Dramatique de l'Ouest*, XXXIX (1961). nv
Knight, G. Wilson, *The Christian Renaissance* (New York, 1962), pp. 341–347. (First published in *Stand*, IV [Summer 1960] as "Ever a Fighter: On Sean O'Casey's *The Drums of Father Ned*")
————, *The Golden Labyrinth; A Study of British Drama* (New York, 1962), pp. 373–380.
Kornilova, E., "Vsegda s Irlandiej, Vsegda s Narodom," *Teatr*, XX, No. 5 (1959), 167–178.
Koslow, Jules, *The Green and the Red: Sean O'Casey, The Man and His Plays*, New York, 1950. (Journalistic)
Krause, David, "The Playwright's Not for Burning," *Virginia Quarterly Review*, XXXIV (1958), 60–76.
————, " 'The Rageous Ossean': Patron-Hero of Synge and O'Casey," *Modern Drama*, IV (1961), 286–291.
————, *Sean O'Casey; The Man and His Work*, New York, 1960. (Derives from a diss.)
Larson, Gerald A., "The Dramaturgy of Sean O'Casey," unpubl. diss. (Utah), *Dissertation Abstracts*, XVIII (1958), 1147–48.

Lennon, Michael J., "Sean O'Casey and His Plays," *Catholic World,* CXXX (1929), 295–301, 452–461.

Lewis, Allan, *The Contemporary Theatre; The Significant Playwrights of Our Time* (New York, 1962), pp. 169–191.

Lumley, Frederick, *Trends in 20th Century Drama,* rev. ed. (London, 1960), pp. 223–225.

Lunari, G., "L'Arcivescovo di Dublino non Am nè O'Casey, nè Joyce," *Il Dramma,* CCLIX (1958). nv

Magalaner, Marvin, "O'Casey's Autobiography," *Sewanee Review,* LXV (1957), 170–174.

Malone, Andrew E., *The Irish Drama* (New York, 1929), pp. 209–219.

Marriott, James W., *Modern Drama* (London, 1934). nv

Merchant, Francis, *A. E.: An Irish Promethean* (Columbia, S. C., 1954), pp. 205–207, 238–239. (Includes an O'Casey letter)

Mercier, Vivian, "O'Casey Alive," *Hudson Review,* XIII (1960), 631–636.

———, "The Riddle of Sean O'Casey," *Commonweal,* LXIV (1956), 366–368.

Morgan, Charles, "On Sean O'Casey's *The Silver Tassie,*" in *The English Dramatic Critics; An Anthology, 1660–1932,* comp. James Agate (London, 1933), pp. 347–349. (First published in London *Times,* October 12, 1929)

Nichols, Beverley, *Are They the Same at Home?* (New York, 1927). nv

Nicoll, Alardyce, *World Drama from Aeschylus to Anouilh* (New York, 1950?), pp. 807–810.

Nordell, Rod, "Cock-a-Doodle Casey," *New Leader,* XLI (November 3, 1958), 20–22.

O'Casey, Sean. (NOTE: Restricted to essays and letters about himself and his work; the autobiographies are fictionalized to the point of unreliability, according to John M. Firth. David Krause is the authorized editor of O'Casey's letters, which should be published within a few years. O'Casey was generous to commentators; many of his remarks on himself appear in the books and articles listed. See also under Colum and Starkie.)

———, "Always the Plow and the Stars," *New York Times Book Review,* January 25, 1953, pp. 1, 23.

———, "*Cock-a-Doodle Dandy* (1958)," in *Playwrights on Playwriting,* ed. Toby Cole (New York, 1960), pp. 247–249. (First published as "O'Casey's Credo" in New York *Times,* November 9, 1958, drama section)

———, *Feathers from the Green Crow; Sean O'Casey, 1905–1925,* ed. Robert Hogan, Columbia, Mo., 1962.

———, *The Flying Wasp,* London, 1937.

———, *The Green Crow,* New York, 1956.

———, "*Kathleen Listens In,*" *Tulane Drama Review,* V (June 1961), 36–50. (Comment by O'Casey on p. 36)

———, "Lettre à Jean Vilar," *Bref,* XLIII (1961). nv

———, "The Play of Ideas," *New Statesman and Nation,* n.s. XXXIX (1950), 397–398.

———, "Sean O'Casey Concerning James Joyce," *Massachusetts Review,* V (1964), 335–336. (Three letters to a professor)

———, *Sean O'Casey Reading from His Works. . . . Recorded at his Home on November 12, 1952,* Caedmon recording. (His excerpts from *Juno* vary from the texts, and are apparently his own revisions)

———, "Tribute to O'Neill," in *O'Neill and His Plays; Four Decades of Criticism,* ed. Oscar Cargill et al. (New York, 1961), p. 96. (First published in New York *Times,* November 9, 1959)

———, *Under a Colored Cap,* New York, 1963.

O'Hegarty, P. S., "A Dramatist of New Born Ireland," *North American Review,* CCXXIV (1927), 315–322.

O'Neill-Barna, Anne, "O'Casey at 80: More Rebel Than Ever," *New York Times Magazine,* March 27, 1960, pp. 26, 90–91.

O'Riley, Margaret C., "The Dramaturgy of Sean O'Casey," unpubl. diss. (Wisconsin), *Dissertation Abstracts*, XVI (1956), 340.

Palitzsch, Peter, *Huldigung für Sean O'Casey*, Wuppertaler Bühnen, Programmblätter für die Spielzeit 1958/59, IX. nv

Paul-Dubois, Louis, *Le Drame Irlandais et l'Irlande Nouvelle* (Paris, 1927). nv

———, "Le Théâtre Irlandais," *Revue des Deux Mondes*, XXVII (1935), 644–652.

Pelegrini, A., "Dalla Tragedia Irlandese e di Sean O'Casey," *Convegno*, XVII (August 1936), 329–342. nv

Pellizzi, Camillo, *English Drama: The Last Great Phase*, tr. Rowan Williams (London, 1935), 236–240.

Peteler, Patricia M., "The Social and Symbolic Drama of the English-Language Theatre, 1929–1949," unpubl. diss. (Utah), *Dissertation Abstracts*, XXII (1962), 4441–42. (Part on O'Casey)

Progressivnaja Literatura Stran Kapitalizma v Bor'be za Mir (Moscow, 1952). nv

Regnault, M., "Sean O'Casey, le Poète de la Rose Rouge," *Lettres Francaises*, No. 810 (1960). nv

Reid, Alec, "The Legend of the Green Crow: Observations on Recent Work by and about Sean O'Casey," *Drama Survey*, III (1963), 155–164.

Rest, Jaime, "O'Casey, Adios al Teatro de la Abadia," *Teatro*, XX, No. 6 (1964). nv

Ritchie, Harry M., "Form and Content in the Plays of Sean O'Casey," unpubl. diss. (Yale, 1960). nv (Not included in *Dissertation Abstracts*)

———, "The Influence of Melodrama on the Early Plays of Sean O'Casey," *Modern Drama*, V (1962), 164–173.

Riva, Serafino, *La Tradizione Celtica e la Moderna Letteratura Irlandese* (Rome, 1937). nv

Rivoallan, Anatole, *L'Irlande* (Paris, 1934). nv

———, *Littérature Irlandaise Contemporaine* (Paris, 1939). nv

Robinson, Eric, "*Juno and the Paycock*: An Introduction," *Use of English*, XI (1959), 111–118. nv

Robinson, Lennox, *Curtain Up; An Autobiography* (London, 1942), passim.

———, *Ireland's Abbey Theatre, a History, 1899–1951* (London, 1951), passim.

Rollins, Ronald G., "O'Casey, O'Neill and Expressionism in *The Silver Tassie*," *Bucknell Review*, X (1962), 364–369.

———, "O'Casey, O'Neill, and the Expressionism in *Within the Gates*," *West Virginia University Bulletin. Philological Papers*, XIII (1961), 76–81.

———, "O'Casey's *Cock-a-Doodle Dandy*," *Explicator*, XXIII (1964), Item 8.

———, "O'Casey's *The Silver Tassie*," *Explicator*, XX (1962), Item 62.

———, "Sean O'Casey: The Man with Two Faces," unpubl. diss. (Cincinnati), *Dissertation Abstracts*, XXI (1961), 2721.

———, "Sean O'Casey's Mental Pilgrimage," *Arizona Quarterly*, XVII (1961), 293–302.

———, "Sean O'Casey's 'The Star Turns Red': A Political Prophecy," *Mississippi Quarterly*, XVI (1963), 67–75.

Rudin, Seymour, "Playwright to Critic: Sean O'Casey's Letters to George Jean Nathan," *Massachusetts Review*, V (1964), 326–334. (A description of them, with excerpts)

Ryan, Desmond, *Remembering Sion* (London, 1934). nv

Sagarra, Juan de, "En la Muerte de Sean O'Casey y Otras Notas," *El Noticiero Universal*, October 2, 1964. nv

Santos, A. Noguiera, "Sean O'Casey, Oitenta Años de Juventude," *Gazeta Musical e de Todas las Artes*, Nos. 109–110 (April–March 1960). nv

Sarukhanian, A. P., "Sotsial'no-Avtobiograficheskaia Épopeia O'Keisi (40–50-s gody)," *Uchenye Zapiski Moskovskogo Pedagogicheskogo Instituta T. 52: Kafedra Zarubezhnykh Literatur*, Vyp. 2 (1956), Stp. 253–277. nv

Saurel, Renée, "Un Dramaturge Inconfortable," *Temps Modernes*, XVII (1962), 1938–44.

Schoen, Ernst, "Der Dramatiker Sean O'Casey," *Theater der Zeit*, IX, No. 4 (1954), 19–21. nv

———, "Sean O'Casey. Ein Dramatiker Unserer Zeit," *Theater der Zeit*, n.s. III (1960). nv

Selz, Jean, "Le Théâtre de Sean O'Casey," *Lettres Nouvelles*, XXXI (1959), 15–17. nv

Sinko, Grzegorz, "Irlandia Daleka i Bliska," *Dialog*, X (1961), 106–117. nv

Smet, R. de, "Sean O'Casey et la Tragédie des 'Tenements,'" *Revue des Vivants*, VIII (August 1940), 411–426. nv

Smith, Winifred, "The Dying God in the Modern Theatre," *Review of Religion*, V (1941), 264–275. (Largely on *The Silver Tassie*)

Spinner, Kaspar, *Die Alte Dame Sagt: Nein!: Drei Irische Dramatiker, Lennox Robinson, Sean O'Casey, Denis Johnston*, Swiss Studies in English, Bern, 1961. nv

Starkie, Walter, "The Plays of Sean O'Casey," *Nineteenth Century and After*, CIV (1928), 225–236. See also O'Casey's reply, "The Plays of Sean O'Casey: A Reply," pp. 399–402.

———, "Sean O'Casey," in *The Irish Theatre*, ed. Lennox Robinson (London, 1939), pp. 149–176.

Styan, J. L., *The Dark Comedy; The Development of Modern Comic Tragedy* (Cambridge, Eng., 1962), pp. 148–153.

———, *The Elements of Drama* (Cambridge, Eng., 1960), pp. 190–195.

Trewin, J. C., *Dramatists of Today* (London, 1953), pp. 56–66.

———, "Lord of Language," *Drama; The Quarterly Theatre Review*, n.s. No. 35 (Winter 1954), 34–38.

———, *The Theatre Since 1900* (London, 1951), pp. 187–191, 288–290.

Verdot, Guy, "Paris Fait Connaissance avec l'Irlandais O'Casey," *Figaro Littéraire*, No. 772 (1961). nv

Vilca, Mario, "Sean O'Casey e o Movimento Dramatico Irlandès," *Vertice*, Nos. 96–97 (1951). nv

Viola, Wilhelm, "Sean O'Casey," *Theater und Zeit*, VIII (June 1961), 96–98. nv

Ward, A. C., *The Nineteen-Twenties; Literature and Ideas in the Post-War Decade* (London, 1930), pp. 73–75.

Wieczorek, Hubert, *Irische Lebenshaltung im Neuen Irischen Drama* (Breslau, 1937), passim.

Williams, Raymond, *Drama from Ibsen to Eliot* (London, 1952), pp. 169–174.

Williamson, Audrey, *Theatre of Two Decades* (London, 1951), pp. 186–189.

Williamson, Ward, "An Analytical History of American Criticism of the Works of Sean O'Casey, 1924–1958," unpubl. diss. (State Univ. of Iowa), *Dissertation Abstracts*, XXIII (1962), 1713.

Wittig, Kurt, *Die Nationalliteratur Irlands in Englischer Sprache von 1889–1939* (Halle, 1945). nv

———, *Seán O'Casey als Dramatiker: Ein Beitrag zum Nachskreigsdrama Irlands*, Halle, 1937. (Publ. diss.)

Woodbridge, Homer E., "Sean O'Casey," *South Atlantic Quarterly*, XL (1941), 50–59.

Worth, Katharine J., "O'Casey's Dramatic Symbolism," *Modern Drama*, IV (1961), 260–267.

Yeats, William Butler, *Letters*, ed. Allan Wade (New York, 1955), passim.

———, *Letters on Poetry from W. B. Yeats to Dorothy Wellesley* (London, 1964), pp. 1, 22.

Zaslawski, Heinz, *Die Werke Sean O'Caseys, Unter Besonderer Berücksichtigung Seiner Zweiten Periode*, Wien, 1949. nv (publ. diss.)

INDEX

A. E. (q.v.), 720, 768, 777, 783, 789, 803, 834, 874, 876

Abbey Theatre, *xii, xiii, xv,* 757–58, 767, 768, 771, 773–89, 791, 798–800, 803, 805–7, 809–13, 815, 832–34, 874, 883, 925, 929, 933, 934

"Afore Night Come" (Rudkin), 944–45

Agate, James, *xi,* 876, 985, 991–92

Aldwych Theatre, 991

"Alice, Where Art Thou?", 663–70

All for Ireland League, 707

Allgood, Sara, *xiv*

American Spectator, 883

"And Evening Star", 890–94

"And So to Bed" (Fagan), 820

Answers magazine, 819

Archer, William, 991

Arden, John, 949

Aristophanes, 944

Artaud, Antonin, 941, 943–44

Ashe, Thomas, *xiii*

ATHEIST, THE, 207–83

Atkinson, Brooks, 880, 919, 990

"At the Sign of the Pick and Shovel", 701–16

Auden, W. H., *xi,* 939

AVREEN, JACK, 967–81

AVRIL, 287–364

BAGNAL, BARNEY, 137–203

"Bald Prima Donna, The" (Ionesco), *xxiv,* 942n

"Bald Primaqueera, The", *xxiv,* 941–953

"Bald Soprano, The" (Ionesco), 942n

"Ballad of Father Gilligan, The" (Yeats), 711

Barlow, Sean, 786

BARNEY, 287–364

Beckett, Samuel, 965

"Bedtime Story", *xvii, xviii,* 505–28

"Behind the Green Curtains", *xvii*

BENTHAM, CHARLES, 5–61

BINNINGTON FAMILY, 531–600

Birrell, Augustus, 715

"Birthday Party, The" (Pinter), 947–48

BISHOP, THE, *xvi,* 207–83

"Bishop's Bonfire, The", *xvi, xxiii,* 918–19, 922–23, 927, 929, 935

"Bitter Sweet" (Coward), 828

"Black Oxen Passing By", 833–35

Blackwood, William, 819

Blasts and Benedictions, xxii, 937–966

"Blessed Bridget O'Coole", 757–61

Boer War, homefront politics of, *see* Political views

"Bonfire Under a Black Sun", *xxiv,* 917–35

Boucicault, Dion, 760; *see also* "The Shaugraun"

BOYLE, JUNO, 5–61

BOYLE, "CAPTAIN" JACK, 5–61, 984

Boys, Richard C., 848–49

Brady, Jim, 827–28

BRENNAN, CAPTAIN, 64–131

BRENNAN O' THE MOOR, 367–434

BREYDON, AYAMONN, *xiv,* 367–434, 987

BREYDON, MRS., *xii,* 367–434

Brighton Rock (Greene), 847

"Bring Forth the Best Robe", 649–656

British Broadcasting Corp. Schools Broadcasts, *xii, xxiii,* 940
Brook, Peter, xvi
Buchanan, Jack, 828
BURGESS, BESSIE, 64–131, 992
Burns, Charles Wesley, 846, 849

"Caitlin ni Houlihan" (Yeats), 769
Carey, Eileen Reynolds, *see* Eileen O'Casey
Casey, Archie (brother), 614–15, 625–26, 631, 645–47, 679–80, 689, 774, 786
Casey, Ella (sister), 614–15, 622, 623, 625–26, 646–47, 658, 730, 731
Casey, John (Sean O'Casey), *xii*
Casey, Michael (father), *xii,* 605–6, 609–11, 617, 621–28, 632, 738, 740
Casey, Mick (brother), 623, 658, 731, 790
Casey, Susan (mother), *xii, xiii, xxi,* 64, 603–28, 630–35, 644–47, 649–51, 657, 663, 704–5, 729–744, 760, 801, 804, 862–63
Casey, Susan (sister), 731
Casey, Tom (brother), 625, 658, 676, 689–90, 730, 731
Casside, Johnny (Sean O'Casey), xx
Casside, Susan, *see* Susan Casey (mother)
"Cathleen Listens In", 758, 775
"Childerness", 851–59
"Child Is Born, A", 603–10
CHREEHEWEL, REV. GEORGE CANON, 287–364
Clarke, Austen, 784
CLINTON, REV. E., 367–434
CLITHEROE, JACK and NORA, 64–131
CLOYNE, 287–364
Cochran, C. B., 799, 802–3, 827–28
"Cock-a-Doodle Dandy", *xiv, xvi,* 435–503, 922
"Comin' of Age", 645–49
Communism, *see* Political views

Connelly, Marc, 814
Connelly, Rev. Terence, 847–49
Connolly, James, 707–9, 711–12, 714
"Cooing of Doves, The", 758
Costello, Ward, 814
"Countess Cathleen" (Yeats), 711
Court Theatre, 798, 803
COVEY, THE, 64–131
Coward, Noel, *xi,* 827–28
"Crabbed Age and Youth", 953–57
Craig, May, 777–78
"Crime and Punishment", 636–44
"Crimson and the Tri-Color, The", *xiii*
Criterion, The, 840
Critic and the Drama, The (Nathan), 785
Criticism, literary, 917–35, 928, 984–92; *see also* the various critics
Cromer, Lord, 827
Cross, The, magazine, 811
Crowe, Eileen, *xiv,* 777, 787
Cummins, Dr. J. D., 366, 778, 828
Cusack, Cyril, 918, 921, 923

Daily Telegraph, 917
Daily Mail, 917
DALY, "JOXER", 5–61
Dartington Hall School, *xxii,* 860
Davis, Thomas, 710, 713
Davitt, Michael, 931–32
"Day the Worker Blows a Bugle, The", 959–64
"Deep in Devon", 859–66
Desmond, Thomas C., 953*n*
DEVINE, JERRY, 5–61
Disraeli, Benjamin, 818
Dolan, Michael J., 776, 786–88
DOMINEER, FATHER, 437–503
Doran, Dr., 897
Douglas, Melvyn, 842
Dovergull, Anthony, 648–78 *passim,* 681
Dramatic Criticisms (Shaw), 784–785

DREAMER, THE, 207–83
"Drums of Father Ned, The", *xvi*, *xvii*, *xxi*, 529–600
Drums Under the Windows, *xx*, 701–28
Dublin, Archbishop of, *xvii*
Dublin International Theatre Festival, *xvii*
Dulanty, John, 877, 887–88
DYMPNA, 367–434

Eagle, The (The Standard), 812
Easter Rising, *xiii*, 789, 992
Edwards, Bridgid, 366
EEADA, 367–434
Eliot, T. S., *xiv*, 840, 858, 926
Emmet, Robert, 720
Encore magazine, 965, 965n
"End of the Beginning, The", 924
"Entertaining Mr. Sloane" (Orton), 949
Ervine, St. John, 803, 827
Euripides, 944
Evening Herald, 813, 815
"Everyman", 926
Exeter Hospital, 898

Fagan, James B., 781, 783, 794–95, 816, 820–21
Fallon, Gabriel, 759, 778
Farr, Florence, 764
"Feathering His Nest", 816–32
"Figuro in the Night", *xviii*
FINGLAS, INSPECTOR TOM, 367–434
FINOOLA, 367–434
"First the Green Blade", 611–16
Fitzgerald, Barry, *xiv*, 758–59, 776–777, 780, 785
Fitzgerald, Sir Edward, 719
Five Great Irish Plays, 990
Flanagan, Father, 928
Fletcher, Bramwell, 843
Fletcher, Dudley, 720
Flying Wasp, The, *xxii*
FLYNN, PETER, 64–131
FORAN, TEDDY and MRS., 137–203

Fortune Theatre, 794–95
Fox, R. M., 784
Freud, Sigmund, 943
Freudianism, in the drama, 942, 949, 984
"Friggin Frogs, The", 806–16

Gaelic nationalism, *see* Political views
Gaiety Theatre, *xvii*, 814
Garnett, David, 778
Gassner, John, 990
Geriatrics, O'Casey's views on, 953–957
Giraudoux, Jean, 921
Gish, Lillian, 843
Glynn, Sir Joseph, 772–73
Gods and Fighting Men (Gregory), 989
GOGAN, JENNIE, *xxi*, 64–131
GOGAN, MOLLSER, 64–131
Golden Bough, The (Frazer), 945
GOOD, FLUTHER, 64–131, 780, 809, 992
Green Crow, The, *xxii*, 917–35
Greene, Graham, 847
Gregory, Lady Augusta, *xiii*, *xv*, 757–71, 787–88, 790, 800, 804, 814, 825, 833, 834–35, 859, 925, 933, 989
Gregory, Robert, 770, 801
Grey, Mary, 795
Griffin, Cardinal, 855
Griffin, Rev. E. M., *xxi*, 739, 792
Griffith, Arthur, 690, 708, 710–15
Gwenn, Edmund, 820

Haddon, Dr., 898, 905
HALIBUT, DANIEL, 507–28
Harvey, Bob, 703–4, 713
Heard, Gerald, 875
"Heartbreak House" (Shaw), 881–882
HEEGAN FAMILY, 137–203
"Hill of Healing, The", 616–20
"His Da, His Poor Da", 621–24
"His Father's Wake", 625–29

Hitchcock, Alfred, 944, 950–51
Hobson, Harold, 949
"Hound of Heaven, The" (Thompson), 926
Hyde, Douglas, 705, 715, 769
Hymdim, Leadem & Co., 645–78

I Knock at the Door, xii, xx, 603–44, 858, 863
"Inishfallen, Fare Thee Well", 787–792
Inishfallen, Fare Thee Well, xx, 729–92
Ionesco, Eugène, xxiv, 942n, 944
Irish Academy of Letters, 806, 883–884
Irish Catholic, 812
Irish and Catholic Power, The, 930–931
Irish Citizen Army, xiii, xv
Irish Drama Critics Circle, 827, 931
Irish Football Association, 927
Irish Literary Society, London, 803
Irish Nation, 715
Irish (Gaelic) nationalism, see Political views
Irish National Theatre Society, 791; see also Abbey Theatre
Irish Peasant, 714
Irish Press, 917, 928
Irish Rosary, 813
Irish Statesman, 778, 783, 803
Irish Times, 804, 815, 927, 931
Irish Transport and General Workers Union, 718
"Is the Priest at Home?" (Tomelty), 930
"I Strike a Blow for You, Dear Land", 689–700
"I Wanna Woman", 967–81

Jackson, Sir Barry, 798–99
Jews, O'Casey's views on, 650–51, 845–46
John, Augustus, 766, 789, 799–801, 824, 834, 878–79

"John Bull's Other Island" (Shaw), 924, 943, 984
Johnston, Denis, xi, 864
Johnston, Moffat, 843
Jones, Bob, 713
Jonson, Ben, 938–39
"Journey's End" (Sherriff), 833, 937n
Joyce, James, xvii, xx, 809, 847, 859, 865, 880, 934
JULIA, 437–503
"Juno and the Paycock", xiii–xvi, xxii, 3–61, 776, 847

KILLSALLIGHAN, TOM, 531–600
"Kincora" (Gregory), 769, 770
"King's Threshold, The" (Yeats), 769
Krause, David, xx

Labour movement, England, 816–820
Labour movement, Ireland, see Political views
Lane, Sir Hugh, 760, 770
LANGON, LIEUTENANT, 64–131
Laoide, Seosamh, 924
Larkin, Jim, xiii, 717–28, 774, 818, 858
Laughton, Charles, 833
Laye, Evelyn, 828
Left-wing opinions of O'Casey, see Political views
Life of Lenin (Stalin), 772
Littlewood, Joan, 966
Logue, Cardinal, 711, 715
Lomonovska, Raissa, 775
"London Apprentice", 793–95
London Daily Worker, xix, xxiii
London *Times*, xxiii, 815, 917, 983
Longford, Christine, 932–33
Lucey, Dr. (Bishop of Cork), 928

McCormick, F. J., xiv, 758, 776, 778, 785, 787, 789, 810–11
McDonald, Dr. Walter, xxi, 814, 849, 924, 928

McElroy, Billy, 823
McGilligan Family, 531–600
McGuiness, Dr., 828
McGunty, Oscar, 531–600
Macmillan, Daniel, 802
Macmillan, Harold, *xxiii*
Macmillan & Co., Ltd., London, 802
Madigan, Maisie, 5–61
Mahan, Sailor, 437–503
Mahon, Christy, 701–4, 713
Malone, Andrew E., 784
Manchester Guardian, xxiii
"Man and Superman" (Shaw), 785, 788
Marion, 437–503
Marlowe, Christopher, 938–39
Marthraun Family, 437–503
Martyn, Edward, 716, 768
"Mary, Mary, Quite Contrary" (Ervine), 758, 776
Massey, Raymond, 799
Maunsel & Son, 729, 732
Maxwell, Forby, 137–203
Mechanics' Theatre, 680–81, 774, 791
Mermaid Theatre, 990–91
Middleton, Georgie, 636–43, 701, 703
Miles, Bernard, 991
Milton, John, 902
Mirror in My House, xx
Mitchel, John, 836, 921
Monican, Susie, 137–203
"Moon Shines on Kylenamoe, The", *xviii*
Mooney, Ria, 778
Moorneen, Sheila, 367–434
Moscow; U.S.S.R., *see* Political views
Mossie, Miss, 507–28
Mother and Child Bill, 930
"Mrs. Casside Takes a Holiday", 729–44
Mullcanny, Peter, 367–434
Mulligan, John Jo, 507–28
Murphy, Dr. J., 814
Murphy, William Martin, 720–23

"Nannie's Night Out", 777
Nathan, George Jean, 784, 812, 816, 833, 883, 887, 918, 919, 921, 990
Nationalism, Gaelic, *see* Political views
New Irish School, 784
New Statesman and Nation, 923
New Theatre, 816
New Times (of Moscow), *xix*, 959*n*
New York, O'Casey's admiration for, *xi*, 835–37, 841–44
New York Times Magazine, 937*n*
Nichols, Beverley, *xi*
Nightingale, Angela, 507–28
"Night Out, A" (Pinter), 947
Norton, Simon, 137–203
"Not Waiting for Godot", 965–66
Nugent, "Needle", 5–61

"Oak Leaves and Lavender", *xix*
O'Balacaun, Roory, 367–434
O'Brien, Dermod, 774
O'Brien, George, 787–88
Observer, 803, 986
O'Casey Festival, 990
O'Casey, parental family of, *see under* Casey
O'Casey, Breon (son), *xxii, xxiii*, 799–801, 804, 806, 829, 858, 860, 891, 898–916 *passim*, 954
O'Casey, Eileen Reynolds Carey (wife), *xiii, xxi, xxii, xxiii*, 134, 798–800, 804–5, 816–17, 820–824, 828, 832, 834–35, 846, 850–58, 860, 868–69, 874–79, 881, 886–90, 892, 897–916 *passim*, 955
O'Casey, Niall (son), *xxii*, 850–58, 860, 891, 897–916
O'Casey, Shivaun (daughter), *xviii, xxi, xxii*, 286, 865, 891, 897–916 *passim*
O'Casside, Michael, *see* Michael Casey (father)
O'Casside, Sean (Sean O'Casey), *xx*, 732

O'Cathasaigh, Sean (Sean O'Casey), xiii
O'Daly, Paddy, 716
O'Donnell, Donat, 923–24
O'Donnell, Frank Hugh, 783
O'Donnell, Peadar, 887
O'Faolain, Sean, 834
O'Flaherty, Liam, 778, 784
O'Hickey, Dr. Michael, xxi, 928
O'Higgins, Fred R., 784, 815, 933
O'KILLIGAIN, JACK, 287–364, 985
Old Vic, 966
Once Around the Sun (Atkinson), 880
O'Neill, Maire, xiv
O'Reilly, Father, 790
Orton, Joe, 949n, 950
Orwell, George, xi
O'Ryan, W. P., 714–15

Parnell, Charles Stewart, 608–9, 632, 707, 711, 717, 780, 785, 791, 812
Pearse, Padraic, 720, 791
People's Theatre, Newcastle, 966
Pictures in the Hallway, xii, xx, xxii, 645–700
Pinero, Sir Arthur Wing, 991
Pinter, Harold, 947, 949
"Plough and the Stars, The", xiii–xvi, xxi, xxii, 63–131, 777, 784, 813, 816, 991–92
POGES, CYRIL, 287–364, 984–87, 989
Political views of O'Casey
  Boer War, homefront politics of, 689–96
  Communism, xviii–xix, 930, 959–964, 984–85
  Gaelic nationalism and the Irish Labour movement, xiii, 699, 705–28, 737, 758, 763, 770, 772–73, 775, 779–86, 789–92, 812, 817, 867, 912, 924, 929–935, 984, 992; see also Easter Rising; "The Raid"
  Left-wing opinions, 913, 983

Moscow; U.S.S.R., xviii, 775, 832, 872–73, 893, 910, 912, 934, 938, 959
  Socialism, 740, 959–64
"Pope in Killybuck, The" (Walsh), 813
"Pot of Broth" (Yeats), 769
"Prometheus Hibernica", 717–28
"Purple Dust", xvi, 285–364, 983, 985, 986, 990
"Purple Dust in Their Eyes", 983–92
Purser, Sarah, 882

Queen's Theatre, 815

Radio Eireann, 924, 927, 933
"Raid, The", 745–57
"Red Laugh of War", 867–74
REDMOND, ROSIE, 64–131, 780
"Red Roses for Me", xii, xiv, xvi, 365–434, 987
"Resounding Tinkle, A" (Simpson), 948
Resurrection (Tolstoy), 850
"Riders to the Sea" (Synge), 764
Robinson, Lennox, 757, 758, 759–760, 776, 777, 786, 787, 798, 800, 814, 834, 925
Rose and Crown, xx, 792–850
Royal Court Theatre, 991
Royalty Theatre, 794
Rudkin, David, 944n, 947
Russell, George, see A. E.
Russia, see Political views
Ryan, Frank, 781

St. Bartholomew's Hospital, 904, 907
"Saint Joan" (Shaw), 882
St. Mark's Ophthalmic Hospital, 613, 616–20, 791
SALVATION ARMY OFFICER, A, 207–283
Sean O'Casey; the Man and His Work (Krause), xx
Selwyn, Archie, 827, 828
"Serjeant Musgrave's Dance" (Arden), 949

"Shadow of a Gunman, The", *xii,*
    xiii, 775, 925, 928
Shakespeare, William, 802, 937–40,
    944, 946, 953, 989, 991
"Shakespeare Among the Flags",
    937–40
"Shame Is a Thief and a Robber,
    The", 656–63
SHANAAR, 437–503
"Shaugraun, The" (Boucicault), *xiii,*
    680, 681, 774, 791
Shaw, Anne, 808
Shaw, Charlotte F., 805–6, 833,
    874–90
Shaw, George Bernard, *xv,* 737, 764,
    766, 784–85, 805–6, 833, 848,
    855–56, 859, 860, 874–90,
    925, 954, 956
"Shaw's Corner", 874–90
Sheedy, Father, 928
Sheehy-Skeffington, Mrs., 781–82
Shelley, Percy Bysshe, 725–26
Sherriff, R. C., 833, 937*n*
Shields, Arthur, *xiv,* 759
SHILLAYLEY, BERNADETTE, 531–600
"Ship in Full Sail", 835–42
Shyre, Paul, *xx*
"Silver Tassie, The", *xv–xvii, xxii,*
    133–203, 795–806, 807, 809–
    815, 825, 833–34, 874, 883,
    917
Simon, Sir John, 819
Sinclair, Arthur, *xiv*
Smith, Ned, 713
Socialism, *see* Political views
"Songs of the Wren", *xii*
SOUHAUN, 287–364
Speaight, Robert, 814
Spellman, Francis Cardinal, 854–55
Standard, The (*The Eagle*), 812
"Star Turns Red, The", *xviii–xix*
Stephens, James, 436, 720
STODDART, CORPORAL, 64–131
STOKE, BASIL, 287–364, 984–87,
    989
"Stop the Clock" (Longford), 932
Story, Mr., 613, 617, 619–20

"Story of the Citizen Army, The",
    xiii, 729
"Story of Thomas Ashe, The", *xii*
Stratford Theatre, 938, 991
"Street Sings, The", 629–35
Sullivan, Father, 846, 848–49
Sullivan, Charlie, 680, 682, 689
Sunset and Evening Star, xii, xx,
    851–94
Symons, Arthur, 764
Synge, John Millington, 764, 780,
    989

Tablet, 813
TAITE, JESSIE, 137–203
Talbot, Matt, 772–73
Talton, Tommie, 679, 682–89
TANCRED, MRS., 5–61
Taylor, Rod, *xxi*
"Temple Entered, The", 771–87
Temple Rodeph Sholem, 845
Theatre of the Absurd, 942, 948–49
Theatre of Cruelty, 941*n*
Three Shouts on a Hill, 737
TINLEY, SERGEANT, 64–131
"To Him That Hath Shall Be
    Given", 671–78
Tomelty, Joseph, 929, 930–31
Tone, [Theobald] Wolfe, 785
Torbay Hospital, 913
Tostal, xvii; see also "The Drums of
    Father Ned"
"Touched by the Theatre", 679–89
Townshend Dramatic Society, 679
Trewin, J. C., 918, 990
Tynan, Kenneth, *xi,* 986–92

Ulysses (Joyce), *xvii, xx*
Under a Colored Cap, xxii, 897–916,
    983–92
"Under a Greenwood Tree", *xxii,*
    897–916

Varian, Dr., 828, 909
Vaughan, Stuart, *xx*

Waddell, Helen, 874–75

"Waiting for Godot" (Beckett), 966
Walker, Rev. Reginald, 928
Waller, Dr. Harold, 828
Walsh, Edward, 836
Walsh, Louis J., 813
Watts, Richard, 990
"Where There Is Nothing" (Yeats), 769
"Where Wild Swans Nest", 761–71
Whitman, Walt, 716, 750, 835
"Who's Afraid of Virginia Woolf?" (Albee), 940

"Wild Duck, The" (Ibsen), 966
Windfalls, 967–81
"Within the Gates", *xv–xvi*, 205–283, 807, 842–50

Yeats, William Butler, *xiii, xv,* 710–711, 720, 759–60, 762, 764–766, 768–69, 776, 779–84, 787–88, 790, 798, 800–810, 812, 814–15, 825, 829–34, 840, 858, 876, 925, 926, 933, 989
"Young Cassidy" (film), *xxi*